THE STORY OF CINEMA

CINEMA

VOLUME TWO

From Citizen Kane to the Present Day

THE STORY OF CINEMA

CINEMA

AN ILLUSTRATED HISTORY

VOLUME TWO
From Citizen Kane to the Present Day

DAVID SHIPMAN

HODDER AND STOUGHTON
LONDON   SYDNEY   AUCKLAND   TORONTO

By the same author

THE GREAT MOVIE STARS:
   Volume 1 – The Golden Years
   Volume 2 – The International Years

THE STORY OF CINEMA
   Volume 1 – From the Beginnings to Gone with the Wind

British Library Cataloguing in Publication Data

Shipman, David
   The story of the cinema.
   Vol. 2
   1. Moving-pictures—History
   I. Title
   791.43'09'4   PN1993.5.A1

   ISBN 0 340 28259 2

Contents

Acknowledgments

WRITING a book on the cinema is to an extent a solitary experience: one watches films without talking, one sits alone at the typewriter. When it comes to investigating or checking facts I do my own research. The job became more social watching movies on television or on the Steenbeck machine, and it became positively congenial when the following were commenting on the text and suggesting changes: Christine Medcalf, Barbara Noble, Philippa Toomey, Bruce Goldstein, Susan Lermon and Felix Brenner. My thanks to the last-named and to Frank Thomas for assistance on the index. Gratitude, too, to the late Keith Roberts, who initiated the project in the first place, and to my agent, Frances Kelly, the jewel of her profession. To my editor, Richard Cohen, and to my designer, Margaret Fraser, special thanks for our tripartite conferences, which will remain among the happiest experiences of my writing career. It has been observed that there is nothing a movie buff enjoys more than the company of other movie buffs: though Richard would come into that category Margaret would not, but I recall with great pleasure her enthusiasm as memories were evoked while we examined thousands of stills for the illustrations.

For their co-operation in supplying us with stills and/or permission to reproduce I am grateful to the following: A.J.Y.M., Avala, R. D. Bansal, Manuel Barbachano, Barrandov Studio, Ingmar Bergman, Ceskoslovensky, Ceylon Studios, Champion, The Cinema Bookshop, Cinetel, Columbia Pictures, Contemporary, Daiei, Dear Film, del Duca, Walt Disney, E.M.I., Film Polski, Filmel, Films de la Boétie, Films du Carosse, Films de la Pléiade, Les Films 13, Filmsonor, Finos, Franco London, Goldcrest, Greenwich Film, Gujarat Cooperative, Hungaro Film, Iéna, Imperia, Igor Film, I.T.C., Lira, Deana Lom, Lux, Mafilm, Merchant Ivory, M-G-M/UA, Mosfilm, John B. Murray, New South Wales Film Corporation, Nikkatsu, Nouvelles Editions de Films, Paramount, Paris Film, Pathé, Ponce, Ponti de Laurentiis, Elias Querejita, R.A.I., Rank, Satyajit Ray, Reggane, Rizzoli, R.K.O. Radio, Rome Paris Films, Safir-Film, Sandrews, Shintoho, Shochiku, Silver Film, Bernhard Sinkel, Sono, South Australia Film Corporation, Sovexport, Spéva Film, Svensk Filmindustri, Tango Film, Titanus, Transcontinental, Toei, Toho, 20th Century-Fox, Uninci, Union Générale, Universal, Vides, Warner Bros., W.D.R. and, above all, the National Film Archive of Great Britain.

Introduction

THE PURPOSE of this book has been to attempt an exploration of the cinema's riches. I was encouraged to undertake so daunting a task because I believed that predecessors in this field had had priorities which were no longer relevant. They loved the cinema and, in the very early days, wanted it to gain respectability; accordingly they tended to overestimate many of those films which they hoped would help it to take its place alongside the other arts. Conversely they tended to overlook the real quality of many of the entertaining films made in the factories of Hollywood. It seemed to me that there was a balancing job to be done. During the Silent era and just afterwards there were published two or three histories of film as an industry, but since then most writing on the subject has been concerned with aesthetics. There was also a growing need to discover what the movies had told us about the twentieth century.

I have thus attempted to juggle three subjects simultaneously – the cinema as art, as industry, and as a reflection of our times. The first two of these factors might have been handled by research among printed sources and only minimal viewings of films, but it was precisely because some commentators seemed so entrenched in their views that I felt the films themselves had to be seen or reseen if there was anything new to be said. Fortunately, as I pointed out in my introduction to Volume One, the world's film archives are being opened as never before. Old, forgotten films are being received by young audiences with enthusiasm while some supposed 'classics' are regarded with indifference or even apathy. So, if it is important to know what had been written when these artefacts were first seen it is equally vital to know how they appear to a generation born long after that.

A film, by its very nature, is practically immutable, and few of those with strong narratives lose their appeal; but one not blessed with that advantage may have attracted the admiration of contemporaries for advocating social change and today seem simple-minded propaganda; another might offer a horrendous mixture of mayhem and melodrama but also an accurate record of the dialogue and decor of the time. In most cinema histories in English, Dovzhenko holds an honoured place but Gerhard Lamprecht goes unmentioned (almost certainly because his films have hardly been seen abroad); in writing Volume One it did not occur to me to compare the two since their work is different and was made for different purposes, but I can see in retrospect that apart from being contemporaries both made films about the poor and underprivileged: and that Lamprecht's realism is infinitely more valuable than Dovzhenko's poetic approach. In coming to my opinions of their films I was, subconsciously at least, using all my knowledge of similar films, as well as looking for films which provided *information* on the Soviet Union and Germany in the Twenties.

Working on Volume One the joy of discovery was frequent – not only Lamprecht, but Sjöström, early Ozu, pre-Hollywood Lubitsch and individual works of many other film-makers whose gifts I thought I knew. It was one thing for research to reveal (with difficulty, for the facts had been hidden or ignored by some writers) that D. W. Griffith was not the innovator that he claimed to be; it was another to find (without difficulty) that most viewers today find his films quaint at best and at worst unwatchable. The essential element in my own appreciation of them – leaving aside the magnitude or ambition of the best known of them – was a comparison with other films made at that time which I was considering long after the event. Volume Two had to be approached differently, for these are the movies of my lifetime; the early chapters deal with films that I first saw uncritically as a child and as an adolescent.

As I have implied, I looked again at as many of these films as possible. For over ten years I watched movies for this history, sometimes two or three a day, occasionally wearily but never, initially, without enthusiasm. There was no other way to go about the task: if the opinions were secondhand – or from memory – they became superfluous. It was necessary to see films in both commercial and specialised cinemas. I saw *The Towering Inferno* in a provincial English city with an audience which let out a huge collective sigh when the interval announced itself; I saw one left-wing film with a specialist audience which almost came to blows over its merits; I saw another – if *Missing* may so be termed – with an enthusiastic audience in what is traditionally 'redneck' country in the United States. I experienced the roar of applause at the end of *Singin' in the Rain* (far from the ears of M-G-M, Gene Kelly or anyone connected with the film) and the intensity of an art-house audience watching *Battleship Potemkin*. On the other hand, there are the walk-outs: my opinion of Dovzhenko is not uninfluenced by seeing his films deplete audiences. I have seen Godard's *A Bout de Souffle* three times, in Zurich, Paris and London, with spellbound audiences; I have never seen his later films without some spectators walking out. So although I accept full responsibility for the opinions expressed in this book it was not written in a vacuum. It reflects the views offered to me by many people opposed to the published consensus on some film-makers. I do not want to anticipate the text too much but here are some of the opinions which first came to me through friends and associates: that most of Hitchcock's films entertain but are not of any profundity; that those of John Ford declined drastically at the end of his career; that those of Lindsay Anderson and

Michael Powell have been greatly overrated; that after Truffaut's superb beginning few of his films have been either substantial or deeply felt.

In the matter of favourites, I concluded Volume One with some lists of popular and admired movies made chiefly at the point where that text ended, so we may start now with two more, reflecting the taste of the present, courtesy of the British Film Institute. In 1982 *Sight and Sound*, the Institute's journal, published its ten-yearly poll of the world's movie critics and in 1983 the members of the National Film Theatre were asked for their choice of preferred movies.

The *Sight and Sound* List:
1. *Citizen Kane*
2. *La Règle du Jeu*
3. {*Seven Samurai*
   {*Singin' in the Rain*
5. *8½*
6. *Battleship Potemkin*
7. {*L'Avventura*
   {*The Magnificent Ambersons*
   {*Vertigo*
8. {*The General*
   {*The Searchers*
10. {*2001: A Space Odyssey*
    {*Andrei Rublev*
12. {*Greed*
    {*Jules et Jim*
    {*The Third Man*

The National Film Theatre List:
1. *Casablanca*
2. *Les Enfants du Paradis*
3. *Citizen Kane*
4. *Singin' in the Rain*
5. *2001: a Space Odyssey*
6. *Some Like It Hot*
7. *Seven Samurai*
8. *Gone with the Wind*
9. *The Third Man*
10. *One Flew Over the Cuckoo's Nest*
11. *Céline et Julie vont en Bateau*
12. *The Graduate*
13. *Death in Venice*
14. *La Grande Illusion*
15. *Brief Encounter*
16. *Manhattan*
17. *Top Hat*
18. *Kind Hearts and Coronets*
19. *Apocalypse Now*
20. *The Searchers*
21. *Orphée*
22. *Cabaret*

Introduction

The two lists reflect those films that these critics and buffs have seen. *Seven Samurai*, which is in both lists, is the best known of the score of Japanese movies which have achieved popularity in the West; very few of those to be discussed later have achieved more than minimal viewings. The only film which I feel should not be in this company is one responsible for multiple walk-outs, *Céline et Julie vont en Bateau*; but the critics' list, although shorter, is nevertheless a disturbing reflection on those asked: no Bergman, De Sica, Buñuel, Ray, Clair, Visconti, Capra, Zinnemann, Mankiewicz, Kazan, Wilder, Cukor, Wajda, Kobayashi, Ichikawa, Mizoguchi, Ozu – to restrict myself to directors of the Sound era. It is warming to find *L'Avventura* there, but *8½*? I once observed that I didn't like the late films of Fellini because I wasn't interested in his fantasies, to which a friend replied that I liked Bergman – before quickly adding that he supposed Bergman's fantasies were universal. Of the other films, the inclusion of *Vertigo* astonishes, with its artificial plot, miscast players and clumsy art direction; I saw it with an art-house audience which laughed at it.

The deification of Hitchcock continues apace, which I find profoundly discouraging. Still, it was good to have available again the five late-period Hitchcock movies, recently reissued. It was even better to have the reconstituted print of Cukor's *A Star Is Born*, and it is a richer film for the restorations, both as a love story and a portrait of life in Hollywood. The cuts were particularly damaging to what was intended: they could have been made, as Cukor himself observed, by trimming instead of ripping out whole sequences. Since I completed Volume One, one of the score of missing films of Sjöström has been rediscovered, and though the three-reel *Sea Vultures* is not one of his masterpieces it gives hope for the recovery of others.

Films are now issued, not unlike books, on videocassette, so there should be no further losses – although as yet most of those produced are those unwanted either by cinemas or television, so there would be no great deprivation if they were. It would be disingenuous of me not to pretend that the video revolution provides the ideal point at which to conclude. In 1983 the last cinema closed on the island of Bermuda, where the population of 40,000 prefers to watch its movies at home, bought or rented from the shop around the corner. Where Bermuda leads, will not Huddersfield and Minneapolis follow? Apart from the growing volume of videocassettes the proliferation of television channels and cables means that more films become accessible all the time. Even so, the backlog of material grows: there were seventy years of film-making to look back upon when I started; now there are over eighty. Interest has also continued to grow in lost, forgotten and overlooked movies, and it is to those – once the classics have been issued on video – that cinemas will have to look for their programming. Since, as I said, I have attempted to search out the cinema's riches, I am well content.

538

21

Kane and Other Citizens

IN AN INDUSTRY geared to the star system there was little real place for any other creative force except the actor – unless its name was Capra or Lubitsch. As for the writer-director that was a concept not unknown in Hollywood but unacceptable to its executives, at least until the new decade, when the situation in Europe indicated both a lessening of foreign markets and growing local intolerance of trumpery melodramas. Foreign invasion was no longer outside the bounds of possibility, and indeed a vast number of citizens thought it had arrived one evening in 1938, as they listened to C.B.S. radio. The panic was caused by a documentary-like version of H. G. Wells's novel, 'The War of the Worlds', and Hollywood promptly sent for the man responsible.

Orson Welles (b. 1915) came to movies after a sensational career in radio and theatre – and with a determination to live up to his reputation. Recommended to R.K.O. Radio by one of its founders and chief stockholders, Nelson Rockefeller, he asked for and was given terms commensurate with that reputation: $100,000 for one film a year, to be produced, directed, written and performed by him, on a subject of his own choosing, with no artistic interference, and the right to refuse executives access to the film till completed. The industry gasped, but according to Welles's then-partner, John Houseman, in his memoir 'Run-Through', 'R.K.O. was a maverick operation . . . its present interim and insecure boss – a former sales manager named George Schaefer – had little to lose and a lot to gain by putting many of his eggs into the hands of the Wonder Boy of Broadway and radio, who might just come up with a

winner for him.' After six months, during which announced plans came to nothing, R.K.O. made it known that, till a final script emerged, salaries would be deferred to the Welles unit, which consisted mainly of personnel with whom Welles had worked in New York. These included an experienced screenwriter, Herman J. Mankiewicz (1897–1963), who relieved Welles of a difficult situation when he came up with an idea called *American*. The screenplay of **Citizen Kane** (1940), as it was eventually called, is credited jointly to them, but according to Houseman and Mankiewicz's biographer, Richard Meryman, it was written by Mankiewicz, assisted by Houseman.

Welles's reluctance to give Mankiewicz credit was due to the fact that Mankiewicz's reputation was at a low ebb in Hollywood – he had only recently been sacked by M-G-M. He was also a production-line writer and therefore his participation might tarnish a glittering occasion. Ever short of money, Mankiewicz had been writing some scripts for Welles's radio show – though the credit went to Welles – and he agreed initially to work on the film uncredited. Mankiewicz poured into the script experience from his days as a journalist, including some autobiographical touches. Mankiewicz said of Welles, 'There but for the grace of God goes God,' which was capped by Dorothy Parker, a friend from the days of the Algonquin Round Table: 'It's like meeting God without dying.' The exact authorship of *Kane* is worth establishing, since Welles's later work – after he left R.K.O. – is so disastrously inferior. He would never lose either imagination or flair; and if Houseman allows the glory of *Kane* to Welles, so

RIGHT: Orson Welles
as the young Charles
Foster Kane in
Citizen Kane, before
he has acquired
Xanadu, ABOVE,
the vast mansion
based on Hearst's
San Simeon.
In it Dorothy
Comingore, as
his mistress and
eventual second
wife, spends most of
her footage being
miserable.

may we, but not without noting that his cinematographer was another great professional, Gregg Toland.

The film is the study of a tycoon; but whereas its model, *The Power and the Glory*, is a conventional tale of a man's thirst for power, this is, as Welles intended, sociology. In the earlier film the posthumous enquiry into the nature of the tycoon is done as a series of recollections, but here it is quite literally an enquiry, as pursued by a reporter. If the build-up in this case (the newsreel obituary on Kane's death; the attitudes assumed by Kane's friends) is extraordinary, it is Welles's own performance which gives the film momentum – gilded youth personified, insolent and self-assured, and still powerful when acting less interestingly as the older Kane. The character was known to be based on William Randolph Hearst, whose relationship with Marion Davies is paralleled here by Kane's relationship with his mistress, whom he promotes, despite critical ridicule, as an opera singer – and it is at that point, in the second part of the film, that it begins to weaken. Not only is Dorothy Comingore poor in the role but, like the discarded wife (Ruth Warrick), she appears only to illustrate some facet of Kane's megalomania. There is nothing to suggest that he has either affection or sexual feeling for her, or that she might tolerate the world he has created. Why is she sitting gloomily doing jigsaws if there are hundreds of guests in the west wing? Why is their home, Xanadu, so hideous and thunder-racked? Is this what Welles wished on Hearst, or is it supposed to be the fate of tycoons? It is, in its gothic manner, effective. We learn about Kane only in dazzling fragments – the dancing with the showgirls, the shrugging-off of responsibility – and the portrait has eventually no more depth than that in *The Power and the Glory*: in both films the underlings are baffled and bemused as they begin to loathe the boss, but coping with the whims of powerful paranoics is not as simple as that. The film is stuffed with irrelevant detail, much of it showing-off on the part of its director. The final effect is one of youthful enthusiasm accompanied by intensity and vitality – qualities not usually then seen in the so-called 'serious' film.

Although in the furore that followed the preview Welles denied that the character of Kane was based on Hearst that gentleman's past had certainly been researched by Mankiewicz: not only do Kane's political ambitions follow the general outline of Hearst's but his speeches and the newspaper headlines that we see are subtle parodies of Hearst's endeavours. Both Hearst and Kane were expelled from Harvard; and if the Comingore character were not based on Davies the source would be Sybil Sanderson, an early mistress of Hearst, whose operatic debut was saluted extravagantly in his *San Francisco Examiner*.

The first person outside the studio to identify Kane with Hearst was Hedda Hopper, the gossip columnist who was the rival of Louella Parsons, Hearst's own Hollywood correspondent. Hopper forced her way into a preview, and her subsequent behaviour was undoubtedly an attempt to persuade Hearst that she would be better in Parsons's job than she was. Both ladies, the one vindictive (Hopper)

and the other stupid, were enormously influential: they believed, not without truth, that they could make or break careers and they now set out to break a film. Parsons told Nelson Rockefeller, a major creditor of R.K.O., at that point in receivership, that she would print an unpleasant story about one of his relatives. Louis B. Mayer intervened, and his boss, Nicholas Schenck of Loew's, offered to refund Schaefer the negative cost, plus all expenses incurred to that time, $842,000. Schaefer declined to suppress the film, but its booking at the company's flagship, Radio City Music Hall, was cancelled. Hearst himself threatened a series of exposés of Hollywood morals in his papers and banned all R.K.O. advertising. When Hearst failed to take legal action, on the grounds that he could not go into court and admit that he recognised himself in the role of the unpleasant Kane, R.K.O. threatened anti-trust suits against the circuits which refused to book the film. Those mainly independent cinemas which did show it took care of the demand to see it which, despite the publicity and warm reviews, was not excessive. The film was nominated for several Academy Awards, but the industry's nervousness about Hearst and renewed resentment against Welles – now that he had lived up to his reputation – ensured that it won in only one category, that of Best Screenplay.

This pattern was to an extent repeated with **The Magnificent Ambersons** (1942), though this time Welles himself was partially to blame. He did not seem to care whether or not his work appealed to a mass cinema audience, which he respected as little as he did the Hollywood system. Houseman has pictured him as a man of whim and great indecisiveness, a genius in a hurry, with quickly waning enthusiasms; and he apparently lost interest in *Ambersons* as filming proceeded and his next project began to occupy his thoughts. He was attracted to Booth Tarkington's novel because it allowed him to re-explore the terrain of *Kane* – the surging, evolving America of the previous half century. Again, there was precedent, in Vitagraph's 1925 version of the novel, *Pampered Youth*, and the similar presentation of a number of sequences suggests that Welles had seen it. The material is a not particularly distinguished family saga, but the film nicely sets the tone: 'In those days, they had time for everything. Time for sleigh-rides, and balls, and assemblies, and cotillions.' The ball is sumptuous, like everything about the Amberson mansion, and the set was constructed to allow the camera to keep moving from room to room. The decor (by Mark-Lee Kirk) – or at least the use that Welles puts it to – alternates between the ornate and the very plain; similarly the camera of Stanley Cortez sweeps and pounces, and then remains stationary, as in the famous kitchen scene between Aunt Fanny (Agnes Moorehead) and George (Tim Holt). If the work has even more bravura than *Kane*, the finished product is more consistent – except for the three scenes at the end not directed by Welles, easy to spot because they entirely lack his combustive energy.

The direction is at its most striking in the interplay between Morgan (Joseph Cotten) and his daughter (Anne Baxter) and that within the Amberson family – which may be because Moorehead and Cotten had been members of Welles's Mercury company in New York. She, with her pinched, unhappy face and that dry, querulous voice has more dimension than most movie spinsters. 'Really, George, I don't think being an aunt is the great career you think it is,' she says, part-fretful and part-malicious. Cotten is the faithful suitor, authoritative in some matters but amiable enough to let a whippersnapper like George put him in his place. Holt's weak looks are right for the role, and he suggests an incipient Fascism: a more dynamic actor might have been better in the part, but this is very much a movie which does not need a centre or a focus of attention.

In this case, the trouble started with the previews. Schaefer had been dismissed, and the new management demanded the running-time be reduced from 148 minutes so that the film could be programmed on double-bills. Welles, on location in Brazil for his next film, telephoned a number of suggestions; other hands were called in to make deletions and insertions, and to clarify the plot, since (it was said) Welles had left a number of points unexplained. Perhaps most regrettable is the loss of two reels of panoramic documentary; at 88 minutes the film satisfied R.K.O., who finally released it to support *Mexican Spitfire Sees a Ghost*, one of a series with Lupe Velez, designed ordinarily to play the lower spot.

Welles, who did not appear in *Ambersons*, was meanwhile acting in but not directing the third film of his contract, **Journey into Fear** (1942). American entry in the War and the box-office failure of *Kane* had made his position in Hollywood uncertain, so he needed to complete another film quickly. The sets used were those constructed for the abandoned *The Heart of Darkness*, from Conrad's novel, which had been announced as his first film venture; as director he chose Norman Foster, because he both admired the Oriental atmosphere of Foster's B-movies and was employing him already on pre-production work for the South American venture Welles had chosen to make a thriller, taking as his source one by Eric Ambler. The plot involves a man in a vast political trap from which he cannot escape: but at that point in Ambler, when the nightmare builds in complexity, the movie simply disintegrates. It is a heavily atmospheric film but gives the impression of having been made in a hurry – for Foster was not given to the endless retakes undertaken by Welles. The film exists in two versions, since Welles on his return from Brazil was appalled by the 69-minute one first released. He re-cut it, and shot a new final sequence, adding thirteen minutes. The faults this time are more clearly his: the screenplay, credited to him and Cotten, picks up ideas and drops them, characters are not developed and the story leads nowhere. Neither does either of them emerge with credit as performers: the Turkish police chief of Welles is sketchy, and Cotten, supposed to be frantic, looks merely frustrated.

The South American adventure ended in debacle. Rockefeller believed that the world situation required America to emphasise its closeness to its Southern neighbours, and he encouraged Welles, in a picture additional to his contract, to journey south with that in mind. Welles envisaged a three-part film, to be called *It's All True*, but had to stop shooting when the new management abandoned the project Welles's three films had proved him 'uncommercial', but it was due to his extravagant working methods that he was viewed with bitterness. Like Von Stroheim before him, he could only work in Hollywood a an actor – at least for a while. The later films (q.v.) he directed have flair, but only intermittently do they suggest that Hollywood let go a great film-maker. Yet *Kane* and *Ambersons* are indelible achievements. It is a sad comment on the Hollywood system that it could not accommodate a maverick, however self-indulgent and undisciplined. These were precisely the qualities which the studios' editors should have been capable of curbing, or using to their advantage – since overshooting would give the team in the cutting-room much more with which to work: which may be why *Kane* and even the mutilated *Ambersons* are so very good.

There was already one eminent writer-director in Hollywood as Welles began *Kane*, and he was to have an equally difficult time. In the Silent era a number of scenario-writers had turned director, invariably relegating the scripting to others. One writer, Preston Sturges (1898–1959), did not care for the treatment that other directors had meted out to his scripts, and he decided to do something about it. Like Welles, he came from a background both wealthy and intellectual, and had been educated, if somewhat bizarrely, in France, Germany and Switzerland. His satiric attitudes may just be discerned in one of the first films he wrote, *The Big Pond*, but are largely absent in the others to which he contributed over the next ten years. The most interesting of them is *The Power and the Glory*, and although Sturges disliked what Mitchell Leisen had done with his screenplays for *Easy Living* and *Remember the Night*, they are still recognisably Sturges's work, certain that the world is divided into the haves and have-nots.

He persuaded Paramount to let him direct **The Great McGinty** (1940), partly by selling them the script for only $10, partly by agreeing to the severely restricted budget of $350,000 – necessitated in any case by its commercially risky subject, political corruption. A foreword informs us that two men have met, one who did one dishonest action in an honest life, and one who did just one honest action in a dishonest life: it doesn't matter in the end who did which, since both end up down-and-outs in a South-of-the-Border bar. 'Everyone lives by cheating everyone else,' says the Boss (Akim Tamiroff), while the Politician (William Demarest)

claims, 'They forget that if you don't have graft you'd have a low type of person in politics. Men with no ambition.' McGinty (Brian Donlevy) marries for the sake of his image, and it is a marriage quite as spurious as that of Citizen Kane; however, he eventually falls in love with his wife, but giving up the Good Life for a Good Woman is not a satisfactory Sturges dénouement.

The films of Capra had created a climate in which Sturges was permitted to express his fierce anti-capitalism. **Christmas in July** (1940) concerns a slogan competition for a coffee manufacturer, Maxford House, with a clerk (Dick Powell) conned into believing that he has won. Says his boss (Ernest Truex): 'I *think* your ideas are good because they seem good to me. I *know* they're good because you won the contest over millions of other people.' Sturges's general view of human greed and frailty becomes more particular in **The Lady Eve** (1941), as two card-sharpers working the North Atlantic, father (Charles Coburn) and daughter (Barbara Stanwyck), prey on a Harold Lloydish young man (Henry Fonda), heir to the Pike's Ale fortune. All is discovered, and in the course of time she turns up at the Pike mansion, posing as a British society girl – and her revenge is one that the changing moral standard has now rendered very tame. However, the freshness and ingenuity for which the film was praised still delight, and it is perhaps the last good example of a dying breed, the screwball comedy.

Sullivan's Travels (1941) is dedicated to 'those who made us laugh . . . the motley crew, the clowns, the buffoons'. Sullivan (Joel McCrea) is an idealistic movie director, weary of turning out trivia like 'Ants in the Pants of 1939' and therefore researching a social treatise called 'Oh Brother Where Art Thou?'. In the course of his travels he has the experience of watching Mickey Mouse with an audience, and changes his mind. 'There's something about making people laugh. It isn't much, but it's all some people have.' He also learns that poverty does not ennoble, as he had thought, and the film becomes oddly poignant when this intelligent man has for his audience only one pathetic and aged half-wit. Sturges's overall view is not as serious as the one Sullivan

Kane and Other Citizens

The world of Preston Sturges: Joel McCrea and Claudette Colbert, RIGHT, feuding husband and wife in *Palm Beach Story*, and FAR RIGHT, Eddie Bracken, centre, the little man caught up in situations too big for him, in *Hail the Conquering Hero*. Both McCrea and Bracken were actors whom Sturges admired and used more than once, but the two with Bracken appeared in virtually every Sturges film and were essential to his world – left, the effeminate busybody Franklin Pangborn, and the marvellously gruff William Demarest.

intended, since the film is often hilarious: but then throughout the film he seems to be crying out for the best of all possible worlds.

Palm Beach Story (1942) has no such preoccupations, being content to chart the amorous adventures of a millionaire (Rudy Vallee, made up to look like John D. Rockefeller III) and his sister (Mary Astor) with a divorcing husband (McCrea) and wife (Claudette Colbert). Among marital comedies there is none better, with dialogue not so much notable for its wit as for its bite and discrimination. Sturges catapults ideas one after the other, as in the superb scene when Vallee is explaining his penny-pinching ways to an artlessly enquiring Colbert. And the slapstick – notably when Colbert is adopted by the Ale and Quail Club – is merely incidental to the comedy, unlike, say, *Bringing Up Baby*, where it is essential to it. In the same tradition, neither McCrea nor Colbert plays for sympathy, and in fact their roles are hardly admirable, have-nots no better than the haves. Yet the lack of any moral centre is one of the film's most invigorating features. James Agee, remarking upon the evasions and cynicism of **The Miracle of Morgan's Creek** (1944), suspected that 'Sturges feels that conscience and comedy are incompatible,' adding that 'it would be hard for a man of talent to make a more self-destructive mistake.'

That talent was in fact evolving: Sturges's first films (i.e. as director) look

back to the social comedies of the Thirties, while both *The Lady Eve* and *Palm Beach Story* are in the tradition which stretches back to Wilde, or even Restoration comedy. But both *Miracle* and **Hail the Conquering Hero** (1944) are contemporary tales, built around the reaction of small-town America to the War, as represented by the military in its midst. *Miracle* encapsulates that period when G.I.s were on the loose for loose girls, and girls were glad to be that way. Possibly the Hays Office insisted that this particular girl (Betty Hutton) marry her G.I., but the wedding is the only event of one wild night that she remembers. The audacity of the resulting situations is encouraging but, apart from the breakneck pace, all that I find to admire is Sturges's view of a world where all well-meant schemes go wrong and opportunists wait on every corner. If *Conquering Hero* looks back to *Christmas in July*, with its protagonist caught up in plots not of his own making, its comment on American gullibility is freely borrowed from *Nothing Sacred*. Woodrow Lafayette Pershing Truesmith (Eddie Bracken) is recognised by a marine sergeant (William Demarest) as 'Hinky Dinky's boy', i.e. the son of an old comrade-in-arms, so he and his buddies phone Woodrow's mother to tell her that he is a hero, which, as someone says, is the least you can do for a mother. The town goes ecstatic, but the squirming Woodrow refuses to wear uniform till someone points out that his grandfather wore his Civil War uniform as long as he lived, so that we could never forget that brother fought brother – which is the most extreme example of Sturges's cynicism. His second half is predictable, as if Sturges, having poked fun at both the cults for military heroics and Monism, was afraid to go any further. However, the film provides Demarest's biggest role in films, and for that it is notable; Raymond Walburn and Franklin Pangborn are also at their best, the other constants of the Sturges stock company – the realist and the two dreamers.

Despite its faults, the film confirms Sturges as far ahead of his peers in light comedy, and **The Great Moment** (1944) proves him level with them in more serious matters – though a number of comic sequences indicate that, long before films like $M \star A \star S \star H$ (q.v.), he found humour in pain. Here the hero is W. T. G. Morton, the nineteenth-century dentist who claimed the discovery of the anaesthetic effects of ether, and he is played by Joel McCrea, Sturges's favourite leading man. Biographies of such figures were generally accorded the greatest respect in Hollywood but Sturges's own interest in Morton, began because he had been a man who had benefited society but had been so little thanked, remembered or admired. In fact Morton's claim was much disputed, and the disappointments of his life would have made a much more ironic – and indeed a more Sturges-like – ending than the happy one the film provides. That is Sturges's own ending, as referred to in the title, but the original structure of the film, as suggested by *The Power and the Glory*, did not attempt a strict chronology. Paramount disliked much of the film, which included in the first frame a shot of Morton's grave, followed by one of a modern operation; Sturges, tired of his disputes with the company, left the recutting to his usual editor, Stuart Gilmore – after which the film sat on the shelf for two years, finally being released in 1944 to almost complete indifference. There is no doubt that it is less than we might expect from one who has been called a genius by some, and though still weighty in comparison with the films on Pasteur, Ehrlich, etc. the writing is similarly conventional.

In *Sullivan's Travels*, when Sullivan tells his bosses that he wants to make serious films, one of them observes, 'Something like Capra, I suppose?' to which Sullivan flashes back, 'What's the matter with Capra?' The film answers the question: nothing, but Sturges lacked Capra's belief that there would always be someone to speak up for the 'little man'. As Capra went to war, Sturges rose, to blaze like a comet, and not till Billy Wilder made *The Apartment* (q.v.) would any American director equal the balance of comedy and seriousness of *Sullivan's Travels*. With Sturges's decline, Wilder, the other great cynic of the American cinema, had emerged as a bright new talent. Like John Huston (q.v.) he was encouraged by Sturges's success to turn director. Sturges's decline was quick. He had become very expensive: whole towns had to be constructed and hundreds of extras employed. He wrote at night, slept mornings, which meant that shooting did not start till the afternoon; and though he shot with few retakes, the longer schedule increased the budget. He had also become autocratic, demanding a place in the commissary for his stock company on a par with deMille's. Nevertheless, when he left Paramount at the end of 1943, and while that company pondered on the box-office appeal of three unreleased films, he was asked to come back. He refused, also rejecting an offer from M-G-M, and with an old friend, Howard Hughes, formed California Pictures. Hughes's interest in the company was the promotion of his latest protégée, Faith Domergue.

He believed that she could become a bigger star than Jane Russell (for whom he had fashioned *The Outlaw*), but the costume film he planned for her, *Vendetta*, with Sturges as producer and Max Ophuls directing, had to be postponed (it was eventually released in 1950, with the direction credited to Mel Ferrer). Hughes's interference and vacillation drove both men 'to distraction', according to Hughes's biographer, Noah Dietrich, but with Hughes's money and independence Sturges 'went wild'. His contract with Hughes called for two more films as producer-director-writer and he conceived the idea of making a film with Harold Lloyd, whom he admired because he had achieved a long career with complete independence. He inveigled him out of retirement (Lloyd had found the fun had gone out of filming while making *Professor Beware*), and **The Sin of Harold Diddlebock** (1947) begins with the last reel of *The Freshman*, for its purpose is to examine the college hero later in life. We find little has changed: he was an accountant and has remained one. However, he is suddenly sacked, and with his savings has his first alcoholic drink, which sends him on a binge, during which he buys an eccentric check suit and wins and loses a fortune – losing it mainly by acquiring a circus. It is a very poor film indeed, and the charge against Sturges is not that he misuses Lloyd, though he does, but that he does not begin to understand him. It is grievous to see the irrepressible young Harold become a failure – the man who surmounted so many plights and dangers now facing the same yet virtually turning away. He is saved by chance and not by his own skill.

Lloyd, Sturges and Hughes were the strangest of bedfellows, and Lloyd, who had been persuaded that the film would be an attack on smugness, loathed it. So did everyone else. After previews it was retitled *Mad Wednesday*, as which it limped around the U.S. for a while, not surfacing in New York till 1951. Its artistic and commercial failure shattered Sturges, as well as the deal with Hughes. Sturges never recovered, and his drinking did not help his later work.

As we saw, Sturges, like Capra before him, paid tribute to the one true independent, Walt Disney (1901–66). His is one of the industry's great success stories, perhaps because he was the antithesis of Welles and Sturges – of artisan stock, low-brow, very much concerned with pleasing his audiences. Like them, however, he put his 'art' before financial consideration, which is not contradictory, for his taste was far closer to audiences than his advisers understood. He made the animated cartoon into an art for the masses, which is why David Low, the British newspaper cartoonist, called him 'the most significant figure in graphic arts since Leonardo'.

He was born in Chicago; a talent for drawing took him into commercial art, and in Kansas City, with Ub Iwerks (1901–71) he began making animated shorts for cinemas. In Hollywood he found buyers for a series of short cartoons called *Alice in Cartoonland*, and with Iwerks

started a series of shorts for Universal called *Oswald the Rabbit*. He, or they, created Mickey Mouse in 1928, beyond which it is difficult to determine to what extent Iwerks was the creative force at the Disney studios. He received credit for the early cartoons, which remain by far the most inventive ever to emanate from Disney, though Disney disliked giving credit – till persuaded to do so for the feature-length cartoons, which were issued with such extensive lists of names that the public only remembered his. He may have been a kindly employer, as has been claimed, but the publicity department created a mystique about him, as though he created the films single-handed. Iwerks left in 1931 and did not return for many years, his work for other companies reputedly suffering from his lack of narrative sense and also, as an independent, the financial acumen of Disney's chief adviser, his brother Roy Disney. It is more than likely that Iwerks had left a durable mark on the Disney team: the quality of the shorts had begun to decline before the end of the decade (and production had by then started on the early feature cartoons, even those released as late as 1943).

The first Mickey Mouse short was **Plane Crazy** (1928) and the second **Steamboat Willie** (1928), to which was added, after completion, a synchronised score. Their immediate success led to Columbia reaching an agreement with Disney to release his films, starting with the synchronised *Plane Crazy*. To anyone who knows only the later, epicene Mickey, these early works are astonishing: he could put his anatomy to amazing use, and he could be ferocious and randy. The screen is ablaze with action, everything is animated, including inanimate objects – usually involved, like the casts of animals, in questionable play. In **Karnival Kid** (1929) the hot dogs are obviously phallic, and one has pants like a foreskin for Mickey to peel back to tan his behind. The anal and the phallic humour were quickly banished – perhaps when the implications were pointed out to Disney; a harsher cinema climate dictated the end of such commonplaces as yowling alley cats and flying chamber pots. The pre-Code Disney films could be called Rabelaisian, but the term does not apply to those made later.

In 1929 the first 'Silly Symphony'

appeared, **The Skeleton Dance**, in which amazing things happen to rattling bones. The series went into colour in 1932, and the first in Technicolor, *Flowers and Trees*, so impressed the Academy of Motion Picture Arts and Sciences that it introduced a new category in its annual awards – Short Subject: Cartoon – which Disney then won annually till the end of the decade, despite his several imitators. This Oscar, however, went only to the Silly Symphonies, and then usually to the winsome rather than the raucous – **The Three Little Pigs** (1933), *The Tortoise and the Hare* (1934), *Three Orphan Kittens* (1935), *Country Cousin* (1936), *The Old Mill* (1937), *Ferdinand the Bull* (1938) and *The Ugly Duckling* (1939). The cartoons, however, were not particularly profitable: when in 1932 Disney moved to United Artists they were guaranteed an advance of $20,000 each from that source, to be set against the manufacturing cost of around $27,500, which almost doubled with the making of prints and shipping. Despite their popularity, their average gross during the first year in release was only $80,000; *The Three Little Pigs*, however, took $125,000 in that time, and twice as much again before being withdrawn. Its phenomenal success bewildered Disney, and since its theme tune, 'Who's Afraid of the Big Bad Wolf?', and the film itself, seemed to mean so much to Depression-hit America, he is said to have screened it constantly to find out why – but there was no discernible message, only a tale of two improvident pigs and their wise brother, whose brick-built house keeps out the salivating wolf (who was at some later point redrawn and re-recorded to remove the characteristics supposedly typical of Jewish pedlars). At the end of the year *The New York Times* 'safely' ventured that it had been 'shown at more theaters simultaneously than any other film, short or feature length'. It temporarily reintroduced the industry's practice of bicycling prints.

As box-office attractions the Disney shorts outdistanced any other item on the bill except the main feature, and audiences roared their approval when the first titles flashed upon the screen. The Mouse, already joined by Minnie, Pluto the Dog and Goofy, went into colour in 1934, the same year that the bad-tempered bird, Donald Duck, made his debut – and he proved so popular that he later 'starred' alone. The public mania for the menagerie meant a flood of comic strips and subsidiary rights of all kinds, from towels to toothbrushes; and highbrow and lowbrow alike had no reservations about Mickey.

Disney's decision to make a feature-length cartoon was born less from a desire to capitalise on this success than from ambition: it had not been done, therefore he would do it – which he did, against almost total opposition, and in addition to foregoing the financial security which would have been his at the time. When the contract with United Artists came to be re-negotiated in 1936 the Disney brothers not only insisted on retaining television rights – a good indication of their farsightedness – but wanted to include the feature cartoon already in production. The directors of United Artists were not interested, and a deal was made instead with R.K.O., which took the shorts at better terms – advancing the total cost of production, with a promise of 50% of the gross receipts when that investment had been recouped – but insisted on a separate agreement for the feature. Virtually Disney's only ally was the manager of Radio City Music Hall, who booked it sight unseen; by the time it premiered there, five years from its inception, the cost had escalated from the original estimate of $250,000 to over $1,700,000, partly as a result of Disney's augmenting his staff to make it. Disney's survival did not depend on it, but many expected him to be crippled with debts for years: the film, however, was a triumph for him, both within and outside the industry.

The film is, of course, **Snow White and the Seven Dwarfs** (1937), and the Disney Organisation has reissued it since at seven-year intervals, to new generations of children, though few can have experienced the same enchantment as those who saw it earlier. I do not believe that it has been bettered in the intervening years, but I have to say that to my own generation it was a completely new experience; many of us had never seen a film, and certainly not television. It is a story with terror and hope, deception and romance, with a special magic in the sequence when the dwarfs entertain Snow White – simply because audience pleasure is balanced by the knowledge that the Queen is planning

Disneyland

The artwork for
*Snow White and the
Seven Dwarfs*, ABOVE
RIGHT, was the basis
for the original
advertising cam-
paign, and has been
used in moderated
form for most of the
reissues – sometimes
in inferior manner,
which is curious for
a company which
specialises in design.
RIGHT, *Pinocchio* and
ABOVE, Mickey
Mouse, of course.

further witchery. Sentimentality is kept at bay by Grumpy – murmuring 'Mush' while Snow White warbles 'Some Day My Prince Will Come' – and the comic stuff remains funny still because the dwarfs are so richly characterised, atoning for the saccharine heroine and the operatic posturing of the Prince. If the animals of the forest are most kindly regarded as being in the taste of the time, the film survives marvellously on its visual qualities, both in its evocation of the Brothers Grimm and the colours of its palette: the luminosity of Snow White as she runs through the forest, the predominantly crimson, fawn, ochre and brown of the dwarfs' clothes and the velvety shimmer of the Queen's gowns and the witch's cloak. The concept of these two ladies – though they are in fact the same – is genuinely astonishing, with the magic mirror, the huntsman's shadow, the transformation scene and the vultures circling as the dwarfs pursue the witch up the rain-wet rocks. (Recent reissues have lost the witch kicking the prone skeleton as she proceeds to her Stygian boat.) These effects were reached by committee – although David Hand is credited as supervising editor – but there must have been elements in the climate of the time for something so imaginative and terrifying to emerge.

Disney's faith in feature-length cartoons was so strong that he had already begun work on **Pinocchio** (1940), which is also peculiarly sinister. From *The Skeleton Dance* onwards, through Pegleg Pete, Mickey's enemy, and such shorts as *The Mad Doctor*, a spoof of Frankenstein, the studio had been practised in the gruesome; and Carlo Collodi's fantasy was ideal material, concerning an innocent in a malevolent universe. On the side of the puppet-come-to-life-Pinocchio are his loving but ineffectual 'father', the insect appointed to be his conscience and the formidable Blue Fairy. Against him are a series of monsters and freaks progressively more terrifying: Honest John the fox and his simple but vicious assistant, Gideon; Stromboli, the puppeteer; the stupid Lampwick, who will lead Pinocchio into corruption and vice; the Coachman, who manages to make Stromboli's greed and malice seem almost virtuous; and Monstro the Whale. The film may be a bastardisation of the book, but it is a black masterpiece, with one sequence – that in which the boys are metamorphosed into donkeys – as terrifying as any ever put on film.

Fantasia (1940) was begun in the wake of the acclaim for *Snow White*, and was a bold undertaking. The Silly Symphonies had demonstrated Disney's interest in the marriage of sound and image; The Sorceror's Apprentice was planned as a short, but Stokowski expressed a wish to conduct the score and suggested a full-length cartoon on similar lines. Disney saw himself as a populariser, and bringing music to the masses became his dream, as it was Stokowski's avowed intention 'that [its] beauty and inspiration must not be restricted to a privileged few.' Whether more than a few would be receptive was another matter, and as it turned out they decisively were not. The critics, however, were fascinated, if polarised between those who considered 'great' music demeaned and those who, like Bosley Crowther, of *The New York Times*, told readers that 'history was made last night.' More cautiously, Frank Hoellering in *The Nation* called it 'a promising monstrosity' and in Britain James Agate found it 'magnificent and trivial, inspiring and commonplace, exciting and tedious'. Today one might wish for the animators to have departed more frequently from the Disney style – at its worst in the interpretation of Beethoven's Pastoral, with sexless centaurs and cute cherubs. The Dance of the Hours is a dullish satire on ballet, with hippopotami and other animals in tutus, and The Nutcracker Suite is variable, at its best in the Thistle cossack dance and that of the Chinese mushrooms. The introduction, abstract patterns to Bach's Toccata and Fugue in D Minor, soars; The Rite of Spring, curtailed and rearranged, astonishes with its vomiting volcanoes and shuddering mountain-quakes, and The Sorcerer's Apprentice, with Mickey Mouse, is equally effective; while The Night on a Bare Mountain does have the quality of Bosch, and in sheer drawing technique is more advanced than the rest of the film – though it is followed by an interpretation of 'Ave Maria' more suitable to a nursery wall. The film cost $2,300,000 and was made under great financial pressure when the profits from *Snow White* were exhausted and the banks refused credit. If Disney had expected it to

Mickey Mouse's most popular rivals were Betty Boop, BELOW, drawn by Max Fleischer for Paramount, and Tom and Jerry, ABOVE, drawn by Hanna and Barbera for M-G-M.

make money it was because he had confidence in all his judgments, as he had every right to have – at least, from the commercial standpoint. But in this case the public was not ready for serious music, and though that situation would change within a few years the first reissues were tentative; not till a decade later did the film start to enjoy a wide popularity, and it is difficult, today, to reconcile it with its former reputation as 'highbrow'.

Meanwhile **Dumbo** (1941) did much to restore Disney's financial standing. Taken from a run-of-the-mill children's story, it was originally intended to be a Silly Symphony and cost only $700,000. Disney resisted pressure to make it longer than 64 minutes and, despite comparatively simple animation, the film is packed with a number of splendid items: the flying elephant himself; the circus train, chugging away in the manner of the Silly Symphonies; 'Pink Elephants on Parade', an arabesque for elephants; and the song of the crows, 'When I See an Elephant Fly', in which the view of Negroes as flash dandies is alleviated by the joyousness of the number itself. **Bambi** (1942), three times as expensive and much longer in preparation, is technically a much more accomplished work. The story of a baby deer and his growing up, from the novel by Felix Salten, its hold on sentiment, when necessary, is equally sure; and the treatment of the forest glades in lightly Impressionist manner indicates an artistry seldom found

thereafter in the studio's work. Indeed, this enchanting film is Disney's last major work.

The decline of the short cartoons had already begun, and it is possible that Disney's artistic judgment faltered under pressure. The popularity of *Bambi* hardly offset its cost, and his losses were such at the time the U.S. entered the War that he was only too happy to take commissions from the government, which realised the propaganda uses of the animated film. Most of the resulting shorts were for showing on service installations; a feature, *Victory Through Air Power* (1943), with Donald Duck, was released to cinemas. Also as part of the war effort Disney toured the southern continent on behalf of the U.S. State Department, and made, with **Saludos Amigos** (1942) and **The Three Caballeros** (1944), hotchpotch assemblies of animated Latin-American travelogues and unrelated short cartoons, linked by the presence of Donald Duck. The second of the two used both drawings and humans, of which supposed innovation the publicity department made much, overlooking the fact that Disney had done that at the start of his career, in the *Alice* cartoons. The method here is a little more sophisticated: settings for humans who are made to look like cartoons, some back projection and some painting on the finished film. The final sequence, as a real girl sings inside an animated flower, has a few abstract designs which recall the best of *Fantasia*.

Disney's fading pre-eminence in the short cartoon was indicated in 1940 when the appropriate Oscar went to M-G-M's Tom and Jerry, the malicious but hard-done-by cat and his cheeky rodent adversary; and though Disney took the award again in the two subsequent years it went to Tom and Jerry five times during the next six years (and on the other occasion to Warner Bros.). Until that time most of Disney's rivals had followed his lead, including the team of Hugh Harmon and Ralph Ising at M-G-M with their 'Happy Harmonies', though they claimed to have used both Sound and serious music (a Strauss waltz) before Disney. Their reign in Fred Quimby's Shorts Department ended as Tom and Jerry rose, giving way to Joseph Barbera (b. 1911) who had started the cat and mouse as a magazine strip, and his partner William Hanna (b. 1920). The two hundred cartoons they turned out over the twenty-year period are seldom as inventive as the Iwerks Mouse, but good enough to supplant the Disney characters as popular favourites. Of the others, perhaps only Bugs Bunny and company at Warners were serious contenders – and probably the Terry-Toons at Fox were the least likely. Most of these rivals were created by defectors from Disney, and Hanna and Barbera are unusual among animators of the time in that they never worked for him.

However, Disney's most serious rival was flourishing when he joined the industry. Max Fleischer (1889–1973) made 'Out of the Inkwell', a series combining live action and animation. With his brother, Dave, as his administrator, he had a success in the early Thirties with Betty Boop, a sexy little flapper, and later a more pronounced one with Popeye, the bellicose but soft-hearted sailor. Paramount distributed, and after the success of *Snow White* agreed to a feature, **Gulliver's Travels** (1939), which uses the first section of Swift's novel for a pantomime about a helpful giant in a warlike kingdom. The film is technically often impressive, but like the Capraesque **Mr Bug Goes to Town** (1941) too slight to do more than mildly amuse. The second film was a complete failure, since Fleischer had never been able to enter the world of children as Disney had, and that was something, apparently, that even adult audiences wanted from full-length cartoons. He did not attempt another, leaving that field free to Disney, who was to have no further rival during his lifetime.

There were in Hollywood at this time four foreign directors who managed to preserve artistic control over the films they made – if only at the cost of moving from studio to studio. Easily the most successful was Alfred Hitchcock, under contract to Selznick, whose reduced activity allowed him to 'loan out' Hitchcock for projects that they both considered suitable. After *Rebecca* Hitchcock made the more characteristic **Foreign Correspondent** (1940) for Walter Wanger, who was more willing to appreciate his particular talent than Selznick. Wanger's interest in foreign politics had led him to buy the memoirs of Vincent Sheean, 'Personal History', to serve as a basis for a tale of an American reporter in Europe; but the early scripts were abandoned as the European situation changed, and it was turned over to Hitchcock to make the film to his British formula – in his own words, 'the innocent bystander who becomes involved in an intrigue'. His starting point was the superb sequence of the assassination in the rain, followed by the windmill hideout. Equally memorable are the scenes where the hero (Joel McCrea) is at the top of Westminster Cathedral with a professional assassin (Edmund Gwenn), and that in which McCrea escapes his own would-be assassins along the hotel parapet in robe but no pants – a suitable garb for a reporter to work in in the privacy of his own room but leading, once down from the parapet, to farcical complications. This is one of Hitchcock's funniest films, as it is one of the most ingenious, and plotted as cleverly as any of Graham Greene's political thrillers. The screenplay is credited to Hitchcock's old associates, Joan Harrison and Charles Bennett, with dialogue by James Hilton and Robert Benchley. Benchley is also in the cast, which is a splendid one: Albert Basserman as a statesman considered able to prevent war; Herbert Marshall as head of the Universal Peace Party; George Sanders as a reporter; and Laraine Day as the heroine. Unfortunately, the last sequences have dated: the shooting-down of the clipper over the Atlantic seems a last-minute idea to remind audiences of the seriousness of war, and McCrea broadcasting to the U.S. – while bombs fall around him in London – now seems banal.

Hitchcock directed **Mr and Mrs Smith** (1941) as a gesture to Carole Lombard, who co-stars with Robert Montgomery. They play quarrelling spouses who philander ostentatiously after parting: Hitchcock claimed that he did not understand the characters, so filmed the Norman Krasna dialogue as written. The sole funny sequence – that in which Lombard struggles into an old dress – therefore may be his. Returning to crime, he was no happier with **Suspicion** (1941), accepting a foolishly simulated England of thatched manor houses. Presumably, however, he was responsible for the screenplay – by Miss Harrison, Alma Reville (his wife) and Samson Raphaelson – which does scant justice to the original novel, 'Before the

Kane and Other Citizens

The fifty-year film career of Alfred Hitchcock has a number of highs and lows: the late Thirties and the Fifties are certainly high points, and he also made some of his most enjoyable films in the first half of the Forties. RIGHT, the assassination in the Netherlands which sets off the events in *Foreign Correspondent*.

Fact' by Francis Iles. That was about a woman who gradually realises that her husband plans to murder her, but who is so much in love that she does not mind, whereas the film is a dotty cat-and-mouse tale, leading to a chase sequence rendered ludicrous by a happy ending. Cary Grant is the cat, and Joan Fontaine, who won an Oscar for the role, the mouse. Hitchcock explained the film's artistic failure by saying 'the producers would have refused' to let Grant be a murderer.

The producers of both films were at R.K.O., but finding another independent producer – Frank Lloyd at Universal – Hitchcock again hit his best form, providing the scenario from which Peter Viertel, Miss Harrison and Dorothy Parker wrote the screenplay. **Saboteur** (1942) significantly is to formula, about a man (Robert Cummings) who flees because he thinks no one will believe his innocence. The crime committed is sabotage in a Californian factory, which leads to the unmasking of a spy ring in New York, on the way to which are such diversions and/or set-

pieces as a seemingly deserted shanty town near Boulder Dam, a chase through Radio City Music Hall and another on the crown of the Statue of Liberty. **Shadow of a Doubt** (1943) gained a reputation as Hitchcock's own favourite among his films, but if he gave that impression, he said later, that was because it caused the least dissatisfaction to those who complained of implausibilities in his plots. The situation is that of a murderer (Joseph Cotten) living in a family, and what happens when his adored and adoring niece (Teresa Wright) finds out. What she does *not* do is go to the local police (when she cannot contact her detective boyfriend); but otherwise this is a clever screenplay as written by Thornton Wilder, Sally Benson and Alma Reville, from a story by Gordon McDonnell, a novelist married to the head of the Selznick story department. Wilder had been invited to participate because he had written 'Our Town', and this particular small town – Santa Rosa, California – has such ordinariness that the presence there of an evil man is the more powerfully

552

felt. It was unusual at the time to go on location when simulation was possible on the back lot; and the film was further admired for the intimations of the murderer's psyche, though these, like the heavy ironies, now seem jejune.

Hired out again, to 20th Century-Fox, Hitchcock made **Lifeboat** (1944), proceeding from a desire to produce a motion picture from limited material – in this case a party adrift at sea, a 'microcosm', as he himself put it. John Steinbeck was invited to write the script, but his efforts proved inadequate and the screenplay was eventually credited to Jo Swerling. On the lifeboat are Kovac (John Hodiak) and other crew-members (William Bendix, Hume Cronyn and the black Canada Lee) of the torpedoed ship; a nurse (Mary Anderson), a millionaire (Henry Hull) and a lacquered and be-minked journalist (Tallulah Bankhead), complete with typewriter. In time they pick up another woman (Heather Angel) with a 'biby', as she calls it, and a German captain (Walter Slezak), whom they christen Willy. They let Willy guide them, and each time he glances surreptitiously at his compass the audience's tensions and suspicions mount. He is, of course, the representative totalitarian, controlled, efficient and calm-in-an-emergency, while the others – a spectrum ranging from the Fascist millionaire to the Communist-inclined Kovac – are in disarray, panicky, self-pitying and self-absorbed. Hitchcock said later that he wanted to show that 'while the democracies were completely disorganised, all the Germans were clearly headed in the same direction. So here was a statement telling the democracies to put their differences aside temporarily . . .' which is an improvement at least on the only other political statement he made in a film – in *Saboteur*, to urge good Americans to look for Nazis in the woodpile. His other comments on the film are as pompous as his direction is expert; he permits no sense of studio-tank or back-projection and although Miss Bankhead is incongruous, both she and Hitchcock know it.

Jean Renoir, less classifiable, had a much harder struggle than Hitchcock. As the maker of *La Grande Illusion* and *La Bête Humaine*, he had no difficulty getting a contract – with 20th Century-Fox, which offered him the 'class' subjects, historical

or European, which Hollywood associated with esteemed directors. He was not interested, especially when he realised that the results would have to conform to the studio's standards – which meant abandoning those methods which had led to his reputation in the first place. Determined to tackle an American subject, he came upon the screenplay of **Swamp Water** (1941), written by Dudley Nichols from a novel by Vereen Bell for John Ford, who had turned it down. Renoir was allowed to go to the Okefenokee region of Georgia to do location work. The film itself indicates that he thought it worthwhile to tell of plain folks against their genuine background, but the screenplay is unequal to the occasion, contrived and, until the climax, blindingly obvious. Even Walter Huston fails to make his character come alive, and Dana Andrews and Anne Baxter are not the screen's most sympathetic lovers. Renoir was at one time removed from the film, when shooting went over schedule, and he was not permitted to do his own editing, which he regretted. He did not work for Zanuck again, and in his memoir sadly quoted Zanuck's opinion of him: 'Renoir has a lot of talent, but he's not one of us.'

In that same memoir Renoir did not mention his experience at Universal, which gave the industry good reason to think again about employing him. The studio had decided that what Deanna Durbin needed at this stage in her career was a European-type movie, and Renoir was given virtual carte blanche, the sole proviso being that she be the central character. He began the film that eventually became *The Amazing Mrs Holliday* (q.v.), concerning Durbin in charge of some Chinese refugee children, but after some weeks of filming he decided that he was dissatisfied with it. He would prefer, he said, to make a modern version of 'The Taming of the Shrew', set in and around a Texas gas station. Both the star and Universal liked the idea, if unsure whether she would be credible as a gas-station attendant; but Renoir himself quickly found that he disliked this idea too and reverted to the original project – which he could not finish since Dudley Nichols had arranged a joint venture at R.K.O. Universal, after six months' filming and no vehicle in sight for its most popular star, were glad to see him go. One of Miss Durbin's writers, Bruce Manning, was given the task of salvaging what he could of the first story. Renoir had, of course, behaved similarly in France over *Partie de Campagne*.

The R.K.O. film, written and produced by himself and Nichols, was **This Land Is Mine** (1943), 'intended to show that life for the citizen of a country occupied by an enemy power was not so simple as Hollywood seemed to think.' That country – unnamed in the film but clearly meant to be France – is at first affected only when teachers are required to tear pages from history books, but when supplies for Germany are blown up hostages are taken. Interest centres on two teaching colleagues (Charles Laughton, Maureen O'Hara) and he, a coward, is forced into bravery. When the Gestapo finally comes for him he is declaiming the Declaration of the Rights of Man – a forgivable ending for local audiences, but when French audiences saw it after the Liberation they laughed, and Renoir was ridiculed by former advocates of his work. Worse errors are the Hollywood-style close-ups of Miss O'Hara and the scenery-chewing performances of Una O'Connor as Laughton's mother and Walter Slezak as the German governor. Laughton, basing his characterisation on Renoir himself, cannot save the film, since Renoir, dis-

trusting his audience, is constantly overstating in an already melodramatic tale – in sum one much inferior to the not dissimilar *The Moon Is Down* (q.v.). The sole indication of subtlety is, surprisingly, the performance of George Sanders as a patriot determined to make concessions to the invaders.

After another long period of inactivity Renoir restored his reputation with **The Southerner** (1945), backed by Robert Hakim and David L. Loew at United Artists, which loathed the film and only took it because Loew had interests in other of their projects. Hakim had offered the screenplay to Renoir, who disliked it; but he admired the book of short stories on which it was based, 'Hold Autumn in Your Hand' by George Sessions Perry, and proceeded to write his own script. It is a wresting-a-living-from-the-soil story, reminiscent of John Ford's rural movies. The touches of melodrama are more in keeping with American taste of the time than with Renoir's French work, but the real failings are elsewhere. The story concerns people who are grindingly poor, but Renoir feels no indignation at their plight. He offers instead affection, a lovely quality but not the one needed. He hardly shows us the anxiety of the young couple (Zachary Scott, Betty Field), but emphasises instead their love and mutual respect for each other. It was not enough to use non-stars and deglamorise them further, though Miss Field is moving as a young woman who has reflected on her lot and come to accept it.

The film won First Prize at the first postwar Venice Festival, and its critical success enabled Renoir to set up **The Diary of a Chambermaid** (1946), envisaged as a vehicle for a friend, Paulette Goddard – whose husband, Burgess Meredith, co-wrote and co-produced with Renoir, as well as performing in the film. It occasioned little interest then and, as with Renoir's other American films, was execrated in France. It has been rehabilitated since, and if flawed by the obvious studio exteriors – even though designed, as with *This Land Is Mine*, by Eugene Lourié – is otherwise among his best work. Octave Mirbeau's novel had long been dear to Renoir, who had echoed it in *La Règle du Jeu*, in the scenes of the servants aping their masters. Celestine (Miss Goddard) is a

Renoir's *Diary of a Chambermaid* gives the chambermaid, Paulette Goddard, a number of piquant adventures – mainly amorous. Here she is between the two chief men in her life – left, Hurd Hatfield, her boss by virtue of his being his mother's son, and right, Francis Lederer, a companion of hers from below stairs.

Paris-born maid whose situation with the family Lanlaire involves her with the vicious Joseph (Francis Lederer), the valet, and the whimsical captain (Meredith) next door. The screenplay follows a dramatised version once done in Paris, and Buñuel's later film (q.v.) follows Renoir's, both of them incorporating Celestine's recollections of earlier employments, but using different ones. In Mirbeau a grandmother encouraged Celestine to amuse her tubercular grandson. Here, Madame Lanlaire (Judith Anderson) wants her to look pretty enough to keep at home her wandering, wayward son, Georges (Hurd Hatfield).

The film begins as a satire on the bourgeoisie: the dominating mistress of the house, whose relationship with the valet is perhaps more intimate than it should be; and the useless master (Reginald Owen), who is sent out on walks or to prune the roses, and is not allowed a word or a penny of his own, although he carries on a petty feud with the retired officer next door. This latter gentleman, lecherous and eccentric, is mothered by his servant (Florence Bates), though if it suits him he locks her up. This playful mood is abandoned when Celestine settles for the valet, his ambitions of more consideration to her than the fact that he is a murderer; and the mood turns black when he uses his whip on the villagers. It should have ended there, with the two lovers riding on, ambition achieved but outcast. However, Celestine turns tail, for a tacked-on 'happy' ending as unconvincing as any in Hollywood history. Somewhere between Mirbeau and Miss Goddard Renoir compromised.

When the film failed Renoir again found himself casting around for work.★ It was now possible for him to return to France, but he wanted to stay in Hollywood – he resided in Los Angeles for the rest of his life – and therefore approached R.K.O. with a view to making low budget films of quality. He found a sympathetic producer here, and R.K.O. offered them a starring vehicle for Joan Bennett, **The Woman on the Beach** (1947); but Renoir had to cope on his own when the producer died, and the original novel – 'None So Blind' by Mitchell Wilson – proved more intractable than he had hoped. The result is a very

★Another project had foundered in 1944, when R.K.O. cancelled *The Temptress* after Jean Gabin had insisted that Marlene Dietrich replace Louise Rainer as his co-star.

ordinary melodrama about a bored, trampy wife (Miss Bennett), her blind, bigoted and selfish husband (Charles Bickford) and a moody marine officer (Robert Ryan). It is not Renoir's worst film, but one without a shred of his character, except that the central situation reflects the pessimism of his previous film. He had reason to be pessimistic, since he would not find work in Hollywood again.

René Clair was more successful in America, by the industry's own standards; but the four films he made there are not among his best. Disillusioned with his experiences in the British studios, he had returned to France in 1939, and had begun work on *Air Pur*, a story of slum children in a summer camp – an idea which had come to him when meeting his own small son at the Gare de Lyon. Shooting was abandoned in August 1939 and most of the unit was mobilised. By the time it would have been possible to resume filming most of the children in the cast had grown too much. Meanwhile Clair signed a contract which called for him to make a film in Hollywood for either R.K.O. or Columbia, and the Ministry of Information discussed with both him and Julien Duvivier the possibility of making French films in Hollywood: that project became impossible after France submitted to Germany's terms, but the two directors were allowed to leave for the U. S.

The first film made by Clair was in fact at Universal, where Joe Pasternak thought he might be the ideal director for Dietrich. Clair was attracted to Norman Krasna's screenplay, since it is set in the then French city of New Orleans, in the nineteenth century, and his sense of irony is apparent in the otherwise wan **The Flame of New Orleans** (1941). He capitalises on Dietrich's lack of range by allowing her to use her best expression – a look of surprise. Here it indicates her astonishment that her imposture (as a countess) should be accepted so easily; and he photographs her as did von Sternberg, with veils.

The film's failure left Clair free to instigate his next project, **I Married a Witch** (1942), based on Thorne Smith's last, unfinished comic novel, 'The Passionate Witch'. A chance remark to Preston Sturges brought him and the project to Paramount, who thought it ideal for its new star, Veronica Lake – whom Clair accepted on Sturges's urging. In the event the studio disliked the finished film and sold it to United Artists when that company was desperate for product. Presumably both were aware of the film's commercial worth – i.e. not much, since whimsy was usually unsaleable, though the names of Lake and Fredric March were. In fact whimsy began to enjoy a vogue during the war years, and like Duvivier's *Flesh and Fantasy* (q.v.) this film was highly regarded. Since the March character is candidate in a gubernatorial election a political aura is established, but the promised satire does not materialise and we are left with the tiresome tale of a respectable man pursued by a sexy vamp. Since she had been a witch and is now a ghost the film recalls Clair's earlier excursions into the supernatural, *Le Fantôme du Moulin Rouge*; the level of humour is little higher.

United Artists were sufficiently pleased with the result to ask Clair to stay, and he made **It Happened Tomorrow** (1943), which he himself thought the best of his American films. Of the three comedies it has the soundest basic idea – a newspaper reporter (Dick Powell) magically finds himself the recipient of the next day's paper, which enables him to make some wonderful scoops and become very rich via his bets at the race track. The early editions continue, but on the third day he reads of his own death and nothing, it seems, can prevent him from being at the appointed place at the appointed time. Powell's smugness harms both the tension and the humour, and as written by Clair and Dudley Nichols the screenplay is superior to the direction. Nichols led Clair to an independent company releasing through 20th Century-Fox, and he wrote the screenplay of **And Then There Were None** (1945), based on the most celebrated of Agatha Christie's thrillers, 'Ten Little Niggers'. Since the story is taller than tall – ten guests are mysteriously killed during one night at an island mansion – some humour is injected, without the characters being any less flat than as left by Mrs Christie. The voice of the dead host on a record is that of Alfred Hitchcock, an in-joke which few filmgoers of the time could have appreciated. However, the humour is not taken far enough: thus when the doctor (Walter Huston) observes 'but this knife I removed from the back of the victim

means only one thing' everyone concerne[d] seems to be in dead earnest. Clair returne[d] to France, and although R.K.O. had [a] financial interest in his next film, *Le Silenc[e] est d'Or* (q.v.), he never seriously consid[e]red working in English again.

Fritz Lang had been long enough an[d] successful enough in Hollywood for th[e] industry to consider him 'one of us' though his reputation had dimmed sinc[e] the days of *Fury* and *You Only Live Once* He worked for two years on a Wester[n] saga, which he saw as the New Worl[d] equivalent of the Nibelungen, to be calle[d] *Americana*; and when the project was aban[-] doned Zanuck, having noticed Lang's in[-] terest in the old West, offered **The Retur[n] of Frank James** (1940), with Henry Fond[a] repeating his role of the younger Jame[s] brother, and then **Western Union** (1941) with Robert Young and Randolph Scot[t] leading the expedition into Indian Countr[y] to wire up the cables. Both are unpreten[-] tious and pleasing in their background au[-] thenticity – in Technicolor; the latter ha[s] more exuberance and a much better scrip[t] by Robert Carson.

Both films might have been made b[y] any good Hollywood journeyman, an[d] Lang's next three films are shaky con[-] tributions to the war effort. The worst o[f] the three is that on which he had complet[e] autonomy, **Hangmen Also Die** (1943) backed by Arnold Pressburger at Unite[d] Artists. As a Resistance story it starts wit[h] an excellent theme – German reprisals i[n] Prague after the assassination of Reichs[-] protektor Heydrich, known as 'the hang[-] man' – but, as Theodore Strauss put it i[n] *The New York Times*, 'as it tries to echo th[e] anguished heroism of a captive people i[t] fails badly both in the script and the per[-] formance.' The script, which contains th[e] classic film-Nazi expression, 'Ve haf vay[s] of making you talk,' is by Lang and 'Bert' Brecht, who were both indignant whe[n] the American Screenwriters' Guild (afte[r] arbitration) insisted on sole credit going t[o] John Wexley, a German-speaking write[r] whom they had brought in to help the[m] with the English. One would hav[e] thought that they would rather have bee[n] glad to let him take the blame. Both **Ma[n] Hunt** (1941) and **The Ministry of Fea[r]** (1944) are set mainly in London, an[d] though they were made respectively fo[r] 20th and Paramount it is a London eve[r] more phoney than usual. The films also have in common particularly uninteresting leads – Walter Pidgeon and Joan Bennett in the former, Ray Milland and Marjorie Reynolds in the latter – and their source in exceptionally strong writers – Geoffrey Household's 'Rogue Male' and the 'entertainment' by Graham Greene. Lang, returning to the thriller genre, is at least at ease, and both films are entertaining. *Man Hunt*, made before the U.S. entered the War, has an anti-Nazi fervour missing from *Hangmen Also Die*; its subject is a Nazi pursuit of a big game hunter who had intended to assassinate Hitler at Berchtesgarten. The film introduces a prostitute, the role played by Miss Bennett – her profession, of course, is never mentioned, though we can tell from her outfit and the saucy way she holds a cigarette – and has many new adventures for the beleaguered hero in London. Lang ensures that the very air of the city holds menace, and that is true of the film of Greene's novel, even though the portrait of a weary wartime London has gone: the best of the film is, however, from Greene – the fête, the seance, the organisation called 'Mothers of Free Nations', which is clearly up to something more sinister. Lang, who accepted the assignment after making an offer himself for the novel, disliked the changes made by the producer-scenarist, Seton I. Miller, but Greene proves stronger than both Miller and Lang.

Lang in turn retrieved his reputation with **The Woman in the Window** (1944), also a thriller, and the only reservations in the reviews concerned the ending, when the nightmare situation in which Edward G. Robinson finds himself turns out to be just that, a dream; but Lang later defended the denouement by claiming that the plot developments would otherwise have been implausible. He fought the producer-scenarist, Nunnally Johnson, over it, and managed to incorporate the apt little coda suggesting that the dream would come true. The film is more typical of Lang's best work than Johnson's, his misanthropy seldom better expressed than when Joan Bennett says off-handedly about searching the corpse, 'It had to be done, didn't it?' Bennett smiles and smiles and plays the villain memorably, while Robinson's skill at playing mild, trapped men should not be taken for granted. They

would play similar roles for Lang in *Scarlet Street* (q. v.), produced independently; this film was made by a new company, International (q.v.), releasing through R.K.O.

The postwar rush to independence began with the small group of individuals working during the War. It must be said that Disney stands apart, and of the others of this period only Hitchcock was a success by industry standards. Wilder would be similarly regarded; the former prestige of Capra and Sturges would be remembered by other producers and directors anxious for autonomy, and they would recall what had happened to Welles, one of the most gifted men to work in Hollywood. Directors did not necessarily do their best work when granted independence, but they often managed to assert in it their individuality; as critics praised *The Woman in the Window* and *The Southerner*, they reflected on the comparatively recent feeble work of two directors once greatly esteemed. The industry might not want Renoir, Welles or Sturges, and it never cared greatly for Lang; but about this time studio executives began to concede that Chaplin and Capra were not the only directors who might be permitted to mould their films as they saw fit.

The high regard in which Fritz Lang is now held was not his during much of his career, and he had been some years in the critical wilderness when he made *The Woman in the Window*. Edward G. Robinson is a professor accosted by a model, Joan Bennett. 'I'm not married, I've no designs on you. One drink is all I require,' she says, and in her apartment he is equally matter of fact, 'I was warned against the siren-call of adventure.'

22

The British at War

THE BRITISH cinema grew up during the War and, as has doubtless been remarked elsewhere, it needed to. In the gravity of the situation – the proximity of the enemy, the Blitz, the successful invasion of most of Europe – audiences demanded either better escapism or more reflective content, and as far as the latter was concerned, the industry began to answer their needs when it re-adjusted after the Blitz. Although Hollywood met the challenge of the War more immediately, it was not until 1945 that it produced any contemporary subjects of lasting worth: yet it is one of the curiosities of film history that American films, when they seem to change with the passing of the years, become either better or worse, while on re-examination British films, if they change at all, only become worse. The tendency of British critics to overpraise local product, as the only mass-cinema alternative to the almighty Hollywood, was natural enough in peacetime, but under wartime conditions the tone became shriller and more urgent. A great many British films were overpraised, but a great number of hitherto promising talents were thereby encouraged to do their best work (as it turned out).

Though the declaration of war in September 1939 closed cinemas for fear of air-raids, they were soon re-opened in the cause of maintaining morale – and the increased attendances, to continue throughout the War, proved the justification for this move. Work in the studios was also temporarily interrupted, to the chagrin of Korda, who on his enforced departure for Hollywood left as legacy **The Lion Has Wings** (1939), conceived on 2 September, the day after the Germans marched into Poland, and released just two months later. Three directors, Michael Powell, Brian Desmond Hurst and Adrian Brunel, worked simultaneously, and Korda, uncredited, directed Ralph Richardson, as an R.A.F. officer, and Merle Oberon, as his wife who joins the Red Cross. The G.P.O. Film Unit was engaged to shoot documentary material, and the newsreel companies were raided, along with *Fire Over England*, for Elizabeth I's Tilbury speech, and a 1937 short called *The Gap*, which imagined an air-raid on London. The plot – dog-fights in the sky and tensions in the Ops Room – is dull, but the long introduction is a valuable example of propaganda, contrasting Britain and Germany, with Hitler ranting while the King and Queen sing 'Underneath the Chestnut Tree', and German pilots being briefed 'in striking contrast to the friendly atmosphere which is Britain's way'. The film cost £30,000, and Korda used his last life insurance policy to complete it; the British were not grateful, but the Americans were, doubtless because it was so much more immediate than newspaper reports.

There was no other serious approach to the War for a while, though there were a good number of Nazis to be seen on British screens – played by the familiar villains of British comedies, and indeed in their customary roles, revealed in reel ten to have swastikas on their underwear. Scriptwriters reworked the same old plots, only our heroes rounded up fifth columnists instead of gangsters, and that was, as they put it, one in the eye for old Hitler! In Walter Forde's **Sailors Three** (1940), Tommy Trinder captures a German battleship; in Forde's **The Ghost Train** (1941) Arthur Askey captures gun-runners, who have become Nazis since the original play and earlier film version; in Marcel Varnel's **Let George Do It** (1940), George Formby rounds up a spy ring in Norway; while in John Paddy Carstairs's **Spare a Copper** (1941), he uncovers a sabotage plot in Liverpool; and in Varnel's **The Ghost of St Michael's** (1940), Will Hay discovers that the ghost is really a Nazi agent. Hay, turning director, worked with Basil Dearden on **The Black Sheep of Whitehall** (1941) and **The Goose Steps Out** (1942), respectively finding spies in a nursing-home and being parachuted into Germany to steal a secret weapon. These harmless comic-cuts were made either by Ealing, where Formby had been joined by Hay and Trinder, the latter a brash newcomer from the music-hall, or by Gainsborough, which hoped that the diminutive, chirpy Askey would take the place of the defecting Hay. Askey's best film is **Charley's (Big-Hearted) Aunt** (1940), directed by Forde, a distant cousin of the play by Brandon Thomas, while the best wartime films of Hay and Formby also had nothing to do with the War – respectively **My Learned Friend** (1943), directed by Hay and Dearden, with Hay as the intended sixth victim of a homicidal maniac, and **Turned Out Nice Again** (1941), directed by Varnel, with Formby as overseer in a ladies' underwear factory.

    Cottage to Let (1941) concerns an unworldly inventor (Leslie Banks), who lives in a Scottish village which turns out to be a hive of espionage activity: everyone behaves suspiciously, and Anthony Asquith always cuts away before we learn why. Carol Reed does something similar with **Night Train to Munich** (1940), taking it at express speed. The Nazi agents include Felix Aylmer as a Hampstead dentist and Rex Harrison as a German officer, except that he is really on the British side. Their concern is a Czech scientist whom the Nazis want to recapture, and like *The Lady Vanishes*, also written by Launder and Gilliat, the climax takes place aboard a train. As in that film, Margaret Lockwood is the bewildered heroine, while Basil Radford and Naunton Wayne are again the foolhardy Britishers abroad.

    The formula was quickly set: **Pimpernel Smith** (1941) also has a British mastermind who is not what he seems, and who at times dons Nazi uniform. Its other ingredients include doltish and Achtung-ing

German officers; a trap to be evaded in the last reel; and a propaganda message for Allied audiences. There is much to be said against turning war into a Richard Hannay-type adventure, but this one is as disarming as it is witty, due in no small part to the direction of Leslie Howard and his playing of the seemingly woolly-minded professor. Howard had disliked being a Hollywood leading man, and had returned to Britain to participate in the war effort. His presence in the British studios gave a lift to the entire industry, while his popularity in the U.S. ensured a hearing there for the propaganda contained within his films. However, **The First of the Few** (1941) has to work hard for contemporary relevance since it is a tribute to R. J. Mitchell, the designer of the Spitfire aircraft, who had died in 1937. Accordingly it features a sequence in which German industrialists in 1934 boast of their supremacy and of the new Chancellor, Herr Hitler. Howard again played the lead and directed, but he served only in the latter capacity on **The Gentle Sex** (1943), bringing deft Hollywood-learnt skills to this composite portrait of the women's army, the A.T.S. The film takes lightly the heartache and bloodymindedness but is otherwise honest (i.e. without comic stereotypes or false heroism), and it has performances to match the title by Rosamund John, Lilli Palmer, Joan Greenwood

The wartime Resistance thrillers were all much of a muchness, but *Pimpernel Smith* is an exception. Its subject is the spiriting away of prisoners from the Nazis in the summer of 1939. Few films of the period knew how to end, since the conflict that was their backdrop continued, but in this one Pimpernel simply disappeared in a cloud of smoke, his voice on the soundtrack assuring the Germans that he would be back. Here Leslie Howard, who also directed, is on the verge of disappearing.

and Joyce Howard. Leslie Howard speaks the commentary and may be seen in the opening shot – which was a last glimpse for audiences, since, after a government-sponsored lecture tour of Spain and Portugal, his plane was shot down over the Bay of Biscay.

Posthumously shown was **The Lamp Still Burns** (1943), solely credited to Maurice Elvey, who had worked on *The Gentle Sex* – and this is similarly a recruiting poster. It is based on an autobiographical book by Monica Dickens, 'One Pair of Feet', and concerns a young woman (Rosamund John) who gives up a lucrative job as an architect for a life of drudgery as a nurse. The War is hardly mentioned, and the plot chiefly concerns the nurse's rebellion against hospital discipline; her dedication eventually triumphs, with no suggestion that she will marry the winsome Stewart Granger when the War is over. Nevertheless the film is typical of Howard's approach, and the sober style is his rather than Elvey's, which tended towards the vulgar and pedestrian. Together the four films demonstrate that the former Hollywood matinee idol might have become an important force in leading the British cinema towards greater honesty and realism.

Howard also appeared in **The 49th Parallel** (1941), along with Laurence Olivier, Raymond Massey, Anton Walbrook, Eric Portman 'and the music of Ralph Vaughan Williams'. Although dedicated to the people of Canada it was aimed at American audiences, and was the most ambitious of the films to do so. Retitled *The Invaders* and distributed by Columbia, unfortunately it was not seen in the U.S. till three months after the War was over. It was a jinxed film from the start, for the Ministry of Information, having been allotted half a million pounds for such ventures, withdrew after an expenditure of £60,000 (and its experience resulted in it spending but little, and gingerly, in future). Part of the trouble was that the female lead, Elisabeth Bergner, after filming locations in Canada, declined to return for the interiors in Britain, preferring the safety of the U.S. Glynis Johns replaced her, after the completion money had been advanced by J. Arthur Rank, who thereby again moved towards production. Michael Powell directed, from a screenplay by Rodney Ackland and Emeric Pressburger, and there is probably no more rabid propaganda movie in existence. This propaganda is sometimes cleverly contrived – as, for instance, when the 49th Parallel is referred to as 'the only undefended frontier in the world'. A group of Nazis, inhuman, Führer-fixated – in fact, a stranded U-boat crew, led by their even more fanatical commander (Portman) – journey across Canada. There they meet a carefree French-Canadian trapper (Olivier); a Hutterite leader (Walbrook), who refuses to declare for Hitler by pointing out that his community left Germany for racial and religious tolerance; and an Indian expert (Howard), who chatters on about a tribe whose barbarities remind him of the Nazis.

Michael Powell (b. 1905) had begun in films with Rex Ingram at his studios in Nice, and he had directed over twenty quota-quickies in Britain before *The Edge of the World* (1937) brought him to the attention of Korda. Because of the similarity of setting he was assigned to **The Spy in Black** (1939), set in the Orkneys, and to help with the script Korda brought in a fellow-Hungarian, Emeric Pressburger (b. 1902), thus initiating a partnership that was to endure for over fifteen years – with joint credit as producers, writers and directors, though Powell usually functioned alone as director. This, their first collaboration, was a far-fetched espionage drama, set in the First World War, and their second, **Contraband** (1940), was more of the same, also with Conrad Veidt and Valerie Hobson but set in contemporary London. *The 49th Parallel* was their first prestige film, but it was **One of Our Aircraft Is Missing** (1942) which made the reputation of the team – incredibly, for this is a 'Boy's Own' adventure about the Dutch Resistance helping a grounded R.A.F. crew, consisting of the usual spectrum of British types. That a country fighting for its existence should offer such lunatic fictions almost beggars belief.

Michael Balcon's Ealing Studios offered two even worse films, both naval dramas. **Ships with Wings** (1941) was directed, ineptly, by Sergei Nolbandov, a former writer who otherwise only produced a few films for the company. This one concerns a disgraced civil pilot who joins a run-down airline on a spy-ridden Mediterranean sland, and who in wartime redeems himself by bombing the German dam – a model so atrocious that Noël Coward regarded it as one of the laughs of the War. The film purports to be a tribute to the Fleet Air Arm, while **The Big Blockade** (1942) hopes to be a semi-documentary account of the British Navy's blockade against Germany. As directed and part-written by Charles Frend, it attempts vignettes of life under the Nazis. 'A fantasy for us – a hideous reality for the conquered nations,' says the commentator, journalist Frank Owen, but the whole film is fantasy. The American journalist Quentin Reynolds also appears, to assure the British that the U.S.A. is with them one hundred per cent – and to remind us that those films not aimed at the Americans were meant to cheer up local audiences.

Ealing had a better moment with **Went the Day Well?** (1942), directed by Cavalcanti from a screenplay by John Dighton, Diana Morgan and Angus MacPhail, all of whom added so much to the original story, by Graham Greene, that the latter refused credit. Perhaps his true reason was that as directed the story simply strains credibility. It is possible that the situation did not seem so improbable then, when 'Careless Talk Costs Lives' was an everyday expression, and quislings were thought to be lurking under every bush but, assuming that a group of Germans could take over an English country village for forty-eight hours, how did they ever get there in the first place? They, of course, are beastly, but the film is interesting in that it takes a while for the British to become heroic, and also because it is accurate in sentiment, as in its comment by one evacuee (Harry Fowler), 'We won't 'arf give those blinkin' jerries the works.' The producer, Michael Balcon, later expressed surprise that it had never been recognised as the important film he believed it to be.

Pastor Hall (1940) deserves a mention as a tale of the Resistance in Germany. Poor in every department, including the direction of Roy Boulting, and solidly British despite the 'herrs' and 'fräuleins' of the dialogue, it nevertheless demands attention for sincerity and for the performance of Wilfrid Lawson in the title role, a priest whose opposition to Nazi doctrine leads him to a concentration camp and death. The source is a play, based on fact,

by Ernst Toller, a socialist who left Germany in 1932, and who committed suicide in 1939, just before a translation appeared, by Stephen Spender (who is not credited on the film). Asquith made **Freedom Radio** (1940) on the same subject, specifically concerning Hitler's doctor (Clive Brook) who runs a clandestine radio station to apprise Germans of the truth, and who until the last minute is misunderstood by his wife (Diana Wynyard), an actress who stage-manages Hitler's rallies. Sober and well-made, it is nevertheless much less effective than *Pastor Hall*.

As far as the other European nations are concerned, it would seem in retrospect that Britain and Hollywood were in competition to see who could make the most idiotic Resistance film. The ingredients were almost interchangeable: the goodies (the occupied people) versus the baddies (the Germans); an ammunition dump to be blown up; a pilot to be smuggled across the lines; hostages to be sacrificed; and quislings round every corner. The British tended to like a note of hope: **Tomorrow We Live** (1942), set in France and directed by George King, and **The Day Will Dawn** (1942), set in Norway and directed by Harold French. In the latter the hostages, in prison, listen for the sound of the firing squad. But what is this? Boats bounding across the sea? A British commando raid? Naturally. The villains are shot, and our British heroes and the entire population of Lungefjord decamp, to spend the rest of the War in Britain.

A year later a note of reality had crept in: 'The truth is that a nation will live only as long as it has people ready to die' are the last words of **The Silver Fleet**, directed by Vernon Sewell and Gordon Wellesley with the co-operation of the Royal Netherlands government and the Royal Navy.

The public, at least, loved **Dangerous Moonlight** (1941), if mainly for the 'Warsaw Concerto', composed by Richard Addinsell with no illusions as to its merits but which was nevertheless a huge factor in the wartime expansion of interest in 'serious' music. The star is Anton Walbrook, with his lionlike but soulful presence and hint of temperament – and the conjunction of him and the music suggests a great romance; but this is a numb, small film, typical of its director, Brian Desmond Hurst, and of Terence Young, who wrote the story and the screenplay. Wal-brook plays a shell-shocked pilot and pian-ist, remembering both Warsaw and an American journalist (Sally Gray); later, in New York, she tries to convince him that he can serve his country better by ham-mering away at that concerto than by join-ing the Free Polish Air Force.

This England (1941) is a panorama of English life – retitled *Our Heritage* for Scot-tish cinemas – as described by squire (John Clements) and labourer (Emlyn Williams) to a visiting American (Constance Cum-mings). The magic of cinema takes them back to 1066, 1588, 1805 and 1918, but there is not much magic in what happens, as Clements and Williams overact their forebears and Miss Cummings variously impersonates their ladies. Williams wrote the dreadful script, and the direction by David Macdonald is of the same level. **The Demi-Paradise** (1943) is an affectionate account of the British at war as viewed by a visiting Russian engineer (Laurence Olivier) and as written by a Russian, Ana-tole de Grunwald, who also produced. It is pleasing enough on its Home Counties upper-crust level, but is neither informa-tive nor satiric – except about a village pageant, which has Margaret Rutherford and Joyce Grenfell as eager participants. Olivier has a discreet romance with a ship-builder's daughter (Penelope Dudley Ward) and makes a speech in which, as Richard Winnington put it, 'he gives us just that line we love, a deprecatory state-ment of our national faults, as a prelude to the big boost which is the absolute peak of inverted smugness.' Since the film was designed as propaganda for the U.S.A., if not the U.S.S.R., it is a shame that it is another which did not arrive there till well after the War, meaninglessly retitled *Adventure for Two*. Anthony Asquith directed. As defiantly English, though not about the War, is his **Quiet Wedding** (1941), adapted and opened out by de Grunwald and Terence Rattigan from a matinee play by Esther McCracken. Mar-garet Lockwood and Derek Farr, as the couple thwarted of a quiet wedding, are colourless, but rendering the mild humour are Marjorie Fielding as the impervious, managing mother, and such players as Athene Seyler, Peggy Ashcroft, Roland Culver, David Tomlinson, Martita Hunt and Margaret Rutherford.

Thunder Rock (1942) proves that better the approach patriotic than the ap-proach philosophic. Robert Ardrey's play was first presented in New York, by the Group Theatre, but it was its success in London which led to its being filmed, with Roy Boulting directing and M-G-M par-ticipating. A young man (Michael Red-grave) has taken refuge on a lighthouse in the Atlantic, having failed to make either the British public or its newspaper prop-rietors aware of the dangers of Fascism. Holed up, and away from the apathy of his countrymen, he conjures up spirits from the names he finds in an ancient ship's log-book – drowned people fleeing from the tyranny of Europe, as represented by the Industrial Revolution, medical bigotry in Vienna and anti-women's suffrage. The spirits realise that they should have stayed to fight, which makes Redgrave resolve to return. This actor gives his usual perform-ance when faced with a moral or emotional dilemma, which is to gaze soulfully at some object just out of camera range; but there is a good, brief appearance by James Mason, as an old friend, and a better and longer one by Frederick Valk as the Aus-trian doctor. Mr Valk was Jewish, and we are reminded that Ardrey ignores the more important issue of racial prejudice; but what renders the piece meretricious is that though it aches with concern it is of the wise-after-the-event kind.

We would not expect it to compete with **Major Barbara** (1941) in brilliance of ideas but nor would we expect this film of Shaw's play to be one of the most stimulat-ing of the war years, since his truths stand revealed as those of a late nineteenth-century reformer. These concern econo-mics rather than politics, as expressed in his preface: 'to wit, that the greatest of our evils, and the worst of our crimes is pover-ty, and that our first duty, to which every other consideration must be sacrificed, is not to be poor.' Eventually the armaments manufacturer, Undershaft, is revealed as one of the privileged who has accepted the world's values in order to provide for the other half, while his daughter Barbara, in a plea for Shaw's new morality, is encour-aged to find 'the way to life through the factory of death' rather than through orga-nised religion. In all of Shaw's plays the confrontation of the upper and lower orders provides some of the best fun and the best argument – even if, on examination, the latter seems specious – and unfortunately here the poor are played with too many a nudge and a wink by Emlyn Williams and Robert Newton, as respectively the hypocritical repentant and the genuine one. It is not an easy piece to handle, with its diverse moods and locations – bound only by the author's rhetoric – and if the scenes with the Undershaft family emerge as the best that is not entirely due to the acting, since it is of many styles. Rex Harrison as Dolly and David Tree as Charles, both playing in impeccable Shaftesbury Avenue manner, at least belong on the same 'stage' as Marie Lohr as Lady Brittomart. Sybil Thorndike is outstanding as the warm and wily Salvation Army general. Along with Mr Newton, the calamity is Robert Morley's Undershaft – the actor was not only too young for the role but played it as a white-bearded, fanatical evangelist. Wendy Hiller as Barbara entirely misses the humour of her priggishness. To blame is Gabriel Pascal who, after the success of *Pygmalion*, got backing again from the Rank-owned General Film Distributors, plus an investment of £20,000 from Shaw himself. Pascal decided to direct, and indeed takes credit, though most of the work was done by David Lean, as then untried, and Harold French who, returning after having been fired, was therefore able to demand minimal interference. The original ten-week schedule doubled, as did the cost – due also to the fact that French brought in Harrison to replace the original Dolly (Andrew Osborne) and to constant air-raids; finally the film did miserably at the box office.

A filmed play much admired was **Gaslight** (1940), from Patrick Hamilton's long-running thriller about a long-time spinster now adrift in an increasingly unhappy marriage and uncertain whether she is going mad. In the role of the scheming husband Anton Walbrook is basically manic, but Diana Wynyard is distracted rather than distraught; moreover the piece loses its effectiveness because the atmosphere of claustrophobia has been lost to make it cinematic, and the wife has become much younger, to accommodate the box office. Thorold Dickinson, directing, has unfortunately concentrated on Victoriana at the expense of tension.

Conversely, **Kipps** (1941), despite dreadful studio exteriors and somewhat excessive Cecil Beaton costumes, is otherwise excellent. The theme of Wells's novel, that kind hearts are worth more than coronets, has dated now, despite the fact that the snobbish Walsinghams are sympathetically treated. Michael Redgrave does not have the right levity for Kipps (and his plebeian accent wobbles), but he is good when trying to improve his knowledge and learning to move into society. As the girl he hopes to marry Diana Wynyard looks and plays like the goddess he thinks she is. Carol Reed directed and Edward Black produced – from a script by Launder and Gilliat – for 20th Century-Fox, one of a series of films this team made for Fox under the auspices of Gainsborough.

Another is **The Young Mr Pitt** (1942), occasioned by the success of Korda's Hollywood film about Nelson, *That Hamilton Woman* (q.v.). It has the gall to start with the elder Pitt defending the American Revolution, and does not stop proselytising till the end, when Pitt makes his last public speech: 'Let us hope that England, having saved herself by her energy, may save Europe by her example.' In between Launder and Gilliat are nothing if not partial: Pitt is meant to be Churchill, and his accession to power to parallel Churchill's in 1940, with the obvious conclusions to be drawn between the belligerent Pitt and the mediocre Addison. This does more than justice to Churchill, whose position in politics before Munich was not comparable to Pitt's, and it does less than justice to Pitt, who cleverly kept England out of European involvement for some years. Nothing is shown of Pitt the appeaser, or of his treaties with Russia and Prussia; at no point is it suggested that Britain is not alone against the devouring might of Napoleon. Such single-mindedness extends to Robert Donat, who makes of this Prime Minister a well-meaning, self-confident and honourable man, with only his cynicism to represent the vices and shortcomings noted by contemporaries. The wartime coalition dictated no mention of Whig or Tory, so we are left to guess at the beliefs of 'Mr Pitt's party' and 'Mr Fox's party' – except that Robert Morley's flamboyant, petulant Fox is portrayed as untrustworthy. As the vain aspirant to Pitt's heart, Phyllis Calvert is toothsomely cloying, but there are good performances by Raymond Lovell as George III; Max Adrian as Sheridan, a snake-tongued charmer; and Albert Lieven as Talleyrand, as Talleyrand ever is in movies – sly, smart and transparent. Most notably, Reed's direction is both economic and elegant.

Among the other historical propaganda films are **The Prime Minister** (1941), Thorold Dickinson's sober study of Disraeli, with John Gielgud in that role, and Diana Wynyard as his wife; **Atlantic Ferry** (1941), also produced by Max Wilder for Warner Bros., directed by Walter Forde, with Michael Redgrave building the first steamship to cross the Atlantic for the eventuality that 'Britain and the United States should be united against a common enemy'; and **Penn of Pennsylvania** (1941), sincere but foolishly scripted, directed by Lance Comfort with Clifford Evans as Penn.

Another British historical, **The Great Mr Handel** (1942), was Rank's second whole-hearted involvement in production. He wanted to make a religious film, but did not want to lose money, the evident concomitant. Having, therefore, no clear aim other than to raise the tone of the cinema, he consulted Norman Walker, director of his previous venture, *The Turn of the Tide*. A contributor to that had been L. duGarde Peach, best known for his radio plays for children – and one of these, transcribed, would provide uplift, thought Walker, with himself directing and Wilfrid Lawson, star of the earlier occasion, playing Handel. The result is effortlessly superior to the European attempts of the previous decade to make romances from the lives of Schubert, Beethoven and Tchaikovsky. These films have in common a protagonist who loves music so much that everything else is subsidiary; but in Handel's case the consequent woes are not amatory, but concern royal displeasure, lack of commissions, debts and personal unpopularity – and these matters are handled with more tact, taste and truth than were usually found in the movie lives of the great. Contemporary appraisals concentrated on the music, the art direction by Sidney Gausden, the colour photography of Claude Friese-Greene and Jack Cardiff, and Lawson's lovable-bear-

at-heart Handel. Business at home was good, and in the U.S. above average for a British film, though Rank, in deciding to use Technicolor and two players with reputations – if small – in America (Elizabeth Allen played Mrs Cibber), had hoped for more.

The script takes pains to point out that, though born a German, Handel preferred the British way, and something similar is the sole proposition of **The Life and Death of Colonel Blimp** (1943) – incidentally, the second of Britain's seven wartime features in Technicolor. Messrs Powell and Pressburger are again very certain of the beastliness of the Hun, if allowing a few good ones, represented through three generations by Anton Walbrook. 'You are fighting for your very existence against the most devilish invention of the human brain – Nazism,' he tells Colonel Blimp (Roger Livesey) in the third part of this chronicle. The first episode, set just after the Boer War, has at its base a good idea, with Blimp in Berlin to negotiate a lessening of anti-British propaganda, but the two that follow prove pointless. Powell and Pressburger juggle with such intriguing matters as the nature of the British, Anglo-German relations and the mentality of the professional soldier, but without having anything to say about any of them. The length (163 minutes), the settings by Alfred Junge, the connection with David Low's newspaper cartoon Blimp – though limited to the physical – and an impression of seriousness, brought a modicum of approval.

In trying to explain the British to themselves and others the documentarist Humphrey Jennings could say more in five minutes than Powell in as many hours. **The First Days** (1939) is a typically perceptive and wide-ranging account of Britain at war, starting with that sunny Sunday when Chamberlain announced the beginning of hostilities, and concentrating on London's preparations for the coming bombardment. Though the direction is credited to Cavalcanti, he was in fact only the producer and Jennings's imprint is stronger than that of his two co-directors, Pat Jackson and Harry Watt. Also in two reels, and apparently co-directed with Stewart McAllister, **Listen to Britain** (1942) is a medley of sounds and pictures meant to illustrate twenty-four hours of life in wartime Britain for American audiences. Munitions workers, miners, servicemen and teachers go about their daily tasks, and a Londoner walks to his office past bomb-damage. Their routines are set to the tunes which Jennings used so eloquently in most of his films, from 'Roll Out the Barrel' at the Palais de Dance to soldiers on a train chorusing 'Home on the Range'. In the factory lunch-break Flanagan and Allen sing 'Round the Back of the Arches' while, at the National Gallery, Myra Hess plays Mozart, her pages turned by an airman while the Queen and Kenneth Clark look on. Mozart continues over views of Trafalgar Square, factories and a field of waving corn till replaced, in diminuendo, by 'Rule, Britannia'. (Jennings's fellow-documentarists did not approve. Their work, John Grierson had stated in 1937, arose not so much from an 'affection' for film but from 'an affection for national education', and one of their number, Edgar Anstey wrote – in *The Spectator* – that 'it will be a disaster if [*Listen to Britain*] is sent overseas'.)

The record that Jennings left of that war is the best available to us – from any film maker, from any country. He saw his job as a morale-booster, but his patriotism was subservient to his interest in people. His portraits of Britain indicate that it was a good place in which to live, but his genius is precisely in the selection, the juxtaposition and the length of his images. His work for the B.B.C. – at the time he began in films – eventually gave birth to **Words for Battle** (1940), an attempt to match the appearance of wartime Britain with spoken sentiment. Laurence Olivier speaks the verse, which moves from Milton and Browning to Blake, with 'Jerusalem' accompanied by evacuees first being herded away and then playing in 'England's green and pleasant land'. London devastated by the Blitz is accompanied by Kipling's poem to the effect that the British have learnt to hate, and the Gettysburg Address by tanks moving past the Lincoln Memorial in Parliament Square. **London Can Take It** (1940) is not a documentary about the Blitz, but a celebration of the British spirit at the time. It shows people walking to work through the rubble and broken glass, clearing up the debris, Civil Defence workers being trained in salvage operation. It is not a film

about nobility but sweetness, not about bravery but doggedness. **Heart of Britain** (1941) is a companion piece, set in the North and Midlands at the time their cities were being bombed, and it emphasises two of Jennings's beliefs – that the obligatory, morale-boosting shots of the King and Queen must be as brief as possible, and that in the midst of chaos orchestras must be seen to play and choirs to sing. At 36 minutes **The Silent Village** (1943) is longer than most of his films, and they are among the most moving in the history of cinema.

The village concerned is in the Welsh valleys, and it is a mining community – and so, a foreword tells us, was Lidice, the Bohemian village obliterated by the Germans in revenge for the assassination of Heydrich, the Nazi governor. Jennings does not identify the enemy, which, beyond a few uniformed men briefly seen, exists only as a loudspeaker on a car. Similar reticence is applied to the villagers, and destruction amounts to a burst of gunfire, a burning building and a stream littered with furniture.

A Diary for Timothy (1945) is a companion piece to *The First Days*, being an anthology of events in Britain and Europe from D-Day to Christmas 1944, when the outcome was no longer in doubt. The less emotional (I speak of effect, not of intention) and evocative films still indicate skill and sympathy of a high order: **The Eighty Days** (1945), the story of the Flying Bomb, and **A Defeated People** (1946), an essay on the British zone of Germany. **The True Story of Lili Marlene** (1944) becomes, with its concluding shot of the grave of the Unknown Soldier, a plea for an end to wars; it is nevertheless interesting as documentary, but the 'acted' scenes do not indicate that Jennings could have moved towards the fiction film. As much may be said of **The Cumberland Story** (1947), though in this case his participants are mining and union officials playing themselves. The film itself is eloquent on the long-lasting divisions within that industry, and it is clear, despite the supposed objectivity, where Jennings's sympathies lie. Perhaps, after the Socialist government took office in 1945, he felt he needed a breathing space. He eventually decided to move his film-making career in a different direction, and was scouting locations in

The British at War

Humphrey Jennings was the only major film-maker to emerge from that misguided movement, the British documentarists. His one feature-length film *Fires Were Started* is a tribute to firemen, whose bravery is all the more moving because they are unaware of it: they are not even particularly aware of saving London, but are merely 'doing their bit'.

Greece when he died on Poros in a fall in 1950. It was appropriate, since he had hymned Britain so brilliantly, that his last film, commissioned for the Festival of Britain, should again be on that subject. **Family Portrait** (1951) has a modest commentary; its choice of men to exemplify the country's quality consists of engineers rather than poets; and the images are as much of town as of country. The ending does not eschew cliché, but transforms it, suggesting a world civilisation, since the British came from many parts of Europe and their truths from Greece, Italy and Israel.

Jennings left one feature-length documentary which, if not the best film made in Britain during the War, is unequivocally the best portrait of the British at war. **Fires Were Started** (1943) (there was an earlier, shorter version, *I Was a Fireman*) was the official tribute to the Auxiliary (then National) Fire Service, and it now has a resonance unconsidered at the time – a record of ordinary people doing extraordinary things. They are not even particularly aware of saving London, but are merely 'doing their bit'. Only one brief scene is out-of-synch, when a telephonist dives under the table at the sound of a close bombing, to emerge and say into the

phone, 'Sorry for the interruption.' It is not that this is phoney – wartime conversations were full of stories like it – but that it exemplifies the stiff-upper-lip platitudes of commercial films to which Jennings never otherwise resorts. The earlier part of the film concerns one particular unit – not the usual liquorice allsorts cross-section – quartered in a converted school and welcoming a new recruit, played by William Sansom, the writer. At night, they wait for the Blitz to start, sing 'Please Don't Talk About Me When I'm Gone' and someone reads Sir Walter Raleigh's dissertation on death. This is dockland, and the ships stand idle. The German quarry is a factory in Trinidad Street, and the unit at first fails to quell the fire started by incendiaries. One man is killed, and his wife, unknowing, listens to the News, 'Fires were started . . . casualties light.'

The Bells Go Down (1943) is also about the Fire Service, the training of three men (Tommy Trinder, Philip Friend, Mervyn Johns) and their (literal) baptism of fire. Basil Dearden's direction and the screenplay are so abysmal that the climax – two men sharing a last cigarette on what is left of the thirteenth floor, as they wait for the building to cave in – is bizarre rather than moving. The film's sole redeeming feature is James Mason's performance as the disciplinarian who trains the recruits. This was a production of Ealing Studios, where Michael Balcon was trying to build a new team to provide the more serious films he thought the times demanded. To this end he brought Cavalcanti in from the documentary movement, specifically to supervise contemporary subjects. Another such is **The Foreman Went to France** (1942), directed by Charles Frend, who had made *The Big Blockade*, and the three films make an appalling trio. In this case J.B. Priestley provided the original story, based on fact, of a foreman (Clifford Evans) who before the Fall of France was sent to prevent some valuable machinery from falling into German hands. His progress to the coast, accompanied by a Cockney tommy (Trinder) and a stranded American (Constance Cummings), features every possible cliché, including that one in which the British C.O. (John Williams) is really a Nazi in disguise.

Balcon also brought Harry Watt from documentary films, and at the very least

Nine Men (1943) is not a betrayal of that movement. Watt wrote his own screenplay, ostensibly from a story by Gerald Kersh but more probably from a Russian picture, *The Thirteen*, which was also the basis for Columbia's *Sahara*. All three films concern a small band of soldiers stranded in the desert; in this version their exploits are related in flashback, a device which looks like padding, since the entire film runs only 68 minutes. The scenes of barrack-room life are admirably done, and the desert sequences made without undue heroics. It is more honest than the major effort of the Crown Film Unit* itself, **Western Approaches** (1944), a feature-length account of a boatful of torpedoed merchant seamen adrift in the Pacific. Pat Jackson, a stalwart of the Unit, directed.

The first really good British war film was made by a consummate and complete man of the theatre. Noël Coward had evinced no interest in the cinema since *The Scoundrel*, and when Lord Louis Mountbatten suggested a film about the Navy at war he said that he would be agreeable if it was based, at least in part, on Mountbatten's own experiences. Coward wrote, produced and acted in **In Which We Serve** (1942), and since he was inexperienced as a director he looked for a collaborator, choosing the inexperienced David Lean (b. 1908), on the basis that the films edited by Lean moved faster than most British films. Ronald Neame was hired as cinematographer. As far as reviewers were concerned, the result was the 'best' (Dilys Powell in *The Sunday Times*) or 'finest' (*Newsweek*) film of the War. 'There have been rumors that a truly great motion picture was coming to New York,' wrote Howard Barnes in that city's *Herald Tribune*. 'They are triumphantly confirmed . . . It is a masterpiece of filmmaking, a stirring testament to men of good will, in whatsoever age they may have loved, fought and endured.' We do not have to disagree, today, to also understand why most naval men saw it with an embarrassment bordering on shame.

'This is the story of a ship,' says the foreword, and as the ship is launched a copy of the *Daily Express* lies sodden in a pool, its headline claiming 'No War This Year' (which is one reason its proprietor,

*As the G.P.O. Film Unit was rechristened, making wartime propaganda movies.

Lord Beaverbrook, pursued Coward and Mountbatten with such hatred through the years). Shipwrecked, the Captain (Coward) and two others reminisce – the Chief Petty Officer (Bernard Miles) and a rating (John Mills) – on the role of the Navy in their lives. On Christmas Day the rating's family joke about the Navy and the Marines in a gorblimey way and toast both; the Chief Petty Officer and family toast the ship itself, H. M. S. *Torrin*; and the Captain toasts the King, while his wife (Celia Johnson) makes an eloquent toast to her rival, the Senior Service. Film critics, but surely not servicemen, might agree with Coward's sentiments at the end '. . . for if they had to die, what a grand way to go, for they lie with the ship we loved so much.' Away from the battle-front sang-froid, the film belongs to the cosy artefacts of the period, but is accurate, for instance, on the grin-and-bear-it attitudes of the Blitz. Reservations are further lessened because of the performances, especially those of Miss Johnson, Miles, Joyce Carey (Miles's wife), Kathleen Harrison and Kay Walsh (respectively Mills's mother and sister), and including Coward's own stiffly self-conscious portrayal. Also admirable is the film's composition, from the first shots of the rivets being driven in to the final view of the surviving officers disappearing into the darkness of the dock at Alexandria.

It was also the most influential film since the outbreak of War. Though the documentary movement had for the first time impinged on the public consciousness with such features as *Target for Tonight* (1941), directed by Harry Watt, and *Coastal Command* (1942), directed by Jack Holmes, only Ealing had responded, though it was hard to tell as much from the results. Coward's film proved to both British and Hollywood producers that the lives of servicemen and their loved ones at home were sufficiently dramatic without Nazi agents and fifth columnists. Its influence can be clearly felt in Anthony Asquith's **We Dive at Dawn** (1943), in its portrait of a submarine crew on leave, and its sober account of the voyage to the Baltic to sink a German warship. The screenplay, by Val Valentine, J. B. Williams and Frank Launder, avoids stereotype by giving the Captain (John Mills) an address book of popsies, and by making its representative

The British at War

Noël Coward, right, with John Mills just behind him, shipwrecked in *In Which We Serve*, and it is while clinging to this raft that the men reminisce, via flashback, to happier days. Although the film was accepted on the Home Front as an accurate portrait of service life, the troops themselves thought its respect towards the Navy exaggerated, and wondered where Coward had found his portrait of uncomplaining cameraderie.

On the other hand, Carol Reed's *The Way Ahead* is much better on the boredom of service life, as it follows a group of recruits from training to induction in battle. Here, looking suitably fed up, are from left to right, Leslie Dwyer, Jimmy Hanley, Raymond Huntley, James Donald and John Laurie.

rating (Eric Portman) particularly sour. But then it loses its nerve and opts for a ridiculous climax, with the latter dressed as a German officer and keeping Hitler's entire army at bay with one machine-gun.

Carol Reed had directed a short for the Army Film Unit, *The New Lot*, showing the induction of one group of civilians into army life, when he and the actor David Niven fell to discussing the possibility of a film on the wartime Army such as Coward's on the Navy. Thus emerged **The Way Ahead** (1944), based on *The New Lot*, one of whose writers, Peter Ustinov, was joined on the new film by Eric Ambler. By a fortuitous stroke of timing it opened in London on the day of the Normandy landings, and if it was in the fervour of the moment that C. A. Lejeune called it 'one of the splendours of the British cinema' the remark is no less true today. We may not now feel, as she did that these actors are so good that we do not think of them as such, especially as many of their faces became over-familiar, usually above a uniform. As with *In Which We Serve* barrack-room banter was never as discreet as this; but this is the Army as seen by the Army, a necessary and benevolent institution, and on its own terms the film's sole mistake is the Chorus of two Chelsea pensioners, representing Tradition. The men do curse and grumble, and if their Sergeant (William Hartnell) is a disciplinarian, underneath he is as fond of them as is their officer (Niven). The men adjust to the food, to beds without sheets; they are invited to a local home, and attend a camp concert that would be of singular ghastliness were it not so typical. The broadest and best portrait is of Davenport (Raymond Huntley), who had 'quite an important job, really', in charge of officers' kit, and thus was accustomed to meeting 'them' on equal terms; disillusioned, he later becomes almost happy, and nothing in a basically true film is better than his joining in with the others as Tessie O'Shea sings 'If You Were the Only Girl'. Having shared such common relaxations as well as common boredom, they share common danger, and we leave them as they disappear in the gunsmoke of battle in North Africa. Reed's mastery is complete: he was a director who lived films, and saw as many as he could, but no particular influence is discernible here. The film is all

the more moving a tribute to the men who humbly helped to play their part in saving Britain in that it sets out merely to record.

It was Anatole de Grunwald who decided that there should be a comparable film for the R.A.F. **The Way to the Stars** (1945) was directed by Anthony Asquith, his usual collaborator, and written by Terence Rattigan, who had been in that branch of the services. It did not come out till the War was over, which may have helped its popularity, for it already looked back to that time as deeply romantic – and the R.A.F. was, in any case, the most romantically regarded of the three services. Dilys Powell said, 'I can only say that now, at this end of a moment in history, the piece is to an ordinary citizen inexpressibly moving,' but it no longer is, precisely because that is what it so wants to be. It is all here: the briefings, the camaraderie of the local pub (as prominent in the story as the airfield), the transient wartime romances, the Yanks who came over and went on to bomb the hell out of the Ruhr, and the people who waited, sometimes in vain. One has the suspicion, as the Yanks take over the film as well as the airfield, that it was made for the American market – an impression confirmed when a huge title, 'August 17th', interrupts the action, followed by a note to the forgetful that that was the date of the 'First U.S. Raid on the Nazis'. The comic misunderstandings between British and Americans are merely coy; the corrective balance of the great romantic films is here common farce; and the direction, though 'sensitive', drains away what life there is in banal two-shots for the endless dialogue. And where *In Which We Serve* has a sufficiency of stiff-upper-lips and *The Way Ahead* has Niven's eternally charming officer, this film is awash with stiff upper lips on the faces of charming officers. John Mills, terribly decent and terribly nice, bears the brunt of the clichés. Trevor Howard, as the brisk C.O., too soon killed, and Michael Redgrave, as another doomed flyer, do manage a bit of personality, if only their own, but Mills has nothing but sincerity to offer. The widow (Rosamund John) is allowed only the wisp of a romance with the American flyer (Douglass Montgomery). It is possible that time may restore the qualities which once endeared this film to audiences – and it was far more popular

The British at War

Gordon Jackson and Patricia Roc in Launder and Gilliat's *Millions Like Us* – 'and millions like you' say the credits, after the cast list. Since this could hardly mean workers in Delaware or Detroit, no American distributor was interested in taking the film, which was a shame, for it was honest (and sometimes funny) on what the War was like for the average Briton.

than Coward's film, or Reed's: but where those are, above all, about people, this is the home equivalent of the films about the Empire, being mainly concerned with such sentiments as love and bravery.

It is better, however, than **Journey Together** (1945), written and directed by John Boulting from a story by Rattigan, and it is perhaps because the sponsor was the R.A.F. Film Unit that only the uniforms reconcile us to the fact that it is about the R.A.F. – it is not even comparable to the already doubtful R.A.F. of the other film. The title refers to both the co-operation given by American and Canadian instructors to the service and the friendship between a Cockney corporal (Richard Attenborough) and a college graduate (Jack Watling). The Cockney flunks his flying test and, like John Garfield in *Air Force* (q.v.), is made bitter and twisted before becoming a hero. The chief interest is the brief presence of Edward G. Robinson as one of the American instructors, having donated his services after an approach from the British Ministry of Information.

The other aspect of the War, the home front, receives its due in **Millions Like Us** (1943) which is, with *Fires Were Started*, the outstanding record of what it was like to live in Britain at this time. The writing team of Launder and Gilliat, after directing a short, *Partners in Crime*, were given the

chance to produce and direct a feature – and in an interesting dual career they did nothing more accomplished. The Ministry of Information suggested the subject. After establishing, in the manner of Jennings, the atmosphere of August 1939, the film follows the fortunes of Celia (Patricia Roc), who longs to be a W.A.A.F. or a Landgirl but is shunted into a Munitions factory by an overworked official. So is the haughty Jennifer (Anne Crawford), who has an inconclusive affair with the foreman (Eric Portman). The stories intertwine, but Celia's is the more remarkable precisely because it is the more mundane, and her romance with and marriage to a young R.A.F. sergeant (Gordon Jackson) is handled with extraordinary simplicity. Miss Roc, never thereafter as good, has a grace in her ordinariness, providing ample reason why she could turn no man's head while considerably interesting viewers. There are also vignettes in the Jennings manner: the Home Guardsman who slips off for a pint; the stories of queueing, of 'before the War'; the air-raid; and, at the end, a 'Workers' Playtime' concert which conveys better than any other film the 'oneness' of Britain at the time.

Launder and Gilliat decided after this experience never to co-direct again, but they continued to co-produce, each usually directing his own script. **Two Thousand Women** (1944) was written for Hitchcock, who accepted it till Launder was persuaded to direct it himself. It might, for box-office purposes, have been called 'Two Thousand Women and Three Men', being about British women interned in France, in a former luxury hotel, and the airmen they are trying to smuggle to waiting Resistance forces. Launder later said that he should have treated the subject more seriously. As it is, this is a good-to-fair thriller, with Miss Roc, Phyllis Calvert, Flora Robson and Co. coping with dialogue some notches below *The Women*.

In **Waterloo Road** (1945) Gilliat, writing and directing from a story by Val Valentine, examines the consequences when a soldier (John Mills) goes A.W.O.L. in search of a spiv (Stewart Granger) who has seduced his wife – only he hadn't really: she was simply fed-up with the cramped quarters of her in-laws. The slot-machine arcade is an art director's paradise, and if the raffish atmosphere of

that part of London is missed Gilliat gets
instead something of the quality of the
Blitz – the nights in the tube, the sea of
uniforms changing trains, the shortages,
the sense of change and flux.

This batch of films emanated from two
companies: *In Which We Serve*, *The Way
Ahead*, and *The Way to the Stars* from Two
Cities; and *We Dive at Dawn* and the Launder and Gilliat films from Gainsborough –
and by the end of the War these were
recognised as the two leading British studios. Two Cities had been founded in 1937
and had received a boost two years later
when Paramount had agreed to co-operate
on its production of *French Without Tears*,
from Rattigan's play to which it owned the
rights, and it had also contributed Ray
Milland. Legal adviser to the company was
Filippo del Guidice (1892–1961), brought
in by one of its founders, fellow-Italian
Mario Zampi, later noted as a comedy
director (q.v.). Del Guidice was instrumental in raising the money for *In Which
We Serve*, including an extra advance from
the distributor, British Lion, when funds
were exhausted. Two Cities films were
thereafter handled by either Eagle-Lion or
G.F.D., both owned by Rank, and it was
Rank who provided additional finance
when needed during the filming of *Henry V*
(q.v.), which gave him a degree of control
over the company, now in fact managed
by del Guidice – who, a keen entrepreneur,
was also associated with Powell and Pressburger, and would take on Launder and
Gilliat when they left Gainsborough Pictures. Gainsborough was also coming into
the orbit of Rank, via his relationship with
C.M. Woolf within G.F.D. – and it was
well worth having, since under the management of Maurice Ostrer and the production initiative of Edward Black it had
become the most financially successful
studio ever to operate in Britain.

Its run of phenomenally popular films
began with **The Man in Grey** (1943),
directed by Leslie Arliss (son of George
Arliss and formerly a writer specialising in
comedy) and adapted by him and Margaret Kennedy from a period romance by
Lady Eleanor Smith. Without exactly intending to, it challenged Hollywood
where it was strongest – in the areas of
escapist entertainment and star performances. Though Margaret Lockwood,
Phyllis Calvert, Stewart Granger and

James Mason (b. 1909) had all been in films
for some time, only Miss Lockwood
might have been termed a star; seen today,
only Mason is at all good, and it was his
suave villainy which carried the film to
success. His part hardly begins to exist – a
grim, grey Regency rake who marries a
ninny (Calvert) for the sake of heirs and
then has an affair with her best friend
(Lockwood) – but he is a supreme example
of an actor who has merely to enter a room
to dominate it. Screen villainy took a new
turn as he sneered at Calvert, sniffed round
Lockwood and finally took a horsewhip to
her. Lockwood, given to frigid smiles and
moods of envy, plays a girl of unamiable
ambition, and the film is as good as any of
the subsequent movies about scheming
women, British and American, to which
the success of this one gave rise.

Fanny by Gaslight (1944), directed by
Anthony Asquith, is based on a much
better novel, by Michael Sadleir, a man
fascinated by the Victorian underworld –
both by the gilt and plush brothels, where
overdressed milords over-drank and over-
ate till they sank into stupor, and by the
hypocrisy, whereby the Church Commis-
sioners preferred not to know that the
rents they collected came from harlots living at poverty level. This is the richest of
Sadleir's three novels on the subject, but
Doreen Montgomery has extracted from it
merely a conventional romance, about the

The auguries for
Fanny By Gaslight
are not good, since it
was directed by the
variable Anthony
Asquith and pro-
duced by Gains-
borough, whose
period romances
so infuriated British
critics. Some of
them, however,
stand up well, and
this one particularly
– partly due to James
Mason, who is
glowering at Stewart
Granger to the left.
Phyllis Calvert and
Jean Kent watch in
alarm.

illegitimate Fanny (Miss Calvert), the high-born swell (Granger) who defies his family to go and live with her, and the evil Lord Manderstoke (Mason), whose footsteps dog their fate – but it works, nevertheless, as well as some of the best Hollywood love stories. Enough of Sadleir remains; and this is the only film ever made to look at the sexual underworld of Victorian Britain, its brothels and dance-halls. The handling of the duel scene would not have disgraced Ophuls, and in both this film and *The Man in Grey* the superb sets give no sign of wartime austerity.

That was part of their attraction, and audience enthusiasm was such that the more homely Lockwood and Calvert were preferred to all but a handful of Hollywood stars. Critics moaned, but despite buzz-bombs and black-out audiences queued for **Love Story** (1944), directed by Arliss, in which a doomed pianist (Lockwood) falls in love with a dashing R.A.F. pilot (Granger), whose sight is failing. The background is Cornwall, the music the 'Cornish Rhapsody' (cousin to the 'Warsaw Concerto'), the outcome, inevitably, that Love Conquers All, even a scheming Patricia Roc.

Although a foreword to **Madonna of the Seven Moons** (1944) assures us that its 'facts' are known to the medical world the plot belongs to the world of Grand Opera – and Italian opera at that, for though Roland Pertwee's screenplay is based on a British novel, by Margery Lawrence, the ingredients include gypsies, fiestas and assorted Latin passions. A convent girl (Calvert) has Something Awful happen to her in a wood. Though happily married – says her husband, Giuseppe (John Stuart), gazing at her, 'Pity Botticelli isn't alive' – and with a grown-up daughter (Roc), all within the space of seconds, she has a mysterious illness which causes her to disappear. When Sandro (Peter Glenville) turns up at a ball, she grabs her jewel-case, snaps a dagger in her garter and takes a one-way ticket to a 'slum' called San Gimignano. There she enjoys an idyll with Nino (Granger), till Sandro tries to rape her daughter. Sandro knifes her and she stabs him, at which point Nino realises the reason for her long absences: but, as she told him earlier, 'A love like ours can't be measured by time.' The direction is credited to Arthur Crabtree who, like every-

one concerned with this production, seems to have aimed it for amateur night at the village hall.

From there Gainsborough could only go up, and C. A. Lejeune of *The Observer* – whose weekly column was the *sine qua non* for all self-respecting British movie buffs – was so startled to find a film from this company which she liked that she called **A Place of One's Own** (1945) 'a fine piece of work'. It is a tale of a girl possessed by a spirit, clearly filmed because of the success of *The Uninvited* (q.v.), but the director, Bernard Knowles, failed to understand the importance of atmosphere in such stories. Distinguished contributors include Rex Whistler, credited with 'additional designs', and Sir Osbert Sitwell, author of the original story, who co-operated on the production – surprisingly, in view of its disregard for the niceties of late Victorian society. Miss Lockwood is the girl; James Mason (who asked for the role) plays the elderly Yorkshire grocer whose wife (Barbara Mullen) engages her as a companion.

Ealing also offered a ghost story, **The Halfway House** (1944), directed by Basil Dearden. It is derivative – and finally trite – and yet quite unlike any other film. Its forebears include 'Outward Bound' and J. B. Priestley's Time plays. The War had created among certain film-makers a more than usual interest in the might-have-been and the hereafter, and it is precisely the War which has created all the problems for these people stranded in a remote inn in Wales. They include a naval wife (Françoise Rosay), a black marketeer (Alfred Drayton), and an officer (Guy Middleton) who has absconded with the mess funds. Angus MacPhail and Diana Morgan wrote the script which, however misguided, did provide evidence of the ideas British cinema was now prepared to tackle.

For audiences satiated with war, Ealing offered **Champagne Charlie** (1944), a fable about the popular Victorian entertainer George Leybourne (Tommy Trinder) and his rivalry with The Great Vance (Stanley Holloway). It is pleasing to find a Hollywood formula – in this case, the backstage story – being used for indigenous factors, and instead of chorus-girls we get the songs straight, the booze-boasting ballads of the era. There is no love affair for George, while the juveniles are dull, and what matters above all are the theatres and bars, marvellously recreated by the director, Cavalcanti, the art director, Michael Relph, and the photographer, Wilkie Cooper. Richard Winnington called Holloway's 'a delicious performance by an actor who is Britain's best film discovery of the war years'; apart from the fact that Holloway had been in films for years he is right.

Only the prologue of **On Approval** (1944) mentions the War, and only then to remind us how remote it is. The film is a valediction by Clive Brook, whose acting career had been faltering since he left Hollywood in 1934. He produced, directed and adapted Frederick Lonsdale's play, doing none of these things well, but it is still a droll piece. That is due to the sharp playing, by himself and Googie Withers (as the couple who go off to Scotland for a trial marriage), and to the sublime performances of Roland Culver and Beatrice Lillie as their scornful chaperones. Miss Lillie is a permanent termagant whose level glare indicates constant affront and suspicion; it was about this time that she turned down a seven-year M-G-M contract – to be near her son – and film history is the poorer because of it.

Another play filmed was **This Happy Breed** (1944). Noël Coward had decided that what the times needed was another of his patriotica, but as the mood had shifted since the days of 'Cavalcade' he wrote not of upstairs and downstairs, but of one South London family, against a background of the Armistice, the General Strike and the Abdication. There can be no question that his heart was in the right place, and that the dialogue, purposely mundane, is often entertaining; but it gives pause when Miss Lejeune approvingly quotes a Flying Officer in the Balkan Air Force who said he had seen the film on three consecutive nights, with Dominion and Allied troops, 'who were seeing England, the real England, for the first time'. *Cavalcade* worked so well because it was part fantasy, and we all knew it; this piece works less well because it is so determined to be on 'our' side. Even so, the film removes much of what was so condescending in the play, Coward having left it in the hands of the creative team of *In Which We Serve*, now assembled as Cineguild, an off-shoot of Two Cities. The screenplay is credited to Ronald Neame,

Anthony Havelock-Allen and David Lean. The latter also directed, sensitively, in Technicolor. In the thankless and demanding role of the mother Celia Johnson is called upon to register as many emotions as any actress since films began, and she never fails us; as the father Robert Newton is less mannered than usual; and Stanley Holloway is a tower of strength as the next-door neighbour.

In the matter of patriotic drama, the major event was **Henry V** (1944). The studios had left Shakespeare well alone since the three attempts to film his plays almost a decade earlier; the incentive this time came from Dallas Bower who, on hearing Laurence Olivier in a radio excerpt of the play, was impressed with its potential as propaganda. The man determined to make the project a reality, however, was del Guidice. As well as playing the title role Olivier agreed to direct when no one else he trusted was able or willing, and in his hands the filming of Shakespeare was revitalised. Wartime economy caused the particular and imaginative shape of the film so that it starts in 'this wooden O', the Globe Theatre, moving on to an equally theatrical Harfleur, based on the Duc de Berri's *Book of Hours*, and thence to 'the vasty fields of France', which are indeed fields. Then, having opened out completely, the film folds again, like the petals of a flower. The budget was huge, just under £500,000; the Battle of Agincourt was re-enacted in Ireland – to avoid aircraft – but these still plagued shooting, as did bad weather. It is an exciting and colourful battle, deploying the full panoply of medieval heraldry and armour. It is not perhaps much like the real Agincourt, for the movie did not aim at naturalism but wanted to show little England overwhelming the immense forces of the foe – and it is that nationalistic interpretation, now often under-emphasised in stage productions, which limits the film today.

It concentrates on Henry's great rallying cries, plus the battle and the reflective sequence which precedes it. 'If the cause be just,' says the English soldier, and in 1944 it seemed so; but in the interim we have come to believe less in the right of kings to go a-conquering. Olivier plays for laughs the sequence concerning the Salic law, as he also plays down the insult of the gift of tennis balls; but we may still feel

that Henry's invasion of France is committed for the most trumpery of reasons. Olivier's own force of personality holds the film together. He plays the king as a correct English gentleman, and only in the exquisite wooing scene does he allow a touch of humour. The acting throughout, in what we may call the Old Vic style, is exemplary – with Leslie Banks as the Chorus, Renée Asherson as the Princess, Esmond Knight as Fluellen and Leo Genn as the Constable. Paul Sheriff's artwork is outstanding, as are the costumes of Roger Furse; and Robert Krasker's camerawork never allows a banal image – which would have been easy among the stylised settings. William Walton's music borrows an air or so from the Songs of the Auvergne, and is thrillingly matched to the images. I have indicated that Olivier's concept is imaginative and, though the final impression is of solid craftsmanship, that is the way – with constant invention – that he led his team.

Understandably, given the moment – and the previous poor screen versions of Shakespeare – the film was widely hailed as a masterpiece; and since it brought much prestige to Mr Rank he had high hopes of **Caesar and Cleopatra** (1945), which Gabriel Pascal had chosen as the third of his Shaw films, this time without directorial help. With two stars who were names in the U.S. market, Vivien Leigh and Claude Rains, he persuaded Rank to provide a budget of £470,000, with the expressed aim of making a dent in the international market. Despite the War, a unit was sent to Egypt to shoot locations, and the cost began to spiral, eventually stopping at £1,300,000, making it the most expensive film yet made. Filming was an unhappy experience for all concerned, and Claude Rains, for one, appalled at Pascal's incompetence, ceased speaking to him. Rank, some months after the premiere, spoke of 'a disastrous loss', and cancelled his contract with Pascal, who was told formally by the Association of Cine-Technicians that he would not be allowed to work again in Britain, except under the most stringent restrictions. Rank could not even comfort himself with prestige, for the film was slaughtered by the British press, and though in America the critics were kinder it did, in contrast to *Henry v*, almost no business there. Shaw had written an intimate comedy, with great historical charac-

ters portrayed as matter-of-fact people: the film is not comic but facetious, and it is certainly not intimate. The action sequences, moreover, are atrociously staged, and when ever anyone moves the camera seems to be in the wrong place – which can hardly have been the fault of Robert Krasker, F. A. Young, Jack Hildyard or Jack Cardiff, since individually on other occasions each showed himself a master of his craft. Oliver Messel's sets are dull, and, in a film costing so much, folds in the backcloth are even less forgivable than usual. Mr Rains and Miss Leigh are efficient; Stewart Granger is a boisterous Apollodorus, about as Sicilian as a Henley coach; Basil Sydney is a spirited Rufio, while Flora Robson, as Ftatateeta, and Cecil Parker, as Britannus, struggle to enliven Shaw's jokes on, respectively, the difficulty of pronouncing her name and woad-wearing Britons.

Mr Rank's wrath may have been assuaged by a modest – but also Technicolored – stage adaptation, **Blithe Spirit** (1945), directed by David Lean for Cineguild. Coward's play, as all good comedy should be, is funny, ingenious and callous. It is also a re-working of 'Private Lives', inasmuch as both pieces concern a man beset with two wives, the second of whom turns up – in this case in spirit form – to bicker with him over what went wrong with the marriage. Rex Harrison is the husband, and his clubman *persona* makes the exchanges even more brusque than they need be; Constance Cummings is Ruth, the second wife. From the stage production come the two definitive portrayals: Kay Hammond as the spectral first wife, petulant, sulkily drawling, delighting in Ruth's discomfiture; and Margaret Rutherford as Madame Arcati, the medium, with her brisk manner, hockey-sticks slang and over-reaching enthusiasm.

Coward's play, though it ran in the West End throughout the War, made no reference to the conflict. Its success was the reason that it was filmed, but unlike, say, *Quiet Wedding*, it was not meant as a relief from ration-books and the air-raid sirens; the War was receding. From 1943 on there are no diatribes against 'old Hitler'; but there were a number of films about England, as if in relief that it was no longer on the brink of extinction. This was not a case of militant patriotism: there was a greater

Laurence Olivier in *Henry v*, offering a straight reading of the role, attempting for instance neither power-complex nor divine mission. One imagines him behaving similarly on the set, for the film gives the impression of having been cared for by all its participants.

The British at War

Given that the British suffered air-raids for most of the Second World War it is not surprising that most of their films were concerned with the War in some way. Towards the end of it, however, they turned from mocking the Germans to a more rewarding series of films, such as *Tawny Pipit*, which were trying to portray the country for which they were fighting. This one had some overt propaganda only when a Russian woman sniper lectures the villagers on Russian cornfields.

awareness of the diversity of the country since people visiting evacuees and doing military service were travelling to parts of the country they had not seen before. In escaping into rural Britain the film-makers were questioning materialism and traditional values. That was the starting-point for Powell and Pressburger in making **A Canterbury Tale** (1944), which is about three young people going to Canterbury for variously idealistic reasons – a Landgirl (Sheila Sim), an army sergeant (Dennis Price) and a G.I. (Sgt. John Sweet of the U.S. Army). Throughout the film, for every good idea there is a daft one – such as the misogynist J. P. (Eric Portman) with a penchant for pouring glue over the heads of young ladies in the black-out. Indeed, as one of the film's admirers wrote to the weekly *Time & Tide*, the plot is 'doolally'; and for all that the native cinema would be poorer without Powell and Pressburger, this film is no exception to the rule that most of their films are terrible.

Tawny Pipit (1944), also celebrates the rural landscape. Charles Saunders and Bernard Miles wrote and directed this kindly film about a rare bird which has laid its eggs in a cornfield, which must therefore be protected from Ministry ploughs and

army tanks by the villagers, including a nurse (Rosamund John) and a convalescent pilot (Niall McGinnis). Lejeune observed, 'It is just for the right to enjoy such things, the film suggests, that we are fighting; and, although conceivably mad, that is the way we are.' In other words, the film celebrates the cuteness of the English.

So too does **Don't Take It To Heart** (1944), written and directed by Jeffrey Dell, a comedy about a stately home and the place of the aristocracy in a changing world. Both films, from Two Cities, are the germs from which Ealing comedy (q.v.) grew.

Ealing itself remained serious, and **Johnny Frenchman** (1945) offered a new slant on the Englishness of the English by contrasting it with the Frenchness of the French – as represented by those age-old rivals, the Cornish and the Bretons. However, the similarities between these peoples is reduced to a latter-day Min and Bill by the writer, T. E. B. Clarke (q.v.), with Françoise Rosay as French Min and Tom Walls as Cornish Bill, and their children as Romeo and Juliet. Paul Dupuis is good as the French boy, but Patricia Roc's Mayfair accent negates her flat heels and pinnies. Charles Frend directed this 'hands-across-the-Channel' effort.

Ealing, for all its postwar reputation, still lagged far behind del Guidice's Two Cities as purveyors of entertainment, but both companies shared a resolve to avoid their old formulae. No longer did the British studios ape Hollywood, or try to make the musicals they did so badly. The comics had been unceremoniously dumped, and gone, too, were the asinine thrillers and tabloid newspaper stories. It was therefore a very changed industry to which Alexander Korda returned, and one much more to his liking – but it was not one to which, with his record, he could gain easy access. To all intents and purposes it was owned by Rank, who in his benevolence would have welcomed Korda: but Korda decided that if he were to be responsible to anyone he would prefer that person to be far away, and he approached M-G-M, anxious to re-activate its British operation. To the mutual gratification of himself and Louis B. Mayer, therefore, London Films and M-G-M-British amalgamated, but after a two-year association and an expenditure of £1 million only one film emerged: **Perfect**

Strangers (1945). The idea for the film was Korda's, despite the fact that some of Metro's money had gone to such esteemed writers as Evelyn Waugh, Graham Greene, James Bridie, James Hilton, A. E. W. Mason and Robert Graves, all put under contract by Korda. Virtually the sole satisfaction afforded Mayer was that it utilised Robert Donat and Deborah Kerr, both under contract but not required under those contracts to work, at that moment at least, in Hollywood.

The film starts at breakfast-time: she (Miss Kerr) is drab, with a sniffle, he (Donat) meticulous, wing-collared and Something in the City. When he joins the Navy she joins the Wrens, and since their leaves are cancelled or do not coincide, and he is torpedoed, they do not meet for three years – by which time neither is sure that they like their old selves, and both are pretty sure that they do not like each other. Though it could be a great deal better – the eventual reunion is much too prolonged – this is a valuable and important film on a subject no other tackled. Hollywood made the most successful film on homecoming, *The Best Years of Our Lives* (q.v.), but this one, far less sober – indeed, it is a romantic comedy – has far more to say, since its subject is the changes wrought by the War upon individuals. Wives changed not only because they joined the services, but because many went out to work for the first time; the experience of going abroad and the rigours of personal combat changed many men; and both sexes had their first chance to mix with people from other social classes. In this film both husband and wife are allowed a discreet romance, and it should be said that the success of the film owes much to these players, who, never notably glamorous, do not have to try too hard for plainness. Clemence Dane, one of the many people to work on the screenplay, won an Academy Award for Best Original Story. Wesley Ruggles was to have directed, but was frustrated by Korda's constant interference with the script, so that Korda himself took over the job.

The last impressive British war film was **The True Glory** (1945), released as the War in the Far East was ending: a British-American co-production, sponsored by the U.S. Office of War Information and Britain's Ministry of Information. Carol Reed and Garson Kanin co-directed this distillation of all the newsreel footage – said to be 6½ million feet – taken between D-Day and V.E.-Day, almost a year later. Thus the Invasion and the battle for Europe is told in newsreel images, but what puts the film ahead of the other war documentaries – except those of Jennings, whose influence is clearly felt – are the troops' voiced impressions of what is happening. The dialogue is spoken by professionals (at least, one recognises certain voices, such as Celia Johnson and Leslie Dwyer), but the credited writers – Eric Maschwitz, Arthur Macrae, Jenny Nicholson, Gerald Kersh and Guy Trosper – surely collected it rather than invented it. An American speaks of Belsen in a neutral tone, 'It was the worst thing I ever saw in my life and I wouldn't have missed it for anything,' and in the ruins of a German town a British soldier comments, 'A German woman said to me, "If only you'd given up in 1940 none of this need've happened." ' It is seldom brave and comfortable dialogue, and it is not free of criticism and complaint, speaking of the Boche without either bitterness or magnanimity, but rather with compassion. Basically the film is a tribute to the common soldier, and above all it offers a more compelling insight into what can only be described as 'history' than any other movie on record. The score, by William Alwyn (who contributed so memorably to *Fires Were Started* and *The Way Ahead*), is here bombastic enough to emphasise the banality of the images, though perhaps that is its purpose. Two of those images are particularly memorable in capturing the moment: the shot of the Fleet steaming across the Channel, and the shot from inside the barge as the men prepare to disembark on French soil to rid the world of Nazism.

23

Hollywood's War Effort

HOLLYWOOD's preparations for war had not gone unnoticed. The War Department was delighted with those films which encouraged recruitment, but the anti-Nazi films provoked less favourable reactions among non-interventionists. In August 1941 Senators Gerald P. Wye and Burton K. Wheeler accused the film industry of having brought the country to the brink of war, as a result of which a Senate investigatory committee was set up. It had not proceeded far when the Japanese attacked Pearl Harbor, at which point – in fact, the very next day – it was disbanded. The Hollywood studios threw themselves into the war effort with vigour, loaning facilities and equipment to make training films, and sending out stars for Defense Bond tours and U.S.O. camp shows. Meanwhile the Motion Picture division of the Office of War Information suggested that Hollywood build its product round one or more of six basic principles:

1. The Issues of War:
   what we are fighting for, and the American way of life
2. The Nature of the Enemy:
   his ideology, objectives and methods
3. The Allies
4. The Production Front:
   supplying the materials for victory
5. The Home Front:
   sacrifice and civilian responsibility
6. The Fighting Forces,
   including the job of the man at the front.

The whole-hearted response of the studios was due partly to guilt at being so far from the field of battle and partly to their customary sense of responsibility as providers of the world's leading communications medium. They were little affected by wartime shortages, for the government recognised the cinema as a prime means of maintaining morale – and indeed during the war years more Americans were regular cinemagoers than at any other time in the industry's history.

Production remained at full throttle to meet the demand, and it was not necessary to mention the War in *every* film despite government decree – for many war-weary spectators would be glad to forget it for an hour or two while watching comedies and musicals. As in Britain, the film companies welcomed new themes and new stories, even if many of them were old ones in disguise. As far as the British were concerned, Hollywood's heart had gone out to them at the time of the Blitz; and after Pearl Harbor the whole of America felt even closer to them in their beleaguered isle. Sentiment was to play a large part in the reception of many wartime films.

Since M-G-M remained the leader of the industry, it was appropriate that it produced the one film which seemed to everyone to represent the common experience of war – if not quite their own experience of it. 'Perhaps it is too soon to call this one of the greatest motion pictures ever made,' said Bosley Crowther in *The New York Times*, 'but certainly it is the finest film yet made about the present war, and a most exalting tribute to the British, who have taken it so gallantly.' He went on, 'One cannot speak too highly of the superb understatement and restraint exercised throughout.' In truth, since the film is **Mrs Miniver** (1942), one cannot speak of them at all. As it happened, Jan Struther's stories of a British family coping with the War had been published in *The New York Times*: Sidney Franklin bought the rights and assigned four writers to the script, including the novelist James Hilton. William Wyler was borrowed from Goldwyn to direct, his last film before joining the U.S.A.F. – which took him to Britain, where he soon realised that the film was inadequate to its subject. In their annual poll the New York critics affirmed the superiority of *In Which We Serve*, but in Hollywood Oscars were showered on the Minivers: Best Film, Best Direction, Best Actress (Greer Garson), Best Supporting Actress (Teresa Wright), Best Screenplay from Another Source and Best Cinematography (Joseph Ruttenberg). Today the two actresses concerned are handicaps in what at least was an honest endeavour, the one relentlessly noble and the other dimpling prettily throughout. The film took at least $5½ million in admissions, the highest-grossing M-G-M film up to that time. Since then Miss Garson rounding up a German flyer in her garden has become a cinema joke. Mr M. (Walter Pidgeon) had taken his little boat to Dunkirk, and it is just after turning in the German that Mrs M. sees it returning in the pretty river at the end of the garden. Doubtless the studio's heart was in the right place, but the war was not like this – even remotely (there is no mention of rationing, which was what concerned the British most after the bombing). However, Winston Churchill said in Parliament that the film had done more for Britain than a flotilla of destroyers.

It was only one of several M-G-M hymns to Anglo-American understanding. The company had always been Anglophile and, since the American public had indicated a weakness for spires and cloisters in *A Yank at Oxford* and *Goodbye, Mr Chips*, it was to be hoped that it would not notice the solecisms of similar films made on the Culver City lot. **Random Harvest** (1942) has the same writers as *Mrs Miniver* and also Miss Garson, as a music-hall star who meets and marries an amnesiac officer (Ronald Colman). The time is Armistice Day, 1918, and the film follows their benighted fortunes till the reunion under the cherry blossom. Mervyn LeRoy directed, but it is Colman's conviction which keeps us watching – and interested – while our intellect is assaulted. It is inferior to the great prewar romances, and one does wonder why 'Loch Lomond' accompanies the sequences in the West

Country; but, at least, unlike *Mrs Miniver*, it does not have exalted ideas of its own importance.

The White Cliffs of Dover (1944) does not feature the wartime song of that title, since presumably it was not classy enough for the occasion: instead the soundtrack throbs with every well-known British air except 'Loch Lomond'. Clarence Brown directed, from a screenplay by two of the *Miniver* writers, Claudine West and George Froeschel, joined by Jan Lustig; and this came from an unlikely but popular source, a long poem by Alice Duer Miller, about an American girl (Irene Dunne) who marries an English baronet (Alan Marshall) and loses both him and their son in the two World Wars. She moves only in the best society – Sir C. Aubrey Smith and the like – and sheep graze in all the country exteriors. While the couple enjoy a holiday idyll in a Dieppe hotel, thousands of men were dying just down the line – but typically there is no indication of that in this gauzy-glamorous film. The plot makes much of the British delight at the U.S. entries into both wars, and the point was not lost on the British that though they may have taken American girls into their aristocratic families, when it came to fighting they needed American men.

Irene Dunne plays lightly, making lines passable which in the mouth of Miss Garson would seem like lead. Of **A Guy Named Joe** (1943), which again stars Irene Dunne, I can do no better than quote a letter I once received from a friend, Donald Wayne Hunt: 'Honest to God, the plot goes like this: Spencer Tracy is a fighter pilot who loves Irene Dunne, a ferry pilot. He gets called to the heaven of dead pilots where God, played by Lionel Barrymore, sends him back to earth assigned to student pilot Van Johnson, who meets and falls in love with Irene. Tracy is invisible, even to her, though the way her eyes mist up we know she *knows* he's there. When Van draws an assignment to bomb a munitions dump, she knows that his number is up because he pulls at his eyebrows the way Spence used to pull at his: so she steals out and takes the plane up, and Tracy is there with her showing her how to work the guns, and her eyes are all misted up. Then he sets her free to marry Van, because a love like theirs shouldn't wither away. One nice thing: she sings

Hollywood's War Effort

Spencer Tracy in Fred Zinnemann's excellent *The Seventh Cross* (1944), made somewhat surprisingly by M-G-M, a company also responsible for some of the worst films about the War. The public discriminated, but not always wisely, and seem to have been put off this by critics commenting that it showed a number of Germans in a favourable light.

"I'll Get By".' Dalton Trumbo wrote the screenplay, a perfect demonstration of Dwight Macdonald's comment that the Hollywood 'Unfriendly Ten' (i.e. those blacklisted in the late Forties) were by and large the Untalented Ten. Blame must also be apportioned to the director, Victor Fleming, for permitting the painted backdrops that masquerade as airfields in the film.

'A highly placed American officer with whom I discussed the matter said that wartime Hollywood had become a pain in the neck to all decent-thinking Americans, and that the boys themselves, meaning the troops, were not amused,' wrote James Agate in 1943. One film they may have had in mind is **The Cross of Lorraine** (1943). The Marseillaise thundering out over the credits announces its intention, and Tay Garnett directed these adventures of a group of Frenchmen from Conscription to Resistance. Gene Kelly represents all those who wanted to fight on while the rest capitulated; Jean-Pierre Aumont pretends treachery in the cause of heroism; Hume Cronyn is the prospective collaborator; Peter Lorre the German sergeant; and Cedric Hardwicke the senior member of the Church. The film concludes with the Germans temporarily vanquished, and the villagers marching to a hide-out in the mountains singing you-know-what.

M-G-M atoned with **The Seventh**

Cross (1944), which shares with the pre war anti-Nazi films a sense of responsibil ity, as if its makers too understood th significance of handling totalitarianism Helen Deutsch wrote the screenplay from a novel by Anna Seghers, and even the titl takes us into mystical areas to whic movies seldom aspire: it begins in concentration camp – the time is 1936 where the film's hero, George Heisle (Spencer Tracy) has been imprisoned fo crimes described as 'political'. We follov the story of his escape and the pursuit, an very few thrillers then and since have dea so honestly with their audience. Wound ed, Heisler goes to a doctor (Steven Geray who says, 'Before I treat you the law re quires me to tell you that I am a Jew,' sentence that can still send a chill down th spine. The only fault in an otherwise flaw less film is a touch of romance at the end though the climax itself is more subtle tha was customary. Comment at the time in dicated that the film was premature i showing good as well as bad Germans what impresses now is that the eviden brutality of the bad ones is not underlined and that the good ones are more rounde than most movie people of the period Tracy, grim and haunted, gives his bes performance in his best serious film. At th time, he astonished the M-G-M publicit department by offering to meet the pres to praise his company. The Viennese-bor director, Fred Zinnemann (b. 1907), ha worked with Robert Flaherty in German in the early Thirties on a documentar which was abandoned: what he learne from that experience he put into practice i a semi-documentary about fisherfol made in Mexico in 1935, *Redes* (or *Th Waves*). It was unusual to find a film maker with a penchant for realism a M-G-M, but in *The Seventh Cross* h achieves, with the aid of his art director Leonid Vasian, a Germany that looks lik Germany. He succeeds far better tha Lang, Renoir and other European direc tors who handled similar themes at thi time; the film has infinitely more dimen sion and individuality than any othe M-G-M war movie and, since Zinneman carried far less clout than Wyler, Brown o LeRoy, that is no mean achievement.

Keeper of the Flame (1942) was als topical, and its screenwriter, Donal Ogden Stewart, reckoned it 'the pictur

I'm proudest of having been connected with – in terms of saying the most about Fascism that it is possible to say in Hollywood'. He also thought it daring to have made it under the nose of Louis B. Mayer, but in fact the possibility of Fascism in America had been discussed far more boldly in *Meet John Doe* and *Confessions of a Nazi Spy*. In view of the current U.S. hostility towards Hitler, it was not courageous to suggest that a man aiming at a similar degree of power should be destroyed. This potential dictator had been a national hero till he took to preaching anti-Semitism: but since he is dead before the film starts any potential argument is stifled. Some interest is engendered when a reporter (Spencer Tracy) attempts to meet his widow (Katharine Hepburn), but matters soon descend to the level of turgid gothic mystery with an insane old mother hidden away and a glowering cousin who swaggers about in riding boots. It is possible that I.A.R. Wylie, who wrote the original novel, and Cukor, who directed, were so entranced by the underlying theory – that idealism can turn to Fascism – that they felt they might find a wider audience by indulging in melodrama. Resemblances have been noted to *Citizen Kane*, but Cukor finds 'no conscious echoes . . . [they] were just an accident. There was something in the air; it was simply the result of the prevailing political climate'; at the time the film was compared, unfavourably, with *Rebecca*.

Coming back to haunt Mayer later was **Song of Russia** (1943), one of a number of American films extolling the Russians made at the height of Allied co-operation. A naive propaganda piece, greeted by the armed services with 'one long howl of laughter' (according to *Time* magazine), it was quickly forgotten till resurrected by the House Un-American Activities Committee in the late Forties: Mayer managed to imply that it had slipped out while he was not looking, and its star, Robert Taylor, testified that he had made it under protest. The Soviet's own movies are not more ardent in their fervour for the Collective way of life: working in the Collective fields, training with the Collective machine-gun, listening to the Collective radio or marching home after a hard day's work with their hoes over their shoulders and their voices raised in song. There is

even an Eisenstein-like close-up in a montage, but on this evidence the director, Gregory Ratoff, had never heard of his distinguished predecessor.

Having foisted this film on to defenceless audiences M-G-M came up with the equally foolish **Dragon Seed** (1944), feeling it incumbent upon them, as makers of *The Good Earth*, to inform the world exactly how the Chinese were coping with the Japanese occupation – or, rather, overcoming it, as Katharine Hepburn, impersonating a Chinese peasant, disposes of the entire Japanese garrison by putting poison into the duck sauce. Under the same slant-eyed make-up are Aline MacMahon and Walter Huston, mouthing such dialogue as 'Wait five hundred heartbeats and then go to her'. Pearl S. Buck again wrote the original novel; Jack Conway directed, with Harold S. Bucquet replacing him when he became ill; and Lionel Barrymore speaks the unbelievably condescending commentary.

Wartime propaganda also turned up in **Madame Curie** (1943), since its aged heroine (Miss Garson, now the studio's biggest star) at the end makes a plea for international understanding. Planned for Garbo, this respectful tribute might with her presence have taken fire, but Garson seems to move in a cloud of sanctity, smiling quizzically to indicate intelligence. Paul Osborn and Paul H. Rameau have taken the facts from Eve Curie's biography of her mother; Mervyn LeRoy, directing, never finds the requisite spirit. The scientific work is well explained, and her private life – there is no mention of her real-life lover – depicted as idyllic till the accidental death of Pierre (Walter Pidgeon). To be savoured is an incredible moment when Van Johnson turns up claiming to be a reporter from Grenoble.

In **Gaslight** (1944) the Swedish Ingrid Bergman, the Frenchman Charles Boyer and the American Joseph Cotten all pretend to be British, Bergman as the frightened wife, Boyer as the sadistic husband and Cotten as the Scotland Yard man still on the trail of her aunt's disappearance. Patrick Hamilton's original play,★ a study in morbid psychology, had been reworked – by John Van Druten, Walter Reisch and

★The British film version had been held up pending the Broadway production, which was so successful that M-G-M bought the rights.

Hollywood's War Effort

John L. Balderston – into a conventional murder mystery with Victorian trimmings, and Cukor, directing, was unable to evince from Bergman the requisite panic and terror. Her Best Actress Oscar was presumably an expression of Hollywood's fascination with her at this time, and could certainly not be justified when Barbara Stanwyck was nominated for *Double Indemnity* (q.v.).

Also set in Victorian London, **The Picture of Dorian Gray** (1945) marked a return to the studio of Albert Lewin, a former Associate Producer who had made *The Moon and Sixpence* (q.v.) for United Artists. His second excursion as writer-producer-director finds Wilde's novel filmed with three virtues: the decor, excessive but splendid; the inserts of the portrait in Technicolor, a rarely used device; and Angela Lansbury as Sybil Vane – a 'vaudeville' performer in this incarnation – plaintively singing 'Goodbye, Little Yellow Bird' in her perky hat while paper snow is thrown over her. As the immaculately silk-hatted Dorian looks at her in the East End dive we know that he will destroy her, and we enjoy a slight *frisson*, contemplating his catalogue of crimes – but they, often left ambiguous in the book, are hardly more explicit here. Drinking in a Ufa-influenced dockside den, listening to his favourite Chopin prelude, or climbing up the rickety stairs, he is without joy. However much Wilde privately flouted Victorian morals, his book upheld them, so doubtless Lewin was correct in showing sin as mirthless – not that Mayer or the Hays Code would have permitted him to do otherwise. And by not specifying the reasons for Dorian's hold over a number of young men Lewin may have been dropping a hint that only one in a thousand of the audiences at the time would pick up. As Dorian, Hurd Hatfield not only reveals no wrinkles but no discernible emotion at all; as Lord Henry, George Sanders is permitted to mouth a number of epigrams borrowed from other of Wilde's works.

Equally an expression of Metro's love affair with Albion is **Lassie Come Home** (1943), directed by Fred M. Wilcox, and the apotheosis of the boy and dog movie, throbbing with sentiment, aglow with Technicolor, and with an ending that James H. Fitzpatrick could not have bettered. It was adapted from a novel by Eric Knight, a Yorkshireman who survived the First World War but died in the Second as a major in the U.S. Army – or so a maudlin introduction tells us. Roddy McDowall plays the boy who loses his dog and never sheds a tear, obviously to accommodate the wartime notion of the British as a titanically stoic race; as for Lassie, she makes her way back from Scotland via Big Sur, Colorado and the swamps of Georgia, not to mention that vast river (a heavenly choir accompanying) which, explains Dame May Whitty,[*] separates Scotland from England. Nigel Bruce is the squire, and Donald Crisp gives his stock performance as the boy's father. And then there is Lassie: what can one say in view of the fact that it took no less than three canines to play the role, all of them male? The question becomes even more confused in **Son of Lassie** (1945), directed by S. Sylvan Simon, which is really Lassie Goes to War, only it is the son, Laddie . . . and like James Cagney in *The Fighting 69th* he doesn't learn the meaning of discipline till the last reel. Canada this time does duty for both Yorkshire and Norway; and the grown-up McDowall is Peter Lawford, as an R.A.F. sergeant in a blue previously unknown to the R.A.F. *Lassie Come Home* is not anyone's idea of a good movie, but it had a certain drive and sincerity: this has neither.

Of the same lineage is **National Velvet** (1944), lifelessly directed by Clarence Brown from Enid Bagnold's whimsical tale about a little girl determined to ride her horse in the Grand National. The film has achieved some fame, partly because it is the only one from Elizabeth Taylor's childhood which anybody remembers. It is also tawdry; the California coast poses grandly as the Sussex downs, and the back-lot village is painted and garish; the quality of hope in the book has become gooey sentiment, except in the performance of the mother by Anne Revere, who rightly won a Best Supporting Oscar. Angela Lansbury offers a pleasing study of adolescence, and Jackie 'Butch' Jenkins is a *Saturday Evening Post* cover child come to life – not English, but not bad; Taylor plays honestly and spontaneously – qualities she never showed as an adult –

[*] Her husband, Ben Webster, plays exactly that here, and it is odd to think of him (the original wearer of Wilde's green carnation, before his days as Shakespearian actor-manager) being in the same film – her first – as Elizabeth Taylor.

582

confirming the truth that some children have a natural talent.

Another talented child actress was Margaret O'Brien, who was the antithesis of Shirley Temple and therefore popular with many critics. She could indeed perform with emotion, if a little too knowingly as time went on. She is pleasing in **The Canterville Ghost** (1944), directed by Jules Dassin and, as updated from Wilde, an uncertain mixture of slapstick, whimsy and homilies on Anglo-American co-operation. Robert Young heads a G.I. platoon and Charles Laughton is 'the most fearsome phantom in all England'. **Our Vines Have Tender Grapes** (1945), as directed by Roy Rowland, is an affectionate study of a Norwegian community in Wisconsin – O'Brien and her cousin (young Jenkins) quarrelling over roller skates and getting lost in the spring floods, and father (Edward G. Robinson) taking her into town in the night to see the circus pass through. C. A. Lejeune was so taken by the child that she thought the film 'one of those rare hours in the cinema that leave you wondering if the thing may not grow into an art some day'.

Such films – the family Americana – were dear to the heart of Mayer, and in the presumptuously titled **The Human Comedy** (1943) they reach an apotheosis. It was written by William Saroyan, whom the producer Arthur Freed had introduced to Mayer, who was so impressed with his conversation that he offered him a contract. Freed also persuaded Saroyan to write the story on which this film was based. Mayer purchased it for $60,000 and gave Saroyan $1,500 a week to be groomed as producer-director, but Mayer then became disenchanted after seeing a short Saroyan made, *The New Job*, so the direction was given to Clarence Brown, Metro's prime exponent of the American way of life. He was seldom more sensitively employed. The subject is the War as seen from a small Californian town, and there are at least a dozen superb scenes, including all those with Frank Morgan as a tippling newspaperman. As it happens, drink is the town's sole vice. Everyone is nice and kind; no one lies or loses his temper, which hardly atones with my idea of the human comedy. Saroyan's view is not merely cosy but dripping with sentiment, and the final sequence, where Mickey Rooney recognises the uniformed stranger as his dead brother's best buddy, lays fair claim to being the most embarrassing moment in the whole history of movies. Time has not changed it, since C. A. Lejeune spoke for all the critics when she said: 'Have you ever seen a film that irritates you, embarrasses you, and yet moves you so much that you stiffen at the criticisms of other people equally irritated and embarrassed?'

It was reputedly Mayer's favourite movie. He did not like **An American Romance** (1944), the third part of the war-wheat-steel trilogy proposed to him twenty years earlier by King Vidor, who claims that the studio ruined it. *The Big Parade* and *Our Daily Bread* (not made at M-G-M) were now ancient history; Vidor was allowed Technicolor, but not the promised stars, Spencer Tracy, Ingrid Bergman and Joseph Cotten – and Brian Donlevy, Ann Richards and Walter Abel are dull replacements. The picture is part documentary and part fiction, and when the first cut called for pruning, the studio started lopping at the main story, whereas Vidor would have preferred losing some of the shots of fields and mills. In fact, these remain the film's sole justification; the rest is garbled stuff from better movies – such as the schoolteacher wife and illiterate husband in *The Power and the Glory*, or the Cotten/Able role, an amalgamation of those Cotten played in *Ambersons* and *Kane*.

One veteran director did provide M-G-M with a good film, and indeed **They Were Expendable** (1945) is one of the best contemporary films about the War. It was John Ford's first film since leaving the navy, and his first for the company since *Flesh* in 1932; it would also be his last for M-G-M. Robert Montgomery, also returning from naval service, plays a character based on Lieutenant Johnny Buckley, who pioneered the use of the P.T. boat in combat, and Frank Wead adapted from a book by William H. White. Since there is little plot the mood is all: the film is a tribute to wartime camaraderie – to the men's attitudes to fighting, to dying and to each other, and the sentiment is more honest than in most of Ford's films. Montgomery and John Wayne are excellent, though the latter's heroics are in the conventional mode.

583

Judy Garland and Robert Walker, right, in *The Clock*, their romantic mood momentarily shattered by a drunk, Keenan Wynn. The critic James Agee paid the film the rare tribute of believing it would be remembered in fifty years' time.

From M-G-M, too, came the best wartime romance, **The Clock** (1945), the story of a G.I. (Robert Walker) and the girl (Judy Garland) he meets and marries on a two-day pass. The director, Vincente Minnelli, used New York, as he said, as a 'third character' when he took over from Fred Zinnemann (whom Garland found unsympathetic), largely abandoning a script in which the characters mouthed banalities instead of what they really thought – a device for which he thought audiences were not ready. Despite some back-projection, the Manhattan of this film is alive, and the comic relief – Keenan Wynn as a drunk, James Gleason as a friendly milkman – forced but accurate. For once in a movie the lovers do seem to care for each other, and Garland handles a number of non-movie emotions, as when her room-mate berates her for letting herself be picked up, or when she experiences the panic and self-pity of not feeling married at the wedding feast. This is an infinitely better (both more interesting and more honest) performance than the one which won Joan Crawford an Oscar that year – and those given by the other nominated ladies.

Garland's other wartime films were musicals, and with the advent of Minnelli M-G-M was to attain a form in this field which demands a chapter to itself. However, we might glance here at **Thousands Cheer** (1943), since it almost shakes with emotion for all things military. The ambiguous title might suggest the army or 'the M-G-M star parade', or the former cheering the latter at the concert which provides the film's climax – a form of self-congratulation pioneered by Paramount with *Star Spangled Rhythm* (q.v.). But apart from songs by Garland and Lena Horne there is little to cheer over. The pre-concert story concerns Kathryn Grayson as the pride of the regiment and Gene Kelly as the rebellious G.I. for whom she falls. Soon involved is Mother (Mary Astor), who had left Father (John Boles) years before because he loved the army more than her – an unconvincing assertion in view of the fact that he is seen to do nothing but fuss about the romance. Kelly eventually learns that teamwork and discipline are as essential to life in the army as they were to his trapeze act – a glimpse of which offers a revealing detail of G.I. life, that they shaved their armpits. It also convinces him: 'I want to be the most important man in the world – a private in the United States Army,' he says, after which it is left to Miss Grayson and a massed choir to sing 'Make Way for a Day Called Tomorrow' before the flags of the Allies.

The United Artists contribution to the all-star wartime film was **Stage Door Canteen** (1943), the brainchild of Sol Lesser as written by Delmer Daves, who later provided the identical story for *Hollywood Canteen* (q.v.). The institutions celebrated served the forces with food and entertainment, as provided by thespians high and low; since U.A. had no contract list Lesser used Broadway players who had appeared at the Canteen and Hollywood stars currently without affiliation – thus we are offered such as George Raft and Alfred Lunt in aprons, Katherine Cornell doling out hamburgers, and Tallulah, cigarette in hand, growling to a G.I. 'You do your job well, and remember, we'll do our job well.' Among the few bearable turns are Yehudi Menuhin playing 'The Flight of the Bumble Bee', Ethel Merman belting out 'We'll Be Singing Hallelujah as We're Marching Through Berlin', and Benny Goodman playing 'Why Don't You Do Right?', with Peggy Lee as his vocalist.

Between turns we are offered some budding romances, such as that between a G.I. called 'Dakota' (William Terry) and an aspiring actress (Cheryl Walker), who after a tiff sit watching the dawn come up over Washington Square, saying things like 'I like hot baths on cold nights' and 'Do you like dogs?' – an apt question with his particular film. Finally the young actress is given a pep talk about doing her bit by no less than Katharine Hepburn: clever lady, she waits till the end and gets the best scene. The once estimable Borzage directed.

One of U.A.'s more memorable additions to the war effort was **That Hamilton Woman** (1941), a pro-British movie released some months before Pearl Harbor; American audiences actually applauded when Nelson (Laurence Olivier) says of Napoleon, 'There are always men who for the sake of insane ambition want to destroy what other men have built up.' It was virtually a British film: Korda produced and directed, and the writers were R.C. Sherriff and Walter Reisch, who had both worked with him at Denham. It was made in six weeks on a low budget, with some improvisation, and was constantly revived over the next few years. It ran throughout the War in the Soviet Union, and Churchill, who loved it, had special screenings for visitors. Today it stands as another of those romantic dramas which betray the truth of human behaviour yet manage, by virtue of dramatic intelligence, to remain moving years after the audiences for which they were made have passed on. As usual, this has something to do with the players, and with this barely-written role Olivier completes his quartet of Hollywood heroes (Heathcliff, Maxim, Darcy), playing each for full-blooded romance in four quite different ways. Here, on his first appearance, he is direct with Sir William and gauche with milady; he even manages to suggest that he is wall-eyed. Later, lacking arm and eye, he establishes himself as a figure grown in authority, but subject to a passion which he tries not to show. Gladys Cooper is the bitter Lady Nelson, and Alan Mowbray has the best role as the cuckolded Hamilton. Vivien Leigh's Emma hardly manages a Cockney accent, and she is too naive; but she is pert and pretty and vital; no wonder the two men refuse her nothing! In the later stages,

listening to Hardy as he tells her of Nelson's death with one unchanging expression of disbelief, she is also moving. The Hays Office insisted that she pay for her sins, so the story was framed by a sequence with her as a derelict in Calais – removed by Korda for later reissues. We are otherwise not shown her darker side – one of her qualities captured by Terence Rattigan in his 'A Bequest to the Nation'. In fact, the 1973 film based on Rattigan's play borrowed and tinted the battle sequence from this film, despite the fact that the ships were obvious models.

Korda continued his Sabu vehicles with **The Jungle Book** (1942), directed by his brother Zoltan, with his other brother, Vincent, providing sometimes superb decor. Its chief demerit is the presence of white actors in dark make-up, but Sabu is a natural Mowgli. Kipling's stories do not too readily lend themselves to adaptation, and Lawrence Stallings's screenplay leans heavily on Edgar Rice Burroughs.

Before returning to Britain – where he was engaged on secret war work for two years – Korda co-produced **To Be or Not To Be** (1942) with Lubitsch, who directed. In Britain, in *The Spectator*, Edgar Anstey observed that they 'here and there abandoned their buffoonery to commiserate with the Poles and Jews, and to make some return for their Hollywood comforts with sequences which they no doubt hope may prove to be anti-Nazi propaganda'; and in the U.S. *Life* magazine sniffed, 'In years to come the fact that Hollywood could convert part of a world crisis into such a cops and robbers charade will certainly be regarded as a remarkable phenomena [*sic*].' Lubitsch was upset when accused of bad taste – notably over a line spoken by Sig Rumann as a German, of Jack Benny as a 'great' Polish actor, 'What he did to Shakespeare we are now doing to Poland.' It is true that his original intention (he wrote the story with Melchior Lengyel; Edwin Justus Mayer turned it into a screenplay) was to show that actors remain actors whatever the circumstances. In the event, the heroic antics of this theatre troupe are neatly balanced against the rottenness of the Nazis, and indeed the latter are so menacing that the advent of Rumann as a cretin is a relief. It should have been clear that Lubitsch's approach was preferable to the daft exploits of the now-proliferating Resistance movies – on which this, if a mite prematurely, is a sharp satire. Benny – who should have made more films – is superb, as is Carole Lombard as his wife (it was her last film; she was killed in an air crash while travelling across the country to sell War Bonds).

With the departure of Korda (and Gold-wyn) the company was so desperately in need of product that it bought a group of B-pictures from Paramount, plus two A-features, *I Married a Witch* and *The Crystal Ball*. It flirted increasingly with Rank, and had big-city successes with *In Which We Serve* and *Henry v*, but there was acrimony over the failure of *Caesar and Cleopatra* – and Rank, anyway, was becoming financially involved with Universal. Of the established U.A. producers, Edward Small continued to turn out usually modest products, including **International Lady** (1941), directed by Tim Whelan, one of several current films concerning espionage and intrigue in London, Lisbon or the North African cities, with in this case the uninteresting team of George Brent and Ilona Massey. For Small, Allan Dwan directed **Abroad with Two Yanks** (1944), which concerned two marines (Dennis O'Keefe, William Bendix) in London, and a sequence of lively comedies based on old stage farces, **Up in Mabel's**

Room (1944), **Brewster's Million** (1945) and **Getting Gertie's Garte** (1946). O'Keefe is the bright but not bril liant farceur in the trio, of which the best i the middle one, since Eddie 'Rochester Anderson is on hand as his valet. Benedic Bogeaus started badly with the compan with **The Bridge of San Luis Rey** (1944) an intolerably slow version of Thorto Wilder's novel as directed by Rowlan Lee, but he picked up with **Dark Water** (1944), a frightened-lady-in-the-old-dark house situation, beautifully directed b André de Toth, who never again cam anywhere near this form; the dreariness o his leads, however – Merle Oberon an Franchot Tone – detracts from the atmos phere he creates.

A concurrent attempt at gothic melo drama was **Guest in the House** (1944) produced by Hunt Stromberg, the mos promising of the newcomers to U.A. since he had given M-G-M some of thei biggest successes, including *The Grea Ziegfeld* and the MacDonald-Eddy musi cals. This one is more typical of his work for U.A., being indifferent in all respect but the supporting performance by Alin MacMahon. John Brahm directed, and i includes a number of quintessential Fortie ingredients, including pounding surf, th house on the storm-beaten cliff, and th scheming woman (Anne Baxter), though by all to be the flower but to be revealed a the serpent under't. Stromberg's health was in fact being undermined by drugs, but he had started well as an independent with **Lady of Burlesque** (1943); his direc tor was William Wellman, who was more than able to evoke the tawdry bustle of backstage life. Barbara Stanwyck is the bump-and-grind star who goes sleuth ing, and she has three amusing buddies, Iris Adrian, Marian Martin and Gloria Dixon – not that they're very close: Stan wyck was ever a cat that walked alone, and here she is more catlike – and laconic – than ever. The source was a novel by Gypsy Rose Lee, 'The G-String Murders', a title which the Hays Office refused to sanction.

Also at U.A. Wellman directed **The Story of G.I. Joe** (1945), for Lester Cowan, described by him as 'a bastard', and an otherwise undistinguished pro ducer. Agee observed that Wellman and his colleagues – the writers are Leopold

Robert Mitchum in William Wellman's *The Story of G.I. Joe*, the first American 'anti-war' film (since the films made during and after the First World War could more correctly be termed 'pacifist'). The new expression was needed since the cinema had almost always hallowed war – and a word was needed for those movies which were more honest.

Atlas, Guy Endore and Philip Stevenson – 'did not regard their job as an ordinary one. They undertook a great subject. It is clear that they approached it with a determination to handle it honestly and to make a masterpiece' – and if it was not that, he concluded, 'I cannot help resenting those films that are.' Its subject is the ordinary soldier foot-slogging it from North Africa to the road to Rome, as witnessed by Ernie Pyle, the war correspondent, who died not long after the film came out and is played in it by Burgess Meredith. 'I have loved many men,' he says at one point, 'but C Company most of all,' and the incidents he describes comprise the film; the doling-out of mail or Christmas chow; the young soldier so alarmed at what he has seen that he bursts into tears in the telling; the rock-like sergeant who succumbs to battle fatigue; the enemy seen only as shadowy figures or as gun bursts. 'But the G.I. lives so miserably and dies so miserably,' says Pyle to the captain (Robert Mitchum). The final sequence Agee thought 'a war poem as great and as beautiful as any of Whitman's': the men, veterans now, sit by the road as other units move on, and the captain's body is brought down the hill at twilight to be laid in a field of new white crosses. As with *They Were Expendable* and *The Clock* it was not until the cessation of hostilities that movies portrayed the serving man with any honesty: Wellman's fine film is the best contemporary American tribute we have in this medium.

In contrast is **Since You Went Away** (1944), produced and written by David O. Selznick – whose inactivity had been of serious concern to his partners in United Artists. In 1941 he had signed a contract with Pickford, Chaplin and Korda for a quarter-share in the company, and had in the meantime toyed with a number of projects which he had sold off to other companies. Looking for something important enough to follow *Gone with the Wind* he came up with what the foreword calls 'the story of that unconquerable fortress – the American Home Front, 1943'. We follow a year on the home front from the departure of Father to the cablegram announcing that he is, after all, not killed. It takes 170 minutes and though smoothly directed by John Cromwell there is hardly one of those minutes which I do not find offensive even now. The American home front was probably the least affected of all the countries involved in the War, but the insult lies in the inference that the events depicted are typical. 'You are what I thought America was,' Mother is told by a refugee (Nazimova), but she isn't, for she is Claudette Colbert, photographed without a wrinkle though she has a grown-up daughter (Jennifer Jones). Apart from taking in a paying guest (Monty Woolley) and praying – to the strains of 'Ave Maria' – she seems unaware of the War – though she does go into a munitions factory at the end. 'I thought we might try out those new hairstyles from *Vogue* tonight,' says Colbert, but Jones refuses. 'Do you mind, Mother, I want to try out those treatments for third-degree burns.' Love plays a great part in their lives, since Mother has an old admirer (Joseph Cotten), sporting a dazzling array of uniforms, and daughter a shy young G.I. (Robert Walker). They are a liberal family, and gladly entertain a fellow-officer (Keenan Wynn) of Cotten's called Solomon. The maid (Hattie McDaniel) has been let go, but wants to work without pay. 'I couldn't let you do that,' says Colbert, but sho'nuff Miss McDaniel is soon waiting at table and dispensing Hattie McDaniel-type philosophy. Relief is provided by Agnes Moorehead as a cocktail-lounge gossip who takes the War lightly, and Colbert, as capable as ever, does manage to make quite moving the scene where she tells Jones that her fiancé is missing: it seems almost like an accident.

The film's cost of $2,900,000 was justified at the box office, and Selznick gave the company another success with *Spellbound* (q.v.); but he left U.A. soon afterwards. There was a third film for United Artists at this time, **I'll Be Seeing You** (1944), directed by William Dieterle, a wan and ridiculous romance about the mutual help given by a shell-shocked soldier (Cotten) and a thief (Ginger Rogers) on parole.

Albert Lewin, in conjunction with David L. Loew, gave the company an odd prestige movie in **The Moon and Six-pence** (1942): M-G-M had owned the movie rights to the novel while Lewin had been scenario editor there, but had not seriously considered wrenching a screenplay from it. We may thus assume a labour of love in Lewin's screenplay and direction – by its fidelity to the original, as far as was

From left to right, Jeanne Cagney, James Cagney, Joan Leslie, Walter Huston and Rosemary de Camp as the Cohan family in *Yankee Doodle Dandy*. Its patriotism may now seem excessive, but James Cagney's ebullience keeps the film, most of the time, several feet off the ground.

possible. Deprived of Maugham's speculations on the Gauguin-Strickland character, the story is thin; and though in that role George Sanders is convincing as bounder and cynic, he is an unlikely painter. Herbert Marshall plays Maugham; and Lewin's respectful treatment brought appropriately respectful notices.

United Artists also provided a haven for James Cagney, tired of haggling with Warners over contracts. Again the idea seems to have been an attempt at less standardised fare, but there is little to be said for **Johnny Come Lately** (1943) and even less for **Blood on the Sun** (1945), both produced by his brother William, and with himself as a tough reporter on both occasions. In the former, directed by William K. Howard, he helps an old lady (Grace George) revive her newspaper, and takes on corrupt politicians; in the latter he tackles what seem to be the entire Japanese army, government and police force. His contempt for all things Japanese may have brought cheers from Allied audiences,

long immune to the presentation of the enemy as one-dimensional villains; but Cagney's behaviour is intolerable, and Frank Lloyd's tired direction does not help. As Cagney returns at the end to face death, for the sake of democracy, and Sylvia Sidney – on our side, after all – sails off with Japan's plans for world conquest, one may conclude that if a nation's intelligence is indicated by its film industry, the U.S. would have been, till recently, in the dunce's corner. Only fourteen years separate *Blood on the Sun* from the first part of Kobayashi's *The Human Condition* (q.v.), but it seems like centuries.

In the last days at Warners, Cagney had been in two more efficient propaganda pieces: **Captains of the Clouds** (1942) and **Yankee Doodle Dandy** (1942), both directed by Michael Curtiz, and respectively waving the Union Jack and Stars and Stripes. The former has a lumbering plot borrowed from earlier Cagney movies; it is in Technicolor, and its setting would be evident to a blind man, since the sound-track thunders with 'The Maple Leaf For-ever'. Cagney hears on the radio Chur-chill's speech, 'We shall never surrender', and wants to join up ('Now there's a guy who knows how to issue an invitation'); but is refused. 'Why don't you go back where you came from?' he snarls to the examining officer, who replies, 'I can't, Mr MacLean. My home was in Coventry' – a line which is touching in that audiences were trusted to get the full import. *Yankee Doodle Dandy* is the story of George M. Cohan, as told in a ghastly framing device to an invisible Roosevelt, and its prevailing tone is set by an early remark, 'I guess I was born with an American flag in my hand.' Cohan's songs are marvellously staged and sung, or whipped into a plethora of mon-tage sequences (arranged by Don Siegel), and the dialogue is mercifully sparse (when the *Lusitania* is sunk, Cohan says, 'And we were worried about the success or failure of our show. Now we've really got some-thing to worry about.') Though the writers (Robert Buckner, Edmund Joseph) do provide correctives – via some characters who despise Cohan's chauvinism – the schmaltz can be overpowering. Cagney's George M. won him Best Actor citations from the New York critics and the Holly-wood Academicians, and the film was the first hugely successful show business biography since *The Great Ziegfeld*. If we accept the two early Jolson Talkies as special cases, only five American films had taken more money – *Gone with the Wind*, *The Birth of a Nation*, *Sergeant York*, *The Big Parade* and *Mrs Miniver*. They were all war stories, which may or may not be coincidental.

Bogart also went to war. With snappy direction, by Vincent Sherman, and an excellent cast (Peter Lorre, Conrad Veidt, Ed Brophy, Frank McHugh, William Demarest, Wallace Ford), **All Through the Night** (1942) is watchable; but after a promising start it descends to high jinks about rounding up Fifth Columnists in New York, with Bogart seemingly un-interested in the anti-Nazi speeches he has to make. In **Across the Pacific** (1942) he single-handedly saves the Panama Canal* from Nippon sabotage but, till then, the piece has much of the savour of *The Mal-*

*Hawaii in the original script, but shooting was overtaken by events.

tese Falcon – understandably, since John Huston again directed and Mary Astor and Sydney Greenstreet repeated their per-formances as mysterious lady and genial if menacing adversary. The screenplay by Richard Macaulay (from a novel by Robert Carson) has the bantering, slangy dialogue he had been providing in films like *Torrid Zone* and *They Drive by Night*, to remind us how much more febrile was Miss Astor than the other independent dames.

Bogart has another memorable partner, Ingrid Bergman, in **Casablanca** (1942) which could never have attained mythic status had it starred the lesser Warner players previously announced. It starts like a B-picture, and by planting a nightclub in an 'Oriental' city it collects at once two staples of movie melodrama; but since the War is on, the situation is more than usual-ly tense, since most of the *dramatis personae* are desperate for American visas. It is their interplay which first indicates that the film is a unique one: Claude Rains, as the cor-rupt and wily police chief; the fawning Lorre, with the stolen visas – 'Now are you impressed with me?'; Veidt, as a visit-ing German officer; Greenstreet, owner of a rival bar and, by his own admission, 'leader of all illegal activities'; and, at their centre, Bogart as Rick, the American with the successful saloon, drinking too much, a former gunrunner and Loyalist fighter who now declines to 'stick his neck out for nobody'. His black pianist (Dooley Wil-son) plays 'As Time Goes By' and in walks Ilsa (Miss Bergman), wife of a Resistance worker (Paul Henreid) but Rick's beloved in prewar Paris. Till then, the film had hurtled along; now it pauses, to give mar-vellous expression to his pessimism and her divided loyalties. The role of Ilsa is written as a *femme fatale*, which Bergman ignores: she is simply superbly right in every way that has to do with beauty, youth, warmth and lack of sophistication and conventional glamour. It is the con-trast between the personalities of Bogart and Bergman which makes their scenes so captivating: the Paris flashbacks of their long ago love affair are tinged with heart-ache. The love scenes were written by Casey Robinson, uncredited, after Bogart refused the script as penned by Julius J. and Philip G. Epstein and Howard Koch (based on an unproduced and apparently poor play); that was why they had no

589

Humphrey **BOGART** · Ingrid **BERGMAN** · Paul **HENREID**

A HAL B. WALLIS PRODUCTION

Casablanca

CLAUDE **RAINS** · CONRAD **VEIDT** · SYDNEY **GREENSTREET** · PETER **LORRE**

Directed by MICHAEL CURTIZ

kind, and it had been fairly but not sensationally popular. It was not till the Fifties that it came to be regarded as the best-loved Hollywood melodrama; it is extraordinary that material basically so artificial should become so holding and so moving.

It was typical of Warners to produce a number of imitations, including **Background to Danger** (1943), directed by Raoul Walsh, with George Raft, set in Ankara, and **The Conspirators** (1944), directed by Jean Negulesco, with Hedy Lamarr and Paul Henreid, set in Lisbon. The contract list was expanded to include several European actors suitable for such tales, including Victor Francen, Philip Dorn and Helmut Dantine – who, together with the inevitable Lorre and Greenstreet, supported Bogart in **Passage to Marseille** (1944). The presences of Rains and a European beauty – Michèle Morgan – plus the flashbacks, further the resemblance to *Casablanca*; Curtiz again directed, from a screenplay by Robinson and Jack Moffit. Bogart is an exponent of Free France, 'a greater patriot', in the words of another patriot, 'than we can ever hope to be'. We first meet him imprisoned on Devil's Island, and his adventures subsequent and previous (i.e. in the flashbacks) are ridiculous even for a Resistance tale. Much better is **To Have and Have Not** (1944), freely adapted from Hemingway's novel by William Faulkner and Jules Furthman, who have introduced into it the Free French and the Vichy French. The setting is Martinique, and Bogart is the neutral observer, an American who runs a fishing boat for wealthy visitors. Much of the action again takes place in a saloon, and Hoagy Carmichael has replaced Dooley Wilson at the piano. Howard Hawks is far too strong a director merely to recreate the atmosphere of *Casablanca*, and he has a whole new cast of characters, headed by Dan Seymour as the fat, effete Vichy inspector, with Sheldon Leonard and Aldo Nadi as his co-thugs. The woman drifter common to most of these movies is like the one Furthman wrote for Hawks in *Only Angels Have Wings*, plus some of the insolence he had written for Jean Harlow in *Red Dust* – and with Bogart responding in the same rueful manner as he had to Astor in *Across the Pacific*. This one is baby-faced, as played by a novice Lauren Bacall, and very self-assured. 'Anyone got a match?' is her

ending until the last day of shooting – and it was the producer, Hal Wallis, who contributed the famous last line. No one involved thought the film exceptional till it won Academy Awards for Best Picture, Best Direction (Michael Curtiz) and Best Screenplay. The reviews had indicated merely that it was above average of its first line, lounging in the doorway of his room. The scenes between them have not dated a jot. She: 'I'm hard to get. All you have to do is ask me.' It is not simply their rapport and pleasure in each other (in life, they fell in love during the film and married), or that she is as cynical as he, but that the characters they created remain so vivid. At such times Bogart seems the best of all screen actors; his impatience of cant was never better expressed than in his response to an official asking his nationality: 'Eskimo,' he says.

The Mask of Dimitrios (1944), like *Background to Danger*, is based on a novel by Eric Ambler, but in this case Frank Gruber's screenplay retains its civilised tone and sinewy quality. The exposition is stunning: the body washed up on the shore of Turkey, supposedly that of Dimitrios, and the interest shown in it by the writer Leyden (Lorre), increasingly troubled by glimpses of the mysterious Mr Peters (Greenstreet). As Dimitrios, Zachary Scott looks right but does not sound it; and despite a ludicrous impression of Paris, a 'European' flavour is well maintained in Negulesco's controlled direction. It revives better than one of the Warners' few sober accounts of War – **Action in the North Atlantic** (1943) – which is about the Merchant Navy's role, with Raymond Massey as a commander and Bogart as his executive officer – but then, Lloyd Bacon's direction cannot conceal the clichés.

For Warners, Errol Flynn also went to war, but the films concerned were the subject of much derision: for years people remembered his gall at the end of **Desperate Journey** (1942), crying, 'Now for Australia and a crack at those Japs!' Raoul Walsh directed, as he did **Northern Pursuit** (1943) and **Objective Burma!** (1945), the former a conventional story of Nazi infiltration into Canada, with Flynn as the Mountie they hope will turn traitor. Since we know he won't, it makes dull viewing. *Objective Burma!*, on the other hand, is a very good film, and it is ironic that jokes about Flynn capturing Burma single-handed should have haunted him to the end of his life. The screenplay makes clear that he is leading a small American group, but the lack of any significant British participation so incensed the British that the film had to be withdrawn a few

days after its London premiere. It was the straw that broke the camel's back, for the newly-liberated European nations were being flooded by the backlog of movies bragging of American heroism. In fact *Objective Burma!* is for the most part a realistic portrait of fighting men, foreshadowing both *A Walk in the Sun* (q.v.) and *The Story of G.I. Joe* – and indeed the character of the war correspondent (Henry Hull), aware of age and fallibility, is based on Ernie Pyle. Two sequences are first-rate in their depiction of men at war; the troops in their planes on the way to the target, and the fear in the night of the survivors, anticipating an attack. But courage fails Walsh and his writers, Ranald MacDougall and Lester Cole, who, trying for the full horror of war, lack conviction: one need not have seen similar sequences in Japanese films to find ludicrous the one here in which the men find their colleagues dead and dying. Walsh, otherwise, does a superb job, confirming that most of his later work was cursory: he keeps the camera low, and drives most of the action towards it, achieving dynamism without pretension.

Flynn's limitations were such that there was little that Warners could do but cast him as the intrepid hero of such films. War films were usually new variations on old shoot-em-ups, and the studios, it seems, were much less interested in informing a public avid for information on the War than in keeping their coffers filled via the usual star vehicles. Thus Flynn is typically grim and purposeful, if an unlikely Norwegian patriot in **Edge of Darkness** (1943), which, as directed by Lewis Milestone and written by Robert Rossen (from a novel by William Woods), attempts to be a serious Resistance epic. While long, it has a hard edge, and looks more closely than most films at the reactions of Occupied and Occupiers. The Norwegians are found to be cautious, and subject to conscience, human error and frailty, while the German invaders (for once, three-dimensional) have that jocular coarseness and lack of feeling which characterised many of them. A wholly American cast does not help; and as the heroics become increasingly far-fetched it is clear that the suffering that was endured and the bravery achieved should not be reduced in this way. Eventually, with Nancy Coleman becoming a whore

Hollywood's War Effort

By now, Bette Davis has had a longer screen career than any other star actress – lasting for fifty years – and one reason is the series of superior melodramas she made for Warner Bros. in the early Forties, astonishing audiences with her range and attack. The films were also so popular that she was once called 'the fourth Warner brother'. RIGHT, with Mary Astor in *The Great Lie*, discussed in Chapter 17; FAR RIGHT, with Claude Rains in *Now, Voyager*; and BELOW, with Walter Abel and Rains in *Mr Skeffington*.

and Ann Sheridan getting raped, war becomes simply a nasty business.

Away from the War, Flynn was James J. Corbett in **Gentleman Jim** (1942), the bank clerk who became one of the famous figures of the fight game. Ward Bond is John L. Sullivan, his rival, Jack Carson his sidekick, and Alexis Smith the haughty lady to whom he aspires (in life, Corbett had three wives); in general the care and thought put into this piece place it way ahead of most films about sportsmen. Walsh directed.

Walsh's companion in favour, Howard Hawks, directed **Air Force** (1943), a project instigated by the Army Air Corps, and the lack of histrionics does again suggest seriousness: it is clear that the aim was to show what it was like to be part of a bomber crew – in the Pacific, at that particular time. But on the screenplay Dudley Nichols was neither inspired nor informed: there is no evidence that he had ever heard any G.I.s talking, and his hero is the usual chip-on-the-shoulder underdog (John Garfield), a gunner resentful because he flunked pilot training – and who of course single-handedly brings down the crate with its undercarriage gone. Hawks is as good an action director as he ever was, but the film is nevertheless a well-intentioned slog until the last reel, when it veers dangerously out of control.

Warners had the temerity to offer not one but two of the patriotic all-star musicals: **Thank Your Lucky Stars** (1943) and **Hollywood Canteen** (1944) are respectively the best and worst of them. David Butler directed the first, chiefly remembered for Bette Davis's sung lament, 'They're Either Too Young or Too Old', but there are other good moments: Ann Sheridan instructing a sorority house that 'Love Isn't Born, It's Made'; and Hattie McDaniel exhorting 'Ice-Cold Katie' to marry that soldier. The score by Frank Loesser and Arthur Schwartz helps; a plot about young hopefuls trying to get into show business does not. One of these is Joan Leslie, and one of the idiocies of *Hollywood Canteen* is that a G.I. (Brian Hutton) chooses her when offered as a prize an evening with any star in Hollywood. Another is that this film city equivalent of the Stage Door Canteen is devoid of any stars but Warners': maybe the other studios were jealous, or maybe

they had read the script – by Delmer Daves, who also directs. The shamelessness of one scene became famous: a G.I. (Dane Clark) dances with a girl who looks like Joan Crawford, and when she confesses that she *is* Joan Crawford, he falls down in a faint; later, he finds that because of that dance he no longer needs a stick, and says, 'All those big shots being friendly . . . That's democracy, all them big guys talking to little guys like me.' Warners produced this memento because Bette Davis had been a prime mover in founding the Canteen; she plays herself without embarrassment, a considerable feat in this film.

This actress has one of her rare 'normal' roles, that of a loyal wife in **Watch on the Rhine** (1943), based on Lillian Hellman's play. Ostensibly about the nature of Fascism, that word and 'Germany' are bandied about, with one fleeting reference to thugs smashing up a local fête as explanation of how Nazism came about. A famous German anti-Nazi (Paul Lukas) and a party sympathiser (George Coulouris) are fellow guests in an 'ordinary' American home, but since there is neither discussion nor confrontation it seems strange, to say the least, that the original play was given the New York Drama Critics Award. The screenplay is by the author and Dashiell Hammett (Hellman's lover), and the director, Herman Shumlin, had done the New York production, as is evident from the film's staginess. Lukas, also in the stage version, won both an Oscar and the New York film critics' award for his performance, and if the thing has any merit it is in his eventually gritty portrait of a man who puts duty before personal safety.

Watch on the Rhine is the only Davis film of this period not to revive well – ironically, since it was well received, at least in the U.S., while the others were usually dismissed as 'women's pictures'. It so happened that I saw **Now, Voyager** (1942) at a press show – in 1972 – and the audience not only broke into applause at the end but cheered at that moment when Davis revolts against her selfish mother (Gladys Cooper). Davis is splendid as 'poor Aunt Charlotte', tense and bruised, a frump in sensible shoes who smokes in the secrecy of her room. Taken in hand by Claude Rains, 'the foremost psychiatrist in the country', after listening to the Whitman lines which give the film its title, she

592

'The Fourth Warner Brother'

becomes glamorous and *soigné* – but Davis from the start sensibly had signalled the qualities of strength and gaiety now established in the character. Paul Henreid is the man she meets on her recuperative cruise, and they fall in love over Old-Fashioneds, to Max Steiner's theme song, later reprised each time they look at, or think of, each other. Irving Rapper directed this worm-that-turned tale, which is perhaps more enjoyable than the better-constructed **In This Our Life** (1942), credited to John Huston, but since he and Davis disagreed on the handling Raoul Walsh directed most of her scenes. Howard Koch wrote the screenplay from Ellen Glasgow's strong novel about a small Virginia town and the family that dominated it. The film is not, as the book was, an indictment of the conditions that arise when the rich are careless of their privileges but, in the words of *The Sunday Times* of London, 'that one about the self-centred girl who wrecks lives and, ultimately, cars.' She is Stanley (Davis), and the film's success is in always making us doubt whether or when the others will see her for the bitch she is. Olivia de Havilland, playing in flippant style, is just the sort of woman to attract the same men as she; and Dennis Morgan and George Brent are foolish enough to go from one to the other.

Miss Davis's ability to give life to these melodramas was not lost upon the public, which had conferred on her a popularity unprecedented in Hollywood for a serious actress. She gave value for money while never misjudging her effects, and it is a pleasure to see her take **Old Acquaintance** (1943) from Miriam Hopkins, an actress who never does a half-gesture when she can do a whole one. The formula is that of the haves-and-have-nots, and, as in *The Old Maid*, she has it not while Hopkins is the successful one who has it and loses it. They are both novelists, Davis the respected one in modest tweeds and Hopkins the flashy bestselling lady. As adapted from the play by John Van Druten, the piece retains its theatricality – but then audiences looked forward to the inevitable 'confrontation' scene of the Davis movies. In **Mr Skeffington** (1944), also very well directed by Vincent Sherman, she is on the receiving end, as a spoilt society beauty who uses those about her.

The film retains the ending of the original novel, by 'Elizabeth', in which the now-blind Mr Skeffington – Claude Rains at his best – continues to think of Fanny as a young woman, and the fact of his blindness was resented by some critics. But it is not for nothing that he is called Job, with patience to match his biblical namesake. Both films are not entirely dishonest as to how certain American ladies conduct their careers and emotional lives, and indeed *Mr Skeffington* is often very funny on the subject of women who place physical appearance above all else, or who take to psycho-analysis because they have nothing else to do. Davis never loses sight of Fanny deep down, who is just like Fanny on top – coquettish and vain, a woman brought up without regard for the realities of life which, when pointed out to her, could not interest her less. It is a superb interpretation of that phenomenon, the famous and fading beauty.

Another well thought of stage play was the source of **The Corn Is Green** (1945), one of the lesser Davis vehicles – and not just because she hardly has a field day as the English teacher who founds, against all odds, a school in a Welsh mining village at the turn of the century. The screenplay relegates to the background the social forces of Emlyn Williams's original, which is further reduced by becoming a tale of inspiration and idealism, with the star pupil (John Dall) going, not like Cinderella to the ball, but to Oxford. Irving Rapper directed, and was presumably not responsible for the reproduction of the village, which marks a nadir in Hollywood's attempts to reconstruct other places and other times. Davis is excellently supported by Rhys Williams and Mildred Dunnock as her colleagues; in the difficult role of the budding Shakespeare Mr Dall has a variable accent; as the Cockney slut who almost brings him down, Joan Lorring almost brings the film down as well.

It is possible that the enterprise might have fared better had Hal Wallis still been at the studio. Casey Robinson – credited for the screenplay with Frank Cavett – is on record as saying that Wallis was responsible for the high quality of the Warners pictures at this time. Wallis had been at the studio since the amalgamation with First National, as producer and then executive producer, and having to make thirty pictures a year, as Robinson put it, he 'needed any help he could get – the type of writers who could prove their worth on the screen . . . And so out of this peculiar circumstance of Jack Warner's pecuniary stinginess' – he refused to pay for rewrites and reshooting – 'and Hal Wallis's need and recognition of talent, there grew up the greatest staff of writers that ever existed in the history of the motion pictures.' Warners had been the most misogynist of studios but, with the rise of Bette Davis, vehicles for the lady stars were needed, and amidst the often tear-jerking formulas can be found qualities common to virtually all the films in which Wallis had a personal hand – sourness, hardness and cynicism.

Wallis meanwhile was determined to leave Warner Bros. He had stepped down from head of production to make a handful of films annually with virtual independence, but found Jack L. Warner both uncooperative and interfering. The last straw was when Warner bounded down the aisle at the Academy Awards ceremony to collect the Oscar for *Casablanca*, since it was one of Wallis's films. Wallis could have gone to any Hollywood studio, and J. Arthur Rank asked him to name his own terms to take over his British operations; but Wallis chose to go to Paramount with complete autonomy over his productions.

A monument to him, to Robinson, and to Sam Wood who directed, is **King's Row** (1942), adapted from a virtually intractable novel by Henry Bellamann – a small town exposé, again set in the early years of this century: but out of this 'trash', as Robinson called it, he found his theme: 'the struggle of young people to grow into manhood and womanhood'. The film has a quality unlike any other small town film, with its cross-currents, the assumption by some of superiority, and the whispers on all manner of things from insanity to self-righteous sadism. Claude Rains is a tortured doctor, and Charles Coburn a brisk one, with little outward sign of evil; Ann Sheridan is the girl from the other side of the tracks, as warm and understanding as any legless man could want for support; and Betty Field is a wounded bird of a girl, desperate for company. As the joint heroes, Ronald Reagan and Robert Cummings are unexpectedly good; but the virtuosity and James Wong Howe's camera-

work cannot disguise the fact that King's Row is a painted town.

The Hard Way (1942) also had excellent construction, a strong narrative drive, and was well thought of then, when it won for Ida Lupino the New York critics' award for the year's Best Actress. Personally, I feel that any film which begins with her committing suicide is off to a good start, but the rest is flashback as she ruthlessly pushes her sister (Joan Leslie) to stardom – 'the John Dillinger of the one-night stands', as Dennis Morgan puts it. Jerry Wald wrote the story, after talking to a certain star's ex-husband following his suicide attempt, and the director, Sherman, admitted that it was based on a famous star and her mother. The screenplay by Irwin Shaw and Daniel Fuchs

At one time the small town movie constituted a genre in its own right, but this sunny picture from *King's Row* is not entirely typical, since the film took a somewhat misanthropic view of its eponymous setting. The stars were Ann Sheridan and Ronald Reagan: he turned to politics as his film career faltered, eventually becoming President of the United States.

595

drops a hint or two that the lady concerned was Ginger Rogers.

On the lighter side – which the company seldom was – the most cherishable of their comedies is **Larceny Inc.** (1942), with Edward G. Robinson, 'flannel-brain' Broderick Crawford and Ed Brophy as three ex-cons who want to go straight, but need cash and therefore buy a shop next door to a bank. Lloyd Bacon directed, sharply, which is more than can be said of William Keighley's work on **George Washington Slept Here** (1942): despite Ann Sheridan and Jack Benny this is a dull version of the Kaufman-Hart play about a couple buying a dilapidated country home – the first of several movies on this theme. **The Male Animal** (1942) raises a serious issue, when a professor (Henry Fonda) wants to read to his pupils a letter written by Vanzetti but is opposed by another (Eugene Pallette), who sees a red under every bed; but it is more concerned with the triangle between him, his wife (Olivia de Havilland) and a superannuated ballplayer (Jack Carson). Elliott Nugent directed, from the listless play that he wrote with James Thurber.

The studio's two most important morale-boosters were both entrusted to Michael Curtiz after his success with *Yankee Doodle Dandy*. **This Is The Army** (1943) was based on the stage revue devised and produced by Irving Berlin, with songs by him. Meant to promote good relations for the army and featuring entertainers currently in battledress, its metamorphosis into film now included a storyline linking it to a Berlin show of the First World War, and since its every sequence is drowned in patriotism it is perhaps appropriate that the father and son leading roles are played by George Murphy and Ronald Reagan, both of whom later took up political careers. The film beams good will, and so, in a different way, does the other film, **Mission to Moscow** (1943), one of the oddest Hollywood contributions to the War. It is an account of Joseph E. Davies's relations with the Soviet Union from his appointment as Ambassador in 1936 to his tub-thumping on its behalf after Hitler attacked. The film was instigated by the Office of War Information, which chose Warners to produce it on the strength of *Confessions of a Nazi Spy*. Recalling the public response to

that, Warners were not enthusiastic and the initial praise turned sour when the handling of the subject matter was attacked. The reservations which Davies had expressed in this autobiographical book were ignored in Howard Koch's screenplay, and Davies himself was criticised for appearing in the film to vouch for its integrity. The distortions include: blaming France and Britain for appeasement, and suggesting that the U.S.S.R. distrusted Fascism, being driven into its arms – the Soviet-German pact – by the conduct of those two countries; Davies visiting a prescient Churchill in 1939, whereas in his book he mentions merely meeting him two years earlier; myriad references to Japanese aggression – whereas a Russian-Japanese non-aggression pact was still in force when this film came out; and a complete falsification of the Moscow trials. The trials were featured in the film because Davies had referred to them in his book, being now intended as implied criticism of the régime to counterbalance the admiration shown for the May Day parades, etc. But where the film Davies (Walter Huston) speaks of 'the integrity and honesty of the Soviet leaders' the real Davies was already privately aware of Stalin's purges. The combination of documentary footage and reasonably re-enacted accounts of Davies's work in Russia, plus Huston's performance, make the film persuasive; and Curtiz and the editing department move the film to a climax where none really exists. Since its purpose was to make Americans understand the Soviets and love Uncle Joe, it may be said to have succeeded.

Adolph Zukor continued to lead Paramount, though the titular chief was a former Georgia showman, Y. Frank Freeman, who according to John Houseman (in his autobiography) was 'respected in the industry, where he had a reputation for "fairness" and financial know-how. In my experience I found him ignorant, bigoted, reactionary and malignant' – notably in trying to ensure that no negroes appeared in Paramount pictures. The Chief of Production remained B. G. (Buddy) de Sylva, who (as we have seen) had succeeded William Le Baron. The latter moved on to 20th Century-Fox to produce mainly musicals and light comedies – which were precisely the genres of films preferred by de Sylva, whose team included many experienced talents in those fields. With some reason Paramount projected the friendliest image of the studios, and it may be seen in **Star Spangled Rhythm** (1942), the first of all the films about Hollywood doing its bit for the troops. A sailor (Eddie Bracken) has both a father (Victor Moore) and a girlfriend (Betty Hutton) working at Paramount, and he accordingly persuades the entire contract list to put on a show for the boys. George Marshall directed, and among the less-dated turns are 'Hit the Road to Dreamland', sung by Mary Martin and Dick Powell, and an old chestnut of a sketch, 'If Men Played Cards as Women Do', acted by Ray Milland, Franchot Tone, Lynne Overman and Fred Mac-Murray. Bing Crosby sings a long patriotic number, 'Old Glory', before a painted Mount Rushmore, while several ethnic groups (despite Mr Freeman) explain why they are proud to be American.

The 'Road' pictures which Crosby made with Bob Hope have turned out – surprisingly, I think – to be ageless. **Road to Singapore** (1940) had been originally planned as a vehicle for Dorothy Lamour, with Fred MacMurray as a wealthy boy fond of the roving life and George Burns as his sidekick. MacMurray decided that he wanted no part of this jungle lore, and the script was seized upon by Hope and Crosby, whose verbal sparring on the golf-course had persuaded them that they should make a film together. Hope's role was built up; as a team they were not yet free-wheeling, but under the same director, Victor Schertzinger, they took off in **Road to Zanzibar** (1941). It was this which established the pattern for the series: they are carnival performers who, forced to flee, find themselves in an exotic spot where they encounter Miss Lamour, for whom – and perhaps some buried treasure or merely a quick buck – they are prepared to double-cross each other and anyone else in sight. In *The New Republic*, Otis Ferguson decided that this was 'the funniest thing I have seen on the screen in years', and in the course of a long analysis on screen humour observed that it 'still has the free and happy air of the spontaneous, the best vein, the laughter shared and mounting'. With **Road to Morocco** (1942), directed by David Butler, they

added sight-gags, puns in abundance, and jokes about Hollywood and themselves for which posterity may need a glossary. The films were easily the most popular screen comedies since Chaplin's peak: the Forties would not have been the same without them. Hope and Crosby take us into their idiot make-believe world, conning and cheating and chasing the girl, and they do it with teamwork that is a high spot in film history; no other film comics ever approached their mutual understanding, and of other screen teams only Hepburn and Tracy matched their timing. It is a nice act to start with, beyond the pleasant personalities founded on greed and lust: the beauty is in the ad-libs and throwaways. The films themselves are not smart or anarchic, and they offer no vision of the world; at the worst, they are amiable, and at the best uproariously funny. The daffiest is *Road to Morocco*, the most inventive narrative the Alaskan adventure, **Road to Utopia** (1945), directed by Hal Walker, and the best gags are in **Road to Rio** (1947), directed by Norman Z. McLeod. The writers are various, and the fair-to-excellent songs by Burke and Van Heusen.

Bing Crosby and Bob Hope in *Road to Utopia*. Much earlier, before the 'Road' films became a series, the *Motion Picture Herald* called Crosby and Hope 'the most successful pairing of comedy talents brought forth upon the screen since Hollywood memory runneth not to the contrary.'

Ingrid Bergman and Bing Crosby in *The Bells of St Mary's* directed by Leo McCarey and a sequel to *Going My Way*, also with Crosby. It takes a high place among the 'spiritual' films turned out at this time, which, if one refers to the earlier film, is a weak compliment; however, the disparity in quality was not remarked upon at the time.

Irving Berlin wrote the score for **Holiday Inn** (1942), which increased Crosby's already huge popularity. Berlin had been trying to build a revue around the American holidays, and when the project did not materialise he sold it to producer-director Mark Sandrich as a vehicle for Crosby, with the possibility of Fred Astaire as co-star. The War had just started, and Paramount, uncertain of its effect upon the box office – in fact, audience numbers increased enormously – only agreed to the salaries involved by economising on the leading ladies, the little-known Marjorie Reynolds and Virginia Dale. If the point of a musical is to be a showcase for the talents of its contributors, this is a great one, as the screen's best dancer and its most popular singer share Berlin's lilting songs, including 'White Christmas', introduced herein. Ease is both the keynote and the manner in which the stars handle an inconsequential plot about amorous rivalry and a country club. It matters not that there are musicals with more zest.

Leo McCarey conceived a film for Crosby, but it was not till he arrived on the Paramount lot that Crosby learnt that he was to play a priest in **Going My Way** (1944), a film which today seems merely an extended P.R. job for the Roman

Catholic Church. Father O'Malley is more Crosby than Crosby, a temple of all human virtues who wears casual clothes, sings popular songs, and enjoys a tot of whisky and a round of golf; Barry Fitzgerald is the irascible Irish elder priest who is converted to his ways – and my own attitude towards both actors is for once reversed, since the latter's grumpiness is welcome in a film whose 'holier than thou' stance is virtually intolerable. Both actors won Oscars, and the New York critics agreed with the Academicians over Fitzgerald, over Best Picture and Best Director; McCarey also won an Oscar for Best Story, and Frank Butler and Frank Cavett for Best Screenplay. Public response made it the most successful film yet made, after *Gone with the Wind*, till overtaken by its sequel, **The Bells of St Mary's** (1945) – which for contractual reasons was made at R.K.O. It is mercifully less sentimental, and both more confident and less insistent in its treatment of religion. The screenplay by Dudley Nichols is more subtle, and Crosby, who in the earlier film rarely seemed human, is very winning here. This time his priest is pitted against a hidebound nun (priests were not new in movies, but nuns were, except in small roles) and to that role Ingrid Bergman brings a discretion which equals Crosby's. At ease in both films, he underplays the better material of this one, and the farewell scene between him and Bergman is touching, despite the arc-lights trained on her nose. The popularity of both players had much to do with the film's success, but the reviews were universally good: Howard Barnes in *The New York Herald Tribune* called it 'inspiring, in the best sense of the word'.

After Crosby and Hope, Paramount's most popular star was Alan Ladd, an inexpressive, slight-of-stature tough guy. Of his many films, less than half a dozen are memorable, but those that are include the first two in which he starred, though made by directors whose other work is largely undistinguished. Frank Tuttle handled **This Gun for Hire** (1942) and Stuart Heisler was responsible for **The Glass Key** (1942), but we may suppose the films' qualities emanate from their original novels – respectively by Graham Greene and Dashiell Hammett (the former with a screenplay by Albert Maltz and W. R. Burnett, and the latter with one by Jonathan Latimer). In the case of the Greene, the book is pictured under the credits, usually an indication of respect: the dialogue and plot are virtually intact. It concerns a hired gun (Ladd) searching for the man who betrayed him; but whereas Greene's Raven had a hare-lip and was hired by a doddery old Jewish millionaire who wants an assassination to start a war in order to grow rich on armaments, in the film he has an injured wrist and is employed by a manufacturer who aims to sell gas to the Japs. What was original in Greene has by a trembling of a leaf become movie-conventional; what was moving – Raven's probing towards a relationship with the girl (Veronica Lake), his comments on his past – often seem glib. Most to be regretted is the substitution of Los Angeles for Greene's shabby, cold Midlands town with its grimy grand hotels, its ABC cafés, the Industrial Revolution railway yards and its one run-down music hall. Notably good are the portraits of the old master-mind (Tully Marshall), and the fat and cowardly connoisseur of chorus girls and candy (Laird Cregar) – both characters to reappear revamped in the American *film noir*. If *The Glass Key* lacks the gallery of characters that made Huston's *Maltese Falcon* so satisfying, here is William Bendix, whose ape-like features, stupidity and Brooklyn accent nicely underscore his deadly endearments, 'You mean I don't get to smack baby?' and 'Little rubber ball does all right, doesn't he?' Veronica Lake again plays Ladd's female foil, and it is difficult to believe that her screen persona was not dreamed up by these writers, for her golden mane and little girl insolence suited this genre as no other.

Another undistinguished director, Lewis Allen, made **The Uninvited** (1944), which, to start with, looks more like Cornwall than do most films loc-ationed at Carmel. The art directors, Han Dreier and Ernst Fegte, managed an exceptionally good haunted house – a house in which the new tenant (Ray Milland) is woken by a sobbing woman, the cat refuses to go upstairs, there is sudden cold, a scent of mimosas in the air, and in the attic a bouquet of roses shrivels. Like all such establishments, it has a malevolent influence on a beautiful girl (Gail Russell), but the film still comes across as one of the best of its type. **The Unseen** (1945) is one of the worst, with an unconvincing London, two children borrowed from 'The Turn of the Screw', and a father (Joel McCrea) whose daft behaviour menaces the children's young governess. The first film has a good screenplay, by Dodie Smith and Frank Pártes, from a novel by Dorothy McCardle, the second an absurd one by Raymond Chandler and Hagar Wilde, from a novel by Ethel Lina White; and Allen has reacted accordingly, the direction of the one being as assured as the other is sloppy. Miss Russell is in both films, and the producers were Charles Brackett for the first and John Houseman for *The Unseen*, whose first film this was in that capacity.

The direction of **For Whom the Bell Tolls** (1943) was entrusted to a freelance, Sam Wood, though originally announced for deMille. It is possible that the author, Hemingway, vetoed deMille, since we know that he recommended the stars, Gary Cooper and Ingrid Bergman – but his advice was not taken in the case of the latter till executives saw the rushes of Vera Zorina in the role. The already huge bud-get was extended to a publicity campaign of like proportions, and the film lasts almost three hours – during which it is mute on the causes of the Spanish Civil War. Indeed, were it not for the cast (com-posed of every nationality except Spanish) and the weaponry at the end, one might take it for an episode in the history of the Hatfields and McCoys. A further quota-tion from the Donne sermon follows the credits, 'Any man's death diminishes me', which provides a moving statement on the existence of the International Brigade, of which Cooper is its chief representative, while Bergman represents the Spanish peasantry. The front office had emascu-lated Dudley Nichols's screenplay, and although the Hays Office had sanctioned Cooper's farewell line to her – 'I am you and you are me. You're all there'll be of me' – audiences had to grasp at its mean-ing. However, sex on the screen did ad-vance when she agreed with a cheery grin that she was shameless. Bergman is odd casting, tall and blonde,★ for a character

★Her cropped hair was a deliberate policy on Paramount's part to counteract the popularity of Veronica Lake's long tresses. In emulation of Miss Lake many women on war work were getting their hair caught in the machines, and Paramount was held responsible.

naively conceived in the first place, and we may find her Maria hardly more real than the surprisingly poor process work; but as Wood subjects her to a battery of smiling close-ups, as if unable to accustom himself to an actress so natural, we may at least, all these years later, understand how he felt.

DeMille's two wartime spectacles are dreadful even by his later standards. **Reap the Wild Wind** (1942) has a tale of amorous rivalry against a background of sailing ships, a battle with a giant squid, and some of those pointless discussion/courtroom scenes which then characterised the more ambitious historical films. It also has a high-spirited heroine who scandalises society; Paulette Goddard's performance only reminds us how much better Vivien Leigh and Bette Davis were in like circumstance. The awfulness of **The Story of Dr Wassell** (1944) is more serious, since it was based on the true story of the doctor who insisted on staying on Java to care for the stretcher cases after the Japanese had landed. Gary Cooper copes with the situation in a way that reduces our memories of Mr Deeds, but the film turns out to be less interested in that than in his youth, settling for a long and cliché-ridden flashback about trying to find the cause of some dread tropical disease in China. The art direction is ghastly; and deMille's vulgarity was never better demonstrated than by the cut from a hospital being bombed to cute Chinese children singing on a small humped bridge.

Paramount had in fact the distinction of being the first studio to make a film about American participation in the War, and **Wake Island** (1942) came out while other studios were still offering hokum like *Across the Pacific*. It tells, 'as accurately and factually as possible', of the first American feat of valour, when a small group of Marines held out against repeated enemy assaults on a former Pan American fuelling base. That they eventually surrendered was known to every American, and the difficulty of ending films on the War by the depressing truth was solved by a commentator assuring audiences that the Marines would return to exact a 'terrible' vengeance. Bosley Crowther saw it on a Marine base, where it was received 'with thunderous applause' – and reported that it would 'bring a surge of pride to every patriot's breast'. It is hard to watch today,

especially for those familiar with the clichés of the First World War movies purloined by W. R. Burnett and Frank Butler for their screenplay: the Quirt and Flagg relationship of the buddies (Robert Preston, William Bendix), the dedicated commander (Brian Donlevy), and the jabbering enemy – who are glimpsed being elated or disconcerted as the case may be. The polished direction is by another variable talent, John Farrow,* who managed beautifully with an even less promising war story, **You Came Along** (1945). Ivy Hotchkiss (Lizabeth Scott) is selected to chaperone three Air Force heroes on a bond-selling tour, and she falls for the one (Robert Cummings) who has leukaemia: 'Promise me one thing, never grieve for me,' he says as he proposes, and they thank God for every day they have together. When his time comes, he gets his buddies to look in on her: 'Here's to the four of us' they say, a lachrymose *menage à trois*, as the camera pans to a sky of silver linings. There is a glutinous theme song and an unattractive cast apart from Miss Scott, showing in her first film the warm and genuine spirit she had before they turned her into a cut-price Lauren Bacall. There are also sequences of charm and humour, as in the other soap operas of Hal Wallis, whose second 'independent' production for Paramount this was.

Mitchell Leisen also made a film about flyers, **I Wanted Wings** (1941), taking over from J. Theodore Reed, and thus saving its producer from certain disaster. It is watchable, which is an achievement in view of the fact that it has the standard plot of all service movies, i.e. the ups and downs of some rookies: the know-it-all rich boy (Ray Milland), the dumbbell (Wayne Morris) and the grease monkey (William Holden). Made before the U.S. entered the War, it has an extraneous prologue assuring Los Angeles that in the event of a blackout the Air Force is standing by. The War in Europe provides the springboard for **Hold Back the Dawn** (1941), one of the last great Hollywood romances, written by Wilder and Brackett for Leisen, their third film for him. They gleefully pursue a sure-fire plot, from a semi-autobiographical story by Ketti

*'John [Farrow] combined the distinction of being a Papal Count with a reputation for sadism practised professionally and individually on the persons of male and female performers' (John Houseman in 'Front and Center').

Frings, starting pleasingly in a Hollywood studio with Charles Boyer as a down-and-out putting a touch on Leisen himself. He, Boyer, turns out to be a former gigolo domiciled in Mexico who nabs the first virginal schoolteacher (Olivia de Havilland) to cross his path, because he needs an American visa – and how blithely she ignores the little indications of the truth of the matter! As the besotted and then disillusioned woman Miss de Havilland was never more winning; Boyer in the second half has little to do but look stricken at his lack of scruples – partly because Wilder and Brackett wrote him out when he refused to play a scene with a cockroach.

After some bland comedies, Leisen succumbed to Paramount's plea that he helm **Lady in the Dark** (1944), part-persuaded by the fact that he had not worked in Technicolor before. He helped design the costumes and, though the Hacketts are credited, wrote the screenplay – from Moss Hart's 'play with music' which had startled New York in 1941. That had concerned a fashion editor undergoing psychoanalysis, but the subject had deterred the Hollywood studios, together with the difficulty of replacing Gertrude Lawrence in the role and staging her dream sequences. Korda had bought the rights, and when Ginger Rogers insisted on doing this film under the terms of her contract, he parted with them for the then–record sum of $285,000.★ A difficult shooting schedule included much temperament on the part of the star – she refused to do the requisite bumps and grinds for the song 'Jenny', because they did not fit her image – and also the jettisoning of much of the Kurt Weill–Ira Gershwin score, including the indispensable 'My Ship', because it was despised by B.G. de Sylva. As offered here, the story is neither comedy nor drama, nor anything between: the problem of the woman's romantic choice is of no interest, and her dreams are merely tastefully vulgar. But then, as C.A. Lejeune observed, the film was 'variously described as the Song of Songs of Every Woman; the Last Word in Beauty, Spectacle, Colour, Music, Romance; the Girl of the Moment with the Loves of the Year in the Picture

of a Lifetime; the Startling Story of a Woman's Secret Love; the Minx in Mink with a Yen for Men; and – rather breathlessly – the Most Beautiful Thing in the World of Motion Pictures from Paramount. Who says so? Guess who.'

Frenchman's Creek (1944) was also expensive, at $4 million the most costly American film made to that time (though concurrently at M-G-M reshooting on *Ziegfeld Follies*, q.v., would push it to that sum). This one suffered a number of mishaps (such as fog during location shooting), but Leisen was also prone to extravagance. He thought Daphne du Maurier's novel 'as dull as dish-water' and the picture 'lousy', and he is not wrong; but in lushness and silliness it reminds us of the days when movie-going was fun. The middle reaches – when the aristocratic concubine dresses up as a cabin boy – are brackish, and that is partly because as her pirate lover Arturo de Cordova lacks any romantic aura; but Joan Fontaine is playful and artificial, just what the enterprise needs. Memorable is another Cornish mansion, created by Dreier and Fegté, for which they won an Oscar.

Dreier's recreation, with Walter Tyler, of eighteenth-century London in **Kitty** (1945) is also outstanding. Leisen was fascinated by the period, and this was one project for which he cared: a tale about a Cockney guttersnipe (Paulette Goddard) who ends up a duchess – from a novel by Rosamund Marshall which combined 'Forever Amber' with 'Pygmalion' – in which role, foppish and elegant, Ray Milland is excellent. Those situations not already exhausted are diverting: 'How will I find her?' asks Kitty, arriving to take tea with Lady Susan (Constance Collier). 'Drunk' is the laconic reply of the butler (Eric Blore), masterful beneath his powdered wig. Cecil Kellaway is superb as Gainsborough, and Reginald Owen gives a magnificent display of decrepit lechery. Miss Collier was seldom better than as the tippling beldame, her bearing masking a complete lack of scruples. The script tentatively suggests that Kitty is the true lady, since she lacks the deceits of society, and her progress is closer to American democratic ideals than the skeletons in the cupboards of the British aristocracy.

The film temporarily halted the decline in Leisen's work which had begun after

---

★Korda made a huge profit, taking advantage of Miss Rogers's intransigence; but in general Broadway successes had more value than best-selling novels. Paramount paid $150,000, for *For Whom the Bell Tolls* the previous year and that was then a record sum for a novel.

Hold Back the Dawn, and with the death of Lubitsch in 1946 there were few other practitioners of the comedy in which they had been supreme. Billy Wilder (b. 1906) had written for them both, and like Preston Sturges he turned director as a result of Leisen's cavalier treatment of his scripts.

Wilder adored the films of Lubitsch, but his own films were more surely shaped by his familiarity with what Sturges had achieved at Paramount – as well as by his experiences as a child and a young man. Born in Vienna to a family of hoteliers he learnt quickly the facts of hotel life; in Berlin during Inflation he was a dance partner, his cynicism increasing as he sought work as a journalist or in films. As we have seen, he emigrated to Paris when the Nazis came to power, and a fellow ex-patriate, Joe May, helped him to get a writing job in Hollywood. His career really began when he was teamed with Charles Brackett on *Bluebeard's Eighth Wife* in 1938, and their great success was another reason that he turned director with **The Major and the Minor** (1942), encouraged against studio opposition by the lady for whom it was written, Ginger Rogers. She plays a country girl who, after twenty-seven jobs in New York, decides to pack it in; but the only way she can afford the fare home is to disguise herself as a small girl. The screenplay is much less witty than the one Wilder and Brackett had written for *Midnight*, and superficially the film is conventional. However the first half contains a number of incidents influenced by Sturges: the lecherous client (Robert Benchley) chasing Rogers round the room; the guy who pricks her balloon; the stumblebum who pinches her change; while the second half contains a number of typical Wilder pre-occupations, such as the continuation of the masquerade (by Rogers). Two subjects which most interested him, however, had to be treated with deference to the Code: the 'Lolita' situation, whereby the Major (Ray Milland) is attracted to the 'child', and the sexuality of the adolescent cadets whom he teaches.

The film was based on a *Saturday Evening Post* story and an unrelated, unproduced play. Wilder's sources would often remain unusual – *Sunset Boulevard* (q.v.) grew from a proposal that *The Royal Family of Broadway*, to which Paramount owned the rights, might be adapted to suit a Hedda Hopper-type gossip columnist – and **Five Graves to Cairo** (1943) is remake of *Hotel Imperial*, as suggested by Lajos Biro, who wrote the play on which that film was based. It takes only the bones of the original – the inn, the maid, the fugitive and the occupying army – which is perhaps why, at the time, no one noticed the resemblance, though there had been a remake in 1940. The fugitive (Franchot Tone) is now English, the army is headed by Rommel (Erich Von Stroheim) and the inn is in the desert. Other ingredients include an impersonation, a body in the cellar, a secret map, a manhunt – and Wilder handles them as though he had been directing thrillers for a lifetime. The wittiest lines go to Von Stroheim, but the Englishman is, as ever, gentlemanly and resourceful; the German lieutenant (Peter Van Eyk) humourless and efficient; and the French girl (Anne Baxter) shrewd and bitter, is prepared to bargain her body for her brother's life. The Egyptian (Akim Tamiroff) is confused and sycophantic, and the Italian general (Fortunio Bonanova) an opera addict and a hopeful lecher the latter is the butt of several jokes in a thoroughly enjoyable tale.

Double Indemnity (1944) was written by Wilder and Raymond Chandler, who later wrote, 'Working with Wilder . . . was an agonising experience and has probably shortened my life, but I learned from it about as much about screenwriting as I am capable of learning, which is not very much.' Their source was a novel by James M. Cain, a devilish thing about a proposal for accident insurance which snowballs into the perfect murder. Its efficacy depends on its twists, but the best sequence is still the tone-setting first meeting between the insurance agent (Fred MacMurray) and his client's bored young wife (Barbara Stanwyck), with his professed admiration for her ankle-bracelet and her riposte to his 'pass', 'There's a speed limit in this State' – her cheap perfume and the smell of that hot, dusty room permeate the rest of the film. The star players here are murderers with no regrets – Wilder had difficulty in finding willing players and commented that he knew he had a good film when George Raft turned the role down. MacMurray has the facile charm, the shifty eyes, the hail-fellow-well-met attitude which does not disguise an iron will as

Barbara Stanwyck, Fred MacMurray and Edward G. Robinson in Billy Wilder's *Double Indemnity*, the latter as the cant-hating insurance man investigating the death of the lady's husband. Robinson later observed, 'It might have been a classic if Wilder had had just a little more heart,' but to most of us it is a classic as it is.

strong as the lady's – to be intermittently observed in the smiling eyes beneath the cheap blonde page-boy of a transformed Stanwyck.

At Universal the career of Deanna Durbin survived the debacle of **The Amazing Mrs Holliday** (1943). Studio executives placed her future in the hands of Felix Jackson, but it hardly endured beyond her marriage to him, since only the first films he produced satisfied the public devoted to the now grown-up Deanna. This venture was popular – the tale of a girl who, to find a home for Chinese evacuees, claims to be the widow of an aged naval commander who is not, as she thought, dead. However, as credited to the writing team of Frank Ryan and John Jacoby, and directed by Bruce Manning, the result is a synthetic and somewhat tasteless mixture of comedy and wartime sentiment. The same combination does work pleasantly in **Hers to Hold** (1943), directed by Ryan, which resurrects only the youngest of the *Three Smart Girls* so that, as headstrong as ever, she can pursue a handsome flyer (Joseph Cotten). At one point she sings 'Say a Prayer for the Boys Over There' to her fellow workers in a munitions factory, but

for all that these are pictures less grovellingly patriotic than most of the period.

There is nothing of the War in **His Butler's Sister** (1943), one of the last Hollywood fairy tales, agreeably directed by Frank Borzage. Pat O'Brien is the butler and the film's best invention has his Park Avenue peers (Akim Tamiroff, Alan Mowbray, Frank Jenks, Sig Arno and Hans Conried) all vying for the hand of the new maid, Miss Durbin. Only her employer (Franchot Tone) takes till the last reel to realise that she is Broadway's best bet in years – but he had missed hearing her topical medley of Russian songs. One reason to like the film is that Walter Catlett has a large role, as a lecherous producer.

'Deanna Goes Dramatic' was Universal's publicity line on **Christmas Holiday** (1944), which is Maugham's novel diluted. He wrote of a confident, bourgeois young Englishman whose values are shattered by a visit to Paris and a meeting with a White Russian prostitute, married to a convicted murderer. 'I've learnt,' he says – as transcribed in the screenplay by Herman J. Mankiewicz – 'a hundred years of living in the past twenty-four hours.' On screen he has become a nice young lieutenant (Dean Harmes) in the U.S. Army, the setting is

New Orleans, the brothel has become a roadhouse and the lady its resident singer. She still has her reminiscences to tell and Mankiewicz, following his work on *Citizen Kane*, has chosen not to relate them in chronological order. Suffice to say that she meets a bounder (Gene Kelly) while listening to the 'Liebestod', and marries him. As both the B-girl listlessly waiting for her man to be released and the sensible, strong young woman too nice to ask all the right questions, Durbin holds both sections of the film together – despite the fact that, according to the director, Robert Siodmak, she 'wanted to play a new part, but flinched from looking like a tramp; she always wanted to look like nice, wholesome Deanna Durbin pretending to be a tramp'. Siodmak (who had known the producer, Jackson, when the latter was a writer with Ufa), does so well with the atmospheric centrepieces which were his speciality, that we hardly notice when the film falls apart towards the end – as Durbin has to cope with a confrontation and declaration of love which would have defeated even Duse herself.

The result, however, pleased all concerned, including the public, but the star decided to return to more obviously escapist fare. Jackson had the good sense to commission Jerome Kern to compose the songs for **Can't Help Singing** (1944) and they were the best she was ever given. She plays a senator's dizzy daughter who pursues her lover to California, taking her pratfalls with a will and acting without any concession to 'charm' or sentiment. A crisp script is plentiful with misunderstandings and subterfuges, bowled along with zest by the director, Ryan. The Grand Canyon and Durbin were photographed in Technicolor for the first time, but with make-up as harsh as any Goldwyn Girl it does not flatter her. **Lady on a Train** (1946) is similarly marred, an otherwise neat whodunnit, from a novel by Leslie Charteris, nicely directed by Charles David (best known, otherwise, as the producer of *Drôle de Drame*), who later became her third husband. In view of the personal relationships, one must assume that both producer and director complied with her own wish to look like a blonde cutie, singing 'Give Me a Little Kiss, Will You, Huh?' in the finger-snapping style of Betty Grable. Given that she intensely disliked

her screen image, her decision to change is understandable. On the other hand, he[r] fans were not pleased, and since, accordin[g] to *Picturegoer*, 'more than most stars he[r] private life has been her public's concern['] a second divorce – from Jackson – di[d] not help matters. Both on screen and of[f] the child to whom the world had give[n] its heart was, after all, just anoth[er] Hollywood star.

Universal took firm action, and re[-] turned to its early formula, an unglamo[r]ised Durbin in light comedy with song[s] but few people liked **Because of Hi[m]** (1946). Richard Wallace directed airily, b[ut] there is not a single laugh in this tale of [a] stage-struck girl (Durbin) who cheats [a] ham actor (Charles Laughton) into helpin[g] her achieve her ambition. One does n[ot] necessarily have to recall *All About E[ve]* (q.v.) to recall how good Hollywoo[d] could be on the morals and mores [of] Broadway. The star herself retained th[e] impulsiveness which had made her s[o] fetching as a child star, and it now sug[-] gested the sort of roles that Carole Lom[-] bard had once played – or Margaret Sull[i]van, since **I'll be Yours** (1947), directe[d] by William A. Seiter, was a remake of *T[he] Good Fairy*. The Preston Sturges script wa[s] used again, but neither the leading ma[n] Tom Drake, nor two usually excellen[t] supporting players, William Bendix an[d] Adolphe Menjou, were of much help t[o] the star.

The film was seen after Universal ama[l]gamated with International Picture[s] (q.v.), whose owners, Leo Spitz and Wi[l]liam Goetz, had made the deal with th[e] primary aim of acquiring Miss Durbin['s] services. She remained, as she had bee[n] since arriving at the studio, its only majo[r] box-office star. She had made the tran[-] sition to adult roles with ease; she coul[d] play both comedy and drama; she could b[e] demure or glamorous; she could sing any[-] thing within a range from opera to swing[.] She was in fact a better actress and a mor[e] effective screen presence than Betty Grab[le] or Rita Hayworth, who were worth for[-] tunes to their studios, respectively 20t[h] Century-Fox and Columbia. But the pub[-] lic which had deserted Miss Durbin afte[r] *Lady on a Train* were not reconverted b[y] the two subsequent films. Spitz and Goet[z] hired Johnny Green, the musician, to sal[-] vage her career but soon lost heart: the had purchased a Broadway show for her, **Up in Central Park** (1948), but filmed it in black and white when the other studios were using Technicolor for musicals. Durbin herself, aware that Judy Garland – they had appeared together in their first film, *Every Sunday*, a short – never stepped before a camera without being surrounded by M-G-M's best talents, pleaded for better material but instead was offered a raise in salary. In 1947 she was the highest-paid person in the U.S., but Universal now claimed, paradoxically, that her fee was too great to accommodate either colour or more popular co-stars. It turned out to be ill-advised penny-pinching; the lady retired to live in France with M. David, and has remained amused but otherwise silent about the whole episode.

In her last poor films her natural but effervescent personality remains as attractive as ever, though one sometimes senses her impatience with the inadequate material. Like Alice Faye she refused to continue struggling with poor scripts and turned her back on the business rather than start again at another studio (for twenty years more her old mentor, Joseph Pasternak, begged her to come to M-G-M). It is sad to see talent driven out by studio executives (other stars – Garland and Marilyn Monroe q.v. – were instrumental in their own destruction), but Miss Durbin had a sweet and satisfying revenge – if we are to believe the constant reports from radio and television stations which deal with requests from the public: for she invariably heads every list.

Universal had acquired another box-office attraction – Abbott and Costello, a former vaudeville team. Bud Abbott is the straight man, wholly without charm, and Lou Costello, short and tubby, the comic. He is a creature to whom things happen; he exists in the middle of slapstick, not contributing. Universal set them to the usual tasks allotted screen teams: they joined the navy, played detective, and so on. They lacked the ability to create their own lunatic universe in the manner of Laurel and Hardy; timing and wit they knew not of. Their real popularity was brief: by the end of the War their films were double-bill fare, but they kept going till the mid-Fifties in a series of 'creepy-funnies' in which their co-stars were ghosts, Frankenstein, the Invisible Man and other

Deanna Durbin in 1948, smiling despite the terrible films she was required to make for Universal.

phenomena. If posterity draws a blank with Abbott and Costello, it warms slightly to another vaudeville team, Olsen and Johnson, and that is because of the three films they made the first is **Hellzapoppin** (1941). The pair had struck lucky with a Broadway revue of this title in 1938, with 'improvisations' which included a gorilla dragging a woman member of the audience from a box, a tout trying to sell tickets for another show, and a man and woman undressing in the stalls. It ran for over three years, and Universal bought the film rights – at least, they bought the title and its two stars, then commissioned from Nat Perrin and Warren Wilson a script to satisfy anyone who had heard of it or them. It starts, literally, with a merry hell that turns out to be a film set, and moves on to a Long Island estate for a conventional musical comedy plot – but H. C. Potter, directing, pushes through the gags at reckless speed: Martha Raye, an overgrown vaudeville star, has only to see Mischa Auer, a phoney Russian count, to start chasing; Frankenstein's monster steps in to give a helping hand; dogs talk, also photographs, and the players to the audience; the film itself slips from its sprockets, part of it is censored,

605

and one reel supposedly gets mixed up with that of a Western. It is a lively experience, and one that must have influenced the 'Road' comedies; what would have been interesting is a filmed record of the original show.

Chief among the studio's other players were Jon Hall and Maria Montez, who starred in a number of Technicolor adventures which found wartime audiences at their most indulgent. Walter Wanger, now a contract producer at the studio, produced the first of them, **Arabian Nights** (1942), clearly inspired by Korda's *Thief of Baghdad*; the credits are promisingly done over a simulation of Persian prints, and they list as writer Michael Hogan, who had worked on some reasonable movies, including *Rebecca* and *The Prime Minister*. He has tried to be light-hearted, but gets no help from the director, John Rawlins – his only A-feature in a career directing Bs – or the two leads. The woodenness of both Hall and Montez may be the reason that the subsequent films in the series are so awkward and inept – astonishingly so among major studio productions. **Ali Baba and the Forty Thieves** (1944), directed by Arthur Lubin, does have a mite of spectacle, and a plot that is one half 'Robin Hood' and one half Resistance drama. **Cobra Woman** (1944) has Montez in a double role, and was directed and part-written by two men who should have known better, Siodmak and Richard Brooks. The former called it 'silly but fun. You know, Maria Montez couldn't act from here to there, but she had a great personality and believed completely in her roles: playing a princess you had to treat her like one all through lunch, but as a slave girl [her dual role here] you could kick her around anyhow and she wouldn't object – Method acting before its time, you might say.'

Siodmak, in his own words, 'had been in Hollywood for three years, doing what work I could get. Then Universal sent me the script of **Son of Dracula** (1943): it was terrible...' His wife persuaded him to take it, in the hope that it would lead to something better, and though there is nothing in it to indicate the major talent responsible for such films as *Abscheid* and *Brennendes Geheimnis*, Universal were sufficiently impressed to offer a seven-year contract. It was not *Christmas Holiday* – much less

Cobra Woman – which re-established his reputation, but a lesser film, **Phantom Lady** (1944), perhaps because it is more obviously redolent of his European work. Some Ufa-like settings and lighting indicate Siodmak's actual control over the material, but that, alas, is poor, despite a good start in which a man (Franchot Tone) whose wife has been murdered seeks to find the woman who can provide an alibi. In the original novel by William March the murderer is not revealed till the end, but he is disclosed here much earlier – and in that role Tone tears at the scenery. The situations are again preposterous in **The Suspect** (1944), though the central idea is also promising: a mild-mannered tobacconist (Charles Laughton) does away with his nagging wife (Rosalind Ivan) and is blackmailed by a neighbour (Henry Daniell). That apart, the tale owes as much to Francis Iles's novel 'Malice Aforethought' as that owes to the case of Dr Crippen. Edwardian London is the usual foggy metropolis, but Siodmak has made the house of murder exceptionally sinister. Both films are handicapped by a pretty but inept actress, Ella Raines – she is particularly incongruous in the Ethel Le Neve role – and at this point only *Christmas Holiday* reveals Siodmak at his best, particularly in the sequences in the all-night café, the too-roomy roadhouse and the punters' bar.

Another European director, Julien Duvivier, also found a haven at Universal, if less permanently than Siodmak, but at least he fared better on Hollywood's own terms than his compatriots Clair and Renoir, as his prestige increased during his time there and theirs did not. Both **Tales of Manhattan** (1942) and **Flesh and Fantasy** (1943) were regarded as 'different' and therefore superior to most American films. The former – made in fact for 20th Century-Fox – like Duvivier's earlier *Carnet du Bal* consists of a series of sketches with a common motif, in this case a tail coat passed from hand to hand. Ten writers are listed as having contributed to story and screenplay, including Molnar and Ben Hecht, but the unacknowledged source is a German film, *Der Frack*, as recalled by Billy Wilder and Walter Reisch. It had been recommended by them to the producer S. P. Eagle, who had not long arrived in Hollywood after a varied career in Europe – he was to have a distinguished one in the U. S. under a new name, Sam Spiegel. Eagle invited Duvivier to do the film, and one of its star players, Charles Boyer, asked Duvivier to join him at Universal, where he was moving on an actor-producer contract (which proved short-lived). Together Boyer and Duvivier produced *Flesh and Fantasy*, which is composed of three disparate stories of the macabre. One is 'Lord Arthur Saville's Crime', modernised and its outcome hardly in doubt since Edward G. Robinson was one of the few stars acceptable as a murderer; another depends for its effectiveness on a mask resembling a face. The creation of the supernatural is unhappily too literal; as in *Tales of Manhattan* the events on screen are artificially treated and not pithy enough in their own right. Despite their all-star casts both films failed to find a large public, so that although the Hollywood moguls admired Duvivier they were not thereafter anxious to employ him.

Lacking as it did any truly creative filmmakers, Universal chose to turn to its own past. Of several remakes the most enjoyable is **The Phantom of the Opera** (1943), though poorly performed under Arthur Lubin's direction by Susanna Foster as the diva and Nelson Eddy and Edgar Barrier as the smirking rivals for her hand. (They sing excerpts from the operas 'Martha' and 'Amour et Gloire', the latter consisting of morsels of Chopin to which someone has laboriously set a French text). The Technicolored backstage sets look exactly right for the Palais Garnier, while the wronged violinist is Claude Rains, whose silky tones invoke the appropriate pity and terror. **The Spoilers** (1942) is the fourth of five screen versions of Rex Beach's novel, produced by Frank Lloyd, as ever showing his fondness for the 'big' picture. The setting is Nome in 1900, where a gold prospector (John Wayne) vies with the crooked commissioner (Randolph Scott) for a dance-hall girl (Marlene Dietrich); as directed lightly by Ray Enright, the famous marathon fight starts in her bedroom and ends some miles down the street. Wayne and Dietrich complement each other in the manner of the best screen teams – he relaxed, steadfast and teasing, she painted, fickle and humourless. She was said to have been considering retirement at this time, perhaps because she had

to wear the same costume in three different scenes.

Broadway (1942) was remade because Warners had had a success with *The Roaring Twenties*, but despite the vintage songs it has not the slightest feel for that particular era. William Seiter's direction has to contend with the fact that George Raft plays himself as a younger man – a hoofer and good egg, true to some idiotic George Raft code that prevents him co-operating with the cop (Pat O'Brien) trying to prove his innocence. He played himself again, more or less, in **Follow the Boys** (1943), 'Show Business's Tribute to Show Business'. There may be no more embarrassing sequence on celluloid than that in which the stars, coyly batting eyelids, volunteer to entertain the armed services. They are all Universal players (with Miss Durbin and Abbott and Costello more gainfully employed), plus a couple freelancing, a scattering of vaudeville names, and the usual bandleaders. The only one to emerge with credit is Dinah Shore, with two suitable songs, 'I'll Walk Alone' and 'I'll Get By'. The 'turns' were mainly done on the back lot, though intercut with location footage when such as Sophie Tucker and the Andrews Sisters were entertaining the troops – and it is a shock now to see the black servicemen bunched together in the audience. Universal was clearly in agreement, since the one black performer, Louis Jordan, is seen playing for an exclusively black unit, though Raft magnanimously joins him. The object of this and similar films was to remind the world of the film industry's contribution to the war effort, but the list of names at the end, headed by Carole Lombard and Leslie Howard, merely adds insult to injury: apart from a few performers who did travel extensively to entertain the troops, the War hardly intruded upon the lawns and orange groves of Beverly Hills.

The executives of Universal should have felt particularly ashamed, since apart from having Abbott and Costello join the Army, the Navy and the Air Force, they virtually ignored the War. If we discount Hitchcock's *Saboteur*, the company's sole war film of distinction is **Corvette K-225** (1943). Some critics at the time considered it superior to *In Which We Serve*, and it can now be seen to be one of the handful of fiction films to give a true indication of what the War was like. The production, by Howard Hawks, and the direction, by a veteran of B-movies, Richard Rosson, utilise newsreels, back-projection and some unconvincing models, but these are subservient to a very fine screenplay by John Sturdy, a lieutenant in the Royal Canadian Naval Reserve. His focus is an escort ship, and though his incidents parallel those of *Action in the North Atlantic* he had had experience denied to the writers of that film. He knew that among the hazards faced by a small craft are the heavy seas that sweep into every cranny; that after a Luftwaffe attack below-decks becomes a make-shift sick-bay; that junior officers may not follow the example of a disciplinarian captain (Randolph Scott); that the tension of living in cramped quarters can be so extreme that even such a small thing as the repeated playing of a phonograph record can cause a row; and that a floating lifeboat may not contain living survivors. The Canadian source is the reason why the corvette and its crew are of that nationality – which is why the film was retitled *The Nelson Touch* for Britain and its then territories.

Columbia also failed to cover itself with glory during the War. The loss of Frank Capra found Harry Cohn at a low ebb, till the public discovered Rita Hayworth and he promoted her into the studio's leading star. Miss Hayworth (b. 1918), a former dancer, had played small roles at 20th Century-Fox before moving to Columbia. She was wondrous to look upon but not much of an actress, so Cohn put her into two musicals, **You'll Never Get Rich** (1941), directed by Sidney Lanfield, and **You Were Never Lovelier** (1942), directed by William A. Seiter. The studio scored a triple coup by bringing in Fred Astaire (not then greatly in demand) and for the scores respectively Cole Porter and Jerome Kern, both of whom loved working in films. In the former, Astaire joins the army and persuades a Broadway producer (Robert Benchley) to put on a show for the troops. In the much better second film – it also has the more memorable songs, including 'Dearly Beloved' and 'I'm Old-Fashioned' – Astaire is an American dancer employed by a South American tycoon (Adolphe Menjou) to woo his frigid daughter (Hayworth). Miss Hayworth observed in

1970 that these were the only two films she made that she could watch without laughing – 'the only jewels in my life' – but presumably she overlooked **Cover Girl** (1944). Astaire turned down the project because he did not want to be again associated with one particular partner; Gene Kelly (q.v.) was brought in, and it must surely be one of the jewels in his life. He has said that by the time he came to the project Cohn was so desperate for a leading man that he acceded to his request to do his own choreography. To assist him on this Kelly brought in Stanley Donen (q.v.), and though neither is credited – Sidney Buchman, also uncredited, produced and Charles Vidor directed – it was Kelly's contribution, as was immediately recognised, which made this one of the great musicals. Of a range of imaginative numbers, composed by Kern, there are such highlights as 'Put Me to the Test', with its impromptu clowning, and 'Long Ago and Far Away', the first ballad since the Astaire–Rogers series to indicate falling in love; but it is the zingy 'Make Way for Tomorrow', with its seeming vivid spontaneity, which opens the way for *On the Town* (q.v.). Kelly is sympathetic, though required to play the usual boorish producer (Bing Crosby was almost the only star actor in musicals never required to be boorish), and Hayworth is the usual model who forgets him and her antecedents when she becomes famous. Because it is in colour, this film is her apotheosis, and the crude tones of Technicolor at this time make it absolutely of its period. Despite that, and its routine book, it revives well.

Flushed with its success, Vidor and Buchman – the latter as writer only – embarked upon a one-time project of Capra's, **A Song to Remember** (1945), a life of Chopin. It should be a camp classic, with Merle Oberon as George Sand in pantaloons and rakish top hat, and with that memorable moment when Technicolor blood drops on the piano keys; but it is arduous to watch, partly because this Chopin (Cornel Wilde) is a dead fish. As his professor, Paul Muni donates enough acting for the two of them, attempting a spectacular impression of S. Z. 'Cuddles' Sakall, and Oberon is merely absurd. 'I hope you like Paris, Monsieur Chopin. I'm sure Paris will like you' she says on her first entrance, accompanied by Liszt and de

Musset – who will be joined on the cast list by other celebrities, including Balzac, Paganini and Delacroix. Columbia was apprehensive of a movie with 'classical' music, and only occasionally is Chopin allowed to play more than a few bars: but the movie public's discovery of his music is the chief reason why this film is so popular.

It was a rare 'class' offering from this company. Miss Hayworth apart, Columbia concentrated on medium-budget comedies. Typical are **They All Kissed the Bride** (1942), directed by Alexander Hall, and **What a Woman!** (1943), directed by Irving Cummings. Both concern career women whose hearts are melted by, respectively, a charming reporter (Melvyn Douglas) and a flip professor (Brian Aherne). In the case of the reporter, his task is eased when the lady (Joan Crawford) takes to jitterbugging and getting drunk at the firm's dance – after which she yearns for simple things like knitting and babies. The moral was salutary at the time when women were increasingly needed for men's jobs, but both films were merely vehicles for important female stars. Crawford, borrowed from M-G-M when Carole Lombard was killed, still could not play comedy; but Rosalind Russell, in the second film, could make palatable such masochistic roles. Given half a chance, as in her drunk dancing scene, she is formidable.

An even better comedienne, Jean Arthur, was in a position to refuse such stereotyped roles; she played in two films directed by George Stevens, which, like *Woman of the Year*, were primarily comedies but indicated a new seriousness. In **The Talk of the Town** (1942) Miss Arthur is a schoolteacher who lets her house to a professor (Ronald Colman), and then discovers a suspected arsonist (Cary Grant) hiding in her attic. The three become allies as the town works itself into a lynching mood, which causes the film to say something pertinent on civic corruption and social duty. Funnier, but less likeable, is **The More the Merrier** (1943), one of several films about a Washington overcrowded because of the War; frenetically sharing a room with Miss Arthur are Joel McCrea and Charles Coburn.

The War otherwise hardly impinged on Columbia's films. An exception is **Destroyer** (1943), but it is at the opposite end of the scale from *Corvette K-225*. William A. Seiter directed, and Edward G. Robinson plays an ex-Navy man restored to his command on the outbreak of war – despite opposition and the distrust of his men. They are led by the Chief (Glenn Ford), who nevertheless woos and wins Robinson's daughter, while Robinson wins over the men by single-handedly repairing the torpedoed ship.

R.K.O., after the collapse of its dreams of glory with Orson Welles, again relied upon Disney and Goldwyn to keep its distribution arm in profit. The studio itself returned to its former policy of programmers and B-pictures interspersed with an occasional A-movie. Its leading director, Leo McCarey, was united with its principal stars, Ginger Rogers and Cary Grant, for the misleadingly titled **Once Upon a Honeymoon** (1942). McCarey had said earlier, 'I'll let someone else photograph the ugliness of the world. It's larceny to remind people of how lousy things are and call it entertainment,' but at this juncture he decided to remind people of the dreadful conditions in Europe in the form of entertainment. This is one of several films in which a nice American girl (Rogers) unwittingly marries a Nazi (Walter Slezak). A reporter (Grant) chases her all over Europe to apprise her of the truth, whereupon she gives her passport to her Jewish maid and in a supposedly comic scene gets herself and Grant arrested as Jews. They are imprisoned in a Jewish transit camp till the U.S. ambassador turns up to rescue them, and the sequence would be offensive even if the film were not operating at that level where Rogers can crack the Nazi cabinet's secret code and later push her husband overboard (to prevent him from converting the U.S. to Nazism). Except for its patriotic fervour, audiences were not expected to take all this seriously, but as a piece of film-making it is as inept as McCarey's previous film, *Love Affair*, was controlled. He would recover some prestige with his 'priest' films starring Bing Crosby, but would never recover his old form.

It was apparently difficult for the American film industry to come to terms with Nazism, and **Hitler's Children** (1943), though more responsible in content is considerably more hysterical in approach. It is one of the few movie dramas – as opposed to thrillers – set in the Germany of the Third Reich, and as adapted from 'Education for Death' by Gregor Ziemer it examines the effect of Nazi ideology on an American girl (Bonita Granville). When she refuses further indoctrination she is threatened with sterilisation, and that brings a member of the Nazi Youth (Tim Holt) to his senses. The film, made on a small budget, was not meant for major consideration, but it became a freak success when taken up by the public (its domestic gross of $3½ million represented a return on investment of just under 1,000 per cent). Its director, Edward Dmytryk, was forthwith promoted to major projects.

Despite the profits from that film, R.K.O. was as usual in the red, and it was suggested that some musicals with Dick Powell might prevent the company going into receivership – an odd proposition, since Powell was no longer a box-office name. Powell himself declined to sing again on screen, fancying himself as a tough guy – and it was agreed that he would play private detective Philip Marlowe in a version of Raymond Chandler's 'Farewell, My Lovely', to be directed by Dmytryk and retitled **Murder, My Sweet** (1944) in case the conjunction of Powell's name and the word 'lovely' suggested a musical. R.K.O. owned the rights, having filmed it with changed names to fit into a B-series as *The Falcon Takes Over* just two years earlier ('The Falcon', played by George Sanders and then by his brother Tom Conway, was a debonair fixer of crime mysteries) – but Chandler's reputation had grown in the interim. Chandler himself thought Powell the best of the screen Marlowes – perhaps because his performance is anonymous throughout. He glowers, but brings neither the character nor tension which Bogart was to bring to *The Big Sleep* (q.v.), but, once that is accepted, we may enjoy the respect accorded the material (as scripted by John Paxton). As the dangerous Mrs Grayle, Claire Trevor fails to measure up to Mary Astor or Barbara Stanwyck in similar roles, but the others are good: Mike Mazurki as the slobbish, beastly Moose Malloy; Esther Howard as the drunken Mrs Florian; and Otto Kruger as the silky psychiatrist quack, Jules Amthor.

Another attempt to make R.K.O. solvent was to invite Val Lewton (1904–51), story-editor with Selznick, to form a new B-unit producing thrillers to take the lower half of double-bills. Lewton decided to utilise budget restrictions by limiting himself to unseen phenomena – to what he called 'dramatisations of the psychology of fear'. He made eleven such films, and the cult admiration that exists today may have begun with James Agee's comment after seeing the first half-dozen, praising Lewton's team 'because for all their unevenness their achievements are so consistently alive, limber, poetic, humane.' On the other hand I find the films disappointing. A B-picture is always a B-picture: the studio's first requirement was not that it should be entertaining but that it should be brought in as quickly and as cheaply as possible. The imaginative touches in Lewton's films are invariably derivative, while there are inadequacies in performing which tend to emphasise the perfunctory nature of the action. The first of them, **The Cat People** (1942), has an ingenious story by DeWitt Bodeen about a man (Kent Smith) whose wife (Simone Simon) believes, with reason, that she turns into a panther at night; but apart from one set – in fact left over from *The Magnificent Ambersons* – the film lacks completely the necessary atmosphere as directed by Jacques Tourneur. An R.K.O. executive, hoping for a sequel, came up with the title **The Curse of the Cat People** (1944), but Lewton refused to capitalise on the earlier film, which is of the 'horror' genre – however mild. Bodeen contributed a story about a child bewitched by her ghostly mother (Mlle Simon), but he admits that the film is really Lewton's work, since Lewton put into it all his ideas on child psychology. Gunther Fritsch and Robert Wise (q.v.) directed. The result is not unlike *The Uninvited*, but if that film is a supernatural feast, even perhaps vegetarian, this is a stale cucumber sandwich. **I Walked with a Zombie** (1943) does manage a passable reconstruction of a Caribbean island, and Frances Dee is a sympathetic heroine; but Tom Conway is poor in a role based on Charlotte Brontë's Mr Rochester and the final effect is only too trivial as directed by Tourneur.

Also brought in to help the studio out of its difficulties was Damon Runyon, but only one film resulted, **The Big Street** (1942), directed by Irving Reis and written by Leonard Spigelglass from what is described simply and modestly as a *Colliers* magazine story: immediately recognisable are the customary muggs with the heart of gold, the two-timing dames and the firm belief that magic can happen in a nightclub. Eugene Pallette (as Nicely Nicely Johnson), Agnes Moorehead, Sam Levene, Louise Beavers, Ray Collins, Millard Mitchell and Marion Martin are likeably Runyonesque; Henry Fonda is kindly and intense as 'Little Pinks', the bus boy 'stuck' on the boss's foul-mouthed doll – a difficult role, and only once before the end does Lucille Ball show any feeling. She is so expert with the cracks that she is engaging without ever being sympathetic. She made one more film at R.K.O. before going to M-G-M for *DuBarry Was a Lady* (q.v.) and her performance here almost compensates for her poor work for Metro.

In another attempt at box-office success R.K.O. brought back Fred Astaire, but **The Sky's the Limit** (1943), directed by Edward H. Griffith, is a mere husk of former glories. Astaire plays a 'flying tiger' with lots of Japanese planes to his credit, a fact not disclosed to Joan Leslie, who tries to fix him up with a job till her boss (Robert Benchley) plays cupid, and she gazes skywards with misty eyes as 'his' plane whizzes past – the end, it would seem, of every other wartime movie. Harold Arlen's score includes 'One for My Baby', the *pièce de résistance* as sung by Astaire in three different bars and concluded by a drunken tap dance.

The songs in **Show Business** (1944) are old ones, used to deck out an affectionate and unpretentious tale of loving and warring vaudeville couples, directed by Edwin L. Marin and produced by Eddie Cantor, who also stars, with the equally agreeable George Murphy, Constance Moore and Joan Davis. Miss Davis was a horse-faced comedienne – described here as looking like 'an umbrella with a broken handle' – with considerable attack; she is very funny with a good line, thus, 'Listen, show me a way to earn folding money and I'd do a fan-dance with a fly-swatter.' Among the minor pleasures here is a montage of railway trains and billboards.

The Enchanted Cottage (1945) is also more successful than it has any right to be.

This late play by Pinero (1922), called him a 'fable', had been filmed by First National in 1924 with Richard Barthelmess and May McAvoy, and it belongs to that era. Resurrecting it while the War was still on appeared foolhardy, since its subject is a man (Robert Young) embittered by his war scars. He marries a 'homely' girl (Dorothy McGuire), and under the spell of their honeymoon cottage they become beautiful, which his meddling mother (Spring Byington) and her equally insensitive husband cannot understand. When the couple meet they are photographed alternately as they are and as they think they are, leaving us to wonder whether they will hold on to their illusions. Owing to the dedication of the director, John Cromwell, and the skills of DeWitt Bodeen and Herman Mankiewicz, who wrote it, this is one of the few pieces of Hollywood whimsy that works. Miss McGuire is here the best of those unglamorous, breathy actresses who linger on the last words of a sentence, even if her transformation does only prove that all she needed was an hour in a beauty parlour; and Young is good simply because he has no false romantic aura. They are beautifully supported by Mildred Natwick as the householder who cedes her place – rather dopily – to maid McGuire, and by Herbert Marshall as the blind friend.

Sam Goldwyn's major contribution to the war effort was **The North Star** (1943), a hymn to the gallant Russians. Russian-born himself, he insisted on compatriot Lewis Milestone as director, though Milestone disliked the script commissioned from Lillian Hellman. When she refused to change a word, Goldwyn sided with Milestone, and an uncredited Edward Chodorov worked over her screenplay. As shot by James Wong Howe, the result looks both epic and European, but in sum is absurdly pretentious, its comments on war emerging as piffling. Among the better situations is that of the humane town doctor (Walter Huston) provoked into killing the German C.O. (Eric Von Stroheim), after telling him that the intelligent Germans are more guilty than the Nazi puppets; while the introduction into the plot of the fact that the Germans took blood from Russian children for their own wounded soldiers is more plausible than most of the atrocities Hollywood dreamed up for them.

They Got Me Covered (1943) is a salutary reminder of the time when every other beauty parlour in Washington was a front for a Gestapo spy ring. This particular ring is rounded up by Bob Hope, playing an otherwise incompetent journalist, and he has quips about such other wartime hazards as the blackout and air-raid wardens. He was borrowed from Paramount, in a deal which included Dorothy Lamour and the director David Butler; when Hope and Butler returned to Goldwyn for **The Princess and the Pirate** (1944) the package included some of Hope's usual writers, Don Hartman, Melville Shavelson and Everett Freeman. Both films are burlesques, a form neglected from the Silent period to the second 'Road' movie with Hope and Crosby – and Hope was to work memorably in this field in the postwar period, with such films as *The Paleface* (q.v.). It suffices to say that *The Princess and the Pirate* is one of Hope's most brilliant films, both fond and funny beyond the knowingness which is all that some recent practitioners have brought to the genre. Clearly, it is a spoof on pirate adventures, and one reason it is so good is the glee with which it re-creates its world of easy death: the bleaker and blacker the milieu, the funnier Hope's craven behaviour.

The only studio constantly to treat the War with comparative responsibility was 20th Century-Fox. Joseph Schenck resigned as chairman in 1941, after being jailed for tax evasion and for bribing film unions during the industrial troubles a few years earlier; the following year the company's president, Sidney Kent, died, to be succeeded by a former exhibitor, Spyros Skouras. Both men had been instrumental in merging 20th Century with Fox, along with Darryl F. Zanuck and William Goetz. When Zanuck joined the army his assistant, Goetz, became his deputy – though Schenck was able to resume a certain amount of power. Both of them were responsive to talent (unlike Schenck's brother, Nicholas, the power at M-G-M), but Zanuck's lieutenant-colonelcy in the Signal Corps did not prevent him from continuing to make his voice heard at the studio. Unlike the other two dynamic studio heads, Harry Cohn and Jack Warner, he brought creative ability to the making of films. He knew how to construct films and had the ability to spot weaknesses in a script; he appreciated intelligence in subject matter and dialogue, while distrusting motivation to the extent that he would have preferred his films to consist chiefly of action. His first instincts were good: his poorest films were often those he worked upon longest and hardest. He was absent, in fact, at war for only eighteen months, until May 1943, when he found his patriotic fervour somewhat less than that for movies, and he asked to be put on the inactive duty list. Any assessment of his work must take into account the fact that although Fox musicals became increasingly stereotyped they were preferred by the troops to those made by any other company.

One of his personal productions, **This Above All** (1942), was directed by Anatole Litvak from a novel by Eric Knight which, like many another bestseller, undoubtedly embodied a number of fine thoughts and unimpeachable values. Joan Fontaine plays a wealthy English girl so earnest about the War that she joins the W.A.A.F.s, quickly falling for a working-class bloke (Tyrone Power) who hates the aristocracy and deserted after Dunkirk. She gives him one of those eulogies on England ('the sound of taxi-horns, the dignity of our ancient cities') of which Hollywood was so fond at this time, and if it is an odd England, it is an even odder W.A.A.F. service: 'Can you get leave?' he asks and she replies unhesitatingly, 'Of course I can, darling.' No wonder that she is fairly ludicrous in uniform. Power makes no attempt at a British accent, but tries hard to suggest a man beset by both neuroses and left-wing yearnings; in support Alexander Knox is a one-armed, pipe-smoking, dog-collared figure of compassion.

Son of Fury (1942) and **The Black Swan** (1942) both prove that Power could not swash a buckle as blithely as did Errol Flynn. John Cromwell directed the first, from a novel by Edison Marshall, about an orphan – played as a boy by Roddy McDowall – cheated of his inheritance in Regency England, and consoled by both a two-faced blonde (Frances Farmer) and a Polynesian beauty (Gene Tierney) encountered on his travels. Henry King directed the other, adapted from Rafael Sabatini's novel by Ben Hecht and Seton I. Miller, a teaming which promised something considerably more lively. Leon Shamroy won an Oscar for his colour cinematography of some obvious model-galleons in full sail against resplendent sunsets. Power, Laird Cregar, a one-eyed Anthony Quinn and a red-bearded George Sanders are the pirates. The heroine is Maureen O'Hara, who plays with 'no more feeling than a load of clams', as fellow crewman Thomas Mitchell says scornfully.

Power's departure for the Marine Corps left Betty Grable and Alice Faye as the studio's chief assets, and they proceeded to make the same film under various titles. When neither was available, as in **My Gal Sal** (1942), Rita Hayworth was borrowed. The film was directed by Irving Cummings from a reminiscence by Theodore Dreiser of his brother, Paul Dresser, 'whose own career was as flamboyant and extravagant as the era he set to music'. As detailed here, it follows the familiar progress of the struggling songwriter (Victor Mature) and his stormy affair with a Broadway leading lady, while Dresser's own songs are supplemented by no less than five new ones by Robin and Rainger. The numbers are mounted with extravagance, if not flamboyance, and during wartime austerity the costumes were a tonic – the ladies in osprey headdresses, candy-striped bustles and diamonds, and the men in duds equally dazzling. Public response to this sartorical display convinced 20th to cover Miss Grable's legs with long skirts for most of **Coney Island** (1943), directed by Walter Lang, in which she is fought over by rival saloon-owners, and **Sweet Rosie O'Grady** (1943), directed by Cummings, in which she bags an English duke while pretending to be a 'class' artiste. Both films are inferior to *My Gal Sal*, though that has nothing to do with the playing; in both Miss Grable is a wised-up showgirl who is at heart a good Joe. The troops adored watching her, especially the famous legs – when they had the chance – and were indifferent to her limited talent. The famous pin-up picture of her is seen under the credits of **Pin-Up Girl** (1944), directed by Bruce Humberstone, an otherwise dim piece in which as a secretary in Washington she dons specs so that the naval hero (John Harvey) will not recognise her. She does have one dance number – with an apache, whose clothes,

bearing and postures would reappear in Gene Kelly's developed style.

The Gang's All Here (1943) is a dire film, but it has an impressive place among the myths and memories of the era, with its G.I. sentiment ('Hearing from you every day would make me feel as though you're marching with me at the head of the column'), Miss Faye sighing gently to the stars, and Carmen Miranda in her fruit cocktail headpieces, bare midriff and platform shoes. The director is Busby Berkeley, whose production numbers have won a belated fame, though at the time 'The Tutti-Frutti Hat' was noticed by *The New York Times*, which thought that 'if interpreted [it] might bring a rosy blush to several cheeks in the Hays Office'. This has much to do with the raising and lowering of giant bananas by a line of scantily-dressed chorus girls, and what it tells us of Berkeley's subconscious hardly bears contemplation.

Two or three seconds of 'Daisy, Daisy', sung on a trolley car in *My Gal Sal*, may have inspired the best number in *Meet Me in St Louis* (q.v.). Certainly the success of the latter inspired Fox to remake **State Fair** (1945), as a musical, and the only one of the time with any claim to originality. Since the piece always was Americana, Zanuck hired the new heroes of that form, Rodgers and Hammerstein, to write the songs, which resemble those of 'Oklahoma!' – updated, perhaps, and made palatable to front office taste. They are splendid, of course, but unenterprisingly done apart from 'It's a Grand Night for Singing'. As directed by Walter Lang, the rest is Forties kitsch. Jeanne Crain's sugary breathlessness has dated as badly as the dirndl skirts and bouffant sleeves she wears, and as her brother Dick Haymes plumbs new depths of charmlessness. The self-conscious air of niceness affects Charles Winninger and Fay Bainter as their parents, as well as Donald Meek and Percy Kilbride, also representing the older generation.

Zanuck, the first to realise how much Technicolor enhanced musicals, would not use colour for **Stormy Weather** (1943), but it is the one most worth preserving, offering as it does the talents of Lena Horne, Cab Calloway, Fats Waller and a sensational dancing team, the Nicholas Brothers. Andrew L. Stone produced and directed this all-black musical, sanctioned after the critical reception given to M-G-M's *Cabin in the Sky* (q.v.), and it is a pity that no white person is ever seen in the night clubs which provide the film's setting.

The best of the studio's pieces of Technicolor escapism is **Heaven Can Wait** (1943), directed by Lubitsch and adapted by Samson Raphaelson from a play by Lazlo Bus-Fékete called 'Birthday', in which, apparently, the hero's birthday was an excuse to reminisce about amorous gambols in his past. It could never have been a distinguished piece, but its wild humour has an air of breathless gaiety which sits well on period comedy. The pleasures of Henry (Don Ameche) range from the French maid in boyhood to the night nurse in his dotage; his wife is Gene Tierney, and she was never again as good – which is true also of Charles Coburn as Henry's indulgent grandfather, Laird Cregar as Old Nick in the framing sequence, Eugene Pallette and Marjorie Main as a couple who communicate only through their servants and Anita Bolster as the lady who at Henry's funeral sings 'Now Is the Closing of the Day' – something he had managed to avoid while alive. The chief joy is Ameche, taking the role of a lifetime and giving one of the great comic performances of the American cinema.

This film and **Cluny Brown** (1946) reveal that Lubitsch was tired of both the famous 'touch' and the eternal triangle. The latter movie, written by another regular collaborator, Samuel Hoffenstein, with Elizabeth Reinhardt, is a straightforward version of Margery Sharp's novel – taking, indeed, its wry tone from that source. Lubitsch had always been amused by protocol, and *Angel* had demonstrated his fascination with the British upper classes; but *Cluny Brown* is, rather, about British snobbery, both above and below stairs, and he could not bring himself to be cruel enough. His Hollywood British cast do not play with sufficient edge, and his leads – Jennifer Jones as a parlourmaid, Charles Boyer as a Czech refugee renowned for his anti-Nazism – are not the first names that come to mind as comedy players.★ These were the only two films Lubitsch completed under his contract with 20th. He prepared a remake of *Forbid-*

★She was cast at the insistence of Miss Sharp, who refused otherwise to sell the rights.

den Paradise, called *A Royal Scandal*, but ill health caused him to hand it over to Otto Preminger; and the latter was the studio's choice to replace him when he died while making *That Lady in Ermine* (q.v.).

Preminger had been a sometime actor and theatre director in Vienna, who had directed his first American film in 1937, at 20th, but did not do so again till the same company asked him to re-stage *Margin for Error* which he had directed on Broadway. Zanuck disliked him, and relegated him to the B-unit, but agreed to let him produce a screenplay by which Preminger held much store – **Laura** (1944), written by Jay Dratler, Samuel Hoffenstein and Betty Reinhardt, from a novel by Vera Caspary. Rouben Mamoulian was to have directed, but Zanuck asked Preminger to replace him after a few days' shooting. His direction is not as ponderous as his later efforts; and the film's unique quality springs both from David Raksin's haunting theme tune, and the acidulous dialogue given to the *bon vivant* Waldo Lydecker (Clifton Webb). When the lady of the title is found murdered, a detective (Dana Andrews) interviews those who knew her – her aunt (Judith Anderson), her fiancé (Vincent Price) and Lydecker, whose protégée she had been. As we move into flashback, an ordinary mystery takes on a certain fascination. Lydecker is a compendium of Alexander Woollcott, George Jean Nathan and other holy horrors. 'In my case,' he tells Laura (Gene Tierney), 'the self-absorption is total.' The film does not divulge the extent of their relationship, but anyone acquainted with Manhattan society will recognise the suave bitchiness of both Lydecker and the fiancé as more than likely homosexual in origin. The acclaimed sophistication of this film is in truth a little simple-minded, but taken as a whole it remains enjoyable.

There is murder, but little mystery, in **Roxie Hart** (1942), the first of three films made at 20th at this time by William A. Wellman; Nunnally Johnson wrote it from Maurine Watkins' play 'Chicago', originally filmed by Pathé in 1928 with Phyllis Haver. That had concerned a travesty of justice when a murderess wins the sympathy of an all-male jury by pretending to be an expectant mother. To pass the Code, the film is about a showgirl who confesses to a murder to get her name in lights –

though she does invent a pregnancy when her thunder is stolen by the more notorious Two-Gun Gertie (Iris Adrian). The evocation of the period is weak, and Ginger Rogers is self-conscious as Roxie. She is at her best chewing gum and with legs ready to shimmy, but not in the same class as Stanwyck in Wellman's *Lady of Burlesque*. Adolphe Menjou is good as the defending lawyer, mainly preoccupied with cash and manipulating the jury, and there is a memorable moment when Roxie's Paw gets back to his rocking-chair and says laconically, 'They're gonna hang Roxie,' to which Maw replies, undisturbed, 'Whatud I tell ya?'

Most of **The Ox-Bow Incident** (1943) is memorable. Certainly its genesis is. A writer, just sacked from 20th, had asked Wellman to read Walter Van Tilburg Clark's novel about a small-town lynching, with a view to turning it – 'You won't believe this,' said Wellman – into a vehicle for Mae West, in an interpolated role as a singer who entertains the cowboys. Since the writer had been unable to interest anyone in Hollywood in either the idea or the book, Wellman was able to buy the rights for $6,500 – and when he too could find no interested producer, he contacted Zanuck (according to him, they had not spoken since a quarrel during the filming of *Call of the Wild*), who said that it would not make a nickel but that it was the sort of movie with which his studio should be associated. After Zanuck was drafted, his deputy, Goetz, cancelled it, but allowed Wellman to remind Zanuck of their agreement.

Thus the film was made, from a screenplay by Lamar Trotti; and after a preview in the presence of the principals, Mrs Zanuck observed loudly that the studio should be ashamed. The entire front office concurred: but Zanuck was able to return to his initial enthusiasm once the notices were in. Audiences, however, by their absence, agreed with Mrs Zanuck, since at that time they were ill-prepared for a subject so uncompromisingly 'depressing', or even a serious subject not bathed in 'uplift'. Two years later, when the War had brought a new seriousness to the cinema, they might have taken it in their stride.

The setting is a small town in Nevada in 1885, where the men gang up to murder someone – anyone – because they are bored. Questions of guilt are secondary. It is a world and an era where nothing is certain: Carter (Fonda) and his companion ride into town to meet with automatic suspicion, but their motive in joining the lynch party is probably to see justice done. Other reactions are equally ambiguous, and since the faces are so much more eloquent than the dialogue it is a pity that the final moralising is so explicit and that there is never any doubt of the innocence of the doomed men (Dana Andrews, Anthony Quinn, Francis Ford). However, there is enough subtlety to counterbalance the self-righteousness, and it is not of great import that the lighting in the night scenes emphasise the film's aspirations to art – though the European influence was no longer Ufa but Marcel Carné.

Buffalo Bill (1944) was one of the studio's recurrent looks at old American heroes, undeterred by the fact that they all led boring lives – boring, that is, as generally rendered. The film has none of Wellman's usual vitality or questioning, and when occasionally the script begins to suggest that Bill Cody may have been a charlatan it quickly veers away to safer concepts. Joel McCrea plays the likeable but uninspiring man of action; Miss O'Hara is incongruous as the enamelled girl he marries.

In **The Immortal Sergeant** (1943) this actress describes herself as a pianist, and one apparently with unlimited clothing coupons. She is remembered in the desert by a British corporal (Henry Fonda), since this was the first film on the Libyan campaign, hastily adapted from John Brophy's novel by Trotti when 20th decided it must make some sort of a bow to the British war effort. Brophy had written about a shy young man who found himself influenced by a rough N.C.O. from the working class – the character of the title, played by Thomas Mitchell in an 'inspirational' glow. These soldiers' adventures resemble the events in a Foreign Legion movie; and the feeling of unreality is increased by poor lighting – the men often have *two* shadows apiece in the desert, a rare fault in a major Hollywood movie. The director was John M. Stahl, who specialised in British subjects for the company.

Holy Matrimony (1943) is a version of the only Arnold Bennett novel which has interested Hollywood, 'Buried Alive' (it had been filmed by Paramount in 1933 as

His Double Life), but neither Stahl nor his writer, Nunnally Johnson, has quite the measure of it, for only once does it offer the moral knot which Bennett provided so generously. Monty Woolley is the artist who takes the place of his own valet (Eric Blore), when the latter dies; Laird Cregar is his dealer; and Gracie Fields, not at all at home, is the woman he marries.

Stahl worked with the writer George Seaton on **The Eve of St Mark** (1944), adapted from a Broadway play by Maxwell Anderson – somewhat drastically, one imagines, since it falls into three sections: home front sentimentality just before Pearl Harbor; stress under fire in the Philippines; and barrack-room badinage. The barrack-room scenes are reasonably authentic, demonstrating that though 20th Century-Fox's war films are not overall better than those produced at other studios, they did try harder.

Stahl was not the director he once was, but was assigned to one of Zanuck's more ambitious projects, **The Keys of the Kingdom** (1944) – working this time with a distinguished producer, Joseph L. Mankiewicz, who had just arrived from M-G-M. Mankiewicz also worked on the screenplay with Nunnally Johnson, but it omits the whole point of the novel, by A. J. Cronin, on which it is based. That concerned a priest who, after a lifetime in China, was more Chinese than Scottish, his Christianity imbued with the teachings of Confucius – which was why his Church failed to understand him: but as played by Gregory Peck he is merely a sincere and questioning individual with a penchant for talking to God. There is an excellent scene where an aged Mother Superior (Rosa Stradner) tells the aged priest what his friendship has meant to her, but the other representatives of the Church are either twinkle-eyed or disagreeably worldly. The film makes several moral judgments, but like most religious films of this period it is not religious at all.

It followed the standard procedure for bringing bestsellers to the screen: dignified advertising, a longish running time and a cast of major character players. There was also a standard trailer, in which the camera tracked along a shelf of successfully-filmed books to pause at *this* one, described in such terms as 'the novel the world has thrilled to becomes the mighty motion picture it cannot wait to see'. The sales and borrowings of books did rise considerably during the War, and there was a reawakening of interest in the works of the Victorian novelists: but the decision to remake **Jane Eyre** (1944) – there had been a version with Virginia Bruce ten years earlier – was probably caused by Goldwyn's successful reissue of *Wuthering Heights*. Hollywood was obsessed with the British and their land of mists and shadows; so after many imitations it made sense to go to one of the prototypes of all romantic fiction. The model adaptation, by John Houseman, Aldous Huxley and the director, Robert Stevenson, deviates from the original with poignancy by having Jane (Joan Fontaine) return to Aunt Reed (Agnes Moorehead) rather than stay with the Rivers'. Stevenson and his photographer, George Barnes, approach their subject with relish, and though they used the studio lights at full tilt the film stays in the memory while the locations for the matter-of-fact 1971 version have faded. It has been claimed that this pictorial style was influenced by *Citizen Kane* because Orson Welles heads the cast: it could be said with more certainty that he was permitted control of his performance, which suggests a Mr Rochester as mad as his incarcerated wife. With Peggy Ann Garner as the child Jane, Henry Daniell as Mr Brocklehurst and Miss Moorehead's complacent, unfeeling Aunt, the first part of the film captures superbly the eerie quality of the novel at that stage, but the remainder is not an anti-climax.

Jane Eyre was one of the films planned by David O. Selznick and sold to 20th Century-Fox, along with its star and director (Stevenson's contract with Selznick was one reason for his inactivity in Hollywood – unlike his compatriot Hitchcock, who both awed Selznick and was in demand elsewhere). Another such deal was done with **Claudia** (1943), together with the services of Dorothy McGuire, who had played the title role in Rose Franken's original play on Broadway. In an attempt to re-create the press interest over the casting of Scarlett O'Hara, Selznick had pretended that he had had no intention of using Miss McGuire, and several important stars were reported as having tested for the role, including Margaret Sullavan – on whose screen image the role was modelled, intentionally or not. Claudia wears flat shoes and a cardigan, her hair is untidy and she slouches or lolls when in a chair; but it is made clear – or as clear as the Hays Office would allow – that her slightly-older husband (Robert Young) finds her sexually irresistible. She is therefore an interesting character to find in movies at this time, since Zanuck was apparently fiercest in the belief – shared by all the studio heads – that women were either whores or chaste. The film otherwise is a smug comedy, set in a never-never Connecticut peopled with comic neighbours: that would be much imitated, but the apple-pie girl who was also sexy would not be common in movies for some years – if ever. The director was the veteran Edmund Goulding – his first film for the studio in which he was to eventually end his career.

The director of **The Lodger** (1944) and **Hangover Square** (1945) was John Brahm, who was German-born, but before arriving in Hollywood he had worked in Britain – a fact which has a certain relevance, since the mists swirling in both films are London fogs. The films also have in common Laird Cregar in sinister roles and George Sanders as Scotland Yard stalwarts; they were produced by Robert Bassler from screenplays by Barré Lyndon – whose other work, like that of the director, is of little or no distinction. The re-creation of Edwardian London, by James Basevi and John Ewing, is outstanding, and the second of the two films is at least extremely well made: in that, Linda Darnell gives real edge to her usual movie role at this time, a floozie, but Brahm managed no similar miracle with Merle Oberon in the first. She plays niece to the folk who house the lodger of the title, and his intended final victim: and as he had seen her on stage doing her version of the can-can we may feel his thoughts of homicide justified. Lyndon follows Hitchcock's Silent version in adding such frills to this story of Jack the Ripper; but the mangling of Patrick Hamilton's novel, for the second film, is more serious, beginning with the transposition of the action from the present day. *Gaslight* (based on a play by Hamilton) and *The Lodger* itself may have proved that London was more frightening some years earlier, while *The Phantom of the Opera* possibly dictated the change of the protag-

onist's profession from motor-car salesman to composer. Bernard Herrmann's concerti for him are impressive, but, as Richard Winnington observed, 'It's always safer to make a homicidal maniac an artist.' With his soft voice and lumbering frame, Cregar is particularly remarkable in this role as a schizophrenic. His powerful personality had helped to promote him to stardom, but since he was hardly leading-man material the studio considered him as its Chaney or Karloff. He so resented the alterations made to Hamilton's novel that he submitted himself to a slimming course so as not to be typed; and it killed him.

Another actor surprisingly to be found at Fox was Jean Gabin, and much care was taken over his American debut, with the eminent John Steinbeck retained to write the screenplay (from a novel by Willard Robinson). But **Moontide** (1942), like *The Ox-Bow Incident*, proved Hollywood's over-readiness to ape Europe

Edwardian London, with its fogs and hansom cabs, had a fascination for movie-makers from the Silent days until the Fifties, usually for stories of murder and mayhem. Two of the best were offered to wartime audiences, *The Lodger*, illustrated, and *Hangover Square*, both starring Laird Cregar, a versatile actor who was exceptionally effective being sinister.

when attempting seriousness: the title is reminiscent of *Sunrise*, and not for nothing are there endless *brumes* engulfing these California *quais*. Gabin is a drunken migrant worker caught between a would-be suicide, Anna (Ida Lupino), and his best friend (Thomas Mitchell) – whose love for him is so extreme that he plans to rape Anna rather than arouse other suspicions in the audience. The film does, at least, begin well: a riverside bar, 'Remember?' on an old phonograph echoing across the bay, and a drunken montage – perhaps the contribution of Fritz Lang, who directed for four days before being replaced by Archie Mayo.

The actual contribution of individual directors under the studio system has always been difficult to assess: **The Moon Is Down** (1943) and **Guadalcanal Diary** (1943) may be added to the list of good films made by mediocrities, the first by Irving Pichel and the other by Lewis Seiler. In each case the original material was superior to most and adapted with respect – the former from Steinbeck's play by Nunnally Johnson, the latter from the book by the war correspondent Richard Tregaskis by Lamar Trotti. *The Moon Is Down* is better than most Resistance films in striving to explore the relationship between opposing nations and ideologies trying to live together, even if Steinbeck misunderstands Nazism; the characters spout attitudes at each other, but the dilemmas of the mayor (Henry Travers) and the German commander (Sir Cedric Hardwicke) are reasonably presented – and the film ends with muted heroism instead of the usual idiocies. Death in *Guadalcanal Diary* also seems not squalid, not quite necessary, and needing courage to confront. The film's strength is that it seems to have been filmed wholly on location; its overriding fault is that its squadron of Marines contains only stereotypes: the kindly chaplain (Preston Foster), the scared kid (Richard Jaeckel), the conscientious sergeant (Lloyd Nolan) and the Brooklyn bruiser (William Bendix). Richard Conte and Anthony Quinn represent the underprivileged ethnic groups, but there are no blacks to be seen.

Lloyd Bacon directed two films about the home front, neither free from cliché, but **The Sullivans** (1944) is as good as **Sunday Dinner for a Soldier** (1944) is poor. The Sullivans were an Iowa family who lost five sons at Guadalcanal, and the film is a tribute to such 'typical' people. The family in the other film lives in a shack and is bone-shakingly cute: when the girl (Anne Baxter) speaks of their poverty the soldier (John Hodiak) tells her that they are the richest family he knows, 'You have the sort of wealth no one can destroy.' A British critic, Winnington, found 'a warmth of honest sentiment that is irresistible', but in the U.S. James Agee felt 'embarrassment rather than simple anger because most of the people who worked on [it] appear to have loved it, believed in it, and had great hopes for its originality and worthiness'.

Lewis Milestone's two war films for the company are also polarised in quality. **The Purple Heart** (1944) was based on an actual incident, when a bomber crew, shot down in Japan, were subjected to a civilian trial in Tokyo for allegedly strafing non-military targets. From the few available facts Zanuck (under the pseudonym of Melville Crossman) devised a story about the bravery of the crew and the beastliness of the Japanese – and though most of the torturing takes place off-screen, the film was censured in the press for marking a new depth in the depiction of cruelty. Today, despite the sobriety of the direction, the film is merely absurd. As the Japanese general, Richard Loo seems to have strayed in from a Silent yellow-peril melodrama; the crew is the usual cross section – Dana Andrews as the fearless commander, Farley Granger as 'the kid', Conte as the Italian, Sam Levene as the Jew – though as in *Action in the North Atlantic* his Jewishness extends only to his name.* The soldiers of **A Walk in the Sun** (1945) have greater individuality, but this was a further example of superior source material – a novel by Harry Brown, written for the screen by Robert Rossen (q.v.). A simple plot follows a platoon from its landing in Italy to the taking of a farmhouse, its men glad of 'butts' (cigarettes) or any minor diversion as they are decimated: under the guidance of their sergeant (Andrews) they are merely doing their job. Milestone produced and directed indepen-

---

*I do not mean to imply that any such quality exists, but that Hollywood, incapable at this time of showing any ethnic group without stereotyped mannerisms, was sensitive on the Jewish issue.

dently, and showed the finished product to Zanuck, who 'raved about it . . . and enthusiastically recommended it to his principals in New York. He accordingly got the release, and the rest is history' – an ambiguous remark, since the film initially failed. 20th did not open it in Britain, but sold it six years later to a minor distributor, who opened it to exceptional notices just after a revival of *All Quiet on the Western Front*.

As hitherto, Zanuck's major projects were assigned to Henry King – and there was none more major than **The Song of Bernadette** (1943), based on the best selling novel by Franz Werfel, a Jew, about the French peasant girl who claimed that the Virgin in person had directed her towards the discovery of a spring with healing properties. It is a handsome film reminiscent of the prints of the period – 1858 – and King creates a not especially reverential mood around the religious controversy engendered by the child's claim. 'For those who believe in God, no explanation is necessary. For those who do not, no explanation is possible' runs the famous foreword, but I think it immaterial whether Bernadette saw the Virgin – the Roman Catholic Church, who made her a saint, obviously believes she did – since the story is strong enough anyhow: one girl's faith against the combined scepticism of the townsfolk and the clerical establishment. George Seaton's dialogue dwindles into a series of discussions in a dusty room, and though King strives for variety by staggering the tempo and changing the groupings he cannot sustain the film over 156 minutes. We cannot blame him for the heavenly choir, but the effect is banal whenever Bernadette sees the Virgin: there are highlights on the young girl's face, while the Lady, surely better unseen by us, is played by Linda Darnell (uncredited) and shimmering like a Rockefeller Center Christmas tree. Jennifer Jones, hitherto unknown, as Bernadette is just a young girl with a piping voice; and the other mistake in an otherwise fine cast is Vincent Price, doing his usual supercilious job as the Imperial prosecutor. There are some poor lines ('So you're the urchin every idiot in France is talking about?'), but it is easy to see why the studio spent its largest advertising budget to this time – despite the fact that starless films seldom did well –

and to see why the public responded so warmly.

Its success encouraged Zanuck to embark on another venture without the guarantee of star players, and indeed at $5,200,000 **Wilson** (1944) was the most expensive film made in the U.S. up until then. It too lasted two and a half hours. The minds of movie moguls are unfathomable, and one cannot imagine what Zanuck hoped to gain other than an Oscar from this study of the chilly twenty-eighth President of the United States, remembered as the man who reluctantly led the U.S. into the First World War and who later sought to rid the country of its isolationist stance by promoting the League of Nations. The War had brought renewed interest in such matters, so at least we can understand Zanuck's claim that if the film failed he would never make another film without Betty Grable. (It did, and he didn't.) Trotti's screenplay reduces any political issues to a magazine summary, while the characters are dummies, carefully made up to resemble the originals, wheeled on and then off after saying their piece. Both Mrs Wilsons smile all the while, but as the President Alexander Knox is admirable, never playing for sympathy. King seems overwhelmed, unable to convey the sense of flux and change and inner struggle which were available in a not dissimilar tale, *The Magnificent Ambersons*.

Zanuck's belief in American democracy was given full play in **A Bell for Adano** (1945), taken from John Hersey's topical novel about the rehabilitation of a defeated people after the War – specifically about the impact of a handful of American soldiers on a small Italian town, left in ruins and without food after the Germans and the Fascists deserted it. It is the task of Major Joppolo (John Hodiak) to accustom them to peace, and he spouts to them of American democracy – mainly to the peroxide blonde Tina (Gene Tierney), who understands what he means by his Bronx upbringing: 'My dark hair was my Bronx. I wanted something very different.' The film becomes banal and anachronistic whenever she appears; Hodiak, however, is excellent, with his Clark Gable moustache, army haircut, incipient double chin and his little boy smile of enthusiasm coping with the preachiness. In

Hollywood's War Effort

Darryl F. Zanuck firmly believed in message movies, especially if they were based on bestselling novels or longrunning plays. *A Bell for Adano* remains one of the most interesting, partly because of its setting, a small Italian town to which the American military personnel are bringing their concept of democracy. The chief spokesman, happily, is the excellent John Hodiak, centre, with William Bendix, left. Among those playing the locals is Monty Banks, the Italian-born Silent screen comic (and Gracie Fields's husband).

the U.S. at least the arguments would have had a reassuring effect on a public shaken by the War. Today we may admire King's smooth direction and the studio-constructed town, meticulously re-searched, and photographed by Joseph La-Shelle in a manner – cobbled squares shown from high above, crowds massing – which was to deeply influence the Italian film-makers themselves.

In return an Italian film, *Roma, Città Aperta* (q.v.), would help to pave the way for a more realistic cinema in America – something that was felt to be urgently required as the War ended. Some of the films we have looked at had brought the industry renewed respect, and it is these which are the valuable records of the time. They were seldom what people wanted, but despite the fact that audiences in-creased enormously under wartime condi-tions public taste was growing closer to the critics: on the home front, at least, many,

busy with war jobs, became selective about what they wanted to see. The troops felt differently, and we should perhaps be indulgent towards the escapism which for an hour or so diverted them. Nevertheless, Hollywood had become more schizo-phrenic than ever about its responsibilities. The tinny, cliché-ridden musicals and daft Resistance thrillers were manufactured to keep the wheels turning and the stock-holders happy; on the other hand, many within the industry felt that, with the world situation so grim, the cinema-going public might be conditioned to think more than hitherto about the quality of the wares. In the meantime, the studios counted record profits, not really alarmed that a few critics in the big cities were for the first time preferring a number of Brit-ish films to the home product. But it was only a mild threat to the American film industry's supremacy; and there were no others to be seen on the horizon.

24

Italy: The Tradition of Realism

FOR MOST FOREIGN audiences the Italian cinema died after the early spectacles. It had apparently produced nothing of interest since – that is, nothing that foreign distributors wished to handle. Therefore, when the first postwar Italian films were seen abroad, they were as startling as Minerva springing full-grown from the brow of Jupiter. They were regarded as revolutionary, with their apparently makeshift location shooting and their unactorish or seemingly amateur players; they considered the vitality of the medium and the worth of ordinary people of primary importance and were therefore to be preferred to the expensive product of Hollywood. 'Shoestring masterpieces' Richard Winnington called them in 1949, also saying, 'Since Rossellini (q.v.) shook the screens of America, France and Britain over three years ago the prestige of the Italian cinema has come to be the highest in the world, equivalent to that of France in the period before 1939.'

The film with which Rossellini shook the screens of America and Britain was *Roma, Città Aperta*, known as *Open City*, but it had impressed neither the Italian nor French critics who had seen it at the first postwar Cannes Festival.* France had been seeing Italian films regularly throughout the Thirties and the War years so there was nothing new in the film to excite them. In the debate that followed between British and American critics and film historians the French remained silent, though Georges Sadoul in 1953 confused the issue (in 'French Film') when he said,

erroneously, that Renoir's *Toni* 'can be traced as the source from which springs the modern Italian school of Rossellini and de Sica'. This movement was called neo-realism, and it was said to have been started by Visconti with his *Ossessione* (q.v.), tantalisingly unseen after the War because it was based on James M. Cain's 'The Postman Always Rings Twice', and M-G-M, which owned the rights, quite justifiably banned showings. *Ossessione* was screened under club conditions at the National Film Theatre in London in 1957, when critics again wondered at Visconti's 'discovery' of the miracle of neo-realism. They were reflecting an article in *Sight and Sound* of the previous year in which Giulio Cesare Castello made such claims for Visconti, and he was supported by Gianfranco Poggi, writing in *Film Quarterly* in 1960. Both can be dismissed as more than partial to the work of Visconti, and the truth became further obscured a year later, when in his book 'Il Cinema Italiano', the director Carlo Lizzani claimed that virtually all the films made under the Fascist regime were worthless.

Thus was the myth of neo-realism established, and even if the prefix does indicate a re-birth, there was only a very brief period during which Italy abandoned the realist tradition, started by the Neapolitan film-makers with such films as *Assunta Spina* in 1915 – and indeed, these were only in accord with the *verismo* school of painters (Segantini, Pellizza) and musicians (Puccini, Mascagni), working to the tradition of peasant drama. At the same time another myth was perpetuated, that of the *telefono bianco*, supposedly the essential prop of the chiefly frivolous comedies or trivial melodramas of the Mussolini

*It was in fact the first ever Cannes Festival, having been postponed from September 1939 due to the outbreak of War: it had been initiated in protest at the rigging of the voting of the Venice Film Festival, begun in 1934 at the behest of the cinema-orientated Mussolini government.

period. The postwar film-makers did not deny this, perhaps because they preferred not to look back to that time, and it was not until 1975, when the Pesaro Festival featured a number of Italian films of the Thirties, that their true quality was available for rediscovery.

The leading realist of the Thirties was Alessandro Blasetti (b. 1900), a former film critic, who in 1928 formed Augustus, a co-operative, intended to alleviate the appalling state of the Italian film industry, bankrupt after the remaking of *Quo Vadis?* by the producer Giuseppe Barattolo. The pioneer Palermi followed that extravagance with a new *Gli Ultimi Giorni di Pompei*, as disastrously expensive. The directors with some reputation – Genina, Gallone – left to work abroad, and in 1926 the government, alarmed that cinemas had only foreign films to show, set up a commission. Blasetti was a supporter of the regime, and the subject of his first film, *Sole* (1929), now partially lost, was the draining of the Pontine marshes south of Rome, a project initiated by Mussolini. It was Blasetti's desire to return to the principles of the Neapolitan school, including shooting on location, which was not new since technicians were accustomed to using sunshine instead of arc-lights; but after a peasant drama, *Terra Madre*, Blasetti turned to more theatrical material, including **La Tavola dei Poveri** (1932), which bears the influence of René Clair.

Both **1860** (1934) and **Vecchia Guardia** (1935) show the influence of the great Soviet propaganda films, and indeed the hero of *1860*, like that of *The End of St Petersburg*, is clearly meant to represent the whole Italian nation. In the same way as the Russian heroes are viewed at some distance from the leaders of the revolution, so Garibaldi is much discussed but not seen. The film superbly encapsulates the major issues concerning the Risorgimento: its inevitability, the people's determination that it could only be achieved with Garibaldi, and their speculation about the government of the country when the fighting was over. A simple story takes a Sicilian partisan to Civitavecchia to make contact with revolutionary forces, and then home again, where he takes part in a battle. The film abounds in a sense of history, and patriotism, and in documentary technique; the leading roles were

played by amateurs, post-dubbed, since Blasetti insisted on using natural light and hence avoided the limitations then imposed by sound equipment. Post-dubbing became general in the Italian film industry, with professionals doubling for both amateur players and stars – to the extent that the true voices of many stars were not known to the public – but with *Vecchia Guardia* Blasetti used natural sound. His purpose was again semi-documentary, showing the rivalry and occasional battles between small town socialists and Fascists, and if the death of the boy Fascist is deliberately modelled on the Nazi propaganda films, Blasetti is by no means vicious, as they were, about his opponents. Indeed, the film is only moderate propaganda, and the sole reason given for this family being Fascist – and it is offered with a shrug – is the fact that the father served in the War. There is a finale involving the March on Rome and military songs, but the film's group heroics and discursive nature are unsatisfactory. The Italian public of the time avoided it.

Also a complete failure was **Il Canale degli Angeli** (1934), directed and co-written (with his brother) by Francesco Pasinetti (1911–49), whose writings had been the inspiration for Blasetti, and who was to be described by Vittorio de Sica (q.v.) as 'our conscience'. Vitally important as teacher and writer on cinema, and later screenwriter and director of shorts, this sole feature allowed him to put his ideas into practice – though the film itself bears a debt to other attempts at realism, notably *Lonesome*. It is lyrical, as were all films on the working classes except Lamprecht's – a simple tale, concerning a young wife and mother tempted to run off with a sailor; it is performed by amateurs (Maurizio D'Ancora, who plays the sailor, later founded the firm of Gucci) and was entirely filmed on location, in Pasinetti's native Venice. The cost – which was not high – was supplied by the government, since Pasinetti, though himself well-to-do, took advantage of the special grant for dubbing, initiated to protect the language.

The directive was really aimed at foreign films, which began trickling through again (after a hiatus with the coming of sound) once they had been dubbed – and a tax on this dubbing was ploughed back into the local industry. This duty saved one of the oldest and in theory one of the most powerful companies, Cines, whose new chief, Emilio Cecchi, decided to film a story by Luigi Pirandello, the only Italian author with an international reputation; and to increase its chances of success abroad he brought in a German director, Walter Ruttmann. **Acciaio** (1933) has little dialogue and, like Pasinetti's film, the simplest of working-class stories – of a young man (Piero Pastore), who returning from conscription, finds his girlfriend (Isa Pola) engaged to his best friend (Vittorio Bellaccini). As may be expected of the man who made *Berlin: die Symphonie einer Grosstadt*, Ruttmann in this refreshing film views the inhabitants and sunny streets of Terni with fondness; he includes the almost obligatory fairground sequence and allows one-third of his running time to the steel-works where the two men work.

Also working at Cines at this time was Mario Camerini (1895–1981), whose films for the company were aggressively working-class. He had entered the industry as an assistant to his cousin, Genina, and had started directing in 1923. His Silent films were a mixed bag but, influenced by the writing of Blasetti, Pasinetti and others, in 1929 he made *Rotaie* in the realistic tradition. *Rotaie*, a stark title, was no more likely than *Sole* to appeal to a basically rural and uneducated population, and the titles of both **Gli Uomini, che Mascalzone . . .** (1932) and **T'Amerò Sempre** (1933) deliberately set out to attract the least sophisticated cinemagoer: beneath both these titles, however, lurk remarkably good films, and as far as the second is concerned the title is ironic – since the heroine (Elsa de Giorgi) is not loved for ever, as she discovers to her sadness in the maternity home. A traditional tale of orphan girl and wealthy seducer develops into an equally conventional tale of an unwed mother, but one transformed by charm and a gift for *verismo*. In an almost extraneous sequence the heroine is invited to a party at the home of her new, bourgeois, suitor (Nino Besozzi), and it is a sequence of extraordinary freshness, if reminiscent of scenes in earlier films by Stiller, Von Stroheim and Clair. In this film Camerini offers a vivid portrait of the heroine's working-day, in a hairdressing salon, and *Gli Uomini, che Mascalzone . . .* is very much centred on the jobs

of its lovers – chauffeur and shopgirl. He (Vittorio de Sica) spots her (Lia Franca) as she leaves for work, and follows her tram on his bicycle through the streets of Milan: the film merely portrays the mainly comic ups and downs of their relationship till he proposes.

Vittorio de Sica (1902–74) came to the fore in Camerini's comedies, and he was particularly funny as a working-class man, underplaying to the extent that a slack jaw was his prime comic gift. In **Il Signor Max** (1937) he is a newsvendor courting the maid (Assia Noris) by day, and at night a fake-millionaire courting the mistress. Camerini said that he intended a satire on the petit bourgeois, as represented by de Sica, but that the film was liked because it was seen as a satire on the aristocracy. Despite his customary geniality it is second-rate; so is **Darò un Milione** (1935), despite a brilliant Clairish beginning in which a millionaire (de Sica) changes places with a tramp. The press takes up the story and everyone in town becomes generous to down-and-outs. The film degenerates into junketings in a circus, and is a particular disappointment as the first screen credit of Cesare Zavattini (b. 1902), who was to be so significant in de Sica's career as a director (q.v.).

Camerini also made a mirthless version

Lia Franca and Vittorio de Sica in Camerini's charming *Gli Uomini, che Mascalzone . . .* The tune they are dancing to, and the film's theme song, helped the film become a big success in France, from where the song passed to the U.S. and Britain as 'Love's Last Word is Spoken, Cheri'. Its popularity did not enable the film to be seen in either country.

of the old Spanish tale, now transferred to Italy, **Il Cappello a Tre Punte** (1935), primarily a starring vehicle for the Neapolitan comic team of Eduardo and Peppino De Filipo, who had been appearing in a stage version, the former as the governor and the latter as the miller. Since the film mocked authority, several sequences were censored, and the film was excoriated in the magazine run by Mussolini's son, Vittorio: Vittorio Mussolini (at least unofficially) controlled the film industry and was involved in the production of many of its propaganda films.

Two of the most famous, **Lo Squadrone Bianco** (1936) and **Scipio l'Africano** (1937) were directed respectively by Augusto Genina and Carmine Gallone, veterans recently returned to work in Italy. Each film has in common a fervour for Italy's intervention in Africa, either from historical right or sheer love of the desert, and a deadly dullness. Genina wrote his film with Joseph Peyre, from the latter's novel about the French Foreign Legion – here Italianised, but since it is Foreign Legion plot Numero Uno, they need surely not have bothered. Rejected by a woman, Mario (Antonio Centa) joins the Legion, where he becomes a hero under the stress of fire and because of the tuition of an admired disciplinarian captain (Fosco Giachetti) – the latter very much a required figure in the Fascist cinema; and we may note that the lady concerned, like any good Fascist, relents when she knows that Mario is in Africa. In the other film, it is not till the final reels that Scipio actually crosses the Mediterranean – but if the events concerned are presented somewhat incoherently they are, as in the Nazi historical films, in accordance with the true facts. The heroine is based on deMille's Cleopatra, and both the crowd scenes and battle scenes were intended to out-Hollywood Hollywood.

Since these films lack the venom of the Nazi propaganda films, it is difficult to feel about them in the same way: Nazism and Italian Fascism were as different as the character of both countries, and a rare 1959 showing of Genina's pro-Franco *L'Assedio dell'Alcazar* (1940) caused the French director Yves Boisset (q.v.) to note a true heroic style and that 'the appalling suffering of the besieged families is communicated with moving restraint.'

However, it is easy to dislike the heroics of two of the films directed by Goffredo Alessandrini, a former member of Blasetti's co-operative, who at one time had helped M-G-M dub its movies into Italian. **Luciano Serra, Pilota** (1937), with Amadeo Nazzari in the title role, stressed Italian patriotism, as we may suppose from the participation of Vittorio Mussolini, who provided the idea for it, combining his love for movies with that of aviation; it was the most popular film in Italy during this period. **Cavalleria** (1936) stresses the glory to be gained from dying for one's country in battle when the cavalry-officer hero (Nazzari) joins the air corps; throughout, the film positively dotes on young men in uniforms and shiny boots, but in the matter of handling his turn-of-the-century bitter-sweet romance Alessandrini proves himself no threat to Max Ophuls.

Nevertheless, the film paved the way for a series of period romances, and filmmakers turned to them gratefully as an alternative to dealing with contemporary Italy, where Mussolini was increasingly endorsing Hitler's policies. Blasetti, after a glorification of the navy in **Aldebaran** (1936), turned first to fantasy, in *La Contessa di Parma*, and then to history, in *Ettore Fieramosca*. In the latter, the Soviets again provided the inspiration, in this case, that of *Alexander Nevsky* – and the same influence lingers on in **La Cena delle Beffe** (1941), a tale of medieval Florence as taken from a dramatic poem first published in 1909. Presumably Blasetti was attracted to it as a compendium of what is expected in medieval tales – revenge, cruelty, lust and rivalry, encrusted with torture, madness and murder. It is a difficult film to like, since the entire dramatis personae is unsympathetic, including the chief protagonist, Nazzari; and as his opponent Osvaldo Valenti is monotonous.★ Clara Calamai, Dietrich-like as the woman who goes from one to the other, has at one point a breast-baring scene, apparently the first in Italian, if not world, film history. The influence of Eisenstein's film is felt also in the earlier **La Corona di Ferro** (1941), another distillation of the old legends, with their intrigues and turns of fate. There are

★In this case life imitated art, since Valenti known for his activities in torturing anti-Fascists, was shot by partisans in 1945.

other influences – *Maciste*, Lang's *Nibelungen*, the Fairbanks *Thief of Baghdad* – but Blasetti and his writers tried to create a legend of their own: they have a magnificent tournament in the middle, after which the action is sufficiently ludicrous as to be riveting.

One of Blasetti's writers was Mario Soldati (b. 1906), master of the period film proper. A successful novelist, he scripted several movies, often for Camerini, regarding the cinema as a means of making money in order to pursue his true occupation. However, turning director, he allows no indication of condescension in **Piccolo Mondo Antico** (1941) – indeed, no better film of the period exists. As with Max Ophuls's *Werther*, which may have influenced it, it tries for a real insight into the way people lived; it is not a romance, but it is romantic, inasmuch as most of the characters are fired by the thought of the Risorgimento – which eventually separates Franco (Massimo Serato) from his wife (Alida Valli). The latter role is exquisitely played, and Ada Dondini, playing Franco's grandmother, is a magnificent villainess. There are also such matters as a secret marriage and a suppressed will, to remind us that the source is the nineteenth-century novelist, Antonio Fogazzaro; the final section, when the couple are separated by grief, is both literary and lacking the momentum of the rest but nevertheless absorbing. With **Malombra** (1942), Soldati turned to an earlier novel by the same writer – and an inferior one, being pseudo-gothic with intimations of Ibsen. Like the other film, this is one detailed, elegant and surprising, but though there are some first-rate sequences towards the very end, Soldati loses interest halfway through the long running time. One handicap is Isa Miranda, a far better actress than most of the Italian ladies of this time but playing passion conventionally and looking more like a modern glamour queen than a nineteenth-century orphan. The role is

The early films of Mario Soldati are notable for their exquisite recreation of period detail. Both *Piccolo Mondo Antico*, with Alida Valli, and *Malombra*, ABOVE, were based on novels by Antonio Fogazzaro and set in and around Lake Garda.

625

that of a self-willed girl so determined to re-live past events that she is prepared to destroy both those who stand in her way and others innocently involved. Andrea Checchi is her major victim, perhaps the natural son of her guardian, and the adaptation seems uncertain as to whether he or the girl should be the chief protagonist. Both films have in common the setting of the Italian lakes, lovingly photographed, and art direction by the brilliant Gastone Medin, responsible for that of every major Italian historical film of the period. Of the two, this is the lesser, but Soldati's quest for realism in this particular subject has resulted in a film like no other – one more taking, but less satisfying, than any Hollywood gothic romance of the time, and far ahead of its French counterpart, *L'Eternel Retour* (q.v.).

One of Soldati's writers was Renato Castellani (b. 1913), who had also worked with Blasetti and Camerini: he in turn made his directing debut with **Un Colpo di Pistola** (1942), with Soldati among his writers. This school of film-making had by now been termed 'calligraphic', meaning that as much attention was paid to the method of telling as to plot, and this particular film, based on a story by Pushkin, is extremely literary, depending for its suspense on two separate if linked episodes told to a French novelist by the chief protagonist. He (Fosco Giachetti) is a Russian officer who thinks he has lost his fiancée (Assia Noris) to his best friend (Antonio Centa), and their separate dilemmas are almost ruined by Miss Noris, who, correctly coquettish in the first half, merely poses as the desperate heroine of the second. She was one of the several somewhat artificial film stars thrown out of work by the return to realism in the postwar period; as the solo-billed star we may regard her as less than an asset to Castellani, whose direction is academic and lacking the spirit of Soldati.

Ferdinando Maria Poggioli (1897–1945), another disciple of Blasetti, came to prominence at this time, after working on short documentaries. **Addio Giovinezza!** (1941) is based on the play by Sandro Camasio and Nino Oxilia which had been filmed at least three times before (twice by Genina). By concentrating on the Torino locations and period detail Poggioli robbed it of much of its senti-

mentality. Unfortunately, Maria Deni was another actress identified with a certain cinematic behaviour, in this case suffering; she is certainly never wholly bad, and in the first half is delightful as the shopgirl who attracts a student lover (Adriano Rimoldi), only to lose him temporarily to a woman of the world (Clara Calamai) – and then permanently as a result of her jealousy. **Gelosia** (1943) starts brilliantly, with a murder, and it turns out that the killer is the Marquess (Roldano Lupi), jealous of the man he forced his mistress (Luisa Ferida) to marry: their eventual fates never involve us overmuch, since Signor Lupi is weak in a role needing the young James Mason, but the evocation of rural Sicily in the nineteenth century is splendidly done. **Sissignora** (1941) is set in Genoa, and recounts the adventures of a serving-maid (Miss Denis), after she has attracted the attentions of her spinster employers' favourite nephew. This is probably the most ingratiating of Poggioli's films, notable for its sequences in market and dance-hall. Every room in a Poggioli film is richly characterised, and **Sorelle Materassi** (1943) offers a particularly interesting villa just outside Florence, where impoverished spinster sisters, again played by Irma and Emma Grammatica, sew to restore the family wealth. This threatens to be devoured by a completely amoral nephew, played in appropriately sullen fashion by Massimo Serato, whose misadventures, financial and sexual, are faithfully rendered from Aldo Palazzeschi's popular novel: but the hero's final pursuit by a wealthy Argentinian (Miss Calamai) belongs to any crass minor comedy, as if the homosexual Poggioli had no interest in seeing his stud hero settle into domesticity.

Another historical subject to be tackled was **La Tosca** (1940), which Jean Renoir was invited to direct. He accepted, because he wanted to 'experience the complicated magic of Italian baroque', and because the French authorities wished to do everything possible to keep the friendship of Italy. The subject was apt: a French play (by Sardou) with an Italian setting, but Renoir had shot only the opening sequence – the galloping horses – when the French ambassador recommended that he leave. Rome was increasingly full of Germans, and the Italian police were turning a blind ye to their strong-arm tactics. Renoir handed over the film to Carl Koch, a colleague who had worked with him in France (and the husband of Lotte Reininger). Obviously, it was safer in the hands of a German, for no one could have missed the analogy of Rome under a foreign-appointed governor – especially with Michel Simon's Scarpia, as petty as he is arrogant. Puccini's music is used in the background, and the only weakness is Imperio Argentina in the title role, always too risky and inadequate in the emotional moments. Renoir said later that it was a pity that Koch never directed another film, which on this evidence it is; however, the film's most striking feature is its use of the Castel St Angelo and the streets and churches of Rome.

One reason for the sudden crop of period films was the existence of Cinecittà, built by Mussolini, and opened in 1937 with the intention of rivalling Hollywood. After the decrepit studios in France, Renoir and his colleagues were amazed by it, while Italian film-makers were only too easily seduced into availing themselves of its facilities. **Via delle Cinque Lune** (1942), though ostensibly set near the Piaza Navone, was filmed entirely within Cinecittà, despite its being a production of the progressive film school, Centro Sperimentale di Cinematografica;* indeed the director of the film, Luigi Chiarini, had founded that in 1935, with Mussolini's blessing. It is an entertaining film, from a sound Balzacian novel by Matilde Serao, about a dragonish woman (Olga Solbelli) who is sexually drawn to her prospective stepson – and the attraction is not only reciprocated, but after the affair has begun he becomes as rapacious as she. In this role, Andrea Checchi once more demonstrates his versatility, and the scenes of the two of them together with the lady's familiar indicate Chiarini's delight in villainy. The film, the best of the half dozen that he made, is another brilliant evocation of the last century, despite a rather ponderous style. Chiarini (later a critic), who became the first professor of film in Italy and director of the Venice Film Festival during the Sixties, was already at this time a theoretician of film. He had published a book on the subject with Umberto

*The prospect of lecturing to its students was another reason Renoir had come to Italy.

Barbaro – who was, with Pasinetti, his fellow writer on this film.

These were the apostles of neo-realism: Chiarini and Barbaro propounded their ideas both in a magazine called *Cinema* and as lecturers at the Centro Sperimentale. **La Peccatrice** (1940), scripted by Pasinetti and Chiarini for the director Amleto Palermi, was considered a step in the right direction, since it was a contemporary story with an implied social criticism. Palermi's *Cavalleria Rusticana* (1939), based on Verga, was also admired, and he himself is a key figure, since he too chose to work with Zavattini, Barbaro and Aldo Vergano. It is not surprising that Barbaro and Vergano, both Marxists, returned to the principles of Blasetti, since they had belonged to his pre-Talkie collective. Students and critics emerging from the Centro Sperimentale, such as (q.v.) Antonioni and Giuseppe De Santis, both future directors, were scornful of the calligraphic school, claiming that its conjuncture of cinema and literature was arid, and at a time when cinema memories were short, such films as *Il Canale degli Angeli* and *Vecchia Guardia* seemed to belong to pre-history. In fact, the essential tradition of Italian films had been maintained, with only a few exceptions, for the working lives of their characters were considered as relevant to the plots as their emotional problems. The demand for a 'new' cinema was not only exaggerated, but the movement must be considered in the light of political frustration. Those mainly concerned disliked both the War and the government, yet, unable publicly to express their feelings about either, knew that the solution for the industry did not lie with period romances. Paradoxically, they admired both the writings and the documentary-like work of Francesco De Robertis (1902–59), who remained as staunchly Fascist as Blasetti and Chiarini had been.

De Robertis, a former naval officer and theatre producer, was appointed head of the naval film service, for which he wrote and directed **Uomini sul Fondo** (1941), an account of a submarine stuck on the ocean during routine manoeuvres. It is entirely staged, or re-enacted, by amateurs picked from the service, and what humour there is is derived from the reaction of the men, while the drama arises from their

627

Italy: The Tradition of Realism

The importance of the Italian neo-realist movement overshadowed all other discussions of international cinema in the postwar period, and since foreign critics saw so few of the films the origins of the movement were wrongly attributed – and were certainly not found to have taken root during the War. One early film of the movement is Blasetti's *Quattro Passi fra le Nuvole* with Adriana Benetti and Gino Cervi. Among other matters, it is set in the milieu of working people, and to the protagonists their means of earning are essential to the plot, as would be true of all the neo-realist films.

anxiety and the mechanics of rescue. When the last men are finally raised from the sea, the waiting fleet gives vent to a show, recalling *Potemkin*, with the crews clustered in similar picturesque fashion on the rigging. De Robertis later supervised *La Nave Bianca*, the first film made by Rossellini, his assistant on *Uomini sul Fondo*, and after the fall of Mussolini organised the remains of the Fascist industry till Venice was taken by the Allies.

Meanwhile, those hoping for a new cinema were also encouraged by de Sica's third film as a director, **Teresa Venerdi** (1941). Though the title refers to the orphan girl (Adriana Benetti) who wins her hero in 'Daddy Long Legs' fashion, the true subject is the love life of the hero, a penniless young doctor, played by de Sica himself. His mistress is a volatile music-hall star (Anna Magnani), and she and her seedy milieu are portrayed as amusingly as are the guardians of the orphanage, while the sympathy extended to the unfortunate girls prefigures the later films that Zavattini, here uncredited, wrote with de Sica.

Zavattini is responsible for introducing satire and feeling into the Italian cinema. Neither quality had been entirely absent, for both were encompassed within the affection Camerini and Poggioli felt for their characters; but other leading film-

makers had tried to be detached, avoidin the cheap tricks by which the makers slapstick comedies and sentimental dram hoped to find their audiences. Moreov Zavattini believed that these qualiti sprang from the everyday, a theory that was able to put into practice in **Quatt Passi fra le Nuvole** (1942), which Blase directed and helped to write – and t result may be considered creatively thei since the customary plethora of Itali screenwriters is often suspect, i.e. they a often friends or relatives of the produc and should only be considered serious when they have other credits. In this ca the film is much warmer than Blasett other work, almost certainly becau Zavattini contributed to both story a screenplay. His stated intention throug out his career was to build a film round o day in the life of an ordinary man. Su films had been attempted before, and th all begin, as this one does, with the ringi of an alarm-clock and someone rising fro bed. Paolo Bianchi (Gino Cervi) is alm aggressively ordinary, a salesman depe dent on commission, in his mid-thirti and with a nagging wife. He sets out for l usual working day, but by a series circumstances, each of them slight yet d tailed, he finds himself by the end of pretending to be the husband of a pregna girl (Miss Benetti) and spending the nig with her in the family home. The title, t 'four steps in the clouds', refers to l sensation at returning to the country, a the movie, charmingly filmed in the ope air, is light-hearted, clever and refreshin Since it was hailed as a triumph of ne realism when shown in Britain and t U.S. in 1948 – the only Italian film of t war years to reach either country at th time – it is worth noting that the scene the coach-passengers all singing in a bus indebted to *It Happened One Night*.

The most significant of all neo-real films is, however, **Fari nella Nebb** (1942), directed by Gianni Francioli (1910–60), who was associated with t avant-garde during most of his stay France. He had returned to Italy to dir one documentary and just one featu prior to this one. Apart from tenuous co nections a decade later – one section of dim, episodic film, *Siamo Donne*, to whi Visconti and Rossellini also contribute and as director of a Zavattini scrip

Buongiorno Elefante! – he has no link with
the movement, nor have any of the several
writers who worked on the script. Violently demotic, set in and around Savona,
it tells of the broken marriage of a truck-
driver, and how the wife is tempted by a
flash-Harry, while the husband (Fosco
Giachetti) takes up with the 'fast' Piera
(Luisa Ferida). This may well have been
the first time European filmgoers – Hollywood's delicacy in such matters was all-
pervading – had seen adulterous lovers in
bed together, and Franciolini is equally
honest with his settings, moving from
cluttered rooms to doleful bars to the ramshackle trucking offices. His direction
fails, however, to inject momentum, and
his ending is particularly poor.

Its significance is in its influence on a
much greater film, **Ossessione** (1943),
with which Visconti introduced an element of subversion into the neo-realist
movement. Mussolini was shown the film
privately, and the censors banned it because they disapproved of the protagonists, a grubby couple who murder the
lady's older husband in order to continue
fornicating. Visconti may have begun his
preparations before seeing Franciolini's
film, and he may have shot some material
before the authorities interrupted shooting; but the credited photographer is Aldo
Tonti, who had shot *Fari nella Nebbia*, and
the two films have much more in common
with each other, both as to tone and visual
quality, than Visconti's does to his source
(its plot-line apart).

Luchino Visconti (1906–76) was of the
ducal family, more interested in horses and
couture till Coco Chanel introduced him
to Jean Renoir, who took him on to the
production team of *Partie de Campagne*. He
had stayed with *La Tosca* after Renoir's
departure, by which time he decided that
he wanted to be a director. It was Renoir
who recommended Cain's novel – already
filmed in France★ – and Visconti had started
work on it, without benefit of permission,
when the censor refused to sanction his
first project, an adaptation of Verga.
Visconti's ambitions determined him to
undermine complacency in the cinema,
but as a Fascist he did not set out to challenge authority; he did not become a
Marxist, at least openly, till it was safe to

★As *Le Dernier Tournant*, from which Visconti also borrowed
details.

do so. In his version James M. Cain's taut,
legal thriller has become an updating of
Boccaccio, though with only two scenes
which could be described as erotic – the
first quick, sudden mating, and the later
reconciliation on the sands of the estuary.
Giovanna (Clara Calamai) is tired, bored
with her husband and with drudgery: she
wastes no time when she sees Gino (Massimo Girotti) and by the following day is not
only rejuvenated but in thrall to sexual
passion. In the book, their relationship
falls apart under the strain imposed by the
investigations; Visconti burdens Gino with
the guilt of a Macbeth and, though he did
not realise it, recedes into convention.

Gino, having persuaded Giovanna to
run off with him, immediately finds her an
encumbrance, and falls in with an itinerant
actor (Elio Marcuzzo), in a relationship
which ends in violence, as would several
such relationships in Visconti's later films
(q.v.). He may have believed that destruction was an element of homosexuality, or
at least a way of making it acceptable to
audiences at the time: the implication is
gratuitous, but confirms what the brilliance of Calamai's performance (the role
was meant for an even stronger actress,
Magnani, who was pregnant) almost disguises – the inference that Visconti was
romantically inclined towards his leading

Massimo Girotti and
Clara Calamai in
Ossessione, the film
with which the
aristocratic Luchino
Visconti hoped to
challenge the Fascist
regime, since its
subjects are infidelity
and murder – social
evils which the
government claimed
to have eradicated
(which is one reason,
since they are the
staples of fiction,
Italian film-makers
had been con-
centrating on period
films). The film was
promptly banned,
but was shown
when Italy was
liberated a few
months later; for
copyright reasons
it was not seen
publicly abroad till
fairly recently.

male character. Everything about Gino is approved of to the point of inconsistency: his rolling-stone disposition; his preparation for the sexual act, posing like a figure in Grand Opera; and his reaction to the permanence of his relationship to his mistress – drinking, and leaving her for bed after a busy day at the inn, with a solitary meal and the debris in the kitchen to be tackled. The film is visually memorable – the small trattoria on the bank of one of the tributaries of the Po, the straight road disappearing into the marshes, and the interiors of the inn, like an opera-set and larger than those in *Fari nella Nebbia*. Against the realistic sound of the amateur concert at Ancona, there are the pseudo-Puccini fugues of doom on the soundtrack. Visconti would both explore the tenets of neo-realism, and become a director of Grand Opera; his films would in themselves represent the eternal dichotomies of the Italian cinema – the realistic on the one hand and the epic and grandiose on the other.

De Sica's **I Bambini ci Guardano** (1944) also examines the consequences of an illicit affair – from the point of view of a small boy (Luciano de Ambrosis). We only glimpse matters which he does not comprehend, such as the furtive sexual relations of other grown-ups which impinge upon his life, or his mother's fascination with her lover. At one point the child's parents are reconciled and spend a vacation in Alassio – which has the same liberating effect on de Sica as the Po estuary had on Visconti, allowing him to make witty comments on the pleasantries in the dining-room and the festivities on the beach. In apportioning no blame to the grown-ups, the screenplay retains the traditional detachment, but it introduces to the preoccupations of the neo-realists that of responsibility, as the title indicates. It was the first film directed by de Sica in which he did not appear. He became a director, he said, from vanity – and a sense of righteousness, after the press had criticised a performance he had given under Gallone's direction and Gallone had refused to listen to his own comments on that performance. In this case he had decided to film a novel by a friend, 'Prico' by C. G. Viola, and he had sought Zavattini's collaboration because of his dissatisfaction with the original screenplay. They had not

known each other at the time both had worked on *Darò un Milione*, but had later met socially, at which time de Sica had been impressed with Zavattini's views on screenwriting.

Nevertheless, Zavattini was still engaged in such trite exercises as **Il Birichino di Papà** (1943), directed by Raffaello Matarazzo, a vehicle for fifteen-year-old Chiaretta Gelli – Italy's Deanna Durbin – and the film's sole virtue is to indicate how well Zavattini understood the construction of the early Durbin films, even if, with these collaborators, he was unable to duplicate it. In June 1943 the word 'neo-realism' had just been coined by Barbaro in an appreciation of *Ossessione*, but feeling that it should lead to the rejection of the light comedies and calligraphic films in favour of Italian films in the manner of *Quai des Brumes*. Meanwhile, shut off from the rest of the world's films other than the French and those of Nazi Germany – which were ignored – Soldati was imitating more recent and far more interesting French cinema. **Quartieri Alti** (1944), a version both of an Italian novel and of Anouilh's play, 'Le Rendez-vous de Senlis', owes much to such films as Autant-Lara's *Douce* (q.v.), with its clever, but artificial, conversations and intrigues.

Inevitably such films were swept away by **Roma, Città Aperta** (1945), which the Italian public liked as much as their critics had disliked it: but would the furore it created abroad have been quite the same had British and American critics known that Rossellini's two previous films, *Un Pilota Ritorna* and *L'Uomo della Croce*, had been, at best, mediocre tributes to the Fascist war effort? Roberto Rossellini (1906–77) had started in films as an amateur, and had been welcomed into the industry as a writer by Vittorio Mussolini; he had assimilated the documentary technique he had learnt with De Robertis, to the extent that *Roma, Città Aperta*, a study of the city during the last days of the Occupation, was said by some foreign critics to have been filmed surreptitiously at that time. Its improvised appearance – due to the shortage of equipment – and its formlessness were considered a virtue; it is certainly facile and often self-conscious, but it is deservedly a monument, as engrossing and exciting now as when it came out. It follows the fortunes of the hunted

Resistance leader (Marcello Pagliero) and a pregnant widow (Anna Magnani), whom one of his colleagues hopes to marry and who is shot down in the street. The film's ingredients also include a kindly priest (Aldo Fabrizi) and a consideration of the German authorities, together with a lesbian collaborationist, and the silly young tart (Maria Michi) led into their circle for the sake of a fur-coat. Whatever its reception at Cannes, the film was rapturously received in Paris; critics everywhere were united in preferring the peasant-like Anna Magnani (1908–73), with her power and humour, to the songs of Bernadette and Betty Grable.

They also preferred **Paisà** (1946) to the well-meaning *Bell for Adano*; like its predecessor, *Paisà* is less a tale of battle than a portrait of Italy at war. One is about the Germans leaving; the other is about the Americans arriving, and it follows them from Palermo to the Po, in a series of anecdotes with anti-climaxes and no easy solutions: an Italian girl leads a group of G.I.s on a night sortie, who sneer when she is killed by German snipers; in Naples, a drunken negro soldier has his boots stolen by an urchin; in Rome, a G.I. (Gar Moore) tells a prostitute (Maria Michi) of the sweet and pure girl he had met on his last visit, failing to recognise that they are the same woman; in Florence, an Italian-speaking American nurse and a partisan move through the beleaguered city with the cool acceptance of death we noted in *Roma, Città Aperta*; in the Romagna, three padres, Catholic, Jewish and Protestant, are received in a remote monastery – the best and only comic episode; and in the marshes of the Po, when the O.S.S. and the partisans are finally routed by the enemy, the former are spared under international convention but the partisans are dumped summarily into the river, bound, gagged and presumably still living. The film fades on this image, and like the one which began the sequence, it offers the most emotional comment on how the Italians felt about the War. The impact of this film remains extraordinary, though to a greater degree than *Roma, Città Aperta* it arouses the suspicion that its virtues are largely due to necessity and chance. Both are tremendous films, and given the jagged nature of Rossellini's contribution, it would be unwise to suggest, as did many observers at the

time, that the major creative force was that of screenwriter Sergio Amidei (b. 1904): yet the brilliance, particularly of *Paisà*, is in the concept and the dialogue.

Amidei worked with Zavattini and de Sica on **Sciuscià** (1946), but the essential contribution seems to have been that of Zavattini, for de Sica, offered the subject by an Italian-American producer, Paolo William Tamburella, initially found it too theatrically treated, particularly since it was based on fact. Like Rossellini's two films, it created a sensation abroad. James Agee found it 'different from almost any other movie you care to name [because it concerns] the ultimate absoluteness of responsibility of each human being' – and it is a responsibility far deeper than that of de Sica's earlier film about childhood, *I Bambini ci Guardano*. De Sica said later that the most urgent necessity of the time was to 'redeem our guilt' for the Fascist years, and as we can read into that film some criticism of a guilty couple – and in the Rossellini films that of a foreign power – *Sciuscià* is unquestionably an indictment of all society. It is therefore a vital addition to the premises on which neo-realism was founded. With its amateur cast, its sour, grim locations and uncommercial subject,

It is now curious to read the contemporary British and American review of *Roma, Città Aperta* and *Paisà* – because, for instance, many critics insisted that all the players were amateurs, which they were not. The director, Rossellini, was widely said to be a genius, a fact disproved by his subsequent films, though these two remain extraordinarily impressive. This is a scene from *Paisà*, with a part-time whore (Maria Michi) taking home a drunken soldier (Gar Moore), who only wants to talk about the girl he had encountered when last in Rome.

Italy: The Tradition of Realism

Andrea Checchi and Vivi Gioi in *Caccia Tragica*, De Santis's haunting study of rural Italy in the aftermath of war. Set in Piedmont, it begins in the muddy lanes and fields where the peasants hope to earn a few lire for food; it ends as shown here, with two criminals trapped in their hide-out, and the director moves easily between realism and melodrama. There are, incidentally, good reasons why this still is reminiscent of the one of *Quai des Brumes*.

de Sica was able to get backing only on the strength of the world reception of *Roma, Città Aperta* – and, as with that film, *Sciuscià* picks its characters from the streets of the capital, the fourteen-year-old orphan Pasquale (Franco Interlenghi), and the younger Giuseppe (Rinaldo Smordini), equally rootless but with an older brother, whose black market dealings will entice them away from shining the shoes of G.I.s and eventually land them in a reformatory. The film is not an object-lesson in what happens to homeless children, but it is about the prison gates that close as adulthood approaches. From the first sad, chance involvement in crime, the boys lose the freedom that is the right of all children, till in jail they are coarsened and lose their sustaining feature, the friendship of their earlier lives. The film allows few culprits: the police are harassed and the school authorities without imagination. A breezy old doctor observes of one chronically sick boy that his solution lies not in prison or in sanatorium but in vagrancy, for then he would have the chance to survive. The lawyers, possibly representing

that section of society which should know better, are depicted as mercenary, shifty and doddery, while the boys are sometimes treated in the sentimental manner of 'Emil und die Detektive'; and it is surely a mistake to use the horse, owned by the boys, as a symbol of the soul – if by no means as blatantly as in *Viva Zapata!* (q.v.), whence it was copied. De Sica's approach was again dispassionate, or seemingly so, and that was what made *Sciuscià* revolutionary among polemical films: the indignation of de Sica and his colleagues was so palpable that they had no need to guide audiences towards the desired reaction.

It is precisely that passion which **Il Sole Sorge Ancora** (1946) lacks. A rural version of *Roma, Città Aperta*, it is a vivid portrait of one small Italian town from the Armistice in 1943 to the rising against the Germans in 1945. The characters are divided into the partisans and their supporters, and those who collaborated with, or tolerated the German occupiers, chief among whom is Major Heinrich, played with monocle and cropped haircut by Massimo Serato. The film is also conventional in other ways; the hint of lesbianism may have been inspired by Rossellini's film, and the opening scene, of the hero (Vittorio Duse) in a brothel, may be a borrowing from or a homage to, the opening of *Acciaio* – since the bordellos in both are incidental to the events that follow. The portrait of the collaborators is the most unflattering yet, which may be a reason why export was discouraged – though the film received some recognition, as *Outcry*, when shown in New York in 1949. It is the best film directed by Aldo Vergano, who had written *Sole* for Blasetti: he believed himself unjustly neglected at the expense of his colleagues, and wrote a bitter autobiography before he died in 1957.

His co-writers on this film included Carlo Lizzani and Giuseppe De Santis (b. 1917), the latter having moved directly from film criticism – he notably savaged Rossellini's *L'Uomo della Croce* – to working on the screenplay of *Ossessione*. He made an impressive start as a director on **Caccia Tragica** (1947), which is even more valuable than *Il Sole Sorge Ancora* in its portrait of the chaos and confusion of postwar Italy. Based on fact, the film follows the consequences when a group of *banditi* have stolen the annual payroll of one of the newly-formed workers' co-operatives. This act was born of desperation, and when the co-operative sets out to pursue the thieves, they come across service veterans marching to protest against the lack of work and bread. The *banditi* themselves, whom we assume at first to have strayed in from a superior gangster picture, turn out to be an assortment thrown together by the times – a German ex-soldier, a girl (Vivi Gioi) called Lili Marlene since she had been a collaborator, and her lover (Andrea Checchi), a victim of the German concentration camps. It is increasingly clear that these two are meant to represent the guilty of Italy, and that they are modelled on the doomed couple of *Quai des Brumes*: Barbaro, who looked to that film for inspiration in defining neo-realism, is one of the writers of this, together with the director, Lizzani, Michelangelo Antonioni and Zavattini. This is perhaps the key film of the movement, with all its strengths and weaknesses. At the same time it is an honest and socialist-inspired portrait of the working classes, and a thriller which can as easily encompass 'grotesque' cinema, as when the hero (Massimo Girotti) finds himself surrounded by children in masks.

Alberto Lattuada (b. 1914), a former screenwriter who had begun directing in the calligraphic style in 1942, took advantage of the new and freer shooting methods to make **Il Bandito** (1946), while aiming for tragedy, though both here and in **Senza Pietà** (1948) the effect is often closer to melodrama. Both films are further portraits of Italy in the aftermath of war, the former concerning the returning soldier (Amadeo Nazzari), who is appalled to discover the falling-away of morals in his native town but is eventually another contributor to this – as driven by his wife (Anna Magnani). *Senza Pietà* is set in Livorno, where a number of American deserters had settled to form a small colony – inevitably of social outcasts – and one among them, a negro (John Kitzmiller) falls in love with a prostitute (Carla Del Poggio). Lattuada's handling, supposedly detached, like that of de Santis recalls Carné: his obvious sympathy for the lovers created problems for its American distributor.

In **Vivere in Pace** (1946) Luigi Zampa returns to the war years and brings comedy to neo-realism. The setting is a village the War has passed by, though that does not mean that its inhabitants believe the local Fascist when he claims that his side is winning it. Two escaped American prisoners arrive, one of whom can be passed off as a local to the solitary German corporal; the other, however, is a negro (Kitzmiller), and must be kept hidden. The inevitable confrontation goes not as expected, since the local wine has had its effect on both belligerents, but it underlines Zampa's purpose throughout, which is the absurdity of war.

The fragility of neo-realism was apparent in Rossellini's **Germania, Anno Zero** (1947), written with Lizzani, and, for the German dialogue, Max Kolpet. The attempt was to portray the former ally and enemy coping in the aftermath of War, and devastated Berlin was to provide the contrast with the well-preserved Italian cities. The protagonist is again a child, Edmund Köhler (Edmund Möschke), the family breadwinner, except for what his sister makes by being friendly to the occupying forces. Father is sick in the apartment which is shared with another family; the brother has never registered, so cannot work. A pederastic teacher (Erich Gühne) uses the boy to sell a record of a Hitler speech to some G.I.s, and he also persuades the boy to dispose of his father, since as an invalid he is useless to society. The boy duly administers poison and then commits suicide, clearly atoning for German guilt, a matter otherwise mentioned only in passing. As Hitler on the record boasts of victory, the camera roams across the ruins of Berlin, and that is virtually all that Rossellini has to say about Germany in the year zero. As Adam Helmer observed at the time in *Sequence*, 'its pessimism, the so-called tragedy . . . is false and concocted, a manoeuvre rather than a conviction.'

It is now clear that **Il Miracolo** (1948) is no improvement. At the time consideration of its merits was overshadowed by its content and the consequent censors' edicts; after being banned outright in Britain, it was, wrote Dilys Powell, 'being talked about as if it were a cross between the works of the Marquis de Sade and the First Epistle to the Corinthians'. The story was

Italy: The Tradition of Realism

By 1948 the Italian cinema was beginning to exhaust the War and its aftermath as a subject, but for many life remained a struggle against poverty, which was what Visconti wished to show in *La Terra Trema*. The actors were amateurs, the *pescatori Siciliani* so proudly announced on the credits: this one played the film's chief protagonist, seen here with his brother in the film.

written by Federico Fellini (q.v.). It tells of a stranger who plies with wine and makes pregnant a shepherdess (Anna Magnani) – she only too willing, since she sees in him a dead ringer for St Joseph, with the consequent belief that the child she carries is the Messiah. As the villagers cast her out, an allegorical point is made, but the piece is merely an anecdote, a vehicle for Anna Magnani, as is clear from the dedication, which is to her 'art'; it was originally part of a longer film called *Amore*, but the other section, a version of Cocteau's 'La Voix Humaine', was lopped off by Rossellini and has hardly been seen since. Certainly Magnani is one of the few actresses convincing as a peasant, and the views of village and sea accorded to the principles of Italian cinema at the time. **La Macchina Ammazzacattivi** (1948) is set in a small

seaport south of Naples and is about a photographer who finds that his camera has magic powers: as he photographs snapshots in his studio, their subjects expire in another part of the town, and he embarks on a scheme to kill the wicked, the greedy and the corrupt. Eduardo De Filippo, with Fabrizio Sarazani, provided the story of this rural whimsy, but in Rossellini's hands it is neither *comédie noire* nor the sunny comedy suggested by the setting. It is merely undisciplined and completely unfunny: Rossellini later referred to it as 'an isolated experiment' and in fact it went virtually unseen. There were some isolated showings★ four years after completion, in 1952, and despite his international reputation it was not considered of sufficient merit to be exported.

Had the neo-realist movement depended on Rossellini, it would have died with these two films, the one artificial and the other quite pointless. However, Visconti was already at work on **La Terra Trema** (1948), which he envisaged as a great new opening for the movement. Indeed, he was so determined to make the most of neo-realism that the dialogue was recorded in the Sicilian patois of its fishermen characters, all of them played by amateurs. That fact limited its commercial reception in Italy, and when Visconti, with aristocratic disdain, refused to re-dub, showings were confined to the film societies. He was also unable to film the other two episodes of what was to have been a trilogy: this one bears its original subtitle, *Episodio del Mare*; the source is Verga's 'I Malavoglio', which Visconti had abandoned before *Ossessione*, and the other two parts were to have concerned the sulphur mines and farming. The running time of just under three hours is as ambitious as the title, with its echoes of revolution: indeed, it was meant to be a revolutionary manifesto, proclaiming in a foreword the truth of the conditions depicted as 'true of all countries where men exploit men'. At the centre is the Valastro family, of Aci Trezza in Sicily, living and working as they have done for generations. They are kept poor by the wholesalers, in an agreement not to offer competitive terms: 'Ntoni Valastrato decides to confront them by going direct

★According to some commentators it was never publicly seen.

to the retailers, and the family support him by mortgaging the house. The elements defeat him; his girl will not speak to him, and his brother is lured away by a stranger in plus-fours who hands round Lucky Strikes. Home gone – squalid enough, goodness knows – and head bowed, he goes to work for the mocking wholesalers. The men and the buildings, the sea and the sky, marvellously photographed by G. R. Aldo, with Gianni di Venanzo as his cameraman, coalesce into one gigantic fresco – a word used advisedly, since the characters are one-dimensional. Visconti's response to the poverty of fishermen was intellectual: they are found to be stoic, long-suffering, hard-working and tolerant – and thus without the anger and greed of the characters of de Sica and Zavattini. If we note that the men are far better looking than the women, and prey to them (according to the commentary) that is not necessarily untrue; in general the film is free of Visconti's operatic graces, and is made with such imaginative grasp that it is powerful for its entire length. It is a rigorous film, and of great purity; it is one of the twin peaks of neo-realism.

The other is **Ladri di Biciclette** (1948), which is also probably the greatest film of the movement. While *La Terra Trema* languished in the vaults, this film of de Sica's opened up vast new audiences abroad for foreign language films. Considered then a great film, partly because it concerned poverty, its sometimes clumsy technique was also admired, though curiously the word most often occurring in reviews is 'flawless'. It is the least formidable of great films; it is transparently honest. Zavattini wrote it from a story by Luigi Bartolini, and as a Marxist he was perhaps grinding an axe; de Sica seems merely to have been content to illuminate a small corner of existence. Its reputation has dimmed, since most people cry during at least part of it and remember it as sentimental – which it is not, even remotely. It is harsh and hard and cold-eyed. Antonio (Lamberto Maggiorani, a non-professional, as were all the cast) gets a job as a bill-sticker provided he has a bicycle, and his wife sells the sheets to get that out of pawn. On the first day it is stolen, and the police are indifferent – an intimation of bureaucracy which accounts for much of the film's success with post-war audiences. With his son (Enzo Staiola), Antonio combs Rome for the thief, who goes into an epileptic fit, which is probably faked, when caught. Before a hostile crowd, Antonio speaks to another indifferent policeman: 'If you knew what this meant to me,' and it must be the most understated plea in the history of films. The boy watching his father's eventual humiliation provides one of the most pessimistic of all endings, and it is odd that Richard Winnington, who admired the film inordinately, should have allowed his left-wing viewpoint to suggest to him that Antonio would get help because he had friends. Discussion is academic: poverty may not have gone from Rome, but the city has changed out of all recognition – this is a mean provincial town, with hardly a car in sight. There are few trees and little cement, since de Sica used locations near the Tiber; he filmed in odd days, often Sundays, over a long period, and the total cost was the equivalent of $25,000 or £9,000, supplied by a consortium of three businessmen after de Sica had failed to get backing from the film industries of Italy, France and Britain – having journeyed in desperation to Paris and London, since *Sciuscià* had been successful in both cities.

Despite the prestige accruing from its foreign success, the Italian film industry continued to loathe it. It rejoiced instead in the success abroad of **Riso Amaro** (1948) – a success which was to damage the industry to the present day, so that it is always looking for ways to recapture the world market. That success was made by the stills of Silvana Mangano, up to her calves in the rice-fields, with huge thighs above black stockings which looked infinitely worth the parting. Sex is certainly provided by the story, during the course of which Mangano divides her attentions between a police sergeant (Raf Vallone) and a small-time thief (Vittorio Gassmann), and the melodrama drives out any serious comment intended on the exploitation of the migratory female workers in the Po Valley rice-fields. Giuseppe De Santis directed, having made a conscious decision to abandon the principles he had preached as a critic and had demonstrated in *Caccia Tragica*. Paradoxically, he said about this time that the Italian contemporary he most admired was Visconti, since he alone refused to consider the world market when making a film – and yet he deliberately

Italy: The Tradition of Realism

also no longer responding to tales of deprivation among the working people. In October 1949, for instance, they were presented with **Il Mulino del Po** and **Cielo sulla Palude**, both good films, but hardly cheerful entertainments. The former is directed by Alberto Lattuada and is set in 1876, adapted from a novel by Riccardo Bacchelli concerning labour unrest when the trade unions come into conflict with the local *padrone*. Lattuada keeps an admirable balance between the principals, the family running the mill on the Po, and the peasantry at large, and if, as a portrait of the past, it lacks the intensity of Sjöström it is virtually as convincing. *Cielo sulla Palude* also concerns the past, as a destitute family roams the marsh country looking for a roof. The director is Genina, whom we may consider the Vicar of Bray of the Italian cinema, but he takes to neo-realism as a duck to water, superbly guiding his amateur cast and conveying the tale in images of great simplicity. The screenplay is by Suso d'Amico Cecchi, daughter of Emilio Cecchi, and Fausto Tozzi, based on the 'life' of Maria Goretti: clearly she did not have much of a life, with little recourse but to pray whenever rape was threatened (she was later canonised, for forgiving her attempted rapist and murderer on her deathbed). That rape and violence arise from poverty and ignorance is a plea the film convincingly makes: and their circumstances are as banal as the final crime, which I intend as a compliment. We may in both films enjoy the photography, of Aldo Tonti and G. R. Aldo respectively; and a visit in each to the local fiesta only underlines the quality of sameness.

aimed *Riso Amaro* at the local audiences which had shunned the later films of Rossellini and de Sica. Yet even as a 'commercial' film, this is a swift descent from *Caccia Tragica*, almost always sacrificing probability for effect; realism has gone, to be replaced by a phoney melancholy which would be copied by others, including Fellini, in the next decade.

De Santis may have argued that sex was not incompatible with neo-realism, since it had been an essential ingredient of peasant drama – and he might have added that the movement did put grave limitations on material. Audiences, in reaction to the Fascist past and postwar confusion, made it clear that they did not want frivolous subjects. Blasetti tried to return to the epic of antique times in *Fabiola*, which was a resounding failure, but audiences were

Contemporary problems were examined in **Il Cristo Proibito** (1951), but audiences had been subjected too often to its twin themes, the difficulties of the returning war veteran (Raf Vallone), and his attempts to sort out exactly what went on in his absence between the collaborators and his partisan brother; some doubted that any sort of realism was really achieved when peasants are so beautifully grouped and photographed. It is the only excursion into cinema of the novelist Curzio Malaparte, who wrote and directed, and it is an absorbing movie – of a genre almost unknown in the Anglo-Saxon cinema, the serious melodrama. On a personal level, the film becomes an examination of the futility of war, and like all good Italian films a celebration of Italy, done with love, pride, wonderment and more than a touch of cynicism.

These qualities are also to be found in two marvellous films directed by Renato Castellani: the aptly-named **E Prima-vera** (1949) and **Due Soldi di Speranza** (1952). Castellani, after his first two films, embraced neo-realism with *Mio Figlio Professore* in 1946. After one more film, he attacked *E Primavera* with what Gavin Lambert in *Sight and Sound* called an almost boundless vitality: it is apparent in his locations, his non-professional perfor-mers, and in the screenplay which grew from conversations with several conscripts on the advantages of amatory adventures when away from home territory. In this particular case, one (Mario Angelotti) takes, with conceit and charm, a wife in Milan and another in Sicily. Castellani's view of his countrymen is to paint them warts and all, and the villagers in *Due Soldi di Speranza* are greedy and grasping. The youthful members of the Communist par-ty are in direct contrast to the priest, who is fat and slothful, and their conflict reflects Italy's greatest dilemma since the War. The setting is a village on the slopes of Vesuvius, and the protagonist is Antonio (Vincenzo Musolino), just back from the War, and without a job to support his two sisters and self-dramatising mother: he would like to work for his future father-in-law, but the old man cannot stand the sight of him. He is enterprising in getting work, and the fact that it turns out to be always temporary is never actually his fault. The title refers to his marrying the girl without either a job or her father's approval, which make for a denouement slightly at odds with the honesty of the rest of the film. Both movies are as funny as they are furiously inventive. Castellani's reputa-tion was such that he persuaded the Rank Organisation to back **Romeo and Juliet** (1954), ravishingly photographed, in Technicolor, in and around Verona. It was, however, not a success, since he failed to get even adequate performances from an amateur, Susan Shentall, his Juliet, or his Romeo, Laurence Harvey. Discouraged, Castellani returned to writing for other directors, and the occasional films he directed are of indifferent quality.

Meanwhile, de Sica and Zavattini had also brought comedy to neo-realism, though the key sequence of **Miracolo a Milano** (1951) is near the beginning, when a small boy is left alone in the world. Later, on leaving the orphanage, all his posses-sions are stolen from him. Even so, he has a 'Buon Giorno' for everyone, and finds friendship in a shanty-town on waste ground outside the city. With his simple goodness, he turns it into a real village, and is much loved: but after the miracle of the title occurs, there is little love anywhere, since the derelicts turn out to be as covet-ous as the tycoon who owns the land. They cannot win against him, and the piece concludes as they fly on broomsticks over the cathedral to a land where 'Good Morning really means Good Morning', on the bitter theory that there is hope for the poor only in heaven. This most cunning of film fantasies has prepared us for this end-ing, with its deliberate references to *A Nous la Liberté*. It had started with the credits superimposed over images from Hieronymous Bosch: there is little Bosch in Clair, but there is much here – the pained despair, the physical ugliness, the greed, and the hopeless fêtes and fairs. De Sica made the film as a favour to Zavattini, whose screenplay was based on one of his own novels and one of which he was par-ticularly fond. For his next project he asked Zavattini to write a screenplay on the subject of old age.

Umberto D (1953) is in fact about an old man's hopelessness, and that is all there is to it. Umberto (Carlo Battisti, in life a university professor) lives in a respectable apartment, albeit in one room, and is neat-ly dressed; he is proud and querulous, and is unable to make up the difference be-tween expenditure and income. He tries to sell his watch, and his books, and he cam-paigns for a raise in pensions outside the Ministry concerned; he gets himself pack-ed off to hospital in order to save a few days' food. We do not know whether he is widower or bachelor; his only friend is the pregnant scullery maid, though whether by the soldier from Napoli or the one from Firenze she does not know. That is her lot, together with the truckle-bed in the hall, the cockroaches above the sink and the letter home. Her relationship with the old man is based on a common loathing of the landlady/mistress, and he is sustained otherwise only by his love for his dog.

De Sica's Compassionate Films

De Sica's reputation has been hurt by his greatness, since people remember being moved by his films (the good ones, that is) and recall them as sentimental. They are not: they are cries of despair that the world is a cruel place for the poor and deprived – though that is not entirely true of the young hero, Luciano de Ambrosis, of *I Bambini ci Guardano*, RIGHT, though his parents disregard him as they pursue their own selfish ends. This film crept into the cinema consciousness, via showings at film societies after the furore caused by *Ladri di Biciclette*, BELOW, when it first appeared outside Italy. As *Bicycle Thieves* in Britain and *The Bicycle Thief* in the U.S. it ran for months, establishing undreamt-of records for art-house showings. With its successors, *Miracolo a Milano*, FAR RIGHT, a comedy, and *Umberto D*, BELOW RIGHT, it established new criteria for foreign-language films.

The players in all
four films were
amateurs. They are
Lamberto
Maggoriani and
Enzo Staiola in *Ladri
di Biciclette*, an
unnamed boy, the
hero as a child, in
Miracolo a Milano,
and Carlo Battisti (in
life, a university
professor) and Maria
Pia Casilio in
Umberto D, which de
Sica dedicated to his
father, whose name
was Umberto.
These three films
were disliked by
Italian critics as
giving a false picture
of Italy, which
partly explains why
Umberto D was the
peak of de Sica's
career and why he
began to decline
thereafter.

Italy: The Tradition of Realism

When suicide seems the only solution, this love may save him. The film is a masterpiece, but like *Ladri di Biciclette* it has suffered from being remembered wrongly – as a story of a man and a dog. Zavattini had wanted to write a film about a man to whom nothing happened, and here he had written about a man to whom nothing much happens, with the enormous exception that poverty is constantly allied to death – though it is very doubtful whether the old man comprehends that.

When this film came out, we felt that there was nothing the cinema could not do, that there was no facet of human behaviour which even merely gifted men could not use to make us understand ourselves and our planet better. After *Ladri di Biciclette* and *Miracolo a Milano* we had expected greatness: we could not have guessed that it was the summit of de Sica's and Zavattini's work both together and individually. Still less could anyone have realised that the humanist film would die, except for such practitioners as (q.v.) Ermanno Olmi and Satyajit Ray. However, it was perhaps not surprising that de Sica and Zavattini became professionally cynical. They struggled to make these films, and though they were artistically and commercially successful abroad, they were execrated at home, either for presenting a false picture of Italy or exaggerating a problem which hardly existed. The future prime minister Giulio Andreotti was among several leading public figures who roundly and publicly condemned them, which made it difficult for them to get further backing. Rizzoli had financed *Umberto D* in the hope of persuading de

Sica to direct *Il Piccolo Mondo di Don Camillo* (q.v.) and its total failure in Italy did not encourage that company to try again. De Sica refused the Don Camillo film, and he is reputed to have refused Selznick's proffered backing for *Ladri di Biciclette*, with Cary Grant playing the leading role as part of the deal. De Sica did finally agree to work with Selznick, on *Stazione Termini* (q.v.), and was forced into a series of compromises which were soon to have a disastrous effect on his work. He and Zavattini remained proud of these three films, but they surely could not have been surprised by their failure in Italy, for despite their humour and an implied compassion in attempting to record the imbalance of society, the overriding mood of each is despair.

Neo-realism was only marginally a humanist movement. It was important technically, in removing the encrustations that increasingly burdened film since the cameras were first taken out into the streets of Paris – the artificiality, the 'glamour', the synthetic tree or mountain which was not as convincing as the real thing. It removed the Italian cinema from the confines of Cinecittà, but its importance inside Italy was relative, since the *verismo* tradition was so strong. Nevertheless, the few postwar Italian films shown abroad had an influence on other cinemas comparable only with that of the Soviet films in the late Twenties. Their value to Italy, and to the rest of the world, lies in their record of a particular time in the country's history – set down with as much fidelity and honesty as was possible at that time.

25

French Cinema during Occupation and Readjustment

FILM PRODUCTION in France halted and hesitated during the early months of the War – a handful of movies was abandoned, first temporarily and then permanently – but once the German Occupation was established the studios returned to full activity. The number of French-language films made in Germany prior to the War is evidence of Dr Goebbels' interest in French cinema. With the Occupation, the offices of Tobis and Ufa in Paris were reopened, and their activities enlarged; the Germans also took over a number of industry properties either Jewish-owned or controlled, including cinemas. Approximately one-third of the industry was German property for the duration of the War. Production recommenced in the 'free' zone, in the studios at Nice, sooner than in Paris, but there, too, Jews were among the early victims. Following a decree by the Vichy government in October 1940, the Comité d'Organisation Cinématographique headed by Raoul Ploquin – producer of *Gueule d'Amour* and *L'Etrange Monsieur Victor*, among other films – issued a list of specific Jewish personnel who could not be employed.

Jewish players were also cut from the reissues which cinema-managers programmed during the film shortages caused originally by the (temporary) closure of the studios and then by the banning of British and American films. Some films, accordingly, no longer made much sense, while *Macao, l'Enfer du Jeu* was partially reshot with Pierre Renoir in the role played formerly by Erich Von Stroheim. As German films replaced American ones as the big attractions on the Champs-Elysées, Goebbels took an interest in their reception – but that, in general, was poor. Fore-seeing similar resistance to French films emanating from Tobis and Ufa, Goebbels set up a 'French' company, Continental, reputedly recommending it to only produce films which were *'légers, vides et si possible stupides'*. Ostensibly, however, Continental allowed artistic freedom to those it employed; a request for the services of a particular player was in fact a command, and many artists spent the war years finding good reasons to be unavailable – usually by pleading retirement or overwhelming prior commitments.

There was indeed no vestige of freedom. All scripts and the finished product itself were examined by both the German censor and that of Vichy – the novelist Paul Morand. Otherwise the industry might be regarded as healthy. Activity increased, to the extent that eighty-two films were produced in 1943 – almost twenty more than the prewar average, and twenty more than were produced in Germany that year. Given the limitations on subject matter – an edict had forbidden any more than forty per cent of the running time being devoted to adultery – it is not surprising that of the 225 films made between 1940 and 1944 only a few had any quality. A great many were thrillers, and the remainder almost all in full flight from reality.

That is in direct contrast to many made in the period immediately before and we might pause for a moment to look at **Menaces** (1940), shown six months before the Germans occupied Paris and containing a riveting portrait of the period September 1938 to September 1939. The director, Edmond T. Gréville, was usually mediocre, but his fellow writers on this occasion were Pierre Lestringuez, who had worked with Renoir, and Curt Alexander, who had worked with Ophuls. The setting is a small hotel near the Panthéon, and at the obvious level this is conventional drama, some way below *Hôtel du Nord*. But most of the guests come from abroad, from a Europe which is clearly disturbed; one of them, a German professor (Erich Von Stroheim), is a refugee from Hitler, and after reflecting on peace and war – he wears a mask to hide wounds received in World War One – he commits suicide. The characters are all pitiable or lost, except for one guest who is French, Denise (Mireille Balin), who is engaged to an English journalist (John Loder) – and the handling of that relationship is clearly symbolic. Guests and staff are increasingly apprehensive as they listen to Hitler on the wireless, and the film ends with the hotel closed for the duration as planes thunder overhead. Gréville changed the script as filming proceeded, and then had to begin again after the original negative was destroyed by fire; the second version was completed as the Germans invaded Poland.

Goebbels found it expedient to forget which film-makers had expressed anti-German sentiments. With the exception of Marcel Carné, France's best-known directors were in Hollywood – Clair, Duvivier, Renoir; and they were joined after the Occupation by Jean Gabin and Michèle Morgan, claiming either prior contracts or leaving by the devious route of 'Free France' and North Africa. (The great actor Louis Jouvet spent the War in South America, after taking a theatre troupe into neutral Switzerland.) To this day controversy surrounds some of the artists who remained: Maurice Chevalier did not make any films, but he did sing to German audiences – though it was later established that that was in return for the protection of Jewish friends; Danielle Darrieux worked for Continental and went on a goodwill tour to Germany with other members of the industry, but in 1942 she retired for the duration.

Marcel Pagnol was making **La Fille du Puisatier** (1941) in Nice when the Germans moved into France, and in the confusion he lost one of his players, Betty Daussmond. He replaced her with Line Noro, and inserted a sequence in which Raimu, Fernandel and Josette Day listen to Marshal Pétain's radio announcement of the end of hostilities – though the artists concerned had already concluded their work on the film. Later, the radio speech was replaced by one by General de Gaulle, and that was the version which was so warmly welcomed by British and American audiences after the War. Some critics felt that Pagnol now tended to emphasise the 'Frenchness' of his characters, and others, with more reason, that the piece lacked the humour of *La Femme du Boulanger*. In France it was said that he had told this particular story once too often – of the pregnant girl (Miss Day) and her angry father (Raimu) – but there are some pleasant variations on it as told in *Fanny* and *Angèle*. She is one of six unmarried daughters, and her father turns her out because of the effect of her influence on the younger ones; her lover (George Grey) is a dashing, well-heeled young man who leaves her to join the airforce. The scenes between Raimu and Charpin, as the boy's father, make up for longueurs elsewhere; and Fernandel is enjoyable as the girl's vain suitor.

Many newcomers entered the film industry. Sadoul has observed that the best film-makers retreated into 'brilliant fantasy' but I think a better term might be 'black whimsy'. It can certainly be applied to **L'Assassinat du Père Noël** (1941), directed by the veteran Christian-Jaque. The action is literally cut off from what was happening elsewhere, being set in a snowbound village in the mountains of Haute Savoie. The characters are crippled emotionally, mentally or physically, and all are involved in personal missions of despair, fantasy or obsession. There is little reality in their everyday lives, but they try to escape from whatever there is. The man who is called Père Noël (Harry Baur), a globe-maker by profession, treats the children to fantastic stories of a Chinese bandit while his daughter Catherine (Renée Faure) makes dolls. The Baron (Raymond Rouleau) insinuates that he has leprosy, though that is only a device to keep people away. Catherine takes pity on his loneliness, and it flowers into love. Pity often merged into love in the films made during the Occupation, but love, when it came, was passionate, perhaps not to last, and these emotions were often associated with dusty baronial halls, candlelight and archaic costume, as in this case. The general mood is fey and uneasy, thus able to encompass the hooded figure who stomps through the village – for it is, despite the trimmings, a thriller. Unfortunately, the direction becomes as banal as the story. The film does, however, demonstrate the French cinema in both its glory and the guise it wore at this time; and it is likely that the crippled boy urged to walk again was meant to represent France itself.

Marcel l'Herbier's **La Nuit Fantastique** (1942) could surely have appealed at no other time. It asks us to accept Fernand Gravet (almost forty) as a student: those who know him only from his two Hollywood films will be relieved to find that in his own language he has a certain charm, if perhaps whimsical – not a disadvantage in these circumstances. He dreams of a white lady, and when he thinks he sees her (Micheline Presle) he follows her, his illusions shattered when he finds her with her father (Saturnin Fabre) and cadaver-like fiancé: and of this grim trio, she, silly and giggling, is perhaps the worst. With the illogicality of dreams, a farce backstage at a magic show is followed by an escape from a madhouse; a love scene set on the rooftops of Paris is followed by a trip to the Caveau des Illusions; the comfort of being drunk or looking at beautiful women is shattered by mental patients clutching at prison bars or by a bicycle race. L'Herbier and his writer, Louis Chavance, may have intended a homage to Méliès, but for all the levity and promise of a happy ending, despair and tragedy lurk round the corner.

This film, together with *Les Visiteurs du Soir* (q.v.) and **L'Eternel Retour** (1942), was one of the three great successes during the Occupation. In the two last named films may be seen the influence of the current films of Blasetti, notably *La Corona di Ferro*, which for some months engaged the attention of artistic circles in Paris. *L'Eternel Retour* was written by Jean Cocteau, his first work for the cinema since *Le Sang d'un Poète*. It is a revamp of the story of Tristan and Isolde (the dramatist Jean Anouilh was currently enjoying success with 'Eurydice', another tragic myth become doomed love story) and this was not the first time that Cocteau had turned to the old legends for inspiration. His avowed reason on this occasion was to make a movie star of his protégé and lover, Jean Marais, who is kitted up in a stunning wardrobe of sweaters and riding breeches;

directed by Jean Delannoy, Marais appears in often identical shots to the Prince in *Snow White and the Seven Dwarfs*. Cocteau succeeded beyond his wildest dreams: Marais became the desired of every other woman in France, and audiences by the million fled their hardships with this gloomy tale – not to the dismay of the Occupiers, who approved both of the source of the film, which could be said to be Germanic, and of the blond Aryan good looks of the lead players. Even in wartime audiences were unlikely to swallow the business of the love potion, so Isolde (Madeleine Sologne) has a pal who specialises in herbal medicines; and the fate of the lovers is sealed by the meddlesome *méchant nain* who is part of the fetid household. Unfortunately, when Isolde observes that matters have become so absurd that she refuses to believe them, she is speaking for modern audiences. Contemporary comment was almost entirely favourable, and even as astute a critic as William Whitebait wrote, for the *New Statesman*, 'a mature work of art that embodies civilisation as surely as do Eliot's "Four Quartets", Britten's Michelangelo Sonnets, and Henry Moore's shelter drawings'. That was in postwar London; a later generation would find it adolescent fantasy and homosexual to boot. It has no sympathy for women: the heroine is as warmly conceived as the plaster cast which her face resembles, and the other women are either malicious or predatory. Only a homosexual, I think, would want to '*boire énormément*' when left alone with the woman he supposedly loves,★ while Marais's response to getting engaged is not to embrace his fiancée but to throw himself on the bed in a mock battle with her brother. We are meant to understand that the brother has a crush on him, since to know Marais was presumably to grovel at his feet.

Le Baron Fantôme (1943) also looks back to Blasetti, as well as to Marivaux; it is linked to *L'Eternel Retour* by a breathlessly romantic sleepwalking sequence and, though a box-office failure, would lead Cocteau to *La Belle et la Bête* (q.v.). He wrote it (and also plays a supporting role) but the scenario is credited to the director, Serge de Polignac. It is set in 1826 in a

★The situation is repeated in John Osborne's play 'A Patriot for Me', in which the hero tries to persuade himself that he can become heterosexual by getting drunk.

haunted castle, and each time it comes dangerously close to being a fairy story, it throws in something humorous, macabre or cynical – the cynicism is so often directed at the film's central characters, a quarrelsome quartet of lovers, that they thereby avoid becoming tiresome.

Les Visiteurs du Soir (1942) is more sprightly than most of the escapist films; it suffers, however, from the presence of Alain Cuny, an unsuitable romantic lead. Marcel Carné decided to emulate *La Corona di Ferro* when the censor turned down each of the contemporary subjects he submitted, and Pierre Laroche and Jacques Prévert provided a script about two of the Devil's creatures sent up to the medieval world. They are Gilles (Cuny) and Dominique (Arletty), *en travestie*, and when each becomes romantically involved with a human, the Devil (Jules Berry) manifests himself. The lovers, Gilles and Anne (Maria Déa), are separated, but their love is so strong that they manage a 'Peter Ibbetson' kind of relationship, and when the Devil, who represents Hitler, turns them to stone their hearts continue to beat – an allegory not lost on French audiences at the time. This is the familiar Carné–Prévert duel between good and evil, the hopeful and the corrupted, but the only good reason for seeing it is Arletty, with her infinite grace and Giaconda smile, the most enigmatic of Devil's envoys.

The influence of the Italian calligraphic films can be seen in **Douce** (1943), which even opens with the panning shot of rooftops as in Poggioli's films. Recourse to a period subject was natural to its director, Claude Autant-Lara (b. 1903), who had worked with both l'Herbier and Clair as art director. Directing infrequently for a decade – including two French versions of Buster Keaton comedies for M-G-M – he had not been successful till *Fric-Frac* in 1939, a polished version of a famous comedy about crooks, with Arletty and Fernandel. *Douce* was adapted – from a novel by Michel Davet – by an experienced screenwriter, Jean Aurenche, and a new one, Pierre Bost (1901–79), who would thereafter work almost exclusively together, and indeed usually for this director. Its subject is three generations – the imperious Countess (Marguerite Moreno), her ineffectual, crippled son (Jean Debucourt) and his perverse, wilful daughter

(Odette Joyeux); their relationships with the governess (Madeleine Robinson) and the groom (Roger Pigaut) provide a certain satire, though we are offered a welter of emotions instead of the clean irony of *La Règle du Jeu*. The characters are enjoyably rounded, speaking in civilised tones, which as we saw in the last chapter was a facet of French cinema much admired by contemporaries in Italy.

The two countries collaborated on a handsome new **Carmen** (1943), vigorously directed by Christian-Jaque, with Viviane Romance in the title role and Jean Marais as Don José: the version to see is the (dubbed) Italian one, in which Don José has a more suitable bass voice. The supreme French evocation of the past is in a film begun clandestinely during the Occupation, **Les Enfants du Paradis** (1945) – and it is the past of Balzac and Eugène Sue, the Paris of theatres and sideshows along the streets and byways. The courtesan Garance (Arletty) and the mime Debureau (Jean-Louis Barrault), meet and fall movingly in love, though she is bound to Lacenaire (Marcel Herrand), a man of doubtful tastes and activities; she is also loved by the actor Lemaitre (Pierre Brasseur) and is the mistress of a nobleman (Louis Salou), but it is for Debureau alone that she feels emotion, an emotion which is part maternal and part concupiscent. Like its predecessor, the film owes much to Arletty's bewitching performance, but it is flawlessly conceived and realised, by Carné and Prévert, on a vast romantic scale. It is a masterwork, and it is to the French cinema what *Gone with the Wind* is to the American – and the peak of Carné's career. It was a tremendous success in France and in every country where it was screened – one of the first French films to be shown abroad after the War.

Prévert's brother, Pierre, had meanwhile made his first film since 1932, **Adieu, Léonard** (1943), and like *L'Affaire Est dans le Sac* it is larky – but professional. Léonard (Carette), a salesman of novelties, turns to crime to maintain his wife's pretensions, and is therefore the blackmail victim of Bonenfant (Pierre Brasseur), who wants him to murder his wife's cousin Ludovic (Charles Trenet). Ludovic is a simple philanthropic soul and an incurable optimist, quite unperturbed at being thought mad and by Léonard's attempts to

644

Arletty, with unnamed player and Jean-Louis Barrault, seated, in *Les Enfants du Paradis*. The fact that it so richly recreates the Paris of the 1820s has somewhat obscured the fact that its theme is the same of the other memorable romantic films of writer Jacques Prévert and director Marcel Carné – of the brevity of happiness and the frustrations of love in an imperfectly designed universe. It is the masterpiece of this team and in 1979 was voted by the French Academy of Cinema Arts as the greatest French film ever made. The runners-up were, in order, *La Grande Illusion*, *Casque d'Or*, q.v., *La Regle du Jeu*, *La Kermesse Heroïque*, *Pierrot le Fou*, q.v., *Hiroshima Mon Amour*, q.v., *Les Jeux Interdits*, q.v., *Quai des Brumes* and *Le Salaire de la Peur*, q.v.

murder him: he eventually triumphs, however, in a quasi-Clair ending that is as pathetic as Trenet's performance. The piece, inventive without being surprising, would have been better if it had all been as sharp and blustery as Brasseur's performance.

Autant-Lara's **Sylvie et le Fantôme** (1945) also needs more asperity; with that quality and its château setting, it might have passed for one of the *pièces roses* of Anouilh. The château is saved by selling the painting of the White Hunter, who leaves behind a ghost (Jacques Tati); Sylvie (Odette Joyeux) loves the White Hunter as if he were real, and matters are complicated by the professional ghost hired from Paris – her father's birthday gift. For such conceits, this film was much admired: William Whitebait thought it audacious to add farce to a wistful tale of a girl's love for a ghost. Alfred Adam, influenced by Giraudoux's 1933 play 'Intermezzo', wrote the story; the direction is as light as air. Mlle Joyeux's co-star is François Perier, but the successful rival for her hand is Jean Desailly, a featured player: that co-stars did not always fall in love was one

reason why French pictures held more surprise than those from Hollywood.

Les Anges du Péché (1943) is one of the rare screenplays by Giraudoux, with dialogue as studied and formal as the film's appearance. The director, Robert Bresson (b. 1907), had been assistant to Clair on his *Air Pur*, abandoned on the outbreak of war, and had directed one unsuccessful film nine years earlier. He had also been an art photographer, and he knew exactly what he wanted when he stepped inside this particular cloister. Convent life is clearly a way of escaping contemporary problems, but other problems arise, and as expressed here – the pride of one nun, and her rivalry with another – they are far more fervid than the austere style at first suggests. Despite its complete lack of humour, the film can just be taken seriously, which is more than can be said for **Les Dames du Bois de Boulogne** (1945), written by Cocteau and Bresson from a story by Diderot, 'Jacques le Fataliste', which had also served D. W. Griffith for *Lady of the Pavements*. The tale is an early example of two of the chief themes of French literature, revenge and destruction

645

of the young by cynical elders, but this modernised version is merely lurid melodrama. Moreover, Bresson's Paris belongs to no known world, and the characters move like puppets through carpetless, echoing rooms: the chic woman (Maria Casares), bent on vengeance, in pearls and black skirts that sweep the floor, contrasting with the girl (Elina Labourdette), in felt hat and raincoat. In the original story the latter is manipulated into prostitution, but here she only does a solo rumba in a cabaret before rushing home where, skirtless, she helps mother entertain young men in white tie and tails with champagne. That hardly makes her unworthy of the man (Jean Marchat) in love with her – and perhaps explains why the film was disliked when it appeared.

Sharing Bresson's misanthropy was another new director, Henri-Georges Clouzot (1907–77), who had been assistant to Anatole Litvak and E. A. Dupont. He had worked in Germany on French-language films; and because of his right-wing views he was not unwilling to work for the German company, Continental, initially as writer on *Le Dernier des Six* (1941), adapted from a detective novel by S. A. Steedman, and directed by Georges Lacombe, with Pierre Fresnay. His adaptation of a novel by Simenon, **Les Inconnus dans la Maison** (1942), was notably well received; a story of a lawyer (Raimu), long past his better days and heavy with drink, who returns to his profession at the behest of his daughter and her lover – a Jew, whose criminal tendencies had caused her to stray from the straight and narrow path. As directed by Henri Decoin, its atmospherics and social criticism made it seem in the prewar tradition, though it did not escape attention that Raimu's summing-up speech quoted, in Sadoul's words, 'favourite catch-phrases of the Vichy Press'. Raimu, whose presence at Continental was considered a coup for the company, asked his agent to find him immediate work elsewhere to prevent him from staying, but Decoin was to make several more films for Continental.

Clouzot adapted another novel by Steedman, **L'Assassin Habite au 21** (1942), and Continental gave him the chance to direct. Few directors made a more brilliant start – literally, since after an opening sequence in which a series of grisly murders is discussed in a bar the camera follows one of its patrons along the street and it is gradually clear to the audience that he is being followed by the killer. Subsequently the detective in charge (Pierre Fresnay) goes to stay in a boarding house where everyone is suspect: they, the guests, are droll, and Fresnay himself has some Hollywood-style sparring with Suzy Delair, his mistress, who has decided to do some sleuthing on her own.

Le Corbeau (1943) is also a whodunnit, but harsher and darker, leaning even more heavily on the style of the late German Silents. In a small town where children play in the sun and the curé is a leading force, a series of poison-pen letters provoke suspicion and unrest: as they mount into hundreds, few people escape – and most of them blame a doctor (Fresnay), accusing him of being an abortionist and a lecher. The doctor's relationships with the spiritual but married Laura (Micheline Francey), and the sexually ravenous – and crippled – Denise (Ginette Leclerc) are unusual, and the latter's attempts to seduce him are strong by the standards of the time: it is nice to be able to reveal that lust wins.

The film was disliked in France for its unflattering portrait of provincial life, which was one reason that the Germans ensured that it was shown in other Occupied countries. It was not, however, shown in Germany, since the authorities there decided that it might cause outbreaks of anonymous letters with which the Gestapo could not cope. That fact was utilised after the War by Clouzot and the film's writer, Louis Chavance, when they were indicted for having contributed to anti-French propaganda; and Chavance was able to prove that not only had he not specifically written the film for Continental but that the screenplay – based on some actual events which happened in Tulle – had existed as early as 1933. However, both he and Clouzot were forbidden to work again in the film industry.

The order was later rescinded, and both men returned with films which were among the greater successes of the postwar period. However, it was with Jean Ferry that Clouzot adapted yet another novel by Steedman, **Quai des Orfèvres** (1947) – and they falter in their task only at the end.

The film's absorption in its chosen milieu is as comfortable as a glove – prewar Prévert superimposed onto postwar Paris. And memorably so: who could ever forget the seedy Menilmontant music hall, filled with tobacco smoke, and Suzy Delair 'avec son tra-la-la', with her toothy smile, or the way she looked in her black underwear? – or Charles Dullin's definitive dirty old man or, above all, Louis Jouvet's wily, tired but relentless detective, coping with a running cold? It is a tale not only of murder but of pimping, ambition, jealousy and passions not then usual in films: when the detective realises why Dora (Simone Renant) has risked so much for Jenny (Delair) he observes that, like himself, she has not been particularly lucky with women.

Jouvet was also in the film which allowed Chavance to work again, **Un Revenant** (1946) – written in co-operation with Henri Jeanson and directed with Christian-Jaque. Jouvet plays a successful choreographer who returns to his home town and is reminded of a youthful love affair. The woman concerned (Gaby Morlay) obliquely suggests a manner in which he can take revenge on those who destroyed their love: eventually, however, he abandons his plans to do so and his cynicism gives way to reflection – and both qualities are, nicely, found within the film.

As with Clouzot, the first feature of Jacques Becker (1906–60) was also a thriller, **Dernier Atout** (1942). He had directed some short films, and had been assistant to Renoir; in 1939, he had started a feature, *L'Or du Cristobal*, but the money ran out and he disowned the result as finished by other hands. *Dernier Atout* concerns American gangsters in an imaginary Latin American city, and it was specifically designed to appeal to those who felt deprived of American films; the plot is over-complicated, but Pierre Renoir is a sour, glowering villain and the tone light enough to be called felicitous. Becker's second success was **Goupi Mains Rouges** (1943), with story and screenplay by Pierre Véry, who had provided the similar mysteries and black humour for *Les Disparus de St Agil* and *L'Assassinat du Père Noël*. In this case a large and self-regarding provincial family closes ranks when one of its members has been murdered. Becker regards them with detachment and one

suspects that his fascination is due to the unchanging ways of country folk – as is demonstrated in the final sequence.

Naïs (1945) is also bucolic melodrama, and yet another modernisation, in this case of Hugo's 'Naïs Micoulin': it concerns the love of a hunchback (Fernandel) for the beautiful Naïs (Jacqueline Bouvier), and how he comes to her aid after she has been seduced by a wealthy wastrel (Raymond Pellegrin). The director is Raymond Leboursier, but the Provençal locations and the approach indicate that Marcel Pagnol was the writer and producer; amidst the clichés there remains his awareness of the complexity of life, and the acting – with the exception of Mlle Bouvier, who was his wife – also contributes to the film's effectiveness. However, Pagnol's time had passed, and the few films he subsequently made aroused little interest.

Le Ciel est à Vous (1944) also offers a convincing portrait of provincial life, in an uncertain tale of a married couple so obsessed with aviation that their home is almost destroyed by it. Begun and abandoned in 1939, the film was finished in 1943, and apparently the dedication of the couple had significance in the final days of the Occupation. Charles Spaak wrote the screenplay from a story by Albert Valentin, and it is the last film of any consequence directed by Jean Grémillon. He planned a number of semi-documentaries, with government aid, on such subjects as the Revolution of 1848 and the Munich Settlement, but none was made. He did make some documentary shorts, and the fiction films he produced revealed only too clearly his loss of interest in that form.

Martin Roumagnac (1946) is also set in a small provincial town and, as stolidly directed by Georges Lacombe, is notable for its assembly of attitudes from prewar Gabin films. Gabin himself plays a builder who falls for a lady known locally as *la veuve joyeuse* (Marlene Dietrich), supposedly an Australian: she marries in name only a diplomat (Marcel Herrand), and after Gabin has been acquitted of strangling her, he is shot by her latest admirer (Daniel Gélin). The film was a failure, but was at the time notorious as the vehicle chosen by the two stars after the debacle of **Les Portes de la Nuit** (1947). Since *Les Enfants du Paradis* had confirmed the ability

647

of Carné and Prévert to provide the French film industry with international success, a great deal of money was invested in *Les Portes de la Nuit* – 80 million francs, or a quarter of a million dollars. Dietrich left the cast after deciding that her role was too small, and Gabin was sacked after complaining about the script and quarrelling with her replacement. Though the public cast Gabin as the villain, Carné's own primadonna temperament and extravagance – he meticulously reconstructed great areas of the Boulevard de la Chapelle in the studio – had made him many enemies, and when this film failed with both public and critics he was cast into a wilderness from which he never really returned. It is not difficult to see why the film was disliked: its gloom and fatalism were only too reminiscent of prewar days, and by wallowing in these qualities as a new era was supposedly dawning Carné and Prévert were either showing themselves reluctant to change or throwing out a challenge to the public. On the evidence available within the film they may have felt that any salute to the new era must wait till the recent past had been examined. Their miscalculation was compounded by having the fatalism personified – by a *clochard* (Jean Vilar) who claims he is destiny itself – and by the unholy mixture of dated romanticism and references to wartime collaboration.

Today the film is as hugely enjoyable as any that Carné made, and it certainly has nowhere to go but down after a dazzling opening – the Métro at Barbes-Rochechouart during the rush hour. Opposed, for the purposes of the plot, are two friends (Yves Montand, Raymond Bussières) and a father (Saturnin Fabre) and son (Serge Reggiani), whose activities have moved from collaboration to the black market; to Kosma's song 'Les Feuilles Mortes' Montand falls in love with a married woman (Nathalie Nattier), daughter of his enemy, while two younger lovers moon and dream on the periphery of the story.

The film's failure caused the abandonment of the next Carné–Prévert film *La Fleur de l'Age*, and they did not work together again. Carné was reunited with Gabin, for **La Marie du Port** (1949), but with his usual team – Kosma for the music, Trauner to do the art direction and with

the addition of Alekan on camera – he failed completely: beyond the locations, in Normandy, there is nothing to suggest that this film was not made by a hack. Carné and Louis Chavance had adapted a novel by Simenon, but fail to capture the atmosphere created by that writer – a dusty, flaked-out people, dying a little each day in their dull little towns. With the exception of *Hôtel du Nord* Prévert had written all of Carné's films, and since from *La Marie du Port* onwards Carné's work would comprise only one above-average film, *Thérèse Raquin* (q.v.), we may well conclude that it was indeed Prévert's influence which made the best Carné films so atmospheric, romantic and teeming with life.

A new hero among directors was Jean Delannoy, and when in 1947 the magazine *Cinémonde* and Radio Luxembourg, Europe's most popular commercial station, asked for votes on the most popular film of recent years, an easy winner was **La Symphonie Pastorale** (1946); it also won the Grand Prix at the first postwar Cannes Festival and an acting award for Michèle Morgan, portraying blindness by giving one of her expressionless performances. Much better is Pierre Blanchar as the pastor who self-indulgently and secretly loves her. The screenplay (by the director and Aurenche and Bost) trivialises everything that was admirable in André Gide's original tale by attempting to turn it into a tragic romance. For **Les Jeux Sont Faits** (1947) Delannoy was able to command the services of Jean-Paul Sartre, an even more impressive cultural figure, in this case writing his first screenplay. Sartre's existential quest caused him to question man's relationship to God and the universe and the film attempts to do likewise, foolishly aiming its half-formed theories at the audience like rockets. The chief question is whether there is life after death: in a fictional country run by a Fascist usurper two people are fantastically reprieved: a wealthy woman (Micheline Presle), poisoned by her husband – one of the dictator's underlings – and a factory worker (Marcel Pagliero), assassinated while attempting to overthrow the régime. They fall in love before dying again, and the difference in their social positions is handled as soap opera rather than sociology. There is a love scene, fully clothed, which is remarkably erotic by the standard of the day and unusually imaginative for Delannoy. Another question raised is whether love and lust are more important than loyalty to comrades, and after the recent work of the Resistance it was presumably an important one.

The reasons for the pessimistic fantasies of the French cinema at this time are obvious, and we may include among such films **La Belle et la Bête** (1946), though that is of more enduring enchantment. Cocteau follows Mme Leprince's tale faithfully, but I do not think you would be wrong to find allegory in this rendering, since Cocteau was always prone to autobiography in his work. At this time homosexuals were pariahs, like the Beast; they were not thought to have feelings, and certainly conventional people were not supposed to fall in love with them. Perhaps that is why the triumph of the film is the Beast, his appearance and character, and the sepulchral tones which emerge from him: he is a carnivorous monster, and you may never forget his anguish after he has killed for food. It is all the more ironic that at the end he is transformed into a golden-haired fairy prince, but we should not mind, since Beauty (Josette Day) clearly does not. The influence of *Snow White* is again obvious, but Cocteau employed Christian Bérard, a designer of genius, whose contribution he warmly acknowledges in his diary on the making of the film. Also unforgettable is the château, with the flambeaux held by magical arms, and the caryatids of the chimney with their moving eyes. Henri Alekan, the photographer, suggested slowing down or increasing the camera speed, which had not been done since the Silent days. Yet the guiding hand was always that of Cocteau: he wrote the screenplay, and as the credited director became the new golden boy of French cinema.

According to an interview published in *Sight and Sound* in 1950, the real director was René Clément (b. 1913). Clément had been a gag-writer (with Jacques Tati), and a maker of documentary shorts; he had started in features as assistant to Yves Allégret, and while 'assisting' Cocteau on *La Belle et La Bête* was concurrently making a full-length documentary on the Resistance, **La Bataille du Rail** (1946). The documentary marked a return from the unreality which had by necessity afflicted the French cinema since the fall of France. A large number of Resistance dramas poured from the French studios over the next few years, to the embarrassment of French critics, who did not know whether to be more incensed by them (because they looked to the past) or by the Hollywood versions which were now arriving. As far as posterity is concerned it is another matter, and nothing in this genre is as funny and as moving as a slight scene in Clément's film when two men in a café watch the retreating Germans and one says, 'Ça arrange, ça arrange'. With France divided, the railways were the only link between the two zones, and Clément, who also wrote the scenario, shows how men were smuggled across the frontier, how messages were conveyed and how acts of sabotage were carried out. Sabotage is the business of this movie, often done by amateurs growing into professionals – and nothing in it is as stirring as that growth, as the men co-operate with the Maquis, the real professionals. The Germans, except for one sequence when they wait for a derailed train to be righted, remain shadowy, or present only via their signs and posters – and indeed, the film begins with one such, to the effect that Jews are not permitted to cross into the Occupied zone. One of Clément's achievements is to involve us in situations instead of with people – with a revolt always gathering force as the railworkers try to prevent German supplies from reaching Normandy after D-Day. A portrait emerges of a nation under stress, co-operating secretly and silently for its freedom. Clément does not theorise between some marvellous shots of trains, being content to show the ingenuity of the Resistance workers and to admire them.

Inevitably Clément's subsequent films were less impressive, but **Les Maudits** (1947) is interesting, if only in its ambitions; it is an allegorical tale of the Nazi collapse – in panic and recrimination after an abortive attempt to found a new Nazi state somewhere in Latin America. France is represented among the Fascist refugees by a collaborator and by the hero, a country doctor (Henri Vidal) who has been shanghaied to tend a wounded man on the submarine in which the Nazis are escaping; the Nazis are uninteresting, except for their leader (Jo Dest), and that is because he is given an acolyte (Michel Auclair) who is obviously something closer than that. There are no other instances at this time of any leading character being overtly homosexual – and this is a particularly unpleasant one, revenging himself sadistically on his friend for a momentary flirtation elsewhere.

The success of *Bataille du Rail* tempted another documentary director, Georges Rouquier, to make a feature, **Farrebique** (1947), which takes its title from a farm in the Massif Central. It invites audiences to spend a year with the inhabitants of the farm, and they play themselves – which is perhaps why we do not get close enough to them. They make bread and they harvest; the children go to school, with packed lunches; in the evening they sit around the lamp, the silence broken only by the ticking of the clock. They want electricity, but must share the cost with an unwilling neighbour; there are bigger dramas when the eldest son falls off the hayrick and when it becomes necessary to share out the farm after the old man dies. For the exquisitely wrought intimation of his death, Rouquier deserved both his Cannes Grand Prix and the Grand Prix du Cinéma Française. He misses a certain dimension – we do not see the family in the bistro or at the market – but his film is worth all the fictions and falseties of his acknowledged influences, Flaherty and Dovzhenko. One sequence beautifully and notably foreshadows television documentary, as the old man uses maps, postcards and old photographs to illustrate his words. Later there would be a place for films like this on television, but there was none, then, in cinemas, despite the warm reception given this one and also to Clément's film in France and elsewhere; distributors regarded them as freak successes, and Rouquier had to abandon plans to make similar features on the workers of Paris and the natives of North Africa. In the Fifties, he made two unsuccessful fiction features and eventually moved over to television.*

Another documentary to be noted is **Paris 1900** (1950), a pioneering assembly of early film by Nicole Védrès. Earlier searchers in the vaults had used their finds

only facetiously, but Mlle Védrès set out to portray an era in this delightful piece. Since the available material was not plentiful she cheats a little, with detail, for instance, of an Art Nouveau Métro station and a sequence or so from some of Zecca's fictions. She offers La Belle Otero dancing and the Seine overflowing, Bernhardt in *La Dame aux Camélias* and the blowing up of a gangster's hide-out; here are Chevalier and Mistinguett, Colette and Willy, Renoir and Monet, Tolstoi and Andrew Carnegie. Here, too, as young women are Yvonne de Bray and Gabrielle Dorziat, whom audiences had seen recently in *Les Parents Terribles* (q.v.) – and to see them now in this film is to be offered an awesome glimpse into the way in which cinema changes historical perspectives: for the Paris of the *belle époque* seems to be closer now than when Mlle Védrès set out to put it into perspective for us in this collage.

Like Rouquier, she remains famous for one film, and the same was true for many years of Roger Leenhardt, who made just two fiction features in a lifetime of making shorts. **Les Dernières Vacances** (1948) was a promising debut; and it is, as the title indicates, a film about growing up. It contains another traditional aspect, for it looks mockingly at a bourgeois family; it is also sunny as well as sad, indications that the French cinema was finally leaving its postwar gloom. Unfortunately the performances are both colourless and strident, making us wonder about the director's sensitivity – but it is on the whole a likeable sensitivity.

Jean-Pierre Melville (1917–73) also found difficulty following his first feature, **Le Silence de la Mer** (1949), based on the novel by Vercors which had been published clandestinely during the Occupation. A lover of film, Melville had directed as an amateur, and this feature, financed by himself, was filmed entirely on location with a small crew over a two-year period. Again, it is very much of its time, with its wintry exteriors, extended commentary and air of melancholy. The latter is certainly appropriate, for the subject concerns an elderly Frenchman (Jean-Marie Robain) and his niece (Nicole Stéphane) during the Occupation and their reactions to the German officer (Howard Vernon, a Swiss-born actor who specialised in such roles) billeted on them. The situation is artificial,

*As this book goes to press, he is making, with American money, a sequel to *Farrebique*.

Jean-Pierre Melville is best-known for his thrillers of the Sixties, and that is partly because his early films were not very successful – including the first, *Le Silence de la Mer*, based on a clandestine bestseller of the Occupation; but that, by 1949, was something that the French preferred to forget. The film, however, is an eloquent if romantic reminder of that time, with Howard Vernon as the German Officer trying hesitatingly to communicate his love of their country to the household with whom he is billeted.

for surely if the two of them welcome the German's visits to their room – which they will not admit – they would have melted before his ardent francophilia: but it is most touchingly done, and with its companion picture, *Léon Morin, Prêtre* (q.v.), proof that Melville's true forte was romanticism.

Maurice Cloche made dozens of films, to be renowned only for **Monsieur Vincent** (1947) – since he was incapable otherwise, said Sadoul, of making a good one. With that in mind, and the strange fact that it was almost wholly financed by parish collections, it may be that Cloche was, literally, inspired. Working from a screenplay by Jean Anouilh and Jean-Bernard Luc, he presents St Vincent de Paul (Pierre Fresnay) as the first social worker of the modern world, while always keeping in mind the underside of hagiography, in this case the do-gooder as masochist. Vincent, the priest, was not well born, but chance brought him into contact with those who were, and he used that relentlessly on behalf of the poor. Setting out to discover the misery caused by poverty, he is appalled, though it still has to be demonstrated to him – which the film shows in such a way as to make socialists of every member of

the audience. '*Je n'en savais rien,*' he says with tears in his eyes. An oddity of the film is its double ending, consisting of Vincent's reflections with Anne of Austria on the differences between their lives' work and his passing on of his creed as he lies dying. For such matters the film was praised – to the mortification of its detractors, irritated by the simplifications and its open proselytising. In that respect, it fulfilled its function: the audiences who flocked to it everywhere were impressed to find a film about dedication and selflessness. For myself, I was moved only once, when Vincent takes the place of a galley slave – for despite the diseased faces and bodies on display, it is, in the end, a comfortable film: yet the audiences were right, for it has a rare humanity.

The readers of *Le Film Français* voted it the best film of the year, while those of *Cinémonde* reversed the position with that of the runner-up, **Le Diable au Corps** (1947), directed by Autant-Lara and adapted by Aurenche and Bost from the novel by Raymond Radiguet – relevant again at this time, since it concerns a married woman who carries on an affair while her husband is at the front. Distancing made it palatable: the time is the First

651

of course, Nastasia Philippovna, now more accessible as relegated to a demi-mondaine, of which the actress offers a traditional portrait – generous, capricious and undoubtedly Garboesque.

Philipe is also an excellent Fabrice in **La Chartreuse de Parme** (1948), playing him with an air of perpetual surprise but suggesting a man tempered by good humour. The film has that quality, too, and at almost three hours' running time is always an enthralling entertainment; the story is unharmed by its being built round the matter of Fabrice's imprisonment and replacing Stendhal's irony with a vaguely sardonic tone. Maria Casares is rightly haughty as the aunt, Gina, and there are splendid performances by M. Coëdel as the conniving police chief, Rassi, by Louis Salou as the tyrannical prince, and Tullio Carminati as the weak-minded prime minister. A weakness is the Clélia of Renée Faure, then married to Christian-Jaque – who directed on Italian locations – but the rococo decor adds to the felicitous result.

If by now the Italian cinema had become the most admired by the press, the foreign-language picturegoers in the English-speaking world still remained loyal to the French. The films of Jean Dréville enjoyed a wide popularity, and though some critics dismissed them, quite rightly, as having too much artifice, for their specialised public they were – it was often said – films which only the French could make. **La Ferme du Pendu** (1945) was particularly attractive, for one of its leading characters was insatiable in his sexual desires – which intrigued a great many Anglo-Saxons and confirmed a number of others in their opinion of the French. The so-called sex maniac (Alfred Adam) comes, rightly enough, to a sticky end, while his elder brother (Charles Vanel) eventually dies so that this provincial family shall not lose its land. The conjunction of sex, death and devotion to the land was further appealing, as was the very plot of **Le Visiteur** (1946), which concerns a famed lawyer (Pierre Fresnay) who evades a murder rap by hiding out in the orphanage of which he is the benefactor; since the boys hero-worship him he must not disillusion them when the police come for him. **Copie Conforme** (1946) is an ironic comedy in which Jouvet plays several roles, but mainly those of an

It is not altogether surprising that a new generation of critics and film-makers should sweep away the literary adaptations which had been a staple of the French cinema since its inception – and it may have been for the best. On the other hand, some of the Thirties and Forties versions of the classics contain both solid craftsmanship and solid entertainment values – like Christian-Jaque's long but fast-moving version of *La Chartreuse de Parme*. Gérard Philipe is Fabrice and Maria Casares the aunt whose attitude towards him is always so equivocal.

World War, with the young man (Gérard Philipe) the most charmingly heartsick of students, and the woman (Micheline Presle) as lacking in conscience as he. The scenes between them have a tenderness rare even in the French cinema.

Gérard Philipe (1922–59) was the first actor of his generation noted for his stage work in the classics. In films, he was drawn to adaptations from literature, and is memorable as Dostoevsky's Prince Myshkin in **L'Idiot** (1946), directed by the otherwise undistinguished Georges Lampin. Charles Spaak's screenplay follows a tortuous route, always aware of matters greater than itself, but by picking the flesh off the bones it concentrates on aspects which best demonstrate Dostoevsky's genius. Philipe is entirely what the latter intended, moving in an odour of sanctity like a half-baked evangelist, but destroying because he fails or refuses to understand that other people are ruled by greed and vanity. Meek of mien and proud of bearing, there is a demonic gleam in his eye. The billed stars are Edwige Feuillère and Lucien Coëdel, whose sketch of Rogogine, the merchant, indicates a man of strong inner momentum. Mlle Feuillère is, unambitious little man who accepts employment with a prominent con-man – who uses him as his alibi when carrying out his jobs.

The later films of Dréville show a marked decline, but there seems no good reason why these particular ones – like many discussed in this chapter – should have lost their place in the international repertoire. The films of Jean Cocteau are usually available, and the best of them surely deserve to be. Most of the others seem to me to be no more than representative of the French cinema of this time, being claustrophobic, fantastical and usually superficial. Contemporary reviewers noted that Cocteau was poet, novelist, dramatist, designer, film-maker, a public figure and even an architect – and thus to some a Renaissance man reincarnate. Few suspected that he was drawn to the studios chiefly to further the career of Jean Marais – and there could be no other reason for making **Ruy Blas** (1948), one of Victor Hugo's lesser plays which Cocteau rendered even less by replacing the verse with flat modern dialogue. The director was Pierre Billon and the designer Georges Wakhévitch, whose triumph it is, since apart from a church and a market-place he had to achieve visual elegance with confined spaces and a small budget. Marais has a double role, as student and nobleman; Danielle Darrieux is the damsel in distress, a Queen of Spain; and Marcel Herrand is the chief of police who would like to trap them both.

Cocteau himself directed **L'Aigle à Deux Têtes** (1948), of the same species, with splendid barbaric decor by Bérard, and Marais in lederhosen as a would-be assassin. His intended victim is a Queen (Edwige Feuillère) till revolutionary fervour turns to love which allows some spectacular emotions, since the piece was designed solely to display the talents of its two stars. They had done it on the stage, and the play had subsequently been received with respect in translation in London and New York. Feuillère at least was worthy of the attention; and was never more Garboesque. The role might have been written for that actress – the royal widow who casts off her weeds for a brief, doomed happiness – but where Garbo's allegiance was to her script and herself, Feuillère's was to her art: in this case that

was not entirely the wrong approach. **Les Parents Terribles** (1949) is meretricious and its author-director is at his most coy when one character remarks that if there were not situations like this there would be no plays. Cocteau had originally written it as a stage vehicle for Marais, based on the latter's hectic relationship with his own mother – a role destined for Yvonne de Bray, who declined it for the stage but accepted for this film version. The mother is furious at the engagement of her son to a young girl (Josette Day) who happens to be the mistress of his father (Marcel André), a gentleman for whom aunt Léo (Gabrielle Dorziat) has long nurtured a secret passion. Both play and film were regarded as a critique of the bourgeoisie, and Cocteau was rightly congratulated for retaining the restricted settings but avoiding the semblance of a photographed play. He may also be complimented for his cast, acting away like mad, but interestingly so.

He declined to direct **Les Enfants Terribles** (1949), based on his old novel, and assigned it to Jean-Pierre Melville on the strength of *Le Silence de la Mer*. The result he considered the best of his films, and certainly Melville has made the most of this material, which considers the odd relationship between Paul (Edouard Dermithe) and his sister Elizabeth (Nicole Stéphan), who live, eat, wash and sleep in the same room, in a state of permanent disorder. Paul is hit in the chest by Dargelos (the name and the incident also occur in *Le Sang d'un Poète*), and has to stay in bed, after which each invites a schoolfriend of the same sex to move in. These newcomers are tolerated only because they provide an audience for the quarrels and tantrums without which the others cannot function, till Elizabeth suddenly marries a wealthy American Jew, who is conveniently killed on his wedding night, for (says the narrator) she had married him for his death. Cocteau himself referred to the piece as 'the no man's land between life and death', and as such it is wryly amusing from time to time. Had he been more honest about the sexual orientation of the pair it might have been more than a diversion: instead we pick our way among a series of hints, such as Paul's pin-ups of boxers and male movie stars, all with the same sulky expression as himself. Der-

653

Cocteau's Fantasies

From youth onwards Jean Cocteau moved at the centre of the artistic life of Paris, his contributions to it seemingly in accordance with Diaghilev's command to astonish everyone. He loved the cinema, and in typical manner toyed with it until 1946 when he wrote and co-directed *La Belle et la Bête*, with Josette Day and Jean Marais, RIGHT. His published diary of the making of the film indicates much hard work, much teamwork and a conviction that the finished result would be a major achievement, but it does not dispel the impression of Cocteau as a dilettante. However, the film is important and it has lost little of its power to astonish.

The penchant for modernising ancient legends has been widespread among French writers for centuries, but it received a new impetus during the war years and just after – when it was triumphantly manifested in Cocteau's *Orphée*, BELOW, Maria Casares, with Edouard Dermithe, being carried by two motorcyclists, and Jean Marais. It deals fairly with its source, is richly autobiographical, and its cinematic tricks remain as rewarding as those in *La Belle et la Bête*.

mithe had replaced Marais in Cocteau's life, and the characters (according to Janet Flanner) were based on one of Cocteau's former lovers★ and his sister. The film leaves an acrid taste, to remind us that its original English title was *The Strange Ones*, and its novelty was accentuated by the innovatory use of baroque music – by Vivaldi – on the soundtrack.

Although **Orphée** (1950) was also based on his youthful material, a play, Cocteau regarded it as the summation of his life's work and 'the fulfilment of those ambitions which once drove me to attempt *Le Sang d'un Poète* with no experience and insufficient technical means. Here, I felt, I wanted to express something that could not be expressed through any other medium . . . and this is to my mind the real task of the film.' As a foreword acknowledges, this is a retelling of an old myth, but it is a great improvement on *L'Eternel Retour*; and has its own unique flavour. When Cegeste (Dermithe) is killed during a café brawl by Death's outriders, Death – the Princess (Maria Casares) – takes instead Orphée (Marais), but allows him to return home in the company of Heurtebise (François Perier) who will fall in love with Eurydice (Maria Déa). Orphée has already fallen unwillingly in love with the Princess, who steals Eurydice to entice him back: but she relents and releases them provided he does not look at his wife; unfortunately, he sees her by accident in a car mirror. Heurtebise, from love of her, agrees to take Orphée back to the Underworld to rescue her, but he himself and the Princess are arrested for failing to conform to the standards of the Netherworld – for allowing Life to go free.

It is a film which lends itself to meanings, all of them clear to anyone with even a perfunctory knowledge of Cocteau's work, such as the '*étonnez-nous*' spoken during the café fight, implying that to astonish is more important than to quarrel: it is the prerogative of the artist. Later, Death says to Orphée, '*Il ne faut pas comprendre. Il ne s'agit de quoi,*' and we may understand the artist's fascination with death, death as a mother figure, mother as a muse, death as a muse – as well as the

artist's need to travel into the unknown, his right to stimulation and his awe at his own dispensability. The film is a marvellous experience, because of its deliberately unreal level of fantasies and passions, and the trickery with which they are executed: the throbbing of drums during the fight and the invasion of the Bacchantes; the motorcyclists, deliberate reminder of Fascist authority, as emissaries of Death; the use of negative on the road to Hades, and the concept of a mirror as an entrance to hell. D'Eaubonne, with an assistant, is credited with the sets (the film is dedicated to Bérard, who died while it was being prepared). The film haunted me for months when I first saw it and it may be a film to see when young. There are films more enriching than this glittering basket of '*étonnez-nous*', these Chinese boxes, but I would wish everyone a film to discuss and argue over and dream about – one which, as Cocteau intended, is timeless.

Clouzot's **Manon** (1949) is, on the other hand, a tract for the time – though set in 1944, which was a convulsive year for France. Just as the heroine of Prévost's 'Manon Lescaut' could not help being a trollop, neither can this one as written by Clouzot and Jean Ferry. There is little to choose between the two ladies as Manon (Cécile Aubrey) moves from collaborationist in Normandy to black marketeering in Paris; but whereas the original Des Grieux was an honest man who accepted degradation because his beloved was wedded to her profession, here, as played by Michel Auclair, he has no quality at all – beyond having been heroic with the Maquis. Both of Clouzot's lovers are absurdly childlike – perhaps the reason he drops the love story some way into the narrative; but there is no compensating insight into the matters taken up instead, which include the Liberation, illegal immigration and the Jewish-Arab War (which provides the desert setting for the finale). *Greed* was as much an inspiration for Clouzot as Prévost, with Manon dying of thirst and exhaustion after days in the desert. The sequence was much criticised as sadistic and it caused much trouble among the world's censors. Today it looks overblown, an early example of the modern trend to visual extravagance offered in the hope that audiences will read significance into it – and only the cynical may be

★The man was Jean Bourgoint, introduced by Cocteau to drugs, and who later became a Trappist monk; Bourgoint's sister contracted gonorrhoea on her wedding night and shortly afterwards committed suicide.

unsurprised that this film was awarded a Grand Prix at the Venice Film Festival. Elsewhere, some were shocked, such as Leonard Mosley in England's *Daily Express*, who could 'not recall a more horrible film . . . everywhere touched with evil'. Reputation preceded it even before its Paris opening, when the police were called to prevent hysterical crowds from fighting; it subsequently flopped, and except for its few and vague comments on corruption, it deserved to do so.

Clouzot followed the customary pattern in such cases, and with Ferry adapted **Miquette et sa Mère** (1950), in fact the third Talkie version of a revered boulevard comedy. The plot is traditional, and concerns the passion felt by young Urbain (Bourvil) for a shopgirl (Danièle Delorme). Because of this, he is sent away by his uncle (Saturnin Fabre) on a theatrical career – with a touring actor (Louis Jouvet) of the fifth or sixth rank. The delights of the piece are less in its mechanics than in the glimpses of backstage life, with the climax set against an absurd historical play concerning Richelieu at La Rochelle: Clouzot was, all the same, happier with the sinister theatre of *Quai des Orfèvres*, but the whole film is as disarming as the bows that the cast takes at the end.

Helping to lift the gloom of French cinema was Christian-Jaque, who first tested public mood with **Souvenirs Perdus** (1950), one of the first of the portmanteau films which would prove so popular with French (and Italian) producers over the next two decades. Inspired by the British *Quartet* (q.v.), these four stories are linked by items in the lost property office, and they are respectively, sentimental comedy, comedy of situation, melodrama and farce. This director also attempted a fairy tale, **Barbe-Bleue** (1951), but all is heaviness surrounding Pierre Brasseur's pleasingly facetious playing of the title role. Also in the film's favour is the castle designed by Wakhévitch, though its splendour is diminished by the limited palette of Gevacolor (this was one of the first French films in colour). The sunny landscapes of **Fanfan la Tulipe** (1951), as photographed by Christian Matras, are an asset, as is the deadpan commentary, written by Henri Jeanson: for this is a comic swashbuckler – another genre to be endlessly repeated in

France and Italy – and an inventive and ingratiating one, with Gérard Philipe as adept with a sword as he is, we assume, in the haystacks and fourposters with the ladies. He helped Christian-Jaque towards his last great success both in France and abroad, and from then on this director declined with a series of historicals and sex comedies.

Occupe-toi d'Amélie (1949) could be termed sex comedy, and when a suitor explains the absence of his trousers to Amélie as a way of saving time, the British censor was so outraged that he refused to pass the film; that a number of local authorities did permit it to be shown hastened the introduction of the X certificate, applied to 'Adults Only' films, of which most of the first batch were French. This film introduced to British and American audiences the work of Georges Feydeau, farceur supreme of the *belle époque*; and they were reminded, for the first time since the strengthening of the Hays Code, that the pursuit of sex can be gloriously funny. Autant-Lara directed, sometimes using theatrical settings and retaining the proscenium arch, at the same time indicating a fondness for both the decor of the period and Feydeau's artlessly simple complications. Danielle Darrieux, Jean Desailly and the rest of the cast have precision and are funny without being vulgar, which, taken together with the breathless pace, so impressed the critics that the film did in fact advance the cause of sex in the Anglo-Saxon cinema.

Occupe-toi d'Amélie and *La Ronde* (q.v.) made the recent work of René Clair seem old-fashioned. Returning from Hollywood, he had made **Le Silence Est d'Or** (1947), set against a background of filmmaking in the Silent era, on which subject he is witty and affectionate. However, he is not at his best with the central situation, that of a young girl, an innocent at large in Paris, attracted to its less orthodox opportunities but prevented from enjoying them by her guardian (Maurice Chevalier), who falls in love with her but unwittingly hands her over to his rival (François Perier). Unashamedly a middle-aged comedy, its melancholy is misjudged because there is no compensating charm in the crucial corner of the triangle – the girl, who is poorly played. **La Beauté du Diable** (1950) is a retelling of Faust – a subject which might well have suited

Gregoire Aslan, trouserless, in *Occupe-toi d'Amélie*, a situation which most of us today would recognise as stemming from Georges Feydeau. There is no such scene in the original play, but when the director Claude Autant-Lara did send his characters out into the street the camera was just as likely to draw back to reveal that street behind a proscenium arch. This film therefore retains the theatricality of French farce while pretending to dress it up in cinematic manner, which means for audiences the best of both possible worlds.

Clair, but he strains for both jokes and significance, though agreeably without pretension. Gérard Philipe is Faust and Michel Simon the mischievous Mephistopheles; the film was made in Italy, for Clair had run into trouble setting up the project. That difficulty was not unconnected with the relative failure of the previous film, one of the first postwar foreign-language films distributed by an American company, in this case R.K.O. It may have been compensation for Clair that in both cases the critics were kinder than the films deserved.

As he began to recover his old form with his next film, so did Carné, for the last time, with **Thérèse Raquin** (1953). The script he wrote (with Charles Spaak) distorted Zola's original story almost as much as it modernised it. Instead of Zola's sweaty animals, Carné offers the usual illicit couple, living now in Lyon, and the man has become an Italian truck driver; he does not murder from lust for Thérèse, but in anger; they no longer live under the eyes of the paralysed Mme Raquin, but guiltily till reunited by the threat of blackmail. Their fate is therefore achieved by circumstance rather than faults within themselves, as in earlier Carné films, and if we compare this one with those we can see

that his narrative skill is as sure as ever. The initial situation is both faithful to Zola and beautifully handled: Thérèse (Simone Signoret) has married in gratitude her cousin (Jacques Duby), a snivelling, petty clerk who cheats at the card game he plays every Thursday with his cronies and his doting mother, who is implacably hostile to Thérèse. In the circumstances, the audience palpably wants Signoret to fall in love with Laurent (Raf Vallone), who looks dependable and handsome – and almost the best aspect of the film is her realisation of the nature of passion. As of old, Carné is helped enormously by his settings: the stuffy apartment above the shop and the deserted suburban dance hall where the lovers meet.

Another reason that the film was poorly received in France was that Carné was supposed to be sustaining a pessimism he no longer felt, and this particular film is best regarded as an excellent thriller, made at a time when the French film industry was beginning to change. The pessimistic mood prevailing in French films for the early postwar years was said by critics to have been dictated by producers, hoping to repeat their prewar successes, but the French had perhaps better reason to make despairing films after the War than before:

657

A number of reputations crumbled in the postwar French cinema, as local critics objected to the continued spate of pessimistic films, suggesting that film-makers were trying to cling to the themes which had made them renowned initially. Abroad, with the promised return to prewar conditions still some way off, critics were much kinder to these films – and since Yves Allégret's *Une si Jolie Petite Plage* remains so enjoyable, Allégret's motives in making it seem unimportant. Also, of course, foreign audiences found the problems of Gérard Philipe somewhat more important than those bothering Cary Grant or Gary Cooper.

the traumas of recent history were not shaken off overnight with the Liberation. In any case, the instability of the industry was hardly conducive to a run of bright comedies; added to that was the uncertainty induced by the failure of *Les Portes de la Nuit*, on which so many hopes had rested. Sadoul attacked the 'postwar imitations' for 'repeating endlessly such faults as [the earlier] films had had, usually in the form of a convention for apeing a "naturalism" far removed from actual life.' He cited as typical two films directed by Yves Allégret, **Dédée d'Anvers** (1948) and **Une si Jolie Petite Plage** (1949). They both are indeed in the tradition of *Quai des Brumes* and *La Bête Humaine* – emotional drama posing as social realism. The Italian neo-realists demanded that audiences consider injustice in society, whereas French cinema really offered escapism – inviting audiences to forget their own difficulties in experiencing the highly romantic problems of their characters who, though ostensibly working class, were not at all like themselves. Nevertheless, these films of Allégret are very entertaining. Both *Dédée d'Anvers* and **Manèges** (1949) feature his then-wife, Simone Signoret, respectively as a prostitute finding brief happiness with an Italian seaman in the dusty cafés of Antwerp, and a perverse, restless wife in French château country. They are mechanical but memorable films, and it is impossible to forget the images of *Une si Jolie Petite Plage* – the ill-assorted guests gathered in the bar of

the ugly resort hotel in winter to discuss a recent *crime passionel*, and Gérard Philipe as the fugitive from justice, wandering gloomily among the rain-sodden dunes and beach huts. Allégret's best work is forceful, and the dingy emotions with which he dealt, usually relating to love and/or sexuality, were refreshing then when considered beside the more anodyne problems of the English-speaking cinema.

Two films at least proved that the lovers caught in the web of fate had had their day. **Les Amants de Vérone** (1949) is set against the filming of a new version of Shakespeare's play, and the lovers (Anouk Aimée, Serge Reggiani) are alone exempt from the universal cupidity and amorality. They, and everyone else, have supposedly been conditioned by the War, so the film presents, among others, the once-famous attorney (Louis Salou) whose wartime associations have made him a drunken, half-crazed hermit, and his war-maddened gun-crazy cousin (Marcel Dalio). Jacques Prévert wrote the screenplay for André Cayette, and though the piece is as melodramatic as, say, *Caccia Tragica*, it is not redeemed by any honest observation of the society which it is criticising. Nor does it have the romantic aura of the Carné–Prévert films – and it was precisely that which was sought by the neo-realist writer, Zavattini, and the director of *Bataille du Rail*, Clément, in their collaboration, **Le Mura di Malapaga/Au delà des Grilles** (1949), made in Italy in both Italian and French versions. The story is a concoction about a seaman (Jean Gabin) who, wanted for murder, jumps ship in Genoa and falls in love with a waitress (Isa Miranda): extensive location work did not rescue the film from seeming old fashioned.

Clément made an indifferent star vehicle with Michèle Morgan and Jean Marais, *Le Château de Verre*, before succeeding with **Les Jeux Interdits** (1952), which the British Film Academy voted 'The Best Film from any Source' and the American Academy its Best Foreign Language Film.* For a few years thereafter it consistently

*Until 1956, when the American Academy committee established the Best Foreign Language Film as a separate category, with five nominations, this was an honorary or special award, in response to members' admiration for developments abroad, starting with an award to Laurence Olivier for *Henry V* in 1946. The other awards, prior to 1956, were to *Sciuscià* in 1947, *Monsieur Vincent* in 1948, *Ladri di Biciclette* in 1949, *Le Mura di Malapaga* in 1950, *Rashomon* in 1951, *Gate of Hell* in 1954 and *Samurai* in 1955.

By the time René Clement made *Les Jeux Interdits* the French cinema had been knee-deep in gloom for almost two decades, but all was exorcised by this one film. It was not the most horrifying film that could be made on the subject of war – which was only peripheral to its central plot – but it was a genuinely strange piece, some of its eeriness springing from the fact that it stressed not only the sufferings of the innocent but the way in which their minds can be twisted. The innocents concerned were Brigitte Fosey and Georges Poujouly, both remarkable in their roles.

headed students' lists of the greatest film ever made – probably because they, like the film's protagonists, had been children during the War. A prologue establishes the flight from Paris in June, 1940: German planes swoop down with machine guns, and a child (Brigitte Fosey) is left an orphan. As she chases after her dog, floating dead in a river, she meets a boy (Georges Poujouly) slightly older than herself, and his peasant parents give her a bed. The boy's friendship enables her to accustom herself to her new surroundings, and then they invent their secret games, which consist of burying the dog, and then mice, chicken and insects, with crosses – after they get ambitious – stolen from the local churchyard. The title puts undue stress on that aspect of the story, since what interested Clément most was the situation of the little girl, suddenly bereft of parents and set down in an alien world. Working from an adaptation by Aurenche and Bost of the novel by Jean Boyer, he directs with humour, sensitivity and sympathy.

The film was admired for such touches as the lovers in the hay, the fat old priest cuffing the boy, and the flies that settled on faces – the appurtenances of realism. But, like a great many other films which the public found significant, its realism merely disguised – despite the chilling ending – a throbbing romanticism. Within France, the significance was much more real. It was the last film which was really close to the experience of the War. Those that came later, whether nostalgic or bitter with recriminations, were historical reconstructions. It also ended, perhaps because it was like no other film, that obsession of the French cinema with doom and gloom which had begun with appeasement and continued through the guilt of the war years and during the shame of the aftermath. As we have seen, comedy was returning to French films, and the tradition of pessimistic drama could not be broken by one film, however cathartic; but the French film-makers at this point lost interest in allegory, symbolism and message. For the rest of the decade they returned to the primary business of entertaining audiences.

659

26

The M-G-M Musical

THE SUPERIORITY of the M-G-M musicals in the postwar period is now an acknowledged fact; they used better talents, better directors, better songs, orchestrations and even better colour than other studios. It was with *On the Town* (q.v.) in 1949 that both industry and critics realised that something exciting was taking place at Culver City, and the excitement was repeated a number of times before the Hollywood musical began to die towards the end of the next decade. By that time it was recognised that all the best M-G-M musicals prior to *On the Town*, as well as those made after, had been produced by Arthur Freed (1894–1973). Since most of them are of enduring quality, and have delighted successive generations, we may speak of him in the superlative – as the most gifted producer in the history of Hollywood. The adjective is well deserved by the man who fostered, encouraged and used to the best advantage the abilities of Judy Garland, Fred Astaire and Gene Kelly.

A former song-writer, he had been with M-G-M since the early days of Sound, and was an early advocate of Garland's talents, one reason why Louis B. Mayer promoted him to producer. Freed initiated *The Wizard of Oz*, and produced the first three Garland–Rooney musicals. Later in his career he produced four non-musical films, and he did eventually become, in theory at least, an independent producer, releasing through M-G-M. He was the first to admit that he was neither creative nor intellectual, but he knew how to choose the talents he needed, and he was wise enough to give them artistic freedom. These were essentially musical talents, and include most notably Roger Edens (1905–70), musical supervisor and later Associate Producer, and Vincente Minnelli (b. 1906), a director whom Freed found on Broadway and trained for two years before putting him in charge of a film. If Edens's contribution can never be properly estimated, Minnelli's work is on screen, signed, and with the exception of his second film, *I Dood It*, all his M-G-M musicals were made for the Freed unit. If Minnelli wanted a particular composer or New York designer, Freed, it seems, was always amenable.

The non-musicals directed by Minnelli are discussed in a later chapter, but they were mainly produced by Pandro S. Berman, who produced two musicals for Metro, one of them *Ziegfeld Girl*. The achievements of the Freed unit are thrown into relief when one compares the musicals created at this studio by other hands, who had the same pool of talent upon which to draw. Also associated with this form at Metro were Joe Pasternak – who had moved from Universal after a disagreement over the handling of the adult Deanna Durbin – and Jack Cummings, a nephew of Louis B. Mayer, whose earlier films had included the *Broadway Melodies of 1938* and *1940*.

It was Edens who, years later, described Garland as 'the biggest thing to happen to the M-G-M musical', something which he and Freed believed from the moment they heard her sing. They nurtured her during the transition from child star to adult player: as a grown-up she came into her own with **For Me and My Gal** (1942), which also marks the screen debut of Gene Kelly (b. 1912), a dancer and, later, choreographer who had achieved Broadway stardom in 1940 in 'Pal Joey'. Busby Berkeley directed for Freed, and though the film is dedicated to all vaude-villians past and present, it is a bit short on the vaudeville side, being heavily involved with the First World War, like *Tin Pan Alley* two years earlier. As the U.S. was now in the War, the film tends towards the patriotic and sentimental. The Freed unit is shown at its best with the first number, the title song, in which Kelly talks Garland into joining him in a dance, and in a med-ley of World War One songs when Gar-land responds to the audience (as opposed to the camera). If you look closely you can see her young face crossed with lines, but her acting is perfect. Kelly's natural charm helps him through a role that requires him to be determined heel in the first half and, despite the plot, a determined hero in the second; also likeable is George Murphy as the guy who loses Garland to him.

Minnelli's first film was **Cabin in the Sky** (1943), based on an all-black Broad-way show. Freed was given a budget of $600,000 ($200,000 less than that for *For Me and My Gal*, and only half the cost of each of his next two films – though these were in Technicolor) since he had con-vinced the front office that it would be a prestige success. M-G-M had had such a success with the all-black *Hallelujah!*, yet in the intervening years nothing had been done to remove the element of gospel singing from negro entertainments; but this one has a cheery plot about the struggle of Little Joe (Eddie 'Rochester' Anderson) between his ever-lovin' Petunia (Ethel Waters) and his weakness, Georgia Brown (Lena Horne). Miss Waters, one of the greatest of all entertainers, can wring your heart with lines like 'Lord, why you let me love him so much he can hurt me so bad?', and her fellow artists – who include Louis Armstrong, Rex Ingram and the Duke Ellington Orchestra – also help to make the material palatable. Freed usually made his own decisions regarding the music, and though he often jettisoned good Broadway songs for new and in-ferior ones, in this case he kept the best by Vernon Duke and John Latouche – the title song, 'Taking a Chance on Love' and 'Honey in the Honeycomb' – while com-missioning three from Arlen and Harburg which are better than those unused. Min-nelli's staging is happier with those in the jazz idiom, and only occasionally does he revert to stage patterns.

Norman Taurog directed **Presenting Lily Mars** (1943) for Pasternak and **Girl Crazy** (1943) for Freed. The former, from a novel by Booth Tarkington, is much like Pasternak's Durbin pictures, with Garland playing with great aplomb a stage-struck brat and having one enchanted sequence, on a darkened stage, when she and a stage-sweeper (Connie Gilchrist) do an impro-vised 'Every Little Movement'. *Girl Crazy* was the last teaming of Garland and Mickey Rooney, whose functions Freed had now defined – when she is not singing, he is clowning: his wide-ranging talent is at its best as he plays a young city slicker bested by the rubes. The source was an old Gershwin show, with the plot – about a co-ed school in the wilds of Nevada – and the score both left more or less intact. The stars have a song, 'Could You Use Me?', which may well be the best comedy duet in films, and it was filmed on location: this was one of the first musicals to go exten-sively outside the studio. The finale is a long extravaganza by Busby Berkeley, and he was also to have directed till replaced at Garland's request – the first recorded instance of her temperament.

On the other hand, Freed mangled both *Lady, Be Good* and *Panama Hattie*, by drop-ping songs, turning the 'books' inside out and adding guest stars: M-G-M badly needed a leading lady in the Ethel Merman mould, and cast Ann Sothern, a B-picture star, who was good, but in neither film quite good enough. So M-G-M signed Lucille Ball, another B-picture star, and put her in both **Best Foot Forward** (1943) and **Du Barry Was a Lady** (1943), directed respectively by Edward Buzzell and Roy del Ruth. Perversely, Freed kept the undistinguished Broadway score of the first, while throwing out most of the Cole Porter songs of the second. Ball is poor in both, and in *Du Barry* neither she nor Red Skelton are substitutes for Merman and Bert Lahr, whose teaming had been the main raison d'être of the original. That had also been rather risqué, and despite the fact that it had pleased Broadway for over four hundred performances, the Hays Office demanded considerable alterations – and the fantasy sequence which gives the film its title is abysmal. For solace, look to the third-billed star, who is Kelly, though then an indifferent dancer in white-tie-and-tails still seeking his individual style.

661

At the last minute he and Virginia O'Brien move in to prevent Ball and Skelton from ruining a splendid song, 'Friendship'.

Broadway Rhythm (1944) is also based on a show, and though as 'Very Warm for May' it was one of Broadway's more memorable flops, that seems little reason for retaining only 'All the Things You Are', with a brief sending up of the other songs from the Kern-Hammerstein score. Originally, like *Babes in Arms*, concerned with some kids putting on a show, the piece now has a clichéd plot about a Broadway producer (George Murphy) caught between a search for 'art' and a big Hollywood star – played by Ginny Simms, a plastic, podgy radio singer who was a protégée of Mayer. It is difficult to decide whether she or the ingenue, Gloria De Haven, is the less talented. Five minutes of dialogue as if by clockwork alternate with five minutes of song, all taking place in night clubs, theatrical agencies, theatres and hotel rooms, to emphasise the fact that, like *Born to Dance*, the film is a *Broadway Melody* in all but name: as was the case with the later Broadway Melodies, del Ruth directed for Cummings, and the otherwise dire guest list includes Lena Horne.

Cummings produced **Bathing Beauty** (1944), one of the first features directed by George Sidney (b. 1916), a former studio all-purpose man with a long experience in short subjects. It was also the first starring picture of Esther Williams, hard-faced and unsympathetic, not yet the smiling girl – she never could act – of her later films. Metro executives, in their wisdom (rightly as it turned out), thought this professional swimmer could be a star attraction, and for the next decade producers and writers were required to fashion stories set around swimming pools. In this one Miss Williams is a teacher at a girls' school, and Red Skelton, also from the downmarket end of the studio's players, is her ex-fiancé and a deviser of water pageants. The finale, conceived by John Murray Anderson, has great fountain leaps to rival the masturbatory fantasies of Berkeley in *The Gang's All Here*.

Clearly, none of these films prepared audiences for **Meet Me in St Louis** (1944), and it was not a project favoured by the front office. Freed had wanted to buy 'Life with Father', but had lost it to War-

ners, and was persuaded instead to buy Sally Benson's stories of turn of the century St Louis, which had also appeared in *The New Yorker*. Mayer agreed to what he regarded as a period Andy Hardy-type film: one jazzed-up screenplay was abandoned when Minnelli, Freed and Garland protested – though she in any case had at first not wanted to appear in the film. Later, she was very proud of it, as were all the participants and the front office as well, since apart from *Gone with the Wind* it was M-G-M's biggest grossing film up to that time. Garland's own magic contributes – as do the sets, designed by Cedric Gibbons,★ Jack Martin Smith and Lemuel Ayers: George Folsey's camera moves through them, timed to the music, in what is the most entrancing co-ordination since *Le Million*. The film is, as James Agee pointed out, a love story between a family and their way of life, and that is beautifully expressed in the opening sequence: Mother (Mary Astor) is in the kitchen making ketchup with the maid (Marjorie Main); Grandfather (Harry Davenport) is singing the title song, and the two older girls (Garland, Lucille Bremer) take up the refrain before mooning about the boy (Tom Drake) next door; the two younger girls (Margaret O'Brien, Joan Carroll) are following the ice cart, while Father (Leon Ames) returns home hot and bad tempered. They are all agog over the romantic phone call expected from New York, and there is a reference to young Lonnie (Henry H. Daniels Jr) going to Princeton. The dinner-table conversation is funny and unforced: every line of the confident screenplay, by Irving Brecher and Fred F. Finklehoffe, adds to our knowledge of and liking for these people. No musical since *Swing Time* had been handled with such grace and sensitivity, but then, there had been no musical like this one: a sole reservation might be that Minnelli allowed Garland to sing 'The Trolley Song' with vivacity but no joie de vivre – and perhaps a second one would be that the finale at the St Louis Fair seems to need a song.†

★Though Gibbons was credited as Art Director on almost every M-G-M film for over thirty years, at this stage he presumably only approved the work of the others, who were working to the specifications of Freed and Minnelli.

†It originally had one, 'Boys and Girls Like You and Me', which Freed had bought from Rodgers and Hammerstein when it was cut from 'Oklahoma!', but it was also omitted here when the film was thought overlong.

Judy Garland and Lucille Bremer in Minnelli's enchanting *Meet Me in St Louis*. The film's visual elegance was not reflected in the studio's publicity material, which reflected great uncertainty as to whether the public would respond to a period musical. That material included the advertisements and sheet music covers, for there was no soundtrack album, but when Garland's record company, Decca, was successful with studio recordings of her songs M-G-M negotiated for Decca to release songs taken directly from the soundtrack of her next film (*The Harvey Girls*). Hitherto only Disney had licensed his soundtracks but in 1946, with *Till the Clouds Roll By*, M-G-M founded its own company to issue recordings from its films. It was not for another ten years that the other studios began to see the advantages of soundtrack recordings, but meanwhile almost all the great M-G-M musicals were commemorated on disc.

Despite the general standard of screen musicals, the fact that *Meet Me in St Louis* was no more than warmly received by reviewers suggests that they were less spoilt than imperceptive; it is equally hard to credit that **Anchors Aweigh** (1945) was overall better liked, but at least most critics recognised that Gene Kelly was becoming a creative force in film musicals. As directed by George Sidney for Pasternak, this one is stuffed with songs and dances, but in a lucky dip manner, since for each good thing there are several duds – the latter including José Iturbi graciously playing himself, as well as 'The Donkey Serenade' and the 'Hungarian Rhapsody' accompanied by an army of pianos, and Kathryn Grayson, whether singing, acting or trying to be charming. Isabel Lennart's laboured screenplay has to do with some sailors meeting Kathryn Grayson in Hollywood, but it is punctuated with Kelly's dances. Because of his success with *Cover Girl* he was allowed to do his own choreography, and not long into the film he and Frank Sinatra bid farewell to their buddies in a marvellously freewheeling number; later his solos are proof that he regarded movies as fantasy bait: obviously he believed that dancing on film could be enhanced by the use of dreams and cartoons – and most people remember this movie for his dance with Tom and Jerry.

For Freed and Minnelli, the success of *Meet Me in St Louis* had been followed by *The Clock*, also with Garland, and the first straight film for all of them. In addition they were euphoric at having coaxed Fred Astaire into a long-term contract, but in proving that he could also dance in balletic style they made a mistake, which is entitled **Yolanda and the Thief** (1945). The leading lady is Lucille Bremer, 'a protégée of one of the studio bosses', said Minnelli later, 'and quite unsuitable'. He also referred to 'the insane plot' – taken from a story by Jacques Théry and Ludwig Bemelmans, about two American con men (Astaire, Frank Morgan) involved in the affairs both of a mythical kingdom and a fey, convent-reared heiress. The attempt of the decor to reproduce Bemelmans' paintbox colours is merely vulgar, while the hillocks and flowers swamp Astaire. He and Bremer do have one halfway good dance, 'Will You Marry Me?', but it is School of Agnes deMille, which does not suit him. This was the first Freed production to lose money, and was perhaps instrumental in Astaire's decision to retire – which, fortunately for the cinema, was later rescinded.

He had already filmed his sequences in the Freed–Minnelli **Ziegfeld Follies** (1946), and their reception must have been a consolation to all three of them: 'This Heart of Mine', in effect his first film ballet, a gay piece about a jewel thief, with Bremer; 'Limehouse Blues', a part-theatrical piece of chinoiserie, also a ballet with Bremer; and 'The Babbitt and the Bromide', the Gershwins' old number, teamed with Gene Kelly. Also in the region of the sublime is 'A Great Lady Has an Interview', giving Garland's wit full rein as a gracious movie queen – and with added piquancy if you know that it was written for Greer Garson. Freed had long cherished the idea of another film celebrating Ziegfeld (M-G-M held the rights to the name), and finally came up with the first purely revue film since the early Talkies, and the last created specifically for film.★ In heaven, Ziegfeld (William Powell) looks down and murmurs something about 'so many wonderful people remaining and so many wonderful people coming along in the meantime': the only Ziegfeld star on display is Fanny Brice, and her sketch is somewhat less unfunny than others with Red Skelton, Keenan Wynn and Victor Moore; a number of other sketches were tossed out during a troubled production history which brought costs to an almost unprecedented $3¼ million. Started in

1943, the film was delayed because its ostentation was thought to be at odds with the wartime mood; it was previewed at the end of 1944, in a three-hour version, and again with cuts and changes the following year. Minnelli, despite being solely credited, directed only the Garland and Astaire numbers and the florid staging of the 'Drinking Song' from 'La Traviata'. George Sidney, whom he originally replaced, directed the opening number, 'Here's to the Ladies', with Lucille Ball and Virginia O'Brien, and many hands worked at the finale – Kathryn Grayson's ballad amid the floating foam – but it cannot be worse than the one originally intended, with Astaire, Bremer and James Melton. We may also wonder about an artistic judgment which threw out an Astaire solo but kept the Esther Williams water ballet. The film did, however, make a handsome profit.

After Roger Edens had seen 'Oklahoma!' he wanted to make a Western musical, and **The Harvey Girls** (1946), intended as a straight vehicle for Lana Turner, became a musical for Garland. The latter had become, according to Gallup, America's favourite female star, after Ingrid Bergman and Bette Davis, and that was partly because of *Meet Me in St Louis*: so that although Freed did not like repeating a formula, he allowed the numbers to be influenced by that film – the wistful love song, the waltz for the girls, and the marvellous opening, 'The Atchison, Topeka and the Santa Fe'. He had always liked unusual performers, but had slotted them into his films usually as specialities till Minnelli (in *Cabin in the Sky* and *Meet Me in St Louis*) had shown that each could have his moment or be part of the ensemble – and George Sidney, directing on this occasion, goes further by integrating into the whole the contrasting talents of Virginia O'Brien, Ray Bolger, Cyd Charisse and Kenny Baker. Nevertheless, it remains Garland's film. Her private difficulties are beginning to show – she is a peaky, unjolly heroine; but her smile, when it comes, could melt the snows of Everest. Her role is that of a mail-order bride-to-be who arrives in a small Western town and joins the Harvey Restaurant girls in their battles with the saloon hussies, led by Angela Lansbury.

Till the Clouds Roll By (1946) was

★Such wartime films as *Thousands Cheer* had proved the form viable, but they had 'books', as did Warner's 1952 *Starlift*. The independently produced *New Faces* (1954) was a record of a Broadway revue, and some compilations of television comedy series have found their way to cinemas.

664

Freed's first bid in that breed known as the biopic, and it is as dreary as any of the others. The composer maligned here is Jerome Kern (Robert Walker), especially when he looks at the Mississippi and is inspired to compose 'Show Boat', or when he says 'I'd rather hear her sing my songs than anyone else in the world,' referring to Lucille Bremer, who in this narrative becomes a big M-G-M star. Real M-G-M stars sing the songs, including two by Judy Garland as Marilyn Miller, which were directed by Minnelli, to whom she was now married. Richard Whorf, a former actor, is credited with the direction, but Sidney handled the finale, a bland pot-pourri of Kern's songs (for which Sidney cannot be blamed) and the majority of the other numbers were the work of Robert Alton; the opening medley from 'Show Boat' at least starts the film well.

Pandro S. Berman produced **Living in a Big Way** (1947), written and directed by Gregory LaCava, who had not made a film for five years – and he would live for five more without making another. He had become an alcoholic, and though the film is lively and well made, it was a flop. Gene Kelly was persuaded into making it because the studio hoped to turn his co-star, Marie McDonald, into another Lana Turner, but he found her 'a triple threat who couldn't sing, dance or act'. He also thought the script dated, and it is certainly mushy on the subject of war veterans; but LaCava is to some extent his old self on a favourite theme, the impoverished citizen (i.e. an ex-G.I.) who becomes embroiled with a wealthy family. Kelly's numbers include a spectacular dance on the rafters of an unfinished house. The film was in black and white, otherwise abandoned for musicals by M-G-M in 1943, which could be one reason for the public's indifference.

Summer Holiday (1947) was also a director's first film in five years and a disaster: he is Rouben Mamoulian, and the producer was Freed. Its source is O'Neill's 'Ah Wilderness!', but it might just as well have been called 'Andy Hardy Gets Drunk': Mickey Rooney is merely brash as a precocious student with a deep love for a poem he calls 'The Ballad of Reeding Gole'. The elders – Walter Huston, Selena Royle, Frank Morgan and Agnes Moorehead – are obviously suitable, but Gloria De Haven is null as Rooney's puppy love and Marilyn Maxwell only a small-time Mae West as the chorus girl alternative. Mamoulian himself liked the sequence where the latter's dress changes from pale pink to scarlet as she and Rooney sit drinking, but here and elsewhere the use of colour does not prevent the film from being vastly inferior to Clarence Brown's earlier version of this play: nor does the passing of song from person to person help it approach the quality of *Meet Me in St Louis*, even if Mamoulian had done that successfully in the past (in *Love Me Tonight*).

The period detail – the time is the Twenties – is somewhat sporadic in **Good News** (1947), but the film is lively, as directed by Charles Walters (1911–82), promoted by Freed after having choreographed for his unit for some years. The cast breaks into song and dance as if it were the most natural thing in the world, and the songs are mainly those of Brown, deSylva and Henderson, whose old college musical has been rather vaguely followed. The students are led with predictable charm by June Allyson and Peter Lawford. She obviously was directed to sing her two ballads with the wistfulness and gestures of Miss Garland.

Garland herself was reunited with Kelly in **The Pirate** (1948), one of their less popular films – for on this occasion Minnelli and Freed were galloping too fast for public taste. Albert Hackett and Frances Goodrich wrote this cod tale of Caribbean romance from a play by S. N. Behrman, originally a divertissement for the Lunts. It is fun but not funny: a daydreaming orphan (Garland) is torn between her chosen fiancé (Walter Slezak) and a strolling player (Kelly), who pretends to be her idol, a notorious pirate. Garland's grasp of the form required is surer than Kelly's, for she only hints at parody, while his attempt to mix the styles of Barrymore and Fairbanks is too broad – which may be why he regards the film as a failure while Minnelli does not. The settings are theatrical without the preciosity of *Yolanda and the Thief*, and the Cole Porter songs include 'Be a Clown', to provide a rousing finale.

The same principals were originally involved in **Easter Parade** (1948), but Freed replaced Minnelli with Charles Walters, since he thought that the Garland–Minnelli marriage, now under strain, might mend if

The *sine qua non* of the musical is a likeable cast, and that the M-G-M musical usually boasted. Beyond that the studio had three stars who were almost certainly the greatest ever to work in the genre – Judy Garland, Fred Astaire and Gene Kelly. She made three films with Kelly, but only one with Astaire, which is why *Easter Parade* is precious. She proved herself no mean dancer, and she could pick up steps immediately – but the purpose of 'A Couple of Swells' was, as can be seen, comic.

they did not work together; and when Kelly broke an ankle, Astaire was persuaded out of retirement. Thus the film stars two nonpareils, and is generally worthy of them – at least, to see it now is to marvel at their talents, and that of Irving Berlin, whose songs, old and new, are bountifully melodious. The staging of the numbers, by Walters and Robert Alton, ranges from the good to the magnificent – in the case of a montage of ragtime done by the stars; and the book, by Goodrich and Hackett, is a serviceable tale of a dancer and his two partners – the other of whom is Ann Miller.

The score of **Words and Music** (1948) is also exceptional, since the title refers to the work of Rodgers and Hart, whose collaboration provided Freed with a more refreshing film than the one on Jerome Kern. The story, as directed by Norman Taurog, is bland. So is Tom Drake as Rodgers, presumably out of deference to the composer; as Hart, Mickey Rooney is merely cocky, self-conscious about his

height, and given to disappearing when lyrics were urgently needed. No hint is given of Rodgers's defection to Hammerstein during the last months of Hart's life, nor of the latter's taste for low-life pick-ups – and his unrequited love is naturally heterosexual. The ending originally had a drunken Hart watching his old flame (Betty Garrett) in a dive where she is singing 'It Never Entered My Mind', but it was cut, presumably as being too strong after the blandness which had preceded it. The numbers are zestfully staged, whether as party pieces or the usual stage routines, and the success of a ten-minute ballet, 'Slaughter on Tenth Avenue', danced by Gene Kelly and Vera-Ellen, was further impetus to the Freed unit to experiment with the musical form.

Kelly and a frequent collaborator, Stanley Donen (b. 1924), provided the original story for **Take Me Out to the Ball Game** (1949), and it is immediately clear that their aim was to use the ultra-masculine world of baseball as an occasion for song and dance. They also choreographed and directed the musical numbers, favouring (apart from one vaudeville duo) 'spontaneity' in natural settings, and an exhilarating collection they are. 'Don't go home yet' sing Kelly and Frank Sinatra to the audience at the end, explaining that the romantic complications have yet to be solved – and their action is an acknowledgment that we did not come to the cinema to see a musical about a baseball team, but these particular people entertaining. That we are more interested in them than in the plot derives from the Hope and Crosby films, but Kelly and Donen would use the concept to bring the film musical to its richest form. This one was directed by Busby Berkeley, and Esther Williams (as owner of the baseball team) does not have a swimming ballet, though she does take a turn or two around a hotel pool.

The Barkleys of Broadway (1949), though in no sense innovatory, does indicate that the Freed unit had become even more confident after its recent successes. The film musical still counted for less than the Broadway musical, though by this time *Meet Me in St Louis* had been recognised as the best since the films of Astaire and Rogers. Since 'Oklahoma!' the Broadway musical had been experimenting in such matters as plot and atmosphere, and its Hollywood poor relation also dropped the traditional comic supporting players, while often remaining lighthearted. In reuniting Garland and Astaire, Freed wanted to capitalise on her way with a comic line, and also to reintroduce the comedy element from Astaire's prewar pictures. A suitable script was commissioned from Adolph Green (b. 1918) and Betty Comden (b. 1919), a team of New York writers whom he had brought to the coast for *Good News*. Like much of their screen work, this one has an element of the biographical, concerning as it does a dancing team which splits up when the distaff half wishes to go dramatic. Ironically, the ailing Garland was replaced by Ginger Rogers – and also ironically she is the reason that the result is hardly funnier than *Easter Parade*. The new ladylike Ginger is not a patch on the young Ginger: tackling a recitation in French of the 'Marseillaise', she does it absolutely straight, for all the world as if she had seen another Oscar in her crystal ball. As a result this film lacks the careless rapture of the films the team made for R.K.O., but as an entertainment it did not disappoint the many cinemagoers who came to see this already legendary couple.

Since the failures of *Yolanda and the Thief*, *Living in a Big Way* and *Summer Holiday*, M-G-M had been reluctant to sanction musicals that did not involve theatre folk, and since **In the Good Old Summertime** (1949) concerns the romance of two shop assistants, its four songs – there is also a lullaby – are bunched in twos, as if removable. Garland sings them all, two at the firm's party, and two in the shop – for fortunately the shop sells music and musical instruments. This is an otherwise straightforward remake of *The Shop Around the Corner*, now set in Chicago in the 1900s, and as directed by Robert Z. Leonard for Pasternak not quite achieving the marzipan tone of the Lubitsch original. Both directors took their cue from their star, and Garland – looking healthier and happier than in the films made either side of it – is very funny as she tries to prove her worth in the shop while mooning about her pen-friend, Van Johnson. (The piece was intended to be one of his teamings with June Allyson, who was pregnant.) The supporting cast includes Buster Keaton, till recently a gagman at the studio – and he has one pratfall which can bring the house down.

On the strength of *Take Me Out to the Ball Game*, Freed allowed Kelly and Donen to direct **On the Town** (1949), and though one of its heroines is a dance student, none of the other principal characters has any connection with the theatre. It is the great liberating musical of the American cinema. M-G-M had bought the property before its Broadway opening because of the enthusiasm of a member of Mayer's staff, who happened to be a friend of the composer, Leonard Bernstein. Mayer and his fellow executives so loathed it, however, that when Comden and Green arrived under contract they were advised to remind no one that they had written the book. George Abbott had directed it on stage, and when Freed invited him to make a film of his choice he chose this – though the project was taken over by Kelly and Donen within hours of Freed's assent. Kelly considers the result his greatest contribution to the film musical, and I think we may assume that the achievement is mainly his. The film recounts the adventures of three sailors in New York; it begins in the Brooklyn Navy Yard as they leave ship at 6 a.m. – and break into song and dance in anticipation. The scene was filmed on location, and the song continued in recognisable parts of New York – if not in fact very many, for M-G-M was nervous about something so novel, and ordered the company and crew to return before they had finished: but the opening is one good reason why the film bowled over every critic who reviewed it. The staging of the numbers was another, and the key to their success lies in Kelly's view: 'If you make it look like hard work it's no good. You've got to make the public believe they can go out and do it themselves.'

In *Anchors Aweigh* there is a moment when Kelly and Sinatra are escorting the girl home, and there is a kidding gaiety about them, because they have had a marvellous evening together: it is a feeling that recurs throughout *On the Town*. Each number seems to be improvised and impromptu – and this was the first time an entire film had been built around this concept. Previous examples had seldom had as much exuberance and hilarity, a feeling of

The Screen's Other Great Dancer

By 1949 Gene Kelly had gained creative control over the musicals he made, bringing the genre to its peak. Together he and Stanley Donen directed *On the Town*, ABOVE, which raised Kelly's speciality, seeming spontaneity, to a new art, and here are, clockwise, Betty Garrett, Ann Miller, Kelly, Alice Pearce, Jules Munshin and Frank Sinatra entertaining impromptu the customers of a Coney Island bar. Minnelli directed *An American in Paris*, ABOVE RIGHT, with Kelly and Leslie Caron in the climactic ballet – the artiness of which was reflected for a brief moment in *Singin' in the Rain*. ABOVE FAR RIGHT, The lady is Cyd Charisse, more rewardingly employed in another sequence, RIGHT, from the same exhilarating number.

Howard Keel in
Annie Get Your Gun,
based on Irving
Berlin's Broadway
musical. When in
1974 M-G-M issued
its compilation film,
That's Entertainment
it was not permitted
to include a sequence
from this particular
musical since Berlin
held the rights and
was smarting from
the cancellation – by
another manage-
ment – of a project
built round his
songs, and one on
which he had
worked for years.
However, he
relented in view of
the film's enormous
popularity, and there
is a scene from *Annie*
in *That's
Entertainment Part 2*.

nice people liking each other – of just being alive on a night like this – and it was never more invigoratingly done than in the anticipatory title song, as rendered by the sailors and their girls, starting at the top of the Empire State Building and continuing into the street. It is one of the new numbers written by Comden and Green with Roger Edens, and good enough almost to justify the rejection of much of Bernstein's score, which Freed did not like. Bernstein's bal-let, 'Fancy Free', which inspired the show, received homage from Kelly in the form of a new ballet to Bernstein's music, 'A Day in New York'. It was recognised as far more modern and cinematic than the only other ballet then conceived for the screen, the British *Red Shoes* (q.v.).

The admiration accorded *On the Town* tended to obscure the fact that it was an adaptation, and indeed the original had run only just over a year on Broadway, while really successful shows ran for several. The price of the film rights had therefore esca-lated and deterred the Hollywood compan-ies from purchasing them, while the whim-sical nature of many musicals prevented

them from reaching the screen.★ **Annie Get Your Gun** (1950) may be considered the first film version in several years of a Broadway musical, and it was a second consecutive triumph for Freed, who had persuaded the studio to pay a record $800,000 for the rights as a vehicle for Judy Garland. Unfortunately, he assigned Bus-by Berkeley, whom she loathed, to direct. When her personal difficulties led to her removal, his footage was thought unus-able and he was replaced by George Sid-ney. Sidney agreed with Freed that he should approach it as one of Broadway's great shows, with a strong book by Her-bert and Dorothy Fields, and a marvellous score by Irving Berlin. It has been filmed as if for a stage audience, with the songs belted at the camera – and it is certainly the right decision, in view of the over-emphatic and enthusiastic approach of Betty Hutton, Garland's replacement. She so clearly wants to be loved and admired that she eventually succeeds, while Ho-ward Keel is a tower of strength as Annie's big-headed beau. It is a carnival film, never losing sight of the milling circus crowds, the galloping horses, the balloons and the banners.

The skills of the Freed unit were appear-ing in the studio's other musicals, and **Three Little Words** (1950), directed by Richard Thorpe for Cummings, could be the definitive 'And then I wrote . . .' movie, detailing the collaboration be-tween song-writers Bert Kalmar (Astaire) and Harry Ruby (Red Skelton). Astaire brings attention and style to very little in the way of plot and choreography, but really needs a sharper partner than Vera-Ellen to make the most of his remarkable qualities. The pairing of Garland and Kelly in **Summer Stock** (1950) is perfect, de-spite the fact that she is stoutish – and was having so many problems in her personal life that sometimes she did not know what she was doing, or so said the director, Charles Walters. Pasternak, the producer, noticed that these did not show in the finished result, and when she finally takes the lead – as we knew she would – in the

★M-G-M bought Lerner and Loewe's 'The Day Before Spring' for $250,000 in 1945, and never filmed it; the much more successful 'Brigadoon', also a fantasy, was purchased by the company for only $120,000 – but not until three years after its Broadway opening, and filming did not start till three years after that; Walt Disney bought 'Finian's Rainbow' but did not film it.

how which Kelly has been rehearsing in her barn, he says with exceptional feeling, 'You're wonderful – everything I ever hoped for in a leading lady.' In each of the films prepared for her since *The Pirate*, a comic duet had been planned, but she did only one, 'A Couple of Swells' with Astaire in *Easter Parade*; Astaire did others with Ginger Rogers and Jane Powell, while her absences during the shooting of this particular film caused Kelly to do this number with Phil Silvers. When Garland left the studio by mutual consent after this film, the front office was relieved, but her colleagues – tried though they had been by her behaviour – acknowledged that the M-G-M musical would never be the same again.

Certainly Esther Williams was no replacement, swimming – and singing – in the *sea* in **Pagan Love Song** (1950), and even if she and Howard Keel do little else for the 76 minutes' running time, that is part of the film's charm, along with its songs and bounteous South Seas locations. Unfortunately the missing plot is telescoped into the last five minutes, destroying the audience's relaxed mood. Robert Alton directed, one of his two films in that capacity, after Miss Williams had complained to Freed that his first choice (Donen) had no belief in her talents. Donen's direction of **Royal Wedding** (1951) and his staging of the numbers is so dire that we may confidently credit Kelly with the energy and inventiveness of the films they made together. Indeed, apart from the contributions of Astaire and the composer, Burton Lane, the film is disastrous, perhaps because Freed had conceived it for two doubtful British acquisitions – some Technicolor footage of the last British royal wedding, and Moira Shearer, the dancer of *The Red Shoes*. Astaire found her an unsuitable partner, and she was replaced by the even less suitable Sarah Churchill, daughter of Winston, and a sometime actress. The screenplay has Astaire falling in love with her while in London with his sister and vaudeville partner (Jane Powell), and as written by Alan Jay Lerner the script is witless.

At the lower end of the studio's musicals are those with Mario Lanza, a temperamental tenor whose career was entrusted to Pasternak. Lanza made two films with Kathryn Grayson, which the public wisely avoided, but 'Be My Love', a song from the second of the two, had been much played on juke boxes. The studio accordingly embarked upon **The Great Caruso** (1951) hesitantly, since a film of operatic excerpts was considered a risk. However, these were by no means unfamiliar to the public, and the box office benefited from a hit song, 'The Loveliest Night of the Year', based on an old waltz, 'Over the Waves', sung to Caruso at his birthday party in one of several borrowings from *The Jolson Story* (q.v.) Lanza's arias are curtailed (unlike this particular song), but confidence in the project is not instilled by the very first shot (Naples with Vesuvius to its north). The real Caruso was short, stout and inordinately vain, though managing a spectacular career before dying after a long illness in Milan at the age of forty-eight. In the film he dies on the stage of the Metropolitan, appropriately so, since it is made to appear the only opera house of any importance – and as played by the bull-like but otherwise negative Lanza it is not a moment too soon. The memoir by Caruso's much younger American wife was the basis for the screenplay, and it comes as no surprise to find that she publicly dissociated herself from the film.

Commercially, at least, the M-G-M musical was at a peak. This film joined *Annie Get Your Gun* to become one of the most profitable the company had ever made, while Freed's next two productions also appeared in the list of the year's highest-grossing films. **Show Boat** (1951) is very handsome: George Sidney's films, including his non-musical ones (q.v.), were increasingly pleasing to look at, and this, with its notable shots of the show boat as it moves down the Mississippi, has felicitous contributions from Charles Rosher, the cinematographer, and the designer, Jack Martin Smith. The orchestrations are by Adolph Deutsch, and though the score has been curtailed the songs seem to come up at five minute intervals, while the rest of the time they may be heard behind the action – which is sometimes choreographed to them, most agreeably when Magnolia and Julie break into their gay little dance. Despite the presence of Miss Grayson as Magnolia, it is the way Kern's music is used which makes this the best of the three film versions – and it has Howard Keel to sing his share of the lyrics.

Those with fond memories of Universal's 1936 version of *Show Boat* did not expect the M-G-M remake to be quite as good as it is – which was almost certainly a challenge to Freed's team. They capitalised on two factors – its incomparable score, splendidly arranged and recorded even when relegated to the background, and Technicolor. It may have been the easiest decision to have the show boat itself move down the (back-lot) Mississippi to the strains of 'Ol' Man River', but it is enormously effective.

Ava Gardner is a magnificent Julie; Marge and Gower Champion have two witty dances; and Joe E. Brown and Agnes Moorehead are the Wilkes. The book has also been better compressed – by John Lee Mahin – than in Whale's version, and Sidney makes it move along with a certain charm.

Equally popular and much more admired, **An American in Paris** (1951) has dated badly, though we may consider it beyond good and evil because Minnelli, the director, and Kelly expected audiences to share their enthusiasm for Paris and modern French art. No one involved seems to have got closer to Paris, re-created in the studio, than any two-day tripper, and Alan Jay Lerner's screenplay about an ex-G.I. (Kelly) staying in the city to paint is exceptionally thin. The staging of the songs, from the Gershwin library, is as self-conscious as it is confident, but the numbers are nonetheless memorable – especially the cheerful 'Swonderful', as sung by Kelly and Georges Guetary, the romantic 'Our Love Is Here To Stay', as

danced by Kelly and Leslie Caron, and 'I'll Build a Stairway to Paradise', a luscious and affectionate parody of Ziegfeld production numbers, sung by Guetary. The final dream ballet, too much influenced by the one in *The Red Shoes*, now seems studied and over-zealous, with its prancing around the mock fountains of the Place de la Concorde. It was filmed last – at a cost of over half a million dollars, just under one-fifth of its total budget – because the studio had reservations: ironically, it was the one musical number (if I may so term it) which the industry most admired★ and it helped the film towards its several Oscars, including Best Picture and a special award to Kelly for his choreography.

On the other hand, the unappreciated **The Belle of New York** (1952), directed by Walters, retains its charms. Freed had been preparing it as a vehicle for Astaire

★In the 1974 compilation of numbers from M-G-M musicals *That's Entertainment*, the commentary still spoke of the ballet 'as their major achievement. As a celebration of these films this one was enormously popular, but a sequel, *That Entertainment 2*, was, despite the linking material provided by Astaire and Kelly, dismissed – quite rightly – as a rip-off.

and Garland when Astaire announced his retirement in 1945: there were script troubles – the film has only a slight connection with the old stage musical of the same name – and they were hardly solved when the project was re-activated. Freed's musicals had been moving towards a loose, inconsequential structure, but the plot – a man about town (Astaire) meets and woos a Salvation Army lass (Vera-Ellen) – found little favour. Astaire said that he is 'mad' that it failed as it is one of his favourite films, and it was fun to make: it is fun to watch, mainly because the numbers show him and the Freed unit at their best, especially in 'The Bachelor Dinner Song', 'Oops', done on a streetcar, and the Currier and Ives number.

By common consent **Singin' in the Rain** (1952) is the masterpiece of the Freed unit, and probably the best musical ever made in Hollywood – the gayest, the funniest, the most affectionate, the most insouciant. Freed had wanted to build a film about the songs he had earlier written with Nacio Herb Brown for the first Talkies, which gave Comden and Green the idea of a Hollywood story about the coming of Sound; and Howard Keel was originally to have starred as a Silent actor adjusting to speech. The film has a silly, entrancing plot about a Silent swashbuckler being converted into a Talkie, with Gene Kelly as its hero and Debbie Reynolds as the chorus girl, whom he wants as his leading lady; Jean Hagen is Lina Lamont, his actual co-star, who reads all the fan magazines and consequently believes that she loves her as much in life as on the screen. Since Lina's voice does not, to put it mildly, match her looks, the moment when she opens her mouth is overwhelming. Miss Hagen's performance is one of the funniest ever put on film, as she ardently and triumphantly quotes the magazine which called her 'a shimmering, glowing star in the cinema firm-a-ment'. As directed by Kelly and Donen, the film is never serious for more than a fleeting second, with good jokes at the expense of Hollywood and that era of wonderful nonsense. Kelly, Reynolds and their cohort Donald O'Connor are captivating together, especially in their 'spontaneous' numbers, while Kelly's usual song and dance to denote his falling in love, this time in the rain, is probably the most beloved sequence in the history

of film musicals. Most of the film has a deliberately drab look, coming vividly to life whenever it celebrates show business, as in the 'Beautiful Girl' number which heralds the coming of the 'All-Singing All-Dancing All-Talking movies', and the ballet, with its scarlets, greens, yellows and whites. The ballet, a salute to old Broadway, is described by Kelly to the producer (Millard Mitchell; the role is based on Freed), who says, *after* we have seen it, 'That's all very well, but I'll have to wait till it's visualised on screen.' The film is replete with such touches, which is one of the reasons few people ever tire of it. It did not, as it happened, get tremendously good reviews – certainly not as good as those for the more innovative *On the Town* and the arty *An American in Paris*, but the public loved it.

Metro's acknowledged supremacy in musicals resulted in the purchase of a number of old Broadway shows, few of which were filmed. **Lovely to Look At** (1952) is one that was, a remake of *Roberta*, and the worst that may be said of it is that it entailed the suppression of the earlier film for two decades. As produced by Cummings and directed by Mervyn LeRoy – except for the fashion parade at the end, which Minnelli directed – it may be enjoyed for the deployment of its score, almost intact, and its handling by Keel, Ann Miller and the Champions. Something similar may be said of **The Merry Widow** (1952), equally sumptuous, for the Danilo of Fernando Lamas is surprisingly effective; he looks very romantic, even if he lacks the charm or comedy sense of Chevalier. Pasternak produced this third M-G-M version of the Lehar operetta, and it was directed by Curtis Bernhardt who, like LeRoy, is not the lightest of directors, in this case foolishly allowing Lana Turner (in the title role) to set the tone.

Lili (1953) was directed by Charles Walters, whose own favourite picture it was: 'We certainly had problems on that one – including two dull leading men – but it all worked out marvellously.' As adapted by Helen Deutsch from a story by Paul Gallico, this film is about a waif (Leslie Caron) who, taken into carnival life, is torn between the magician (Jean-Pierre Aumont) and an embittered puppeteer (Mel Ferrer) – a matter she resolves after a couple of dream ballets. With the exception of Miss Caron, the cast – which also includes Zsa Zsa Gabor and Kurt Kasznar – is not one to be employed when attempting winsome charm; the puppet scenes are cute; the one song is plugged to death; and the settings are the worst kind of Hollywood France. Caron's performance has honesty and a quiet vitality; against all studio advice she insisted on drab clothes, and by not playing for sympathy she almost makes this film bearable. Walters and Deutsch must have agreed with the interpretation, for the Cinderella Caron plays for them in **The Glass Slipper** (1955) is described as 'not exactly an amiable child', and the hostility shown to her is understandable. For such reasons this is one of the better films for children, but they – and indeed, anyone – would be bored by the dream ballets choreographed by Roland Petit. The producer of both films was Edwin H. Knopf, who also came up with a new version of *Waterloo Bridge* with Caron, the ghastly **Gaby** (1956), directed by Curtis Bernhardt.

Meanwhile, since Astaire's only two failures for M-G-M had been without a show business background, Freed commissioned a theatre story from Comden and Green. **The Band Wagon** (1953) is cousin to *Singin' in the Rain*, since it is also about turning a flop entertainment into a success, and is also built round some old songs, by Arthur Schwartz and Howard

Dietz (who was a 'house' man, in charge of the studio's publicity). The characters played by Nanette Fabray and Oscar Levant are based on Comden and Green themselves; the theatre director *wunderkind* played by Jack Buchanan is based on Minnelli; and Astaire plays a washed-up Hollywood song and dance man who had once starred in 'Swinging Down to Panama'. Some of his lines reflect his unease at still playing in musicals in middle age, and while in-jokes, rare in movies at this time, proliferate (there is a parody of the auction scene in *The Star* q.v.) the darts are not particularly well aimed. The musical numbers are among the best ever put on film, whether 'improvised' or as part of the stage show. Astaire is in incomparable form, and when Cyd Charisse wraps her arms and legs around him as they dance you may forgive her for seeming to read her dialogue from cue-cards. As directed by Minnelli, everything about the film has style.

That is not a word to be used about a new version of **Rose Marie** (1954), as produced and directed by Mervyn LeRoy, whose attitude seems to have been that people who like operetta will like anything. In this case they were offered neither the original plot nor score, though the new songs are an improvement on the old ones omitted. They are sung by Keel, Ann Blyth, Fernando Lamas and Bert Lahr, but are so poorly staged as to minimise both singer and song. The original setting of the Canadian Rockies remains, since the studio found the subject suitable for its first CinemaScope (q.v.) musical, but the location work only emphasises the painted studio mountains which alternate with it. Another CinemaScope remake, **The Student Prince** (1954), directed by Richard Thorpe, is sometimes revived, presumably since it features 'The Singing Voice of Mario Lanza'. Relations between Lanza and the studio had reached a point of no return, the star having given the word 'temperament' a new meaning, according to Pasternak. M-G-M owned the song-tracks, already recorded, and replaced him in front of the camera with Edmund Purdom, who does little to improve matters. Towards the end he goes into the cathedral to sing, with Lanza's voice, 'I'll Walk with God' (a number of religious songs had been getting into the hit parade), and you

One of the reasons that Fred Astaire's career at M-G-M was so rewarding was that Freed was determined to show even more of his extraordinary talent than had been revealed during his days dancing with Ginger Rogers at R.K.O. He was pushed towards the balletic, and in *The Band Wagon* was engaged in an enjoyable number taking off thick-ear private eye thrillers. The lady is again Cyd Charisse, going from brunette to blonde and back again to prove herself deadly to the male.

would be well advised to walk out of the cinema – if, by chance, you are still there.

Though *The Student Prince* is handsome in the M-G-M fashion, it is hard to believe that it and *Rose Marie* were in production at the same time as **Kiss Me, Kate** (1953) and **Seven Brides for Seven Brothers** (1954), since these are among the best M-G-M musicals – and they were produced by Cummings. *Kiss Me, Kate* was made in 3-D, like CinemaScope then being used in an attempt to prevent audiences from defecting to T.V. A three-dimensional effect was achieved by having each spectator wear special glasses, and the system was exploited by ensuring that a fair number of things were hurled at the audience. The decision to make this property in that gimmicky process may be one reason why Freed was not involved – for he was a friend of Cole Porter, whose greatest stage success it had been. The show was unsatisfactory only because the Sam and Bella Spewack book lacked wit, and Dorothy Kingsley's screenplay is little improvement. A famous acting couple, once married, are reunited for a musical version of 'The Taming of the Shrew' – of which we see a potted version between their bickering and other backstage nonsense. As most of the content consists of a stage performance it can only transfer uneasily to film, and George Sidney directs with no firm control. However, the musical numbers make it a feast if not a banquet – at least to admirers of Keel and Cole. Keel is notably good with the point numbers, and his Petruchio is a luscious piece of braggadocio. As the virago of a leading lady, Kathryn Grayson improves mightily over her simpering soubrettes, but is an inconsiderable artist and insufficiently stylish. Ann Miller has five numbers, including two duets and two excellent dances shared with Tommy Rall, Bob Fosse and Bobby Van – 'Tom, Dick and Harry' – and the interpolated 'From this Moment On'. 'Brush Up Your Shakespeare', done with amateur buck and wing by Keenan Wynn and James Whitmore, is still a show-stopper, despite some bowdlerisation of the lyrics.

Seven Brides for Seven Brothers was made in CinemaScope, and at this point it may be said that its extra cost and its temporary achievement as a box-office attraction caused some studios to avoid Technicolor

for a cheaper colour system. M-G-M owned Anscocolor, and used it for this film, which, with painted backcloths, makes it often visually depressing, though, when Keel breaks into 'Bless Yore Beautiful Hide' it is clear that Stanley Donen, the director, has found a style to match the hope of the song's lyric, the jauntiness of its music, and the masculine strength of the singer. The screenplay was written by Albert Hackett, Frances Goodrich and Dorothy Kingsley, working from a story by Stephen Vincent Benét. Keel plays a mountain man who takes a wife (Jane Powell, in her best screen work), whereupon his six brothers are encouraged to emulate the rape of the Sabine women by forcibly abducting their chosen brides. Keel has a song about that event, 'Sobbin' Women', and Powell has a similar one, 'Goin' Courtin'', which whirls itself into a joy we seldom see; but the film's tour de force is the virile, balletic square dance, as exhilarating as any sequence ever put on film.

Though Donen's work on this occasion achieves something as good as his films with Kelly, he plummeted again with **Deep in My Heart** (1954), one of the two films produced by Roger Edens (independently of Freed). There is in theory no reason why two supposedly forward-looking artists should involve themselves

Seven Brides for Seven Brothers is another landmark of the M-G-M musical. It was the last one which was critically admired and hugely popular – with the exception of *Gigi*, which was recognised as a late flowering. The end of the M-G-M musical is one of the mysteries of cinema, for the financial return on *Seven Brides* was enough to offset the two or three failures that followed. A planned follow-up, with Howard Keel as a singing Robin Hood, was cancelled: Keel is virtually the only one of the leading players not in this picture, and it is Matt Mattox whom the others are admiring.

with a biography of Sigmund Romberg, even if that composer was not then well out of fashion, but this humourless enterprise damns both of them. The guest turns, notably those of Ann Miller, Gene Kelly (and his brother Fred), sometimes help, but the film is mainly a bonanza for José Ferrer as Romberg: he is presented not only as dedicated composer but prankster, lover, dancer, high liver, conductor and idealist, at one point miming a whole musical comedy in the manner of Danny Kaye.

Also unsuccessful were Minnelli's **Brigadoon** (1954) and **Kismet** (1955), both in CinemaScope, a process which robbed musicals of their intimacy and which he himself disliked. He was not interested in transferring Broadway musicals to the screen, and only did the second one in return for receiving assent to his proposed film on Van Gogh, *Lust for Life* (q.v.). He had disliked *Brigadoon* on stage, and it is with incredulity that one learns that Alan Jay Lerner objected to the changes that Minnelli and Kelly proposed making to his daft, solemn book. On stage it had been billed as 'a whimsical musical fantasy': two Americans stumble on a small Scottish town which materialises only once every hundred years, and one of them falls in love, thus willing the town to reappear. Kelly had liked it on stage but lost interest when it was decided to film it in the studio; at the time Freed said, in a widely-quoted remark, that he had gone to Scotland and found nothing that resembled Scotland, while a further plan to shoot on location at Big Sur was abandoned in an economy drive. However, the sets – a brave attempt by Preston Ames at lochs and hills – are the least of its failings. The cast, which includes Cyd Charisse and Van Johnson, was clearly of no help, and Minnelli misuses Kelly's particular talents, as he admitted; and most reviewers found the performance forced. Helping to reduce the whimsy in the original show was the male chorus dancing – increasingly important in Broadway musicals and hence a heavy influence on *Seven Brides* – but the wedding reel in the film is glum. Agnes de Mille's final chase ballet was restructured for film, but comes too late to save the situation. Furthermore, for the first time in his career Minnelli often positions the camera in the wrong place, as he does again in *Kismet*.

With the exception of the Caliph's wedding procession – 'Night of My Nights' – and 'Baubles, Bangles and Beads' the numbers in *Kismet* are not so much staged as merely delivered. Keel and Dolores Gray perform with verve, but Ann Blyth and a sluggish Vic Damone slaughter 'A Stranger in Paradise', in a garden set which looks like a Macy's window display, while 'And This Is My Beloved', shorn of its multiple rhythms and voices, is a mere shadow of its old self.

Kelly also gave Freed two consecutive musical failures, but **It's Always Fair Weather** (1955), directed with Donen, revives better than contemporary opinion suggests. The starting point was *On the Town*: Comden and Green wondered what had become of the three sailors – who became soldiers when Frank Sinatra refused to be part of the project – and decided that civilian life had made them cynical, smug and hypocritical. This is a musical of disillusion and disenchantment, and to everyone involved 'most friendship is feigning, most loving mere folly.' It does show talent evolving, and also on the credit side are the use of the wide screen and Kelly's solo dance on roller skates, using passers-by as props, as he once used a rainstorm. Against these must be set the muddy colour, a weak score by André Previn, some broad satire at the expense of television and advertising, and the fact that alone of the cast Dolores Gray is good, playing a phoney, schmalzy T.V. star; as Kelly's old buddies, Dan Dailey and Michael Kidd are well cast.

Kelly's original intention with **Invitation to the Dance** (1956) was to salute American dancers, but the studio, having cautiously agreed to an all-dance film, insisted that he himself appear in it and then, to keep costs down, that it be made in Britain. Production began in 1952, and though the delay in completion was due to the fact that one sequence required animation, the studio so disliked Malcolm Arnold's score for 'Ring Around Rosy' that Previn wrote a new one, working from the images on the screen. Another sequence was abandoned because Freed disliked the rushes, but as a tribute to Tin Pan Alley it would surely have been more 'commercial' than what remained. These are: 'Circus', a commedia dell'arte romp, with Kelly as a white-faced clown and some splendidly energetic male dancing; 'Ring Around Rosy', a version of Schnitzler's 'La Ronde', which is neither as funny nor as sophisticated as it should be; and the animated 'Sinbad the Sailor', which alternates between failure, as in Kelly's pas de deux with the cute princess, and success, as with the witty and fantastic harem guards. Kelly himself thinks the film failed because there was too much dancing to absorb, but the reviews were universally bad. It had cost almost $1½ million, and in the U.S. took only $200,000.

Also finding little degree of acceptance were the low-budget experimental musicals produced by Cummings, usually with the studio's lesser talents. The dancing of Marge and Gower Champion saves Donen's **Give a Girl a Break** (1953), but there is no redeeming feature in Richard Thorpe's weird **Athena** (1954), about a nice young lawyer (Edmund Purdom) who becomes involved with a family of California cultists and a Mr Universe contest. The huge success of *Seven Brides* restored studio confidence, leading directly to **Jupiter's Darling** (1955), produced by George Wells, a studio writer and producer of three minor musicals. The props and costumes from *Quo Vadis?* were in store, and the studio owned Robert E. Sherwood's 'The Road to Rome', an historical spoof adapted here by Dorothy Kingsley without wit; the score is also poor. The result is pleasing, partly because George Sidney makes the most of the costumes and spectacle, and partly because the players seem to be enjoying themselves – Esther Williams, the Champions and Keel, who, as Hannibal, has a self-glorification song copied later in 'A Funny Thing Happened on the Way to the Forum'.

The film failed, while Pasternak's conventional musicals found favour, at least with the public. **Hit the Deck** (1955), directed by Roy Rowland, is based on an old Broadway show, and though the subject matter is not dissimilar to that of *On the Town*, the discrepancy is wide – a fact not unassociated with the standby cast, including Jane Powell, Debbie Reynolds, Tony Martin, Vic Damone and Russ Tamblyn. There is also Ann Miller, tapping away in the finale in front of hundreds of sailors, as Eleanor Powell once did: the song is 'Hallelujah!' and if the choreography of Hermes Pan is unworthy of it,

Grace Kelly was one of the nicest things to happen to M-G-M in the Fifties – if briefly, since she had been only five years in films when she went off to become Her Serene Highness Princess Grace of Monaco. She didn't exactly happen to the M-G-M musical, but she did sing a few notes with Bing Crosby in *High Society*, earning herself a Golden Disc in the process when the soundtrack recording of 'True Love' had sold over a million copies.

the score as a whole – taken from several shows by Vincent Youmans – atones for much.

Recent failures had made the M-G-M management unreceptive to musicals, but there was no hesitation in producing **High Society** (1956), because it united so many fine talents and indeed this remake of *The Philadelphia Story* is a drawing-room comedy interspersed with songs. If the performance is of no more than of repertory standard that is because Walters's direction seems non-existent. The four leads are otherwise solid gold, with Bing Crosby and Frank Sinatra offering lazy charm instead of the rather frenzied approach of Grant and Stewart; Grace Kelly (q.v.) has eagerness and coldness where Hepburn was extravagant and disdainful, but her presence is refreshing; and Celeste Holm, though given too little to do, is quite delicious. Louis Armstrong has two guest turns, including a duet with Crosby, 'Now You Has Jazz', one of the four superb songs slapped into the centre of the film. There are not many others, but they are all by Cole Porter, and if they do not seem directed either, this is one occasion when leaving well alone★ achieves gratifying results.

The director of the original, George

★Too well, since this is the only Hollywood film I know where the microphone may be glimpsed; it was made quickly to allow Miss Kelly to marry her prince.

Cukor, made **Les Girls** (1957) for the same producer, Sol C. Siegel, responsible for musicals good and bad during his tenures at Paramount and 20th Century-Fox. On this occasion Cukor's handling of Porter's songs (it was his last score) and the backstage scenes is as assured as those in his version of *A Star Is Born* (q.v.), while one number in particular, 'Ladies in Waiting', has a panache which – as rarely in their screen treatment – belongs completely to Porter's world of musical comedy. However, like *High Society*, this is less a musical than a story punctuated by songs, concerning as it does a libel trial at the Old Bailey, and what may or may not have happened among some members of a dancing troupe in Paris. Vera Caspary wrote the original story and John Patrick did the screenplay, making nothing out of much. A subdued Kelly is the head of the troupe, in dispute between Taina Elg, Mitzi Gaynor and Kay Kendall. Miss Kendall (1926–59) is gorgeous, with those intimations of civilised zaniness which so beautifully recall Carole Lombard, and as long as she is front and centre the film is fine.

Kelly requested a release from his contract, which was granted; and, since musicals were now frowned upon, Howard Keel was allowed to go. Though both continued to work in films (and elsewhere), the great days of their careers were over, even if at this stage they may have been more popular than those stars important in box-office statistics (Rock Hudson, Yul Brynner, Burt Lancaster, Glenn Ford and William Holden): they are certainly more fondly remembered. Kelly may have been drained artistically and marked by both the failure of his ballet film and the traumas of its making. He had also at one point been making a musical version of *Huckleberry Finn*, which was abandoned, and Donen has said of their last collaboration that it was 'one hundred per cent nightmare. Gene didn't get on well with anybody. It was the only picture during which the atmosphere was really horrendous.' Since *The Band Wagon* had been made in similar conditions – partly due to Astaire's worry over his wife's illness, and Jack Buchanan's nervousness at working with him – the personal factor should be considered in the decline of the M-G-M musical, a reason perhaps why the talents involved agreed with the bosses that it was

dying. The artistic failure of several of these films may have sapped confidence and indeed the safe, unimaginative treatment of Broadway musicals at other studios was proving more satisfactory to the public.

Then there were the performers. Apart from Doris Day, none of the other women stars still under contract at the studio was worth building a musical around, and she made only *Love Me or Leave Me* (q.v.) for M-G-M at this time – though she returned to Warners, where Donen co-directed her in *The Pajama Game* (q.v.). The male stars were ageing, a fact taken into account by Edens as he prepared **Funny Face** (1957) for Astaire and the much younger Audrey Hepburn (b. 1929) – and she, significantly, was not known as a singer or a dancer, though she had sung and danced on the London stage before arriving in Hollywood. This was Edens's second film credited as producer – and his last, despite its success. It was planned at M-G-M but, when the Gershwin score that Edens wanted was sold by Warners to M-G-M, the whole package was bought by Paramount, who owned both Hepburn's contract and a commitment from Astaire. Donen directed, and unlike the other film he made for Edens, this is, or was, considered chic. What was then thought to be imaginative in the pictorial treatment has long since been assimilated into movies, and you may blanch at the juxtaposition of tourist Paris and fashion plates. Neither Astaire nor Hepburn could be less than entrancing, but Donen has refrigerated the air around them – though Kay Thompson's occasional asides warm the whole self-conscious enterprise. Leonard Gershe's screenplay is feeble, supposedly poking fun at the fashion world and people talking intently in left-bank cellars – and Hepburn is merely playing a new version of the classical-music-playing dame who takes off her specs and starts to jive. When she dances with Astaire in the Pré Catalan they are surrounded by turtle doves and primroses, which are unnecessary embellishments for artists of this quality. You would, however, not want to miss a second of him singing the title song, her version of 'How Long Has This Been Going On?', or the two of them joining Kay Thompson to rejuvenate that business of singing in the streets, 'Bonjour Paris'.

Astaire danced on the screen for the last time in **Silk Stockings** (1957), but in spite of this and the Porter score it was another nail in the coffin of the M-G-M musical. This is *Ninotchka* by way of Broadway, supposedly more topical than ever, but the anti-Russian jokes give an impression of mindless superiority. The stockings of the title replace the hat to which Garbo succumbed; Ninotchka is now sent to Paris to retrieve three composers retained by an American film producer. Freed chose the Russian Rouben Mamoulian to direct, against the advice of his unit (remembering the failure of *Summer Holiday*), and a degree of misplaced confidence is obvious – on the part of Mamoulian, for instance, in discovering 'satire' in the script by Leonard Gershe and Leonard Spigelgass, from the Broadway book by George S. Kaufman, that gentleman's wife and Abe Burrows. Mamoulian supposedly wanted to tell the story through dance, which simply does not happen: people lumber on from one side of the (wide) screen and go off the other, behaving as though trapped in Greek tragedy. Since Hermes Pan's choreography seems to be serviceable, the lifelessness of Astaire's numbers with Charisse must be blamed on both directorial incompetence and her lack of presence. Foolishly, she attempts Garbo's accent while speaking Garbo's lines. Astaire does a rock 'n' roll number which both he and Porter loathed (it was commissioned for the film in a panicky effort to attract 'modern' audiences), but there are isolated pleasures, as when Astaire breaks into the lyrics or sings 'Stereophonic Sound' with Janis Paige, playing a dumb movie star anticipating her first non-swimming role.

Gigi (1958) was a last success for the team of Freed and Minnelli, aided by the co-operation of Lerner and Frederick Loewe, whose success with 'My Fair Lady' brushed off on this film – with the M-G-M management, the public and Academy voters, who awarded it nine Oscars, including Best Picture. Its achievement is undeniable, and if it is studied and heartless these are qualities not alien to the subject, for Gigi, after all, is a little girl being trained to be a *poule de grand luxe*. The only interests of its characters are money, gossip and *l'amour*, in that order, and when the film was praised for its charm, it was the charm of a Paris motivated by three ruling

passions – by money, gossip and *l'amour*. Lerner's screenplay, based on Colette's story, attempts Wildean epigrams ('Bad table manners, my dear Gigi, have broken more households than infidelity'), but, as usual, his lyrics are smart; Loewe's music mines the same Viennese seam he used for 'My Fair Lady' – less melodically, but efficient in context. Cecil Beaton's costumes and decor are exquisite, and graceful use is made of the Palais de Glace, Maxim's and the Bois: the piece evokes the painters and writers of the era, so that Gigi in the Bois is Proust's Albertine, and the beach scenes are Boudin. Attempting all this has defeated Minnelli, who misses when he strives for insouciance in 'The Night They Invented Champagne'. Filming in Paris was fraught with difficulties, and when he remained there to work on another film, Walters re-shot in Hollywood a number of scenes which had been disliked at previews. Leslie Caron is the most adorable of little girls, and Louis Jourdan's wooden good looks blend into the fabric of the whole; the major asset is Maurice Chevalier, a practised charmer in such situations – and it was significant to observers of the musical form that he was the only real singer in the cast and though Caron can dance, she was not called upon to do so (and her singing was dubbed).

The film proved to be the one exception to the industry rule that the public would only 'buy' film versions of Broadway hits – a rule typically self-protective and self-

Gigi was the final triumph of Freed and Minnelli – at least statistically, for it made a lot of money and won a fistful of Oscars. However, some of it seemed forced, and the sum was less than the parts – the latter notably including a nostalgic duet for Hermione Gingold and Maurice Chevalier, 'I Remember It Well'.

deceptive, since audiences had liked both *Seven Brides* and *Funny Face*. M-G-M laid claim to one Broadway success, **Bells Are Ringing** (1960), because the book was by Comden and Green. It is a daffy piece about a meddling telephonist, and was written for their old colleague, Judy Holliday (1922–65), with lyrics by Sammy Cahn and an excellent score by Jules Styne. Both Cahn and Comden have said that the film should have been much better, and Cahn said of the leading man, Dean Martin, 'He blew it away.' They should have got a better singer or a better actor.' The CinemaScope camera sits before obvious sets, recording too-broad performances, and as we watch them we may decide that the real culprits are Freed and Minnelli. After the failure of *Kismet*, they should have realised the pitfalls of playing to non-existent footlights. In that film at least there were vestiges of Minnelli's penchant for smart decor and his ability to handle ambitious numbers, but the big ones here are reduced to dowdiness – while three of Holliday's best numbers in the show have gone. She was unhappy during filming, and wanted to buy herself out – and she is certainly badly treated on screen, coiffured and dressed as no telephonist ever was. That she remains marvellous is no credit to anyone but herself.

Minnelli directed no more musicals for M-G-M, while Freed spent the last years of his life planning *Say It with Music*, to have been built round Irving Berlin's songs, a project which was cancelled during the several changes of management in the late Sixties. Edens was Associate Producer on what are, in effect, the last M-G-M musicals, **Billy Rose's Jumbo** (1962) and **The Unsinkable Molly Brown** (1964), both directed by Charles Walters, getting the utmost from the material, and both at times worthy of the heyday – especially in the production numbers for *Jumbo* (Billy Rose managed to get his name in the title because he had presented the original show on Broadway). This has a Rodgers and Hart score, and because of its circus setting had been at first bought by Freed as a possible follow-up to *Annie Get Your Gun*; the project was resurrected because Doris Day, then the reigning box-office queen, had indicated that she would like to sing again and owed a commitment to M-G-M. She is fine, but Stephen Boyd, an exceptionally dreary leading man, sinks the enterprise. The powers that be, however, decided that the film failed because audiences did not want to see Day in musicals and *Molly Brown*, bought for her, went to Debbie Reynolds. Miss Reynolds throws herself about like a dervish, clowning, singing, dancing, and even emoting heavily, but is as interesting as a slice of stale angel cake. This time there is a stalwart leading man, Harve Presnell, but the fortunes of the piece, as on Broadway, were not increased by a banal score by Meredith Willson, who had seen in the leading character, a late nineteenth-century eccentric, a promising subject to follow his success with 'The Music Man' (the film, q.v.).

The M-G-M musical had really died with *Bells Are Ringing*, and it was an unexpected way to go – mishandling an above-average Broadway show and its star. It is sad to reflect that Freed and Minnelli, responsible for so many triumphs in the musical field, should have seemed with that project as tired as any of the hacks who had ever toiled in Hollywood's poverty row. No excuses have ever been forthcoming, nor, I think, could there be. All the great and good things had been done, and all the good things in this particular Broadway show had been copied from M-G-M musicals – which is surely why Minnelli showed so little interest in transferring them to the screen. His influence, and that of Kelly, would continue to be felt: there would be half a dozen goodish musicals in the decade to come. They would not, however, have Kelly, or Garland, or Astaire.

27

Postwar Hollywood:
The Directors in Their Brave New World

THE FILM-MAKERS who had served in the War returned to California very much changed. They had discovered honesty and reality, and they wanted to make films that were honest and real. William Wyler had served in Europe and had also made two documentaries on the Air Force's contribution to the War, *The Memphis Belle* and *Thunderbolt*. He found the subject of **The Best Years of Our Lives** (1946) in a verse novel by MacKinley Kantor, which he asked Goldwyn to buy – though the publicity maintained that the idea came from Goldwyn himself and Mrs Goldwyn. Its subject is service veterans readjusting to civilian life, and the first half hour remains moving, especially the sequences involving the young sailor amputee – a role played by Harold Russell, who had lost his hands, and whose only previous acting experience was in an army documentary. (In the original story, the character was a spastic on the verge of alcoholism, but Wyler considered that a spastic was both too difficult and too easy to portray.)

A film which offers such a situation is not spun of the usual web of dreams and there are impressive passages: the sergeant (Fredric March) discovering that his children have grown up while he was away; the bombardier (Dana Andrews) becoming disillusioned with the wife (Virginia Mayo) he knew for only twenty days. She sings in the usual Hollywood-sized night club and like the sergeant's wife (Myrna Loy) is positioned to catch the highlights on her face and well-coiffed hair; the sergeant – a bank teller in civilian life – lives in a mansion-sized apartment, indicating that Wyler's desire for honesty and reality was either insufficient or curtailed by Goldwyn. The film, in any case, settles for triteness – as when the sailor rejects his fiancée because he fears pity, a situation already used in the British film *The Captive Heart* (q.v.); and it is hard to believe, for instance, that the bombardier, reduced to his old job of soda-jerking, would be sacked for defending the amputee in an argument with a civilian blowhard.

Few reservations were expressed at the time and the film was widely received as proof of the new maturity expected of Hollywood. It won seven Oscars, including Best Picture, Best Direction and Best Screenplay (Robert E. Sherwood), and there can be no doubt that it spoke more directly to Americans than any film yet made. After the turmoil of war it was encouraging to find that the country had not changed – if only in the Hollywood scale of things.

Frank Capra also offered reassurance, reiterating his vision of America in **It's a Wonderful Life** (1945). He had spent the war years on a series of documentaries called *Why We Fight*, and this new film was intended to be an extension of the arguments put forward in those documentaries, as it hymns a regular guy (James Stewart) saved from suicide by a guardian angel and his nursery version of Donne, *viz.* 'Remember no man is a failure who has friends' and 'Each man's life touches some other lives.' Capra found his fable on a Christmas card, where it was called 'The Greatest Gift', and R.K.O. had already commissioned several other (unused) scripts – since by coincidence it owned the poem. To his delight, it was offered to Capra – who is credited with the screenplay with Albert Hackett, Frances Goodrich and Jo Swerling. According to his

Postwar Hollywood: The Directors in Their Brave New World

memoirs, he considered the result not only his best film, 'but the greatest anybody ever made' – and it remains his (and Stewart's) favourite. But critics and public liked it much less than Wyler's more topical treatise, not appreciating their similarities – for both kept intact the myth of an America that was cosy, understanding and loving. Capra borrowed situations from his earlier films too readily (John Doe's contemplated suicide, Mr Deeds's 'sharing out'); the film was old fashioned, and whimsy was at odds with the postwar mood – which accounts for its failure. In Europe, and especially in Italy, film-makers were reasserting the central belief of the realistic film, that the meek shall not inherit the earth – a view untenable in Hollywood, even if already tentatively expressed by Preston Sturges. Capra certainly was not making a realistic film, though he too was trying to indict the system, with one man's restored idealism shown as the only alternative to the evils of capitalism. The latter is represented by a honky-tonk town of dives and strip joints, which, apart from the assumption that ordinary people disapprove of booze and sex, demonstrates a failure by Capra and his hero to face up to the world. This particular sequence is an antidote to the sweetness and light of the rest of the film. As the good time girl turned whore Gloria Grahame is virtually the only Hollywood player allowed to be explicitly so since the tightening of the Hays Code in 1934.* The prevarications at the heart of the film are the more insidious because it is so entertaining and beautifully crafted; it has a superb cast, and James Stewart was the best possible choice to play Mr Goody Two-Shoes.

Capra had returned from the War more than ever imbued with the idea of 'one man, one film', convinced that the public was hankering for quality after the 'anything goes' policy of the industry during the war years. Since the three most successful films in more than a generation – *Gone with the Wind*, *The Bells of St Mary's* and *The Best Years of Our Lives* – had each been produced by an independent, almost every Hollywood figure of importance

was forming his own company. With Samuel Briskin as secretary-treasurer, Capra had formed Liberty Films, and Wyler and George Stevens were invited to join, each with autonomy as producer-directors; a deal was made with R.K.O. for nine films, with facilities to be advanced in exchange for distribution rights. When, in industry terms, *It's a Wonderful Life* was 'less than a smash', R.K.O. baulked at the high budget ($2,800,000) of **State of the Union** (1948), which Capra intended for Gary Cooper. M-G-M, however, picked up the project because Spencer Tracy coveted the leading role, an aircraft tycoon, chosen as presidential candidate by a Republican newspaper proprietor (Angela Lansbury). He deceived himself that he can win, despite the political chicanery of his sponsors and their opposition to such demands as universal Medicare, more housing and more internationalism. As written by Anthony Veiller and Myles Connolly, the film is witty and apparently sharper than the original Pulitzer Prize-winning play by Howard Lindsay and Russell Crouse; it has little remarkable to say about political immorality, but on that subject a restatement of the obvious is always welcome.† Tracy's final stand, reunited with his estranged wife (Katharine Hepburn), may echo other Capra dénouements, but the film is a fresh departure for Capra and proof, despite the weaknesses in the material, that he believed in 'worthwhile' subjects.

The volatile public mood had again veered towards escapism and though it was ready to accept a number of 'serious' films, the reception for this one proved little warmer than for other political films in the past. The wind blew bitterly towards Liberty, and a decision was made to sell the company to Paramount, with the properties it had acquired and the services of its directors. Stevens was against the deal and was proposing to join Leo McCarey, when he discovered that McCarey was also considering the sale of his company to Paramount. The disintegration of Liberty was undoubtedly regarded by the studio bosses with

*The Hays administration finished in 1945, and the Breen Office, as it then became known, was later officially titled the Motion Picture Association of America or M.P.A.A. Hereafter I shall refer to it as such, and to the Hays Code by its official designation, the Production Code.

†I saw it at the height of the Watergate scandal, and Tracy's line, 'I forgot how quickly the American people smell out double-dealers and crooks,' brought a prolonged round of applause.

682

satisfaction. Others who surrendered their independence at this time, after virtually only one film apiece, included Fritz Lang, Mervyn LeRoy, the Cagney brothers, Frank Borzage, Garson and Michael Kanin, and Gary Cooper. Wyler and Stevens settled in at Paramount, but Capra, in his own words, 'drank the hemlock of champions: the bitter, souring realisation that part of what made [me] great was dying'. The loss of his independence was made even more painful by an edict from Barney Balaban, the studio's head, that no film should cost more than $1½ million. Balaban could point to the fact that attendance figures in the U.S. had dropped from eighty million patrons weekly in 1946 (an all-time high) to only sixty-two million in 1948, but we may suspect a certain wish to humiliate the fugitives now once again under control.

Among the properties Capra could not make for the required sum were several which became successful for other directors – *Roman Holiday* (q.v.), *Friendly Persuasion* (q.v.), *Westward the Women* and *A Woman of Distinction*. He thought a new version of *Broadway Bill* could be kept within the budget – though that is why **Riding High** (1950) has a rather inadequate leading lady. He had had reservations about the original, because Warner Baxter had been afraid of horses, and Bing Crosby, who loved them, was, like himself, under contract to Paramount. Since Crosby was the more ingratiating actor, the result, as Capra claims, is an improvement, with Crosby's songs fitting easily into Robert Riskin's original screenplay, kept more or less intact. In their original roles are Raymond Walburn, Margaret Hamilton, Clarence Muse, Douglas Dumbrille, Ward Bond and Frankie Darro, while what Capra called 'the greatest collection of time-saving, sure-fire entertainers ever assembled in one film' also includes Charles Bickford, James Gleason and Oliver Hardy.

A warm reception did nothing to alleviate Capra's unhappiness. He was offered **Here Comes the Groom** (1951), another Crosby vehicle, and took it, intending a spectacularly entertaining swan song. He should have scrapped the opening (as he did with *Lost Horizon*), where Crosby sings to a bunch of orphans in Paris something about hanging 'the dreams you want

as pictures on the wall'. Once Crosby arrives in the U.S. to recapture his ex-fiancée (Jane Wyman) the fun is lively – and it includes 'In the Cool, Cool, Cool of the Evening', as sung by them strolling round an office desk and down into the street. The number sparkles, which Capra thought partly due to his refusal to pre-record the songs, then a long-standing practice; it makes one regret that he never attempted a real musical. He made no further fiction films for a decade, working much of that time on scientific documentaries for the government.

Meanwhile, Wyler took years to find a subject to follow *The Best Years of Our Lives*, and in contemplating its lack of contemporary relevance it should be borne in mind that at that time versatility was an even more prized quality. **The Heiress** (1949) is a faithful version of Henry James's 'Washington Square', as written by Ruth and Augustus Goetz from their own Broadway adaptation. The story is theatrical – the shy, clumsy Catherine (Olivia de Havilland) is courted by a man (Montgomery Clift) whom her father (Ralph Richardson) believes is a fortune hunter – and so are the effects: she waits for the carriage that never comes, and slowly puts out the lights at the end. The crisp, ironic lines which punctuate an already good text – 'Father, talk to him about me – you know me so well, it will not be immodest of you to praise me a little,' and 'Cruel? You forget, aunt, I have been taught by masters' – require master players, and Richardson, cold, gently ironic, self-centred and unfeeling, never gave a better performance. The role of Catherine has many subtleties – for example, the possibility of her knowing that Morris is rotten, and not caring since her real aim is to get away from her father – and Miss de Havilland won an Oscar for it; she is particularly good in the later scenes, where uncertainty has hardened into a never defined vindictiveness. She was, I think, greatly helped by Wyler, whose usual quest for perfection caused him to exceed the Hollywood average of takes per shot – but his attention to detail helps to make this an enduring entertainment. He could do little with the far too modern Clift (q.v.), who is not a man you could ever imagine buying real chamois gloves.

Wyler changed genres again with

Detective Story (1951), also adapted from a Broadway success – of the genus 'Street Scene', in which audiences are invited to witness a series of actions in a supposedly realistic milieu. Adapted by Philip Yordan from Sidney Kingsley's play about life in a police precinct, this was stale stuff even then; Kirk Douglas is a tough detective who has to cope with a couple of burglars, a shoplifter (Lee Grant), a suspected abortionist (George Macready) and his own, hysterical wife (Eleanor Parker). The complete absence of background music was considered an asset at the time.

Returning to period drama, Wyler made **Carrie** (1952) mainly for the opportunity to portray an interesting time in American history. Hollywood had long flirted with Theodore Dreiser's novel, but had hesitated, since its protagonist is a loose woman who suffers no retribution after one man has ruined himself because of her. The screenplay by the Goetzes makes Carrie (Jennifer Jones) reluctant to become a kept woman and at the end she feels such remorse that she searches for Hurstwood (Laurence Olivier) in the hope of taking care of him. Dreiser wrote of the new, teeming cities, and of the girls seduced by carriages and restaurants, so much to be preferred to damp tenements and tramways, but Wyler, whatever his motives, has merely made a version of All for Love, or the World Well Lost – yet this, because of Olivier, is a moving document. His Hurstwood is elegantly mannered and attired, with only an occasional pinched look to indicate an unhappy marriage: when he meets Carrie he reacts like a thoroughbred puppy, but his sadness returns fleetingly when he is not with her. Technically, this actor is always a marvel, revealing Hurstwood's degradation by the slope of the shoulders, a pulled down Homburg, and unkempt moustache and blank, dead eyes. In the generally dire reviews this great performance was noticed by only a few critics – and did nothing to prevent box-office failure, for audiences, if occasionally approving of sad endings, tend to avoid films which move downhill all the way. That fact further emphasises the novel's limitations as screen material: to say that they are not overcome and that this is, nevertheless, one of Wyler's best pictures is to demonstrate his position among film-makers. Like Dreiser himself, he is a first-rate artisan; and though his attachment to verisimilitude, to the details of the commonplace and the minutiae of personal behaviour sometimes blinds him to the larger passions, he cared greatly for both his stories and the intelligence of his audience.*

Of the three Liberty directors, George Stevens took the longest to return to work; when he did, it was on loan to R.K.O., which owned a popular play which he wanted to film. This was **I Remember Mama** (1948), which John Van Druten had adapted from a memoir by Kathryn Forbes about her Norwegian family. Van Druten was too old a hand to persuade himself that the material was fresh, but no one was more adept at artfully presenting everyday activities in a way which would delight Broadway audiences. There are no family eccentrics – with the possible exception of fearsome Uncle Chris (Oscar Homolka); father is neither lovable drunk nor improvident inventor and there is no juvenile romance. Rightly, therefore, the qualities which Stevens brings are also negative – reticence and discretion; the result is arguably the least cloying family film since *Meet Me in St Louis*. It has charm, inevitably, since Mama is played by Irene Dunne. Barbara Bel Geddes is the girl remembering, and her well-scrubbed face is as pleasing as anything in movies. Also refreshing are the views of San Francisco, with its clapboard houses and steep streets with the cable cars sweeping up and down, while women climb the hills slowly, the wind ruffling their hair and feather boas. Stevens otherwise uses the standard 'quality' approach to stage material – one large set comprising all the cluttered rooms, and a mobile camera to follow the family from one to another.

Thus did Hollywood's brave new world offer sentimental valentines to the American past. On the other hand, George Stevens's **A Place in the Sun** (1951) was considered an important film in America, and it was thought significant when Chaplin, in a rare public statement, pronounced it 'the best film ever to come out of Hollywood'. It went on to win four Oscars, including Best Direction and Best Screenplay from Another Source – the source

*Wyler later cited this film as one he regretted making 'because it didn't make a penny'.

being Theodore Dreiser's 'An American Tragedy'. The story has been reset in the present and, like Wyler's treatment of this writer, has been reduced to a 'tragic' love story. Moreover, this adaptation sins even more grievously, for in removing Clyde's antecedents, and therefore his reasons for wanting a place in the sun, it also does away with all of Dreiser's comments on materialism. Montgomery Clift as Clyde – renamed George Eastman – is both the film's greatest asset and biggest liability. He plays with intensity and sensitivity, a rare combination in American actors at this time, but he suggests neither a seducer nor a pushy young man: if the American tragedy is a will to succeed at all costs, including murder, then this lugubrious film is not an example of it.

The most interesting change makes the victim shrill instead of stupid, though in the performance of Shelley Winters she remains pathetic; as the rich girl for whom she is dumped, Elizabeth Taylor suggests one of no intellect at all. In the book she refuses to have anything more to do with Clyde after the murder, but here she turns up in prison in a chic outfit to assure him that she will always love him – while to Franz Waxman's relentless and swelling 'love-theme', close-ups of their kisses are superimposed over the image of his face as he walks to the Chair. Abroad, the film was at least admired for its visual style, but in fact the slow dissolves and cunning use of shadow were derived from von Sternberg's long-unseen version of this tale, as Stevens privately acknowledged. Had the film adhered to the spirit of the novel, the M.P.A.A. need not have worried so much about the situation of sex outside marriage: this was permitted for the sake of 'art' and Hollywood maturity, and the film's reception did in fact result in further relaxations.★

Among the younger directors permitted a certain choice of material was Billy

★Up to this time, the situation had, as if statistically, been limited to one film a year, and then only when germane to the plot, as in (q.v.) *The Sea of Grass*, *To Each His Own* and *Letter from an Unknown Woman*, each of which is set in the past, when supposedly different values prevailed – but even so assumed merely one lapse, and the woman clearly suffers because of it. *Johnny Belinda* (q.v.) concerns a rape, and *Not Wanted* an unmarried mother: the M.P.A.A. recognised serious purpose in both films, and the latter, an independent, low-budget film, was thought likely to pass unnoticed by sensation-seekers – as indeed happened. Cases where audiences presumed illicit sexual relations were, of course, something else again.

Wilder, also at Paramount, and that was because of **The Lost Weekend** (1945), a project for which he and his producer and co-writer, Charles Brackett, had overcome front office opposition. It went on to win the chief Oscars – Best Picture, Best Direction, Best Screenplay/Adaptation and Best Actor – and was widely regarded as one of the films which helped Hollywood grow up. Certainly it is one of the rare dramas of the period which may be taken as seriously now as then. Agee thought it 'unusually hard, tense, cruel, intelligent and straightforward', but we would agree with him that it does not enter deeply enough into the world of the alcoholic, failing to examine the hurt caused by the majority of alcoholics. In Charles Jackson's novel, an attempt was made to probe into the childhood of Don Birnam (Ray Milland), and the conclusion was drawn that his trouble was caused by a refusal to accept homosexual tendencies; Wilder and Brackett settled for the most obvious censor-free motivation, that he is a writer without inspiration. Since writers are prone to drink, it is a good premise, though we are not encouraged to believe that the talent is a major one – nor does Milland suggest a character basically flawed. Certain sequences remain unsurpassed – the trudge along Third Avenue trying to sell the typewriter, the theft of the handbag, the exchanges with the sour bartender (Howard da Silva). Wilder had insisted on the then rare luxury of New York locations, and audiences were impressed by the sight of an apartment that was for once small and cluttered.

Turning about, Wilder decided to emulate his idol, Lubitsch, and **The Emperor Waltz** (1948) has a delicious framing device and a role for Joan Fontaine modelled on the young Jeanette MacDonald – that of a countess, prim at first, who succumbs to an uncontrollable passion for the leading man. He (Bing Crosby) is no Chevalier, so Brackett and Wilder have given him a randy mongrel who sexually assaults the countess's prize poodle – which at this time was somewhat outrageous. The studio shelved the film for over a year, even though Crosby was its leading box-office star. Wilder was actually too sophisticated to make a vehicle suitable for this actor, and the film, little liked when it appeared, is hardly more likeable now.

685

Three lost Hollywood souls in Billy Wilder's *Sunset Boulevard*: Gloria Swanson as the forgotten Silent star dreaming of a comeback, William Holden, centre, as the screenwriter who accepts her hospitality as the bailiffs close in, and Erich Von Stroheim as her one-time director, now her chauffeur, who writes the fan letters she still expects to receive daily. Holden looks uncomfortable, for heroes even in Wilder films were not expected to become gigolos.

It is doubtful whether many today would agree with Agee that much of **A Foreign Affair** (1948) is 'in rotten taste'. Wilder laid his comedy among the ruins of Berlin, and a jeep speeds through them as the soundtrack offers 'Isn't it Romantic?'. At the Brandenburg Gate, the troops are engaged in activities unthinkable on Main Street, such as purchasing each girl in sight with one candy bar or a pack of Camels. It was not until the arrival of Preston Sturges that the American film had satirised others than the rich and famous: Wilder was to go much further, and this study of the occupying armies and the defeated is his first flowering. 'Sometimes I wonder whether it wasn't a waste of money to import eleven thousand ping-pong tables for you men,' says the General (Millard Mitchell), reprimanding the hero (John Lund) for his affair with a singer (Marlene Dietrich); and after explaining to a committee of visiting congressmen that four million Displaced Persons had been resettled, he adds that on the day the gas was reconnected there were 160 suicides. Wilder and his co-writers Brackett and Richard L. Breen also refurbish the cliché of the plain jane who takes off her glasses and falls in love – in which role Jean Arthur takes top billing, the man and the film from Dietrich.

Its topicality was not much admired, as that was not then considered a requirement of the American screen, despite recent suc-

cesses such as *Mrs Miniver* and *The Best Years of Our Lives* – not to mention the excitement currently engendered by the Italian cinema. Indeed, Wilder's greatest critical success to date was set in a Hollywood even less in touch than usual with the contemporary world or indeed anywhere but itself. **Sunset Boulevard** (1950) begins with a body in a pool, and the body tells the story. He (William Holden) is just another minor screenwriter in a sports jacket, fleeing the bailiffs – after which Hollywood fact Hollywood fantasy takes over, as he finds refuge in the mansion of a dotty and singularly humourless Silent picture queen, Norma Desmond (Gloria Swanson). 'You were big once,' he says irreverently. 'I am BIG,' she replies, 'it's the pictures that got smaller.' She dreams of a comeback, but hates 'that word. It's a return – a return to the people who've never forgiven me for deserting them.' She has written a script, 'Salome': 'They'll love it in Pomona,' he observes, to be interrupted with 'They'll love it everyplace.' She projects for him her old movies (among them *Queen Kelly*, one of the few Swanson Silents not made by Paramount, but directed by Von Stroheim, here playing the butler); plays bridge with cronies (Buster Keaton, H. B. Warner and Anna Q. Nilsson); the young man stays and they tango on the floor where Valentino danced. 'As long as the lady's paying,' says the tailor's salesclerk, and for an instant Wilder's subtlety deserts him. 'Twenty press-agents working overtime can do terrible things to the human soul,' says Cecil B. deMille, as himself, recalling that at seventeen Norma had 'more courage and wit and heart than you could possibly imagine', but in the film she is always pathetic. If Holden merely suggests an all-American boy going to seed, Swanson is magnificent, assuming the gestures associated with the Silent screen but vulnerable beneath the snake-like exterior and imperious manner. The woman is a shell; under the bombast there is nothing but hurt. She is not of the stature of Lady Macbeth or Cleopatra – and similarly the movie is classic but not a masterpiece. It has dated only in the most perfunctory way; and its strongest quality, permeating the entire film, is its veneration for an earlier age of motion pictures.

The screenplay was written by Brackett

and Wilder (with D.M. Marshman Jr) and the severance of their partnership at this point was not connected with the film's commercial failure. It was, nevertheless, unexpected – at least by Brackett, who moved to 20th Century-Fox and never recovered from the break. Wilder chose Lesser Samuels and Walter Newman as his co-writers on **Ace in the Hole** (1951), sometimes known as *The Big Carnival*; it was rechristened after its initial failure – a failure that again was gratifying to those who regarded Wilder as attacking their professional ethics. The profession in this case was journalism, and there were few good reviews. Unbiased critics recognised it as one of a number of superior films then being made which combined the thriller form with a glancing thrust at American society: in this, with the exception of a newspaper proprietor (Porter Hall), everyone is avaricious, particularly one journalist (Kirk Douglas). Learning that a garage man has been trapped in a cave-in, he turns it to his advantage. The facts of the film are reminiscent of the Floyd Collins case of 1925 (Collins had won a Pulitzer Prize for his coverage of a mine disaster). Among other things, the journalist persuades the victim's bored, sluttish wife (Jan Sterling) to remain at the site. 'I met a lot of hard-boiled eggs in my time, but you, you're twenty minutes,' she says, and as much might be said of the touts and hucksters who flock in to prey on the tourists.

Only a mite less misanthropic is **Stalag 17** (1953), which was much liked only in the U.S., where the Broadway original – by Donald Bevan and Edmund Trzcinski – had prepared audiences for a view of P.O.W.s which found them anything but noble. As in *A Foreign Affair*, the soldiery are a conniving bunch, headed by Sefton (William Holden), who runs a black-market trade and appears to be in cahoots with the Germans. Wilder likes the film as much as any he has made, 'perhaps because there were eight minutes which were any good' – and he may be thinking of the Christmas party, where the men dance together; he liked to ignore Hollywood taboos and he does so on this occasion with wondrous tact. In the matter of taste, there is also the one-legged prisoner who stores contraband in his empty pants-leg – further compensation for the soft ending,

a fault only avoided in Wilder's films of this period by *Sunset Boulevard*.

Sabrina (1954) is soft to start with, and Wilder chose it as his last film for Paramount because it gave him a chance to direct Audrey Hepburn. Its source is a comedy by Samuel Taylor, apparently influenced by *Sunny Side Up*, and as written for the screen by the two of them, with Ernest Lehman, it has ideas of democracy as naive as the fairy tale which surrounds them. As Sabrina, the chauffeur's daughter, Broadway audiences had loved Margaret Sullavan, and Miss Hepburn is just as enchanting, with grace and a sombre, little-girl intensity. That she attempts suicide in an eight-car garage is a typical Wilder touch, as is the younger scion (Holden) having the debris of champagne glasses picked from his rear. Humphrey Bogart, playing the elder son, disliked both players, Wilder and the film; he is too old for his role, and though too good an actor to be miscast, this was not his finest hour. When the piece came out, it seemed too long and big for its frail little tale, but it pleases intermittently today.

Among other directors pleasing audiences – if less often – was John Ford, who fulfilled his commitment to 20th Century-Fox with a Western, **My Darling Clementine** (1946), notable mainly for Henry Fonda's tight-lipped performance as Wyatt Earp, though the relationship with Doc Holliday – mistrust ripening into cagey friendship – would be more interesting with a better actor than Victor Mature. That relationship is based on one in *The Westerner*, as is the barn-dance sequence; and in returning to the Western for only the second time since the Silent days, Ford also borrowed from Renoir's *The Southerner*. **The Fugitive** (1947), another of his attempts at the Great American Art film, was influenced by Eisenstein's Mexican material – though the photographer, Gabriel Figueroa, may be exonerated, since his later work for Buñuel has none of the pretension apparent on this occasion. The screenplay by Ford and Dudley Nichols follows its source, Graham Greene's 'The Power and the Glory', and succeeds now and again on the level of elementary suspense. Dolores del Rio is allowed Madonna close-ups which are more spectacularly lit than those in all the churches in Rome. She is not, as in the Greene novel,

687

John Ford directed many excellent movies, but he was also as opportunist as any who ever toiled in the Hollywood vineyards, making a number of disastrously arty films and then, when they failed, incorporating 'Fordian' sequences in his more honest enterprises. He did not coin the adjective, but when certain admirers drew attention to aspects of his work, he repeated them for effect – rewardingly in, say, the recreation of a certain atmosphere, but foolishly, as in the repetition of funeral sequences. One such appeared in the otherwise splendid She Wore a Yellow Ribbon with, in the foreground, Ben Johnson, John Wayne and Frank McGrath.

living with the priest (Fonda), nor would the M.P.A.A. allow him to be alcoholic – which eliminates any point in making the film. The retention of the original ending is nullified by the standard of the whole (an alternative 'happy' ending still precedes Greene's conclusion in the final print) and though Mexico is credited for providing production facilities, the story is no longer set there. Whatever religious or political pressures were put on Ford, he himself claimed that 'It came out the way I wanted it to – that's why it's one of my favourite pictures – to me, it was perfect.'

Critics and public thought otherwise and the film was a dismal beginning for Argosy, the independent company Ford had formed with Merian C. Cooper, with whom he had worked at R.K.O., which distributed the film. Its failure, and the arrival of Howard Hughes as boss, caused Cooper to make an agreement with Republic, whose owner, Herbert J. Yates, used the company mainly to promote to stardom Vera Hruba Ralston, whom he later married. Since My Darling Clementine had confirmed renewed popularity for the Western, Ford concentrated almost exclusively on that genre for Republic – and indeed for the rest of his career. His Westerns of this period, underrated then and subsequently overvalued, are nevertheless – with the exception of The Grapes of Wrath – his most enduring films. Heroes are good

for the nation, he observed, and these films are tributes to the pioneers. You will not find an authentic portrait of the Old West, and you may be disappointed by the puppet-like characters (why else would he have used Maureen O'Hara?), by the gleaming neatness, and by the 'Sons of the Pioneers' singing on the soundtrack. Many spectators see only the clichés and the mawkishness. His expositions are often weak, his climaxes careless, and his situations – reflective of sentiment, camaraderie and dalliance – often ritualistic.

Fort Apache (1948), written by Frank S. Nugent from a story by James Warner Bellah, is a Cavalry vs. Indians tale, set in a stockade in Monument Valley commanded by a Patton-like Fonda; John Wayne is his second-in-command, Pedro Armendariz the Spanish-speaking sergeant and Shirley Temple and John Agar the tiresome juveniles. **Three Godfathers** (1948) was made by Argosy for M-G-M, which owned the rights, having done the last of the four previous versions in 1936; Ford himself had made one of these in 1919, with Harry Carey, to whom the 1948 version is dedicated. Harry Carey Jr is in this film, with Wayne and Armendariz, and they are three bank robbers lumbered with a baby in the Mojave desert. The naivety and Christian symbolism belong to an earlier age, but it is a film to be experienced, as filmed on unearthly locations by Winton C. Hoch, in colour – Ford's second venture in that process. Hoch's Technicolor photography for **She Wore a Yellow Ribbon** (1949) was based on Remington, and won an Academy Award, but the story by Nugent and Laurence Stallings, again from a novel by Bellah, is of less interest. As the Indian-fighter captain, nearing retirement age, Wayne is an asset, but the reverse is true again of the juveniles – Agar, Carey Jr and Joanne Dru – and you must be Ford-indulgent to enjoy the shenanigans of Victor McLaglen as the fist-happy, softhearted and hard-drinking Sergeant Quincannon, a character common to several films in this group.

When Willie Comes Marching Home (1950), an assignment at 20th Century-Fox, concerns a small town boy (Dan Dailey) who becomes a local hero when he is the first to enlist, only to become an object of scorn when he fails to get an overseas posting; as written by Mary

Loos and Richard Sale from a story by Sy Gomberg, this is a long way after *Hail the Conquering Hero* and Ford's not dissimilar comedies with Will Rogers – and, except for William Demarest as the boy's father, indifferently cast.

Ford himself provided the self-indulgent storyline of **Wagonmaster** (1950), which concerns two horse-traders (Carey Jr, Ben Johnson) taken on by a Mormon leader (Ward Bond) to guide a wagon train heading West. **Rio Grande** (1950), together with *Fort Apache* and *She Wore a Yellow Ribbon*, is said to complete Ford's cavalry trilogy, and the setting is once more Monument Valley at the end of the Civil War. Wayne is again in command and again untypically moustached (seemingly a badge of office for those in charge in Ford's films), coping with Indians, an estranged wife (O'Hara), and a son (Claude Jarman Jr) expelled from West Point.

However, the ambivalence we feel towards Ford's writers does not extend to his superb photographers – not only Hoch, but Bert Glennon and Archie Stout, either individually or in pairs – or to Wayne, who was seldom more authoritative and relaxed. Despite the occasional presence of Wayne, who was finally achieving huge popularity after almost twenty years in films, all these movies were at best middling successes at the box office, or, in the cases of *Three Godfathers* and *Wagonmaster*, outright failures – as was a remake of the Silent **What Price Glory?** (1952) at 20th Century-Fox with James Cagney and Dan Dailey. It was planned as a musical, but Ford declined to use the score – which could only have improved it.

He felt no such inhibitions about the soundtrack itself of his films, and **The Quiet Man** (1952) pounds away with every overfamiliar Irish air. Ford, observed Richard Winnington, 'enthusiastically joins the great company which, aided by the Irish themselves, insists on viewing Ireland's aimlessness, poverty and disease through a mist of begorras and blarney . . . this must be the work of any good Hollywood hack.' Elsewhere, astonishingly, it was called 'Shakespearian' (by Lindsay Anderson in *Sight and Sound*), presumably because it attempts the lyrical and has recognisably Irish versions of Beatrice, Benedick and Dogberry. Even a better

film would have been ruined by these studio exteriors, and close-ups which jar with their surrounding shots. Ford is unhappily trapped between a misty-eyed obsession with the auld country and the quest for a heroic concept such as he had already attempted in *The Informer* and *The Fugitive*. Most of the cast is Irish distilled in Hollywood, including McLaglen as the squire, Barry Fitzgerald, and Ward Bond and Arthur Shields as rival priests. Only Wayne is at ease as an American returning to his native land to woo a pre-Raphaelite O'Hara, for whom he engages in a donnybrook borrowed from *The Spoilers*.

That battle was instrumental in the film becoming the biggest success in the twenty-five-year existence of Republic (which abandoned production in 1957, with Miss Hruba Ralston as far from popularity as ever). Ford followed it with a 'little' picture – a policy, he claimed, which enabled him to relax. **The Sun Shines Bright** (1953) is a return to the 'Judge Priest' stories, of which three were gathered into a screenplay by Stallings. Ford later cited it with *The Fugitive* and *Wagonmaster* as 'coming closest to what I wanted to achieve', and it certainly demonstrates his handling of mood and composition; it also resembles rather closely other Ford films but not much, as usual, real life. Among several strands of plot is one where the judge (Charles Winninger) coolly turns away a mob hunting a black boy accused of insulting a white girl; in another he arranges for a madam 'a funeral with all the trimmings', though it puts his re-election in jeopardy – and virtually the only moment of genuine sensibility is that when her 'ladies', in black bombazine, sit upright in their carriage to counteract the indignation directed at them. The film was unsuccessful, but since it was 'personal' it endeared itself to those about to drag the *auteur* theory into film criticism. Ford was on the verge of achieving a recognition such as he had never known – and he was ready for it, growling out a macho, no-bull philosophy which, as with a number of American writers, contrasts with the inherent sentimentality of his work.

Alfred Hitchcock was another to benefit from the *auteur* theory. Aided by a 'concerto' by Miklos Rozsa and a dream sequence designed by Salvador Dali, he had another big success with **Spellbound**

(1945). He told a disappointed Truffaut, who admired the film, that it was 'just another manhunt story wrapped in pseudo-psychoanalysis', but in claiming to be the first to put psychiatry on the screen he clearly did not think of Pabst. Credited to Ben Hecht, from a novel by Francis Beeding, the screenplay is about an amnesiac (Gregory Peck) only able to clear himself of a suspected murder if he can recall his past – which he cannot do because of a traumatic incident in childhood. Leo G. Carroll is the head of the clinic, Ingrid Bergman is the doctor trying to help Peck, Rhonda Fleming is a nymphomaniac who hates men, and Wallace Ford a man in a hotel lobby who pesters Bergman sexually – understandably, we may feel. She, as so often, provides the main interest: a severe hairdo, glasses and a concentrated expression can neither hide her beauty nor suggest 'a dedicated scientist', but she admirably portrays a woman in love.

She is less convincing at the start of **Notorious** (1946), having turned to men and martinis because her father was a traitor – but the plot makes her atone when a government agent (Cary Grant) recruits her to infiltrate the household of one of her father's friends (Claude Rains). The relationship of the three has piquancy: Rains, the older man uncertain of his luck in getting a beautiful bride; Bergman, caught between love – for Grant – and duty; and Grant, deeply resenting the claims of the latter. Indeed, this is a classy example of the thriller, and its key sequence – Grant's stealing away from a reception to get into the wine cellar – is one of Hitchcock's finest essays in suspense. The two stars also have a kiss which broke records in screen length – and that, as its publicity-minded director intended, made the film very famous at the time.

It had been prepared by Hitchcock and Selznick, but was sold by Selznick before production to R.K.O. for $800,000 and half the profits – which were again considerable. The two men collaborated for the last time on **The Paradine Case** (1948), with a screenplay credited to Selznick. He had once persuaded M-G-M to buy Robert Hichens's novel as a vehicle for the Barrymore brothers and Diana Wynyard, later purchasing it himself for another star – but as one of his memos sadly states, 'Miss Garbo has always had an aversion to the story'. This film proves her to have been right: a happily-married lawyer (Peck) falls in love with his client (Alida Valli), believing in her innocence despite the enmity of her murdered husband's valet (Louis Jourdan), later revealed to be her lover. This is the sole enigma in a two-hour plod which stops abruptly when it is announced that the valet has done away with himself (in exactly those words) and the beautiful client confesses her guilt. Most of the cast is ill-equipped to breathe life into it: of the stars only Charles Laughton, as the judge, is good, and only Valli – whom Selznick fancied as a new Garbo – is forgivable, since it was only her second film in English. John Williams can be spotted in the courtroom, with never a line of dialogue : later, in *Dial 'M' for Murder* (q.v.) Hitchcock would give him his first major screen role – and we may suppose that had he thought (or been allowed) to cast him in the part played here by Peck, this would not be so unreservedly Hitchcock's own worst American film.

Despite its reception, Hitchcock was in a better situation than most to become independent, and he formed Transatlantic Pictures with Sydney Bernstein, an old acquaintance of his British days, head of the Granada circuit in the U.K. Preserving his autonomy and most of the profits, he supplied the talent and Bernstein the money; the subjects were chosen with special attention to the company's name. There is no other good reason why the action of **Rope** (1948) should have been transferred from Britain to the U.S., even if Patrick Hamilton's play had been inspired by the Leopold–Loeb murder case. As restaged in a palatial Manhattan penthouse, the piece loses much of its fetching grisliness – as well as (because of censorship) Hamilton's hints at the exact relationship of these degenerate young students (John Dall, Farley Granger) who 'killed for a thrill'. That the piece survives is due to the acting – though not that of James Stewart, miscast as the professor who guesses their horrible secret – and the dialogue: it is almost all dialogue. For this film, Hitchcock used the much-touted 'ten-minute take', purportedly to allow sequences to build to a dramatic climax. He assuredly had fun devising the camera movements, but otherwise the technique resembles that of the early Talkies – or of T.V. drama, with which audiences were then becoming familiar. In fact, the only thing that prevented the film from looking like television was Technicolor; and it is perhaps because of television that Hitchcock dropped the device after one more film.

This was **Under Capricorn** (1949), and the publicity 'push' was not the ten-minute take, but that he was returning to Britain with the biggest star of the time, Miss Bergman. Hitchcock's own attitude to this homecoming with Bergman he later categorised as 'childish', and it was presumably that which caused him to choose a subject suitable to neither – though the dramatist James Bridie, working from a novel by Helen Simpson, almost makes it work. The setting is Sydney in 1831, and as on past occasions the director is unhappy with a historical subject. Equally ill at ease are Joseph Cotten as Sam Flusky, ex-convict, and Bergman as his wife, an Irish aristocrat turned alcoholic. Since she attempts an Irish accent on top of her Swedish one, the casting is one of the reasons why people find this film preposterous. Margaret Leighton, as the evil housekeeper, drops one H in three – and reminds us of *Rebecca*, as does the crux of the film, when Bergman confesses that she is a murderess. The piece is not at all bad on such matters as ladies who marry beneath them and on the difficulties for a once-convicted man to acquire respect; there are also several sequences of the sort Hitchcock always does with relish (e.g. dinner parties) and, overall, we may find the result somewhat more enjoyable than contemporary opinion allowed.

Warner Bros. released both films, and their failure found Hitchcock working out a contract made directly with that company. He remained in Britain to make **Stage Fright** (1950), based on a novel by Selwyn Jepson, which he later admitted had attracted him only because several reviewers had observed it to be suitable for a Hitchcock film. A drama student (Jane Wyman) helps a man (Richard Todd), who tells her that an actress (Marlene Dietrich) has murdered her husband and involved him, whereupon she poses as a maid in order to investigate on his behalf. Hitchcock partly blamed Miss Wyman for the film's failure, claiming that she refused

to deglamorise herself for the impersonation – a remark which quite understandably bewildered that lady. In fact, the film has only two frail strands of suspense – when will the police put a stop to the girl's snooping and how long will it be before they discover that the actress is the real killer? More crucial to our disappointment is the fact that Hitchcock cheats. When Agatha Christie in an early mystery novel broke a similar rule, her audacity surprised her readers – but the camera should not lie, even in flashback. The suspect roles are uninteresting as rendered by Dietrich and Todd; Wyman and Michael Wilding, as the detective, are pleasing; Alistair Sim, as so often, brightens the proceedings – but when Truffaut told Hitchcock that he disliked the performance, Hitchcock replied, 'Here again is the trouble of shooting a film in England. They all tell you, "He's one of our best actors; you've got to have him in your picture." '

Strangers on a Train (1951) was the long-delayed return to form – and the plot at least is a classic one, written by Raymond Chandler and Czenzi Ormonde from a novel by Patricia Highsmith. On a train, Bruno (Robert Walker), wealthy mother's boy and psychopath, proposes to Guy (Farley Granger) that they exchange

Like John Ford, Alfred Hitchcock decided early on that he wanted to be noticed as a director, and he was also sufficiently gifted to realise what he could not get away with. But after he had succeeded in Hollywood in a way no other British director had done, he began to make bad movies. One was so poor (*The Paradine Case*) that the two independent pictures that followed could only be improvements: but they were hardly better liked, and Hitchcock returned to the cleverly-plotted thriller which had made him famous, *Strangers on a Train*, with Robert Walker as the killer. His victim was played by Patricia Hitchcock, the director's daughter.

murders, as each wants someone out of the way. Guy does not take the matter seriously, but since this is a set-up for the perfect murder it is tempting to regard the film as the perfect murder story. It does not, unfortunately, repay close examination, but the set pieces are among the director's best: Bruno, losing self-control during his demonstration of strangling at a party; the tennis match that Guy must win in order to get away to the scene of the crime (why didn't he just throw the match?); the murder itself; and the finale – the fight on the carousel. For Hitchcock himself, the flaws included 'the final script', and 'the ineffectiveness' of the leading players. Walker's performance is generally regarded as brilliant, suggesting neuroses beneath a level-headed charm, while Granger's indication of weakness satisfies the spectator's need for logic, explaining why he does not go to the police.

To consolidate the renewed interest in his work, Hitchcock spent a long while preparing **I Confess** (1953). The locations were filmed in Quebec, a city of dark mansions and gloom as seen by him – which pleases those of his commentators looking for a sense of guilt which they say can be traced to his Jesuit upbringing; we might remark instead that his only early successful films were those dealing with crime, and that he therefore developed an interest in stories within that genre. This particular one first saw the light of day in 1902 as a play by Paul Anthelme – and it was recommended to Hitchcock by Louis Verneuil. Discussing it, Hitchcock observed that 'most of the material submitted to me is generally wrong for me' – and it is surely significant that, working within what is in itself a second-rate field, he avoided the first-rate within it (Chandler and Hammett). He was really only interested in displaying the Hitchcock 'genius'; nothing was allowed to get in the way of that. This is technically one of his most brilliant films, with every shot precise and well judged. The premise is appealing: a murderer confesses to a priest (Montgomery Clift) who, later accused of the crime, is unable to break his vow of silence. He does behave, as the detective (Karl Malden) puts it, 'with too much mystification', and though that is later justified, the course is strewn with the usual red herrings of pulp fiction, including

missing clues, a wrong police diagnosis and a confession by an old girlfriend played by Anne Baxter, forced on Hitchcock by Warners in place of Anita Björk (whom he had already signed), and acting so badly as to detract from the priest' dilemma.

Movies in this genre usually trade probability for tension, and Hitchcock was certainly aware of the pitfalls in his branch of the trade; moreover, he did not take himself as seriously as some of his admirers do. He could be very entertaining, as he is here, but given that he had more freedom of choice than most Hollywood director it is sad that all the expertise was now expended on something more worthwhile. After watching all his films again at close intervals for the purposes of this book, I was only too aware of the tricks lies and cheating involved in creating that tension: but perhaps, in the end, it is enough that a dozen or so of them do repay watching a second time.

After earning his living for four years as an actor, it was with a Hitchcock-like thriller that Orson Welles returned to directing. He was engaged to play one of the leads in **The Stranger** (1946), which John Huston had written and was planning to direct; but Welles persuaded Sam Spiegel to let him direct it as well. Huston departed amicably, and the screenplay is credited to Anthony Veiller: whoever wrote it, it is deeply rooted in years of Hollywood junk. A good prologue introduces Edward G. Robinson as an agent tracking down Nazis in the U.S. – and this actor subsequently holds the film together; it also 'establishes a small Connecticut town, in wintry sunshine, and Russell Metty's photography would later serve Welles's increasingly flashy style. Welles himself plays a Nazi disguised as a professor, 'till the day we strike again'; Robinson recognises him when he claims 'Marx wasn't a German, he was a Jew', and the pursuit that follows includes his new wife (Loretta Young) watching newsreels of Auschwitz, but otherwise behaving with the illogicality of most film heroines by deliberately courting death. Welles looks so panic-stricken and wild-eyed that he gives himself away in the first reel.

Even worse is **The Lady from Shanghai** (1948), which Welles had talked Harry Cohn into letting him make, claiming that he could bring in a class film on a low budget. He was also at the time married to Rita Hayworth, Cohn's biggest star, and as the marriage was already on the rocks, Cohn felt that a professional collaboration could not worsen the situation. Cohn loathed the rushes, and when the cost reached $2 million, shooting was hastily wound up; Welles had nothing to do with the final print, into which badly-matched close-ups of Hayworth had been inserted to justify its existence. On this admittedly doubtful result, Welles's earlier films seem flukes: not only does this thriller not thrill, but when it is straightforward it is un-believable and for the rest of the time incomprehensible. It has to do with a mys-terious blonde (Hayworth), the Irish sailor (Welles) she encounters while being mug-ged in Central Park, her crippled, older husband (Everett Sloane), and his partner (Glenn Anders), who also has a crush on her. Redeeming features are the naturalis-tic trial and the famous shoot-out in the hall of mirrors.

Further persuasion by Welles found Re-public financing **Macbeth** (1948), on a budget of $800,000 – roughly the cost of a Vera Hruba Ralston vehicle (which sel-dom made a profit anyway). It was shot in the summer of 1947, in three weeks, but due to dubbing problems not shown till late 1948 – and in a few cities only; with-drawn for re-dubbing, it did not open in New York till the end of 1950. Despite ignominious reviews it has survived, usually defended as visually imaginative – since no other claim can be made for it. The opening sequence promises well, with swirling mists, but they clear too soon, re-vealing the backlot sky. Macbeth's castle, all papier-mâché cliffs and stairs that go no-where, has puddles on its black marble floor; the equally pretentious costumes (Welles designed those of the men) include a series of headgear for Macbeth purloined from *Alexander Nevsky*. Aurally, the occa-sion is even less rewarding. The dialogue was recorded in Scottish-English, in Brit-ish-English, and in Transatlanticene: what was finally used seems to be a blend of all three. It hardly matters, for the text has been so mutilated as to suggest that the screenplay was compiled from a dictionary of quotations, with interpolations which are pure doggerel. The cast, which in-cludes Welles in the title role, is abysmal.

Undeterred, he did an **Othello** which borrows from Olivier's *Hamlet* (q.v.) by beginning with its hero's funeral: other comparisons are supposedly allayed by Welles's own description, 'a motion pic-ture adaptation'. He began the planning in Rome, while making another film there, and started shooting with inadequate funds. He sank his own money into it, and any more he could beg or borrow – the bulk of it coming from a financier in Casablanca (which is why the film has Moroccan nationality) where he had made *The Black Rose* (q.v.). Filming was not only interrupted by his work on other films, but by a nervous breakdown and a London production of the play (under Oli-vier's management). The film was pre-miered at the Cannes Festival in 1952 and won the Grand Prix, but United Artists did not release it in New York till 1955. Lea Padovani, Cecile Aubrey and Betsy Blair had all had a go at playing Desdemo-na, but were either fired or frightened away; Suzanne Cloutier, who finally acted the role, was French-Canadian. The in-fluence of Eisenstein is apparent, especially in the opening scene, with black-cowled monks against the sky. The Venetian scenes are hurried through – the Ca d'Oro and the Bovolo staircase for Desdemona's home, the Miracoli for the wedding, the Scala dei Giganti for the conclave with the Duke; the rest seems to have been photo-graphed at the fortress in Mogador. There are two good sequences: Iago planting the seeds of suspicion in Othello's mind as they are pacing the battlements, and Roderigo's attempted murder of Cassius in a Turkish bath. But though Welles has worked out the action in film terms, it is clear that without the aid of the Hollywood cutting rooms he has no sense of narrative. His gifts as an actor should have been sufficient to make up for deficiencies elsewhere, but he makes matters worse by offering an Othello with only one pained expression. The net result is a dreary one-dimensional tale, moving in fits and starts to an im-probable ending. In the circumstances, Michael MacLiammoir is an acceptable Iago; Fay Compton is an execrable Emilia.

Welles provided Chaplin with the idea of **Monsieur Verdoux** (1947), and the latter seems to have been attracted to Landru, the French Bluebeard, for his 'mes-sage' value – for Verdoux's murders, the film claims, are hardly worse than the mass murdering done by nations; at his trial – supposed to take place in 1938 – Verdoux claims that the gains from his crimes are as nothing to those to be made in the forthcoming conflict. Verdoux is a meticulous dandy, with a voice so high-pitched as to be androgynous. His rapport with people and the scrapes he gets into are entirely those of Chaplin the Tramp – and considering how ruthless the Tramp could be it is no surprise to find Chaplin only physically transformed; he kills solely for the sake of his crippled wife, though with the added incentive of revenging himself upon a society which had sacked him after thirty years in the same job. The best scenes are those involving Martha Raye, who distrusts him as much as his other wives but will forgive everything for some slap and tickle – or more: in no other film of the period does a woman so lust after her man. There is also a waif (Marilyn Nash, perhaps the most amateurish of all Chaplin's discoveries), and his dialogues with her are the essence of later Chaplin – naive philosophies passed on as truths, e.g., on death, 'I guess if the unborn knew of the approach of life they'd be just as terrified.' In his memoir, Chaplin claims this to be 'the cleverest and most brilliant film I have yet made', and though it is muddled, overlong and sometimes mistaken, he is probably right. Most American critics took the view of Howard Barnes in *The New York Herald-Tribune*, that it was 'something of an affront to the intelligence'. In cinemas, the debacle became a rout: catcalled in some, it was withdrawn in others. The intelligentsia was pro-*Verdoux*, either on its own merits or because Chaplin could do no wrong, while a number of people, especially in the industry, were determined that the public should not see it. His personal stock was near to zero. A much-publicised morals trial, though it acquitted him, had harmed his image, and the situation was not helped by his marriage to the very young Oona O'Neill and the objection to the marriage by her father, the playwright Eugene O'Neill. Chaplin's pro-Soviet stance during the War was recalled to make him a target for rightists. In short, a great number of Americans regarded *Verdoux* as subversive – a view which could be sustained only if they had not seen it.

In Britain, which had a Socialist government, the political bent of the film was hardly remarked upon; in France, the left-wing weekly *L'Ecran Français* returned to it constantly with newer and better superlatives. The situation had changed little by the time Chaplin offered **Limelight** (1952), for though on this occasion American reviewers approved, hostility in other quarters had hardened: the State Department made it clear that if he left the country to attend the film's British premiere there would be no guarantee of re-entry. (He had remained a British citizen.) Chaplin went to London, and then settled in Switzerland with his young family; his personal situation may have been one reason why the film was ecstatically received in Europe. If anyone saw it as evidence of decline, which it surely is, it was not mentioned.

The plot is slim: Calvero (Chaplin), a once-famous clown, saves from suicide a young dancer (Claire Bloom) whom he nurtures into success; she helps him to one last triumph, and goes on dancing, his creation, as he dies. As with *Verdoux*, the screenplay is a compendium of a lifetime's reflections – on such matters as audiences, success, love, art, fame and poverty. One is momentarily intrigued when Chaplin's own face appears from behind the mask inadvertently, as in the situation of the girl's love for a much older man. This parallels his own life at this time, but of course young girls are better box office than old girls. And though the decline of Calvero cannot be autobiographical, it is presumably a musing on what might have happened had Chaplin not left Fred Karno's company. When Calvero is a success with the same act he once flopped with, we assume audiences to be conditioned by factors (time, place, publicity) which have nothing to do with talent or the essential being of an artist – but the point is made so unobtrusively (unlike most of the film) that I am not sure that Chaplin was aware of it.

Limelight reaffirms Chaplin's belief in the innate goodness of mankind: the realisation of this vis-à-vis Chaplin's own situation undoubtedly affected reviewers then, but it should not blind us now to the fact that this is all the picture has in common with his earlier films. It soon soured in the memory, with its cheeseparing sets nd the glutinous theme tune, composed by Chaplin, ubiquitous on the airwaves for year afterwards; and then Chaplin withheld the film from us for twenty years. It was indifferently received when revived – pleasant enough 135 minutes but unexceptional, except perhaps in the music hall ct with Buster Keaton. Some observers ind it hard to forgive Chaplin for cutting, s we now know, Keaton's footage in this cene, but one had remained a star while he other had not – and Keaton was glad to vork. In the interim we had had the chance o assess the achievements of them both, nd the film now sours not afterwards but vhile watching it.

A King in New York (1957) was made n Britain and, on Chaplin's orders, not hown in the U.S. Considering that his ɔurpose was to attack that country, this vas self-defeating; doubtless he thought hat deprivation would be some punishnent for its treatment of him. It was beause of that treatment that much was xpected of this riposte: the reaction of the Britisih press was one of baffled disappointnent. It was finally shown in the U.S. in 971, when it was generally ignored. Chaplin himself passed over it in his autoiography, but is reported as saying 'I was lisappointed in the picture. I meant it to be o up to date and modern, but perhaps I lidn't quite understand it.' He was sixtyight when he made it, and obviously out ɔf touch. Television commercials are such asy game that he cannot be congratulated ɔn being amusing in that direction; but he s not funny on movie trailers, rock 'n' roll nd such old targets as social climbers, ɔlastic surgery and room service. Where ıe should be sharpest, on the thenımerican obsession with reds in their nidst, he is feeble; and the views of demoracy put into the mouth of a schoolboy ıre only too infantile. When he had made *Modern Times* he had said, 'There are those vho always attach social significance to ny work. It has none. I leave such subjects o the lecture platform.' This is ingenuous; t might just be true of his films till then, ɔut it certainly is not true of those that ame afterwards. The message of this one, ıuch as it is, might not be so diminished vere the film not so appallingly executed, vith its ancient stock shots and London andmarks standing in for Manhattan.

Preston Sturges is equally disappointing with **Unfaithfully Yours** (1948), the first of two films he made for 20th CenturyFox. Unlike Chaplin, Sturges was an accomplished satirist, but this screenplay is devoid of wit. A bad-tempered musician (Rex Harrison) is given cause to think that his wife (Linda Darnell) is unfaithful: while conducting – Rossini, Wagner, Tchaikovsky – he fantasises on her infidelity and his revenge. The uneasiness is not lessened by Darnell and Barbara Lawrence in roles which required players of the calibre of Constance Bennett and Ina Claire. Perhaps Lucille Ball was needed for **The Beautiful Blonde from Bashful Bend** (1949) – but it has Betty Grable, as a brassy saloon singer, rather too quick on the draw. 'Nice clean world,' she muses, 'no drunks to roll, no salesmen to listen to,' but it is not her line, nor was she adept at knockabout comedy. Zanuck, stung by the terrible reviews her films received, had made an effort to find her better material: Sturges wrote and directed from a story by Earl Fenton, cribbing wildly from 'L'il Abner'. The result is not good Sturges, nor a satire on Westerns, but its sly humour is at least a partial return to form – though it fared no better with audiences than did its predecessor.

Many of the later films of Fritz Lang found little more favour. After the success of *The Woman in the Window* he formed a production company with Walter Wanger and Joan Bennett, and in **Scarlet Street** (1945) they set about emulating that film. Edward G. Robinson is again the infatuated older man and Bennett the woman who embroils him in her affairs; once more they are supported by Dan Duryea, up to no good. Dudley Nichols, who had written *Man Hunt* for Lang, did the screenplay, from the same novel which had been the basis of Renoir's *La Chienne*. Lubitsch had held the rights for years, but could not get a workable script; Lang felt that it would be possible if Greenwich Village were substituted for Montmartre. That it is not is the fault of the Production Code: *The Woman in the Window* had been just a murder mystery, but this is a study of relationships – made implausible right from the start since the Bennett character cannot be designated an out-and-out prostitute. The M.P.A.A. did not, for once, mind the hero getting away with murder, but he has to suffer from guilt instead; the ending is mere bathos, whereas Renoir's was an ironic twist. **Secret Beyond the Door** (1948) was based on an old script that Wanger had in his files, and the project, dogged by ill fortune, wound up the Wanger-Bennett-Lang company. Lang had no good word for it, and it is surely one of the worst of the many Forties films about murderer-husbands. This particular one collects rooms where famous murders occurred, and the title refers to a replica of the heroine's own bedroom. Michael Redgrave has tried hard to find a motive for the man's behaviour, but the role defeats him.

Lang's reputation did not recover with the films he made for other companies. **Cloak and Dagger** (1946) is a Hitchcockian adventure about a mid-Western professor (Gary Cooper) sent into Switzerland during the War to discover whether or not the Germans are developing the atom bomb. Lang said that Warners would not permit any comment on the latter, but his attempt to make something more than a Resistance thriller was foiled by an absurd script by Albert Maltz and Ring Lardner Jr. Equally contrived is **House by the River** (1950), made at Republic, as adapted by Mel Dinelli from the novel by A.P. Herbert. Louis Hayward is both colourless and unsubtle as an unsuccessful author who finds involvement in murder a sure way to sell his books, and Lang responds to his material only in the courtroom climax and in his handling of the gloomy Edwardian mansion in which most of the mayhem takes place. **An American Guerilla in the Philippines** (1950) concerns Tyrone Power and Tom Ewell hiding from the Japanese occupiers, frequently reminding each other that MacArthur promised to return: when he eventually does, someone says, 'He said he'd return.'

'Hate, murder and revenge' is said, or rather sung, throughout **Rancho Notorious** (1952), to remind us that it set new standards for violence in a Western; it is also a precursor of later Westerns in keeping its tongue firmly in its cheek. It did not prove influential (apart from a theme song integrated into the action, a device immediately copied by *High Noon*, q.v.), nor was it an attempt to extend the range of the Western – for this tale of an ageing dance hall girl and an old gun-hand was conceived as a vehicle for Marlene Dietrich.

Since Lang found her 'very, very disagreeable' on the set, it seems apt that she should be its chief weakness, masklike and humourless – yet at the same time she gives the piece a flavour, dealing cards with cigarette dangling, or intoning a song. As gun-slinger, Mel Ferrer has an insolent smile but is as likely as Pegleg Pete waiting table in a gay bar, and Arthur Kennedy is not the most convincing actor to play relentless avenger. But in dealing with matters which include rape and wholesale slaughter, Lang works with greater confidence than in years. This renewed vigour is also apparent in his second film for R.K.O., **Clash by Night** (1952), adapted by Alfred Hayes from a play by Clifford Odets – and though Jerry Wald, the producer, admired Odets, it is difficult to see why he thought this tired eternal triangle situation worth another whirl. It entertains by its sheer awfulness, as when a jaded Barbara Stanwyck returns to her home town, observing 'I don't remember a lot of things.' Knowing that she had done this sort of role too often, she plays down the histrionics; as the dull man she marries Paul Douglas does a deal of teddy-bearing but is convincing in the harsher moments, and Robert Ryan was seldom better than as the smart-ass pal she falls for. In the play the husband killed the lover, but in the film the wife finally discovers the husband's True Worth. The film also transferred the action from Staten Island to Monterey; it was Wald's idea to use a fishing village and the documentary material that Lang shot gets the film off to a good start. Later scenes of pounding surf and scudding clouds indicate that he knew the level of his material, but with a stronger milieu than he had had since *Fury*, he responds magnificently: the Sunday afternoon dance, the beer halls, the shore, the quayside.

There are some promising foggy exteriors in **The Blue Gardenia** (1953), but it is otherwise stale. A girl (Anne Baxter) goes to a man's apartment while drunk and then thinks she has murdered him. When an esteemed director takes on such tales, it is either for the twists or for opportunities with *mise-en-scène*: but since neither is apparent, we may suppose Lang still nourished a desire for independence – which he had retained, in the main, over his recent films, despite the involvement of the major companies as distributors. Lang would not be the first or last to equate independence with a vague but cynical notion of what the public wanted, the result in this case being a film of no quality at all. Its failure, and the consequent blow to what was left of his reputation, caused him to move to Columbia for a programmer, **The Big Heat** (1953) – and ironically it was that which restored him to critical favour. A cop (Glenn Ford) investigating a suicide begins to suspect that it was murder; as he probes deeper, an attempt is made on his life and his wife is killed – then he discovers a nest of corruption which includes a number of high police officials. Civic corruption in movies had, since Capra, only been hinted at, and it was refreshing to see the subject handled again at this time, from a story by Sydney Boehm, who also contributed some crude but excellent dialogue. The film's violence was much commented upon, especially that directed at the gangster's moll (Gloria Grahame). Lang's response was intense, and this is, simply, a superb thriller, looking more intently at the roots of crime than any other film of the time.

Human Desire (1954) was Lang's second attempt at remaking one of Renoir's films, and the idea was Wald's, since he had loved *La Bête Humaine*; it was originally to have been made with the same stars as *Clash by Night*, but Wald took the property with him to Columbia, who cast Ford and Grahame. Renoir's film is a black, engulfing drama; Lang's is a footling little melodrama about adultery. He has reacted well to the grey industrial town where it takes place, the bar where the husband (Broderick Crawford) goes to drink, the suburban home with television and flying ducks on the wall, but the story does not work in this American setting. Glenn Ford fails completely as both a potential murderer and a man motivated by an *amour fou*, and in his role Crawford has neither the necessary guile nor the intelligence.

Moonfleet (1955) was produced by John Houseman, British-reared and therefore familiar with the hundred and one boys' adventure stories on which it was modelled; since it has little in common with J. Meade Faulkner's half-forgotten classic of the same name, we may assume that the writers, Jan Lustig and Margaret Fitts, poured into it every breathtaking convention of the genre. Lang disliked the story (though he was flattered to be asked back to M-G-M), but brought to the film the strong atmospheric qualities that Houseman hoped for. As the boy hero, Jon Whiteley is a huge asset, grave and courageous, unflinching at revelations of his idol's villainy; in the part of guardian and smuggler chief, Stewart Granger found his best screen role; George Sanders is a milord; Joan Greenwood his treacherous wife; and Viveca Lindfors is the common-law wife from the Indies. M-G-M loathed the film and threw it away as the lower half of double bills – to the indigation of many, savouring (for what would be the last time) the director's old panache.

While the City Sleeps (1956) and **Beyond a Reasonable Doubt** (1956) are both pulp thrillers, needlessly well made. The first has a newspaper background and a cast including Dana Andrews, George Sanders, Ida Lupino, Vincent Price and Thomas Mitchell; the second has a more intriguing plot about a husband who has theories about a murder which are turned against himself, and it has Andrews and Joan Fontaine. Lang may have had no illusions about the basic value of his material, nor qualms about the way these films too were thrown away by R.K.O., a company then in its death throes. He was no longer interested in working in Hollywood; he said later that as old age approached he was certain that it was no longer worth the ulcers.

At this time, Lang's reputation was outstripped by that of Robert Siodmak, who had had fewer setbacks with his own strongly atmospheric melodramas. After the success of *The Suspect*, Universal bought for him another English period melodrama, by Thomas Job, **The Strange Affair of Uncle Harry** (1945), but as adapted by Stephen Longstreet it was now set in the present day in New Hampshire. Siodmak is able to make little of 'the typical small town' promised in the foreword, but he clearly enjoys the cluttered mansion which is the setting for Harry (George Sanders), a mild draughtsman, and the neurotic sister (Geraldine Fitzgerald) whose passion for him threatens his engagement. There is another large house in **The Spiral Staircase** (1946), and the time is again the turn of the century. Written by Mel Dinelli from a novel by Ethel Lina White, this is less a whodunnit than a who'lldoit: several physically handicapped girls have been murdered, and a deaf mute (Dorothy McGuire) is expected to be the next victim. A shadowy figure spies upon her as she leaves for the house where she is a servant, and is later glimpsed within it. 'Oh, it's you,' says Blanche (Rhonda Fleming) to someone we cannot see in the cellar, 'You quite frightened me.' In time the deaf mute is alone in the house, and a storm rages without . . . The art direction is appropriately splendid, and the film was rapturously received. Selznick produced, and this was one of the films he sold in pre-production to R.K.O.

Returning to Universal, Siodmak made **The Killers** (1946), which disposes of Hemingway's story in so tense and eerie a ten minutes as to make the remainder an anticlimax. There are ninety-five more to go, and their substance was devised by the producer, Mark Hellinger, in conjunction with Anthony Veiller and John Huston. (As with *The Stranger*, Veiller gets sole credit, but in this case because Huston's contract with Warners forbade mention of his name; Veiller later worked on some of Huston's own productions.) An insurance investigator (Edmond O'Brien) is called upon to examine the past of the murdered man (Burt Lancaster) and his involvement with a gang boss (Albert Dekker), a detective (Sam Levene) and a two-timing dame (Ava Gardner). Lancaster, in his first film,

performs in a manner which suggests th... he learned his lines phonetically; but he not ineffective.

The Dark Mirror (1946) permits Sio... mak no atmospheric shots, since the actio... is virtually restricted to an apartment and consulting room. That also suggests bot... considerations of cost – the film was mad... for International (q.v.) while in the proce... of amalgamating with Universal – and belief that the story is sufficiently strong. concerns seemingly respectable twin sis... ters, both played by Olivia de Havillanc... one of whom is suspected of murder – an... the plot is engrossing till it is obliged t... reveal which one of them is guilty: fro... that point Siodmak and his producer writer, Nunnally Johnson, try to sustai... interest by such devices as Miss de Havil... land handing articles to Miss de Havillan... or embracing herself with both profiles t... the camera.

Siodmak dismissed most of his subse... quent films as potboilers, but connoisseur... of the *film noir* of the Forties cherish **Cry o... the City** (1948), made for 20th Century Fox, and **Criss Cross** (1949), made fo... Universal. Both are imitative of old War... ner Bros. thrillers, but are deficient wher... their prototypes were strongest – in thei... leading men. In *Cry of the City* Richar... Conte and Victor Mature are uninterestin... as gangster and detective respectively... There is, however, a superb job lot o... supporting characters: a shyster lawye... (Berry Kroeger), a psychotic jail-cleane... (Walter Baldwin), a sadistic guard (Rolan... Winters), a friendly hooker (Shelley Win... ters), a tough nurse (Betty Guard) and... bull-dyke masseuse (Hope Emerson), wh... is revealed to be the Miss Big of the opera... tion at the heart of the plot. *Criss Cros... concerns a guy (Burt Lancaster) who turn... crook when he discovers that his wif... (Yvonne de Carlo) has moved in with... bounder (Dan Duryea). In this case it i... less the subsidiary characters who ar... memorable as the settings: it begins in a ca... park outside a dance hall, soon revealed a... a tacky room behind a long, low an... smoky bar; by day sunlight filters into i... while cars bake in the Los Angeles heat... 'There's so much you can't control,' sai... Siodmak to explain his loathing of shoot... ing on location: but you would not know i... from his use of it.

He was invited to go to M-G-M to tak...

Yvonne de Carlo and Burt Lancaster in *Criss Cross*, a conventional crime story of the sort now seen nightly on television. What distinguishes the film is the direction by Robert Siodmak, whose reputation fluctuated from his first film in Berlin in 1929 to his death over forty years later. That was why his material was often undistinguished, but there were occasions, such as this one, when his handling made it seem much better than it was.

over **The Great Sinner** (1949), with a screenplay by Ladislas Fodor and Christopher Isherwood – but with no credit offered to Dostoevsky. Gregory Peck plays a nineteenth-century Russian writer who becomes involved with, among others, a countess (Ethel Barrymore) based on the countess of 'The Gambler' and a pawnbroker (Agnes Moorehead) from 'Crime and Punishment'. M-G-M was not a natural habitat for Dostoevsky, as Siodmak discovered when he tried to cut a screenplay which would have run for six hours. He managed to bring in a three-hour version, but it was 'heavy and dull', mainly due, he thought, to Gregory Peck, whose normally slow speech became even slower, so overawed was he by acting in Dostoevsky. 'Now the story didn't even make sense. By the first preview we had cut it down to two hours ten minutes . . . At that point I washed my hands of the film, and heard nothing until a message came that they – at M-G-M it was always "they" – had decided that what was needed was a new and stronger love story.' Since Siodmak refused to return, Mervyn LeRoy did the reshooting, and though Siodmak claimed that he did not recognise the finished result, it retains a European feeling. It is set around the Casino in Wiesbaden, and the action gathers momentum whenever we get to the tables: the dozens of films featuring roulette and chemin-de-fer were to the taste of industry executives rather than audiences, and this one was rare in making these scenes exciting. The rest of it is hardly Dostoevsky but not despicable. Ava Gardner is miscast as a Russian countess, and some other performers are left floundering – Walter Huston as her father, Melvyn Douglas as her fiancé, and Frank Morgan as an inveterate gambler.

Like *Criss Cross*, **The File on Thelma Jordan** (1949) has a brilliant opening, and it is placed in palm-lined California, where all motives are ambiguous and even the oranges are sour. Thelma (Barbara Stanwyck) is new in town; it is possible that she may not be all she seems to be when the Assistant D.A. (Wendell Corey) kisses her goodnight and she is then pulled into the shadows by a mysterious stranger. Corey, with his bow ties and wintry smiles, is the decent man embroiled in the machinations of a scheming woman – who protests her

innocence seemingly without guile. Ketti Frings wrote the screenplay (from a story by Marty Holland), and Hal Wallis produced for Paramount; without being particularly convincing, it is always interesting – and that is due entirely to Siodmak. With the exceptions of *The Spiral Staircase* and *The Dark Mirror*, both carefully plotted, he was dealing with material with few ideas but with characters who were perverse or criminally-minded: building upon that, he found contradictions and tensions not only in these people but in the bars and apartments they inhabited. Today his unpretentious films are preferred to some of the stuffed albatrosses of the period: but at that time content was all, and by specialising in crime stories Siodmak not only failed to enhance his reputation but virtually ruined it.

Like Melville in France, he remained at heart a romantic, and welcomed the offer to make **The Crimson Pirate** (1952) for Burt Lancaster's company. That actor appears before the credits, advising us to believe only half of what we see, and Siodmak moves easily between spoof and the lightheartedness of the best old swashbucklers – and the climax is a straight steal from *The Black Pirate*. Roland Kibbee wrote the screenplay, and the action is inventive and high-spirited, as Lancaster and Nick Cravatt, his old circus partner, do their stunts; the cinematographer, Otto Heller, manages to convey the tang of the sea in his images. Though set in the Caribbean, it was filmed in the Mediterranean, and Siodmak remained in Europe to work; after a remake of *Le Grand Jeu* in France, he filmed mainly in West Germany. Like Lang, and for the same reasons, he abandoned Hollywood, but of the dozen or so films he made at this period, including three in English, I can find little of interest. Presumably he, too, found the German film industry temperamentally sympathetic but artistically stultifying.

As Siodmak moved towards the end of his American career he helped Max Ophuls begin his – with **The Exile** (1947). Ophuls had arrived in Hollywood, via Switzerland, in 1941, and he had been one of the directors working for Howard Hughes on *Vendetta* before being fired. Siodmak recommended him to Douglas Fairbanks Jr, then preparing his second film as producer – and it is a pity that Fairbanks did not choose his writer with the same discrimination. He had written the screenplay himself, a trifling episode of Charles II's Dutch exile, but wisely left the visual aspects to Ophuls, who combined his knowledge of Dutch painting (including the costumes in the portraits) and flair for the *decoratif* to produce remarkable results.

The film's visual beauty, if nothing else, attracted attention, enabling Ophuls to direct **Letter from an Unknown Woman** (1948), as instigated by Howard Koch, remembering *Liebelei*. Koch wrote the screenplay from a story by Stefan Zweig (filmed earlier as *Only Yesterday*), and it became a labour of love on the part of both of them and John Houseman, who produced. It is a synthesis of old Vienna, and that is all. A girl (Joan Fontaine) falls in love with a pianist (Louis Jourdan) in the same tenement: they are separated, and she has his baby to cherish till they meet again . . . You might say that she is a silly little ninny, but you would be reckoning without Miss Fontaine, who is exquisite, in one of her three great screen performances. And you would be reckoning without Ophuls, and his love of an idealised past – of champagne and chandeliers and horse-drawn carriages, of the gleam of gaslight and jewellery, of waltzes and romance and heartbreak that is almost, but not quite, a game. In a railway carriage in the Prater, painted scenes of Venice flash by; at a last dance at dawn, the all-woman orchestra is impatient to go home; and in a small square in Linz an engagement is celebrated to the oom-pa-pa of the local band. Franz Planer photographed, as he had done for *Liebelei*, and Alexander Golitzen's sets include a narrow circular stair with iron railings: it is looking down the stairwell that the young Fontaine sees the pianist bringing home a girl, and we see it from the same angle when it is she whom he has brought home.

In the U.S. the critics deplored the film, and the public avoided it, suspecting escapism (then unfashionable), rather than the romantic film it is – or so thought Houseman. In Britain, Universal sold it off to a minor distributor, who booked it into a suburban hall, and there it was tracked down by Richard Winnington, whose notice began its rehabilitation.

As Ophuls's reputation began to be slowly restored, the newly-formed Enterprise Studios (q.v.) offered him the direction of **Caught** (1949), a triangle story written by Arthur Laurents (then, a promising Broadway playwright who had just done the screenplay for *Rope*), from a novel by Libbie Block. Another dreamy heroine (Barbara Bel Geddes), marries a millionaire (Robert Ryan) and regrets it – especially when trying to start a new life as receptionist to an East Side doctor (James Mason). 'The film,' said Ophuls, 'goes off the rails towards the end. Up to the last ten minutes, though, it wasn't bad,' and he is probably referring to the handling of the girl, the tycoon and their motivations, all carefully worked out. As the camera rakes every banister of the millionaire's claustro-phobic mansion, we may be reminded of James Mason's words on Ophuls's tech-nique:

A shot that does not call for tracks
Is agony for poor dear Max,
Who, separated from his dolly,
Is wrapped in deepest melancholy,
Once, when they took away his crane,
I thought he'd never smile again . . .

Mason also had some pertinent remarks to make about Walter Wanger, who pro-duced the last one of Ophuls's four Ameri-can films: he was 'a man who wanted to be a European. He didn't know how to be a European, so this was the kind of film – I suppose, like *Brief Encounter* (q.v.) – that he wanted to make.'

The film concerned was **The Reckless Moment** (1949), and it was to have been another alliance between Wanger and Jean Renoir. The latter, however, was anath-ema to Harry Cohn – Wanger was now with Columbia – and Ophuls was brought in instead. 'It was just another magazine story, not very well written,' said Mason of this tale of a woman (Joan Bennett) who covers up for a near and dear one, directing suspicion to herself because she thinks a murder has been committed; Mason himself plays a blackmailer. Bennett is exceptionally good, chain-smoking dis-tractedly while not finishing some sen-tences and not hearing others: the overall portrait of family relationships, so differ-ent to that of *Caught*, is nevertheless simi-larly honest. Both films are evidence of Ophuls's mastery, and this one was suf-ficiently successful for Wanger to get inde-pendent backing for a version (to be filmed in Europe) of *La Duchesse de Langeais*, with

Mason and Garbo; but when it became clear that Garbo did not have the courage to resubmit herself to the scrutiny of camera, Ophuls accepted a French offer to direct *La Ronde* (q.v.), the start of the brilliant climax to his career.

The misshapen career of Robert Flaherty finished with **Louisiana Story** (1948), the story of a boy of the bayou. 'His name is Alexander Napoleon Ulysses Latour' says a Voice Over, and you might as well leave if you do not fancy another 76 minutes of poetry. Men arrive to disturb nature with their oil wells, and when Father sings to them they laugh, in the forced manner of T.V. interviewers. The public remained indifferent, despite the usual furore among the critics: 'Films like Robert Flaherty's don't turn up often enough in the lives of film-critics to keep flexible their personal standards of what is worthwhile in the cinema,' (E. Arnot Robertson in 'The Penguin Cinema, 1950'). Of course, it was a change from Vincent Price and Lynn Bari; and had not Flaherty so often tried to compromise with the industry to no avail? And had he not obtained financing for this one from Standard Oil and then shown the oil companies in an unflattering light? At least Virgil Thompson's music is splendid.

A good film about children is **The Search** (1948), directed by Fred Zinnemann for M-G-M and Praesens of Zurich. M-G-M's unlikely involvement in European production was due solely to the enthusiasm of Arthur, one of the younger members of the Loew family: thus, Loews distributed *Goupi Mains Rouges*, the first continental film shown in the States after the War. The company later promoted *The Last Chance*, a Swiss film made partly in English, about a British-American team of soldiers helping refugees cross the border. The producer was Lazar Wechsler and though M-G-M International was short-lived (since it had been started only under sufferance), Wechsler persuaded Loews to co-operate on *The Search*, an original screenplay by Richard Schweizer, with additions by David Wechsler and Paul Jarrico.

For those who judge a movie on content or intent it is a great film; in subject matter at least it dwarfs virtually every American film of the period – for it concerns the rehabilitation of the children who survived the concentration camps. Less pure than *Sciuscià*, it is equally an essential footnote to World War Two. In an UNRRA camp in ruined Germany an American woman (Aline MacMahon) is wearily interviewing children, including a Czech boy (Ivan Jandl); he panics and flees, but is eventually befriended by a G.I. (Montgomery Clift), who takes him under his wing. The introduction of the boy's mother (Jarmilla Novotna) brings an element of suspense (will they be reunited?); and there is a ghastly moment when the boy asks, 'What is a mother?' As against that, there is a moving sequence of the child lost, wandering among the rubble, bewildered by another small boy behind a wire fence; the words 'German' and 'Nazi' are never used, and the war and the concentration camps mentioned only in passing. For its creators, including Zinnemann, this film may be a way of thanking the Americans, as represented by two people – a middle-aged woman and a carefree young G.I. – for their unselfishness in the aftermath of war. Miss MacMahon is never tearful or indulgently smiling, and Clift is better than any other screen G.I. that I have seen – chewing gum, shirt bulging from his pants, sprawling (never sitting) in a chair.

Notable in Zinnemann's **Act of Violence** (1948) are characters more rounded than was usual, including the protagonists – a good bad man (Robert Ryan) and a bad good man (Van Heflin), respectively a killer with a justified vengeance and a decent man with a guilty war secret. A gun before the credits and the nebulous title indicate a thriller; as such, it has its moments, especially when Heflin and his wife (Janet Leigh) are cowering in the darkness, listening to Ryan's gimpy foot moving round the house. Both the actors are excellent (Ryan in particular), but the best thing in the movie is Mary Astor. Hollywood had not allowed a whore in a leading role since before the Code, and hers is superbly realised: she has a heart of gold, but she is middle-aged and sad, cheering herself up with lines like 'I got my kicks. I got along.' Robert Surtees's photography includes some notable views of downtown L.A. at night, deserted except for a wind-tossed newspaper – which was not yet a cliché.

The Men (1950), like *The Search*, is a

The Films of Fred Zinnemann

As a contract director at M-G-M Fred Zinnemann began to make interesting pictures as soon as he was permitted and his first films as an independent were notably courageous. *The Men*, RIGHT, was a study of war-wounded paraplegics, notable for its sobriety and the performances of Everett Sloane, right, and Marlon Brando, the latter reminding us how he revitalised American acting – though it must be said that none of his rawness and vibrancy rubbed off on Teresa Wright. Those who were moved were not many, and Zinnemann had to wait till *High Noon* FAR RIGHT for his first big popular success – and that too has dated little, as its frequent revivals testify. In the centre of the picture are Grace Kelly and Gary Cooper, and no one who has seen the film will need to be told at what point this scene occurs. However, *The Member of the Wedding*, BELOW, with Julie Harris, Ethel Waters and Brandon de Wilde, is Zinnemann's favourite among his own films.

Postwar Hollywood: The Directors in Their Brave New World

study in rehabilitation, in this case G.I.s handicapped by paralysis. It concentrates on one ex-officer (Marlon Brando) whose bitterness has to be eradicated before he will agree to marry his fiancée (Teresa Wright). It was partially filmed at the Birmingham Veterans Hospital near Los Angeles, where preliminary studies had been done, and Zinnemann insisted on his cast being thoroughly rehearsed in the subject. It is clear that the film means to be more honest than most hospital films – as the doctor (Everett Sloane) lectures to the patients' wives on the malfunctioning of bladder and bowels; he turns out to be unlike other movie doctors, being salty-tongued, gritty in his humour and capable of being testy. The hospital scenes are hard and edgy, for example, using little dialogue to indicate the way in which the sullen hero responds to his fellows. Unable to compete in sexual frankness with the much later *Coming Home* (q.v.) this film nevertheless moved its audiences more – but the wedding night sequence (picked out for special praise by Richard Winnington in *Sight and Sound*) is now crude in forcing emotion, partly due to the writing and partly to the equally conventional playing of Teresa Wright. The brilliance of Marlon Brando (b. 1924) only serves to emphasise her inadequacy. This was his first film after his Broadway success, and to see it now is to be reminded how he changed the course of American acting, with his shifts of moods and darting energy. The film falters in other ways, as in its opening plea for pacifism, but it is always free from the weaknesses of *The Search*. Both were foremost among the films which gave Hollywood renewed respect in itself; and since Stanley Kramer, the producer, and Carl Foreman, the writer, though often serious minded, did little of worth outside their work with Zinnemann, we may suppose the achievement to be mainly his.

Despite the protestations a few years earlier, Zinnemann seemed now the only Hollywood director concerned with contemporary problems, and with **Teresa** (1951) he attempted to study the adjustments needed to be made by the G.I.s' foreign wives. Returning to M-G-M and producer Arthur M. Loew Jr, he persuaded them to allow him foreign locations, still a rarity, and a cast of unknowns.

Louis B. Mayer had been ousted in favour of Dore Schary precisely because Schary had been associated with contemporary subjects; but *Teresa* is only too typical of the customary approach to such matters, and too much action is piled into it because many of those involved had no confidence in a simple subject. Alfred Hayes, with firsthand experience of the army in Italy, wrote the story with Stewart Stern, but the latter's screenplay enmeshes its mixed-up hero (John Erickson) in swathes of war guilt and family guilt which were not exactly typical of those G.I.s and their brides who did have difficulty in readjusting and settling down. Zinnemann, unlike most of his confrères at the time, believed that the way to involve audiences was to suggest that it was filmed as it happened, but Stern's screenplay seems to have unnerved him. Zinnemann makes *Teresa* 'better' than most American films of the time, but only by emulating de Sica or Emmer – two of the players here were in *Domenica d'Agosto* (q.v.) and the bride, Pier Angeli, was discovered in a film made by Leonide Moguy.

Zinnemann returned to form with **High Noon** (1952). The conjunction of the theme music and the railroad stretching into the distance is an indelible cinema experience; you know that something will happen when the train arrives at high noon. Gary Cooper is the friendless sheriff who waits to confront the killers out of his sense of duty, and the Code of the West was never expressed with less pretension. In Zinnemann's own words, it is about 'a man's crisis of conscience'. Foreman wrote the screenplay, and because he was black-listed thereafter, political references have been read into it; there was certainly dissension between him and Zinnemann on incidentals, and Zinnemann himself thinks the prime contributions are those of Floyd Crosby, who photographed and Dimitri Tiomkin, who composed the score. It was not until Tiomkin had persuaded Frankie Laine to record the song that U.A. lost their reservations about the film. It was an instant classic: 'quite on a par with *Stagecoach*' said John McCarten in *The New Yorker* – and it has not dated nearly as much.

The Member of the Wedding (1952) confirms Zinnemann as a man of taste and meticulous craftsmanship, but the fact that it is his own favourite amongst his films tells against him as a film-maker, for it is in the Broadway-American literary tradition of tales about people to whom life has not been particularly kind – and Carson McCullers's fragile novel had been successful in a stage version. As on Broadway, Julie Harris's performance deserves superlatives, but the theatre still clings to it; the backcloth of this child's backyard looks like a backcloth with imported Spanish moss. The best sequence was not in the play – when she is picked up by a drunken boy G.I.: suddenly the book's central subject, adolescence, is presented without coyness, and Zinnemann's feeling for the terror and romance of night-time America comes across with force. Harris's precocious, wayward and loquacious tomboy is accompanied by the black servant (Ethel Waters) and the solemn younger boy (Brandon de Wilde): together on screen, they move the film towards magic – but it is the magic of the theatre, even when transcended by Waters singing 'His Eye Is on the Sparrow' before what must be the Second Act curtain.

Zinnemann had persuaded Kramer to buy the play – to the disgust of Columbia, whose contract with Kramer allowed them no control over his material. The film's complete failure was one of the reasons why Kramer returned to United Artists. Zinnemann remained at Columbia to direct **From Here to Eternity** (1953), grateful for the chance to 'go commercial', as he put it. James E. Jones's novel had Tolstoyan ambitions; he did not write well and he wrote too much, but the cumulative effect was of something torn from life – a bitter tale of the peacetime army, the ox-like regular servicemen, their limitations and the degradations inflicted upon them. Since the situations and language were then considered 'raw', the industry had hesitated; Daniel Taradash finally came up with a workable screenplay, but it is a glossy summary of some aspects of the book, over-explaining, and without understanding. The affair between the officer's wife (Deborah Kerr) and the sergeant (Burt Lancaster) has become real love, despite the still-famous clinch amidst the foam; and Lancaster is given the impossible task of both loathing his officers to the point of self-destruction and making glowing tributes to Service life. Lorene (Donna Reed) is no longer a whore, but is

allowed Madam's sitting room and sofa for the long *conversations* she has with men. The stars remain stars, and in that respect are almost all inferior to the players in the 1979 T.V. adaptation; an exception is Montgomery Clift as the rebel, his thought processes getting in the way of a man who worked on instinct, but undoubtedly strong. All the artists billed above the title were nominated for Oscars, and the film collected a bevy of awards; it was popular everywhere, but not much admired critically outside the U.S. Nevertheless, it helped to break down taboos in the American cinema, and Zinnemann managed some aspects of Service life beautifully: the aimless wandering around the barrack room, the high spirits as the men prepare for a night out – a motley group, with small aims and vices, an aptitude rather than a taste for drunkenness and an apathetic attitude towards each other.

Like Capra, Stevens and Wyler, John Huston's war service included a number of government-sponsored documentaries, sufficiently touted for him to return to Hollywood with reputation enhanced. **Let There Be Light** (1946) remains an impressive study of the rehabilitation of soldiers mentally scarred in battle. His first postwar work was writing for other directors. He returned to directing with **The Treasure of Sierra Madre** (1948). Most of it was shot on location in Mexico, with Humphrey Bogart urging Huston on to film as he liked; Warners viewed the result with distaste, and released it with indifference – to be surprised at its pattern of praise and awards: Best Motion Picture and Direction from the New York critics; Best Screenplay and Direction from Academy members. The film was liked for being unconventional, by implication because the leading players were unshaven and unheroic; and because greed and other chicaneries plague the progress of these treasure hunters it was thought to have some significance. It is dated today by Max Steiner's thundering score, dissipating the tension built up by the direction; the studio sets, though few, do not help, and Huston's screenplay – from the novel by B. Traven – needs humour. For virtually the only time in his career Bogart lacks conviction; as the seedy, suspicious and small-minded Fred C. Dobbs he has to disintegrate – literally – before our eyes, and he seems to have been unnerved by the prospect. In any event he would have been outclassed by Walter Huston, as the wily old prospector who talks in gusts, in his own shorthand – a character realised as we are seldom privileged to see on the screen.

Key Largo (1948) was Maxwell Anderson's rejigging of the *The Petrified Forest*, and James Agee thought the Huston–Richard Brooks screenplay an improvement on the Broadway version; but he added, 'Some of the points Huston wanted to make were cut out of the picture after he had finished it, and I rather doubt anyhow whether gangsters can be made to represent all that he meant them to – practically everything that is wrong with postwar America.' The film seems to me, rather, to pose the gangster as an anachronism in the postwar period – Johnny Rocco (Edward G. Robinson), boasting of the time he bought and sold state officials, is a stale survivor: at the end, when he is dead, Lauren Bacall opens the shutters to (aaagh!) let the light in. Opposing the gangster is a disillusioned war veteran (Bogart, repeating his role in *Dead Reckoning* q.v.). Huston's flair for depicting eccentricity of character is exemplified here by the gang: the bullying and deceptively friendly Curly (Thomas Gomez); Toots (Harry Lewis), baby-faced and capable of a torture that hints of castration; Angel (Dan Seymour), moon-faced and observant; and the moll (Claire Trevor), doing a rotten job on 'Moanin' Low' for the price of a drink – probably the first lady lush in Hollywood history actually to be well dressed and made up.

Huston's first film as an independent – he had formed a company with producer Sam Spiegel – was a failure. **We Were Strangers** (1949) is a story of revolutionary activities in Cuba, and in this way an unlikely couple (John Garfield, Jennifer Jones) are brought together. Trying to say too much, the film says little, and in the matter of illegal motives Huston is much happier with the petty criminals of **The Asphalt Jungle** (1950). He wrote the script with Ben Maddows, from a novel by W. R. Burnett, and directs with a strong feeling for time and place – a small mid-Western town, where a German doctor (Sam Jaffe), a drifter (Sterling Hayden) and a shady lawyer (Louis Calhern) combine for a heist. We had not seen mascara

running in movies before, which happens here with the pathetic tramp (Jean Hagen), nor for years a relationship like that of the lawyer and his baby-faced girl (Marilyn Monroe, q.v.), given the difference in their ages and her pouting note of sexual anticipation. For that matter, the dénouement – the crooks falling out and apart – was a revelation, and if that has dated, like the cop's earnest comment on his role in society – this remains one of the best of all crime films.

It was made for M-G-M, after Huston had begged release from *Quo Vadis?* (q.v.), which had originally interested him as an allegory on modern dictators. He remained at Metro for **The Red Badge of Courage** (1951), which provided an experience as disastrous as his involvement with *Quo Vadis?*. Louis B. Mayer loathed the project from the start, but Huston and Dore Schary (q.v.) had the backing of Nicholas Schenck in New York. Mayer seemed to have been proved right when the preview audience catcalled, and in panic the film was reduced to a mere 69 minutes, with an explanatory commentary, and touted as a version of an American 'classic'. What remains surely catches the feel of Stephen Crane's strange evocation of the near past and one frightened young man's experience of war; nor does Huston betray Matthew Brady, whose photographic record of the War he emulates without pretension. The cuts do not show, but with a longer running time – and hence more cumulative force – the film might have become the masterpiece it has sometimes been said to be. The press perhaps reacted to the accounts of the production as published in *The New Yorker* (and later in book form, as 'Picture') by Lillian Ross, who had decided that it might be an interesting one to follow. None of the principals involved emerged with much credit, but Gottfried Reinhardt, the producer, correctly assessed the film's failure: 'We do not have a great picture. There is no story because we do not show what the youth is thinking. It is not in the script. John said he would put it on the screen. It is not on the screen.'

Huston missed the later quarrels, having gone to Africa to shoot **The African Queen** (1951) for his own company: location work was both difficult and uncomfortable (because of heat and insects). A further drawback was that the only box-office factor was the presence of Bogart, which represented for Huston the sort of risk he liked to take. C. S. Forester's novel had been bandied about for some time – once as a starring vehicle for Bette Davis and John Mills – so it is worth remembering how well the film endures.★ It is classic adventure stuff – a crazy trip down an African river because the spinster (Katharine Hepburn) is determined to do something for the British war effort, to its wild, illogical ending. The book concludes more reasonably, but Huston could not kill off his stars. Neither the novel nor, according to him, the screenplay (by himself and James Agee) originally had much humour, and that only arose after he had suggested that Hepburn model her role on Eleanor Roosevelt. An additional factor was that Hepburn and Bogart realised that they enjoyed working together.

A love affair between a stubborn spinster and a feckless, drink-sodden Cockney (Canadian in the film) had been originally done by Maugham (in 'Vessel of Wrath'), but here it is accompanied by their growing also – in daring, in understanding – into heroes; their love is bound up in their acceptance that they are unlikely to come out alive. His grudging 'Yes, miss' becomes 'Of course, Rosie', but he catches her determination just as she learns from him dependence and humility in the face of privation. Whether sitting on the porch with dry tears for the death of her brother (Robert Morley) or pouring away her partner's gin, she has us mainly on her side; when she says, 'Dear, what is your first name?' no one in films could match her look of apprehension, but he has several different looks of apprehension. There is no other screen romance as rich as this.

Moulin Rouge (1952) was further proof of Huston's eclectic taste. Its justification could well have been that no one had yet made a film of an artist's life that was not risible. However, the basis for the screenplay – by himself and Anthony Veiller – was a novel by Pierre LaMure of incredible banality, and the worst of it has not been entirely banished: 'I have a friend, maman, he is a painter. His name is Vincent

★In 1967 readers of the Los Angeles Times voted it their favourite film, and four years later those of the (London) Sunday Times considered it the one they most wanted to see again.

Van Gogh,' says Lautrec (José Ferrer). The film does ask compassion for Lautrec as artist and cripple: he was not, in fact, an outcast from the society into which he was born, but the concept of him as an embittered and misanthropic dwarf is valid enough. His relationship with one woman is borrowed from 'Of Human Bondage', and another, with an older woman, is platonic: thus he is driven into brothels to satisfy his needs, and thus the great movie public is supposed to forgive him. The famous opening of the film, in the Moulin Rouge, does suggest very strongly that in this milieu this man finds both inspiration and companionship and the piece overall is most successful in its visual representation of the *belle époque*, as photographed by Oswald Morris. Ferrer's technical achievement (walking on his knees) results in a bloodless performance, but he is his usual self in doubling as Lautrec's father.

Again changing direction, Huston offered **Beat the Devil** (1954), written with Truman Capote from a novel by Claude Cockburn, a quirky black comedy of a type that became popular later. Its detractors (Bogart, the star, was one) hoped for a thriller, and complained with more justice that the plot was not clear: what matters is both the upending of the usual rules in stories of mayhem and the eccentricity of the characters – a British couple (Jennifer Jones, Edward Underdown), seemingly veddy County, though

John Huston's predelections led him to more full-blooded and gritty adventure stories than were common in Hollywood at the time. Perhaps the most admired – and most loved – of all his adventure films is *The African Queen*, with Robert Morley, Humphrey Bogart and Katharine Hepburn.

she is a congenital liar; an American adventurer (Bogart) and his Italian wife (Gina Lollobrigida), obsessed with all things British; and his associates – fat, cowardly, *toujours la politesse* (Robert Morley), foppish (Peter Lorre), and the minute, bowler-hatted ex-Indian major (Ivor Barnard), ever ready with a knife. The film's wry humour is entirely typical of Huston – though we had seen it only infrequently at this point. This was his third film in Europe; and only when interior shooting is necessary has he since returned to the American studios (except for *Annie*, q.v.).

Elia Kazan (b.1909) came to the fore during this period. A graduate of the Group Theatre, his reputation was such that 20th Century-Fox negotiated a contract that stipulated only an occasional film. The first was **A Tree Grows in Brooklyn** (1945), from Betty Smith's best-selling novel about a Brooklyn family in the earlier years of the century. Hard up working-class people seldom found their way to the screen: the novel had conveyed the sense that they were only one remove from fact, and that was a quality kept by Kazan and his writers, Tess Slessinger and Frank Davis. That the film is moving, when the feckless father (James Dunn) dies of alcoholism, is due chiefly to the performance of Peggy Ann Garner as the daughter. In Kazan's own words, 'she was not pretty at all, or cute or picturesque, only true'; he said, rightly, that Dorothy McGuire was miscast as the working-class Catholic Irish mother, but it is a pleasing performance within the conventions of the time, and there are some excellent supporting performances, especially Lloyd Nolan as the local cop and James Gleason as proprietor of the bar the father frequented.

Kazan's handling of material which could have been rendered sentimental is admirable, but he did not distinguish himself when he took on **The Sea of Grass** (1947) for the chance of working with Spencer Tracy and Katharine Hepburn (the back-projection work, on the wheatfields which give the film its title, had already been done by the time he arrived on the project). They and he seem depressed by this nineteenth-century saga about a land baron and a wife so bored that she slips into sin with his mortal enemy (Melvyn Douglas); the son from this liaison

grows up to be so dissolute that his antics bring her back to the neighbourhood and, for an unconvincing finish, into her husband's arms. Kazan loathed the material (and Metro), and immediately took on **Boomerang** (1947), one of 20th Century-Fox's factual series which had begun with *The House on 92nd Street* (q.v.), using real locations in Stamford, Connecticut. In Richard Murphy's screenplay the accused man (Arthur Kennedy) is innocent, despite the number of eye witnesses who declare him guilty; but the D.A. (Dana Andrews) is on his side. Kazan has said, 'I think it's a good film. I thought everything *worked*. It was a piece of mechanism, a fairly effective piece of story-telling mechanism.' Not everything works now – nor did it work then, for the accused man is a war veteran, and it would be some time before a veteran could be shown as anything but perfect. The real culprit is laughably obvious, but against that, Kazan has given fresh thought to the methods of the police and the reporter (Sam Levene). The film's reception by the press secured Kazan's reputation, which leapt further when his next film won Oscars for Best Film and Best Direction.

The Academy Awards of the postwar years seemed to Hollywood to confirm its new social conscience. There remains merit in *The Lost Weekend*, and at least it is possible to see why contemporaries admired *The Best Years of Our Lives*; but **Gentleman's Agreement** (1947) is based on a false premise, and audiences today find it, at best, quaint. It is difficult to accept Gregory Peck's Galahad of a reporter – so high-principled, so dedicated, so charming – and even harder to believe that he could have reached his age without any awareness of anti-Semitism, especially as his oldest friend (John Garfield) is a Jew. He seethes with indignation and starts research for an article to be called 'I Passed for a Jew for Six Months'. The original novel was by Laura Z. Hobson, and Zanuck – the only Gentile among the heads of the major studios – was much praised for acquiring it. The screenwriter, Moss Hart, was a Jew, and also too intelligent (on other evidence) to have penned these platitudes without intending to satirise Hollywood's crusading heroes. He does have a moment or so of honesty: Dorothy McGuire trying to persuade Peck to drop the pretence for his first visit to her sister; June Havoc hiding her Jewishness under a Gentile name; Sam Jaffe as a professor much amused by his Jewishness; and Garfield deciding to move his family to Connecticut because someone has to break down the barriers. (The outstanding performance is that of Celeste Holm, as a breezy and understanding fashion editor.) In fact, the barriers had been down for years: anti-Semitism, rife enough in the States by the Twenties, began to fade as news filtered through of Hitler's Germany and was dealt a severe blow when wartime conscription revealed the extent of prejudice and discrimination against blacks. Hollywood was, as ever, years behind, but Zanuck caught up somewhat with his own film on that particular racial problem, **Pinky** (1949), about a black girl so light-skinned that she could pass for white: again Zanuck compromised, by casting a white actress, Jeanne Crain – or so said Kazan, who does not regard this as one of his own films, since he took it on when John Ford fell ill after a few days' shooting. The writers, Philip Dunne and Dudley Nichols, working from a novel by Cid Ricketts Summers, offer their heroine an identity crisis but refuse to deal with racial prejudice; the film's only superiority over the other racial dramas of the time – *Lost Boundaries*, *Home of the Brave* – is in its half-decent depiction of the Southern black's miserable lot.

Kazan found his style with **Panic in the Streets** (1950) – or was helped to it by Joseph Macdonald, the photographer. Macdonald and Norbert Brodine between them had photographed almost all 20th Century-Fox's 'factual' movies, and Kazan used their skill dynamically, adding to the city's chiaroscuro harsh natural sound and furious editing, suggesting a corner of life as experienced by someone with raw and jagged nerves. It was a style entirely suited to the subject – the search for a murderer with bubonic plague. It is a chase story, pure and simple, well written by Richard Murphy and well acted by Paul Douglas as the police officer in charge of the case, Richard Widmark as the city medical officer, and Barbara Bel Geddes as his wife.

Kazan had directed **A Streetcar Named Desire** (1951) for Broadway: 'The Pulitzer Prize-Winning Play and recipient of the New York critics award' say the credits, by way of preparing audiences for what was then unusual cinema fare. Both film and play for once deserved that favourite adjective of publicists, 'sensational': Blanche duBois (Vivien Leigh), a seemingly well-born teacher, is revealed as frequenting the infamous Flamingo Hotel not merely for money, and her brother-in-law Stanley (Marlon Brando), having discovered this, ravishes her the night his wife Stella (Kim Hunter) gives birth to their baby. It no longer shocks, now that rape and nymphomania have become commonplace on the screen: as they were, of course, though in more decorous fashion, before the Hays Office clamped down. In this instance the M.P.A.A. bowed to the play's reputation, resisting only Blanche's brief reference to her husband's homosexuality and insisting that Stanley be punished for his uncontrollable lust. As it happened, screen audiences were not immensely taken with *Streetcar*, perhaps because of Tennessee Williams's baroque, poetic approach; but the matters with which it deals could then only be found in textbooks on psychology. Its greatest truths are in the relationship between Stella and Stanley. The warm, practical Stella and the ape-like, self-possessed Stanley *enjoy* each other – the way the other looks and talks – and when they kiss, you can sense the sexual pleasure; it is in direct contrast to Blanche's sleazy past and Stanley's donning of his best pyjamas when he has decided to take her.

Brando and Miss Hunter are wonderful, and their performances move into a region which takes no account of concepts of 'theatre' or 'cinema'; from the Broadway production, Karl Malden – as the hoped-for suitor – is almost as good, but most of his scenes are with Blanche, and she is a very theatrical lady.

At the last minute Kazan decided to film the play as written, jettisoning a free adaptation,. a wise decision, since both Stanley and Blanche are larger than life; though the cinema can absorb without difficulty his half-articulate slobbishness. Blanche is a coquette of airs and graces, her speech remembered from cheap novels and primers on etiquette: she represents something of the author's fascination with Southern belles and sex for sale, but she is also a very real character – and one going mad. To have put both her and the gradual

709

Postwar Hollywood: The Directors in Their Brave New World

Early in his career as a director Elia Kazan made a handful of films which remain as powerful as contemporary opinion maintained. Among them are *A Streetcar Named Desire*, RIGHT, with Marlon Brando, Vivien Leigh and Kim Hunter all repeating their stage performances, and *Viva Zapata!*, BELOW, with Brando. Kazan understood exactly how to harness Brando's personal magnetism to the brutish Stanley of *Streetcar* and the rebel leader in *Zapata* – and this leader was certainly unlike heroes played by Cooper, Gable or Tracy.

insanity into acceptable screen terms would surely have destroyed the qualities of the original; instead, her artificiality is emphasised by dressing her in fussy nets and tulles, so at odds with the clothes of Stella. Miss Leigh is the only Blanche I can ever imagine or ever want to see. Kazan says that she was so imbued with her theatrical interpretation (as directed by Olivier for the London production) that he had difficulty in getting her to act for the camera – unsuccessfully, one imagines, since she is constantly in the middle of a speech, or even a word, when the camera angle shifts slightly via a cut, suggesting that the performance was assembled in the cutting room. The film is nevertheless a masterwork in some indefinable middle ground which is neither quite stage nor screen. Kazan uses huge close-ups, he uses a jazz soundtrack (by Alex North, the first time jazz had been so used in a dramatic film), he shows cluttered interiors and peeling exteriors; out of mist appears the woman selling flowers for the dead, and

710

when Blanche tells Mitch of her past, mist shrouds the light across the bay. The style is the right one, and Williams has paid tribute to Kazan's creative contribution to his work. There is no more *filmic* record of an American play than this one.

Another admired writer provided the screenplay and, alas, the 'poetic' dialogue of **Viva Zapata!** (1952). The project grew from a conversation between Kazan and John Steinbeck. (Since Zanuck had achieved much prestige with *The Grapes of Wrath*, this, too, became one of his 'personal' productions.) Their view of the brigand who became President of Mexico was romantic, and though not solving the enigma he represents in the history of his country, this film appeared to aim for greater veracity than most Hollywood biographies. While it was true that few people outside Mexico could question the accuracy, it could be claimed that Zapata had to be made into an acceptable revolutionary hero.

His indiscriminate killings and pillaging, and his twenty-six bigamous marriages are omitted; but the most serious simplification is the suggestion that he relinquished the presidency after a few months, to return to country life (in fact, he ruled jointly with Villa for eight years, and his reasons for leaving were far more complex). However, the film was courageous by Hollywood standards and extraordinarily exciting to all who saw it; some sticky symbolism is one reason it revives less well, but with virtually no competition it remains the best cinema study of revolt between *October* and *La Battaglia di Algeri* (q.v.). Taking liberties, chances, and sometimes leave of its senses, it offers the contrast between an illiterate and inert peasantry and a vicious militia – and between the dead lives of the former and the battles and intrigues of the latter; Kazan moves incisively, claiming that he learnt from *Paisà* 'to jump from crag to crag, rather than going all along the valleys'.

For once, the tensions of a revolutionary's life are understood, and Brando plays him as the inarticulate underdog, as in his earlier films, and the man of destiny which he would often play later; he has both personal magnetism and a sullen expression, disguising his surprise at being caught up in these events. The film was designed to expose the ineffectiveness of idealistic

revolutionaries. Kazan has explained, 'I believe that democracy progresses through internecine war, through constant tension – we grow only through conflict. And that's what democracy is. In that sense, people have to be vigilant, and the vigilance is effective. I truly believe that all power corrupts . . .' Such is probably the thinking behind every 'political' film made in Hollywood.

The comment (though made years later), and the film itself, were meant to justify Kazan's co-operation with the House Un-American Activities Committee, investigating Communist affiliations with the film industry.

To emphasise his fitness to be part of a de-Communised film industry, Kazan accepted a political subject from Zanuck, **Man on a Tightrope** (1953), the story of a circus in conflict with the State, specifically Czechoslovakia. The commissars complain that the clowning of Cernik (Fredric March) lacks commitment; and although the point is hammered home that under Communism no artist is allowed freedom, the film was regarded merely as an indifferent chase thriller by contemporary critics – who commented adversely, if at all, on the dialogue by Robert E. Sherwood (working from a novel by Neil Paterson). To this high-flown script Kazan brought 'European' direction – Ufa lighting and groupings from *Varieté*, which had had a not dissimilar story: despite or because of that he attains a singular conviction in his deployment of the circus itself and the (German) locations. For anyone with a taste for irony there is the arch right-winger, Adolphe Menjou, at his best as a left-wing commissar, moustache drooping seedily and his front speckled with cigarette ash.

Kazan's films (though *Streetcar* was made for Warners) contributed much to the reputation of 20th Century-Fox as the boldest of the studios. So, increasingly, did those made by Joseph L. Mankiewicz, whose stint as a writer for Paramount had been followed by what he called 'the black years', producing for M-G-M.★ Only cynicism can explain his Joan Crawford

★He left after a row with Louis B. Mayer over his relationship with Judy Garland. His contract, which had some time to run, was assigned to Fox, then being run (Zanuck was in the army) by Joseph Schenck, who was so pleased to get Mankiewicz that in a unique deal for the time he was allowed to produce, direct and write, or any one or two of the three.

vehicles, and though he also made such films as *Three Comrades* and *Woman of the Year* few could have forecast his achievements at Fox. His contract guaranteed him the opportunity to direct and, sidetracked into producing and writing *The Keys of the Kingdom*, he had worried over Stahl's handling of it. Although he disliked the derivative novel (by Anya Seton) on which **Dragonwyck** (1946) was based, he agreed to direct and script it as he would be working under the supervision of Lubitsch, his friend and mentor at Paramount. (The novel had been purchased for Lubitsch as a change from comedy, but after the heart attack which had caused him to relinquish the direction of *A Royal Scandal* he had decided to accept the less strenuous job of producing only.) Mankiewicz stresses the American-Dutch elements of the setting in order to play down the pseudo-Gothic plot, but as soon as we see the mansion illuminated by lightning we know the new governess (Gene Tierney) will take up the candelabrum for a midnight prowl; as soon as the nice young doctor (Glenn Langan) opposes the mysterious master of the house (Vincent Price) we know which one will be holding her in his arms at the end. At least Mankiewicz gets Tierney and Price to resemble real people.

As far as Mankiewicz was concerned, he was acquiring an unobtrusive directorial style. **Somewhere in the Night** (1946) is a melodrama about an amnesiac army veteran (John Hodiak) – and by a process known only to Hollywood, amnesia can turn a nasty guy into a nice one.★ He sets out to find his identity in the familiar world of *film noir*: a dusty rooming house where a hooker lurks in the hall; a Turkish bath with a surly attendant; a fortress-like mental home. There is also the girl, played by Nancy Guild with the looks, voice and talent of a combined Tierney and Veronica Lake, proving again that no star ever made it who was a copy of just another one – or two. She has to say 'Things don't happen like this,' which does not excuse Mankiewicz or his fellow screenwriter, Howard Dimsdale.

The next three films were written by Philip Dunne, whose screenplays for them are verbose but – at least as far as the first two are concerned – intelligent: in both

respects they reflect Mankiewicz's later, more personal work. **The Late George Apley** (1947), adapted from the play by John P. Marquand and George S. Kaufman (from the former's novel) is an aimless comedy about a Boston blue-blood (Ronald Colman) who in middle age has to learn that there are values other than his own. **The Ghost and Mrs Muir** (1947), adapted from a whimsical novel by R. A. Dick, concerns a widow (Miss Tierney) who falls in love with a deceased sea captain (Rex Harrison). Neither is promising material, but by treating them as witty observations on social behaviour and putting justified confidence in the charms of his leading men Mankiewicz makes elegant entertainments of both. Rex Harrison, as it happens, persuaded Zanuck to sanction **Escape** (1948) for him, as he had admired the 1930 film version of Galsworthy's play with Sir Gerald du Maurier: shooting on location on Dartmoor gave the company an opportunity to use funds 'frozen' by the British government and to use two British contract-players (the other was Peggy Cummins) whom American cinemagoers were not exactly taking to their hearts. The plot hoarily supposes that an escaped convict (Harrison) can easily find a car to steal, a hut to hide in, a spirited girl (Cummins) to help him, and so on: it is accompanied by dialogue in which are embedded some nuggets of wisdom, equally dated, and though Mankiewicz handles all matters in a smooth style there is nothing to suggest that his next film would be so very good.

A Letter to Three Wives (1948) established Mankiewicz as a brilliant director and screenwriter – it won him Oscars in both capacities – and as a social comedy it has dated hardly a jot. As a director he relies much on good faces and good furniture, and as a writer he has an aptitude for lines both funny in themselves and able to illuminate the quirks and whims of character. His subject is marriage: three ladies ponder on theirs, as the voice on the soundtrack (Celeste Holm, uncredited) informs them that she has run off with the husband of one of them. Mankiewicz is not particularly interested in the country-club couple (Jeanne Crain, Jeffrey Lynn) and their wartime marriage, but he dotes on the others – whose stories to an extent intertwine. They are a soap-opera writer

---

★The idea, however, had been used earlier by Jean Anouilh in 'Le Voyageur sans Bagage'.

(Ann Sothern), her poetry-pop-quoting husband (Kirk Douglas), and the girl (Linda Darnell) from the wrong side of the tracks who is using every wile to get her boss (Paul Douglas) to the altar. A dinner party involving the four of them, plus a slovenly maid (Thelma Ritter) and a monstrous sponsor (Florence Bates), is as funny as the similar sequence in *Alice Adams*.

The film's producer, Sol C. Siegel, interested Mankiewicz in **House of Strangers** (1949), adapted by Philip Yordan from a chapter of a novel by Jerome Weidman: Mankiewicz rewrote the script but declined to share the credit with Yordan and was consequently denied any by the Screen Writers Guild. The story, derived from the biblical tale of Joseph and his brethren, concerns an Italian barber (Edward G. Robinson) who becomes a bank tycoon by managing the affairs of other immigrants, all the while singing the praises of spaghetti and opera, and finally allowing his favourite son (Richard Conte) to take the rap for embezzlement. The piece itself is not unoperatic, but there is a feeling that it should have been about a Jewish family* rather than an Italian one and indeed Jewish talents were involved. The film was a box-office failure, but Mankiewicz's twin Oscars were a contributory factor in Zanuck assuming the producer credit on Mankiewicz's next three films. This was an usurpation of command, but Zanuck did institute **No Way Out** (1950), which he considered, rightly, a more creditable addition to the brief cycle of racial dramas than *Pinky*. For Mankiewicz it was a belated return to the mood of *Fury* (which he had produced), and similarly a good crime story is buttressed with indignation at social injustice. But if Mankiewicz and his co-writer, Lesser Samuels, start with some impeccable and understated points about the behaviour of blacks in the face of racial prejudice their young doctor (Sidney Poitier) is, in the end, too noble, too impervious to danger. 'Maybe someday some autopsy can analyse that mind,' says the head doctor (Stephen McNally) of the thug (Richard Widmark) determined to kill Poitier. Sidney Poitier (b.1924) would become the first black movie star since Paul Robeson,

and though not required to play 'Sambo' roles he would, for most of his career, play a number of fellows so noble that they have little dimension.

Meanwhile, Mankiewicz wrote and directed **All About Eve** (1950), which was popular at the time – at least with the carriage trade – and now causes most people to stay home whenever it is on television. Its durability confounds those who thought it too talky and too static. The exposition is swift, the dialogue smart, the characters appealing – theatre-obsessed, egotistical, virtually incestuous in their loves and hates. Mankiewicz set out to examine – with no conclusions drawn – the psychology of a successful actress; he ended with a symposium on the theatre as witty as it is deflationary, encapsulating all one might care to know on the subject. His comments are put into the mouths of people with the rare virtue of having a life independent of what they are doing on the screen – with the exception of the critic, Addison de Witt (George Sanders), whose function is not unlike that of the Greek chorus, and his 'protégée', Miss Caswell (Marilyn Monroe), 'a graduate of the Copacabana School of Dramatic Art'. However, the film's ace is in its portrait of the actress concerned: actresses have always revelled in playing actresses and for more than two generations Bette Davis's rendering of this one, Margo Channing, has been definitive.

The events recounted in Mary Orr's original story happened to Elisabeth Bergner. The star originally contracted was Claudette Colbert, who broke her back, and it was then offered to Gertrude Lawrence, whose agent wanted her to sing a song in the party sequence – a suggestion Mankiewicz declined. Davis, by a quirk of fate (she had broken a blood vessel in her throat and was forced to speak in a lower register) discovered that everyone thought she had based her portrait on Tallulah Bankhead; she has said that Margo is not like herself, but there must be something personal to explain the sense of heartbreak, which is as sure as any put on film. Margo's suspicions, her need for comfort and reassurance, her realistic attitude towards her job, all lead to a number of clashes with her entourage. That is one situation; the other tells how Eve (Anne Baxter) schemes to take over her friends, her man

*Weidman's novel had originally concerned a Lower East Side Jewish family but he had changed it before publication to an Italian one after criticisms of his treatment of the Jewish community in 'I Can Get It for You Wholesale'.

713

Joseph L. Mankiewicz had been writer, then producer and finally director before handling all three functions on some films fondly remembered – and in the case of *All About Eve*, still much admired. Its subject is the theatre, and for a while its clever remarks are those one might expect from a bright Hollywood boy who had been an occasional observer of the Broadway scene. That it becomes something more is due partly to the portrait of an ageing actress by Bette Davis, seen here with Gary Merrill.

(Gary Merrill) and certainly her next role. Margo is as wary of her as of everybody, and though there have been aspiring actresses as vulpine and unscrupulous as Eve, I find it hard to believe that even sentimental theatre folk would be taken in by her as played by Miss Baxter. The years have done nothing to diminish Davis, Celeste Holm and Thelma Ritter (as best friend and dresser respectively), but Baxter now seems just another plastic puss, unable to convey shades of meaning: only the drive of Davis even off-screen prevents Baxter's scenes from falling apart – yet Davis's is, if marginally, the lesser role. Mankiewicz reflects the general belief of the time that audiences were more intrigued by smart little schemers than ageing actresses – which is why it is all about Eve and not all about Margo.

With fistfuls of Oscars and other awards, it was inevitable that his next film would be an anti-climax, and **People Will Talk** (1951) was not popular. The acclaim had been such that he had nothing to con-

sider but his own talent, and he put it at the service of doctors as *Eve* had put it at the service of actresses. His source was an old German play and film, *Dr Med Hiob Praetorius*, by Curt Götz and it was used, as Mankiewicz explained in an interview, to prove that 'psychiatry is as necessary to the doctor as anatomy itself, and that medicine should be more than pills, serums, and knives.' The minimal plot concerns a humanitarian, all-wise doctor (Cary Grant, who never had a better chance to express himself) who marries a pregnant girl (Jeanne Crain) and triumphs over a jealous colleague (Hume Cronyn) who has been sniping at him; but the plot gives Mankiewicz the chance to air such topics as free medication, quackery, the idiocies of habit, the decline of standards and academic backbiting – the last of these being a reference to the current H.U.A.C. witch-hunts. In its form it is an unsatisfactory film. It proved to Hollywood that Mankiewicz could make a serious film with the sort of intelligent dialogue for which he was now noted; he uses Brahms and Wagner to prove that good music is as essential to civilised living as good conversation. As for the heroine's pregnancy, that was a challenge to the childishly restrictive M.P.A.A. Mankiewicz claimed that without that situation the film could not have been made, but the plot would not have suffered had the girl been a widow instead of unmarried. Like all of Hollywood's leading talents, Mankiewicz wanted movies to be more realistic: so Miss Crain, who had not bothered to get married, is not punished but rewarded – with Mr Grant.

Mankiewicz had one film left under the terms of his contract. He had no intention of renewing it, since he disliked Zanuck's helping himself to the producer credit; Zanuck, though he felt it vital to the company's prestige to keep Mankiewicz, disliked his status as 'producer' being so obviously subservient to a now-renowned writer-director. Mankiewicz found a way out of the impasse by suggesting **Five Fingers** (1952), scheduled for Henry Hathaway, as his last assignment – and since the project already had a nominal producer and a writer (Michael Wilson) Mankiewicz would relinquish credit for both activities, though he did virtually rewrite the script. In the event he again proved himself at ease in a milieu – the diplomatic set – which had often defeated film-makers. The diplomats are for once played by the correct nationalities, and the locations are those of the original incident – Ankara in 1944, when the Albanian-born valet of the British ambassador sold secrets to the Germans for what turned out to be counterfeit money (among the documents he photographed were the plans for the Normandy landings, which the Germans ignored). The facts were set down by L. C. Moyzisch, a former German attaché, in 'Operation Cicero', a book published in 1950, and the film starts with the British government's admission of its accuracy. Wilson's addition of an impoverished countess (Danielle Darrieux) was resented by some critics, but her verbal sparring with the valet (James Mason) is of an urbane level – and so superior to Wilson's other efforts as to confirm Mankiewicz's hand. Darrieux plots secretly and pouts deliciously; Mason is superb, both proud of his wit and humble calling, if not much like the shifty and shabby original. That gentleman was alive when the film came out, and never told his own side of it: I doubt whether that would include the final chase from Ankara to Istanbul, which provides a perfect climax.

As with Mankiewicz, the films of George Cukor are civilised, if not sophisticated. He also brought to above-average material the correct furnishings, photographing them (whether faces or props) without pretension and keeping most of the action in medium close-up. He was fastidious over his choice of material, and it was four years after *Winged Victory* that his name appeared on a film – since in the interim he refused a credit for his work on **Desire Me** (1947), which starred Greer Garson as a Breton war widow whose first husband turns up after she has remarried – a situation taken in this case from Pirandello. (Among others who toiled on it was Mervyn LeRoy, but it went out without a director credit, the only major Hollywood production to do so between the Silent era and the present.) Cukor would not have been foolish to have also disclaimed credit on **A Double Life** (1948) and **Edward, My Son** (1949), two superficial studies of paranoia. He admitted that he could not direct melodrama, and he chose in both cases a style that is of the theatre but not theatrical. The former, in fact, concerns the theatre, and was written by Garson Kanin and his wife, Ruth Gordon. It was one of the postwar bids for independence, produced for Universal by Kanin's brother Michael – and since Kanin had no wish to return to directing, Cukor (who had worked with Miss Gordon on *Two-Faced Woman*) was borrowed from M-G-M. When Kanin calls the film 'terrible', he may be thinking of its central idea – that some actors are so overwhelmed by an emotional part that they allow it to affect their private lives. This one (Ronald Colman) is currently playing Othello,★ but no further suggestion is forthcoming for his Jekyll and Hyde behaviour. Colman, as Cukor said, had no sense of the demonic, being merely moody and uncharacteristically wild-eyed; the Oscar he was accorded for this performance may have been due to sentiment, or to the voters' customary admiration for anyone in a double role – or capable of speaking Shakespearian verse. Nor is Spencer Tracy at his best in *Edward, My Son*, though reverting to his old role of the self-made tycoon who destroys all about him: his wife (Deborah Kerr) becomes an embittered alcoholic and his son a wastrel. These tired themes had been rejigged into a British play by Robert Morley and Noel Langley which had a mild success on Broadway, suggesting to Metro an ideal way to use funds blocked in Britain. Donald Ogden Stewart's screenplay retains the gimmick of the original, which never allowed us to meet the Edward so much talked about.

Adam's Rib (1949) was written by Kanin and Gordon for Tracy and Katharine Hepburn, drawing upon characteristics of all four of them – and it is a movie which inspires affection for its leading players, partly because the affection between them is manifestly there. As a team their characters had been established in *Woman of the Year* (which Kanin, uncredited, had initiated): they have a greater number of domestic scenes here, and the same professional rivalry – they are lawyers, he prosecuting and she defending Doris (Judy Holliday), who had shot at her unfaithful husband (Tom Ewell); they are opposed,

★Othello's offstage homicidal tendencies had already been examined in a Matheson Lang vehicle, 'Carnival', filmed in 1921 and 1931, and *Men Are not Gods*.

715

Postwar Hollywood: The Directors in Their Brave New World

The early Fifties were clearly a happy time in Hollywood, with the directors gaining more power and the studio bosses not yet panicking as television began to eat into cinema attendances – or so we may suppose, for George Cukor was yet another director whose work of the time is both confident and relaxed. Though mainly associated with drama, he concentrated on comedy with the aid of some very bright scripts by Garson Kanin and his wife Ruth Gordon. *Adam's Rib* was written for Spencer Tracy and Katharine Hepburn, right, but it contained a large supporting role for Judy Holliday, centre, who had scored a Broadway hit in Kanin's play 'Born Yesterday'.

equally wittily, over what is now called women's lib. Miss Holliday (1922–65) had appeared on Broadway in Kanin's 'Born Yesterday', and there was a conspiracy to throw scenes her way so that Columbia could not avoid putting her in the film version (q.v.) of the play; these scenes – her deposition and appearance on the witness stand – are notable for the unselfishness of the other players and her own skill. The supporting cast includes David Wayne, singing a ballad by Cole Porter.

After directing Hepburn and Holliday, Cukor turned to the vacuous Lana Turner: Isobel Lennart's screenplay for **A Life of Her Own** (1950) was ordinary, he once admitted, but bearing in mind that it was a star vehicle, he thought he could do a useful job. It is quite lively, especially on the practical difficulties and mechanics of a model's life, accepting the sort of facts which good movies (let alone soap operas) were still ignoring – that girls who take up this career are ambitious but not too bright, and that the men who take up the girls are likely to be elderly. The subsidiary characters similarly have more life than we

might expect – the sour-faced pianist acknowledging an offered drink with a nod, the bustling fat concierge turning the men out of the mezzanine of the hostel, the fashion editor with the cigarette holder and exaggerated English accent. What Cukor could not manage was to get a good performance from Turner, but she is not – for once – a dead loss. Preview audiences disliked her suicide at the end, so that was changed; but the same fate was allowed to Ann Dvorak, stunningly good as a girl who knows the score yet is pathetically involved with a playboy.

Judy Holliday did get to repeat her stage role in **Born Yesterday** (1950), and Cukor, borrowed from M-G-M, once again used unobtrusive skill in translating high quality theatrical dialogue – reworked from his own play by Kanin, though for various reasons he let credit go to a lesser writer who had worked on one of the drafts. This story of an education is sometimes sententious, since the education begins with lectures on Tom Paine and Jefferson, and there are even indications that we are meant to see Billie (Miss

Holliday) as a free democratic spirit escaping from the tyranny of Brock (Broderick Crawford) the scrap dealer who keeps her. In fact, Billie is one of the great comic creations, moving between the two moods learnt from experience – suspicious and defensive, with a matching armoury of phrases. Her philosophy is summed up thus: 'If he don't act friendly, I don't act friendly. As long as I know how to get what I want, I'm all right.' To watch Holliday begin to learn, understand and warm to her tutor (William Holden), is a wonderful thing; and to that extent the story is a combination of Cinderella, Pygmalion and the worm that turned. Holliday's performance, touchingly vulnerable, childishly triumphant, is to be endlessly studied and savoured, from her surprised 'What d'ya know!' to her crumpled 'I did look it up and I still don't know.' Brock has only two things to say to her – 'So shut up' and 'All right, I'll buy it for you' – and Crawford is bull-like, lacking the vestigial charm Paul Douglas brought to the role on stage. Perhaps it is as well that there seems no sexual attraction between them – though that is an odd omission in a piece about a kept woman. Nor is there any sex when she says to her tutor, 'Are you one of those talkers or would ya like a little action?', which is the creed of a woman who owes her wellbeing to her body.

It is clear that Cukor and/or the Kanins were happier with domestic love: **The Marrying Kind** (1952) was written expressly for Holliday and this, the third of their comedies together, is more serious than the theatrical froufrou of the earlier two. Its roots lie in the American working-class comedies of the early Thirties, and there is in it a quality of hurt which would not be found again in an American comedy till Billy Wilder's films of the early Sixties. Florence (Holliday) and Chet (Aldo Ray), are in the process of divorce, and flashbacks fill us in from their meeting in Central Park to the present: an anniversary that goes wrong, an accidental death, a radio quiz show, hospitalisation, interfering relatives and, in the end, too many rows. We see the past as it was, while each remembers only what most favours themselves: the laughter is wrought from reality. Only the dream sequence grates and it confirms a suspicion that the Kanins worked with their heads and memories of other movies

rather than with their hearts. The breakup of a marriage needs more compassionate handling than it gets here. Cukor supplies the balance, and Holliday and Ray go a long way towards supplying the missing dimension. She is again incomparable, funny and touching in every line and gesture; he, especially in a too-large lounge suit, is never like a movie star, while a gravel voice and a certain reticent eagerness make him equally likeable. Neither player makes us feel that this is a great love match, but this tale of two nice ordinary people who marry and are happy and then unhappy is a big achievement among the movies of the time.

Meanwhile Kanin and Gordon had written **Pat and Mike** (1952) for Tracy and Hepburn. He plays a dubious sports promoter and she an all-round sports-woman who resists his 'advances' till she contemplates life with her dull fiancé. Despite the success of *Adam's Rib*, M-G-M hesitated over the material – not surprisingly, since there is no plot, and thirty of the ninety-three minutes' running time are taken up with a golf game. Cukor himself seemed disinclined to develop the authors' tentative situations and was clearly happier on **The Actress** (1953), written by Miss Gordon from her autobiographical play, 'Years Ago'. It is about the desire of Ruth Gordon Jones (Jean Simmons) to go on the stage – after seeing 'The Pink Lady' with its star, seen by her and by us as a remote

After Judy Holliday made the film of *Born Yesterday*, *The Marrying Kind* was fashioned for her, to prevent her from being typecast as a dumb blonde – though as Aldo Ray's wife she was not exactly supposed to be an intellectual genius.

717

deity, which is the sort of right, elegant touch one expects from Cukor. The setting is a small town before the First World War, and he rescues it from the morass of sentimentality, Technicolor and Jeanne Crainisms that we had met hitherto; family life has not only affection but meanness and smallness. The interiors are cluttered and cramped, the exteriors wintry – and the final effect is similar, despite the charm of Miss Simmons, in her best performance up to that time. She is a sloppy, starry-eyed dream of adolescence, her constant high spirits somewhat mocked; as her sea dog father, Tracy never plays for sympathy, but his softhearted conversion to her ambition makes for longueurs in the second half.

In **It Should Happen to You** (1954) July Holliday's ambition to be 'somebody' inspires her to hire a huge sign in Columbus Circle to spell out her name, 'Gladys Glover'. Kanin's screenplay, from his own story, falters towards the end, and well before that it is clear that he could not decide whether he wanted a satire on mini-celebrities (which is what Gladys becomes) or a Holliday vehicle. It is often witty and charming, and this actress justifies his every word, whether handling an ad agency with varying expressions of wariness, or gazing at her poster in a state of euphoria. She is hurt and bewildered when Jack Lemmon (b. 1925), in his first film, yells 'What sort of fruitcake are you?' – and at the same time indignant, 'No sort of'. The sequences between these two players are among the most likeable in the whole canon of American cinema. In the admittedly inferior *Phffft!* (q.v.) they are less effective together, thus emphasising Cukor's usual careful tension between the cinema's ability to charm and entertain and its responsibility to truth.

This balance between entertainment and truth can be found in the work of all these directors, but since it is not necessarily the right balance for serious drama, it is the comedies which wear best; and as Cukor and Mankiewicz made the most accomplished comedies it is ironic that some of their films, with no discernible directorial flourishes, should best represent that age when the American director was for the first time in thirty years being recognised as the prime creative force in film-making.

The modesty of Mankiewicz and Cukor is endearing – *Adam's Rib* even uses a puppet theatre to disarm criticism of its theatricality – but then they were content to stay within their fields of social satire, while other directors had statements to make. The other memorable films of the era – *Letter from an Unknown Woman, A Streetcar Named Desire, The African Queen, The Asphalt Jungle, High Noon* – represent different movie conventions; though it must be said at once that Billy Wilder as ever is *hors série* and *The Search* is an almost wholly successful attempt to emulate the European movie. Most of the directors at this time were influenced by, or at least interested in, what was happening in Europe; they, too, wanted to startle with their 'art'. And the most admired films of the time were those that did so – like *A Place in the Sun*, which seemed to reviewers to presage Hollywood's snatching the crown from Europe, that America, after years of stagnation, complacency and Production Code stifling, would once again make the most exciting movies in the world. Contemporaries were wholly right to admire Stevens and Wyler rather than, say, Cukor, since he was conservative and they were trying to expand the boundaries of cinema – though not, as we have seen, towards the contemporary realistic dramas anticipated in the immediate postwar period. That expansion is the keynote to this time: spurred on by the example of Europe, praise from critics and commercial success, the leading directors were challenging the ever reluctant executives to make the sort of films which they wanted to make – and there is hardly a film discussed in this chapter which was not debated intensively by people who took the cinema seriously. Time has reversed a number of judgments, and may do so again. Meanwhile, we may note that Cukor and the Kanins did not work together again (and the latter were unable for some years to sell scripts in Hollywood), and that Cukor left M-G-M, as did Hepburn and Tracy. The much-desired independence, after a false start in the late Forties, was becoming a necessity a few years later; for the first time since the Twenties the structure of the industry was changing.

28

Postwar Hollywood: The Studios

BY LOOKING FIRST at the leading directors we have covered most of the important American films of the postwar period – if by 'important' we mean those which contemporaries regarded most highly; yet the less prestigious names pointed Hollywood towards its most significant direction of the time – the return after two decades to filming in the streets.

Since the beginning, the cinema had been in the thrall of literature and the stage – which is why it was considered an art form subsidiary to both. For years it had been thought suitable mainly for the frivolous, as the novel had been. In England and America, Dickens, with his social purpose, made the novel virtually essential reading, and the greatness of the Victorian novelists generated a century of fiction. Novel-reading reached a peak during the War, and it could be argued that with the end of the War the decline of the novel began. Escapism became less important, realism more so. The Italians, as we have seen, were the first to respond to the new mood. In Hollywood this happened before American critics began praising de Sica and Rossellini, though few noticed at the time.

Henry Hathaway, the veteran director, was mainly responsible, and he did it without much support from 20th Century-Fox, his studio. He came across the script of **The House on 92nd Street** (1945), to be produced for the company by Louis de Rochemont, one of the founders of 'The March of Time' (a series for the cinema which had been examining current affairs since 1934) – and since these formed part of the supporting programme, Zanuck was confident that the same distinctive approach could only be used for B-movies. The lone predecessor in adopting the 'March of Time' technique (*Confessions of a Nazi Spy*), had not been successful, and the script that Hathaway pleaded to do was also concerned with German espionage activities in the U.S. – in this case seeking the formula for the atomic bomb. The F.B.I. vouched for the film's authenticity and gave full co-operation, which was a coup; but Hathaway underlined the 'authenticity' by shooting on location – as he said, the 'feel' of the script demanded it, and in any case he had always done so with Westerns. The critical reception was such that Hathaway used the same approach for **13, rue Madeleine** (1946): which again included a foreword vowing truth, the shots of filing cabinets, maps and briefings as prelude to a tale of American spies training for action in Nazi-occupied Europe – and despite the presence of James Cagney as chief instructor, a film quite unworthy of its forerunner.

Meanwhile, Hathaway had made **The Dark Corner** (1946) in conventional Hollywood fashion, an excellent thriller about a private eye (Mark Stevens) confronting the New York art world as represented by Clifton Webb and his thuggish aide, William Bendix. Resemblances may be found to the ambiguities of *Laura*, and under the titles we note the presence of 'Street Scene', an orchestral piece to be repeated in the other Fox thrillers of the period. The spy lode could not be mined indefinitely, but the F.B.I. framework was too valuable at the box-office to be thrown aside. The reviews of *Boomerang* once more proved to Zanuck the value of actual locations – and memories of his days at Warners prompted him to commission a 'social conscience' screenplay from Ben Hecht and Charles Lederer for Hathaway to direct. In **Kiss of Death** (1947), the F.B.I.'s quarry is its old enemy, the gangster. Victor Mature is the kid from the back street who just cannot help going to the bad; Richard Widmark (in his first film) is naturally evil, pushing a crippled old lady downstairs; and Brian Donlevy is the lawman convinced that Mature can go straight. The title has no relevance unless it is meant to refer to Mature's performance.

The F.B.I. paraphernalia was, as yet, of more importance than the filming in natural surroundings, but as Hathaway came up with **Call Northside 777** (1948) – with James Stewart as a reporter trying to prove the innocence of a convicted killer – Universal released the first 'imitation', *The Naked City* (q.v.), filmed almost entirely in the streets of New York.★ The press called them 'semi-documentaries' for want of a better word, and was so overwhelmingly favourable that there was no going back. The postwar mood was right for the thriller, and with a large number of petty crooks in the news, the public was appreciative of seediness and intimations of weakness in the screen's larger-than-life gangsters: they would not have supported the return of the flashy paranoiacs, but they responded to Richard Widmark in **The Street With No Name** (1948), as a sniggering weakling with nasal inhaler and floor-length overcoat. Zanuck's acquisition of Widmark was good enough reason to revive the underworld film, but in any case this one would have justified the revival. William Keighley, another veteran, directed and, despite having made no recent films of interest, rallied vigorously to the style set by Hathaway. His work is taut and tense, and he positively revels in this portrait of a dull small town, with its poolhalls, gymnasiums, seedy hotels and run-down all-night diners. J. Edgar Hoover, the head of the F.B.I. himself, presents the introduction, indicating that on occasion his organisation needs to send in an undercover man (Mark Stevens): the film then follows the complicated business of manufacturing a fake criminal career, after

★The title of Universal's film was taken from a best-selling book of photographs by the photo-journalist 'Weegee', whose pictures of seamy life were a great influence on all these films.

which it deals in suspicions and tip-offs till the final shoot-out in a deserted factory.

The battle, if battle it was, was won: except for interiors, the days of studio shooting were numbered. When Jean Negulesco arrived at 20th Century-Fox (from Warners) he was offered **Road House** (1948) because Zanuck had noted his flair for location; and the small town atmosphere is excellent. When Cornel Wilde tells Ida Lupino, 'There's small pickings in this town,' you know it is true: as manager and chanteuse, they fall in love amidst stale cigarette smoke, beer-guzzling and bowling – people still young, but with sapped spirits, making a last effort to shake off spiritual isolation. 'All I want to do is hang around someone on Sunday,' she says. As the cashier, Celeste Holm suggests another sort of loneliness, that of a nice girl who simply wants company; as the owner, Widmark is another lost soul – till he turns psychopathic at the end, a disappointing development.

Jules Dassin came from Universal to make **Thieves' Highway** (1949), thrown away on double bills but a good deal fresher than his lauded *Naked City*, with a feeling for night-time San Francisco beyond the scene of the immediate action: the fruit market, where a truck-driver (Richard Conte) is out to get the Big Man (Lee J. Cobb) who ruined his Pa. By this time night scenes were obligatory, but these have a dusty, melancholy quality, achieved without either menace or mood music. There is also an understated rendering of the life of a trucker, as might be expected from A. I. Bezzerides, who had written *They Drive by Night*, and his dialogue again crackles, till the advent of the rather woebegone whore (Valentina Cortese). With her we see the European influence being at last felt in Hollywood: not Rossellini, but prewar Carné.

Fourteen Hours (1951), from a screenplay by John Paxton and a story by Joel Sayre, is based on an actual event when a would-be suicide stood on the ledge of a skyscraper. Some of the incidents in the crowd are box-office trimming, but others are pleasing: the cab driver, annoyed at first at the delay, laying bets on when the man will jump; the reporters, fed up with the mother's hysterics, getting some 'man-in-the-streets'; the hotel guests adjusting to the disruption of service with irritation and grim curiosity; and the exasperated police chief (Howard da Silva) reacting to telephoned advice from his superiors. There is not much merit to the psychological interpretation – that the man (Richard Basehart) has a dominating mother (Agnes Moorehead, seizing her showy moments with sharp judgment) and a weak father (Robert Keith); but once the film starts gently to send up the enthusiastic psychologist (Martin Gabel) it deserves nothing but praise. Especially good is Paul Douglas, as the traffic cop who happens to be first on the scene and gains the man's confidence.

The subject of Hathaway's next film was even more difficult: **The Desert Fox: the Story of Rommel** (1951). Germans were still unpopular, and a sympathetic portrait was a box-office risk; the difficulty of screen biography increases when names like Goering and Montgomery are bandied about by actors pretending to be their contemporaries. Nunnally Johnson based his screenplay on the biography by Desmond Young, cunningly introduced (and played by Michael Rennie) as a man honourably interested in Rommel's mysterious death. The story proper starts with Rommel (James Mason) receiving instructions to hold out at El Alamein, and details his various periods in hospital, including the crucial one when the ex-mayor of Stuttgart (Cedric Hardwicke) tries to warn him that Hitler is paranoic. The exchanges between the two men are literate and thoughtful, as are those with von Rundstedt (Leo G. Carroll, who is particularly good) – and yet sufficiently sparse. The sobriety of Hathaway's approach works beautifully as we move towards Rommel's disgrace – to the extent that Churchill's panegyric, quoted at the end, is oddly moving.

The Snake Pit (1948) contributed further to the esteem in which 20th Century-Fox was held. It followed *The Lost Weekend* and the studio's own *Gentleman's Agreement*, seeking to interest the public in a pressing social problem. Perhaps critics, in praising these rare Hollywood excursions into life's darker side, were clutching at straws, and it may not be irrelevant that all three films were adapted from middle-brow novels (*The Snake Pit* is based on one by Mary Jane Ward). Nevertheless *The Spectator* spoke for many people when it called *The Snake Pit* 'a memorable and profoundly disturbing film', for none before had attempted a serious portrait of conditions inside a mental home. Inside, Anatole Litvak's direction is sober, careful and concerned to a degree, but when dealing with the heroine's past it is often heavily over-emphatic (like the music). The famous process shot of the inmates viewed as in a snake pit no longer impresses. The film's real subject is a nervous breakdown, and when its causes are finally revealed they are the expected business of an over-loving father and an antagonistic mother. The jolly analyses made by the psychiatrist (Leo Genn) are dramatically weak, and it does not help that he, the understanding husband (Mark Stevens) and the other doctor (Glenn Langan) are merely ciphers. The heroine's confession of love to the last-named is only a device with which to finish: the film ought to have ended with the beautifully-observed dance sequence and its moving rendering of 'Going Home'. Olivia de Havilland's role is one of the most demanding in the history of films, and she always has it under control, excellently supported by Celeste Holm, Ruth Donnelly and Beulah Bondi.

Another sombre enterprise, **Twelve O'Clock High** (1949), begins with an ex-U.S.A.F. officer (Dean Jagger) hearing ghostly choruses of 'Don't Sit Under the Apple Tree' and 'Bless 'em All' on a deserted East Anglian airfield. He recalls the young C.O. (Gregory Peck) whose belief in discipline caused his officers en masse to ask for transfers – till he himself proves his valour on a bombing mission. Unfortunately, as written by Sy Bartlett and Bierne Lay Jr the action takes place in a vacuum: there is a reference to the awful weather, but none to Betty Grable or the local pub. The only character with any dimension is Jagger's moderator, and he won a Best Supporting Oscar; but reviewers of the time took the film at its own valuation.

Henry King's direction cannot hide a certain smugness, but together with **The Gunfighter** (1950) it brought his reputation to its highest point since making *Tol'able David* thirty years earlier. Zanuck regarded *The Gunfighter* as suitable only for prestige, and allowed King to take his own time in evoking the atmosphere of a sleepy little town, galvanised by the presence of Peck as a has-been gunfighter (at thirty-five) – an object of disapproval by the town's matrons, of awe to the children, and of aggression to punks who fancy themselves as his equal. When he is killed, one of them will take his place – and a rotten tradition will have been passed on. It is a thesis too pat for a film otherwise more complex than most Westerns of the period; when the busybody ladies appear – a device favoured by John Ford – it is clear that King has achieved more feeling and more suspense than is available in any Western that Ford ever made.

Yellow Sky (1948) and **Rawhide** (1951) are also good examples of the genre, with William Wellman and Hathaway responding to sound, unpretentious material. Both films concern innocent victims in the clutches of bank robbers, and the former has the nastier villains – Widmark, John Russell and Henry (later, Harry) Morgan – with only Jack Elam to match them in *Rawhide*. Wellman's film can also boast more blood and guts than was usual at the time, as well as Joe Macdonald's photography of a ghost town in Death Valley. Both films are unfortunate in their leads: Peck is conventional in *Yellow Sky* as the bank robber with decent feelings, and as the prisoners in *Rawhide* neither Tyrone

In the postwar period 20th Century-Fox made a series of thrillers which found urban America a grim, seedy place. The studio also made a number of more serious pictures with an equally pessimistic view, the most interesting of which is *Nightmare Alley*, with Tyrone Power and Joan Blondell and directed by the veteran Edmund Goulding.

Power nor Susan Hayward is able to creat tension.

Peck was not under exclusive contrac to the studio but had become Zanuck' first choice for almost every leading role including **The Razor's Edge** (1946) Zanuck, however, changed his mind and became Power's first postwar film. I needed an actor of more ability than eithe to give meaning to Somerset Maugham' hero Larry, who leaves a comfortable lif and his fiancée (Gene Tierney) to seek i Europe and elsewhere his own holy grail He does not find it, but Maugham – play ed, as in *The Moon and Sixpence*, by Her bert Marshall – concludes, 'Goodness i after all the greatest force in the world. But if that was what the book was about the film keeps it a secret. George Cuko was to have directed from a screenplay by Maugham himself, but when Zanuck found it unusable Edmund Goulding re placed Cukor, with a revised screenplay by Lamar Trotti, the best of which is in the commentary, a prolonged series of opin ions and asides taken directly from the book. In uttering these, Maugham appear: as an idealist, and his dislike of his nouveau riche friends remains discernible, but the original text is otherwise unrecognisable apart from Clifton Webb as Elliott Tem pleton, the Europeanised all-American snob. Marshall is good, and would seem even better if everyone did not say 'Mr Maugham' as though *he* were the holy grail. Goulding uses very long takes, directing – according to the cinematog rapher, Arthur Miller – as if for the stage, though his camera moves subtly among the cast; Miller also recalled that he unsuc cessfully implored Zanuck to change the appalling backdrop in the Indian scene. This was another film in which *Life Maga zine* took a special interest – in return for which 20th Century-Fox advertised it heavily in that journal.

A lesser novel, by William Lindsay Gresham, provided a better film for Goulding and Power, as written for the screen by Jules Furthman. **Nightmare Alley** (1947) reaches into terrain where Hollywood seldom ventured – murky areas of cruelty and ambition, the occult and religious sensibilities. Stan (Power) is an orphan who has wandered into the job of carnival barker, and when you see him watching the geek in the first scene you know that that is how he will end up. (A geek is a man who eats live chickens because he is in an advanced state of alcoholism and that is apparently the only way to get his bottle a day.) He starts out by using Zeena (Joan Blondell), half of a phoney mind-reading act, and moves onwards and upwards till he meets his match in Lilith (Helen Walker). She is quite as unscrupulous as he, but unfortunately portrayed as the usual movie predator, with bags of self-confidence and a chic wardrobe. Nor is Power good enough; having returned from the War with a new seriousness, he begged for the role and plays conscientiously: but in place of ambition he offers only deviousness, and for blarney only a fast-moving dimple. Goulding keeps the carnival scenes tacky, and at its best this film is reminiscent of the German Silent studies of low life; it is a pity it is not better, for it is Goulding's last important film and also the last important one that Furthman wrote.

Henry King directed Power in **Captain from Castile** (1947) and **Prince of Foxes** (1949), historical extravaganzas based on the imaginings of Samuel Shellabargar – and the first since Silent days to make extensive use of locations, the former among the Aztec temples and volcanoes of Mexico, and the latter among the towers of Volterra, though Volterra, because of the cost and comparative failure of the earlier film, did not rate Technicolor. Power is the captain from Castile and, as in *Son of Fury*, he sails away from injustice to seek his fortune, followed by a laundress (Jean Peters): 'You'll join the women with the army,' Cortez (Cesar Romero) greets her, 'hoping to find a husband?' – which is Hollywood's way of dealing with one of the more awkward historical facts. Power survives tropical disease and an embarrassing fandango to marry her – because, after all, they are in the New World, home of democracy. The thirty-seven companions who helped Cortez conquer the Aztecs have become a huge concourse of extras. The title of *Prince of Foxes* refers to Cesare Borgia (Orson Welles), and Power here is one of the followers who turns against him when ordered to drive a wedge between the fair Camilla (Wanda Hendrix, pathetically miscast) and her elderly husband (Felix Aylmer).

With **Fallen Angel** (1946) Power's erst-while co-star, Alice Faye, gave up the battle against typecasting and retired. She did on this occasion play, and very well, a timid spinster whose insistence on marrying a blackguard (Dana Andrews) prompts him to plot both a getaway with her money and the murder of her rival, a hash-house waitress (Linda Darnell). The script, by Harry Kleiner from a novel by Marty Holland, has a degree of frankness rare at the time, if only in implying Andrews's lust for Darnell and Faye's for him. A better director than Otto Preminger might have made more of this, but aided by Joseph La Shelle's photography he does achieve a keen portrait of a one-horse town; Ann Revere offers an intriguing study as Faye's sister, recognising the man for what he is and trying to adjust to that fact.

A more conventional look at the mysterious husband and the frightened wife was available in the first of two films for the company directed by Robert Wise (b. 1916), an editor with R.K.O. before becoming a director with Val Lewton's unit. In **The House on Telegraph Hill** (1951) the wife (Valentina Cortese) is an impostor, having taken a friend's place in Belsen (a situation treated so unpretentiously in the prologue that it is quite acceptable). Arriving in San Francisco, she is confronted by a hostile governess and a room into which her husband (Richard Basehart) forbids her to go. Wise's other movie for Zanuck at this time is **The Day the Earth Stood Still** (1951) – the day in question being that when a messenger arrives from another planet to warn of the dangers of a nuclear war. Michael Rennie plays the role, and as he seldom seemed human it is good casting; as the boarding-house neighbour who befriends him Patricia Neal is too good for such storm-in-a-teacup melodrama. But both films, particularly the first, are good examples of the Fox movies at this time. Between 1946 and the advent of CinemaScope in 1953, the studio made some of the most visually satisfying of all movies, in crisp blacks and whites, with locations simply but expressively used. The scenes are, for the most part, shot in medium close-up; the settings were seldom ornate or mannered; the performances were not overburdened with technique, and as a result plots like the basically daft one of *The House on*

Telegraph Hill seem better than they are.

Not in this category is **Leave Her to Heaven** (1945) – if only because it was one of the few melodramas of the time to be filmed in Technicolor – as adapted by Jo Swerling from a novel by Ben Ames Williams. C. A. Lejeune's review reminds us that its sponsors described it as 'the sum total of human emotions . . . You will know you are in the presence of a great moment in screen history,' but she felt, rather, that 'the entertainment lies in seeing what new sin the lady can get up to.' There is just one variation on the other wicked lady dramas of the period, in that it takes Gene Tierney an hour to show her hand. The principals – the others are Cornel Wilde, Jeanne Crain and Vincent Price – are not the ones to portray 'a great moment in screen history', and the director, John M. Stahl, once adept with such material, was clearly dispirited.

As a work of fiction **Forever Amber** (1947) towered above such pieces, having garnered in book form a notoriety which had made it an enormous bestseller. The Legion of Decency led the organisations militant at the thought of a film version, and the chances of getting a workable script were remote. Shooting eventually began under Stahl, with the wildly unsuitable Peggy Cummins in the title role (unlike Scarlett O'Hara, it was a role no one wanted to play): both were dropped by Zanuck after the expenditure of two million dollars, and replaced by Otto Preminger and Linda Darnell. (Zanuck preferred Darnell to Preminger's choice, Lana Turner, because he was unwilling to make overtures to M-G-M for Turner's services.) Zanuck also refused to concede Preminger's point that the material should be mocked because its mediocrity matched its reputation; the result amply demonstrates Preminger's own claim that he was otherwise not interested. Nor were there enough patrons to justify the final $6 million cost, and it may be said that those who did turn up were disappointed. As eviscerated by Philip Dunne and Ring Lardner, Jr, Kathleen Winsor's heroine is still a forward hussy, and if almost forgotten now, it would then not have been necessary to remind anyone that her adventures were conducted in and around the court of Charles II (George Sanders). 'I've been fire-fighting all afternoon down at the docks . . . Perhaps my guests might be interested. It's been such a dull season,' he says to indicate why he was called the Merry Monarch. He (of course) becomes one of her conquests, though she continues to pine for her first love (Cornel Wilde); in the end she is deserted by all, a moral lesson to us and an echo of Scarlett O'Hara.

Zanuck's persistence with such stuff is an enigma: under his aegis Fox was now turning out a higher proportion of good movies than any of the other studios, but it was also perpetrating some which could not possibly have looked good, even on paper. Unlike Warner, Cohn or Mayer, he was a creative producer, capable of going far beyond an assent or refusal to the ideas put to him, and in addition he had a great deal of practical experience behind him. However, he also believed as much in quantity and variety as in excellence. Since the system demanded a biblical 'epic' from time to time – and having studied the profits of deMille's *Samson and Delilah* (q.v.) – he decided to make **David and Bathsheba** (1951). Indeed, it was one of his personal productions, with a superior director, King, and with a writer, Philip Dunne, capable of rising to the occasion: since part of the exercise was to outsmart deMille, they stuck to the Old Testament, with dialogue unrhetorical though also flat and predictable, except for a moment when David is described as 'exposing himself to the enemy'. King seems to have decided that the only way to film it was to move the people in and out of the (excellent) sets like puppets, and his attitude may have been induced by watching Gregory Peck and Susan Hayward reverentially enunciate what they seem to regard as holy writ. He, she and the script deserve each other, and it is noticeable that the climax succeeds well without them, as King does an imaginative job on a flashback of the boy David slaying Goliath.

When Hollywood had need of one of nature's aristocrats it sent for Peck. He is miscast as the hero of **The Snows of Kilimanjaro** (1952), based on Hemingway himself – as he would later be miscast as F. Scott Fitzgerald in *Beloved Infidel*. Peck looked Ivy League, but is unconvincing as a writer since his expressions are so consistently bland – and indeed becomes quite ludicrous (which was not his fault) by banging on about bullfighting and big game hunting while never leaving the soundstage. The film's popularity is unfathomable, unless the Second Unit material deceived audiences into believing that Hollywood was moving out into the world (it was, but this film was a regression). Hemingway's original story was of a man (Peck) critically ill who recalls his misdeeds: Casey Robinson's screenplay gives him plenty of flashbacks deriving from the Hemingway ethic – as well as one cherishable line, spoken to Peck, sick on safari, by Susan Hayward, 'I'm going to shoot some game. The larder's almost empty.' Towards the end, he says, 'I had it all and what did I have? My picture in the papers'; in the interim all *we* have had is Ava Gardner, till she disappears to Madrid where 'that wretched Civil War is on'. She is the love of his life, the only indication he shows, beyond his tweed suits, of good taste – and the only person to emerge from this thing with credit; certainly King, the director, does not.

Anna and the King of Siam (1946) is based on the novel by Margaret Landon, described on the credits as a biography, and in fact based on a memoir by the English widow who in the 1860s went out to teach English to the sons of the Siamese king. Because of this film and the musical – *The King and I* (q.v.) – based on it, most people know the tale, but it was an unusual subject for the cinema then: as the magazine *Time* said, it 'flies in the face of established Hollywood precedent by ignoring young love, and it proves that a movie can be lively entertainment even if boy doesn't get – or even meet – the girl'. There is much that is spurious – the settings, the starlets as Siamese wives, Rex Harrison's make-up as the king – and you may feel your emotions being manipulated; but it is also entertaining and, for a moment or two, touching. That has much to do with Irene Dunne, as conscientious in trying an English accent as preparing for a close-up, and performing with what I can only call a loveliness of spirit. The film keeps Anna's difficulties in sight – being publicly humiliated, summoned at all hours of the night, treated as one of the harem – and they have been rendered with a degree of truth by the writers, Talbot Jennings and Sally Benson. The direction offers one of the last chances to appreciate the sensi-

tivity of John Cromwell, resisting, he recalled, requests to jazz it up: 'D.F.Z. was wondering whether you couldn't punch up the love scenes, inject a little more comedy . . .' It is funny, however, despite Harrison's lack of ease – querulous where Yul Brynner would be insensitive; as his aide, Lee J. Cobb hams, but does suggest a complicity with Anna in dealing with the complex character of the king – which is one of many happy touches.

Zanuck's admiration for the British movies based on Somerset Maugham's short stories (q.v.) resulted in **O. Henry's Full House** (1952), introduced by John Steinbeck, whose reading of a few snatches indicates why Henry does not translate into film terms – though few of this cast are able to render him effectively. The best of the five stories is 'The Ransom of Red Chief', directed by Howard Hawks, with Fred Allen and Oscar Levant as kidnappers of a ghastly small boy; but it is enjoyable less because of Allen and Levant than for the parents' quiet acceptance of their son's enormities. Allen, a unique radio comedian, made too few films; however, he did appear for Fox in what is also the best episode of **We're Not Married** (1952), with Ginger Rogers, as radio stars whose private life is very different from the one projected. Edmund Goulding directed all the episodes – which are predictable from the film's title. The public reception of both films – remarkably inexpensive despite the casts – put into serious doubt the concept of omnibus films in Hollywood.

20th Century-Fox remained literary with **Les Miserables** (1952), tautly directed by Lewis Milestone, who said that he regarded it merely as a job; he also proves to be one of the few directors able to prevent Robert Newton – playing Javert – from hamming. Richard Murphy's screenplay is not overly burdened with fustian, and of all the screen versions (there have been at least ten since 1909; this is the ninth) it could be the best. Michael Rennie plays Valjean directly, never resorting to that raised-eyebrow charm he used in his British films, and is supported by Edmund Gwenn as the bishop, Elsa Lanchester as his housekeeper and Sylvia Sidney as the unfortunate Fantine.

Titanic (1953), another period piece, is not to be despised, as directed by Jean Negulesco and written by Charles Brackett, Walter Reisch and Richard Breen, fresh from their success on *Niagara* (q.v.). On this occasion they bring too much taste and too few details to the tragedy of the *Titanic*, though the actual sinking is as well done as expected. The long fictional frontispiece chiefly concerns a failing marriage, with an American wife (Barbara Stanwyck) taking her children back to the States to rid them of the values learnt in the salons of the old continent: that it works so well is also due to Clifton Webb as the husband, really showing his mettle in a serious role. Some actual names are used – the 'Molly Brown' character is there, played by Thelma Ritter – but the only one of the now legendary incidents used is that concerning the elderly Jewish couple who refused to be parted: perhaps because we know it to be true, it is the only moving moment.

I Can Get It for You Wholesale (1952) is a contemporary drama about the garment industry, based on a novel by Jerome Weidman which had been around for some time. The decision to film it had much to do with *All About Eve*, in which an ambitious schemer tramples her way to the top: common to both films is George Sanders to tempt the lady concerned. She is played by Susan Hayward, a better actress but less mesmerising than Joan Crawford in such roles. Only in Marvin Kaplan's performance as the cocky young clerk is there a strain of the Jewish comedy which, I imagine, was such a feature of the book. The screenwriter, Abraham Polonsky, and the director, Michael Gordon, were both to be victims in the McCarthyism then raging in the industry.

The Star (1953) concerns another dominant lady, and its own star, Bette Davis, recognised Joan Crawford as the source – as its writer had once worked for that lady. In the film, as produced independently for Fox distribution, she has become a has-been, played by Miss Davis quivering with intensity. 'Come on, Oscar, let's you and me get drunk,' she roars at her statuette, but beyond this storm at the film's centre it is a quiet piece. Stuart Heisler's pacing is weak, and he makes his performers seem awkward, including Sterling Hayden as the man the star finds she would like to come home to. The film tries to find something unsaid in *Sunset Boulevard* and *All About Eve* on the

loneliness of stardom and the difficulty of ageing, but while it may be nearer the truth it is not in the same league as either.

20th Century-Fox's own leading star remained Betty Grable, still heading all the box-office polls. In her first postwar film she and June Haver played **The Dolly Sisters** (1945), the Hungarian immigrants who in real life had become the rage of New York, London and Paris for their vaudeville act. The film had been planned for Grable and Alice Faye, who had played a sister act in *Tin Pan Alley*, and it comes as no surprise to find this history of the Dollys is merely a rehash of the equally dire Fox musicals of that time, even to having John Payne join the army. Neither Grable nor Haver look remotely like their originals; nor do their talents appear comparable. Irving Cummings directed (his penultimate film) and clearly he was tired. However, with the troops now demobilised, Zanuck realised that the Grable vehicles needed an injection of originality if audiences were to leave their homes to see them. **The Shocking Miss Pilgrim** (1947) used four unpublished songs by George and Ira Gershwin and a story about a demure but feisty stenographer in old Boston: and if the result is hardly more attractive than Grable's other films this is due to the direction by George Seaton. **Mother Wore Tights** (1947) tells, with the aid of flashbacks, of a vaudeville couple trying to combat their daughter's snobbery. The vaudeville stages still have Fox's polished glass floors and shimmering curtains, but the milieu was reasonably unfamiliar – as were musicals with plots comparatively as strong: the public discerned in it qualities concealed today and under Walter Lang's direction it restored Grable to favour after the failure of *Miss Pilgrim*, as well as providing her with a regular screen partner in Dan Dailey.

There are two Grables in **That Lady in Ermine** (1948), one the captive hostess of an Hungarian commander (Douglas Fairbanks, Jr) and the other an ancestress who descends from a portrait on the wall: for this is operetta, directed by Lubitsch, no less, and scripted by his old collaborator Samson Raphaelson. Lubitsch died during shooting and the film was completed by Otto Preminger, leaving an impression of some agreeable fantasy but basically poor material. It failed, as did *The Beautiful*

Blonde from Bashful Bend, already discussed, and Zanuck returned Miss Grable to clichés as her appeal gradually faded.

There were other occasions when the musicals of this studio attempted to get out of the rut, but they were usually copies of those being made at M-G-M. **Centennial Summer** (1946) is so modelled on *Meet Me in St Louis* that it is hard to believe that it was originally planned as a straight film. The songs (by Jerome Kern) were added, claimed the publicity, because of the success of *State Fair*: but when this family (Dorothy Gish, Walter Brennan, Jeanne Crain, Linda Darnell) sings 'Up With the Lark', passing it around in the manner of the Smiths of St Louis, they only prove that they are not a family you would care to sing along with. The plot has them anxious about the visit of an aunt, and as she is played by Constance Bennett audiences may echo Gish when she wonders 'whether she's still as stunning': but she is not, and we are left to wonder which of her nieces will fall to her 'companion', Cornel Wilde. The fair in this case is the one held in Philadelphia in 1876 (footage of which turns up as the Chicago World's Fair in *Wabash Avenue*) and the director is Otto Preminger.

Margie (1946), therefore, is all the more surprising, being as good as those two films are bad. Henry King's direction never strives or is self-conscious in this affectionate, sketched-in picture of high-school life in a small town in midwinter: the tale of a girl (Miss Crain) who has a fumbling boyfriend (Alan Young) and a crush on the new French teacher (Glenn Langan) in the days of the Stutz Bearcat and the Charleston. This was the first post-contemporary Hollywood film about the Twenties to look like the Twenties; the songs of the period – this is not really a musical – are used delightfully, and so is the star: in King's hands she remains winsome but is for once very appealing.

The level of Zanuck's musicals did not rise when Danny Kaye was imported to play two roles in **On the Riviera** (1951), a revamp of that plot which had seen duty as *Folies Bergère* and *That Night in Rio*, with a good many of its *double entendres* surprisingly intact. Kaye could not have been inspired by his leading ladies – Corinne Calvet and Gene Tierney – but he does have one very bright number, 'Popo the Puppet'. The film was directed by Walter Lang, who was also responsible for the studio's most popular musical of this period, **With a Song in My Heart** (1952), based on the life of Jane Froman, the singing star who was permanently crippled in a wartime air disaster. Susan Hayward plays the role conventionally, but the songs were dubbed by Miss Froman herself – and I trust it is the warmth and richness of her voice which move me, momentarily, as she sings, towards the end, a medley of 'Back Home' songs to the troops at the front.

Lang also directed **Call Me Madam** (1953), sensibly keying the proceedings to Ethel Merman, its star, who had made the original a Broadway hit. On the film's release she observed that at last she was a success in Hollywood, and planned to stay, but it did not work out that way. She is both what is right and what is wrong about this film: vital and vivid, very much a star, but theatrical in gesture and timing, always playing to the gallery. Lang has had to slow the whole thing down to suit her; one admires her button-bright eagerness, even if her charm is as tightly corsetted as her figure. In addition to her role – that of a vulgarian Washington hostess appointed by President Truman to the embassy of a small European country (based on fact: the hostess was Pearl Mesta and the country Luxembourg) – the show has a good Irving Berlin score and a lively book, combining Ruritanian nonsense and some heavy satire on American aid to Europe.

The Fox comedies of the period are no more endearing than their musicals; in the most famous of them, **Miracle on 34th Street** (1947), an elderly eccentric (Edmund Gwenn) insists that he is Kris Kringle and is hired for Macy's Thanksgiving Day parade; kept on, his recommendation of Gimbels and other rival stores makes him either a goodwill asset or a candidate for Bellevue. Such things may recall Capra, but there is an almost clinical impersonality about this film, and the only one of the players to match Gwenn's lightness is Thelma Ritter (in her film debut) as a satisfied mother. Gwenn's old-world charm is hard-pressed to sustain **Apartment for Peggy** (1948), as a widowed professor who finds new reason for living after being inveigled into letting his attic to a G.I. couple, William Holden and Jeanne

Crain. She, jabbering enthusiastically, is meant to carry the film, which sometimes goes beyond cosiness to wisdom, as when Gwenn speaks about teaching: 'You make a lot of people through the years a little more enlightened. You have contributed something.' Both films were written and directed by George Seaton.

There are similar homilies in his **Chicken Every Sunday** (1948), and in **Cheaper by the Dozen** (1950), directed by Walter Lang, two more of the seemingly endless family reminiscences started off by 'Life with Father': the former has Dan Dailey as an impractical dreamer, Celeste Holm (who is excellent) as the managing little woman, and Colleen Townsend as the girl who wrote it all down; the latter has Clifton Webb as the eccentric efficiency expert who carried his business ideas into his home, Myrna Loy as the managing wife, and Miss Crain as the young authoress. It also rated Technicolor and a sequel, **Belles on their Toes** (1952), directed by Henry Levin and equally innocuous. Clearly these entertainments met public demand – most of them are adapted from popular books – for in a fast-changing society, audiences wanted to be reminded of a time when families coped only with gentle changes, such as the excitement of the first automobile and the first phonograph; it is no coincidence that most of them depicted a stern father unwilling to accede to new ideas.

In the same mould are **Mr 880** (1950), directed by Edmund Goulding, with Edmund Gwen as a lovable counterfeiter and Burt Lancaster as the eventually-disarmed F.B.I. man, and **The Jackpot** (1950), directed by Lang, with James Stewart as a suburbanite who wins a quiz-show. One of the most popular of Fox's comedies was **Sitting Pretty** (1948), directed by Lang, about a middle-aged bachelor (Clifton Webb), who becomes an unconventional nurse to the bratty child of Robert Young and Maureen O'Hara. Dreary as many of these family films sound, it should be explained that the public mood five years after the War was different from that which had given rise to Jean Harlow and Carole Lombard.

Come to the Stable (1949) concerns two nuns (Loretta Young, Celeste Holm), one of whom is noticeably wearing lipstick. They are French, and have turned up in the U.S. since they swore during the war years to build a church there; having no money but much faith, they win over a bishop (Basil Ruysdael), a gangster (Thomas Gomez) and an embittered songwriter (Hugh Marlowe). The film sells Christianity, but with more humour than is customary in such circumstances; it also has Dooley Wilson, a mastiff called 'Orson' and Elsa Lanchester as something out of 'Mother Goose'. It is necessary to experience them, and the brisk Miss Holm, to understand why this is one of the movies' more bearable ventures into religiosity. Henry Koster directed, and the artful writers were Oscar Millard and Sally Benson, from a story by Clare Boothe Luce.

The less sentimentally-minded will prefer **I Was a Male War Bride** (1949), which returns comedy from the parlour to the bedroom, an analogy not disqualified by its being the first American comedy filmed extensively on European locations. Its mainspring is that old kick-off, non-consummation of marriage – as suffered by a lieutenant (Ann Sheridan) in the W.A.C.S and an officer (Cary Grant) in the U.S. army. He is called Henri Rochard, and as the screenplay, by Charles Lederer, Leonard Spigelglass and Hagar Wilde, is based on a story by someone of that name we may assume a basis in fact. It sags towards the end, when Grant is looking for somewhere to lay his head in Bremerhaven, but otherwise he runs the gamut of expressions, as usual when directed by Howard Hawks, while Sheridan was one of the few actresses of the Forties who could appear to be having a ball. The plot of **Monkey Business** (1952) involves a rejuvenation formula invented by Grant, which takes him and his wife (Ginger Rogers) back to adolescence and then childhood. The writers are Lederer, Ben Hecht and I. A. L. Diamond, all of them, like Hawks, experienced enough to know that crazy comedy either works at once or never. It makes one wonder why they did not abandon this one during production. Ignored at the time, it achieved a slight fame later because of the presence of Marilyn Monroe (1926–62), in a small role as Charles Coburn's secretary. She has only five lines or so, but the camera lingers on her primping and glowing, because it was clear that this woman had an extraordinary appeal. Zanuck could not see it, but said that she could be shoved into any movie which could use a sexy blonde.

When finally convinced that she was not a nine days' wonder he gave her star roles in **Niagara** (1953), and **Gentlemen Prefer Blondes** (1953), films he judged to be as cheap and vulgar as her appeal. The difference between them, however, is infinite, and *Niagara* is one of the great cod melodramas, as directed by Henry Hathaway and produced by Charles Brackett, who wrote it with Walter Reisch and Richard Breen, two other former associates of Billy Wilder. The way Monroe walks (photographed from behind) and dresses (skintight, and obviously without underwear), and the way she half-closes her eyes and half-opens her mouth at moments of passion seemed sensational; and the writers had concocted a story to indicate that on her honeymoon she is already carrying on with another man – and she is egging on the new man to kill her husband (Joseph Cotten). Overall, she is effective, but not really good; but in *Gentlemen Prefer Blondes*, perfectly cast as Lorelei Lee, the Cinderella of gold-diggers, she proves that with a good line she can move mountains. Jane Russell is her partner, and Zanuck's contempt is indicated by an extremely poor cast, with the exception of Charles Coburn as Sir Francis of the roving eye. The film has only a tenuous connection with Anita Loos's book, being catapulted from the Twenties into some contemporary limbo; and it has little more to do with the 1949 Broadway musical version, retaining just three songs and hardly more of the lines. The new songs are poor, unevenly distributed, and staged with the pointless rushing-about and flouncing of skirts characteristic of Fox musicals: as directed by Howard Hawks this ranks among the most crass films he ever made.

Between Zanuck and his best directors – Mankiewicz, Kazan, King and Hathaway – 20th Century-Fox did respond to the postwar mood with a more mature range of subjects than the other studios. Paramount, however, obliged only by making its melodramas a little more weighty. This studio had always prided itself on being purveyors of 'entertainment', but with the shining exception of Wilder's *A Foreign Affair* did not choose to reflect contemporary problems. The War, however, remained useful for romance.

To Each His Own (1946) starts during the London blitz, as a middle-aged Olivia de Havilland reflects on her small town American past, which turns out to be a combination of *Back Street*, *Only Yesterday* and, later, *The Old Maid*: the First War takes her lover, and the Second brings back her illegitimate son. **Golden Earrings** (1947) also adopts flashback, to show a British colonel (Ray Milland) on the run from the Nazis in 1939, though it is less a thriller than a comedy drama about a stuffy Britisher humanised by an earth mother – a gypsy (Marlene Dietrich). Mitchell Leisen directed both films, and if Charles Brackett's script for the first had a little more humour it would be a classic of its kind; the second is high tosh, and the start of Leisen's run of increasingly poor films. He insisted upon casting Dietrich, against Paramount's wishes, since he wanted a really glamorous woman under the make-up to make the romance work. She may say that she has garlic on her breath and cod liver oil in her hair, but she remains Dietrich with an unusual Max Factor job.

Leisen's last decent picture was **Dream Girl** (1948), based on a play by Elmer Rice which had been a stage vehicle for his wife, Betty Field. In her role, that of a wealthy girl with aspirations to culture, Betty Hutton is miscast and monotonous; as the reporter who persuades her that the world would be a better place if we stopped dreaming and started living, MacDonald Carey does not provide the colour she lacks. It could have been satiric on either New York intellectuals or pseudo-intellectuals, but a novel called 'Always Opal' is the height of its satiric daring, and it is much less pointed on the foibles of the rich than almost any prewar comedy. With these reservations, there are reasons for seeing this film: some small bite in the dream sequences; some funny lines given to the bride's mother (Peggy Wood); and a delicious cameo by Zamah Cunningham as her singing teacher. The film failed to duplicate the play's success, and its failure with the public hastened the departure from the studio of both Hutton and Leisen.

William Dieterle, another of Hollywood's better directors, was also involved in a romantic war melodrama. In **Love Letters** (1945), written by Ayn Rand from a novel by Chris Massie, a soldier (Joseph Cotten) goes in search of the girl (Jennifer Jones) to whom he wrote the letters, finding her both an amnesiac and the murderess of the man she *thought* wrote the letters. He marries her, despite the enigmatic comment of her aunt (Gladys Cooper), 'I interfered once and lived to regret it' – which is no help in untangling the plot, described by James Agee as 'factitious'. The word for Miss Jones's performance, said *The New York Times*, is 'fatuous' and that Selznick thought her 'absolutely sensational' is proof again that love is blind: the role, however, is impossible, all giggles and walking on walls. So is the portrait of England, with Nelson's Column looming just outside the window of an apartment, and a wedding in the ruined church (other quaint notions include rationbooks for porridge and dropping in on the nearest bishop whenever you have a problem) – and indeed, all the studio exteriors are painful.

In that respect there was a change when Dieterle came to make **September Affair** (1950), among the first American films made extensively on European locations, its Cook's Tour taking in a bit of Naples, a *trattoria* on the slopes of Vesuvius, and much of Florence. The lovers lease what must have been the largest *palazzo* in that city, the M.P.A.A. leaving unclear whether or not they have separate rooms – and the film is exactly what cynics might expect of a Hollywood version of *Brief Encounter*, with Joan Fontaine as a celebrated concert pianist and Cotten a very wealthy, unhappily married, engineer. Homage to the British film may be intended in the use of the same Rachmaninoff Piano Concerto, often enterprisingly blended with Neapolitan airs and/or Kurt Weill's 'September Song'. This song is also intelligently used, the verse as well – firstly as the lovers listen to Walter Huston's recording, and again as it is taken up in a restaurant by a rather drunken G.I. (Jimmy Lydon) – and that, together with the locations, explains why many people have a weakness for this film.

It is one of a series of highly artificial stories produced independently by Hal Wallis, each of them characteristic of this period inasmuch as infidelity was allowed to go unpunished, but not to end happily, and Freudian explanations were tentatively offered for such matters as possessiveness, mother-domination, buddy-buddy crushes and even criminal mentality. They were inspired by the Bette Davis melodramas which Wallis had produced at Warners, and usually starred two other 'strong' actresses, the veteran Barbara Stanwyck and the young Lizabeth Scott. You will not believe a word of either **The Strange Love of Martha Ivers** (1946), directed by Lewis Milestone, with Stanwyck, Scott, Kirk Douglas and Wendell Corey, or **Desert Fury** (1947), directed by Lewis Allen, with John Hodiak, Mary Astor, Burt Lancaster, Wendell Corey and Miss Scott – the words in both cases supplied by Robert Rossen, a former Warners writer – but just try to look away. Wallis's men are a new breed – Douglas and Lancaster, with restless energy, to be later joined by Charlton Heston, sharing with Lancaster a new Hollywood anomaly of broad shoulders and asexuality.

Wallis brought to Paramount an old Warners colleague, Anatole Litvak, to make **Sorry, Wrong Number** (1948), which may remind you of that *New Yorker* cartoon of a theatre patron observing, 'If this is supposed to be a realistic play, how come the telephone always works first time?' The sole character of Lucille Fletcher's celebrated thirty-minute radio play is an invalid who, chancing on a crossed line, hears a murder plot whose victim she has reason to believe is herself. In opening out the play, Miss Fletcher's screenplay is less faithful to the original than to what audiences expected of Stanwyck, playing a rich bitch ('When I want something I fight for it and usually get it') who pursues poor boy Lancaster ('What's a dame like you want with a guy like me?'). The second half loses impetus, as is true of **Dark City** (1950), where murder also stalks, on account of an out-of-town salesman (Don Defore) who has committed suicide after gambling away a cheque for $5,000. Heston is the gambling-den boss, out to foil these murders, and his light-toned virility is neatly counterpointed by Scott, crooning 'I Don't Want to Walk Without You' in an almost-baritone. Dieterle directed, and both films manage that Forties ambience we noticed in those of Siodmak: lonely, rainy streets at night, over-furnished rooms with parties going on, pay-telephones in grimy diners, and men in shirtsleeves sitting around in bare rooms.

Most of these films of Wallis belong to what was later recognised as the American *film noir* (and for its first scenes, *Dark City* is as good an example as exists). A masterpiece of the genre is **The Blue Dahlia** (1946) which was also greeted only politely when it appeared. John Houseman produced and George Marshall directed Raymond Chandler's only original screenplay: a South Pacific veteran (Alan Ladd) returns to find, firstly, his wife (Doris Dowling) flaunting her relationship with another man (Howard da Silva), secondly, her corpse, and thirdly, himself as the prime suspect. He tries to get the murderer before the police get him, a favourite plot of the time, remoulded for Chandler's sour, disjointed world, and populated by such as the cool-as-cucumber heroine (Veronica Lake), the seedy hotel dick (Will Wright), the boarding-house proprietor (Howard Freeman), and the veteran's buddy (William Bendix), liable to uncontrollable rages. One of these was not the villain intended by Chandler, and it is worth quoting him on the film's chief weakness, 'Ladd is hard, bitter and occasionally charming, but he is after all a small boy's idea of a tough guy.' With Ladd and Lake one hardly cares what happens to them: for this material really to take off, another team was needed (and that team – Bogart and Bacall – was at Warner Bros.).

It is also difficult to feel anxiety for the man on the spot in **The Big Clock** (1948), for he is both smug and self-sufficient – qualities often inherent in the acting of Ray Milland, who plays him: however, Jonathan Latimer's screenplay thoughtfully refers to the first quality and the plot requires the second. Milland is the editor of a crime magazine, part of the publishing empire of Charles Laughton, who is autocratic, bad-tempered, ill-mannered and pathetic because, as is pointed out to him, he has not a friend in the world. When his mistress (Rita Johnson) is murdered, Milland's situation will remind you not only of *The Blue Dahlia* but of Graham Greene and Hitchcock, with a dash of Hammett and Ambler: the race for the truth, the formidable opponent, the eccentric minor characters. Moving everything at a fast clip, John Farrow confirms the impression of *You Came Along*, that his interest could

be kindled by a comic barman or a crowded restaurant.

Farrow's best film is **Two Years Before the Mast** (1946), and if Agee thought the screenplay – by Seton I. Miller and George Bruce – falsified Dana's contempt for his fellow-seamen, these have not been reduced to stereotypes – with the exception of Barry Fitzgerald in his *Sea Wolf* performance as the Irish cook. Dana (Brian Donlevy) sets out to investigate life at sea, and is duly shown keeping a journal indicating that it consists of flogging, speed and scurvy; the inevitable mutiny is, of course, led by the shipowner's shanghaied son (Ladd). This is not the sort of script that actors can do much about, jogging up and down on some corner of the Paramount lot, and Ladd, after a good start as the cocky young swell, finally becomes a very wan fellow indeed; but the excellence of the film stems directly from the delineation of Captain and First Mate. As the former, Howard da Silva is not so much wicked as content in isolation; William Bendix is the unblinking, unquestioning Mate, a man whose subservience to the Captain goes to the bottom reaches of his soul. Once on dry land, the story tails away with references to Dana's 'scandalous' book, as if the writers could not

There have been books written on the American *film noir*, a genre to which its practitioners did not know they were contributing. Nevertheless, there is a certain similarity between several Hollywood crime films made between 1940 and the late Fifties, even if the same elements may be found in the faster-paced thrillers of the pre-Code era. Many of the later films were influenced by the novels of Raymond Chandler, who wrote the original screenplay of *The Blue Dahlia*, which starred Alan Ladd, seen here escaping from the clutches of Don Costello.

Postwar Hollywood: The Studios

decide how to handle the question of the reforms it occasioned, and the climate at Paramount was not conducive to the discussion of serious matters.

As a result of the film's success, Farrow was assigned to **California** (1946), which was the studio's idea of 'serious'. It hymns, as the title suggests, the State Of, starting with several postcard views in Technicolor and a eulogy, one of several sickly songs, including 'Gold', which accompanies Eisenstein-like shots of greedy faces. Barbara Stanwyck does her own singing, and plays her usual wilful but essentially good woman; Milland can be no one's idea of an action hero. You know from the start that it will be a concocted story, and Farrow clearly shows his lack of interest.

They might as well have handed the subject to deMille, whose **Unconquered** (1947) is about the men 'who push ever forward the frontiers of man's freedoms', as represented by a dour Gary Cooper and a gauche Paulette Goddard. Incidentals include da Silva, excellent again, as the villain; Mr Mason, Mr Dixon and George Washington chuckling at the thought that Pittsburgh, 'this little village . . . will sprout into a city of maybe four or five thousand folk'; a waterfall rescue pinched from *Our Hospitality*; and a climax which gives Goddard a big moment as the Scottish pipes are heard, 'It is! It is! Chris got through!' For all its awfulness, the film demonstrates that reaffirmation of the principles of democracy deemed necessary after the recent world conflict – to which extent it differs from deMille's earlier pioneer dramas which, like his biblical epics, offer a more Victorian view of the triumph of the virtuous over the wicked.

He revived that genre with **Samson and Delilah** (1949), and since the tale had almost no relevance in the postwar world, we may assume its audience was attracted by the prospect of sin and spectacle. It broke every record except those held by *Gone with the Wind*, and yet its vulgarity is transcendent but dreary – except when Samson (Victor Mature) fights the lion, in close-up a moth-eaten old rug, while in long-shot the Samson does not remotely resemble the actor concerned. Since he was claimed to be Hollywood's beefiest man, and Hedy Lamarr its most beautiful woman, casting was thought to be ideal, but as her sister, Angela Lansbury alone of

the cast reassures. The collapse of the temple provides a climax, if a dim one.

The time had not yet come when the contempt of critics could harm such highly-publicised films and when deMille's next film garnered good notices – the first in a decade – it, in turn, became the second most profitable film ever made. **The Greatest Show on Earth** (1952), obviously a circus tale, also won a Best Picture Oscar – presumably since little was expected of deMille. Barnum and Baileys and the Ringling Bros. had just amalgamated, but that was not enough for deMille, who offers documentary footage and several parades – which are fine for those who like decorated floats. The plot concerns primarily a trapeze artist (Betty Hutton), the surly manager (Charlton Heston), and the guest star (Cornel Wilde), professional rival of the one and amatory rival of the other, muttering '*Nom de chien*' in lieu of a convincing French accent. Then there is Buttons (James Stewart), a murderer – a *good* one – hiding out in clown's make-up and redeeming himself by performing an emergency operation after a train crash (the coaches crumble like match-boxes, and one's concern is lessened by a jolly voice calling, 'Here's another corpse'). The film then finishes with the Show Going On, as they put it, 'under God's big top', by which time 153 minutes have passed, seemingly like hours. DeMille's final film, *The Ten Commandments* (1956) lasts 222 minutes, and I have never had the courage to see it. The public queued as before, and even in this age of television other studios were encouraged by its success to invest in projects equally grandiose: it was reasoned that other film-makers could do better, given big budgets and with a minimum of effort – and such indeed was the case.

Paramount's aversion to seriousness was traditional; one of its few topical films was based on a Broadway comedy, Norman Krasna's **Dear Ruth** (1947), as adapted by Arthur Sheekman and directed by William D. Russell. The situation set forth concerns a lieutenant (William Holden) who arrives to woo his pen-pal (Joan Caulfield), only to find that the letters were in fact written by her younger sister (Mona Freeman). Audiences presumably enjoyed Billy de Wolfe as the stuffed-shirt fiancé, and were titillated by the fact that

732

the correspondence was reportedly 'hot', but today it is hard to see why the piece ran so long on Broadway or why the film was popular enough to give rise to two sequels.

Paramount's most important stars remained Bing Crosby and Bob Hope, overwhelmingly everyone's favourites in the postwar era. Since Hope's later films would be so poor, he needed to be rediscovered by a yet later generation – and he almost certainly benefits by putting his comic persona in the context of the War. He is frequently clumsy and cowardly when confronted with death, and his mock-heroic behaviour was probably a relief to audiences when the War was over, as in dazed reaction they wondered how they had coped. His popularity was enormous, and rather like that of Harold Lloyd, but unlike Lloyd his films tell us nothing about his time. A string of gags was built around his vanity and cowardice by, most notably, Jack Rose, Melville Shavelson, Don Hartman, Edmund Beloin, Melvin Frank and Norman Panama; his was a limited talent, and one of the joys of his films is that it is utilised to the full. He never doubts – such is his uncertain place in the world – chicanery all about him; advancing into middle age, he remains desperately anxious to be liked and is never fazed by innumerable rebuffs to his vanity and denigrations of his sex-appeal: one of the reasons he is so good with Crosby is that the latter's simple cunning is too subtle for such an innocent.

As we noted with his two wartime films for Goldwyn, *They Got Me Covered* and *The Princess and the Pirate*, Hope's writers had discovered that he was particularly effective in burlesque. In his prewar films it had been established that he was funny when faced with sudden death, but it was not until *The Ghost Breakers* that an element of spoofing was introduced, in that case on the 'old dark house' genre. The second 'Road' film was a burlesque of adventure films, and about the same time audiences laughed at a send-up of *The Thirty-Nine Steps*, *My Favorite Blonde*, which he made with Madeleine Carroll. He did two more in this splendid series, **My Favorite Brunette** (1947), directed by Elliott Nugent, with Dorothy Lamour, and **My Favorite Spy** (1951), directed by Norman Z. McLeod, with Hedy Lamarr. Miss Lamour is the brunette, a mysterious woman whose sanity is doubted by, *inter alia*, Peter Lorre, a deadly knife-thrower boning up on his examination for naturalisation, and Lon Chaney Jr, parodying his own performance in *Of Mice and Men*. Hope himself plays a baby photographer with aspirations of becoming a private eye: 'I'd rather be caught dead,' he exclaims, before realising what he has said. In *My Favorite Spy* he is set down in a singularly glamorous and inaccurate Tangier, to constantly dodge marksmen lurking behind doors, double-crossing women or even simply eavesdroppers. He plays a comic impersonating a master-spy – and if the description of the latter sounds like Ian Fleming planning the creation of James Bond, the film itself can be seen as a send-up of *Casablanca* and its imitations.

In **Where There's Life** (1947), directed by Sidney Lanfield, Hope is the target of a number of assassination attempts since he is the unwitting heir to a revolution-torn European kingdom; in **The Great Lover** (1947), directed by Alexander Hall, he is the butt of the boy scouts he is supposed to be squiring on an ocean liner, the panting aspirant for the love of a beautiful woman (Rhonda Fleming), the dupe of her impoverished father (Roland Culver), and best of all, the prey of a homicidal maniac (Roland Young). 'I always wanted to be a man about town' is his response to the prospect of dismemberment, and the line is from one of the two Damon Runyon films, **Sorrowful Jones** (1949) and **The Lemon-Drop Kid** (1951), both directed by Lanfield. Shyster and braggart, he fits absolutely into Runyon's world: 'You never heard my courage questioned,' he says to Lucille Ball, who shoots back, 'I never heard your courage mentioned' – and because she is a more forceful lead than Marilyn Maxwell, the earlier film is better. Both are remakes of films Paramount had done in the Thirties – the first as *Little Miss Marker* – and these late versions are, against the odds, sharper-eyed and harder-faced than their predecessors.

Monsieur Beaucaire (1946) puts Hope into Valentino's old swashbuckling role, and is rich in both incident and invention as directed by George Marshall; but the same director's **Fancy Pants** (1950) is a strident remake of *Ruggles of Red Gap*, not improved by the introduction of Miss Ball as a hoydenish heiress. This particular film

733

owed its inception to an earlier Hope excursion to the old West, **The Paleface** (1948), his most celebrated burlesque and his biggest success after the 'Road' films. He plays a dentist who discovers, as he says 'What Horace Greeley meant' on encountering Jane Russell. He is funny discovering that he is a hero, and there is an amusing sequence in a morgue (and a good song, 'Buttons and Bows'); but the plot thereafter lacks development. One of its writers, Frank Tashlin, blamed the director: 'I'd written a satire on *The Virginian* and it was completely botched. I could have killed that guy,' but Tashlin himself made a hash of the sequel, **Son of Paleface** (1952). Hope was instrumental in Tashlin becoming a director after shooting some sequences, uncredited, on *The Lemon-Drop Kid*. Earlier, Tashlin had worked on Warners' cartoons, and he tries to turn Hope into Bugs Bunny, making him skid through a series of doors, to emerge flattened, and so on. The film is crazy – but not in the manner of, say, *Million Dollar Legs*, which preferred its ineluctible view of the universe to a gag for its own sake.

Later, *Blazing Saddles* (q.v.) would try both approaches; Tashlin's jokes prefigure Mel Brooks, as when Roy Rogers says he prefers horses to women and Hope looks askance and steps aside. In failing to understand the nature of Hope's world and his persona, Tashlin did nothing to halt the decline of screen comedy: indeed, if the sequel is compared to *The Paleface* it may be said rather that he accelerates it. For Woody Allen (q.v.) a weekend 'of pure pleasure . . . would be to have half a dozen Bob Hope films and watch them, films like *Monsieur Beaucaire*.' In the light of the films made by Allen and Brooks, most of Hope's middle-period films can indeed be viewed with 'pure pleasure': it is a treat to see comedies so highly tooled, in which everything works.

Crosby's postwar films are not, on the other hand, a happy lot. In its time, **Blue Skies** (1946) wowed audiences: Crosby, Astaire and twenty Irving Berlin songs – plus Technicolor – were enough, since musicals were expected to have mindless plots. Like an earlier Berlin musical, *Alexander's Ragtime Band*, this one is about a romantic trio over the years, and like *Holiday Inn*, much of it is set in night clubs: but

with little period detail and nothing in the way of humour we are left, between songs, to study the familiar contours and colouring of the stars. Crosby is so much more interesting and charming than Astaire (Joan Caulfield's preference is quite understandable) that we may suppose Astaire was directed – by Stuart Heisler – so as to pose no real threat to Paramount's chief asset; Astaire, freelancing, is certainly given less to do. He announced his retirement while making this film, perhaps because he was only getting offers like this, as Bing's side-kick; M-G-M made him change his mind, and he never again appeared to such disadvantage.

Crosby's next few films owed much to *Going My Way*, including the two in which he was again teamed with Barry Fitzgerald: **Welcome Stranger** (1947), directed by Elliott Nugent, as rival doctors against a background of small town politicking *à la* Capra, and **Top o' the Morning** (1949), directed by David Miller, a dire tale about the theft of the Blarney Stone. In the Thirties Crosby's songs – 'I've Got a Pocketful of Dreams', 'Pennies from Heaven' – suited both him and the times, but as Father O'Malley he had delved deeper into the realm of homespun philosophy, 'In the Land of Beginning Again', 'Aren't You Glad You're You?'; thus, after the credits of *Welcome Stranger* he's enjoining us to 'Smile Right Back at the Sun', and in **A Connecticut Yankee in King Arthur's Court** (1949) he is found telling a crowd of children what to do 'If You Stub Your Toe on the Moon'. This film is clumsily directed by Tay Garnett, and hideously decorated, destroying any lingering fantasy in Mark Twain's old tale. Attempting to take on Will Rogers's mantle was not wise, and Crosby reverted to a more natural role as a Broadway star of his own age in **Mr Music** (1950), a loose remake of *Accent on Youth*, with Nancy Olsen as the younger girl with a crush. Standing apart from her and taking its tone from Crosby's easy manner, Richard Haydn's direction is sluggish and the staging of the numbers so tired and overdeliberate that one of Bing's best scores (by Burke and Van Heusen) remains unknown to this day. Crosby seems to have been not so much a poor chooser as a modest one, perhaps leaving too much to the Paramount team, which over-calculated: on the other hand, his musicals of the Thirties remain simple and pleasing.

Paramount's most important female star at this time was Betty Hutton, whose popularity surprised the front office: taken on as a singer and character comedienne, she soon graduated to leading roles. She is remembered for three show business biographies, and indeed it was the popularity of the first of them, in conjunction with *The Jolson Story* (q.v.), which opened the floodgates for films in which stars of the past were revived against a background of their songs, a largely fictional summary of their unhappy love lives, and a usually sketchy portrait of their times. In **Incendiary Blonde** (1945) Hutton is Texas Guinan, nightclub queen of the gangster era; in **The Perils of Pauline** (1947) she is Pearl White, Silent serial star; and in **Somebody Loves Me** (1952), Blossom Seeley, speakeasy singer. She loves and is ill-treated by three dull leading men – respectively Arturo de Cordova as a gangster, John Lund as an actor, and Ralph Meeker as a nonentity trying to get on in the business. As directed by George Marshall, the first two films have a certain gusto, and an affection for the days of tatty touring companies and Silent serials. *Incendiary Blonde* was the first film to treat the subject since *Hollywood Cavalcade*, and its other embellishments were also then rare, including an unhappy ending which is comparable only with that of the Astaire-Rogers film about the Castles, and much better judged. The star herself can be appealing when she sings, either noisily or wistfully, and as an actress her eagerness and enthusiasm are initially touching; but she cannot, for instance, sit in the gallery and watch one of Lund's performances without making moues of approval all the time. Nor was she anything like the ladies she portrayed – for old films reveal Guinan and Seeley to have been tough old birds. The three movies do not represent a trilogy, since that suggests a certain dynamism, and the last of them, as written and directed by Irving Brecher, is exceptionally tired. It demonstrates Paramount at its most commercial, unimaginative and opportunistic, since Hutton was also scheduled to play Mabel Normand, Sophie Tucker, one of the Duncan Sisters, and so on; but she quarrelled with Paramount over her next director and walked out. Her

appeal was probably exhausted, since she did not make a career in television, as did Hope and Crosby when their film popularity waned. Apart from one programmer for an independent she did not film again, evidence that defiance of the studio ruined her career, probably the last example of such an outcome, since the studio system itself was crumbling.

The stars themselves now began to realise that they did not need long-term contracts to survive; they could earn more by moving around, and perhaps prolong their careers by choosing freely (the major grievance was not being tied *per se*, but being forced into uncongenial projects or loan-outs on which the studio made huge profits on their fees). In their turn, the studios found, as audiences deserted them for television, that they were paying players whose actual drawing power was small. At Warners, during the late Forties, around thirty of them could expect to have their name above the title but a mere handful could be called popular. In 1945, almost all studio activity centred on these – Davis, Bogart, Flynn, Lupino, Crawford, Sheridan and Garfield: most of them had been there since 1938. But by 1952 they had left – and already gone or going were those who had come up in the meantime – Doris Day, Kirk Douglas and Jane Wyman.

The dominant figures were Davis and Bogart: her success mesmerised the front office, which had under contract a number of similarly 'strong' actresses – to associate Warners in the public mind with 'women's pictures', and to take over the scripts that she turned down. Bogart was less easy to replace: Cagney and Robinson, the obvious choices, were reluctant to return. Thus the majority of Warner films were vehicles for their women stars.

A Stolen Life (1946) was originally written by Margaret Kennedy to allow Elisabeth Bergner the chance to show her talent as twin sisters. Davis chose it as her first 'independent' production under a new contract. The sisters are rivals in love, the men in their lives including a surly painter (Dane Clark) and a ferryman (Glenn Ford), whose sudden promotion to a business career in Chile is the sort of leap that only films like this can make. What makes it interesting is Davis, as the impostor, encountering classic situations as in the later *Dead Ringer* (q.v.), not knowing which door to use, the dog not recognising her. As directed by Curtis Bernhardt, she tries no great feat of differentiation, being reasonable and straightforward as the heroine and hardly less so as her shallow rival. **Winter Meeting** (1948) confirms her as the best actress of her time. In her imperious moments she is mannered, but in her quieter moments there is no one as relaxed or as able to suggest a thinking woman. She plays a spinster publisher involved with a naval hero (Jim Davis) – a relationship probably futile, since he wants to be a priest. This actor's lumbering integrity is very convincing, but at the time he shared in the opprobrium cast upon the film by reviewers, possibly bewildered by a suggestion of depth and an almost complete lack of melodrama. The ending is trite, but under Bretaigne Windust's direction the film is sharp on certain strata of New York society, and Catherine Turney's dialogue (as in *A Stolen Life*) avoids clichés.

The vibrant intelligence of Davis could make endurable, if not save, a film as bad as **Deception** (1946), directed by Irving Rapper: so we cannot therefore disregard his claim that in fact she directed the films on which they worked together. This one is about good music, and at Warners, where good music was concerned it was class all the way. Just before Joan Crawford romanced John Garfield in the ritziest of apartments in *Humoresque* (q.v.), Davis shot Claude Rains on the grandest of grand staircases in *Deception*. Since her penthouse must be the biggest in New York, the emotions on display are of the same size. She has deserted the world-famous conductor (Rains) for an old love, a violinist (Paul Henreid); when the former turns up at the wedding reception, Davis says feebly – if that adverb could ever be applied to her behaviour – that there had not been time to send an invitation. With poise, she continues to eat her meal, while he observes that the caviare is over-chilled: but they do not ignore the situation. 'Have one husband, have eight,' says Rains in his matter-of-fact fashion, 'but you'll come back to me.' Memorable moments in movies have often nothing to do with life, but the pleasure of this one is that, while it is wholly artificial, there is the nagging thought that this woman, having deceived both her men, might just continue to wolf down her smoked turkey as if nothing had happened.

The director of **Beyond the Forest** (1949) is the once-great King Vidor, and it is a long way behind its contemporary films, such concurrent items as *The File on Thelma Jordan* and *The Reckless Moment*, surely equally synthetic on paper. Davis must take some of the blame – for the absurd décolletage, the hip-swinging and the Charles Addams hairdo. It was she who had started the 'wicked lady' cycle, and this was the last in a decade rich with them: a better actress than others who played these ladies, her performance of this small-town tramp compounded the miscasting. She loathed Vidor and the whole production, believing herself too old – and not the person to hesitate if she wanted to go to Chicago (a device on which the plot hinges); she also thought Eugene Pallette would have been more suitable than Joseph Cotten as the cuckolded husband. 'You're something for the birds, Rosa,' says one of her victims, and so is the film. It ended (by mutual consent) her eighteen years with Warners. Perhaps only the association between M-G-M and Garbo has left a more worthwhile record of an actress and her art.

Writing at the time, Jympson Harman is the London *Evening News* would appear not to agree: 'Nothing seems to happen to disturb my impression that Joan Crawford is the best dramatic actress on the screen today. Bette Davis is a fine runner-up, but her performances are always impregnated with the B.D. personality' – and you wonder how and why he could ever have imagined that the Crawford roles were not 'impregnated' with the 'J.C.' personality. Curtis Bernhardt, the director of the film in question – *Possessed* (q.v.) – observed that it took Crawford twenty minutes to emerge from any given expression after a take, and I must say that that sounds more like her. Her limitations are legendary, and may today be mesmerising – for instance, in the curious way she speaks to domestic servants in her films, as if incredulous that she is not in their place. But was it for such reasons audiences went to watch her play the same monstrous woman in what must often have seemed like the same film? After leaving M-G-M she sat around at Warners for a couple of years before making **Mildred Pierce** (1945), playing a woman who works her claws to the bone for the sake of her daughter (Ann Blyth), who gets meaner by the minute. As written by Ranald McDougall from a novel by James M. Cain, there is a certain fascination in the vicissitudes of these two ladies, and Michael Curtiz gets excellent performances from Warners' not-always-reliable second-stringers, Jack Carson, Zachary Scott and Bruce Bennett. As Crawford's employer and friend, Eve Arden is much more alive and interesting than she is, but nevertheless Crawford won an Oscar as Best Actress and entered a new period of popularity.

In **Humoresque** (1946) she is a bored society dame and John Garfield is a violinist. 'He's rather what you find in a Van Gogh painting,' she says, 'a touch of the savage.' She tells him, 'I have the reputation of knowing about good clothes, good food and good wine,' adding, 'Do you like martinis? They're an acquired taste, like Ravel.' Clifford Odets (reworking an unused screenplay he had written for *Rhapsody in Blue*, q.v.) and Zachary Gold pro-

vided these words, or mined them from a novel by Fannie Hurst; Jean Negulesco directed, failing to persuade his 'strong' star team that they were acting in the same film. It is not that their styles are different, but Garfield has little to do but look dedicated to his violin, and she little but to look dedicated to him: since clearly neither of them felt that way it is a very ho-hum humoresque. While he plays a transcription of the 'Liebestod' – called here 'the love music from "Tristan"' – she walks out of her beach-house into the sea, just like Norman Maine except for the shimmering evening-gown. Why, is not clear, but as Oscar Levant had put it earlier, 'She's as complex as a Bach fugue.' The last word is Levant's, and it comes early in the film: 'Schmaltz? You want schmaltz?'

In the course of **Possessed** (1947) Crawford tries desperately to cling to a man who doesn't love her, marries a man she doesn't love and tries by fair means and foul to prevent her step-daughter from seeing her old flame, and when that doesn't work, shoots him dead. As the film starts she is in a catatonic trance, and as she recalls her past we discover that she has suffered from hallucinations, brainstorms, persecution mania, homicidal mania, schizophrenia, paranoia, and traumas, not to mention various attacks of jealousy and false accusations of guilt – all in ankle-strap shoes and the Adrian shoulder-pads which she herself thought as passé as 'the improbable corn' of **This Woman Is Dangerous** (1952). She left Warners because of *This Woman Is Dangerous*, but it is difficult for most of us to find any distinction between her films of this period. In this one, directed by Felix Feist, she is a high class gangster's moll and criminal mastermind, and it has to be admitted that she does try for a new expression – a sort of agonised apprehension appropriate for someone on the verge of reformation. Yet she can be surprising: as a housewife in R.K.O.'s *Sudden Fear* (q.v.) she is hard-bitten, but as a cooch-dancer in **Flamingo Road** (1949) she is demure. Flamingo Road is the local version of Nob Hill, to which cooch-dancers can make it if ambitious enough; with a good villain (Sydney Greenstreet), a touch of civic corruption and some of Curtiz's best-paced direction, this is the most reasonable of Crawford's Warner melodramas.

Ann Sheridan was promoted from light roles to similar parts. In **Nora Prentiss** (1947) and **The Unfaithful** (1947), the warmth of her personality almost nullifies the most grotesque wardrobes and coiffures ever landed on a queen of soap opera. Vincent Sherman directed both, using the streets of San Francisco and Los Angeles respectively in the way demonstrated by 20th Century-Fox – if only tentatively – and realism extends no further: both are excellent examples of films where no one makes the obvious remark or asks the obvious question. Warners, unrivalled in recycling old material, surpassed themselves on both occasions: the screenplay for the former, by N. Richard Nash, borrows from 'Sister Carrie', *The Blue Angel*, Dr Crippen, *Phantom of the Opera* and *Brief Encounter*, being about an unhappily married doctor (Kent Smith) who falls for a nightclub singer (Sheridan) and tries to start a new life; the latter, though boasting an 'original screenplay' by David Goodis and James Gunn, is recognisable as *The Letter*, the infidelity in this case caused by the separations of war.

War was a useful ingredient in these women's pictures, reminding the still-serving G.I. audiences of the problems of their women at home. Warner writers did not forget the War as quickly as those at other studios, revealing a residue of that old social conscience; and it is probable that their strong, managing heroines struck a chord with those returning servicemen who were having difficulty in adjusting. Barbara Stanwyck drew two of the lighter assignments. In **Christmas in Connecticut** (1945) she is a phoney cookery expert whose editor (Sydney Greenstreet) demands that she entertain a wounded veteran (Dennis Morgan) for the festive season; but as directed by Peter Godfrey matters deteriorate after a promising start. In **My Reputation** (1946) she is a war widow who changes her mind about remarrying after meeting a major (George Brent), though assuring her sons that she will never forget their father. She is seen going into the major's hotel room, but again, as directed by Curtis Bernhardt, the distance from real life is enormous, and there is no suggestion that anyone had ever heard of a bed: it must seem bizarre to a generation not reared on such films.

Ida Lupino never reached the stature of the other Warners ladies, but for those sufficiently perverse she may be enjoyed in **Devotion** (1946). Richard Winnington wrote: 'As one who has spent hours pondering on the aching enigma of the Brontës in front of Branwell's badly painted and beautiful portrait of them in the National Portrait Gallery, I found *Devotion* painless. It never got nearer to the subject than names and consequently didn't hurt.' Here, Charlotte (Olivia de Havilland) learns the bitter truth from Thackeray (Sydney Greenstreet), that 'Wuthering Heights' was created from Emily's frustrated love for the Reverend Arthur Bell Nicholls; here, Charlotte is a self-centred, scheming coquette, revelling in the attentions of London society (whereas in fact she was so shy that she became physically ill). Here the three sisters dress not in drab parsonage clothes but in magnificent crinolines for the ball. Lupino plays Emily, another fate Emily did not deserve; the unbending and unattractive Nicholls is played by the 'charming' and unattractive Paul Henreid, with an Austrian accent – while Branwell (Arthur

Kennedy) has an American one. When the truth is so astounding and heart-breaking, why could they not have used it? The chief culprits are Keith Winter, who wrote it, and director Bernhardt, who later compounded his crime by saying, 'This is the kind of film I like to do. I'd always been interested in the Brontës.'

It would be nice to think that Warners had doubts about the film, for it was one of several whose release was delayed for a couple of years. Another was **Saratoga Trunk** (1945), made by Gary Cooper and Ingrid Bergman on completing *For Whom the Bell Tolls* at Paramount, with Sam Wood again directing – and refusing to take seriously this pseudo-epic of the early days of the railroad. Edna Ferber's novel about a Creole adventuress had been bought in the hope that Vivien Leigh would play it, and certainly Bergman is not as good as she – or Bette Davis – would have been, for she was not a 'scheming' actress. However, her scenes with Cooper work – he seeing through her plotting, and she knowing that he does – partly because of his sure sense of comedy. Like the Warner films of another era, this one is always prepared to sacrifice probability for humour. It played in army camps in 1943, but was withheld from public exhibition till audiences were flocking to see Miss Bergman in *Spellbound* and *The Bells of St Mary's*, presumably on the assumption that they could then better appreciate her versatility.

Warners though that in Viveca Lindfors they had found a new Bergman. She was Swedish also, and **Night Unto Night** (1949) was intended to make her a big star. She is discovered, clearly disturbed, in a house in Key West, when Ronald Reagan comes along: 'I'm a scientist,' he tells her pal – Broderick Crawford as a kitsch William Blake. 'One of those atomic-bomb fellas?' asks Crawford, but it turns out that he is on the side of humanity – creating, not destroying. He too, is sick, subject to 'low-grade epilepsy', which means that he has seizures; Crawford has an exhibition of his paintings, and Lindfors has a nymphomaniac sister (Osa Massen), who, like all such ladies in movies, is also a drunk. The direction is by Don Siegel (b. 1912), former chief editor for the studio – in which capacity he was responsible for some of its most renowned montage sequences.

From the ranks of Warners' second leads, Jane Wyman found a huge popularity with **Johnny Belinda** (1948) as a deaf-mute victim of a rape. It seems to me a sober and decent picture, despite the melodrama and a self-conscious attempt at poetry. Warners had bought the play by Elmer Harris, and assigned it to producer Jerry Wald and director Negulesco, both of whom recognised its true worth but felt that with tact a good movie could be wrested from it. Jack Warner loathed the result so much that he shelved it and sacked Negulesco, which indicates that working on location (in California), Negulesco did things very much his own way: certainly this Nova Scotia community is tenderly evoked. Charles Bickford and Agnes Moorehead are believable as people who have spent their lives tilling the soil; as the rake turned rapist, Stephen McNally is rightly just a village bully, and Jan Sterling is his complement as the girl who marries him. Lew Ayres makes an admirable centrepiece as the doctor, and Miss Wyman blessedly underplays (she studied for the role at a school for the dumb, and used wax in her ears on the set). She won a famous Oscar and, if not giving evidence of overwhelming talent, succeeds marvellously in what I think with anyone else would have been a lesser picture. It is worth adding, because it is seldom revived, that it was in its day a great success with both critics and public.

At Warners Miss Wyman made only one other worthwhile film, **The Glass Menagerie** (1950) the screen version of Tennessee Williams's first stage success. It was poorly received, and I have never come across anyone with a fondness for it apart from myself. As Williams knew, the mood was Tchekhovian – well-meaning people but forlorn, saturated in yearning, frustration and faded dreams. If the actors can only show their concern for each other, where appropriate, the piece plays itself, as it does here under the direction of Irving Rapper. As the painfully shy and lame Laura, Miss Wyman smiles meekly, speaks in a whisper, and betrays occasional panic: she is very likeable, which may not be said for Arthur Kennedy as her brother or Kirk Douglas as the consciously charming Gentleman Caller, but the piece does not depend on them for its effectiveness. As the mother, the role in which Laurette Taylor had made her celebrated return to the stage, Gertrude Lawrence made one of her rare screen appearances, and it was not difficult for this actress to suggest a woman who once had great charm before she lost heart.

Warners' interest in Broadway brought them **Life with Father** (1947), based on Clarence Day's reminiscences of his stern and eccentric father as published in *The New Yorker*; the dramatised version by Howard Lindsay and Russell Crouse had opened in 1939, and Warners were forbidden to release their film till its run finished, which is still a Broadway record for a straight play. The late appearance of the movie did not affect its popularity in cinemas, but there were too many imitations for it to be of much interest today. Cosy, unadventurous, it offers family drama and comedy but, despite the direction of Michael Curtiz, not enough of either. Its chief pleasures are the performances of William Powell and Irene Dunne; and if he plays with the twinkle necessary for sympathetic audience reaction she, commendably, does not.

Broadway was also raided, after a fashion, for **Rhapsody in Blue** (1945). George Gershwin had been dead for only seven years but, as an acknowledged folk hero, was a sure subject for film treatment – which in this case includes a laudable concentration on his serious music, though apart from this audiences must endure a long movie of stupefying banality. After a fair portrait of a vaguely Jewish family, it depicts Gershwin's career as the usual toss-up between jazz and serious music, with his off-duty moments split between the chorus girl (Joan Leslie) who is his one endearing love, and the society beauty (Alexis Smith) who dallies with him at the height of his fame. He is portrayed as inordinately vain, but it is hinted that this is only a passing phase: certainly as played by Robert Alda he has no more character than have the two ladies. Ferde Grofe, who worked with Gershwin, did the arrangement of the Rhapsody, and Walter Damrosch and Paul Whiteman appear to conduct the pieces as they had originally done. Jolson appears as himself, to be thanked sycophantically for singing 'Swanee', and the original Bess (Anne Brown) is made to sing 'Summertime', which is not one of Bess's songs in 'Porgy and Bess'; more questionable is Oscar

Levant's appearance as himself, since he was supposed to be a friend of Gershwin.

On the lighter side, Warners offered **Always Leave Them Laughing** (1949), a saga of a big-headed and second-rate vaudeville comic, played by Milton Berle, who had been in vaudeville and who was otherwise known for supporting roles in a few movies. In 1948 he went into T.V., the new medium, and became known as 'Mr Television'; his popularity was the alleged reason for the upsurge in the sale of sets (numbering around 190,000) by the end of that year. Much care went into packaging him for the cinema public. Roy del Ruth directed, and Melville Shavelson and Jack Rose wrote the screenplay, which leaves no facet of Berle undemonstrated. He might have had a longer cinema career had they done otherwise; the quick failure of this film caused the other Hollywood studios to look askance on T.V. 'stars' for at least another decade.★

Warners did not have a female star for musicals of their own, though that did not prevent them from turning out several musicals every year, often with the duo of Dennis Morgan and Jack Carson, who were some light years behind Crosby and Hope. A band singer, Doris Day (b. 1924) eventually arrived, with pretty, healthy looks, a natural smile and a fetching gawkiness, as well as a singing voice which was not only very much in the fashion of the time but relaxed and increasingly versatile. Warners could only see her as a surrogate Betty Hutton, and thus she was in her first film, **Romance on the High Seas** (1948), an attempt by Curtiz (producing and directing) at a Lubitsch-style marital musical. Immediate public response enabled Day to get away from the Hutton curls, and she appeared to advantage in **Tea for Two** (1950) and **Lullaby of Broadway** (1951), both directed by David Butler. In the wake of M-G-M's success, Warners had realised that the public was tiring of the backstage formula, and if both films are better than most of their predecessors, they are still not good enough. *Tea for Two* uses some songs from 'No, No Nanette' and is set in the Twenties, but apart from a mild Charleston makes nothing of the period; we can,

★Warners had another failure with a T.V. name, Liberace, in *Sincerely Yours* in 1955.

however, recognise that Harry Clork's screenplay aspires to 'musical comedy'. *Lullaby of Broadway* also has several old songs, comedy relief, and a fair screenplay (by Earl Baldwin) on the subject of a girl (Miss Day) suspected of being an old man's darling. Gladys George is her mother, and Gene Nelson was promoted from the earlier film to leading man, but although a good dancer he lacks star quality as an actor.

I'll See You in My Dreams (1951) is one of the last and best of show business biographies as written by Shavelson and Rose and directed by Curtiz, as ever providing pasteboard characters with some dimension. Its subject is Gus Kahn, and it was observed that since Hollywood had run out of composers it was turning in desperation to the lyricists. His life apparently differed little from the composers, and one would have liked more on his collaborators – who included Gershwin – and perhaps greater honesty on his 'managing' wife (Miss Day). Danny Thomas plays Kahn as a schnook, but for all that the film is low-keyed and affectionate.

Young Man with a Horn (1950) was adapted from Dorothy Baker's novel based on the life of Bix Beiderbecke, who died at the age of twenty-eight with a reputation as one of the great white jazz musicians. As renamed Rick Martin (Kirk Douglas), he moves from a jazz-obsessed childhood to a society marriage to alcoholism – from which he is rescued by a band singer (Day) and 'Smoke' (Hoagy Carmichael), an experience which makes him 'a bedder person' as 'Smoke' confides to the camera. It is a good film, except for the interlude with the society girl, superficially written and then misinterpreted by Lauren Bacall. Douglas is not entirely taking, especially when reeling down Third Avenue at dawn – the inevitable ending of such tales, already featured in *Swing High, Swing Low* and *Blues in the Night*. Curtiz makes the major contribution; he always placed his camera for the utmost effect and in this case he uses it for the expression of the music, honing in on, or moving away from, dance halls, jazz-joints and Village bars. The music includes more great songs than in any other movie I can think of, for instance, 'Someone to Watch Over Me' and 'Can't We Be Friends'. They are not reproduced in the manner of the period –

Harry James ghosted the trumpet – but for once it does not matter.

'At fifteen,' says Miss Day in **The West Point Story** (1950), 'I was singing with a band, one-night stands. At seventeen I had a Hollywood contract. I'm a commodity now, not a woman,' but after this promisingly harsh start the story turns into a compound of those of *Varsity Show* and *Flirtation Walk*. James Cagney repeats his role in *Footlight Parade*, that of the hustling show director who, when crossed, becomes a bouncing ball of fury: but the pugnacity sits less easily on a thick-set, middle-aged man. No one could resist his younger self, but here he is for admirers only. Roy del Ruth directed, and apart from Day and Gordon MacRae he and Cagney lack the skilled co-players of their great days at Warners.

Cagney had returned to Warners for **White Heat** (1949), which was occasioned by Zanuck's imitations of their own early gangster films. Twenty years later a gangster's life has become more difficult, and Jody Garrett (Cagney) is reduced to hiding out in a cold, tacky bungalow with his gang: Ma (Margaret Wycherly), his cheap wife (Virginia Mayo), his aide, Big Ed (Steve Cochran) and a man whose face is a mess of bandages. As directed by Raoul Walsh, the mood is sour and grim; the prison sequences are the best that Warners ever did, and it is impossible to forget Garrett's epileptic fit or his final shriek as the police snipe at him above the oil tanks, 'Top of the world, Ma, top of the world!' It is an ironic postscript to *Public Enemy*. The mother in that film was motherhood sanctified, but the one in this is even more demoniacal than Cagney; his wife gets only a kick in the butt when she takes up with Big Ed – because 'All I ever had is Ma.' This Oedipus complex was Cagney's own idea: in his memoir he is insistent that most Warner scripts were 'the same old thing', and that he did what he could to give them individuality* – in this case conceiving the idea of modelling the gang on Ma Barker and her boys. Miss Wycherly is superb, and the others are good, including Edmond O'Brien as an undercover man and Fred Clark as a criminal

*I once came upon a copy of *L'Express*, reviewing this film on a Paris revival in 1963 and devoting its flattery to the director: ironically in its two-page review it did not see fit to mention Cagney's name.

After emerging as the biggest star on the Warner Bros. lot Humphrey Bogart never quite forgave his employers for keeping him so long as a supporting actor. And it was hard to blame him, for they seemed incapable of finding a worthy vehicle after *Casablanca* – except for three that he made with Lauren Bacall, *To Have and Have Not*, *The Big Sleep* and *Key Largo*. There was a fourth, *Dark Passage*, illustrated here because this picture conveys something of their appeal as a team.

mastermind: but one comes away pondering on the appeal of the star, here at the end of a lifetime of crime.

The writers for *White Heat* were the team of Ivan Goff and Ben Roberts, who also wrote **Come Fill the Cup** (1951) for Cagney. He plays an alcoholic reporter rehabilitated by an 'ex-alkie' (James Gleason), asked in turn by his boss (Raymond Massey) to help his nephew (Gig Young), a composer, whose drinking prevents him from finishing his concerto; the latter is also married to the reporter's ex-girlfriend (Phyllis Thaxter) and the climax has a gangster forcing the two men to get drunk at gunpoint. Virtually every review evoked *The Lost Weekend*, but here the intelligent beginning gives way to matters more lurid. It remains well directed, by Gordon Douglas; Cagney is at his most subdued and humorous – probably the most likeable of his later performances.

He moves close to self-parody in **A**

Lion Is in the Streets (1953), as uncertainly directed by Walsh. Cagney is at the same time the film's strength and weakness, playing with characteristic intensity and attempting gestures that a lesser actor would not dare. The role is not easy: it is that of a pedlar with an obsessive interest in law whose ambitions – not credibly deployed – lead to the governor's mansion. Adria Locke Langley's original novel, like 'All the King's Men', was based on the career of Huey Long and is reputedly more accurate; Columbia, which had made a film of that book (q.v.), sued Warners for plagiarism (it is surprising that the Hollywood studios were not suing each other all the time), but the films are dissimilar except in outline. The Columbia film was in newsreel style and this is in Technicolor – both to attract audiences which had seen that and to present the story in appropriate picture-book manner: the American dream gone sour, Huck Finn grown up and gone bent.

Apart from the films he made with John Huston, Humphrey Bogart also fared uneasily during his last years at Warners. He is at his peak in **The Big Sleep** (1946), returning to his most satisfying incarnation, the private eye. There may be distinctions between Sam Spade in *The Maltese Falcon* and Philip Marlowe in this film, but Bogart is superb as both: each film is so strong that it is impossible to confuse them. The confusion that arises in *The Big Sleep* has to do with the narrative. The director, Howard Hawks, said that no one could follow it; the author, Raymond Chandler, when appealed to, could not enlighten him; and William Faulkner, Leigh Brackett and Jules Furthman, writing the screenplay, were unable to clarify it. Whatever the convolutions – and I have never heard anyone express the least dissatisfaction with this film – the result is recognisably Chandler. It may not be visually distinctive, but there is nothing equivocal about the environment or, except where necessary, the characters: the multi-millionaire (Charles Waldron), living in an orchid hothouse to survive; his vulpine daughters, the thumb-sucking nymphomaniac (Martha Vickers) and the insolent divorcée (Lauren Bacall); the bland and cringing bodyguard (Elisha Cook, Jr); the pince-nezed librarian (Dorothy Malone), a rare Forties example of the quick lay; and the various black-mailers and scroungers, all-American footballers gone to seed. Bogart has some searing dialogue, notably his exchange with John Ridgely which builds to the latter's 'I could make your business my business,' and Bogart's rueful response, 'You wouldn't like it, the pay's too small.' The rather déclassé savoir-faire, the sardonic humour, the hunch-backed acceptance of these appointments with fear: Chandler might have created Marlowe for him.

Bogart and Bacall make a self-mocking, inexorable team, but the studio clearly had no idea how good they were together: reunited in **Dark Passage** (1947), she has a role that could have been played by any contract actress, and they are simply not given the teasing dialogue which was a feature of their earlier films together. The source, a novel by David Goodis, is clearly inferior, and Delmer Daves, writing and directing, is merely ponderous. The story concerns a convicted man trying to prove his innocence; Bacall attempts to help him, and Agnes Moorehead is her silly, loquacious sister. The latter takes whatever honours are going, but Bogart is hardly eligible, being seen only in longshot or shadow for the first thirty-five minutes, and then in bandages for the next twenty.

Returning to villainy, he was even less interesting. Capable of a wide range from pettiness to paranoia, he was not a natural wife-murderer, though Warners, having failed with him in **Conflict** (1945), had him at it again in **The Two Mrs Carrolls** (1947). The first, directed by Curtis Bernhardt and adapted from a story by Robert Siodmak and Alfred Neumann, has Bogart bewildered as mounting evidence suggests that the wife is alive after all; the second film sins more grievously, since the wife is Barbara Stanwyck and this is the only time she and Bogart appeared together. The teaming should have left us some tough, slangy drama instead of this cheerless enterprise, drawn from a West End thriller already over a decade old. In the original, there is some doubt as to whether Mr Carroll had murdered the first Mrs C., but this version throws away even that mild bit of suspense. Peter Godfrey directed but, unlike his work on *The Woman in White*, fails to offer a plausible England.

The Enforcer (1951) was Bogart's last film for Warners, and as with Cagney in *White Heat*, an excellent return to beginnings. The British title, *Murder Inc.*, is more telling – and, I should have thought, more enticing to prospective patrons. Notably well constructed – despite flashbacks within flashbacks – it starts on the night before an important trial, with the Assistant D.A. (Bogart) protecting his only witness – a vital one. Raoul Walsh apparently directed most of the film, though the credited director is Bretaigne Windust. A largely unfamiliar cast add to the authenticity, but we may also enjoy some actors we know: Everett Sloane is the mastermind, Zero Mostel the one who cracks; and Bogart is admirable, despite his claim that he had played the role so often that he did it mechanically.

Errol Flynn, another Warner veteran, continued his career in mainly indifferent vehicles. Among the more ambitious is **Silver River** (1948), directed by Walsh. It is set in the West, but Flynn wears silk hat rather than Stetson, since this is one of the many tales of nineteenth-century cattle barons and their ambitions. Ann Sheridan is Bathsheba to Flynn's David, an analogy given emphasis in the script by Harriet Frank Jr and Stephen Longstreet, from his novel. The film did not halt Flynn's waning popularity, so it was courageous of Warners to pour money into **The Adventures of Don Juan** (1948), another example of the studio returning successfully to a particular genre after a long break. The settings are among the most lavish ever, and the costumes among the most sumptuous – owing much to Velázquez, though internal evidence places the action between 1558 and 1603. Vincent Sherman directed, lightheartedly, and the merely serviceable plot provides multiple opportunities for action and intrigue. The writers were Harry Kurnitz and George Oppenheimer, who said 'It's like a piece of Venetian glass,' to which Jack Warner replied 'To hell with that. You know Flynn, he's either got to be fighting or fucking.' Sherman has said that Flynn was no great swordsman, but that he could appear so, adding that he was 'an incipient homosexual' (he designed his own costumes, insisting upon unnaturally tight tights). Sherman also observed that Flynn was more conscientious than he pretended to be, and one can sense behind the breezy charm a sad man – his drinking problem was now extreme – trying to do his job. That is the nearest the film gets to Mozart's opera, from which Max Steiner borrows some of his themes; just as the duels borrow from Olivier's *Hamlet* (q.v.).

Peter Lorre, a deceptively timid villain, and Sydney Greenstreet, jovial and menacing, had become a star team – much to the credit of Warners, even if their films were allotted only medium budgets. In **The Verdict** (1946) it was clearly expedient for Don Siegel – in his first film as a director – to shroud Edwardian London in a fog even thicker than was usual, since that prevented the expense of exterior settings. Greenstreet is a Scotland Yard man with a guilty secret, Lorre is a hard-drinking artist – and Joan Lorring is a music-hall artist for whom Frederick Hollander has provided songs which are more Dietrich than Marie Lloyd. **Three Strangers** (1946) is also fogbound, with Geraldine Fitzgerald joining Lorre and Greenstreet to form a curious trio holding a sweepstake ticket; John Huston wrote the genuinely weird screenplay, and Negulesco takes it to a certain pitch.

Also set in a phoney London is **Confidential Agent** (1945) which Graham Greene thought the best American film of one of his novels – not necessarily a good adaptation, but an interesting film in its own right. Robert Buckner, the producer and writer, has kept the original premise – it could have been adapted to conventional espionage – that a Spanish republican (Charles Boyer) arrives in London to prevent the supplying of coal to the opposite side. I find, even in this painted Britain, the plangent Greene notes: the hotel skivvy whom the Spaniard befriends; the languages school for a form of Esperanto, where he meets Lorre; and the aristocratic girl (Lauren Bacall) too drunk on first meeting to prevent his being beaten up. She does not attempt an English accent – and Boyer, Lorre, Victor Francen and Katina Paxinou are hardly Spanish. Under Herman Shumlin's direction the result is crude, but not negligible.

Greene's novel, though set before the War, could have provided a platform for a discussion of contemporary problems. No more than the other companies were Warner Bros. interested in such matters –

buoyed up as the industry was with the box-office returns for the mindless entertainments which predominated as the War ended. As we have seen, certain directors toyed with postwar problems, but as far as the front office was concerned these were usually to be considered in terms of genres acceptable to the managers of the circuits. It is in this context that we should consider **Storm Warning** (1950). Warners' social reform melodramas had petered out, though Zanuck had remembered them and had recently emulated them. It was his films which prompted Jerry Wald to institute this one, based on a script by Richard Brooks and Daniel Fuchs which had been lying around for some time. It roundly condemns the Ku-Klux Klan as 'a group of wicked men' and with equal lack of subtlety offers a portrait of a town too self-absorbed, as in *Black Legion*, to be aware of the canker in its midst. The members of the Klan are merely 'a lot of hoodlums dressed up in sheets', as the D.A.'s deputy says, admitting that he had once been one of them. To this reasonable presentation – the town appears to have no racial problems – is added the situation of a model (Ginger Rogers), who witnesses a murder while visiting her sister (Doris Day) and recognises her brother-in-law (Steve Cochran) as the killer. She does the obvious thing – rare in such films – and tells her sister, but has a crisis of conscience on the witness stand. Her dilemma is foolishly resolved: we had noticed certain situations borrowed from 'A Streetcar Named Desire' and the film dallies with others from that play as it rushes downhill. Stuart Heisler's direction borrows from its prototype, *Fury*, and is further interesting in subduing Miss Rogers, who 'acts' less than in most of her straight roles, with a consequent gain in credibility.

King Vidor, once concerned with social questions, turned up at Warners, for whom he made three of his late quartet of melodramas: *Beyond the Forest*, already discussed, **The Fountainhead** (1949) and **Lightning Strikes Twice** (1951). 'Perhaps no other director has gone off the rails quite so spectacularly,' observed Gavin Lambert of the fourth, **Ruby Gentry** (1952), made independently and released by Fox. Though Vidor himself disliked *Lightning Strikes Twice*, which is about a girl (Ruth Roman) who refuses to believe that a dour Britisher (Richard Todd) is a wife-killer, he thought the others constituted 'a trilogy of modern American life'; and he scribbled on the script of *Ruby Gentry*, 'Motion pictures are an art form', to which Selznick retorted that this one at least was a commercial enterprise. *The Fountainhead* was written by Ayn Rand from her own novel, with dialogue as high-flown and fly-blown as the plot: an idealistic architect (Gary Cooper) is the object of a smear campaign waged by a newspaper tycoon (Raymond Massey) and a journalist (Patricia Neal) – who seduces the architect but marries the tycoon. On trial for blowing up one of his own buildings, the architect, like Mr Deeds, refuses to defend himself till the last minute, whereupon Massey realises that his wife loves him and shoots himself after one last commission: 'Build it as a monument to your spirit – which could have been mine.' The film ends with Neal symbolically going up in an elevator on the building-site where Cooper is symbolically waiting.

Ruby Gentry concerns a girl (Jennifer Jones) from the wrong side of the tracks who wears tight sweaters and jeans to indicate her wild spirit. The love of her life is Boake (Charlton Heston), who says, 'No woman like her – fightin', scratchin', next moment sweetest woman alive,' but marries another. Ruby, in the manner of her forebears Scarlett and Amber, cannot reconcile herself to losing him, so in revenge accepts the marriage proposal of her foster-father (Karl Malden): 'You and me's the sort of people . . . We're mongrels.' He is soon lost at sea, and the rumours grow till a crowd assembles outside her mansion to scream 'Murderess' – which provokes her to vindictiveness towards all and sundry, especially Boake, who understandably refuses to become her lover again, but later rapes her in revenge for having flooded his land. This director, let it be reminded, once made *The Crowd*.

Vidor's film with Gary Cooper is typical of Cooper's vehicles of this period, which include almost a dozen more unhappy ventures for Warners. **Distant Drums** (1951) is set in Florida, with Cooper as an Indian fighter commissioned to clear the Everglades of the Seminole. The screenplay by Niven Busch and Martin Rackin makes him even more monosyllabic than ever, and his lack of interest was surely increased

by Mari Aldon, his leading lady, an ex-ballerina. She starts almost every scene leaning on a palm tree and gazing at the moon, presumably on the direction of Raoul Walsh, whose work here is of definitive ineptitude. In his long career there was only one period when his work was consistently good, from 1939 to 1945, his first few years at Warners – during which time the studio had probably the most proficient script department in Hollywood and the most skilful editors. This film, however, is completely without tension – the action scenes unroll as if by chance – the sort of hack job which made many people lose interest in Hollywood in the late Forties.

The matter of apportioning blame and credit in most studio films is a vexed one. Walsh 'signed' *White Heat* at a time when all his other films were mediocre, while Curtiz reached a last peak before he too declined – coinciding with his departure from Warners; but if it was the Warners' cutting-room which bailed out Curtiz, why did the editors not do the same for Walsh? All that is certain is that **The Breaking Point** (1950) is the best screen Hemingway since Borzage's *A Farewell to Arms*. Warners played down the Hemingway connection, since this was a remake of *To Have and Have Not* – though as faithful to the novel as the earlier film was not. It tells of a fisherman forced into transporting illegal immigrants; one major change from the novel is the substitution of California for Florida. A line of white-painted inexpensive bungalows shelters under a stormy sky, the first of Ted McCord's memorable compositions of harbours and boats, a large deserted waterfront restaurant, smoke-filled bars. Ranald McDougall's screenplay manages at times to parody both Hemingway and the star, John Garfield – for example, 'A man alone ain't got no chance.' The film is slick, but always pleasurable: the credit may not be due entirely to Curtiz, but some is certainly attributable to the good-time girl of Patricia Neal, taunting and confident, leaving the other vamps of the time at the starting-post.

Speaking of vamps, Columbia had one: 'There never was a woman like Gilda!' said the ads. 'Blimey! there never was,' said C. A. Lejeune, noting that after a while boy-gigolo manner, is unable to suggest ambiguity. When the boss – based on the Clifton Webb character in *Laura* – returns from distant parts with a wife (Rita Hayworth), the relationship between the two men changes – ostensibly because Ford had been in love with her years before, but clearly because the boss demands the return of the key to his bedroom. The role of Gilda was supposed to prove Hayworth a serious actress, and though most critics were unimpressed, she does project – for the last time on screen – a sort of silky earthiness. Her hair was ever her most alluring feature: she makes her first appearance from the bottom of the screen shaking it and later caresses her scalp as she sings 'Put the Blame on Mame'.

By the time she made **Affair in Trinidad** (1952) her charms had flown. This was *Gilda* revamped – an attempt to reestablish her after her years in Europe, loving and losing Aly Khan amidst great publicity. Ford is her co-star and Alexander Scourby is the suave older man; a sole back projection may be Port of Spain, but the film offers the standard South-of-the-Border nightclubs and mansions. The only interest is provided by a foreshadowing of the Cuba crisis: Scourby plans to establish rocket bases which 'will make Pearl Harbor seem like a slap on the wrist'. In *Gilda*, Macready schemed to master the world, and it is only too typical of Hollywood to have taken the worst of that film for this new edition: there is nothing in Vincent Sherman's direction to show that he knew what the worst of it was.

Salome (1953) boasted the cinema's love goddess in Technicolor as one of history's infamous women – no matter that the love goddess was by now too old and that the biblical Salome could hardly provide a full-length film. DeMille had turned Hedy Lamarr into Delilah, so Harry Cohn made Hayworth into Salome, even commissioning one of deMille's writers, Jesse Lasky Jr, to provide the story – which interestingly reveals that it was in fact Herodias (Judith Anderson) who demanded the head of John the Baptist (Alan Badel), so annoying Salome that she runs off with her Roman lover (Stewart Granger), a Christian, to listen to the Sermon on the Mount. The conception of Salome as a misunderstood and well-meaning

It is now a little difficult to appreciate that Rita Hayworth in *Gilda* represented the height of Hollywood eroticism, though she was certainly very effective singing 'Put the Blame on Mame' – or, more correctly, mouthing it, since her singing voice was dubbed.

there is 'a suspicion, subsequently confirmed, that nothing is going to happen except Miss Hayworth'. Richard Winnington thought that to anyone uninterested in that lady 'it will look like one of the worst films in living memory'. Yet **Gilda** (1946) lives on, despite a director, Charles Vidor, and writers, Marion Parsonnet and Jo Eisinger, whose other credits show little else with a claim to immortality. The plot is a wild thing, consisting of skulduggery in and around a Buenos Aires nightclub, but in what is essentially a triangle drama the two men concerned seem to have been more than room-mates. The relationship is unprecedented in an American film, and that it then went unremarked may be attributed to the fact that most people were unprepared to consider the implications of the dialogue. 'You've no idea how faithful and obedient I can be,' says Glenn Ford to his boss (George Macready), and it must be said that this actor, with his bright young lady could have been funny, but Miss Hayworth's interpretation is no laughing matter. William Dieterle directed as though he had a respectable script, which was a mistake, and a good (British) supporting cast follows his lead: Cedric Hardwicke (Tiberius), Basil Sydney (Pontius Pilate), and Charles Laughton, whose Herod is not as rich as was his Nero.

Columbia's dependence on Miss Hayworth is almost all there is to say about the studio at this juncture. However, **The Jolson Story** (1946) was the company's biggest success at that time. It was the project of Sidney Skolsky, a newspaperman, who braved the indifference of the film industry and eventually sold the idea to Harry Cohn. Jolson wanted to play himself, so it was much to his chagrin that they chose a contract player, Larry Parks, to play the role. The movie uses only cliché as he goes from boyhood to the break-up of his marriage to Ruby Keeler, here called 'Julie Benson', since Miss Keeler refused to allow her name to be used; Evelyn Keyes's manicured performance is little like the original. Alfred E. Green directed, but was replaced by Henry Levin on **Jolson Sings Again** (1949), though that belongs less with the original than to something like *Freaks*. It starts with Jolson as half-forgotten (though only he himself is permitted to refer to his faded popularity) and describes his restitution via a film of his life. Parks plays himself as well – a mite less convincingly than his ungalvanic impersonation of Jolson – and undreamed-of heights are achieved when he goes with Jolson (Parks) to a preview of *The Jolson Story*: though if Levin had tried harder he could have got three Jolson/Parks on the screen at the same time – the two in the audience watching the one in the film. That might have been preferable to what seems to be a total reprise of the songs from the earlier film – yet the Jolson songs and the Jolson voice were the ingredients which made these two films so popular.

All the King's Men (1949) was the studio's first responsible film since Capra; it was written, produced and directed by Robert Rossen (1908–66), a former screenwriter, whose second film as director, *Body and Soul* (q.v.), had received much praise. This one is based on the Pulitzer Prize-winning novel by Robert Penn Warren, and is based on the life and times of Huey 'Kingfisher' Long, Governor of Louisiana, but with as much interest in the myth as in the man, and also with a few backward glances at Mussolini. During filming Rossen improvised in an attempt at spontaneity. He was unable to get everything in and unwilling to leave anything out, and the result is chaotic. Such conventional characters as the discarded wife and the dissolute (foster-)son (John Derek) are less rewarding than the members of the demagogue's retinue, including the reporter (John Ireland) who degenerates into an acolyte, and the vicious, equally cynical secretary (Mercedes McCambridge). Indeed, the keynote is cynicism, with too much hysteria and too little analysis – though we may enjoy the manipulation of the crowds ('You're a hick and I'm a hick. We're all hicks') and their blind faith in Huey, here rechristened Willie Stark. Willie's rabble-rousing, his contempt for public ethics and his black book of enemies also provide fascinating material, but eventually the cliché-ridden commentary and lack of organisation put the film far below its model, *Citizen Kane*. Unlike that film, this appealed to the industry, which voted it a Best Picture Oscar; Broderick Crawford's bull-headed but empty performance as Willie also won an Academy Award. Hollywood's approval of Rossen was short-lived, and he was blacklisted when he refused to admit past membership of the Communist Party to the House Un-American Activities Committee. He did return to filming in the mid-Fifties, with uneven results (q.v.).

Meanwhile foreign critics did not receive *All the King's Men* with the rapture of their American colleagues. Today it seems hardly superior to a programme picture like **Bad for Each Other** (1953), 83 minutes of vacuous good intentions about an ex-army doctor (Charlton Heston) who dallies with a mine-owner's daughter (Lizabeth Scott) before realising that his place is with the miners. This echo of *The Citadel* was written by Horace McCoy (author of 'They Shoot Horses, Don't They?') and Irving Wallace, later a best-selling novelist. Irving Rapper directed, and the film was developed but not produced by Hal Wallis, who imposed the property and the two stars on Columbia as part of his price for releasing Burt Lancaster to do *From Here to Eternity*.

Miss Scott may also be seen in **Dead Reckoning** (1947), with Humphrey Bogart: 'He set the pace. He would arrive on the set totally unprepared at nine. He would then proceed to learn his lines before his martini and lunch. Then he would work till five and leave, the scene completed or not . . . These were his rules and although I was equally the star of the picture, I abided by them, as did the crew, the director, the producer and the studio.' Bogart made several films for Columbia (choosing the company to handle his independent productions as a deliberate snub to Warners) and this is the best of them, concerning a tough hero, a double-dealing dame and various heavies. The *films noirs* of the Forties are ritualised, and in this one the writers (Oliver H. P. Garrett and Steve Fisher) hold our attention by the lengths to which Bogart will go in challenging the very dangerous villain. John Cromwell, better known for romantic dramas, times each sequence for the utmost tension; it was his last film before he was blacklisted for suspected left-wing sympathies.

Bogart is also superb in **Knock on Any Door** (1949), as defence counsel for the pleasant youth (John Derek) who is indeed the killer he says he is not: but the touted suggestion that there is one like him in every home is typical of the film's approach – and of the equally superficial juvenile delinquent stories set off by its (albeit mild) success. Nicholas Ray directed, a new man whose work at R.K.O. at this time (q.v.) also indicated a modicum of skill; but **In a Lonely Place** (1950), after a good beginning, proceeds downhill at an alarming rate, unhindered by Ray's handling. For once it is difficult to enjoy Bogart, since as a Hollywood writer suspected of murder he behaves in so guilty a fashion as to forfeit all patience.

The United Artists were foundering; of its originators, only Chaplin and Pickford were left. The postwar surge to independence should have benefited the company above all others, and that it did not may be due to what Selznick in 1945 referred to as the 'insupportable tyranny' of the Chaplin–Pickford faction; both he and other spirits bent on independence found a warmer berth at R.K.O., and by 1951 U.A. was operating deeply in the red, due to the dearth of product and the low profits on what there was. The financial squabbles between Chaplin and Pickford were increasingly acrimonious, and for this reason they both sold the majority of their holdings to a syndicate in 1950. When *The African Queen* and *High Noon* had made the company prosperous again, they took the opportunity to sell their remaining interests.

Few U.A. films of the period are of more than passing interest, and with a couple of exceptions their producers were at best undistinguished. Miss Pickford herself produced **Sleep, My Love** (1948), a thriller which almost revels in its lack of suspense as directed by Douglas Sirk. Claudette Colbert is the bride whose marriage brings hallucinations, and Don Ameche is the suave husband; a third performer is their Sutton Place mansion, if second-best to the one in *Gaslight* where such antics started.

Benedict Bogeaus, a former real estate dealer, and Burgess Meredith, co-producers of *Diary of a Chambermaid*, were reunited for **On Our Merry Way** (1948), one of Hollywood's rare episode films. Two of the three stories were directed by King Vidor, who described the result as 'a synthetic hotchpatch'; the third and best was directed, uncredited, by George Stevens, from a story by John O'Hara about two musicians (Henry Fonda and James Stewart) who, down on their luck, plan to 'throw' a contest to the mayor's son. Leslie Fenton directed the prologue, in which a wife (Paulette Goddard) urges her husband (Meredith) to write a story about the influence of babies in people's lives. It is laboured, as is the tale of movie extras (Dorothy Lamour, Victor Moore); the final story plagiarises O. Henry's 'The Ransom of Red Chief' and is about two con-men (Fred MacMurray, William Demarest) who manage to get themselves kidnapped by a horrible child. That the anecdote could soon reappear in *O. Henry's Full House* is evidence of this film's failure.

Somewhat more successful is **Champagne for Caesar** (1950), though it was less so at the box office, since the stars later sued the producer, Harry M. Popkin, for their deferred fees. They are Ronald Colman and Celeste Holm, usually joyous in comedy, but struggling to make bricks without straw under the direction of

In Europe the episode film, i.e. one consisting of short stories either tenuously linked or not at all, has long been popular, but there are probably less than half a dozen in all Hollywood history, partly because most of those failed. The depth of the failure of *On Our Merry Way* can be gauged from the fact that it was retitled *A Miracle Can Happen* while in release, and it is still today known under both titles. Its failure was three-parts deserved, but the fourth part was a very funny tale about two unemployed musicians, incisively but casually played by Henry Fonda and James Stewart.

Richard Whorf. The film is notable, however, in being one of the first to recognise Hollywood's new rival, television, though its real target is quiz-shows, which were outstandingly popular on both T.V. and radio at the time. Colman plays a mastermind who enters a quiz-show, and Vincent Price is very funny as its pretentious and humourless sponsor.

The Marx Brothers had more or less retired as a team after *The Big Store*, but David L. Loew tempted them back with the incentive of a cut of the profits. **A Night in Casablanca** (1946) is at least funnier than their last film for M-G-M. It is a spoof of wartime spy stories, with Sig Rumann as one of several people in search of Nazi treasure in the Hotel Casablanca, of which Groucho is the new manager. Chico is first discovered running an outfit called 'Chameaux a Piloter Soi-Meme'. Archie Mayo, usually a careful director, approximates the ramshackle atmosphere of their early films, and they appear glad to be back

in it. Harpo has a good comic duel, and when he is kissed one realises that Disney's Dopey was based on him – both the coyness and fierce determination. Harpo cannot, however, sustain **Love Happy** (1949); since dumbness is basically unfunny – a fact the other films managed to hide. Harpo, who (according to Groucho) saw himself as a creative genius, wrote the story, which gives him the leading role as a tramp (the script's word for him) who steals food for an impoverished theatre troupe and has the baddies after him because a sardine-can contains the Romanov diamonds. Chico joined the project because he needed the money, and Groucho was enlisted when no backer proved interested in a film with only two Marx Brothers. Groucho has less than ten minutes of screen time – memorably with Marilyn Monroe, then unknown, who complains that she cannot stop men following her. The screenplay is by Frank Tashlin and Mac Benoff; David Miller directed; and Miss Pickford and Lester Cowan produced, accumulating extra cash by selling advertising space* to companies whose names may be seen on the neon signs in the final sequence. The film was not well received or at all popular – and is surely only revived for fans curious to know why this is so.

Red River (1948) was U.A.'s only spectacular at the time and, with the exceptions already noted, its only popular success, though high production costs involved in the location shooting cut the profits. It is entertaining but completely unsurprising; its appeal to admirers of the director, Howard Hawks, must be because they recognise familiar themes, especially the relationship between the ageing John Wayne and his protégé, Montgomery Clift: 'You really love him, don't you?' says the spunky heroine (Joanne Dru) to one or other of them from time to time. There is much talk of loyalty and man's inheritance, and lots of wide open spaces: but no amount of cattle stampeding or unshaven faces can make us believe the Old West was like this – and Clift (1920–66), a Broadway actor in his first film, does not give the impression that he was the sort of guy to enjoy sleeping rough.

This film and *Arch of Triumph* (q.v.), made by Enterprise (q.v.), were the only major United Artists films of 1948, by which time it was operating on a mere dozen or so releases annually. The new management did increase this to over a score by 1952, but, with the exceptions of the producer Stanley Kramer and John Huston, whose work has already been discussed, the company's reputation deterred other important independents from joining. Consequently the only other U.A. film of this period of interest is **He Ran All the Way** (1951), produced by Bob Roberts for John Garfield – they had earlier made two films (q.v.) at Enterprise – and directed by John Berry. The title is a misnomer, since the 'he', a small-time hood (Garfield) runs only at the beginning, spending the rest of the time holed up with the family of a girl (Shelley Winters) who had befriended him. Like Berry's earlier *From This Day Forward* (q.v.), this was intended to be a rare account of proletariat

New York, but the Winters menage is rather like that of Joan Crawford in *Mannequin* – close to the truth but not close enough. Garfield, who had complained of type-casting under contract, chose to give his usual chip-on-the-shoulder performance. This particular film was made under stress, since the principals were under investigation by the House Un-American Activities Committee. Roberts and Berry were subsequently blacklisted, while Garfield's fatal heart attack at the height of McCarthyism has been attributed to tension caused by Hollywood's rejection; Roberts made no more films, but Berry continued his career in France.

Two new companies were set up in the Forties to challenge the established major studios – the first attempt to do so since Zanuck and Joseph Schenck had founded 20th Century Pictures. International Pictures was the first, and since it was formed in 1944 it preceded the postwar trend to independence. The founders were two alumni of 20th Century-Fox, Nunnally Johnson and William Goetz, together with Leo Spitz, an ex-president of R.K.O. That company was to release International's films, originally intended to be two a year.

The first was **Casanova Brown** (1944), produced and written by Johnson from a play by Floyd Dell and Thomas Mitchell, already filmed as *Little Accident*. Gary Cooper plays a professor who, on the verge of marrying, learns that he has become a father by a previous marriage. The sequences of his going gaga over the baby are not very winning, but this actor knew how to use his personality to make a comic point and he has some funny scenes under the direction of Sam Wood (their fourth film together in two years). Frank Morgan is as ever superb as the prospective father-in-law, scornful that his pal Cooper must marry the daughter he loathes and resentful that though he himself had married for money he has hardly seen a penny of it.

When International's second film, *The Woman in the Window*, did well, production was stepped up, but there was short welcome for both *It's a Pleasure*, with Sonja Henie, and *Belle of the Yukon*, with Dinah Shore and Randolph Scott. Commendably the company attempted a drama supposedly topical in the postwar world, but **Tomorrow Is Forever** (1945), as written

---

*The practice became prevalent in the Sixties, when airlines became particularly susceptible to seeing the characters of a film fly in one of their planes.

by Lenore Coffee from a novel by Gwen Bristow, is only 'East Lynne' with pretensions. Orson Welles is a soldier so scarred in World War I that it is not till after the Anschluss that he returns to Baltimore and his wife (Claudette Colbert), now remarried and unable to recognise him. Miss Colbert, though over-gracious, remains likeable, and perhaps for that reason the film is not quite loathsome with its earnest conversations about militarism going on in a house where the French windows are always open and the children quote Patrick Henry. Irving Pichel directed, and Welles, in beard and heavy glasses, gives what Dilys Powell in the London *Sunday Times* found 'a performance of such sensitivity that I cannot believe the make-up is of his own choosing' – but we know better (cf. *Confidential Report*, *Histoire Immortelle*, q.v., both directed by him).

Welles's *The Stranger* was the last International film released by R.K.O. The company's last two films, *Temptation*, directed by Pichel, with Merle Oberon, and Siodmak's *The Dark Mirror* were released by Universal, which became Universal-International when that ailing company was taken over by International.

Enterprise was not so fortunate. Its chief founders were Charles Einfeld, formerly head of publicity at Warners, and David Loew, of Loew's Theatres, who had also produced some films for United Artists. That company was to distribute the Enterprise films domestically, and M-G-M overseas (because David's brother, Arthur Loew, was the head of M-G-M International), but Enterprise did not intend to be merely a supplier for long: with the help of $10 million in revolving credit from the Bank of America, huge premises were commandeered in Los Angeles and a grandiose programme announced, including the return to the screen of Norma Shearer. That did not happen, nor did the projects for other names like Joan Crawford and Ginger Rogers, attracted not by independence but a share in the profits – a practice which had been becoming reasonably common for major talent just before the War and was being revived.

The first Enterprise film was a Western, *Ramrod* (1947) with Veronica Lake and Joel McCrea. The second was a melodrama, **The Other Love** (1947), produced by David Lewis, who had just moved over from International. He had earlier produced *Dark Victory*, and clearly liked heroines dying from unmentionable diseases. She (Barbara Stanwyck) is a concert pianist, and as she tells the clinic's chief doctor (David Niven), 'There have been many men in my life – Bach, Brahms, Beethoven.' 'Your music belongs to the world,' he responds, 'you've got to get better for that.' When later she finds herself deceived she flees to Monte for one last fling with a racing driver (Richard Conte) but comes to her senses after an attempted rape by a croupier (Gilbert Roland). We leave her with neither hope nor despondency about the future, and such endings, supposedly honest, had become common in the postwar period – usually for dreadful films. The painted mountain backdrops place the setting as Switzerland; the superior score is by Miklos Rozsa, and André de Toth directed from a story by Erich Maria Remarque, as written for the screen by Ladislas Fodor and Harry Brown.

Lewis had a fondness for Remarque, which was to prove fatal to Enterprise. A huge budget of $4 million was set for **Arch of Triumph** (1948) and because of his success with Remarque's *All Quiet on the Western Front*, Lewis Milestone was set to direct. The script credited to him and Harry Brown was overlong, he said later, but the Enterprise executives refused to shorten it since they had paid a vast sum for the rights, and had contracted two important stars. In addition, they hoped to duplicate the success of *Gone with the Wind*, which had just been reissued. The book was a portrait of refugees at a time when France was uncertain both of its future and its attitude towards appeasement, whereas the film is only about a doomed affair between a German refugee surgeon (Charles Boyer) and a lady (Ingrid Bergman) of little virtue. It manages to hint that he scrapes a living by performing abortions, and there were further M.P.A.A. restrictions imposed on *her* problem, which was whether she should live in poverty with the man she loves or in luxury with several men she doesn't – an unsympathetic dilemma, made no more palatable by dressing Bergman as the usual movie *poule* (in mac and beret) or her inability to express coquetry. When the public decisively rejected the film, it was said that it chose not to see Bergman in such a role; but the film itself is glib and gloomy, and disappointingly short on Paris. Milestone managed some sequences well, particularly those in hotel rooms, but it seems that he and Enterprise had different films in mind.

Though the trade reviews were favourable, the studio chiefs had doubts about the film. They were contracted to deliver to United Artists, which threatened to sue if they did not. As far as United Artists was concerned, the quarrels between Chaplin and Pickford had resulted in many banks withdrawing backing. Added to a ten per cent drop in admissions at home was the virtual closure of the British market (boycotted by the American film industry in retaliation for the seventy-five per cent *ad valorem* duty imposed by the financially-troubled Labour government). Enterprise in turn could not afford to delay release while legal problems were settled, as almost all its capital was bound up in the film. The writing was on the wall since only one of Enterprise's first half dozen films had shown a profit.

This was **Body and Soul** (1947), directed by Robert Rossen and produced by Bob Roberts as a vehicle for John Garfield, who plays an unscrupulous prizefighter. The writer was Abraham Polonsky, whom Roberts promoted to director on **Force of Evil** (1948), which Polonsky scripted with Ira Wolfert, author of the original novel, 'Tucker's People'. Garfield is an ambitious young attorney involved in the numbers racket and though, like the earlier film, it has a rough and edgy texture it is again too stereotyped to hold the interest. It was shown as Enterprise closed its doors, and it was one of the three films to be released worldwide by M-G-M – in return for a small injection of cash, which had been managed because of the Loew family connection. The seventh film due to United Artists under the original agreement was never made, and Enterprise returned its studio to its owners, though the lease had not expired. It was announced that the company would be restarted if its last three films were successful, but the public showed no more interest in *No Minor Vices* (1949), a comedy with Dana Andrews and Lilli Palmer, directed by Milestone, than it had in *Force of Evil*. Hopes held out, after previews, for

Ophuls's *Caught*, but it proved the eighth failure out of nine films. It is a pity; the director Robert Aldrich (q.v.), who worked at Enterprise, said that it was a particularly happy studio, with probably a better *esprit de corps* than elsewhere; it had 'everything in its favour except one thing: it didn't have anybody in charge who knew how to make pictures.'

The situation at Universal was little happier, since the studio was turning out more than its fair share of failures. When, in 1954, the Bank of America sold the entire Enterprise output to General Teleradio Corporation – a subsidiary of General Tires – for television transmissions (for $2,350,000) it added twenty-one other films which had not repaid their loans, almost all from Universal and R.K.O. (and one or two each from Republic, Eagle-Lion, International and United Artists).

Among the few Universal films that the public did want to see was **The Egg and I** (1947). Betty MacDonald's account of the experiences of herself and her husband in running a chicken farm was less a bestseller than a publishing phenomenon; and audiences presumably went to this film to revel in their favourite incidents – each predictable, even to one chancing upon them for the first time, and ranging from the funny (the yokels and Claudette Colbert at the village hop) to the sentimental (the neighbours rallying round after the fire). The dilapidated farmhouse had done service in *George Washington Slept Here*, but audiences like the tried and true – which included the stars, who indicated that they had been doing this sort of thing for far too long. The husband is a war veteran, which at this time meant that a number of ageing actors – here Fred MacMurray – could get up to a number of tricks for which they were much too old; Miss Colbert, who had just played June Allyson's mother, wears bouffant sleeves and has a baby. Chester Erskine directed, and the support includes Marjorie Main and Percy Kilbride as Ma and Pa Kettle, she slovenly and raucous but good-hearted, and he slyly borrowing articles which he has no intention of replacing. These two artists later appeared in a B-series built around these characters.

Two further exceptions to Universal's

The studios relentlessly copied each other, as it was their business to do if they were to provide the varied entertainment required by the exhibitors who hired their films. Throughout the Thirties, however, Warner Bros. alone was associated with prison melodramas, but when they lost interest Universal came up with one of the strongest, *Brute Force*, with Howard Duff and Burt Lancaster.

run of failures were **Brute Force** (1947) and **The Naked City** (1948), both produced by Mark Hellinger and directed by Jules Dassin. The former is a late example of a once-popular genre, the prison melodrama, with the usual cross-section – the rebel (Burt Lancaster), the honest Joe, the squealer, the psychopath – shuffling for our attention till the breakout at the end. The director and the equally promising writer, Richard Brooks, strive for greater realism but only make matters nastier and more jejune – as in the character of the guard (Hume Cronyn). He has taken upon himself a Nietzschean mantle, and for a spot of beating-up is half-undressed, with Wagner on the turntable and a print of one of the Michelangelo slaves on the wall. The M.P.A.A. would not have permitted anything more explicit, but this is an instance of Hollywood's gradual return to the often sleazy realism of its pre-Code melodramas. *The Naked City* was much praised for advancing the cause of realism in the matters of New York locations and the notion that its subject, an ordinary

crime, is taken from police files. Indeed, Hellinger introduces the film in self-congratulatory tone by claiming that New York is its 'star' The piece is dull indeed till the climactic shoot-out on the Williamsburg Bridge, and as with *Brute Force* the direction is always sharper than the material: Dassin is to be particularly congratulated on having kept Barry Fitzgerald, as the detective, under control – to his obvious irritation.

Conversely, both **All My Sons** (1948) and **Another Part of the Forest** (1948) are stagey, studio-bound presentations of Broadway plays, the former by Arthur Miller, a study of a war profiteer (Edward G. Robinson) directed on screen by Irving Reis; and the other by Lillian Hellman, a tale of Southern greed with Fredric March as the paterfamilias, directed by Michael Gordon. Both suffered additionally from inadequate performances among the younger players – Burt Lancaster as Robinson's son and Ann Blyth as March's daughter, a role played earlier by Bette Davis (in *The Little Foxes*, which covers

753

the *later* fortunes of this particular family). It was partly because of these two films that Universal's losses continued to mount, but also pushing the company into the red in 1948 were the late, lacklustre Deanna Durbin films, *Letter from an Unknown Woman* and some of the films produced by Walter Wanger.

Only **Canyon Passage** (1946) proves that Wanger had not quite lost his touch – and that is mainly due to the Technicolored Oregon locations and the snatches of Hoagy Carmichael's song, 'Ole Buttermilk Sky'. Jacques Tourneur, the director, once observed that William K. Howard on his deathbed advised him not to make his own mistake of turning down so many scripts – and he has not: 'Indeed, how is one to know what can be done with a script?' But there is no indication that Tourneur did more than tell the actors which chalk lines to stand on. As a pioneer drama this is no better or worse than most, though the exposition is notably long-winded; Dana Andrews is a sullen hero and Susan Hayward flounces to negative effect. (A credit, 'Introducing Patricia Roc', remained in the British release print, though she was one of Britain's most popular stars; her presence in the film was due to pressures by Rank, then a large stockholder in Universal, who wanted to get his own contract artists better known in the U.S.)

The worst Wanger film for Universal-International (as it now was) is **The Lost Moment** (1947), based on 'The Aspern Papers' – which few could ever have imagined as a vehicle for Susan Hayward and Robert Cummings. There is a further bad omen in that it is the only film directed by an actor, Martin Gabel. It was the first screen version of any story by Henry James, though in Leonardo Bercovici's screenplay only the central situation remains. Miss Tina (Hayward) has become young, beautiful, sensual and schizoid – a situation cured after a visit to a 'funiculi-funicula' dance hall with a nice American (Cummings). John Archer plays the man after the letters and Agnes Moorehead is the elder Miss Bordereau: the film's publicity centred solely on the rubber mask used to make her into a centenarian.

It is hardly surprising that at this stage the studio abandoned any project that smacked of class – with the exception of the films of James Stewart, who arrived with a financial agreement often said to be unique, which it was not, but which was certainly not as prevalent as it was to become in the Fifties. Universal had always been plagued by its lack of box-office stars and with audiences now beginning to shrink it was financially unsound to have stars under long-term contracts. So, Stewart, who usually commanded $200,000 per film, was offered, as the studio's official history puts it, '50 per cent' of **Harvey** (1950) and *Winchester '73* (q.v.), the latter the first of a series of successful Westerns this actor made for the company. *Harvey*, directed by Henry Koster, was a big success, as had been Mary Chase's Broadway play on which it was based. Its subject is an amiable drunk (Stewart) whose best friend is an imaginary six-foot rabbit, and your attitude towards it will depend on your taste for whimsy, if leavened with an occasional funny line. In any case the piece is only made bearable by Stewart's underplayed performance and that of Cecil Kellaway, as the head of a sanitorium increasingly unwilling to believe that Stewart belongs inside it.

Otherwise Universal-International concentrated on low-budget action films, usually in Technicolor, and the series with Francis, the Talking Mule (who co-starred with Donald O'Connor) and with Ma and Pa Kettle. As can be seen from his work with 20th Century-Fox and his later independent productions, such films were not to the taste of William Goetz, who had been production chief since the merger; he and Spitz moved out in 1951 after selling their shares. The purchaser was Decca Records, who the following year acquired the controlling interest by buying the shares of J. Arthur Rank. Milton Rackmil became president of both companies. Over several years Rackmil cautiously instituted a programme including only eight pictures with large budgets, up to $1 million, eventually bringing to an end a dark period in the company's history.

In the immediate postwar period several memorable films were made, such as *Letter from an Unknown Woman* and those directed by Robert Siodmak which were also looked at in the last chapter. To them I would tentatively add **Take One False Step** (1949) and **The Senator Was Indiscreet** (1947), two vehicles with

William Powell. The former is a comedy-thriller, the genre in which Powell excelled, and he plays a professor suspected of murdering a blonde (Shelley Winters) with whom he had had a tumble during the War. The film is often implausible, but it entertains as directed by Chester Erskine from a screenplay by him and Irwin Shaw. The other film was an independent production by Nunnally Johnson, who persuaded George S. Kaufman to direct – his only film in that capacity. 'The people we call satirists now,' Dorothy Parker once remarked, 'are those who make cracks at topical subjects and consider themselves satirists – creatures like George S. Kaufman and such who don't even know what satire is.' This piece is assuredly satire – though Kaufman did not write it; Charles MacArthur did – his first screen credit since 1940 – from a story by Edwin Lanham, and it concerns an exceptionally pinheaded senator (Powell) who loses his diary. That brings to his side his opponents while causing other politicians to prepare for flight to Outer Mongolia or the other two countries with which the U.S. does not have extradition treaties. After noting that Kaufman himself was once entrapped by the revelations of Mary Astor's famous diary, we may say that this film is choppy and self-indulgent; but it is refreshing and it is comforting to know that the senator's claim, 'There's a rule in our state – if you can't beat 'em, bribe 'em,' caused Senator Joe McCarthy to denounce the film as 'traitorous' and 'un-American'.

At R.K.O. the situation was also gloomy. In 1946 the film industry achieved a record turnover of $1,692,000,000.* Wartime conditions had increased dependence on the cinema as the country's major leisure pursuit, and it remained so for returning servicemen and their families. That it might fall back to its prewar position worried no one, for that had also been astoundingly healthy. The ten local television stations which had been closed for the duration in 1942 resumed operations, but these were enjoyed by only a minute fraction of the population – and it occurred to only a few in the film industry that the programmes might one day improve. More worrying was the Justice Department's

*The figure was not approached again till 1974, and that was mainly due to much higher seat prices.

order for the severance of the film companies from their theatre chains – a situation to be examined in more detail when we come to consider M-G-M at this period, for the simple reason that Loews fought longer and harder against the decree than any other of the companies.

Under the management of Floyd Odlum, R.K.O.'s precarious financial position had finally steadied, and the deliberately unambitious production schedule of Charles M. Koerner had put the company modestly in profit as the War ended. However, then R.K.O. made a huge sum from its release of *The Bells of St Mary's* and when Koerner died in 1946, his successor, Dore Schary (1905–79), a former screenwriter, was instructed to woo those talents capable of bringing in similarly successful films. Existing agreements with Goldwyn and Disney (and International) boosted the receipts of the distribution arm and, since the R.K.O. circuit would eventually have to be hived off, the health of what was left of the company would be more sound if it handled other successful independents. Hence the agreement with Liberty Films and the flirtation with Selznick.

R.K.O. seldom made a profit from distributing Disney's films, despite their popularity – which was one reason for persevering, since exhibitors appreciated R.K.O.'s links with Disney. The high cost of the films themselves kept the Disney studio in a parlous financial situation (not to be ended till he entered the field of live action films, which enabled him to form his own releasing organisation, Buena Vista, in 1954). During the War, only government contracts for national purposes had kept the studio open, and though in no doubt of the value of re-issuing the full-length cartoons Disney hesitated to embark upon more. He compromised by offering **Make Mine Music** (1946) and **Melody Time** (1948), assemblies of short cartoons linked by music, to be split up should the public not respond. Both films may be regarded as collections of Silly Symphonies or *Fantasia* re-done for the original child audiences of *Snow White* and *Pinocchio*, tentatively thought of as adolescents with no interest higher than popular music. Neither has ever been re-issued, but my unfond memories of both were confirmed when I was able to see *Make Mine Music* recently. It is by turns saccharine, vulgar and cute, with relief from the unimaginative draughtsmanship provided by only two numbers, 'After You've Gone', an abstract on piano keyboards to the playing of Benny Goodman, and 'The Whale Who Wanted to Sing at the Met', a narrative sung by Nelson Eddy, which is vintage Disney.

Indecision also brought about two features divided into two, **Fun and Fancy Free** (1947), about a circus bear called Bongo, followed by a version of 'Jack and the Beanstalk' with Mickey Mouse and friends, and **The Adventures of Ichabod and Mr Toad** (1949), based on stories by Washington Irving and Kenneth Graham. The Graham tale is, of course, 'The Wind in the Willows', in as nasty a betrayal of a classic story as the cinema has yet achieved. The *Ichabod* half was a version of 'The Legend of Sleepy Hollow', narrated by Bing Crosby, with the Headless Horseman himself worthy of vintage Disney 'terror' – perhaps because Ub Iwerks did the special effects.

For years Disney had been considering live action films, but with **Song of the South** (1946) he hedged his bets: announced as the first of a series of films combining animation and actors, it has a slight and unexceptional framing story, directed by Harve Foster and prettily photographed by Gregg Toland, in part about a small boy (Bobby Driscoll) and the black Uncle Remus (James Baskett). The latter's stories are illustrated, and though Brer Bear sounds like Lennie in *Of Mice and Men*, he, Brer Fox and Brer Rabbit are interchangeable with any other cartoon animals of the period; even the Tar Baby is disappointing. Public acceptance was sufficient for Disney to offer a wholly live action picture, *So Dear to My Heart* (1948) and then *Treasure Island* (q.v.), both with Master Driscoll – who would die, unDisneylike, a drug addict at thirty-two.

Samuel Goldwyn's postwar efforts, apart from *The Best Years of Our Lives* and other more coquettish attempts to probe the spirit of the American home, were directed towards the star vehicles of Danny Kaye, a former Broadway and nightclub comic. Kaye has a daft smile, a gift for mimicry, an undoubted ease with a gibberish song but no recognisable comic weakness. **The Secret Life of Walter Mitty** (1947) remains his most celebrated

early film partly because it is based on James Thurber's masterly anecdote and partly because it gives Kaye opportunities to do several impersonations, including an intrepid R.A.F. flyer and a Mississippi gambler. The original tale has been enlarged and glamorised under the direction of Norman Z. McLeod, and brightly it shows that those close to Mitty either despise him (his boss) or despair of him (his mother). But stuck in the sort of situations in which Bob Hope often found himself – pursued, for instance, by a homicidal maniac (Boris Karloff) – Kaye has none of Hope's resources and is simply bland and energetic.

The only other Kaye/Goldwyn film often revived is **Hans Christian Andersen** (1952), a long-cherished dream of the producer who, uncertain of his approach, finally settled for 'a fairy tale about this teller of fairy tales'. Charles Vidor directed, from a screenplay by Moss Hart and a story by Myles Connolly, and to these usually estimable names we may add those of Richard Day, who provided the blowsy, cheap-calendar decor, and Frank Loesser, whose inventive songs do sometimes catch the spirit of Andersen. But otherwise this seems to me one of the nauseous mixtures ever concocted. A British film with an Andersen connection, *The Red Shoes* (q.v.), had been such a success in the States that Goldwyn decided also to incorporate ballet into his film, with the same star, Moira Shearer; and when she became pregnant her role went to the current rage of Paris, Renée Jeanmaire, whose husband, Roland Petit, tagged along to do the choreography. The result, eagerly categorised by the publicity department as a magic mixture of Broadway, Hollywood, Paris and Copenhagen, is deeply dispiriting.

David O. Selznick also devoted most of his attention to one star, Jennifer Jones, whom he eventually married. For her he fashioned **Duel in the Sun** (1946), adapted from a novel by Niven Busch, on which he himself took screenplay credit. The credited director is King Vidor, with whom he quarrelled, and so most of it was done by William Dieterle who (inexplicably) wanted credit; other sequences were handled by Sidney Franklin and Josef von Sternberg, the latter unofficially employed as colour consultant. It was Selznick's first production since *Gone with the Wind*, and he employed similar methods, but without much conviction that he could surpass himself. The critics soon informed him that he had fallen far short, but the public, led to expect something steamy, made it the biggest money-maker in cinema history, apart from its predecessor and *The Best Years of Our Lives*. Indeed, Selznick capitalised on its reputation – it was widely known as 'Lust in the Dust' – and dropped the original 'dignified' ads for something more lurid. Miss Jones plays a half-caste, Pearl, sent by her father (Herbert Marshall, the first actor in history to get star-billing for a three-minute role) to live with an old flame, Laurabelle (Lillian Gish), her husband (Lionel Barrymore), and their two sons – the noble Jesse (Joseph Cotten), who realises that he loves her only after she has been frequently ravished by the lecherous Lewt (Gregory Peck). It may be the l'il old debbil bequeathed by her maw, but Pearl sho' is a puzzle – wanting to be a lady like Laurabelle, but wearing off-the-shoulder blouses guaranteed to give any man ideas. Apart from Miss Gish and Walter Huston (as an evangelist, a role cut to pieces after protests by religious groups) the film is vilely acted and today it tends only to amuse – particularly when one extremely bilious studio sunset evokes the comment, 'What a strange light this evening.'

Selznick, disappointed by the critical onslaught, was further confused by the reception for **Portrait of Jennie** (1948), based on Robert Nathan's wistful novel, about an artist (Cotten) who falls in love with the strange girl (Miss Jones) he meets in Central Park. Miss Jones is appropriately fey, but where in the original she was unreal here she remains a Hollywood star. Miss Gish is a Mother Superior and David Wayne is Cotten's pal – a good instance of artists in movies always having garage mechanics as pals instead of other artists. Dieterle directed; originally there were sequences in sepia and Technicolor, while at the end the screen grew bigger and was tinted green – in a few of the few cinemas which booked it. Due to bad weather on location and Miss Jones's absences due to emotional problems (she was still married to Robert Walker) the cost had mounted to a huge $4 million, and after the original screenings Selznick spent another abortive

$250,000 refilming the storm sequence. Both this and *Duel in the Sun* were in fact distributed by the Selznick Releasing Organization, which he had set up just after the War, and which was now forced to close. The company had always been plagued by lack of product – though he had turned down the chance for it to handle *Red River* on the ground that that was just another Western: his self-confidence was further shaken when it made a fortune at the box office. Apart from *The Third Man* (q.v.), the only films in which he was subsequently involved were a handful with Miss Jones, ending with *A Farewell to Arms* (q.v.) in 1957.

Four of his other projects had been sold to R.K.O., all successfully. We have already looked at the two thrillers, *The Spiral Staircase* and *Notorious*; the other two are comedies – and the comedies of the Forties are not to everyone's taste: fires burn in the grate, breakfast is in bed, lamps are dotted round the room and Ethel Barrymore looks more knowing than the wise old owl. They tend to the mechanical, like both **The Bachelor and the Bobby-Soxer** (1947), directed by Irving Reis from a script by Sidney Sheldon, which has Cary Grant and Shirley Temple in the title roles with Myrna Loy as a judge, Temple's sister, who cures her of her crush on Grant; and **The Farmer's Daughter** (1947), which has Miss Barrymore as a politicking matriarch whose maid (Loretta Young) stands against her own candidate, and who is revealed to be a Fascist by omniscient Ethel, having encouraged him to get drunk in order to expose him. We are not required to condemn her for having hitherto been wrong, but are supposed to be indignant about a bigot in our midst and then amused when, Capra-style, he is exposed. H. C. Potter directed, cosily, and presumably Miss Young won her Best Actress Oscar for her maintenance of a Swedish accent.

Magic Town (1947) is a Capra film without Capra, produced independently for R.K.O. release and written by Robert Riskin, clearly in the hope that Capra would direct. William Wellman, a close friend of Capra and a good substitute, took on the project, but the result indicates how much vitality the genre had lost since the War – perhaps because of it – for the small-town myth was fading, as Capra's own *It's a Wonderful Life* had already suggested. When this one is found to be the most 'typical' town in the whole country, a city slicker (James Stewart) arrives to exploit it, but has a change of heart when he realises that this is also the intention of the town bigwigs; so with the aid of the local teacher (Jane Wyman) he sets out to prove that they are ruining it. The film is crowded with incident but awash with cliché and sentimentality, demonstrating just how far Riskin was dependent on Capra.

Leo McCarey's **Good Sam** (1948), written by Ken Englund from McCarey's own suggestion, concerns a disarmingly kind man (Gary Cooper) sucked dry by leeches, but again it is really a copy of Capra, leavened with the superficial 'do good' ethics of McCarey's two Father O'Malley movies with Bing Crosby. All comes right after Cooper gets drunk in a downtown bar, to remind us that Capra-esque heroes, unlike the rest of us, only get drunk in moments of desperate depression. McCarey's decline is further indicated in one of the several subplots, in which Cooper and his wife (Ann Sheridan) are impeded in their desire for 'marital relations'. This situation, long familiar in farce, had now invaded domestic comedy – and would notably feature in *Room for One More*, with Cary Grant – and there is no reason why it should seem so much more distasteful except that in this case McCarey cannot resist a smirk, taking advantage of the amiability of his star players.

Another theme which McCarey treats is the dream home, undoubtedly a matter of interest to many postwar couples: but his are not in their first youth, nor is that couple (Grant, Myrna Loy) of **Mr Blandings Builds His Dream House** (1948), which describes some misadventures of a New York family settling in Connecticut and is quite nonchalant about mortgages and escalating costs. H. C. Potter directed, from a lively screenplay by Norman Panama and Melvin Frank, based on a book of 'The Egg and I' school. Nevertheless, it all seems to belong to the prewar world, as does the scatty lady novelist, always good for a laugh in Thirties Hollywood: in **Without Reservations** (1946) Claudette Colbert is such a one, and John Wayne is the marine flyer she pursues because she wants him for the film of her book.

Mervyn LeRoy directed for Jesse Lasky – who was attempting another come-back – and he tries briefly to be serious about postwar conditions; in particular, the plight of Mexican immigrants.

The Long Night (1947) does reflect the contemporary unsettled mood after the war years – paradoxically, for it is a remake of *Le Jour se Lève*. It is by no means as inferior as was thought at the time, though that had much to do with the (false) claim, which infuriated critics, that all copies of the original film had been destroyed. This version suggests a postwar disillusionment, a world where all is not black or white; the transference to a small American coal town works quite well, and the only major changes are taken care of in the casting, with the girl (Barbara Bel Geddes) quite innocent and the man (Henry Fonda) going off at the end to face his trial with hope. His dilemma becomes a smaller one – a mulish inability to distinguish between kinds of love; otherwise the screenplay, by John Wexley, and the camera set-ups are virtually the same as in the original. Anatole Litvak directed for Raymond and Robert Hakim, producers who had left France when the Nazis arrived. Earlier, they had done a more thorough plundering job on Decoin's 1939 *Battement de Coeur* (in itself the remake of an Italian film made a few months earlier), even pillaging footage: **Heartbeat** (1946) is a hybrid as directed by Sam Wood (there is no screenplay credit, though Morrie Ryskind is named as adapter), but these exploits of a teenage pickpocket among the diplomatic set might just amuse for their ingenuity, were it not for the miscasting of Ginger Rogers. Far from being artless, she was the knowingest dame in movies, far too old, and no substitute for Danielle Darrieux in the original.

The most important among other independent productions handled by R.K.O. was **Joan of Arc** (1948), produced by a company owned by Walter Wanger, Ingrid Bergman and her doctor husband. The film was based on Maxwell Anderson's 'Joan of Lorraine', which Bergman had earlier played on Broadway. She admitted to a fixation on Joan, and had asked William Wyler to direct to no avail; the result suggests a vanity production, recalling other occasions when the star's husband, also amateur, interfered – it is certainly not as professional as we should expect of Wanger, or Victor Fleming, who directed. It cost $5,600,000 and needed to take $8 million to break even, but according to *Variety* it grossed only $4,100,000, and in her memoir Joan Bennett, Wanger's wife, records that she resumed her career to help pay off the debts incurred. Miss Bergman worried for years that the film hastened the deaths of Fleming and the photographer, Joseph Valentine, neither of whom long survived its completion. In such circumstances it would be nice to find something to praise, but all is disaster: Anderson's screenplay is flat, the production garish and the playing one-dimensional. Bergman's honesty and fervour are not enough.

A comparable decision almost wrecks **From This Day Forward** (1946), since Joan Fontaine is an unlikely working girl from the Bronx, wife of a lathe-operator (Mark Stevens). As a returning serviceman, he looks back on their marriage, their numerous in-laws and the uneasy employment market of the late Thirties. John Berry directed, and Garson Kanin did the adaptation, with less insight than he put into *The Marrying Kind*, Hollywood's next important attempt to portray working-class life. This one does show husband and wife in bed together – by special dispensation of the M.P.A.A. which was beginning to realise that the War had changed the popular view of the cinema's priorities. **Crossfire** (1947) is also about servicemen, in this case drinking and wandering aimlessly in a town strange to them, Washington, till brought up short by the knowledge that one amongst them is a murderer. In Richard Brooks' novel the victim was a homosexual, but since the M.P.A.A. would not sanction that he has become a Jew (Sam Levene), thus providing this film with its reputation as the first to attack racial intolerance. As a polemic, it is infinitely better than *Gentleman's Agreement*, and it remains a good thriller, despite the fact that the detective (Robert Young) seems modelled on Hammett's fictional Nick Charles. John Paxton wrote the screenplay, Edward Dmytryk directed, and it is well acted by Robert Mitchum and Robert Ryan as two of the G.I.s, Ryan as the confident Jew-hater, with an odd look of panic in his eyes in unguarded moments.

The reception of both films, especially that for *Crossfire*, encouraged Dore Schary to put into production **The Boy with Green Hair** (1948), the adventures of an unfortunate war orphan (Dean Stockwell) among a lot of twinkly-eyed Americans. Whichever way you look, there's a message: war is bad, racial intolerance is wrong, and so on, rather predictably. There is no reason why such matters should not be wrapped in whimsy, but this one is too heavy-handed, as written by Ben Barzman and Alfred Lewis Levitt and directed by Joseph Losey. Losey later admitted that he had been unable to deal with the 'unrealistic scenes' but claimed more surprisingly, 'I'm not ashamed of it.'

Many of the talents fostered by Schary fell foul of the House Un-American Activities Committee. Dmytryk was found guilty in 1947 of Communist affiliations and jailed for a year, after which he directed two films in England; in 1951, again before the Committee, he incriminated Adrian Scott, the producer of *Crossfire*, who then left the industry, and John Berry, who went to Paris. Losey was also blacklisted at this time, and he made a new career in England. Dmytryk's imprisonment had been an embarrassment to Odlum, whose dissatisfaction with R.K.O. increased when, at the end of 1947, it was found to have lost $2 million, a large sum, since the company had been in profit for the preceding four years. (The biggest contributors to that loss were Ford's *The Fugitive*, and Dudley Nichols's appallingly stagey version of O'Neill's *Mourning Becomes Electra*, which attracted only minimal audiences.) To add to the imminent divorce of studio from circuit and the growing threat from television was the fact that several foreign governments, including Britain (at that time Hollywood's best foreign market) had frozen American earnings. Odlum decided to sell R.K.O., and he found a buyer in Howard Hughes, whose fascination with the film industry had been unaffected by the failure of *The Outlaw*. He paid $9 million in May, 1948, and Schary soon returned to M-G-M (where he had once been a writer), to the relief of both men; he and Hughes had quarrelled incessantly.

Schary believed in uplift and Hughes in entertainment, and during Hughes's regime at least every other R.K.O. release was a melodrama. Schary had established a series of such films as they could be made cheaply and were usually profitable. **Out of the Past** (1947) is about a private eye (Robert Mitchum), now working in a garage in Lake Tahoe, a paranoiac millionaire (Kirk Douglas), and the latter's missing mistress (Jane Greer). After a good start it falls apart, as written by Geoffrey Homes (also known as Daniel Mainwaring) from his own novel; Jacques Tourneur's otherwise skilful direction shows a touching devotion to cliché. Nevertheless, the film is often cited as a good example of that accidental form, the *film noir* – which **They Won't Believe Me** (1947), despite some claims, definitely is not. When the commentary speaks of seedy, hideaway bars, they turn out to be Hollywood's customary plush nightclubs. Irving Pichel directed from a screenplay by Jonathan Latimer which has more twists than a corkscrew and concerns a playboy (Robert Young) with one woman too many. The most engaging of them is Miss Greer, whose tremulous, lived-in young face and clear tones should have made her a much bigger star than she was.

Also to be classified as *film noir* is **They Live by Night** (1948), which Hughes disliked so much that it was shelved for a while. Nicholas Ray, the director, had been brought to the studio by John Houseman, invited to produce a film of Edward Anderson's novel 'Thieves Like Us', and its quality was recognised when it was released to play some B dates. The protagonists are a deprived and inarticulate young couple (Farley Granger, Cathy O'Donnell), and though they move through what Richard Winnington called 'a haze of bank robberies, cheap hideouts and stolen cars', the film concentrates less on crime than on their doomed romance. That it no longer moves us may be due to Mr Granger, whose character does not suggest years of hardening in prison; we may enjoy the action sequences and the depravity of the rest of the gang. Ray's work on occasion was masterly, as this is evident from the action-atmospheric opening of **On Dangerous Ground** (1951), his sixth picture, again produced by Houseman. The film was a failure, owing perhaps to the fact that the public had just seen a fist-happy cop hero in *Where the Sidewalk Ends*, though this one (Robert Ryan) is not so much violent as disillusioned. There is another impressive sequence where he sets out in the snow to find the child-murderer, but the tiresome nature of the rest of it is due to Ida Lupino's playing of a blind girl, gazing blankly at anything but Ryan and the camera, and looking as if she were party to the wisdom of ages.

According to Josef von Sternberg, the credited director, Ray directed almost all of **Macao** (1952), to which Hughes had assigned von Sternberg as a peace offering after the debacle of *Jet Pilot* – which, begun in 1949, was subjected to so many revisions by Hughes that it did not surface till after he had closed the studio. Von Sternberg was removed from *Macao* after a few days' shooting, and Ray presumably used his set-ups, for the film is visually strong – which is just as well, for the story needs all the help it can get. Robert Mitchum and Hughes's protégée, Jane Russell, were meant to rival Bogart and Bacall, but only he can handle the slangy – if inferior – dialogue. When she asks him whether he caught her nightclub act, 'I didn't exactly fracture the people, did I?', we do not blame the people.

Angel Face (1952) is among the most attractive melodramas of the Hughes regime, due mainly to the performance of Jean Simmons (q.v.) in the title role, a woman not so much vicious or scheming as living in a sad little world of her own. Otto Preminger, the director, called her 'wonderful in the film', and his work on this occasion is both astringent and economical; he had been borrowed from Fox because Hughes knew he could work quickly and Simmons was available for only eighteen days during a six-week period, because of litigation over her contract. Rank had sold that to R.K.O. without consulting her, after previously loaning her to the studio for **Androcles and the Lion** (1952), which provided a disastrous and protracted start to her Hollywood career. Gabriel Pascal, unable to work in Britain, had persuaded Hughes that films of Shaw's plays would give R.K.O. a touch of class, but with the incompetence of the one and the interference of the other, filming turned into a two-year ordeal. James Donald (signed to play the captain) got fed up waiting for filming to start and returned to Britain, to be replaced by Victor Mature (Harpo Marx and Frank Sinatra tested for the role of Androcles; both Rex Harrison and George Sanders turned down the role of the Emperor). At least Pascal did not direct: Chester Erskine did that, and also wrote the script, but the material is lifeless as rendered by a seemingly bored cast – which also includes Alan Young and Elsa Lanchester as Androcles and spouse, and a palpably stuffed lion. There is hamming by Maurice Evans as the Emperor and Robert Newton as the convert Ferrovius, against painted backcloths and between inserts culled from *The Last Days of Pompeii*. The result was universally unappreciated, and Pascal, spurned by the film industry, spent the last years of his life peddling a musical 'Pygmalion' to Broadway producers.

Hughes's other attempt at grandeur (his *King Kong*) was **The White Tower** (1950), a mountaineering drama, a species Hollywood had always left well alone. It was unprecedented for an R.K.O. team to photograph on foreign locations (around Mont Blanc), and this was only the fourth studio production in colour.★ Ted Tetzlaff, a former photographer, directed, from a screenplay by Paul Jarrico based on a novel by James Ramsay Ullman, and their characters are strictly from stock: the girl (Alida Valli) wanting to revenge her mountaineering father's death; the cynical ex-G.I. (Glenn Ford); a British scientist (Cedric Hardwicke); an alcoholic French writer (Claude Rains) and a Nazi bigot (Lloyd Bridges). Given that there remain too many backcloths and the fact that the downward journey is done in less than a second, the film did not live up to Hughes's expectations.

The studio reported a loss of just over $4 million in 1949. In desperation Hughes brought in Norman Krasna, a writer, and Jerry Wald, the successful Warners producer, at large salaries and with promises of complete autonomy. Of the twelve productions announced by this new team, only four were made, including *Clash by Night* and **The Blue Veil** (1951), the latter an effective remake of *La Maternelle*,

directed by Curtis Bernhardt, with Jane Wyman in the Gaby Morlay role. It is a wonder that any films emerged at all, given the reigning chaos at the studio: those that did were given short shrift by critics and public, and the distributing arm had to draw comfort from an occasional independent production. Among these was **Sudden Fear** (1952), directed by David Miller, which is about a wife (Joan Crawford) who learns of her husband's plan to murder her: it defeats belief that she never even considers going to the police, but the film achieves a certain panache when she fights back in her own way. In **The Thing** (1951) a group of isolated Arctic scientists is threatened by the creature of the title; the film is remarkable for Charles Lederer's naturalistic dialogue and the unforced direction, reckoned to be by the producer, Howard Hawks, rather than the credited Christian Nyby.

By juggling with the figures, Hughes managed during these years to show that the company made a small profit. In 1952 he sold his interest to a five-man syndicate whose sole concern seems to have been to sell off the backlog of films to T.V. When the deal was leaked to the press and their credit disallowed he was left with only their $1½ million downpayment. By 1954 he was unable to disguise losses totalling over $40 million, and with production down to thirteen features, he arranged to buy out all other stockholders – at $2 more per share than had been the price when he had taken over the studio. Therefore he paid over $23 million for the sole ownership of the company which he had single-handedly demolished – and that, industry observers felt, was twice as much as its assets were worth. However, he was thought to have made a $10 million profit when in July the following year he sold the company for $25 million to General Teleradio which, as we have seen, had entered the film industry by buying a bunch of unprofitable films and selling them to television. Six months later the new company, now called R.K.O. Teleradio Pictures, sold the T.V. rights of over 700 R.K.O. films to C & C Cola for $15 million. It also announced full-scale production, but those films still in release – including *The Conqueror*, with John Wayne as a Mongol warrior, begun by Hughes and eventually costing over $5 million – performed so

★Since the end of the War, the other major studios had allocated Technicolor to twenty-five to thirty per cent of their product, usually musicals and historical subjects. R.K.O.'s sole Technicolor films to this time were *The Spanish Main*, *Sinbad the Sailor*, produced by Douglas Fairbanks, Jr, and *The Boy with Green Hair*.

disastrously that the programme was abandoned. Those in development likely to make money, such as *The Naked and the Dead*, were made and handed over to Universal-International for distribution. The studio itself was dismantled and the premises reopened for television; in 1958 it was purchased by Desilu Productions, a T.V. outfit owned jointly by Desi Arnez and his wife, Lucille Ball – who had once been an R.K.O. bit player.

M-G-M was also having trouble, but this was not, for the moment, caused by unsuccessful films. The difficulties began in Washington, where for a long time there had been unease at the situation whereby a single organisation controlled production, distribution and exhibition, resulting in such restrictive practices as block-booking. The companies owning the circuits had a considerable advantage over those which did not – and Universal, United Artists and Columbia continued to fight for the bookings they wanted. In 1938 the Department of Justice had begun an investigation which was interrupted by the War; and the anti-trust suits instituted when it was over were as much an incentive to independence as was frustration with the hide-bound methods in operation at the major studios. Films were not automatically booked into thousands of cinemas but were to be bid for on merit – except for the moment in Loews' theatres, for that company fought on till the end, not bowing to the inevitable till 1952. Loews decided then to keep its cinemas and divested itself of M-G-M.

Although, as we have seen, M-G-M's distributing company was concerned with some films with which members of the Loew family were connected, it put on a fiercer front against the independents than any of the others. Louis B. Mayer was utterly opposed to independence of any sort, and Metro continued to operate as it had always done. With Clark Gable back on the lot, it was almost as though the War had never been; but after four years fighting for his country M-G-M showed its gratitude by clobbering him with **Adventure** (1945) and a slogan he loathed, 'Gable's Back and Garson's Got Him'. As a gift for the world's first postwar Christmas the film was 'one of the most outstanding pieces of twaddle in a month

of Sundays' as C. A. Lejeune put it. Gable's return to M-G-M was as momentous as that after his absence making *Gone with the Wind*, and just as that was followed by *Strange Cargo* he was again required – obviously due to his pre-eminent status – to be part of a muddled statement about God's importance to mankind. Portents of this eventual message appear in the early part of the film, which mainly concerns the bickering of seaman Gable and librarian Garson – a sure sign that That Slogan represents the plot. They fall in love under a bush while stealing a neighbour's chicken, which at least allows her to be other than bossy, bad-tempered or tearful. Under Victor Fleming's direction Gable does not show how dispiriting he reportedly found acting with her, but he never really recovered from this film: he stayed off the screen for eighteen months and never again played a devil-may-care adventurer.

Admittedly, he starts that way in **The Hucksters** (1947), but he finishes as an executive with integrity: and the postwar Gable no longer prefers the Harlow kind of woman, charmingly played by Ava Gardner, but the prim widow (Deborah Kerr). In Frederic Wakeman's novel this lady is an unfaithful army wife, so hot for the hero that she is happy to be with him in a hotel little better than a whore-house – a situation turned about in the screenplay by Luther Davis, so that she leaves him flat because he has unfortunately chosen such a hotel. As in the book the romance is dreary and all the commercial sequences splendid, their detail on the advertising world as directed by Jack Conway making this one of the better postwar films. Gable plays a service veteran attempting to re-establish himself in his old profession, and Sydney Greenstreet is his monstrous client (a character based on Walter Hill of American Tobacco).

The starry cast (it also included Adolphe Menjou, Keenan Wynn and Edward Arnold) was an indication of the studio's hope of repeating the era when its films were the talk of both industry and cinema-goers, and there was another such backing Gable in **Command Decision** (1948) – Van Johnson, Walter Pidgeon, Brian Donlevy, John Hodiak, Edward Arnold and Charles Bickford. In charge of both this and *Homecoming*, Gable's previous film, was Sidney Franklin, the studio's most valued producer, another indication of Gable's continued standing. *Command Decision*, directed by Sam Wood and based on the Broadway play by William Wister Haines, has far more guts and intelligence than the not dissimilar *Twelve O'Clock High*. Gable plays a high-ranking officer undecided as to whether the bombing of German factories (known to be manufacturing a new long-range aircraft) is worth the heavy casualties among his own men.

When the public failed to appreciate this further contemporary situation Gable was put into lighter fare, with former co-stars, ladies of his own generation, and you would have thought, considering their ages, that they would not have waited till the last reel to get married. **To Please a Lady** (1950), directed by Clarence Brown, casts him as a famous midget-car racer and Barbara Stanwyck as a needling journalist; **Key to the City** (1950) has Gable and Loretta Young as rival mayors at a convention. In one scene he is locked out of his hotel room searching for his trousers in a Little Lord Fauntleroy suit – a situation which implies that the hotel has no extra keys nor he extra pants, and which would have been far more suitable for someone like Joe E. Brown. George Sidney directed.

Another formula was needed, and **Across the Wide Missouri** (1951) and **Lone Star** (1952) were Gable's first Westerns since joining Metro over twenty years earlier. Mayer had never cared for the genre, but was persuaded that *Across the Wide Missouri* was an epic of the pioneers – of the days when their Technicolored Eden was marred only by marauding Indians. Gable is a trapper, seemingly the only American; his best friend (Adolphe Menjou) is French, and there are innumerable Scotsmen, including one (John Hodiak) who has taken up both Indian costume and their way of life – and when Gable does the same, we may acknowledge a rare example of the pro-Indian film. As directed by William Wellman, it is one which loves the wide open spaces and the people who move through them so clearly aware of their splendour. Their unconventional behaviour and the film's length – a mere seventy-eight minutes – indicates that the cutting-room made the best of a bad job of Wellman's free-and-easy location work. *Lone Star* has a story

and screenplay mainly by Borden Chase, co-founder with Howard Hawks of the Motion Picture Alliance for the Preservation of American Ideals – some of which may be hazily found in this tale of tempers running hot at the thought of Texas joining the Union. There are some fair scenes between Gable, in a replay of Rhett Butler, and Ava Gardner, as a newspaperwoman militant against annexation; Broderick Crawford is a cattle baron and Lionel Barrymore, in his penultimate screen appearance, is Andrew Jackson (as he had been in *The Gorgeous Hussy*).

Gable made three more films for the company, including *Mogambo* (q.v.), which reawakened the company's interest in him, but he knew that the front office had planned to drop him, and he left in bitterness. Few filmgoers could remember a time when there had been an M-G-M without Gable.

Greer Garson left about the same time: with Gable and Judy Garland, she had been one of Metro's most popular stars in the immediate postwar period, but by the time of **Julia Misbehaves** (1948) her lustre had dimmed, and the film was titled in this way in the hope that everyone would know that a new Greer was on display. The trouble was, there wasn't: she has a chic wardrobe and tells lies for the fun of it, but underneath she's just the same old Greer with the same old problems. Based on Margery Sharp's light-hearted novel 'The Nutmeg Tree', the film is not funny, nor is she, nor Walter Pidgeon, as the husband she re-meets at her daughter's wedding. When a number of sentimental dramas with Pidgeon failed to find a public, M-G-M tried another comedy, **The Law and the Lady** (1951), based on Frederick Lonsdale's 'The Last of Mrs Cheyney', which it had filmed twice before. The new prologue, which is quite long, works better than what is left of Lonsdale, since the director, Edwin H. Knopf, cannot handle a comedy of manners; Miss Garson, raven-haired as the jewel-thief, is arch, and no match for Michael Wilding as her accomplice, who (seemingly undirected) floats into view, says his lines effectively and floats out again.

A decade later almost all remakes would become musicals – a thought that may occur as you watch a reworking of *Grand Hotel* called **Weekend at the Waldorf**

(1945), 'suggested by a story by Vicki Baum'; Guy Bolton as adapter and Sam and Bella Spewack as the writers are content simply to disguise the source. There is a sad little film star (Ginger Rogers), so busy making movies and money that she has had no time to live, and a sad little soldier (Van Johnson), so badly shot up – apparently (or, rather, not apparently) – that his hospital treatment is a matter of life and death. Will they find love and happiness during this weekend at the Waldorf? Yes, but not with each other: M-G-M have picked for her an ace war correspondent (Walter Pidgeon) and for him a peachy-looking stenographer (Lana Turner). The smaller roles are excellently played, and Robert Z. Leonard marches the cast on and off the sets with his usual dexterity: unfortunately the two central situations are awash on a sea of absurdity. The plot is more faithful to the original than it sounds, but the chief virtue of that was its misanthropic view. This film has no point of view at all, unless it is opportunism or postwar sentimentality – as when Johnson has the band play a tune by his dead buddy for the folks back in Iowa.

Thus did the postwar world impinge upon M-G-M, but since the other studios did no better it did not need to feel ashamed. Indeed, its defenders could point to *The Search* and **The Beginning or the End?** (1947), the latter a study of the development of the atom bomb, a subject, as directed by Norman Taurog, more interesting than the relationship between the scientists and service personnel involved. M-G-M had retained its sense of responsibility, but its primary commitment was towards heavyweight bestsellers, such as the films of **Cass Timberlane** (1947), by Sinclair Lewis, and **B.F.'s Daughter** (1948), by John P. Marquand. Both concern social inequality in marriage. In the former, a judge (Spencer Tracy) marries a poor girl (Lana Turner), to the consternation of his country-club friends, and the marriage is predictably endangered when one of them (Zachary Scott) makes a play for her during rehearsals of 'The Barretts of Wimpole Street'. The characters include a war veteran (Tom Drake), who drinks both because he cannot settle down and because his father's firm has benefited from crooked business during the War. 'At the time we thought we were making a

great picture,' said the director, Geor Sidney, '[but] on television it comes ov like soap opera.'

War looms larger in *B.F.'s Daughte* because war-work separates wife (Barba Stanwyck) and husband (Van Heflin), assistant professor at Columbia. In view his pronounced, indeed infamous, social stance it is, to say the least, insensitive her to purchase a Connecticut palace wit out consulting him – but then he is not to proud to object to her allowance from h father (Charles Coburn). In one sequen the couple prefers to go to 'Hamlet' rath than the latest Broadway musical smas and awe at their daring is made appare by all concerned, including the direct Robert Z. Leonard.

Head and shoulders above M-G-M other serious films is **Intruder in the Du** (1949) which, as directed by Claren Brown and photographed by Robert Su tees, has an intensity and harshness qu untypical of the studio at this time. This William Faulkner's novel, scripted by B Maddow with some speciousness b much suspense, about some townsfo bent on lynching and the stand against the taken by an old negro (Juano Hernande and his stalwarts – a boy (Claude Jarm Jr) and his lawyer uncle (David Brian), indomitable spinster (Elizabeth Patterso and the victim's one-armed father (Port Hall).

'My favourite picture ever, though, **The Yearling**,' (1946) Brown has sai He directed from the novel by Marjor Kinnan Rawlings about an Everglad family haunted by poverty. Mother is u feeling, and the boy, Jody, is closer Paw – for he has just started to hunt an tend the crops, and when Paw is took si with a snake-bite, he takes over his dutie M-G-M had tried to film the book in 194 with Spencer Tracy and Anne Rever directed by King Vidor, who was replace after a month by Victor Fleming: accord ing to Brown, the footage was 'lousy', b as far as I am concerned the adjective is to kind for his version, with its Technicolo cloudscapes and heavenly choir. Jane Wy man as the mother looks plain and car worn, but is permitted a tear and a smi when no one is looking; no amount corn-pone dialogue ('Leave off, Mav Aint 'nuff trouble fallin' out the sky wit out the family quarrellin'?') can mak

Gregory Peck (Paw) other than ludicrous. Claude Jarman Jr as the boy is capable, but, like Peck, directed for charm. Paul Osborn's screenplay decks every scene in irony, jokiness and sentiment: this is not the simple tale of a boy and his pet, a fawn, but a multi-million dollar investment. It was successful and well-liked at the time, while *Intruder in the Dust* had difficulty getting bookings – and not only in the South. It is difficult to believe that both films were made by the same man.

M-G-M continued to make pictures starring Lassie the collie, but the canine's career had begun to falter when he, she or it supported – how are the mighty fallen! – Jeanette MacDonald in **The Sun Comes Up** (1949). Both were under contract, as was young Jarman, so for them the author of *The Yearling* concocted a plot about a dog-owning singer who does not want to adopt the boy who hangs around the country home where she Has Gone to Forget. At the end dog rescues boy from fire, and as directed by Richard Thorpe this is one of the most renowned of those films demonstrating that M-G-M had no shame.

Miss MacDonald had returned to the studio under a two-picture contract at the behest of Joe Pasternak, the producer; and doubtless the title **Three Daring Daughters** (1948) will remind you of his earlier *Three Smart Girls*: instead of daughters trying to unite parents, they are trying to separate mother from her new husband, José Iturbi (as himself), and who could blame them? The director is Fred M. Wilcox, responsible for a number of Lassie pictures and one very good film, **The Secret Garden** (1949). As adapted by Robert Ardrey, Frances Hodgson Burnett's novel for children provides a field day for those who like tales of old houses with secrets and severe housekeepers and noises in the night, but the director makes enough of all this and the Yorkshire moors to suggest that on this occasion he was the one inspired. The sequences in the garden itself are in colour, and a good cast includes Herbert Marshall as the misanthropic guardian, Gladys Cooper as the housekeeper, Elsa Lanchester as the maid, Reginald Owen as the gardener, and, as the children, Margaret O'Brien, Dean Stockwell and Brian Roper.

Little Miss O'Brien's intensity is well used in **The Unfinished Dance** (1947), as an obsessed ballet student whose crush on the premiere dancer (Cyd Charisse) leads her into planning an accident to the visiting ballerina (Karen Booth). This is an inferior remake of Jean Benoit-Levy's 1937 *La Mort du Cygne*, based on a story by Paul Morand. The producer and director, Pasternak and Henry Koster, had once brought us Deanna Durbin's arias, but are less courageous with ballet: the big number is based on 'Holiday for Strings', danced on glass floors like no stage outside a sound-stage. The scenes with the children are good, because they are all so precocious: though, like Miss O'Brien's performance, I am not sure that it was what was intended.

It is a relief to turn to **Lady in the Lake** (1946), one of the best attempts at filming Raymond Chandler – and perhaps almost too faithful as rendered in Steve Fisher's screenplay, for there is so much plot that the direction concentrates on that at the expense of the necessary atmosphere. A good cast includes Audrey Totter as the magazine editor who commissions Marlowe, Leon Ames as its owner, and Lloyd Nolan and Tom Tully as cops; Robert Montgomery is Marlowe, and (with the exception of George Montgomery in *The Brasher Doubloon*) the least of the screen Marlowes, beaming smoothly whenever we see him. This is not often, for this is the famous occasion where the 'I' is the camera, with Marlowe seen only in mirrors except when speaking directly to the audience. This was Montgomery's own idea, directing a film for the first time, but Chandler does not need gimmicks.

Another classic thriller met a worse fate: that **The Postman Always Rings Twice** (1946) has occasionally been named as one of the best *films noirs* of the period – presumably by people who have never read the novel – is a tribute to James M. Cain's novel, which is taut, atmospheric and riveting; the film, faithful only in outline, is full of holes. As the husband victim, Cecil Kellaway ambles through his role, and Lana Turner, though she has a trashy, cheap quality, is no better under Tay Garnett's direction than she was under anybody else's. As the lover-accomplice, John Garfield is, for once, hardly more expressive: just when we should be most concerned about their fate, there arrive Leon

Ames and Hume Cronyn, two real actors, as the opposing lawyers.

Under Louis B. Mayer, the studio continued to show little orientation towards thrillers or action films, but his days as prime arbiter were numbered. Since the death of Thalberg, everything had to receive his assent; as the old guard left – the more vigorous-minded producers, like Hunt Stromberg and Joseph L. Mankiewicz – M-G-M films were increasingly a reflection of Mayer's taste, and he was a man of formidable likes and dislikes. When, in 1946, Loews, Inc., made a record net income of $18 million, Mayer's position was unassailable; but two years later the figure had shrunk to just over $4 million (the lowest figure since 1933) and the studio was operating at an estimated loss of $6½ million. With the loss of the theatres imminent, the front office panicked, and decided that what was wanted was a new Thalberg. The job was offered to Arthur Freed, who declined it, and then to Dore Schary, who arrived in July 1948: the individual producers were to be responsible to him rather than Mayer, and he was to be responsible not to Mayer but to New York – not a situation congenial to him, because of Mayer's reaction, and even less congenial to Mayer. At this uneasy juncture, the company celebrated its twenty-fifth anniversary.

The anniversary films were lavish and Technicolored. Mervyn LeRoy's **Little Women** (1949) is inferior to Cukor's version, but you may become reconciled to it if you accept that the Jo of Miss June Allyson is as anxious to be liked as that of Katharine Hepburn was not; there is, however, good representation of the older generation – by Mary Astor (Marmee), Lucile Watson (Aunt March), C. Aubrey Smith (Mr Lawrence), Leon Ames (father) and Elizabeth Patterson (the maid). **The Three Musketeers** (1948) also suffers from uneven casting: on one hand Gene Kelly, a marvellously agile D'Artagnan, Frank Morgan and Angela Lansbury as the King and Queen, and Keenan Wynn as the valet; on the other, Van Heflin a too-sober Athos, Miss Allyson a sugary Constance, Vincent Price a too-knowing 'President' Richelieu (in deference to Catholics he was not allowed cardinal's robes) and Lana Turner, a void as Milady. Kelly's avowed inspiration was the elder Fairbanks, and

the decorators have provided him with sets evocative of the Fairbanks version of this story – narrow Paris streets, rose-covered inns, marble ballrooms; the duels are both ingenious and funny, but there is no sense of respect for the material. Fairbanks knew better, but the chief trouble is Robert Ardrey's screenplay, which has not succeeded in taming a long novel, and under George Sidney's direction the film flies off at every angle.

The anniversary line-up was led by **That Forsyte Woman** (1949) – appropriately, for it is the quintessential M-G-M film: stately, star-studded, sumptuous and pointless. It continued the studio's love affair with Britain, for it is, as the credits clarify, 'Part One of John Galsworthy's "The Forsyte Saga"', a study of the late Victorian moneyed classes. The Forsytes prided themselves on being exactly what they were, on thinking exactly as they thought, and doing exactly as they wished, but as Soames, their chief representative, Errol Flynn is merely gruff and grim, and as Irene, Greer Garson is all suffering graciousness; the true relationship between this ill suited couple is beyond either performer. As the two others who challenged the complacency of the Forsytes, Walter Pidgeon as Young Jolyon is a conventional black sheep, and Robert Young as Bosinney is twenty years too old and completely without Bohemia in his soul. Whether the novel had more merit than other family sagas filmed in the Forties is not clear from the screenplay, by Jan Lustig, Ivan Tors, James B. Williams and Arthur Wimperis, or the direction by Compton Bennett, a Britisher – on loan from the Rank Organisation – who prided himself that he never raised his voice on the set.

Schary was fully aware that the studio's reputation depended on such entertainments. Some thought was given to remaking *Trader Horn*, but it was decided that **King Solomon's Mines** (1950) would make a stronger African adventure. Rider Haggard's story provides only the framework: a wife or widow (Deborah Kerr) hires Alan Quartermain (Stewart Granger) to go into dark unexplored regions in search of her husband. Helen Deutsch wrote the screenplay, leaving out the business of the eclipse (perhaps because it had recently turned up in *A Yankee at*

King Arthur's Court) and making it just another trek through the jungle. The film was very popular, so the studio must have thought their money well spent. Like *Trader Horn*, it was filmed in Africa, and, unlike the Gaumont-British version, it uses a real African tribe; the climax among the Watusi is memorable – and Umbopa, the guide who turns out to be a king, was played by a real one, Siriaque. As against this, audiences roared with laughter when Miss Kerr, having washed her hair in the jungle, looked as though she had just popped out of the studio beauty parlour – which may be the fault either of Bennett, again on loan to M-G-M, or of the second-unit director with whom he was compelled to share credit, Andrew Marton.

Stewart Granger, according to Bennett, was 'monstrously difficult' to work with, but this British acquisition was ideal material for Schary's plan to remake two of the company's Silent successes, **Scaramouche** (1952) and **The Prisoner of Zenda** (1952) – and Lewis Stone, who had had leading roles in them, was again featured as a sentimental gesture at the end of his long career. The writers of *Zenda* were John L. Balderston and Noel Langley, the first of whom had worked on the 1937 Selznick version – of which, frame by frame, this is a copy, a fact obscured by Richard Thorpe's plodding direction and the addition of Technicolor. With the exception of James Mason's bullet-headed and insolent Rupert, the cast is inferior: as the King, Granger is arrogant and over-weening, and as Rassendyll he has British Imperial integrity and a good profile – but as was proved again by the 1973 *Lost Horizon*, Ronald Colman films should not be remade without Ronald Colman. Nor could Granger manage the laughter of Rafael Sabatini's Scaramouche. The other leads are again weak, including Mel Ferrer as the smiling villain – the hero's brother and not, as in the earlier version, his father. There is only an approximation of seventeenth-century France, but George Sidney's approach is even more spirited than on *The Three Musketeers*, perhaps because he has a better screenplay, by Ronald Millar and George Froeschel: the sequences in the Assembly and the Commedia dell'Arte are splendid, as are the swordfights – and the climactic duel all over the theatre, all seven minutes of it and devoid of any

sound but the clash of rapiers, may well be the best ever put on film.

Sidney's films were usually fast-paced and visually handsome, but his name appears on **Young Bess** (1953), which is neither. Margaret Irwin's novel had been owned by the studio for some time, and this film was rushed into production after the accession of Elizabeth II – an M-G-M candy for the Coronation. Clumsily adapting the book's viewpoint, but ignoring its comment on the nature of Seymour's ambition, the film presents Elizabeth (Jean Simmons) as a teenager with a crush on one of the male teachers, watched tolerantly by her grown-up rival, Catherine Parr (Deborah Kerr). Seymour becomes, in Stewart Granger's handling, the usual Granger hero, but with one memorable line, 'I wish that Italian fellow were alive . . . Leonardo. He knew how to paint a woman like you.' At such moments it is clear that the Hollywood historical was determined not to grow up: there had been vast advances in education since such dialogue was common, and the Tudor period is so alive with death-tinged intrigue that there was no need to add or subtract anything. The writers were Arthur Wimperis and Jan Lustig, the former one of the writers of Charles Laughton's Henry VIII, and in repeating that role Laughton improves upon it by indicating the king's cruelty.

As puzzling as Sidney's unevenness is the work of the cutting-room, and we can only conclude that the editors of *Young Bess* were not supplied with the material to bring it anywhere to the level of *Scaramouche*. Similar assumptions may be made about **Kim** (1950), which is credited to Victor Saville, though there is no internal evidence of its having been directed. The camera merely records the actors speaking their lines and their actions, the pieces then being assembled to form a narrative. Without the essentials which made up Kipling's novel – its mixture of mysticism, high adventure and feeling for India – the editors evidently had no chance to make a decent movie. Dean Stockwell has spirit in the title role and, what is rarer among child actors, intellect; in the smaller role of Red Beard, Errol Flynn is lively.

M-G-M's historicals include *Ivanhoe* (q.v.), made in Britain, which proved again that the profits were commensurate with the cost. Since the company was, in

767

Postwar Hollywood: The Studios

At the time Vincente Minnelli was an incomparable maker of musicals he also made some good serious films, including *Madame Bovary*, with Jennifer Jones. She was so perfect that it was no surprise to learn from Minnelli's autobiography that she herself was partly Emma.

financial terms, only limping along, it looked again to its past – specifically to *Ben-Hur*, but the chance to remake that was passed over in favour of **Quo Vadis?** (1951), from an equally venerable novel which the studio had owned for some time. With Schary's approval it was given to producer Arthur Hornblow and John Huston. Mayer argued against their 'intellectual' approach in favour of a deMille spectacle, going over their heads to Nicholas Schenck in New York. Accordingly the project passed to producer Sam Zimbalist and Mervyn LeRoy, with the then stupendous budget of $10 million – to be spent in Italy, where costs remained lower than in California. Eventually the film was only just behind *The Greatest Show on Earth* among box-office successes, but in spite of a number of reissues it had earned only $12½ million before being sold to T.V. Now that the days of the monster biblicals have gone, it is hard to regret the expenditure. What is to be regretted is the script, by John Lee Mahin, S. N. Behrman and Sonya Levien, with its religiosity and a wishy-washy romance between a feebly acted Roman general (Robert Taylor) and a Christian (Deborah Kerr). There is a Jewish Paul (Abraham Sofaer), a Scottish Peter (Finlay Currie), and a host of other British players, including Peter Ustinov, whose Nero almost saves the occasion – exuberant, larger than life, petulantly and naively in awe of his own genius. This is another Metro film which seems to have been assembled rather than directed, but, unlike the later attempts in the genre, the climactic moments do not fail: the two decades of experience were not lost in filming the scenes in the arena.

With M-G-M's pool of talent to draw upon, Schary instituted a scheme he had been fostering at R.K.O., which was to encourage directors to make low-budget films of their own choosing. The directors concerned were veterans, like William Wellman, who made *The Next Voice You Hear*, the next voice being God's – in a radio broadcast – or newcomers, like John Sturges, whose *The Magnificent Yankee* is a biography of Oliver Wendell Holmes (Louis Calhern). As the series proved unsuccessful, it turned towards the thriller, and one of the last was Sturges's **Jeopardy** (1953), as unpretentious as the title, a tense little tale about an escaped convict (Ralph

Meeker) and a woman (Barbara Stanwyck) whose husband (Barry Sullivan) is trapped as the tide is rising.

One of the best serious M-G-M films of the time came from Arthur Freed, who had admired the work of writer Richard Brooks and brought him to the studio for **Crisis** (1950), which, with the compliance of Cary Grant, Brooks directed, from his own screenplay. Its credited source was a story by George Tabori, about a surgeon (Grant) forced to operate on a foreign dictator (José Ferrer): a British film with an identical plot was simultaneously on view, *State Secret* (q.v.), and the fact that there was no report of litigation may be because the situation had already been used in a little-known play by Karel Čapek, 'Skeleton on Horseback'. Both films are thrillers, and the American one is more sober; the British one, by identifying its setting as a Balkan state indicates a Communist dictator, but this film is more cagey – unwilling to admit that there might be a Communist state in the Western hemisphere, even though the setting is South of the Border. (Prophetically, the dictator wears a Castro-like beard.) There are implausibilities, but *Crisis* is carefully worked out; Grant, in one of his last serious performances, is excellent and Ferrer is amusing, self-congratulatory and prone to tantrums.

Freed's most famous protégée, Vincente Minnelli, did poorly with his first serious film, **Undercurrent** (1946), produced by Pandro S. Berman and renowned at the time as Robert Taylor's first postwar film. Taylor plays a deranged captain of industry who marries an unworldly girl (Katharine Hepburn) and decides to murder her when she proves a gauche hostess and over-curious about his brother (Robert Mitchum). There are a number of the customary, infallible scenes, such as the one where she tries to flee and the car will not start, but the result is high tosh, for which Taylor was singularly unequipped.

Berman also produced **Madame Bovary** (1949), since he wanted to make a film about adultery, in the manner of current European films, and had been advised that a version of a 'classic' was more likely to be passed – with the M.P.A.A. helpfully adding that it stood a better chance with an actress like Jennifer Jones rather than Lana Turner. To appease the censor even more

768

the film has a prologue and epilogue in which Flaubert (James Mason) defends his work and attempts to justify Emma's behaviour. The unexpected triumph is Miss Jones's Emma, exactly the sort of girl who has fed her adolescence with tales of romantic love and marries the first man to come along. The screenwriter, Robert Ardrey, and the actor (Van Heflin) have missed the point of Charles Bovary, who was not merely an affectionate nonentity but devoid of imagination; Louis Jourdan is a tired fop rather than the uncouth, selfish squire; and Christopher Kent – Sweden's Alf Kjellin renamed – is simply awkward. The film omits the sexually-charged airings in a closed carriage, but none of the changes damage its purpose. The critic of the *Manchester Guardian* observed that it used 'exceptionally fine material to add yet another competent film to the many competent American films which are made just as easily from novels of much less literary worth', which is absolutely true, so it is a comment on the relative strengths of the two media that there are scenes in the film which must be memorable even to the least attentive spectator: the ball marking Emma's debut in society, with the camera holding her giddy, gliding excitement; the coach for her planned elopement moving past, leaving her stranded; and her ineffable appreciation of the opera at Rouen. Minnelli's overall understanding is remarkable, as is the transformation of Metro's famous village* into Normandy.

Minnelli directed **Father of the Bride** (1950), which is a chronicle of the funny things that surround a wedding, scripted by Frances Goodrich and Albert Hackett from a book of comic essays by Edward Streeter. Matters are entirely predictable, from father's realisation that his dove is about to flee the nest, to his contemplation of the guest list: 'It's no longer a question of insulting people, but of survival.' The direction is heavy, and Minnelli cannot make the young couple (Don Taylor, Elizabeth Taylor) anything but ninnies. However, all is right when Spencer Tracy is on screen, talking to the audience in a

*Recognisable by its stream and humped bridge, despite often drastic work by the art department, it featured in virtually every M-G-M film of this period which was set in Europe, e.g. *Till the Clouds Roll By* (English), *The Green Years* (Scottish), *Desire Me* (French again).

wry, not-to-be-defeated tone. This actor is reputed to have had doubts about every film he accepted, so it is hard to understand why he made **Father's Little Dividend** (1951), which is living, or rather, dead proof that sequels are seldom good. Its subjects is an expectant mother, and there was nothing in it, incidentally, to offend *Picturegoer*, which a few months earlier had complained that the continental tendency to show pregnant women as pregnant was extending to the U.S. – a 'disgusting' practice which, it was hoped, would not spread to British films.

The Bad and the Beautiful (1952) is perhaps Minnelli's best non-musical film, and it is the cinema equivalent of the *roman-à-clef*, stuffed with Hollywood folklore as it recounts the exploits of an all-time heel. Charles Schnee wrote it from a story by George Bradshaw, John Houseman produced it, and its structure is the same as the most famous film on which he worked, *Citizen Kane*; in it a producer (Walter Pidgeon), a director (Barry Sullivan), a star (Lana Turner) and an author (Dick Powell) each remember a former colleague (Kirk Douglas). The film picks at its victims, refusing to dig beneath the surface – which is perhaps why the industry did not loathe it as it had loathed *Sunset Boulevard*. It is circumspect, for instance, on sex, with just one representative dame to be nice to producers, with just a hint of men passing on their women: one extra complains to her boyfriend that getting on 'depends who you *live* with' (my italics). Oscars went to this movie for costume design, set design and Robert Surtees's cinematography (as well as to the screenwriter), evidence of Minnelli's flair for the visual: the camera rakes across a studio floor, catching details in pools of light, and it trails the guests at a cocktail party, catching snatches of conversations. The film is even more enjoyable if one knows its victims: the Turner character is mainly Diana Barrymore, daughter of John, and part Turner herself, 'wooden, gauche and artificial' as described by Leo G. Carroll, playing a very British director; while the Douglas character is mostly Selznick, part Thalberg, and a little Val Lewton – though his faults all seem to stem from Broadway's Jed Harris. Among the extras may be spotted a dead-ringer for Lubitsch, a plaintive chantoosie looking like the 1948 Judy

Garland, and a Joan Crawford-like star who speaks lovingly of her fans; collector of trivia may care to note that the film in this movie called 'The Proud Land' can be seen on a 42nd Street marquee in Minnelli's next film, *The Band Wagon*.

'Jealous – in London! Forbidden – in Rome! Dangerous – in Paris!' read the ad for **The Story of Three Loves** (1953) and though at least two of the three adjectives are lies, you know what sort of film this will be. Sidney Franklin produced it after searching for a vehicle for the new continental actresses under contract, Leslie Caron and Pier Angeli; not coming up with anything, he put them in two separate stories and added a third, with Moira Shearer. Minnelli directed the Caron sequence only, in which she plays a governess loathed by her charge (Ricky Nelson) till he visits a witch (Ethel Barrymore) who tells him that if he gets up to some jiggery-pokery at bedtime he can turn into Farley Granger. The direction flounders in whimsy, and the whole enterprise was far from being the equal of the European art movies intended.

It was not a success, nor was *Crisis*; it is no wonder, then, to find the studio panting for the return of Joan Crawford, directed in **Torch Song** (1953) by Charles Walters: 'When you make a Crawford picture you've got to go all the way. *She's* the picture and she dominates. I remember stealing ideas from her personal life to fit the character in the picture . . .' John Michael Hayes and Jan Lustig wrote the script, and Crawford must surely have recognised that of all the bitches she played this one at least was based on herself – though of course it is hard to tell, since she had a humourlessness that bordered on the bizarre. She plays a song-and-dance girl, still holding up her skirt as she did in *The Hollywood Revue of 1929*. 'You're the times in Times Square, you're the broad in Broadway,' says her agent, but she is bored. So bored. After glowering at her blind pianist (Michael Wilding) for ten reels, she discovers that before his accident he wrote of her 'gypsy madonna hair' and the film ends with her arms around him, less protectively, I thought, than as if she were about to devour him.

We may wonder why such films hung on so long, anachronisms in the postwar world. Hollywood was slow to acknowedge that a considerable portion of its audience was spilling over into the art houses, to see films like *Ladri di Biciclette* and *La Ronde* (q.v.) – and the industry's attitude is understandable when much-praised films, *and* in English, were failing to attract more than minimal audiences. When these films lost money, the industry and M-G-M could not decide whether it was because they were the wrong films or because the publicity representatives – and hence, exhibitors – were flummoxed when faced with what they considered to be films untypical of M-G-M. Of the films for which Schary was personally respons-ible, only one was enormously successful – *Battleground* (1950), a World War II drama, directed by William Wellman – and it was in the wake of that that Loews Inc. re-affirmed its faith in Schary by finally forc-ing Mayer from the company he had helped to found. Mayer's belief that films should be made for the entire family had been successfully challenged by Schary, who had reintroduced Westerns and action films, but it is doubtful whether he be-lieved in them. If he believed in anything at all, it was the 'message' film in rather chi-chi form – in violent contrast to Zanuck, the most astute studio head at this time, who believed in 'message' only if the 'entertainment' ingredients were right. Arthur Freed certainly believed in his musicals, and so popular was the M-G-M musical at this time that it kept profits

buoyant and prolonged Schary's regime.

Mayer's reactionary stance was neither more nor less reprehensible than Schary's inadequate attempt to break new barriers: however far apart they seemed to each other, they were at heart commercially-minded industry men. The film industry itself had been stable for so long that it could not comprehend the changes which were about to be wrought upon it. Audi-ences were falling and the threat of tele-vision was growing. Such things were understood, and each studio was not un-willing to dispense with the huge number of players under contract. The business-men and executives had refused to under-stand the drive for independence by crea-tive talents – who in turn had not under-stood its failure. At the heart of the matter was the volatility of audiences, restless after the War, who were finding new calls on their leisure time. Critics and public had had little impact on each other in the Thir-ties, but their views were seldom far apart – though paradoxically their preferences grew further apart as more and more cinemagoers turned to reviewers for guid-ance. A trend had begun, which would continue till the late Sixties, for poor films to attract crowds and good films to pass unnoticed. The majority of the box-office successes of the postwar period are not worth a dime either on television or at revival houses, while many of the failures have passed into folklore.

Production in Austerity Britain

IN BRITAIN, the end of the War meant the end of air-raids and the black-out; servicemen returned to Civvy Street, but conscription continued. So did the rationing of petrol, fuel, clothing and most foodstuffs. In the bitter winter of 1946–7 the government forbade the cinemas to open before four p.m. because of the fuel crisis. At the same time, the television service resumed, for the few thousand sets which had been in operation before the War. Despite the poor quality of the programmes transmitted by the B.B.C. (then a monopoly) the service made much greater headway than in America, partly because of the televising of Princess Elizabeth's wedding in 1947 and of the Coronation in 1953: during that time there was a significant falling off in cinema attendances. The person most concerned was J. Arthur Rank, who owned two-thirds of the nation's cinemas and its leading production and distribution companies. The resurrection of Alexander Korda's London Films presented competition but no rivalry, since Korda was a creative producer and Rank mainly a financier, dipping into the profits from his flour-mills to retrieve his film interests where necessary – which happened frequently, owing to the poor economic health of both the country and the film industry. The government had imposed an Entertainment Tax, on cinema admissions, so that the industry was crippled where it was traditionally strongest, in exhibition. Someone once observed that Rank's family motto should have been *Panem et Circenses*, and his ambitions with regard to the latter caused him to make repeated expensive forays into the American market.

Unfortunately Rank did not understand cinema – nor, incidentally, have any of his successors at the Rank Organisation to this day. The creative force in the company at the end of the War was Filippo del Guidice who had gathered there the most talented film-makers in Britain. Rank allowed them creative freedom, but del Guidice's position was weakened as, one by one they deserted to Korda, impressed by his immense personal charm, and a greater enthusiasm for the medium than Rank possessed.

Del Guidice was eventually ousted, not long after giving Rank **Hamlet** (1948) which received praise unprecedented for a British film. It won awards throughout the world – including Oscars in Hollywood for Best Picture, Best Direction and Best Actor, overshadowing the prestige gained by *Henry V*. Since that time del Guidice had been cajoling Laurence Olivier into undertaking another Shakespeare film and it is typical of Olivier's career that he should take on the challenge of filming what many consider the greatest play ever written. He rejected 'Macbeth' and 'Othello' because Orson Welles had expressed an intention of doing both; as far as the box office was concerned – and exhibitors quaked at the thought of programming Shakespeare – *Hamlet* was marginally the best known of the three titles. Alan Dent's adaptation chopped away many of the play's complexities, to leave a firm story line and to allow Olivier to develop this 'tragedy of a man who could not make up his mind' – a statement which prefaces the film, together with the 'So oft it chances in particular men' speech. Olivier as the prince is less interested in his contemplative moods than his sardonic humour

Physically, it is not easy for him to look vacillating, so he starts as a student withering away in aimlessness, but when the ghost directs him to his destiny he becomes misanthropic and suspicious, a focus for the court around him. As director, he imparts an atmosphere of danger and propels the narrative towards its powerful and exciting climax, the duel; and there are other elements as impressive as they are harmonious – the music by William Walton, the photography by Desmond Dickenson and the cavernous sets designed by Roger Furse. It was clear then that Olivier and his collaborators understood the Bard better than any of the others who had attempted to present him on screen – and if we extend the remark to include Olivier's own *Richard III* (q.v.), it takes care of all other efforts in the meantime. Roman Polanski, later to film *Macbeth* (q.v.), is only one of several filmmakers to have spoken warmly of the influence of *Hamlet*: and its position today,

after some years during which the initial reaction was thought excessive, is unassailable. It is a very satisfying film, because it takes very great material and interprets it with honour, imagination and intelligence.

It marks a peak in postwar British production, as does *The Best Years of Our Lives* in American cinema. Neither, as different as they are, was typical: the British studios showed as little interest in classic plays as basic material as their Hollywood counterparts did in contemporary subjects. As far as the latter were concerned, the demand for topical material declined sharply with the end of the War. It had been easy enough to construct thrillers around the gangsters of the Depression era and the Resistance fighters of the War; but relief that the War was over prevented anyone from suggesting that there might be discord within the current mood. Nevertheless Britain could not return to the trivial thrillers and comic cut-ups of the prewar

The praise accorded Olivier's three Shakespeare films, especially *Hamlet*, indicated that they were regarded as important cultural artefacts, with the result that their reputation has fluctuated over the years. They have always been popular on revival – when they can be judged for what they are, superbly-crafted versions of classic plays. Olivier as Hamlet is in the chair, with Eileen Herlie as Gertrude and Basil Sydney as Claudius; to the right is Terence Morgan as Laertes.

773

Production in Austerity Britain

Margaret Lockwood, *The Wicked Lady* herself, could not resist going to the hanging of the lover and partner that she has betrayed: but in the view of the letter handed to her by Ivor Bonard, left, she clearly wishes that she hadn't. The critics loathed the film, but the public loved it, while it was the other way round with *Brief Encounter*, OPPOSITE. The public soon reversed its judgment, but if *Brief Encounter* has become one of the most beloved of all films, *The Wicked Lady* is really not that bad at all.

years. European critics, seeing British films for the first time in five years, were astounded by the improvement, while the American cinema seemed virtually unchanged – a fact gradually dawning on some American critics, who used British cinema as another stick with which to beat Hollywood.

The new Labour administration was undoubtedly the inspiration for making **Fame Is the Spur** (1947), based on Howard Spring's novel about a Socialist politician (played in the film by Michael Redgrave) – a thinly-disguised Ramsay MacDonald, the first Labour prime minister. Nigel Balchin's screenplay has in common with *Goodbye, Mr Chips* the early death of the wife and the protagonist's lonely if honoured old age: but since it leaves vague the extent to which he regrets his betrayal of his youthful ideals the result is hardly more than a rags-to-riches story. The accompanying attempts at 'art' and significance, as directed by Roy Boulting and produced by his brother John, are typical of the time.

Moving from Rank to Associated British, the Boultings brought similar ability to **Brighton Rock** (1947) or **The Guinea Pig** (1948), but these are, nevertheless, distinctive films. The former was scripted by Graham Greene from his own novel (the credits claim as co-writer Terence Rattigan, who said that his contribution was small and that he did not work with Greene), and this is possibly why the film is agreeably raffish, with seedy seaside streets, tacky cafés, deck-chairs on the promenade – a world of Woolworth teacups, bottled ale and wind-up gramophones. The cast fits splendidly into it, except for the boy killer (Richard Attenborough), either posed or posing, and the direction always signals the action. Roy Boulting also directed *The Guinea Pig*, a further copy of *Goodbye, Mr Chips*, and more reasonably, since it is based on Warren Chetham Strode's public school play. The subject was topical, in that the Labour government was expected to abolish these seats of privilege, and it specifically concerns a grammar-school boy sent to one of them. His dilemma is treated in a patronising half-hearted way, and for a climax the film has the effrontery to offer his tobacconist father (Bernard Miles) arriving to say that the house system is partly responsible for Britain's greatness. The boy – played by Attenborough on one note of quivering lip – has the impudence to use the word 'arse' to a master, and much fuss was made because the censor let the word pass.

The British public was otherwise indifferent, preferring undisguised fictions, and indeed, as the War in Europe finished, it was watching James Mason drive Dulcie Gray to drink in **They Were Sisters** (1945), unperturbed that Dorothy Whipple's novel had been falsified to further Mason's popularity as a villain. Gainsborough's romances now exuded the confidence brought by success, and this one catches well the British upper bourgeoisie of the Twenties, as three sisters (Phyllis Calvert, Anne Crawford, Miss Gray) marry diversely; it is also a vast improvement for Arthur Crabtree, who had directed *Madonna of the Seven Moons*. **The Wicked Lady** (1945), again demeans its source, Magdalen King-Hall's pastiche account of one of the eccentric seventeenth-century miladies, who in this case takes to larceny on the king's highway. The writer-director, Leslie Arliss, added elements of 'Vanity Fair' and 'Forever Amber', but also some wit, moving it through gracious settings at a tremendous clip. He certainly provides a field-day for Margaret Lockwood, flashing her eyes and curling her lips with wild improvidence – indeed she owed much of her popularity to the fact that English lady stars had not hitherto been allowed such high-flown passions. Audiences recognised in her the Hollywood heroines who had thrilled them in like manner, but the only other of the major players not gauche is Mason as a highwayman. Any other faults escaped the notice of the public. It was the most popular British film up to that time; in the U.S. market, despite much refilming to meet M.P.A.A. requirements over the matter of Miss Lockwood's cleavage, it failed to make the least impression.

Brief Encounter (1945) opened in London the same day, to the reverse reception – critical praise and indifference from the audience. Now it is constantly revived while *The Wicked Lady*, though undeniably a junk classic, is half-forgotten. It did not take long for *Brief Encounter* to become loved – and imitated – though none of the subsequent cinema encounters have been as touching (and many of them have dated far more). Noël Coward adapted it from his one-act play, 'Still Life', viewing the situation only from the outside – the difficulties of meeting, the fear of what neighbours might think – but thereby matching his characters, who are middle-class Britishers. Laura Jesson and Alec Harvey are not frustrated or despairing; they have all their lives done the 'decent' thing, and they respond to each other when they laugh at the inmates of the station buffet, the Donald Duck cartoon and the pince-nezed lady in the Kardomah coffee-house. He has a Galahad quality: she is left breathless by his insistence on seeing her again and by his quixotic solution, which is to emigrate. Celia Johnson and Trevor Howard generously fill in the emotions between the lines; the comic passages – Stanley Holloway and Joyce Carey in the buffet – are by no means as far-fetched as they may later seem; and David Lean's direction is exemplary.

At this point he and his collaborators at Cineguild – the producer Ronald Neame and associate producer Anthony Havelock-Allen – turned from Coward to Dickens for further examples of the British ethos for world audiences. Both **Great Expectations** (1946) and **Oliver Twist**

(1948) are superb, from the mystery and disquiet seen at the outset to their galloping finales. (Both have been done again, in colour and with music,* though the addition of songs to Dickens's teeming plots must be at best superfluous.) Lean has absolute faith in his author, with Guy Green on camera and John Bryan, the designer, integrating and exploring every aspect of their crafts – even to a slight overheating, but that is exactly the sort of virtuosity required. Of the other Dickens films, only Cukor's *David Copperfield* approaches the excellence of this pair, partly because his casting, too, was near-perfect. As the grown-up Pip and Estella, John Mills and Valerie Hobson are no more appealing than Dickens made them, but as children they are well played by Anthony Wager and Jean Simmons; Martita Hunt is the memory-haunted, nocturnal Miss Havisham; Freda Jackson and Bernard Miles are the Joe Gargerys; Finlay Currie is Magwitch, most alarming of convicts; Ivor Bonard is Wemmick, Hay Petrie Uncle Pumblechook, O. B. Clarence the Aged P., Alec Guinness Herbert Pocket and Francis L. Sullivan is Jaggers. Sullivan

*In the case of the 1974 *Great Expectations* the songs were, however, cut from the release print.

Celia Johnson and Trevor Howard in *Brief Encounter*. The prestige of J. Arthur Rank was at its peak; he was the financier, a benevolent despot to the film-makers working in the companies he controlled. Gainsborough Pictures, making melodramas like *The Wicked Lady*, OPPOSITE, brought in huge profits, while Cineguild – an offshoot of Two Cities – reaped fine notices and awards. In 1946 the New York critics voted Celia Johnson the best actress for *Brief Encounter* and Laurence Olivier best actor for Two Cities' *Henry V*, the first time they had cited players for films not made in Hollywood.

Production in Austerity Britain

In retrospect, the praise meted out to British films in the Forties does seem justified. No one has filmed Shakespeare as well as Olivier, and no subsequent version of Dickens has been a patch on the two made by David Lean – and this is *Great Expectations*, with Jean Simmons and Anthony Wager as the infant Estella and Pip, and Francis L. Sullivan as Jaggers. Film-makers today leave the handling of such classics entirely to television, which may or may not be a pity.

is Mr Bumble in *Oliver Twist*, so well matched by Mary Clare in their early sequence that it is a joy to see them unhappily wed; Ralph Truman is the mysterious, brutish Monks; Gibb McLaughlin and Kathleen Harrison are the Sowerberrys, with Diana Dors as the drudge and Michael Dear as uppity Noah Claypole; Henry Stephenson is the kindliest of Mr Brownlows and Anthony Newley the most artful of dodgers; Robert Newton is a frightening Sykes, and in the title role John Howard Davies is a little too well-spoken and self-effacing. Alec Guinness enjoys himself as Fagin, whose presentation in this tale, though unavoidable, caused high blood pressures in the Jewish-dominated American film industry, necessitating some cuts and a three-year delay in its being shown in the U.S.

776

Lean's run of fine films ended with **The Passionate Friends** (1949), H. G. Wells's 1913 novel modernised by Eric Ambler, who also produced. 'The important thing is the situation,' he said of his adaptation, 'and that could have happened at any time.' Yes; but not, surely, like this. The happy ending is a violation of Wells's intention, and far from there being a suggestion of free love, we are not party to Mary's sexual relations with either husband (Claude Rains) or lover (Trevor Howard): if they are more than friends, passionate or otherwise, why does Mary (Ann Todd) show not an iota of feeling? C. A. Lejeune suggested that the box-office failure of *Brief Encounter* made Lean have his characters 'wear dressier clothes and move in smart settings' but I suspect that he wanted (it is not uncommon among European directors) his star, who was also his wife, to be shown off in Hollywood-like glamour. Neither the Swiss locations nor her extensive wardrobe are objectionable, but her mask-like face gets many a glistening close-up and gives nothing in return.

The Cineguild team had split by this time, and Neame and Havelock-Allen, together and separately, tried to turn the clock back with some thrillers only too depressingly reminiscent of prewar British programme-fillers. However, **The Small Voice** (1948), produced by Havelock-Allen and directed by Fergus McDonell, is a well-paced and well-cut piece about convicts keeping a lonely household prisoner – a situation common in Silent Westerns, and to be used again in several films of the Fifties. Neame turned director, and a prosaic one, bringing to his subjects neither vulgarity nor vigour. Two literary adaptations are agreeable: **The Card** (1952), written by Ambler from Arnold Bennett's novel, and **The Million Pound Note** (1954), by Jill Craigie from Mark Twain. The former does not catch the flavour of the Five Towns, but is better than most British comedies because Bennett was more resourceful than most people who write comedies for Alec Guinness (b. 1914). This is a vehicle for Guinness, a stage actor then establishing himself in a series of mildly eccentric screen frolics. He is likeable, if not pushy enough, as the deceivingly inventive Denry, well-abetted by Glynis Johns as a conniving minx

and Valerie Hobson as a democratically-minded countess. The Twain tale has Technicolor, Joyce Grenfell as a society hostess, and concerns an unusual banknote offered by two clubland pranksters to a penniless American – played by Gregory Peck, brought across at great expense by Rank in yet another belated attempt to break into the American market.

The decline and disintegration of Cineguild is symptomatic of the British film industry at that time. During the War and just after, Lean and his colleagues had made a handful of films worthy to set with the world's best; also under the Rank umbrella, other bright talents were making the films which were recognised as having greater vitality than those arriving from Hollywood. Inevitably among those tackling unhackneyed subjects were Powell and Pressburger – though in the case of **I Know Where I'm Going** (1945) an old one was tricked up to make it seem like new. Their first film together had been set in the Hebrides, and they returned to the Isles for this story of a girl (Wendy Hiller) who finds that love is more important than money. She learns her lesson through the Islanders and their customs, including Highland reels and falconry; and she is also subjected to the kilted charm of the laird (Roger Livesey).

The producer of Lean's Dickens films was Ronald Neame, who himself shortly thereafter turned director and in *The Card* turned an Arnold Bennett novel into a pleasing Ealing-type comedy. Alec Guinness, seen here with Glynis Johns, was already associated with Ealing comedy and the public relished his ability constantly to change his appearance. He was the first star daring enough to do so without the benefit of an outsize personality, like Laughton or Olivier.

Production in Austerity Britain

It is a slight and charming film, but the three films which followed it are remarkable for the courage of their excesses. Powell and Pressburger claimed that their films were entirely collaborative efforts, and it was not disclosed till later that Powell was the actual director and that Pressburger contributed little once the film was on the studio floor. More than their earlier films together this bizarre trio calls into question the nature of their collaboration, and an examination of the films they made before they teamed up suggests that Pressburger is a writer of European sensibility while Powell may be relegated to the ranks of work-a-day directors. (After the team split up he made an almost appallingly silly horror film, *Peeping Tom*, but even that had a moment or two of visual flair.) Yet the faults of **A Matter of Life and Death** (1946) are so thorough that there is no apportioning blame. It is as platitudinous as it is ambitious. There is no other film quite like it, even if it follows the European tradition of whimsy (e.g. *Death Takes a Holiday*) and borrows some dim ideas from a dim picture – the dead pilots' receiving room in heaven from *A Guy Named Joe*. While a pilot (David Niven) struggles for life under anaesthetic, his doctor (Livesey) – after mounting an endless staircase leading to a heavenly courtroom – pleads for his life before a Jewish judge (Abraham Sofaer). Many of the arguments concern the differences between Britain and America (their cultural values represented respectively by broadcasts of a cricket commentary and 'Shoo Shoo Baby') – the excuse being that the pilot has fallen in love with an American girl (Kim Hunter). The prosecuting counsel (Raymond Massey) is an American, and though there is evidence of Powell and Pressburger's customary pride in Britain the specious arguments set forth show much kowtowing to the country on the other side of the Atlantic. There were economic reasons for that and for the presence of Americans in the cast: the film cost so much that only with American acceptance could Rank get his money back. He did not get it. It was treated with great earnestness – a fact that must give pause to anyone coming upon it now for the first time. For that reason it has a minor place in the history of postwar Britain – along with the fuel crisis of 1947 and the 'Britain Can Make It' exhibition – and also because it was selected for the first Royal Film Performance.

'One is starved of Technicolor up here' is typical of the humour, since the trial scenes are in monochrome; but Powell and Pressburger elsewhere seldom starved audiences of Technicolor. **Black Narcissus** (1947) is visually ravishing as photographed by Jack Cardiff and designed by Alfred Junge; it was filmed entirely in Britain and the process work simulating the Himalayas may be described as miraculous. The setting is a convent and the screenplay is quite faithful to Rumer Godden's novel as it charts the quarrels and rapports of the nuns (headed by Deborah Kerr and Flora Robson) with two princes, father (Esmond Knight) and son (Sabu), and their British agent (David Farrar). Our doubts may arise when the jealous nun (Kathleen Byron) doffs her wimple for a spot of raving nymphomania, but this time I intend an unqualified compliment when I say that there is no other film quite like it.

The same is not entirely true of **The Red Shoes** (1948), with its formula backstage plot – a dancer torn between composer and a Svengali-like impresario;[*] it also manages to parallel the Hans Andersen tale – which itself turns up in the climactic ballet. And as the first English-language film to deal almost exclusively with ballet it attempts several large statements on the nature of art and the artistic impulse. As the dancer, the Sadler's Wells star Moira Shearer is gazelle-like, badly made-up and completely without humour; Marius Goring is the dullest of composers and Anton Walbrook the most demonic of impresarios; the presence of Massine, Robert Helpmann and Ludmilla Tcherina helps to lend authenticity to the backstage scenes. The combination of the familiar and the fervid made the piece popular in the U.S., where the profits made up for the losses on *Stairway to Heaven* (as *A Matter of Life and Death* had been retitled). Indeed, the film's success in America was greater than that of any other British movie of the time, thus encouraging Rank's ambitions in that direction – ironically so, for at one point during shooting, when the budget was exceeded, overtures were made to Korda

[*]The inspiration was, like the 1931 film, *The Mad Genius*, the relationship between Diaghilev and Nijinsky.

to take over the project. Korda declined, but in view of Rank's trepidation it is not surprising that Powell and Pressburger made their next films for Korda.

Frank Launder and Sidney Gilliat also followed their wartime successes with one equally interesting film, **The Rake's Progress** (1945), which they wrote and Gilliat directed. It 'anticipates the first British satire of the screen' thought Richard Winnington, contemplating this study of a typical playboy (Rex Harrison) of the Thirties – from being sent down from Oxford (for placing a chamber-pot on one of the dreaming spires) to killing his father (Godfrey Tearle) in a drunken motor accident. His first job, as befits the black sheep, is with the British in South America, where cricket is more important than work, and attendance at the club more important than either – a condition satirically handled, but a poor reason for his cynicism and philandering. He marries an Austrian half-Jewish girl (Lilli Palmer) to help her escape the Nazis – a situation used to dramatic advantage and also interesting since the plight of European Jews had mainly escaped the attention of filmmakers. His kindness is short-lived, but at the end he is redeemed by the love of a good woman – after which, in the epilogue, he becomes a war hero. C. A. Lejeune was one of several reviewers who objected to the implication that this was 'the type who won the War': today we are more likely to agree with her contention that the film shirks 'the responsibility of a really rotten hero'. Apart from bogeymen, the screen would not see a wholly reprehensible protagonist till Wilder's *Ace in the Hole* (q.v.).

Launder and Gilliat returned to roots with two thrillers, but as we may expect from the writers of *The Lady Vanishes*, both are superior examples of the genre – and, indeed, **I See a Dark Stranger** (1946) has a number of similar twists as it charts the progress of an Irish girl (Deborah Kerr) from her spying for the Nazis to her conversion by a British officer (Trevor Howard); Launder directed from their screenplay. Gilliat directed **Green for Danger** (1947) based on a novel by Christianna Brand – which is classic, inasmuch as a great number of skeletons are dragged from cupboards as each of the major characters is suspect in turn after murder in the

operating-room. The suspects (Howard, Leo Genn, Sally Gray, Rosamund John, Megs Jenkins, Judy Campbell) wear their uniforms as though striding the wards for years, but it is Alistair Sim, smug and infuriating as the Scotland Yard man, who transforms a good thriller into a remarkable one. Gilliat was much less skilful in **London Belongs to Me** (1948), reducing to stereotypes the inhabitants of Norman Collins's South London boarding house – for this is a version of that author's Grand Hotelish bestseller.

It was becoming clear that Launder and Gilliat were unlikely to fulfil the promise of *Millions Like Us* and *The Rake's Progress*. **Captain Boycott** (1947) takes an engrossing subject, the landlord (Cecil Parker) who drove the nineteenth-century Irish peasantry to extremity, but since it portrays him as merely misguided the film suffers from a lack of conflict. It was further compromised by Stewart Granger, in a narcissistic performance as the Errol Flynn-like hero; the fact is that it was rewritten thus after he had expressed an interest in playing the role. Admittedly without him Rank would not have backed the venture, since it required expensive location work. So did **The Blue Lagoon** (1949), which was also primarily Launder's film. 'Crusoe-and-soda' Claude Cockburn described de Vere Stacpoole's antiquated bestseller, and because of

One particularly admired British partnership of the time was that of Launder and Gilliat, who had begun – as writers – modestly on quota quickies in the Thirties and would become disappointing journeyman film-makers in the Fifties. *The Rake's Progress*, however, with Rex Harrison and Lilli Palmer, is one of several Launder and Gilliat films of the Forties which revives strongly.

watchful censorship boards it was even sillier on screen: the couple (Jean Simmons, Donald Houston) stranded on a desert island are no longer cousins, and before the baby is born they read to each other the marriage ceremony as found in a convenient-to-hand book of etiquette! As intended, the palmy beaches and sunsets did help to lighten the gloom of postwar Britain, but the country's critics ungratefully termed the film more than usually irrelevant. Americans for once proved uninterested in desert island romance, and since it had been financed with more than an eye on the American market it was Launder's second failure for Rank. He and Gilliat also departed to work for Korda.

Carol Reed followed *The Way Ahead* with **Odd Man Out** (1947), and as the earlier film had established him as the country's leading director it was both fitting and typical that he should choose as his source F. L. Green's novel: it was clear to this movie buff film-maker that the bleak, sad story of a hold-up in an Irish city could provide affinities with certain classic films, e.g., *The Informer, Quai des Brumes*. For most of its length, it is very fine indeed as a straightforward thriller: but when it deserts the streets for the decaying mansion – where a mad, drunken artist (Robert Newton) wants to paint the eyes of the dying Johnny (James Mason) – it splurges into the surreal. Reed then tends to lose control and move towards pretension, but in that respect the film is more subtle than most of its contemporaries. It was certainly regarded as unreserved proof that the British could make a 'great' picture.

Reed's first two films for Korda consolidated his unrivalled position. **The Fallen Idol** (1948) and **The Third Man** (1949) were both written by Graham Greene, the former from his published story and the latter from a novella written expressly for screen adaptation. *The Fallen Idol* is about a small boy (Bobby Henrey), the son of an ambassador whose butler, Baines (Ralph Richardson), is his idol and surrogate father; Mrs Baines (Sonia Dresdel) is the embassy Carabosse – and the child's mainly innocent world darkens further with the discovery of adultery and a death. The Belgrave Square locations remain vividly in the memory. For *The Third Man* Reed used what seemed like most of Vienna, a city of ruin and shadows harbouring felons

more sinister than usual – cold-war opportunists and black marketeers. It is a second tale of disillusion, this time experienced by a writer (Joseph Cotten) in search of a mysterious friend, Harry Lime (Orson Welles), now a profiteer. Assisting the writer is a laconic British major (Trevor Howard) and not helping him is a ballerina (Alida Valli), with strong convictions about the Harry she once loved. Enhanced by its haunting zither theme music, the film was a great success the world over – though less so in the U.S. It was a co-production between Korda and Selznick – for the Americans were resuming their prewar interest in the British film industry.

Both films retain their powerful individuality, even though *The Third Man* was imitated, conspicuously by Reed himself (see below); but, after three critical successes, Reed disappointed all the more with **An Outcast of the Islands** (1951). The cinema has seldom tackled Conrad, and William Fairchild's screenplay reveals that he was the wrong man for the task, since after an uneasy exposition nothing much happens. The rigours of filming on location (Ceylon, not the Malaya of the novel) may be one reason why Reed accepted some dreadful performances: Robert Morley, a buffoon as Almayer; Richardson (who was superb in *The Fallen Idol*), orotund as the captain; and George Coulouris and Kerima, who as natives seem to have strayed from a Maria Montez epic. Only in Trevor Howard's Willems and Wendy Hiller's Mrs Almayer are there intimations of the film that might have been. Its failure forced Reed to backtrack. He had once told an assistant, Guy Hamilton, 'When in doubt, do a comedy-thriller. You may lose some of the laughs and some of the thrills, but you'll get something': but there is little of either in **The Man Between** (1953). The script commissioned from Harry Kurnitz is reminiscent of *The Third Man*; but Reed's snowbound Berlin has none of the eeriness of his Vienna, and James Mason, as the enigmatic Ivo, cannot escape from the shadow of Harry Lime.

Reed then made a more serious mistake in tackling something new. Both he and Korda believed that that was the business of film-makers, but Korda had doubts about **A Kid for Two Farthings** (1955), written by Wolf Mankowitz from his own short story. A patronising concoction of

Carol Reed's Shadowland

We may also feel that the later films of Carol Reed are not so good, but the promise of his prewar films was more than fulfilled by his films of the Forties, including *Odd Man Out*, ABOVE, with James Mason and F. J. McCormick, and two versions of Graham Greene, *The Fallen Idol*, ABOVE RIGHT, with Bobby Henrey, and *The Third Man*, RIGHT, with Orson Welles. Reed was the first film director to be knighted, and whether or not one agrees with the British honours system that is indicative of the prestige he brought to the native industry. He is also the only British film director to be so honoured to date, if we accept Olivier and Richard Attenborough as primarily actors and Chaplin and Hitchcock as American film-makers – and both of them were knighted towards the end of their lives.

Petticoat Lane philosophy, humour and fantasy, it is played by a bunch of show business Cockneys bearing as much resemblance to the real thing as Christmas tree glitter to snow – an analogy I use to give some indication of the decor. Few major directors ever miscalculated so horrendously.

David Lean's films for Korda also show a falling-off – though at the time **The Sound Barrier** (1952) was much admired and actually voted by the British Film Academy as superior to, q.v., *Rashomon*, *The River* and *Casque d'Or*. The film opened at the time the first jet passenger plane, the Comet, made its early flights, and was therefore bang up to the minute, with its discussions on the conquest of space and its then-unprecedented aerial photography. Terence Rattigan's screenplay toys with the idea that scientific idealism is compatible with human sacrifice, but is otherwise soap opera, with its fanatical aeronautics tycoon (Richardson), bravely-waiting little woman (Ann Todd) and phlegmatic test pilots.

Lean, like Reed, turned about, unearthing **Hobson's Choice** (1954), Harold Brighouse's old play. It concerns the cobbler's daughter (Brenda da Banzie) who sets about marrying the meek employee (John Mills) and unseating pa (Charles Laughton). The photography of the exteriors is a celebration of Edwardian Salford, but its fussiness in the cramped interiors is communicated to both the screenplay and some of the performers. Nevertheless, Lean's direction seems more personal than in his two previous films and in the one that followed.

That is **Summer Madness** (1955), a mating of two wonders, Katharine Hepburn and Venice – and Lean seems to have been content to let his camera stare starry-eyed at both. It has subsequently proved impossible for many to be a tourist in Venice without recalling this film (if only because the quintets in the Piazza San Marco still perform its theme tune) – and, of course, few cities have a better claim to be captured in colour for the screen. It is seen through the eyes of a hopelessly enthusiastic tourist, played by Hepburn – who despite some actressy tricks makes touching a woman's loneliness and what may be both her first and last affair. The screenplay, by Lean and H. E. Bates, is not with-

out wit and acerbity, as based on Arthur Laurents's Broadway play, 'The Time of the Cuckoo'; the film's American title is *Summertime*; Ilya Lopert and United Artists joined Korda in backing it. Lean's career henceforward was to owe more to Hollywood than to Britain.

American interest proved fatal to Powell and Pressburger; they had made **The Small Back Room** (1949), for them a rare excursion into monochrome, which Powell believes is his best film. Unfortunately, Nigel Balchin's novel of the darkest days of the War featured two aspects already hackneyed – meddling civil servants and an embittered war hero (David Farrar), a scientist with a tin leg who wants to go back on the booze. There followed, in Powell's own words, two 'disastrous films', **Gone to Earth** (1950) and **The Elusive Pimpernel** (1950), for which Korda had welcomed the participation of Selznick and Goldwyn respectively. Selznick's excessive interference in the former was due to the fact that Jennifer Jones was in the lead, while Goldwyn was involved in the latter because the other star, David Niven, was under contract to him. Powell later observed, 'If you're making a film between Goldwyn and Alex Korda . . . you get ground to powder.' *The Elusive Pimpernel* had been planned as a musical, and 'it never went right,' according to Powell, 'because there were relics of the musical idea still in it.' Whoever was responsible, direction, acting and writing are of an appalling level, despite the excessive cost of £450,000, which became half a million with the retakes demanded by Goldwyn, who, in the end, decreed it below the standard necessary for the U.S. market. (A small independent outfit managed to get it a few dates there four years later.) Selznick felt the same about *Gone to Earth*: the British premiere was delayed by the insertion of close-ups of Miss Jones, while the American version, rechristened *The Wild Heart* and shortened by twenty minutes, was extensively re-shot and re-cut by Rouben Mamoulian. In this instance the difficulties were partly due to the source material, a novel by Mary Webb, reduced to a sex triangle between the wicked squire (Mr Farrar), the new minister (Cyril Cusack) and a fey girl (Miss Jones) who keeps a pet fox.

To retrieve their reputation, Powell and

Pressburger accepted a suggestion from the conductor Sir Thomas Beecham, who had helped on *The Red Shoes*, to film **The Tales of Hoffman** (1951). At that time Italy was exporting a number of black and white opera films, with the camera seemingly set in the stalls; Powell, of course, went to the other extreme. The prologue and the Olympia sequence are often imaginative, but vulgarity – always just at bay in his work – sinks the Giulietta sequence beneath its pink Venetian waters, while the Antonia section, placed last, is a dull and muddy anti-climax. The special effects are inspired by Cocteau, while the decor by the variable Hein Heckroth, Powell's invariable collaborator, only renders Offenbach's masterpiece as Festival of Britain kitsch. The film's comparatively low cost was not enough to endear Powell and Pressburger to the industry when the public failed to respond, and they were absent from the studio till Associated British backed **Oh . . . Rosalinda!!** (1955), a modernisation of 'Die Fledermaus' influenced by Peter Ustinov's play 'The Loves of Four Colonels' – an attempt at satire on the Allied powers occupying Vienna. The level of the humour is exemplified by the Russian colonel claiming that a book entitled 'Five Thousand Ways to Say No' is a standard work in his country, while the performances, aspiring to the 'naughtiness' suggested by the new title, are bloodcurdling – with the definite exception of Anton Walbrook as the bat and the possible one of Anthony Quayle as the Russian. Indeed, as a catalogue of disasters this is an *embarrass de richesses*, though *The People* newspaper proved that chauvinism was not dead by declaring, 'This film puts British musicals on the map at last!' That map did not include the U.S., whose distributors refused to handle it after studying the other reviews and the domestic receipts. Nor does it appear in that curious phenomenon of the present day, Powell retrospectives.

It is ironic that despite the more benign atmosphere reigning at Korda's studio none of these film-makers managed to maintain the standard of their earlier work. Since not one of them (I exclude Laurence Olivier, a special case) has a better film in his future we may conclude that the confident days of the British film were over. Launder and Gilliat started the period well but were spent forces by the end of it. It should be noted that though their first two films for Korda are excellent, neither is exactly forward-looking. **State Secret** (1950), written and directed by Gilliat, has a plot not unlike those they tackled in *The Lady Vanishes* and *Night Train to Munich*, involving a man (Douglas Fairbanks Jr), whose life depends on crossing the border to a free territory; he is now in one of the iron curtain states, and as in the concurrent *Crisis* he is a surgeon who has operated on a dictator.

The Happiest Days of Your Life (1950) concerns the billeting, due to a Ministry blunder, of a girls' school on a boys' school. As directed by Launder and written in collaboration with John Dighton (the author of the play), the consequent chaos is worked out logically and is wonderfully played, from Alistair Sim and Margaret Rutherford downwards. They are the head teachers, and their battle is titanic – she lips-pursed determined, righteousness personified, blissfully unmindful of her eccentricities and those of others; and he abandoning his armoury of pouts and nervous giggles to shudder before a new onslaught perpetrated by her or her girls, his eyes quivering like fried eggs. In any other film Joyce Grenfell and Richard Wattis, getting a laugh with every line, would be called scene-stealers: this is one of the funniest of all screen farces.

Gilliat was engaged on an ostensibly more lavish Korda production, **The Story of Gilbert and Sullivan** (1953), which was issued to celebrate the twenty-first birthday of London films. The account of the famous partnership is limited to the pompous Englishness of Gilbert (Robert Morley) and the yearning of Sullivan (Maurice Evans) to write serious music; but the excerpts from the operettas are so abundant and so charmingly presented that the flatness of the rest of it becomes unimportant.

Launder returned to the schoolroom with **The Belles of St Trinian's** (1954), but where *The Happiest Days of Your Life* galloped towards an organised chaos, here only confusion reigns. The screenplay by himself, Gilliat and Val Valentine catches the macabre note of Ronald Searle's cartoons, with girls competing with mistresses (Miss Grenfell, Hermione Baddeley, Irene Handl, Joan Sims, Beryl Reid and Mr Sim – in drag) in monstrousness; but the joke becomes wearisome. It was popular, and Launder and Gilliat made a number of sequels as their joint careers faltered. At that time what turned out to be their last film for Korda was **The Constant Husband** (1955), directed by Gilliat from a screenplay by himself and Valentine, with Rex Harrison playing a confirmed bigamist. That it is so much worse than any of Launder and Gilliat's previous films may be due to the speed with which it was assembled. Korda sold it to American T.V. for its world premiere, claiming it was a bold experiment but in fact evidence of his financial troubles. *Variety* commented kindly that it was unlikely to do much for the cause of British pictures in the U.S.

The Boulting brothers were also with Korda for one film, and it is their best. **Seven Days to Noon** (1950), directed by John from a story by Paul Dehn and Anthony Harvey, concerns a professor (Barry Jones) who threatens to blow up central London with a nuclear bomb unless the premier (Ronald Adam, chosen because he resembled Attlee) bans the manufacture of such weapons. It begins as a thriller and ends part-documentary as London prepares for devastation; the final scenes are a pastiche of wartime moods and situations, from the evacuations of children to 'crisis' speeches, justly borrowing from Humphrey Jennings for an effect both powerful and moving. There is a touch of moralising, and of course implausibility, but the casting is superb – the heroine (Sheila Manahan) looks, for instance, more like a duck than a starlet: and most notable is Olive Sloane as the ageing soubrette who unwillingly shelters the professor. The players are also fine in a follow-up, **High Treason** (1952), directed by Roy Boulting for Rank, which is a story about Scotland Yard's efforts to prevent the destruction of Battersea Power Station by a group of Communist saboteurs.

Korda's first production after the War was **A Man About the House** (1947), but despite the foreign (Sorrento) locations, then a rarity, he found it unworthy to launch his postwar programme and it was released without the London Films logo. The producer was Edward Black and the director Leslie Arliss, who, as fugitives from Gainsborough, knew how fond British audiences were of the past – not the Imperial past or the historical past, both of uncertain advantage despite the recent victory, but that specific period of prosperity and safety which began in the reign of Victoria and ended with the First World War. Audiences were constantly offered ladies in bustles going about the business of adultery or murder – but in this case it is the Italian husband (Kieron Moore) who is suspected of poisoning one of the two schoolteachers (Dulcie Gray, Margaret Johnston) from North Bromwich. Adapted from Francis Brett Young's novel, British superiority fades under Italian resource and British frigidity succumbs to Italian charm: that the film even partially succeeded is mostly due to Mr Moore who, though a failure later as Korda's much-touted new star, is impressive here as the enigmatic Italian peasant.

Thus **An Ideal Husband** (1947) reintroduced London Films, and it was also Korda's farewell as a director. The Englishness of the Irish Wilde particularly appealed to him, though this was a less happy choice for filming than either 'The Importance of Being Earnest' or even 'Lady Windermere's Fan', both of which had recently enjoyed successful revivals. Cecil Beaton designed the costumes, which are shown to advantage in Technicolor. Bedecked in a number of them is Paulette Goddard, to whom Korda owed a commitment – and Mrs Cheveley is probably the only character in Wilde for which she was suitable. She plays her nevertheless as an absurdly obvious schemer – in direct contrast to Michael Wilding, whose superb, underplayed Lord Goring did not apparently please Korda, perhaps because he was trying to approximate a stage production. Once that is accepted, the other performances may be enjoyed, especially those of Diana Wynyard and Hugh Williams as that insufferably priggish pair, the Chilterns.

Vivien Leigh, like Miss Goddard, was a close friend of Korda, and he talked her into doing a new **Anna Karenina** (1948) – against her better judgment, as she later admitted. She does provide a centre, but it is of the nature of Dresden porcelain. The justly drubbed Vronsky (Kieron Moore) could have been of no help to her, but confronted with Ralph Richardson's excellent Karenin she proffers only well-bred prettiness. Far more of the story is retained than in the M-G-M version, which seems crude beside this one – except, of course, that it was transformed by Garbo's intensity: at best this is just another triangle drama in a handsomely reproduced Russia. Jean Anouilh's original screenplay had relocated it in the Paris of the *belle époque*, which Korda would not sanction, but the script was eventually credited to Anouilh, Guy Morgan and the director, Julien Duvivier. Duvivier and Korda had worked quite harmoniously on *Lydia*, but their quarrels on this occasion were so fierce that Korda himself had to take over on those days when Duvivier refused to go on the set. Despite these crippling circumstances the major scenes have dramatic pitch, and presumably both decided to keep the camera off Vronsky wherever possible – a positive virtue.

Korda had reverted to his prewar policy of employing the best British talent available and attracting any names which had any meaning for American exhibitors. He brought from Hollywood the director Gregory Ratoff, who seldom made a good film – but who could be relied upon in turn to attract American stars unwilling to be handled by British directors whose work they did not know. A further ploy was to offer the stars pleasing locations. Thus resulted two dreadful films: **That Dangerous Age** (1949), in which Myrna Loy, in Capri, is attracted to a man who is not her husband, and **My Daughter Joy** (1950), with Edward G. Robinson, in San Remo, obsessed by his daughter to the point of paranoia. Also common to both films are Richard Greene and Peggy Cummins, British-born players who had starred in some American movies.

Also from Hollywood came two Britons, David Niven and director Robert Stevenson, contracted for **Bonnie Prince Charlie** (1948), which became the greatest disaster of Korda's career. Stevenson had worked on the project for eighteen months and directed for just over one when he left after a quarrel with Korda, who took over before assigning Anthony Kimmins, the credited director. The credited writer is Clemence Dane, but she was only one of many. The hapless prince (Niven) was doomed not to leave the studio at Shepperton, whose rocks and crags ill match the

unit photography; the film, which in fact cost a fortune, looks as though it had been made by a fly-by-night Wardour Street operator hoping to make a quick buck. Disjointed and dull, it is a contender for the worst film ever made, and – if it is not a contradiction in terms – one of the least profitable.

Still, at this time Kimmins did provide Korda with one of the few London Films to get good notices. The critic Richard Winnington considered **Mine Own Executioner** (1947) fit to be bracketed with *Great Expectations*, *Brief Encounter* and *Odd Man Out*, only missing 'as in the book from which it is taken, an overriding poetry'. It seems to me that what is missing is plausibility, intelligence and craftsmanship, not to mention seriousness – though that is the one quality its makers clearly thought they had. This film stands with its contemporary, *Spellbound*, as the two major movies to deal with psychiatry, and it was customary for the British to congratulate themselves on handling something soberly which Hollywood had treated romantically. In this case Nigel Balchin's screenplay, from his own novel, would appear to have been penned after perusal of a magazine article on the subject, and his plot ('Physician, heal thyself') seems taken from something similar.

Anthony Asquith, who had directed some of Anatole de Grunwald's successful films, was reunited with him for **The Winslow Boy** (1948), and it is one of London Films' enduring entertainments. De Grunwald had originally commissioned the screenplay from Terence Rattigan after *The Way to the Stars*, and when he rejected it Rattigan refashioned it for the stage – where its success enabled him to ask much more for the screen rights. It is not an exemplary film, because it is all talk – and sententiously so in discussing British fair play; but the acting is satisfying and the material somewhat more than that. It is based on the Archer-Shee case of 1910, when a Dartmouth cadet was expelled for a petty theft: one advantage over similar dramas is that this one is less concerned with injustice than the process by which the boy was vindicated in law. As the advocate, based on Sir Edward Carson, Robert Donat nobly heads a cast including Cedric Hardwicke, Margaret Leighton and Kathleen Harrison.

Production in Austerity Britain

Donat was also a participant in one of Korda's less fortunate schemes, when three leading actors were invited to turn director on modestly-budgeted projects of their own choosing. **The Cure for Love** (1949) had been one of those regional farces – in this case by Walter Greenwood – that used to take root in Shaftesbury Avenue. Donat repeated his stage role of the returning soldier trapped by the tarty and rapacious blonde (Dora Bryan) who wants to marry him, and the nice girl (Renée Asherson) he wants to marry. The camera reveals him too old for the role and also exposes the painted sets. Similarly, most of **The Last Days of Dolwyn** (1949) occurs in the open, but it never uses a location when it can opt for a painted set. Emlyn Williams, as accomplished an actor as writer, starts off with the excellent idea of a Welsh village about to be flooded in order to provide a reservoir for the English; its inhabitants are to be rehoused and recompensed, but the chapel caretaker (Edith Evans) refuses to go, after discovering that she owns her cottage in perpetuity. Unfortunately, Williams's own performance as an erstwhile villager bent on vengeance is as wildly melodramatic as the motivations of his characters. Ralph Richardson, like Donat, also selected one of his stage successes, **Home at Seven** (1951) about a clerk who finds himself suspected of a double murder committed during his twenty-four hour amnesia. R. C. Sherriff's play could never have made a good film, but it just might have provided an interesting picture of suburban life. Shooting was done in fifteen days, for this is one of several low-budget films instituted by Korda during 1951–2 in the hope of offsetting his losses. He himself supervised while Jack Hildyard, one of the credited photographers, planned the shooting; Richardson restricted himself to giving tips to the actors. All three films seem equally directionless.

Korda's fortunes, as parlous as ever, were temporarily restored by **The Wooden Horse** (1950), directed by Jack Lee, a former documentary director who had made one minor film for Rank (like Anthony Asquith, he subsequently declined to work for Korda again). The film, from a novel and screenplay by Eric Williams, concerns a break-out from Stalag Luft III: but as recounted here this true

happening becomes a schoolboy jape – and one with little tension. Nevertheless the British public lapped it up, and when Rank had a similar success with *The Blue Lamp* (q.v.) it was officially declared that there was no longer any urgent need to angle films for the American market. Doubtless Korda was sincere in agreeing with the statement – and doubtless he had to, since the British Film Production Board (q.v.) was no longer prepared to countenance his extravagance. Even so, the American market remained tempting, especially after the success there of **The Captain's Paradise** (1953), which featured one passé Hollywood name, Yvonne de Carlo, and one art-house attraction, Alec Guinness. Certainly there was little merit in the film itself, good American reviews notwithstanding – a comedy, directed by Kimmins, about a sailor with wives (the other is Celia Johnson) in two ports.

Korda accordingly approached 20th Century-Fox for participation in **The Deep Blue Sea** (1955), though the initiative in this case came from Vivien Leigh, who had implored him to find a film for her – and he acceded to her request for this particular property, though he thought it wrong for her. So did Kenneth More (1914–82), at that point becoming Britain's most popular star. He was repeating his stage portrayal of the breezy ex-R.A.F. type attempting to extricate himself from a love affair gone sour, and the film is only notable for its preservation of that performance. Fox insisted upon Anatole Litvak as director and the use of Cinema-Scope (q.v.), which factors, plus the miscasting of Miss Leigh as the older woman, all but destroyed Rattigan's intimate drama. Like *Summer Madness*, also a co-production with Hollywood, the film failed at the box office.

Hardly more popular were two African stories, but both are honourable and interesting – as superior to most of Korda's postwar output as the Imperial adventures among his prewar films. In both cases the superiority is due almost entirely to the source material. It should be noted, however, that with **Cry, the Beloved Country** (1952) Zoltan Korda was permitted, to his satisfaction, to be more realistic than on previous African excursions. The country of the title is South Africa, and the film is a plea – as written by Alan Paton from his own bestselling novel – for racial integration. That plea nests easily within the framework of the plot, which chiefly deals with a black priest (Canada Lee) whose son has gone to the bad, and a bigoted white man (Charles Carson), who disapproves of his own son's efforts on behalf of such people. Since the film would have no point did he not see the error of his ways, it is to its credit that the conversion is more subtly done than in most didactic films – despite naiveties elsewhere. John McCarten noted in *The New Yorker* that 'the picture is obviously more interested in getting the problem on record than in providing a hard-and-fast solution'; it does provide a dossier on the huge unbridged gap between the black shanty-towns and the comfortable white suburbs.

George More O'Ferrall (the first British director recruited from T.V.) brought little more distinction to **The Heart of the Matter** (1953), but it is a reasonable condensation, by Lesley Storm and Ian Dalrymple, of Graham Greene's major novel. Set in an East African township during the War, among the traders and the British community, it observes one man (Trevor Howard), the deputy police commissioner, as he so compromises his professional and private lives till suicide is the only solution. It is Howard's understanding of the role which makes the film worthy of its original: only a resonance in his declaration of love recalls his doctor in *Brief Encounter* and only his bearing that of the officers he played elsewhere: for this is the complete Scobie, 'the typical second man', and one of the best performances ever recorded on film.

The same may be true of Laurence Olivier's interpretation of the title role in **Richard III** (1955), and that was the intention. His career was, by his standards, in the doldrums, so he sought to put on record his much-praised, definitive performance. The play was renowned as a vehicle for great actors, but was not entirely suitable screen material – and Korda's backers would not underwrite the battle sequences★ as Rank had once lavishly financed Agincourt. A foreword notes that this is one of the 'legends' that surround the English crown, and the crown is always central to the piece, offered by Olivier, if not Shakespeare (there is no

★They were filmed in Spain as an economic measure.

screenplay credit, but it was Olivier's decision to incorporate interpolations by Colley Cibber and Garrick, and to start with the Coronation scene which concludes 'Henry VI, Part 3'), as a prize which perverts and corrupts all those subservient to it. Utilising Otto Heller's camera and Roger Furse's sets (cf. *Hamlet*) to underline the intrigue – and with William Walton's score emphasising the melodrama – Olivier's direction is full of master touches (even if most of them are to enhance his own performance): this wittiest of actors sees Richard as the wittiest of villains, delightedly sinning his way to the throne. He is a compendium of perfidy – jealous, hypocritical, petty, scornful; and as demanded by the text he is a whole menagerie of animals from the dark side of the moon. Yet by looking into the camera he makes us share his arrogance and delight in his own scheming, so that at the end we pity him, alone and helpless, as he fights on to the finish. Three other actor-knights support him: John Gielgud looking apprehensive as 'false, fleeting, perjured' Clarence; Cedric Hardwicke, a benign Edward IV; and, most notably, Ralph Richardson as Buckingham, a blandly-smiling, secret opportunist. Claire Bloom is the Lady Anne; the termagant Margaret has been sensibly removed and Jane Shore has been added – with only one line, but in the tantalising person of Pamela Brown.

The film restored Olivier to his pre-eminence among British actors. He went on to play Macbeth at Stratford – which in common with most people who saw it I consider the greatest of all his performances. He spent a great deal of his own money on preparation for a film version, but backing was not forthcoming, though he had gone cap-in-hand to Rank, to the American companies and the British government. Korda had just died; *Richard III* had been his final financial wave-of-the-wand, composed partly of $500,000 from N.B.C. Television for its American premiere, in a complicated deal which included a repayment of $300,000 if earnings in cinemas exceeded $350,000. But *Richard*, though as warmly reviewed as *Henry V* and *Hamlet*, was not as popular as either and therefore could not help London Films survive the death of Korda.

Though Korda's postwar regime produced more worthwhile films than the prewar one, it had been equally disastrous financially: it would be easier to list the films which had made money than those which lost it. At the outset the losses on *An Ideal Husband*, *Bonnie Prince Charlie* and *Anna Karenina* were such that when the government set up the British Film Production Fund in 1949 it immediately allocated one million pounds to settle Korda's debts. Another two million followed from the same source, as *The Third Man* proved that he could produce a money-making film, but both the sum and the film only staved off disaster; nor were the coffers filled from the proceeds of those movies made to keep the studio ticking over. Closure was only avoided by the sales of the Olivier and Rex Harrison films to American T.V. and the prewar London Films library to the new British independent television channel. That no other British producer had a large collection of films to sell may be a fitting epitaph to Korda's achievement.

Financially these years were no better for J. Arthur Rank, and they were calamitous artistically – though that was not something which interested him too much. He was sufficiently chauvinistic for us to suppose that he would have found some way of holding on to those talents which had made him internationally famous had Korda not been there to take them on. But Rank was primarily a financier, and as owner of two cinema circuits he knew that cinemas could be filled with run-of-the-mill product. Chauvinism was his downfall: just as he could not see that lavishly assembled British films could not compete with Hollywood on its own terms, so he failed to appreciate that it was Hollywood's packaging that made ordinary stories so attractive. He began the period with two producers who did understand such matters – Filippo del Guidice at Two Cities and Edward Black, working under the auspices of the Ostrers at Gainsborough; but they were replaced by people much less expert.

Admittedly at that point his chief task was the administration of the studios, production companies and distributors which, though nominally independent, were under his financial control. The rational solution was for them all to be brought under one umbrella, the J. Arthur Rank Organisation. The distribution arm remained known as General Film Distributors, at least for the present, since it was with that company that Universal had signed an agreement for the release of its product in Britain. G.F.D.'s involvement with Universal encouraged Rank to buy Universal shares, till at one point he was the largest individual shareholder with twenty-five per cent. One outcome of this was the proposal for a jointly-owned American circuit so that Universal could compete with those companies which owned their own, but the plan was unfeasible with the government's anti-trust laws pending. Instead, in 1945, Rank and Universal announced the joint formation of United World Pictures, with an annual distribution programme of eight British and eight American productions. The American films were not to come from Universal, but from a new company, International (then releasing through R.K.O.) – and the attractiveness of International's offerings were to compel American theatre owners to take the Rank films as well. But since, as we have seen, the new laws were designed to prevent the practice of block-booking, this project was also aborted. United World was disbanded, and Universal and International amalgamated – though Rank was appeased by a new agreement by which the Universal-International distribution offices would annually handle twelve of his films. He was convinced that since British cinemagoers had long learned to love American films, the reverse would ensue once Americans were accustomed to British accents, and therefore the Universal-International dozen would be insufficient for American requirements. In the event that company failed to find a dozen it thought suitable for its audiences – which left Rank with another American outfit that he had optimistically started, Eagle-Lion.

The name came from what was to have been a worldwide distribution organisation started in 1944 but absorbed by G.F.D. in Britain two years later: it was applied to a now defunct American company, Producers Releasing Corporation, specialists in B-movies – and once again the initial programme was to consist jointly of American and British product. Under its American management, Eagle-Lion was also to produce films, but since these were little better than the rock-bottom

B-pictures made under its former name, it was hardly a prestigious outlet for Rank's British-produced movies (Rank eventually closed it in 1950). A further attempt to reach American cinemagoers was made in a deal with R.K.O. based on the theory that they would learn to love British stars by seeing them acting alongside their R.K.O. favourites. Accordingly, R.K.O. sent Edward Dmytryk to Britain to direct an Anglo-American cast (including John Mills, Trevor Howard, Richard Carlson and Martha Scott) in **So Well Remembered** (1947), based on James Hilton's novel about a small-town newspaper; but there were no successors. Rank was able to develop a circuit in Canada, but below the border had to content himself with a New York showcase, the Winter Garden, because of the decree divorcing exhibition and distribution. With the exception of Olivier's Shakespeare films and *The Red Shoes*, *The Seventh Veil* (q.v.) was the only British film to rouse American audiences during that period which finished with the announcement that Rank and Korda would no longer try to woo them. In 1951 *Variety* reported that both impresarios hoped to build upon the unexpected popularity their old films were finding on American television (then as yet without any significant Hollywood competitors).

Rank's obsession with the American market began during the War, when critics on both sides of the Atlantic observed that such films as *In Which We Serve* and *Henry V* not only equalled but surpassed those emanating from Hollywood. Thereafter Rank constantly put his faith in the wrong projects; after *Caesar and Cleopatra*, which failed to appeal despite star names and spectacle, he aped Hollywood with a musical, **London Town** (1946). Wesley Ruggles had come to Britain to work with Korda but had quarrelled with him, and therefore he proposed this film to Rank, to star a West End comic, Sid Field. The plot, about an understudy waiting for his chance of stardom, managed to include Field's best-known routines. Ruggles brought over a number of his colleagues from Holly-wood, including the songwriters Burke and Van Heusen. The numbers are staged with definitive incompetence, often moving between a variety of styles, and Ruggles's work as producer and director was such that he could not find work again after

returning to the U.S. The film was eventually shown there, much cut and retitled *My Heart Goes Crazy*, in 1953: it was said in the meantime to be the greatest item in Rank's posted loss in 1946 of £1,700,000.

Also contributing to that loss was **Men of Two Worlds** (1946), which was directed by a proven talent, Thorold Dickinson. Dickinson was allowed £600,000, three years, location-shooting and Technicolor to make this an examination of the British responsibility to its Empire, as exemplified by a district commissioner (Eric Portman), a doctor (Phyllis Calvert) and an educated African (Robert Adams) trying to come to terms with the primitive nature of his people. Dickinson's first film had been a high-pitched African melodrama, and this was an attempt to make amends; but it is as patronising as earlier British films which sent Paul Robeson to battle with the witch-doctor – and even dumber and duller. The crêpe-paper banana-trees may have contributed to its delay in reaching the U.S. – in 1952, retitled *Kisenga, Man of Africa*. Another contemporary subject was poorly handled in **School for Secrets** (1946), written, directed and co-produced by Peter Ustinov. It involves back-room scientists or boffins (a word much bandied about at the time) and their difficulties in developing radar – the boredom of which is only relieved by that bugaboo of early wartime movies, the secret raid into Germany led by Ralph Richardson.

Both films were considered important, but two romantic films adapted from second-rank novelists proved more durable, even if interpreted by directors of lesser stature (both promptly disappeared) – Stanley Haynes with Compton Mackenzie's **Carnival** (1946) and Charles Frank with Sheridan Le Fanu's **Uncle Silas** (1947). *Carnival* concerns the doomed romance between a Cockney dancer (Sally Gray) and a dilettante artist (Michael Wilding), and though neither player has quite the romantic aura found in the best Hollywood love stories, she has a sweet toughness and a springlike look when her hair is down, and he has the *désinvolture* which explains his irresolution. The film's chief contribution comes from Paul Sheriff, whose sets are a far better reproduction of Edwardian London than was customary. The standard of British art direction – certainly in historical films – was outstanding

789

at this time, perhaps reaching a peak in Laurence Irving's Gothic mansion for *Uncle Silas*, which he also produced. Irving's illustrious career in the theatre had left him little time to work in films, where his efforts had been confined to the design of two films for Fairbanks Sr and *Pygmalion*. The screenplay credit on this occasion is unexpected, being Ben Travers, the writer of the celebrated Aldwych farces. Le Fanu's tale, of an heiress (Jean Simmons) terrorised by uncle (Derrick de Marney) and governess (Katina Paxinou), makes an entertaining film in its particular genre.

These films were produced by del Guidice, clearly in emulation of the Gainsborough melodramas, which remained profitable for Rank: those made between 1943 and 1946 earned twice their cost, but by 1946 the Gainsborough management had changed. Edward Black had left after a quarrel with Maurice Ostrer, joining first M-G-M and then Korda; it was he, just before he died, who instituted the *Bonnie Prince Charlie* which caused Korda so much grief. As the Rank-owned companies grew closer together, Ostrer resented the interference of del Guidice and resigned. He subsequently produced **Idol of Paris** (1948), a melodrama in the Gainsborough mould, and left the business forthwith, since its reception indicated no other course. Del Guidice remained till the end of the decade, when Rank compared his extravagance with the tight economies practised at Balcon's increasingly successful Ealing Studios (q.v.). A replacement was found for Gainsborough, Sydney Box, who with one film proved himself adept at making the sort of 'women's pictures' for which Gainsborough was noted.

That film was **The Seventh Veil** (1945). 'BRITISH – and a WINNER all the way,' said the *Daily Mirror*, an attitude which helps to explain the popularity of certain native films. This one was unusual, as written by Box and his wife Muriel, since it suggested that a disturbed mind might be cured by psychoanalysis; it also flattered audiences that they could be attentive to 'good' music; and it was James Mason's moment. The film is now, initially, tedious and unattractive, but just as you are about to reach for your hat it takes on a grandeur, composed of the melodramatic elements of 'Trilby', 'Jane Eyre' and 'The Constant Nymph'. That effect was

accidental, happening only after Mason replaced the infinitely less romantic Francis L. Sullivan: as the guardian, Mason suavely suggests a misogynist drawn towards his ward (Ann Todd), and simultaneously drawn the impresario to his protégée. Audiences loved his sadism (*Deception* and *The Red Shoes* would confirm this particular view of the practitioners of classical music) and clearly the ingredients were right for both the time and the director, Compton Bennett, perhaps the most assured of the second-rank local directors. His aspirations were clear when he and Box made **Daybreak** (1946), but the film was not released until 1948 due to censorship problems over the love scenes and its indictment of capital punishment. It again stars Ann Todd, who looks like Michèle Morgan, and the film, a triangle drama chiefly set on a barge in the Thames, resembles several prewar French ones: but Bennett was much less successful in this respect than Reed had been with *Odd Man Out*.

As head of production for Gainsborough, Box's position was strengthened by **Holiday Camp** (1947). Holiday camps were a postwar phenomenon: petrol was still rationed and few people could afford to go abroad; war had both staled the memory of boarding-houses and accustomed much of the population to live in regimented fashion. Like *Bank Holiday* this film looks at a cross-section, but, unlike that, it always opts for the cheapest emotion, the easiest laugh: it was clearly put together for people who love holiday camps by people who would not be seen dead in one; Ken Annakin directed from a story by Godfrey Winn. Its huge popularity resulted in three more films built around its leading characters, Mr and Mrs Huggett (Jack Warner, Kathleen Harrison), who had caught the imagination of the public. The intention was a British equivalent of the Hardy family but more down-to-earth, since that is how the British saw themselves in comparison with their American rivals. In the event, the press reception for the first of these follow-ups ensured a speedy end to the series – except that the assembly-line production methods forced upon Box meant that the third film was already shooting.

The industry was in serious trouble, which began with the dollar shortage. Since Britain was both impoverished

Production in Austerity Britain

(because of the War) and Hollywood's best export market (in 1947 over $18 million went to the American film companies) the Exchequer was rumoured to be considering a twenty-five per cent *ad valorem* tax on all American films arriving in Britain. The Hollywood companies hastily suggested leaving their earnings in Britain to finance production – which Rank regarded as a threat to his virtual monopoly while also fearing retaliation in his attempts to market his films in the U.S. The government listened to neither side and levied a tax of seventy-five per cent. The American companies immediately withheld their films, leaving their British subsidiaries to dig into their small stockpile and make attractive packages of reissues (neither, of course, subject to tax); but if the cinemas themselves were to survive, British studios had to fill the gap. The government did not want them to close, since it extracted a large revenue in Entertainments Tax.★ Rank was asked whether his studios could supply the demand, and with over two-thirds of the country's 2,100 cinemas of his own to be programmed he arranged for bank loans of over £9 million. In November 1947 a programme of forty-seven films was announced, but that was insufficient for his ambitions since as distributor and exhibitor he knew how much Hollywood earned from the supporting programme. He had already started an animation unit with David Hand, a Disney alumnus, in charge, as well as a British equivalent of 'The March of Time' called 'This Modern Age' – but when a year later a loss of £3½ million was announced on production alone it was clear that neither would survive. Under the Ostrers, Gainsborough had delivered a handful of films annually; the reviews were marginally better for most of Box's twice-monthly films, but few appealed to the public.

The only success – at least, critically – of the Box regime was **Quartet** (1948); four Somerset Maugham short stories adapted by R. C. Sheriff for four different directors. The short story form had been virtually neglected by the screen – and none of calibre equal to Maugham's had appeared

in their original, abbreviated form. The Old Party himself conferred his imprimatur by introducing them, but neither here nor in the two sequels, **Trio** (1950) and **Encore** (1951) were the best stories included – perhaps because he wished to reserve those as likely to be the basis of a full-length film. The treatment of the ten stories in these three films does not begin to compare with any of the series made later by British television, but the changes wrought upon the texts tell us something of the mentality of those who made them. All opportunities for comic pantomime are zealously taken; sex is as resolutely erased – 'The Facts of Life' and 'Gigolo and Gigolette' have become meaningless titles – although British censorship was much more relaxed than American. The whole point of 'The Alien Corn' is lost, since the family is no longer either Jewish or nouveau riche; but it should be said that 'The Colonel's Lady' is almost intact, tersely directed by Annakin and lovingly acted by Norah Swinburne and Cecil Parker.

Box's Gainsborough saw the rise and fall of David Macdonald, originally considered Rank's most distinguished director after the defection of the best of the others to Korda. Macdonald had made some respectable thrillers before the War and had come into prominence with a number of wartime documentaries. His first postwar film, **The Brothers** (1947) was adapted from a novel by the worthy L. A. G. Strong and beautifully photographed under the glowering skies of the Hebrides: it benefited from having an unusual subject – or so it seemed, for in fact it embodies almost every cliché of bucolic melodrama, including rape – and that the heroine (Patricia Roc) and the rapist (Maxwell Reed) secretly loved each other conformed to British movie ideals of the time. So did the mainly seedy set of characters on display in **Good Time Girl** (1948), which follows the downward path of a teenager (Jean Kent) through Soho hat-checking to reform school to a liaison with – final degradation! – two American G.I. deserters.† Critics' doubts about Macdonald became certainty with **The Bad Lord Byron** (1949), whose wisely-uncredited screenplay culminates in the revelation

★ In 1948 'from a net box-office receipt of £70 million the British producers were left with £7½ million. But since production costs had amounted to nearly twice that (£14 million) the tax was taking from the film industry nearly ten times as much money needed to enable it to break even.' ('The Great British Picture Show' by George Perry, London 1974.)

†The film was inspired by the case of Betty Jones, who eventually, with an American deserter, went on trial for murder.

791

that the celestial judge appointed to examine the life of Byron (Dennis Price) is none other than the poet himself. By the time the film had insulted the intelligences of critics and the few spectators who had ventured to see it Macdonald was in the midst of shooting **Christopher Columbus** (1949), Rank's latest expensive intended-assault on the American box office. To that end Fredric March and Florence Eldridge were brought over, she to play Queen Isabella and he to suffer every indignity available to the historical film: 'You'd never see a civilised man doing that,' he says on seeing Indians smoking – and since critics ridiculed this and other dialogue, written by the Boxes (with Cyril Roberts), Rank's disenchantment was complete. Box left, but the films of Two Cities, Gainsborough and the Rank 'independents' became, if anything, even more standardised.

Those covered in the next few pages seem to me symptomatic of the ills of the Rank Organisation – or, much less numerous, of interest for their own sake. The latter do not include **Trottie True** (1949), a Technicolor musical. The failure of *London Town* still rankled, and this film was meant to prove that the lesson had been learned – for, like the much-praised *Champagne Charlie*, it did not ape Hollywood in telling its tale of an old-time music hall star. In that role Jean Kent proves that she would hardly have made it to the chorus in an American film; its total lack of success is also due to the perfunctory direction of Brian Desmond Hurst.

Hurst was one of the most trusted of the Rank directors, as was John Paddy Carstairs, who specialised in films of Shaftesbury Avenue comedies. **The Chiltern Hundreds** (1949), written by William Douglas Home (of the political family), attempts to come to grips with the 1945 General Election, one of the watersheds of modern British history. Home was bright enough to realise that there was a new flexibility among the classes, and offers a number of pro-left jokes. His plot and conclusion are, however, depressingly prewar: the scion (David Tomlinson) of an aristocratic family decides to stand as a Socialist, while his butler (Cecil Parker) opposes him as a Tory – till the latter realises both that he would rather buttle and that it is part of the appointed order

that a milord should represent the county. **Fools Rush In** (1949) is of the *Quiet Wedding* genus, with an uncertain bride (Sally Ann Howes), a reprobate father (Guy Rolfe), and the bridegroom who forgets his pants – a joke Carstairs felt so funny that it is repeated in **Tony Draws a Horse** (1950), which prefigures 'Equus' inasmuch as a boy needs psychiatric treatment because of a horse fixation.

Psychiatry is also the subject of **The Astonished Heart** (1950), adapted from the short play by Noël Coward, who replaced Michael Redgrave in the lead during shooting. Coward had earlier written that the play concerned 'the decay of a psychiatrist's mind through a personal sexual obsession', but the film is simply an arch triangle drama, with Celia Johnson as the wife and Margaret Leighton as the mistress. All concerned were thoroughly ashamed of it, with good reason. The co-directors, Terence Fisher and Anthony Darnborough, also collaborated on **So Long at the Fair** (1950), based on the classic mystery of a disappearance at the 1889 Paris Exposition. David Tomlinson is the one who vanishes, and his sister is Jean Simmons, the only reason for seeing the film. 'I would say, without hesitation,' said C. A. Lejeune, 'that England has never had a nascent film star and I stress the word *star*, which is not necessarily synonymous with actress – of her quality.'

Roy Baker was one of the more promising directors who came to prominence with Rank. **The October Man** (1947) has atmospheric sets designed by Vetchinsky – a Home Counties common with a shabby-genteel boarding-house on the edge of it; it is also notable for its heroine, played by Joan Greenwood, generous with feeling. Train whistles screech in the night and a distraught John Mills – suffering from amnesia and suspected of murder – is inexorably drawn to bridges overlooking the tracks. But, since the police pursue their investigation in the usual dim movie manner, this is not the best screen work of the usually admirable writer, Eric Ambler, who also produced. In **Morning Departure** (1950), a submerged-submarine drama, Baker has Mills, Kenneth More and others sport upper lips so stiff that one suspects rigor mortis; and Richard Attenborough, the coward, is similarly afflicted after a pep-talk.

Public approval of these naval heroics replenished Rank's coffers, and since G.F.D. released Ealing's films Rank was also the beneficiary of the enthusiasm for police work demonstrated in that studio's *The Blue Lamp*. The much-vaunted 'realism' of both gave rise to **White Corridors** (1951), though many would regard the British movie tradition of steely devotion to duty as another cliché. This portrait of hospital workers has Googie Withers and James Donald as doctors who put romance second; nor is it significantly more authentic than the American *Vigil in the Night*. It is well directed, by Pat Jackson, whose work in the documentary field had brought him an M-G-M contract – but he made only one programmer during the five years he languished in Hollywood. *White Corridors* seemed to presage a new career, but subsequently he did little of note.

It is also a film with an original screenplay, and that is the virtue – if virtue it is – of almost every film made at the time by the Rank Organisation. Certainly adaptations of well-known novels were few, but the two films produced by the actor John Mills for Two Cities are versions of H. G. Wells and D. H. Lawrence, **The History of Mr Polly** (1949) and **The Rocking-Horse Winner** (1950) respectively. Mills's own self-conscious performances, as the dreamy draper's assistant and the Cockney groom, are not endearing, and the direction by Anthony Pelissier reduces the material to a plod. But the selection of the stories does credit to Mills. Wells's collection of minor eccentrics is admirably realised, and Megs Jenkins is touching as the homely innkeeper with whom Mr Polly finds bucolic tranquillity; in the Lawrence, there are good performances by Valerie Hobson as the mother and John Howard Davies as the boy with a knack for picking the horses.

Even Anthony Asquith abandoned his apparent plan to film the Complete Works of Terence Rattigan (including his screenplays) for an original by an unknown writer, John Cresswell, **The Woman in Question** (1950). Though an unexceptional whodunnit, it does have an interesting central idea – of tracing the varying viewpoints of a woman (Jean Kent), now dead, by five people who knew her. The camera as a seeing-eye with different points of view had been used by the Ger-

man and Russian directors who had so influenced the young Asquith, but it had not before been the basis of an entire film (coincidentally Kurosawa was doing something similar in *Rashomon*, q.v.). Asquith returned to Rattigan for **The Browning Version** (1951), which the dramatist himself extended to feature-length from his one-hour play, about a middle-aged schoolteacher whose career and marriage are simultaneously revealed as failures. The mechanics are apparent, but the piece does not lack pity, as when the wife's lover (Nigel Patrick) berates her for her treatment of her husband. 'I think he's been as deeply hurt as a human being can be.' (The similar dialogue in 'Death of a Salesman', across the Atlantic, reminds us that both compassion and the failed hero were late in coming to English-language modern drama.) As the dry, apparently insensitive teacher, Michael Redgrave is as imposing as was Eric Portman on the stage (and he was superb), but the casting of Jean Kent removes the original's poignancy, since this is no longer the question of an embittered middle-aged woman throwing herself at a younger man. Miss Kent is not only too young, but plays in conventional 'wicked lady' manner; and, as befits a Rank star, her clothes are more suitable for Ascot than for Open Day. Otherwise Asquith, sensitive, if often bumbling, is at his most professional.

The Rank Organisation had a number of box-office successes in the Fifties – though few in proportion to what emerged from its studios – yet it is difficult to find respectful reviews, let alone admiring ones. *The Kidnappers* (1953) is an exception, though its director, Philip Leacock, who began as a documentarist, did little else of note. Neil Paterson wrote it, from his own story, and it concerns two young boys sent to live with their fierce granpappy in the Nova Scotia of the 1900s. His dialogue for the adults was much less good than that for the children, who were played winningly by Jon Whiteley and Vincent Winter (Whiteley is the taller one).

He attempts only filmed theatre with **The Importance of Being Earnest** (1952), and in the opening sequence Redgrave and Michael Denison aim their dialogue at some non-existent balcony. Edith Evans's famous Lady Bracknell, perfect on the H.M.V. recording, is so given to over-emphasis that both accent and character are vulgar. Asquith simply will not leave Wilde's lines to the players but constantly cuts for reaction shots – so that Gwendolin and Cicely share their tea-party with the butler's raised eyebrows. However, there are two perfect pairings: Margaret Rutherford's Miss Prism, enchantingly scatter-brained, with Miles Malleson's urbane Chasuble; and Joan Greenwood's splendidly jaded Gwendolin with Dorothy Tutin's Cicely, superficially as 'simple, unspoiled' as Lady Bracknell considers Gwendolin, but in fact equally coquettish and grasping. In view of these four performances, this version might be said to be nearly definitive; interestingly, though by far the best of Wilde's plays, it was the last of them to reach the screen.

The Young Lovers (1954) concerns a cold war Romeo and Juliet – a U.S. embassy official (David Knight) who meets a Soviet bloc ambassador's daughter (Odile Versois) at Covent Garden: but with this premise established the screenplay has nowhere to go – one reason why Asquith's respectful handling is disappointing. It leaves *The Importance of Being Earnest* and *Genevieve* (q.v.) as the last interesting films from Rank for many a year.

Rank himself by now relinquished the running of the organisation to John Davis, an accountant, who decreed that profits were the first of his priorities – and that meant popcorn in the cinema foyers (those that were not closed down) and less films on the studio floor. The trouble with Davis was not that he made fewer films but that those that he sanctioned were formula pictures involving mediocrities both fore and aft of the camera. The Rank films of the Fifties were among the dreariest ever made, which is why some people in the industry do not have fond memories of Davis. The government was not much help. The discriminatory tax against American films was so clearly a mistake it was lifted after a few months – and those that flooded in from Hollywood did nothing to benefit the British industry when, as a result of American pressure, the forty-five per cent quota requirement (to show British films) was lowered to forty. The Entertainments' Tax was reduced slightly and to counter criticisms of the amount that the government took from the industry a system of loans and subsidies was established by which, as we have seen, £3 million went to Korda. Harold Wilson, then President of the Board of Trade, made that decision, refusing all other applicants – including del Guidice, who otherwise might have continued independently in films. In 1950 the quota was adjusted again, to the more sensible thirty per cent, and money was taken 'voluntarily' from exhibitors to go into a pool from which producers could borrow. All the while some independents worked on without attracting the headlines that accompanied the problems of Korda and Rank.

The most successful – by far – was Herbert Wilcox. He had been promoting his wife, Anna Neagle, with varying degrees of success for over a decade, till, in the later war years, there were no takers; then he found a story with the right ingredients to re-establish her, **I Live in Grosvenor Square** (1945), for which he found financing without recourse to Maurice Cowan, its author, who was to have been a partner on the production. It concerns an English girl (Neagle) torn between the British and U.S. armies as represented by Rex Harrison and Dean Jagger, and it was followed by **Piccadilly Incident** (1946), with Michael Wilding as the man Neagle loves and loses in the chaos of war. The British loved that and, equally unexpectedly, found they loved the stars, who were therefore teamed in a series of curious films (all with London place-names in their title) – snobbish, sentimental, cliché-ridden and, with one exception, inept. Since they were also old fashioned their popularity may have had something to do with the wish of audiences to escape from the realities of postwar Britain. Miss Neagle, like Joan Crawford, impresses by her very lack of talent: never as wholeheartedly absurd, she as ardently believes in her tinny stories, flashing her regal airs but unbending now and then to offer a little song or two. She wears elbow-length gloves and picture-hats, and on one memorable occasion was to be found with a large hat *and* flowers in her hair, sipping Cassis through a straw. Towards her Mr Wilding adopts a tone of light-hearted gallantry or downright frivolity, having decided that that is the only way to treat the lady: you cannot call it a technique, but he is the saving grace of these films – apart, that is, from some unintentionally funny lines, such as when Neagle says, 'Father, are you subject to apoplexy? – I'm thinking of going on the stage.'

The line occurs in **The Courtneys of Curzon Street** (1947), which repeats *Piccadilly Incident* in that the stars marry, are separated and reunited while she is singing to the troops, but the rest of it is so much like 'Cavalcade' that Coward might have sued for plagiarism had he felt so inclined. **Spring in Park Lane** (1948) is for many the only watchable Neagle film, and certainly the only Wilcox film of this period to be well received by the press. A trifle about a young milord posing as a footman, it has an unexpected gaiety, but when Wilcox remade it in Technicolor, with borrowings from his earlier *Irene* and now titled **Maytime in Mayfair** (1949), he substituted facetiousness for what had been occasional wit. He left Wilding aside for **Elizabeth of Ladymead** (1949), in which Neagle is discovered as a young aristocrat waiting for a returning husband in 1946: since Wilcox was so quick to borrow, one ought to have expected something from *The Best Years of Our Lives*, but instead she is whisked back to 1854, 1903 and 1919, when each soldier husband returns to find her a Different Woman. In 1919 she is a flapper, and when the husband finds Ladymead deserted, you know – with relief – that she will not sing to him; but she does not deny us a few sedate steps of ragtime.

Returning to her prewar urge to play the famous women of history, she had the title role in **The Lady with the Lamp** (1951). Lytton Strachey's study draws a comparison between the Florence Nightingale of popular conception and the lady of fact, concluding that the latter was the more interesting – which of course is not the one Neagle attempts. Warren Chetham Strode's script, from Reginald Berkeley's 1929 play, is reasonably accurate in outline; the film is too genteel to get to grips with the horrors of Scutari, but the mattwork is notably good; so is the supporting cast, which includes Wilding as Sydney Herbert. Sybil Thorndike (who played another famous nurse, Edith Cavell, for Wilcox in 1928, in *Dawn*) is Miss Nightingale's secretary at the end, and it is curious to see a good, aged actress playing scenes with a poor one pretending to be old.

In 1953, for the Coronation, Neagle had appeared in a stage enterprise entitled 'The Glorious Days', in which she had reprised her Nell Gwynn, Queen Victoria and various musical comedy actresses, cobbled together with other situations from her films, with songs. The press reception – Kenneth Tynan's review was one of the wittiest ever penned – did not prevent Wilcox from filming it, as **Lilacs in the Spring** (1954), with no screenplay credit and Errol Flynn imported to play the male lead, his Hollywood professionalism having appropriately disappeared en route. The result is a film for connoisseurs, a camp classic, but for Wilcox, it was no laughing matter – the first of a series of box-office disasters which were to lead to the bankruptcy courts. Other ageing filmmakers have been luckier: they were only employees, and merely faded away. But there was no public sympathy for Wilcox: lively and innovatory in the Twenties, he had since simply followed in the wake of others, borrowing and repeating, finally unaware of the changing taste of audiences.

He sought redemption with **The Beggar's Opera** (1953), but not without a degree of opportunism, since the star was to be Laurence Olivier and the director Peter Brook, the most discussed man of the theatre of his generation. Brook had not made a film before, and no one involved had any experience in filming eighteenth-century musicals. Whenever Macheath (Olivier) launches into action or a song it is clear that the sequence has been choreographed for maximum visual effect – but unfortunately the strain shows, and the high spirits intended are often dampened by Macheath's obvious doubts as to the life he is leading. The uncertain grasp of the material also extended to Dennis Cannan, who adapted John Gay's libretto, with additional dialogue by Christopher Fry. The score, arranged and conducted by Sir Arthur Bliss, is marvellously sung – and dubbed, except by Olivier and Stanley

Holloway, singing for themselves. The exceptional cast also includes Dorothy Tutin as Polly, Daphne Anderson as Lucy, George Devine and Mary Clare as the Peachums and Athene Seyler as Mrs Trapes. The decor by Wakhevitch uses primary colours against the drab grey of the prison walls and they positively glow. However, the film was dismissed by a number of critics as looking like an animated Yardley's perfume ad and its faults stressed – so that what is withal a hugely entertaining film became a total failure; the industry, uneasy with such 'highbrow' subjects, sent *enfant terrible* Brook back to the theatre and returned to its inane light comedies and war films.

Associated British, apart from backing Wilcox's first two 'London' films, had been more or less quiescent, its few A-pictures falling by the wayside. Production was stepped up after the success of **My Brother Jonathan** (1948), produced by Warwick Ward, the former actor, and directed by Harold French from Francis Brett Young's 1928 saga about the trials and tribulations of a young doctor. It has a homely British quality, and were it possible to believe in it for an instant it might make us fonder of qualities such as self-sacrifice and the will to fight hypocrisy as personified by Michael Denison – whose sincerity certainly benefits the film. The company made a bid to become a major force in film-making with **The Dancing Years** (1950), directed by French (to his admitted shame), a Technicolor version of one of Ivor Novello's Viennesy stage musicals. In Novello's own role, Dennis Price's embarrassment communicates itself to the audience – though any members persevering will find pleasures not dissimilar to those of *Lilacs in the Spring*. Associated British did better commercially with **Angels One Five** (1952), a title bearing tones of *Twelve O'Clock High* and set on an airfield existing in a similar vacuum. If it says little about the Battle of Britain, its portrait of the R.A.F. is less risible than usual, and the direction by George More O'Ferrall has a certain energy.

With **The Queen of Spades** (1949) Associated British achieved a critical success. The film's instigator was the playwright Rodney Ackland, who hoped to direct, but he received only a co-writing credit in the end and Thorold Dickinson

directed. As designed by Oliver Messel, photographed by Otto Heller and finely cut, it is a handsome film, but it is also boring. Much of the point of Pushkin's tale is lost, since we are shown matters which he only implied: Herman stakes his all on either a ghost or a figment of his imagination – it matters not, since he is mad: but he does not become mad in this film. In that role, Anton Walbrook is miscast, and in a rubber mask Edith Evans is uninteresting as the old countess.

For Associated British J. B. Priestley contributed a rare original screenplay, **Last Holiday** (1950), but it went unnoticed, on the assumption – thus was the cinema regarded – that if he had considered the material important he would have made a novel or a play from it. This is a typical piece, overly concerned with the 'little man' (Alec Guinness) and convinced that all would be right in this world if the running of it were left to him: in this case the man has a fatal illness which gives him new courage to help his fellow holiday-makers. They are variously eccentric, or conventional types, but Priestley sees them in the round, so that when they co-operate to get dinner we may smile at this ingenuous Utopian view, but we may also find it attractive. As directed by Henry Cass, Kay Walsh brings memorable warmth to the role of the caretaker, and Guinness vaults easily from timidity to life-and-soul of the party.

Cass also directed **Young Wives' Tale** (1951), about two couples sharing because of the housing shortage. The situation is hardly original, but it has Audrey Hepburn in one of her first roles, Athene Seyler as the most indulgent of nannies, and Joan Greenwood, who, recognising the material as rightfully hers, floats as confidently through it as she had surely done on stage. She creates her own world, as did Keaton and Beatrice Lillie, a world in which her fantasies sustain her as her good intentions are misunderstood, her dinners burn and her nannies are always taking umbrage. **Laughter in Paradise** (1951) also features two players who could enrich any comic situation: Alistair Sim, as a self-effacing writer who publishes lurid fiction under several pseudonyms, and Joyce Grenfell, as his gawky naval fiancée. He is one of a number of heirs required to do uncongenial jobs before they can inherit a fortune: the opening sequence is reminiscent of *If I Had a Million*, but the jokes that follow are strictly British, even if ordered by an Italian, Mario Zampi, who directed several British comedies with similarly strong basic situations. In Britain this was the year's most popular film.

British National offered one film of interest among its entertainments for middle-aged ladies, **No Room at the Inn** (1948), directed by Daniel Birt from a screenplay by Ivan Foxwell (who produced) and Dylan Thomas, not then earning much from his poetry. Since Joan Temple's play about evacuees was seriously regarded, it should be noted that the film is like a dark, charcoal version of 'Hansel and Gretel' – preposterous, yet extraordinarily vivid. There were indeed people like Mrs Voray (Freda Jackson), a hard-drinking good time girl who accepts a houseful of kids for the money they brought in. The core of the story concerns the refined little girl who might eventually be corrupted by her or by her other charges – and since the role is priggishly played it is hard to sympathise; yet one experiences a shock, if cheaply motivated, when the child's father proves less interested in her complaints than in Mrs Voray's sexual advances. Miss Jackson at times finds a sense of humour in this woman, but in rendering her monstrous almost chews the scenery; her neighbour, a gin-soaked harridan as grasping as any in Dickens, is played by Hermione Baddeley, who, as ever in the business of overplaying, spurts home an easy winner.

Renown, hitherto best known for its sponsorship of the Old Mother Riley comedies, made three versions of classic novels. The first, **Tom Brown's Schooldays** (1951) was filmed mainly *in situ*, at Rugby, but the director, Gordon Parry, mismanages the scenes of bullying by making them both unpleasant and trivial; he gets a good shot from Robert Newton as Dr Arnold. Still, I suspect the film was made mainly to exploit the prepubescent charms of John Howard Davies, who had been David Lean's Oliver Twist. Both **Scrooge** (1951), directed by Brian Desmond Hurst, and **The Pickwick Papers** (1952), directed by Noel Langley – who had a hand in the screenplay of all three films – only serve to recall the superiority of Lean's Dickens films. As Scrooge Alistair Sim sets his face into a scowl, resembling nothing but a nice man with a bilious attack. Nor do the members of the Pickwick Club – James Hayter as Mr Pickwick, Nigel Patrick as Mr Jingle, James Donald as Mr Winkle – leave much impression; but headed by Kathleen Harrison as Miss Wardle, the Pickwick ladies come off somewhat better: Miss Grenfell as Mrs Leo Hunter, Miss Baddeley as Mrs Bardell, Athene Seyler as Miss Witherfield and Hermione Gingold as Miss Tomkins.

Just about everybody is in **The Magic Box** (1951), the industry's collaborative effort to celebrate the Festival of Britain. Ronald Neame produced, John Boulting directed, and Eric Ambler wrote it, immediately soothing a contentious matter by claiming in the preface that its hero, William Friese-Greene, is but 'one of the inventors of cinematography'. Robert Donat plays Friese-Greene, and like the film is likeable without having much fire; his wives are Maria Schell, smiling through her tears, and Margaret Johnston. The sixty or so stars are listed only at the end; the one everyone remembers is Olivier, who turned down the lead but accepted the plum among the other roles – that of the Holborn policeman who was the first in the kingdom to see moving pictures.

By this time the American companies had begun to return to Britain. 20th Century-Fox had honorably led the way as early as 1946 with *Meet Me at Dawn*, with two second-rank stars, William Eythe, an American, and Hazel Court, a Britisher, but it was not a success. During its quarrel with the British government, Hollywood's expressed desire to help the British industry resulted in no more than a handful of films, but as audiences everywhere began to shrink, if slightly, by the end of the decade it was realised that filming in Europe was cheaper – and British technicians spoke English.

Before that Warner Bros. released **They Made Me a Fugitive** (1947), having retitled it – the original novel was called 'A Convict Has Escaped' – to remind audiences of their old movies (for the U.S. they renamed it *I Became a Criminal*). It was claimed to be Britain's first gangster film, since the crooks in prewar movies were usually forgers or race-track 'fixers'; but during the War, and hardened by it, the

Production in Austerity Britain

black market attracted the criminal element. The story is about a disaffected R.A.F. type (Trevor Howard) who joins a black-market operation; but the film is neither a realistic portrait of the London underworld nor a good thriller, and the direction by Cavalcanti is lumberingly slow, making the American-type wisecracks in Noel Langley's script even worse.

Night and the City (1950) attempts the same tack, its Soho seen by an American writer, Jo Eisinger – adapting a novel by Gerald Kersh – and an American director, Jules Dassin. Dassin moved about town for locations, but his is merely a film about ugly people – a club boss (Francis L. Sullivan), his wife (Googie Withers), and a dreary little con (Richard Widmark). There is also Gene Tierney, doing little, but included for the sake of the U.S. box office. The producer was 20th Century-Fox, the most active of the major studios in Britain, sending over a number of important directors and stars: among them was Irene Dunne, and as Queen Victoria, being phlegmatic with her cheeks stuffed with cotton wool, she is not to be believed in **The Mudlark** (1950), directed by Jean Negulesco. And it is a shock to find James Stewart living in a council house in **No Highway** (1951), even if he is the archetypal absent-minded scientist and described as having lived in Britain for some years. This version of Nevil Shute's novel was directed by Henry Koster, and it was thought to be a mature film because Stewart shows no romantic interest in either airhostess Glynis Johns or fellow passenger Marlene Dietrich (who, facing certain death when she hears their plane has metal fatigue, is as unbelievable as Stewart). Another Fox miscalculation is **The Black Rose** (1950), in which two Saxons (Tyrone Power, Jack Hawkins) set out on the road to Cathay and, like Hope and Crosby, acquire a girl, Cecile Aubrey. Aware that audiences had grown up since mindless swashbucklers like *The Mark of Zorro*, Fox offered a real historical background, some serious implication, e.g. racial intolerance, and numerous locations – among which the director, Henry Hathaway, was overwhelmed.

It was the American acceptance of Disney's **Treasure Island** (1950) which warmed the Hollywood companies to the British studios. Disney was using blocked funds, but it made sense to him to make a British classic with British players. This was his first wholly live action film, directed by Byron Haskin, and it offered the two most familiar ingredients of his cartoons, incident and visual beauty. Alas, today, the painted backcloths are all too visible; and an otherwise good cast starts horrendously with Robert Newton overacting as Long John Silver, and cutely with American Bobby Driscoll as Jim Hawkins. **The Sword and the Rose** (1953) is a Disney remake of *When Knighthood Was in Flower*, with Glynis Johns in Marion Davies's old role of that playful princess, Mary Tudor, who was forced to marry the aged Louis XII by her brother, Henry VIII – in which role James Robertson Justice roars and winks to the point of alienation. The hapless hero, Richard Todd, was also cast in the title role of **Rob Roy** (1953), with the same co-stars, but Disney this time made amends – for at least this is a stirring version of Sir Walter Scott's novel as directed by Harold French.

M-G-M also had a success with its version of Scott, **Ivanhoe** (1952), scripted by Noel Langley and directed by Richard Thorpe, with Robert Taylor uneasy in the title role. The performance by Elizabeth Taylor is justly famous, but, as Rowena, Joan Fontaine is almost as bad – and hers is the more serious fault, for she could act when she tried. **Never Let Me Go** (1953) stars the other ageing Metro idol, Clark Gable, as an American correspondent in Moscow who marries a Russian dancer (Gene Tierney), an unimaginative idea which under Delmer Daves's direction amounts to little. Of the cast only Kenneth More, as Gable's English confrère, is able to get away with the anti-Russian sentiments.

Warners used their frozen funds for **The Hasty Heart** (1949), though in Britain it was released as a production of Associated British, a partially owned subsidiary. It was a splendid example, at least commercially, of Anglo-American harmony. The original Broadway play was by an American, John Patrick, who had based it on his wartime experiences with a British ambulance unit. Warners sent over a director, Vincent Sherman, and a writer, Ranald MacDougall, both adept at handling superior soap opera, which this is; they were accompanied by Patricia Neal, to play a Canadian nursing sister, and Ronald Reagan, to play 'Yank' – both inmates of a British field hospital in Burma. A relatively-unknown British actor, Richard Todd, played superbly the leading role, that of an arrogant and embittered young Scots corporal who does not know that he is dying. He gets the backs up of the men in his ward, and since the piece concerns the breakdown of mutual hostility it should be pointed out that it only does so by ignoring or transgressing virtually every rule known to any Medical Corps in any army; but the scene in which the black African with no English shows that he likes the Scot provided a comforting message to the postwar world.

Bette Davis crossed the Atlantic for the British-backed **Another Man's Poison** (1951), though insisting on an American director, Irving Rapper. With flaring nostrils, those wide eyes widening, a cigarette in one hand and a riding-crop in the other, she strides about in jodhpurs, commits double murder, tries to send a man to his death in a jeep without brakes, steals her secretary's boyfriend, and has a fixation on a horse called Fury. Incredulity sets in within a minute of the credits. You might feel similarly about **Pandora and the Flying Dutchman** (1951), produced, written and directed by Albert Lewin, apparently under the influence of 'Omar Khayam', though one might probably be grateful to him for bringing Ava Gardner with him, to be as lovingly photographed by Jack Cardiff in Technicolor as the Spanish locations. She is Pandora, a nightclub singer; the spirit who loves her is a glowering James Mason.

Hollywood's tentative and self-interested foray into the British cinema did not stem the overall decline in quality, yet as the decade turned the films from Ealing Studios continued to improve – as they needed to, from their dreadful but well-meaning productions of the war years. The War had given Michael Balcon's company a sense of direction. Until then he had had no policy such as he had had as head of production at Gaumont-British, but by 1945 Ealing consisted of a dedicated group identifying itself with its native hearth. The lessons of documentary had been learned, and are charmingly pleasant in a slight tale of life on the barges, **Painted Boats** (1945), directed by Charles Crichton, and made as a supporting feature. Nevertheless there remained for some years a fallacy at Ealing that good films resulted from taking the camera out into the open, preferably the streets of the East End: it was only by studying Hollywood that Ealing realised that a strong story was also needed.

Eschewing for the moment the sunny fields and dark satanic mills, the studio came up with **Dead of Night** (1945), a compilation in the manner of Julien Duvivier's *Flesh and Fantasy*. The directors were Crichton, Cavalcanti, Basil Dearden and Robert Hamer (1911–63), working from a number of writers including H. G. Wells and E. F. Benson. The most truly macabre is the tale of the ventriloquist's dummy who takes over his master (Michael Redgrave), but for those who have seen *The Great Gabbo* it is as predictable as the rest. One sequence recalls *Friday the Thirteenth*, which Balcon had produced, and he ordered a revamp of that, **Train of Events** (1949), in which four assorted flashbacks explain why these people are travelling on this particular train; but as directed by Dearden, Crichton and Sidney Cole they make negligible entertainment.

For the moment Ealing stayed with artificial drama, though **Pink String and Sealing Wax** (1945), based on a popular stage play, has more on its mind than the murder at its centre. Hamer, directing, intended a compendium of Victoriana – the gin-palace, the heavy father, concerts on the pier. The dramatic construction is weak, and the sets, though attractive, are very obviously sets. Accordingly Charles Frend manages slightly better another period piece with the same actress, Googie Withers, **The Loves of Joanna Godden** (1947), skilfully photographed on the Romney Marshes. Miss Withers plays a tough lady farmer, and the film's chief flaw – which is not the fault of the actress – is that by failing to communicate her feeling for her land, sheep or men, the story creeps into inertia. Notwithstanding that the film is set in Edwardian England, it does reflect the fact that women could play a more important role than hitherto in British society. It has been suggested that this may also be found in the Gainsborough melodramas, but the roles played

Production in Austerity Britain

by Margaret Lockwood and Phyllis Calvert are basically imitations of those played by Hollywood's important female stars – and apart from Gracie Fields the British had not before had any popular lady movie stars. Miss Withers's following was not in the same league; and as their films prove, the talents at Ealing were more alive to contemporary feeling than those at Gainsborough.

Nicholas Nickleby (1947) had the misfortune to be released while Lean's *Great Expectations* was fresh in the memory; it is not one of Ealing's successes. John Dighton's screenplay brought some order to the long and disorganised plot, and Michael Relph's decor is impeccable. But Cavalcanti's direction often makes the distinguished cast look awkward – even Cedric Hardwicke as Ralph Nickleby and Stanley Holloway as Mr Crummles. As Nicholas and Kate Nickleby, Derek Bond and Sally Ann Howes are well cast, being players without discernible personalities: but that does not help the film at all.

Turning to a contemporary subject, in fact the War, **The Captive Heart** (1946) followed the adventures of some P.O.W.s in Germany and their homecoming: the actual scenes of their ship docking, a sequence not (as far as I know) duplicated in any other fiction film of the time, is very moving. The central character is a Czech (Michael Redgrave) who has successfully till now impersonated a British officer –

and though the situation is *ersatz* it i[s] nicely directed by Basil Dearden. The other P.O.W.s are, however, strictly from stock: they include Basil Radford, Mervyn Johns, Jimmy Hanley, Gordon Jackson (as a sensitive young Scot afraid that his fiancée will not want him now that he is blinded, cf. *The Best Years of Our Lives*) and Jack Warner (as a Joe Blunt Cockney). These particular actors appeared so often in Ealing films as to suggest they represented certain kinds of Britishness to Balcon, though a doubt persists that Ealing ever cared much for either performers or the characters necessary to its stories.

That Warner's reassuring middle-aged persona turns out to be a traitor in **Against the Wind** (1948) indicates that the film was meant to be more honest than others on the work of Resistance fighters and those who were parachuted into Europe to help them. But the other characters, who include a Belgian woman (Simone Signoret) and a partisan priest (Robert Beatty) are conventional, and their adventures are pallid beside *Bataille du Rail*, though the film has aspirations in that direction. Crichton directed, from a screenplay by T. E. B. Clarke (q.v.), who was so important in the development of Ealing comedy.

'Would *you* take Frieda into your home?' asked the advertisements for **Frieda** (1947), directed by Dearden from a West End play. It concerns an ex-officer (David Farrar), his German war bride (Mai Zetterling), and the various reactions to this viper in the nest. His sister (Glynis Johns), who lost her husband in the War, is compassionate; his aunt (Flora Robson), about to stand for parliament, is a kind woman, but uncertain whether there is anything in the German character to be kind about – a view apparently confirmed when Frieda's Nazi brother (Albert Lieven) turns up, to send Frieda rushing down to the weir like Rebecca in 'Rosmersholm'. Till then the film is serious; and audiences approved of the scene where Frieda insists on watching the newsreels of the Nazi concentration camps in order to share German guilt.

Despite its topicality, the film, with its small-town setting, fails to reflect the austere Britain of Sir Stafford Cripps, the Chancellor of the Exchequer. That can be found in no film of the period – in the way that *Millions Like Us* reflects wartime Britain – but **It Always Rains on Sunday**

(1947) takes us back to the time when Dad put on three-piece suit and watch-chain to go to the pub on Sunday and a bunch of daffs could be bought for half-a-crown. Young men could not take girls to their rooms, records spun at 78 r.p.m. and, more germane to the plot, petty spivs operated in the arcades and dance-halls of Bethnal Green. They are less East Enders than West End actors pretending, and there are occasional notes of archness between the opening (raindrops at dawn near the railway-arch) and the hackneyed climax (a chase at night through the railway yard). The virtues include Miss Withers, as a married woman whose former lover (John McCallum), a convict on the run, wants to hide in the air-raid shelter, now a tool-shed, and the dialogue, adapted from Arthur La Berne's novel by Angus Mac-Phail, Henry Cornelius and Hamer, whose direction has gusto. As with *Dead of Night* and *The Captive Heart* the notices were warm, and it was, in addition, Ealing's first great popular success.

All the same it is not to be compared to *The Street with No Name*, and it was the 20th Century-Fox films of that school which taught Ealing much about filming in the streets. London is splendidly used in **The Blue Lamp** (1950), a tribute to the Metropolitan police, directed by Basil Dearden. It was enormously popular, but it is difficult now to say whether it was once a good film. There is a scene in which a couple quarrel about a film they have just seen, and he says that the only laugh he had was when the baby died: and some of us may feel that way about the scene in which the young P.C. (Jimmy Hanley) has to inform a stoic police wife of the murder of her husband (Jack Warner). For like most Ealing films, this one insists on whimsical, unsentimental niceness. All the bobbies on display are cheerful and understanding, with a quip for a small boy, a helping hand for an old lady, and their choir carols 'Nymphs and Shepherds'. The film exudes moral fervour, but is closer in tone to *Rebecca of Sunnybrook Farm* than *The French Connection* (q.v.) – or, to take, more suitably, a contemporary, *The Asphalt Jungle*.

The same troubles beset **The Cruel Sea** (1953). Ealing's prestige was such by this time that Rank, as distributor, was happy to find the huge financing needed for the rights to Nicholas Montserrat's whopping bestseller. During the period of austerity and the junketings of the Festival of Britain the War had been partly forgotten, but Montserrat's book began a nostalgia for the War years, as if it were time to take stock. That did not include the brothel scenes, missing from the film, though a vital element in the book's success, and Eric Ambler's screenplay turned personal reminiscence into the clichés of the wartime movies – so that one officer has a flighty, faithless wife and another a very nice one, who accompanies him for the inevitable picnic on the downs. As directed by Charles Frend, the characters are complacent and bloodless, as might have been surmised from Frend's earlier study in British heroism, **Scott of the Antarctic** (1948). The screenplay by Ivor Montagu and Walter Meade refuses to acknowledge that Scott's expedition was at best foolhardy and mismanaged, and it chauvinistically plays down the fact that Amundsen had beaten Scott to the Pole. Its dispassionate tone is demonstrated in the shots of feet tramping in the snow, offered in lieu of any explanation of how the men coped; and even in the location shots there is no steam on their breath (to show this in his run-of-the-mill *Dirigible*, Capra caused the actors to suck dry ice – and one of them lost three teeth and part of his jaw). As Scott, John Mills is just another kindly C.O., his motives unexplained, while Christmas in the Antarctic turns out to be just like Christmas in a P.O.W. camp in any British P.O.W. movie; nor is there the slightest sense of adventure.

It was made in Technicolor, as was **Saraband for Dead Lovers** (1948), and the simultaneous release of these two expensive productions was intended to demonstrate that Balcon now considered Ealing a studio of world class. *Saraband*, like Cineguild's earlier *Blanche Fury* – also with Stewart Granger – was yet another attempt to demonstrate to Gainsborough that at least one British studio could treat an historical subject with both flair and accuracy. The source was Helen Simpson's novel on the amours and intrigues of the Hanoverian court, and as directed by Basil Dearden it was with some justice critically trounced.

It is nevertheless more watchable than Ealing's three 'Commonwealth' adventures, the first of which, **The Over-**

landers (1946), was much praised. Balcon and Harry Watt had discussed a film paying tribute to Australia's war effort, and Watt pointed out that reconstructed documentaries had been rendered obsolete by the several features composed of newsreel footage, such as *Desert Victory*. He was also struck by the fact that that 'huge, exciting, hard country' had not been used by filmmakers, and his determination to utilise it himself was strengthened when an official of the Ministry of Information mentioned an incident which could provide the basis for a film combining fact and fiction in equal measure – specifically, the driving of 100,000 head of cattle across the country in 1942. Unfortunately, Watt and his writers deal with this situation only in thundering cliché. Among others, Richard Winnington had reservations, but he was excited about the prospect of the Commonwealth being used as Hollywood had used the great spaces of the American West. So was a South African conglomerate, which approached Ealing for a similar film on Africa. After a preliminary sortie, Watt suggested a film based on the work of the Kenyan conservationist, Mervyn Cowie. Three writers are credited with the script of **Where No Vultures Fly** (1951), but their ideas on conservation are on the level of a vapid Shaftesbury Avenue thriller. It was chosen for the annual Royal Film Performance – an institution about to fall into disrepute, due to the kind of dish the industry saw fit to set before the King – and was popular enough to necessitate a sequel, even more stilted, **West of Zanzibar** (1953). Neither is in the same league as the M-G-M *King Solomon's Mines*, which they hoped to emulate.

The actors concerned, not in the first place of the highest quality, clearly received little help, and a study of all three films does nothing to solve the mystery of why Watt was considered one of Britain's leading directors. A similar enigma surrounds Thorold Dickinson, despite his apparent intelligence and love of the medium. The best of his handful of films is **Secret People** (1952), though by an odd circumstance it shattered his reputation. Simultaneous with the premiere there was published a book about the production, 'Making a Film', written by Lindsay Anderson with such admiration that the critics lost their balance – a view at least

tenable after a re-reading of the reviews, which are negative and almost totally untrustworthy. For instance, Valentina Cortese's performance, far below her best work, was much praised, while most complained that the film was incomprehensible – which, for all its faults, it is not. Gavin Lambert's review in *Sight and Sound* speaks constantly of 'style' – which is wholly lacking, despite some action sequences so well achieved that they make up for the gaucheness elsewhere. The subject is terrorism, as practised in London by some foreigners hoping to assassinate a Fascist dictator, and Dickinson's script (written with Wolfgang Wilhelm from his own idea) says unequivocally that those who resort to violence, from whatever motives, are thugs. Yet Winnington thought the message only 'tentative'; he is on surer ground concluding that since the innocent (Cortese) caught up in the scheming is in no sense politically active the film had no point, and 'Sir Michael Balcon was much perturbed over this vital flaw.' In the final analysis this is a fair attempt at a political thriller, less tense than Hitchcock's not dissimilar *Sabotage*, but more mature.

Significantly, Dickinson was the only outside director invited to work at Ealing, whose films in general made little out of much. Balcon's team approached interesting ideas in a prissy, pussyfooting and peculiarly British way. **Lease of Life** (1954) wears its Englishness like a halo. It is a study of a country parson (Robert Donat), directed by Frend from a screenplay by Eric Ambler, and it has points to make on ecclesiastical promotion, mortality, the interdependence of a middle-aged couple – even village busy-bodies. Donat plays with the correct blend of humility and theatricality; the film, though sincere and likeable, suffers from a lack of guts. Ealing's basic trouble was that it made its films by committee. Old hand Balcon encouraged his bright young men to throw out ideas, and they hammered at them until all individuality had gone. To Balcon the image of the studio was more important than the ideas of any particular filmmaker, and as a result it is impossible to distinguish the work of one Ealing director from another.

That was exactly what was intended. It was not a writer's studio either, as we may see by examining the Ealing films written by Jack Whittingham (b. 1910), whose previous work, including (especially) *The Dancing Years*, was of little account. His first film for Ealing was no better – **Cage of Gold** (1950), with which Balcon hoped to please Mr Rank, since it was a vehicle for Jean Simmons, playing a girl caught between a respectable doctor (James Donald) and a rotter (David Farrar), the usual former R.A.F. officer adrift in the post-war world. Dearden directed, clearly depressed by the screenplay, so it is a surprise to find that **Pool of London** (1951), made by the same team, is one of the most successful of all Ealing pictures. (The writer John Eldridge conceived the idea and was working on the script with T.E.B. Clarke, but Clarke found himself handling the seemingly obligatory 'criminal element' as a joke. His ideas were developed into *The Lavender Hill Mob*, q.v., and he was replaced by Whittingham.) It follows, in the manner of *Grand Hotel*, some merchant seamen during one summer weekend, especially the quick-talking, philandering Dan (Bonar Colleano) and his Jamaican chum, Johnny (Earl Cameron): the latter falls in love with a cinema cashier (Susan Shaw), quite discreetly, but this is nevertheless the first inter-racial romance in an English-speaking film.* The 'crime' ranges from the smuggling of nylons to a diamond heist; and the piece is not without coincidence. But I know no more vivid portrait of London – its pubs, its trams (soon to be done away with, as someone says), its music halls (one grand and one seedy) and the silent empty streets of the City and Dockland.

A similar formula is applied to probation officers in **I Believe in You** (1952), directed by Dearden and written by him, Whittingham, Nicholas Phipps and Michael Relph, who also produced. Relph was one of the stalwarts of Ealing, as art director, Dearden's usual producer and in the case of this film son of the actor George Relph, who gives a touching performance alongside Celia Johnson, Godfrey Tearle and Cecil Parker as the other probation officers. The piece is conventional both on their dedication and the delinquency of their charges. **The Divided Heart** (1954) is even more high-minded, and as modest in conception as it is lofty in aim, i.e. it

denounces war with particular attention to the havoc it wreaks on the innocent – to whom it refuses a happy ending. Whittingham's story and screenplay, based on an actual event, concern a war orphan (Michel Ray) whose foster parents, a Bavarian couple, discover that a Slovene woman (Yvonne Mitchell) has applied to the Allied High Commission for custody · in the certainty that he is her son. By concentrating on the court case the film hopes it avoids sentiment; but as directed by Charles Crichton it is sometimes arch and occasionally plodding.

Its inspiration is obviously *The Search*, just as there are echoes of *Ladri di Biciclette* in **Hunted** (1952) in the relationship of a murderer (Dirk Bogarde) on the run and unwanted small boy (Jon Whiteley). Crichton and Whittingham balance that relationship with the 'chase' element, and tug neatly at our emotions when the boy – the performance is as worthwhile as any in movies – recites 'The Owl and the Pussycat'. C. A. Lejeune said, 'This is a film with a great deal of heart for its small size, and I think it should command affection.' It also commands respect, but it was not made for Ealing, since the crowded production schedule would not permit it; it was made by one of Rank's production companies. But it is of the Ealing level, workmanlike and well-meaning. Only two of Ealing's directors made considerable films elsewhere, Henry Cornelius with *Genevieve* (q.v.) and Alexander Mackendrick with *Sweet Smell of Success* (q.v.). Balcon was paternal and protective: the outside world was very cold.

The Ealing comedies reflect this, being insular, if in the best sense, with a sharp eye for the foibles of the British – even if they are reduced to such stock types as plucky Londoners and cunning country-folk. The scripts are *gemütlich*, but are, in general, inventively developed. The films are the British cinema's most original and influential body of work – too influential, which is why they revive variably. The first of them, **Hue and Cry** (1947), was less a comedy than a boys' adventure with laughs, an unusual film to make in the climate of British cinema at the time: it cost little, and had it failed it could have been expected to recoup its cost at children's Saturday matinees. Crichton directed and the script by T. E. B. Clarke (b. 1907), by

---

*Always excepting, that is, the dusky maidens who enslaved white men in such jungle melodramas as *White Cargo*.

The Ealing comedies came as a tonic to austerity Britain – and indeed the world, notably finding a new audience for British films in the U.S. The cuter, more homely ones were so much copied that some of them seem dated today, leaving as the peak *Kind Hearts and Coronets*, a stylish black comedy perhaps too good to be imitated – a proposed remake in 1976 was cancelled after a storm of protests. Almost certainly they could not have found players to match the originals, including Joan Greenwood and Dennis Price.

far the most individual of Ealing's writers, started by reworking 'Emil und die Detektive' against London's blitzed buildings: a gang of Cockney kids sets out to trap some black marketeers, with a timid writer (Alistair Sim) of blood-and-thunder stories caught between them. Encouraged by the film's reception, Balcon initiated work on three more comedies rooted in national and regional life, and they each opened in London a week apart: **Passport to Pimlico** (1949), directed by Cornelius from an original screenplay by Clarke; **Whisky Galore!** (1949), directed by Alexander Mackendrick (b. 1912), an American-born former scriptwriter for the company, from a screenplay by Angus MacPhail and Compton Mackenzie, from the latter's novel; and **Kind Hearts and Coronets** (1949), directed by Robert Hamer, and written by him and John Dighton from an Edwardian novel by Roy Horniman.

It is significant that both MacPhail and Dighton had worked on scripts for George Formby and Will Hay, and *Passport to Pimlico* takes its basic idea from *Look Up and Laugh*, which Gracie Fields had made for A.T.P., Ealing's predecessor. Updated, it provides a bombsite and an old charter to prove that one area of London belonged to Burgundy – a fact seized on by its inhabi-

tants, anxious to be free of ration books and other restrictions imposed since 1939. The spirit of the blitz prevails: 'It's because we are English that we're sticking to our rights to be Burgundians' used to get the biggest laugh. For later audiences, perhaps, the fun has faded – bureaucratic bunglers, lend-lease parcels, postwar spivdom; but it remains a sweet film, winningly performed by everyone, from Stanley Holloway (owner of the local hardware store) and Margaret Rutherford (the historian authenticating the charter) downwards. On the other hand, *Whisky Galore!* wastes Joan Greenwood, the most endearing of English comediennes. The film itself is an under-nourished account of a shipwrecked cargo of whisky which disappears, and the efforts of the red-tapebound authorities to prise it from the locals. As *Tight Little Island*, it was a particularly big hit in the U.S., presumably with those who find crafty Highlanders hilarious in themselves.

Kind Hearts and Coronets is the best of the Ealing batch, the only one with a claim to greatness. I can only think of one movie like it – Carné's *Drôle de Drame*, and that, in contrast, is less an ironic comedy than farce. Guitry used irony and irreverence towards the matters handled here, families and murder, but nothing in British cinema prepares us for it except perhaps *On Approval*; Lonsdale and his peers might have created its hero – flippant, imperturbable, unable to speak except in epigrams. Every other line has a double meaning, whether known to its speaker or not, and though a certain elegance is attained, the visual style is not always of an equivalent standard; nevertheless after several viewings the film manages to surprise, and it keeps before us a cast of characters who, when they are not sublimely foolish, are selfish, self-centred and heartless. As the young man who murders the family which stands between him and a dukedom, Dennis Price is good enough to make one regret that his screen career gave him no other similar chance; Alec Guinness, in a celebrated tour-de-force, is several members of the family; and Miss Greenwood and Valerie Hobson are their women, a match of scheming cupidity and condescending stupidity.

Ealing did not try to duplicate *Kind Hearts and Coronets*, but the chorus of praise for all three films resulted in **A Run for Your Money** (1949) and **The Magnet** (1950), where the incipient larkiness and cuteness of *Passport to Pimlico* and *Whisky Galore!* have been somewhat extended. The regional interest pertains to Wales and Liverpool respectively, and though both films are more modest and less amusing, they are, as directed by Charles Frend, immensely likeable. *A Run for Your Money* follows two Welsh miners up for the international rugby match at Twickenham, and it has that Ealing device of most of the cast haring over most of London. It has excellent contrasting performances by Donald Houston, desperately wide-eyed as one of the miners, and Guinness, as the gardening correspondent reluctantly accompanying him, a meek man whose assertiveness is limited to his moustache. The best scene involves Joyce Grenfell as an excruciatingly gauche dressmaker, and it is too good to be spoilt by Moira Lister, playing her usual role of a gold-digger with all the subtlety of a ten ton truck. *The Magnet* concerns a small boy (William Fox, who changed his Christian name to James as a grown-up actor) who covets a magnet belonging to an even smaller boy, and who, having deceived to get it, is ashamed, and unable to dispose of it as he hopes. T. E. B. Clarke wrote it, and the film is one of the best ever made for children.

Clarke's most celebrated script, for **The Lavender Hill Mob** (1951), directed by Crichton, starts with a plan to rob the Bank of England by a staid, humble bank clerk (Guinness), but he can think of no way to hide the bullion till a manufacturer (Stanley Holloway) of geegaws comes to live in the same boarding house . . . Alas, the film is now almost threadbare. Making mugs of the police in comic chases goes honourably back to the Keystone Cops; but although the ploy had been intermittently used it became a cliché with this film. So did the situation of Cockney criminals and/or lovable eccentrics planning and executing a heist: no other Ealing comedy was as much copied.

For that reason it revives less well than **The Man in the White Suit** (1951), directed by Mackendrick, in which Guinness amused us at about the same time. It is no longer particularly funny, but alone of the Ealing comedies it remains relevant (if any of them were) – for it is a comedy of

the boardroom, and like *The Solid Gold Cadillac* (q.v.) it is one of the few films to stray in that direction. The prospect of an everlasting dirt-free fabric might then have been a gleam in a boffin's eye – which may be why the single-mindedness of Guinness, as its inventor, is still so effective. The spectacle of the manufacturers uniting to suppress the cloth is revealing, and the concern of the workers about redundancy a real one. The screenplay by Dighton and Roger Macdougall, from an unproduced play by the latter, rightly withholds from both sides the fact that they want the same outcome: and if in other ways it is careless (as good American comedies never were) it juggles its complications inventively.

Though it is easy in retrospect to pinpoint weaknesses in all these films, the first time contemporary critics did so was with **The Titfield Thunderbolt** (1953). Britons at the time were chuckling over Emmett's cartoons of whimsical railways in *Punch*, and since these were dedicated to the notion that machines were quaint a union was inevitable, since the Ealing comedies felt the same way about people. Clarke's screenplay repeated the view of *Passport to Pimlico*, that when the British are up against it they lose their reserve and with cheery optimism team together in opposition. In this case, faced with the closing of a branch line, they combine to operate a railway – led by the vicar (George Relph), delighted to indulge his life-long passion for steam-engines. There are felicitous incidents and, this time, Technicolor, but the qualities peculiar to Ealing comedy are used without restraint. These are not evident in **The Love Lottery** (1954), also directed by Crichton, though the idea is typical: a movie star (David Niven) is offered as first prize in a lottery. A Hollywood writer, Harry Kurnitz, was brought in to polish up a script attempting satire on big business and movie stardom (in particular the 'sexy Rexy' aspect attached to Rex Harrison's image): together with the international star name (Niven) and exotic locations (the Italian lakes) this represents the company's one excursion into mainstream comedy, and it is a disaster.

The participation of Americans in *The 'Maggie'* (q.v.), on release simultaneously, was essential, but meanwhile American interest was helping to destroy Ealing. The popularity in the U.S. of the comedies,

Production in Austerity Britain

Genevieve was not strictly speaking an Ealing comedy, but the director, Henry Cornelius, had worked for the studio, and the screenwriter, William Rose, would subsequently do so. Since its four leading-players were little known, there was no advance publicity and the critics were as surprised as they were delighted. Kay Kendall and Kenneth More both became stars – and the film itself still holds the record for reissues in Britain: *Gone with the Wind* has played the circuits more often, but not in such a concentrated period.

especially those with Guinness, revived Balcon's competitive spirit, recalling the inroads made into the American market during his tenure at Gaumont-British. He was cautious since he appreciated that Ealing's success depended on its parochial approach, but increasingly Rank tried to dictate policy – and the more successful and ambitious Balcon became the more he was dependent on Rank's financial support. The accountants who had taken over at the Rank Organisation had stultified production at the studios already controlled by them, and they attempted to prevail at Ealing without having the least understanding of Balcon's creative policy. As Balcon capitulated, Ealing's films became indistinguishable from those of the Rank studios, and his position was weakened by the increasingly indifferent reception accorded them – and by the inevitable defection of the members of his team. In 1955 Stephen Courtauld, who had managed Ealing's financial affairs since the arrival of Balcon, decided to retire. Balcon resolved to finance the immediate projected batch of Ealing films from the National Film Finance Corporation – as Harold Wilson's production fund was now called (as a member of the board he had not wanted to call on it before). In order for the loan to be repaid

he accepted an offer from B.B.C. television for the Ealing studio itself, for £350,000, on the understanding that the two new soundstages being built at Pinewood were to be for the exclusive use of the Ealing unit. For John Davis, the situation provided an opportunity to bring Balcon even further under Rank control, for Balcon was to petition for studio space at Pinewood like any other Rank producer. Balcon accordingly dissolved the 1945 agreement by which Rank distributed his films, and he signed a new one with M-G-M, which recognised Ealing as a company with a world-wide reputation. But Ealing, to all intents and purposes, was dead; a disheartened team made some films for M-G-M as weak as the later ones for Rank, including the final Ealing comedy, *Barnacle Bill* (q.v.). In 1959 what was left of Ealing became Michael Balcon Productions, though briefly, and he himself later served in advisory capacities with Bryanston (q.v.) and British Lion. The Ealing catalogue passed to Associated-British – a more valuable item than its own.

If we except *Barnacle Bill*, the comedies ended on a high note, though the best of them, and the most spectacularly successful, **Genevieve** (1953), was made directly for Rank when (as in the case of *Hunted*) the

Ealing schedule was too full. The script was by an expatriate American, William Rose (b. 1918), who had hitherto contributed to some nondescript British films; the director, Henry Cornelius, had served as editor and writer at Ealing but was otherwise only known for his handling of *Passport to Pimlico*.★ The film has such Ealing characteristics as a quaint central idea – the Old Crocks' rally to Brighton and back – and an amused but affectionate view of such local types as obtuse policemen and kindly but unhelpful landladies. What Rose added was malice and sex: it has a bite which recalls the Hollywood comedies of the Thirties – not least, as Richard Winnington pointed out (in one of the unanimous rave reviews), because it was unique among British films in regarding its main characters as sexual beings. They are a husband (John Gregson) and wife (Dinah Sheridan), their best friend (Kenneth More) and the model (Kay Kendall) he hopes to bed when they arrive in Brighton. In appearance and attitudes they are, for the first time on screen, the affluent postwar generation; and though the marital squabbles are beautifully managed, it is the other couple who take the screen. More, with his desire to combine the London-Brighton run with 'a really beautiful emotional experience', goes further than Gregson in arrogance and adolescent delight in old cars; and the film was the first to exploit the gift of Kay Kendall (1927–59) for remaining soignée while being bumped or slapped around. None of these players had been well known hitherto: but they were seen frequently as the film had an unprecedented number of circuit re-issues over the next few years. Abroad its reception was rather 'caviare for the general', but it is constantly revived the world over.

Rose's next two screenplays were written for Ealing, and **The 'Maggie'** (1954), like *Genevieve* and his later *It's a Mad, Mad, Mad, Mad World* (q.v.) is about getting from one place to another – in this case as

experienced by an American (Paul Douglas), who wants some £4,000-worth of equipment transported to his new island home in the Highlands. The concept came from Rose's fellow-American, Mackendrick, who also directed, and like his *Whisky Galore!* its chief subject is Scots canniness – in this case more than a match for American ingenuity. Both aspects are handled with charm and discretion, as when Douglas discovers that he enjoys both the open life and the battle of wits. Perhaps because the cast includes so many dour Scots it lacks insouciance, but the second Rose-Mackendrick collaboration, **The Ladykillers** (1955), can hardly be faulted. Like *Genevieve*, it builds inventively; like *Kind Hearts and Coronets*, it is *comédie noire*; and like all the Ealing comedies its keynote is a coy irony. As with *The Lavender Hill Mob* its band of comic, incompetent crooks (Guinness, Cecil Parker, Peter Sellers, etc.) would be much copied, yet they are both too original and too much indebted to the cartoonist Charles Addams (with acknowledgment: cf. Guinness's make-up) to be entirely equalled. And no one could use again the enchanting situation of the lavender-and-old-lace landlady (Katie Johnson) who innocently proves more than a match for them.

This film was on release when the break with the Rank Organisation was announced. For M-G-M, Balcon, Frend, Clarke and Guinness made **Barnacle Bill** (1957), about a retired sea-captain who takes charge of a seaside pier, but it only proved that confidence had crumbled; the dispersed team of Relph and Dearden made the infinitely better *The Smallest Show on Earth* (q.v.), with a script by Rose, for British Lion, and with it the age of Ealing comedy was over. By that time, for the first time in almost three decades, Balcon was no longer a force in British filmmaking. Korda, his rival of the prewar years, had died while Balcon was negotiating his escape from the Rank Organisation – which was left, alas, as the only potent force in the British film industry.

★Balcon's excuse for not finding studio space for *Genevieve* was apparently that Cornelius was no longer on the payroll.

30

Luis Buñuel and his Followers

TILL THE END of the Forties most of the foreign-language films shown around the world were French, with a smattering from Italy, Russia and Germany. The situation began to change in 1950, when the Mexican *Los Olvidados* (q.v.) and the Japanese *Rashomon* (q.v.) were warmly received at the Cannes and Venice Film Festivals respectively. The Mexican film was the work of a name then hallowed only in film societies, themselves few in number: Luis Buñuel.

He had lost interest in making films after *Las Hurdes*, but rather than live on family money he returned to Paris to supervise the dubbing of Paramount's films for the local market. He went on to do the same for those of Warner Bros. in Madrid, and was also executive producer on some minor Spanish films. On the outbreak of the Spanish Civil War he offered his services to the Republican government in Paris, who sent him to Hollywood to advise on any movie project favourable to its cause: he did work on one such project, at M-G-M, but it was abandoned when it was clear that Franco would be the victor. Iris Barry got him a job at the Museum of Modern Art in New York, supervising Spanish versions of American films for Latin America; and when he was forced to resign – because someone discovered that he had directed the still-scandalous *L'Age d'Or* – he found similar work with the U.S. Army. That too was terminated when a report appeared that Salvador Dali had described him as an atheist. Warners either did not know or did not care, for they took him on to dub their pictures for the Latin-American market, and at one point considered assigning him to the direction of *The Beast with Five Fingers*. His

preparatory work on the film revived his taste for filming, and he went to Mexico to prepare a version of Lorca's 'La Casa de Bernardo Alba', to be shot in France, but the necessary financing was not forthcoming. A Mexican producer, Oscar Dancigers, offered him a straightforward commercial job, **Gran Casino** (1947), starring two popular singers, but when it failed to confirm their reputation Buñuel received no further commissions. However, he had established a good relationship with Dancigers, who encouraged him to submit an idea for a film for children. Instead, Buñuel suggested a film *about* children, which became *Los Olvidados*; Dancigers promised him 'a degree of freedom' if he would first do a comedy of the type popular in the Latin-American market.

This was **El Gran Calavera** (1949), based on a play, with a screenplay by Luiz Alcoriza, who was to work on many of Buñuel's subsequent films. Its subject is a family versed in deception and headed by an ageing widower (Fernando Solar) who gets drunk every night, to the indifference of his sponging relatives – who are, in fact, the reason for his drinking. When they eventually realise that he may drink away his fortune they trick him into believing that he has lost it. To get his own back, he is faced with the necessity of reform, which he miraculously achieves overnight – undoubtedly to the amusement of Buñuel, a dedicated and unrepentant alcoholic (by his own admission, but possibly not at this particular time). Till that point in the plot the film is a celebration of drink, but Buñuel's expressed aversion to the bourgeoisie is otherwise confined to giving the prospective mother-in-law a not inconspicuous moustache.

His contempt for middle-class values is the abiding theme of his career, but it is nevertheless absent from **Los Olvidados** (1950), which reintroduced him to cinemagoers who remembered him only as the director of two much earlier surrealist films. That contempt would not have been amiss, if only as a side-line, for Buñuel here is concerned with the state of the poor – which he discusses in terms as compassionate and pessimistic as in *Las Hurdes*. Unlike that film, this is fiction aimed at the mass market, for since de Sica's *Sciuscià* there had been several much-discussed and popular films on juvenile delinquency. Buñuel's foreword is unoriginal ('the problem is left to the city . . . and the progressive forces of our time') and the whole is not without some moralising in the manner of *Boys Town* as it ranges through the underside of 'a certain Mexican city', finding overcrowding and promiscuity the essential accompaniments to poverty – together with religiosity, superstition and violence. The children are corrupt and devious – a far cry even from de Sica's protagonists; but it is not till the end, when the blind man they have robbed is revealed as no longer pitiable but lecherous and vindictive, that the film becomes more than a careful and well-photographed study. At that point we recognise the voice that is uniquely Buñuel's, mordantly convinced of human weakness.

Before the film achieved its success at Cannes he had embarked on another purely commercial chore, which, like those that immediately followed, was not expected to travel far beyond the Mexican border. Later he sometimes pretended to forget their titles – while remarking that of his entire output there were only two or three films that he did not like. On another occasion he said, 'I have always been true to my surrealist principles: "The need to eat never excuses prostituting one's art." In the nineteen or twenty films I have made there may be three or four which are frankly bad, but in no way have I infringed my moral code. To have a code at all is childish to many people, but not to me.' That code is discernible in these films, clumsy as they are and often poorly acted, for they picture bourgeois families emotionally crippled by religion and tradition. Their members quarrel and scheme against each other, as the plots slide from melodrama to farce;

and these stories usually depend on that great divider, sex, rendered never as tenderness but as lust and jealousy, always ambiguous and usually farcical as well. **Susana** (1951) is a rural tale of the cuckoo in the nest – the new maid who agitates all the male members of the household in turn. The piece is not without its ironies, as when someone observes, in fact wrongly, that the name Susana means 'charity' – for charitable she is not, and anyone taking her deserves all he gets. She, like the film, is not subtle, but it is interesting as a blueprint for the more mature *Le Journal d'une Femme de Chambre* (q.v.); it would also have been improved, as Buñuel himself observed, with a different ending, presumably one in which she is not simply forgiven for her sins.

La Hija del Engaño (1951) is a remake of one of the films Buñuel had produced in Spain, the 1935 *Don Quintin el Amargao*. Don Quintin (Fernando Solar) casts his wife out on discovering her infidelity, and she retaliates by screaming that their child, a daughter, is not his. Later, when he has become the successful but embittered proprietor of a gambling den, she tells him

Luis Buñuel – seen here with shooting script and parrot – had the strangest career of any major director, so that we are fortunate to have the masterpieces of his late middle-age. After establishing a reputation with *L'Age d'Or* in 1930 it was almost two decades before he directed again. *Los Olvidados* re-established him in 1950, but he was to spend most of the subsequent decade working on commercial Mexican films – though as handled by him they are not routine. Here he is on the set of another of his important films of that time, *The Adventures of Robinson Crusoe*.

Luis Buñuel and his Followers

Subsequent to *Los Olvidados*, few of Buñuel's Mexican films were intended for audiences abroad, and most of them have only been seen at retrospectives of his work. Of the few that were widely screened overseas at the time *El* was perhaps the best received, and it remains a powerful study of an obsessional jealousy. Arturo de Cordova played the husband so afflicted, and, as you may have guessed, it is he on the right of the picture.

that she lied – and he learns that the girl has fled the peasant family with whom he deposited her, because of their cruelty. The film is an odd mixture, at its most acrimonious and comic in the gaming sequences, which contain the only really characteristic Buñuel touch. A young clerk is suicidal because of his gambling debts, but later he becomes a confirmed addict: the irresistible attraction of vice was something that Buñuel would feature in many later films. **Subida al Cielo** (1952) has for its hero a young bridegroom who succumbs much too soon to the advances of a whore. It is Buñuel's most personal film of this period, with its haunting, surrealist dream sequence and a cast of characters – passengers on a bus – mainly corrupt or treacherous. The film merely follows their antics, and those of the bus itself, as it travels from one place to another. 'This is the other Mexico of the tropics,' wrote Tony Richardson in *Sight and Sound*, 'with its rich fruitfulness and lazy Indians, and it has never been so spontaneously caught as in this enchanting film.' However, it is too crude and uneven for complete enchantment. **Una Mujer sin Amor** (1952) must surely be one of the

films that Buñuel dislikes, rambling from the predicament of a young mother who loves another man then later to the two grown-up sons who quarrel as a consequence: the bourgeois family torn apart by dissension is a typical theme, here muted by exceptionally poor playing. The source is a story by de Maupassant, 'Pierre et Jean', adapted by Jaime Salvador, who also wrote *Susana*.

The flimsy construction of all these films contrasts sharply with the intense narrative drive of **El Bruto** (1953) and **El** (1953), both written by Buñuel himself and Alcoriza, the second from a novel by Mercedes Pinto. They are unquestionably melodramatic, but the difference between a Buñuel film and one made by anyone else on the same subject is that he pushes every aspect to its limit (or that permitted by the censors) while never overstepping the bounds of probability. Against his will, *El Bruto* underwent lengthy script changes, but it remains fascinating. Pedro (Pedro Armendariz) is the brute of the title, a slaughterhouse worker who becomes the willing tool of a tatty but ruthless old landowner (Andres Soler); and the abattoir and butcher's shop provide the back-

810

ground for a tale of lechery and senility, of opportunism and exploitation of the poor. The film is particularly critical of the landowner's degenerate family, but on this occasion the relationship of the brute and the waif does not seem to have interested Buñuel. Such relationships had provided movies with a theme since the time of D. W. Griffith – and Buñuel would also return to it, but his later lechers would be much less gross than on this occasion.

In *El* the situation is reversed, since the man is in thrall to a woman. He is the 'el' of the title – Don Francisco (Arturo de Cordova). The woman is again the more innocent, the weaker of the two: but his strength is destructive, for he is jealous to the point of paranoia. Despite his belief in his own infallibility he is neither vicious nor irredeemably vain, and when, finally, he has no one to turn to but his valet, we see that he is essentially pitiable. Doubtless comforted by a foot fetish, he has nevertheless missed so much in life: people who only half-live, suggests the film, do not live at all. Which is, we may suppose, only to be expected of an aristocracy vitiated by centuries of self-indulgence and God-worshipping. Both the glimpses of a priest-ridden society and the charting of Don Francisco's relationship with his wife demonstrate a new energy in Buñuel: unlike *El Bruto* this film has a visual sense as striking as its narrative drive, and both qualities were seldom to disappear from Buñuel's work.

Not till he returned to Europe – and not always then – would he have the advantage of first-class working conditions, but **The Adventures of Robinson Crusoe** (1954) was made in Spanish and English versions, in colour and with an American actor, Dan O'Herlihy, as Defoe's desert-island hero. The international success of *Los Olvidados* had proved to Buñuel's producers (including Dancigers) that Mexico could make a film for world markets, but he himself was unenthusiastic when this project was suggested to him, till he realised that his subject could be solitude, accompanied by despair. Dealing with Crusoe alone as he conditions himself to life on the island and to loneliness, Buñuel finds an almost intoxicating purity of tone but, with the advent of Friday (Jaime Fernández), the film becomes perfunctory, only hinting at equivocation in the master-servant relationship. Buñuel ignores the implications of how two men from entirely opposing cultures can learn to live together, while Friday vacillates between being the 'noble savage' and just a nice guy.

Begun prior to *El*, *Robinson Crusoe* was not premiered until Buñuel had made two more films for local consumption, one of which, **Abismos de Pasión** (1954), transposes the plot of 'Wuthering Heights' to a Mexican setting. The other, **La Ilusión Viaja en Tranvia** (1954) is a pleasant film and, though not typical of Buñuel's oeuvre, has a companion piece in the darker **El Rio y la Muerte** (1955), since both look critically at contemporary Mexican society. Indeed, the earlier of the two films admits in a foreword that its view is 'sincere and somewhat trivial'. It is an urban comedy about a tram, due to be scrapped, that is taken on a final pirate ride by its maudlin driver and conductor. The second film, a rural melodrama, concerns feuding families, and it is only slightly superior to its European contemporaries about peasant vendettas. Both films reach the same conclusion, that man is the product of his immediate society. The driver and conductor rebel, run amok, but must finally conform; and so must in the other movie, the doctor from the city, despite his intellectual rejection of the primitive rules of the village.

Man retarded by his environment was the true subject of *El*, the archetypal Buñuel film of this period, and therefore the one to be seen at all costs; but there are a number of witty variations in what might be the second choice, **Ensayo de un Crimen** (1955), which is best known by its English title, *The Criminal Life of Archibaldo de la Cruz*. The 'crime' of Archibaldo (Ernesto Alonso) is his compulsion to murder, from which he is invariably prevented by fate. Rodolfo Usigli's black comedy provided Buñuel with one of his most congenial subjects, but what matters is the startling way in which he has worked it out, interweaving boyhood traumas and fetishism into a tale of sex and death, and including one splendid scene in which an army officer, a priest and a government official go into orgies of self-rapture about the patriotism involved in all ceremonials – including funerals. The film's triumph, as with *El*, is in its leading character, self-absorbed and selfish, again a representative of all that is wrong in bourgeois society. He may be impotent, but more than any other film I know this one is a masturbatory fantasy. We find him at one moment fondling a brassière and silk stockings: we do not know why, but it does not matter.

A year or so earlier Buñuel had remarked that he would like to film in France, because 'it is easier to make good films there'. The international acclaim accorded *Los Olvidados* and *Robinson Crusoe* gave him the chance to return to make **Cela s'Appelle l'Aurore** (1956). With Jean Ferry he adapted a novel by Emmanuel Robles, and the film, which is poorly shaped, concerns a doctor (Georges Marchal) who begins an affair with an Italian woman (Lucia Bosè) while his wife is away. He also becomes involved again with a peasant friend (Gianni Esposito) of the war years, who has been evicted by his landlord. According to Freddy Buache (in his 1970 monograph on Buñuel), the film 'advocates subversion and makes statements that are very rarely to be heard in the cinema', and he further notes that the title is drawn from the final line of Giraudoux's 'Electre', with its reference to day breaking and everything pillaged or lost – and so ends this otherwise unremarkable film. It is a solid commercial venture very much of its period; de Sica's *Umberto D*, for instance, is far more subversive, and that is only part of its purpose. One sequence, however, is reminiscent of de Sica (and Renoir): two peasants, the sacked one and his replacement, make the best of the cruel situation – one brought about by (of course) the self-opinionated, hedonistic *petits bourgeois*. The film's chief theme is loyalty, be it marital, amatory, patriotic, local, between old comrades or employer and employee. The acting of Marchal, a fading matinee idol, and Bose, who was pretty but of no great ability, is of little benefit: Buñuel did not return to France first-class.

La Mort en ce Jardin (1956) and **La Fièvre Monte à El Pao** (1960) were Franco-Mexican productions, and so inferior to the intervening *Nazarin* (q.v.) as to emphasise that both were again purely commercial chores – though they do share resonances with it. The setting in each case is a squalid, totalitarian banana republic, but since in melodramas like these such

matters as police brutality, political imprisonment and injustice are used for routine dramatic effect the moral point is lost – along with Buñuel's own interest, if it can be judged by his indecisive approach and the sagging narrative shared by the two films. *La Mort en ce Jardin* concerns a small mining town run by the French, and the loyalties that divide when the militia arrive; and although the prostitute (Simone Signoret) parading in the jungle in evening gown and jewels may be a comment on the follies of human behaviour in adversity – anticipating *El Angel Exterminador* (q.v.) – the sequence might as well belong to any down-market jungle movie. The second film is 'Tosca' with twists, and its main interest lies in its leading characters – the governor's lady (Maria Félix) with the instincts of a whore, the president (Jean Servais) who has abused his revolutionary ideals, and the Cavaradossi figure (a miscast Gérard Philipe), whose idealism is of wrong-headed and muddled as that of the protagonist in *Nazarin*. The last-named is prefigured in *La Mort en ce Jardin* by the character of the priest (Michel Piccoli), who responds to the laws both of the jungle and those made by man (often in the name of Christianity) with his own daft interpretation of Christian ethics – which, when lost in the jungle, is ridiculous. At that point in the plot there is a hint of Ingmar Bergman's favourite theme, the refusal of God to reveal himself: the fact that it is only a hint may reflect Buñuel's indifference or his confusion. Nevertheless he was steeling himself for a confrontation with the subject of Christianity.

That comes in **Nazarin** (1959), which is a masterpiece. Like Bresson's earlier *Journal d'un Curé de Campagne* (q.v.), it is the study of a failed priest, but, as adapted from a late nineteenth-century novel by Benito Pérez Galdós, is more complex. The screenplay by Buñuel and Julio Alejandro has transferred the action from Spain to Mexico, and some important shifts in emphasis may be explained by Buñuel's own comment, 'As a young man I was able to glimpse something that, on the spiritual and poetic plane, goes far beyond Christian morality. I'm not so presumptuous as to want to make the world over . . . It is possible to be *relatively* Christian, but the *absolutely* pure, the *absolutely* innocent man – he's bound to fail. He's licked before he starts.' Don Nazario (Francisco Rabal) is absolutely pure and absolutely innocent. In the ranks of the church he is of the lowliest, existing in abject poverty, without a parish or permanent post. Anticipant of charity, he is stoical because he has gone hungry before and most likely will again; he deflects abuse; he endures. He is a Christian penitent who receives a pittance substituting occasionally for the fat-cat Father Don Angel, even rolling his cigarettes for him. There ought to be better ways of being a priest than this – servile and parasitic, one of society's failures. Don Nazario faces each fresh humiliation and insult with the Gospel prescription to love, unprepared to discover that there are other forms of love – mainly profane ones. Those who duly laugh at Buñuel's anticlerical references – and there are several sharp ones here – will find that this film is essentially a questioning of that 'love', though Nazarin's humility may be preferable to the smug self-assurance of Don Angel. As in de Sica and Preston Sturges, the meek shall definitely not inherit the earth. We leave Nazarin – unlike the original novel – moved because charity has been given to him as a man rather than as a priest, and we cannot know what that act has done to his faith. Many of Buñuel's endings are open to various interpretations, and of this film as a whole he remarked that it is 'strange and ambiguous. The style is ambiguous and that's what interests me. If a work is obvious, as far as I'm concerned it's finished.'

The Young One/La Joven (1960) starts keenly, as a boat puts in to a small tropical island: a Negro (Bernie Hamilton) gets out to meet Miller (Zachary Scott), the island's warden, as well as the newly-orphaned Evalyn (Kay Meersman), all three of them very conscious that she has just passed puberty. It is an open question which one of these honourable men will seduce her. It is Miller who does so: but that his own sexual conduct is unlawful does not prevent him from joining in a false assumption that the black man is a rapist. The film by this time has fallen apart, and since the black man is being chased through the swamps by a nigger-hating Fascist, we have to seize on small matters – such as the character of the prim, well-meaning priest – to remind ourselves that we are not watching a steamy Holly-

wood B-movie. The racial overtones extend our knowledge of Buñuel, but the quality of debate is distressingly trite. One often suspects that this director plays down to his audience, and the fact that this film was made in an English version, that is, for wider consumption, may be one reason it lacks the bite or ambiguity of even his least Mexican film. It was not a success, and Buñuel remained a shadowy figure outside the Spanish-speaking world, known only for his early films and *Los Olvidados* and *Robinson Crusoe*, plus the three French films which few had liked (*Nazarin* had not yet been seen outside Mexico).

It was **Viridiana** (1961) which permanently re-established him, and those who had hoped for the return of his anarchic spirit, as evidenced in *L'Age d'Or*, found it stronger than ever. The film itself is a virulent attack on Christian ethics, and

Francisco Rabal in *Nazarin*, Buñuel's complex study of the priesthood – a subject whose success is not assured, but is perhaps explained by Buñuel's own remarks on the film: 'The style is ambiguous and that's what interests me. If a work is obvious, as far as I'm concerned it's finished. As for the religious problem, I'm convinced that the Christian, in the pure and absolute meaning of the word, has no place on earth.'

Luis Buñuel and his Followers

Fernando Rey and Silvia Pinal in *Viridiana*, which re-established Buñuel. He made it in Spain, invited back by the government, but in anarchic spirit chose a subject of which he could hardly have expected the government to approve, for it not only questions Christianity but throws rocks at it.

because it was made in Franco's Spain many were astonished – not least Buñuel himself, and the whole episode appealed mightily to his sense of humour. A young Mexican producer had proposed a co-production with Spain to Buñuel, who consented only because some young film-makers, such as Luis Berlanga (q.v.), were trying to wrench Spanish cinema free from the stranglehold of cheaply-produced musicals and melodramas. The censor in Madrid duly asked for some changes in the screenplay, and when Buñuel agreed the Spanish government dropped its guard. Buñuel moved to Paris to complete his editing of the film, which he was invited to take to the Cannes Film Festival, since he was attending in a personal capacity. Spain had not entered a film for the competition, and the assumption that *Viridiana* was an official entry gained credence when a government spokesman failed to deny that it was. It was awarded the Palme d'Or, but the government earned no consolation from the implication that the film revealed Franco as more tolerant of 'free speech' than was generally thought: for everywhere it proved impossible to discuss the film without reference to the facts that it was banned in Spain and that the government had been hoodwinked. The film's effect on audiences and critics was – to use correctly for once the most-abused word of movie publicists – sensational.

As I said, *Nazarin* had not been seen in Europe, so it was not recognised that

Viridiana was a progression from that film. Viridiana (Silvia Pinal) is soul-sister to Nazarin – an ex-nun whose belated 'education' is the subject of the film. Alejandro again wrote the screenplay with Buñuel, from their own original story – but we may assume that Galdós was at least an inspiration, for its plot much resembles that of *Tristana* (q.v.), another of his novels that Buñuel filmed. There are also echoes of earlier films, notably *El*, in that a man (Fernando Rey) is obsessed with a young girl, though in this case it is because she can be persuaded to re-enact the eroticism of his dead wife. When he dies, Viridiana devotes herself to charity and self-sacrifice, only to be brutally awakened to the realities of life by his bastard son (Rabal). She submits to his way of life, though whether from carnality, self-knowledge or a sense of futility is unclear: the only finality, the only solution, is sin. Goodness is equated with smugness, hypocrisy and destruction. Viridiana destroys; her victims include both the beggars she tries to help and the old man – destroyed as much by her as his own fantasies. The son is realistic and survives: he knows that religion is no substitute for a rich, full life.

Viridiana, even more than *Nazarin*, underlines the paradox in Buñuel's approach to Christianity. The more violently he attacked the Church, the more his 'religious' characters are shown to be subject to the temptations of the flesh and the devil. It is as though he recognised in some people a natural aptitude towards holiness and sanctity, which he found himself compelled to defile. *Viridiana* was accused of blasphemy, whereas what Buñuel himself considered debasing is the divorce of the Christian religion from many of the things which make life worth living.

This passionate enquiry into the nature of clericalism is continued in **El Angel Exterminador** (1962), made in Mexico. Alternatively, the film may be regarded as a wry look at a fatuous aspect of human endeavour and aspiration: the society dinner party. It opens as the party ends, when the guests find themselves incarcerated in the dining room, apparently overcome by lassitude and cowardice. They remain for several days, discussing their dilemma and agreeing that it is not logical, and all the while their hold on their morals and emotions is ebbing away. The situation is treated as both ordinary and extraordinary, the clues to Buñuel's purpose emerging as pinpricks: 'A key is anything that opens the door to the unknown,' says someone. As 'society' breaks down it becomes vicious, an attitude adopted by many satirists before Buñuel, and what happens at the end should hardly be of much relevance to those brought up in the freer-thinking Protestant tradition. On repeated viewings this allegory retains a horrible fascination, and nothing in it is entirely alien. Buñuel's own reflection on the film is found in his remark that 'people always want an explanation for everything. It's the logical result of centuries of bourgeois education. And when they can't explain something, they end up by turning to God. But what good does that do them? They then have to explain God.'

Buñuel returned to Spain after com-

pleting the film; the government indicated that its difficulties with *Viridiana* were forgotten, and that it would like him to make another Spanish film, but at the last minute permission to shoot *Tristana* was withheld (he was not to make it till 1970). Accordingly he went to France to find backing for **Le Journal d'une Femme de Chambre** (1964), from the novel by Octave Mirbeau which had been the source of Renoir's film of 1946. In the history of screen remakes there is no parallel case of two great directors using the same source material, each moulding it to his whim – though as David Robinson has pointed out, *âpre* (bitter, harsh, violent) was Mirbeau's favourite word, and the quality is as much to be found in Renoir's version as, more expectedly, in Buñuel's. The original story is related in the first person by Célestine, a housemaid newly employed

There is no other film quite like *El Angel Exterminador*, whose meaning is not yielded until the final sequence. Meanwhile, these dinner guests have lingered on. 'We are all victims of a joke in bad taste' says one of them, and that turns out to be a comment on two thousand years of Christianity.

815

Luis Buñuel and his Followers

Jeanne Moreau and Georges Géret in *Le Journal d'une Femme de Chambre*. The same novel had provided a film for Jean Renoir, and though there are other cases of good directors using identical material, in no other instance can the results be said to be so outstanding.

by a wealthy bourgeois couple. Each film uses different incidents from her past to embellish her progress in this household. Buñuel's screenplay – written with Jean-Claude Carrière, collaborator on all his French films thereafter – is the record of a girl determined to make headway in the world of her 'betters'. Jeanne Moreau's performance beautifully suggests a woman of limited imagination but unlimited experience – and very much her own mistress. She guardedly but obediently obeys the instructions of madame, and deftly parries the amorous advances of monsieur (Michel Piccoli); she gamely reads to madame's father and wears the boots as required by him; she is repulsed but yet attracted to the gamekeeper (Georges Géret), who may be a child-murderer and is certainly a great patriot and religionist. Finally, she marries the neighbouring captain (Daniel Ivernal) who is no better than any of them. The bourgeois, in fact, get a thorough beating: these people writhe like maggots in their own deceit and pettiness in the pursuit, usually, of sexual fulfilment, but having to settle for *certaines caresses* – which, as madame admits to the prurient priest, is all that she permits to monsieur. What Célestine sees and deplores, she inevitably becomes. Buñuel's irony was never more effective, but he had never before directed actors of this quality. Technically the film is superior to even his most polished

previous work – adroitly shaded visually and psychologically.

Buñuel returned to Mexico to make **Simón del Desierto** (1965), an anecdote about a man who emulates St Simeon Stylites. In all the annals of hagiography there can be – even according to the precepts of the time – few more ridiculous figures than a man who spent the last thirty-seven years of his life on the top of a pillar, and he inspires Buñuel to some donnish jokes. His Simón (Claudio Brook) is, like Nazarin, a foolish figure, one of society's rejects, while his theory that asceticism is the bridge to God is regarded with bemusement. Only in relation to the people below does he have any stature – figuratively and literally – but they are unhappily ungrateful for his act of devotion, while the Church, also to his dismay, sees in him a threat to its own power. The Devil appears, in the guise of both Christ with a lamb and a typical Buñuel heroine, exposing her stocking-tops: and when Simón succumbs to her, he is transported to a New York *boîte*, where the world frugs and twists without heed or need of his sacrifices or those of any other saint. The film is short – 45 minutes – and the ending is abrupt and unsatisfactory: despite the low budget, the money ran out, thus robbing us of another full-length portrait of one of Buñuel's lame-duck protagonists.

Among the pleasures of **Belle de Jour** (1967) is its portrait, unlike that in any other film, of a brothel. The film stands chronologically between the old, romantic view of such matters, as in *La Viaccia* (q.v.), and the realistic attitude of *The Last Detail* (q.v.). Whether or not Buñuel shared what seems to be the universal fascination with the oldest profession he depicts it here with relish. The brothel concerned is situated in a small street near the Opéra, and it is clinically furnished – not unsuitably, since we see it only during the equivalent of office hours: for it is then that Belle (Catherine Deneuve) slips away from married respectability and memories of a Catholic childhood. The subject – an upper middle-class wife who turns to whoredom – must have appealed to Buñuel, though he disliked Joseph Kessel's original novel (published in 1929). The critic John Simon, admitting an aversion to Kessel, wrote, 'I gather the dream fantasies are Buñuel's, as is that elusive ending. So, too, is a daydream in which an ageing, crazed duke performs on Belle de Jour a mock ceremony involving incest, necrophilia, onanism and sacrilege; perversity coupled with anti-Catholicism is as dear to Buñuel as to de Sade.' But, Simon concluded, 'Buñuel or Kessel, it is all trashy because superficial' – and I would agree only inasmuch as fantasy and perversity were to provide the starting-point for Buñuel's worst film, *Le Fantôme de la Liberté* (q.v.). As a documentary on the activities of a brothel, *Belle de Jour* is both audacious and reticent; Buñuel works with wit and clarity on what may be considered the opposite of these qualities – the ambivalence of human behaviour. Certainly, as narrative it touches a number of nerves – will the husband (Jean Sorel) find out? How will she react when, inevitably, a friend of his appears? To what degradation will she sink?

Since the ending, with Belle punished, is moral, we look in vain for a trace of Buñuel the anarchist: the producers (the Hakim brothers) eliminated some minor details and the film had virtually no trouble with censors anywhere in the world – undoubtedly due in part to Buñuel's reputation. He himself called it 'pornographic . . . by that I mean *chaste* eroticism', and though we might prefer him to have provided unchaste eroticism, his purity of style is remarkable. It is the perfect counterpart to Mlle Deneuve, as glacial as ever: unable to express much beyond a slight wonder, her thoughts remain for us to guess; her white underwear and long blonde hair are both virginal and sensuous at the same time. It is this balance, maintained throughout the film, which is Buñuel's finest achievement. We, the cinemagoers, are forced more than by most films to be voyeurs, and just at the point when we are enjoying it most Buñuel asks us to take a moral view of what Belle is doing. The result is one of his most enjoyable and accessible films, and though in France the critics did not like it, the public did. Undoubtedly it was its subject, as with *Never on Sunday* (q.v.) which brought it a popularity beyond the art house the world over; and since Buñuel was now commercial the industry itself could finally regard him as a 'great' director on the lines of Bergman

and Fellini – the irony of which could not have been lost on the old surrealist.

He retaliated, typically, by offering **La Voie Lactée** (1968), whose deliberate obscurity – except to the initiated – endeared it to neither critics nor public. The Voie Lactée is the route taken by pilgrims to Santiago de Compostella, and as two *clochards* journey south they are involved allegorically with the six central 'mysteries' of Catholic doctrine and the heresies which have grown up around them. The concept is too cerebral, but some of the incidents find Buñuel at his most brilliant and dexterous; for example, the argument between the Fascist policeman and the priest who turns out to be mental, and the two sixteenth-century students who arrive

Francis Blanche, impatient client, and Catherine Deneuve, whore, in *Belle de Jour*. She is a respectable wife who does not have to do this for a living – which is, as it happens, the subject of the film.

in the present day and are befriended by a priest whose interest is more than fatherly. Elsewhere the piece lacks buoyancy, leaving the audience uncertain whether to regard Catholic teaching as mumbo-jumbo or God's truth – and that cannot have been the intention.

The Spanish government finally granted Buñuel permission to film **Tristana** (1970) – in Toledo, the quintessential Spanish city, and one virtually unchanged for centuries. Since the film's themes are familiar throughout his work, we may suppose that it was the Spanishness of Galdós's novel that most appealed to Buñuel and therefore the reason he did not, as with *Nazarin*, transfer the action to another country. He has, however, brought the action forward to the Twenties. Its subject is the relationship between Tristana (Mlle Deneuve), an orphan, and Don Lope (Fernando Rey), an impoverished but fiercely independent middle-aged gentleman. She is not essentially his opposite, though she is devout, unworldly and young. They are drawn together – she for protection and he from lechery – and presumably a symbolic bond is intended by successive close-ups peering over the tops of her stockings and the garters on his socks. His attitude towards her is alternately paternal and conjugal, the implication being that this can only happen because they are Spanish or, rather, that because this is Spain it is the sort of thing that happens. He destroys her by gradually draining her of freedom – not that she was free in the first place, but she could, as she says, choose which of two streets to walk down. Seducing her and then not permitting himself to marry her is a violation of her Spanishness, as is the decision by the young artist (Franco Nero) to marry her though she is not a virgin. Don Lope must therefore marry her to keep her in his power: she survives him, to become bitter, crabbed – and amputated, a situation which seems to have little to do with the film's arguments, except that no one can again spy at her stockings (and it is a reflection of the fate meted out to Belle de Jour). In Buñuel's Mexican films the men survive, but in the later films it is the women who confront us at the end – and we cannot tell whether they (Viridiana, Célestine, Belle, Tristana) are the happier for it.

Everyone survives in **Le Charme Dis-**

cret de la Bourgeoisie (1972), despite i‹ background of anarchy and revolutior gunned down, these remnants of *El Ang‹ Exterminador* – bishops, ministers, ambas sadors and their wives – perk up agair which we may suppose is the prerogativ‹ of their class. With sangfroid, they con tinue their rituals and chit-chat, their ir sistence on the importance of good foo‹ and good manners, backed up by the un holy alliance of Church, state and th‹ military (the police are so long entering th‹ scene that it is almost a relief to find th‹ Buñuel had not forgotten them – and, ‹ course, they prove as adept at violence a the others). The film slips into its myria‹ fantasies with deceptive ease, calml‹ accepting the chaos it conveys – and tha we may take to be Buñuel's prerogative i his old age. He fails to build to a climax ‹ any sort, but huge audiences neverthele‹ delighted in seeing him take pot shots a the bourgeoisie and its sacred cows though the laughter, plentiful to sta‹ with, is later sparse. The film won a Oscar for Best Foreign Language Pictur‹ and did very well for 20th Century-Fo‹ who released it in most territories. Fo happily handled **Le Fantôme de I Liberté** (1974), but though Buñuel ha‹ become too fashionable to reap the poo notices the film deserved, it was shunne‹ by the public. It was, noted the critics surrealist and subversive, and thoug‹ Buñuel had said that he would nev‹ attempt another *L'Age d'Or* (since worl‹ events had proved to him the emptiness ‹ his attempts to be outrageous) the simila 'shocks' of *Le Charme Discret* had found whole new audience for him. I believe tha this *Fantôme* was flung contemptuously i the face of the public – that public whic‹ did not patronise his better films. It con tains a ragbag of favourite themes, offere‹ without surprise or wit, filled out with ba‹ taste jokes borrowed from lesser directo‹ – Godard,★ Polanski, Bertolucci – an‹ with a perfunctory salute to contemporar‹ terrorism.

Urban terrorism of many varieties i present in the background of **Cet Obscu‹ Objet du Désir** (1977), causing som‹ observers to consider it relevant to its cen tral theme – which, once again, is th‹ nature of obsession. Having failed with *L Fantôme*, Buñuel abandoned the shock

★For Buñuel's opinion of Godard see page 1019.

Buñuel's last film, *Cet Obscur Objet du Désir*, returns him to a favourite theme, that of sexual obsession. Fernando Rey, at the left, is the man obsessed, and Angela Molina is the object of desire, not too obscurely: her plan, at this point, is to increase his frustration by making love with a man of her own age, David Rocha.

and fantasies of his last two films for a relatively straightforward tale which he had long wanted to film. This was Pierre Louys' 'La Femme et le Pantin', and at one point he had been the proposed director of the 1959 version which Julien Duvivier eventually made (earlier, von Sternberg had filmed the story as *The Devil is a Woman*). Fernando Rey is again the man obsessed, though dubbed by Michel Piccoli, a popular and eminent actor who had already made four films for Buñuel: playing a Frenchman, Rey cannot have a Spanish accent, but the casting also suggests that Buñuel regarded Rey as his alter ego (as von Sydow was to Bergman). The Spanish ambience of the original has been retained by setting the film partly in Seville; and the object desired is played by two actresses, one Spanish and one French – which is not especially gimmicky, though the actresses, contrarily, are not required to represent different aspects of the character. Neither is very interesting, and though she, Conchita, perversely leads on Rey and then repulses him there is little variety in her provocation. Rey's gnawing frustration is not, therefore, interestingly drama-

tised and when, at the end, he becomes violent as she taunts him by having sex with another man before his eyes, the effect is disappointingly mild. It is ironic if the one director always so far in advance of usual movie concerns should be overtaken by younger men often emulating him, but had this film been made by anyone else it would not have caused a ripple.

For at least ten years Buñuel had been proclaiming his intention to retire – an intention circumvented by Serge Silberman, the producer of his last three French films; and during that time the cynicism often apparent in his work had become more and more obtrusive, culminating in *Le Fantôme*. *Cet Obscur Objet* is more insolent, and indeed its refusal to offer denouement, climax or even ending is breathtaking – for, like the work of many inferior film-makers it does not conclude but simply stops, with an explosion. Even in *Tristana* the old master had begun to lose interest before the end; but then, when left to himself – i.e. not working from a novel – in all his later films he is inclined to disintegrate, being wayward, jokey, and hitting out at his old favourite targets with both an obvious symbolism and with private jokes. It is probable that the jaded polemics of *Le Charme Discret* will delight audiences as long as those of *L'Age d'Or*; but I believe that his most lasting monument will be his studies of man's illusions – *El, Nazarin, Viridiana, Le Journal d'une Femme de Chambre* and *Tristana*, films as good as any ever made. Buñuel died in 1983.

Apart from Buñuel, the Spanish cinema has made little impact on the international scene. Once in every half dozen years a Spanish film enjoys success in other parts of Europe and in the U.S., offering evidence of a national cinema of some vitality. In the Fifties, while Buñuel was in Mexico, both Luis G. Berlanga (b. 1921) and Juan Antonio Bardem (b. 1922) enjoyed a measure of international acclaim. Serious Spanish cinema may be said to begin with them, as they chose to move away from the stereotyped musicals and melodramas which had emanated from the studios in Madrid.

They trained together at the Instituto de Investigaciones Cinemátograficas, and collaborated on a number of shorts before writing and directing their first feature, **Esa Pareja Féliz** (1951). Its acknowledged influences were Becker's *Antoine et Antoinette* and the writings of Zavattini, but it also owes a debt to Clair and Capra. The title is ironic, since the couple are happy neither before nor after they are chosen by a soap company offering them Madrid at their feet for a day. The prospect is exciting for them, but almost everything goes wrong and they end the day in a police station. Their adventures are almost charming and sometimes funny. The film's lack of ambition is to be admired, as is its assurance that everything about Madrid – especially its entertainments – is second rate. Berlanga and Bardem then wrote **Bienvenido Mr Marshall** (1952), which Berlanga directed. It was sent to the Cannes Film Festival in 1953, after which it enjoyed a success in most countries – and it remains Berlanga's best-known film. The setting is a small town in Castile, where the only excitement is the weekly cinema showing of an old Western – till, that is, news arrives of the impending advent of Marshall Aid. For a while, everyone is greedy; then the townsfolk decide that they should welcome the Americans – whom they expect in person – with

appropriate fanfare. They elect to trans form the place into the traditional Spanis town, even to the extent of erecting fals façades and building a bull-ring. The fil strongly bears a resemblance to Ealin comedy, as do Berlanga's next film though in each case there are also oth influences at work: in **Novio a la Vist** (1953) there are shades of *Les Dernièr Vacances* and in **Calabuch** (1956) there a traces of *Seven Days to Noon*. *Novio a Vista*, set in a small resort town in 191 deals with a group of children who revo against their parents and go to live in separate camp: they include the tombo who at the end of summer opts for adul hood and romance. *Calabuch* proposes a atomic scientist so ashamed of his re searches that he goes into hiding – in small Spanish fishing village, where h becomes involved in making fireworks fc the local celebrations. The professor played by Edmund Gwenn, and th romantic leads are Franco Fabrizi an Valentina Cortese, both stars in their na tive Italy: but the film, with good reasor did not repeat the success of *Bienvenido M Marshall*.

Indeed, that was a freak success. Ber langa's films to this time are pleasant, bu too local in interest. Another influence Pagnol, but Berlanga lacks Pagnol humour. He changed course with **Plácid** (1961), undoubtedly influenced by th writer Rafael Azcona, who was to collabc rate on all his future scripts. *Plácido* elabc rates on the theme of the earlier films – th provincial town transformed by commer cial interests – but it has a blacker satiric thrust. A firm of soap manufacturers bringing a trainload of film stars fror Madrid for the Christmas Eve festivities which also include the poor being invite into the homes of the rich for a meal: bu as with *Esa Pareja Féliz*, nothing goes a planned. **La Boutique** (1961) was a ambitious project, filmed under inadc quate conditions in Argentina. Its interest ing central situation involves a philanderin husband (Lautaro Murua) who decides t indulge his mild little wife (Sonia Brunc on learning that she has not long to live she decides to open a boutique, allow herself to be seduced by its designe and is soon making her husband fe unimportant.

El Verdugo (1963) enjoyed some inter

820

national success. It is based on the lively notion of a young man (Nino Manfredi), who takes on the occupation of his father-in-law, that of public executioner, only for the sake of the new apartment that goes with it: he intends to retire at the prospect of the first garrotting, but that is to be in Palma, and his wife has always wanted to holiday there – and, says her father, the man is bound to be reprieved. The film is an attack on capital punishment, its satiric intent weakened by Manfredi, who plays the hero, a vain and fraudulent Latin type, for sympathy. Sitges is the setting for **Vivan los Novios!** (1970), and as bikini-clad tourists stare at a black-garbed funeral procession Berlanga and Azcona are making their own comment on the old and the new Spain. Both the middle-aged hero (José Luis López Vázquez) and his bride-to-be (Lali Soldevilla) represent the old Spain, but he, with so many blondes about, is tempted to try the new Spain. The film otherwise is a rather strained black comedy, and I do not think **Grandeur Nature** (1974), also known as *Life Size*, is any more successful. It concerns a dentist (Michel Piccoli) who becomes obsessed by an inflatable life-size plastic doll; he loses his wife, and it becomes clear that his obsession can end only in madness or death. It is a film about loneliness and fetishism – about 'masturbation de luxe', in the words of Jean-Claude Carrière, who wrote the screenplay from an original story by Berlanga and Azcona. Carrière's contribution may be one reason the film is richer than Berlanga's other films; and it may be why Buñuel (or a semblance thereof) appears in its final shot. Buñuel certainly approved of fetishism: but this film is as much a condemnation of the Spanish mentality as is *Viridiana*. Like *El Angel Exterminador* it does not reveal its meaning until the end – when the dentist's Spanish servants and their friends (the film is set in Paris) are revealed as crude, animalistic, and so stupid as to treat the dentist's aberration as normal (so does his mother, but Buñuel never showed much affection for mothers, either).

The film, made in France, was not shown in Spain till censorship was relaxed after the death of Franco. Berlanga was expected to be one of the most vocal critics of the Franco regime, and **La Escopeta Nacional** (1978) is virtually a compendium of the faults, vices and stupidities of the ruling classes. It lacks the subtlety of *Furtivos* (q.v.), without being any less derivative than usual: it is no more than a mixture of *La Règle du Jeu* and *Le Charme Discret de la Bourgeoisie*. It is also noisy, frenetic and scatological – all reasons why it was not seen outside Spanish-speaking territories, although it was one of the biggest successes ever shown in Spain. That fact called for a sequel, and Berlanga and Azcona had the excellent idea of bringing its leading characters, the decadent marquis and his family, into Madrid in the hope of breaking into court life. The earlier film was set in the last days of Franco, and **Patrimonio Nacional** (1980) in the first days of King Juan Carlos. There is every reason to suppose that these two social satirists should have made one of their best films, but on the contrary this is an anything-goes farce, and a rather tired one at that. Both films indicate that Berlanga, despite years of trying otherwise, had become strictly a local director.

His old colleague Bardem elicited some international interest after their collaborations. **Muerte de un Ciclista** (1955), Bardem's third film as a solo director, was one of the revelations of the Cannes Festival. It was more accomplished than Berlanga's films to this time, and seemed more impressive than it was, since few outside Italy at that time had seen Antonioni's *Cronaca di un Amore* (q.v.), its inspiration. In both films Lucia Bosè is an adulteress, and it is the accident of the title, caused by her and her lover, which occasions the guilt and consequent reassessments of the corrupt society around her. The society of **Calle Mayor** (1956) is provincial, as the title indicates: a gang of pool-punters plan to trick a plain spinster (Betsy Blair) into believing that she is to be married – and the elected fiancé (José Saurez), not the brightest of schemers, finds the situation far more difficult to get out of than he had expected. Bardem was in the middle of shooting this film when the authorities, disliking *Muerte de un Ciclista*, found an excuse to jail him, and he was there when it won the Critics' Award at Cannes. The foreign success of both films established him as Spain's leading director, but **La Venganza** (1958) was so mutilated by the censor as to become only a travesty of what had been intended. The export of his

Luis Buñuel and his Followers

Among Spanish directors, Carlos Saura is among the best known outside his own country, perhaps because many of his films feature Geraldine Chaplin, who has an international reputation (if hardly that of her father, Charlie). Here she is in *Peppermint Frappé*, with another of Saura's favourite interpreters, José Luis López Vázquez. The film itself is reminiscent of the work of both Buñuel and Resnais, but Saura's work, when not highly individual, is clearly emulating only the best.

films was discouraged, and a film magazine that he had founded was banned for nine issues. As the prime figure in bringing Buñuel to Spain for *Viridiana* he again angered the government, and it would seem that these battles sapped his creative energy. A co-production in English, **Les Pianos Mécaniques** (1965), with James Mason and Melina Mercouri, was poorly received.

Virtually the only other Spanish film of this period seen widely abroad was **El Cochecito** (1959), after scoring a success at the Venice Festival for its Italian-born director, Marco Ferreri. He had undertaken various jobs in his native film industry before a Spanish producer decided to finance this venture. It was in fact his third film, written in collaboration with the author of the original novel, Rafael Azcona, who had not at that point linked his fortunes to those of Berlanga. The film purports to be a black comedy, as an old man (José Ibert) discovers that he lacks the love and honour which should accompany old age, and that his troops of friends are the cripples of the streets. He decides that he would like a motorised wheelchair like his friends, but this promising material – the setting (Madrid), the bourgeois family – is reduced to a cipher. Ferreri returned to

Italy to make a series of films on equally eccentric situations – *L'Ape Regina*, *La Grande Bouffe* (made in France with Azcona), *L'Ultima Donna* – but lacking point or narrative form.

Carlos Saura (b. 1932), like Berlanga and Bardem, studied at the Institute of Cinema Research in Madrid, and his first feature, **Los Golfos** (1959), is as blighted as those films of the academically-trained directors of the Soviet bloc, though it is far from an endorsement of this equally totalitarian regime. Indeed, its portrait of a group of young, impoverished drifters from the outskirts of Madrid is an implied criticism – and its form self-confessedly influenced by the Italian neo-realists. There is, however, no discernible personal statement, and Saura was to re-examine his approach after meeting Buñuel – still *persona non grata* in Spain – when *Los Golfos* was sent to the Cannes Festival in 1960. For the next few years Saura taught at the Institute in Madrid, until his contract was allowed to lapse. His scripts were all turned down by the censor, but in 1964 he deliberately set out to make a purely commercial film, *Llanto por un Bandido*. That enabled him to make, for the producer Elias Querejeta, **La Caza** (1965), an account of four gentlemen rabbit-hunting, each old enough for their vague references to 'the War' to have a meaning. The film is a parable of the Civil War, if examined closely enough, and was described by Buñuel as the most completely achieved work he had seen in a while; it is clear, however, why his words were not warmer, for the film has talent and energy but insufficient discipline or imagination. It won prizes at both the San Sebastian and Berlin Festivals, and at Berlin **Peppermint Frappé** (1967) won for Saura a Best Director award, a consideration echoed by the Spanish Screenwriters Guild, who also voted it Best Script: but in fact neither film was seen widely in Spain – though government policy encouraged their export, to indicate how liberal the regime had become. Neither film was more than tentatively subversive – and *Peppermint Frappé* is chiefly notable for its slavish imitation of Buñuel, to whom it is dedicated. As it is a successful imitation, with suspense and some wit, it entertains considerably, and is beautifully acted by José Luis López Vázquez as the forty-ish, bald, celibate doctor from Cuenca who becomes obsessed with two women, one of whom, his nurse, he attempts to re-mould in the image of the other. Both women are played by Geraldine Chaplin, who became Saura's chief interpreter and wife.

La Prima Angelica (1974) is dedicated to 'Charlie and Oona'. In it Miss Chaplin plays the present-day Angelica and, in the flashbacks to 1936, her mother; in **Cria Cuervos** (1975) she plays the present-day Ana and *her* mother. Much of *Peppermint Frappé* revolves round memory, and these later films are devoted to that subject. They are both more complex, reminiscent of the gothic puzzles of Leopoldo Torre Nilsson (q.v.). Significantly in *La Prima Angelica* the leading character, a Barcelona businessman (López Vázquez), considers Proust and the madeleine as he takes a journey into the past while in Segovia to bury the ashes of his mother: he recalls the outbreak of the Civil War and, bemused by memories of his cousin Angelica as she was, and is now, he leaves without being able to reconcile past and present. *Cria Cuervos* is set in a well-to-do suburb of Madrid, with the grown-up Ana recalling incidents before the death of her parents – which have mainly to do with the infidelities of her military father. Saura, writing a screenplay unaided for the first time, has worked diligently, though it is difficult to find his own personal despair in the film. It may be found in the superior *Angelica*, but the weakness of the later film really lies in the infant Ana, played by an intense child called Ana Torrent. Saura admitted that he was fascinated by her, and is, I think, rationalising wildly when he claims that she, he and we are 'victims of modern society'.

Mama Cumple 100 Años (1979) stars Miss Chaplin, who had recently appeared in Altman's *A Wedding* (q.v.) – of which this is a rehash, plus the inevitable borrowings from Buñuel (*El Angel Exterminador*) and in this case Berlanga (*La Escopeta Nacional*). Family gatherings, if they cannot be original, should at least contain either likeable or amusing participants.

Deprisa, Deprisa (1981) is a return to the milieu of *Los Golfos*, and it is one of Saura's best films. It charts the progress of three young thugs, from stealing cars to robbing banks: they are joined by Angela, the adolescent mistress of one of them, who in Franco's Spain would have been a virgin and attended church daily. Now she embraces drugs, guns and the accompanying thrills – and I would like the film more if it did not imply that such appurtenances are essential to youngsters today anxious to break the monotony of daily life. It is one thing to be objective, but there is no great film-maker, including Saura's idol, Buñuel, who was not also a moralist. The particular quality of the film is due partly to the locations: the suburbs of Madrid and the scrubbish countryside around Segovia. The brilliant photographer involved is Teo Escamilla, who also worked on *Mama Cumple 100 Años* and Saura's **Bodas de Sangre** (1981), a brief account (72 minutes) of a dance version of Lorca's 'Blood Wedding', as adapted and choreographed by Antonio Geddes. The producer, Emiliano Piedra, had so admired Geddes's flamenco ballet that he commissioned Saura to film it, and Saura, uninterested in filming the production, has restaged the work in a rehearsal room. He observed that he disliked adaptations, 'as they represent a kind of betrayal', an odd remark from one whose work has been so derivative. But the film is exhilarating.

Saura's usual producer is Elias Querejeta, who has been responsible for some of the most distinguished Spanish films, including **El Espiritu de la Colmena** (1973) – *The Spirit of the Beehive* – directed by Victor Erice from a screenplay by Francisco J. Querejeta. It takes place in 1940, in a remote village of Castile, and recalls another first feature about childhood, Truffaut's *Les Quatre Cents Coups*. As Erice is another film-maker obsessed with movies, the action devolves round the visit of the child (Ana Torrent) to Whale's *Frankenstein*. It has an air of mystery which many films on childhood lack, but that mystery seems borrowed from other cryptic films rather than observed from life; it thus destroys the faint comment it proffers on the country after the Civil War.

It has in common with all the films produced by Elias Querejeta an allusive quality. His influence may be judged by **A un Dios Desconocido** (1977), since he wrote the screenplay with its director, Jaime Chavarri. It purports to examine the dilemmas confronting a middle-aged homosexual (Hector Altiero) in contemporary Spain. The Argentine-born Altiero

823

Luis Buñuel and his Followers

The death of Franco effectively released the Spanish film industry from its shackles – which had restricted it to safe themes and certainly no criticism of the regime. The best films since have examined this recent Fascist past, or attempted to make a statement on the division between right and left which still exists in the country. Among these is *Furtivos*, directed by José Luis Borau, who also played a supporting role as a provincial governor. Once again the film is so good as to make one regret that we have since seen too little of a clearly revitalised industry.

won a Best Actor award at the San Sebastian Festival for his performance, but it consists of little but allowing a singularly glum expression to break into an occasional smile. It is difficult to sympathise with him – but that is also because the script is less interested in him than in its symbolism. It begins with the death of Lorca, but the man's obsession with Lorca, an interesting theme, is hardly developed. At the same time the piece works best in those sequences, perhaps influenced by Saura, in which the past impinges on the present.

Sexual irregularity is also discreetly handled in **Mi Querida Señorita** (1972), the tale of a middle-aged spinster (López Vázquez) who attempts, unsuccessfully, to come to terms with the sex 'she' was born with, i.e. male. The director, Jaime de Armiñan, treated another unusual subject in **El Nido** (1980), the relationship between a fifty-ish widower, a landowner (Altiero), and a twelve-year-old village girl (Miss Torrent). It is an accomplished film, with luminous photography by Escamilla; but the spirit of Buñuel lies heavily over both films. These were not subjects which attracted him, but his influence descends via Berlanga and Bardem to Saura and José Luis Borau – and Borau produced and wrote *Mi Querida Señorita* with de Armiñan before becoming a director himself. These films have Buñuelesque

qualities: a far-fetched story, usually one of passion, told in such a manner as to seem reasonable; a critical look at Spanish society, especially its authoritarian aspects and if not an unhappy ending, a sense of impending doom. Generally lacking however, is his sense of humour.

There is humour in Borau's **Furtivos** (1975) – *The Poachers* – which became the most popular Spanish film seen abroad after *El Espiritu de la Colmena*. Borau's voice, amused and acrid, is recognisable in *Mi Querida Señorita*, and that piece is to be preferred to his own first directorial effort **B. Must Die** (1973), incautiously aimed at the international market – though its humour makes it rare among its breed, that of the political thriller. It is set, ostensibly, in a South American country, where a Hungarian truck-driver (Darren McGavin) comes up against the system and winds up dead; en route he lives with a plain, ageing widow (Patricia Neal), and is persuaded by a fellow boarder (Burgess Meredith) to seduce the mistress (Stéphane Audran) of an industrialist troubled by labour unrest. There are ruthless police and anarchist bombers, but the film offers insufficient parallels with Spain for it to have worried the authorities. However, the censor, though by this time more liberal, refused at first to pass *Furtivos* without cuts, allegedly because of its erotic content. The plot is darkest bucolic, not too far from 'Maria Marten' – the faithful husband, Angel (Ovidi Montllor), the flighty wife (Alicia Sanchez), the jealous mother-in-law, the bandit lover who suddenly turns up – and it sometimes seems saved only by the luminous photography of Luis Cuadrado (who later went blind), also responsible for *La Prima Angelica* and *El Espiritu de la Colmena*; but, like them, it sets its figures surely in a landscape, and bears its double meaning with ease. To Borau himself, the film is summarised by the sequence in which the governor emasculates Angel – who is also his foster-brother – by making him a game warden, punishment for having shot the stags he wanted to bag himself. Buñuel had left – in his Mexican films and *Viridiana* – a tradition of the clerical and bureaucratic haves, as against the peasant have-nots, but Borau has refined it; this governor, played with wit by Borau himself, is fastidious, shallow, self-important and above all, petty –

and there is a great, suppressed cry for freedom emanating from Angel, from his wife, mother, the bandit and the governor, locked as they are in degrees of fear, possession, position, rivalry, ingratitude and several sorts of love. 'Spain is a cruel mother who devours her children,' said Borau, and *Furtivos* is a cruel film. There was a chance that it would not be publicly shown in Spain, and the censor only relented when it was chosen as the country's official selection for its own festival at San Sebastian, where it carried off the Grand Prix. It subsequently became the most successful Spanish film ever shown in its native cinemas. Borau refused to see it as a turning point; he did, however, concede that there was a new movement headed by Erice and Saura.

The film's popularity benefited from the death of Franco, since in the new, immediate, freedom there were no restraints on either showing or publicising it. **Camada Negra** (1977), a product of the post-Franco era, caused an uproar, because it deals with a situation labelled political; and I fancy it would have done so in any country alive to the threat of the extreme right to the progressive left in this era of youthful terrorists. The film is quirky, violent, and vastly entertaining; it says little that is controversial and nothing profound, partly because it is woven with fantasy, adopted for once with humour: but there are dazzling intellects behind it – those of Borau and Manuel Gutiérrez Aragón. They had also written *Furtivos* together; Borau this time acted only as producer, and Aragón directed. Their thesis centres on a group of young men who sing publicly as a choir and clandestinely plan to destroy any manifestation of the left: their first target is a left-wing bookshop – and the location used was a bookshop savaged by rightist hooligans some months before this film started shooting. The fiercest of these Fascist partisans is one too young, in fact, to join the clan, the angelic-looking Tatin (José Luis Alonso), whose sex life is as impotent as it is brutal. A director who plays with symbolism to the extent that this film does should be fast and subtle, and Aragón is.

His limitations were revealed, however, in **El Corazón del Bosque** (1979) and **Maravillas** (1981), co-written with and produced by Luis Megino. Escamilla's contribution to the former is paramount, since his photography gives the film a dreamlike quality. Nevertheless, the film would be better were its style keyed to its essentially simple plot, concerning a hunt for a guerrilla leader who has been hiding in the mountains of Asturias since the end of the Civil War. *Maravillas* is a black comedy about an adolescent girl in present-day Madrid. Once again in a Spanish film the piece consists of quirkish behaviour, constant allusion – often to the Civil War – and borrowings from Buñuel and Berlanga.

Earlier Aragón had been the co-writer on the successful **Las Largas Vacaciónes del 36** (1976), with its director, Jaime Camino. It was made before Franco died (which coincided with the conclusion of shooting), and was the first film to deal both overtly and at length with the Civil War. Camino described it as a memory piece, dealing with the War seen by the children of two Catalan families, but despite a number of sickening sequences the title's closeness to *Summer of '42* (q.v.) is not inapt, for what begins as a record of unusual times becomes gradually the usual adolescent chronicle of sexual encounter. For all that, it is a vast improvement on **Jutrzenka** (1970), the only other of Camino's films that I have seen, a stultifying account of the Chopin-George Sand affair.

My attitude is undoubtedly ungrateful, since *Jutrzenka* is one of the few Spanish films I have seen not bearing the influence of Buñuel. He was, as I have said, a great director, but these few of his compatriots have demonstrated sensitivity and skill to the extent that they should be able to turn in other directions. Perhaps the Spanish cinema is too young to be assured, despite *Furtivos* and *Camada Negra*, films of astonishing maturity.

31

A Picture of India:
The Films of Satyajit Ray

INDIA PRODUCES A vast number of films every year, almost all of them for local consumption. Those we see in the West are usually quiet stories of village life, with occasional excursions to Bombay and Calcutta. They are hardly representative of Indian production, which likes to cram several lifetimes and a couple of continents into one film. One of these extravaganzas was seen in the West when offered to distributors by its producer, emboldened by the fact that it was the first Indian film in colour and the knowledge that the West enthusiastically accepted *Rashomon*. In this case the press and the public regarded the film as a curiosity, and to this day it is the only film of its kind to have been widely seen.

Its title is **Aan** (1952), sometimes known as *The Savage Princess*, and it was directed by Mehboob, one of several Indian film-makers who start with an outline and let the plot develop during shooting. Although set in the distant past, 'when civilisations rose and fell', there are motor cars on view and a villainess who wears jodhpurs and a hacking-jacket. She, the savage princess, comes between a peasant boy (Dilip Kumar) and his sweetheart, while her brother usurps the maharajah's throne. They act out their adventures in a farrago of duels, chases, murders, assassination attempts and intervals of song and dance, as they move from palace to gypsy camp to torture chamber to lion's den. They do not kiss, since the censor forbids the touching of lips, but they embrace; and there are several left-wing messages in the 180 minutes running-time (150 minutes on its original Western showings).

The musical numbers were in Indian films since the coming of Talkies, when it

was discovered that audiences mutinied if they were not included. Earlier Indian films are accordingly less extravagant than *Aan*. The father of the Indian cinema is reckoned to be D. G. Phalke (1870–1944), who gave it his first success, *Raja Harishandra*, in 1913. Only one reel now survives, but I have seen *Childhood of Krishna*, made six years later, and Phalke's daughter as Krishna is not the only reason that the film seems like a very bad home movie. **Light of Asia** (1926) is an enormous advance on this, as made by Himansu Rai and his German co-director, Franz Osten (who remained to film in India till 1935). The film's source is a once-popular Victorian poem about the life of the Buddha, who is played by Rai. The credits on the existing English print inform us that what follows is 'as seen at Windsor Castle by Royal Command' – which may be the reason it ran for ten months in the Philharmonic Hall and was voted the third Best Film of the year by the readers of the *Daily Express*.

Up until 1955 ten per cent of Indian films were Bengali made. From the beginning they were largely based in the Bengali literary tradition, rather than song and dance epics ubiquitous in the rest of the subcontinent. Since the popular novels tended to be vacuous and the films themselves inert, there was a movement that began in the Thirties towards making 'social issues' cinema which faltered, only to be resumed in the Fifties. If to Western audiences Indian cinema means the films of Satyajit Ray (b. 1921) that is not necessarily an injustice, since he towers over his contemporaries. The son of the writer, painter and photographer Sukumar Ray, Satyajit Ray was educated at Calcutta University. He started his career in the

826

A Picture of India: The Films of Satyajit Ray

Calcutta branch of a British advertising agency, and developed an interest in film while living in London as a young man. He says that he liked the films of Wyler, Ford, Capra and Stevens, and thought himself fortunate in London to catch up with the work of Clair, Duvivier and Renoir. On his return to India he founded the Calcutta Film Society, and engineered a meeting with Renoir when he was in the country to make *The River* (q.v.). He cites Renoir and de Sica as the governing influences on his own work, along with a fellow Bengali, Bibhuti Bhushan Bannerjee, whose autobiographical novel he had illustrated for publication. It was after seeing *Ladri di Biciclette* that he determined to make a film of Bannerjee's book, which he eventually started with his own and his wife's money. Just when it seemed that he might have to abandon it, Monroe Wheeler of New York's Museum of Modern Art, visiting India to prepare an exhibition of Indian art, saw some stills and promised to premiere the film at the museum in conjunction with the exhibition. In the climate of Indian cinema, Ray knew that foreign showings were essential for the film's acceptance and for his own financial wellbeing. The government of West Bengal were sympathetic to his aims, and gave him further money. The film, **Pather Panchali** (1955), went on to triumph at Cannes, and Ray decided to make two more from the same source material, **Aparajito**/*The Unvanquished* (1956) and **Apur Sansar**/*The World of Apu* (1958), for which he was able to obtain private financing.

We know the three films as 'The Apu Trilogy', from Apu, their hero. *Pather Panchali* means 'Song of the Open Road', but it is this film which should have been called 'The World of Apu', for it is about the world of a young boy, centred on the derelict home with its fine courtyard, except when his sister (Uma Das Gupta) takes him across the cotton fields to see the trains. His father (Kanu Bannerjee) picks up a job here and there, between dreaming and writing plays; his mother (Karuna Bannerjee) is thrifty and perpetually worried; Auntie (Chunibala) is an old crone tolerated rather than loved, surviving poverty and infirmity by retreating into her fantasies. Apu (Subir Bannerjee) goes to school, watches a play, raids his sister's toybox; his aunt and then his sister die, and

his mother only gives way to grief when his father returns from the city. As they leave to live in Benares a snake weaves its way into the deserted house, and as they huddle in their wagon they look out at the rain but do not see it. Ray loves his people, but never patronises or sentimentalises them. He lingers on a moment of humour, on a faded hope, on reeds on the lake, the wind ruffling the water-lily leaves, the boy dawdling on the way home from school, the sweet-seller jogging by the river. There is a timelessness which evokes the dead lightness of time in the tropics, of everything suspended listlessly in the warm air; and with it is conveyed a series of perceptions that come to us all as we are growing up. It is my view, although aware that the analogy is not particularly apt, that the Apu films are to cinema what Proust is to literature: they are simply richer and more universal than most films ever made.

Aparajito begins with Apu (now played by Pinaki Sen Gupta) in the train to Benares. In the village he had played with bow and arrow, but in the city he reads, choosing a book about Livingstone, who at that time – 1920 – was a gigantic figure in the Empire saga. He sleeps in a room with an electric light, he has a toy globe on which he can locate Calcutta; eventually he

Satyajit Ray, the first Indian film-maker to have gained a world-wide reputation. A lover of movies from his youth, he determined to make films in Western style – that is, without the spectacle and songs expected by local audiences. His films are therefore too austere for India, and few of them have been overwhelmingly popular there. Some also appear too austere for the West – at least, they have not always received the acclaim that should rightfully be theirs.

The Apu Trilogy

It was the praise for the Apu Trilogy at film festivals in the late Fifties which gained Ray recognition. The three films are among the noblest works of the cinema, which has few experiences as absorbing or richly rewarding as following the progress of Apu from boyhood to manhood. The fact that he is, inevitably, played by several different actors passes unnoticed. BELOW, Subir Bannerjee as the boy Apu in *Pather Panchali*. FAR BELOW, Pinaki Sen Gupta, who shared with Smaran Ghosal the role of the growing Apu in *Aparajito*, and, RIGHT, Soumitra Chatterjee in *The World of Apu*.

is able to explain to his mother the workings of the heavens. The boy's awareness in the earlier film is partly replaced by doubts and a growing sense of responsibility, in particular towards his widowed mother, who needs his love and protection. In this respect the film is more perceptive than any other study of adolescence that I know. Ray's calm and subtle method of charting the boy's progress allows the spectator to become aware of the most important moments in Apu's life; for instance, that his ailing mother will not see him again, and that the acquisition of learning is the most important goal in life.

Nevertheless, in *Apur Sansar* he is forced to leave college without graduating. Encouraged by his friend Pulu, he tries to make a living as a writer, and it is for the sake of Pulu's family that he replaces a chosen bridegroom who has been discovered to be mentally sick. His marriage is idyllically happy until his wife (Sharmila Tagore) dies in childbirth. He refuses to see his son and loses all interest in the world until finally prevailed upon to see the child. *Pather Panchali* ends in defeat and *Aparajito* in death, but in echoing their closing sequences *Apur Sansar* ends in hope: this is 'The Unvanquished'. Despite the physical dissimilarity of the three Apus (in *Apur Sansar* played magnificently by Soumitra Chatterjee, who would become Ray's favourite interpreter) one becomes more than ever involved in Apu's world: as in childhood, the dingy room with the flapping curtain to keep out the rain; the train whistle, symbol of his (and India's?) progress; and his love of Wells's 'Outline of History' because he finds it revelatory. When he speaks of the novel he is planning he says of his hero, 'His hardship, his education broaden his mind and sharpen his wit. He feels the seed of greatness within him . . . The whole point of his life is facing up to life, not turning his back on humanity.' That, modestly offered, is the philosophy behind the trilogy, since Pulu laughs, not impressed, and Apu shrugs, seeming to agree. The comment is at once touching and ridiculous, symptomatic of Ray's approach throughout, which is to appear detached while being tremendously involved.

By the same token – and Ray is aware of this – *Apur Sansar* does not have the purity of the earlier films. He made it after their world-wide success, which he must have wanted to emulate. He makes no concessions, but after the gentle opening, with its references to the past, he moves to a more exotic India, with the wedding ceremony and the consequent melodrama revolving around the mad bridegroom. Other works about growing up come to mind, whose authors remembered their childhood with artless fidelity but recalled their adult life somewhat less convincingly. The portrait of Apu, with his hopes, aspirations, sorrow and striving, is matched by those of the people around him. They are caring and kind. So is Ray. He has said that he considers himself by instinct and education caught between East and West, but that being a Bengali and working in that country have given him an ability to understand it. In 'The Apu Trilogy' he evinces a love of his homeland and his fellow-countrymen unequalled by any other director.

While working on the trilogy, he made two films designed primarily for domestic audiences, **The Philosopher's Stone** (1957) and **Jalsaghar**/*The Music Room* (1958). Ray's love of children's stories led to the first of these, from a tale by Parasurum about a sacked bank clerk who finds a stone that can turn metal to gold but does not bring happiness with it. It was Ray's love of music which caused him to make *Jalsaghar*, from a Chekovian story by Tarashankar Bannerjee, about an impoverished landowner or *zamindar* (Chabi Biswas) who has mortgaged his decayed palace to the local Lopahin. His last three hundred rupees are spent on a musical entertainment, after which, at dawn, he goes to a drunken and bravura death on his trusty steed. Both films, despite their simplicity, are somewhat clumsily constructed – for instance, the early death of the wife and daughter in *Jalsaghar* renders much of the subsequent action anti-climactic: but it is still a haunting, elegiac piece.

The Philosopher's Stone was not seen much abroad, but *Jalsaghar* was successful in most countries, confirming Ray as one of the greatest living directors; but in my opinion **Devi** (1960) is even more remarkable. He adapted a story by Prabhat Kumar Mukherjee, based on a theme by Tagore, which deals with a man who loses his wife to a god; a foreword to the film remarks that in India it is not uncommon for a

A Picture of India: The Films of Satyajit Ray

woman to suppose herself to be the reincarnation of the goddess Kali. The time is that of the Raj, when cultured Indians were adapting themselves to the West and awakening to the world outside India. 'Why is it so important to learn English?' someone asks, but although there is no answer, the husband (Soumitra Chatterjee) is happily adapting, while his wife (Sharmila Tagore) is drawn towards the past. As a rational man, he rejects reincarnation, but his inability to take a firm line with her proves fatal; she is encouraged by his father who, unlike him, is part of the fabric of old India (and like the old man in *Jalsaghar*; the same actor plays both), and, similarly, takes a long time a-dying. Even more than the trilogy, *Devi* reveals Ray's preoccupations with British influence on India and the Indian temperament, which he finds by turns vain, vacillating, bad-tempered and foolish. Mr Chatterjee's performance as the weak but amiable husband is unforgettable, as are the views of the wide river and the religious festivals, the clanking verandahs of the palace and the scenes of the 'goddess' receiving her flock.

Ray's involvement with Tagore, who was a family friend, has enriched the medium, not least in a documentary, **Rabindranath Tagore** (1961). The government commissioned several artists to contribute works to celebrate the centenary of Tagore's birth, but hesitated before approaching Ray because he was not a historian. It was Nehru who insisted that Ray be asked, but Ray found himself hampered by the contract, which called for an hour-long film to send abroad and a two-reel condensation for local consumption. In this hour Ray combined still-photographs, newsreels, views, interviews and re-enactments of Tagore's youth in a way which would become standard procedure in television documentary. His aim was to prevent the result from being static, and he believes that he worked harder on it than on any three of his features. He stresses Tagore's well-born origins, his stance as a man of peace, and his belief in the importance of the dialogue with the West while treasuring all that is best in Indian life; he emphasises that Tagore, city-born like himself, grew to love the country, which he claimed he himself hardly knew until he came to make *Pather Panchali*. He has also said 'uniqueness and universality are what I try to convey through my films', and these are qualities found in both the subsequent films based directly on Tagore's stories.

The first of these, **Three Daughters** (1961) contains three separate tales. It lasts three hours, and it is advisable to adapt to its pace, containing as it does the slowness of life itself, the meticulous selection of incident and a fond look at our follies. There are again scenes from provincial life, about good intentions, hopes too brave and love which does not quite work out. In 'The Postmaster' Nanda (Anil Chatterjee) arrives from Calcutta, hangs the family group photograph on the wall and starts to stamp the letters. He is drawn to his housekeeper, Ratan (Chandana Bannerjee) – an eleven-year-old who is in some ways already a woman – and she to him: but despite that, and their loneliness, they are unable to help each other. 'Monihara' is a ghost story, though we may accept it as another of Ray's studies of a marriage. He himself excised it for showings in the West, but the film is richer for being a triptych. Phanibhusan (Kali Bannerjee) brings his wife to the house that he has inherited, but the marriage disintegrates as she frets over her childlessness and fears that his family do not like her. *Devi* is recalled even more strongly in the last

The riches of Ray's films seem sometimes inexhaustible, and his adaptations from Tagore are equally as enthralling as the Apu Trilogy. *Three Daughters* (1961) is an 'omnibus' film, with three separate stories. All are good, but the first, 'The Postmaster', is outstanding. Chandana Bannerjee is the new maid, and Anil Chatterjee the postmaster himself, trying to adjust to rural ways.

story, 'Samapti', with Soumitra Chatterjee again as its Westernised hero, complete with a portrait of the King and Queen on the wall, a watch-chain on his waistcoat and suspendered Argyle socks and brogues under his dhoti. Amulya, his examinations passed, has returned to his remote village home on the Ganges, but refuses to accept the dumpling of a girl his mother chose as his bride. If he must marry, he says, he will have the village tomboy (Aparna Das Gupta): but, having rejected an arranged marriage for himself, it has not occurred to him that she could do the same. He spends much of their hilarious courtship angrily stomping through the mud to see her before she changes her mind.

Kanchenjungha (1962) was Ray's first original screenplay, and where certain other great film-makers (Renoir, Bergman, Antonioni) only came into their own when working from their own material, Ray had already established his mastery. There is nothing startlingly original about the film's theme, which is that of a group of people whose lives are changed by a catalyst within their society and an outside event. They, gathering on the hilly paths of the town, include a daughter who is trying to avoid an arranged marriage; her sister, whose arranged marriage has come apart; their brother, a philanderer; and the outsider, Ashoke (Arun Mukherjee), with his B.A. degree and cheerful disposition. As Ray himself said, the cinema can be the place for a conversation piece, provided the conversation is good: 'The quality of a good wordy film does not consist in the words alone, but in the way the words are combined with significant action, details of behaviour.' *Kanchenjungha* is as such satisfying, and if it lingers in the memory it is because of the use made of Darjeeling, the town the British built as a summer retreat across the valley from Kanchenjungha. However, the location shooting seems to have impaired his players (Anil Chatterjee, superb in *Three Daughters*, is awkward as the philanderer) and Ray's usual cameraman, Subrata Mitra, was inexperienced in filming in colour. For these reasons the film may have been neglected; it was not publicly shown in Britain until more than ten years later, when it appeared on television. It was seen in the U.S. in 1966, due to the enthusiasm of an elderly distributor, Edward Harrison, whose constant belief in Ray's work was never affected by the indifference of American audiences.★

Abhijan (1962), virtually unknown in the West, was a huge success in Bengal. At 150 minutes it may move too slowly for Western audiences, but while that is by no means a fault, it does emphasise what seems to me the flaw in Ray's talent – that he cannot make a narrative point (as opposed to an emotional one) with economy. Like *Jalsaghar*, the source is a novel by Tarashankar Bannerjee, suggested to him by a producer: Ray agreed to write the script, but only decided to direct after he had seen the locations, a plain scattered with gigantic rocks. Soumitra Chatterjee again demonstrates his range, as Narsingh, the member of a high-caste family in reduced circumstances and now a cab driver. His mournful mien and monotonous life only lighten when overtaking other cars on the road, until he is befriended by both a Christian family and a prostitute, people of goodwill who are anxious to love him. They live in a village very different from those in Ray's other films, with its miserable drinking den and poorly-lit restaurant, where there is talk of trafficking in drugs and whores: life for these people is only alleviated by a visit to a film-show or a twopenny circus.

Waheeda Rehman, who plays the whore, was a star in her own right, drawing a fee of 250,000 rupees (approximately £18,600) a film – which had been more than the total cost of each of Ray's films before he made *Kanchenjungha*. Ray has said that all of his films except *Aparajito* have been profitable, but obtaining the financing has not always been easy, coming from various orthodox production companies, philanthropic institutions and wealthy individuals. He has turned down numerous offers to work abroad. (Asked whether he would make a film about an Indian family living in Britain, he said he would do so only if convinced there was no British Indian able to make it.) He works for a flat fee, a remarkable decision in view of his creative participation, which ranges from writing and directing to

★This is one example – we shall examine others – when the influential opinion of *The New York Times* was wholly destructive, since Bosley Crowther did not like Ray's films, starting with *Pather Panchali*, which he thought 'so amateurish that it would barely pass for a rough cut in Hollywood'.

A Picture of India: The Films of Satyajit Ray

Charulata is another version of Tagore, serving Ray again for a study of a marriage and of a Westernised Indian, here played by Sailen Mukherjee, with Madhabi Mukherjee as his wife. She appears neglected, and is: but the film is about much more than that.

composing the music (Ravi Shankar had provided the scores for his first few films) and later doing his own camerawork. He is also his own producer, inasmuch as he initiates his projects and selects all the creative elements and the locations: but he does not think of himself as a producer, because he is not interested in the bureaucracy involved in arranging distribution and foreign screenings. In the matter of locations, incidentally, he says that he is primarily a studio director, and the fact that so few people can notice when a sequence moves from a real city street to a simulated one is a tribute to his photographers, designers and lighting directors.

In the early Sixties four of his films were financed by a producer new to the business, R. D. Bansal, with help from the government-funded Film Finance Corporation. At least two of those films are flawless (*Kapurush-O-Mahapurush* and *Chiriakana* have never been seen in the West, and Ray does not intend that they ever shall be). **Mahanagar**/*The Big City* (1963) and **Charulata** (1964) are both about marriage, but that is all they have in common. *Mahanagar*, taken from two stories by Narendra Nath Mitra, concerns a wife (Madhabi Mukherjee) who breaks with tradition and takes a job because her husband (Anil Chatterjee) cannot make ends meet on his salary as a bank clerk. He

is a graduate, and a recurring theme in Ray's work is that teaching and the university degrees are of little aid to advancement. Once again he presents a detailed but selective picture of 'earning a living', and again this is a study of change, as the timid wife adjusts to both life in the office and selling knitting-machines door-to-door. She is helped by a jazzy colleague (Vicky Redwood), an Anglo-Indian, 'that race left by our ex-rulers' says the boss, as he sacks her. *Charulata* is from a story by Tagore, in which the husband is Bhupati Dutt (Sailen Mukherjee), a well-off Calcutta man whose passions in life are local politics and those abroad, which involve Mr Gladstone, one of his heroes. As the publisher of an influential journal of small circulation which takes up most of his time, he provides company for his wife (Miss Mukherjee) by arranging for her brother and sister-in-law to live with them; but it is a cousin, a character based on Tagore himself, the student Amal (Soumitra Chatterjee), who furnishes the company she needs, and as he teaches Charulata to write she falls in love with him. The sequences in which this happens are among the most delicately observed in all cinema, and they are entirely of Ray's making, for the love is only hinted at in the original. The fact that the story was autobiographical and that the lady concerned did commit suicide may have inspired Ray to emphasise her emotions, almost at the expense of Tagore's study of a British-orientated literary-political society. Less positive than the conclusion of *Mahanagar*, *Charulata* ends on a note of hope, instead of bleakly as in Tagore's novel. Charulata, Amal and Bhupati join Ray's gallery of beautifully-realised characters, but it is Bhupati who most interests him, a man completely Anglicised but deeply conscious of being Indian: it is typical of him that he celebrates Mr Gladstone's victory with a concert of traditional local music.

Charulata is Ray's own favourite among his films, because 'it has the fewest flaws'. It was the twelfth he had made in the first decade of his work in the industry, and at least nine of the films are masterworks – which constitutes a record perhaps only equalled by Bergman. Leaving aside the two films he refuses to be shown abroad, it may still be said that his next two films are minor. **Nayak** (1966) is a pleasant enough tale of a movie star (Uttam Khumar) and of his brief acquaintance, on a train journey, with a young student reporter (Sharmila Tagore); interwoven with their conversations are amusing flashbacks to the star's usual routine and vignettes of their fellow passengers, most of whom wish to return to the days of the Raj. **The Adventures of Goopy and Bagha** (1968) is Ray's adaptation of a folk-tale by his grandfather, Upendrakishore Roychowdhury, which takes its two ne'er-do-well heroes from the granting of three wishes to a 'Gulliver's Travels'-like conclusion. Despite some stunning locations, it soon becomes stale; every creative director is allowed one mistake, and this is Ray's.

He has said that his major films exhausted him, and that he was learning to relax with less demanding material: accordingly, while making *Goopy and Bagha* he was gearing himself for **Days and Nights in the Forest** (1969), based on a novel by Sunil Ganguly. It is a study of four wealthy Calcutta men who spend a week's vacation in a forest lodge, with no ambition other than to laze away the days and drink away the evenings – till, that is, they become involved with a Calcutta family of their own class and with the villagers, whose women drink and work 'just as in Western society'. The men do not really communicate, even between themselves, since their only common bond is an obsession with money. The symbols are not writ large, and the restating of old themes – chiefly of people whose lives touch for a while – has here a new-found pessimism. That quality is even more apparent in **The Adversary** (1971), based on a book by the same novelist. The title is ironic: the protagonist, a failed medical student, Siddhartha (Dhritiman Chatterjee), has a friend who is an anarchist, but if he himself is opposed to anything it is bureaucracy – or, subconsciously, a society which does not need him. His life is a round of futile interviews, gossiping with friends and meandering, until he finally takes a rotten job in a fly-blown small town outside Calcutta. The forlorn ending may come from the original novel, but we are a long way from *Il Posto* (q.v.), which Ray surely had in mind. Ray is always less lighthearted than Olmi, and our sole consolation is that Siddhartha is a younger version of the

usual Ray protagonist: he has the same preoccupations as the most sensible of the young men in *Days and Nights in the Forest*, he is a modern Apu, the movie star in *Nayak*, the various husbands: overdog or underdog, they may sin and accept defeat, but they are all for life, understanding and compassion.

They are also, even the young Siddhartha, throwbacks to the Raj. The young men in *Days and Nights* pride themselves on their deft English phrases, and try to imagine that they are vacationing on the French Riviera: they ape the Britishers of the past or their movie heroes, but the young protagonist of **Company Limited** (1971) is entirely of 'the new India'. He is Shyamal Chatterjee (Barun Chanda), a personable young executive with large glasses. Like his predecessors, he sighs for what might have been (in his case continuing his earlier vocation as a schoolteacher in Patna), but he knows that the good things in life are in Calcutta. His past and present take on renewed vividness when he is visited by his wife's sister: he asks her twice whether she thinks that he has improved as well as changed, and neither time does she answer. He drinks whisky, and copes with office problems: he confronts crises by combining a native cunning with Western notions of unions and strikes – and since the result consists of no

Sharmila Tagore and Soumitra Chatterjee with, between them, Robi Ghose, another favourite interpreter of Ray's, in *Days and Nights in the Forest*. The two men are among a party of Europeanised friends enjoying a week's vacation, and Miss Tagore is a widow, also from Calcutta, with whom they become involved. Here they are visiting the village fête as it winds down towards the grey evening.

red ink in the ledgers and a directorship, it is a good conjunction. He does not really comprehend the moral surrender involved in the inevitability of Europeanisation, a process which Ray views as inescapable, with reverberations of the India that was and the one that is to come.

The Middle Man (1975), like *Company Limited*, is based on a story by the novelist Shankar, and with *The Adversary* they make an unintentional trilogy about life in contemporary Calcutta. Ray has observed that all three films were based on 'second-rate' novels but with fascinating elements 'which were retained and then the rest was transformed in the process of writing the screenplay.' The middle man is Somnath (Pradip Mukherjee), another young graduate who cannot get a job and therefore engages himself in buying unneeded goods to sell to uninterested parties. He is not a very special fellow, and he bends with the wind, eventually turning to pimping, a matter which troubles him only because the girl concerned is the sister of a friend. Ray regards the conclusion as pessimistic but essential since 'the main mood is one of cynicism: it deals with corruption.' Yet while clearly condemning the bartering of flesh for contacts, he is aware that it is a step up for Somnath, preferable to driving taxis. One reason for Ray's superiority over virtually every other director working today is his ability to take a moral stand, and yet be both sympathetic and humorous – qualities necessary in portraying such people as Somnath, occupied with his own useless company as a status symbol and finding that doing business, if not reliable, can be agreeable.

These three films were made in answer to those Indian critics who constantly accused Ray, as the country's leading film-maker, of avoiding contemporary issues – and that may be why he worked from three sources for which he had no great respect. He has since said that he is only really interested in making films about the problems of the rural areas, in which respect he is echoing Gandhi, who observed that those who want to know the real India must go to the villages. In the midst of making the three Calcutta stories, he turned again to Bannerjee, the author of *Pather Panchali*, for **Distant Thunder** (1973). The setting is a remote village in 1943, and the title refers to the War –

something which no one understands, beyond the fact that King George is fighting the Japanese. The fact that Singapore has fallen is regarded as a grave matter, except that no one knows where it is. The schoolmaster hero (Soumitra Chatterjee) says that it is in another province, which might have ended any speculation on war till rice becomes scarce and, as a result, law and order break down. An astounding final shot is followed by a title epilogue with the information that over five million people died in what became known as the 'man-made' famine in East Bengal in 1943. I believe that this film was also made as a reply to Ray's critics, but that, once away from the city, he found himself incapable of the requisite harshness. He does not flinch from portraying the ugly mood in the latter part of the film, but his customary humour and affection are apparent whenever he contemplates the teacher, feckless and kind, with his odd little white lies and innate decency, and his wife, touchingly loyal and kind. He pauses for a sudden expression on their faces, as he does for a shot of a flower, of a field with a bank of clouds over it, of a stream flowing through a wood or a snatch of overheard conversation. Thus he shares with us some images from one man's small existence.

It was Ray's first film in colour since *Kanchenjungha*, and he was to use colour with each film from **The Chess Players** (1977) onwards. This was Ray's first film in Hindi and made in Bombay ostensibly because it required a larger budget than usual and Hindi films are more widely distributed than those made in Bengali. In fact, Ray's autocratic attitude had made him unpopular with the self-regarding Calcutta film industry, but he could point to the fact that the original story, by Munshi Premchand, was in Hindi. Its subject is two chess-playing nabobs, and there is a sub-plot about the East India Company trying to manipulate the abdication of an effete ruler. The latter is but a pawn in the game of taking over India, and we may assume that his lack of will and the indifference of the nabobs were contributory factors in India becoming a red mass on the map of the British Empire. However, the film is decorative rather than political, and when it attempts to explain it does so in primer-style, filling in the background with long duologues between the British commander (Richard Attenborough) and his aides. Ray had one of his greatest successes in the West with this film, but I find that it neither flows nor breathes. More surprisingly, the relationship between the nabobs (and their wives) lacks shading – that shading which had hitherto made his work so infinitely rewarding. In his studies of married couples, of Calcutta businessmen, of students and graduates he had always conveyed the minute pressures, the small compromises, the growing (or receding) consciousness which constitute for all of us ways of coping with life.

The Chess Players seems to me less good than the three children's films that he made at this time. The first of them, **The Golden Fortress** (1974) is two and a half hours of enchantment, and while I appreciate the difficulties involved in programming long, subtitled films for children, I do not understand why this one has not been seen in the West outside the festivals. Based on a serial Ray wrote for the children's magazine which he edits, it is the reverse, let it be said, of *Goopy and Bagha*. When its young hero, Mukul (Kushul Chakravarty), is seen reading Tintin, we know what to expect; like Tintin, Mukul sets out on his adventures with some motley friends, including a bodyguard detective (Soumitra Chatterjee), and there is many a cross and double cross before the villain is unmasked in the golden fortress itself, Rajasthan. **The Elephant God** (1978) is an enjoyable sequel, and **The Kingdom of Diamonds** (1980) consists of the further adventures of Goopy and Bagha, which are considerably more colourful than those in the earlier film. Ray's feeling for his characters and for the vastness of India – particularly strong in *The Golden Fortress* – are among the reasons these are some of the very best films for children.

They were extremely popular on their home territory, and Ray has observed that his unit had great fun in their making. During this time he also made some documentaries, but none of this work does he consider as major. That he has been so much less prolific in recent years is due to his refusal to undertake any project which does not interest him wholeheartedly. He has recently made two short films, one for television in France (a country in which his films are having a belated success), and it is heartening to know, as I write, that he is embarking upon *The Home and the World*, from a story by Tagore which he had originally intended to make before *Pather Panchali*.

Ray was a great admirer of Ritwik Ghatak (1926–76), whose first film, **The Citizen** (1952), pre-dates *Pather Panchali*. Ghatak was born in that part of Bengal which eventually became Bangladesh, and the Partition haunted him all his life. He started writing plays at college, and joined the Indian People's Theatre Association, but decided that as a Communist – and, like Ray, prompted by *Ladri di Biciclette* – films offered a greater platform for his political views. Ray, paying tribute to him after his death, said that his most valuable and distinctive characteristic was that he was 'a Bengali director in heart and soul, a Bengali artist'; he also said that he admired him for there was nothing of Hollywood in his work, despite the fact that these were almost the only foreign films seen in India during their formative years. Ghatak had, apparently, seen the Soviet Silent classics, and Ray detected the influence of these in Ghatak's films, along with 'theatre, in the dialogue, content and conclusions of his films'. *The Citizen* is theatrical, in the manner of the Group Theatre, and understandably so, since Ghatak's work in the theatre had involved him in American left-wing plays. Unlike de Sica, Ghatak in *The Citizen* tempers realism with poetry, in the repeated symbol of the pavement violinist. Its few scenes in Calcutta bars and offices are lively, but he is less intense and less sensitive than Ray in dealing with the poverty-stricken family at the centre of the film. Prostitution beckons for the girls; the family's hopes are centred on Ramu (Satindra Bhattacharya), alternately optimistic and depressed as he regards his university degree, which he finds is no passport to employment. That is only one of the several themes in this film which was to turn up in Ray's later work, but that may be because poverty in Calcutta is unchanging.

Ray may not have seen the film. It was an entirely cooperative effort, made with friends (many of the players became important stars), and a revolutionary project for India: the studio, the laboratory and the supplier of film stock all contributed, but though passed by the censor the film came into the hands of a dishonest businessman and was not seen publicly till after Ghatak's death. Following Ray's example with *Pather Panchali*, Ghatak applied to the government of West Bengal for the financing of **The Mechanical Man** (1958), which became a great favourite with local audiences. It was submitted to the committee of the Venice Film Festival, which turned it down, thus denying Ghatak an opportunity to win international fame and the attendant benefits – and world audiences of seeing a superb film. In a series of gently amusing episodes it deals with Bimal, a rural, drunken cab driver, and his even more unreliable but beloved taxi, which has, to put it mildly, seen better days. The ending of the film is undeniably sentimental, but technically this film is so accomplished that it should be required viewing in film schools.

None of Ghatak's other films is as satisfactory, starting with **The Runaway** (1959), about a small boy who flees to Calcutta for a series of adventures of varying quality. The film has a dreamlike quality and Calcutta has no reality: for the boy, it is, like dreams, by turns benign and disturbing, and absolutely nothing turns out as he expects – at least in human terms, as adults are revealed as anything but what they seem at first. Consequently the boy's perceptions are both heightened and limited, evidence enough that the film itself is more perceptive than most films on childhood. Ghatak's next two films seem to me unsatisfactory, partly due to the performances of Supriya Choudhury in the leading roles. **The Hidden Star** (1960) is not unlike *The Citizen*, about an impoverished family dependent on the daughter (Miss Choudhury). She loses her amiable fiancé to her sister and subsequently finds after all her sacrifices that she has a fatal illness. The film is beautifully made, but the autobiographical **E Flat** (1960) tries to say too much, and it does not say it well. Its subject is the rivalry between avant-garde theatre groups, to which is attached the relationship between the idealistic chief (Abanish Bandyopadhyay) of one and an actress (Miss Choudhury) in the other. Both of them are victims of Partition, and are drawn together because of it.

Partition is the subject of Ghatak's most complex film, **Subarnarekha** (1962), which manages to combine some bravura passages, both beautiful and melodramatic, with much social criticism, directed mainly at the methods of small-minded businessmen. The film's central characters have been left stranded by Partition: Ishwar is helped by an old friend to get a job at an iron foundry in the country, and he takes an abandoned small boy whom he educates. The boy, grown-up, wants to marry his foster-sister, but as he is thought to be of a lower caste the bosses intervene, and the young couple run away to Calcutta, where she is eventually forced into prostitution. The tale of these three people culminates in violence, but the film's ending is of hope, not unlike *The World of Apu*. Ishwar himself is a tragic figure, but like many another protagonist in the Indian cinema so weak that he can be easily destroyed by stronger forces.

The film was not shown till three years after it was made. A number of other projects were begun and abandoned, partly because Ghatak's reputation as an alcoholic and as undependable frequently prevented him from getting backing. He did make *A River Named Titus* in Bangladesh not long before he died of tuberculosis and chronic alcoholism, and he knew that he was dying when he made the autobiographical **Reason, Debate and a Tale** (1974). He himself plays the leading role, that of a man whose career and marriage have been ruined by drink. With some equally aimless companions he goes to visit his wife, before becoming involved with some terrorists. Ghatak's inspiration was Fellini's *8½* (q.v.), and for a while it is more pointed; but, like much of the work of alcoholics, it is self-pitying, boring and eventually incoherent.

Ghatak's preoccupation with Partition is shared by M. S. Sathyu, whose first film, **Hot Winds** (1975), is sufficiently like *The Citizen* as to suggest a homage to Ghatak. Sathyu, coming from the theatre, is an uninspired but careful craftsman, and the achievement of *Hot Winds*, which is considerable, lies in its screenplay by Kaifi Azmi and Shama Zaidi, from an unpublished story by Ismat Chugtai. It focuses on the plight of one Muslim family left in Calcutta after Partition, the increasing hostility around them, the difficulty of continuing in business (they own a small shoe factory) and the temptation to join other members of the family who have

A Picture of India: The Films of Satyajit Ray

M. S. Sathyu's *Hot Winds* is one of several Indian films of the Seventies which examine the effects of Partition, in this case on a Muslim family which remains while all their friends have gone to Pakistan. The effect is profound on the daughter (played by Gita) who loses both of the young men she loves (this one is played by Jalal Agha), and this film is almost unique in its delicate linking of romance and polemic.

emigrated to Pakistan. Emotional problems caused by Partition drive the daughter to suicide, which seems a dramatic device rather than a matter deeply felt, but the ending, in which the remaining members of the family find that they cannot leave India, is superb. The film was much reviled and discussed when it came out, but was popular with audiences. It was seen at the Cannes Film Festival and deserves to be more widely known.

The most political of Indian filmmakers is Mrinal Sen, whose didacticism has sometimes alienated even those who share his left-wing views. His early films were influenced by Brecht and the *nouvelle vague*, and by the time of his third movie, *Akash Kusum*, in 1965, his work was dismissed by Ray, who can be a severe critic of the films of his colleagues. It is ironic therefore that Sen had an enormous popular success with **Bhuvan Shome** (1969), though it should be noted that it was made in Hindi rather than his native Bengali, unlike his earlier films. This one was backed by the Film Finance Corporation, and was so profitable that the government entered the film business on a large scale, to

the extent that the country's annual output was doubled (India made 396 films in 1970, which had risen to 742 in 1980, many of them made for the linguistic minorities, hitherto accustomed to Hindi films with subtitles). *Bhuvan Shome* is little more than a character study of the eponymous hero, a railway official who learns to relax and become more human on a hunting trip. Chiefly responsible for his conversion is the fiancée (Susasini Mulay) of one of his employees, a man to be sacked or reprimanded for taking small bribes. Miss Mulay is reason enough for seeing the film.

For Western viewers, it has a Godardian friskiness which is tiresome, and the exposition is clumsy, a fault Sen has not always managed to overcome in his later, better films. Among these are **The Royal Hunt** (1976) and **The Outsiders** (1977), both rural tales in which the villagers are harassed, harried and deprived of any real livelihood by the landowners or their representatives. The first film concerns the headman's son, a hunter, and his friendship with the white district officer whom he considers a god. When the landowner's

837

agent kidnaps the hunter's wife for sexual purposes he murders him before telling his white friend – a rather unconvincing denouement in view of the latter's fondness for the couple. The outsiders of the second film are an unruly old man and his son, whom he encourages to be idle and to steal, like himself, rather than submit to the iniquitous system imposed upon the other villagers. Again, the climax is ridiculous, as the young man sits by and lets his wife scream during the labour pains that kill her, but Sen makes a point from that, as the two men beg for the fees for the funeral. Something is wrong with a society that has money for death but not for life: it is a powerful ending if you take the cynical view that Brecht and others have taught us that the message must be simple-minded.

And Quiet Rolls the Dawn (1979), Sen's only film to be widely seen in the West, was criticised for its didacticism, but if it is occasionally nudging it is subtle enough as a feminist tract. Based on a story by Amalendu Chakravarty, it is, like Ghatak's *The Citizen*, in the tradition of tales about families living in poverty in large decaying tenements (once mansions) in Calcutta. As in the earlier film the rest of the family depends on one member, the daughter Chinu (Mamata Shankar), for its livelihood, and the action solely concerns

the one night when she does not return. There are fears that she has had an accident, and the elder son (Tapan Das) goes to the police station, the morgue, a hospital; the suspicion that she may have been with a man becomes a certainty, if to her family but not to audiences, and yet again the ending lacks conviction. Overall this is a sweet, unpretentious film, with some telling vignettes of the family, of neighbours, of officials – all of them, as is usual in Sen's films, beautifully acted.

Sen lacks the intellectual rigour of Ray and Shyam Benegal (b. 1934), though Benegal shares his indignation, particularly in regard to conditions in the rural areas. All three of them are trying to tell us about their country, but where Sen makes his habitual condemnation Ray and Benegal ask for an understanding to be extended. Ray wants us to love his people as much as he does, finding chinks of hope; Benegal seems dismayed that conditions remain so feudal, and does not express much hope in change. He has, like Ray, stated his preference for filming in what he calls 'the remote corners of our land. The glitter and glamour of the few cities that most of us are a witness to are not in reality our way of life.' His first four films form a remarkable quartet.

He is a Hindi, born in Hyderabad, where he also attended university. He worked on documentaries before turning to fiction with **Ankur**/*The Seedling* (1974) – a fiction, however, based on events that he had witnessed as a student, about a young man, Surya (Anant Nag) who is sent to oversee a remote corner of his father's estate and finds that he cannot cope. **Night's End** (1975), also based on an actual incident, is set in 1945 and concerns the abduction of the new schoolteacher's wife by the family of the *zamindar*, one of whom is sexually attracted to her. **The Churning** (1976) is founded in events told to Benegal while making one of his documentaries, about the efforts of some city-dwellers to bring a cooperative to a backward village. **The Boon** (1978), conversely, is whimsical. Its hero, Parasuram (Mr Nag), believes that he has been granted divine powers, which prove to have terrible consequences when he is forced to use them.

The themes of the four films are interchangeable, but whereas *The Boon* concen-

The films of Shyam Benegal are too little known, and the best of them are worthy to rank with those of Ray. *The Churning* concerns a city man, marvellously played by Girish Karnad, right, who attempts to persuade a rural community to adopt more modern methods. He is a kindly man, but that was not the quality required and he retires at the end defeated.

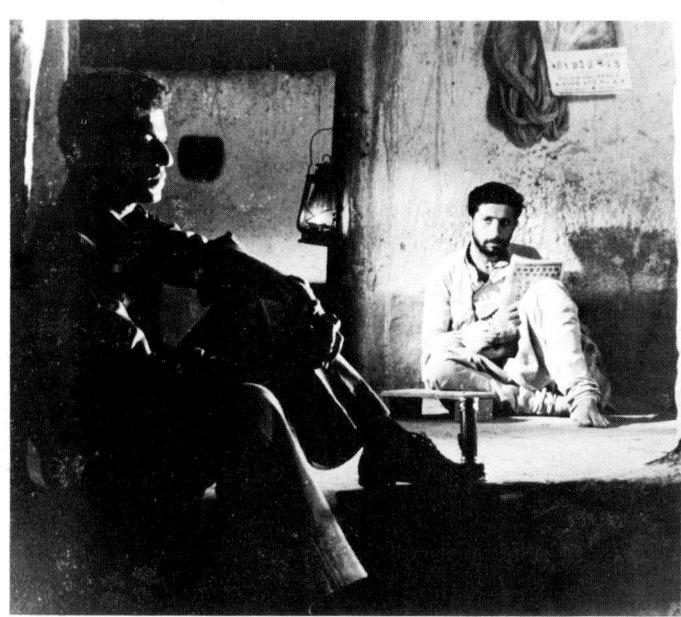

A Picture of India: The Films of Satyajit Ray

trates on the effect of superstition and the misuse of religion its most brilliant sequences concern the family of the *zamindar*. The iniquities of the *zamindars* provide the most sustained of the themes throughout the quartet: they are greedy, self-indulgent and indifferent to the wrongs they do, while the police who support them are lazy and corrupt. The peasants are slothful and resigned, unlikely to respond to the teachers and townsfolk who want to help them and who in any case have their own shortcomings – pomposity, divided goals, lack of money and an inability to overcome centuries-old prejudices and mores. In *The Seedling* Surya's 'kindness' to his housekeeper, a woman of lower caste, leads to his complete isolation, as do the teacher's rightful claims for his wife in *Night's End*. In Benegal's films violence and rapacity are always in prospect, which is one reason we could never confuse them with Ray's.

The first two of the quartet were backed by Blaze Enterprises, a successful producer of advertising shorts run by two journalists. *The Churning* was financed, the credits inform us, by '500,000 farmers of Gujarat', that is by the milk cooperatives of that province, each member of which provided two rupees towards its making. Since milk production creates the staple income in most smallholdings, the government formulated its plans on the cooperatives in an attempt to end the exploitation of the peasants by the landowners: but from the radio broadcasts heard in the film it is clear that Benegal does not think the government entirely blameless. This is a true socialist film, if less vehement than Sen's similar tales, more contemplative and richer and more honest. It is the best of the quartet, of which only *Ankur* has been publicly seen in Britain.

Ironically, two of Benegal's lesser films have been publicly shown in London. **Bhumika/*The Role*** (1977) is too long at 140 minutes for its content – which is close to soap opera, despite the director's claim that 'it is about the problems of women in our society, the search for their own identity, their desire to achieve independence'. He himself contributed to the screenplay, based on an autobiographical book by Hansa Wadkar, a film star of the Thirties. This film begins then, but mainly concerns the years of success of the star,

Usha (Smita Patil), and her manipulation by her husband (Anant Nag), who is also her manager. Unfortunately Benegal does not let us know to what extent the man controls Usha's career and instead offers some affectionate satire on the Indian movies of the time. Escaping her husband, the woman has casual sex with a stranger and goes to live with him, finding the domesticity she always craved but an even greater restriction on her freedom – and it is at this point that the film at last becomes powerful. **Junoon** (1979) has an even stronger situation, but Benegal is simply overwhelmed by it. Its source is a nineteenth-century story, 'A Flight of Pigeons', by Ruskin Bond, about the plight of an Anglo-Indian family at the time of civil disorder. The actor Shashi Kapoor produced, on a large budget, and plays the lead, that of a Pathan nabob obsessed by the daughter of the family. Benegal lacks the courage to be full-bloodedly romantic, as demanded by the subject, and makes instead small and tactful points about British rule and Indian submission which in the end amount to very little.

Ascending Scale (1982) would seem to confirm that Benegal is at his best dealing with contemporary issues. His subject is once more the power of the landowners, which was hardly shaken by the government decree of 1967 that the peasants must be given three out of every five shares of land. That power, and local superstition, plus an inefficient bureaucracy and an often corrupt judiciary, are all evidenced in this film, and it is therefore almost startling to find that it was sponsored by the government of West Bengal, using the cinema's powers of persuasion as they had seldom been used since the Soviets at the time of Eisenstein. There are parallels in the portrait of the effete landowners, and the solidarity of the workers (at the elections; during the Great Bengal Flood of 1977), while the main plot concerns the ten-year struggle, often in the courts, of Hari (Om Puri) to claim the land that is rightfully his. Two subplots concern relatives who because of poverty go to Calcutta where one, Hari's brother, becomes involved with crooks and anarchists, and the other, a girl, becomes a kept woman before going mad. Her story in particular is melodramatic, but that is possibly because unsophisticated audiences could

839

A Picture of India: The Films of Satyajit Ray

hardly be expected to be wholly taken up with Hari's legal battles – and the film was clearly made *pour encourager les autres*. It is an important, powerful and absorbing one, and if it firmly establishes Benegal as a polemic film-maker he remains primarily a humanist.

One reason that Mr Kapoor had produced *Junoon* was that as one of India's leading film stars he had become disillusioned with the 'rubbish' that was being offered him – and the word is that of his wife, Jennifer Kendal, whom he had met and married while acting with other members of her family in *Shakespeare Wallah* (q.v.). He produced **36 Chowringhee Lane** (1981) as a starring vehicle for her, and in it she plays an Anglo-Indian teacher living in Calcutta. She is a spinster, and lonely because her niece has recently married an Australian; she befriends a young couple (Debashree Roy, Dhritiman Chatterjee), who respond in order to be able to use her cluttered apartment to make love, and she is consequently disillusioned when marriage means that they no longer need her. This is a delicate, touching film, and all praise is due to those concerned, which include the Film Finance Corporation (the cost was two million rupees, or the equivalent of £117,000, as opposed to six million or £350,000 for *Junoon*). There are jejune touches, such as the shots of the Calcutta poor against 'Silent Night' on the soundtrack, and Miss Kendal's otherwise lovely performance is spoilt by a tendency to over-react: but perhaps Aparna Sen did not care to 'direct' the producer's wife. Miss Sen also wrote the screenplay, performing both functions with the blessing of Satyajit Ray, for whom she had made her screen debut in *Three Daughters*. The Indian censor, incidentally, passed the nude and the usually-banned kissing scenes on the grounds that this was an 'English' film: in fact, the lovers speak Bengali to each other, and certain other scenes seem to have been filmed in that language and dubbed.

Since America has been inhospitable to Ray, we do not need to ask why Benegal's films have only been shown in that country at festivals. As far as Britain is concerned, the praise of a handful of critics who have championed Indian cinema is offset by the others, who have been mainly indifferent – with art-house audiences apparently agreeing, as explained by one distributor who had failed several times with the work of the Singhalese director, Lester James Peries (b. 1921). The same distributor observed that he had made losses on a couple of Ray's films – and Ray, said Peries, 'is a far greater director'. This is true, but that might still mean that Peries is a very good one. There are a number of interesting films among his work, but his first film, **The Line of Destiny** (1956), is not one of them – despite its acclaim at the time in Sri Lanka (then Ceylon). At that time the available 'Singhalese' films were made in Madras, by Tamils, with painted scenery and no knowledge of Sri Lanka except for the language. They were very long, with musical episodes. Peries, a former journalist (like Ray, he had worked in London for some years), was engaged on filming documentaries for the government, and he asked two colleagues to join him on a true Singhalese film, which, incidentally, went into production as Ray was finishing *Pather Panchali*. He wrote the screenplay himself, since there were no suitable works for adaptation (those available were either didactic or in the style of nineteenth-century melodrama), and it is about a small village boy who is thought to have magic powers, which turn against him when the area is afflicted by drought.

If *The Line of Destiny* fails to illuminate village life, Peries had become much more accomplished by the time he made **Gamperaliya** (1964), his third film. It is the story of an arranged marriage in a village in southern Ceylon just after the turn of the century, and, with reason, it won the Grand Prix at the Delhi Film Festival. I am not sure that it reveals 'the inner life' of its characters, which Peries claims is one of the virtues available to those who make films. The otherwise interesting **Between Two Worlds** (1966) fails on that account, as it follows the doubts of a wealthy playboy (Tony Ranasinghe) when he knows that his family intend that a servant should take the blame for a hit-and-run accident for which he is responsible. Peries's slow pacing is tiring (as Ray's is not, for his films are more richly detailed) and **Five Acres of Land** (1969) is overlong at 132 minutes. Otherwise it marks another advance for Peries, both in the skill with which it is made and the material itself, which is built round a young man (Milton Jayawar-

A Picture of India: The Films of Satyajit Ray

lena) who is being educated at a college in he city. He is a nice young man, lonely at irst, and conscious of the sacrifices being nade by his humble family: yet he falls in ove with the bourgeois girl with whose amily he is lodging and loses his chance of bettering himself.

The title of **The Treasure** (1972) refers o both a human being and gold, insofar as t exists. The hero's confusion between the wo is one reason why this is a very appealng story. The hero is Willie (Gamini Fonseka), a penniless landowner. He has a dream of becoming rich: legend says that reasure is buried in a deserted temple in a forest, but can only be unlodged by someone sacrificing a virgin. Willie dreams about a virgin with certain birthmarks, sees her in the flesh, and offers marriage. He treats her as father rather than husband, till he realises that he loves her, but Willie is caught up in a train of consequences which lead to tragedy. A framing device gives dimension to this somewhat dubious story, written by G. B. Senanayake; the screenplay is by Tissa Abeysekera, Peries's usual collaborator at the time, and M. S. Anandan's photography is as luminous as it was for *Five Acres of Land*. Fonseka's detailed performance is magnificent, as is that of Malina Fonseka as the bride. She is as meltingly beautiful as Madhabi Mukherjee in *Charulata*, to which Peries pays homage in one scene. Despite the shortcomings of the plot, this is a film of almost the same quality.

The Eyes (1972) confirms that Peries came into his own by this time. A simpleminded village man (Joe Abeywickrema) marries a blind girl (Srijani Amarasane), and is then not sure whether he wants her to be cured by the holy man (Ravendra Randenija). **Enchanted Island** (1976) is a simple tale of a youth so wild and destructive that he alienates his parents and the kindly schoolteacher (Mr Abeywickrema) to whom he is sent for correction. He cultivates a desert island so successfully with a friend that the crown agents allow them to keep it. **White Flowers for the Dead** (1976) somewhat resembles *The Treasure*, and within its complex past-to-present structure is an affectionate portrait of a doctor (Mr Ranasinghe) whose bitterness after his wife's death is lessened as he becomes caught up once more with the members of her family. Peries's direction,

after the confidence of *The Treasure*, becomes hesitant again, a fact somewhat disguised by his superlative team of players and a series of photographers of the same quality.

Peries did make two expensive and unqualified failures. **The God King** (1974) was financed by a Briton, who offered him the subject, an historical fresco set in the fifth century, and the largest budget ever offered by the West to an Asian director (Ray had failed to make a projected film with Peter Sellers; Kurosawa had walked off *Tora! Tora! Tora!*). Peries was so flattered that he ceded control over casting (three British actors were blacked-up to play Singhalese) as well as script and editing (his wife's cut was not accepted). The Rank Organisation, which was due to release the result, lost interest, as did the minor British company which took it up after a test engagement in Liverpool for the Indian and Pakistani population, who quite reasonably were not interested in a Singhalese film. The failure of **Rebellion** (1978) is Peries's own, indicating that he has no aptitude for the epic form (I cannot say the historical film, since his second film, *The Message*, was historical and so popular that the negative and all remaining copies were worn out, so that it does not exist for valuation). The film's subject is Veera Puran Appu (Mr Randenija), the Singhalese outlaw and patriot who led a revolt against the British in 1848. Local critics disliked the film because of its

Like most Asian directors, Lester James Peries has been influenced by Satyajit Ray, and they have a common goal, to depict the everyday life of ordinary people. When Peries has been more ambitious he has sometimes failed, and his best films have all concerned wealthy bourgeois families in his native country, Sri Lanka. His best film is *The Treasure*, a study of a strangely motivated marriage between a landowner (Gamini Fonseka) and a girl (Malina Fonseka) from another class. Both players, who are not related, are superb.

841

A Picture of India: The Films of Satyajit Ray

unpatriotic climax (the revolt had been unsuccessful), but the anti-British stance of it is both justifiable and well expressed. Elsewhere Peries seems to have no control, but it is interesting for once to see British colonials as the villains.

British Ceylon is the background to **Village in the Jungle** (1980), based on Leonard Woolf's novel of the same name, published in 1913. Its subject to an extent resembles that of *Ankur*, for it finds a weak landowner's son banished to a remote village as overseer, but who himself contributes to the greed, superstition, prejudice and depravity that he finds there. A comparison of the two films shows Peries unable to make his characters as full-blooded as those of Benegal, though he is equally critical of rural life. As with Ray, Peries is found wanting by some local critics who claim that his films are not sufficiently political; left-wing Indians and Singhalese who recognise both directors as powerful communicators are heartened by the demotic subjects they choose but are disappointed by the end product. Although Peries has echoed Ray in saying that the only material which really interests him concerns the conditions in the rural areas, he has returned to the bourgeoisie of *Gamperaliya* for his most recent work. When he set out to make that film he was unaware that the original novel, by Martin Wickremasinghe, was the first part of a trilogy, 'The Changing Village'. The popularity of *Gamperaliya* in Germany encouraged one of the country's television channels to finance the further two parts, of which the first, **Kaliyugaya** (1981), has already been shown. The circumstances of its being made clearly restored Peries's confidence, for this is his most masterly film since *The Treasure* and *The Eyes*. It takes up the fortunes of the family of *Gamperaliya* some twenty years later (with flashbacks, which of course are in monochrome), and finds them now living in the city and somewhat more affluent. Its chief theme is the alienation of the son, who went to live in London when the family disapproved of his chosen bride: at the end of the film he breaks off all communication with his widowed mother, leaving us to wait for Part Three to know whether this family solves its difficulties.

We may also regard the American, James Ivory (b. 1930), as a disciple of Ray.

He studied film in California, where he was born, and as a documentary filmmaker was sent to India by the Asia Society of New York. There he met Ismail Merchant, who became his partner and who operates the commercial end of their production company, tapping various unlikely sources for financing in many countries. One reason for this is the uneven quality of Ivory's work – and hence its eventual reception at the box office – but his first film, **The Householder** (1963), is good and the second, **Shakespeare Wallah** (1965), something more than that. Ivory's co-writer was the German-born* novelist, Ruth Prawer Jhabvala, who was to receive sole billing for the screenplays of most of Ivory's later films. *The Householder*, based on one of her novels, is reminiscent of both *The World of Apu* and *Mahanagar*, being a study of the first year of marriage of a city couple (Shashi Kapoor, Leela Naida). It is slight and unspoilt, even if derivative. From an indigenous couple Ivory turned to an English family in *Shakespeare Wallah*, a band of actors in an India that no longer really wants them. They had come out years before, as idealists, trailing across the subcontinent to play Shakespeare in halls, gardens, private homes, till interest has dwindled to an occasional princeling, an indulgent school and the British who have remained. The film is a tender postscript to the British love affair with India; the Darjeeling that we see is not that of *Kanchenjungha* but of British hotels, damp and decaying. It is a film of resonance and nuance, not least because Geoffrey Kendal and Laura Lidell were virtually playing themselves; at the end their daughter Felicity leaves for England – as she did in life, later to become one of Britain's brightest stars of stage and television. Her portrait of adolescence is as touching as that in Renoir's *The River*, and this is, like that, a special film, one for which many people have a fondness.

It is clumsily and often amateurishly made, faults not always eradicated in Ivory's subsequent and more expensive films. **The Guru** (1969) was also made with love and it also has some acute perceptions about the British in India – the modern, young British, that is, for it con-

*Her parents were Polish; she was educated in England and married an Indian architect.

cerns a pop-singer (Michael York), who comes to study the sitar. 20th Century-Fox were the backers – this was not long after the world-wide success of *Un Homme et une Femme* (q.v.) – but they did not, in view of the returns, care to repeat the experience. An Indian businessman financed **Bombay Talkie** (1970) and Ivory's first American feature, **Savages** (1972). *Bombay Talkie* proposes an engaging new version on the theme of East versus West, and on real emotions as opposed to pretended ones, since its leading characters are all engaged in the media. A much-married and bestselling American novelist (Jennifer Kendal) is attracted to both a penniless and honest poet (Zia Mohyeddin) and a good-natured but vain film star (Mr Kapoor): the opening sequence between the three of them is especially well balanced. Thereafter the film moves downhill to a conclusion which is anything but. For sheer pointlessness and melodramatic idiocy it would be hard to

equal it, but Ivory managed this in *Savages*, which follow a group of primitive beings as they invade a deserted mansion, become civilised and then regress to their original state.

The film needs, but does not have, the cinema's twin bogies, sex and violence, which is also true of **The Wild Party** (1975), a pastiche tale of Hollywood in the Twenties, with James Coco as an Arbuckle-like clown. Its source is a melodramatic narrative poem by Joseph Moncure March, its emphasis weakened by overstatement. The backers this time were American International Pictures, whose version was refuted by Ivory in letters to a number of leading critics, claiming that many of his discarded sequences had been inserted in 'a cheap attempt to over-exploit everything exploitable'. Since not one single scene worked on screen, the film only served to underline Ivory's position as a dilettante among film-makers. However, **Roseland** (1977), three separate

The director James Ivory made his best film at the beginning of his career, *Shakespeare Wallah*, about the adventures of a group of strolling players, seen here arriving in a small town in the hills.

843

A Picture of India: The Films of Satyajit Ray

stories of lonely people drawn together at New York's famous dance-hall, finds him in finer form than at any time since *Shakespeare Wallah*. This film and that have in common some lonely, unwanted people in a somewhat faded and déclassé setting, and perhaps that is where Ivory's sympathies really lie.

Returning to India, he made **Hullabaloo Over Georgie and Bonnie's Pictures** (1978), financed by a British T.V. company. The subject is fascinating. An aristocratic English collector (Peggy Ashcroft) and an American dealer arrive to prise away from a bankrupt young maharajah (Victor Bannerjee) his inheritance, a group of paintings the two con-artists believe would be of more benefit on gallery walls. Eventually both the Englishwoman and the American discard their selfishness and find new values, but that theme, apart from being an unoriginal one, is hardly explored. Turning to Henry James, Ivory reveals in **The Europeans** (1979) a lack of narrative sense or rhythm, thus failing to do justice to the material. He seems to believe that camera movement and editing can make a movie, which perhaps in the days of the studio system they could; but his players, if likeable, have no life beyond the set, and since this is a costume picture one readily imagines them taking their clothes from wicker baskets just before parading in front of the camera. The experienced Lee Remick acts at best moderately well, and only Lisa Eichhorn seems deeply immersed in her performance. As beautiful as both ladies are the yellow and red leaves of the New Hampshire Fall. James did not call for these, but his story is just strong enough to survive.

Perhaps because of his own life in India or his peripatetic adventures as a film-maker Ivory has been drawn to tales of people adapting themselves to strange environments, to expatriates, to people passing through, and this penchant led him to the Anglo-American colony in Paris in the Twenties, in **Quartet** (1981). Its source is Jean Rhys's cynical, autobiographical novel, founded on her relationship with Ford Madox Ford. The characters based on the two of them are played by Isabelle Adjani, whose limitations are of no help to the piece, and Alan Bates; his wife is played by Maggie Smith. The characters around them are somewhat more interesting, with their double options and conflicting, if usually selfish, emotions. The Paris of the time is as attractively caught as the Hollywood of the Twenties in *The Wild Party* was not. And, unlike *The Europeans*, Ivory has not betrayed his source material.

Anyone who cares for civilised cinema – particularly as it seems to be disappearing – would want Ivory to succeed as well on every occasion. Returning to India he did so, with **Heat and Dust** (1982), the first time that Ms Jhabvala has adopted one of her novels for Ivory since their collaboration began with *The Householder*. Side by side it examines the India of today, as a British woman (Julie Christie) seeks information on the life of her great-aunt, and the India of the Raj, when that lady, as a young woman (Greta Scacchi), first arrived to join her husband. Christie finds an India of teeming people, fake American pilgrims, bus-rides and offices; Scacchi's India is of elegance, idleness, ceremony, of dressing for dinner and of picnics with a romantic nawab (Shashi Kapoor) distrusted by the British. The film is too schematic and has moments of overemphasis, but Ivory's handling shows a confidence missing from some of his recent films. His best work has always been that which reflected a more glorious past or that in which two cultures try to come to terms with each other. There is no one theme in the film, which is, as the title implies, about India – and it is one of the most loving and accomplished on that huge subject ever made.

It reminds us that in his first two films he also added to our understanding of India. Ray, incidentally, had been instrumental in their production, lending members of his unit and his photographer, Subrata Mitra. Perhaps he influenced them more than we know. Benegal, Peries and Sen have acknowledged their debt to Ray, who has also been an inspiration to other realist, humanist film-makers in Third World countries or those few who work with honesty while mired in an industry dedicated largely to inanities. But Ray's greatness as a film-maker goes beyond his influence. The moral complexities of his characters and the notion of 'right living' may be found in the great writers of the world, from Jane Austen to Tchekhov; but in very few film-makers.

32

Hollywood in the Age of Television: The Directors

THE AMERICAN FILM industry had not ex-pected cinema attendances to hold to the record level of 1946. Its major preoccupa-tion in the years that followed was in learning to accept the separation of exhi-bition from distribution and production, thus ending those practices which made the majority of films profitable. But once the smoke had cleared, it was evident that the decline in audiences could not be halted, for they were becoming selective. Increasingly the public began to echo the age-old cry of critics that Hollywood films were inferior to those from Europe; and television was proving itself a more formidable rival than the industry had ever considered. The large companies were horrified at the thought of leasing or sell-ing their films to television,★ but the small independent companies had no such qualms. The laughably low quality of old British films on television did not seem so funny when patrons were being lured away from their sets to see the latest Ealing comedy – if, as yet, only in the big city art-houses. Other television entertainment might also be derisory, but the living-room armchair began to take precedence over the effort required to see the latest Betty Grable vehicle. The habits of a life-time were being broken, and Hollywood was vulnerable for the first time since the Depression.

Its answer was three-fold. The most important and least remarked upon was the greater autonomy allowed to indi-vidual film-makers – a move that the moguls regarded with magnanimity, hav-ing crushed or frustrated the postwar de-sire for complete independence. The least significant, at least for the moment, was the poaching from television of product and talent. The other, inevitably much publicised, was the use of devices denied to the pocket-sized black-and-white screen in the corner of the living room.

In the graveyard of important but half-forgotten old movies is a tombstone called **The Robe** (1953) – a noteworthy tomb-stone, since it was the first film made in CinemaScope. This system, invented by Professor Henri Chrétien (1879–1956), re-placed the customary box-shaped screen with one of panoramic proportions. The image projected was two and a half times as wide as it was high, an effect achieved by compressing a wide angle of vision on to a strip of 35mm film and expanding it again as it moved through the projector. The system dated back to 1927, when Chrétien had adapted the distorted lens he had de-vised during the First World War for tank periscopes. The following year Claude Autant-Lara had used it for a short, *Pour Construire un Feu*, but Hollywood had passed it over when making its own hand-ful of wide-screen (70mm) films in 1930–1, and it had lain dormant till brought to the attention of 20th Century-Fox in 1952, amidst speculations in the industry about films requiring several projectors and/or special eye glasses for three-dimensional effects. CinemaScope was relatively simple, but there remained the possibility that exhibitors would refuse, as they had twenty-two years earlier, to make the nec-essary expensive conversions. Darryl F. Zanuck and Spyros Skouras, by now con-vinced that CinemaScope was the sole solu-

★It has been claimed that Walt Disney was the only producer in the prewar period whose contract specified the possibility of television showings, but Paramount's lawyers seem to have been equally farsighted, if not sanguine, about that ever happening.

845

Hollywood in the Age of Television: The Directors

With the growing popularity of television, Hollywood decided that colour alone was insufficient to combat the public's fondness for the new medium. The home screen was small and in black and white, so it could easily be put to shame by the industry's new systems – the third-dimensional film, the wide screen and stereophonic sound. The first 3-D film most people saw was *House of Wax*, TOP RIGHT, but the use of special glasses was a barrier to really wide acceptance, and the industry moved over to the wide screen when 20th Century-Fox introduced CinemaScope a few months later. BOTTOM RIGHT, you can see how they advertised the new techniques, and this piece of promotion material was issued to emphasise how much more audiences were getting for their money. As it happened, *The Robe* did not use the wide screen well.

tion to the problem of declining audiences, decided to minimise the risk by offering a biblical spectacle, always a certain crowd-puller. *The Robe* was based on an 'inspirational' bestseller by Lloyd C. Douglas; the novel's triteness and mawkishness have been retained with awesome fidelity in Philip Dunne's screenplay. 'When it comes, this is how it will start – some obscure martyr in some forgotten province' says the Emperor Tiberius (Ernest Thesiger) as a Roman centurion (Richard Burton) is converted to Christianity for the sake of a childhood sweetheart (Jean Simmons). Vast numbers of people found in the film exactly what they knew, or wanted to know, about Christianity, undeterred by the fact that the director, Henry Koster, had adopted a camera-in-the-stalls approach.

It was considered that the public would accept neither close-ups nor imaginative cutting in the use of the wide screen, a timidity comparable with the cinema's early days and the coming of Sound. This was in accord with the reverence required by the subject, but studio executives were so excited by the early rushes that the green light was given for a comedy in Cinema-Scope, **How to Marry a Millionaire** (1953). Jean Negulesco directed this re-tread of Fox's familiar tale of three girls in search of wealthy husbands, having regard to the new system by stringing his stars – Marilyn Monroe, Lauren Bacall and Betty Grable – across the wide screen, for example by making them lounge horizontally in their penthouse apartment. Despite Monroe's short-sighted dumb blonde and Bacall's stylish divorcee, the film is only mildly amusing today, but its popularity confirmed that CinemaScope was not a flash in the pan. The profits of 20th Century-Fox rose to a record level, and though it was tempting to retain Cinema-Scope for its exclusive use (the company owned the patent), it did not do so because that would have been contrary to the interests of exhibitors. They were expected to install Stereophonic Sound, the essential accompaniment to the wide screen – although Skouras later capitulated on that requirement. He also announced that all Fox films would be in 'Scope and colour (thus ending the particularly rich but unpretentious visual aspect of its monochrome films of the time), and other

studios jumped on the band wagon till they began to develop wide-screen systems of their own. Skouras balanced the increased budgets by eschewing Technicolor and using a cheaper colour system, De Luxe; the other companies acted similarly, but it was admitted later that Warnercolor and M-G-M's Anscocolor and Metrocolor were merely versions of Kodak's Eastmancolor. Only Paramount stood aloof, retaining Technicolor and using its own patented VistaVision, which used depth of focus in something like the old ratio, so that the exhibitor had the option of increasing the size of the projected image without loss of clarity. The action was restricted to the centre of the ribbon, so that the film could be projected on screens of any width. However, as the standard screen ratio was changed at this time to accommodate exhibitors with screens of variable length, Paramount decided that VistaVision was redundant. Although Technicolor Inc. introduced Technirama, its own wide-screen process in 1957, by the mid-Sixties all films intended to benefit from a panoramic image were using the more economical Panavision.

Like the wide screen, the three-dimensional film had been given experimental showings in the early Talkie era, and in 1953 M-G-M reissued some old 3-D shorts in a package. The wearing of special glasses (disposable, with one cellophane eye green, the other red) did not appear to be offputting – indeed the profits reaped by the first 3-D feature, **Bwana Devil** (1953), a meretricious jungle drama written and produced by an independent, Arch Oboler, were highly encouraging. To even larger and more appreciative audiences Warners offered a remake of *The Mystery of the Wax Museum*, **House of Wax** (1953), directed by André de Toth and starring Vincent Price. These audiences, cowering under an onslaught of ping-pong balls, the legs of can-can dancers, and other missiles, moved on to ooh and aah their way through a few better films, including *Dial M for Murder* (q.v.) and *Kiss Me Kate*. But later films made in 3-D were issued 'flat', to no public protest, and the trade turned its attention to CinemaScope – except, that is, those who believed that the answer to television was Cinerama.

Since Cinerama required the wholesale and costly conversion of a cinema, it was

OLD STANDARD SCREEN

CINEMASCOPE

only selectively adopted and never really looked like the road to salvation. Invented by Fred Waller, it called for a wrap-around floor-to-ceiling screen to take slightly overlapping images from three separate projectors. Its sheer size and the obvious joins limited its use for showing fiction, and the travelogues which clogged the converted cinemas for years on end – they had to, if a profit was to be made – were more effective on scenic railways and run-away trains than on visits to the Vatican. There were some thrilling trips above and across the world's terrain in the series of spectacles which began with **This Is Cinerama** (1952), but a decade later diminishing returns led the Cinerama Company into an agreement with M-G-M for two narrative films. *How the West Was Won* (q.v.) seemed to indicate that there was a future for the process, with takings of $23 million, but at the same time *The Wonderful World of the Brothers Grimm* managed to earn only a meagre $6½ million. While its failure proved that Cinerama was not in itself a box-office attraction, hopes for improving the system were pinned on a single-lens system, used initially for *It's a Mad, Mad, Mad, Mad World* (q.v.). However, though the images were exceptionally well-defined across the giant curved screen, the screen itself detracted from the film's merits (few as they were). Once the size of the screen was reduced, Cinerama became just another wide-screen process and was abandoned after another failure, *The Greatest Story Ever Told* (q.v.).

Cinerama had only ever been a practicable attraction when confined to one theatre within a large catchment area: the requisite higher prices and advanced booking added to the circus-like sense of occasion, causing some showmen to recall the infrequent cinema 'road-shows' which had begun with the early Italian epics and continued till *Gone with the Wind*. Some dozen films a year were exploited in this manner – at least in the big cities – and when the practice was abandoned it was because of the War. A Broadway entrepreneur, Mike Todd (1907–58), decided that the time was ripe for its revival, and persuaded Rodgers and Hammerstein to partner him in filming *Oklahoma!* (q.v.), an epoch-making musical for which they had so far refused all film offers. The 'wide open

spaces' of the stage original were resplendent in a wide-screen system called Todd-AO, and certainly the public's response was sufficiently encouraging for Todd to embark upon **Around the World in 80 Days** (1956). Jules Verne was chosen to emulate the Cinerama travelogues, and among the locations selected (by William Cameron Menzies, the associate producer) were Paris, the temples of Rangoon, the bull ring in Almeria and Mount Fujiyama. James Poe, John Farrow and S. J. Perelman wrote the screenplay, and the director was Michael Anderson, a hitherto little-known Briton. He handles the travels of Phileas Fogg (David Niven) as though they were a stroll around the block, and although he may have been taking his tone from the relaxed manner of his star, the great enterprise is thereby reduced. The film does, however, use its guest stars amusingly. The practice of cramming several names into one movie had been abandoned after a Korean war re-run of the all-star revue – Warners' excruciating *Starlift* – but Todd revived it for publicity purposes. The first guest contracted was Noël Coward, on the correct assumption that if Coward sanctioned the project, others would follow, for less than their customary fees. The range of names goes from Marlene Dietrich to Fernandel and includes, most enjoyably, Buster Keaton as a railroad conductor, Beatrice Lillie as a Salvationist, John Gielgud as Fogg's valet, and Ronald Colman as an Indian railway official (and what a Fogg he might have been!). Todd's gift for publicity was rewarded at the box office and, cynics might think, by the Academy of Motion Picture Arts and Sciences, which voted this the year's Best Film.

The film's success mesmerised the industry. Musicals and biblicals were one thing (deMille's *The Ten Commandments* came out around the same time), but the public was now prepared to pay high seat prices for other spectaculars, most of them requiring a whole evening to see. By the early Sixties about half a dozen films were opening annually, on an advance booking basis, and complete with 'Overture', interval and souvenir programmes. Since 'more' seldom means 'good', the arrangement only survived by virtue of a few huge public successes. The most memorable of these were musicals – the screen versions of the Rodgers and Hammerstein Broadway shows – and it may be rewarding to examine them as a group.

The composer and lyricist were involved in the productions of **Oklahoma!** (1955) and **South Pacific** (1958), which may be why neither seems to have lost a syllable or a note from the original. Both are canned theatre, despite the balmy breezes ruffling the real corn sheaves and palm trees that were only painted on Broadway. *Oklahoma!* has the better director, Fred Zinnemann, and the better cast, headed by Gordon MacRae as the cowboy and Shirley Jones as the girl. Zinnemann handles his material sensitively, but seems to have overlooked the fact that everything that had been innovatory about it in 1943 had in the interim been surpassed on the screen by the M-G-M musical. On the other hand, Joshua Logan treats *South Pacific* as earnestly as if he were handling Greek tragedy – doubtless because he had also directed it on the stage. Logan and Rodgers and Hammerstein had only themselves to blame for the dreary Mitzi Gaynor and Rossano Brazzi in the roles played originally by Mary Martin and Ezio Pinza. As the American nurse who falls in love with a French planter, Miss Martin had provided the show with its greatest charm, though there were those who appreciated the robust chorus of half-naked sailors of whom Logan seemed so fond. Tossing off 'There Is Nothing Like a Dame', they provide a sturdy opening to the film, but when it arrives at the song about Bali Ha'i the screen turns magenta and puce; as cued by a line in the lyric, 'A Cock-Eyed Optimist' is photographed through a filter of canary yellow – and similar procedures are followed till the end of the film. Consequently one longs for the songs to finish so that natural colour will be restored. Nevertheless, the film ran for months in some cities – and for five years at one large London theatre.

The hallmarks of Rodgers and Hammerstein – the unusual choice of material, the ineluctable welding of song and book – did impress anew in **Carousel** (1956) and **The King and I** (1956), both filmed by 20th Century-Fox, who owned the plays on which the shows had been based. As directed respectively by Henry King and Walter Lang, each film is an admirable reflection of Hollywood craftsmanship at its most skilful. The texts are, again, over-faithful, but there is compensation in the Maine harbour settings of *Carousel* and the studio Siamese palaces of *The King and I*, photographed in CinemaScope 55, a high-definition process so expensive that it was immediately abandoned, despite the popularity of both films. The yachts bob on the water and there is an elaborate mating dance to 'June Is Busting Out all Over', which is just one of the songs in a score that I have seldom found less than entrancing. Gordon MacRae and Shirley Jones splendidly head the cast, but *Carousel*, like its source, 'Liliom', concludes in whimsy, which is rendered here with an arty and saccharine ballet likely to destroy the goodwill of all but the most indulgent audiences. The leads are also admirable in *The King and I*, based on *Anna and the King of Siam*: Deborah Kerr is basically theatrical but sincere as the indomitable governess, while Yul Brynner as the king shows warmth, humour and authority, qualities that were rarely apparent in his later screen work.

When Rodgers and Hammerstein's *Flower Drum Song* was converted from mild Broadway success to outright film failure by Universal, in 1952, Rodgers wisely decided – his partner had died – that **The Sound of Music** (1965) would be more safely berthed at 20th Century-Fox. As creative spirits and entrepreneurs this partnership had dominated the musical taste of Broadway for two generations; their taste coincided with that of the public to a marked degree, flattering it in subject matter and never shattering its complacency (even with the then-unusual anti-racialist song in 'South Pacific'). *The Sound of Music* was based on the last of their Broadway shows, which had been disliked by most reviewers. The true story of the von Trapp family offered a certain novelty, featuring nuns, Nazis and a handful of troublesome children, but as interpreted it was undeniably schmaltzy. In an attempt to counteract this, 20th Century-Fox offered the direction in turn to Billy Wilder and William Wyler,★ without success. The screenplay was entrusted to Ernest Lehman, also considered one of the more sophisticated men working in films; his

★Wyler in fact accepted, but then decided that he would prefer to do *The Collector* (q.v.).

Hollywood in the Age of Television: The Directors

The Sound of Music was seen by more people than any other film for more than a generation. One reason was Julie Andrews (with her arm raised); another was the direction of Robert Wise, who beyond the 'favourite things' and the Do Re Mes had audiences panting with Austrian patriotism at the end of a mediocre song called 'Edelweiss'. Here is the inevitable 'Do Re Me' that Miss Andrews is singing, accompanied by Charmian Carr, far left, and the other children.

partner on *West Side Story* (q.v.), Robert Wise, turned down the direction three times, and each time the offer of profit participation was increased; yet he accepted only when the illness of Steve McQueen (q.v.) caused the postponement of *The Sand Pebbles* (q.v.). The result is awash with common sense, good advice and 'inspiration'. It has not dated an iota, because it was already old fashioned – with a story similar to several that Mary Pickford did; at one point, as she leaves the convent, Julie Andrews even looks like Pickford.

Julie Andrews (b.1934), is the film's great good fortune, carrying it through the quagmires of taste by seeming thoroughly to enjoy herself and making every half-funny line count for far more than its worth. She lights up the screen in a proverbial manner, the more so because she is surrounded by a lacklustre cast. Christopher Plummer plays the baron with a smug chill rather than what was needed – the charm of the young Anton Walbrook. As the countess who hopes to win him – Blanche Ingram to Julie's Jane Eyre – Eleanor Parker overacts with every eyebrow and elbow, and Richard Haydn is auntish as the family friend. After Miss Andrews, what matters is Salzburg slumbering in the sun, and the lakes and mountains which surround it. The helicopter shot that starts the film, moving

from the crags to the mountain field where the young novice is singing her head off, is one of the great moments in films – and is typical of the care that went into its planning. Many of the other songs are carolled all over the environs – mimed, in fact, to be fitted together later: but instead of being mechanical, Andrews and the children give them an air of spontaneity. We have her word and that of the director that every line of dialogue was examined several times before shooting, and if there are still times when the unwary feel like crawling under their seats that is in the nature of the beast. As far as the industry was concerned, someone did something very right, for the film was to supersede *Gone with the Wind* as the most financially successful film yet made. Unlike the films that overtook both movies a decade later, this was a considerable achievement, for seat prices in the Sixties were not significantly higher than those for Selznick's film on its initial high-price release.

Hollywood itself regarded *The Sound of Music* as a miracle film, voting it six Oscars including Best Picture and Best Direction. Not the last part of the miracle was that an expenditure of $8 million had, by 1969, brought in over $115 million. There were two subsequent reissues in the U.S., and a television showing, before the film was licensed to N.B.C. for a twenty-year period – which would bring a further $25 million – in all, over 1,750% return on investment. The myriad expensive attempts to find the same market failed, but then *The Sound of Music* was an anachronism – it was the last melodious musical, and the children who first saw it grew up to prefer a very different sort of tune.

Despite the felicities in these Rodgers and Hammerstein packages, especially in *Carousel* and *The Sound of Music*, with each of these films the cinema died a little. With the wide screen, the American film became stultified, at least for a time – as will be seen in the next chapter, which takes up the continuing fortunes of CinemaScope. The quality small film – economically budgeted, without star names, in black and white – also made its appearance. The cycle began with **Marty** (1955), which won the most important of the year's Oscars – Best Picture, Best Director, Best Actor, Best Screenplay – and proved that there were big pickings to be had from the simplest ideas. It was written by Paddy Chayevsky (1923–81) from his television play. The play had been seen by someone at the Hecht, Hill and Lancaster organisation who thought that a large screen version would provide both prestige and a means to submit a tax loss in order to offset excessive profits. There was little reason to suppose that it would appeal to more than a minority, since in its own parlance it deals with a couple of 'dogs': an amiable and aimless mother-dominated thirtyish bachelor butcher (Ernest Borgnine) and a painfully shy and awkward spinster (Betsy Blair) whom he meets in a Brooklyn dance hall. With a sympathy rare among writers, Chayevsky observed the nuances of speech, the uncertain interplay of characters not brought up to command the world. Admittedly *On the Waterfront* (q.v.) had already introduced an inarticulate hero, but for the first time in films Brooklyn and Bronx accents were no longer confined to floozies and cab drivers.

Since Chayevsky's style – 'What'ya doin' tonight, Marty?' – was so much parodied, it is astonishing how well his films revive, and I like even better **The Bachelor Party** (1957), made by the same team which included Delbert Mann, who had also directed both television versions. He moves the action from poky flat to Greenwich Village loft to subway to a men's toilet; we had never seen them before, at least not like this, and what most impresses is the delineation of the daily grind. Four accountants accompany a fifth on a bachelor party – away from wives and night school – yet despite the occasion their individual worries are never quite suppressed. These are best summed up by the oldest and most respectable of the group, Walter (E. G. Marshall), who, drunk, is more than ever conscious of his doctor's recommendation to move to Arizona: 'What does it all mean? . . . "Sound and fury" . . . yeah, I read a book. You think I ain't read a book? Everyone thought I'd be the first Catholic president.' The morning after the bachelor party, nothing has changed: we are a great remove from Clifford Odets, since these people are as far as ever from knowing what they want from life.

The success of *Marty* encouraged a slew of television dramas refashioned for the large screen until, low costs and high praise notwithstanding, they failed to arouse much activity at the box office. Many of them were worthy, but lacked Chayevsky's affectionate yet pessimistic attitudes. His effect upon the choice of subject matter was strong, but too often the films emerged as fictionalised versions of agony-column problems – infidelity in *Strangers When We Meet* (q.v.) and abortion in *Love with the Proper Stranger* (q.v.). Chayevsky's real influence was not truly to be felt till the Seventies, when young talents coming into the industry tried again to treat everyday problems with more honesty.

The American cinema stagnated during the Eisenhower years. At their onset, McCarthyism was so harrying the industry that few could consider it calmly enough to turn it to dramatic account (even in allegorical form), and by the time the country was reflecting upon the consequences of the Korean War, Hollywood was engrossed in its contest with television. Later, the assassinations of John and Robert Kennedy and Martin Luther King were too terrible to be assimilated quickly, and as the nation began to absorb the horrors of Vietnam and political corruption, Hollywood occupied itself with its own collapse – the staggering losses, and struggles for control over the faltering studios. The television-inspired small-budget dramas – there is no generic name – were, during this period of confusion and false calm, the sole exemplars of responsible cinema – that is, apart from the works of the major directors.

Given the autonomy then granted to this group of film-makers, in retrospect the results can be seen to be not nearly as good as they should have been. The battle against crass producers had been fought and largely won. There is a significant line in *The Big Knife* (q.v.) stating that the only reason for being in films is to work for 'Wyler or Wilder, Stevens, Kazan, Ford or Zinnemann'. Such directors were, in the main, intelligent men working on projects aimed at intelligent audiences. They were still hampered by censorship, but they undertook their work with the responsibility which was Capra's legacy to them. They tried to make films which, if not of any marked social import, were more entertaining than the studio products –

and the growing number of discerning filmgoers looked forward to these movies and discussed them avidly afterwards. Still, the tastes these directors displayed were almost as limited as those of the moguls thirty years earlier – precisely because it was at that time that most of them had started to work in films. There were probably few brighter or younger filmmakers than John Huston or Joseph L. Mankiewicz, and they too had been in films since the early Thirties.

That statement in *The Big Knife* should certainly have included Mankiewicz, who, when he left 20th Century-Fox, in 1953, was admired as no other film-maker since Capra. He moved to M-G-M to direct **Julius Caesar** (1953) for the producer John Houseman, who had persuaded the company that a Shakespeare film could be made comparatively cheaply (the *Quo Vadis?* costumes in Rome had only to be shipped across). Houseman did not want the drama to be swamped by production, so he refused the offer of Technicolor, but though adopting the contemporary 'black and white of newsreel and television screens' the film refuses to draw political parallels. Mankiewicz, renowned for his handling of dialogue and players, was an ideal choice. Despite all the care taken in selecting the cast, he thought its members sufficiently disparate to insist upon three-weeks' rehearsal (almost unheard of in Hollywood) – during which time, apparently, John Gielgud's expertise and encouragement set the tone of the production. It is a film of quiet excellence, faltering only in the later moments when budget restrictions hampered the handling of the battle sequences. As Brutus, James Mason is somewhat self-consciously noble, but his scenes with Gielgud's superb Cassius are particularly splendid, negotiating the verse as in no other Shakespeare film to date except Olivier's, and as effortlessly projecting thought and feeling. The Antony of Marlon Brando is astonishingly convincing and there are sound interpretations of Caesar and Casca by Louis Calhern and Edmond O'Brien respectively. Greer Garson (Calphurnia) and Deborah Kerr (Portia) were cast to bolster the film's box-office chances. It did extremely well, and though some Hollywood companies have been involved in the occasional Shakespeare films made since

then, none has been made in America as a major studio production.

Mankiewicz failed to agree with M-G-M on the two other projects for which he was contracted, and so United Artists agreed to finance two films which he would write and direct for his own company. Since he had made a wise and witty film about a Broadway star, *All About Eve*, there was considerable interest when it was known that **The Barefoot Contessa** (1954) was about a movie queen. As with *Eve* Mankiewicz used a favourite device, the flashback, to tell the tale with the wisdom of hindsight. The story chiefly involves three people: the star (Ava Gardner) – a role based partially on Rita Hayworth – with peasant beginnings, sensuality, a kind heart and a complex about men; her director and discoverer (Humphrey Bogart), an ex-alcoholic who finds that he can be bought – by a Howard Hughes-like producer – when confronted with lies and innuendo; and the European aristocrat (Rossano Brazzi) whom she marries. The result, however, is an overlong thesis on movie stardom, its parts not relevant to the whole nor referring to each other. 'In a nutshell,' as Bogart puts it, 'the plot is that life louses up the script' – which is clever, since Mankiewicz points to the confusion experienced by such people. As Mankiewicz moves from movie people to international society he appears to pursue gossip for its own sake, but in his own opinion the second part of the film is weakened by the casting of Brazzi (James Mason turned down the role) and the fact that he could only hint at the character's impotency.

To an extent **The Quiet American** (1958) is a very good film. The Saigon of Graham Greene's novel, with its seedy restaurants and apartments, is superbly conveyed, and much of Greene's dialogue has been retained. 'Twenty-two million people: all they need is to survive,' observes the Englishman (Michael Redgrave), obstinate but vague in conscience, pitting himself against the American (Audie Murphy), all puppy-eagerness, patronising and devious. The Englishman betrays him to the Communists, supposedly from jealousy, at which point the film makes nonsense of what has gone before and of Greene's powerful criticism of entrepreneurs like the American and his countrymen's intervention above and below the line. Greene's furious letter to *The Times* irredeemably damaged the film's chances in Britain, where success might have compensated for its failure in the U.S.

The Barefoot Contessa had failed equally, and after both instances Mankiewicz surrendered his independence, working respectively for Sam Goldwyn and Sam Spiegel. Goldwyn had outbid all competitors for Frank Loesser's Damon Runyon musical, **Guys and Dolls** (1955), and added to the then-record price of $800,000, plus residuals, he set a budget of $5 million. It was his first film in three years, and just as Mike Todd had hired Zinnemann for *Oklahoma!* he engaged a director associated not with musicals but with prestigious films. Mankiewicz, who wrote his own screenplay, enjoyed working with Goldwyn, but between them they made two errors. A musical is not, or should not be, a story punctuated by songs, but a celebration of a time when life is cosier and happier – and the only way to express yourself is to burst into song. This film is more respectful of Runyon than Loesser, even dropping three of the songs (including that incomparable expression of dawn in Manhattan, 'My Time of Day'). The settings are largely plastic-abstract, except for Miss Adelaide's nightclub, where Hollywood's usual lavish decor replaces the cheerful tattiness it had onstage. At least Vivian Blaine's Miss Adelaide and beaming, chubby Stubby Kaye's Nicely Nicely Johnson are retained; and as the Salvation Army lass, Jean Simmons also shows that she was having a wonderful time. Marlon Brando's★ way of playing comedy is to raise a supercilious eyebrow, and Frank Sinatra, lacking all the gutsiness that Sam Levene had in the role, is simply bland.

Spiegel, who regarded himself as a latter-day Goldwyn, had bought a one-act play by Tennessee Williams, who wrote the screenplay with Gore Vidal. So, for the first time in a decade, Mankiewicz worked on a film only as director (he had fashioned the screenplay of *Julius Caesar*): **Suddenly Last Summer** (1959). Not for nothing is

★For the role Goldwyn had wanted Gene Kelly, who wanted to play it, but his contract was held by M-G-M, whose boss, Nicholas Schenck, harboured grudges against both Goldwyn and Mankiewicz. Ironically, a deal was made for M-G-M to release the film.

the exposition set in a hothouse, complete with Venus flytrap, but the direction is always in control of the excesses. The play had been a study of hysteria, of the suppressed emotions apparently common to many people; there may have been no need to add cannibalism to incestuous love and neurotic imbalance, but it is not dramatically invalid. Unfortunately, the film shows in flashback what the play only mentioned and, as the hysteric, Elizabeth Taylor discloses so little feeling that we do not care whether her outburst is a quest for truth or mere vindictiveness. Before witnesses, she and the mother (Katharine Hepburn) of the dead Sebastian argue over the suspicion that his passion for young men led to his being eaten on an African beach. The M.P.A.A. had refused to allow the Brazzi character in *The Barefoot Contessa* to be homosexual, and had in the interim refused similar implications in the film of Williams's *Cat on a Hot Tin Roof* (q.v.), but it was permitted in this instance.

Mankiewicz then began moulding Lawrence Durrell's Alexandria Quartet into a screenplay, until called upon to rescue **Cleopatra** (1963) – the making of which is considerably more interesting than what finally emerged on screen. Two books have been written on the subject, one by Walter Wanger, who was returning to large-scale production. Wanger first announced the project in September 1958 as a modestly-budgeted spectacle starring either Joan Collins or Dana Wynter, but then decided that he preferred Elizabeth Taylor – whose agent put her fee at one million dollars. Both she and 20th Century-Fox liked the attendant publicity so much that neither cared that the contract drawn up stipulated much less – that she did earn much more was due to expenses and huge fees when shooting went over schedule. That began in September 1960 at Pinewood, on a budget of $6 million, with Rouben Mamoulian directing, Peter Finch as Caesar and Stephen Boyd as Antony. When Mamoulian abandoned it the following spring – with Taylor's illness a contributory factor – $7 million had been spent, with only twelve minutes of film to show for it, which Mankiewicz, taking over, considered unusable. Filming recommenced in Rome, with Finch and Boyd replaced in turn by Rex Harrison and Richard Burton. Eventually Wanger was

Hollywood in the Age of Television: The Directors

sacked, Spyros Skouras fired as head of 20th Century-Fox, and as the final cost came to around $37 million, Mankiewicz was taken off the film. He could not therefore oversee the editing, but was later permitted to carry out some minor adjustments at Pinewood in the spring of 1963, two months before the film's premiere. There were a number of million-dollar lawsuits over the film, but all were dropped or settled out of court. One of them accused Taylor and her paramour, Burton, of devaluing the film by their behaviour – but the charge itself is debatable, since Taylor's defection from her then husband, Eddie Fisher, provided a bonanza of publicity. However, the fact remains that while this dull film might just have been acceptable with another actress, it was doomed when she was cast. For almost four hours we are subjected to the whims, ambitions, amours, tantrums and follies of the Egyptian queen, yet not for an instant does she command interest or sympathy. 'You have broken out of your nursery to irritate the adults' says Caesar – and that is fair comment.

Mankiewicz did not like sharing the screenplay credit with Ranald MacDougall and Sidney Buchman, who had worked on it before he arrived: but equally they must share the blame for some jarring modern idioms – which, since Mankiewicz wrote and rewrote, often on the set, he had neither the will nor the stamina to avoid. His direction is so graceful, however, that it seems unfair that the film's reception should have dented his considerable reputation. 20th Century-Fox had persevered with this project after a series of flops, hoping that it would do for them what *Ben-Hur* (q.v.) had done for M-G-M's finances, but it did not turn a profit till sold to television, and has proved to have no revival value.

Mankiewicz once commented that the film was 'conceived in a state of panic, shot in confusion, and wound up in blind panic', but he has since refused to discuss it publicly. He is equally unhappy about **The Honey Pot** (1967), with which he returned to independence, since the distributor, United Artists, insisted on removing the framework of the original script (in which an American theatre owner discusses aspects of the script with the film's leading actor), and then almost twenty

minutes were cut after the London premiere. It remains much too long, a protracted joke about a modern Volpone (Rex Harrison) who sends for three former mistresses to tell them that he will leave one of them his fortune. They are inexpertly played by Susan Hayward, Edie Adams and Capucine, but even the scenes between Maggie Smith (as the secretary of one of them) and Harrison are strained, despite some typically civilised dialogue. As the Mosca character, a former gigolo (though the reference to this is no longer in the present version) and the actor who is stage-managing the deception for Harrison, Cliff Robertson was encouraged to impersonate Mankiewicz himself. The film is much richer than either the (modern) play or the novel on which Mankiewicz based it, but nevertheless it confirms that he was in love with his own talent. He had every reason to be: but he was a better film-maker when he was less so.

His experiences on both films convinced Mankiewicz not to direct his own scripts again – and with **There Was a Crooked Man . . .** (1970) it is interesting to see him at the service of a strong screenplay by David Newman and Robert Benton. It was their first credited work after *Bonnie and Clyde* (q.v.), and their purpose was the same: to destroy the old myths while creating new ones – in this case that of the Old West. The men stink downwind and have no loyalties except unto themselves. The film, much aided by Henry Fonda's performance as the corruptible governor, is more subtle and polished than the similar *Cool Hand Luke* (q.v.), also backed by Warners, with Mankiewicz's cynicism providing a neat gloss to the enthusiastic script. **Sleuth** (1972) was written by Anthony Shaffer from his long-running play, and any cynicism would have destroyed its simplistic cat-and-mouse twists. The play's renown was reason enough to attract Mankiewicz, together with the casting of Laurence Olivier and Michael Caine as cat and mouse respectively. Apart from their participation however there was no good reason to go and see it. Mankiewicz's subsequent retirement has not been voluntary, but among the projects he has turned down is *The Front Page* (q.v.), which Wilder took on after Mankiewicz decided that the material had lost its freshness.

854

With more reason, the reputation of George Stevens did not survive this period intact. Riding on the crest of his success with *A Place in the Sun* he made **Something to Live For** (1952), which failed, though in my opinion it is better than the earlier film and those he made thereafter. Its lush Victor Young score and Dwight Taylor's screenplay imply that soap opera was intended, as a husband (Ray Milland) is tempted to leave his wife (Teresa Wright) for an actress (Joan Fontaine). The lovers teeter on the edge of a precipice, not because of infidelity but because of their shared alcoholism, a terror which Stevens conveys with understanding. He also understands both Manhattan, pictured alternately with acrid realism and glamorous virtuosity, and his stars, stripping from them the fossilised and film-starry mannerisms they had learnt to use under other directors. Few films better illustrate the changes that can be wrought on substandard material by sensitive and polished direction.

Shane (1953) was acclaimed as a classic Western from its first appearance. Two aspects separated it from other essays in the genre: its deliberately mythic treatment of the stranger (Alan Ladd) who rides in, stays to help, and then moves out again into the blue, and the related viewing of events through the eyes of a child (Brandon de Wilde). Stevens was much congratulated on choosing a 'superior' Western novel – by Jack Schaefer – to which was added an excellent script by A. B. Guthrie, Jr, and 'picturesque' photography by Loyal Griggs, who was awarded an Oscar for it. What the film lacks is momentum, and one gets the feeling that life has been crushed out of it by its production values. The suspicion that Stevens gave precedence to producing over directing was confirmed in **Giant** (1956), a formless version of a novel by Edna Ferber. The title refers to Texas, but if Stevens had any feeling about the way the discovery of oil had coarsened and changed its society, it is lost in the welter of themes – commerce vs. agriculture, racial prejudice, female emancipation, the *nouveau riche*, the emptiness of ambition . . . As the central couple, Elizabeth Taylor and Rock Hudson are not players of sufficient calibre to engage our attention for three hours (the over-long running time), and as they age, their hair becoming bluer, they hardly resemble real people. The role played by James Dean – in youth the outsider, in middle-age the magnate – is poorly motivated and interpreted. *Shane* at least has an innate simplicity and a spirit of adventure; *Giant* has neither, and having raised a large number of questions, it suddenly stops, as if hoping that sheer length has bludgeoned audiences into approval.

Shane had been Stevens's last film for Paramount; *Giant* was to have been the first of several projects for Warner Bros. Both studios regarded him as a prestigious director, whose invariably warm notices were reflected in the box-office takings; but the profits of both films, though considerable, were eroded by his increasingly fastidious production methods. Accordingly he moved to 20th Century-Fox to make **The Diary of Anne Frank** (1959), working, alas, from the stage version by Frances Goodrich and Albert Hackett, who also wrote the screenplay. They have added a commentary, from the young Dutch girl's own words, but even with that addition the film is pallid. It merely plods through the routines and small events of the Frank and Van Daan families hidden away at the top of the warehouse in Amsterdam, and in the process destroys an earlier inference that they are meant to represent all the Jews marked out for elimination. The use of Cinema-Scope, albeit in black and white, contradicts the fundamental feeling of claustrophobia and intimacy, and a more serious error was the casting of Millie Perkins as Anne. This ex-model was chosen, sensibly, so as not to associate Anne with a known actress, but Miss Perkins has a jarring accent (even to American ears) and the gamine looks fashionable in 1959. The direction is expectedly careful and tasteful, but again lacking in feeling: a book which haunts all who have read it has become a forgettable film.

The same accusation may be levelled at **The Greatest Story Ever Told** (1965). It was Stevens's not unambitious intention to chronicle the Gospel better than the admittedly poor previous screen attempts. Since his screenplay, written in collaboration with James Lee Barrett, was based on Fulton Oursler's bestseller, critical expectations were not high, even with Carl Sandburg as artistic adviser. As costs rose during the years of preparation, 20th Century-Fox lost interest, and sold the project to Cinerama, who arranged with United Artists to share the eventual budget of $24 million. It was the second most expensive film (after *Cleopatra*) made by a U.S. company, and at 225 minutes the longest since the days of Von Stroheim.

Stevens had gone for broke and lost: faced with disastrous notices, the 'exclusive' Cinerama showings were abandoned – in favour of Ultra Panavision 70 – in an effort to recoup costs before the public realised how bad it was. United Artists began whittling away at the length, eventually arriving at 141 minutes, thereby removing some of the guest stars – but not, alas, John Wayne's centurion, whose delivery of his one line ('This truly was the sahn of Gahd') is of staggering banality. Many of the others are hardly better. In Max von Sydow the film has an austere, sincere Christ; and in taking pains to duplicate nineteenth-century religious paintings Stevens presumably achieved his object in giving the least offence to most people. But the film is as dull as it is reverent, with a particularly crass ending: 'The fuss will all be forgotten in a month's time' says someone, and the answer comes back quickly, 'I wonder . . .'

The resounding failure of this film affected Stevens far more than that of *Cleopatra* had hurt Mankiewicz, since at least a number of patrons had turned up to see *Cleopatra* out of curiosity. But it was the star of that film, Elizabeth Taylor, who enabled Stevens to work again by insisting that he direct one of her films, thereby proving as loyal to her colleagues – she had similarly tried to help the actor Montgomery Clift in his sad last years – as she is uninteresting on screen. A former child player, she had stayed in the public eye by virtue of good looks and a number of highly publicised marriages and divorces. Her film appearances made considerably less impact on the public until she began to have some isolated box-office successes just before and after *Cleopatra*; yet her films had already begun to fail★ by

★The paucity of female stars was one reason that Hollywood hoped Taylor would remain popular. The industry was similarly blinkered with the equally untalented Natalie Wood and Debbie Reynolds, also being paid huge salaries long after the public had lost interest. Earlier, scripts passed from Taylor to Audrey Hepburn to Marilyn Monroe to Shirley MacLaine (or vice versa), and it is hard to imagine four more disparate personalities or talents.

the time 20th Century-Fox agreed to let Stevens direct her in **The Only Game in Town** (1970). Her ability to create headlines apparently meant more to this studio than the notices of critics, which had seldom been kind. The terms granted her on this occasion were even more farcical than usual, starting with the $500,000 20th Century-Fox paid for Frank D. Gilroy's original play before it opened on Broadway (where it ran for one week). Despite the evidence of its own *Cleopatra*, the company decided that Taylor's presence in the film would help it recoup its investment and a deal was worked out whereby she and Richard Burton, now her husband, were to share $2½ million for her appearance in this and his in *Staircase*. At their request, and despite the fact that the settings were respectively Las Vegas and London, the films were to be made in Paris – at much extra cost (as was pointed out at a stockholders' meeting) since everything down to door handles had to be imported. Eventually *The Only Game in Town*, with a cast of only two and having virtually only one set, cost $8 million. The studio disliked the result so much that it was kept on the shelf, with not even a token showing to qualify it for the Academy Awards. When at last it did open it took a meagre $1½ million; that at least was considerably more than the earnings from *Staircase*.

Such plot as there is concerns an ageing, aimless showgirl and her relationship with a compulsive gambler (Warren Beatty). Stevens, who had hitherto coaxed two reasonable performances from Taylor, on this occasion only ensures that she does not fluff her lines. She remains a dull, shrill woman, her dead eyes giving no reason why she had chosen this particular profession. Apart from this, the piece seems very well directed, with the smooth mixture of intimate detail and bravura that distinguished *Something to Live For*: it is pleasing to see an old master return to such form in his last film.

Concentration and confidence were also the qualities most evident with William Wyler, who made one of his best late films with an actress of a different quality, Audrey Hepburn (b. 1929), making her Hollywood debut after some small parts in Britain. The film is **Roman Holiday** (1953) – a reversion to that old movie staple, royalty travelling incognito. Ian

McLellan Hunter and John Dighton wrote the screenplay, and Wyler's touch is neither light nor in any other way reminiscent of Lubitsch; that the piece serves romance better than comedy is due to this actress of heartbreaking enchantment. Miss Hepburn won a Best Actress Oscar as the princess escaping from protocol, grave, wistful and unworldly but very sure of herself. As the American reporter who doesn't let on because he wants her story, Gregory Peck is at his best. Wyler was equally dependent on his leading players in **The Desperate Hours** (1955), but the requirements were vastly different. Humphrey Bogart, in one of his gratifying appearances as a man with no redeeming quality, is one of a criminal gang which holes up with an ordinary suburban family, headed by Fredric March. The material, as adapted by Joseph Hayes from his Broadway play, is not otherwise very effective, and its inferiority to most that Wyler handled reveals his shortcomings at this stage of his career. Despite his attempt at realism, there is nothing beneath the surface: the characters behave convincingly but cease to exist once the cameras stopped turning.

Wyler's shortcomings are also evident in a better film, **Friendly Persuasion** (1956), his first independent production, made under the auspices of Allied Artists, formerly known as Monogram. The name had been changed in 1953, and two years later Walter Mirisch, the company's vice-president, courted three of Hollywood's most admired directors in an effort to move into the major league. He was unsuccessful, although, in the end, Wyler's film was not as great a failure as Wilder's *Love in the Afternoon* (q.v.) – after which the company decided not to proceed with John Huston's *Typee*.

Friendly Persuasion also created a number of problems. Jessamyn West's novel about a Quaker family in the Civil War had been originally – like *Roman Holiday* – one of Capra's projects at Liberty Films. A law suit was brought by Michael Wilson, claiming that the current screenplay – by Jessamyn West and Wyler's brother Robert – was based on the one he had prepared earlier at Capra's behest. As Wilson had been blacklisted in the McCarthy purges of 1951, Allied Artists counterclaimed that his name was a commercial

liability – and so the film went out without a screenplay credit. The budget had risen to double the $1½ million originally estimated, and the film looked like being a disaster, until it won the Grand Prix at Cannes. Business improved further when Pat Boone's recording of Dmitri Tiomkin's title song charmed its way into the hit parade. Mr Boone's voice accompanying the credits is part of Wyler's calculated assault on audience sensibilities. As with Stevens and Capra, the failure of Liberty Films influenced each decision Wyler made thereafter, but in striving for popularity he has made this family, under their sombre garb, as saccharine and cuddlesome as the Hardys. Gary Cooper and Dorothy McGuire are pleasing enough players and the social milieu is more interesting than in many American films of the time: but it might have been just as well to leave the Quakers to themselves instead of turning them from plain to fancy.

William Wyler continued to hold his pre-eminent position during his later career, choosing his subjects with care and handling them with skill and affection. If his work became overly academic it is because his pace is in direct contrast to his early films. *Roman Holiday* would have benefited from that speed, but it is nevertheless engaging, partly because of Audrey Hepburn, as a princess befriended by American journalist, Gregory Peck.

Given Wyler's attitude, it is no surprise to find that **The Big Country** (1958) is only too aptly named. Inside this long, inert and grandiose movie is a small, short and entertaining story about earnest pioneers and greedy cattle barons. Its major defects are its pretentiousness and the performance of its star – elements which come together in the person of Gregory Peck, who co-produced with Wyler (a relationship which ended in bitterness). In Wyler's only major sound Western, *The Westerner*, Gary Cooper allowed himself to be used: the stars of Peck's generation consented only to being handled. Peck is well cast in *The Big Country* as an Easterner, a man of good will who tries to bring peace to the big country, but his nobility is, as always, tiresome. There are also too many close-ups of him appearing wise and given to philosophies which are at once self-aggrandising and much too modern for the film's supposed period. As his opponent, Charlton Heston is given very few close-ups or homilies.

The bigness of **Ben-Hur** (1959) was a different matter. When financial tremors shook M-G-M in the late Fifties, its new president, Joseph R. Vogel, promised shareholders a new *Ben-Hur*. Thinking big usually brought commensurate results: the company had done so with *Quo Vadis?*, whose producer, Sam Zimbalist, was assigned to this project. To direct he wanted Wyler, who resisted, but because of the chariot race (though already under way with the second unit, headed by Andrew Marton and Yakima Canutt) finally accepted; as he said later, 'Basically, of course, it was an adventure yarn.' The chariot race *is* tremendous, but otherwise an 'adventure yarn' is treated as holy writ, making heavier weather of its nineteenth-century moralising than the infinitely superior Silent version. One might have supposed it directed at Sunday-school teachers – though of course the plot ensures the Jewish vote. By what seems like mischance, Wyler keeps the heavenly choir silent till the final shot, and he did bring in Christopher Fry (to whom the Screen Writers Guild would not allow a credit) to make decent language out of Karl Tunberg's screenplay. However, some people were impressed, among them those who vote for the Hollywood Oscars, of which it won eleven, including Best Actor

(Charlton Heston), Best Picture, Best Director and Best Supporting Actor (Hugh Griffith). The $15 million investment (until the advent of *Cleopatra* it was the most expensive film made) had yielded a profit of approximately the same amount by the time it was sold to television. Vogel had been justified. Others were merely grateful that the *nouvelle vague* was now rising: it was not to drown dinosaurs like this, but it would keep them in their place.

It was in the wake of such films – not to mention those of Antonioni and Bergman – that **The Children's Hour** (1962) was foisted upon audiences. Wanting to do a 'little' film after *Ben-Hur*, Wyler chose to remake *These Three*, restoring the lesbian theme. The property was purchased from Goldwyn for $350,000, and Lillian Hellman, author of the original, was engaged to write the screenplay – but upon the death of Dashiell Hammett the job was assigned to John Michael Hayes. Miss Hellman loathed this film, and Wyler respected her reasons: 'I had been too faithful to the original and made no attempt to modernise and bring it up to date.' Her stage play, like many of the time, depended on confrontations, hidden secrets and revelations, with characters to root for and characters to detest: consequently *These Three* is enjoyable, but this film version, slow and serious, only emphasises the meretricious nature of the material. Wyler was initially hurt and surprised by the film's reception, feeling that he had been brave in filming a story about a community shocked by the discovery of lesbianism in its midst, but neither the play nor this film goes further than *thoughts* of deviant love on the part of one of the teachers. Shirley MacLaine plays this decent, ordinary girl. As the other, Audrey Hepburn looks like a model, and as the man who walks into their relationship James Garner looks less like a doctor than someone advertising beer.

Wyler tried to make amends with **The Collector** (1965), again demonstrating care but little regard for the sensibilities of modern audiences. He had found himself 'fascinated' by the unsolicited screenplay sent to him by Stanley Mann and John Kohn, based on John Fowles's novel, in itself an English variation on the Proust-Albertine situation. The result, with little resemblance to Fowles, rests uneasily between suspense story and contemplative melodrama, while the casting of little-known players – Terence Stamp, Samantha Eggar – is insufficient proof of integrity. **How to Steal a Million** (1966) was written by Harry Kurnitz, and is ample demonstration of Kenneth Tynan's observation that his real-life wit seldom found its way into his screenplays. Once, memorably, Wyler took Audrey Hepburn to Rome, but here they are forgettable in Paris – except that she is, as ever, a pleasure to watch, if hardly varying her inevitable comedy role, the wide-eyed innocent. As her co-star, Peter O'Toole is, in the words of the critic John Gillett, 'more winsome than winning'.

Having turned down *The Sound of Music*, Wyler accepted a second offer of a screen version of a Broadway musical, **Funny Girl** (1968). The producer of the show and the film was Ray Stark, whose (deceased) mother-in-law, Fanny Brice, was the funny girl of the title. It is a meat-and-drink role: a ghetto girl who becomes a Ziegfeld star, in the process getting hooked on a no-good gambler. Fanny is (as in life) undoubtedly and unashamedly Jewish, and thus in the film becomes the first Jewish heroine (since the Silent era) to express herself in the East Side dialect. Her quick, put-down humour is marvellously conveyed by Barbra Streisand (who had played the role on Broadway) and that, coupled with the razz-matazz numbers in Jules Styne's superb score, makes the first half of this long entertainment quite enjoyable; but her moping in the second half is wearing. Acting straight, Streisand is so completely without feeling that by the time she gets to her *pièce de résistance* – 'My Man', rightly interpolated – one could not care less, even if her squealed rendition were not far below Garland, Faye, Mistinguett and Miss Brice herself. Almost all the songs not done by her in the original have gone (including the marvellous 'Who Taught You Everything You Know?'), while others have been elaborated to make her shine even more brightly. The battles between her and Wyler during shooting were due, it was said, to her experience of audience reaction to her best effects, and they are in the film for all to see – glaringly.

The film's popularity heartened Wyler, but its reception by reviewers confirmed

the impression that he was *passé*; trying to rectify that, he did a tale about a contemporary social problem, **The Liberation of L. B. Jones** (1970), based on Jesse Hill Ford's novel on racial prejudice in southern Tennessee. Since Stirling Silliphant had recently won an Oscar for his not dissimilar script for *In the Heat of the Night*, he was assigned to this one. In its excellent exposition L. B. Jones (Roscoe Lee Brown) wants a divorce, and since his wife wants alimony, he is forced to cite a white cop (Anthony Zerbe) who, together with his lawyer (Lee J. Cobb), is determined to prevent this. The result increasingly resembled overheated melodramas like *The Chase* (q.v.) and, when it was dismissed as old fashioned, Wyler decided to retire. However, the film has merit, and he had proved, like Stevens and Mankiewicz in their very last films, that his old skill and sensitivity remained intact.

Frank Capra also found himself redundant and made his exit, though in his case he refused to compromise or submit to the exigencies of the stars concerned. He had been engaged on scientific documentaries for some years when offered **A Hole in the Head** (1959) in partnership with its star, Frank Sinatra. Arnold Shulman adapted his own Broadway play about a small-time Florida wheeler-dealer, but at the insistence of star and director the characters were changed from Jewish to Italian – and given a happy ending. Whether Sinatra plays Jew or Italian is immaterial, since he acts in his own leading-man style – i.e. with quizzical, casual charm – which is hardly what this particular wheeler-dealer needs. Capra did manage the sentiment and comedy adroitly, and virtually for the first time humour seemed compatible with the wide screen.

The film made a small profit, but since it did not, in Capra's opinion, re-establish him, he embarked upon a remake of his *Lady for a Day* (paying Columbia $225,000 for the rights, as opposed to the $15,000 originally paid to Damon Runyon). **A Pocketful of Miracles** (1961), as the film was called, is pleasant, but unnecessarily attenuated, being half an hour longer than the earlier version. Glenn Ford is bouncy, though not miscast as Capra implies in his memoir; Bette Davis makes the same mistake as May Robson – after the transformation the old lady is too regal.

Hollywood in the Age of Television: The Directors

Thomas Mitchell and Edward Everett Horton are among the veterans in support, and Peter Falk – Capra's 'joy, my anchor to reality' – has Ned Sparkes's old role of right-hand man. He is also the anchor of the film. Capra had looked upon it as a gamble, because the subject was old fashioned, and considers that United Artists did not market it properly. 'My people,' he said, 'did not come' – because he had compromised: 'this was not the film I set out to make; it was the picture I chose to make for fear of losing a few bucks. And by that choice I sold out the artistic integrity that had been my trademark for forty years.' He goes on, 'When Glenn Ford made me lick his boots – I had lost that precious quality that endows dreams with purport and purpose.' Earlier Capra had bowed out of a filmed life of Jimmy Durante when he realised that his stars, Frank Sinatra, Bing Crosby and Dean Martin, had reserved the right to co-produce so that all decisions were subject to the agreement of all parties. Later he left *Circus World* when John Wayne preferred another script to the one that he had prepared. But his memoir makes clear that it was his experience with Glenn Ford which scarred him.

Capra's old idol, Walt Disney, became richer as his films became worse. In 1954 he began the first of his hugely successful forays into television; the following year he opened Disneyland in California (Walt Disney World was opened in Florida in 1971, five years after his death). Disney also increased his live-action programme to some half dozen or more films a year – many of them popular, if negligible as entertainment. His catalogue of feature-length cartoons proved literally invaluable, as it became clearer than ever that they could be reissued at intervals to new generations of children – a mixed blessing, since the later cartoons are as poor as the early ones are good. Stylistically they wander from self-plagiarism to strip cartoon, and seem to have little care for colour or the integration of the cute and coy creatures set to gambol in the foreground; mediocre songs are simply thrown in (no less than seven people adapted Tchaikovsky for *The Sleeping Beauty*) amidst the tired whimsy and uninspired knockabouts. Singularly objectionable are Disney's half-hour cartoons based on A. A. Milne's Winnie-the-Pooh stories, since the animation vulgarises Ernest H. Shepard's original illustrations. ★

In over thirty years only two of Disney's full-length cartoons have been well received: **The Lady and the Tramp** (1955) and **One Hundred and One Dalmatians** (1961), both with largely canine casts. I for one find the former highly resistible on the whole: no advantage is taken of the wide screen, the settings are cheapest Woolworth Christmas card, and the romantic leads, a spaniel and a mongrel, absolutely deserve the future they were to have as miniature china ornaments. The film does have an occasional *frisson* of horror and two amusing songs, written and sung by Peggy Lee – one as two haughty Siamese cats and the other as a blowsy blues singer. Such moments of taste and invention occur gratifyingly often in *One Hundred and One Dalmatians*, which, along with *Alice in Wonderland*, is the only Disney cartoon since *Bambi* worth preserving. Extra care may have been taken because of the remarkably bad reviews for *The Sleeping Beauty*, or possibly the Disney team was inspired by Dodie Smith's story, the strongest plot line since the heyday of the studio, concerning the kidnapping of some puppies and the subsequent chase over half the English countryside. The villainess is loathsome in the right way, and wittily drawn; and there are rare touches of satire – as in the Osbert Lancaster-inspired London, replacing the particularly insipid one which had appeared in *Peter Pan*.

Mary Poppins (1964) is live action except for one animated sequence, of the customary visual level, seemingly influenced by the British adverts for Babycham. The film's source is another stout English original – P. L. Travers's stories of the flying governess who, in her own words, is 'practically perfect in every way'. As crisply delivered by Julie Andrews, the line brooks no argument, and indeed she is irresistible as the self-confident nanny who offers her charges a life of enchantment. Directed by Robert Stevenson, the film is a mite heavy, but like *One Hundred and One Dalmations* it demeans neither its subject nor its audiences – which may be why it was the most

★Which under a licensing agreement the Disney organisation now controls, and while not suppressing them is able to flood the book market with its own inferior imitations.

financially successful of all the Disney films.

Another veteran entertainer, Alfred Hitchcock, increased his hold on the public, who in the Fifties again felt that his name guaranteed an evening of enjoyable mayhem. Many of his admirers find this his richest period, but I find almost all of his later films lumbering, literal and not nearly as clever in evoking thrills as they think they are. In fact, seeing his films of the Fifties again has been for the most part a disappointment, except for the presence of Grace Kelly (1928–82), the cool, elegant blonde for whom he had been subconsciously searching for years. In **Dial M for Murder** (1954) she is an intended murder victim who turns the tables on the assassin (Anthony Dawson) hired by her husband (Ray Milland). Aided by a crisp performance by John Williams as the Scotland Yard man, the film's twists are enjoyable – despite a cheap back-projection London and the fact that it is no more than a filmed play. Frederick Knott wrote it – and sold it to Korda for £1,000 before it became a success on both sides of the Atlantic; his chagrin when Warners bought it from Korda for a much larger sum was presumably mitigated when he was hired to write the screenplay.

Hitchcock moved to Paramount – with an unusually advantageous contract – taking Miss Kelly with him. In **Rear Window** (1954) and **To Catch a Thief** (1955) she has to radiate sexual attraction for James Stewart and Cary Grant in turn. Since she was both subdued and intelligent, the dialogue perforce required a certain sophistication, and Hitchcock found in John Michael Hayes the man to write it. What goes on around it is of the usual confected order, and *To Catch a Thief* concerns an outbreak of cat burglary on the Côte d'Azur – views of which considerably help its purpose as a smart entertainment. *Rear Window*, after an exceptionally plodding exposition, is eventually light-hearted about a morbid interest in murder. Stewart, chairbound with a broken leg, is convinced that one of his neighbours across the courtyard is a killer. His nurse (Thelma Ritter) relishes gore, creating a combination of the funny and the macabre, unusual at the time. Stewart is, after all, a voyeur, and he sees some suspect goings-on – usually of a sexual nature

– featuring the honeymoon couple, a frustrated spinster who picks up a man, and a 'Miss Torso' constantly entertaining men. These are only minor aspects of the script, but their acceptance by the M.P.A.A. demonstrates the influence of Hitchcock's impish sense of humour on Hollywood's growing-up. An additional factor in that respect is the 'atmosphere' between Miss Kelly and her leading men.

There are views of London and Marrakesh (replacing St Moritz) in the remake of **The Man Who Knew Too Much** (1956), with Doris Day and James Stewart as the parents who get caught up in international espionage. Hitchcock has extended the set pieces of his earlier version, such as the projected assassination in the Royal Albert Hall, and as a result the film dies. In **The Trouble with Harry** (1956) it is Harry who is dead – buried in a New England wood in all its autumn glory. The film's irreverent attitude to beds and bodies found little appreciation at the box office, though an additional reason may have been the nice, but unstarry cast – Mildred Dunnock, Mildred Natwick, Edmund Gwenn and the then-unknown Shirley MacLaine (as Harry's widow). There is no other film quite like it. It was followed by **The Wrong Man** (1956), which is, conversely, one of the most humourless films ever made. Hitchcock made it for Warners, partly because he felt that he owed them a film (having given them three failures of the five movies he made there, he took no fee), and partly because they owned the property – based on the true story of a man wrongfully arrested that he had read in *Life* in 1952. Maxwell Anderson and Angus MacPhail turned it into a screenplay, Henry Fonda plays the man, and Hitchcock used the actual locations where possible. His long-held fear of the police was one reason he was attracted to the subject, and the film is detailed on police procedure: but the result, as he said himself, is one of the 'indifferent' Hitchcocks.

He returned to the rich and glamorous in **Vertigo** (1958), but with John Michael Hayes no longer on hand the laughter is against the film rather than with it. The screenplay is by Alec Coppel and Samuel Taylor, from a novel by Boileau and Narcejac, who wrote it with Hitchcock in mind after learning that he had liked *Les*

Hollywood in the Age of Television: The Directors

Hitchcock, the old master of suspense, hit a winning streak again in the Fifties, virtually never faltering in his choice of material and its execution – though we might accord a nod to fortune, who so obligingly supplied him with the ideal Hitchcock heroine in Grace Kelly. And there must have been a slight element of luck in finding in Robert Bloch's novel *Psycho* the perfect horror story for him. Anthony Perkins stands on the steps and the house still stands on the Universal lot – and of all the old dark houses in movie thrillers it is probably the most memorable.

Diaboliques (q.v.). The plot is a mighty con job, but may be enjoyed by those not knowing the twist; however, 128 minutes of James Stewart and Kim Novak mooning around San Francisco is self-defeating. He is fine as the ex-cop hired to study her strange behaviour, but ludicrous when supposed to be in the grip of an *amour fou*. The film has a dreamlike quality, but also much flashy use of colour and camera. The reviews were uniformly poor, which may be why Ernest Lehman apparently made an intensive study of the more successful early Hitchcocks before writing the screenplay of **North by Northwest** (1959), which they made at M-G-M. The mistaken-identity victim comes from *The Man Who Knew Too Much*, the hero-in-a-trap from *The Thirty-Nine Steps* and *Saboteur*, the climax on the national monument from *Blackmail* and *Foreign Correspondent*. In any case Eva Marie Saint is a more acceptable substitute for Grace Kelly (by now Princess of Monaco) than all the other actresses Hitchcock hoped would be. As one of the villains, James Mason is stylish; as the hero Cary Grant muggs somewhat.

By this time Hitchcock sponsored a television series, 'Alfred Hitchcock Presents . . .', some episodes of which he directed. His spoken introductions made him a household name which, with his gift for self-publicity, he exploited to the hilt each time one of his films was to be launched upon the world. This weekly television series caused him to move away from accepted 'Hitchcock' material, to try a cinema essay in that admittedly grubby genre, the horror film. He admitted that his approach to **Psycho** (1960) was as to a television film, but he took particular delight in matters unlikely to be sanctioned for television in a million years (or so it seemed then). He was attracted to Robert Bloch's original novel – based on a newspaper item about a man who kept his dead mother in the basement – because of the early, sudden murder in the shower.★ Being murdered in some unknown stop-off place by a stranger runs second only to the nightmare of having dared to commit embezzlement and being discovered at it.

★The designer Saul Bass planned and edited this famous sequence, a fact not generally acknowledged until after Hitchcock's death.

Hollywood in the Age of Television: The Directors

The film then shifts into different gear, but is always nasty, skilful and self-consciously clever. The plot is preposterous and is rounded off with an absurd piece of amateur psychology, but the film grips even on repeated occasions, which is no mean achievement when its initial impact depended on the element of surprise (it was not uncommon for members of the audience to scream).

It was Hitchcock's last film for Paramount. His agent, M.C.A., was associated with his television series and still, at that point, affiliated to Universal, with whom a deal was made stipulating that he was not required to seek approval for any film budgeted at $3 million or less. As it turned out, **The Birds** (1963) was his last estimable film. Evan Hunter wrote the screenplay, transferring the action of Daphne du Maurier's short story from Cornwall to California, and considerably fleshing it out – since attacks by birds on people would hardly sustain a two-hour feature. Those attacks required much planning and pre-production (as well as a budget of more than $3 million). The film is smoothly entertaining, and Rod Taylor is a tower of strength as the hero.

The heroine, Tippi Hedren, was an ex-model chosen because Hitchcock thought he could mould her into another Grace Kelly. In **Marnie** (1964) she plays a kleptomaniac and Sean Connery a man with a compulsive desire to bed her – the element of the plot which appealed to Hitchcock on reading Winston Graham's novel. Neither player is up to the demands of the film, which dallies with an *amour fou* in the manner of *Vertigo* before drifting into matters reminiscent of another of Hitchcock's worst films, *Spellbound*. Deservedly, it failed, and he returned to stars and more familiar material in a Cold War thriller, **Torn Curtain** (1966). On this occasion, the earlier films plundered included *Psycho*, *North by Northwest* and *The Lady Vanishes*, plus two not by Hitchcock, *State Secret* and *The Man Between*. The credits nevertheless claimed an 'original' screenplay – which makes it the first that Hitchcock had directed since *Notorious*. He subsequently dismissed its writer, the novelist Brian Moore, as the wrong man for the job, and also in public was less than gracious to his stars, Julie Andrews and Paul Newman.

Since *Torn Curtain* did only a little better than *Marnie* he determined never again to work with stars – who did, after all, deflect attention from him. Just as he had given up John Michael Hayes for some lesser screenwriters (though, to be fair, Hayes's other credits are of unequal quality), so he relinquished Bernard Herrmann, whose music had contributed to so many of his films. Without the cost of stars he did not need to seek budget or subject approval, though it was Universal which suggested **Topaz** (1969) when he could not settle on a property. Whatever the merits of Leon Uris's original novel, based on a true espionage affair, the film emerged as a showy exercise in Hitchcockism, moving its setpieces from Harlem to Copenhagen to Cuba to Paris. The last two films are equally mechanical and much more old-fashioned than such concurrent formula films as *Dirty Harry* (q.v.). **Frenzy** (1972), about a London sex killer, was based on a novel by Arthur La Bern, who wrote to *The Times* denouncing the film. **Family Plot** (1976), written by Ernest Lehman from a novel by Victor Canning, is set in California and involves two pairs of crooks (William Devane and Barbara Harris; Bruce Dern and Karen Black) whose paths cross, with fatal results for the less cunning of them.

Although Hitchcock in old age expressed discontent over the projects which, he said, his backers would not sanction, he failed to take any of the risks open to the world's most famous director. Because of his position, his decline was less inevitable than most, and it is probably no coincidence that his films became less interesting as his fame increased because of television and the over-lauding of some cinéastes. Daniel Gélin, working with him on the remake of *The Man Who Knew Too Much*, reports that Hitchcock used to chuckle over the *Cahiers du Cinéma* theories, for ever claiming unwarranted complexities in his films, but there is sad evidence that the old man eventually began to believe them. A disservice had been done to an entertainer whose long career encompassed some enjoyable films.

Another veteran, George Cukor, made one of the most enduring films of the period, **A Star Is Born** (1954), intended as a showcase for the talents of Judy Garland by her (second) husband, Sid Luft,

Personal difficulties kept Judy Garland off the screen for four years before *A Star Is Born*, and although it was among the biggest money-making films of 1954 reports of her temperament – denied, however, by her director George Cukor – marked her as a star best avoided: a loss both to the industry and cinemagoers. One of the themes of this particular film is star quality, as explained by James Mason in the film, 'That little bell that rings inside your head, that little jolt of pleasure . . . You've got that little extra something that Ellen Terry talked about.'

whose inexperience as a producer contributed to the film's excessive budget. Another cause of overspending was the decision by Warners to scrap the initial shooting and recommence in Cinema-Scope. CinemaScope had not till then been used with imagination; here the opening sequence, a Hollywood premiere, is handled by Cukor as a whirling bubble of self-importance and hysteria, while Garland supplies the intensity dissipated elsewhere by the wide screen. This is intimate drama, and she plays the star who rises while her husband (James Mason) wanes. Reworking the screenplay of the earlier version, Moss Hart considerably strengthened the satire of the first half, while leaving intact the tragedy of the second. Cukor handles both with virtuosity, understanding the glamour and viciousness of Hollywood, and knowing that as a show-business tale it is entitled to wear its heart on its sleeve. The faults are minor: alcoholism is pictured as not disagreeable while the kindness of the studio head (Charles Bickford) and the malignancy of the press agent (Jack Carson) each seem

exaggerated (would the latter have been quite so nasty to the husband of his most important client?). Of the two leading players, Mason may be the better, since he submits himself to the material while Garland dominates it. But that is half the point: her acting is allowed greater range than hitherto, and her handling of the songs – particularly 'The Man That Got Away' – unparalleled in Hollywood history. Mason and Cukor observed that the film was better without the twenty-minute song sequence, 'Born in a Trunk', interpolated after Cukor had moved on to his next project; and they and others who saw the original three-hour film have testified to its superiority over the two-and-a-half hour version which was put into release.★ There had been no longer American film since *Gone with the Wind*, but Warners got cold feet when it was clear that it would not do commensurate business. In the event, it turned a small profit.†

Cukor's years with M-G-M concluded with a more orthodox musical, *Les Girls*, already discussed, and **Bhowani Junction** (1956), produced by his old colleague, Pandro S. Berman, from John Masters's novel about the plight of Anglo-Indians at the time of the British withdrawal. This was clearly a more responsible view of the Raj than Hollywood's prewar adventures, and the locations again demonstrated Cukor's mastery of the wide screen. But, in his own words, 'the story went wrong'; it succeeds neither as political thriller nor action tale, and it is hard to like or understand the characters in the foreground, who include Stewart Granger as the C. O. and Ava Gardner as an Anglo-Indian subaltern. We may feel the same way about those in **Wild Is the Wind** (1957), since they include Anthony Quinn as a son of the soil, Anna Magnani as his mail-order bride, and Anthony Franciosa as the adopted son with whom she falls in love. These players provide no justification for disinterring this revamp of *They Knew What They Wanted*.

Cukor's response to the theatre sequences in *Les Girls* was repeated in the de-

★In 1983 most of the lost footage was restored and the reconstituted version was endorsed by critics and audiences.

†Warners did not proceed with the next two pictures called for in their contract with Garland, presumably because her unreliability and Luft's inexperience were given more weight than the film's good business and her glowing personal notices.

lightful re-creation of nineteenth-century drama in **Heller in Pink Tights** (1960). He was attracted to the subject, a theatre troupe in the old West, and although he admitted that there was no real story, he felt that it would be serviceable. It is hard to believe that the troupe's leading lady (Sophia Loren) would prefer her morose fellow-thespian (Quinn) to the attractive outlaw suitor (Steve Forrest, on this occasion transformed from his usual dull screen self). Or that, in this metier, she would experience such remorse at promising sex – in return for favours – that she would flee from each aspirant. Restrictions had recently been lifted on depicting such matters, so perhaps Cukor was working from an old script; it was the last one written by Dudley Nichols (with Walter Bernstein, from a novel by Louis L'Amour). The exteriors are imaginative and the interiors authentic in a way which was unprecedented. Cukor was always anxious to praise Hoyningen-Huene, credited as 'colour co-ordinator' on several of his films at this time – and it is for their visual quality that they are memorable – as opposed to the urbanity of most of his earlier work. There is little of either quality, however, in **Let's Make Love** (1960), a supposed satire on theatre people written by Norman Krasna. Cukor seems to have been depressed by the presence of a British 'pop' singer, Frankie Vaughan, playing a Broadway star, while both Yves Montand and Marilyn Monroe are wan as a multimillionaire and the singer he falls for.

20th Century-Fox made the film, and later threatened to sue if Cukor did not fulfil his other contracted commitment to them. He solved the problem by agreeing to make **The Chapman Report** (1962), based on Irving Wallace's novel about a Kinsey-like examination of selected Californian women. Cukor had always claimed to be a commercial director, and he later defended this rather salacious film by observing that the novel 'presented something contemporary (at the time) about outwardly respectable women who were frigid and took lovers and went to psychiatrists'. Zanuck, returning to the company as head of production during the troubles with *Cleopatra*, stopped work on all projects, including this one – but he nevertheless produced it, under an agreement with Warner Bros. This meant two

front offices making cuts and changes – and the censor also interfered. Blaming them for the resulting version, Cukor said 'I know one always talks this way when a picture doesn't turn out, but in this case it was definitely so . . . The picture did have some virtues.' As it stands, its chief virtue is Jane Fonda, even if her inexperience shows as a young widow troubled by her frigidity (a subject only elementarily handled). Shelley Winters is conventional as a married woman with a passion for a man who regards her as just a passing fancy, and Glynis Johns is lamentable as an arty wife who seeks experience with an unlikely beach boy (Ty Hardin) – thus ruining the intentionally comic section of the film. Claire Bloom punishes herself for her nymphomania by committing suicide after being gang-raped – a situation new to American films. Such words as 'foreplay' and 'frequency' (of orgasm, a word not mentioned) are bandied about, but few commented on the film's frankness. Conditioned by *Peyton Place* (q.v.), whose source was an even more meretricious novel, the public seemed to think that it was time Hollywood accepted the facts of life.

Few of Cukor's films since *A Star Is Born* had made much public impact, but his reputation remained high – and it rested chiefly on movies which made him, in his own phrase, a 'wise choice' for **My Fair Lady** (1964), based on the most successful musical in Broadway history. Unfortunately, Jack Warner insisted on a replica of the stage show, insofar as it was possible, and he had, after all, paid an unprecedented $5 million for the rights. The Shaw Estate apparently refused any further excisions in what had once been 'Pygmalion', and not only was Alan Jay Lerner disinclined to cut his own libretto, but he even added to it, drawing on Shaw's additions to the 1938 movie. Consequently, the material was both overfamiliar and too thin for a three-hour film, a fact undisguised by Cukor's mobile camera and command of the big screen. He said that they were aiming at a fairy-tale London, but it is heavy and graceless, while Cecil Beaton's celebrated costumes are too theatrical for the screen. Still, these are offset by Rex Harrison's definitive Higgins and Audrey Hepburn – even if, like most Elizas, she is not

865

too comfortable before the transformation and over-enthusiastic after it.

Cukor took over **Justine** (1969) in mid-production. 20th Century-Fox had struggled for ten years to fashion a screenplay from Lawrence Durrell's Alexandria Quartet. After the debacle of *Cleopatra* Mankiewicz was not invited to return to his version; one by Durrell himself was turned down, and the film eventually went ahead with a script by Lawrence B. Marcus. The original director, Joseph Strick, had been chosen as the result of two art-house semi-successes, *The Balcony* (q.v.) and *Ulysses*, but when the company disliked the footage arriving from Tunisia, Cukor was asked to replace him – and he reshot as much as was possible. Since the chief virtues of the four novels were descriptive, it is rewarding to see Alexandria as it should be, with teeming streets and houses with hot, untidy, dirty rooms. It may not be quite as Durrell portrayed it, but it is a clever updating of that old Hollywood hunting ground, the cosmopolitan city of intrigue, now populated by transvestites, trollops and deviates. They – French, English, Greek, Jewish, Coptic Egyptian – move from brothel to embassy, united only in contempt for the native population and each other. Trying to pin down something of the original, the plot flies off in all directions, with Cukor racing through such setpieces as the carnival in bravura style. An unusually uneven group of players revived his reputation as an actors' director: Anouk Aimée as the mysterious Justine, Dirk Bogarde, Anna Karina, Philippe Noiret and John Vernon. If the exposition remains clumsy, Cukor's overall rescue job is a triumph, unrecognised by the press for the achievement it is. Audiences today are no longer concerned whether Durrell has been betrayed, caring more for a director at the peak of his form.

Nevertheless, Cukor's style was unable to make amends for a poor screenplay fashioned from Graham Greene's novel **Travels with My Aunt** (1972); and a miscast Maggie Smith, who replaced Katharine Hepburn at the last minute, does not improve matters. Nor did Cukor emerge with much credit from **The Blue Bird** (1974), except that he seems to have been the only one of the American principals to have had any regard for their Russian co-workers. This first Soviet-American co-production was the brain-child of Edward Lewis, a former writer who had produced for the companies of actor Kirk Douglas and director John Frankenheimer (q.v.). Reports on the shooting suggest that very few of those concerned had a good word to say for Lewis (several of the more catastrophic films of this time were produced by independent operators). The hapless studio involved was 20th Century-Fox, but much of the $15 million budget was put up by the Russians, who also provided production facilities in Leningrad. A prime mistake was the choice of Maeterlinck's dated play; the two child actors involved are uninteresting, and Elizabeth Taylor is a banal presence. Unfortunately, she has three roles, and in the most important, the Fairy Light, lacks beauty and magic – though Jane Fonda, as Night, and Ava Gardner, as Luxury, are little better. Luxury's party reveals some of Cukor's old flair, but there is one scene, as Light waves her wand to bring on various balletic elements, which is exactly like parents' night at the local dance school – an effect emphasised by dialogue in rhyming couplets.

Cukor's civilised talents were more suitably engaged in **Love Among the Ruins** (1975) and **The Corn Is Green** (1979), both with his old friend Katharine Hepburn, who is a little too consciously radiant for the circumstances. The first is an autumnal teaming with Laurence Olivier, giving a witty performance as a one-time lover now defending her in a breach of promise case. James Costigan's screenplay (written for the Lunts) would have benefited from the old Hollywood treatment, resulting in more point, humour and body than it presently has. The second film is a remake for Warners of their old movie, superior because of its views of Wales, a sensible attempt to improve the dialogue and the performance of Ian Saynor as the miner-student.

Both films were made for television, following the disastrous reception of *The Blue Bird*. With the outstanding exception of *My Fair Lady*, Cukor's movies of his last two decades were unsuccessful, so it said much for his standing within the industry that he became, at eighty-two, the oldest director ever to be entrusted with a major film, **Rich and Famous** (1981). It was the second Bette Davis film that he had re-made in a row, for it had once been *Old Acquaintance*; but more importantly, it was another rescue operation, with Cukor brought in after Robert Mulligan (q.v.) had not seen eye to eye with the producers, who included Jacqueline Bisset, one of the stars. She plays the highbrow novelist, Candice Bergen the friend who writes trashy bestsellers, and David Selby the man who marries the one but wishes he had married the other. Gerald Ayres's script was, said Cukor, 'witty, intelligent' and therefore 'irresistible', but despite that there were glib references to Yeats and Eliot and some cheap touches, such as Bisset allowing a nineteen-year-old pick-up to make love to her (in the Algonquin). It was another commercial failure, perhaps because it remained too much like the films Cukor had made on first arriving in Holly-wood; but overall it bore impeccable witness to the unobtrusive skills he had acquired in the fifty years' interim.

The late films of John Ford, another old master, bear witness to all that he had learnt in a similar period, but unlike Cukor, his energy, if not his craftsman-ship, diminished as the years went by. **Mogambo** (1953), a remake of *Red Dust*, is one of his brightest pictures, but perhaps because M-G-M paid handsomely for African locations the flora and fauna take precedence over John Lee Mahin's screen-play. The bantering, taunting dialogue be-tween Clark Gable and Ava Gardner is less amusing and outrageous than that Gable shared with Jean Harlow, but both players are superb.

Mister Roberts (1955) is one of Ford's finest achievements, or so it seems after examining the contentious shooting his-tory, which ended with the Directors Guild insisting on a shared credit with Mervyn LeRoy. Thomas Heggen's novel had been adapted and produced for Broad-way by Joshua Logan, whose contract specified the direction of any eventual film. Since he owned twenty-five per cent of the property, he ceded to Ford, who was Warners' choice, agreeing that the result was likely to be more profitable thereby. John Patrick wrote the screenplay, but Ford brought in Frank S. Nugent (the former critic, his son-in-law and a regular collaborator since *Fort Apache*) to make further changes to what he always referred to as 'a homosexual play'. Thus the contin-gent of nurses in the original was increased from one to six, but Henry Fonda, who had earlier played the title role on Broad-way, felt that the changes vulgarised the material. After an altercation between the two, Ford got drunk and, according to Logan, stayed drunk. The actor Ward Bond directed some sequences before LeRoy was called in, and Logan himself directed some – for which he was consoled with a writing credit. But the visually magnificent exteriors which comprise most of the film are superior to the forced comedy of the scenes inside the ship, and they are all Ford's work. Fonda is excellent as the exceptionally nice officer beloved by the crew, as is James Cagney as the vicious captain; William Powell is the doc and Jack Lemmon the amorous ensign – and it is pleasing to see together these two supreme light comedians of different generations. The American public loved the film, with its portrait of service life as a mixture of boredom, horsing around, drunkenness and petty-mindedness. The British critics were scandalised almost to a man, a telling comment on the dishonesty of British movies on service life.

Ford continued on form with **The Searchers** (1956), written by Nugent from a novel by Alan Le May about the early settlers and marauding Comanches. There are flaws and irrelevancies, but once John Wayne sets out on his dual mission, of revenge and quest for his captive niece (Natalie Wood), the film's epic ambitions are sustained. This was the level at which Ford was expected to work, now that he was no longer restrained by crass pro-ducers; but neither **The Wings of Eagles** (1957) nor **Gideon's Day** (1958) are of the standard of his early commercial chores for Fox. The former, based on a true story, deals with a dedicated naval man, Frank Wead (Wayne), who takes up writing screen-plays, including *Ceiling Zero* and *Hell Di-vers*, after being crippled. *Gideon's Day* is a half-hearted account of a Scotland Yard man (Jack Hawkins), which was produced in London by Lord Killanin (who was also responsible for Ford's Irish venture, *The Rising of the Moon*). John Creasey's novel was adapted by T. E. B. Clarke, writer of *The Blue Lamp*, which shares with this film the obvious premise that the police are as human as the rest of us.

The Last Hurrah (1958) was the last spurt of an old runner. As no American film on politics had succeeded at the box office since *Mr Smith Goes to Washington* (and this was to prove no exception) it was surprising that Columbia wanted to film Edwin O'Connor's novel. As the 'engaging rogue' who stands for re-election, Spencer Tracy was never more richly human. He had not worked with Ford since his first film, and the occasion snared some of the great character actors among their contemporaries: Pat O'Brien, James Gleason, Wallace Ford, Frank McHugh, Basil Rathbone, Basil Ruysdael and Edward Brophy. The material might have yielded better results in the hands of a more sensitive director, but no one could have treated these people – both the roles they play and hence the subject itself – with more affection.

Ford continued making films for another ten years, each one worse than the last. As with Hitchcock and Cukor, some buffs held him in an admiration which amounted to idolatry, but where Cukor justified it by stretching his talent, Ford, like Hitchcock, fell into self-parody. He made John Ford movies, each lethargic, often plotless, with cardboard characters bashing away at one another in a manner meant to be light-hearted. Admirers claimed that he had earned the right to be self-indulgent, but others were bored by these formless melanges of masculine camaraderie and sentimentality. **The Horse Soldiers** (1959) and **Two Rode Together** (1961) both treat the over-familiar rivalry between old hand and young upstart. These are played by John Wayne and William Holden in the first, and by James Stewart and Richard Widmark in the second. **Sergeant Rutledge** (1960), set in cavalry days, yet again, more interestingly concerns a black (Woody Strode) on trial for rape and murder – though never for a moment is it doubtful that he is blameless. It is evident that Ford, with customary cynicism, saw the theme as a way of establishing himself with a new generation as a liberal, caring film-maker – whereas, equally clearly, he was not really interested. **The Man Who Shot Liberty Valance** (1962) – which marks, incidentally, a last return to black and white – has Wayne in his usual role, Stewart (unbelievably, given his age) as a

novice in the West, and Lee Marvin as the villain. Wayne and Marvin fight each other over a number of beaches and bars in **Donovan's Reef** (1963) – this is an Hawaiian *Quiet Man*. Like *Liberty Valance* it is tired to the point of dropping, and both films were made worse by sequences with cute native kids.

Ford, Henry Hathaway and George Marshall shared the direction of the M-G-M Cinerama Western, **How the West Was Won** (1962), with its several episodes and thirteen star names – the whole, as scripted by James R. Webb, adding up to an anthology of pioneering clichés. Of its various spectacles, only one succeeds* – the train robbery – and that is due to Eli Wallach's gleeful little bandit rather than the speeding train on the triple-panel screen. Said Hathaway: 'That goddamned Cinerama . . . Cinerama was a joke anyway. I laid out that film; it was my conception to break it into four sections. I shot "The Rivers" and "The Plains" and then I had to reshoot most of George Marshall's stuff, "The Trains". I didn't touch John Ford's Civil War stuff even though it looked a little stagey. He shot the whole sequence on a sound stage and it was no good, frankly. It looked shabby. It was the most expensive film I've ever made: nearly ten million dollars.'

Its producer, Bernard Smith, went into partnership with Ford, and despite Ford's poor box-office record in recent years, found backing for what turned out to be his last two completed films. The first, **Cheyenne Autumn** (1964), was very expensive, its appeal like *Sergeant Rutledge* predicated on a liberal point of view. Webb wrote it, from a novel by Mari Sandoz, and it is about the return of the Cheyenne in 1868 to their native territory – a journey of 1,500 miles – escorted by a squadron of cavalry. Not only is it pro-Indian, but the cast includes some Quakers to plead the pacifist cause, asking such questions as, 'Does it matter who fires the first shot?' No one concerned seems to have been remotely interested in the answer, and the film is hindered by a number of familiar faces lurking under the wampum beads and warpaint. Cuts were made in the original running time of 170 minutes, but it was still a flop. **Seven Women** (1966)

*Perhaps I should say succeeded, since Cinerama is no longer with us.

might have been acceptable if made thirty years earlier, but as it is, audiences were reduced to giggles when the agnostic doctor (Anne Bancroft) saved the ladies of the lay mission by swallowing poison and 'giving herself' to the Chinese warlord. It was 'a hell of a good picture' commented Ford later, in his sad decrepitude.

Earlier illness had forced him to cede **Young Cassidy** (1965) to Jack Cardiff, the former cinematographer, whose direction complements a script superior to most that Ford worked with. It was written by the dramatist John Whiting, from Sean O'Casey's first volume of memoirs, 'Mirror in My House', and it conveys well O'Casey's instinctive protest against the poverty around him. It is ambivalent on the subject of the patronage of Lady Gregory (Edith Evans) and Yeats (Michael Redgrave), but clever with regard to its effect on him. Accordingly it ranks high among films about writers; its re-creation of Dublin at the time of the Troubles is outstanding; and though 'A John Ford Production', it is his one 'Irish' film in which the soundtrack is not weighted down by the most hackneyed Irish airs. In the title role, Rod Taylor is not only physically the antithesis of O'Casey but more sympathetic.

Almost everything that may be said about Ford's last films may be said about those of Howard Hawks. An epic of antique days, *Land of the Pharaohs* (1955), was, with some reason, so badly received that Hawks took several years off to contemplate 'how we used to make pictures'. That did not include the provision of plot, as Leigh Brackett observed after being commissioned to write **Rio Bravo** (1959) with another old and valued colleague, Jules Furthman. What plot there is derives from *High Noon*, but since John Wayne had loathed that film (because no one had come to Gary Cooper's aid) he is given three assistants plus a girl (Angie Dickinson) in the vein of earlier Hawks heroines – when they were so much better played by Jean Arthur or Lauren Bacall. **El Dorado** (1967) 'could have been called "Son of Rio Bravo Rides Again" ', said its writer, Miss Brackett. Its easy superiority over *Rio Bravo* is partly due to the casting of Robert Mitchum, both a more likeable drunk than Dean Martin and a more challenging partner for Wayne. The casual bantering tone

of Hawks's early work reappears with ideal interpreters, and this is his best film in two decades. Sadly, Hawks's other late films are negligible – *Hatari!* (1962), *Red Line 7000* (1965) and *Rio Lobo* (1970); there was also **Man's Favorite Sport?** (1964), with Rock Hudson, who later said 'He'd made very many brilliant films. But it was like he'd given up. And therefore it was quite disillusioning. All the jokes and comic sequences in that film were repeats of things he'd done in his various other films.'

The later films of John Huston are more eclectic, including some as uninspired as lesser Ford and Hawks but many which are, at least, satisfactory entertainments. His most ambitious project to that point, **Moby Dick** (1956), ended up between the two extremes. With his photographers, Oswald Morris and Freddie Francis, Huston evolved a colour scheme approximating that of old whaling prints, but despite extensive location work at sea we are all too often aware of the studio tank – not to mention the synthetic Moby. The film manages some fine moments in Nantucket and aboard the *Pequod*, but Melville's thundering mysticism has become an occasional eeriness, and that is partly because of the portrayal of Ahab. Huston favoured Laurence Olivier, but accepted Warners' suggestion of Gregory Peck, a sounder box-office name for what was a risky venture; and since he had coaxed a performance from Audie Murphy (in *The Red Badge of Courage*) he was confident that he could do the same with Peck. But Peck is neither pitiable nor indomitable; he is never vengeance incarnate. Leo Genn's Starbuck is no more interesting, and Richard Basehart is a bland Ishmael. The screenplay is credited to Huston and Ray Bradbury, who has claimed that it was his work alone.

Despite its shortcomings, the film added to Huston's reputation for making 'art' movies, but with forethought he knew that a failure with a similar project would leave him vulnerable. To prove that he remained at the service of the industry rather than vice-versa, he signed a contract with 20th Century-Fox for three films. The subjects were not necessarily of his choosing, but he was to have autonomy during shooting. **Heaven Knows, Mr Allison** (1957) follows the adventures of an American marine (Robert Mitchum) and an Irish nun (Deborah Kerr) on a Pacific atoll in wartime. It has the enchantments of other coral island stories rather than those of *The African Queen*, of which we are initially reminded; and since the central relationship raises the issue of romance, which it then avoids, we may see this as an example of Huston's ability to take an unlikely or unlikeable subject and convert it into a reasonably sophisticated entertainment. He directed **The Roots of Heaven** (1958) for Zanuck, whose independent company produced for 20th Century-Fox release. After quitting as head of production, Zanuck made his headquarters in Europe and turned out films usually featuring one of his several French mistresses – in this case Juliette Greco, who can sing, in her fashion, but cannot act. This one, Huston admitted, 'wasn't a very good picture', but if it achieves the dubious distinction of being the best of Zanuck's batch that is due to Trevor Howard's sincere and energetic performance as a man fanatically opposed to the destruction of elephants. The script, by Romain Gary and Patrick Leigh-Fermor, from Gary's novel, was an acknowledged mess when shooting began, and it suffered the further indignity of having chunks omitted when the African locations proved too arduous or when Errol Flynn was too drunk to remember his lines and improvised.

Many of Huston's films were battlegrounds: he worked with many stars who were roisterers or difficult, as later in the cases of Marilyn Monroe and Montgomery Clift. He and John Wayne detested each other on **The Barbarian and the Geisha** (1958); Wayne was as professional as he was popular, and relations deteriorated as he realised that Huston, a recognised maverick, was making a semi-documentary instead of a star vehicle. The 'barbarian' of the title is Townsend Harris, accepted under duress in 1856 by the Japanese as the first American consul, after two centuries spent avoiding European influence. The screenplay sidesteps all the issues and opts instead for pretty panoramas. That there is a genuine feeling for the Japanese past probably stems from the participation of the veteran director, Teinosuke Kinugasa, credited as 'script supervisor'. The result is not an enthralling entertainment, though it does not provide

evidence of the decline spotted by contemporaries, admittedly with *The Roots of Heaven* fresh in their minds.

After these far-flung American adventures, Huston decided to return to American roots, if not to Hollywood (and he avoided shooting there for another two decades). The experience of his last two films had taught him that he needed good screenplays, and two were at his disposal, both set in the West. **The Unforgiven** (1960) was adapted, by Ben Maddow, from a novel by Alan Le May, in which he reversed the situations he had used in 'The Searchers': in this case it is the Kiowa Indians of Texas who want the return of a girl they consider their own. As the girl, Audrey Hepburn is miscast but nevertheless an asset; Burt Lancaster (whose company produced) is the man of the house; and Lillian Gish the matriarch. Franz Planer's Panavision photography greatly aids what is essentially an attempt at the epic, but if the result is sometimes self-conscious Huston, typically, has 're-thought' the West: he offers the necessary neighbourliness (when possible) and the logistics of living so close to Indians in an area of almost supernatural vastness, with incandescent days and long nights of vaulted, fearful darkness.

The second film with a Western setting was **The Misfits** (1961), written by Arthur Miller for Marilyn Monroe, to whom he was married at the time. Great coverage was given in the press to the troubled shooting, due in part to the break-up of the Monroe-Miller marriage and culminating in the death of her co-star, Clark Gable, a few days after filming finished. The character of Roslyn, naive and caring, was based on Monroe herself, but Miller was not writing exclusively about her: this was a New Yorker – not a Westerner – looking at the land beyond the Rockies and the sort of people it produces, and wondering why and how it differs from the old West and its myths. These misfits find odd pockets of compassion for each other. Gable is beautifully cast as the man with two kids somewhere, nothing guiding him beyond the hatred of a nine-to-five job and a longing for the days when the hills were full of mustangs. Montgomery Clift, so weak as a Westerner in *Red River*, easily manages the aimless, simple-minded Pete, obsessed with loathing for his stepfather; Eli Walach is Guido, a former bomber pilot; and it is only Thelma Ritter, the divorcee, who allows her past to catch up with her, forcing her to desert her new-found friends. The rounding-up of the mustangs accelerates the break-up of the party, till its violence gives way before the spirit of Roslyn. As this poignant creature, Monroe gives no hint of the comedienne – which at this point she was considered to be. The film itself has grown in stature with the years, justifying Huston's faith in the screenplay, which was not generally admired.

The filming of **Freud** (1962) was also fraught with trouble. Huston and Charles Kaufman had wanted to make a movie on psychoneurosis since 1946, the year they had made *Let There Be Light*, a documentary for the War Department. By 1957 Wolfgang Reinhardt and Jean-Paul Sartre had joined the project. Sartre's proposed screenplay would have run to ten hours' screen time, however, and the one eventually used is credited to Reinhardt and Kaufman, from a story by Kaufman. Universal backed it, since at that time the company was making an effort to return to 'quality' films, but difficulties with Clift (Universal sued him, and he countersued) sent the budget and shooting schedule soaring. A 240-minute print was whittled down to 139 minutes, and then to much less on release. According to Robert LaGuardia, in his biography of Montgomery Clift, this film was Huston's 'dream of a lifetime', but his inability to understand the subject was 'embarrassing' – or so Kaufman told him. Apparently Huston approached the subject in ignorance, and later 'puritanically' took out much that was best in the script. The result is very much like the screen biographies Warners made when Huston was a writer with them: it is craftily made, dark, handsome and sober, with no serious anachronisms. Freud's thirteen documented cases are reduced to one and a half, but his growing understanding of the troubles of that one patient (Susannah York) makes interesting enough entertainment. The dream sequences renew one's respect for Huston, but there are some sentences of the 'Siggy, you're working too hard' variety, and the film eventually disappoints because its 'revelatory' climax on sexuality in children is no revelation for the great majority of its audience.

After an inadequate joke-thriller, **The List of Adrian Messenger** (1963), Huston tackled a play by Tennessee Williams, and after *A Streetcar Named Desire*, **The Night of the Iguana** (1964) is the best film of a Williams drama. In reworking his short story for the stage, Williams had moved close to self-parody, but Huston's screenplay (written with Anthony Veiller) eliminated those facets of Williams with which he had no sympathy. Gone is the half-squeamish fascination with decadence, in favour of what had attracted him ever since *The Maltese Falcon* – the interplay of assorted individuals: the drunken ex-priest (Richard Burton), grandiloquent and sardonic; the warm-hearted innkeeper (Ava Gardner), with her young male escorts; the untalented but resolute spinster (Deborah Kerr); the lesbian chaperone (Grayson Hall); and her young charge (Sue Lyon) who cannot wait to jump into bed with the priest. The images – palm tree, shore and shutters – are as heady as the text, but as photographed by Gabriel Figueroa they manage to remain a knife edge away from cliché.

Huston accepted the challenge of **The Bible . . . in the Beginning/La Bibbia** (1966) offered by Dino de Laurentiis, who intended it to be the culmination of the recent spate of religious epics. Originally several other film-makers were to have been involved, each with artistic control over their own sections – Robert Bresson (for The Creation), Orson Welles, Fellini and Visconti – but there were quarrels over Christopher Fry's draft screenplay. Even with a sole director in control, the project seemed one of the most risible in cinema history, but Huston, mindful of his reputation – since with it went his independence – approached it with care and vigour. The result is one of his finest achievements. A series of episodes from the Old Testament, visually impressive, is accompanied by a text which is an excellent pastiche of the King James Version. Solutions have been found to virtually insurmountable problems, marvellously so in the cases of the Flood (Huston himself played Noah) and the Tower of Babel; but unfortunately the ninety-minute story of Abraham, rounding off the second half, is no more than a scripture lesson. There are, too, occasional banalities, but also few shots which do not carry the mystique of

871

Hollywood in the Age of Television: The Directors

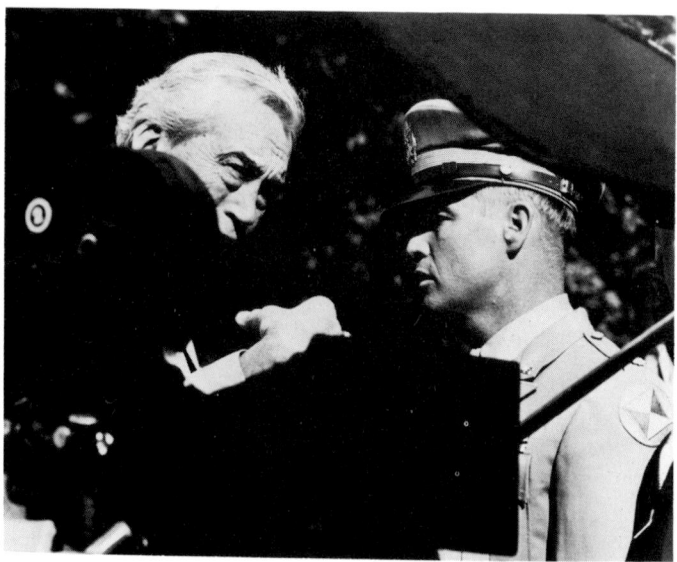

Of the major American directors, only George Cukor had a longer career than John Huston, and Huston's career is the more interesting, since he has shifted from genre to genre with frequency, even to finally making a musical, *Annie*. His films of the last three decades have not been uniformly good, but he has succeeded with some notoriously difficult subjects – not least with the overheated world of the novelist Carson McCullers, *Reflections in a Golden Eye*. Here he converses with Marlon Brando, the film's leading actor.

the text, if in the manner of Victorian illustrations: to that extent it is superior to Wyler's *Ben-Hur* and Stevens's *The Greatest Story Ever Told*, but if you had read the reviews you would not have supposed it so much better. Stevens's film was instrumental in lessening public interest in the genre, but this one found its own – rapt – audience.

Nor were American reviewers kind to **Reflections in a Golden Eye** (1967), but it was liked elsewhere. Carson McCullers's novel, a quadrille for two army couples, contains risky matters for the screen, and the screenplay by Chapman Mortimer and Gladys Hill, Huston's secretary,★ adds yet another – the officer horsewhipped in front of guests by his flighty wife. Huston ignores the difficulties and brings his sardonic humour to bear on three interrelated studies: the sickly, withdrawn wife (Julie Harris) and her camp, sycophantic houseboy; the colonel (Brian Keith), engaged in an affair with the major's wife (Elizabeth Taylor); and the major (Marlon Brando), with his fixation on an enlisted man. The major gazing at a photograph of a nude statue or applying rejuvenation cream seems a naive approach to homosexuality, and no more

★There is no doubt that Huston contributed to virtually all the screenplays he directed, whether credited or not, but by this time Miss Hill so clearly understood his requirements that he was happy to let her take sole credit for most of the writing they did together.

than in *The Night of the Iguana* does Huston seem sympathetic to the preoccupation of the Williams-McCullers school in such matters; but he had decided, irrespective of what other film-makers were doing, that it was time they surfaced in films – hence, similarly, Freud's identification as a Jew in that movie, at a time when Jewish characters were rarely recognised as such in films. For the deficiencies in both films Huston atones in this one with a superb scene in which Brando waits for the soldier, as tense as one of Buñuel's shoe fetishists, irrevocably committed to a meeting he knows is foolish. Brando's performance is the definitive study of a military man – a hopeful martinet everywhere but in his own home, where he uncertainly accepts humiliation. Brian Keith is equally good because he is equally stupid underneath his virility, and Julie Harris completes a trio of excellent performances.

Huston said later that he had made 'only three good films in the last decade', citing this one, *Fat City* (q.v.) and *The Man Who Would Be King* (q.v.). He liked, he said, 'to jump around in life and in films . . . Perhaps my greatest contribution has been that of keeping certain films from being mediocrities instead.' He blamed the failure of **Sinful Davey** (1969) on himself, explaining that he had lost interest before filming began – which is not surprising, given the derivative script by James R. Webb for this Scottish *Tom Jones* (q.v.) and the inadequate casting of the then unknown John Hurt in the title role. **A Walk with Love and Death** (1969) also has deficiencies in the script and leading performances – Assaf Dayan (son of the Israeli statesman) and Anjelica Huston (the director's daughter); the setting, however, is well realised. The challenge of re-creating Moscow may have attracted Huston to **The Kremlin Letter** (1970), or he may just have wanted to try his hand at a spy thriller. He wrote the screenplay with Gladys Hill, from a bestseller by Noel Behn, and it has that rueful humour and ruthlessness that we recognise as his hallmarks. The basic plot, about a team of experts operating behind the enemy's lines, is as old fashioned as Phillips Oppenheimer, if decorated with such elements as Cold War commissars, perversion and drugs.

By this time Huston was much in

demand as an actor – having been invited to make his debut in Otto Preminger's *The Cardinal* in 1963. One may have supposed that his career as a leading director was behind him, and the last three films tended to confirm this. Nothing, even in his best films, prepared the public for **Fat City** (1972), as freshly observed as if made by a newcomer. None of his contemporaries had managed to come to terms with the changed cinema of the Seventies in the same way. Huston had taken Leonard Gardner's naturalistic novel and tossed it around in the fashionable fragmentary style, but, more importantly, he imbued the film with all the perceptions that are fascinatingly possible in life but that were not available in movies when Huston started his career. It consists of a series of vignettes in the lives of two small-time boxers, one (Stacey Keach) already over the hill at thirty, and the other (Jeff Bridges) just starting on the same path. They hang out in Fat City – Stockton in Northern California – in grubby bars and sweaty little halls, doing deals over hamburgers or the pool table. The youngster marries the girl he has got pregnant, and is probably as happy as the next man – but, if that man is Keach, playing marvellously, he keeps his thoughts to himself. The public had never cared for films about losers, however compassionately treated, and despite rapturous notices this was no exception. Aware of this, Huston had agreed to direct two films with Paul Newman. Both **The Life and Times of Judge Roy Bean** (1972) and **The Mackintosh Man** (1973) feed on old movies, written in the first case by John Milius and in the second by Walter Hill (from a novel by Desmond Bagley), both newcomers who were later to become directors. Neither film was well received, and the $400,000 paid for the screenplay of the former, about lovable eccentrics in the old West, was not money well spent. *The Mackintosh Man*, a man-on-the-spot tale in the Hitchcock mould, manages both tension and surprise, with the director's humour surfacing as he follows the rules of the game.

It was Newman's partner, John Foreman, who found the financing for **The Man Who Would Be King** (1975), an expensive project Huston had planned twenty years earlier for Humphrey Bogart and Clark Gable. Kipling's well-nigh-unfilmable short story had been turned, by Gladys Hill and Huston, into a long (130-minute) screenplay, which is remarkably faithful in spirit, though that is not enough to make it work. It is not remotely mysterious, despite or because of the mountain locations (Morocco deputising for the Khyber Pass); and what in Carnehan's recollection is elusive or fantastic becomes only too literal on the screen. The fault lies in the stars: 'I use actors with strong personalities, ones who are like the characters they play,' Huston said, of Sean Connery as Dravot and Michael Caine as Carnehan, adding that he marvelled at Olivier, but 'that's a kind of virtuosity that does not serve my purpose'. Connery, however, has everything for the role but the one essential quality – recklessness – and Caine, on this occasion, is quite hopeless.

The film, though not a gigantic success, restored the industry's confidence in Huston, but instead of the major projects he was being offered, he chose to make **Wise Blood** (1979), the first time in his career he worked without a major studio or distributor behind him. That, and the film itself, would be remarkable in any Hollywood director; it is even more remarkable in one of his generation. The producers were amateurs, friends of Flannery O'Connor, whose novel provides the source, and the producers' son, Benedict Fitzgerald, wrote the screenplay, which is mainly about Hazel Motes (Brad Dourif), who may or may not be a lay preacher. Motes is volatile, basically bruised and introspective, but he cannot be said to be stupid, as everyone else is. I am not sure that Huston has conveyed Flannery O'Connor's questioning views on Southern religion, but as in *Fat City* he has gone to a forgotten part of America, where the buildings are bleak and the roadways seem endless, where there is a deadness in the air except in the almost gothic rooming houses.

Huston's next two films, **Phobia** (1980) and **Victory** (1981), indicated no great interest on his part; the first, a Canadian horror film, was an assignment done at a time when his health had deteriorated to such an extent that no insurance company would accept him as a client during the usual shooting schedule. He had obviously recovered by the time he made **Annie**

873

(1982), into which producer Ray Stark and Columbia poured some $25 million, including $6½ million for the screen rights – the highest sum ever paid (the reported figure was $9½ million and a final cost of $40 million, but these were the 'hype' sums, according to Columbia's president, Frank Price). Clearly it was hoped that *Annie* would repeat the success of *The Sound of Music*, but the score is poor, and the book, based on a comic-strip about a cute little orphan in the Thirties, includes such dubious conceits as a singing F. D. R. There are past examples of prestigious directors failing with the musical form, but Huston had always shown himself able to learn from past mistakes, his own included. In addition, he had recently proved himself to be as much in tune with the times as any film-maker fifty years his junior – if that was what was needed. What he has done to *Annie* is a matter of conjecture: he has tried to treat its dull 'book' lightly – and Carol Burnett gives an outrageous, but funny, performance as the orphanage gorgon. Ann Reinking handles some songs and dances with ease, but as 'Daddy' Warbucks Albert Finney lacks the necessary villainy and geniality. Huston observed that since this was his first musical he would leave the handling of the numbers to those expert in such matters. The numbers, however, are memorable only for the inefficiency with which they have been staged, with the camera constantly cutting away as they try to work up steam. One, 'Let's Go to the Movies', takes place in Radio City Music Hall,★ with its platoon of ushers and the Rockettes; but it is even niggardly in using them. Columbia in desperation advertised the film as 'The musical of Tomorrow' – a reference to its only known song – but it assuredly was not.

Huston's reputation as a maverick and his record of occasional box-office (and artistic) failures has not prevented him from almost uninterrupted employment with the major Hollywood studios. Orson Welles, on the other hand, has not been prolific; he worked frequently as an actor for Zanuck, who on other occasions expressed the warmest regard for Welles's work. Welles's reputation in fact grew as

Citizen Kane retained its stature in the eyes of each new generation of movie buffs. He began innumerable projects, usually in Europe, often with distinguished participants, but the money either ran out or the film was abandoned, temporarily and then permanently, when Welles accepted an acting job. 'I started at the top' he observed in 1982, 'and worked downwards' – and the films he did make prove that he has only himself to blame. He persuaded a consortium of Swiss and Spanish businessmen to finance **Confidential Report** (1955), the shooting of which took cast and crew to Munich, Juan les Pins, Tangier, London, Chillon, Segovia and Paris (the action takes place in another half dozen exotic cities, but the regional shots were, presumably, from stock). The film is a rehash of *Citizen Kane*, with some mayhem thrown in; it has the same intricate structure, but the tycoon whose life is examined is European – perhaps based on Kruger, the match king. But in Europe, Welles is just a tourist: his script has nothing to say about wealth, international business or indeed anything. As the tycoon he looks ludicrous, and acts no better than anyone else in the cast. Warner Bros. bought the film for American distribution, but did not open it in the U. S. until seven years later, as *Mr Arkadin*.

Universal employed Welles as director on **Touch of Evil** (1958), apparently at the insistence of the star, Charlton Heston, who refused to believe that Welles had been hired only to act in the film. Welles's own performance, as a crooked district attorney, is, as usual, weird – and his direction of like quality. A simple thriller has been given an extraordinary surface: as ever, Welles is able to achieve striking visual effects, but only at the expense of the plot, which is often obscure. The version released was not Welles's own conception: a different management kindly issued that in the late Seventies, but it did not prove to be superior. To date, Welles has not directed another film for a Hollywood studio.

In France he made *The Trial* (q.v.), and then again with Swiss and Spanish backing he directed **Chimes at Midnight/Falstaff** (1966), which he adapted from both parts of 'Henry IV', plays that have been regarded as the greatest celebration of England and Englishness ever penned. The

---

★Which is playing *Camille*, which was not shown there, one year before it opened. The montage of scenes from that film is another of this one's miscalculations.

film has been so affected by the gaunt, cold walls of Castile, where it was filmed, that Welles hoped to fend off criticism by calling it 'a lament for Merrie England'. The plays have been savagely cut, but, unlike his earlier Shakespeare films, cut with understanding. John Gielgud is the old king, and Welles wisely left it to this admired exponent of the Bard to carry every scene in which he appears; elsewhere, much redubbing was necessary to bring the film to the level of the occasion. The battle sequence is magnificently conceived, outstripping in effectiveness that in *Richard III*, but its purpose seems less to honour Shakespeare than the film's producer-director-star. As Falstaff, he is not very merry, and he lacks heart. Keith Baxter is an excellent Prince Hal, and Norman Rodway a lusty Hotspur, though the role has been much reduced. All the performances are superior to those in Welles's *Macbeth* and *Othello*. In sum, the film was encouragement to those who wished to believe, despite evidence to the contrary, that the Welles of *Citizen Kane* was not dead.

Although *Kane* and *Ambersons* remained in the repertory of many art-houses, there was little interest in Welles as a director. In the mid-Fifties interesting film-makers were working in Hollywood, and those people who a decade earlier had looked to Welles to make the best films now turned above all to Elia Kazan. Rightly or wrongly, *Man on a Tightrope* was quickly forgotten, and the man who had made the acclaimed earlier films could still tackle anything that appealed to him. He himself was certain that *Panic in the Streets* was his best film, and he set to work with the playwright Arthur Miller on a not dissimilar subject – and one much to the fore at the time, about the troubles in the Longshoremen's Union in New York. Columbia was to have produced but Miller lost interest and the script was finally written by the novelist Budd Schulberg (b. 1914), the son of B. P. Schulberg, the founder of Paramount. Schulberg's screenplay for what became **On the Waterfront** (1954) was based on some magazine articles by Malcolm Johnson; it was to be filmed in New York, partly because the locations demanded it, and partly because Kazan, like Huston, Mankiewicz and Zinnemann, believed

that the atmosphere of Southern California was detrimental to his work. He was still angry about the cuts Zanuck had insisted on in *Man on a Tightrope*, but nevertheless *On the Waterfront* was destined for 20th Century-Fox until Zanuck decreed that audiences were not interested in labour problems. The project was taken on by the independent producer, Sam Spiegel, who arranged a deal with Columbia, and whose help in all ways was 'tremendous', according to Kazan.

The film reunited Kazan with Marlon Brando, whose performance as Terry Malloy, ex-pug and longshoreman, is one of the best ever recorded on celluloid. A foreword claims that the film 'will exemplify the way self-appointed tyrants can be defeated by right-thinking people in a vital democracy', thus avoiding the main problem, which is how tyrants achieve power in the first place. Malloy defeats them not by persuasive convictions about democracy but by the old movie standbys, revenge and the strength that comes from love. The film's rich texture and dialogue disguise the fact that Malloy is activated by a familiar maxim, 'A man's gotta do what a man's gotta do', but, as Brando makes clear, he is not accustomed to thinking. As events crowd in on him he uses his hands

A familiar face looks at us from a Spanish film – or at least one filmed in that country: and perhaps it is wisest not to enquire where Orson Welles gets his financing or why he films – as a director, that is – in so many different countries. We should pass discreetly over the films begun and to date not completed, leaving this one, *Chimes of Midnight*, the sole triumph of his later career – or, if it comes to that, the only wholly successful film he has directed since *The Magnificent Ambersons* over twenty years earlier. He played Falstaff; the lady behind him is unnamed in the cast list.

875

Hollywood in the Age of Television: The Directors

Eventually Elia Kazan's *On the Waterfront* falls into most of the traps lurking to ensnare film-makers of reforming zeal, but its virtuosity is undeniable – be it the words unheard under the ship's hooters or the shuffling conversation in the taxi, devices which were then new in films. The film, though often imitated, still retains its power, not least in the taxi scene, where Marlon Brando, right, tells his brother Rod Steiger that he coulda been a contender.

desperately in gesture or is forced back on an insolent grin; he under-reacts in contrast to the admittedly striking histrionics of Rod Steiger as his brother, of Lee J. Cobb as the corrupt Union boss and a rather dotty Karl Malden as the local priest. Brando is most memorable in the love scenes with the equally impressive Eva Marie Saint, playing the neighbourhood girl who encourages him in a quietly bantering way which effectively contrasts with the excitement of the rest of the film. It can be enjoyed as a thriller about corruption – at least, till the denouement, when Malloy becomes a Capra-like hero and testifies before the Crime Commission, and is ostracised by his colleagues – but rises from a beating-up to martyrdom and atonement. The subject is emotional and volatile, filmed in a style appropriate to the occasion; Leonard Bernstein's score is theatrical, but offset by Boris Kaufman's photography of Hoboken across the river, white with winter mists and steam drifting from the manholes.

The film's seven Oscars included awards to Kaufman, Brando, Kazan for direction and one as Best Picture. Its popularity re-established Kazan after the box-office failure of his previous two films. He identified with Malloy ('he felt proud and ashamed of himself at the same time. He wavered between the two, and he also felt

hurt by the fact that people – his own friends – were rejecting him. He also felt that it was a necessary act').★ And he chose his next film, **East of Eden** (1955), for autobiographical reasons – he had always felt that his father preferred his brother to himself, and he found a similar theme in John Steinbeck's novel. As O'Neill turned to the Greeks, so Steinbeck turned to the Bible, resetting the Cain and Abel story in the Salinas Valley of California during the early years of the century. Adam (Raymond Massey) is of a Bible-punching righteousness, but the behaviour of Cal (James Dean) would alienate the most patient of fathers, being fey, attention-seeking, erratic, vindictive, selfish and otherwise tiresome. Cal finds that his brother's girl (Julie Harris) enjoys being with him, but the pangs of despis'd love worsen when his brother, like his father, turns against him; he eventually gets revenge on his brother by taking him to visit their mother (Jo Van Fleet), thought dead, who runs a brothel in Monterey. Kazan disliked Dean, but used every facet of his 'unpredictable' behaviour for the role. Nevertheless, Dean is too cute for Steinbeck's pretensions, which were otherwise followed in the screenplay by Paul Osborn, commissioned by Kazan. The use of colour and CinemaScope complete the impression of trivial situations being treated in epic proportions.

With the equally meretricious *Splendor in the Grass* (q.v.), *East of Eden* was Kazan's last commercial success, but with good reason his next two films were much admired. His reputation and that of Tennessee Williams enabled **Baby Doll** (1956) to be made in defiance of the Code, but denunciations by the Roman Catholic church proved detrimental at the U.S. box office. Kazan constructed the film from two of Williams's short plays, and though Williams is credited with the original screenplay it would seem to have been their joint work. When Archie Lee (Karl Malden) burns down the cotton-gin of Vacarro (Eli Wallach), the latter sets out to seduce his virgin child-bride (Carroll Baker). The mixture is familiar: the Deep South is still deep in decadence, with

★Many left-wingers regarded the final sequence as Kazan's own comment on having given evidence before the House Un-American Activities Committee, which many former colleagues had refused to do.

mansions crumbling and leaves falling, but there is probably normal life continuing beyond the central trio playing their own cruel sex game. At least, they seem to be playing a game, although in fact the bride is a case of arrested development, Archie Lee is unaware of what is going on and Vacarro is motivated less by sensuality than revenge. The situation is dramatically effective, since it involves suspense and the promise of a cataclysmic change in relationships if Vacarro succeeds in his aim – but those elements have more to do with the audience's own erotic expectations than anything in the film, which is one reason why it is so powerful.

Kazan worked with another former collaborator on **A Face in the Crowd** (1957) – Budd Schulberg, whose screenplay was based on his own short story about a popular television personality who develops megalomania.★ There have been a number of films on this theme, including *Citizen Kane* and *Network* (q.v.), as well as *The Great Man* (q.v.), which preceded Kazan's film by a few months – and we should note a new urgency in the subject, as television was creating a new breed of demagogue. Lonesome Rhodes (Andy Griffith) is an Arkansas hillbilly singer who moves from local radio in his home state to television success in Memphis and eventually national fame in New York: the adulation is such that his advice is sought not only by advertising agents but by a senator with presidential ambitions – and since the girl who discovered him, Marcia (Patricia Neal), realises that he is virtually a Fascist, she determines to destroy him. Her sexual fascination with him, which begins only with his climb to power, is one strand in a film rich in detail – and these include references to Nixon's 'Checkers' speech and Will Rogers, a Marilyn Monroe look-alike model, 'This is Your Life', a sycophantic Sammy Glick-type agent (Anthony Franciosa) and Walter Winchell (the number of unpleasant people playing themselves in cameo roles may be an in-joke). The voice of conscience is a cynical writer, played by Walter Matthau, then little-known, and since he is plain and bespectacled and the closest the film comes to a romantic hero much of what he has to say may be forgiven. Kazan himself says

★Schulberg wrote the story after discussing the television star Arthur Godfrey with William Roland, his producer.

that the film is 'over-explicit' and equally correctly it had remained in my memory as somewhat hysterical; the ending, borrowed from a film Schulberg's father produced with Emil Jannings, is grandiloquent. Nevertheless, in humour and intelligence this film is probably the best on this particular subject.

These movies, and those that Kazan made up to and including *The Arrangement* (q.v.) were released by Warners, but **Wild River** (1960) completed his contract with 20th Century-Fox, whom he blamed for its failure, since they hardly bothered to promote it. The film, 'one of the one or two purest I've made', arose from a desire to say something about the work of the Tennessee Valley Authority. After trying his hand at his own script, Kazan again commissioned one from Paul Osborn based on two novels, 'Mud on the Stars' by William Bradford Huie and 'Dunbar's Cove' by Borden Deal. The result unfortunately reflects the disparate sources, combining a romance between the T.V.A. agent (Montgomery Clift) and a Dogpatch-like lady (Lee Remick), and some community-conscience sequences about an old woman (Jo Van Fleet) to be evicted in the course of building the new dam. The piece meanders so much that it is eventually hard to care about the fate of the old lady, despite Miss Van Fleet's affecting performance.

Usually categorised as poet or realist, Kazan used **Splendor in the Grass** (1961) to demonstrate that he was, rather, someone who went to the heart of any subject that interested him, which in this case was the conflicting moralities of the Twenties. He has been at pains to point out that the film is not just about the traumas suffered by a boy (Warren Beatty) and girl (Natalie Wood) because they cannot sleep together, but as no other point is discernible it would seem that he did not get to the heart of this particular matter. The erosion of moral standards may well give rise to tragedy, but William Inge's original screenplay – the recipient of an unaccountable Oscar – is merely the forerunner of later, more opportunistic movies which were to encourage the younger members of the audience to 'do their thing'. The film's reception diminished Kazan's reputation, which was not restored by two ventures, **America, America** (1963) and

The Arrangement (1969). Both are based on autobiographical novels he had written: the first follows the adventures of a young Anatolian Greek immigrant (Stathis Giallelis) at the turn of the century, and the second recounts the various breakdowns endured by a middle-aged man (Kirk Douglas) because of his family, his adultery and his high-powered job in advertising. *America, America* begins with a portrayal of racial intolerance in Turkey, which colours the rest of the film and its hero's desire to escape; the individual sequences are powerful and possibly more effective now than then. On the other hand, *The Arrangement* is merely top-heavy with ideas which do not coalesce into a whole; and it is a pity to see this master film-maker borrowing the flashy cutting from the *nouvelle vague*. Further, the film is not helped by the fact that the Douglas character is drawn with self-loathing but is designed to elicit sympathy. (The film might have been better with Brando, who at the last minute relinquished the role.)

Experimenting with 16 mm, and with a cast and crew of friends, Kazan made **The Visitors** (1972), about some Vietnam veterans, but the result suggested that he had not regained his creative force, a view confirmed by **The Last Tycoon** (1976). He had been invited back to Hollywood by Sam Spiegel, but there was no echo here of their collaboration on *On the Waterfront*. Neither the direction nor Harold Pinter's screenplay shows the least understanding either of Hollywood or Scott Fitzgerald's unfinished novel. It must be the most po-faced film ever made about the movie industry, at the same time rejecting Fitzgerald's outline for the continuation and conclusion of the plot in favour of cliché. Its box-office failure may be added to what Kazan called his 'six colossal disasters' since *On the Waterfront* (the exceptions being *East of Eden* and *Splendor in the Grass*, which were popular, and *The Visitors*, which did not try to be). It is a sad comment on someone who had given Hollywood a handful of its most memorable movies.

Fred Zinnemann, unspectacularly, weathered the years better. Having risked – and almost lost – his reputation with *Oklahoma!*, he had another close shave with **A Hatfield of Rain** (1957), based on a sensational and specious Broadway play about drug addiction by Michael V. Gazzo, whose screenplay, written with Alfred Hayes, is no improvement on the original. The grainy photography of a wintry New York was then rare, and the players are convincing as ordinary people in extraordinary circumstances: Don Murray as the 'junky', Eva Marie Saint as his wife and Lloyd Nolan as his father.

The Nun's Story (1959) is based on Kathryn Hulme's bestselling autobiographical novel and much of the 151-minute running time is a documentary account of convent life, so organised as to let us draw our own conclusions about the system. Elsewhere we are invited to examine the conscience of Sister Luc (Audrey Hepburn) during her struggles for humility, the back-breaking work and the decision, reached after much heartache, that she is not suited to the calling. There are contrivances in Robert Anderson's screenplay, and Franz Waxman's insistent score is appropriate to Zinnemann's style: with a lesser director the result would be pompous or ponderous, but this one respects his subject and his audience. He wanted to use monochrome for the Belgian sequences and colour only for those in the Congo, but Warner Bros. decreed the use of Technicolor throughout. Miss Hepburn was the one actress of her generation who could convey intelligence and dignity, and Zinnemann uses her personality to intensify the script's intentions – as do the other actresses, most memorably Peggy Ashcroft and Edith Evans as Mothers Superior of limited imaginations.

At the time **The Sundowners** (1960) was regarded as the best Australian picture yet made, if, in principle, it should be difficult to accept Robert Mitchum and Deborah Kerr as denizens of the Outback. They act so attentively that their portrait of a happy marriage has freshness, while their relationship to this terrain – is the film's chief theme – is achieved by the meticulous and optimistic Zinnemann despite a sprightly Tiomkin score, such expected fauna as kangaroos and koalas, and a Cockney saloon owner, carelessly played by Glynis Johns. The casting is central to the failure of **Behold a Pale Horse** (1964), a fact that Zinnemann realised too late, after casting Gregory Peck as a Spanish guerrilla leader and Anthony Quinn as a captain in the

Guardia Civile. In the circumstances Zinnemann's sympathies for Spain* in the aftermath of the Civil War went for little.

The subject of **A Man for All Seasons** (1966) is the intransigence of Sir Thomas More. Robert Bolt, adapting (and improving upon) his very successful play, had more on his mind than the king's bedding and wedding, though both are relevant to More's quarrel with the king. At the centre of these matters is Paul Scofield's exquisite portrait of More, a man of sweetness and strength, thinker, reader and unwilling courtier, with unbounded faith in his own intelligence and integrity. Watching his destruction – and his efforts to prevent this without compromise – make the film a compelling experience, despite some simplifications in the characters of Cromwell (Leo McKern) and Wolsey (Orson Welles); and purists may have preferred Henry VIII as the physically bloated, middle-aged man that he then was to the golden, youthful figure that Robert Shaw makes of him. Given aptly presented confrontations audiences will enjoy history and religion, but the film was also helped to success by six Oscars (including Best Picture, Best Direction, Best Actor and Best Screenplay) – and it was a deserved success, for Zinnemann has placed More beautifully in his time and setting; the Thames runs at the foot of his garden and is depicted in all its moods, especially those of night and twilight, times of contemplation.

This film and *The Nun's Story* are rare demonstrations among Hollywood artefacts, if so we may term them, of good intentions not gone awry; if we add to Zinnemann's record just *The Search* and *The Men* it is evident that this most modest of film-makers felt that he had much to live up to. After several years' pre-production work on *The Old Man and the Sea* (q.v.) and *Hawaii* (q.v.) he was dissatisfied, and left both to be made by other directors. In 1969, on the morning that shooting was scheduled to begin, the new management of M-G-M cancelled *Man's Fate*, based on the novel by André Malraux, on the grounds that it was unlikely to recover its considerable cost. Zinnemann also

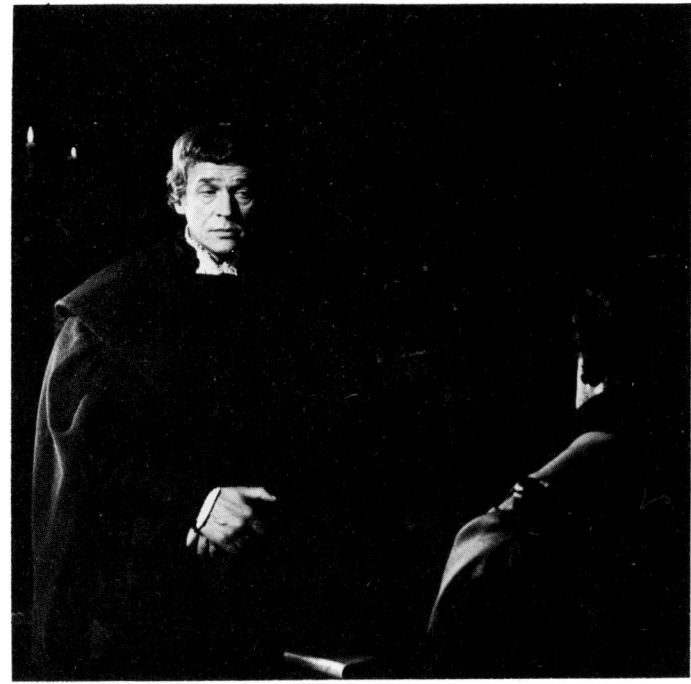

worked for some years with various writers in an attempt to find a way to film *The French Lieutenant's Woman* (q.v.), also eventually made by another director. These four aborted projects were all based on popular books, but they are not contradictory to the themes most apparent in Zinnemann's work – courage, obsession, integrity held in the face of adversity. Since these subjects also interested Kazan, another liberal-minded director, we might note two further analogies between the two men: both disliked Hollywood (Zinnemann had lived in London since the Fifties) and both returned to commissioned work after more than two decades of acclaim. But whereas *The Last Tycoon* did not turn out well, **The Day of the Jackal** (1973) and **Julia** (1979) showed that Zinnemann had moved with the times. His former academic style had given way to one more elliptical but not otherwise influenced by current European fashions; with the exception of Huston, Zinnemann was the only one of his contemporaries to realise that modern audiences liked to draw their own conclusions.

The Day of the Jackal is a thriller, from Frederick Forsyth's novel, with Kenneth Ross's screenplay carefully examining the

Fred Zinnemann apparently abandoned the contemporary problems with which he had made his reputation – but we cannot tell for sure, since he worked on several projects which he left before their completion when he doubted the quality of the final result. His search for perfection has, however, served the cinema in a curious way, for he is another who has succeeded where other American directors have failed – with the re-creation of history, for example, *A Man for All Seasons*, with Paul Scofield as Sir Thomas More.

*The Spanish government did not feel the same sympathy: the film was banned in that country, and as a mark of displeasure Columbia's films were refused distribution in Spain for several years.

various people involved when a professional assassin (Edward Fox) is engaged to kill De Gaulle. *Julia*, written by Alvin A. Sargent from Lillian Hellman's 'Pentimento', a memoir of people she had known, is chiefly about that childhood friend whose passionate but illogical political beliefs – the role was well taken by Vanessa Redgrave – culminate in her disappearance while fighting Nazism in Berlin. The tale is padded out with references to the relationship between Hellman (Jane Fonda) and Dashiell Hammett (Jason Robards), to the success of her first play, and a train journey sequence familiar from movies like *Night Train to Munich*. The disturbing ending is partly the director's triumph, with Hellman's disquiet at a mystery unsolved, at events, a friendship, which she knew she should have handled better. Both films were made on myriad European locations, but **Five Days One Summer** (1982) is set chiefly in Switzerland, in the Thirties, for it is there that a Scotsman (Sean Connery) brings the girl (Betsy Brantley) who is ostensibly his bride. Zinnemann had long had an affection for Kay Boyle's original story, which on this evidence is rather slim. It is an old-fashioned film – a throwback to the German 'mountain' movies, but particularly pleasing in regard to the other films on offer at the time; it should have been more successful than it was.

Stanley Kramer (b. 1913), who had produced three of Zinnemann's most distinguished early films, became a director, but is chiefly remembered for those movies and a handful of others emanating from his production company. A former film researcher and writer, he formed this company in 1948, releasing through United Artists, but with the exceptions of his second production, *Champion*, and *High Noon*, most of his films were failures, if honourable ones, like **Cyrano de Bergerac** (1950). Michael Gordon directed – one of the rare American attempts to film 'classic' European drama – on budget limitations reflected in the cast and settings. In the title role José Ferrer was awarded an Oscar but roundly trounced by British critics, who had lately seen Ralph Richardson play it on the stage. Ferrer can speak the verse, and he has panache and glee but no sense of pathos – nor of modesty, so that he is still showing off in his technically correct death scene.

For Kramer, Laslo Benedek directed **Death of a Salesman** (1951) and **The Wild One** (1953). Born in Budapest in 1907, Benedek worked in Germany as assistant to Joe Pasternak, who was later to give him a chance to direct, at M-G-M in 1948, with *The Kissing Bandit*, a musical with Frank Sinatra. Like Benedek's later American films, it is of no interest, but *Kinder, Mutter und ein General*, made in Germany in 1955, has quality, as have the two for Kramer. *Death of a Salesman*, from Arthur Miller's play, has Fredric March overacting as Willy Loman, the salesman, but is otherwise well performed, by players chiefly drawn from the original Broadway production; Mildred Dunnock's Mrs Loman is especially good. The permanent, composite set used on stage gives way to a cinematic device whereby Willy is able to walk into his past, which is quite powerfully done. *The Wild One* was called *The Cyclists' Raid* in production, and that is what it is about in John Paxton's factually-based screenplay, as two rival bands of motorcyclists gradually take over and terrorise a small town. Till the halfway point, the piece is frighteningly convincing, and as it becomes trite it becomes clear that the chief character's troubles are a ragbag of those listed later in the song, 'Gee Officer Krupke', in 'West Side Story'. However, Marlon Brando's performance

As a producer Stanley Kramer made a name sponsoring films attacking the evils of modern society, but when he continued to do so as both producer and director it became clear how much the earlier films had owed to their directors, particularly Fred Zinnemann and Laslo Benedek. Benedek, however, is a puzzle, for his first Hollywood films are poor, and so are the later ones he made; but *The Wild One* with Marlon Brando, centre, is splendid.

makes a lasting claim on our attention. This tin Napoleon is different from the hero of *On the Waterfront*: he has the same difficulty thinking and articulating, but what Brando conveys is the shifty mentality of the master-boy. 'What're you rebelling against, Johnny?' asks the town blonde, and he replies, 'What're ya got?', which to some makes him the forerunner of the rebels in all the youth films that followed. Fearing that young Britishers might emulate these gangs, the British censor banned the film, the first major American movie to be so treated since the early Thirties.★

The first of these two films was released by United Artists and the second by Columbia, for Harry Cohn was looking for 'quality' films to swell his company's product. An agreement was made with Kramer for thirty films, each with complete autonomy and a budget ceiling of $980,000 unless Cohn agreed to further expenditure. As each flopped (the worst was a musical fantasy, *The 5,000 Fingers of Dr T*, which returned only $249,000 of its $1,631,000 cost), Cohn's disenchantment grew, and Kramer's contract was annulled after only ten films. Kramer was determined to make one last film a success, and in fact **The Caine Mutiny** (1954) wiped out the accumulated deficit, making a gross of $11 million on an outlay of $2½ million. Cohn had agreed to the budget because Herman Wouk's novel had been a bestseller, and Stanley Roberts's screenplay is an exemplary model of how to cut a long text – even if it still allows too much time to the priggish young ensign played by Robert Keith. Edward Dmytryk directed, and the film itself is a fine entertainment from the mutiny onwards. Humphrey Bogart's performance as the disciplinarian Captain Queeg, shifty-eyed, weak-jawed and finally paranoic, is one of his most notable achievements. The film's foreword claims that there had never been a mutiny in the U.S. Navy, but subsequently one such commander, carrying discipline to idiotic lengths, was court-martialled during the Vietnam War.

Disbanding his production team and turning director, Kramer arranged distribution through United Artists and chose another bestseller, **Not as a Stranger**

(1955), about the medical profession, with a hero (Robert Mitchum) so ambitious that he destroys a number of people in his path. So much goodwill was felt towards Kramer that the film was dismissed as merely disappointing, so that it was not until **The Defiant Ones** (1958) that he was taken seriously as a director – at least in some quarters. The plot involves a prejudiced white man (Tony Curtis) with an understanding black (Sidney Poitier), because they are convicts chained together; their eventual concord is one of those messages always worth restating, but the path to it is strained, not least in the introduction of a lonely young widow (Cara Williams) who seems neither to know nor care that there are dangerous escaped convicts in the neighbourhood. The physicist Dr Linus Pauling told Kramer that he had saved the world with **On the Beach** (1959), an adaptation by John Paxton of Nevil Shute's novel in which atomic fall-out brings about the end of humanity – clearly not with a bang but a whimper, as a naval commander (Gregory Peck) moons over a dipso nympho (Ava Gardner). At the end, vistas of deserted streets (the film was made in Australia) and an abandoned banner, reading 'There is still time . . . Brother', only serve to remind us of the superiority of *Seven Days to Noon*.

Inherit the Wind (1960) starts with the disadvantage of having a subject inherently without tension: 'The Monkey Trial' in Tennessee in 1925, in which a teacher was tried for instructing his pupils in Darwin's theories of evolution. This circus became a Broadway play by Jerome Lawrence and Robert E. Lee, well-intentioned and with no (obvious) concessions to public taste, and as such was a logical subject for Kramer. In re-creating a similar cause célèbre in *Ace in the Hole*, Wilder used satire, but Kramer fights his old fight with earnestness but no insight into either the town concerned or the era. Of the opposing attorneys, Fredric March is in his element as the showy and pompous William Jennings Bryan, but Spencer Tracy takes the film as the more thoughtful Clarence Darrow (though neither of these names was used in the film). Kramer's inability to *construct* a film is one reason this film is so boring. **Judgment at Nuremberg** (1961) may be his most watchable film, because he had the unofficial assistance of George

★The ban was lifted in the mid-Sixties.

881

Hollywood in the Age of Television: The Directors

Roy Hill (q.v.) who had directed the original television version. That was written by Abby Mann, whose three-hour screenplay is exactly double its length. Inevitably during that time it makes an occasional worthwhile statement on German war guilt, but they are mainly in the nature of notes for further study – such as the fact that there are 'good' and 'bad' Germans – and the Auschwitz newsreels have been doctored so that they are not too painful. The whole would be decent enough on some distressing matters had it not been stretched out, inflated and star-studded. There are thoughtful performances by Tracy as the judge, Maximilian Schell as the prosecuting counsel and Judy Garland and Montgomery Clift in cameo roles as victims of the Nazis. Richard Widmark is good, Marlene Dietrich is unlikely, and Burt Lancaster out of his depth as one of the elderly accused.

To prove his versatility, Kramer presented **It's a Mad, Mad, Mad, Mad World** (1963), typically planned as the biggest comedy ever made – 3 hours 12 minutes – in Cinerama (not in itself a disadvantage, but laughter and awe – at the all-enveloping views – are not suitable bedfellows). Everything goes on too long, and the Sennett-like destructions ignore what Sennett himself knew – that destructiveness for its own sake is not funny. That may have been in Groucho Marx's mind when he observed that one reason no one laughed at this film is because it is not about anything – other than greed and chasing about in cars – which reminds us wistfully of *Genevieve*, from which William and Tania Rose have cannibalised two or three gags. With Tracy heading the cast, and some genuinely funny men among the huge cast of 'comics' – Peter Falk, Terry-Thomas, Eddie 'Rochester' Anderson, William Demarest *and* Buster Keaton – the film was a box-office success, but it is doubtless significant that no one tried to make another three-hour comedy in Cinerama.

Ship of Fools (1965) lasts 150 minutes, not, apparently, having lost a comma from the Katharine Anne Porter novel on which it is based. She looked at the Old World as the Nazis came to power, believing that her account of it might help us all; and certainly Kramer and Abby Mann were the right people to put it on the screen. But unlike older movies about transatlantic liners, this is the most tedious of crossings. 'There are a million Jews in Germany. What are they going to do – kill all of us?' asks the Jew (Heinz Rühmann), who happens to be the most understanding, warmest and cutest little chap on board. The general overstatement is offset only by the relationship between the ship's doctor (Oskar Werner) and a drug-addicted countess (Simone Signoret); because the roles are interesting, these two non-English players are more at ease than anyone else in the cast. Vivien Leigh plays a woman regretting her fading beauty and a famous marriage that failed: 'We put up a wonderful front. In private it was different.' That she could say such autobiographical lines with no apparent feeling is another reason why this film is better forgotten.

If **Guess Who's Coming to Dinner?** (1967) does not deserve the same fate, it is because the stars are Katharine Hepburn and Spencer Tracy, in the last of their teamings. Kramer, to his credit, was the only producer to find work for the aged Tracy; in desperation, knowing that he had not long to live, Kramer turned to William Rose, who remembered an old, unproduced play in a drawer and turned it (just) into a screenplay (but later admitted privately that it was insufficient for the occasion). Hepburn and Tracy play a couple confronted with the prospect of a black son-in-law – the casting of whom, the improbably perfect Sidney Poitier, made the whole even more specious. The popularity of these three players ensured a great box-office success, about which Kramer declared, '[but] I don't think we made it with the intellectual idiot fringe because they were already ahead of us' – a remark symptomatic of his aspirations.

By the time he made this remark he was smarting from the successive failures he had had since that film. After he had discussed them on television one reviewer wrote: 'According to Mr Kramer, he didn't really make any mistakes. It was just that the American public, inexplicably, perversely, chose not to appreciate certain movies Mr Kramer thought would be good for them, those big-budget, big-idea jobs thrust upon us, like cough medicine for a sore conscience. Really, now, Mr Kramer *produced* some pretty good movies; he *directed* things like *The Defiant Ones, On the Beach, Judgment at Nuremberg* and *Ship of Fools*. All those big ideas – race hatred, nuclear war, evolution, genocide – running around in that tiny mind gives me cramps.' Interestingly, that appeared in *The New York Times* (in 1975, written by the paper's television reviewer, 'Cyclops'), but the films listed had all appeared in that journal's Ten Best of the Year lists, as chosen by its critic of the time, Bosley Crowther. After acknowledging that the period would not have been the same without Kramer's tombstone Messages to the World, it must be said that Crowther, as critic of the nation's most influential newspaper, could make or break any movie with any pretension to seriousness. Consciously or not, other reviewers followed suit. Since he supposedly represented the views of the New York intelligentsia, he often influenced the voters of the Academy Awards. He had a knack of liking the films which impressed the industry itself – including those of Otto Preminger, another mediocre film-maker whose reputation did not survive Crowther's departure from *The New York Times*.

Apart from *Laura*, Preminger's early films had attracted little attention and the fact that **The Moon Is Blue** (1953) did so had nothing to do with its quality. It traces the attempts of an architect (William Holden) to seduce a fey girl (Maggie McNamara), and is precisely the sort of comedy (one set, four characters) which twenty years later might be seen on television any night of the week. The Legion of Decency, knowing the Broadway original (which Preminger had 'produced'), threw up its skirts in horror, and the M. P. P. A., having seen words like 'virgin' and 'mistress' in the script, refused the film its seal – which in theory meant that no cinema in the U. S. could book it. It was Preminger's first independent production, and he went ahead courageously, if on a small budget: the reams of press coverage persuaded exhibitors to show it and the public to see it – thus taking the first steps towards the crumbling of the industry's own censorship.

Preminger returned to 20th Century-Fox, where he had been a contract director, to make two films in CinemaScope. **River of No Return** (1954) takes the situation of *The African Queen* to the Old West, but he was not the director to get sparks from these supposedly incompatible companions in danger, a gambler (Robert Mitchum) and a showgirl (Marilyn Monroe). **Carmen Jones** (1954) takes Bizet's opera to the Deep South, as adapted by Oscar Hammerstein II for Broadway. The film starts magnificently, as the sauntering Carmen (Dorothy Dandridge) goes into her Habañera – 'Dat's Love' – and taunts Corporal Joe (Harry Belafonte) by, at one point, brushing his pants, a peak of eroticism at the time; but from then on it proceeds at ponderous pace.

An all-black musical was still considered daring, and since with two of these three films Preminger had succeeded in drawing attention to his advanced thinking, he did so again with **The Man with the Golden Arm** (1955), sensibly retaining from his last film Saul Bass, whose posters and credit titles did so much to get Preminger's films discussed. In this case, a still rare jazz score – by Shorty Rogers – also helped. The subject, taken from Nelson Algren's novel, was drug addiction, which had been taboo in the movie industry since the era of *Broken Blossoms* – to which, most of the time, this film seemed to belong. Only for a brief moment, when its hero (Frank Sinatra) needs a fix, does it have the force or legitimacy of *The Lost Weekend*, which it was patently emulating.

Following previous example, **Anatomy of a Murder** (1959) introduced a number of banned words, such as 'contraceptive', 'rape' and 'spermatogenesis'. Respectability was triply confirmed by a Duke Ellington score, by the fact that the original bestselling novel had been penned by a judge (under the pseudonym Robert Traver) – who felt that the readers of fiction should for once be told the truth about real-life murder and trial – and by the casting of a much-respected lawyer, Joseph N. Welch, as the judge in the film. Wendell Mayes wrote the screenplay, and for Preminger this is an accomplished film, but 160 minutes is too long to attend to characters – lawyers, witnesses and the accused – for whom we could not give a damn.

Porgy and Bess (1959) is an ignominious step in Preminger's career, since, with the compliance of Sam Goldwyn, he virtually destroyed one of the major works of this century. Goldwyn, for what was to be his last film, had signed Rouben Mamoulian, who had directed the original stage production. The two could not get along, so Goldwyn substituted the director of *Carmen Jones*, who but gingerly moves his Todd-AO camera within the horrendously theatrical setting. Except for a picnic sequence which is derived from *Carousel*, the piece dies from inertia, its talented cast reduced to amateurs. I have seen William Warfield as Porgy and Leontyne Price as Bess on the stage, and in place of Warfield's soaring, majestic voice, a light tenor has been dubbed to Sidney Poitier's conscientious and dull performance; and where Price was a superb slattern, Dorothy Dandridge's dubbed Bess is a mere waif tossed on the breeze.

Although foreign critics, especially those in Britain, looked askance at Preminger's work*, *Porgy and Bess* was sufficiently applauded in the U.S. for him to acquire (or have bought on his behalf) the expensive rights to bestsellers. **Exodus** (1960) is an overblown account of Leon Uris's tale of Jewish refugees settling in Israel, but Allen Drury's novel, **Advise and Consent** (1962), provides the basis for what is by far Preminger's best film. Bass's credits promised to lift the lid off Washington, and certain observers recognised the characters' real life counterparts – as well as the juggling for power, the party rivalry and the skeletons in the closet. The skeletons turn out to be Communism and homosexuality, and if Wendell Mayes's screenplay has a fault it is its inability to see the comic aspect of setting up these particular bogies. Homosexuality as a fact of life had at last been acknowledged in a Hollywood film, after insinuations in a number of others, but this was the first to stage a sequence in a gay bar, and to portray a homosexual both overtly and sympathetically. He (Don Murray) is a happily married senator being blackmailed to do something of which he disapproves (we may find it difficult to believe that any politician would prefer suicide to

*Goldwyn waited through the five years' London run of *South Pacific* to get the Dominion Theatre for *Porgy and Bess*, and in Paris he waited a similar period for a cinema caught up with *West Side Story* (q.v.); but *Porgy and Bess* failed to repeat the success of either film and after dreadful notices was withdrawn in a matter of weeks.

compromising his integrity). Given Preminger's opportunistic attitude towards the liberalisation of the screen, I do not think he deserves credit for retaining this element from Drury's novel, but he is to be acknowledged for telling his story plainly and rejuvenating the veteran cast of Lew Ayres, Henry Fonda, Franchot Tone, Walter Pidgeon, Paul Ford, Peter Lawford and Charles Laughton. This is Laughton's last film, and as the wily Southern senator he walks away with it under his arm.

The renown of these films, if somewhat self-engendered, served to obscure one resounding failure in their midst, a stolid version of Shaw's **Saint Joan** (1957), waywardly cut by Graham Greene, if we are to believe the screenplay credit. A solid English cast supports an American teenager, Jean Seberg, whose total inexperience is only too obvious. A few years later, Preminger's reputation ebbed to nothing – not overnight, but from *The Cardinal* (1963) via *In Harm's Way* (1965) to *Hurry, Sundown* (1967). With Hollywood censorship gone, there were no more taboos to break, and he was revealed more than ever as a lumbering showman drawn to overblown bestsellers. However, **Bunny Lake Is Missing** (1965) embodies, for the most part, the straightforward virtues of *Advise and Consent* and such early contract films as *Angel Face*. It is Preminger's contribution to the grotesqueries that followed *Psycho* and *Whatever Happened to Baby Jane?* (q.v.), and it finds him in charge of the two greatest names in the twentieth-century British theatre, Laurence Olivier and Noël Coward, one as a no-nonsense Scotland Yard man, the other as a witch-like landlord.

The eminence of both players seems to have protected them from Preminger's on-set rages. He did not, as the saying goes, run a happy ship, and many actors, having once worked with him, refused to do so again. Among his last films is **Such Good Friends** (1972), a comedy about smart and promiscuous New Yorkers which followed a number of others such. Louis Gold's reputedly autobiographical novel was the basis of the screenplay by Elaine May (q.v.) – under the pseudonym of Esther Dale – and the dialogue is as pointed as the situations are distasteful. It starts with the pleasing premise of a wife (Dyan Cannon) confronted with her husband's infidelities as he is dying; the scene in which she goes down on a doctor (James Coco) and he spatters on her nose shows Preminger unchanged with the years.

A more sincere seeker for significance was Robert Rossen, though the two films he made after *All the King's Men* both flopped – **The Brave Bulls** (1951), made in Mexico, and **Mambo** (1954). With the advent of CinemaScope, the studios took a renewed interest in epics, and Rossen persuaded United Artists to back **Alexander the Great** (1956), which with *Helen of Troy* (q.v.) is the best of a bad bunch – and coincidentally the only other Greek subject among a plethora of Romans. Both films use uncluttered texts and look impressive: in this case the veteran art director André Andreyev achieves a superb pastiche of Greek architecture with economy – but the harsh Spanish locations could persuade no one that they are in Macedonia or Asia Minor. Rossen's original three-hour script became, after intervention by U.A., only 135 minutes on the screen, in the end neither a comic strip nor the intended psychological study. Its only merit is its responsibility to the subject, and it might be less dull if Richard Burton, though graceful and authoritative, could suggest any complexity of character.

Rossen's commitment to substantial subjects was sufficient reason for Zanuck to engage him for **Island in the Sun** (1957), written by Alfred Hayes from Alec Waugh's novel about life in the British West Indies. The tenets behind the tale are sound – that it is time for the black people to take over government – but any interest that Rossen may have felt is deflected by the starry cast and exotic locations, seemingly the essential requirements of CinemaScope. The major problems touched upon in reel one are reduced to a couple of interracial romances. Harry Belafonte plays the key black role, a young lawyer and opportunistic labour leader – in fact, a nonsensical amalgamation of two characters in the book. His love scenes with Joan Fontaine, though confined to some hand-holding, were the subject of much comment in the press and were regarded by the industry itself as a great step forward in this area. Thus, yet again, a bestseller freed Hollywood from its Victorian morals – a point reinforced by the fact that no one commented (publicly,

at least) on the clinch, earlier in the film, between John Justin and Dorothy Dandridge, probably the first white-black kiss⋆ in the American cinema.

Independently Rossen made **They Came to Cordura** (1959), which attempts to examine courage and cowardice as it follows a trek across the desert. Led by Gary Cooper, in one of his late masochistic performances, it was, deservedly, a failure, and Rossen was planning to recut it when he died in 1966. If we ignore, as we should, his last film, *Lilith*, we find his uneven work capped by one excellent one, **The Hustler** (1961). Here he is marvellously in control of the script he had written with Sydney Carroll, faithfully based on a novel by Walter Tevis and concerning the small-time Charlies whose aspirations rise and die in the shadowy world of pool rooms. As a young man Rossen had written an unperformed play on the same theme, which is perhaps why he responds so well. It was a subject that films had ignored, at least in the U.S., and his portrait of the seedy night city stands alone between *Act of Violence* and *Fat City*. The film is memorable for the well acted performances of Paul Newman, George C. Scott, Piper Laurie, Jackie Gleason and Myron McCormick.

⋆There were of course occasions when white actresses played half-castes. However, the difference was that Dorothy Dandridge was black, and not a white actress in dusky make-up.

Jackie Gleason and Paul Newman in *The Hustler*, which finally fulfilled the promise of Robert Rossen's early movies. He had worked as a writer on some of Warner Bros. more distinguished melodramas before turning to direction in 1947. He made only a handful of films in that capacity, including *All the King's Men*, which established him as a major writer-director, but it was not till *The Hustler*, ten years later, that he found a subject as congenial to his talent.

Hollywood in the Age of Television: The Directors

The cinema's battle for audiences included a vast number of musicals and historical spectaculars, with many of Hollywood's leading directors tempted to work on them, as well as some of the lesser lights, like Anthony Mann, who directed *El Cid*, with Charlton Heston, left. The producer was Samuel Bronston, who supplied the apparent need for such films from Spain, where the costs were cheap – including those of the hundreds of extras needed for soldiers. After a while, however, the public decided that the reserved seats/higher prices/separate performances system was not worth the boredom of spectacle without content. Bronston went bankrupt, leaving *El Cid* as the one watchable film he made.

As a producer of epics Samuel Bronston achieved a brief eminence, and we might pause to look at the two directed by Anthony Mann, best known for such action tales as *Winchester '73* (q.v.). Mann began *Spartacus* (q.v.), but was replaced by Stanley Kubrick, and was thus free when called to Spain by Bronston for **El Cid** (1961). Bronston had produced one Hollywood film in 1943, and resurfaced in 1959 after a trip to Spain, during which he learnt that filming in that country was economical since wages were low, and that many American companies had funds there blocked for reinvestment. Both *John Paul Jones* and a new version of *King of Kings* had 'name' casts and were taken for distribution by the Hollywood companies, which encouraged Bronston to pay the star salaries demanded by Charlton Heston and Sophia Loren for *El Cid*. As Spain's legendary hero Heston has stature, but his comic-strip face is incapable of much emotion. However, he is involved in adventures which are the very stuff of boys' fiction, often detailed with visual imagination – especially in the final sequence, the battle on the beach and the siege. Public

response caused Bronston to embark upon the building of a studio near Madrid, and after the failure of *55 Days at Peking* he recalled Mann for **The Fall of the Roman Empire** (1964), whose harsh winter colours again confirm his visual flair. Not since *Intolerance* had so many individuals been seen in such grandiose settings but when they come to talking only James Mason among the leads is not reduced to a waxwork. Bronston had a second flop with *Circus World*, and when at the same time his principal financier withdrew, he left the industry in a flurry of lawsuits.

Neither Rossen nor Mann were familiar names to the public at large, nor was, or is, Robert Wise, despite the success of *The Sound of Music*. Wise is typical of this period in that he rose from contract director to independent producer-director, by dint of choosing above-average material; but his conscientious and often shrewd craftsmanship cannot – at least with hindsight – disguise the hollowness of much of it. **Executive Suite** (1954), for instance, has some quaint notions about big business, insisting that it is less interested in profits than keeping the workers happy and turning out good products. In this boardroom struggle for power, the issue is between two directors – young, idealistic William Holden, seen in overalls doing something unspecified on the factory floor, and ageing, avaricious Fredric March, who even before Holden's Capraesque speech is generally despised by the other members of the board. The film's precepts were hardly questioned, since it moved away from stereotyped areas of screen fiction – and it was much praised for dispensing with background music. Ernest Lehman scripted, from a novel by Cameron Hawley; and another presumably honest man, John Houseman, the producer, had brought Wise to M-G-M, who offered a contract.

Wise moved briefly back to Warners for **Helen of Troy** (1955), and it has to be said that with Homer to guide him he had an easier task than Rossen with *Alexander the Great*. However the dialogue does not strike a note equal to the high matters on display, and the leads – Jacques Sernas as Paris, and Rosanna Podesta as Helen – are etiolated. Nevertheless, helped by Harry Stradling on camera and the decor of Roger Furze, Wise attacks the big scenes with vigour and imagination, getting closer to 'The Iliad' than was appreciated by reviewers. More justifiably, the critics did not care for **Tribute to a Bad Man** (1956), which suffered from the substitution of James Cagney for Spencer Tracy during shooting. Tracy was by this time a gruff bear, but Cagney retained his bantam-like persona; for all his authority the piece really needed something of the godlike stubbornness that Tracy brought to *Broken Lance* (q.v.) – for this is a Western with conscience, needing an heroic centre. It was typical of the films produced at M-G-M under Dore Schary's regime, one of the last of which was **Somebody Up There Likes Me** (1956). It was one of several based on confessional bestsellers, in this case by Rocky Graziano, who assures us in a foreword that what follows is accurate, a comment at odds with the title song, which offers the sort of syrupy self-satisfaction that had remained the keynote of M-G-M. The locations used are strong and 'realistic', but the piece is bathed in a romantic glow to facilitate approval of the fact that an admired prizefighter (Paul Newman) had been a juvenile delinquent.

Ernest Lehman wrote the screenplay, and it is surprising to find that he considers it his best; he also regards the film itself – the second of the four he made with Wise – as the most satisfactory of those with which he has been connected.

Wise does not seem to agree: at least, when he came again to tackle a factual, contemporary subject – after three unexceptional, if pleasing, pictures – he allowed no compromise. **I Want to Live!** (1958) is the story of Barbara Graham, a small-time party girl whose life ended in a gas chamber in San Quentin in 1955, after being convicted of murdering an old lady during a burglary. Walter Wanger initiated the project, which was produced by Joseph L. Mankiewicz's company because his nephew Don (son of Herman) had written a screenplay from the material provided by Ed Montgomery, a Pulitzer Prize-winning journalist who had doubts about Graham's guilt. After Wise agreed to direct, the material was reworked by the novelist Nelson Gidding – who, Wise said, should have received a sole writing credit. The film's first hour sets out the details of Graham's grubby life, and the second follows her time in jail. A further half hour charts all the grisly minutiae necessary for Graham's death and is a harrowing plea for the abolition of capital punishment: if we accept the polemic and the fact that crime must be followed by punishment, this section causes the film to tower above the other crime dramas of the time. Instead of the types assembled in the gangster films of the Thirties, Wise cast players who resemble the people we meet in the street; and though he overstates elsewhere he does not do so when it really matters. He is let down only by his leading actress, Susan Hayward, who never tried harder but was incapable of portraying anyone but the usual movie broad – sharp-tongued and chip-on-the-shoulder. Because of her the film is not moving but only well-intentioned and gruelling.

Unlike Stanley Kramer, Wise did not take the film's favourable reception as evidence that more significance was needed in the cinema, but behind the heist thrills of **Odds Against Tomorrow** (1959), produced and directed for Harry Belafonte's company, is a plea for racial tolerance. Slater (Robert Ryan) has, as the film puts it, pre-Civil War ideas about blacks, and the heist turns on the fact that one of his partners (Belafonte), accepted unwillingly, is black. This mixture of message, seediness and crime is as skilfully managed as that in *I Want to Live!*, but it is less well balanced – which may be why audiences were not interested.

Nevertheless, both films pointed to Wise as the logical choice for **West Side Story** (1961), given its attitude to the backstreet gangs which are at its centre. It had been a triumphant Broadway achievement directed and choreographed by Jerome Robbins (who accepted co-director billing on the film after initially refusing to go to Hollywood just to re-create his dances). Wise, who had not directed a musical before, observed after United Artists had sacked Robbins (for going over-budget and over-schedule) that the film remained their joint effort, since Robbins had rehearsed all the numbers with the cast. Robbins had shot the opening sequence, 'The Jets' Song', before leaving, and it is so electrifying that we are a long way into the film before realising that the rest of it is not exactly compelling. Certainly the moralising of the screenplay (by Lehman, from Arthur Laurents's original) is now tedious, the street gangs too much like chorus boys, and the Romeo and Juliet lovers cloying as played by Richard Beymer and Natalie Wood; but the choreography and much of Leonard Bernstein's score remain exciting. The film was as enthusiastically received as the original and went on to win Oscars for Best Film and for its two directors.

Wise followed with two modest black and white films, **Two for the Seesaw** (1962) and **The Haunting** (1963). The first had been a Broadway two-hander by William Gibson, coming to the screen virtually unchanged – and, alas, uncut – and therefore heavily dependent on its players, Shirley MacLaine and Robert Mitchum. The second film was based on a novel by Shirley Jackson, which on this evidence has a weak exposition ('What is a poltergeist?') and an even sillier denouement. This was Wise returning to sources, since he had directed his first film for Val Lewton; but in following Lewton's principles on horror, he raises never a frisson, unaided by mannered performances from Julie Harris as the frightened girl and Claire Bloom as a predatory lesbian.

The problem after *The Sound of Music* was to find another musical for 20th Century-Fox and Julie Andrews. The associate producer on that film and *West Side Story* had been Saul Chaplin, who is the credited producer on **Star!** (1968), a project mooted around Hollywood for two decades and by this time resolutely old fashioned. It is the story of Gertrude Lawrence, 'probably the most beautiful and entrancing creature who ever walked on the English stage', as she is described in the film by her famous partner, Noël Coward – impersonated by Daniel Massey with Coward's own (uncredited) intervention on his dialogue. The rest was penned by William Fairchild, a British writer with an undistinguished record. Opening with a newsreel in the manner of *Citizen Kane* (on which Wise had worked as editor), the screenplay brings not a modicum of wit or intuition to Miss Lawrence's fairly uninteresting life. Julie Andrews plays with style, clearly most at ease in those aspects which parallel her own career, which is why the first half is the better. She is also winning when the songs are done simply or in keeping with the period (as in the two excerpts from the Coward plays); but too often they are staged in the manner of this studio's musicals of the Betty Grable era. There was a particularly ugly advertising campaign, and Wise, reflecting on its failure, felt 'we had got ourselves mislaid somewhere along the way. There wasn't quite the documentary feeling about it that I had intended.' Others felt that the public did not want to see Miss Andrews as a bitch goddess, hard and lacquered. Wise has worked intermittently since, but with no marked degree of success.

Another R.K.O. alumnus who has enjoyed a long career is Robert Aldrich (b.1918), purveyor of the wittiest and most indiscreet interviews in Hollywood – and some of its worst films. He became a director in 1953, and came to the fore with two adventures for Burt Lancaster's company, **Apache** (1954) and **Vera Cruz** (1954), the latter chiefly notable for playing down Gary Cooper's ageing hero in favour of Lancaster's grinning villain. Aldrich's penchant for Hollywood stories was first apparent with **The Big Knife** (1955), filmed in the wake of *A Star Is Born* but, unlike that, bland and hysterical at the same time. James Poe's script goes further than Clifford Odets's original play in indicating an endless supply of blondes and booze, but if it is eloquent on Hollywood's ruthlessness it is weak on the search of one poor little star (Jack Palance) for integrity. Aldrich later admitted that it was difficult to feel sorry for a man making $5,000 a week; and the drama further suffers from the fact that the balance of power had changed so much since 1949, when the play was written, that few stars were still dependent on the whims of producers.

The film demonstrated no directorial style at all, unless it was over-emphasis at the more demanding moments, but it could be said that Aldrich had achieved a certain florid manner by the time he came to make his most famous film, **Whatever Happened to Baby Jane?** (1962). Obviously he saw in Henry Farrell's thriller a chance to make his own *Sunset Boulevard*, for its subject is two Hollywood stars (Bette Davis, Joan Crawford) after the glory faded. The camera pokes about their Santa Monica home for over two hours, which is a long time to watch two old ladies locked in depravity. Their environment is admirably conveyed, but the chief interest, as in the follow-up, **Hush . . . Hush, Sweet Charlotte** (1964), is in watching Bette Davis give point and meaning to the grotesques she plays. A third exercise in Grand Guignol was meant for Davis, **Whatever Happened to Aunt Alice?** (1969), but she was replaced by Geraldine Page, with Ruth Gordon as the other obligatory ageing star. Aldrich turned over the direction to Lee H. Katzin, whose flair for the genre atones for the absence of Miss Davis.

With a war film, **The Dirty Dozen** (1967), Aldrich had a success comparable to that of *Baby Jane*, and this seemed to confirm his view that he should never suggest when he could emphasise, especially when handling the more sensational aspects – in this case repeated violence. His handling was not perhaps detrimental to another Hollywood tale, **The Legend of Lylah Clare** (1968), but it was in any case a failure, for which he blamed himself. 'There are twenty-five cop-outs' he said, 'who cared about Peter Finch, and is Kim Novak a joke in her own time? . . . [but] if the director-producer can't, with no limitation on money, communicate to an audience what he wants them to be interested in, fascinated in and/or amused by, then he has failed. Then he shouldn't have made that picture.' The source was a television play about a lightly disguised Marilyn Monroe, but the film, in his words, involves 'an amalgamation of myths', which we recognise also as Dietrich, Joan Crawford, Harlow and perhaps Garbo. Unfortunately, they emerge less as myths than ideas – ideas desperately in search of a script. Novak is for once almost adequate trying to portray them, but Finch is absurdly miscast as a von Sternberg-type of director – and at this time looks absurd in only removing his shirt before throwing himself on the bed to make love. Even so, as thriller or Hollywood gossip, the film has something, which may not be said of another show-business tale, **The Killing of Sister George** (1968). Frank Marcus's original play had been both funny and touching as it followed a B.B.C. star of soap opera whose professional and private lives fall apart simultaneously. On the stage in London and New York, Beryl Reid as Sister George had been bad-tempered, selfish, piggish and particularly nasty when drunk (which she habitually is), yet somehow sympathetic: but in the film Miss Reid becomes simply another of Aldrich's grotesques. As her sullen, childish lover, Susannah York is negative, while as the B.B.C. official who comes between them, a mailed fist in a velvet glove, Coral Brown is only bitchy. These two ladies have a love scene – the first in a respectable industry film – claimed to be essential to the argument, though it had originally been at a different point in the script and between York and Reid – till the latter refused to play it.

Loud accusations of vulgarisation were levelled by the novelist Joseph Wambaugh after he had seen Aldrich's version of his tale of the L.A. police force, **The Choirboys** (1977). There was much talk of lawsuits and Wambaugh insisted thereafter on creative control of any of his novels bought for filming. We may assume Steve Shagan felt the same about **Hustle** (1975), since his hero (Burt Reynolds) is a younger version of the one he wrote for *Save the Tiger* (q.v), romantically-minded, aching with nostalgia and with a stubborn belief that chivalry and compassion can counter contemporary malaise. He is a cop and is

889

constantly humiliated, for instance by listening to the conversations of his callgirl mistress with her clients. Whereas by this time even the least crime movie attempted subtlety, Aldrich reverted to the style of *Kiss Me Deadly*, explaining and then underlining; this is presumably why it was one of the few Reynolds vehicles to fail at the box office – as indeed did most of Aldrich's films of the Seventies.

It is agreeable, at least for a while, to turn to Stanley Donen, who seldom sought other aims than to divert us. After *Funny Face* he returned to directing in collaboration at the behest of Warners, who brought George Abbott from Broadway to re-stage **The Pajama Game** (1957) and **Damn Yankees** (1958) with the original casts – apart from the two leads who were replaced by Doris Day and Tab Hunter respectively in the interests of the box office. These are the best records we have of Broadway shows, since in spite of a mobile camera and much reshaping, often for the open air, their origins shine through, especially in the musical numbers. The effect is frequently exhilarating, and credit must be shared with Bob Fosse, reworking his Broadway choreography. The music and lyrics by Richard Adler and Jerry Ross (who died during the second show's New York run) often lack the 'heart' which is extolled in one of the best songs. Both books were based on the premise, then current, that the most suitable subject for a musical was the least likely – that is, a wage dispute in a pyjama factory, and 'Faust' with a baseball background; the latter has the advantage of Gwen Verdon's emissary from Below, 'a ravishingly beautiful witch', whose obvious and inept vamping is a high spot in the decade's musicals.

But musicals were going out of fashion and Donen turned to comedy. **Kiss Them for Me** (1957) was written by Julius Epstein from a play of the same name by Luther Davis, based on 'Shore Leave', a novel by Frederick Wakeman. The result is just another comic World War II movie (the spate of these was due both to nostalgia and to America's involvement in a rather more squalid war, in Korea) which tries to examine the attitudes of some participants and non-participants. The bitterness of the climax, however, is merely spurious, and Cary Grant is miscast as a giddy young rip. Despite the film's failure, Grant and

Donen formed their own production company, but the films it made (all comedies) – and those made by Donen without Grant – were equally badly scripted and often featured players with no gift for the genre (though in this case Jayne Mansfield and Suzy Parker were forced on Donen by 20th Century-Fox).

Donen was certainly no Lubitsch, but **Indiscreet** (1958) has its pleasures, not least of them Cary Grant making bricks without straw as a diplomat involved in an affair with an actress – played by Ingrid Bergman, whose smile alone compensates for the fact that she was not a natural comedienne. The setting is London, as scripted by Norman Krasna from his Broadway play. In **Once More with Feeling** (1960), Harry Kurnitz, adapting his own play, also relocated the action to London. The subject here, long absent from movies, is warring spouses, played by Kay Kendall and Yul Brynner. Brynner's only resource in comedy is to look bright and pleased with himself, and since Donen, aiming for the skittish, allowed Brynner's steamroller approach to dictate the tone, the film is almost a total disaster. With Grant in the cast, **The Grass Is Greener** (1960) is an improvement, but compares unfavourably with his prewar comedies – though it goes further than they could in suggesting physical infidelity, when a hitherto blameless wife (Deborah Kerr) is drawn to an interloper (Robert Mitchum). Cary Grant is the husband, Jean Simmons the other woman, and the setting is one of the stately homes of England – the country where Donen settled, though he continued to make Hollywood or Hollywood-style movies.

The best of these are **Charade** (1964) and **Two for the Road** (1967) – indeed they are among the best-remembered films of their era. In both Donen was working again with Audrey Hepburn, and once more he settles for chic; his confidence atones for a certain lack of subtlety. *Charade* is imitation Hitchcock, depending on European locations (mainly Paris), the twists in the plot (which are often good), and the playing of Grant and Hepburn (who are splendid – he quizzically underplaying and she having the time of her life). In *Two for the Road* Hepburn and Donen were allied with two more realistic Britons, Albert Finney and the novelist

Frederic Raphael, with results more rewarding than usual in such circumstances. Raphael had cleverly devised a study, fairly abrasive and in non-sequential order, of a deteriorating marriage set against the roads of France, where the couple first meet – and neither Miss Hepburn nor the Côte d'Azur was ever more appealing.

It is best to draw a veil over some of Donen's other films, which are closer in quality to *Once More with Feeling* than to *Singin' in the Rain*. Indeed, as each came along, one began to wonder exactly what his contribution to the films made with Gene Kelly and George Abbott had been. There was a singularly unfortunate music-al, **The Little Prince** (1974), with music by Frederick Loewe and book and lyrics by Alan Jay Lerner – who in his memoir blames Donen's handling for the film's complete failure. However, **Movie Movie** (1978) is sheer delight, cleverly written by Larry Gelbart and Sheldon Keller. The spoofing of old movies had been a staple of television comedy, and sometimes in the Sixties there seemed to be half a dozen spoofs of old Hollywood musicals playing off-Broadway at the same time – all of them dreadful. *Movie Movie*, reasonably, looks back primarily at old Warner Bros. movies, one on boxing, 'Dynamite Hands', and then a musical, 'Baxter's Beauties of 1933' – and between the two is shown an equally sharp take-off of a trailer of the period. Donen and his collaborators are both affectionate and accurate, but not slavishly so – both sections, for instance, gain from the use of colour.★ *Movie Movie* lacks only heart and drive, qualities also missing from George C. Scott's performances as veteran boxing trainer 'Gloves' Malloy and Broadway producer 'Spats' Baxter. Audiences, not associating Scott with light entertainment, and having perhaps been 'bitten' by those off-Broadway shows, stayed away; it was their loss.

The very nature of *Movie Movie* reinforces my belief that many of the lighter entertainments prove more enduring than those sweating for uplift or message. There are some good serious films in this period, and those that failed did so not because of the temerity of producers and

distributors, as in the past, but because of the inadequacy of the talents tackling them. There was one director who remained light-hearted, but he is a social satirist of a high order. Billy Wilder o'ertops all other American film-makers at this time, and some half dozen of the films that he made then are likely to be around as long as there are screens on which to show them.

If one of them proves to be **The Seven Year Itch** (1955), that will be because of Marilyn Monroe, curiously thought to be 'too substantial for dreams' by the critic of *The New Yorker*, who added that she reduced the picture 'to the level of a burlesque show'. The level was hardly high to start with, being a Broadway farce of the same species as *The Moon Is Blue*, but much less smirking and twice as funny. Its author, George Axelrod, wrote the screenplay with Wilder, involving a grass widower (Tom Ewell) whose erotic thoughts wander to the girl upstairs. In the role of the girl, a combination of two comedy standbys, old and new – the innocent in the big city, and the kook – Monroe seems oddly cast at first glance: looking as she does, she is hardly likely to be either. But in a way that was hers alone – for she never seemed to have a particularly strong, definite personality – she makes the girl warm, funny and sexy, to the extent of overwhelming the little man with the seven-year itch. That may be just as well, since Ewell is over-reliant on leers and cunning grins.

For his second film as an independent, Wilder accepted Jack L. Warner's offer of **The Spirit of St Louis** (1957), based on the first solo transatlantic flight. In writing the screenplay with Wendell Mayes, from an adaptation by Charles Lederer of Lindbergh's memoirs, he found it difficult to 'reach' the flyer. The film was a challenge, since he had never tackled an 'outdoor' subject, nor could he rely on his sardonic humour. He resolved his difficulties triumphantly, by simply and soberly re-creating the experience – the events leading up to departure and the flight itself, with its perils and wonders. Above all – with the aid of the superb images caught by Robert Burks and J. Peverell Marley – it is the awe that he has captured: of clouds, sea, mud-flats, tiny planes in the distance; of mist and darkness and sunlight peeping into the

---

★On its original cinema release 'Dynamite Hands' was in black and white.

cockpit; of the crowds in Paris which take on the quality of a seething, roaring, unknown beast. At a cost of $6 million the film was the most disastrous flop in the studio's history; years later in his memoir Jack Warner was still pondering on the matter. A contributory factor may be the performance of James Stewart, over twenty years too old for the role, with hair waved and blonded, and seemingly daunted at playing a living hero. But the truth probably is that in the jet-age Lindbergh's flight was no longer of interest, especially as everyone knew the result.

Wilder's imagination and understanding were more expectedly on display in **Love in the Afternoon** (1957). These qualities were needed, since these post-meridian sessions overlooking the Place Vendôme are between a dewy-eyed student (Audrey Hepburn) and the middle-aged roué (Gary Cooper) whose amours preoccupy her private detective father (Maurice Chevalier). As is apparent from the gypsy band kept at hand to aid amorous conquest, this is Wilder again attempting the Lubitsch style, though the film is for much of its length a straightforward remake of Czinner's *Ariane*. Both versions are about double standards, but Wilder obscures that. In this, his first collaboration with I. A. L. Diamond (who was to partner Wilder on all but one of his subsequent scripts), they manage to suggest that the girl is quite compliant, but in not making the lover the cold fish that he is in the original – it was presumably important to retain Cooper's charm – they are conventional where Czinner was poignant. To keep Czinner's magical ending then requires an unconvincing line to the effect that all planes are grounded. When the public failed to find any virtue in the age discrepancy of the lovers, Wilder fell back on a thriller, **Witness for the Prosecution** (1958), based on Agatha Christie's courtroom play. The script, which he wrote with Harry Kurnitz, has added some necessary humour. Wilder's puckish approach is most apparent in the portrait of the testy defending barrister, splendidly hammed by Charles Laughton, but it is hard to care whether Tyrone Power is acquitted or convicted, and Marlene Dietrich is ludicrous both as a thirtyish singer and in impersonating a Cockney.

The Diamond connection obviously

stimulated Wilder, and they started a splendid run with **Some Like It Hot** (1959), again a risky subject and again developed from an antique German film. It was, in box-office terms, the most successful comedy ever made, and it is one of the near perfect ones, the wit of its lines only exceeded by the bizarre quality of the situations – which involve, as perhaps the whole world knows, two men hiding in drag with an all-woman orchestra. Marilyn Monroe's band singer, with her realistic estimate of her voice and her yen for bootleg hooch and saxophone players, is one of the cinema's most endearing creations; Wilder matches the innocence he found in her with that of Jack Lemmon and Tony Curtis, from the first moment we see them disguised, purse-lipped and tottering on high heels. Unlike Curtis, Lemmon does not, for his own reasons, yearn to get back into men's togs, despite his lech for Marilyn; this actor's playing in most comedy is virtuoso but here it has to be, and indeed is, inspired.

Flushed with success, Wilder and Diamond mounted another assault on the accepted sexual themes permissible in the cinema. **The Apartment** (1960) concerns a nice young man (Lemmon) who lends his flat to his bosses for assignations, and a nice young woman (Shirley MacLaine) who willingly goes to such places with one of them (Fred MacMurray). She is, admittedly, made to suffer in the way of female transgressors, by being deserted and attempting suicide – but that enables Wilder to add poignancy to what was otherwise a conventional mélange of situation comedy and satire. Whether or not it was his intention, he gets closer in tone than hitherto – certainly closer than in *Love in the Afternoon* – to the bitter-sweet continental romances of the early Talkie period. And in that respect, he was aided, paradoxically, by a compendium of the relaxed but wary attitudes of New Yorkers – towards the office party, loneliness in a crowd, smart little bars in which to get blotto, assumptions about hit shows, and the tragedy in the neighbouring apartment. These, and more, are superbly expressed by Lemmon and MacLaine, both managing those odd curves between farce and pathos which make this film unusual. The source, Wilder has admitted, is *Brief Encounter*, since he began to wonder about that apartment which was almost used for adultery.

The source of **One, Two, Three** (1961) was a one-act play by Molnár, unrecognisable here as performed and directed *molto furioso*, with the jokes coming a dozen a minute. In the circumstances, it is not surprising that some do not work, and others hit obvious targets – e.g. Russia and Communism, Germany and its lack of war guilt, the U.S. and Coca-Colonisation; but most are smart (there are several cinema references), some utilise a knowledge of the famous international *sous-entendres*, and many of them are wonderful. The film is built around, and takes its frenetic speed from one of the great players, James Cagney, in his last film before retirement:* he plays a rough-and-tumble businessman up against it when his ward – a batty Southern belle, deliciously played by Pamela Tiffin – falls in love with a bare-footed and rabid red (Horst Buchholz).

After three superlative comedies – though the last of them was not particularly popular – Wilder tackled **Irma La Douce** (1963), which had been the first French musical in generations to become an international success. This was due to Marguerite Monnot's score and a book which celebrated the whores and pimps of Pigalle. Wilder jettisoned the score because he said that he could not make a musical, but that left him with a risqué story which censors would find hard to ban, since it had been acclaimed in several of the world's more sophisticated cities. The screenplay did try to appease Middle America by making Irma (MacLaine) turn from unrepentant whoring and by making Nestor (Lemmon) a pimp by accident. Doubtless Wilder was amused at making the first American film in which the baby is born on the altar steps, but it is only because this was the first major American film on prostitution in fifty years that it was popular. It was Wilder's biggest financial success, which amuses him, for he likes it least of all his films. In my view, it is as bad as any film could be that is directed by him and stars these particular players. Lemmon and MacLaine remain resolutely American, and though Wilder hired Alexander Trauner to design a studio Paris to match

the comic-strip humours, the Frenchness of the original eluded him.

Wilder had always taken care with casting, knowing that likeable playing is a palliative to outrageous behaviour: but in **Kiss Me Stupid** (1964) we are constantly invited to confuse the character played by Dean Martin – a smug, semi-alcoholic and lecherous singer – with Martin himself. Passing through a small, remote Western town, he meets two songwriters who will stop at nothing to have him sing one of their songs. They are two ordinary Joes so obsessed with the American dream that they resort to pimping – and that is but one of several frontal attacks on sacred cows: the image of the television personality; a climactic melée in which a wife and a hooker (Kim Novak) swop roles and like it; and an implicit suggestion that the only fun place in town is the local brothel – 'The Belly Button' – 'Drop in and get lost.' Since the line is typical, it is clear that the film is not greatly dependent on wit. Like all good farces – the source this time was an Italian play, 'L'Ora della Fantasia' – it depends on surprise or, in the case of Wilder and Diamond, the extent to which they dare go. The dialogue here is single-minded, concerned with the hopes and hypocrisies with which society surrounds copulation. Everyone is cheapening sex hereabouts, perhaps because that is in the nature of the beast. The message did not get lost; not since the heyday of Mae West had there been such an outcry against Hollywood's 'immorality', and United Artists hurriedly dissociated itself from the film by passing it to a minor distributor (in fact, owned by them, and used to handle foreign-language product). Wilder, to his eternal shame, issued a public apology. Elsewhere, the gaminess was remarked upon, but nobody got upset – but then, it was not their society that Wilder was satirising with such acerbity.

The Fortune Cookie (1966) is even denser and richer, a film of astonishing black humour. When Harry (Jack Lemmon) is hospitalised after being struck during a ball game, his brother-in-law, Whiplash Willie (Walter Matthau), is determined to sue everyone in sight: that brings to Harry's side his ex-wife (Judi West), as grasping as Willie, and the kindly Boom-Boom Jackson (Ron Rich), the ballplayer responsible for his troubles in

*From which he emerged, twenty years later, to appear in *Ragtime* (q.v.)

893

The Comedies of Billy Wilder

The first film that Billy Wilder directed was a comedy, but there were dashes of a mordant sense of humour in the mainly serious films he made after that. Since *The Seven Year Itch*, RIGHT, with Marilyn Monroe and Tom Ewell, he has concentrated again on comedy, but not without notes of seriousness, as in *The Apartment*, BELOW RIGHT, with Shirley MacLaine and Jack Lemmon, and *The Fortune Cookie*, BELOW, with Lemmon and Walter Matthau. When both films sidestep the laughs they offer some pertinent if pessimistic comments on human behaviour, and even in those films devoted solely to laughter Wilder seems uncertain whether he likes the human race. His most beloved movie is *Some Like It Hot*, BELOW FAR RIGHT, with Jack Lemmon and Marilyn Monroe, and his most brilliant is, perhaps, *One, Two, Three*, ABOVE FAR RIGHT, with Hanns Lothar, James Cagney, Horst Buchholz and Pamela Tiffin. Wilder is on record as saying that he enjoyed directing Cagney, and many of us would say something similar about watching these Wilder films, among the most endearing – and enduring – in the history of film.

894

the first place. 'The pressures on Wilder to help maintain the American dream are probably immense,' wrote Hollis Alpert in *Saturday Review*, but after chipping away for years this was Wilder's second full-scale assault on that dream. There is Willie, dedicated to dunning; the wife, moving from one crummy flat to the next for a chance in show business; Harry, hoping to be reunited with that awful woman; and Boom-Boom, sobbing and defeatist. It is Boom-Boom who at the end walks away with Harry into the sunset – a fact unremarked upon at the time, though Wilder was surely aware that he had made the first Hollywood love story between two men, or at least the beginning of one. Boom-Boom is also black, and, though rich and famous, happy to return to the black-white relationship of a hundred years earlier: when he cooks dinner for Harry and his wife it does not occur to them to ask him to join them – but we can be sure that that also occurred to Wilder.

Wilder may be a cynic, but his later films reveal a compassion absent from those he wrote and/or directed from the Thirties to the Fifties (with most Hollywood filmmakers, the reverse is true: their work reveals less feeling as they age). Lemmon and MacLaine are mere babes in the wood in *The Apartment*; in *Kiss Me Stupid* the cheap, sad hooker is battling against the forces of darkness which are the respectable townsfolk; the lovers in *Avanti!* (q.v.) have been repressed till the onset of middle age. The best that we can say for Wilder's other sympathetic characters (as against those played sympathetically) is that they are vacuous and unworldly – like Tiffin in *One, Two, Three*, or Monroe in *Some Like It Hot*. The boss in *The Apartment* is completely self-centred; others – Cagney in *One, Two, Three*, Matthau in *The Fortune Cookie* – are opportunistic, as were Holden in *Sunset Boulevard* and Douglas in *Ace in the Hole*. When Buchholz in *One, Two, Three* finally and joyfully opts for the capitalist way of life, it is just another joke: for its values, as depicted here and elsewhere, are as offensive – if more subtle and luxury-lined – as the Communist slogans he formerly spouted. Wilder is moralist as well as cynic, the cinema's heir to Voltaire: Candide would be at home in any of his films. But the American public, after laughing at *Irma La Douce*, turned its back.

The time was wrong, between the assassination of John F. Kennedy and Watergate, for a critique of American society.

Wilder turned away to the past, to pastiche. He had held the rights to Conan Doyle's characters since 1957, and he and Diamond wrote some new exploits for the famous detective (Robert Stephens) and Dr Watson (Colin Blakely) in **The Private Life of Sherlock Holmes** (1970). Only two of the four projected adventures reached cinemas, though all of them were filmed; the plot(s) may be as far-fetched as the films of Wilder's youth, but with a decreasing impetus. Filming on British locations seems to have put Wilder into a mellow mood, though he cannot resist a desire to shock, even slightly, with hints of drugs and sexual perversion. **Avanti!** (1972) is even more relaxed – and perhaps again Wilder succumbed to his setting, Ischia. A hyperactive American businessman (Jack Lemmon) finds himself surrendering both to old Europe and British rationality, in the person of an overweight, 'not very attractive' London girl (Juliet Mills), the daughter of his father's mistress. They have come to the island to claim the corpses of these parents, he at first shocked by the adulterous relationship of the deceased, and then re-enacting it. There are a few bad jokes, a few outrageous ones, and a touching sequence in the morgue; as the film works towards full-blown romantic comedy it is handicapped by the very ordinariness of Miss Mills, but the result is one of the rare pleasures among the films of the period.

Wilder's reputation for handling 'bad taste' caused him to be asked to remake **The Front Page** (1974), after the producer, Paul Monash, had seen a revival at the National Theatre in London. Raciness was considerably and pointlessly added; given that Wilder had been at one time a newspaperman, we may not find the four-letter words inappropriate, but the coarsening was often unfunny, as in making the fastidious Bensinger into a guy given to fondling young men and complaining that his toilet roll had been stolen. Lemmon and Matthau were the best possible choices for Hildy and Burns respectively, the latter gloomy and deadly, at times erasing memories of Cary Grant in *His Girl Friday*. Wilder knew that he had that film to beat but the chases – especially after those in *One, Two, Three* – reveal a man devoid of confidence. That may well have been the result of his string of failures: but this was the only one which deserved its fate.

Wilder could not get backing for **Fedora** (1978) in the U.S., and it was made in Munich – with little subsequent interest after a Cannes unveiling, though United Artists did later open it in the U.S. The instinct was to love this problem child, especially as it had become increasingly clear during Wilder's decade of bad luck that his earlier films – constantly revived – were amongst the most enduring ever made; but John Coleman in the *New Statesman* could not resist calling it 'old hat', and in a basically kind review pinpointed the trouble, '. . . I hardly believed in the brittle plot.' The source is a novella in Thomas Tryon's collection, 'Crowned Heads', and as presented here it concerns a desperate Hollywood producer (William Holden) confronting a series of Chinese boxes as he tries to persuade a reclusive Garboesque star to make a comeback and thereby get him the backing he needs. Some reviewers evoked *Sunset Boulevard*, and clearly Wilder had reasons for his jokes about the current state of the industry; the mood is rather that of *Avanti!*, and once you have swallowed the plot you may be entertained in the manner of *The Major and the Minor* or *Sabrina*. I cannot say how well it may stand up, but I can say that I would rather see it again than most of the films of this period.

Buddy, Buddy (1981) is another matter. Two producers at M-G-M, Alain Bernheim and Jay Weston, wanted to help Wilder off his losing streak, and Jack Lemmon said that he would always be there if the director needed him. Lemmon plays a would-be suicide (because his wife has left him) and Walter Matthau is the hit man in the room next door, unable to prepare for his killing because of Lemmon's antics. On internal evidence the script was hastily assembled and filmed while these actors went from one engagement to the next. Basically the film is a straightforward remake of *L'Emmerdeur* (q.v.), with few extra jokes – despite such targets (hotel life,

posses of police) as had delighted Wilder in the past. Some scenes in a sex clinic – it was an ordinary clinic in the original – fail completely, but otherwise this is one of the few unfunny comedies which is nevertheless pleasant. Diamond observed in an interview that Wilder had turned down *Victor/Victoria* (q.v.) because he hated to repeat himself, but much of *Buddy, Buddy* is reminiscent of *The Front Page*, including a final gag about someone running off with someone of their own sex.

If Wilder, in the end, is in decline, he is in good company: most of the leading directors of his generation had done their best work by the end of the Fifties – yet in the following decade he was to make some of the boldest and most mature films in the history of the American cinema. In this profession (or industry, whichever way you prefer to regard it) age seems to take a toll of talent. As the Fifties started, only Welles and Chaplin trailed clouds of critical glory, but though both were professionally active – at least in theory – for most of the following two decades they did little to justify their reputation. Some of the other admired American filmmakers made only one or two good films apiece: Stevens, Ford, Disney, Hawks, Wyler and Hitchcock, plus Capra and Rossen, whose output was severely limited. It may be that the academic films of Wyler and Stevens will look better in ten years' time; it may be that Hitchcock's films of the Fifties, which seemed so enjoyable then, will further diminish in effectiveness (even on their own chosen level). I would not want to be categorical about this, since I would not want to follow *Cahiers du Cinéma* with its 'pantheon' of admired directors. In fact, I start from a different premise, that as far as the American film industry is concerned the important directors were those who were willing to risk their reputations in making films above the average. By that token the modern American cinema was made by Kazan, Mankiewicz, Zinnemann, Cukor, Huston, Wilder and, to a lesser degree, Robert Wise. While the moguls worried and fretted about the size of screens, they strove to make movies for intelligent people.

33

Hollywood in the Age of Television: The Decline of the Studios

IN 1947 THE WEEKLY cinema attendance in the U.S. averaged 87 million, but this had dropped to a mere 15 million by 1969, the year when Hollywood faced its own Armageddon, with most of the major studios convulsed by their financial losses. By then the industry had accustomed itself to the fact that television had become the country's favourite leisure activity. In the Fifties Columbia and Warner Bros. had been the first studios to acknowledge the vitality of the growing rival by becoming suppliers of television programmes; 20th Century-Fox made potted versions of its famous movies for the new medium and Universal moved in via its acquisition by M.C.A. At the end of this chapter I shall list the more radical changes, since they are better discussed as applicable to the industry as a whole than to individual studios. For the last time we shall look at films which are primarily studio artefacts – either because they were typical or of more than passing interest. The studio system still operated so well that few of them were made, if planned, in panic, but they were designed to lure back those patrons who had succumbed to the small screen at home. The liberalisation of attitudes to sex was to play a vital part in the battle.

Although the introduction of Cinema-Scope had enabled 20th Century-Fox to dominate the industry, the system itself proved of only temporary benefit, partly because it was not well used. Audiences were often given the impression that they were watching as through a proscenium arch, with the entire cast lined up across the screen for longish periods. Almost all the contemporary subjects seemed to consist of people talking in rooms, with some token views (usually of New York's skyline) thrown in. **Three Coins in the Fountain** (1954) was no exception. This was the studio's perennial about three girls in search of rich husbands, but it had been re-set in Rome, with manifold picture postcard views of that city interrupting the 'action', if so it may be called. A title song destined to blare from every juke-box in the country helped it to a huge popularity, encouraging the studio to send the film's director, Jean Negulesco, on to Hydra for **Boy on a Dolphin** (1957), which offered underwater photography and some equally spectacular views of Sophia Loren in a wet dress. By this time the studio had become much less cautious about using CinemaScope, and Westerns, in particular, benefited from the photography of the wide open spaces.

Initially, because of the success of *The Robe*, the wide screen was thought ideal for historical spectacle and the courts of Napoleon (Marlon Brando) and Elizabeth I (Bette Davis) were on display in **Désiree** (1954) and **The Virgin Queen** (1955) respectively. As directed by Henry Koster, who had made *The Robe*, the two stars were below their best, but these were personalities able to overcome the staginess apparently inherent in filming in Cinema-Scope. The first musical in the process was **There's No Business Like Show Business** (1954), built, like the studio's *Alexander's Ragtime Band* of old, round a bevy of Irving Berlin's songs old and new. Strung across the screen is a show-business family – Ethel Merman, Dan Dailey, Donald O'Connor, Mitzi Gaynor and Johnny Ray – all of them resistible performers as directed by Walter Lang. Acting with them, Marilyn Monroe is patently amateurish, but in her case it matters little.

The archetypal professional, Fred Astaire, is in **Daddy Long Legs** (1954), which is also unappealing – or as much so as any film could be in which he appears. It had been planned for Dailey and Gaynor, but they were dropped and Leslie Caron was borrowed from M-G-M. Under Negulesco's direction she is relentlessly cute, and the old story is not improved by insisting that there is nothing a French orphan could want more than to be brought up in the U.S. The colour and settings are poor but, to compensate for two derivative ballets choreographed by Roland Petit, there is one splendid dance for Astaire, 'Sluefoot', and a pleasing song, 'Something's Gotta Give'.

The songs in **The Best Things in Life Are Free** (1956) are from the catalogue of deSylva, Brown and Henderson, who are impersonated in it by Gordon MacRae, Ernest Borgnine and Dan Dailey. Show-business biographies were going out of fashion – and not a moment too soon – but this one was made just after *Carousel* and *The King and I*: the extra care taken with them was reflected at the box office, so something similar was done in this case. Most of the numbers are stylishly handled, and the film marks a return to form for Michael Curtiz, whose direction had sometimes been slack since leaving Warners. José Ferrer directed **State Fair** (1962) and, according to Alice Faye – returning briefly to the screen to play the mother – he gave no help whatsoever to the cast, which may be why three of the four young players are so poor – Bobby Darin, Ann-Margret and Pat Boone. Pamela Tiffin is the other, but despite her and Miss Faye the apple-pie feeling of the 1945 version is missing; and it is grossly inferior to Henry King's original version.

The success of M-G-M's *Gigi* inspired 20th Century-Fox to film **Can Can** (1960), a Broadway musical which had not interested Hollywood when produced seven years earlier. That concerned an upright young judge who one drunken night finds himself loving the flesh-pots of Montmartre; the film script, by Charles Lederer and Dorothy Kingsley, substitutes smuttiness for sophisticated corruption and, though the characters have not become virtuous, they are dull in their vices. The seductress *d'un certain âge* is now the scrubbed, young, all-American Shirley MacLaine, while

Louis Jourdain (the judge) and Maurice Chevalier repeat their double-act of *Gigi*, and Frank Sinatra his role from *Guys and Dolls*. Walter Lang's direction takes no advantage of the Todd A-O screen, which was preferred to CinemaScope on this occasion, and some of Cole Porter's score has been omitted to accommodate four of his most hackneyed songs. Since the same thing happened at Columbia on *Pal Joey* (q.v.), whose 'book' was also bowdlerised, we should note the presence on both occasions of Sinatra, who was certainly powerful enough to insist on changes (or prevent them). The can-can within the film cannot compare with those in the movies by Renoir and Huston, though it created a minor sensation during the filming when the Soviet premier, Krushchev, denounced it as immoral – somewhat ungratefully, as it was staged for him on his visit to the studio, Hollywood's official welcome during his American tour.

The film's failure, though deserved, was one reason why the studio took special care with another Broadway hit, **Hello Dolly!** (1969). The production and screenplay were entrusted to Ernest Lehmann, who had done both for *The Sound of Music,* and the direction to Gene Kelly, considered the most knowledgeable practitioner of the musical form. Together they strove to emulate the verve of the M-G-M musical in the production numbers, but at the same time the lack of originality suffocated the piece. The Broadway Dolly, Carol Channing, rightly thought it 'like a version of *The Sound of Music* only more ponderous. *Hello Dolly!* should crackle, snap, never stop moving.' The title song, on stage a *tour-de-force* for her, has in Barbra Streisand, her screen replacement, only a lank, mechanical pivot, while elsewhere this actress attempts to be an adenoidal Mae West. Less expectedly, Walter Matthau, as the object of her attentions, cannot disguise the fact that the material is less than brilliant. The cost was $24 million – including $2½ million for the reconstruction of New York's 14th Street on the back-lot – which made it the studio's most expensive film ever, apart from *Cleopatra*. Yet even as it was clear that the response was not warm enough for it to recover its costs, 20th Century-Fox was pouring $25 million into *Tora! Tora! Tora!*, a re-creation of the bombing of Pearl Harbor. This was yet another attempt to repeat one of the studio's past successes, and it was an even greater failure than either *Can-Can* or *Hello Dolly!*

The earlier film concerned is **The Longest Day** (1962), adapted from Cornelius Ryan's best-selling documentary account of the Normandy landings. At the time when Zanuck had quit the studio to become an independent producer, it had produced another film on this subject, *D-Day, the Sixth of June,* which had passed unnoticed. Nevertheless, from his base in Europe Zanuck decided that *The Longest Day* would crown his career, and he even directed the American interior sequences himself. The other credited directors are Ken Annakin, responsible for the British interiors, Bernhard Wicki, responsible for those with the Germans, and Andrew Marton, who filmed the American exteriors; Eric Williams was 'co-ordinator of the battle episodes'. It lasts three hours; it has a star, or at least a 'name', in fifty or so leading roles. (Most of them were paid $25,000 for two or three days' work, except John Wayne, who refused his role because of his experience at this studio on *The Barbarian and the Geisha*; he finally relented when offered $250,000.) The film is well organised, but suffers from presenting only stereotypes: the British are casual and stiff upper-lipped, the Americans democratic, somewhat cynical and given to reminiscing about the folks back home; the French are wily and excitable; and the Germans the same rule-book lugheads of the wartime Resistance movies. Zanuck himself was wrestling with a drink problem, and the film went over budget. It nevertheless made a huge profit – which was one reason why Zanuck was urged to return as production chief.

The film was made in black and white; the studio had originally relented on the question of monochrome with Cinema-Scope when the producer Charles Brackett considered colour unsuitable for **Teenage Rebel** (1956), a drama about the reunion of a mother (Ginger Rogers) and a daughter (Betty Lou Kim). Brackett and Walter Reisch wrote it, Edmund Goulding directed, but they had all become tired. So had Nunnally Johnson, writing and directing **The Three Faces of Eve** (1957), based on another best-selling book and also in black and white: but the film was much discussed as one of the few contemporary American movies to deal with a situation based on fact. Its subject is the treatment by a doctor (Lee J. Cobb) of a schizophrenic, by turns a drab housewife and a whorish slut who, in either guise, still shrinks from sexual contact. When she is cured of both manifestations a third personality emerges – an Eve who resembles every other film heroine. In the role(s) Joanne Woodward fills in the gaps left by the inadequate handling, deserving her Oscar for Best Actress.

The Young Lions (1958) and **Compulsion** (1959) were also thought unsuitable for colour, the first because it is set in World War II and the second since it centres on one of the grimmer aspects of the Jazz Age. *The Young Lions* is Irwin Shaw's synthesis of the experience of war as set down in the ironic terms prescribed for best-sellerdom. The book is faithfully followed in Edward Anhalt's adaptation which resulted in a better film than *From Here to Eternity* (though that had better source material and a better director) because in the five years between the two the M.P.A.A. had lifted considerable restrictions on the portrayal of such matters. Edward Dmytryk's direction shows him unbothered by his many and far-flung locations and by the fact that the paths of his three chief protagonists will not cross until the final reel. Dean Martin and Montgomery Clift are the Americans and Marlon Brando the German – attempting to encompass in his performance a suggestion that the Germans were not the only guilty ones. The film's polemics manage to incorporate the word 'ovens' during the sequence of the concentration camp, but it is reticent on a subject which much concerned Shaw, anti-Semitism in the army. Indeed, it plays down the fact that the Clift character is a Jew. Similarly, the Jewishness of Leopold and Loeb is hardly referred to in *Compulsion,* but the M.P.A.A. permitted hints of their homosexuality; the emasculation of Meyer Levin's brilliant – and by its very nature sensationalist – book seems to have been the decision of the producer, Zanuck, since the film leans over backwards to be sober and respectable. As directed by Richard Fleischer and written by Richard Murphy, the gaps and flaws prove its undoing, and these include the lack of period sense, the book's painstaking descriptions of the police investigation and Levin's pervading sense of incredulity that this once had happened – that two wealthy young men (Dean Stockwell, Bradford Dillman) killed a young boy simply for the excitement of it.

That both **Peyton Place** (1957) and **From the Terrace** (1960) were also set in the recent past – the Forties – was clearly irrelevant to Mark Robson, their director. John Michael Hayes and Ernest Lehmann respectively wrote the scripts from novels by Grace Metalious and John O'Hara, with Hayes retaining at least some of the former's 'profundities': 'Time should not pass: it should be used.' The film 'lifts the lid off' one supposedly typical Pennsylvania town to find everyone seething with sex – or the lack of it, as in the case of the heroine's frigid mother (Lana Turner). The book's enormous popularity meant further encroachments of the Production Code, as 20th Century-Fox persuaded its guardians to permit reference to mixed nude sunbathing and youngsters sending for one of those manuals which arrive in plain brown wrappers. The effect is prurient; but the three years elapsing before the equally meretricious second movie brought further frankness, enabling it to be matter-of-fact about the infidelities of the hero's wife (Joanne Woodward) and mother (Myrna Loy).

Robson also directed **The Inn of the Sixth Happiness** (1958), from another best seller, 'The Small Woman', based on the life story of Gladys Aylward, who spent more than thirty years as a missionary in China. Ingrid Bergman, who plays the role, is very obviously *not* small, and also references to her throughout as 'the Englishwoman' are inconsistent with her accent. But her saintly no-nonsense enthusiasm sits well on this Gladys and as a more practical, older co-worker Athene Seyler is superb, and Robert Donat, in his last screen performance, is the mandarin. Wales doubles for China, whose people Robson clearly did not understand; but this is a pleasant, accomplished movie, even if the book should have yielded something different.

The same stricture may be applied to **The Sun Also Rises** (1957) and **Tender Is the Night** (1962). *The Sun Also Rises,* written by Peter Viertel from Heming-

way's novel, was one of the films Zanuck produced independently. It may have been his decision to treat it with the reverence usually bestowed on classics – not a good idea, given these characters, a bunch of irresponsible drifters. As played by Tyrone Power, Errol Flynn, Mel Ferrer and Eddie Albert, they are the dreariest of drinking companions; Ava Gardner glitters but is wrongly cast as Lady Brett. Zanuck did a disservice to himself in asking Henry King to direct, for King responds to neither the European locations nor the material. Since the reviews pointed this out, King did himself a disservice in tackling Fitzgerald's novel, as adapted by Ivan Moffatt. He starts *Tender Is the Night* well, with Jennifer Jones making a brave stab at Nicole and Joan Fontaine stagey but enjoyable as her sister; but as Dick Diver, Jason Robards lacks both charm and style in a story reduced to that of a dull man not knowing what to do for the best. The film brought King's distinguished career to a sad end.

M-G-M and then David O. Selznick had earlier owned the rights to 'Tender Is the Night', and Selznick had sold them to 20th Century-Fox with the proviso that Miss Jones play the lead. He relinquished them also because of the disappointing experience of **A Farewell to Arms** (1957), which 20th Century-Fox released. Apart from *Stazione Termini* (q.v.), it was his first film in eight years, and the last he produced. In this case the rights to 'A Farewell to Arms' had passed from Paramount to Warners (in exchange for *A Connecticut Yankee*) when Warners had planned a version to star Humphrey Bogart and Ingrid Bergman as a projected follow-up to *Casablanca*; it was never made, and Selznick in turn obtained them in exchange for his rights in *A Star Is Born*. He commissioned a screenplay from Ben Hecht, and John Huston directed till receiving one of Selznick's longer memos, which confirmed his gloomy suspicions that Selznick saw the film primarily as a vehicle for Miss Jones. Whether handled by him or his replacement, the opening battle scenes are good; but thereafter in re-creating the Italian campaign Selznick seemed to think that he was burning Atlanta over again. Hemingway's self-congratulatory lovers were tiresome enough on the page, but with Miss Jones's determined smile and

Anatole Litvak, another veteran, directed **Anastasia** (1956), presumably chosen because he was Russian-born, but there is no internal evidence that he worked hard at the job. As written for the screen by Arthur Laurents, it is a study of the woman who claimed to have survived the massacre at Ekaterinburg and it finds its level with the Grand Duchess (Helen Hayes) playing cupid to her and the man (Yul Brynner) who trained her. As Anastasia, Ingrid Bergman reminds one that she was never the actress to suggest mystical inspiration; the several awards she won for this performance may have been tokens of pleasure at finding her back on the English-speaking screen after the scandal that began with *Stromboli* (q.v.).

With Bergman and Deborah Kerr (for *The King and I*) in competition that year for the Oscar (which Bergman won), 20th Century-Fox was not interested in promoting the chances of Marilyn Monroe, so that she was not even nominated★ for a performance with more bite than either. The film is **Bus Stop** (1956), and though her vulnerability in the role now contributes to the legend, this was the first time audiences were aware of the full extent of it. Curiously, the part in William Inge's original play is much more like the naive vamp enacted in *The Seven Year Itch*, whose author, George Axelrod, wrote this screenplay. He is not one from whom pathos was normally expected and, as the film is more serious than the play, it is possible that he was inspired by qualities that Monroe had which had not yet been shown on the screen. She may also have inspired the director, Joshua Logan, as this is more surely handled than his *Picnic* (q.v.), also from an Inge play: it is equally diffuse, but more successful in being romantic about second-rate people. The view it offers of the U.S. – materialistic and seedy – was one seldom then seen in movies, but the situation, of the reluctant bride, is from classic comedy. As the brash cowboy who pursues Monroe, Don Murray achieves depths unsuspected on first encounter. There are also nice performances

When Marilyn Monroe made *Bus Stop* she had been off the screen for a year, due to quarrels with the studio and personal difficulties. She returned with a new gift for pathos, playing a small-time show girl, ekeing out a living by wiggling her hips for cowboys and dreaming of being 'discovered' on the corner of Hollywood and Vine.

Rock Hudson's blankness they exhaust our patience early on; the film is twice the length of the earlier Borzage version, with none of its intimacy.

Another remake, **An Affair to Remember** (1957), is also inferior to, and longer than, the original, *Love Affair*, but in this case Leo McCarey was again in charge. The ease of Cary Grant and the delicacy of Deborah Kerr are no substitutes for Charles Boyer and Irene Dunne; and it ends mawkishly with children carolling 'There's a wonderful place called Tomorrowland, and it's only a dream away'. McCarey directed two more films, neither of distinction. In fact, he made only four films in the last twenty years of his life, which was summed up succinctly by Peter Bogdanovich (q.v.): 'A bright, happy first half of life that led to sadness, tragedy. A near-fatal auto accident. Drink. Drugs.'

★The studios are not supposed to be influential in either the nominations or the winners, but a certain amount of lobbying goes on, and the studios are allowed to remind potential voters of the films by advertisements in the trade press. There is general agreement within the industry that certain performers won chiefly because of canvassing in the trade press.

by Eileen Heckart as Monroe's solicitous pal and Betty Field as the brassy proprietress of the bus-stop diner.

There is little to be said for the early CinemaScope comedies, but **Will Success Spoil Rock Hunter?** (1957) is the best of Frank Tashlin's career. It was directed and adapted by him from Axelrod's play, a satire on advertising and Hollywood – to which Tashlin constructively added television. Says the copywriter, 'What has success to do with talent? If it had, Brooks Brothers would go out of business, T.V. studios would be turned into supermarkets' – an unexceptional remark today, but not then. The tone is sour in the Manhattan manner and the piece remains hilarious. Jayne Mansfield, whom the studio hoped would replace the temperamental Monroe, plays the dumb blonde movie star based on Monroe, and the fact that Mansfield herself soon became a joke may be one reason that this film is denied the reputation it deserves. Tony Randall, accomplished as he was, later played roles which turned him into a poor man's Jack Lemmon, while Tashlin disappeared into a welter of Jerry Lewis comedies. Tashlin emerged only notably with an amiable farce, **Bachelor Flat** (1962), written by Bud Grossman from his own play. It has just two comic notions, girls popping out of cupboards and a man bereft of pants – in which role Terry-Thomas, as a British professor running around a Californian beach with rolled umbrella, is an inspiration to his countrymen everywhere.

Gene Kelly directed **A Guide for the Married Man** (1967), one of the first comedies to take advantage of the relaxation of the Production Code. Frank Tarloff's screenplay, from his own book, starts with a quotation from Oscar Wilde, 'The one charm of marriage is that it makes a life of deception absolutely necessary for both parties,' but that is its highpoint. Walter Matthau is the man desperate to be unfaithful to his wife, and Robert Morse is the neighbour only too anxious to help him. Both try to rise above the film's leering attitude towards women, as exemplified in the recurring images of wiggling bottoms. The view that all women are aching for a roll in the hay is at least put more wittily in **The Secret Life of an American Wife** (1968). As written and directed by Mr Axelrod, this is a variation

on his theme in *The Seven Year Itch*, in which a man thinks about sex the moment his wife leaves for a vacation, an acceptable situation in the post-Kinsey era, and this film was only possible now that the Code was defunct. Here a Connecticut housewife (Anne Jackson) fantasises about sex with a movie star (Matthau) and sets out to put her dream into practice the instant her husband leaves for the office. Axelrod, a genuine satirist – he is very funny on the pandering to movie stars' whims – has much to say about the battle of the sexes, which puts his comedy on a higher level than those of the time which relied upon salacity for its own sake.

Sex had always been box office, and the denial of the M.P.A.A. seal of approval to *The Moon Is Blue* and the British-made *I Am a Camera* (q.v.) had not prevented American exhibitors from booking them. In the meanwhile the art-houses were doing turn-away business with the films of Brigitte Bardot (q.v.), and those turned away were returning the next day instead of making a bee-line to the circuit theatre down the street. Also withheld from the Hollywood companies was the money that could have been earned from those sitting at home before their television sets – and sex was something that T.V. did not have. In the face of falling attendances the studios and exhibitors were delighted at the gradual erosion of the Code, though few acknowledged the fact publicly, and in 1966 it was finally abandoned. Instead the M.P.A.A. substituted a series of ratings certificates meant to separate the men from the boys – except in such cases where 'Parental Guidance' was needed.

But if that meant that sexual conduct could be shown instead of merely implied – and few could have guessed that the M.P.A.A.'s new regulations would lead to the graphic depiction of sexual acts – it was not only needed in the cause of frankness. By this time people were reacting against the mindless, cosy domestic comedies which television stations had been transmitting for more than a decade – 'sitcoms' of such patent phoniness that they may be one reason why family life in the Sixties fell apart for many of the post-T.V. generation.

These changes were eventually reflected in a number of films celebrating the hippie movement, but they may be found in more subtle form in **Pretty Poison** (1968), produced by 20th Century-Fox less because of any desire to reflect the general disorientation than because of the success of *Bonnie and Clyde* (q.v.). This chilling film concerns two youngsters caught in a web of fantasies which endanger a society misfit (Anthony Perkins) with arson in his past and a girl (Tuesday Weld) with matricide in her future. The setting is Massachusetts, its particular beauty at odds with the evil beneath the surface as the murderers go about their business as calmly as the citizens go about theirs. The film was written by Lorenzo Semple Jr from a novel by Stephen Geller, and directed by Noel Black, neither of whom was to repeat their achievement of this, their first film.

The graphic portrayal of violence marched hand in hand with the new sexual leniency. **The Detective** (1968) was one of the first films to employ both. Within seconds of its opening, a cop (Frank Sinatra) is stating 'Penis cut off', as you or I might remark on the weather (except that the actor's delivery is somewhat self-conscious). The victim is a homosexual and his killer turns out to be a married man – whose discovery of his sexual orientation might have been more credibly handled. But then the writer, Abby Mann, and the director, Gordon Douglas, are busy detailing such ingredients as semen stains on the sheets, a cop who 'won't lick ass' and an estranged wife (Lee Remick) who has galloping nymphomania. Sinatra is exceptionally kind to black cops until one (Al Freeman Jr) steps out of line, when he behaves ruthlessly. Such was the new realism; but, like its hero, this film flaunts 'concern', it does not feel it. It is preferable, however, to **The St Valentine's Day Massacre** (1967), a re-creation of the era of Al Capone (Jason Robards) and Bugs Moran (Ralph Meeker), directed by Roger Corman without flair.

This was virtually Corman's only film for a major company. His speciality was horror films on small budgets, some of which helped him gain a cult reputation. He was chief among some idiosyncratic movie-makers whom the major studio executives did not really understand and, when he failed to achieve a success for them, he was forced back into independence. It was symptomatic of the panic of

this time that the studios were prepared to employ exploitation movie-makers while still deploring their work. After Corman's departure Russ Meyer was hired by 20th Century-Fox. He had begun making pornographic movies in 1959, and was the most successful practitioner in that field as more and more cinema houses, desperate for business, succumbed to demand. When the abolition of the Code led to the introduction of hard-core pornography, Meyer remained with soft-porn and was thus sufficiently respectable for 20th Century-Fox to take him on.

Beyond the Valley of the Dolls (1970) reflects no credit on him or its co-writer, Roger Ebert, a Chicago film critic, or the studio. *Valley of the Dolls,* based on Jacqueline Susann's sleazy best seller about young hopefuls, had been a box-office success, so the studio prepared a sequel. She was to have turned the outline into a book, but refused when executives balked at her demand of $1½ million for the rights to 'The Love Machine'. They were accordingly left with a title and an outline, which Meyer was required to turn into a 'non-Hollywood' film, i.e. one without star players and as much sex as the ratings system would allow (which would mean an X, so that no one under seventeen could be admitted). The cast includes a brazen nymphomaniac and several other women apparently with the same inclinations; a man who sports a German S.S. uniform and another in a leopard loin-cloth; while the sex includes much nipple-fondling and lingering kisses amongst the women and a weirdo homosexual trying to arouse another male. Halfway through, a harmonium erupts on the soundtrack, in a vain attempt to link the film to the unrealities of soap opera: like the bloody ending, the device seems desperate, and audiences laughed at the film instead of with it. When Meyer's second film for the company, *The Seven Minutes,* also failed, it was decided not to experiment further along these lines.

We have looked elsewhere at the M-G-M musical and there is little else of distinction to note as its forty-year reign over the industry drew to a close. Amid fluctuating profits and continual boardroom battles the studio chiefs never sank as low as 20th Century-Fox, but they too were desperate.

M-G-M was still clinging to the system of long-term contracts as the Sixties dawned, but few of its stars or directors were of more than passing interest.

Stewart Granger was one of their last stars, at one point specialising in remakes of Silent swashbucklers. **Beau Brummell** (1954) was based on an unvenerable antique by Clyde Fitch which had seen service for John Barrymore. It concentrates on the Beau's friendship with the Prince Regent, played by Peter Ustinov as a temperamental booby, but one with taste. Robert Morley is George III, and there was an outcry when this movie was chosen for the Royal Film Performance, thus ensuring that the Queen watched the antics of a mad ancestor on her annual public cinema outing. That, together with Curtis Bernhardt's direction and Elizabeth Taylor's performance, rather obscured the film's virtues, which are real. In leaving the behaviour and character of Brummell an enigma, Karl Tunberg's screenplay anticipated the coming trend in drama; but he was unwise to adhere to the foolish climax of the Fitch play.

The film was made in Britain, and M-G-M, the only company with its own studio there (since 1948), no longer gave the impression of a wealthy relation conferring a favour. The advantages were the relative cheapness of shooting, the army of high-quality supporting players and, when necessary, convenient locations. After *Ivanhoe* had shored up Robert Taylor's waning popularity, producer Pandro S. Berman and director Richard Thorpe sent him to Tintagel for **Knights of the Round Table** (1954) and to Chambord and Chenonceaux for **The Adventures of Quentin Durward** (1956). The settings cannot disguise the dullness of this actor, and *Knights of the Round Table* has in addition a wooden Arthur and a miscast Guinevere (Ava Gardner) – which may be why it reminds one of cut-out paper figures placed before a cardboard set; at the same time, this was the first 'British' film in CinemaScope, a process which seems to have terrified Thorpe. The veteran art director, Alfred Junge, tries to evoke the pre-Raphaelites here and more especially in *Quentin Durward*. That the last is the most entertaining of the trio is due to Robert Ardrey's screenplay and the presence of Kay Kendall as the lady in distress.

Another durable boys' adventure, **The Time Machine** (1960), also has good art direction and a superior screenplay, by David Duncan, as well as a likeable time-traveller in Rod Taylor. In this case H. G. Wells's London and future world were created in Hollywood, at the instigation of George Pal, who produced and directed. He was one of the few film-makers with a continuing interest in the cinema's capacity for fantasy, and had already produced some science fiction films, including *War of the Worlds* (q.v.); for M-G-M he also produced and directed *tom thumb*. Another semi-classic, **Green Mansions** (1959), emerged less convincingly as directed by Mel Ferrer. Selznick had originally bought W. H. Hudson's novel in 1931 as a vehicle for Dolores del Rio and M-G-M had acquired the rights in 1946 for the singer Yma Sumac. A version with Pier Angeli was started and abandoned in 1954, and it says much about the changes at the studio that like-thinking did not prevail on this occasion, with inadequate B-picture back projection and studio jungle. There are strange performances by Anthony Perkins as a revolutionary and Lee J. Cobb as the grizzled grandfather of Rima the bird girl – in which role Audrey Hepburn (then married to Ferrer) darts about like a Disney fawn. The music is by Villa-Lobos, except for one ditty sung by Perkins to a guitar, 'In this land of eternal spring/Where humming-birds can learn to sing/And green grow the mansions of love'.

M-G-M had disdained Westerns since the Silent era, but a number were made during the Schary regime, of which the best is **Escape From Fort Bravo** (1953). We may admire John Sturges's fresh handling of some old themes: the wilful, independent heroine (Eleanor Parker), travelling through perilous territory – Arizona – with several trunks of Helen-Rose-designed gowns; the captain (William Holden) whose sense of duty rankles with both his Union colleagues and the Confederates; the dance; and the prisoners crooning at night. The lengthy climax, with a party ambushed in the desert by Indians, moves this film to classic status. However, it was **Bad Day at Black Rock** (1954) which deservedly made Sturges's reputation. Like all his films, it has a simple aim, seeking only to entertain by creating great tension. He finds menace in a couple of

Hollywood in the Age of Television: The Decline of the Studios

deserted gasoline pumps or reflection in a plate-glass window, and he emphasises the smallness of his central figure against the Arizona mountains and the shacks that constitute Black Rock. That figure is a one-armed Spencer Tracy, arriving in this middle of nowhere on a government mission, to find hostility from everyone, especially Robert Ryan, Ernest Borgnine and, even more villainous, Lee Marvin.

It was Tracy's last film for the company; Clark Gable also left, but Gary Cooper arrived to make his penultimate film, **The Wreck of the Mary Deare** (1959), in which he and a taciturn Charlton Heston try to salvage a wreck in the Channel; those up to no good include Richard Harris as a sarcastic first mate. Eric Ambler wrote the screenplay from a novel by Hammond Innes, and Michael Anderson directed after Hitchcock abandoned the project.

Glenn Ford was the last important male star ever to be under long-term contract to M-G-M, but he was not one to fill the shoes of the great departed. He was assigned to several military comedies, made in a bid to attract diminishing audiences with nostalgia; but it is significant that in the Eisenhower years these films reaffirmed the message which the U.S. had given to its allies and defeated enemies ten years earlier. **The Teahouse of the August Moon** (1956) is set during the

American occupation of Japan, and the humour lies in the consistent outsmarting of the sophisticated Americans, led by Ford, by the primitive and resourceful villagers as represented by Sakini (Marlon Brando). What starts amusingly soon degenerates into maudlin sentimentality on the differences between East and West; among those responsible are Daniel Mann, who directed, and John Patrick, who adapted – with few changes – his own long-running and Pulitzer Prize-winning play, mined in turn from Vern Sneider's novel.

It was not only that CinemaScope was as much blight as boon in its first years, forever slowing down the action; there was a blight too in the artistic climate of the studios, so that films emerged trying to be all things to all men. **Don't Go Near the Water** (1957) strives to be comedy, spectacle and a vehicle for Ford; much footage is expended in establishing his niceness. He plays a sceptical junior officer who brings democracy to a far-flung Pacific island – in fact by blackmailing an odious reporter (Keenan Wynn) to get a native school built: but then in the cause of democracy anything is possible. The dialogue has real bite as written by Dorothy Kingsley and George Wells from the book by William Brinkley; Charles Walters directed. Ford is superbly supported in the first of these films by Paul Ford and in this one by Fred Clark, both playing superior officers with solid bone where the brain should be.

Walters worked almost exclusively in comedy, more reliant than most directors on the quality of his scripts. In **The Tender Trap** (1955) he is never incisive enough to surmount the excessive length, stagy settings, CinemaScope and the self-conscious charm of Debbie Reynolds. She plays a starlet bent on marriage, stealing Frank Sinatra from Celeste Holm, though it is made clear that he had only encouraged this older lady as long as she tolerated his philandering. With this one-time Broadway play Sinatra instituted a series of comedies about 'swinging' bachelors with large pads and large champagne glasses, and very soon he and rivals would not have to wed the girl to bed her. The prevailing mood was one of self-satisfaction, replacing the moralising inherent in previous Hollywood comedies on philandering, since they had always been derived, if

Among the spate of service comedies of the Fifties is *The Teahouse of the August Moon*, in which Marlon Brando, left, as a wily Japanese villager, outwits the American army as represented by Paul Ford and Glenn Ford (no relation). Their puritanism is overcome and the teahouse built: here they are on the site of it.

906

on occasion somewhat distantly, from Schnitzler and his contemporaries. Gone too was the mordant wit and repartee which had once enlivened American comedy, though an exception is **Ask Any Girl** (1959), about an innocent in New York, played with a battery of ingenuous expressions by Shirley MacLaine. She wins the sternest and strictest of her admirers (David Niven), while the two philanderers (Gig Young, Rod Taylor) end up on the shelf. Walters directed, and the superiority of this film is presumably due to its source, a book of comic essays by Winifred Wolfe.

Five years on, the innocent concerned rather wanted to lose her virginity, which is what makes this **Sunday in New York** (1964) different from the one spent by Judy Garland and Robert Walker in *The Clock*. Rod Taylor as the womaniser and Jane Fonda as the girl are pleasing company – she sharp and shrewd but, like Carole Lombard, able to assume naïvety when required. As directed by Peter Tewksbury and written by Norman Krasna from his own play, this is as funny as any of Krasna's scripts twenty years earlier. **Designing Woman** (1957) is a rehash of the idea behind *Woman of the Year,* but is directed lamely by Vincente Minnelli. Lauren Bacall has a stylish comedy sense rather than comedy technique, and Gregory Peck is not a light comedian of the quality of James Stewart, for whom the role was written.

The picture was personally produced by Dore Schary, and was his last film for the company. Joseph Vogel, the president of M-G-M, dismissed him with the explanation that he was disliked by the board, that he was unable to work as a member of a team and that he had too many political interests. But in fact they had clashed earlier when Schary had refused Vogel, then head of the Loews theatre chain, a private screening of an unfinished film. On that occasion Vogel had sworn that he would sack Schary if given the chance. *Designing Woman* had been planned for Grace Kelly, whose films made on loan were so superior to the one she made at her home base, M-G-M – **Green Fire** (1954), a puerile adventure tale with Stewart Granger, directed by Andrew Marton. She had turned down many projects and did this one under protest – and its reception only exacerbated her discontent. Since the press took up the cudgels on her behalf the studio did prepare a number of more promising films, but most of them were made with other actresses after she went to live out her own Ruritanian romance. As she married Prince Rainier of Monaco audiences could see her in something similar, **The Swan** (1956). They were not, with reason, unduly appreciative, but seeing it now on television (i.e. robbed of its CinemaScope frame) it gains in intimacy to become one of the most pleasing comedies of the period. Based on Molnár's play about a royal wooing, it has a Lubitsch-style opening and if, after that, the director Charles Vidor fails to add much in visual terms he moves with ease among these European aristocrats – who include, apart from Miss Kelly, Alec Guinness and Louis Jourdan.

Miss Kelly's popularity was such that her loss was a blow to M-G-M, which had continued to uphold its tradition of fashioning vehicles for the leading female stars – at this point becoming an endangered species, which was why the practice was abandoned by the other studios. June Allyson made her last film for the company in 1956; Debbie Reynolds remained until the Sixties; Ava Gardner was unwilling to return to fulfil her commitment. M-G-M were delighted to have Doris Day on a non-exclusive basis, particularly after the success of her first film for them, **Love Me or Leave Me** (1955). Charles Vidor directed this biography of Ruth Etting, whose songs Miss Day sings in very different manner. Etting's old recordings were reissued as the film came out, and on the album cover she looks demure (with a voice to match her appearance); but in playing her Miss Day is hard and whorish, perhaps because Etting had been a dime-a-dance girl. With that exception – and that the small-time hood (James Cagney) she married made her a star – the facts in the film and those on the record sleeve bear little relation to each other. The situations are dramatic ones in principle, but the film muffs most of them, despite Cagney's cocky and oddly touching performance. The real Ruth Etting must have been either more ambitious or more naïve, and surely she could not have loathed her man quite so much.

Film biographies of the lost souls of show business proliferated, owing to the success of **I'll Cry Tomorrow** (1955) as both book and movie. Lillian Roth's memoir followed her life from starring in the Follies to Alcoholics Anonymous, via two drunken husbands and a spell on the Bowery; but neither the script nor Daniel Mann's direction is able to illuminate the problems of alcoholism. Since Susan Hayward was not an actress to compensate for their deficiencies (and as she was not a singer, like Miss Day, there are few songs), the chief point of interest is Jo Van Fleet as a stage mother.

In theory this was the sort of 'thought-provoking' drama that Schary had been brought in to foster, but he became cautious as the profits on the studio's musicals showed the public in the mood for light entertainment: no more than during Mayer's regime was M-G-M regarded as a studio interested in social problems – and the few that were made were the work of the writer-director Richard Brooks, who was only sometimes adequate to the task. He adapted **The Blackboard Jungle** (1955) from Evan Hunter's novel about his teaching experiences in New York, but retained only a few nuggets of fact or genuine emotion in an often superficial essay. Glenn Ford is the teacher who refuses to accept the indifference of his colleagues and Sidney Poitier the most delinquent of his pupils, with a chip on his shoulder because of his colour. The film is mostly remembered for a song played by Bill Haley and the Comets, 'Rock Around the Clock', which was to lead to a radical change in popular music. Brooks only directed **The Catered Affair** (1956), which Gore Vidal scripted from Paddy Chayevsky's T.V. play, but with a note of contrivance more pronounced than usual in filming this writer. The title refers to a Bronx–Irish wedding, and the family quarrels it provokes sound truthful enough; but in emphasising that this is not the usual movie tale of young love Brooks makes heavy going of the bride's unattractive parents. They are played by Ernest Borgnine and Bette Davis, who, moving into character roles with a vengeance, is too broad for the setting.

In his pursuit of 'important' issues, Brooks wrote and directed **Something of Value** (1957), obtaining the endorsement of Winston Churchill, who appears to introduce it: but its portrait of British Africa

in its death throes is as cliché-ridden as its David and Jonathan relationship between white (Rock Hudson) and black (Sidney Poitier). Brooks turned to Dostoevsky, but if his own adaptation of **The Brothers Karamazov** (1958) is a fair summary of its events, it reveals little understanding of the concern behind them. In any case, the project was foredoomed by the casting of Yul Brynner as Dmitri and Maria Schell as Grushenka.

Nor did Brooks do justice to Tennessee Williams with either **Cat on a Hot Tin Roof** (1958) or **Sweet Bird of Youth** (1962), missing the cadences of passion and corruption in an attempt to provide 'adult' drama. At least *Sweet Bird* preserves Williams's tumbledown hotel and the Broadway performances of Geraldine Page and Paul Newman. As a has-been star Miss Page is even more flamboyant than Davis in *All About Eve* and Swanson in *Sunset Boulevard* – and she manages to convey the fear that lurks in every celebrity even better than they did. Newman is more workaday as the exponent of the American dream gone sour, returning to his home town not as the movie star he hoped to be but gigolo to another – and now less an ageing bisexual opportunist than a golden-beauty ne'er-do-well. The Production Code, still in operation, dictated that the castration become a beating-up and that the abortion be glossed over – changes which should in theory have improved the piece, but it is still often too lurid. *Cat on a Hot Tin Roof*, a better play, has become even more tawdry in Brooks's hands, with whipped-up hysteria and a camera constantly picking up meaningless images. Newman is Brick, managing well his scorn and self-pity as he sinks into alcoholism; Elizabeth Taylor spits out defiance but conveys neither Maggie's sexuality nor her frustrations. Williams observed kindly that she was not his idea of Maggie the Cat, and he loathed the film, which refuses to allow that Brick's affection for the dead Skipper had caused his impotence. Instead, that is blamed on Maggie's infidelity with Skipper, but it hardly matters since little of it makes much sense.

Such films, even with bowdlerisations, were boldly made in an effort to maintain M-G-M's domination of the industry. Similarly, at this time, this company was prominent in filming on location in

Europe. Making the transatlantic trip were Arthur Freed, for his last produced film, **The Light in the Piazza** (1962), and John Houseman, another of Metro's better producers, for **In the Cool of the Day** (1963). The setting of Freed's film is Florence, where Olivia de Havilland is uncertain whether to tell a wealthy and amorous Italian (George Hamilton) that her daughter (Yvette Mimieux) is mentally retarded. Guy Green's direction and Julius J. Epstein's script dilute some of the points which Elizabeth Spencer made in her novel, but ambiguities still remain. *In the Cool of the Day* is a combination of *Dark Victory* and *September Affair*, its lack of originality not disguised by the screenplay or the direction, by Robert Stevenson. Jane Fonda plays a fey creature who leaves her husband to disport herself over much of Delphi and the Acropolis with a British publisher (Peter Finch). The theme of Americans in Europe might still have provided valuable material, but Hollywood was impressed by the inroads into its audiences made by European films. The increase of tourism created audiences eager to relive their vacations; and the Duomo in Florence and the Parthenon were relatively new subjects for the wide-screen cameras to focus upon.

At the same time, in an exotic locale, M-G-M's fortunes were again in the balance. In the wake of Dore Schary's departure, the company suffered its first annual loss* since its inception and, as we have seen, Vogel saved the situation with the remake of *Ben-Hur*. Since that was happily filling theatres, the decision was reached to remake another of the studio's past successes, **Mutiny on the Bounty** (1962) and, on the principle that only the biggest stars are suitable for the biggest pictures, Marlon Brando was approached to play either of the two chief roles. After turning down the project several times – during which the salary offers rose to a final $500,000 against 10 per cent of the gross, plus $5,000 a day overtime if shooting continued beyond the specified schedule – he decided that he might inject some message for humanity into the role of the hero, Fletcher Christian. He then realised that what interested him was the fate of the survivors on Pitcairn Island and, according to the producer, Aaron Rosenberg, was granted 'consultation rights on that part of the picture'. A dozen different endings were written and shot, and any of the other eleven must have been better than the one that was used. Till that point, the film is often entertaining, and the wide screen views are breathtaking even as it is clear that events are conforming to the jungle princess formula. The original writer and director, Eric Ambler and Carol Reed, distinguished British names, were replaced by old Hollywood professionals, Charles Lederer and Lewis Milestone, after two months' shooting, with only one sequence finished. The views of billowing sails and scrubbed decks were done by second-unit directors, but if most of the first half – the voyage out of the *Bounty* – is credit to Milestone's skill, we know from his own account that he gave up: 'Since Brando was going to supervise it anyway, I waited till someone yelled "Camera!" and went off to sit down somewhere and read the paper.' Accordingly Brando may be blamed for his own dreadful performance as an aristocratic fop who becomes tough and heroic under changed circumstances. It is an interesting concept, but he is never the equal of Trevor Howard's blunt and blinkered sea-dog, Bligh. Since this actor is given much less footage, the expected clash of eagles never occurs. The costs had mounted from $10 million to $19 million, but Technicolor and Ultra Panavision notwithstanding, the earlier version is preferable, as the returns indicated to M-G-M's book-keepers.

Vogel resigned the following year and was replaced by Robert O'Brien, who had been executive vice-president of Loews since 1957. His ignorance of the movie-making process was obscured when *Doctor Zhivago* (q.v.) gave the company a good year; and there were several reissues of *Gone With the Wind* to fill the coffers. During his tenure few worthwhile films emerged, and **The Comedians** (1967) is not among them, despite the fact that Graham Greene wrote the screenplay from his own novel. Mauritius and Dahomey deputised for Haiti, but for all the use made

*The situation had been so critical in 1957 that thought had been given to selling the company, which was saved by the popularity of a low-budget vehicle for the rock singer, Elvis Presley, *Jailhouse Rock*. It made up for the losses on *Raintree County*, a bland Civil War epic with Elizabeth Taylor and Montgomery Clift, instituted by Schary as a traditional M-G-M feature. Ironically, one of his first actions on arriving at the studio had been to cancel an earlier version based on the same novel.

of them the film might have been shot on the back-lot. With the local colour and the original sense of menace gone, the tale looks dangerously like self-parody, especially when a dour Richard Burton makes a reference to either faith or death. As his mistress, Elizabeth Taylor has no passion and substitutes an indefinable accent for the German one in the book. Greene said later that the experience was one which he hoped never to repeat, but as a former film critic he should have been wary of producer-director Peter Glenville, whose many poor films include another failure for M-G-M, an unfunny version of a Feydeau farce, **Hotel Paradiso** (1966), with Alec Guinness.

With such films did the once-mighty company wither and die. Its lingering self-respect was surely shattered with **The Singing Nun** (1966), the tale of a Belgian Dominican (a pertly pious Debbie Reynolds), whose singing brings her to the height of anyone's ambition – appearing on the Ed Sullivan Show. She had existed, but this attempt to repeat the success of *The Sound of Music* exists in no real world as directed by Henry Koster. Had it been made in the Forties, the time to which it spiritually belongs – when Hollywood's way with such tales was often as naive as opportunistic – it would still be one of the worst films ever made. Audiences recognised it for the anachronism it was and stayed away, as they did from most M-G-M films at this time.

Paramount survived much better the onslaught of television, though once again not with any consistent policy unless it was an insistence on light entertainment. Profits continued to be satisfactory, mainly due to the comedies of Martin and Lewis produced by Hal Wallis, whose other films were the studio's sole concessions to seriousness. After the departure of Wilder, Wyler, Stevens and Capra, Paramount made no attempt to attract the leading film-makers, apart from Hitchcock, whose films also helped to keep the company prosperous. So did deMille's *The Ten Commandments,* but with his death, and the withdrawal of Hope and Crosby, Paramount no longer seemed like Paramount.

The last films that Hope and Crosby made for the studio are not among their best but they themselves are not blameless, since they were to various extents involved in the production. **Road to Bali** (1952) is the only 'Road' in colour; a later one, *The Road to Hong Kong* (q.v.), was made for United Artists, and if either had been the first it is doubtful whether there would have been another. As directed by Hal Walker *Bali* is careless in both senses of the word, and its humour depends on how much you know about its predecessors.

It was 20th's musicals rather than the airy M-G-M product that Paramount followed for the style of two mechanical and incohesive films, **White Christmas** (1954) and **Anything Goes** (1956). As far as the ingredients are concerned, Paramount had also looked to its own past, for these are rehashes of previous Crosby vehicles. Maybe there were inhibitions, as he was by now virtually a national monument. Perhaps that is why he is again cast as a world-famous entertainer, even if one surrounded by some of the ugliest sets and costumes ever devised. The songs are by Irving Berlin and Cole Porter respectively. In fact the Berlin film was planned to reteam Crosby and Astaire, with a screenplay (by Norman Krasna, Norman Panama and Melvin Frank) which draws on the earlier films they made together, plus a dash of *This Is the Army*. Astaire read it and refused it, and when the second choice, Donald O'Connor, fell ill, Danny Kaye stepped in. As directed by Michael Curtiz, Kaye's 'look at me' niceness does not help an occasion that Scrooge might have cited to justify his attitude. O'Connor did co-star with Crosby in *Anything Goes*, which restores much of the score jettisoned in Paramount's earlier version, plus some new songs by Cahn and Van Heusen which are, again, inferior versions of numbers which Crosby had done with Hope. The sole connection with the original 'book' is the shipboard setting, and the new one, by Sidney Sheldon, is as damp as Robert Lewis's direction.

Crosby did make two decent pictures – in black and white since they were serious subjects – **Little Boy Lost** (1952) and **The Country Girl** (1954), both written and directed by George Seaton. The former was adapted from Marghanita Laski's novel about a journalist looking for the son he had left in France at the beginning of the War, while the latter was founded in a Clifford Odets drama about a drunken actor making a come-back – and with its show-business background the apparently obligatory songs for Crosby were less intrusive. Odets's theme was not new and his customary hyperbole might have passed in a metier where exaggeration is the accepted norm: but many of his scenes are ludicrous, such as that in which the play's director (William Holden) forces a kiss upon the actor's wife (Grace Kelly). However, Seaton's amendments are often telling and original and, if at first it is strange to see Crosby, an entertainer of legendary success, playing one having to audition and afraid of accepting stardom, there is not one emotional scene in which he is not thoroughly in command – even when the words he has to say are disproportionate to the feeling he brings to them. Miss Kelly's inexperience in a demanding role is a prime example of cardigan and glasses convincing the New York critics and Academy voters that they were watching a Best Actress.

Bob Hope's final movies under his contract are tired. Attempting to establish a more serious image, he remained with Paramount for two more films which he produced – **The Seven Little Foys** (1955) and **Beau James** (1957). Written by Jack Rose and Melville Shavelson, who also directed, these are factual tales whose protagonists have attributes not entirely distant from Hope's accepted screen persona, that of a wily opportunist. But it is also clear that the originals in both cases were extremely unpleasant and the sentimental approach further destroys promising material. Despite an attempt to make him charming, Eddie Foy in *The Seven Little Foys* can be seen to be a bad-tempered, misogynistic small-time comic, fussing about billing and exploiting his children until they mutiny and the case ends in court. Mayor James J. Walker in *Beau James* has become a lovable scoundrel whose downfall is brought about when he advances his mistress (Vera Miles) at the expense of his wife (Alexis Smith). The many distortions in this case are exasperating – Walker did not say 'So long, sweetheart' as he left New York for exile, but 'So long, suckers' – even allowing for the fact that the film's model is *The Eddy Duchin Story* (q.v.) rather than many predecessors on corrupt politicians.

Paramount envisaged the much less

volatile Rosemary Clooney as a replacement for Betty Hutton, casting her as a brassy saloon singer in **Red Garters** (1954), originally planned as a spoof Western with Jane Russell and Danny Kaye, to be directed by Mitchell Leisen. After several false starts and cast changes it was clear that Leisen was no longer able to satisfy Paramount executives as he once had and he was replaced by George Marshall, who had had some great successes in this vein; but on this occasion his slow pacing only emphasises the double cuteness of the jokes and of the leading man, Guy Mitchell, a popular singer, in the role intended for Kaye. The stylised one-colour sets (inherited from Leisen) aroused some admiration but, considering that the film was a failure, it is a surprise that Paramount allowed something similar with **Li'l Abner** (1959). The antics of Al Capp's strip-cartoon hayseeds are assimilated into a bright book, mainly about the choice of Dogpatch, 'the most useless place in America', as a testing area for atomic bombs. There are references to Washington corruption and to the vanity and impotency of Abner, played by Peter Palmer with what might not be simulated naivety. Two Paramount writers, Norman Panama and Melvin Frank, had written the show for Broadway, where it had been very successful: they were allowed to return with most of the New York cast, vivacious and energetic on film, especially Stubby Kaye as Marryin' Sam and Julie Newmar as Stupefyin' Jones, a robot-like sex-object. They exult in a lively score, by Gene de Paul and Johnny Mercer (who had written *Seven Brides for Seven Brothers*), and some frenetic choreography, from Michael Kidd's original. Frank's direction unimaginatively reproduces the Broadway show, but at least he learnt from this mistake: when producing another comic-strip musical, *A Funny Thing Happened on the Way to the Forum* (q.v.), he got someone else to direct it.

Panama and Frank, like Shavelson and Rose, another team which had written for Bob Hope, provided Paramount with several old-fashioned comedies at this time. With such stars as Danny Kaye and Sophia Loren, these films prove these writer-directors no match for the LaCavas and McCareys, who understood that stars shone brighter when expressed through

In the days when Marie Dressler coped with a boozing husband, both she and the situation were comic: consequently the more realistic *Come Back, Little Sheba* was regarded as a new departure for Hollywood. Shirley Booth's magnificent performance won her an Oscar, while Burt Lancaster's first 'character' role gave his career a new impetus – a mixed blessing, as it turned out.

situation and dialogue rather than as personalities for their own sake. Another team at Paramount, William Perlberg and George Seaton, also produced several comedies, including two with Clark Gable, *Teacher's Pet* and *But Not for Me*. They were also responsible for one of the few contemporary films on the Korean War, **The Bridges at Toko-Ri** (1954), which Mark Robson directed. It concerns an admiral (Fredric March) with a weakness for young men who resemble his dead son, and a World War II veteran (William Holden) who fills that bill: during this new war Holden becomes less embittered at having had to don uniform again, after accepting March's thesis of the domino theory in South-East Asia. The bridges of the title are symbolic, intended to show the Communists that 'we' shall not give in, but on the evidence of this film James A. Michener's original novel was not useful propaganda.

Hal Wallis was otherwise, as I said, the sole guardian of Paramount's contact with the real world, and he only really liked that if filtered through Broadway. The post-Miller/Williams school of American drama was not entirely congenial to cinema-goers, and to the possible losses on film

versions Wallis could point to the success of his formula films with the rock singer Elvis Presley or those of Martin and Lewis, arguably the most excruciating comedy team in the history of cinema.

Nor, I think, will posterity be entirely grateful to Wallis for the films concerned. The one obvious exception is **Come Back, Little Sheba** (1952), directed by Daniel Mann, since it enshrines Shirley Booth's Broadway performance. Because she was neither young nor glamorous the film was regarded as a new direction in cinema: 'It is essentially *about* the sad business of making the best of a bad job' said *Sight and Sound*, mentioning 'the sort of relationship that carries on quietly in one corner of a Chekhov play'. Lola (Miss Booth) shuffles about in a dressing-gown, listening to soap operas, spying on the young couple in the parlour, and hoping that her husband will not relapse into alcoholism, and even if the character had been much copied, that does not detract from its truth. She does not understand what drove him to drink in the first place, but unfortunately we do – he abandoned his medical studies to marry her when she became pregnant. It is only too clear to us that he

will again resort to the bottle, because of
the antics of the pretty student (Terry
Moore) and her beau (Richard Jaeckel),
one of the Adonis-like creatures that tend
to crop up in the works of William Inge
(who because of this play was taken as
seriously as Tennessee Williams and
Arthur Miller). If Doc's alcoholism is trite-
ly conveyed, it has an appropriate interpreter in Burt Lancaster, who is quieter even
than Spencer Tracy at his quietest, but
self-consciously so, always forcing himself
on the audience's attention. Coupled with
the film's refusal to offer even a fragmentary portrait of small-town life, we are left
only with Miss Booth, heart-rendingly
offering a portrait of a woman who has not
made a success of being a wife.

Shirley Booth won an Oscar, and Wallis
immediately cast her in **About Mrs Leslie**
(1954), a curious and almost splendid film.
It has the same director and the same
screenwriter, Ketti Frings (in this case working with Hal Kanter, from a novel by Vina
Delmar). The problem of finding a suitable
vehicle for this dumpy, middle-aged lady
was solved by involving her in a middle-
aged love affair. She keeps a boarding
house in Beverly Hills and he (Robert
Ryan) is an executive who snatches a
few weeks every year away from wife
and boardroom. Ryan has just the right
mixture of shyness and decency, while
Miss Booth is good natured and humble
(she is much too flattered to rebuff his first
pass), having developed a sturdiness and a
touch of waspishness after a number of
life's knocks. The film failed with both
press and public, so it was some years
before Shirley Booth next worked for
Wallis. In **Hot Spell** (1958) she plays a
mother trying to cope, a conventional role
that she tackles with her usual lack of
self-indulgence. The piece itself is of the
Inge-Williams school, written by James
Poe from a little-known play by Lonnie
Coleman. The film's failure in this case
seems to be due to the fact that without a
Broadway reputation to guide it, the public was not yet ready for dramas in which
mamas and papas were not remembered
fondly. There are faults here in writing and
execution, but there is a rare harshness
in the fights between father (Anthony
Quinn) and son (Earl Holliman), as well as
a funeral done without the usual movie
sentimentality. Some humorous, but bit-

ter, scenes between mother and a friend
(Eileen Heckart) are not at odds with the
rest of the film. Mann again directed.

The cast includes Shirley MacLaine,
who supported Shirley Booth again in
The Matchmaker (1958), directed by
Joseph Anthony from Thornton Wilder's
play (itself derived from a nineteenth-
century Austrian farce). It had been a success in London and New York for Ruth
Gordon, whom I saw in the role. I have
also seen it as transformed into 'Hello
Dolly', and it had, apart from this version,
struck me as a mediocre work. As farcical
comedy it has little wit, but the situations
spring mainly from the motives of the
characters – who are wonderfully played:
Paul Ford as the pompous and miserly
merchant; Anthony Perkins and Robert
Morse as his assistants; MacLaine dimpling prettily as the milliner; and Miss
Booth in the title-role, her chins and
cheeks permanently wobbling, her eyes
darting hopefully from the merchant's face
to somewhere beyond camera range. Her
four screen performances are touched with
magic because she works with that combination of truth and professional instinct
which is the hallmark of all great players.

The film was produced by Don Hartman, a former comedy writer, who shared
many of the principles and pretensions of
Wallis. He was also responsible for **Desire
Under the Elms** (1958), which is *not* notable for its performances – Sophia Loren as
O'Neill's mail-order Phaedra, Burl Ives's
over-ripe New England farmer and Perkins as his tic-afflicted son. Delbert Mann
directed, unfortunately stressing O'Neill's
sophomoric tragic values. The film was
redundant in any case, since Wallis had
recently produced another with the same
situation, *Wild Is the Wind,* with Anna
Magnani.

To capitalise on the Oscar that Magnani
had won for that film, Wallis bought the
rights to **The Rose Tattoo** (1955), a concoction that Tennessee Williams had written for her but which she had refused to do
on Broadway. Williams was a good writer
with the instincts of a hack and his screenplay contains a number of puerilities, not
to mention two dream figures with little
more dimension than photographs in a
physique magazine, a young sailor (Ben
Cooper) and an ageing but still hunky
truck-driver (Burt Lancaster). The young

913

lovers are, admittedly, supposed to point up mother's frigidity, which has to melt before the truck-driver, and Daniel Mann's direction accentuates the most attractive aspect of the piece, its pervading sexuality. In this respect, Magnani also contributes, despite the fact that she spends most of the time shouting at her daughter (Marisa Pavan), the neighbours and the whores; and at one point is seen struggling into a corset. Lancaster is more than willing in situations beyond him; he is his usual ineffable self in **The Rainmaker** (1956), as a peripatetic con-man who stops just long enough to teach an ageing virgin (Katharine Hepburn) the meaning of life. The then novice director, Joseph Anthony – he had staged N. Richard Nash's play on Broadway – allows this actress uncontrolled authority and tears; and he cannot hide the namby-pamby but derivative nature of the material. The obsession with sex in such plays (cf. the works of Arthur Miller) helped liberalise Hollywood, since the M.P.A.A. had difficulty in forbidding what sophisticated New York had applauded. If Wallis saw them primarily as vehicles for the 'strong' actresses he had long favoured, they were also regarded as among the more civilised entertainments to be seen in a cinema.

He was also partly responsible for the return to favour of the Western. That was due to a few good ones as opposed to the genre as a whole, and his **Gunfight at the O.K. Corral** (1957) is expectedly sound and vigorous. The script by Leon Uris – not then a best-selling novelist – retells the feud between the Earp family and Doc Holliday on one hand and Billy Clanton and his gang on the other – the latter bunch acted by some choice bad men, including John Ireland, Dennis Hopper, Frank Faylen, Lee Van Cleef, Lyle Bettger, Jack Elam and Ted de Corsia. As Earp, Burt Lancaster offers in physical bulk what he lacks in virile delivery, while as Doc Holliday Kirk Douglas conveys a real sense of menace, doubtless developed by the expert director, John Sturges. As Frankie Laine warbles a Dmitri Tiomkin ballad, we may be reminded of *High Noon*, a film that helped to redefine the Code of the West.

One-Eyed Jacks (1961) is a frontal attack on that ethos as produced by Marlon Brando and directed by him (after a dispute with Stanley Kubrick, q.v.). The hero (Brando) is stupid, cunning and vicious, finally shooting his enemy the sheriff (Karl Malden) in the back. It is a story of revenge at a time of rough justice, of racial prejudice, of no morals, set in a country where drab-looking girls wait in run-down, deserted saloons, where the desert is vast and lonely and where there is a whipping-post for the hero. That particular sequence may reveal masochism or an intimation of a Messiah-complex on the part of Brando himself; the whole film is an early example of the self-indulgence that was to run rife once the studio system had completely broken down. At the same time it is accomplished, clearly influenced by both John Ford and Kurosawa and, like *Viva Zapata!*, veering back and forth from the romantic to the realistic (the men wear duds as seen in the photographs of the time – 1880 – which movies had forgotten since Tom Mix had introduced his more photogenic outfits). That Brando has not been given another opportunity to direct may be due to the huge final cost, which was only just recovered at the box office.

Despite much publicity and comment, the film was far less influential than Sam Peckinpah's not dissimilar *Ride the High Country* (q.v.) a programmer of the following year. That moved the Western decisively away from Monument Valley and introduced both more violence and older, more robust characters. One of its descendants is **True Grit** (1969), to date the last really popular Western. Credit for its quality is due to the author, Charles Porteous, rendered so capably by Marguerite Roberts in her screenplay, and the veteran director Henry Hathaway. Other recent collaborations with Wallis, the producer, and the equally venerable cinematographer, Lucien Ballard, had not augured a Western of this quality, so we may suppose Hathaway by this time to be only as good as his script. A fat, ageing, one-eyed drunken marshal, Rooster Cogburn (John Wayne), a guileless, rather fey but wary girl (Kim Darby) and a sassy young Texas Ranger (Glenn Campbell) set out amidst yellow saplings and green firs to pursue a killer – and so disarming is their interplay that the villains, led by Robert Duvall, arrive with ferocious suddenness. Only the bad men – Richard Jordan, Anthony Zerbe – are good in an opportunist sequel, **Rooster Cogburn** (1975), directed by

Stuart Miller because Hathaway now considered himself too old for the location work. Wayne and Katharine Hepburn are parodies of their former selves in a pseudonymous script (Wallis and his wife were among the contributors), which is a Wild West version of *The African Queen*. Audiences were not interested in this first teaming of two legendary but aged stars and, unlike its two progenitors, this film was a box-office disaster – the last of several which Wallis had had with Universal, to whom he had moved after a quarrel (q.v.) with Paramount over a film with Richard Burton; and he forthwith retired.

From Paramount came also the Western programmers produced by A. C. Lyles in the early Sixties, and fancied by some buffs since they featured bevies of names from an earlier era, many of them now toupéed, corseted (or unfortunately not), with drooping jowls and, it would seem, in an advanced state of alcoholism. Also from Paramount was a Western musical, **Paint Your Wagon** (1969), persuaded into the project by Alan Jay Lerner, who had written the 1948 Broadway show with Frederick Loewe. After several failures the industry was chary of musicals, but this one offered the opportunity, as with *The Sound of Music,* of attractive locations; and there were leading roles for two of the biggest box-office stars, Lee Marvin and Clint Eastwood (though neither could sing) plus another, supposedly with a certain European clout to help it in that difficult market for musicals, Jean Seberg. Costs rose to over $20 million during the extensive location shooting – often due to difficulties with the director, Joshua Logan. He was a strange choice, since most reviewers had suggested that both *South Pacific* and *Camelot* (q.v.) would have been better with someone else in charge. On this occasion his vulgarity is restrained, despite the opportunities in the story – about sex-starved miners and a *ménage à trois*. Paddy Chayevsky wrote it when Lerner decided that his original book would not do, but he himself wrote the screenplay; when Loewe refused to write any new songs (because he had retired) André Previn contributed two, in a needless Sixties rock idiom. The money was at least well spent when the green valley comes alive with the miners carolling the title song and 'There's a Coach Coming

In'. The singers are self-conscious, but so is the film – including a farcical, destructive climax, pleasantly reminiscent of *Steamboat Bill Jr.*

The film was more popular in Britain than the U.S. (though that did not help it recover its cost), and so, unsurprisingly, was **Half a Sixpence** (1967), a musical version of 'Kipps' which had duplicated its success on Broadway and whose prime virtue, its star, becomes its chief liability on film. Tommy Steele substitutes teeth for talent: after 146 minutes of his grin in close-up, one cherishes all the more Buster Keaton's stone face. Steele has star quality but no reticence, compounding his exuberance with a nasal, grating singing voice and is all the more obtrusive since his leading ladies – Julia Foster as the humble Ann, and Penelope Horner as the haughty Helen – lack personality. Some of their elders (Pamela Brown, Cyril Ritchard) have the requisite style, but this enterprise is only saved from total disaster by the American director, George Sidney. He makes this perhaps the prettiest of all period musicals and has staged the poor numbers with skill and vitality. He is also alive (as the book is not) to H. G. Wells's original novel.

Wells also provided the basis for **The War of the Worlds** (1953). Except for some Z-budget serials, science fiction was ignored by Hollywood from the Silent era until 1950, when George Pal made *Destination Moon* for Eagle-Lion. The not dissimilar *Rocketship X-M* followed soon after, and, if we regard *The Thing* as primarily a horror item, Paramount was the first of the major studios to venture into the field when it financed Pal's Technicolor productions of **When Worlds Collide** (1951) and *The War of the Worlds*, directed respectively by Rudolph Maté and Byron Haskin, with B-picture casts playing dedicated scientists with virtually unspeakable dialogue. The budget for the live-action sequences of the latter was $600,000, an inconsiderable sum, but Paramount was sufficiently encouraged to allow $1,400,000 for special effects. These in their day were good, but the transportation of Wells's novel to contemporary California robs it of much of its appeal without adding to the thrills.

A very different war was the background to Paramount's first European co-production, **War and Peace** (1956), and it became involved because it had first call on the services of Audrey Hepburn. The film industry had always considered Tolstoy's novel too big and too 'highbrow' – with the not surprising exceptions of Korda and Orson Welles, who had planned a production during the War. David O. Selznick and then Mike Todd announced their own versions in the mid-Fifties, as did the Italian team of Carlo Ponti and Dino de Laurentiis, both of whom harboured ambitions outside Italy. They interested King Vidor and Miss Hepburn, the latter to play Natasha with her then husband, Mel Ferrer, as Prince Andrei. As she was so clearly the perfect choice the other producers hesitated, and Paramount agreed to support Ponti and de Laurentiis. The adapters have approached Tolstoy's novel about the French invasion of Russia as though it were *Gone with the Wind*, giving us most of the content, a little character, some motivation, but no complexity. The result is without crassness or sanctimoniousness and, if the characters hardly seem Russian, they are perhaps more alive than in most historical movies. Certainly Miss Hepburn is, whether mooning over the men going to war or revelling in a trip to the country. The other triumph is the photography by Jack Cardiff, with second-unit work by Aldo Tonti. The rest of the acting varies, from Barry Jones (Rostov), Jeremy Brett (Nicholas) and Henry Fonda (a thin and Omaha-accented Pierre), to Ferrer, John Mills (Platon) and Anita Ekburg (Helena) at the other end of the scale.

Hepburn made a number of enjoyable films for Paramount, including *Breakfast at Tiffany's* (q.v.), whose screenwriter, George Axelrod, also scripted **Paris When It Sizzles** (1964), based on Duvivier's *La Fête à Henriette*. She plays stenographer to William Holden, and they are joined by Noël Coward, Marlene Dietrich and Tony Curtis in guest appearances. There are in-jokes, a film within a film, echoes of *Funny Face,* and Eastmancolor, all advantages denied to Duvivier, but of no obvious help to the director, Richard Quine.

Holden was Paramount's primary male star at this time, taking the plum parts and leaving to the equally handsome and dull Charlton Heston the programmers made

for the studio by the production team of Pine and Thomas, who liked the tried, the true and Technicolor. Among the veteran stars who filmed for Paramount at this time is Spencer Tracy – and one of the reasons that he left M-G-M was its refusal, because of cost, to sanction **The Mountain** (1956), based on Henry Troyat's novel. In the interim he had made *Broken Lance* for 20th Century-Fox, from which he brought the director Edward Dmytryk and Robert Wagner. Neither actor makes a convincing French peasant in *The Mountain* and it is equally hard to accept Wagner, thirty years his junior, as Tracy's brother. The moral issues raised as they climb the mountain are simplistic, as rendered in Ranald McDougall's screenplay. He adapted **We're No Angels** (1955), in which another of the great stars, Humphrey Bogart, plays a Frenchman. The Broadway version of this French play goes unmentioned in the credits, but the direction by Michael Curtiz – Wallis's old Warner Bros. colleague – does little to disguise the source. As escaped convicts in an emporium on Devil's Island, Bogart, Peter Ustinov and Aldo Ray enjoy themselves and amuse us and, since this is a comedy, it comes as no surprise when at the end they elect to return to jail.

Comedy had never been Curtiz's forte, and he seems to have been chosen for **A Breath of Scandal** (1960) on the basis that, like its author, Molnár, he had been born in the Austro-Hungarian Empire. Molnár's play – 'Olympia' – is about a hussar officer who takes revenge on an arrogant princess who has spurned his advances. However, this adaptation (by Sidney Howard, who had died in 1939; there is no screenplay credit) concerns a haughty princess suspected of having an affair with an American car salesman. Sophia Loren is no one's idea of a Hapsburg princess, and neither she nor John Gavin are natural farceurs, leaving only Isabel Jeans, as Momma, with the right style, which suggests that Curtiz gave little help to two other experienced players, Maurice Chevalier, as Poppa, and Angela Lansbury, as Loren's jealous rival. Among his later films, only **The Scarlet Hour** (1956) is reminiscent of his Warner Bros. melodramas – made, like this, in black and white. It tells of an unfaithful wife (Carol Ohmart), the lover (Tom Tryon) who is an employee of her husband (James Gregory), and what happens to the two of them when they overhear some men planning a robbery. The night clubs are seedier than they used to be, the bars darker; and much of the action takes place in parked cars.

This sharp and unpretentious movie was not typical of the Paramount films of the time; nor did the company care to follow up its one excursion into filming an admired T.V. play, *Fear Strikes Out* (q.v.). One 'serious' enterprise deserves to be recalled, but only as an object of scorn. This is **The Buster Keaton Story** (1957). As far as Hollywood was concerned, Keaton was one of the derelicts of show business and therefore the fitting subject of a film. The producer-writers Robert Smith and Sidney Sheldon, who also directed, show not the least admiration for Keaton, reducing him to a silly little man and an unfunny minor comic. Their story-line is almost totally fictional, but what is most repugnant is that it violates everything for which Keaton stood. It must surely have saddened him to see some of his sublime numbers vulgarised by adding inane slapstick of which he was incapable. In fact, the film was too cheaply made to re-create his routines well, so that that of *Cops* uses only one set and ten cops. Acting as technical adviser, he was well paid for teaching Donald O'Connor to flap his arms. Keaton loathed the film and must have seen it as Hollywood's last attempt to do him in.

Later, as a novelist, Sheldon's model was to be Harold Robbins. Robbins's best-sellers were unlike those Hollywood used to film, being throw-away airplane reading – consisting often of glamorous beings in highly-charged sexual activities. Paramount's co-productions with Joseph E. Levine are among the more shameful moments in its history. **Where Love Has Gone** (1964) offers two hours with unprincipled and unpleasant people, with Susan Hayward as a sculptress, one of the most curious manifestations of Hollywood casting. 'In the field of sculpture', says someone, 'she's one of the greats.' She herself has such lines as 'I used sex as you used alcohol' as her marriage breaks up, and 'Oh Sam, the United Nations!' on receiving a commission from that source. Her husband, Michael Connors, later attempts to rape her fully-clothed, at which point you may decide that the once-

excellent director, Edward Dmytryk, is as cynical as everyone else involved in the enterprise. He makes little attempt to disguise the fact that his film is a series of conversations, but these at least receive a charge whenever Bette Davis enters the luxurious settings – and she is some consolation as Hayward's snobbish mother. For those interested, Robbins's starting-point was the occasion when Lana Turner's daughter tried to stab her mother's gangster lover. Later movie attempts to duplicate Robbins's paperback sales produced only flops, till by the late Seventies Hollywood had lost interest in him and his imitators. **Sidney Sheldon's Bloodline** (1979) was a last lone flowering, its odd title meant by the author or his agent to remind the industry that one of its hacks had become a best-selling novelist. The film failed more abysmally than a predecessor, *Jacqueline Susann's Once Is Not Enough*, so Paramount soon reduced its ads to minute size, leaving only the title and, to meet contractual requirements, the name of the director, Terence Young. Hence the ads contained the two names likely to deter discriminating patrons, while omitting those of such popular players as Audrey Hepburn, James Mason and Ben Gazzara. Typical of the reviews was David Denby's comment in *New York Magazine*, that 'poor Michelle Philips gets her knees nailed to the floor for not paying her gambling debts. Paramount may have to do the same thing to get audiences to stay through this movie.'

Only one studio did not panic at this time, and that was Warners, whose television Western series were bringing in a reasonable income. Perhaps the prevailing calm is one reason why only Warner Bros. of the major companies offered a homogeneous group of films during this period, projecting the image of middle-class America – usually cosy, unless the requirements of the original, often a best-selling novel, decreed otherwise. Such had ever been Hollywood's intention, and at this time the films may reflect Jack L. Warner's taste more than at others during the company's history. Warners' great periods were moulded by Zanuck and then Wallis and, with the defection of Jerry Wald in 1951, there was no longer a strong or innovative producer at the studio: the only veteran was Henry Blanke, whose productions ranged from the dire (*Sincerely Yours*) to the noble (*The Nun's Story*).

Despite the failures of *Always Leave Them Laughing* and *Sincerely Yours,* Warner himself still believed that patrons could be induced to see their fireside favourites on the big screen, and Jack Webb was hired to direct and star in a cinema version of his T.V. series 'Dragnet'. It enjoyed a mild popularity, encouraging Webb to remain to make **Pete Kelly's Blues** (1955), again functioning in both capacities. The formula of this fondly-remembered film was simple – jazz and gangsters, the latter ever a speciality of this studio; it was the first film to re-create both aspects of the Twenties with any degree of fidelity, and it did so with a pervading melancholy then rare. Webb's own rather uninspired work includes his individual style of narration as used in 'Dragnet' (and parodied in *The Band Wagon*); Richard L. Breen's screenplay is sporadically witty, and the songs are sung by Peggy Lee (in a role which combines the second wife of *Citizen Kane* with Ophelia) and Ella Fitzgerald who, with hardly a muscle moving, sets the pulse racing with her version of 'Hard-Hearted Hannah'.

The Twenties were revisited by Warners for **The Helen Morgan Story** (1957), yet another standardised biography of a great star, palely impersonated by Ann Blyth. Had she used her own soprano voice, she might have managed an approximation of Morgan's style; she is ghosted by the richer voice of Gogi Grant and, because the songs are often superb, the film has its moments. Directing, Michael Curtiz is at his most professional, presenting in the bootlegging scenes an occasional echo of the old Warner gangster movies.

Act One (1963) is another show-business story, based on Moss Hart's memoir, a classic rags-to-riches account told wisely and wittily. Dore Schary, adapting, producing and directing – one of his few films after leaving M-G-M – has tampered only to cut, but his reverent approach destroys the exuberance of Hart's text. The matters dealt with are chiefly Hart's relationship with George S. Kaufman – leading to the triumphant first night of 'Once in a Lifetime' – and in that role Jason Robards rises above the treatment, as well as managing a good physical

resemblance. Hart is played by George Hamilton, whose gleaming good looks are not matched by his talent.

Hart's Jewish youth is played down; and when Warners insisted on diluting the essential Jewishness of Herman Wouk's characters in **Marjorie Morningstar** (1958) the screenwriter, Everett Freeman, sought (unsuccessfully) to have his name removed from the credits. Gutting the novel, he has concentrated on Marjorie's experiences as 'dramatic counsellor' at a summer camp in the Catskills and her fascination with Noel Airman *né* Ehrman (Gene Kelly), philanderer and little-theatre genius. Despite the changes, Natalie Wood's performance as the heroine and Harry Stradling's too lyrical colour photography, the film is better than some of the other novels filmed by Warners at this time. It is odd to see any of them on T.V. today, with only the clothes and the slowness of pace to indicate that they had not been made years earlier. Wouk's **Young-blood Hawke** (1964) is especially relishable, as rendered in Delmer Daves's screenplay and direction. The central character is based on Thomas Wolfe, and it is hard to know which is less convincing – the performance of James Franciscus, the palatial publishing offices, or his relationship with a scheming entrepreneur (Geneviève Page) who goes off to England, as she puts it, 'to look over some Shakespearian actors'. Wolfe's own romance with his mistress is bastardised, and the film's only contact with reality is in Mary Astor's original study of a kindly, but fading, Broadway star.

A more famous novel became a duller film, **The Old Man and the Sea** (1958), a co-production between its author, Ernest Hemingway, Leland Hayward (then a Broadway producer) and Spencer Tracy – whom they agreed should star. Fred Zinnemann began the filming in 1956, but left the project with little footage in the can, due to the difficulties of filming on the ocean. A great tank was constructed on the Warner lot (during which Tracy made another film), but the result, as directed by John Sturges, recovered little of its $6 million cost. Since its sole subject is the old man's pursuit of a giant fish, it depends much on Tracy, but even his skill cannot overcome the fact that the sky behind him is too often painted; and his

Among the brighter stars of the Fifties and Sixties was Doris Day, who was sunny, energetic and natural. These qualities were never better used than in *Calamity Jane*, probably the best film she made. Its makers saw the famous female gunslinger as a tomboy, torn between her fiancé, Philip Carey, left, and Howard Keel, right, playing Wild Bill Hickock.

speaking of the third-person commentary cannot rid it of its pretension.

Buying best sellers, Warners came up with **Sex and the Single Girl** (1964), Helen Gurley Brown's advisory essays. They have been transmuted into a comedy about a Helen Gurley Brown (Natalie Wood) whose best seller on sexual matters causes a battle with the publisher (Tony Curtis) of a scandal magazine. The roles require a technique which the players do not have, making it doubly sad to find superior artists in supporting roles as brawling neighbours. In the event, Henry Fonda and Lauren Bacall publicly repudiated the film, claiming that the director, Richard Quine, had reneged on his promise to build up their roles. The plot borrows from innumerable sources, as scripted by Joseph Heller, who wisely has not written a film since, and David R. Schwartz, whose only other worthwhile credit is a gangster spoof, **Robin and the Seven Hoods** (1964). Gordon Douglas directed and Frank Sinatra produced it to star himself and his 'clan', one of several films engendered thereby. It is brightened by Peter Falk, as a gang leader, and Bing Crosby, as a deceptively quiet do-gooder.

Crosby has the best song, 'Style', or, rather, he steals it from its fellow performers, Sinatra and Dean Martin. Elsewhere the Cahn-Van Heusen score is pleasantly satirical.

Warners had not been noted for their musicals since the early Thirties, so **Calamity Jane** (1953) was a surprise – all the more so, since it borrowed so heavily from 'Annie Get Your Gun' and 'Oklahoma!' As one critic put it, in the *Financial Times,* 'It manages the impossible by making a repeat performance seem as fresh and cheerful as its predecessors.' That is partly due to the stars, Doris Day and Howard Keel, and partly to the songs, staged with vivacity by Jack Donohue; David Butler directed. The film was enormously popular and still delights audiences on its rare revivals.

Miss Day later returned to Warners for *The Pajama Game,* the success of which – and the Rodgers and Hammerstein movies – dictated the style of **The Music Man** (1962) and **Gypsy** (1962). Both are theatrical in their new 'natural' settings, hoping thus to harness some of the energy which had contributed to their stage success. The first came to the screen with its Broadway

Hollywood in the Age of Television: The Decline of the Studios

star, Robert Preston, and director, Morton da Costa; in *Gypsy* Ethel Merman ceded to Rosalind Russell, and the direction was handed to Mervyn LeRoy. Both are, I think, great originals, with scores which in the Broadway cast albums remain enlivening. Meredith Willson wrote that of *The Music Man,* as well as the book, which follows the adventures of a fast-talking con-man in a mid-Western town. Jules Styne composed the music of *Gypsy,* with words by Stephen Sondheim, and a story based on Gypsy Rose Lee's memoir – which is mainly about her dominating, stage-obsessed mother. The thesis in *The Music Man* is that all should be forgiven those who bring life and happiness to those around them and, though da Costa has not solved the problem of restaging Willson's witty numbers, their work is infectious – if, that is, one can take folksiness in full flood and yet another return to the days when all men wore straw hats and the women carried parasols. Even if Preston was a mite old for the role, he is still wellnigh irresistible. In *Gypsy* the only good numbers are those – 'All I Need Is a Girl', 'Gotta Have a Gimmick' – featuring the original Broadway players. As Gypsy, Natalie Wood's striptease would titillate nobody and Miss Russell is broad and hammy: dubbed most of the time by Lisa Kirk, the singing lacks the thrilling urgency of Merman's. Sidney Lumet (q.v.), in explaining why he wants to remake this film, says, quite rightly, that it is a disaster: but without Merman,* *Gypsy* is not *Gypsy.*

Despite favourable reviews, *The Music Man* failed outside the U.S., but Jack L. Warner still outbid the other studios for the rights to two other Broadway successes, both by Lerner and Loewe – *My Fair Lady*, discussed earlier, and **Camelot** (1967), directed for the screen by Joshua Logan. Noël Coward's remark (apropos the Broadway original) that it was longer than 'Parsifal' but without the laughs is a comment on Alan Jay Lerner's earnestness in fashioning a tribute to Goodness from T. H. White's pastiche of the Arthurian legends. As in the film of *Paint Your Wagon,* the theme is the love of two friends for the same woman, none of them wanting to hurt each other, and it is touchingly

*I have, however, seen it well acted with Angela Lansbury and magnificently sung by Dolores Gray.

rendered by Richard Harris as Arthur, who 'grows' beautifully from irresponsible youth at the beginning, by Franco Nero as Lancelot, and by Vanessa Redgrave as Guenevere – though she lacks the merriment of Julie Andrews's Broadway performance, which gave the piece an entirely different dimension. David Hemmings's Mordred is not one of the classic villains and the other knights only grasp at the English comic tradition. The castles are Spanish – the huge pile of Coca stands in for Camelot itself – and John Truscott's art direction, fusing Arthur Rackham and the Pre-Raphaelites, is so attractive that it distracts from the ponderous direction and the relentless chopping-up of the songs. For once, the money that went into these super-musicals was well spent, but the public was not overly appreciative.

Warners co-operated with the American Broadcasting Co. to produce **Mame** (1974), as that company was closing down its film-making operation. One of the reasons it was so short-lived was that A.B.C. always made the wrong decisions, and it never made a worse one than in casting Lucille Ball as Mame. Her singing is a mere croak and, since it has difficulty settling on the right note, it is hardly a pleasant croak; her dancing consists of a few whirls, and she has failed to grasp that Mame is an impulsive, spontaneous, eccentric lady, by turns bitchy and softhearted. She manages the bitchiness, but if she ever understood the other qualities she had forgotten them long since. Gene Saks's direction is of no help, and Robert Preston, as Mame's Southern beau, has too little to do to save the day. New York's fondness for Auntie Mame (hitherto heroine of a novel, a straight play, a film and the Broadway original of this movie) helped to break records at Radio City Music Hall during the first week of the run; but word-of-mouth drastically reduced its figures the following week. Elsewhere, the film's reception proved that few loved Lucy, and its failure was another nail in the coffin of the Hollywood musical.

Before *Camelot* and after his tentative attempt to save *Mister Roberts,* Joshua Logan had directed **Sayonara** (1957) for Warners. Paul Osborn wrote the screenplay from James A. Michener's novel about the American occupation of Japan and the servicemen (Marlon Brando, Red Buttons) who find themselves drawn into relationships with local women. In the book both romances end unhappily, but only one does in the film. The subject of mixed marriages conformed to the studio tradition of expounding liberal attitudes, and Logan underlines the significance; but since, as usual, he wants at the same time to be visually striking the only lasting impression is of pretty cherry blossoms. Some may prefer the only unambitious film that Logan directed, **Tall Story** (1960), a few college japes largely memorable for the performance of Jane Fonda (in her film debut) as a girl bent on marrying the star athlete, Anthony Perkins. Perkins appears nude, if rear-view and briefly, and was probably the first player to do so in a major American film.

The film was based on a Broadway play, as was **The Dark at the Top of the Stairs** (1960), adapted from William Inge's original by Harriet Frank Jr and Irving Ravetch, whose other pieces of Americana include *Hud* (q.v.) and *The Cowboys*. Robert Preston is father, a fast-talking travelling salesman, and Dorothy McGuire repeats, fifteen years on, her role in *A Tree Grows in Brooklyn*; Eve Arden plays in her usual style – which, however pleasing, would jar in a better movie; but the film is taken from them by Angela Lansbury as the husband's beautician friend. Delbert Mann directed this mixture of *Life with Father* and early Tennessee Williams; there are references to anti-Semitism and middle-aged sex (or lack of it), daring at the time, but the effort went unregarded.

The studio tradition of social melodrama was only really revived in **Rebel Without a Cause** (1955), a primary text on juvenile delinquency. The Warner approach to social problems had always been excitable, and the screenplay by Nicholas Ray, who directed, builds from *The Blackboard Jungle* and *The Wild One* (both recently approved of by adolescent patrons) to a dotty climax reminiscent of *The Song of Songs*. His characters are stereotypes, with the important exception of James Dean in the title role, perpetually intense, bewildered, shy-serious, by turns garrulous and inarticulate and with an odd mixture of foolishness and idealism in his adolescent defiance of society. With the

actor's death, the film was raised to cult status by sub-teenagers. It was also the first of many movies in which the young were sympathetic and the middle-aged either venal or contemptible or both. We knew that Andy Hardy and neat little girls in peep-toe shoes were not the truth about childhood, but neither was this lurid tale: nor is it any more on the side of youth than was Louis B. Mayer. At the time the film was either dismissed or considered inferior to Frankenheimer's more honest account of a bourgeois misfit, *The Young Stranger* (q.v.). The producer, David Weisbart, went on to make a number of teenage musicals at 20th Century-Fox.

After a change of management – Jack L. Warner sold his interest in the company to Seven Arts (q.v.) in 1967 – there appeared **The Sergeant** (1968), one of the first films on homosexuality: but in the event that is a subject on which the director John Flynn and the writer Dennis Murphy (working from his own novel) seem to have no opinions. This lack is emphasised by the almost non-existent plot, about a sergeant (Rod Steiger) with a hang-up on one of his men (John Philip Law). Apart from his loneliness and the fact that he had killed a German soldier during the War we are told nothing about him to put his 'weakness' into context. Rejected, the sergeant shoots himself and we are left only with an idle comment on the misuse of authority (the man had been seconded to the sergeant's office). The film is equally reticent on army life, but its portrait of a damp northern France – and Steiger's performance – suggest that the director might have had a more distinguished career.

Earlier, Warners had produced a film of Tennessee Williams's novel, **The Roman Spring of Mrs Stone** (1961), in conjunction with Seven Arts. Williams had apparently situated Rome deep in the Mississippi delta, but he had managed a perceptive portrait of a disillusioned and lonely American fascinated by the decadance of old Europe – represented, poorly, in the film by Warren Beatty's gigolo and the fawning but grasping countess of Lotte Lenya. Under the direction of José Quintero, from Broadway, each scene is designed as if for the stage, and an atmospheric, tenuous novel has become a rather obvious tale. As the lady who takes up with the gigolo, Vivien Leigh has not a

Roman spring, summer, autumn or winter, since she is either obviously doubled or works against a painted blackcloth. In an unbecoming blonde wig, she moves through the piece as if opening a bazaar, substituting a barely perceptible spark of malice for emotion. As in *Ship of Fools*, she presents a self-portrait of the former Lady Olivier, lonely and not liking the once-beautiful face which stares back from the mirror – and unnecessarily established in the tale as a rotten Shakespearian actress.

Also among the Warner grotesques is **Dead Ringer** (1964), with which Bette Davis returned after her success for the studio in *Whatever Happened to Baby Jane?* She plays twins in this second gobbet of Grand Guignol, which is sufficiently well-plotted to lend itself to admirers of the genre. Whether it is to be recommended to admirers of this actress is another matter: as directed by a former co-star, Paul Henreid, she is magnetic but bereft of her once subtle gift for establishing character.

The last Warner movie I think of, chronologically, as a 'studio' product – as opposed to a director's film made at Warners – is also in this category, and an unexpected success as directed by Terence Young from a run-of-the-mill stage thriller, by Frederick Knott. It is **Wait Until Dark** (1967), in which a blind girl (Audrey Hepburn) is beset by a gang of thugs (who include Alan Arkin). The twists of the plot are handled with efficiency; but it is because of one moment which always evokes screams from the audience that it belongs to the screen's most memorable thrillers.

Columbia had not only been astute in forming its television subsidiary, Screen Gems (q.v.), but had begun to distribute European films – not with any marked degree of success. There was no longer any doubt that Columbia was a major studio, but it could only continue to be so if there were enough leading film-makers to work for Harry Cohn. In 1953 he approached Jerry Wald, who had left Warners to form an independent company with Norman Krasna, its product to be released by R.K.O. Wald decided that on balance Cohn was preferable to Howard Hughes – especially as Cohn was to appoint him Vice-President in charge of production. After three unhappy years, Wald joined 20th Century-Fox – as did Buddy Adler,

who had been producing for Cohn since 1948. By the same token, Fred Kohlmar left that studio for Columbia in 1952 and was there when Cohn died in 1958. Between them, Wald and Kohlmar produced all the studio's memorable films at this time, with the exception of its most acclaimed and profitable film to date – *From Here to Eternity*. Adler was actually responsible for that, a fact which Cohn sought to minimise by adding his name to the publicity for the first time in the company's history.

The success of that film was followed by those of *On the Waterfront* and *The Caine Mutiny*, both produced independently within the organisation, demonstrating to Cohn the benefit of welcoming independent producers, and in that matter Columbia was second only to United Artists. But that was only for a brief period, since by the mid-Fifties it was clear that all the studios would have to follow their example.

Of the independent films, David E. Rose's **The End of the Affair** (1955) is yet another mangling of a novel by Graham Greene – as written for the screen by Lenore Coffee and directed by Edward Dmytryk. The piece is no longer about guilt, belief and several kinds of hatred, leaving only the skeleton – a tale of a woman (Deborah Kerr) who gives up her lover (Van Johnson) and his attempts to understand why. No less tolerable than Johnson are two British actors, Peter Cushing as the husband and John Mills as a detective. Belgravia is now the setting instead of that South London common – a loss almost too much to bear – and the atmosphere of wartime London is quite absent. The same is true of **The War Lover** (1963), produced by Arthur Hornblow. It was also filmed in Britain, but in this case with a British director, Philip Leacock. Its subject is American servicemen or, rather, one of them, a psychopathic airman, played by Steve McQueen with leers and smug grimaces. As with *Twelve O'Clock High* no interest is shown in placing these G.I.s in this alien setting, and it is difficult to learn whether John Hersey's novel had any point to make. Both films had been made because the originals had been much praised and popular, but have been so treated as to appeal to as many and offend as few as possible.

On the other hand, **The Strange One** (1957) retains the acrid qualities of the original novel, 'End As a Man', Calder Willingham's attack on military academies. Sam Spiegel produced – his only film between *On the Waterfront* and *The Bridge on the River Kwai* (q.v.). Book and film are different in plot, for Willingham's screenplay was based on a Broadway version as improvised by Actors' Studio personnel under the direction of Jack Garfein. He also made the film with the same actor, Ben Gazzara, as Jocko de Paris. Jocko is peculiar: where his fellow students wear track suits for such after lights-out activities as gambling, boozing and bullying, he disports himself in his cap, a Hawaiian shirt, black shorts, socks and garters and a long cigarette holder. He forces an egregious colleague on his girlfriend (Julie Wilson) and encourages a creepy young man with a crush on himself. These grown men touch each other and help each other to dress: in the book they were more obviously adolescent, which is why the film is the more disturbing. It falls apart at the end, with the kangaroo court, and it lacks depth. Gazzara, shiftily smiling in this film debut, remains its strongest feature. Seeing it again leaves unresolved the question why he never became an important movie star.

The Harder They Fall (1956) also offers an unflattering portrait of one aspect of American life: the fight game. In adapting his own novel, Budd Schulberg has harked back to his screenplay for *On the Waterfront* and allowed an exaggerated crusading attitude to overtake the action. Humphrey Bogart, in his last film, is the once-renowned columnist who succumbs to corruption until his integrity is restored. The boxing scenes are remarkable, as photographed by Burnett Guffey and directed by Mark Robson, who had made a somewhat better film on the same subject, *Champion*.

Wald was the producer, and it is to him that we also owe **The Eddy Duchin Story** (1956), which is romantic goulash, nicely photographed on New York locations by Harry Stradling. Tyrone Power is Duchin the pianist (his playing dubbed by Carmen Cavallero) and Kim Novak the first of his two wives. Sam Taylor's screenplay is dotted with the Statements that graced films at this time – for example,

'No one gets the big jackpot more than once' – and George Sidney directed. Sidney brings imagination and sympathy to **Jeanne Eagels** (1957), also an examination of one of the unfortunates of show business – but made in monochrome since *I'll Cry Tomorrow* had demonstrated that to be more suitable for alcoholism. Robert Planck's photography is always revealing and Daniel Fuchs's screenplay seems more accurate than in other cases (it provides a chance for Frank Borzage to play a Silent film director). Among Sidney's many borrowings is the ending from *Prix de Beauté* which, if inaccurate and sententious, is nevertheless pleasing in this context. He shows a genuine regard for Eagel's plight, while coaxing from Novak what is possibly her most acceptable film performance. Even so, she is less potent with speech than Eagels was when Silent; as her mentor and lover Jeff Chandler is more Yiddish than Italian and insufficiently volatile.

Sidney's forte at M-G-M had been musicals, but the two he made for Columbia are both betrayals of their Broadway originals – which is virtually criminal

Among the films of the Fifties which suggested a new order in Hollywood was *The Strange One*, which looked at life in a military school and didn't like what it saw. Here is Ben Gazzara, left, in the title role, with Paul E. Richards, taking advantage of the latter's crush on him.

in the case of **Pal Joey** (1957). When the original 1940 production had been dismissed as sordid by some critics, Hollywood had shown no interest until the 1952 revival not only rehabilitated it but reaffirmed its brilliance. Columbia, however, decided not to take advantage of the relaxations of the Production Code and removed what social comment there was, and the sexuality, reducing it to the tale of a heel and two ladies. Of Rodgers and Hart's dazzling score, gone are the daring, *intime* ballads ('What Is a Man?', 'Take Him', 'Our Little Den of Iniquity'), while the rousing songs written for the night-club production numbers have been relegated to background noise. There is no consolation to be gained from the four interpolated songs – only one of which is appropriate – and in any case we had heard Frank Sinatra sing them often before. Otherwise, cocky and brash, he goes some way to saving the day, not helped by Rita Hayworth as the older lady or Kim Novak as the younger one – and in that role her inadequacy quickly became legendary. **Bye Bye Birdie** (1963) also suffers from Ann-Margret, a cute, brash, ingenue, while Janet Leigh in a black wig is no more than likeable in the role in which Chita Rivera had been outstanding. The original had also had satirical points to make about show business and the hysteria surrounding pop singers (and in particular Elvis Presley's call-up): but it was now aimed at pleasing the very teenagers who were part of its original target; again the score has been savagely cut.

Kohlmar produced both films (returning to Columbia for the latter) and it was he who invited Joshua Logan to make **Picnic** (1955), as he had directed on stage. Logan's film experience was limited to one movie co-directed in 1938 and his work on *Mister Roberts*. In *Picnic* he tends to let his camera stand immobile while the players emote in the pretty mid-West locations. William Holden is too old and too withdrawn to play a light-fingered youth of braggart mentality, while Rosalind Russell is also miscast as a man-hungry spinster. The character she plays shares with Logan a penchant for bare chests, and her attempt to rip off Holden's clothes comes high on the list of risible movie moments. The film is over-pitched, though William Inge's small-town play was his most successful blend of Tennessee

Williams and Tchekhov. The ending is even changed for the film, allowing the heroine to follow Holden instead of relapsing into dull routine. She is Miss Novak, cherished in memory as she sways in tune to 'Moonglow' in a pink dress against a velvet night: actually she moves awkwardly and looks both bovine and heavily corseted.

For a brief period Novak became the glamorous star for whom Cohn had been searching since the defection of Rita Hayworth. His only other female star of note was Judy Holliday – and both ladies were rivals for Jack Lemmon in **Phffft!** (1954), a sex comedy commissioned from George Axelrod after his success with 'The Seven Year Itch'. Holliday and Lemmon are much too likeable to play Axelrod's heartless and smart-alecky people; but comparing the several situations similar to those in Cukor's Holliday films it is clear that Mark Robson is a lesser director.

At one time Richard Quine seemed to be Columbia's leading director. After a long apprenticeship with the company he made his mark on loan to Universal for **So This Is Paris** (1954), a blatant and charmless imitation of *On the Town*, with Tony Curtis and Gloria de Haven. Its vitality encouraged Cohn to entrust Quine with an expensive musical, **My Sister Eileen** (1955). When Miss Holliday twisted her ankle, Betty Garrett substituted; other M-G-M alumni were Janet Leigh (borrowed for the occasion), Tommy Rall and Robert (Bob) Fosse, who also did the choreography. The numbers accordingly have the spontaneity and sunniness of those of the best M-G-M musicals and, if they have much in common with the Broadway musical 'Wonderful Town', that is because both pieces have the same source, Ruth McKenney's *New Yorker* stories about her sister Eileen (who was married to Nathaniel West and died with him in a car crash). Columbia owned the film rights to those stories and the play based on them, but Cohn was too mean to buy Leonard Bernstein's score for 'Wonderful Town'. He commissioned a new one from Jules Styne and Leo Robin, which did nothing to ensure the success of the film. Nevertheless, it is one of the best of musicals, and if it has only one premise – everyone's preference for Eileen over Ruth – Miss Garrett's way with a self-deprecatory line makes it always funny. 'Wonderful Town' remains unfilmed, and Betty Garrett's touching and often whacky talent was not seen again in a major movie because the industry looked charily at a lady married to Larry Parks, who was found by the House UnAmerican Activities Committee to have been a Communist.

Quine did direct Miss Holliday in **The Solid Gold Cadillac** (1956) and **Full of Life** (1957), both of which re-established her as a working-class American. At least in comedy, few screen heroines since Jean Arthur had actually been seen working: Miss Holliday in *The Solid Gold Cadillac* does work hard, but only after making a nuisance of herself in the boardroom. In adapting the play by George S. Kaufman and Howard Teichmann, Abe Burrows has changed the role from that of an old lady to a young one. Presumably we owe the view to all three writers that those who run large corporations are mainly concerned with making their piles and saving their skins. The film is often extraordinarily funny as Holliday bests the board with that blend of daffiness and singleness of purpose which was her movie stock in trade. As her chief opponents, John Williams and Fred Clark are joyous, though Williams's discomfiture is less rewarding than Clark's explosions of unsurprised disgust; Paul Douglas is the one honest board member. In *Full of Life*, Holliday is a pregnant wife – and pregnancy was a new subject for Hollywood comedy. With Richard Conte coping with her and his idiosyncratic father (Salvatore Baccaloni) the film tries to be original but is only sentimental.

Quine's reputation for handling this genre increased with a fast-paced army comedy, **Operation Madball** (1957), but promptly went in the other direction with **Bell, Book and Candle** (1958). The former pits Jack Lemmon, as the wiliest soldier ever, against the egomaniac and cunning captain of Ernie Kovacs; the latter film wastes Lemmon and gives Kovacs only brief footage as a world-weary alcoholic author. On the stage, John Van Druten's play about some modern witches had had charm and stylish playing by Rex Harrison and Lilli Palmer: any funny lines it had are not retained in Daniel Taradash's screenplay, which Quine has foolishly treated as a Manhattan love story in the manner of *The Eddy Duchin Story*.

Whatever allure or talent Miss Novak had shown in her earlier films had already gone, and James Stewart is miscast in Harrison's role.

There was a return to form with **It Happened to Jane** (1959), in which a businesswoman widow eventually routs a greedy tycoon (Kovacs). Since the community finally joins together to help the heroine – and the shenanigans concern a train – we may be reminded of Ealing comedy. We certainly think of Capra, though Norman Katkov's script is more obviously an amalgam of *It Should Happen to You* and *The Solid Gold Cadillac*. Judy Holliday was appearing on Broadway and so the heroine is played, incisively, by Doris Day. Lemmon is, again, the exasperated beau, and Kovacs's mean, satisfying villain emphasises Columbia's superiority in comic talents at this time. Quine's imaginative direction and the green Maine settings are also assets, but the public was not interested – even though it was to flock to the inferior Thirties-style comedies (q.v.) which Day was to make for Universal.

Quine's decline was quick, and it began with his first serious picture (there had been some programmers earlier), **Strangers When We Meet** (1960), in which Novak and Kirk Douglas inexpressively portray adulterous suburbanites. His excuse is that his wife (Barbara Rush) takes no interest in his work; hers is that her husband fails to react when she sends the kids away for the night and pushes down her blouse to reveal her bra. An effort seems to have been made to treat the subject in the frank manner of *Brief Encounter*, but Evan Hunter's script, from his own novel, is cliché-ridden. Tedium is averted by Kovacs as a writer in a perpetual state of nerves and by Walter Matthau as a malicious, lecherous neighbour.

We have already looked at Quine's *Sex and the Single Girl* and *Paris When It Sizzles*. **The Notorious Landlady** (1962) is equally disappointing, but **How to Murder Your Wife** (1965) is a partial return to form. Both are black comedies with Jack Lemmon, the former concerning American diplomats in a Hollywood England; the presence of Fred Astaire and his 'A Foggy Day' on the soundtrack hardly compensate for Miss Novak in the title-role. *How to Murder Your Wife* also has a weak leading lady – Virna Lisi – but the first hour, at least, is a good George Axelrod jape about a confirmed bachelor (Lemmon) who marries when drunk and regrets it. Axelrod produced (for U.A.), and it is possible that he curbed Quine's style, by now strident and limp – for this is the only one of his later films to recapture any of his early fluidity.

After Cohn died, Columbia did not invite Judy Holliday to make the last film of her contract (she was, incidentally, one of the few people with a genuine regard for him). She herself resented Hollywood's neglect at this time, feeling, quite rightly, that she was a better comedienne than Doris Day. Ironically, therefore, Columbia was imitating Day's Universal sex comedies with **Under the Yum Yum Tree** (1963) and **Good Neighbour Sam** (1964), both with Lemmon and directed by David Swift, from television (to which he soon returned). The first is particularly distasteful, since Lemmon is both lecher and voyeur; the second at least has a genuine comic idea – of a girl (Romy Schneider) who borrows another woman's husband (Lemmon) in order to inherit a fortune. One would wish for more asperity and less reliance on supposedly amusing decor and the beds – unlike earlier films, there is no doubt what these are for. Lemmon single-handedly tries to salvage both films. Best cast as a reasonable man in desperate circumstances, he often goes to the limit of his resources in order not to disappoint. If he were not the best light comedian we have, he would still be exceptional.

Divorce, American Style (1967), like the concurrent *A Guide for the Married Man,* took advantage of the relaxation of the Code while trying to be honest about the modern American ménage, consuming too many Martinis amidst too much gadgetry. Divorce lawyers and marriage counsellors wait to pounce; a colleague takes the husband to a call girl, and every Sunday there is confusion as to which kids have to be sent to their other mummies and daddies. Alimony is the name of the game. Debbie Reynolds and Dick Van Dyke play the divorcing couple and, under his Ivy League glow and her doll-like smile, they would seem to be fairly nasty people. With the exception of Jean Simmons, as the other woman, few of the principals have

charm, which may be one reason why the film is only mildly amusing – and therefore only a half-success for its writer, Norman Lear, and its director, Bud Yorkin. It is better than the other films made by this team, who were to make their reputations with some popular 'social' comedies on television.

Cat Ballou (1965) is one of the very few successful comedy Westerns and an isolated achievement for its director, Elliott Silverstein. He sometimes forces the pace and if Lee Marvin deserved his Best Actor Oscar for his double-act – the shambling dipso Kid Shelleen and steel-nosed gunman Strawn – he gets a close-up too many. Jane Fonda, returning from her European sojourn, is really the best of it, a round-eyed Alice in Wonderland, enjoying every moment of the derring-do. Her schoolteacher heroine has an eager naïvety which enables her to upset the Code of the West; and there is the double-act of the young outlaws (Michael Callan, Dwayne Hickman), cowards and college boys, who go from each other's arms to hers.

Among Westerns, **3.10 to Yuma** (1957) starts from *High Noon*, the point being not whether the killers will get off the train but whether this one (Glenn Ford) will get on it. The excellent screenplay is by Halsted Welles and the splendid black and white photography by Charles Lawton Jr. The film is directed, self-consciously but without frills, by Delmer Daves, who returned to his customary standard with **Cowboy** (1958). This is based on Frank Harris's 'Reminiscences of a Cowboy' and, since these were mainly apocryphal, they were a curious source for a film attempting a more authentic picture of the West than was usual. The book was foolishly adhered to, so that the film has no narrative drive. Jack Lemmon is likeable as Harris, but Glenn Ford lacks the necessary force as a drunken cattle-driver. Again, Lawton's (colour) photography is an asset, and the film, while not a critical success like *3.10 to Yuma,* brought Daves some prestige. After more than two decades in Hollywood, the success of these Westerns enabled him to become producer as well as writer and director; he then proceeded to make some overblown romantic dramas.

Among adventure tales, Columbia offered several films produced by Charles H. Schneer, who specialises in fantasy.

The credit for them rightly belongs to his special-effects man, Ray Harryhausen (b. 1920), who had been fascinated by *King Kong* as a boy and later worked with Willis O'Brien on *Mighty Joe Young*. Harryhausen's partnership with Schneer began in 1952 with *It Came from Beneath the Sea,* and their work includes many other equally unpromising titles. Mainly disregarded by the press and often with second-string players and directors, their films remain in the repertory as useful items for children's matinees. The acting is invariably wooden, the dialogue fustian, the situations closer to comic strips than their sources suggest, yet Harryhausen creates magic. Sometimes one can see the strings; not all his effects work well: but he cares not only for the cinema's capacity for fantasy but also for the mysteries that existed for the ancients. In filming Swift, Jules Verne, the Greek myths and the Arabian Nights he sends his heroes on sea voyages, to unknown islands where strange creatures lurk. He likes sails and decks, deep waters, awesome landscapes and, above all, monsters – who arrive at regular intervals. The Swift tale is **The Three Worlds of Gulliver** (1960), directed by Jack Sher, and the Verne **Mysterious Island** (1961), which is somewhat better: the director is Cy Endfield, blacklisted in Hollywood ten years earlier and whose first subsequent credit this was. He had been living in Britain, which became the headquarters for Schneer and Harryhausen, because of its proximity to Europe and lower costs. Among the dozen Harryhausen films to be enjoyed are **The Golden Voyage of Sinbad** (1973), directed by Gordon Hessler, and **Jason and the Argonauts** (1963), directed by Don Chaffey. The latter film began Harryhausen's collaboration with the British writer, Beverly Cross. Cross is married to Maggie Smith – who with the equally illustrious Claire Bloom and Laurence Olivier played Olympians in **Clash of the Titans** (1981), directed by Desmond Davis. Obviously this was no low-budget production: it was several years in the making, and in fact handled by M-G-M. The conception of Olympus is the usual one, of swirling mists and columns, and some effects, e.g. the Gorgon's head, are not as frightening as they could be. But there are some superb ingredients, such as the destruction of Argos, Perseus (Harry Hamlin) on the back of Pegasus, and the Kraken rising from the sea. If we regard *Superman* (q.v.) as filmed comic-strip we can claim *Clash of the Titans* as the best cinema fantasy since Korda's *The Thief of Bagdad*.

A less respectable but equally enjoyable action tale is **Diamond Head** (1963), a cross between *Aloma of the South Seas* and a Deep South novelette. Set in Hawaii, it concerns a white girl (Yvette Mimieux) whose love for a native boy (James Darren) arouses the wrath of her proud, land-owning brother (Charlton Heston). Watching it, I was reminded of the minotaur's head which used to betoken opinions in the film reviews of *L'Ecran Français*, his expressions going from sheer joy to abject depression: he had one of surprised glee, which he would surely have used for this film, as the clichés mount without pausing for breath. The director was Guy Green, who was handed many more such banalities in **A Walk in the Spring Rain** (1970). In the words of Stirling Silliphant, who provided them, they were aiming for a new version of *Brief Encounter*, as Anthony Quinn, a middle-aged Zorba, pursues a still-radiant Ingrid Bergman. 'There's a lot of woman left in ya,' he exclaims when she protests that she is a grandmother. And he says quite seriously, 'A man's gotta do what a man's gotta do' when accused of adultery.

Middle-aged passion is also the theme of **Middle of the Night** (1959), as a garment manufacturer (Fredric March) becomes involved with a young employee (Kim Novak). Paddy Chayevsky wrote it, from his own long-running Broadway play and, as with *Marty* and *The Bachelor Party,* the director is Delbert Mann. Apart from these three films little of Mann's work is impressive, though as the writer-director Paul Schrader (q.v.) has pointed out the distinctive style of Chayevsky's films was contributed by Chayevsky.★ The authenticity of the working-class dialogue is matched by the settings, but the final effect is as wintry as the bare trees frequently on view. Despite a tagged-on happy ending, a vein of pessimism runs through the piece, not least in the often moving performance of Mr March, which Chayevsky himself preferred to the more warm-hearted one

★The only other recent writer of such 'strength', said Schrader, was Neil Simon (q.v.).

given on Broadway by Edward G. Robinson. To acquire the rights, Columbia had been compelled to make **The Goddess** (1958), based on an original screenplay by Chayevsky, who insisted that John Cromwell direct (Cromwell had returned to Broadway after being blacklisted in 1951). When both films failed, Hollywood rejected Chayevsky's work for years – and it loathed *The Goddess* to start with, for it is about a girl (Kim Stanley) who becomes a star by sleeping with producers. She uses her body and anyone who happens to be handy, developing a protective shell that leaves her devoid of feeling. Eventually she is alone and alcoholic, having alienated everyone except her protective and probably lesbian secretary. The film is verbose and as unfeeling as its central character. Chayevsky labours too hard at the iniquities of ambition, corruption and self-destruction to permit a glimpse into the Hollywood system, thereby ending merely with a thesis. Miss Stanley is a Kim of a different hue from Miss Novak, going through every emotion, except love, that can be asked of an actress. She suggests, as few contemporaries did, an interesting woman – though one not much like Marilyn Monroe, Chayevsky's supposed model: certainly he used his knowledge of her, and of other stars who destroyed their careers – though Joan Crawford would seem the most likely candidate.

The question of source also arises at Universal-International, since the title of **The Great Man** (1956) refers to 'America's most beloved humorist'. As in *Citizen Kane,* the film is a quest for the true nature of someone whose name had been a household word: he did not say 'rosebud' as he died, but the sort of word then only found on lavatory walls. His vices were the usual ones – he is greedy and grasping and drives his wife to drink. The sharply idiomatic script is by Al Morgan, who wrote the original novel, and José Ferrer, who directed unimaginatively except in finding close-ups of his star – who is also himself. He plays a television reporter planning a tribute to the dead man, with a last-reel change of heart, so that he tells the truth – which so impresses the sponsors that, without a trace of irony, he becomes the dead man's successor. It is an ending which contradicts everything we know about the

television industry, and it is a pity the film never has the courage to dissect media popularity. An excellent cast includes Ed Wynn, superb as the man who gave the great man his start, his son Keenan, Jim Backus and Dean Jagger. When Julie London mimes to her own record the film offers the quintessential feeling of the time – hard, gritty, the blues, not too bright.

This was virtually Universal's only serious film in more than a decade, and because it failed at the box office the company reverted to its policy of bland programmers. **The Man of a Thousand Faces** (1957) may be an exception, since it is a biography of Lon Chaney with James Cagney – Hollywood legend as Hollywood legend. This is an improvement on other sunshine-and-showers screen biographies, for it is reasonably accurate – except in suggesting that Chaney's sole motivation in life was frustrated father-love; but the direction by Joseph Pevney is rather heavy.

Among the few other large-budgeted films at Universal were those with James Stewart, all of which are Westerns except for the popular *The Glen Miller Story.* They and it were directed by Anthony Mann, and the Westerns at least show his fine visual sense. However, except for the first of them, *Winchester '73* (1950), the incidents are both ordinary and handled in similar fashion.

The producer Ross Hunter and the German-born director Douglas Sirk first worked together on two pleasing period films with stars no longer shining as brightly as they once did. **Take Me to Town** (1953) is a Technicolor musical with Ann Sheridan as a saloon singer of questionable virtue, and **All I Desire** (1953) shows what happens when a vaudeville star (Barbara Stanwyck) returns to the family she deserted years before. Then the still popular Jane Wyman, under contract for one film, insisted that it be a remake of **Magnificent Obsession** (1954). Sirk, unable to get through the original novel, asked for a treatment based on Stahl's film version, and he found 'a combination of kitsch and craziness and trashiness'. But, working with that in mind and without Stahl's lightness of touch, his film is not to be mentioned in the same breath. Rock Hudson is less bumptious than was Robert Taylor; the sympathetic Miss Wyman smiles too much, but that is part of the Hunter-Sirk approach. The locations, the colour, the fashions, the furnishings, the emotions are 'beautiful' – but plastic-wrapped, as attractive as sandwiches in an airport lounge. The film's success – it cost $800,000 and the gross profit was more than $12 million – encouraged Hunter and Sirk to continue making slushy soap operas. Audiences often laughed at them, and they still do.

Written on the Wind (1956) is about a playboy (Robert Stack) and his nympho-maniac sister (Dorothy Malone), both drunks, and their involvement with their surrogate brother (Rock Hudson) and a smart New Yorker (Lauren Bacall). The background of the Texas oil-fields clearly interested Sirk less than the two small towns of his first films with Hunter, and the piece is flat, slick and characterless, but not badly made. Sirk himself has observed that he is bewildered by the cult following these films have; asked about that, Miss Bacall observed that on the set he was uninventive in staging and unhelpful when the players demanded less unspeakable dialogue.

As public taste for Hunter's tearjerkers declined – there were several with Lana Turner – he found a new formula when a comedy with Doris Day and Rock Hudson, **Pillow Talk** (1959), proved extremely popular. As directed by Michael Gordon, it was an attempt to return to an earlier period of comedy; in it, and those that followed, Miss Day went to bat for her virginity, always in luxurious settings. The art of seduction had been bowdlerised but not banished during the enforcement of the Production Code: that it could return to movies, in terms of basic farce, had much to do with the magazine *Playboy*. These films are only too much like *Playboy*'s leering yet sanitised view of sex (as it was then), with orgasm promised more often than achieved. They offer candy-floss salaciousness instead of wit. Sex in *The Apartment* had been touching, cruel, desperate and funny, but the only despera-tion here is in the jokes – at rock-bottom level in **The Thrill of It All** (1963), when the ageing maid (Zasu Pitts) screams 'Rape' on seeing her kindly master (James Garner) in the doorway of her bedroom. An exception is the experienced Cary Grant in **That Touch of Mink** (1962),

directed by Delbert Mann (and the film is the antithesis of *Marty*, which made his reputation). Hudson is no more adept than Garner, but they are more interesting than Miss Day, whose natural charm gets lost in an artificial welter of hairdos and chic clothes to match the decor. As she con-tinued to remain *virgo intacta* comment became derisive – poetic justice since the films raked in as figures of fun anyone who might ever have had a sexual thought. The writers ape the *Playboy* cartoonists, some-times aspiring to Peter Arno, with no talent other than to exploit the new per-missiveness. They underline the deterio-ration in American comedy when it was uprooted from New York and Chicago to settle in Californian comfort.

We have already looked at other com-edies influenced by these. Universal made several with heroines other than Miss Day, and she, when advised by her manager-husband, moved to other studios to make similar movies. Ross Hunter, after two decades of popular films, had become one of the most powerful producers in the industry; yet when, in 1972, he elected to move to Columbia to make a musical ver-sion of *Lost Horizon* it was a flop of such proportions that – with absolutely no critical reputation to save him – he lost his position overnight and retreated into television.

It Came from Outer Space (1953) and **The Incredible Shrinking Man** (1957) are among Universal's more enduring films, both medium-budget science-fiction tales directed by Jack Arnold. His work does not, here or elsewhere, suggest more than journeyman talent. The first is adapted from a novel by Ray Bradbury, and the second was written by Richard Matheson – an eerie idea about a man who, caught in a radioactive cloud, contracts to the point where he battles spiders with pins and is thought by his family to have been eaten by the cat. Both films would have benefited from bigger budgets (an expen-sive 1981 revamp, *The Incredible Shrinking Woman*, with Lily Tomlin, was disastrous-ly received), since such tales depend on their special effects. But at least the amor-phous one-eyed monsters in *It Came from Outer Space* are imaginatively conceived – and the film itself gained from being orig-inally made and released in 3-D. If it looks somewhat primitive that is because

929

Kubrick revitalised the genre with *2001: a Space Odyssey* (q.v.). The idea of 'them' taking over 'our' bodies was also used with variations in *Invasion of the Body Snatchers* (q.v.) – and it could be said that *Close Encounters of the Third Kind* (q.v.) is a loose remake of *It Came from Outer Space*. We are told that the bright young directors of the present day prefer to make the sort of films they enjoyed when they were growing up – and of course *It Came from Outer Space* is so much easier to improve upon than *All About Eve*.

In time, Universal's executives gave thought to the films the studio was turning out. With the growth of television the market for their anodyne entertainments (few of them, incidentally, shown to the press in Britain) was decreasing, and in 1958 a loss was announced of $2 million. The annual output of approximately thirty-six features was halved in 1959, and overtures were made to artists with their own production units who might contribute box-office films – most notably with Kirk Douglas and *Spartacus* (q.v.). In February 1959 the plant was sold to the Music Corporation of America for $11,250,000, with the right to rent back facilities for future production. M.C.A., once a talent agency, needed space for its T.V. subsidiary, Revue Productions but, when in 1962 it acquired Universal itself, it was forced by government decree to dispose of its agency. In fact, Decca had by that time become virtual owner of Universal, and it was the record business which interested M.C.A. Yet during the intervening three years the film company prospered mightily for the first time since the heyday of Deanna Durbin and Abbott and Costello. The reason again was comedy, especially Miss Day's. Lopping off the second half of the name Universal-International, the company embarked on a carefully-planned programme – few films of which are actually memorable.

One is **Lonely Are the Brave** (1962), an 'art' Western venture which more than half succeeds as directed by the usually undistinguished David Miller. Dalton Trumbo wrote it on the thesis that the world of freeways, jeeps and helicopters has little use for cowboys, as exemplified by one (Kirk Douglas) who is mistreated by the society that is served by them. The film's earnestness is endearing and not, as

is usual in such cases, tiresome, but when Douglas gets holed up in the mountains in the manner of Bogart in *High Sierra* he has better reason for being there and is more genuinely one of society's outsiders.

Like most of the leading stars of this era, Douglas had a hand in the production, as did Gregory Peck with **Cape Fear** (1962). Peck had recently worked with the director, J. Lee Thompson, on *The Guns of Navarone* (q.v.), perhaps the biggest success of both their careers, and he had also worked several times with both the producer, Sy Bartlett, and the screen writer, James R. Webb. It could be said that he selected talents on his own level, except that his co-star is Robert Mitchum – and any sensitive person would be rooting for Mitchum's mean villain rather than Peck's noble hero. The villain has sworn vengeance on Peck, a lawyer, by planning the rape of his wife and daughter. Thus an old-fashioned thriller takes advantage of the new permissiveness, its essential sleaziness not offset by a comment or so on the sanctity of the home. Rape is also threatened in **The Night of the Following Day** (1969), since one of the kidnappers (Richard Boone) fancies the English teenager (Pamela Franklin) whom they have locked up in a house on the dunes near Le Touquet. Other kidnappers include a blond, black-garbed Marlon Brando and a jittery, drug-addicted Rita Moreno. The director is Hubert Cornfield, who wrote the screenplay with Robert Phippeny, from a novel by Lionel White, and it is easy to see why he has not been more prolific – for he constantly misuses the camera. But his enjoyment of his setting makes this a thriller unlike any other. (The T.V. version shows even more of France, as this is one of the films which Universal padded to eke out its length: irrelevant detail, obviously filmed later, adds twenty minutes to the original running-time, while at the same time cuts have been made affecting Moreno's addiction and her relationship with Brando.)

Airport (1970), one of Ross Hunter's last productions for the company, was adapted from a cross-section novel by Arthur Hailey. The most fastidious of filmgoers may enjoy its organisation and its use of the artefacts of aviation to provide the excitement. That is presented in an assured and unpretentious manner, but the credited director, George Seaton, who wrote the script, fell ill and most of the film was directed by Henry Hathaway who, out of friendship for him, refused both billing and salary. Its popularity ensured a sequel, **Airport 1975** (1974), with Jack Smight directing and Charlton Heston succeeding Burt Lancaster at the controls. Jack Lemmon took over – the most thankless task of his career – in **Airport '77** (1977), and his passengers were the usual ageing stars and semi-names, cast on the assumption that familiarity with them will ensure our anxiety that they conclude their fraught journeys. The plot this time is borrowed from another 'disaster' movie, *The Poseidon Adventure*, with the unfortunate aircraft, a 747, lying on the ocean bed. It is a marvellous example of Hollywood knowhow – a thin, impersonal, wholly manufactured film, but providing a frisson or so that you will not find in, say, *Providence*.

Like Universal, United Artists prospered during this time. Mary Pickford and Chaplin had sold the company to a law firm representing an Eastern circuit of cinemas, and two lawyers with experience of the industry were put in charge, Robert S. Benjamin and Arthur Krim. They were assured of 50 per cent control if they could turn a profit in their first year – 1952–3 – and they took full control five years later, with an executive team which remained basically the same till they were ousted in 1978. Under their leadership United Artists, in my opinion, succeeded 20th Century-Fox as the company making the most interesting pictures; but it would be unwise to assume that Benjamin or Krim were creative managers, since for a long while they merely encouraged acknowledged talents to work for them. United Artists had always functioned that way, but after a decade of successfully choosing films for the company to distribute, and successfully counselling the producers of those films, Benjamin and Krim – or their team – began to initiate productions themselves.

For the first few years of the Krim-Benjamin regime United Artists continued to release low-budget films – with the exception of *Moulin Rouge* and some British movies. With *The Moon Is Blue* Otto Preminger began to supply the company with popular films, but the decisive

factor in U.A.'s rise to affluence was Burt Lancaster. With his partners, Harold Hecht and James Hill, he produced a number of money-making movies starring himself, including *Vera Cruz* and *Trapeze* (q.v.). The Hecht, Hill and Lancaster company also produced *Marty* and *The Bachelor Party* – the achievement of which is all the more striking when compared to **Separate Tables** (1958), also directed by Delbert Mann. If the two Chayevsky films were renowned for their honesty, this is as false as its Hollywood-constructed English resort hotel. Terence Rattigan's two one-act plays, a success in London and New York, have been dovetailed, and the material, thin to start with, loses theatrical contrivance with no consequent gain; and what had been a star turn for Eric Portman and Margaret Leighton, in two roles each, becomes – unlike Mann's earlier films – a star vehicle (for four stars). Burt Lancaster and Rita Hayworth (who was married to Hill, her fifth husband) are poor, and unlikely Americans to be in this particular hotel; Deborah Kerr is more successful as the plain and nervous spinster, but David Niven's performance is a mere shadow of Portman's. His Oscar for Best Actor was presumably due to the fact that he allowed himself to be cast unflatteringly, as a bogus major who molests women in cinemas; thus one more curious aspect of human behaviour was accepted into films with the help of an acclaimed Broadway play.

In this respect 1956–8 marked the watershed – with *Baby Doll, The Great Man, Lust for Life, Edge of the City* (q.v.), *Twelve Angry Men* (q.v.), *Fear Strikes Out, The Young Stranger* (q.v.), *Love in the Afternoon, The Strange One, Full of Life, A Hatful of Rain, A Face in the Crowd* and *Paths of Glory* (q.v.). Not all of them are good films and some of them are more superficial and immature than their makers thought they were: but the least of them is to be preferred to any *Magnificent Obsession*, since they are trying to say something about the human condition without the aid of film starriness or beautiful settings – or, for that matter, any of the traditional glamour of the American film. The statements made were not always new, but they had not been allowed in films since the immediate pre-Code days, when they had been expounded with the same gritty realism.

Hecht, Hill and Lancaster's **Sweet**

Tony Curtis and Burt Lancaster in what is probably the best film either . made, *Sweet Smell of Success*, about the power of a gossip columnist. It made few Ten Best lists in the U.S., since columnist Walter Winchell remained powerful – and Lancaster's glasses were of course an allusion to Winchell's trademark. In the film he is sanctimonious, self-righteous, vindictive, petty and cynical, while Curtis's press agent is cringing and fawning, with just enough gut-sense to keep going.

Smell of Success (1957) is redolent of several Warner Bros. movies of that era, with its central character, a Broadway columnist, fixated on his sister – though that also provides a narrative thread, as he attempts to destroy the young man in love with her. As played by Lancaster, the journalist is modelled on Walter Winchell and recognisably so, which was only possible because Winchell's power was lessening – as, on the evidence of this film, it deserved to. It reveals a world without virtue: with everyone motivated by self-interest, corruption is rampant in night clubs and newspaper offices. The press agent (Tony Curtis) is sleazy, opportunistic and sycophantic, with no qualms about pandering his girlfriend to a client in his drive for success. The script by Ernest Lehman and Clifford Odets, from the former's novella, has contrivance but also sour, brilliant dialogue, and the British director Alexander Mackendrick took to night-time New York with assurance.

Mackendrick was expected to have a brilliant Hollywood career, but after starting **The Devil's Disciple** (1959) for Hecht, Hill and Lancaster he was replaced by Guy Hamilton. One of the virtues of *Sweet Smell of Success* was its refusal to allow Lancaster to be in the centre of the screen, but Hamilton apparently flinched at the prospect of directing his producer, for he does not seem to have done anything at all. Lancaster as Pastor Anderson and Kirk Douglas as Dick Dudgeon appear to be having a ball, perhaps because they had relegated to third billing and a supporting role an actor generally regarded as far superior – Laurence Olivier.★ Since Janette Scott is inept as Mrs Anderson it is left to him to save the day, which he does – at his most stylish and authoritative as General Burgoyne. As this role has become slightly more important, few would complain that the play has been altered – and the film, admittedly made in Britain, is a vast improvement on the two previous American attempts to film Shaw.

Douglas's own company had a rousing and unexpected success with **The Vikings** (1958), a synthesis of the Sagas as given to children to read, half Eddas and half Li'l Abner. Portents appear in the sky (the daughters of Odin ride across the moon), men are thrown to the wolves, and the returning warriors dance on the oars as their ship comes to harbour in the fjords.

★Olivier had walked out of *Separate Tables* after Lancaster had tried to tell him how to play the role.

ome critics complained about the vio-
ence, surely more acceptable on this occa-
ion than on some others; one could com-
lain with more justice about the heavy
American accents of Douglas, Ernest
Borgnine, Tony Curtis and Janet Leigh.
However, the director Richard Fleischer
eeps their performances trim, and his
riumph is shared by Jack Cardiff, whose
hotography emphasises the marine aspect
f Viking life.

United Artists also benefited from the
ilms produced by the Mirisch Company,
or Walter Mirisch chose U.A. to handle
is movies after Allied Artists – of which
e had been executive producer – folded in
957. Mirisch's most successful films for
Jnited Artists included several directed
y Billy Wilder, including *Some Like It
Hot,* and *West Side Story.* Also deservedly
opular were two adventure films,
The Magnificent Seven (1960) and **The
Great Escape** (1963), admirably directed
y John Sturges. The former transfers the
lot of *Seven Samurai* to Mexico, but
vhereas in Kurosawa's film the seven were
leadbeats down on their luck, here they
re professional gunmen thirsty for adven-
ure. Yul Brynner is the leader of a likeable
unch, including Steve McQueen, James
Coburn and Charles Bronson. These three
ctors were reunited in the other film,
mong the British and Canadian P.O.W.s
letermined to tunnel their way out of the
amp.

The Broadway producer Paul Gregory,
fter working with Charles Laughton on
he stage, went to Hollywood to make
The Night of the Hunter (1955), which
Laughton directed (his only film in that
apacity) and wrote, with James Agee,
rom Davis Grubb's novel. With the eagerness of novices they have loaded it with
ymbols and allusions, evoking the world
of children's horrors. It is not coinci-
lental that it is set during the Depression
- West Virginia in 1930 – a land devastated
oy poverty and where terror stalks in the
person of a preacherman (Robert Mitchum), who is prepared to kill two small
children for some treasure he thinks they
have (he has already married and murdered
heir mother, played by Shelley Winters).
The river setting and the dead-drunk
Uncle Birdie are from Mark Twain;
the children begging for food are from
Dickens, as is the spinster (Lillian Gish)

who takes them in; the children's song
is pure 'Silly Symphony' and there are
touches of the Bible, Grimm, Andersen
and Aesop. The film has images as clumsy
as they are striking, but it is also unique,
an idiosyncratic mixture of black comedy
and social comment; it was poorly received at the time, but its quality was
soon to be recognised.

The director Alexander Singer had an
isolated success with **A Cold Wind in
August** (1961). Partly due to the exigencies of the star system, there were many
movies about ageing men in love with
younger women, but this one and *The
Stripper* (q.v.) were virtually the only
ones made in America in which an older
woman is the predator.★ She (Lola
Albright) is a stripper and he (Scott Marlowe) the janitor's boy, who leaves her as
lonely as she was when he eventually returns to his own generation. The script
has its weaknesses, but Singer's handling
is so fresh – especially in two 'idyllic'
sequences, in which he turns the mood to
laughter – that several reviewers suggested
that the American cinema might have a
New Wave of its own.

Another one-of-a-kind film is **Lonely-
hearts** (1959) and in this case it is just as
well. Nathaniel West's story, like the
better-known 'The Day of the Locust', is
about the destruction of souls, but the
producer-writer Dore Schary apparently
felt the need to step in and save them – so
that it is no surprise to find the film ending
with the hero about to begin a new life (in
the novel his death is a *coup de grâce*).
Vincent J. Donahue, a Broadway director
– who never made another film – manages
for the first half hour to convey some of the
hatred expressed in the original; as the
Shrikes, Myrna Loy and Robert Ryan convey their mutual hostility well, while
Maureen Stapleton is superb as the woman
who paves the way for the hero's ruin. He
is the gossip-columnist of the title, played
by Montgomery Clift with unaccustomed
exuberance, easily encompassing the problems of a man hanging on for a while
with the hope of booze and sex. His sharp
girlfriend (Dolores Hart) has been turned
into a Florence Nightingale, and since,
by the halfway mark, West's situations
have been rendered conventional, the film

★*The Graduate* (q.v.) is about sex, not love.

933

deserved its failure, adding yet another significant figure to the many mishandled by film-makers unequal to the task.

United Artists seemed chary of comedy, but Bob Hope found a niche there for two films, reunited with old colleagues from Paramount – Norman Panama and Melvin Frank (as writers, with Frank directing) and with Lucille Ball, in **The Facts of Life** (1961), which somewhat surprisingly catches both the charm and amiability of the comedies that he made at the start of his career. Its splendid notion is that a married man and a married woman set out to commit adultery but are plagued by difficulties at every turn. Panama and Frank also wrote, and Panama directed, **The Road to Hong Kong** (1962) which, if not as lackadaisical as *Road to Bali,* is still to be recommended only to the most fervent admirers of Hope and Crosby, at their best with the guest appearance of Dorothy Lamour, elsewhere replaced by an ineffectual Joan Collins as the girl they scrap over. Budget-consciousness seems to have been the

reason for making it in Britain and in black and white. Panama and Frank did not work again as a team, but each has a subsequent credit on a film for which the other was mainly responsible. Frank produced and directed **Buona Sera, Mrs Campbell** (1968), which has some good ideas, including the plot, about an Italian woman (Gina Lollobrigida) who has been receiving paternity cheques for the same child from three ex-G.I.s (Peter Lawford, Phil Silvers, Telly Savalas) – now returning to the scene of the conception. Since Lollobrigida had sabotaged Frank's *Strange Bedfellows* each time she had had a funny line we must wonder why he cast her. It is also unclear whether she is meant to be as unsympathetic as she is. The same is true of the tense and viperish Glenda Jackson in **A Touch of Class** (1975). She plays a British divorcee involved in an adulterous affair with an American (a manic George Segal) living in London: this is both a reworking of *The Facts of Life,* as nothing goes quite right, and an affectionate spoof of *Brief Encounter* (which the couple are found watching at one point). Frank advances from both those films by showing the couple actually fornicating (which provides a joke, since the man's back gives out at the first thrust), but the film is nevertheless schmaltzy and lacking in point.

While Frank persevered, with an occasional big success, George Axelrod made only *The Secret Life of an American Wife* after directing a failure, **Lord Love a Duck** (1966) – his first film in that capacity. He wrote it with Larry H. Johnson, from a novel by Al Hine. It is close to his own novel, 'Where Am I Now that I Need Me?', in its execration of almost every facet of contemporary American society – where all values are surrendered to youth, beauty, gadgetry, fame, success or wealth. The progress of Barbara Ann (Tuesday Weld) towards movie stardom is helped by a genie (Roddy McDowall), and perhaps it is the whimsy which alienated audiences: but Axelrod's satiric potshots, sometimes jaded in his book, are always well-aimed.

It may be that cinema audiences did not care for satire at this time, for **How to Succeed in Business Without Really Trying** (1967) signally failed to repeat its success on the stage. Based on Shepherd Mead's Christmas-gift 'funny' book, it is not satire of a high order, as David Swift,

Among filmed Broadway musicals *How to Succeed in Business Without Really Trying* holds a high place, being so invigorating that its theatricality did not matter. Here, singing a love song to himself, is Robert Morse, making his way to the top: it is uncertain whether he is funnier in glee at his success or in abject repentance when one of his tactics is exposed.

directing, realised. His comic-strip style works better here than in his previous films, and this is one instance in which a Broadway musical, preserved and encapsulated, is invigorating on the screen. Its virtues are those of the original, and chief among them are Frank Loesser's witty score and lyrics and Robert Morse, as the little guy who will literally stop at nothing to get to the top. Looking like a cross between the cover-boy of *Mad Magazine* and a benighted cherub, he has an armoury of glances, falsely humble towards his superiors and gleeful towards us, letting us share his double-dealing. His diminutive stature allows him to fawn on the executives in puppy fashion, in contrast to his equally sycophantic rivals, much more 'square' and much less gifted. As the chief of these Anthony Teague is all teeth and glasses above his Ivy League suiting; as the boss, Rudy Vallee has a dignity only exceeded by his fatuousness; as his secretary, Maureen Arthur looks like an auburn, simian version of Monroe and sounds like Carol Channing; and Michele Lee is warm and winning as the secretary determined to have our hero at any cost.

At Republic, on the point of extinction, **Come Next Spring** (1956) is another one-time movie, for in a long career R. G. Springsteen directed nothing else of note. It is set in Arkansas in the Twenties, with all the hallmarks of the rural dramas of the Silent era, including sentiment and a thrill a reel. After eight years, Matt (Steve Cochran) returns to his wife (Ann Sheridan), who is as sceptical as the townsfolk of his reformation. The central situation is whether, or when, marital relations will be resumed, and it is understated. Elsewhere, despite a tornado and a donnybrook, the material has been infused with enthusiasm and affection. Cochran is likeable and Miss Sheridan is brisk and severe without losing her underlying warmth.

Joan Crawford is at her most grandiloquent in **Johnny Guitar** (1954), a bilious Western directed by Nicholas Ray. The characters are cardboard, even if the women are tougher than the men, and the goodies turn out to be the baddies and vice-versa. An occasional bizarre moment – Crawford tinkling the ivories, the posse turning up dressed in black – hints at an attempt to make a gothic Western, but

even on that level it is damply depressing.

As Republic gave up the ghost, its place as the foremost of the minor studios was taken by Allied Artists, the former Monogram, which had changed its name in an effort to redeem its past. Monogram had specialised in B-pictures and, however much these may have enthused the young Jean-Luc Godard, audiences in what the trade called the more discerning halls greeted its logo with groans. With unwonted perspicacity the executives of Monogram foresaw the B-film as doomed when television began to attract the mass audience, and they stopped using the name in 1952. They had been using the title Allied Artists since 1947 for their more ambitious product, but it took some years and the advent of Walter Wanger to produce one of note. Wanger's career as a major producer had ceased in 1950, when he was convicted for shooting at Jennings Lang, the agent who represented his wife, Joan Bennett, thinking him her lover. He found a haven at Allied Artists after his sojourn in prison – an experience which occasioned **Riot in Cell Block 11** (1954). The director, Don Siegel, has said that it is entirely Wanger's film. The mixture of action and well-meaning polemic is uneasy, and if the story is less rigged than in the old prison melodramas, it hardly digs any deeper. Ironically, it is most notable for the work of Siegel, hitherto an uninteresting director. Here he first displayed his grasp of narrative technique and incidental detail – qualities more strikingly to be seen in **Invasion of the Body Snatchers** (1956), also produced by Wanger. This is a low-budget science fiction, shot in eighteen days, mainly on location; its eerie fascination is partly due to its story – from a *Collier*'s serial by Jack Finney – about a doctor (Kevin McCarthy) who gradually comes to realise that the erratic behaviour of his fellow townsfolk has its source in a mysterious extra-terrestrial invasion.

The Phenix City Story (1955) also attracted attention to Republic, as well as to itself, since there was some controversy as to whether its violence (exceptional for the time) was necessary. There was admiration for its portrait of a small town in which gambling and prostitution are big business, its council controlled by racketeers while the police look the other way.

Just as in France some film-makers were tired of industry film-making so was the actor John Cassavetes, who got together a group of friends to make *Shadows*: they improvised and he directed. It has natural (New York) locations, obscurely placed cameras, overlapping dialogue – and the roughness and readiness of life. Ruefully humorous on a certain milieu – the literary set, minor show-business figures – such plot as it has concerns a couple, Anthony Ray and Lelia Goldoni, whose love scene, discussing the loss of her virginity, was remarkably outspoken.

Even so, the film came somewhat tardily after its inspiration, Kefauver's Senate investigation and his subsequent book on the subject, 'Crime in America' (published in 1951). The director, Phil Karlson, did little else of note, but credit is due to him and his colleagues for a semi-documentary flavour. The locations are splendid: this is a featureless small town of great atmosphere, and as the crowds mill around in search of their evening pleasures one can almost smell the hot dogs. The bad guys include some interesting fatties and weirdies, while as the lawyer pursuing them Richard Kiley has a receding hairline and more intelligence than usual.

Among independent productions **Martin Luther** (1953) demands attention, not only because *The New York Times* thought it one of the best films of the year but also because it was the first time a predominantly Jewish industry had shown interest in a religious figure who was neither biblical nor Roman Catholic. Irving Pichel directed the chiefly British cast and Louis de Rochement produced, claiming accuracy and expecting controversy. It does whitewash Luther (Niall MacGinnis) and is hard on Catholics, headed by a fat and pettish Pope who complains, 'How we are to pay Michelangelo for the Sistine Chapel we don't know!' The commentary says of the 95 theses: 'None could know that this was to be one of the most widely read documents in all history,'

and that exemplifies the approach of this well-meaning picture.

There had always been groups prepared to back religious films, and those who invested in *Luther* could anticipate a continuing income from 16-mm showings in church halls. Otherwise minority cinema in English was not feasible till art houses multiplied and began to cater to wider audiences. At the end of the Fifties a number of young film-makers began to gamble on the cost of a film being recovered from this source. The surge to independence was also spurred on by the *nouvelle vague*, obviously working on minute budgets, and so there appeared three films with private investment: John Cassavetes's **Shadows** (1960), Shirley Clarke's **The Connection** (1961) and Joseph Strick's **The Balcony** (1963). John Cassavetes, an established film actor, used his own money and that of friends, till a mention on television of the project brought in enough to complete the cost of $30,000; Miss Clarke got her vital $167,000 from private sources on the strength of the original play's success in New York; and Strick, by virtue of having Shelley Winters in the promised cast, raised $165,000 from one backer, an art-house distributor, Walter Reade. Reade believed that the art circuit was ready for minority films in English, but when *Shadows* opened in New York nine months after its premiere at the National Film Theatre, it failed to repeat its London triumph. *The Connection* also did poorly in New York, opening eighteen months after its warm reception at the Cannes Film Festival.

In truth, Cassavetes's film is the only interesting one of the trio, both for its technique and its decent statement on black–white relations.★ It grew out of a series of improvisations at the Variety Arts Studio in New York and involves a couple who sleep together but part when he discovers that she is black. *The Connection* spends its entire time with a group of junkies awaiting their fix in a derelict attic, and though it has merit – harsh black and

★Among his Ten Best of the year Bosley Crowther chose *A Raisin in the Sun,* a specious black family drama filmed virtually as a photographed play. The huge British acclaim for *Shadows* probably told against its reception in the U.S., and Hollywood at first only gingerly welcomed Cassavetes into its ranks of directors. However, the film was unquestionably influential in Britain and in Europe and, if inevitably it now seems slightly amateurish, it retains the freshness which gave it such an impact.

white photography, skilful direction, a jazz soundtrack – it so lacks insight into the characters that we could not have cared whether they were waiting for Godot instead of heroin. *The Balcony* takes us behind the scenes in Genet's brothel for a number of charades, perversions and fetishistic impersonations, while a revolution takes place outside; it is a hollow piece, indifferently filmed and demonstrating that adaptations of *outré* European plays were not the way forward for independent American cinema.

The choice of subject was ironic, since at the time – or so it seemed – American literature was experiencing one of its most vital periods; so too was the European cinema, for the first time since the 'neo-realist' period in Italy. Clearly there had to be an American system which could rely on the stimulation of new ideas rather than glamour and spectacle – but the 'alternative' cinema offered often turned out to be lunatic avant-garde experiments like **Hallelujah the Hills** (1962) – an alienating experience written and directed by Adolfas Mekas.

David and Lisa (1962) and **One Potato, Two Potato** (1964) proved, particularly the first, that there was a public beyond the art houses willing to support no-star, small-scale, black-and-white movies without benefit of the ballyhoo of the major distributors. A number of Americans may have patronised *David and Lisa* simply because it represented a force against the Goliath of Hollywood. Frank Perry directed, from a screenplay written with his then-wife, Eleanor, and it is clear from internal references that they like the best museums and the best (foreign) movies. The piece is transparent in manipulating its central couple – a boy (Keir Dullea) and a girl (Janet Margolin) in a mental home – and, because of its setting, unpalatable. *One Potato, Two Potato* handles equally delicate material – the difficulties of a mixed marriage, specifically between a white factory-worker divorcee (Barbara Barrie) and a black white-collar worker (Bernie Hamilton). Friends are embarrassed, a cop calls her a hooker, and her ex-husband turns up, appalled that his child is to be brought up among blacks. Eventually Hamilton's performance and Larry Peerce's direction lose out to a screenplay bent less on conviction

than making points about racial prejudice.

Both Perry and Peerce were invited to work in Hollywood, now alert to the tone of the individual artist. Earlier Raymond Chandler had written, 'The future of the motion-picture industry is in the hands of that small group of people who will break their necks to achieve something beautiful in the almost certain knowledge that it will be spoiled by vulgarians': but the small group was gaining ground and the vulgarians disappearing. In the past, successful European directors went to work in Hollywood, but in the Fifties the American companies began financing projects to be filmed on their home ground. After David Lean had made some extremely popular films for Hollywood, United Artists backed Tony Richardson's *Tom Jones* (q.v.) and M-G-M Antonioni's British-made *Blow-Up* (q.v.) – both to extremely profitable figures. Subsequent adventures with Richardson and Antonioni failed. As profits began to waver and fall for the first time in its history, large-scale failure became a fact for the industry to ponder upon. An industry which had always thought in big terms now learned to suffer on an appropriately grand scale. With television now the nation's chief diversion, it would not have survived had the massive number of flops not been offset by a few very successful films.

The *only* studio that was consistently successful was that of Walt Disney, its policy unchanged with his death. Its unambitious films for children and family audiences made money till the late Seventies, when their old-fashioned subject matter at last began to fail to attract potential spectators: but during the time the Disney films were popular, attempts by the other studios to emulate them only ended in losses. Since the major companies also failed at the other end of the scale with their tentative attempts at the 'adult' films which were coining money for the various independents (some of them little more than amateur efforts), they persevered in their own known territory, the middle ground. But, as one producer, Richard Zanuck (q.v.) put it in 1970, 'The rule book has been thrown away. Today almost anything goes. Frankly, I go on what pleases me personally because I just can't tell what pleases the audience any more.'

Hollywood in the Age of Television: The Decline of the Studios

Hollywood had survived two world wars and actually had thrived on them; it had survived the coming of Talkies and the growth of television – indeed the latter, once an enemy, became a friend, as each company formed a subsidiary turning out programmes or series for the networks. It was a way of using studio space and personnel, though it was not always as straightforward as that, as we noted when M.C.A. bought Universal. Alone of the big studios Universal continued to prosper and doubtless the reason it has been the most consistently successful of the majors was due to M.C.A.'s decision to have the studios move into the new medium.

Columbia was the first movie company to go into T.V. production, via its Screen Gems subsidiary in 1952; Warners followed in 1955, with cut-rate versions of movies like *Casablanca* (with Charles McGraw in the lead) and *King's Row* (with Jack Kelly); 20th Century-Fox followed with forty-five minute condensations of its most famous films, but often with star names. In fact, movies could already be seen on the home box: even in the late Forties you could have tuned in to such Silent pictures as *The Eagle*, or to Monogram's B-movies featuring the detective Charlie Chan. The networks bought packages of British movies and, in 1955, Republic sold its entire 1937–48 backlog. A year later, in November 1956, M–G–M allowed *The Wizard of Oz* a single airing on Ford Star Jubilee for the sum of $1 million – a cost justified by the viewing figures; the Wizard became a perennial, licensed only for short periods for similar fees, which has remained a popular television practice. By 1958 the networks would pay up to $100,000 for less exceptional fare, but the trade press thought it foolish to accept, since *For Whom the Bell Tolls* had taken $800,000 on its 1957 reissue. The studios were shortsighted: Warner Bros. sold its entire pre-1948 library for $21 million – a figure reached when the deal was done in the Twenty-One Club – to Associated Artists Production Corporation, which two years later sold it to United Artists. Two years later U.A. estimated that they had made $21 million from licensing the short cartoons alone. (In 1982 Warners was prepared to pay $95 million to recover its heritage, though the films concerned had seldom been away

from television screens; the figure was said to be a bargain, interesting only to U.A., since that company was in desperate financial straits – and the deal fell through as that situation ameliorated). In 1958 Paramount was reported to be considering an offer of $50 million from M.C.A. for its pre-1948 library, and Universal $23 million – though Universal wisely changed its mind. Not only did people stay at home when old movies were aired, but it stimulated an interest in the cinema's past then unthinkable outside film societies. Also in 1958, *Variety* reported that some post-1948 movies had been sold to T.V., including *High Noon* and *Moulin Rouge*: the trickle soon became a flood.

It was Harry Cohn's nephew, Jack Cohn, who founded Screen Gems by arranging to produce thirty-nine dramatic programmes to be sponsored by the Ford Motor Company, which contributed 75 per cent of the finance for one showing and an option for more; within five years Screen Gems was becoming as important a money-maker as Columbia itself. In time the production and distribution arms became subsidiaries of Columbia Industries Inc., and the studio, under production chief Michael J. Frankovitch, was for some years one of the most stable. But in 1971, as losses on unsaleable films began to mount, the studio property itself was sold and Columbia moved into Burbank alongside Warners – an extension of relations abroad, where the two companies shared distribution facilities. Hopes were pinned on a few expensive films, such as *1776, Young Winston* and the re-make of *Lost Horizon,* but when the public would have none of them, losses for 1972–3 were reported (in *Variety,* 29 August 1979) as over $82 million. In 1977, however, a gamble was taken with the expensive *Close Encounters of the Third Kind* (q.v.) and, when that proved justified, Columbia was itself again – at least for a while. Over the next five years there was only one success, but it was a big one, *Kramer vs. Kramer* (q.v.): but with that ratio of success to failure, Columbia continued to limp along with either few films in production or strict budget limitations on those that were.

CinemaScope did not help 20th Century-Fox for long, and its finances in the late Fifties were helped mainly by the discovery of an oil-well on the back lot. We have already looked at the company's losses on *Cleopatra,* its profits on *The Longest Day,* and the comings and goings of Zanuck. On returning to Hollywood in 1962 he became the company President with his son Richard in charge of production – and it was under their control that 20th Century-Fox enjoyed the unprecedented success of *The Sound of Music.* In quick succession *Doctor Dolittle* and *Star!* failed to recover much of their respective budgets of $18 and $10 million – though their failures were partially offset by the success of *Planet of the Apes* (q.v.). Then, when in 1969 it was clear that *Hello Dolly!* would not recoup its cost – $24 million, of which only $11 million were recovered at the box office – both the Zanucks were moved 'upstairs': Darryl becoming Chairman and Richard President. Both were forced to resign two years later, and Richard became a successful producer, but Darryl Zanuck, after almost fifty years of profitable film-making behind him, left in a welter of failure. The titles involved included *The Only Game in Town, Justine, The Great White Hope* (q.v.), *Staircase, The Kremlin Letter, Che, The Games, Hello Goodbye, The Magus* and *The Undefeated,* which individually lost sums of between $2 million and $7 million. In 1969–70 the company's losses totalled $101,637,000 and they were not unwarranted. A number of traditional entertainments subsequently helped the company to recover – *Butch Cassidy and the Sundance Kid* (q.v.), *The Poseidon Adventure* and **The Towering Inferno** (1974), the last named, incidentally, backed jointly with Warners, when it was discovered that both companies planned films on the same subject, a skyscraper on fire. Stirling Silliphant was commissioned to write a screenplay from the two novels concerned and obviously it did not matter what was rejected, for the fire was the chief element: it breaks out just minutes after the film has started, which is one reason why audiences preferred it, as directed by John Gillerman, to other 'disaster' movies of the time – since in most of them they had to wait till the climax for the thrills. This was the first such studio co-operation in Hollywood history, but that was to become a common practice as inflation pushed up budgets until they became too unwieldy for the financing banks to entrust them to a single concern.

As the number of independent producers and backers multiplied, turning to the old majors for distribution, the latter might take on the film concerned for certain territories only. As European investors, including Britons, financed or part-financed American production in return for distribution rights, films travelled abroad under varying logos. The companies were often eager for films to handle; distributors of foreign films began to handle American films. The proliferation is such that we may only note the earlier instances, such as American International continuing in its chosen field of 'youth'-oriented, low-budget films till the declining demand caused it to move upmarket at the end of the Seventies. Founded in 1955, American International began to make itself heard five years later, just as a former exhibitor, Joseph E. Levine, was heavily promoting an undistinguished Italian adventure which he had rechristened *Hercules Unchained*: from that he progressed to backing some Italian films starring Sophia Loren. Under the name Embassy, his American films were originally distributed by Paramount. Shortly after becoming his own distributor he was bought by the Avco Corporation, whose main business is insurance, and the company was renamed Avco-Embassy (it became Embassy again in 1982 when Avco sold its interest). The three U.S. television networks took advantage of the break-up of the power of the major studios to enter film production in the late Sixties; but none of them, after sustained losses, stayed long. A.B.C. began by buying the assets of the Cinerama Corporation, which had ended $18 million in the red; but even the success of *Cabaret* (q.v.) did not encourage it to continue. Profits on that film were, in any case, shared with Allied Artists – a company increasingly involved with television, though occasionally prepared to back a big film, such as *Papillon* (q.v.).

Avco was not the only giant company looking towards American films capable of vast profits, and with assets, such as property and subsidiary rights in music and records, to which could be added other resources like publishing companies. It was possible at last, by the late Seventies, for one company to control a film from its appearance in author's typescript via hard-cover and paperback editions to the record of the film's score and its appearance on television. In 1966 Paramount was bought by the vast oil-based conglomerate Gulf+Western, and the intrusion of this outsider into the industry was almost as great a shock as that of losing ground to television, although that had been more gradual. In the event, Gulf+Western had little effect on Paramount's fortunes: at least that company had been modestly profitable for some years and when, in 1970, it produced some hugely expensive and unpopular films – *Darling Lili* (q.v.), *The Molly Maguires* (q.v.) and *Catch 22* (q.v.) – Gulf+Western absorbed the losses. At a mere $22 million Paramount's inventory write-down was much more modest than those of the other companies.

In 1966, Warners was bought by Kinney National Service Inc. – best known for its parking lots – though as we have seen, this was no longer the Warners' Warners. One of the first things Kinney did was to drop the Seven Arts which had been hyphened to it by the Hyman brothers, Eliot and Kenneth. Eliot had been one of the first people to see the advantage of selling motion pictures to television; and among the films with which he had been associated were *The Misfits*, *Lolita* (q.v.), *Whatever Happened to Baby Jane?* and *Moulin Rouge*. Kenneth's credits as a 'packager' are less distinguished, but certainly it was by making films the public wanted to see that Seven Arts had grown big enough to swallow Warners. However, the programme inherited by Kinney consisted of a great many films the public did not want to see, including *There Was a Crooked Man*, *Flap*, *Rabbit Run*, *The Ballad of Cable Hogue* (q.v.), *Which Way to the Front?*, *Start the Revolution Without Me*, *Performance* and *The Last of the Mobile Hot Shots*. Warners was actually the first of the companies to go under, with an industry write-down of over $59 million in 1969, and the following year fifty-five out of sixty-two pending projects were cancelled at one fell swoop. The films begun by Kinney – now renamed Warner Communications – performed better and the company's standing within the industry was made clear when the new independents chose to be aligned: First Artists, part-owned by Paul Newman, Steve McQueen, Barbra Streisand and Sidney Poitier; Orion, a company organised by the former long tenants of

United Artists after their differences with the new owners; and the Ladd Company, formed by a group which had been successful at 20th.

Those former United Artists executives, Robert Benjamin and Arthur Krim, had finally faltered after two decades of success – and they no longer owned the company since, following the absorption of Paramount and Warners by conglomerates, they had sold it, in 1968, to the Transamerica Corporation, another insurance company which felt it might project a benign public image as owner of a Hollywood company. It was soon disillusioned as, almost two years later, in 1969, U.A. had had its own inventory write-off of $50 million. The titles responsible include *The Secret of Santa Vittoria*, *Gaily Gaily*, *The Hawaiians*, *Women in Love* (q.v.), *Ned Kelly*, *Leo the Last* (q.v.), *They Call Me Mister Tibbs*, *The Landlord* (q.v.), *Queimada!* (q.v.), *The Happy Ending*, *Born To Win*, *Doc* (q.v.), *The Private Life of Sherlock Holmes*, *200 Motels*, *Halls of Anger*, *Mrs Pollifax – Spy* and *One More Time*. Bolstered by a number of successes, including the James Bond (q.v.) goldmines, the company enjoyed an equable situation for more than a decade, when differences over policy between Transamerica and the company management sent the latter, as I have said, into the arms of Warners.

But it was the mighty M-G-M, the acknowledged leader of the industry, which suffered most – which, as Myrna Loy said, was something that no one had thought possible, even in their wildest dreams. Throughout the Sixties the company was beset with boardroom troubles, increasingly reflected in its films, until by 1969 all except a handful of Metro productions seemed wilfully unattractive. The battles to oust Robert O'Brien had begun in 1967, as it was clear that only David Lean's *Doctor Zhivago* (q.v.) and the re-issues of *Gone with the Wind* had kept the company solvent. In 1970 Lean's *Ryan's Daughter* lost money for M-G-M, but meanwhile Edgar Bronfman of Seagrams Distilleries had acquired control, with O'Brien promoted to Chairman. Battle immediately ensued between Bronfman and Kirk Kerkorian, of Tracy Investments – whose chief interests were in Las Vegas hostelries – and Kerkorian won. He appointed James T. Aubrey, the former head of C.B.S., president – the third in eleven months – and losses were posted of $35,366,000, though that included some cancelled projects, among them *Man's Fate* and *Say It with Music,* on which the respective sums of $3 million and $1 million had already been spent.

Under Kerkorian's aegis, Aubrey began to dispose systematically of M-G-M's assets, including part of the studio grounds, sold for real estate, and the prop department and its contents, including costumes worn by Garbo and Judy Garland's ruby-red slippers from *The Wizard of Oz.* The British studio was closed and a ceiling budget of $2.3 million was put on every film – but these turned out to be even worse than those made during the O'Brien regime. In 1973 it was announced that M-G-M was going out of business except for its television interests, though there would almost certainly be some 'highly selective quality films and other leisure and entertainment activities' – the latter including the newly opened M-G-M Grand Hotel in Las Vegas, its walls hung with portraits of Garbo, Gable and Garland. M-G-M's remaining foreign cinemas were to be sold and its distribution offices closed – with its library and current product handled on home territory by United Artists and overseas by Cinema International Corporation, a company owned jointly by Paramount and Universal.

Looking back to the M-G-M films discussed in this chapter and remembering some of the horrors foisted on us over the years, few of us still cannot help feeling sad – and therefore glad when, in 1980, the company rose from the ashes. It had acquired a new President in Frank E. Rosenfelt, the first of the new moguls (or the old ones, for that matter) to believe in the value, artistic as well as financial, of the films lying in the vaults. By a judicious reappraisal of their worth and by licensing *Gone with the Wind* to television for a twenty-year period he was able to capitalise on the company's past, and in the best possible way, by restoring its glory.

In 1981 Rosenfelt announced that M-G-M was returning to full-scale production, and about the same time he revealed the acquisition of United Artists,

its library, assets and projects, for $380 million. This was the fourth of the real industry thunderbolts, following the death of R.K.O., Paramount's absorption by Gulf+Western and the auction of M-G-M's props. As it happens, R.K.O. is currently returning to the film business, as are the American television companies – but I am anticipating, since these matters belong at the end of the book. So does the apparent end of United Artists and, for the moment, it may be said that that was brought about by the failure of one film. What had been threatened by *Cleopatra* and the 1962 *Mutiny on the Bounty* – the folding of one of the major companies – had finally been achieved by *Heaven's Gate* (q.v.). In the event M-G-M and United Artists amalgamated, and were said in 1982 to have debts to the banks of $650 million, due to a number of unprofitable films put in hand by both managements. *Heaven's Gate* had been written off, but the figure M-G-M paid for United Artists should be compared with the $722 million paid a few months later for 20th Century-Fox by the millionaire Marvin Davis.

When such figures appear in the press we are reminded more than ever that the cinema is an industry and that the people now in control are no longer creative. Doubtless among those calling themselves producers there are those who buy properties – since most of them are ex-agents. It was reported that when Krim and Benjamin were ousted from United Artists the new management bought Gay Talese's book, 'Thy Neighbour's Wife', for $2½ million to prove their clout. This was, it was said, to provide the basis for two films – even if most experienced movie people felt that it would not even provide the basis for one (and, in the event, nothing more has been heard of the project). The studios now exist as production facilities and offices to which talent – stars, directors and writers – take their projects, depending on their attitude to their occupants. The studios exist to do deals. When we return to Hollywood it will be to look at the films initiated by their directors. It may not, in fact, be evident that the demise of the studio system gave rise to better pictures.

34

Ingmar Bergman:
The Quest for Understanding

WHEN IN 1959, the Swedish Institute published an introduction to Swedish cinema, it needed only a few bridging paragraphs, referring to the 'artistic deterioration' of the Thirties, to pass from Sjöström to Ingmar Bergman – Sjöström's heir and the man who has dominated his native cinema for almost forty years. The intervening period was a time when serious films were out of favour, and there was a decade of tedious melodramas and unfunny comedies (Bergman has said that though they seemed bad at the time they are now rather charming). The best light films were made by Gustav Molander, a contemporary of Sjöström – but he also made the best serious films as well. Few were seen abroad (though one of them launched Ingrid Bergman on her American career), but, when, during the postwar period, Swedish films began to trickle across the sea, they became synonymous with gloom and sex – frequently intertwined, since it was often the one night of passion which led to the unwanted baby.

Such, after all, has been the tradition of rural stories the world over, and Swedish films only reflected the national dichotomy of believing deeply in the pleasure of the sex act itself – but unwilling to cast off the puritan spirit. This was the theme of one of the first postwar Swedish successes, **One Summer of Happiness** (1951), in which the castigations of the pastor against a young couple (Folke Sundquist, Ulla Jacobsson) lead inevitably to tragedy. It was directed solemnly – by Arne Mattsson – which was absolutely what audiences expected; many of them had gone to see the nude bathing scene, though that survived intact in very few countries.

Prior to that, many had been impressed by **Hets** (1945), known as *Frenzy* in Britain and *Torment* in the U.S., which transposes a similar story to an urban setting, inasmuch as the student hero (Alf Kjellin) again finds sex irresistible. In this case, the girl (Mai Zetterling) is promiscuous, and the tormentor is the boy's teacher (Stig Järrel) who, since he is also her lover, is the professor of *The Blue Angel* in reverse. Alf Sjöberg (1903–80), the director, makes much of the atmosphere – the echoing school, the over-stuffed home of the boy's parents, the girl's squalid flat – but the result is melodramatic, despite what seems to be an effort on the part of both the director and writer to achieve something a little deeper.

Sjöberg, after making his first film in 1929, had spent most of the subsequent decade directing for the theatre, though he remained obsessed with movies. Few Swedish films were being made, but production was increased when the War isolated Sweden. Accordingly he was able to return to films in 1940. Two years later he attempted to revive the spirit of Sjöström's rural dramas with **The Road to Heaven**, visually influenced by the nineteenth-century primitive religious paintings. Most Swedish films looked back to an earlier era, partly because there was richer source material in the films and plays of the Twenties. *Hets* is, in fact, much more typical of that time than is *The Road to Heaven*: so it is ironic that it was regarded as a statement on behalf of the younger generation, rebellious at what they considered Sweden's inward and backward-looking predilection. It established Sjöberg as a figure equally important to the cinema as he was to the theatre, and he went on to make a number of accomplished films. **Iris and the Lieutenant** (1946) could not claim originality in subject matter, though it recounts the love affair between a servant girl (Mai Zetterling) and a young nobleman (Kjellin) with a warmth and tenderness rare in Sjöberg's work. His screenplay has only a hint of the satirical tone in Olle Hedberg's original novel but, with the collaboration of the author Ivar Lo-Johansson, he captured absolutely the cruel world of the novelist's much-admired **Only a Mother** (1949) – one of his series on the plight of exploited farm workers on huge country estates. Sjöberg was delighted with the film's success, since he believed in the cinema above all as a force for social change. Eva Dahlbeck is magnificent as the woman whose life story the film traces.

Though *Iris* (under that title) was seen briefly in London, Sjöberg was known abroad only for *Hets* when **Miss Julie** (1950) was awarded the Grand Prix at Cannes (jointly with *Miracolo a Milano*). Sjöberg's screenplay was recognised as a brilliant extension of Strindberg's play, introducing by way of flashback some scenes of Miss Julie's childhood and seizing the obvious opportunity to wander into the fields and gardens for the midsummer night's frolic – brilliantly photographed by Göran Strindberg (the playwright's grandson). That the film remains enthralling is partly due to Sjöberg's tenacious hold on the central relationship, from the time Miss Julie (Anita Björk) first humiliates the valet Jean (Ulf Palme) to their separate traumas as each broods on the consequences of their love-making.

The film's international success encouraged its producer, Sandrews, to invest heavily in Sjöberg's version of Pär Lagerkvist's novel **Barabbas** (1953), to the extent of filming abroad – rare for a Swedish film – in Israel and Italy. Despite Mr Palme's magnificent performance in the title role, the film was hardly seen outside Scandinavia: nor was **Karin Månsdotter** (1954), with which Sjöberg returned to Strindberg, basing the central episode on his play 'Erik XIV'. Inspired by his successful additions to *Miss Julie*, in this screenplay Sjöberg frames Strindberg's drama with other events known of the mad King Erik (Jarl Kulle) and his peasant-born queen (Ulla Jacobsson). The prologue, in colour, is a burlesque of Silent comedy

showing their meeting; the epilogue follows their adventures after the king has been deposed. At the start the film has a certain humour, but the tone has been set wrongly: the court intrigues are uninteresting, and the relationships between the king, queen and his commoner adviser (Palme) are marred by the two-dimensional playing and writing. The piece is visually striking, but did not appeal to audiences or critics. The same judgment was passed on Sjöberg's subsequent handful of films, leaving his international reputation to rest on *Hets* and *Miss Julie*.

Hets was one of Sjöberg's few films that he did not write himself. His commanding position in the theatre and the reception accorded *The Road to Heaven* had caused Carl-Anders Dymling, the head of Svensk Filmindustri, to invite him to make a film to celebrate the company's silver anniversary. *Hets* was considered suitable, even though the screenplay was by someone with no previous film experience – an ambitious young theatre director, Ingmar Bergman (b.1918). He had based it on one of his own short stories influenced by his schooldays, and he so wanted to be in cinema that he accepted Sjöberg's offer and took on the lowly job of continuity boy. Some months later, when directing his first film, *Crisis* (q.v.), he was due to be sacked after three weeks because the results were so bad, and the movie was to be

Between the films of Sjöström and Stiller in the early Twenties and Ingmar Bergman in the Fifties only a handful of Swedish films were seen outside Scandinavia. The director Alf Sjöberg had two international successes, the second of which was a version of Strindberg's play *Miss Julie*, which effectively combines lyricism with as much eroticism as was permissible at the time. Anita Björk and Ulf Palme are the mistress and servant who too soon come to regret their moment of lust.

restarted by another director. But Victor Sjöström, as artistic adviser to Svensk, insisted that Bergman reshoot the work, and that he himself would assume full responsibility for its quality. Thus Bergman believes he owes his career to his two great predecessors. Always venerating Sjöström, he regarded Sjöberg as a friend and mentor until his death.

Bergman is the son of a Lutheran minister. While still a boy he had built several toy theatres for himself and by the time he was sixteen had read all fifty-five volumes of the collected works of Strindberg. He was educated at the University of Stockholm, where he was able to develop some of his theories on drama. He was artistic director of the theatre at Hälsingborg when Carl-Anders Dymling, impressed by Bergman's screenplay for *Hets*, offered him the direction of **Crisis** (1945). 'An out-and-out bit of whoredom', said Bergman later, referring to the fact that he disliked the play on which it was based ('Moderdyret' by a Dane, Leck Fisher) – and also perhaps because it was made as a star vehicle for Dagny Lind, a middle-aged actress who specialised in suffering. He also said that 'more than anything else I was longing to make films', but today he mildly approves of only one sequence – that in the beauty parlour. I think he underestimates its portrait of provincial life which, like those in the films of Stiller, is both chilly and amusing. The plot concerns Nelly (Inga Landgré) who, living with her foster mother (Miss Lind), is fascinated by her real mother (Marianne Lüfgren), a Stockholm beautician who is keeping company with a callow young actor (Stig Olin). Nelly finds him more seductive than the foster-uncle who is wooing her, and the rejection of her provincial 'family' prefigures later Bergman films where love will lose ground or go unrequited. With hindsight too, we can see that Bergman already had a predilection for wearing a hairshirt in films, so it may be that the young actor is a self-portrait. Lorens Marmstedt, a theatre owner and distributor, met Bergman while he was making *Crisis* and it was he who produced, and to some extent chose the material for, the next three films Bergman was to direct. **It Rains on Our Love** (1946) also introduced Bergman to the gifted young actor Birger Malmsten and the Stock-

holm drama critic and writer, Herbert Grevenius, who was to collaborate with him for the next few years. The film itself, based on a Norwegian play, is typical of Scandinavian cinema at this time – its theme is the plight of two lovers (Malmsten and Barbro Kollberg) with all the world, or most of it, against them. Their enemies and occasional friends are the grotesques who were so frequently to people Bergman's films for another decade: that none of them is tiresome is due to the confident handling, positiveness of dimension and the setting – a vacant summer villa. Allied to the fact that Marmstedt later gave Bergman the opportunity to direct one of his own screenplays, *Prison* (q.v.), Bergman was also grateful to him for constantly reminding him that he was not Carné nor Malmsten Jean Gabin.

This film is too Nordic for us to make a comparison, but the mark of Carné is on **A Ship to India** (1947) – as is that of Michael Curtiz, whose films Bergman was studying at the time. The film is a melodrama, but less of one than *Mildred Pierce* – for the characters here are much more convincing. What brings the film within reach of greatness, in my view, is its visual richness. The director of photography was Göran Strindberg, whose compositions are without parallel (until the Japanese took to the wide screen): but they are always, and only, used for dramatic effect. Briefly stated, the plot – taken from a play by Martin Söderhjelm – involves a war between father (Holger Löwenadler) and son (Malmsten). Father, a retired sea captain, operates a small salvage barge, but prefers to spend his days whoring, boozing and fighting; the son, a hunchback, dreams of going away to sea and, after one of their incessant fights, gets drunk and attempts to rape his father's mistress. The true tragic figure is the mother, who suffers the rows and the presence of mistress on board, and always forgives; but she is virtually ignored and is passed over completely in the prologue and the epilogue, set some years later, which puts the boy's youthful traumas into perspective.

'It was a silly little film, but my first popular success,' said Bergman of **Night is My Future** (1948) (the Swedish title translates more accurately and less sensationally as *Music in Darkness*). It is about blindness and, if it is not the best film on the subject, Malmsten's performance is the most convincing portrayal on film of a blind man. The ending, with its echo of 'Jane Eyre' and the suggestion that blindness is hardly an affliction if there is someone to care, may be why Bergman dismisses the film – passing over its interesting exposition and magnificent middle section. When Bengt (Malmsten) becomes blind, he stays with a family friend, and there is a chance that he will marry her maid's daughter (Mai Zetterling) – especially as her concern for him is accompanied by erotic feelings. His disappointment is twofold: he cannot marry her because class differences prove too great, and he is rejected by the Stockholm Academy of Music. He becomes a pianist in a small provincial café, where he is subjected to the bitterness of his violinist partner (Gunnar Björnstrand), the whims of the drunken proprietor and the depredations of the landlady's young son. The view of provincial power is darker than that of Stiller or *Crisis*, though we shall find the same view recurring as late as *The Touch* (q.v.).

Port of Call (1948) is set in Gothenburg and is a realistic account of an affair between a merchant seaman (Bengt Eklund) and a girl (Nine-Christine Jönsson) more sinned against than sinner. The romance does not go smoothly, because the girl is on probation – just one aspect of a fairly miserable existence. Love, in Bergman's films, is always a battlefield, but hitherto he had followed such dramatic convention as coincidence, misunderstanding or commitment to the wrong partner. Molander had just directed a screenplay written by Bergman along those lines, **Woman Without a Face** (1947), a straightforward tale of a man (Alf Kjellin) who deserts his wife for a floozie (Anita Bjork). *Port of Call*, however, brings social forces into play, reflecting Bergman's ever-ready ability, at this time, to assimilate what other important film-makers were doing: like de Sica, he believed that individual suffering was caused by the defects in society. At least that view is tenable in *Port of Call*, but he presumably came to believe that the ills of Italian society were not those of Sweden, for none of his other films blames poverty *per se* for the misery of people's lives.

The fault, suggests **Prison** (1949) – also known as *The Devil's Wanton* – lies with

ourselves and, since the film is autobiographical, it is as well to take into account Bergman's volatile nature. He had left home in his teens after a row with his parents; at thirty, his second marriage was in ruins; and the film industry was wary of, rather than impressed by, his energy, which was why he had written and directed films but had not been allowed to function in both capacities at the same time. Having established a good relationship with Svensk Filmindustri, Bergman returned to Marmstedt, who allowed him to direct his own screenplay. *Prison* begins in a film studio where a director (Hasse Ekman) and a writer, Tomas (Malmsten), discuss a film about evil with a reference to the atom bomb, thus reflecting Bergman's own uneasiness about Swedish neutrality (he had produced an anti-Nazi 'Macbeth' at the time Norway and Denmark were invaded). Tomas comes up with an idea for a film about a prostitute (Doris Svedlund) he had once interviewed, whose sister was in league with her pimp (Stig Olin)

Ingmar Bergman at the time of *Persona*. He had been directing films for almost a decade before becoming widely known outside his homeland – and since then his reputation has fluctuated at the dictate of newspaper critics, able to keep audiences away by writing of gloom and depression. The more serious critics – those, that is, who write in the specialist cinema magazines – have seldom wavered in their loyalty and at least twenty of his thirty-odd films are in the permanent international repertory.

to keep her working. Then he, Tomas, drinks himself into gloom and decides to put an end to the bickerings with his wife (Eva Henning) by murdering her and committing suicide. Instead, he meets up with the prostitute and they flee to a boarding house where, in the attic, he finds toys from his childhood, including a cinema projector. The final result of the film is undiluted *angst*, but it contains some unexpected diversions – the gaiety of the scenes with the projector, the comedy of the murder that isn't and the purity of the scenes of Malmsten by the river, contemplating suicide.

We can see now that the writer, the pimp and the director are all aspects of Bergman. *Prison* impressed a number of critics, but was regarded as a failure. Bergman accordingly turned again to Grevenius for a screenplay, and they settled on some short stories by Birgit Tengroth for what became **Thirst** (1949), in which Miss Tengroth herself plays a secondary role. That the two films have so much in common indicates the understanding between the two men (though they drifted apart later, when Grevenius was converted to Catholicism): both centre upon an unhappy married couple played by Malmsten and Henning, and crucial to their unhappiness is the loss of a baby. *Thirst*, like so many later Bergman movies, features a train journey, and as the train goes from Basle to Stockholm it traverses a Germany that prefigures the unnamed country in *The Silence* (q.v.), not merely in ruins but with a ghostly eeriness. Throughout the journey Rut (Henning) and Bertil (Malmsten) bicker, causing her to recall a supposedly happier relationship, with an army officer (Eklund) who did not tell her that he was married until she had informed him that she was pregnant. Rut's present and past troubles are interrupted by some simultaneous events back in Stockholm, concerning Viola (Birgit Tengroth), who is having an affair with a doctor (Ekman). He miscalculates the extent of her dependence on him, so that she is alone on midsummer's night when she meets Valborg (Mimi Nelson), a friend from Rut's days with the ballet. Viola realises that Valborg's need is for something beyond friendship, but at the testing moment she rushes out to wander, like so many Bergman protagonists, down along

the river. These episodes constitute not a narrative, but a thesis – that it may be hell being together but it is better than being apart. Viola's suicide has been unnecessary, for living is preferable to death, even if it means suffering a slippery philanderer or a predatory lesbian. Being single – lonely (as opposed to being merely alone) – is the one great impossibility; an unsatisfactory love is better than none. A similar view is found in the French existentialists, and Bergman has admitted that both this film and *Prison* were influenced by contemporary writing.

When shooting was finished, Malmsten and Bergman took a trip abroad, during which time Bergman began to feel romantic about 'my then marriage, that is to say the one I'd just taken extreme delight in ripping to pieces in *Thirst*.' He also became sentimental about the symphony orchestra he had worked with in Hälsingborg; consequently marriage and music are the twin subjects of **To Joy** (1950), whose hero is a mediocre practitioner of both (Bergman had begun to consider 'how I wasn't such a genius as I'd imagined'). The film centres on two members of a provincial orchestra, Martha (Maj-Britt Nilsson) and Stig (Stig Eriksson), who marry; the years pass and Stig takes solace in a sordid affair – till brought up short by the presence of a lodger (Malmsten), who is also in the orchestra. Stig decides that he is surrounded by mediocrity, and that he will try at least to make his marriage first-rate. Bergman calls the film 'suspect – but with some nice bits in it', and by that he is referring, I imagine, to the scenes of rehearsal, with Victor Sjöström playing the conductor – and offering, as of old, a character in which authority, sympathy and weakness are equally matched.

Otherwise the piece is unsatisfactory, partly because Bergman's fighting spouses were becoming tiresome. It is no less jejune and occasionally melodramatic than Bergman's other films up to that time, but it is interesting as a foretaste of one of the themes of his middle period: the responsibility of the artist. It also lacks the sheer zest of his other early films, which for all their faults still prove him to have been one of the most exciting directors working anywhere in the world.

Till he had achieved international recognition his films were largely confined to

Scandinavia. **Summer Interlude** (1950) is the first Bergman film to have entered the international repertoire with any permanency. Both this and **Summer with Monika** (1953) are about adolescent love affairs – the one to end in death, the other to founder because of the girl's perfidy. 'Has life any meaning?' asks the bereaved heroine (Maj-Brit Nilsson) in *Summer Interlude*, and the answer comes back, 'No, not in the long run.' Years later, when she is a successful dancer, the protagonist is entrapped between a sinister ballet master (Olin) and a boorish lover (Kjellin); similarly the increasingly impoverished and unhappy lovers (Lars Ekborg, Harriet Andersson) of *Monika* have finally the option of moving from one mouse-trap to another. Monika turns out to be both perfidious and sexually unfaithful, which Bergman's heroines, despite their failings, had not been hitherto. The film itself might be said to be the first screen presentation of his burgeoning misogynistic streak; and it is pertinent to remark that six marriages do not seem to indicate great emotional contentment.

Professionally, both films were important. In tackling the subject of a doomed love in a sylvan setting he was following Swedish film tradition, but in *Summer Interlude* he felt, for the first time in film-making, that 'it all worked', while *Summer with Monika* is one of his few early films that he likes and is 'always glad to see again.' The first marked the last time that he worked with Grevenius, and the second and virtually the last time that he worked with any collaborator or adapted from another source; he did later work on screenplays to be directed by Sjöberg and Kjellin, but increasingly he saw each film as a work wholly by Ingmar Bergman. He tended then, and now, to work as far as possible with the same team, once observing that twenty people crammed into one small space called for harmony.

He wrote the screenplay for **Waiting Women** (1952) while the Swedish film industry was idle due to dissatisfaction with its inadequate financing methods. He had been making commercials and wrote this, waiting for matters to right themselves, in 'bad temper, sheer temper . . . My finances were in shreds and my marriage badly frayed.' In common with most of his films at this time, it is built round a

Summer Interlude, ABOVE, and *Summer with Monika,* LEFT, have more in common than the similarity of their titles, for both concern adolescent romances, in which the couples concerned live their idylls among lakes and pine forests. Beyond that, they have little in common, for *Summer Interlude* is an early Bergman attempt to come to terms with the importance of artistic endeavour. She, Maj-Britt Nilsson, is a dancer, and the lover gazing at her is Birger Malmsten. *Summer with Monika* is only about an affair – and it is not idyllic for long – as may be seen here, for Harriet Andersson does not seem overwhelmed by the visit of Lars Ekborg.

Ingmar Bergman: The Quest for Understanding

series of flashbacks, with three women recounting to each other the particular moment when they saw their husbands in a new or different light. The first episode is about a wife (Anita Björk), whose casual infidelity with a friend (Jarl Kulle) leads her husband to decide, after his initial fury, that an unfaithful wife is better than none at all. The second concerns seduction – not this time by a Swedish lake, but in a Paris hotel – when a girl (Maj-Britt Nilsson), disenchanted by her G.I. fiancé, meets a romantic fellow-Swede (Malmsten); and the third involves a pompous, rather drunk man (Björnstrand) who, stuck in a stalled lift with his wife (Eva Dahlbeck), confesses to infidelity and then makes love to her. Bergman says he was delighted by the gales of laughter which greeted the film – presumably only the final, frivolous episode – but to non-Swedish ears the humour is only mildly funny.

Gycklarnas Afton (1953) – *Sawdust and Tinsel* in Great Britain and *The Naked Night* in the U.S. – was another film made, according to Bergman's own report, at a time he felt emotionally humiliated. It was also a film made for its own sake, a situation which has usually resulted in his less interesting work. It bears witness to its inspiration, *Varieté*, in an unappetising tale about a circus couple (Ake Grönberg, Harriet Andersson) trying to escape from their relationship, he to the wife he deserted long ago, she to an effeminate and possibly sado-masochistic actor (Hasse

Ekman). A flashback at the beginning – based on one of Bergman's own dreams – in which a husband is humiliated while his wife cavorts in the sea with some half-naked sailors looking on, accurately foreshadows the film as a whole: it is brilliantly done, but hollow.

The film's rejection by Swedish critics caused Bergman to run for cover and, recalling audience delight at the Dahlbeck-Björnstrand episode of *Waiting Women*, he fashioned **A Lesson in Love** (1954) for the same players. Most of it takes place on a train to Copenhagen, and the use of a journey to revive old memories is a frequent device. A number of the flashbacks are excellent, especially that with the aged parents which anticipates *Wild Strawberries* (q.v.), but slapstick is not Bergman's forte. The rest is ponderous and joylessly optimistic, proving that Dahlbeck and Björnstrand were unlikely ever to rival Hepburn and Tracy.

A similar pretentiousness is echoed in the opening sequence of **Kvinnodröm** (1955) – *Journey into Autumn* in Britain and *Dreams* in the U.S. – set in a photographer's studio; but it is quickly succeeded by one of Bergman's most virtuoso passages, a rail journey at night. The subsequent plotting is evidence of the textural richness of which he was now capable, and the dialogue is alternately ironic and tender. His personal preoccupations were also clearly stated: man's sexual subjugation to woman, the vain hope that love endures and the examination of its possibilities outside marriage.

Smiles of a Summer Night (1955) contrasts the sexual intrigues of the middle-aged with the idealism of the young rather in the manner of Jean Anouilh, though Bergman has claimed that his inspiration was the earlier dramatist, Marivaux. It was Marivaux whom Renoir had in mind when writing *La Règle du Jeu* and superficially the two films are alike.* But, unlike Renoir (and Ophuls and Lubitsch – whose period comedies were an inspiration also) this film has little kindness; indeed, the screenplay is not only heartless, but defiantly so. Again Bergman had returned to comedy after a failure – *Kvinnodröm* – but, he says, 'head office told me it had been a dreadful

*Bergman thinks Renoir over-rated and one of the reasons he dislikes *La Règle du Jeu* is because he thinks it badly acted.

Jarl Kulle, Gunnar Björnstrand and Margit Carlqvist in *Smiles of a Summer Night*, a film neither smiling nor summery, but often quite pointed on the matter of sexual liaisons. It is a Nordic version of Anouilh's 'Ring Round the Moon', and it was that play Harold Prince and Stephen Sondheim had in mind when they began to prepare the Broadway musical that became 'A Little Night Music': when they were unable to purchase the Anouilh rights they bought those to Bergman's film instead.

948

Ingmar Bergman: The Quest for Understanding

miscalculation. The film wasn't funny. It was stylised. It was too lame, and too long' – all of which is true.

The film was, nevertheless, entered for the Cannes Festival – though Bergman says that Swedish films were then only entered at festivals so that the producers could enjoy a free trip. He was astonished when it won the Grand Prix and it was this that ensured it international distribution; but it had no more success than had *Gycklarnas Afton*, earlier dismissed in both New York and London as heavy and overdrawn. It was **The Seventh Seal** (1957), finally, which made his world-wide reputation. The film's concept is impressive: the knight (Max von Sydow) playing chess with Death for his life; the chiaroscuro both visual and dramatic – the contrast between the knight's quest and the drunken cavorting of the people, between religious experience and the harsh facts of poverty and pestilence – indeed the whole panorama of medieval life and superstition. The final effect is less of pretension than of muddle – clarity sacrificed to a joke or private image. It is a divertissement by one whose father had been a preacher, a series of abstractions remembered from hours of boredom in church as a boy.

Many spectators who held out against this film were converted by **Wild Strawberries** (1957). Its starting point is childhood or, rather, a search for the state of childhood, which was triggered off by a drive Bergman took to the town in which he had grown up. His protagonist would be 'a tired old egocentric, who'd cut off everything about him – as I'd done': he is a professor, and the film is a record of his journey to Lund University where he is to be honoured. With him is his daughter-in-law (Ingrid Thulin), and they pick up three students, one of whom is enacted by Bibi Andersson, who also plays the old man's childhood sweetheart. He reminisces, and dreams of death; his regrets are those of an old man who has spent his life compromising. If Bergman had any purpose other than the cinematic equivalent of a sketch for a portrait, it becomes fleshed out by the fully rounded performance of Victor Sjöström, looking blinkered and misanthropic; but the contours of his face nevertheless express contentment and tolerance. Bergman found it 'marvellous, having this inexhaustible wellspring to

hand every day', though he admits that the lessons to be learned from Sjöström were contained in the great films which he had directed years ago – 'his incorruptible demand for truth, his incorruptible observation of reality. His way of never for a moment making things easy for himself, or simplifying or skipping things or cheating or settling for mere brilliance.' For the first time Bergman expresses his love for his country as Sjöström did, in a film richer and more mature than any he had made up to that time. Its reception consolidated his reputation, though neither here nor in *The Seventh Seal* is there much to suggest the substance of the great films to come – although in *The Seventh Seal* we may note the knight's remark, 'I want God to show Himself to me.'

Favourite preoccupations emerge in what is otherwise a straightforward tale of a maternity ward, **Nara Livet** (1958) (*So Close to Life* or *The Brink of Life*): the relationship of women away from the world of men; the omnipresence of death; the inconsequence and consequence of our sexuality. Its source is a novel by Ulla Isaksson, who is credited on the film itself as sole screenwriter, though Bergman elsewhere shares the credit. Released in the same year, **Ansiktet** (1958) (*The Face* or *The Magician*) is the most deeply personal film he had yet made. 'Fraud is so common that those who tell the truth are usually

Though *The Seventh Seal* made Bergman a name on the art-house circuit it was his next film, *Wild Strawberries*, which brought respect into admiration. He felt similarly for Victor Sjöström, who played the old professor in the film, for Sjöström was not only the mightiest figure in the early days of the Swedish cinema but as artistic director of Svensk Filmindustri had been greatly encouraging during Bergman's own first films as a director. With Sjöström here is Bibi Andersson in a scene from the film.

949

Ingmar Bergman: The Quest for Understanding

Naima Wifstrand, Ingrid Thulin, Max von Sydow and Åke Fridell in *Ansiktet* (*The Face* in Britain; *The Magician* in the U.S.) When it was first shown, Bergman was known only as a weighty film-maker, so it was a surprise to find him enjoying himself in creating the terrors of a horror film. It was immediately recognised that there was more to it than that, but it was only when we had seen more of his work that it could be seen as one of his most personal films.

branded as liars,' says the wife (Ingrid Thulin) of the magician (Max von Sydow). The film is about the nature of truth, and it is a homage to the artist who creates the illusion, as the only member of our society permittèd overt concealment. Vergérus (Gunnar Björnstrand), foremost of the bourgeoisie in judging these charlatans and mountebanks, says 'It is distasteful if science has to accept the miraculous' and, later, 'You represent what I hate most – something I cannot understand.' The hypocrisy of his committee is contrasted throughout with the legerdemain of the actors – and though their leader is undoubtedly something of a fake, he is also something of the Christ, both in appearance and suffering. He fights the lonely battles of Jesus, who, like the artist, told the truth and was branded a liar; he dies and is resurrected; and is finally accepted when patronised by royalty – as Christianity was adopted by Constantine.

The film cheats us as much as the magician, Vogler, deceives his audience, since the terror in the attic is caused by cinematic trickery. 'Haven't I done everything to offer you a sensation?' asks Vogler, and that is also Bergman speaking. No earlier film better expresses his approach to directing: 'I make my pictures for use! They are not made *sub specie aeternitatis*; they are made for now and for use . . . Also, they are made to put me in contact with other human beings, to whom I give them and say, "Please use them. Take what you want and throw the rest away." My impulse has nothing to do with intellect or symbolism; it has only to do with dreams and longing, with hope and desire, with passion.'

By this time Bergman had achieved a fame outside Sweden that far exceeded that of any other Swedish director, including Sjöström, and his self-confidence permitted him a number of disquisitions on the silence of God – as in **The Virgin Spring** (1960), for example, where He does not step in to prevent the rape of a young girl. This film is a return to the medieval world, with a screenplay credited to Miss Isakkson, and described by Bergman as 'an aberration, a touristic, lousy imitation of Kurosawa'. **The Devil's Eye** (1960) he

Ingmar Bergman: The Quest for Understanding

described as 'my little game . . . My intention (if any) was to play, for the amusement of the beloved and feared audience' – but few were amused by this Nordic whimsy about Don Juan (Jarl Kulle) sent back to earth by the Devil to deflower a pastor's daughter (Bibi Andersson): 'One of hell's tiny triumphs is more significant than any great success of heaven's' as its final statement puts it. This was, incidentally, the last of Bergman's films to be photographed by Gunnar Fischer; since then his cinematographer has been Sven Nykvist, with whom he had worked intermittently before.

The next three films Bergman regards as a trilogy, since each defines more clearly his views on man's relationship with God. **Through a Glass Darkly** (1961) is about a man (Gunnar Björnstrand) who tells his son that God manifests Himself in love; in **Winter Light** (1962) a clergyman (Björnstrand) loses his faith and tries to believe that God is love; and in **The Silence** (1963), God has deserted the world. Since *The Virgin Spring*, critical esteem for Bergman had been ebbing, and the first two of these films were poorly received – rightly so, in my opinion, in the case of *Through a Glass Darkly*. It portrays a family of tortured souls ruminating beside a gloomy sea – and the love manifested is that of the seduction by a mentally sick girl (Harriet Andersson) of her younger brother. The family's rampant misery here seems shallow, but *Winter Light* springs from deeper doubts. The pastor cannot help himself; too late he has realised that his isolation from the real world began while working as chaplain in Portugal during the Spanish Civil War, and he has therefore no consolation for Jonas (von Sydow), whose melancholia is caused by the world situation. He cannot respond to the lumpy woman (Ingrid Thulin) who became his mistress after he was widowed, and who tells him that he will die in hate. The film makes a number of both oblique and trenchant comments on the Church, but were we to ignore Bergman's preoccupations this would still be a remarkable study of desperation; its events are as harsh as the landscape outside, where the snow is whipped furiously by the wind.

The Silence is set in a strange foreign city, where tanks pass through on their way to a probable war. In a deserted hotel

Gunnar Björnstrand in *Winter Light,* LEFT, and Jörgen Lindstrom and Gunnel Lindblom in *The Silence,* BELOW, which with *Through a Glass Darkly* Bergman regards as a trilogy, since each is an attempt to understand man's relationship with the Deity. *Through a Glass Darkly* was made first, and since it often verges on self-parody it was not well received – a fact which perhaps led to the undervaluation of *Winter Light*, which is masterly even by Bergman's own standards. Happily, *The Silence* was accorded the recognition its merits deserve.

Ingmar Bergman: The Quest for Understanding

two women express their obsessive, self-hating interest in the other, and their indifference to the child with them. One (Thulin) seeks solace in vodka and masturbation,★ and the other in casual promiscuity. They may be sisters or lesbians; the hotel and the no-man's-land they are in may reflect that unreal state which can mark the onslaught of a nervous breakdown. Bergman had been using symbolism in his work for years, and since the advent of Antonioni and Resnais had furthered its use in films, he could push even further his own penchant for the allegorical.

The Silence marked a resurgence of overwhelming critical favour, doubtless because the film's mysteries were in tune with the current climate; and as its two predecessors had been dismissed or misunderstood, few commented on its title – though no one misunderstood its preoccupation with God's presence. Bergman himself said later that *Winter Light* was his last film on God: thenceforward 'We have nothing to do with each other.' However, a clergyman, the Rev. Robert E. Lander, writing almost two decades later in *The New York Times* on *Autumn Sonata* (q.v.), found him as 'hooked on God' as ever: 'Simply stated, [his] theme is the struggle of human beings to communicate love in a world in which God is silent. The meaning and value of that struggle are made precarious for Mr Bergman by the presence of death.'

In 1961 Carl-Anders Dymling became mortally ill, leaving the staff of Svensk Filmindustri without guidance. Bergman was among those on the committee to keep the Rasunda studio functioning and he devised **The Pleasure Garden** (1961) for Alf Kjellin to direct. It was basically a vehicle for Björnstrand and Sickan Carlsson, a rather beefy comedienne on the brink of middle age, who, to this time, had usually played teenagers (and who, according to Bergman, has not filmed since). Björnstrand plays David, a provincial school teacher, whose past catches up with him when a local columnist, Lundberg (Stig Järrel) reveals him as the author of a book of juvenile love poems. Both men have mistresses: David's is a waitress

★Almost certainly the first time this had been shown – via the actress's expression – in a non-pornographic film. Bergman's reputation was sufficient for the censors of most nations to pass the sequence.

(Sickan Carlsson) who confesses herself the mother of a twenty-year-old daughter (Bibi Andersson). David decides to be seen publicly with both – for which he is ostracised by the town, but defended by Lundberg's mistress, the local bookseller, who decides that his action is the logical progression from the feelings expressed in the poems. Local hypocrisy is further shattered when, though unknown to all but the audience, the young curate is so overcome by lust for the daughter that he would seduce her there and then. Otherwise, this young couple is idealistic, in contrast to the two older men, whose complacency towards their women is severely shaken. But most original is the role that is played by the book of poems: the film states that it is possible for our attitude towards a work of art to change under circumstances – that critics are fallible, that even a neophyte work can be valuable, that the meanest creative work should not be written off if it can find a response in one sensitive soul (i.e. the bookseller). The screenplay is by Bergman and Erland Josephson, who had played a small role in *So Close to Life* and who, at the end of the decade, was gradually to replace von Sydow as Bergman's preferred male interpreter (partly because von Sydow's fame as an international actor made him less often available for Swedish films).

The screenplay was publicly credited to the pseudonymous Buntel Ericsson, and some sources list this name as the author of **Now About All These Women** (1964) directed by Bergman. The two films have in common a number of comments on the critic *vs.* the artist, especially the 'littleness' of the former compared to the purity and dedication of the latter. 'Genius,' says the film several times, 'is an ability to make the critic change his mind.' The artist, as the film begins, is dead; a critic, Cornelius (Jarl Kulle) is so angry at not being granted an interview before he died and also at being unable to duplicate his success with women, that he plans revenge – to destroy the deceased's reputation. The piece is slapstick, with stylised mock baroque sets, and the women wearing pretty costumes of the Twenties. It was Bergman's first film in colour (though he had done some tests for *Through a Glass Darkly*). It is not a funny film, and it is – again – hard to disagree with Bergman, who described it

952

as 'glossy, sophisticated, swift, hard and poisonous'. It is mean-minded, partly because by this time he had established himself as so much greater than most film-makers and therefore above his critics. His own voice speaks loud and clear, as ever, but what he is saying is unworthy of him.

The film was catastrophically received, and the welcome was not much warmer for **Persona** (1966), now regarded as one of his finest films. **Hour of the Wolf** (1968), he has said, is one of his most personal pieces. Its title refers to an hour at dead of night, and both this and the preceding film are protracted nightmares. The first concerns an actress (Liv Ullman) who has dried up, suffers a breakdown and finally turns to her nurse (Bibi Andersson), finding in her a mirror image. The film is of complex structure – partly in its choice of images – but its theme is simple: if we look too deeply at ourselves, or the world, the awfulness of both are such that they are intolerable to all but those able to turn away or find someone with whom to hide.

Johan Borg (von Sydow) tries to turn away in *Hour of the Wolf*, and he still has a nervous breakdown. In resuming the themes of *Ansiktet*, Bergman does so with bile, allowing the film to move nearer to Fellini in that no distinction can be drawn between reality and fantasy. Borg speaks for Bergman the artist in making a statement on his fears for his own creativity and his response to the society which has made an outcast of him: 'Nothing is self-evident in what I create – except the compulsion to create it . . . I feel megalomania waft about me, but I think I am immune.'

The Rite (1969) is a dissertation on Bergman's commitment to his art, his fellow artists and his audience – and the three actors undergoing examination by a judge are all aspects of himself. This is a jape, made for television in nine days, and Bergman has said of it that he is equipped with his own angels and devils. This time we cannot share them – perhaps because this was for television, and he did not care whether audiences understood or responded.

On either side of this minor piece he made the two films with which, at last, he takes his place as one of the great creative figures of this century. The title of **The Shame** (1968) refers to the experience of war, and its effect on people; it may also

refer to Sweden's traditional neutrality. Though the specific war is a civil one, and it is probably taking place in Sweden. The couple (Liv Ullman, von Sydow) whose fortunes we follow are called Rosenberg, which may not be a Jewish name in Sweden, but Bergman knows that to the world it is Jewish. They are concert violinists who became farmers when the war destroyed their living. As the conflict spreads to the remote island where they live, they are confronted with the multitude of shaming experiences that war can bring: from the inability to act in the name of humanity and the uselessness of any artistic credo in such circumstances, through the humiliation of killing, of compromising, of being forced to suffer propaganda . . . to the experience of sitting and waiting in an office in an overcoat. As they drift out to sea, in the end, with dead bodies floating around them, the wife speaks of a dream and says, 'I knew I ought to remember something that someone said – but I've forgotten what it was.'

This finale is used as a dream sequence in **A Passion** (1969), also known as *The Passion of Anna*, but then this film abounds in references to his other films, be it repeated names – Vergérus, Andreas, Winkelman – or the same Vietnam War report watched on television in *Persona*. The setting is the same desolate island of the last few films, and the countryside is uneasy, this time due to a maniac who attacks animals at night, to kill or to maim. Thus the central plot again takes place against unnatural events, for God's purpose is turned upside down. Eva (Bibi Andersson) says that she thinks she believes in Him, but she would not instruct her children to believe – a statement which is an urgent, unspoken desire for the Manifestation of God, as if that might put an end to the unhappy writhings and strivings. If Bergman's films are about the implacable silence of God, they are also a quest for the meaning of existence. At first sight, Winkelman (von Sydow) is a happy man, and Anna (Liv Ullman) is more immediately unhappy: starting a relationship, they are contrasted with a happily married couple, Elis (Erland Josephson) and Eva – but she is rootless and more deeply disturbed than she first appears. As the relationships deteriorate – even more painfully than those in the earlier films –

Ingmar Bergman: The Quest for Understanding

Liv Ullman and Max von Sydow in *A Passion*, with which Bergman confirmed his position as one of the greatest of contemporary directors – if not the greatest of all. Those who have followed his career with enthusiasm might be permitted to say that it is in decline, for this film has been succeeded by a number of lesser works; but such is its stature that they were almost inevitably lesser.

the lies grow larger, the undiscussed matters more menacing, the sense of needless waste and loss more overpowering. Winkelman, at one point a man caught by vultures, is finally free but lonely – aimless, stricken, not knowing which way to turn.

We may conclude that Winkelman is Bergman, to the extent that both believe in 'complications which will bring on mental disturbances which will bring on, in their turn, physical and psychical violence.' It is notable that at this time he only used von Sydow when his leading male character was sympathetic (at other times he used Kulle and Björnstrand), but that he rarely made him appear twice in the same guise. Interviewed on film, during the film, von Sydow tells us, the audience, that he has difficulty playing a man without expression – which is plainly untrue, both as regards the character and his own magnificent acting ability. The other three players are equally enigmatic, but the film itself is not. The allusions are there to grasp, while Bergman's technical mastery was by now extraordinary. 'What is this deadly poison which corrodes all of us?' cries Andersson, 'leaving only the shell' – which may be an expression of Bergman's personal dilemmas. If so, it was having the reverse effect on his work.

The Touch (1971) furthers this examination of the loneliness and littleness of man, though it also has affinities with the mood and theme of some of his early films, when some people did come

together, did try to achieve love and did then fail. A woman (Bibi Andersson) is only middlingly happy with her very nice husband (von Sydow), so it is easy for a foreign-born archaeologist (Elliott Gould) to come between them. He, David, is a Jew born in Germany and brought up in the U.S. Like the woman's husband, he is a kind man, and it is possible that the woman allows herself to be destroyed by him because, like Sweden, she remains neutral to the suffering of those around her – specifically that of her husband. She seems unaware of any predicament other than the mechanics and ruses involved in committing adultery. For the first time since *Summer with Monika* Bergman is not generous towards his heroine. His obvious fondness for the von Sydow character may be a valediction, since Erland Josephson would, from the next film onward, replace this actor as Bergman's chief male protagonist (as long as he remained in Sweden); and the film's attitude towards the Gould character is to the end undefined. The presence of Gould did not bring the attention or the audiences that the film deserved – despite the fact that its largely English dialogue is both apposite and idiomatic. American producers had been offering Bergman backing in exchange for world rights, and he had always turned them down, but he relented, and this was a co-production with ABC television, during its brief foray into making films for cinemas. It is also Bergman's second consecutive film in colour, which he would use henceforth.

Earlier, the success of *The Silence* had caused United Artists to make a deal to handle world rights for the next few films, a happy proposition for Svensk Film-industri; but as the films involved had successively less appeal to the American art-house audience, the arrangement had come to an end with *The Shame*. As I have implied, the fluctuations of Bergman's reputation have been constant throughout his career, and I believe that to be because many critics failed to respond to or recognise the demands he made upon them. With the exceptions of *Now About All These Women* and *The Rite* he made what are to me a series of masterpieces between 1962 and 1971 – beginning with *Winter Light* and ending with *The Touch*, seven films in all. Yet it was the reception accorded **Cries and Whispers** (1972) that raised Bergman's reputation to the plateau on which it has remained since. The 'cries and whispers' of this family portrait are the usual preoccupations, but compared with the last few films this is chamber music to their tone poems – exquisitely wrought, but flawed. It is set at the turn of the century, with the past aspirations and present fantasies inexorably mixed; but sequences involving lesbian incest and sexual mutilation verge on self-parody.

It would have been surprising had Bergman not been drained after his great films, and perhaps significantly he worked in television for the next few years, where matters are usually dealt with on a smaller scale. He himself was fascinated by the technology of television. When asked years later whether his work could be seen as a force for social change he said 'Honestly, no', adding that he believed that television had usurped the cinema's position in this respect. His attitude does, I think, explain the nature of his subsequent films, since he observed that the cinema could help in personal matters: 'It is the director's job above all to reach out and touch people.' This is also true of his work for television.

Bergman wrote and directed two television series, the first of which he compared to 'Winnie the Pooh': A. A. Milne wrote his stories and found the world buying them, and 'it was the same with this. I wrote it just for fun and didn't know what to do with it.' Both series were shown in cinemas in different versions which we shall look at in a moment, but we should first note his production of **The Magic Flute** (1975), which was also released to cinemas. It is a small-scale delight, less theatrical than many screen versions of stage pieces, if using artifice to achieve the necessary magic but with the music as the unifying force.

Bergman also wrote a play for television, 'The Lie' – written in fact for Eurovision, which meant that it was telecast simultaneously in local productions in most of the Western democracies. It was an attempt to find the truth about a disintegrating marriage, and that is the subject also of **Scenes from a Marriage** (1974), which is not remotely like 'Winnie the Pooh'. Bergman has also said of it that it is very private, and we may suppose it to

be a distillation of personal experience. It should more aptly be titled 'Scenes from a Divorce', since after a long discussion on the complacency involved in a happy marriage it moves to even longer sequences of anguish and hurt. As played by Liv Ullman (who had lived with Bergman and borne his child) and Josephson, this couple, nice at heart, are stripped emotionally and, more cruelly, ethically before our eyes: the result is very much like a public expiation.

While planning **Face to Face** (1976) Bergman found himself suffering from anxieties which he could not pinpoint, so that there are parallels with his own life in this study of a psychiatrist (Ullman) moving towards a nervous breakdown. He sent a letter to members of his unit explaining that though the film concerned his usual subjects – life, death and love – he wanted to be more rigorous than usual. Without being as accessible as *Scenes from a Marriage* it is less baroque and allusive than the films which precede the two television series: in those Bergman seems to be speaking for humanity, but in these merely for himself. There are nevertheless enthralling sequences in *Face to Face*, notably Ullman's dreams, those of a would-be suicide, and her breakdown itself; but the inclusion of male homosexuality would seem to have been made as the one form of emotional behaviour with which Bergman had not previously dealt. It is surprising to find this humanitarian depicting the prancing, preening gays of films like *La Dolce Vita* (q.v.), and though they are supposed to be counterbalanced by the kindly professor (Josephson) the character is poorly defined. When the psychiatrist accuses him of wanting to seduce her, she is making one of the least of her mistakes, but a significant one, for she of all people is expected to understand emotional responses. Her failure to cope with herself means that the film is a variation on 'Physician, heal thyself', and we may see it as a cry of frustration on Bergman's part: for, like her, he was better equipped than most – after years of public psychoanalysis in his work – to expunge his personal devils and yet was still unable to do so.

Scenes from a Marriage was a six-part T.V. series cut to a movie of 168 minutes, that is, it contained just over half the original material. *Face to Face* was a four-part

Ingmar Bergman: The Quest for Understanding

serial, but after the acceptance of the earlier film in theatres, its cinema version was prepared simultaneously. More debatably, it was shown abroad in some countries in an English version, with Bergman's consent (he had for years controlled the English titles of his films), but to no particular commercial advantage. At least Ullman and Josephson spoke their own lines, in rhythm to the original image, so the dubbing was less barbarous than usual. Bergman had been offered backing by Dino de Laurentiis in Hollywood, and his next film was made in English in conjunction with that producer, but under very different circumstances. In 1976 Bergman had been literally hauled out of the theatre in which he was working for alleged tax offences, and his passport was confiscated: while waiting for the necessary public apology he went into self-imposed exile. With the backing of de Laurentiis, he had his choice of the major film-making countries; he chose Germany, and the resulting film, on Germany in the Twenties, was one he had long contemplated. The leading characters of **The Serpent's Egg** (1977) are trapeze artists, indicating once again the influence of *Varieté* – and the film also contains several none-too-oblique references to Lang's *Dr Mabuse* films. Many reviewers raised the name of Kafka, and those who disliked the film mentioned *Cabaret* (q.v.); indeed, the stage version of that musical may have provided Bergman's starting

point of a society drifting, inert, unaware. Both Manuela (Ullman) and Abel (David Carradine) are aliens, he the more so as an American Jew, and it is hard to understand why they remain in a Berlin increasingly hostile and potentially lethal for them. The nightmare eventually depends too much on *Caligari*. In fact the plot is rigged – to an extent unknown in Bergman since *Ansiktet* – and, as if this were a horror film, flesh is made to creep. Still, Bergman does transcend his material, if only once, when Abel goes berserk at the notion that it is because he is Jewish that he is (falsely) accused of several murders. At that moment Bergman reveals an understanding of the resentment that some Jews may feel at being Jews; and throughout he has a view of the Germans, who, with the possible exception of the inspector (Gert Froebe), emerge as a most unpleasant nation. Büchner's comment 'Man is an abyss and I turn giddy when I look down in it' was quoted by Bergman to justify the film, and if he had used it as a foreword he might have avoided the many unfavourable reviews he received.

Perhaps the strain of making films for over thirty years was beginning to tell: he had worked at the rate of one a year, with an intensity unknown in any other artist working in this medium. By this time he no longer pretended – if pretence it was – that his films were a summer diversion between his more serious winter work in the theatre, directing other people's plays. It would have been miraculous if he could have stayed at his highest level – miraculous if he could continue to dig deeply into himself every time. If the strain were to show, it would be preferable in an 'entertainment' rather than in one of the more personal films. **Autumn Sonata** (1978) is not personal, inasmuch as it was a vehicle for Ingrid Bergman, keeping a promise made to her some years earlier. Nevertheless, the customary themes are present – in his own words, 'the presence and absence of love, the longing for love, love's lies, love that is deformed and love that is our sole chance of survival.' The film's mother-daughter relationship springs from Bergman's feeling that this is a subject neglected by both literature and the cinema, but at the core of the piece is an argument on the consequences of choice – as experienced by a woman (Miss

Bergman) who put her career as a concert pianist before her children. The script is largely a duologue between mother and daughter (Liv Ullman), and after a mellow opening, promising reflection rather than dissension, the bitterness seems occasionally contrived. But there is a distinctive mood, unlike that of any other Bergman film, and the acting alone makes its thoughtfulness absorbing. Ullman is a great actress under Bergman's direction, and Ingrid Bergman, in her native tongue, emphasises how rarely her American films allowed her to display the full extent of her talent.

Aus dem Leben der Marionetten (1980), made in German, strikingly demonstrates Bergman's weaknesses when making a film for its own sake. *The Serpent's Egg* represented the first time that he had dealt extensively with crime (if we except *This Can't Happen Here*, a secret-agent thriller made 'for money' in 1950, which he declines to regard as one of his films), and this one begins with a particularly horrible crime: a successful fortyish businessman (Robert Atzorn) has murdered a prostitute and then committed anal intercourse upon the body. It is no surprise to discover that the cause is a latent homosexuality, as in *Il Conformista* (q.v.), among other films, and when the reason for this is revealed as being in his childhood, with an accompanying final shot of a boyhood toy, *Citizen Kane* springs inevitably to mind. Like *Kane*, this film is an investigation into the man's character and an analysis of his actions – a theme derived (at least) from Dostoevsky, but dealt with much in recent films, notably Imamura's *Vengeance Is Mine* (q.v.). Imamura's particular obsession with appearance and reality has also occupied Bergman, who here handles the series of interviews, examinations, dreams and reminiscences with a virtuosity which at least is not dependent on other films. The factors which prevent the man from recognising his homosexuality – a strict upbringing, a successful social life with his wife – suggest a more repressed time, earlier in the century. Bergman has certainly chosen a perverse way to acknowledge the bisexuality in all of us, and the counterbalancing figure of the gay man – the wife's partner and confidant – is no more satisfactory than the one in *Face to Face*. The actors concerned, like the screenplay, fail to convey the essence of the Bergman we have come to know through the artistry of Malmsten, von Sydow and Josephson – but, frankly, apart from the *angst*, I cannot find Bergman in this film. He had hitherto given more of himself than we had any right to expect, but by the same token we had not asked it of him.

The film was poorly received, meaning that only one of Bergman's three 'foreign' films could be counted a success. The Swedish government having apologised to him, he returned to make **Fanny and Alexander** (1982), with money provided by the Swedish Film Institute and the French company, Gaumont. As an expensive production, it was pre-sold to television in a five-hour version; the three-hour one available to cinemas shows Bergman again at his best. In the words of Derek Malcolm, 'It is a summing up devoid of all *angst*, but full of the old magician's most attractive tricks . . . drawing on the mastery of a lifetime'. The film starts with a family Christmas in 1907, perhaps influenced by *Il Gattopardo* (q.v.), for it celebrates a way of life, with no incident unrecorded. The Ekdahl's are an extrovert theatrical family, loving the good things in life, including food and sex; when one of its members dies, his widow (Ewa Fröling) remarries into a family which is the reverse – and the two young children of the title find life cruel. The new husband is a bishop, so here is the opposite side of the Swedish character – puritanical, spiritual, repressed, authoritarian. The children are spirited away by an ageing Jewish ex-lover (Erland Josephson) of their grandmother's, and with him appears the third influence on Swedish life and Bergman's work, also providing stimulus – the foreign and the fantastical. It is in this context – the old man and his nephews – that Bergman refers to *Wild Strawberries, Ansiktet* and *Persona*; the strain here is of the outsider, the one that moves between the other two, capable of profundity and yet unreal. Perhaps that is Bergman's final message, that he has spoken but we are not to take his words too seriously.

The Josephson character has something of Prospero, still capable of magic but intending to retire: perhaps this way, caught between the secular and the religious, Bergman wants us to remember him – for he had announced that this would be his last film and was quoted (by *The Times*, London) as saying that the Bergman era was over – I trust with a sense of humour. It is doubtful whether most of us have thought of the past forty years in these terms, since he has been the least influential among great film-makers – because he is the most personal.

Nevertheless he overshadowed his Swedish colleagues, though Arne Sucksdorff (b.1917) enjoyed a brief degree of international fame. A former photographer, he had written, directed, photographed and edited some short documentaries, including **A Divided World** (1948), a study of the savagery of forest animals. He returned to this theme in the feature-length **The Great Adventure** (1953), though it is peripheral to the central story of a small boy and his pet otter. It enchanted one generation – admittedly a generation to whom animal documentaries meant either complete lack of imagination or Disney's jazzed-up 'True Life Adventures', but today the blending of fact and fiction looks very contrived. Though working deftly with colour, wide screen and stereophonic sound, **The Flute and the Arrow** (1957) was merely a hackneyed tale of a tiger which threatens an Indian village, and **My Home Is Copacabana** (1965) was a completely artificial study of homeless children in Rio de Janeiro. Indeed, Sucksdorff seemed to confirm the invalidity of the semi-documentary in comparison with fiction told with the insight that de Sica brought to *Sciuscià*.

Earlier, only a few people outside Sweden went to see **The Pram** (1962), the story of a girl and boy who make love too soon and pay the consequences; or **Raven's End** (1963), the tale of an adolescent growing up in the depressed Sweden of the Thirties. But Bo Widerberg (b.1930) achieved world fame with **Elvira Madigan** (1967), a remake of an earlier film and based on a true case towards the end of the last century, when an aristocratic soldier (Thommy Berggren) ran off with a circus tightrope walker (Pia Degermark). In the film they spend an idyllic summer, haunted by the plangent second movement of Mozart's 21st Piano Concerto (which made the hit parade as 'The Theme from *Elvira Madigan*'). Then their money runs out and they are reduced to subsisting on berries. The film is visually exquisite, but, as George Cukor once observed, 'The moment you're aware of something, like the photography is great, it usually means something else is lacking.' Widerberg may be the most guilty of all current practitioners – certainly of those drawn to the more serious issues. **Adalen 31** (1969) and **The Ballad of Joe Hill** (1971) respectively concern a strike and strike breakers in a small Northern town in the early Thirties, and the Swedish immigrant (Berggren) who became one of America's early labour martyrs. Both are unsuitably pretty – which would matter less if Widerberg paid as much attention to the script as to the photography. He dumps an inadequate number of facts before us, and, with an abrupt statement, assumes that he has our sympathy because he is on the side of the people.

His friend and contemporary, Jan Troell (b.1931), has also been disappointing, after his beautifully realised first feature, **Here Is Your Life** (1966), which he adapted from Eyvind Johansson's novel about a boy growing up in the earlier years of this century. The boy goes from pillar to post, and he is the usual wistful, weak adolescent of such films, so that this picaresque story is of little originality; but the discoveries of adolescence have seldom been as sympathetically portrayed. Continuing his theme of an unsatisfactory life in **Who Saw Him Die?** (1967), a schoolteacher (Per Oscarsson) is unable to control his pupils, and Troell is as indecisive as his principal character. That he was happiest with images was borne out by **The Immigrants** (1971) and **The New Land** (1972), a two-part story of a Swedish couple (Ullman, von Sydow) and their adventures in America – and significantly it was only in the two countries concerned that the films were liked. Troell's American film, **Zandy's Bride** (1974), with Liv Ullman, was admired nowhere.

Bergman himself helped to produce **Summer Paradise** (1977). It was directed by Gunnel Lindblom, one of his actresses, who collaborated on the script with Bergman's former associate, Ulla Isaksson, on whose novel it is based. Centred on a middle-aged woman doctor (Birgitta Valberg), it examines both her not too satisfactory life and the members of her family during their summer vacation. The influence of Bergman lies no heavier on it than on other Swedish films, including those of the Finnish-born Jörn Donner (b.1933), who has written and lectured on Bergman, and who is married to Harriet Andersson. She and Berggren were the stars of Donner's first feature, **A Sunday in September** (1963), a study of marriage in its year of disintegration. This may have been the first non-pornographic film to show a couple in the act of copulation – if only from the waist up – but that guaranteed it few audiences outside Sweden.

And that brings us full circle, for apart from Bergman, the Swedish cinema continues to mean sex and gloom – though since 1963, or thereabouts, most nations have been producing their own sex films, and they are not interested in importing the gloom. The Scandinavian cinema as a whole has inclined towards rustic tales of everyday rape, only too often reminiscent of 'Cold Comfort Farm'. Also, since the populations of the four Scandinavian countries are comparatively small, so are the audiences and hence chances for film-makers. Almost certainly the best Finnish film of this time, and probably ever, is **The Unknown Soldier** (1955), the tale of men at the Front during the Winter War of 1940. Its theme is their adaptability. Edvin Laine's direction is notable for its honesty and integrity no matter how much he may have borrowed from some famous war films and no matter that the narrative is weak and the steady tempo monotonous.

During this period Carl Dreyer made three films in Denmark (and one in Sweden, which seems to have disappeared), all adapted from plays: **Day of Wrath** (1944), **Ordet** (1954) and **Gertrud** (1964), and as offered, all entirely trivial. Poor Dreyer simply forgot how to direct in his decades between films. His admirers may invoke 'integrity' to excuse the paucity of his work, but he is plainly incapable of bringing his characters to life, or sustaining any degree of narrative force or rhythm; furthermore it was foolish to choose such blatant melodramas for which he clearly had no conviction. *Day of Wrath* is about seventeenth-century witch hunts, and *Gertrud* is Ibsen-and-water – from a play by Soderberg, a contemporary of Ibsen – clearly bereft of his intellectual fibre and his gift for plot. *Ordet* is another

matter: the subject is merely listless. But it was powerful enough in Molander's 1943 Swedish version – in which Sjöström played the paterfamilias, the rural Montague who, for religious reasons, refuses to allow his son to marry into the Capulets. The creator of this conceit was Kaj Munk, a Danish country parson, and the title means 'The Word' – *i.e.* the word of God. Both Bergman and Sjöström in their films felt the need to have God speak to them – an importunity which seems to be a quintessentially Scandinavian preoccupation.

The Swedishness of both Bergman and Sjöström we have already noted, and Bergman's debt to Sjöström, but whereas these two turned it to triumphant account, it has inhibited their fellow film-makers – most seriously those of Bergman's own generation and after. They seem to feel that there must be seriousness of purpose and seriousness of manner, which often results in a commonplace view of the mundane at a snail's pace. There is also a certain coldness, as if the directors at heart disliked the characters they are offering to us. So, perhaps, does Bergman; and though interviews indicate a cheery and good-natured man, his films would seem to intimate that he is disenchanted with himself. If so, he has turned that concept to magnificent, magisterial account.

He is unquestionably among the greatest film-makers, though that may be seen as a comment on some of the others, since the word 'great' is often applied to those who could better be described as purveyors of good entertainment. Clearly that is no mean achievement, but those whom I think most deserving of our admiration are those who have tried to illuminate our society. Bergman is not the first name that comes to mind in considering films on political abuses, the origins of war or the ills of the deprived, though he has touched on all these matters. He has, instead, cried out against the relationship of the sexes, against the demands society makes upon the artist, and the very nature of God. No one has better expressed our difficulties with each other or with the Deity, in the films that I referred to as masterpieces. But even some of the earlier, relatively journeyman pieces remain as stimulating as when they were first made: his is a unique and astonishing body of work.

35

The Japanese Masters

IT WAS SATYAJIT RAY who pronounced them 'the Japanese masters', and as there are few opportunities to see their films in India, he may have based his assessment on only a few of the titles that we shall be examining in this chapter – which are, in turn, only a small proportion of the total. In this book I have restricted myself in general to those movies shown throughout the world, but the Japanese cinema requires special consideration. Ever since Kurosawa's *Rashomon* appeared in the West – magical harbinger of a mighty film industry – most of his other films have been accessible outside Japan; some of those of Ozu and Mizoguchi have been shown commercially and entered the international repertory, as is true of a handful made by Ichikawa and Kobayashi. These are undoubtedly great film-makers – so good that we may assume that they tower above their confrères, tantalisingly unknown to most of us. Yet festivals and retrospectives arranged by such bodies as the Japan Film Council have indicated that Japan's cinema heritage is one of the richest in the world. For instance, Heinosuke Gosho made over one hundred films, not one of which has been shown commercially in the West: yet the few that I have seen demonstrate a skill and perception the equal of his internationally acclaimed colleagues. Further, the country's decorative tradition is so strong that even the most plodding of its film-makers is capable of work of a satisfying visual beauty. I am therefore going to discuss most of the Japanese films that I have seen.

I cannot imagine any true lover of the cinema missing an opportunity to see any Japanese film of the Fifties or early Sixties made in the wide-screen process – whether in colour or black and white. Unlike most Western directors, those in Japan mastered the new width immediately, deftly adhering to the graphic tradition of the *makimon* (i.e. the scroll paintings which unroll horizontally). The wide screen did not arrive – as in the West – at a time of desperation, for television did not become a threat to Japanese cinemas until the late Sixties; moreover, it came into use at a time when the country's leading directors were experimenting with film form. They did not think of themselves as innovators, and as soon as any new narrative form was introduced – as, say, the intercutting of past and present – it was immediately adopted by others. These film-makers considered themselves artists, still rigidly applying the rules of master-pupil relationships to themselves and their assistants or followers, but they were realistic enough to consider their own needs subservient to those of the industry as a whole. Audiences, unlike most of those in other countries, recognised the director as a factor when choosing the evening's entertainment, but the studios were sufficiently powerful to control even the most famous. There were constant pressures to maintain budgets and schedules, so that in the peak year of 1956 the industry produced 514 films. It says much for the Japanese temperament that under these factory conditions a number of outstanding films resulted – and the Japanese cinema of this period can be seen as one of the most impressive in the history of this industry. As we can date the major creative eras of other national industries, so this one begins *circa* 1950: then, as the major directors of this magnificent decade aged, so in the Sixties the quality declined. Their achievement may not be known outside

Japan, but many of them are among the greatest ever to work in the medium.

Some of the accolades for the later films of Yasujiro Ozu are, however, ill judged. By the time he and the century were in their early fifties his style had become ossified, and his camera, stationed knee-high at distances from four to six feet from the actors, *never* moved; worse, he appeared to be making the same film again and again. Nevertheless, his first two postwar films are very fine, reminiscent of his most reflective and delicate earlier work, stories of the poor and deprived told without sentimentality. Both **The Record of a Tenement Gentleman** (1947) and **A Hen in the Wind** (1948) deal with situations current throughout the country and many parts of Europe at the time, where daily life had been disrupted by the War. Respectively they deal with a child left homeless by the War, and the wife (Kinuyo Tanaka) whose husband returns to be confronted by her wartime infidelity. Despite the title and the fact that the tenement gentleman is played by Chishu Ryu – who remained Ozu's favourite interpreter – the central situation of the first film chiefly concerns a crusty old lady whose heart is melted by the boy. In the second, the wife prefers the pavement to the breadline: the film makes clear that there was no government provision for the wives of soldiers who were missing, still trying to make their way home from those parts of the mainland where they had once been conquerors. Nevertheless, both films border upon nineteenth-century traditions of melodrama which Japanese cinema seemed reluctant to relinquish.

Late Spring (1949) is based on a story by Kazuo Hirotsu, and it must have been the tale for which Ozu had been searching all his life – for he remade it, with variations, many times. After a lapse of fifteen years he was reunited with Kogo Noda, who earlier had contributed to some of his screenplays; thereafter they collaborated on each of Ozu's films. Both this and **The Munekata Sisters** (1950) are unusual among his work, since they are not based on original screenplays, and in both cases Ozu found it difficult to cope with the author's intention and the moulding of it to his own interpretation. Yet, working thereafter from his own material, characters and situations became increasingly

two-dimensional. He also began to slacken his pace – most of his late films are over two hours long – and audiences can pick up his points faster than he realised. Both these films look at the marriage plans of young people and their impact on the family; and it is not too much to say that virtually the only difference between *Late Spring* and **Early Summer** (1951) is that the latter is thirty minutes longer and Mr Ryu plays Setsuko Hara's brother instead of her father.

It was not until **The Flavour of Green Tea over Rice** (1952) that Ozu eventually expressed an opinion on arranged marriages, by contrasting a middle-aged marriage grown stale with the attitude of the wife's niece, who resists the idea of the *o-miai* – the formal introduction to the chosen fiancé. Both in this film and **Tokyo Story** (1953) Ozu's feeling for people trapped in their environment is much revitalised, in the latter instance perhaps because of a change of subject: a middle-aged couple visit their children in Tokyo, only to be disillusioned, for they find their children no longer interested in them. But **Early Spring** (1956), another new departure, is lifeless. At least, it is not so much a new departure as a return to the studies of office life he made so brilliantly many years before: they had been shot in two weeks, and it is probably significant that he laboured three years over this. It was made under the influence of Kurosawa's *Living* (q.v.), and was clearly meant to be a definite statement on the life of an

The later films of Yasijuro Ozu give a new meaning to the expression 'much of a muchness', but his first two postwar films are remarkable. Both concern contemporary problems, *A Hen in the Wind* being specifically about a soldier's wife (Kinuyo Tanaka) who, having received no money from her husband during his absence, resorts to prostitution to pay the hospital bills of her small son. She sins but once, but is too honest not to tell her husband (Shuji Sano) when he returns – and, clearly, the matter causes a rift between them.

961

ordinary clerk. He said, 'I wanted to show the life of a man with such a job . . . his hopes for the future gradually dissolving, his realising that, even though he has worked for years, he has accomplished nothing . . . It is the longest of my postwar films, but I tried to avoid anything that would be dramatic and to collect only casual scenes of everyday life, hoping in doing so that the audience would feel the sadness of this kind of life.'

His own life may have been sad. He never married and lived with his mother all his life, so that these films about fathers might be a wish-fulfilment. Significantly – as in the case of several other directors who have worked out their fantasies or problems on film (Bergman is the outstanding example) – he has chosen the same actor, Chishu Ryu, to be his mouthpiece. Increasingly in these late films Ryu may be seen drinking with cronies in bars – for long sequences – pondering on their relationships with their children and the meaning of marriage. When, in contrast, the father has less admirable qualities, as in **Equinox Flower** (1958), Ozu's first film in colour, he is played by Shin Saburi. This film and **Tokyo Twilight** (1957) do glance at subjects other than arranged marriages, and **Ohayo**/*Good Morning* (1959) providentially focuses on a small suburban community and in particular on the two young boys in one family.

All these films, with the exception of *The Munekata Sisters*, produced by Toho, were made by Ozu for Shochiku, but a move to Daiei for one film only, **Floating Weeds** (1959), proved refreshing. This remake of his tersely constructed early film about tensions in a theatrical troupe is now much too long – and also unconvincing – but there are compensations, especially in the picture-postcard views that constitute his style on location. Daieicolor is a great improvement on the Agfacolor Ozu had been using, and instead of his usual photographer, Yushan Atsuta, he has Kazuo Miyagawa, who did amazing work with Kurosawa, Mizoguchi and Kobayashi. On the other hand, Ozu's last three films resume his old preoccupations, with an increasing staleness: **Late Autumn** (1960), **The End of Summer** (1961) and **An Autumn Afternoon** (1962). As the titles indicate, his integrity has now been combined with melancholy;

his formal visual style may still be deceptively subtle, but if we knew him only through these films we might regard him as a cold, academic director. Only rarely do we glimpse the marvellous observer of his Silent films – he had become either timid or obsessed to the point of eccentricity – but seeing his faithful players for the last time – Mr Ryu, Saburi and Miss Hara – is like saying goodbye to old friends.

If Ozu's vision contracted as he aged, the reverse is true of his contemporaries, though that has less to do with ageing than with the War. At a time when the country was at its most militaristic, a significant number of Japanese film-makers were trying to express humanist values. There is, I think, a schism in the Japanese character, a dichotomy – on the one hand there is the mentality which led to the conflict in the Pacific, and on the other the concern for human life and values which is reflected in virtually every Japanese film. Both may usually be found in the *jidai-geki*, or historical subjects, using the one to point up the other. Those film-makers who had attempted to criticise the regime felt themselves justified by its complete collapse, but they now had to consider the whole experience of War, the atomic bomb, defeat and Occupation. Mizoguchi said that his postwar films represented the working-off of 'a sense of resentment' which had been accumulating during the War, and even today these films remain astonishing (it was not till the Seventies that his work of the immediate postwar period was seen in the West). As in the prewar years, he and his colleagues were still subject to the dictates of a military mentality – in this case those of the Americans, who as the occupying force, were quite definite about the films which the Japanese could and could not make. Subjects concerning rehabilitation and the democratisation of Japanese life were likely to be acceptable, but certain to meet with disapproval were any which glorified the military, the Empire and outmoded codes of honour. If we refer again to the prewar Japanese cinema, we can see that these rules did not put too heavy a burden on the best film-makers; they often met the challenge with great honesty and a searing power.

Mizoguchi's first postwar film was **The Victory of Women** (1946), hastily made for Shochiku, which needed product. The company had no other directors at its Ofuna studio and Mizoguchi worked from an already prepared script by Kogo Noda and Kaneto Shindo. It centres on the personal and professional relations between Hiroko (Kinuyo Tanaka), a female lawyer, and her Fascist-minded brother-in-law, also a lawyer. He was responsible for her fiancé's wartime sentence as a political prisoner, and now they are to fight in court, she as the counsel for defence, over a poor woman who has accidentally strangled her baby. Hiroko believes the responsibility for this act lies with the armaments manufacturer who had sacked the woman's husband, so it is clear that the film has a moral tone acceptable to the American authorities. (It also has an inconclusive ending which alone would put it ahead of most contemporary Occidental films.)

The Americans also approved of the fact that the chief protagonist was a woman in a profession usually associated with men, and Mizoguchi's next two films, **Five Women Around Utamaro** (1946) and **The Love of Sumako the Actress** (1947) are also about the emancipation of women. Yoshikata Yoda, reunited with Mizoguchi, wrote them under rather difficult conditions, since both are *jidai-geki* subjects, to which the Americans were opposed. However after much tampering with the scripts it was decided that, on the whole, the films would be beneficial. Both are biographical, but at the opposite end of the scale to such concurrent Hollywood products as *Devotion* and *Song of Love*. The painter Utamaro is portrayed as a man of the people with a modern attitude towards the rights of women; and Sumako was the actress who first played Ibsen's Nora in Japan. Despite Mizoguchi's training as an artist and his work with actors neither film is particularly strong on the artistic process, and *Sumako* is at its boldest in the relationship between the actress (Miss Tanaka) and her married professor (So Yamamura). *Utamaro* at least reflects its subject matter in being exquisitely beautiful, and contains memorable portraits both of the artistic life of Tokyo in the eighteenth century and of Mizoguchi himself – for Yoda based his characterisation of Utamaro on him.

On the other hand, **Women of the Night** (1948) is a cry of pain: like *Sciuscià* and *Paisà* it is an unreasoned, instinctive outburst, blaming the War for the current chaos in the cities, yet aware that War should have blown the old system away. The first impression is of an unsettled population, struggling to survive, uncertain where loved ones are or whether they are alive; and some, haunting the bomb sites looking for pick-ups, are both desperate and vicious. When, at the beginning, the heroine (Kinuyo Tanaka) is told by an old crone that there are other ways to survive than by selling clothes, we are aware that the plot-line will be much like the German prostitute films of the Twenties (made also by a country in defeat). But this is not like them, nor like Mizoguchi's own geisha films; his vision is darker than it was – moving towards the misanthropy of his later masterpieces – and very much at the centre of the whore's life are such matters as pregnancy and syphilis. When the heroine bitterly talks of infecting her clients in revenge, we are not sure whether it is because her lover has slept with her sister or whether it is because he has given her a venereal disease. The double reasoning and the use of implication were present in Japanese cinema long before they were in ours and it is possible that in this case Mizoguchi avoided a factual statement because he did not wish to sensationalise the subject.

In **My Love Has Been Burning** (1949) the heroine is again played by Kinuyo Tanaka, and once more she is an exponent of women's rights. She is a liberal, and the film is remarkable as a portrait of society in an age of political turmoil, towards the end of the last century. It centres on a group of activists, with their printing presses, their attempts at solidarity with strikers, their imprisonment and subsequent election to power; but in contrast to his public views, the Westernised hero (Ichiro Sugai) is not so advanced in private, and Miss Tanaka, in an echo of 'A Doll's House', finds herself forced to leave him when she discovers that he has merely 'used' his other mistress. We may also note that it would have been extraordinary in a Western film of the time to hear a woman say that she enjoyed sex. Yoda and Shindo wrote it, from a story by Kogo Noda based on an autobiography by Hideko Kageyama, and it was Mizoguchi's last film for Shochiku, who had refused to back *The Life of*

963

O-Haru (q.v.). Shintoho agreed to do so, provided that Mizoguchi would first direct **Portrait of Madame Yuki** (1950), based on a popular novel. Madame Yuki (Michiyo Kogure) is an aristocrat, married to an uncouth, somewhat older man (Rijiro Yanagi) who flaunts his mistress before her: that she cannot bring herself to leave him is almost certainly due to sexual attraction. The film has an exceptionally beautiful end – as the camera tracks back and forth across the lake we are aware of a suicide – but it is essentially a hollow tale.

While waiting to make *O-Haru*, which was to be the first of his masterpieces, Mizoguchi made one very good film, **Miss Oyu** (1951), and another that is almost a great one – **The Lady from Musashino** (1951). The latter, set during the last days of the War, has a line to the effect that that event was caused by a panicky government in conjunction with mentalities left over from the Meiji period. *Miss Oyu*, set in the Twenties, is an examination of the effect of such mentalities on three people – a man and two women – whose defiance of the feudal laws governing sex and marriage leads to the destruction of their relationship. *Musashino* centres on a group of friends, scrutinising them like flies in amber in a way that recalls Virginia Woolf. They are worldly people but struggling for identity, voluntarily and involuntarily hurting each other as they try to settle emotional problems which are beyond their understanding. It is a rare achievement in cinema – one which Bergman later managed, but with a Nordic intensity rather than the elegiac feeling with which Mizoguchi endows the subject here. Later, Ray was also successful, and, in a different fashion, Antonioni (q.v.) – but before them Mizoguchi and his compatriots were using an allusive style then unknown in Western cinema.

Mizoguchi himself thought this film 'didn't quite work' because it dealt with too many themes – among them the uncertainties of the postwar world, the break-up of family life, the responsibility of arms manufacturers and the personal dilemma of a professor who is, significantly, an authority on Stendhal. It is the best of Mizoguchi's contemporary films, marred only by the ending – which, as is so often the case with this director, involves a suicide; moreover, in this instance it is only

too predictable. The Musashino of the title is a region near Tokyo much loved by two of the characters, and we see it through their eyes. This is an example of style and content in perfect cohesion.

Mizoguchi's mature style first became apparent in *Utamaro*. That was the first time he had gone further back in history than the Meiji period, but the world portrayed was fundamentally tranquil and his treatment selective. Before the War, in *Oyuki the Virgin*, with its background of turmoil, he had used a more probing camera, and *My Love Has Been Burning* was another Meiji drama which required a style to match the turbulence of a time when violence, rape and revolt were apparently common occurrences. The camera sweeps up, past and down on crowds and groupings, whereas in *Miss Oyu* he returned to what we might call his contemplative style. There, his people are found in medium or long-shot, often still, in pools of light; he lingers on a moonlit garden, on the shimmering waters of a lake, mists rising from the fields. The two styles coalesce marvellously in Mizoguchi's four masterpieces, **The Life of O-Haru** (1952), **Ugetsu Monogatari** (1953), **Sansho Dayu** (1954) and **Chikamatsu Monogatari** (1954). These are, simply stated, stories of love and suffering in feudal times. Japan remained an oligarchy well into the last quarter of the nineteenth century, and if three of the four films are set in the early eighteenth century (to the West, of course, an age of elegance) they echo the more remote era of *Sansho Dayu*, set in the eleventh century. The foreword to that film states that it was a time 'when mankind had yet to awaken to his humanity'. The population, especially those people living in rural areas, had to be alert against the depradations of warriors, of marauding armies which could in minutes destroy their livelihood, burn their homes and rape the women. Mizoguchi's disposition led him not to tales of heroism, but to tragedy – except of course that tragedy, by definition, concerns the great – and his people are either the poor professional and merchant classes, or the impoverished nobility, families of disgraced samurai.

These historical tales, adapted for the screen chiefly by Yoda and/or Matsutaro Kawaguchi, have their sources in literature.

Chikamatsu Monogatari is searingly faithful to the then advanced drama by the eponymous eighteenth-century playwright. It lacks the tragic intensity of *Sansho* and *O-Haru*: it is 'Romeo and Juliet' to their 'King Lear', with the lovers thwarted by conditions and circumstances, while the protagonists in the latter films struggle on in a universally hostile and savage world. They struggle because there is hope: 'Compassion is what makes men human,' says the father to the son in *Sansho*. 'Be merciful even at a cost to yourself' (but he may say it because this film is the only one of the four to have its origins in a work of the twentieth century). O-Haru herself and the family in *Sansho* suffer – through deprivation, prostitution, injustice, rape, poverty, war, the ambition and greed of others and, indeed, all that flesh is heir to – but they have hope, compassion and varieties of love to sustain them. We may at times be tempted to think of Chekhov's Trofimov and his two-and-twenty misfortunes; the lot of O-Haru is so miserable that a positive reaction to the film can best be made by considering the content of its fellows.

Chikamatsu, since it is set in a time of peace, is the quietest of the quartet, and *Ugetsu* perhaps the most remarkable, since it most consistently blends its mysticism and beauty with barbarism and cruelty. It is also the most magical, especially towards the end, when its hero returns home, a Ulysses with hallucinations. When Mizoguchi died, Kurosawa commented that there were very few directors left able to view the past clearly and realistically, and we may add, in all its complexity. These films are richly satisfying experiences and visually magnificent: Mizoguchi's photographer was Kazuo Miyagawa, whose work we noted on *Floating Weeds*. Miyagawa's other films include *Rashomon*, with Kurosawa, and *The Human Condition* (q.v.) with Kobayashi; yet his films with Mizoguchi alone would proclaim him a genius in his field. The leading players in the four films include Kinuyo Tanaka, Masayuki Mori, Machiko Kyo and Eitaro Shindo.

Although **Shin-Heike Monogatari** (1955) and **The Empress Yang Kwei-Fei** (1955) are taken from traditional tales of feudal times, neither is of a similar quality. Kaneto Shindo, in discussing Mizoguchi,

commented that he had poured everything he had into *O-Haru*, and that these two films represented a decline, 'for he was in need of money at that time and was bent upon making some out of his last films'. They are both in (Eastman) colour, and it is perhaps superfluous to say that it is exquisitely used. It may be that Mizoguchi's energies all went into the design, for there is something relatively lifeless in the telling, as if he had no interest in the intrigue which surrounds the main threads of the plot – respectively about the son of a warrior searching for his real father, and an emperor (Mori) whose love for his favourite concubine (Machiko Kyo) is destroyed because of her family's ambition. (The latter, set in China, was a co-production with Hong Kong.)

During these years Mizoguchi made two more films on geisha life, **Gion Festival Music** (1953) and **A Woman of Rumour** (1954), which, while slight, take on added resonance when placed beside the

Unlike Ozu, Kenji Mizoguchi became more interesting as he aged, and just before he died he made some magnificent historical films. *The Life of O-Haru* features Kinuyo Tanaka, who worked for him often during her career. Here she plays a woman buffeted by fate. She is seen with Toshiro Mifune, who pays with his life for daring to fall in love with such a high-born lady.

rather better **Street of Shame** (1956), his last film. All three look with regret on the changes in the geisha world and on its downgrading in the years since the War. After the War many geishas became prostitutes, and *Gion* concerns one such (Michiko Kogure) fighting to retain her dignity. The film is not a remake of *Sisters of the Gion*, as has been claimed, but the situation is similar – with the elder geisha, trained in the traditional way, and her younger companion, of more fiery disposition. There are two women in *A Woman of Rumour* and, as in 'Mrs Warren's Profession', they are mother and daughter – the latter, incidentally, modelling herself on Audrey Hepburn. She falls in love with her mother's lover, a young doctor, who does not, in the circumstances, behave as admirably as we had reason to expect. *Street of Shame* has more in common with *Women of the Night*, since it is simply about prostitution. All these films infer, if not state, that these women have chosen their profession out of poverty; that their lives are being destroyed by varying emotional needs and that they will be available as men need them. The garish brothel in *Street of Shame* is called 'Dreamland', and the Yoshiwara we see outside shows the influence of the now departed G.I.s, with its glaring neon signs. Miki (Machiko Kyo), ex-mistress of a G.I., dresses and acts like an American cutie – a striking contrast to the gentle Michiko Kogure in *Gion Festival Music*. Miss Kogure – who was also Mizoguchi's Madam Yuki and is, perhaps, his most enchanting actress – also works in 'Dreamland', but only to support her family. Another inmate (Ayako Wakao) is a cheat and a money hoarder; her attempted murder is as near to violence as any instant in Mizoguchi's contemporary subjects except for *Women of the Night*. Unlike the kindly madam of *A Woman of Rumour*, this one is mercenary and vicious, and the customary male owner, often benevolent in earlier films, is hypocritical and greedy.

The prevailing bitterness in this film is not surprising, for Mizoguchi was a life-long frequenter of geisha-houses and, as I said earlier, believed that he was therefore responsible for his wife's mental instability; he also knew that he was dying of leukaemia. The film itself is less hermetic than his others on this subject, and it is possible that at a time when Japanese films were trickling through to the West he thought he could abandon his contemplative style.

Because of its subject matter, *Street of Shame* was seen in London not long after it was finished and in New York three years later. Initially both cities (and hence their respective countries) proved hospitable neither to Mizoguchi nor to Ozu. The first of the latter's films to arrive was *Ohayo*, which was put into commercial distribution in America some seven years after it had been made, and in Britain after another gap of seven years. *The Life of O-Haru* was, in fact, the second postwar Japanese film seen in the West when, following the success of *Rashomon*, it was sent to the Venice Festival in 1952, but it failed to reap the same acclaim. The following year the Japanese selectors submitted a contemporary subject, *Children of Hiroshima* (q.v.). After a festival showing in 1954, one New York distributor launched *Ugetsu* to an indifferent response. However, the French critics, right for once, began to praise Mizoguchi, and within a few years of his death in 1956, he became an established name in Paris art cinemas. In 1962, when the British magazine *Sight and Sound* published its international critics' poll of the best films ever made, *Ugetsu* was sufficiently known worldwide for it to be voted fourth, in a tie with *Greed* – whereupon a British distributor arranged for its first public showing in this country. It was not until the Seventies that as many as a handful of Mizoguchi's films were seen commercially in Britain. The situation is little different in the U.S., though a number have sneaked into art-houses and campus screenings without benefit of press shows. More recently the same has happened in America to the films of Mikio Naruse.

Naruse is an unassuming film-maker whose work becomes more appealing as it becomes more familiar. And, like Mizoguchi, he seems to have moved from early mediocrity to mastery towards the end of his career. He specialised in *shomin-geki* subjects,[*] and with **Repast** (1951) re-established the theme of everyday lower middle-class life, which, apart from Ozu's films, had been out of favour since the

---

[*]As explained earlier, *shomin-geki* is a modern working-class subject and *jidai-geki* is a story set before the abolition of feudalism in 1871.

War. The subject – a failing marriage – is one that Ozu treated twice and the resemblance is heightened by the presence of his favourite actress, Setsuko Hara; but Naruse's film is at once more richly detailed and more deeply felt than Ozu's. Naruse, like Mizoguchi, was a pessimist, certain that none of us gets what we want in this world. His study of a family, **Mother** (1952), leaves us in doubt as to whether the mother, no matter how beloved, is truly happy; the young tour guide in **Lightning** (1952) decides against marriage after contemplating her sponging brother, her weak-willed brother-in-law and her sweaty suitor – though she is uncertain of the alternative; and the retired geishas in **Late Chrysanthemums** (1954) live only in regret. Naruse returned to this theme in **Flowing** (1956), which is even richer: his people as ever are trapped – making do, carrying on, locked in vain hopes and aspirations.

Perhaps because he uses the wide screen and colour in **The Summer Clouds** (1958), Naruse's world seems less glum – but that is partly because humour, a rare trait, is allowed to intrude. The film concerns the landowners who were dispossessed by the 1946 reforms, its heroine a war widow who accepts as her lot both her ungrateful mother-in-law and the fields she has to farm singlehandedly. Her family is drawn to the larger towns, while her affair with a married journalist suggests that she herself should grasp at any possible change in a life of poverty. The film contains a wonderful portrait of a rural community, even though the leading actress, Chikage Awashima, gets a number of starry close-ups, and a 'sad' ending which seems intended mainly to please her fans. Certainly Naruse envisaged **Her Lonely Lane** (1962) as a vehicle for Hideko Takamine, one of his favourite players, but her rather unforceful performance does not overly involve us in this character and her singularly unfortunate emotional life. It is based on a memoir by Fumiko Hayashi, whose work also provided the basis for *Repast*, *Lightning* and *Late Chrysanthemums*. Hayashi was the daughter of itinerant workers which was why Naruse, with his deprived childhood, was attracted to her work. Possibly his instinctive urgency had lessened by this time, and certainly he is at his most compassionate in

Flowing, the one film of his I have seen which can be set with those of his peers.

The films of Heinosuke Gosho are even richer. Like Naruse, he is sentimental, but the dusky pessimism of his characters is gently tempered by both humour and introspection. A pupil of Shimazu, he had directed his first film in 1925, and his style eventually became as formularised as that of Ozu, except that the vast number and composition of his images – aided by the occasional rapidity of his cutting – allow for greater fluidity. Those of his films that I have seen are more lovingly crafted than those of any other director I know – including his colleagues – and that in itself makes them very satisfying to watch. It is perhaps necessary to add that he uses his settings brilliantly – the industrial Tokyo of **Four Chimneys** (1953), and the hotel and its surroundings of **An Inn in Osaka** (1954). The former is a comparatively simple tale of a childless couple and someone else's unwanted baby, and the latter a study of a group of people who realise at last to what extent their lives have been changed by a guest in the hotel, Mr Mita (Shuji Sano). Hotel life was a particularly congenial subject for Gosho, for he liked to manipulate a dozen characters at the same time, contrasting their always different moral dilemmas.

He returned to a hotel setting in **The Fireflies** (1958). The plot involves a neglected wife (Chikage Awashima) and the inn's proprietor, who in middle age develops a passion, quite platonic, for a brave

Mikio Naruse is not one of the great directors of Japanese cinema, but he is only a little below them – which means that most of his work is very good indeed. His best film is *Flowing*, a haunting and penetrating study of life in a geisha house, which tells how modern changes are affecting an ageing geisha, who is also beset by financial difficulties. She is played by Isuzu Yamada, right, and to the left Kinuyo Tanaka supports Haruko Sugimara. All three actresses are among the best-known to Japanese audiences, and Miss Yamada, like Miss Tanaka, had a very long career as a star.

The Japanese Masters

That the genre stories worked so well in Japanese films was due to the director. Gosho's *An Inn in Osaka*, adapted from a novel by Takitaro Minakami, is a complex study of life in a boarding house. Shuji Sano is the catalyst, and like many Japanese heroes he is a well-meaning man whose good intentions turn out badly. He helps a geisha, Nobuko Otawa, who drinks too much and is involved with a friend – but that does not stop her from falling in love with this Galahad.

young man (Miki Mori). Like Naruse's *The Summer Clouds*, this film could be regarded as another occasion for audiences to watch Miss Awashima suffering, but the embroidery is rich: the lazy husband obsessed with cleanliness; the sister who runs off with the travelling conman; and the mistress who hopes to make capital on the – false – claim that she is pregnant. Moreover, the brave young man, Sakamoto, is a liberal who was (in life) assassinated in 1867 for his attempts to overthrow the Tokugawa regime. Japanese audiences expected *jidai-geki* films to be connected with actual events. This one, though considerably less subtle than *An Inn in Osaka*, manages to suggest overwhelming forces determined to put an end to feudal Japan. The hotel receives samurai working for rival tribes, and the bloody struggle when they meet manages to be a comment on life as it is lived in this backwater. It also proves that Gosho, usually considered a miniaturist, was the equal of any in the handling of action sequences.

One of the miracles of Japanese cinema

is that these films, angled to appeal to every taste, could still be complex. However by the time Gosho directed **Our Wonderful Years** (1966) he was required to treat an equally vast canvas with more simplicity. It was one of the last films he made before retiring, and since television was making inroads into the once huge Japanese appetite for cinema, the producers were looking askance at the power wielded by the director. The industry had been founded upon the individual director and his attendant establishment, but that was something the producers had never been entirely happy about. Their attitude changed somewhat when Kurosawa proved that a foreign market existed for the work of certain directors, but by the mid-Sixties even Kurosawa found that the studios were using the threat of television to back only what they considered to be sure-fire successes. In Gosho's case, he was known abroad only for *Four Chimneys*.

Our Wonderful Years is typical of Gosho's work, in that it is an honest and unmelodramatic *shomin-geki* account of a large family. It is as pleasing as *The Summer Clouds*, with which it has a number of common elements: the action takes place on a farm near the sea, it is a tribute to a managing mother and it is set against recent events. Like many other Japanese films, it is based on a memoir, allowing for a nostalgic but not necessarily rosy summary of past happenings – in turn implicitly commenting on the changes in society, an essential of the *shomin-geki* films. The sameness of subject and treatment in Japanese films is remarkable – and would probably be insupportable in the hands of the myriad less gifted directors.

Like Gosho, Shiro Toyoda (1906–77) had benefited from the strict and intense teachings of Shimazu. He also began to direct in the Silent era and leaned towards the *shomin-geki*, dealing predominantly with women. However, whereas his contemporaries sometimes moved close to Western emotional dramas, in which women are tested and tortured by love and duty, he was always concerned with women's place in society. **Sweet Sweat** (1964) is a study of a prostitute, not unlike Fellini's earlier *Notti di Cabiria* (q.v.) but with considerably more realism and complexity. Unfortunately it is victim to the slightly mechanical quality which can develop in most veteran directors, and is certainly a minor work compared to **Marital Relations** (1955), which is less about the situation of women than the interdependence of men and women within society. The title is ironic, since the couple are not married, and that gives rise to most of their difficulties. It is the case history of a love affair, of its joys and its reversals – caused, not by the prejudices of society, but by the particular character of the young man (Hisaya Morishige). As his sister says, 'He has been pampered and spoilt, but he is still a very nice man.' In 1955 no Western film had been as perceptive on either family or adulterous relationships; indeed, I know of no Western film like it.

Another constant concern in Japanese cinema is the transitory nature of life: and in the films of Tomotaka Tasaka, who made *Five Scouts*, events end with journeys, usually by train, for life to start anew. Fortune is precarious and innocents may get buffeted, as in **The Maid** (1955), when the woman of the title is sacked for caring too much for the child in her charge, or in **A House in the Quarter** (1963), in which the lovers are separated when circumstances force the girl to work in a

Kyoto brothel. Tasaka works with the same sympathy and attention to detail as his contemporaries, but unlike many of them he is less adept at concealing the old-fashioned nature of the situations so frequent in the *shomin-geki* films.

Daisuke Ito continued to be sharper and more bitter, as in **The Chess Master** (1948), which is more persuasive and more reticent than Western biographical films of the time – though restraint is not a quality found in its star, Tsumasaburo Bando, who specialised in playing roguish working men. Ito was drawn to the historical epic, and **The Conspirator** (1961) is a tale of civil war and revenge as enthralling as any *jidai-geki* subject we have seen.

Even finer is **Killing in Yoshiwara** (1960) directed by Tomu Uchida (1897–1970), who, on this evidence alone, was the equal of Mizoguchi and Kinugasa, both cronies of his. Based on one of the *bunraku* (puppet) plays of Chikamatsu, it is a story of love betrayed: a wealthy merchant (Chiezo Kataoka) is rejected by the geishas because of his scarred face, but accepted by a whore (Yoshie Mizutani) – for whose ambition, to become a geisha, he sacrifices his fortune and, indeed, everything he has. By the early Sixties the

Tomu Uchida's *Killing in Yoshiwara* is one of the most splendid of all Japanese historical films, beautifully photographed in colour for the wide screen, and with a narrative of considerable intrigue. Traditionally the Japanese film moves at a sedate pace interrupted by small flurries of action – but action in the historical subjects can become prolonged and violent. In this particular film Uchida handles the battles brilliantly, as here, where Chiezo Kataoka, centre, fights off his enemies.

969

The Japanese Masters

West had shown a huge liking for *jidai-geki*, with its exciting duels and battles, so it is surprising that neither of these examples was widely distributed abroad. The reason may be that we did not much care for Toho's expensive version of an old perennial, **Chusingara** (1962) or *The Loyal Forty-Seven Ronin*, remade for perhaps the fortieth time, to celebrate the studio's fiftieth anniversary. This was another example of a Japanese film company misunderstanding the taste of the West: they had made the film very pretty – like an Edwardian production of 'Madame Butterfly' – but the potential audience in the West had become accustomed to the more austere beauty of the films of Kurosawa. Its director, Hiroshi Inagaki, although prolific, also tends towards the stolid; he is a mediocre film-maker and in Toho's view 'commercial' – so it is entirely understandable that a number of his samurai films have been put into distribution in the U.S.

A superior exponent of the genre is Kosaburo (or Kimisaburo) Yoshimura (b. 1911), whose **Tale of the Genji** (1951) was made to mark the tenth anniversary of Daiei. The writer was Kaneto Shindo – his usual collaborator before he also became a

director – who cleverly compressed the fifty-four volumes of the eleventh-century stories of the amorous Prince Genji. In its portrait of the period and its cinematic style it is so much like the subsequent historical films of Mizoguchi as to suggest that it was well studied. These directors did not baulk at borrowing, and to copy at this level is a matter of intelligence and taste rather than straight imitation. Shindo, after all, had worked with Mizoguchi as the latter's style matured – and the contribution of the photographer was also extremely important. If we knew Yoshimura's earlier films we might see what he had learnt from Mizoguchi; what may be said is that working with Mizoguchi's photographer, Miyagawa, and again with Shindo, his **Sisters of Nishijin** (1952) is disappointingly prosaic. Yoshimura was another of Shimazu's pupils and, like most of his colleagues, admired William Wyler's ability to move from one genre to another; but he seemed unresponsive to this modern subject, uneasily juggling its twin themes, the failing fortunes of an industrial family and its consequent difficulties with its workers.

The textile industry of Kyoto is the background of **Night River** (1956), known also as *Undercurrent*, and it is much more vividly detailed. Sumie Tanaka wrote the film from a novel by Hisao Siwano, and it weaves together beautifully the heroine's affair with a married man and her day-to-day existence – which is concerned with dyeing fabrics. Since colour is essential to the heroine's art, Yoshimura and Miyagawa decided to make the film in colour, even though the system they used was not entirely satisfactory.

The first Japanese colour film shown in the West was **Gate of Hell** (1953), directed by the veteran Teinosuke Kinugasa, using the Eastman system. Karel Reisz, then a critic, observed that colour 'is employed to better effect than perhaps ever before in a film'. As one of the early few Japanese films to arrive in the West, its savagery and splendour were overwhelming; even today, it remains impressive. The story, again taken from classical literature, is about a samurai (Kazuo Hasegawa) determined to have at all costs the lady (Machiko Kyo) he has rescued during a revolution, with the inevitable tragic results.

Among Kinugasa's modern subjects at this time is **Actress** (1947) made at the same time as *The Love of Sumako the Actress* and is perhaps even better than Mizoguchi's film. The subject of both is Sumako Matsui (played here by Isuzu Yamada), who, after two failed marriages decided to go on the stage and became renowned for her left-wing views. She is regarded as the first liberated Japanese woman – and all these aspects were dealt with in this film, which is notable for its constant use of nuance to make its points.

These veterans all shared very long careers. The second generation of Japanese directors began during the war years and their work is happily more accessible than that of Uchida, Yoshimura and Kinugasa. Of them, Miyogi Ieki seems the least inspired, and the quality of **The Half Brothers** (1958) may be due to the contribution of Yoda, Mizoguchi's writer, working with Nobuyoshi Terada from a novel by Torahiko Talmiya. The film follows the fortunes of a military man (Rentaro Mikuni) from the late Twenties to the Armistice in 1945. He rapes his maid (Kinuyo Tanaka) and, forced to marry her, continues to treat her with contempt, idolising his own equally militarist sons while the two he has by her are disappointments to him. The film sets out to demolish the standards by which he lives, and does so by virtue of some telling vignettes; it is also actually touching on the subject of this strange marriage, due partly to what may be Miss Tanaka's most brilliant performance. Ieki's early films were, by government decree, of an entirely opposing stance.

Tadashi Imai (b. 1912), a former scriptwriter, also made militaristic films during the War and became a Communist when it was over. It should be axiomatic that left-wing directors in democracies are equipped to provide above-average films, since the capitalist bosses under whom they operate will put a brake on blatant propaganda, while being prepared, at the same time, to accept their more sophisticated skills than those of purely commercial film-makers. Imai is a film-maker committed to sympathetic studies of the poor and deprived, but his work is too often cerebral and misogynist. **And Yet We Live** (1951) is an account of a family on the bread-line, and a number of similarities

reveal that it was prepared under the influence of *Ladri di Biciclette*. However, it lacks not only the compassion of de Sica's film but also the calm emotiveness of Ozu's prewar films about poverty. It was criticised at the time because its players had been selected from a theatre company – albeit a left-wing one. On other occasions it has been clear that because of his political views Japanese critics admire Imai above all his contemporaries.

Imai did realise a noteworthy humanist film with **Kiku and Isamu** (1959), the study of two children living with their grandmother, who makes a meagre living from silk-worms. Their mother is dead and their father (now back in America) was a black G.I., which is why other children regard them as freaks. Imai's best film is probably **Shadow in Sunlight** (1956), also known as *Darkness at Noon*, an enthralling account of police pursuit through the Tokyo underworld. The self-confessed murderer is bullied into implicating his gang, who are completely innocent – and Imai is clearly on their side against the law. He may have learnt from the Italian neo-realists how to be passionately partisan while, at the same time, appearing theoretically objective; and in adopting the thriller form for his purpose he predates the films of Costa-Gavras (q.v.). The story was based on fact, and the film caused a sufficient stir for the Supreme Court to order a re-trial in 1957.

Imai admitted that he was happier with contemporary subjects, and it was not until **Night Drum** (1958) that he tackled an historical theme, written by Kaneto Shindo and Shinobu Hashimoto from a play by Chikamatsu. It is set at the time the country was under the sway of the Tokugawa shoguns and it concentrates upon a minor court official (Rentaro Mikuni) whose wife (Ineko Arima) has been unfaithful. He is unwilling to exact the punishment demanded by society, but does so: he instructs her as she commits hara-kiri; equally reluctant he sets out to find the man who cuckolded him. An epilogue reveals him a ruined man and the final close-up shows him in anguish at having to bow to the absurd code. Imai uses a quiet, reflective style – unlike that of most of his modern stories – but cuts abruptly from past to present as the husband is faced with mounting evidence of his wife's infidelity (in view of Imai's misogyny, it is not surprising that she turns out to have been the aggressor). The varying accounts told to the husband indicate that the film is emulating *Rashomon*, but otherwise the abrupt time-shifts are much in advance of Western narrative technique. Since, outside Japan, such devices were first associated with the *nouvelle vague*, we may suppose that Resnais saw this film, or heard it discussed, when he was in Japan making *Hiroshima mon Amour*. Certainly *Night Drum* and Kinoshita's *The Snow Flurry* (q.v.) are the only precedents I know for *L'Année Dernière à Marienbad* (q.v.).

Imai returned to an historical theme with **A Woman Called En** (1971), based on the true story of a seventeenth-century woman who, after spending most of her early life in prison (she was forty-four when released), refused her lord's command to remarry and earned her living by her medical knowledge. The subject seems more a concession to local women's libbers than another traditional movie examination of women's place in society, but that may be because once again Imai seems rather remote from it. **Takiji Kobayashi** (1974) is a biography of the proletarian writer who died not long after being taken into police custody in 1933, and we may therefore suppose it to have more relevance to Imai. It was his most ambitious film for many years, but on this evidence he had lost his former passion.

Imai finally relinquished his own film company, set up in 1948, and went to work for Toho on **Mon and Ino** (1976), an odd choice for a director once noted for social concern. Also known as *Brother and Sister*, the tale had been previously filmed by Sotoji Kimura in 1936 and Naruse in 1953: a girl has been seduced, and her loutish brother turns on the gentle and gentlemanly student responsible. Hints of incestuous passion jostle awkwardly with the brother's old-fashioned notions of morality, and a comparison with Kimura's version reveals that the story no longer has much relevance. As a concession to the Seventies the family occupation has been changed from fishing to riverside catering, and in handling this environment Imai reveals fragments of his former skill. For that reason alone he deserved his Grand Prix at Delhi. As a result of the award the film was bought for British distribution – to no critical interest whatsoever. It was only the second of his films to be seen publicly in the West, more than twelve years after *Bushido* in New York in 1964.

It is even more to be regretted that the films of Keisuke Kinoshita (b. 1912) remain largely unseen. Imai, when asked which of his contemporaries he most admired, named Kinoshita, adding that it was 'peculiar' that he was unknown outside Japan. None of Kinoshita's fifty-odd films has been seen commercially in Britain, but three have reached New York, including the first Japanese colour film, **Carmen Comes Home** (1951) – the Fujicolor used proves to have been, at the time, the truest colour system after Technicolor. Kinoshita wished to take advantage of the countryside around Mount Asami, and he himself wrote this light comedy of a returning showgirl and her effect on the villagers. It brings to mind the work of Pagnol in its affection and elegiac sentiment, but Kinoshita himself regarded it as a reflection of his admiration for René Clair. He had deliberately set out to restore satire and comedy of character – for both had been largely absent since early Ozu – and he is more successful with the second quality than the first.

Like Yoshimura, Toyoda and Gosho, Kinoshita was a pupil of Shimazu, and his work is further evidence of Shimazu's firm schooling. If a number of his first films are clumsily handled, it may be because their subjects were chosen for him by the government. He was still relatively unskilled when he made **A Morning with the Osone Family** (1946) which is nevertheless a fascinating film. It was designed to be palatable to the American occupation forces, dealing as it does with a liberal-minded – and, it is implied, Christian – family and its attitude towards the War. The film indicates that the country, in defeat, now shares the stance of the family – but that is of little consolation to them, as three of the sons have been killed. The Italians made movies about partisans, but not for twenty years would the Italian film industry allow films to examine the Fascist past; similarly after both wars the German cinema failed to examine Germany's role in the two conflicts; but this film is in the tradition of prewar Japanese cinema in its care for human values. The family is so affectionately and intelligently handled that it atones for the film's didacticism and the overdrawn portrait of the militarist uncle.

By the time of **A Japanese Tragedy** (1953) Kinoshita had become one of the masters of world cinema. The film is not dissimilar to *A Morning with the Osone Family*, being also an example of the *babe-mono* or 'mother-love' story, stunningly set against the events of contemporary history. This mother (Yuko Mochizuki) is rejected by both her children – the daughter preferring to live with a married English teacher, and the son with one of the doctors with whom he is studying. Likeable though they are, both are selfish, able to justify their actions by citing the loose life that their mother had been leading, but the true implications are clear: had there been no War there would have been no widowhood, and hence no 'immorality', no rejection and no final tragedy. The title is by no means pretentious, because the film is representative of Japan at a time of upheaval, showing the country as it moves decisively from the alternating moods of doubt and complacency. The material is sufficiently absorbing to start with, but what is remarkable is Kinoshita's handling, for he makes implications only – as opposed to statements – about his leading characters, pre-dating Antonioni, who introduced the form into Western cinema. He also pre-dates Western techniques by cutting swiftly into the narrative such background matters as the black market and student riots, often in time-shifts.

The intercutting of past and present was developed by Imai, as we have seen, in *Night Drum*, but Kinoshita used the technique even more brilliantly in **The Snow Flurry** (1959), employing it perhaps to add vitality to an otherwise lacklustre story. It is another tale of mother-love, set during the War years and their aftermath in a rural community, and it examines particularly the hardships wrought by the 1946 Land Reform Acts. Chiefly about the sufferings of a mother and son at the hands of a bourgeois family like themselves, the piece, unlike *A Japanese Tragedy*, is not without touches of sentimentality, but once again Kinoshita's selection of detail and incident is astonishing. He wrote the original screenplay, and if, because of the subject, the final effect is minor, it still

dwarfs most contemporary Western films.

The other two Kinoshita films seen in New York exemplify his fascination with stretching the possibilities of film as narrative. **She Was Like a Wild Chrysanthemum** (1955) is evidence of his strong attachment to Japan and the past, but, since his framework is unusual, he doesn't display both at the same time. The title refers to an old man's first love, as he revisits the town in which he grew up, and the flashbacks are enclosed within oval white frames to suggest photographs of the era. **The Song of Narayama** (1958) is set in a remote mountain area where the privations are so great that the people traditionally take their aged to the peak to die; one old lady (Miss Tanaka) is convinced that her time has come and has to persuade her son of it. Kinoshita decided that the exigencies of the subject, bordering on the mythic, required an absence of realism, and chose a style borrowed from the Kabuki, with 'magical' transformations of scenery in the theatrical manner. Since he is, above all, a stylist, the effect is hypnotic – but it is even more remarkable because he was working in wide screen and colour for the first time. In its visual qualities *The Snow Flurry* is even more accomplished, and both films disclose Kinoshita's revitalised creativity. I cannot consider this handful of Kinoshita's movies without being puzzled by their lack of recognition in the West – beyond the fact that those

Of the acknowledged Japanese masters, the least known outside Japan is Keisuke Kinoshita. Isolated showings of a handful of his films suggest that there are riches in the other fifty he has made. *A Japanese Tragedy* is one of the most distinguished of the films which attempted to chart the unrest that followed the Second World War, and comparable to the best of the Italian neo-realist movies. The title also translates as *The Japanese Tragedy*, and it is a particular story which reflects the lives of others in that troubled period – a tale concerning a family, with Yuko Mochizuki and Uteko Katsuragi as mother and daughter.

which reached America were subjected to a group of uncomprehending critics.

This is a vitally important question. If our ignorance of Kinoshita is, as Imai said, peculiar, our admiration for Akira Kurosawa (b. 1910) is justified. Kurosawa, as he has been the first to admit, has been much luckier – having had solid acclaim in Europe before his films were assessed by American critics. When the taste for Japanese prints began in the last century, American collectors, even before the French, led the world in their enthusiasm. But in general American taste-makers have been impervious to the Japanese cinema – despite the fact that New York, at least, has had more opportunities to discover it than any other leading city outside Japan. When in the late Fifties American distributors realised there was an art-house market for samurai films, they began importing subtitled prints, and most of these films have remained in the art-house repertory. Not all of them were reviewed; and during the two decades 1950–70, *The New York Times* – as I said before, the key to serious acceptance in the U.S. – included only four Japanese films on its Best of the Year lists. One was Kobayashi's *Kwaidon* (q.v.); the other three were directed by Kurosawa – and they appeared only when there was a separate category for Best Foreign Films and only after critical acclaim in Europe. Even today, many serious American filmgoers believe that the Japanese cinema begins and ends with Kurosawa – a fallacy which does not, of course, diminish his immense stature.

Having failed to make a living as an illustrator, Kurosawa joined P.C.L. studios as assistant to Kajiro Yamamoto, his only master – though he acknowledges the influence of Capra, Ford, Wyler and, later, Antonioni. He wrote scripts and while at Toho asked to direct the version of a novel by Tsuneo Tomita, **Judo Saga** (1943), a story of the rivalry between judo and jujitsu. It is also a study of the awakening of a young man who, like later Kurosawa protagonists, theorised, practised and did not act until he was fully prepared. Kurosawa made a sequel in 1945, and in the meantime had composed an almost documentary study of a number of factory workers, **The Most Beautiful**. He wanted to make an historical film, but horses were proscribed for movie pur-

poses under postwar restrictions and, further, he was allowed only one set. **Tora-No-O** (1946), also known as *They Who Step on the Tiger's Tail*, is a medieval anecdote, based on fact, and in the repertory of both the Noh and the Kabuki. The American authorities banned it, because of 'the feudalistic idea of loyalty expressed' and it was not shown until 1953. Then it was immediately bought by several Western distributors in the hope that it would appeal to the patrons of *Rashomon*; but it is by no means of equal interest (and since it runs less than an hour is not easy to programme). In the interim Kurosawa had made nine films, most of which are notable. **No Regrets for Our Youth** (1946) is based on the 'Takikawa Incident' of 1933, when a professor was dismissed from the faculty of Kyoto for alleged Communist leanings. The narrative is unsatisfactory – Toho exacted changes in order to differentiate it from a similar story being filmed simultaneously – and the action hazily focuses on the professor's daughter (Setsuko Hara). It does, however, reveal Kurosawa making his way towards his (to me) miraculous style, with its travelling shots and incisive cutting.

Drunken Angel (1948) marks Kurosawa's enfranchisement and, working with new confidence, he captures admirably the curious postwar mood as he examines the relationship between a local doctor and the hoodlum he treats for tuberculosis. The roles are played respectively by Takashi Shimura, a gentle, middle-aged actor, and Toshiro Mifune (b. 1920), who was making his first film. Mifune's sheer energy encouraged a more Western method of acting – and a more robust style was what would help Japanese films find acceptance overseas. There had been other 'rogue' actors in the Japanese cinema, but they would not, or could not, be disciplined in the way that Kurosawa was able to control Mifune. Mifune and Shimura became Kurosawa's preferred actors throughout his career, and at this time he featured them in three more films consecutively. In **The Quiet Duel** (1949) they play doctors, father and son, the latter adjusting to civilian life after some years in the army, and in **Stray Dog** (1949), they are detectives, with Mifune as the junior, searching for his stolen gun. Obviously a thriller, this film tries to put the younger man in the context of the postwar world.

More clearly in **Scandal** (1950) Kurosawa reverted to the social preoccupations of his previous films, this time attacking press ethics – which Kurosawa considered were degenerating as the Occupation came to an end – with a plot about a painter (Mifune) and a singer hounded because of an imaginary affair. He evokes Capra at the end when the lawyer (Shimura) puts probity above his career.

Kurosawa had wanted to make **Rashomon** (1950) for years, and in fact moved from Toho to Daiei to do so. In it, he perfected his technique – which so startled the West – with its gliding camera and dynamic rhythm. It was a style wholly dictated here by the film's source – two stories by Ryunosuke Akutagawa, one of which suggested the framing device, and the other, the central story. It is a study of conflicting testimonies concerning a rape and a murder, and as each version is re-enacted, the nature of truth itself is put in doubt (simultaneously, in Britain, Asquith's undistinguished *The Woman in Question* was predicated on the same theme). The situation belongs absolutely to a country riven by civil war, and with even more virtuosity than in Mizoguchi or Kinoshita, violence is contrasted with a transitory tranquillity – in this case the sylvan setting – and peace is more deceptive because in the undergrowth lurks the bandit (Mifune) bent on rape. The resultant horror is made worse since the deed is witnessed by the husband (Masayuki Mori) who, like us, cannot be sure that his wife (Machiko Kyo) did not enjoy it. The film is spellbinding and, like all great works of art, still holds its mysteries. Neither the executives at Daiei nor Japanese critics liked it, though audiences were sufficiently fascinated to make it financially successful. When Venice requested a Japanese film for the 1951 festival, *Rashomon* had not even been considered, but it was chosen by a representative of Italiafilm in Tokyo, and sent despite the opposition of Daiei. Kurosawa did not even know that it had been entered, and when it was awarded the Grand Prix he observed that he would rather have been honoured for a modern subject, mentioning *Ladri di Biciclette* as the sort of film he had in mind.

However, borne aloft by his prize, he chose not a subject of social awareness but

'art', and persuaded Shochiku to back a version of Dostoevsky's **The Idiot** (1951). Clearly meant to be no ordinary film, it ran to 245 minutes, but Shochiku, by this time agreeing with Daiei that *Rashomon* had been a fluke, cut it to 166 minutes. It was badly received both in Tokyo and on its first Western outing in New York, two years later. Even if it is intermittently powerful and fascinating, it is essentially unsatisfactory. Kurosawa transferred the action to Japan but attempted to express the story in Western terms and in so doing failed to distinguish between tragedy and melodrama. The result is an array of agonised expressions and histrionic confrontations, stagily contrived. As the Rogozhin character, Mifune over-reacts; Setsuko Hara as Nastasya, modelled on the Casares character in *Orphée*, assumes – even more foolishly – Joan Crawford mannerisms; and Mr Mori is simply ineffectual as Mishkin. Kurosawa used the northern island of Hokkaido because of the snow and its Westernised furniture. When he came to film Gorki's **The Lower Depths** (1957) he realised his earlier mistake and did not this time attempt to compromise; but in removing the action from its quintessential

Akira Kurosawa was the first Japanese director widely known to Western audiences, and he remains the best known – though he himself, and Japanese critics, regard both Kon Ichikawa and Masaki Kobayashi as of equal mastery. Indeed, they once teamed with the equally distinguished Keisuke Kinoshita in a doomed bid for independence from the powerful Japanese studios.

Russian milieu to one purely Japanese the piece eluded him even further.

Ikiru (1952) is generally known in English as *Living*, though at one time it was titled *Doomed*, not inappropriately, since it follows the reactions of a minor civil servant (Shimura) on discovering that he has only a few months to live. The theme is nothing less than an examination of Man's reason for living, and the last section consists of the long wake accompanying his funeral, in which all the ironies of his life are exposed. These become a series of anti-climaxes, and though the earlier part of the film lays emphasis on the man's vain dependence on booze and sex – he is a widower – and the lack of understanding between him and his children, these are not great discoveries for a film director to make. The portraits of bureaucratic life and of the Ginza are engrossing, but as a whole the film lacks the urgency and compassion of de Sica's *Umberto D*, with which it has a number of affinities.

These qualities are, however, to be found in **Seven Samurai** (1954), which was made expressly to entertain. It is also humorous, especially in Mifune's performance as the lowly born samurai, and has tremendous tension. The ambience is a primitive one of carnage, misery, self-interest and evil, in the midst of which is just one point of redemption – the honour and idealism of the samurai code. A singularly luckless village employs seven warriors to defend it against pillaging freebooters, though, as is apparent, these are samurai who have seen better days. Both sides fight with desperate courage, the samurai plotting and harassing till there is hope of victory – achieved strikingly in the same strategic manner as was used by the feudal warriors in the West, reminding us that we have no similar film. Our fondness for this led to a Hollywood interpretation as a Western, *The Magnificent Seven* (q.v.). The original version of 200 minutes is even more impressive than the 160-minute rendition usually in circulation.

Both films reflect Kurosawa's own acknowledged quest – to examine the reasons why mankind is incapable of living in harmony. In the wake of new nuclear experiments by the Russians and Americans he felt obliged to make **I Live in Fear** (1954), also known as *Record of a Living Being*, a study of an elderly industrialist (Mifune) determined to emigrate to South Africa to escape the threat of atomic warfare. The film was Kurosawa's greatest commercial failure to that time, and though he himself thinks it is before its time – 'no one was thinking seriously of atomic extinction' – it is a deeply flawed work. Having elected a young man, Mifune, to play an old one, he prevents us from peering too closely, and as a consequence we never know the man. His fears are not dramatised. As a modern-day Lear he is the one sane man in a world gone mad, but beyond the fact of Tokyo in a hot summer, this world does not seem mad. His own descent into madness is merely verbose. Kurosawa observed that he intended to make a satire and found himself making a tragedy, but it is difficult to see what he is satirising unless it is the bickering, grasping family, representing a society on the brink of disaster.

Shakespeare was indeed in Kurosawa's mind, and **Throne of Blood** (1957) is based on 'Macbeth'. It is an infinitely more successful adaptation than *The Idiot*, but it also reduces its source, which, robbed of its poetry and argument, becomes a tradition-ridden, bleak adventure story. As the samurai warrior who plots to rule, Mifune does not develop; his wife (Isuzu Yamada) is small and baleful, and the weighty reasons for killing the overlord become simply 'Without ambition, a man is not a man.' The defeat of Macbeth in Shakespeare satisfies our desire for a return to law and order, but in Kurosawa it is merely the fitting end to a cautionary tale. This is ironic, in view of the magnificence of the conception. As in Shakespeare, civil war has destroyed the countryside and evil lurks at every corner – or rather, in the dark, damp huge forests or within the swirling fogs and mists. The soundtrack uses the whinnying of horses – the sound of fear – and *musique concrète* to reinforce the searing deeds of this protagonist. Macbeth dies – in one of the most pulsating and terrifying climaxes ever filmed – in a flight of arrows, pinioned to the wooden walls of his castle.

Kurosawa's technical mastery was now complete. He said that he turned to *jidai-geki* because he thought most other such films 'historically uninformed', but almost certainly he preferred this form because it

976

gave full rein to his powerful visual imagination. He did say that he resisted the use of colour to keep the feudal world in charcoal blacks and subtle whites, and whatever the narrative shortcomings of *Throne of Blood* it is a haunting film, eerie and unearthly. He used the wide screen for **The Hidden Fortress** (1958); and for the hero (Mifune) the world remains a grim, sinister place, with no succour from either the poor, who are cowardly, naive opportunists, or the powerful who are greedy and ruthless. Still, as with *Seven Samurai*, Kurosawa injects a degree of humour, resembling the films of Douglas Fairbanks in both the settings and the resourcefulness of Mifune – he even sweeps up the princess-heroine on to his horse as he rides past, to escort her through the enemy lines. However, this is the only scene where Kurosawa allows humour to relieve the tension of dangerous situations.

Despite the failure of *I Live in Fear*, Kurosawa was determined to devote his efforts to a contemporary story of 'some social significance' for his first production as an independent (releasing through Toho). **The Bad Sleep Well** (1960) is about corruption in big business, and the connection with Shakespeare this time is 'Hamlet', although the hero, Nishi (Mifune), has a sardonic humour rather stronger than that of the Danish prince. His revenge is directed not against a usurping uncle, but his father-in-law (Masayuki Mori) who, Nishi believes, was responsible, with his colleagues, for the death of his father. Company funds had been misappropriated, and no one will tell the truth since company loyalty is not so far removed from the old samurai loyalties. As a cat-and-mouse thriller, the film is superb, but such devices as ghosts and sleeping draughts seem at odds in a contemporary context, and the tragedy of the ending is unsatisfactory.

Mifune's understated performance is delightful, especially since the success of *The Hidden Fortress* with the Japanese public identified him with heroic roles. Elements of that film and Mifune's role in it were, therefore, incorporated into **Yojimbo** (1961), Kurosawa's second independent production. It too was phenomenally popular, and when Toho asked for a sequel, Kurosawa obliged with **Sanjuro** (1962), later observing

that he considers only the earlier film a major work. The term *yojimbo* means 'bodyguard', and Sanjuro is the name of this master swordsman whom Mifune makes into one of the cinema's great creations. He is shabbily dressed, somewhat theatrical, cautious; and, though by no means a modern man, not unlike the uninvolved, sardonic heroes played by Humphrey Bogart. When underdogs are endangered, however, his innate chivalry comes to the fore. He is a professional, a killer, available to oppressors and oppressed alike, who, in terms of stupidity and evil, are a match for each other. Reunited with Miyagawa as director of photography for the first time since *Rashomon*, Kurosawa creates images like those of Goya's etchings, evoking a stench of rotten, decaying corpses and charred wood. *Yojimbo* has a precision, a sense of inevitability and a harsh beauty that we recognise as requisite to this director, while *Sanjuro* is shorter, and the opposing sides somewhat shallower. Mifune, still aloof, is allowed to blunder; when he eventually triumphs, he strides away, as in *Yojimbo*, spurning the congratulations of his fair-weather allies.

High and Low (1963) is based on Ed McBain's novel 'King's Ransom' and is about the kidnapping of the young son of an industrialist (Mifune). Its long and detailed exposition, as the police enquiry gets under way, is reminiscent of Kurosawa's early films, but he continues to strive for the complexity of his recent work, especially in his account of Mifune's relationships with the police on the one hand and his colleagues on the other. As a social realist, Kurosawa makes the contrast between the rich and the kidnapper, who lives in a shanty town, and it is this aspect which gives the film its title, which in Japanese means 'Heaven and Hell'. Though a superb thriller, this is probably not among Kurosawa's greatest works, while **Red Beard** (1965) most assuredly is. Its canvas is vast, as, set in the nineteenth century, it seeks to delineate a bridge between the feudal world and the modern one. Mifune again plays a right-minded, noble spirit, living in the midst of squalor; he is a doctor, running his own clinic, and passing on his wisdom to a younger man (Yuzo Kayama) – a tradition which has been the theme of many medical dramas. If

978

Kurosawa's Japan: Feudal and Modern

These pictures celebrate not only Kurosawa's artistry but also his popularity in the West: LEFT, *Seven Samurai*; BOTTOM FAR LEFT, *Throne of Blood*, with Toshiro Mifune; BOTTOM LEFT, *Rashomon*, with Machiko Kyo and Mifune; BOTTOM RIGHT, *Red Beard*, with Terumi Niki and Yoshio Tsuchiya, and BELOW, *Ikiru*, with Takashi Shimura in foreground.

this has any affinity to a Western work, it is to Antonioni's studies of young men's self-discoveries, for the arrogant young doctor here learns that the old man has skills and an awareness of which he had not even dreamed. But it is also about a dedicated humanitarian who has chosen to live out his life among the flotsam and jetsam of mankind. The running time is over three hours, the aim being to 'push the confines of movie-making to their limits', and it is wonderfully designed and orchestrated. It is no coincidence that Kurosawa likes filming rain, for he prefers to compose in horizontals and verticals; but, unlike most Western directors whose images may be as forcefully or as carefully composed, his are never arbitrary, but always subordinated to the subject, often as a continuation of it.

As with all great directors, Kurosawa's films plead for involvement. **Dodeska-Den** (1970), in which he returns to a shanty town, similar to *The Lower Depths*, features derelicts no more appealing than those in the earlier film, and with fantasies even less so. The title refers to the noise made by the young hero as he pretends to be a tramcar, and the source is a story by Shugoro Yamamoto, whose work had also provided Kurosawa with *Sanjuro* and *Red Beard*. His first film in colour, Kurosawa brings to it the same warmth as Jean Renoir did when he began to use colour, but unfortunately the settings are theatrical. The film, initially, was to have been over three-and-a-half hours long and even at one hour less it drags: a monumental miscalculation. The public had never cared for tales of gutter survival or for stagy settings, and the combination was a disaster for Kurosawa, who had pooled resources with Kinoshita, Ichikawa and Kobayashi to make completely independent films, which Toho was to distribute. The complete loss of its production cost, and the annulment of his agreement with his colleagues following a quarrel with Mifune and the severing of their partnership, caused Kurosawa to attempt suicide.

During the next few years a number of projects fell through, partly because Kurosawa's attempt at independence had been viewed unfavourably by the industry. But Toho came to his aid after he had persuaded Mosfilm (of the Soviet Union) to back **Dersu Uzala** (1975), based on the books by Vladimir Klavdievic Arsenyev

which he had read years before. In 1902 Arsenyev had led an army unit making a topographical survey of the forest land approaches on Russia's Pacific seaboard, across the straits from Sakhalin, and in the course of his work he had met a hunter, a member of the forest-dwelling Goldi people, named Dersu Uzala. The title role is played by Maksim Munzik, and the army captain by Yuri Solomin; and probably the 'noble savage' syndrome was never more impressively expressed. The captain's admiration for the hunter is due to Dersu's many qualities, chief of which is his instinctive co-existence with the life of the forest, which the captain hopes to acquire himself. Since the man is alone and superstitious and his life is hard, the captain later gives him a home, throwing into relief the extraordinary forest scenes. In these sequences Kurosawa eschewed his swirling camera movement and virtuoso cinematic techniques for a stillness reflecting the nature of the forest: the stereophonic sound and the wide screen, which had never been better used, find us alert to any noise and unexpected movement. Kurosawa surpasses himself in the creation of tension, and the ending in particular reminds us that his films have always been richly imbued with humanity.

The Russians suggested a further project, but did not care for the subject of the script submitted to them. Another screenplay found no backers in Japan, but Toho agreed to a third, an historical film, **Kagemusha** (1980), but not to its estimated budget of $7 million, the highest of any Japanese film to date. Kurosawa, while on a visit to Hollywood, mentioned this to Francis Ford Coppola and George Lucas, and as a result 20th Century-Fox contributed $1½ million in exchange for world rights outside Japan.

At 159 minutes the 'international' version is twenty-two minutes shorter than Kurosawa's original, and although we have been assured that only battle scenes have gone, something more integral seems to be missing. *Kagemusha* is no more than a good historical story, like one of the lesser Mizoguchis; Kurosawa's own historical films usually dealt with power and the responsibility that goes with it, which is precisely what this film would seem to be about, but is not. The screenplay is based on fact – a sixteenth-century shogun named Shingen who used a double to deceive his enemies. In the film Shingen's double – the *kagemusha*, or shadow warrior – is a thief, and both roles are played by an unrecognisable Tatsuya Nakadai, who had played Mifune's foe in *Yojimbo* and in *Sanjuro*. After Shingen's death, the thief, aided by the ruler's brother, assumes the lord's role and in Kurosawa's brilliant exposition the thief, craven at first, begins to settle into the deception and to enjoy it. The dead man's illegitimate son, however, becomes restive on seeing his father's triumphs being enjoyed by so ignominious a creature. The story at this juncture promises a serious comment on the uses of power for good or evil, but nothing interesting materialises: the thief is booted out when he is no longer useful, but he so identifies with the lord's clan that he goes to his death after all the other members have been massacred. It is possible that Kurosawa lacked confidence after fifteen years of disappointments; for even *Dersu Uzala*, with all its critical acclaim, had failed to attract a large foreign audience. However, apart from some minor theatrical lapses, the film is visually magnificent and, because of 20th Century-Fox's handling, has probably been seen by more people than any other Japanese film hitherto.

In the West, the best known of Kurosawa's contemporaries is probably Kon Ichikawa (b. 1915), who was drawn to the cinema by the early films of Walt Disney. He wanted to be an artist and did become an animator, later studying filming under Yutaka Abe. He made his first film, with puppets, in 1946, but the American occupation forces refused to allow it to be shown. His second film was unfinished, but he began directing regularly in 1948 and the following year started his collaboration with the screenwriter Natto Wada, whom he married. They tended to concentrate on comedy, with satiric intent but a supposedly objective approach; their criticism of Japanese society, *i.e.* other people, is imperfect, the individual always commands respect, even if he himself may be no better than those around him. **Pu-San** (1953) was based on a contemporary cartoon and was made in response to Japanese re-armament (sanctioned by the Americans because of the Korean War). Ichikawa feared that public apathy would permit a resurgence of militarism and he

tries, not too successfully, to depict the country in a state of despair and flux – seen through the eyes of a bumbling schoolteacher who loses his job. The effect is rather as though Monsieur Hulot (q.v.) had stumbled into *Umberto D*, but the film is remarkable for its economy of detail, avoiding the irrelevant and concentrating on the informative. The Japanese cinema, as I have said, used omission tellingly, long before the West did, and **The Heart** (1954) not only omits for the sake of discretion, but because Ichikawa thought it unnecessary for us to know the precise extent of the two relationships at the core of the film. Yukio Mishima's 'Confessions of a Mask', had been published a few years earlier, and may have led Ichikawa to an older novel by Soseki Matsume – who died in 1926 – about a man confronting his homosexuality. The relationships concerned are those between Nobuchi (Masayuki Mori) and a friend, now dead, and between Nobuchi and a student. When Nobuchi's wife challenges him about the student he commits suicide (as in the contemporary novels which were timidly raising this subject in Western society), but not before advising the student to seek a happier life through self-knowledge. It is doubtful whether Nobuchi himself ever acquired this knowledge, a matter conveyed stylistically by Ichikawa, moving from the recticent present into flashbacks.

The small military unit at the centre of **The Burmese Harp** (1956), taken from

Kon Ichikawa first became known in Japan as a satirist, but the West became acquainted with him via *The Burmese Harp*, which recounts the odyssey of one young soldier stranded in Burma after the capitulation of Japan in 1945. Ichikawa ignores a number of important subjects – an army in defeat, another army coping with it, the needs of the native population – for one which he clearly considers even more vital, the futility of war; and by emphasising the camaraderie his film is romantic, and absolutely successful in its attempt to be epic.

an original story by Michio Takeyama, is treated elliptically and sentimentally by Ichikawa. There are a number of other flaws, such as the superfluous montage of suffering to indicate the agony of the hero, Mizushima (Shoji Yasui): but these are too minor to mar what is a very big film indeed, and one clearly meant to be epic. It is about a soldier making his way home through South-East Asia after the end of the War. He is a pacifist, and after donning the robes of a Buddhist monk he feels compelled to bury or burn the bodies of the dead. Unlike some stories in Western literature, the donning of the monk's robes does not change Mizushima, and his attitude to religion remains ambivalent: he is of a particular mentality, which Ichikawa constantly has to underscore in order to prevent the film from becoming an expression of a mystical experience – but it may still have become that for many of the audience.

Fires on the Plain (1959), also deals with a soldier after defeat, and concerns, not guilt and expiation, but survival. It is the harshest of all war films, and there is no more degrading shot in all cinema than that of its protagonist, Tamura (Eiji Funakoshi), with his mouth, chin and chest covered with human blood. The civilised world has been turned upside down and Tamura is co-existing with two others whose bestiality includes cannibalism: but he makes his final gesture for humankind – perhaps a useless one. In Shohei O-oka's original novel Tamura returned to Japan to enter a mental home, but in the film he dies; and that is his salvation, as Ichikawa once remarked. War is the greatest sin, he said, able to change the nature of man, and he contrasts what man has done with God's work – the calm beauty of the plains of Leyte. Where in *The Burmese Harp* he offered the spiritual peace of Buddhism and the singing of 'Home, Sweet Home', here there is the image of the cross on the deserted village church.

A third young hero in **Conflagration** (1958) reveals the extent to which Ichikawa differs from Kurosawa as a moralist: it is possible, according to Kurosawa, to struggle on into middle-age with hope for a better society, but in Ichikawa's view hope is destroyed in the young. The screenplay, derived from a novel by Mishima that was, in turn, based on fact, is set

not long after the War and concerns Goichi, the student priest who, deformed by a stutter and crippled by an inferiority complex, deliberately set fire to the Golden Pavilion temple in Kyoto. The temple represents to him all that he is not, and in burning it down he destroys not only his enemy but also himself. Ichikawa chose the subject as a means of showing the poverty, both economic and spiritual, of Japan at the time, again using flashbacks to indicate what led Goichi to the burning. His dispassionate style contrasts with the more partisan approach to social problems taken by Kurosawa and Kobayashi, and it seems to owe much to the photographer, Kazuo Miyagawa. This was the first film in the wide-screen process for both of them and they employ it to extraordinary effect; Ichikawa believed that the camera should take an active part in the action, but left the details to Miyagawa. They worked together on several more films at this time, but not altogether happily, since Ichikawa, far more interested in the directing of actors, was, according to Miyagawa, 'rather vague' about what he wanted.

Ichikawa's interest in the intellectual and mental sickness of society led him to **Kagi** (1959) or *The Key*, a deeper study of sexual irregularity than *The Heart*; in this instance it is not accompanied by love, which is part of the problem. Corruption surfaces in the dishonesty of a family and the young doctor (Tatsuya Nakadai) whom they involve in their relationships. But worse than corruption is their refusal to face up to the truth, acting as they do under a system of double and triple standards, yet still being considered by their fellows – and this is 'the key' – an integral family and ultra-respectable. As human beings, they were spiritually dead before they died; the ending, when the servant poisons the three survivors, was not in the original novel by Junichiro Tanizaki but is, said Ichikawa, his own judgment on them.

Two family dramas, **Bonchi** (1960) and **Her Brother** (1960), reinforce his expressed belief, already evident in *Kagi*, that each member of the family must respect the individuality of the others. A *bonchi* is the eldest son, and the film is an enquiry into one such person, set against a background of recent history, while *Her Brother* deals with the relationship of two siblings in prewar Japan. *Her Brother* is the slighter of the two films, but as the children have a self-centred, and Christian, mother, it is an even more virulent attack on a matriarchal society. **Being Two Isn't Easy** (1962) is, by contrast, a fond look at family life, just avoiding cuteness and false drama as it views the world through the eyes of a baby; one must assume that Ichikawa took it on as a challenge – as he was to with *Alone on the Pacific* (q.v.). Since that, and the two films made on either side of it, represent the art of the director at its most triumphant, I shall discuss them together below. Of his films made subsequently only a few have been seen in the West and they are not of great interest: **To Love Again** (1971) is a trite love story in the manner of *Un Homme et une Femme* (q.v.), dealing with a French boy and a Japanese maiden, and **The Wanderers** (1973) is a tale of the *toseinin* – an amoral brigand breed, runaway, peasant-born rogues – told in an anti-heroic manner. Both of these later films are, of course, well made, but watching them is almost an affront since the subjects are so unworthy of a great director.

Ichikawa was seldom attracted to the *jidai-geki* and **An Actor's Revenge** (1963) is more swashbuckler than history. Because the actor of the title works in Kabuki, Ichikawa was prompted to use a theatrical style, which means one highly stylised – cutting into elegant panoramas for detail, trailing through a stage copse, allowing lights to quiver or grow bright, and confining himself to horizontal and vertical movements throughout the whole. He uses a number of angles from Kinugasa's 1936 version, and the same actor in the lead, Kazuo Hasegawa (who had been known as Chojito Hayashi in the prewar film). The role is a dual one, that of a leading transvestite actor and of a thief, his guardian angel. The actor is seen only in female garb and is referred to as 'half-man half-woman', able to take on the characteristics of each. Hasegawa's interpretation of both roles is faultless. He is, in the role, an actor in life, on the stage and consciously a player acting for the camera, a symbol of deception as also celebrated by Renoir in *The Golden Coach* (q.v.) and scrutinised by Bergman in *Ansiktet*.

He is also the Ichikawa epic hero, the man obsessed with a difficult or impossible mission; and we might say that this film

and the two that followed it are studies in determination. In 1962, after several years' planning, the twenty-three-year-old Kenichi Horie crossed the Pacific in a small yacht, which had never been done, as he says, by a Japanese – and indeed should not have been done at all: in almost the first line of dialogue in **Alone on the Pacific** (1963) we learn that small craft are forbidden on the open sea. The film is based on Horie's logbook and its star, Yujiro Ishihara, also the producer, clearly saw in it an excellent role for himself. It starts with Horie's clandestine departure at night, moving backwards to his preparations. Past and present alternate until he is well into his voyage, and Natto Wada's screenplay, even by her own high standards, is marvellously crafted. Horie is obviously an otherwise unremarkable young man; he is not even articulate on his obsession and is, in the event, less well prepared than he thought. He anticipated the loneliness, but not the fear. The film, magically, gains in intensity as Horie becomes inured to poor winds, boredom and his inadequate diet. He cries, he gets drunk. He behaves childishly when spotted, once by a plane which he pretends to photograph so that its occupants should not think he is in need, and once by a tanker, whose offer of food is rejected out

Ichikawa's career reached a peak in the early Sixties, with three remarkable films, *Tokyo Olympiad*, a documentary, *Alone on the Pacific*, a re-creation of actual events, and *An Actor's Revenge*, an historical film as unlike them as they are unlike the rest of his work. All three are masterpieces and unique experiences. *An Actor's Revenge*, as the title implies, is a melodrama, about a Kabuki actor (Kazuo Hasegawa) determined to revenge himself upon the respectable merchants who drove his father to suicide and his mother to madness. Here he is with the chief of the villains, played by Ganjiro Nakamura.

of some notion of pride. As land is glimpsed through the mist, he decides to spend the night outside the Golden Gate, in the same mistaken pride which inspired the venture in the first place. In the early-morning light San Francisco – of which he is more terrified than the open sea – rises majestically: for an instant it seems wrong to show us its traffic, to lose, for the first time, Horie's point of view, until we realise how unsuspecting is the city of this transoceanic traveller – and that henceforth Horie's life will be an anti-climax. Ninety-four days at sea, and he is a hero for one day more.

Ichikawa views the man's fanaticism and odd practicality with the bemused detachment which he employs for the athletes in **Tokyo Olympiad** (1965); he also conveys the same sense of awe, and the film is even more extraordinary. Under Miyagawa's supervision over one hundred cameras were used to record the eighteenth Olympic Games, and Ichikawa edited the footage into 130 minutes' celebration of sport and the international spirit. The first, breathtaking section celebrates the carrying of the torch from Athens, tracked by a fluid camera through mountain passes and followed by a portrait of the idiosyncrasies of the nations at the opening ceremony: the final part records the marathon with such intensity and concentration that the closing ceremony is inexorably an explosion of exultation and joy. It is succeeded by these words: 'Night, and the fire returned to the sun . . . to meet again in four years' time. Is it then enough for us – this infrequent, created peace?' They emphasise what had been evident from the start, that Ichikawa was not interested in sport *per se*. His long middle section is an essay on the aspiration, the endeavour, the competitive spirit, the sanity, the magnification of working musculature, the beauty of movement and the fundamental brotherhood of man, and he has done it with great wit and the imaginative use of every single trick at the disposal of the film-maker. But that was not what was required by the Olympic Committee, which had commissioned it and thereby prevented it from being shown except in those countries which had contracted for the rights before the event. The version shown in the U.S., for instance, bears little relation to Ichikawa's and consequently

Americans have not had the chance to see one of the masterpieces of modern cinema.

Fate seems to have meted out a like destiny for what, in my opinion, is unequivocally the greatest film ever made, **The Human Condition**, directed by Masaki Kobayashi (b. 1916), a film-maker of the same humanist persuasion as Ichikawa and Kurosawa. He is equally a great director, for it takes an exceptional film-maker to take and fill every second of over nine-and-a-half hours. The film consists of three parts, *No Greater Love* (1959), *Road to Eternity* (1960) and *A Soldier's Prayer* (1961), each over three hours long – in itself an obstacle to commercial distribution. In Japan they were shown separately over a period of years to great popular success; but when the first two parts were shown at European film festivals they were criticised for both length and content. However, enough British critics were sufficiently impressed to guarantee them a showing in London. Unfortunately the venue, a club cinema which had been recently experimenting with sex films, was unsuitable and they were largely ignored. In the U.S. only the first part was shown to the New York critics and, as Bosley Crowther of *The New York Times* disliked it, it quickly disappeared. (Today all three parts are in circulation in the U.S., but the complete work has been seen in Britain only at the National Film Theatre). In *Sight and Sound*, John Peter Dyer spoke of 'titanic journalism', but he also observed that 'no normal, informed person enjoys seeing films about slave labour camps and the inhuman practices of war. There is an understandably general feeling about such films that their message, since it is obvious, is superfluous.'

Were that so, the United Nations would never have been needed and the Nobel Peace Prize would have been discontinued long ago; and that award, in all justice, should have been given to Kobayashi for this film and to Jumpei Gomikawa, on whose six-volume novel it is based. The film, with a screenplay by Kobayashi and Zenzo Matsuyama challenges all normal – as opposed to literary – concepts of capitalism and militarism. It is an epic, or the word has no meaning, awesome in ambition and achievement – in subject matter alone ahead of any Occidental film to this day.

The Guinness Book of Records lists Kobayashi's *The Human Condition* as the longest film ever shown, though that source does point out that it was in three separate parts – shown originally in Japanese cinemas over as many years. The film has many another claim to fame, not least in its ambition, which on one level is to pay penance for Japanese aggression in the Thirties and Forties and on another to condemn fascism in all forms. Kobayashi's achievement is immense, so it is ironic that the only available illustrations are rather like this, showing its hero, Tatsuya Nakadai, in contemplation. This is a scene from Part One, as he considers the action to be taken against the cruelty of the guards towards the P.O.W. labourers.

Its hero, Kaji (Tatsuya Nakadai), endures privations which would have defeated Job, and he faces trials more arduous than those which confronted Hercules. Kobayashi understood that to keep us engrossed for so long a time we must love Kaji wholeheartedly; and Kaji is a dedicated humanist.

The Japanese historical film indicates that the humanity of its heroes, from *Sansho Dayu* to *Red Beard*, is alien to the characters who surround them, and we know from *The Human Condition*, which starts in the Thirties, that the word 'humanism' entered the Japanese language unaltered immediately after the War. Kaji lives in a world where he alone knows what it means. He is an avowed pacifist, the opponent of brutality in any form; he believes in the innate dignity of his fellow man, of whatever persuasion, and it is the affirmation of that belief which constantly brings him into conflict with his superiors and with society, and his obstinacy in pursuing his beliefs which makes him both fool and saint. Irony besets his life; he is always misunderstood when acting on behalf of the common good. As late as 1961, even to so perceptive a critic as Dyer, it seemed 'obscure' to present a hero of contradictions: but Kaji, to go no further back, is

like Buñuel's Nazarin, a man whose belief in the society around him constitutes his weakness. Like all of us, he is fallible – and he has the misfortune to be conscripted in 1943. We first meet him some years earlier working for the South Manchurian Steel Company, as labour supervisor at one of the company mines and determined to be compassionate to the six hundred prisoners of war who had been seconded there. He survives denunciation, just as in Part Two he survives barrack-room brutality and in Part Three defeat by the Russians and starvation. He is proud, clever and resourceful, which is why he is so long in succumbing to death.

Kobayashi's length in telling the story is as necessary as that of 'War and Peace', essential to encompass what has to be said: as it progresses, gathering force like a huge river, there is hardly an aspect of contemporary life on which it does not touch. A film that calls itself *The Human Condition* has to incorporate man's capacity for self-destruction, which, in the largest sense, always means war: the barrack room is a microcosm of the larger battlefield, and since the men cannot live in peace in one room it cannot be expected that they can do so elsewhere. Kobayashi, like Ichikawa, finds that war reduces men

The Japanese Masters

Kobayashi's *Rebellion*, like many of the other great samurai movies, seems to have taken its cue from the films of Douglas Fairbanks – building tension slowly, with little action, till suddenly all hell breaks loose. It is also a brilliant picture of feudal life, literally concerning a rebellion, when one family pits itself against all those in authority over them. The cause is love, when a young wife is called to the castle now that her illegitimate son, by the deceased lord, has become an heir. Supporting her and her son is Toshiro Mifune, left, called upon to fight Tatsuya Nakadai, a friend in former happy times.

to beasts, but he goes further than Ichikawa or Kurosawa (whose war films are all set in the past): by concentrating on violence and cruelty he is attacking not only Japanese imperialism and aggression in the Thirties and Forties but Fascism in whatever form it is found. It is not profound of him to show that war and destruction degrade the human spirit, and he can be heavy when making a point, as with his one-dimensional villains; and subtlety is lacking, but that does not disqualify *The Human Condition* as a work of art – but I would state that after nine-and-a-half hours during which I have been awed, entertained, thrilled, harried and harrowed for every second my critical faculties are lowered, I have no doubt, however, that just as Kaji is the definitive hero of this century, so this powerful epic dwarfs every other film made up to the present.

Kobayashi had begun directing in 1952 and the following year made *The Room with Thick Walls* about war criminals. Shochiku delayed release for four years while Kobayashi made what he termed 'sweet domestic dramas' in the manner of his master, Kinoshita – but the eventual success of the 1953 film led to *The Human Condition*. Understandably, after that he made a comedy, **The Inheritance** (1962), and only at his most cynical could he claim

that its theme is the individual's response to the problem created by his environment, which he has said is the subject of all his films – since it concerns people whose worries are caused by the modern pursuit of money and materialism. It is not in the manner of Clair and Lubitsch, whom he so much admires, but is black comedy, not far in spirit from 'Volpone', involving a number of intriguers gathered around a dying man. The film holds one's attention, but is hardly funny.

Harakiri (1962) is Kobayashi's first *jidai-geki* film, and is magisterial. It moves the anti-militarist argument of *The Human Condition*, as well as the actor Nakadai, into a seventeenth-century feudal setting. Tsugumo (Nakadai), like Kaji, grows progressively more humane: as a samurai he accepted the code of *bushido*, but just as conditions exposed Kaji to a new set of values, so poverty changes Tsugumo, and he awakens to the code's absurdities. The Tokugawa dynasty brought peace to Japan after 250 years of civil war; but although some *daimyo* remained established in their castles, some samurai had lost both their overlords and their homes and were reduced to a state of ronin. Tsugumo arrives at the castle of Iyi clan and pleads for a corner in which to commit the honourable act of hara-kiri, only to face Saito (Rentaro Mikuni), deputising for the lord, who believes that some samurai have adopted this 'threat' as a form of begging. Just as *The Human Condition* shows the survival of the samurai spirit, so this film tries to destroy whatever lingering beliefs there were in its worth. In the final sequence the whole code is turned upside down, irony piled upon irony until its ethos is demolished. (There is even irony in the casting of Mikuni, an actor accustomed to playing heroic and, indeed, reasoning roles.) The great Japanese directors have always loved irony, but I suspect that what attracted Kobayashi here was the form of the film. It lasts 134 minutes and as the outcome is never in doubt he must have enjoyed filling them. There is much savagery (the film would be unthinkable in colour), but the style is austere, except for the justly celebrated duel on the heath.

Kwaidan (1964) is Kobayashi's first film in colour, his declared aim to make 'a gorgeous multi-coloured scroll painting based on the lines and tones of an Indian

Kobayashi's *Kaseki* begins in Paris, and few films have looked so lovingly at that city – indeed, the first half of the film is a superb exploration of European culture as experienced by a Japanese business-man, Shin Saburi. With him is Keiko Kishi as Madame Marcellin, the wife of a Frenchman and, as it turns out, the Shadow of Death – but as such she is realistic rather than malign or upsetting.

ink painting'. To that end he worked entirely within the confines of the studio to create the seas, forests and swirling mists, in a visual style of great intensity. The film is in four parts, each consisting of a ghost story derived from Lafcadio Hearn's versions of traditional Japanese tales; since a fair number of ghosts materialise magically it is clear that the cinema's capacities for fantasy and mystery are exploited to the full.

Kobayashi returned to the historical film with **Rebellion** (1967), a tense account of a samurai (Toshiro Mifune) who rejects a specific feudal code, is dishonoured thereby, and who waits, as ever, to revenge himself upon those who have cast him out. Chief among these is Kobayashi's own preferred actor, Nakadai, while Mifune, who produced for Toho, is at his most magnificent; it is no disservice to Nakadai to speak of the director and the actor-producer as a matching of giants.

That these three last films were available in the West would seem due to our fondness for samurai and ghosts; as *Rebellion*, in particular, was popular it might have been supposed that we would be shown Kobayashi's next films. However, there was in fact a gap until **Kaseki** (1974), whose commercial chances were reduced

by its length (3 hours 40 minutes) and unsatisfactory colour – due to its being culled from a series made for television (with Pan American Airways as one of its sponsors). It is a return to the subject of mortality, and, as in Kurosawa's *Ikiru*, its hero (Shin Saburi) is a modest man. A manufacturer on business in Paris, he suffers the twin pangs of a thwarted love affair and intimations of death. He pauses to contemplate the Romanesque carvings of Vézelay and reflects on the French who have died for its fields – experiences which are absolutely relevant to himself and which help him to put order into what is left of his life. Kobayashi pauses, too, his pacing more apparent now that he avoids the virtuosity of his work hitherto. The mixture of European culture, Japanese big business, the supernatural and the acceptance of the inevitability of death does result in an unusual and enriching experience.

The greatness of these directors influenced many lesser ones, such as Kenji Misumi, whose rather plodding **Zatoichi Monogatari** (1962) nevertheless contains a certain pictorial splendour. He follows the standard formula of late *jidai-geki* – detailed exposition, with several strands of plot coalescing into one, and between the scenes of contemplation and dialogue only

987

one flurry of action before the climactic battle. The author of the original story is Shugoro Yamamoto, whose work was used by Kurosawa. The hero, Zatoichi (Shintaro Katsu) is much like the swordsmen portrayed by Mifune, an outsider of exceptional skill and integrity, somewhat flamboyant, yet doomed to be employed by, and fight for, chieftains and clansmen much his inferior. As so often, the central struggle is between two leaders for local supremacy, and Zatoichi becomes friendly with the champion of the other side, once a great samurai from Edo, now fatally ill. Zatoichi himself, a gambler and masseur when not a warrior, is blind; and it is a measure of Katsu's abilities as an actor that we never doubt that his blindness is a terrifying handicap when fighting in battle.

Katsu has made a career of this role, later taking on both production and direction. (He was replaced by Nakadai in *Kagemusha* when he was found to be monitoring his performance on a T.V. set, since Kurosawa decreed that there was only one director on that project.) The popularity of Zatoichi has resulted in over thirty sequels, and there have been a number of T.V. series, but, unexpectedly, the very first one is reputed to be the best. **Zatoichi and a Chest of Gold** (1964), directed by Kazuo Ikehiro, is equally enjoyable, but memorable mainly for the visual compositions in wide screen and colour by the great cinematographer, Miyagawa. Zatoichi is only one of several legendary swordsmen beloved by Japanese audiences, but unique in having been invented expressly for the cinema. His predecessors include Musashi Miyamoto, based on a real person, whose distinction was that he preferred art and philosophy to fighting, and the fictional one-armed, one-eyed Sazen Tange. They have been the subjects of innumerable films, including trilogies – and which are known by the generic name of *chambara*, a colloquial expression for *ken-geki* or sword-theatre. We have already considered Mizoguchi's film on Miyamoto, *The Swordsman*, and there is at least one good film on Tange, called **Sazen Tange** (1953), directed by Masahiro Makino, which has a labyrinthine plot, intrigue conveyed by conversations interrupted by bursts of action, some social conscience, historical perspective and characters of complexity.

The great Japanese directors built on the groundwork of such films with ferocious virtuosity (including Mizoguchi himself, whose later work is superior to that of *The Swordsman*). In the Sixties two more series vied with Zatoichi for attention, and it is interesting to see vestigial evidence of high intent in even the least of these films, made by various directors usually associated with purely commercial products. Tange was not resurrected during this period, but like him, Kyoshiro Nemuri originated in popular modern fiction. Nemuri's singularity, apart from his reddish hair, was that he was born of an illicit affair between a Portuguese missionary and a lady of the court, from which springs his particular detestation of Christians. The *chambara* films go back to the earliest days of Japanese cinema, but owed this new lease of life to the success of *Yojimbo*. Toei, which had last featured Miyamoto in 1954, initiated a five-part series in 1961 for the company's most popular star, Kinnosuke Nakamura, and its best-known director, Tomu Uchida. Daiei followed suit with the prolific series based on Zatoichi and on Nemuri, who was the subject of eleven films between 1962 and 1969, originally starring Raizo Ichikawa, and, after his death in 1969, Hiroki Matsukata.

I have seen a number of both the Miyamoto and Nemuri films, and, in addition to their striking compositions and invincible heroes, they have a number of other features in common, including the always treacherous court officials and ladies. The scenarios have been constructed with care and flair – for instance, pitching the climactic battle in an unusual terrain. **Musashi Miyamoto: Duel at Ichijoji** (1964) follows the same plot as two earlier versions in trilogies directed by Inagaki. I have not seen them, but cannot imagine that the final battle is as inexpressibly exciting as the one staged here by Uchida – the hero, wielding a sword in each hand, takes on the odds of seventy-three to one in the lanes between the paddy fields. I also cannot imagine why all these films have not been more widely disseminated in the West – they are infinitely superior to the sword-and-sandal spectaculars then being made in Italy – but I must also add that, the action scenes apart, Uchida's handling on this occasion does not seem worthy of the director of *Killing in Yoshiwara*.

The first Japanese film dealing with a contemporary theme to be seen in the West was **Children of Hiroshima** (1953), made independently by Kaneto Shindo (b.1912), a prolific screenwriter turned director. As a native of Hiroshima he hastened to make this film as soon as the American occupation ended. The Americans had prohibited publication in Japan of detailed photographs or documents of the destructions of Hiroshima and Nagasaki by the atomic bomb, and although everyone knew of the slaughter, little was publicised about the mutilated, burnt or diseased survivors. As a device Shindo uses a young teacher returning to her native city, to learn from survivors what happened the day the bomb fell; and the teacher also becomes involved with a former employer of her father, now a blind beggar, who is trying to find his small grandson. One does not need to be aware of the tremendous cries of rage later raised by Ichikawa and Kobayashi to find much of this too mild and rather picturesque. However, a more committed film on this subject might have been too horrifying to sit through, and we must admit at least that this one is grave and concerned.

Shindo had been assistant to Mizoguchi, but **Onibaba** (1964), his own adaptation of a folk story, does not have his master's distancing, his eeriness or his ability to transform historical fact into legend; nor does it bear out Shindo's claim that his class-consciousness causes him to concentrate on tales of ordinary people. In the tall reeds by a lake, at a time of civil war, two women, one old and one young, rob stragglers of their armour and leave their bodies to rot in a pit. The women grieve for the death of a soldier, son to one, husband to the other: but when a comrade-in-arms arrives, the younger woman throws herself at him while the older writhes in sexual frustration. The film is hysterical in manner and, whatever Shindo's claims, is close to (soft) pornography – which is why it had a certain success with Occidental audiences.

Although Shindo is not as profound as some of those with whom he had worked, there is some merit in **The Life of Chikuzan** (1977), a biography of the famous, half-blind *shamisen* virtuoso, who appears in person to introduce it. Exquisitely photographed by Kiyomi Kondo, in win-

try landscapes and on seashores, it balances grinding poverty and misery against joy in music, physical freedom and movement. Domestic audiences found the film tired and over-familiar, but even though Western cinema had achieved a sophistication equal to that of the Japanese, this was still a more mature biography than most made anywhere else at the time.

Shindo had continued to write occasional screenplays for other directors, such as **The Elegant Beast** (1962), a verbose attempt at social satire centring on a family of scroungers and set entirely in their apartment, which was directed by Yuzo Kawashima. Kawashima, who died the following year aged forty-five, was a strong influence on his contemporaries, among them Yasuzo Masumura, a former assistant to Mizoguchi and Ichikawa. Masumura had been directing for ten years when he made **The Wife of Seishu Hanaoka** (1967), written by Shindo from a story by Sawako Ariyoshi based on the life of a nineteenth-century physician. Accordingly, it follows *Red Beard*, but the films are not alike, this one being a sentimental family chronicle, with births, deaths, illnesses, etc., and just enough conflict for it to be considered a comment on human affairs. It is skilfully made, but is basically a vehicle for three immensely popular players – Raizo Ichikawa, Ayako Wakao and the veteran Hideko Takamine.

Shindo's left-wing views are also common among his contemporary filmmakers. Satsuo Yamamoto's most commercial films are always virulent propaganda, like **The Travelling Players** (1955), which centres on a Kabuki troupe who best their capitalist boss by adopting his principles. Among the other younger directors working in the great tradition, using sensitivity and observation, is Koreyoshi Kurahara: his **Flame of Devotion** (1964) is a beautifully crafted, but much too pretty film about two lovers separated when the boy is conscripted. **Shadow of a Flower** (1961), directed by Yuzo Kawashima, is the study of a bar hostess with too many lovers, which is both a critique of Japanese society and an event for ladies who like to cry in cinemas. The same could be said of **He and She** (1963), in which a housewife finds her suburban world of little account when she meets an improvident rag-picker. The role is played by Sachiko Hidari, the wife of the director, Susumu Hani; the film is principally a star vehicle for her. Much better is **Home from the Sea** (1972), written and directed by the less heralded Yoji Yamada, about a young seaman who is forced to give up his job and move to the mainland. Yamada clearly shares the boy's regret at changing values and handles with loving care the facts of his day-to-day existence.

Except for Hani, these directors are almost unknown in the West, but we have seen several films of their contemporaries, in which the posturing and posing, always present in Japanese cinema, have taken over completely: their films are visually striking, but incoherent to a degree. The artificiality of Yoshige Yoshida's **Coup d'Etat** (1973) destroys a potentially interesting subject, a study of a right-wing professor of the Thirties. A formalised visual splendour robs two historical subjects, **Double Suicide** (1969) and **Himoko** (1969), of any sense of human involvement. Both were directed by Masahiro Shinoda (b.1931) who clearly hopes to throw off the yoke of the past by emphasising the image – but he does it at the expense of characterisation and theme. He adopts an intense theatricality in telling **The Scandalous Adventures of Buraikan** (1970). The diffuse screenplay by Shuji Tereyama concerns a layabout (Tatsuya Nakadai) who joins a theatrical troupe at the time of the Tempo Reformation in 1842. By setting each scene against paintings, tapestries and huge prints Shinoda does achieve a unity, but it is not an interesting one.

His work is at least polished – something that could not be claimed for the films of Nagisa Oshima (b.1932). Like many equally ungifted European directors, he has experimented with explicit sex and violence. We may sympathise with his expressed desire to avoid the idioms and techniques of his predecessors, but they are surely better models than Godard and late Fellini. 'I try to start out with the problems of the individual,' he has said, 'and these problems should be meaningful to anybody in the world.' Presumably he was not referring to **Three Resurrected Drunkards** (1969), the clownish adventures of three students, a film which, two-thirds into its exposition, repeats its beginning and continues unchanged – not that the

events are any more comprehensible the second time around. And it would be a rare person who could find anything 'meaningful' in the seemingly endless and mindless discussions of orgasm which constitute **Diary of a Shinjuku Thief** (1969). 'Sexual inadequacy,' said the director, 'is a political inadequacy in itself.' References in the film placing the protagonists in the upheavals of 1969 are not something, apparently, with which audiences are sympathetic, since this is a film always accompanied by the banging of seats being vacated. **The Boy** (1969), a traditional story of a child growing up in poverty, is for the most part professional, if frequently sacrificing conviction in pursuit of visual effects.

Fortunately, the post-Kurosawa generation of film-makers had an imposing exponent in Shohei Imamura (b.1926). After a conventional start he went on to express a commitment to social reform with more intensity than any of his predecessors or colleagues. He had become an assistant to Ozu in 1951, but there is not the least influence of Ozu by the time he came to make his fourth film, **My Second Brother** (1959). This was a studio assignment based on a bestselling diary written by a young girl as she and her brothers and sister struggled against deprivation during the Recession of 1953/4. Magnificently photographed in monochrome by Masahisa Himeda, its portrait of a small seaside mining town in Kyushu is more eloquent than its narrative, proving that Imamura remained faithful to the traditions of treating sentimental stories with extreme harshness: like its contemporary, Imai's *Kiku and Isamu*, it has at once a soft-heartedness and a realism which should have value for posterity.

Hogs and Warships (1961) is a better example both of Imamura being a film-maker before a polemicist and his penchant for working on a large canvas. It is stunningly organised and orchestrated, set in the port of Yokosuka where the civilians working with the U.S. Navy have local live-in mistresses and the sailors get drunk in the red-light district. The Americans supply drugs, and are presumably responsible for the fact that gang warfare is infinitely more vicious than at the time of early Ozu (Imamura was a boy when Ozu made his last gangster film). There are several Mr Bigs, and so many rivalries that the 'business' changes hands frequently: challenging the older mob is a bunch of young punks. The youthful hero hopes to escape poverty by resorting to crime; his pure girlfriend gives in to it, and is soon getting drunk and going to a hotel room with three American sailors. Imamura's rather heavy, sardonic humour (though on this occasion he had no hand in writing the script) is apparent as a small boy reads a book about Japan's unique culture still being able to absorb the finer aspects of Western civilisation.

Imamura's obsession with sexuality found clearer expression in **The Insect Woman** (1963) and **Unholy Desire** (1964) – though both are profoundly feminist – which, like many other important Japanese films of this time, reflect the changing role of the woman in marital relations. The title of *The Insect Woman* refers to the life of its heroine, Tome, grubbing like an insect to survive in post-war Japan. The action starts at the end of the First World War, and for a while is incomprehensible. It improves as Tome finds a way to earn a living by exploiting the contacts she made as a servant in a brothel. She loves her protector and is 'used' by him; her daughter sleeps with him and uses him – but ends unrepentant and happy. *Unholy Desire* describes the pitiful attraction a woman feels towards her rapist, a situation not dealt with (at least in Western cinema) since the Silent period. The man concerned is insignificant, a musician playing with a small combo; the woman is not extraordinary, and our emotions are manipulated as we increasingly loath her husband and his mistress, hoping that the wife will take advantage of her semi-infatuation for her own sake. The film is long, sumptuously photographed by Himeda, and in its combination of black humour and melodrama, typical of this period in Japanese cinema. Since it was also a period of greatness, it should be emphasised that this film is entirely worthy of it.

The Pornographer (1966) is less satisfactory, though that may be true only of the export edition which was prepared by Imamura's customary employer, the Nikkatsu Studio. The film is subtitled 'An Introduction to Anthropology', and claims the co-operation of the sex researchers, Phyllis and Eberhard Kronhausen. Its simple thesis is that the trade of pornography is corrupting and degrading. Plied by Subu (Shoichi Ozawa), a former vendor of medical instruments, it is not well paid; he is constantly harried by the police and rival gangs, and the porn film actors are indifferent and unreliable – so he turns his hand to pimping and the peddling of sex drugs. As always in the films of Imamura, the pressures of poverty lead to the disintegration of family life: his stepson makes off with mother's savings, his step-daughter becomes a prostitute or worse (i.e. is prepared to offer herself for nothing). Subu takes an assistant, also a sexual misfit, uncertain whether he prefers sex with himself or unemotionally with his sister. Subu gradually withdraws from the world, but since he cannot withdraw from his job, he tries to manufacture a life-size doll, in order that men can function sexually without emotion.

The three films, with their common themes, constitute an unintentional trilogy: there are implications throughout that Imamura is becoming impatient of fictional narrative. Ichikawa had dispensed with it in two of his great films, and questioned the worth of it in *An Actor's Revenge*. Antonioni in *Blow-Up* (q.v.) had debated the function of the camera as an instrument of truth, and Imamura himself had begun to question this in *Unholy Desire*, as the mistress stalks the lovers with a camera, and in *The Pornographer*, in which, in the porn film being made, the viewer will see only what he wants to see – and, indeed, will command such movies to order, requiring even more than usual fabrication on the part of the pornographer. Imamura's musing on the subject resulted in **A Man Vanishes** (1967), which is solely concerned with the nature of truth. The man who has vanished has been charged with embezzlement, but that provides only one clue to his disappearance. At first we may suppose the enquiry is being pursued by the police, or by the press, but it turns out that the film itself is the investigation – a documentary. What we, the audience, thought was fiction was actually fact. But it makes little difference, for Imamura is so intent on examining theories that the film dies.

Aware of its failure, he moved to a new theme, or at least seemed to. **Legends** from a Southern Island (1968), also known as *The Profound Desire of the Gods*, is his initiation to colour, and is set on a tropical island almost untouched by civilisation. Its oldest family is primitive in a way that gives added meaning to the word – riddled with superstition, incest, nymphomania, supernatural cunning, mental deficiency and existing at a level hardly higher than animals. That is how they are regarded by the pasty-faced engineer from Tokyo sent to run the local factory. We may see them as akin to the characters of *Tobacco Road*, until Imamura decides to show them – and, eventually their surroundings too – through their own eyes, revealing the island as a paradise that should remain unspoilt. It does not, and the epilogue reveals the native family being endowed with a mythic status for the delectation of the tourists, a status in which truth and legend are mingled until they are indistinguishable.

Following this film, which is as haunting as it is ambitious, Imamura retreated to familiar themes in History of Post-War Japan as Told by a Bar Hostess (1970). Like *Hogs and Warships* it is set in the red-light district of Yokusuka; the title is reminiscent of the theme of *The Insect Woman* and like *A Man Vanishes* it consists of personal recollections of past events. Its form is a combination of newsreels and interviews, with Imamura himself on camera asking his bar hostess whether she is telling the truth. Her misplaced trust in her own destiny is contrasted with her cynicism towards such matters as the Imperial wedding and photographs of atrocities in Vietnam; both attitudes are contrasted with a more general portrait of society, seemingly forever disturbed by train crashes and revolutionary fervour. But the general and the particular aspects of this film do not really fuse, which is why I think it a pity that it is this director's only film to be widely seen in the West. It is much less riveting than Karayuki-San (1975), a relatively simple documentary about a woman who, kidnapped in her teens, has spent her life in a series of brothels in Malaya. It is part conversation with the old lady herself, part reconstruction of her past, and part dissertation on the subject of prostitution. Imamura made this film for television, his chosen medium at this time, finding it preferable for the

examination of a number of his preoccupations – and there were several further studies of the War and its aftermath.

Imamura returned to feature films with Vengeance Is Mine (1979), based on a novel by Ryuzu Saki, in turn based on fact, and once again his protagonist is formed by the environment, postwar Japan. Enokizu (Ken Ogata) is a multiple murderer with no redeeming feature except his sense of humour and, as in his earlier films, Imamura lays a number of unpleasant facts before the audience, inviting it to reach some conclusions of its own. He offers an explanation, since Enokizu suspects his wife of an incestuous relationship with his father (the incest frequent in Imamura's work is seldom between blood relations), and then withdraws it. He refuses to show compassion – the usual excuse for sex and violence on the screen – though he does detail the conditions, usually induced by poverty, which can produce a morally malformed character. Enokizu is captured and hanged, but there remains one murder unexplained by its perpetrator, his captors, or the events that we have seen: and the effect is chilling. Since I believe that Imamura had earlier inspired less talented directors to use sex and violence on the screen, his object may have been merely to show them how to use these ingredients. Indeed they are portrayed so graphically as to be indefensible, were it not for his consummate skill.

The film reaffirms Imamura's claim to be considered the principal heir to the Japanese masters, but his next film, Eijanaika (1981), signally fails to support this claim. It is his first exercise in *jidai-geki* – and Japanese film tradition and history are too powerful for the term to be avoided, even at this stage. The film is set immediately before the Meiji restoration and Imamura wished to draw comparisons with the situation then and that existing today. The title may be translated as 'What the hell!' and is the name given to the supposedly spontaneous riots of 1867, which occurred all over Japan in an attempt to overthrow the Tokugawa Shogunate, as many of the clans resented its fraternisation with foreigners. Imamura wonderfully conveys a society in flux: the 'invaders' with their import-export offices, the disillusioned samurai, the occasional national in Western dress.

The central character is Genji (Shigeru Izumiya), who returns to Japan with rudimentary English after being shipwrecked. His wife meanwhile has become involved with the criminal underworld, and the two of them are among a large cast of characters, all whipped on and off the screen so quickly that they remain shadowy. In this case Imamura's preference for a broad canvas defeats him: even at 151 minutes it telescopes both particular and historical events too much for comprehension. Himeda's photography has never served this director so well, but the chance has been lost – the chance, that is, to get a major film by Imamura into distribution in the West,* where audiences have shown a preference for *jidai-geki* subjects.

I believe the film fails because Imamura tries too hard: even he finds it daunting to invite comparisons with a great generation of film-makers – despite the fact that his contemporary subjects demonstrated a revitalisation after the achievements of Ozu, Shimazu, Gosho, Naruse and Imai. Those film-makers had found that the restrictions of the genre film were an advantage – but when the bounds were breached by Kinoshita and Mizoguchi, all Japanese directors found themselves confronting greater truths in both modern and historical subjects, pointing the way for the great films of Kurosawa, Ichikawa and Kobayashi. When questioned, these directors have preferred to remain mute about their successors (I hope in the case of Imamura because they regard him rather as a contemporary), but they have been vocal enough on the subject of their industry, which they insist has never been more constricting and less adventurous. On both issues they must feel betrayed.

When Richard Griffith wrote 'The Film Since Then' in 1956, he had had but a glimpse of Japanese cinema and, helped by secondhand accounts from other writers on cinema, briefly noted some twenty-eight films. This was enough for him to think we were on the verge of making a great discovery. I have seen over two hundred Japanese films, but I would make the same observation. The Japanese cinema started moving towards greatness in the late Forties, to reach its peak in the Sixties. It is easy enough to list the Japanese masters – and let me make it clear that I regard Imamura as belonging with those mentioned in the preceding paragraph – but I have included, where possible, the work of other directors of whom our knowledge is incomplete. Almost the only Japanese film to enter the international repertory in the Seventies was Oshima's absurd, but sexually explicit, *In the Realm of the Senses*. Yamada, who made *Home from the Sea*, remains unknown outside his own country; Imamura is known mainly from festivals and retrospectives organised by the cinematheques.

But if we are forced back on those Japanese directors whose work we do know thoroughly there are still assessments to be made. They made masterpieces, and at the very least we can say that they never confused or misled audiences in the construction and composition of their extraordinary images. These are the great storytellers and the great stylists and it is with wonder that I recall the sheer density and excitement of their historical films. And it is with gratitude that I think of the humanity with which so many of the rest are imbued.

*As this book goes to press, *The Song of Narayama*, a remake of Kinoshita's film, won the 1983 Grand Prix at Cannes.

993

36

France: Before and After the Nouvelle Vague

TO THE POSTWAR generation, the foreign-language cinema meant predominantly the French. The Italians were impressive, but Anglo-Saxon importers remained wary – and, besides, art-house audiences were familiar with French players and directors. The French cinema was established as presenting a more civilised view of life than was to be found in most American and British movies. Its devotees were accustomed to films which would be uncommercial in English – but what was not readily apparent was that French cinema was moribund, decaying in imaginary gloom. With the hindsight of over three decades this becomes evident, especially because in the interim there was an explosion of talent which changed not only French cinema but all cinema. It was the nouvelle vague or new wave, supposedly washing away the established French film-makers. Most of those did become redundant, but not entirely with justice.

In movies at that time to be civilised meant, above all, to be witty about sex – and the supreme exponent of that was Max Ophuls, returning to work in France after his years in Hollywood. After the modest success of *The Reckless Moment*, its producer, Walter Wanger, tried to set up a production of *La Duchesse de Langeais* in Europe, with Ophuls directing Garbo and James Mason. But while the lady hesitated – which was why the backers eventually balked – Ophuls received an invitation from France to film Schnitzler's 'Reigen', with a glittering cast. Whatever the weaknesses of Schnitzler's text, **La Ronde** (1950) is a triumph from the instant the credits fade: Anton Walbrook, elegant, suave and blasé, strolls on to a set which is neither studio nor stage but a dreamlike

fantasy of how Vienna should have been. Jean d'Eaubonne designed it and Christian Matras photographed it, complementing the text, which if not high wit is at least in the tradition of such moralities. The characters are puppets as they act out their *vie amoureuse* – the whore (Simone Signoret), the soldier (Serge Reggiani), the chambermaid (Simone Simon), the student (Daniel Gélin), the married woman (Danielle Darrieux), her husband (Fernand Gravey), the *grisette* (Odette Joyeux), the poet (Jean-Louis Barrault), the actress (Isa Miranda) and the count (Gérard Philipe), who meets up with the whore to complete the circle. Since their sexual needs differ, the outcome of each relationship cannot be predicted. The loneliness, the frequent degradations and the lack of satisfaction have scarcely been transmitted by Ophuls, who in using period conventions could only function in this *décoratif* way. However, his obvious understanding of such matters provides the work with its unique texture, and its enchantment has not diminished with the years, even if its piquancy has gone. Audiences were not then accustomed to such sexual frankness, and it is doubtful whether the film could have played in Britain had the censor not recently introduced the X certificate for such fare. Denounced by the popular press and praised by the critics, *La Ronde* ran even longer in the West End of London than the unprecedented twelve months of *Ladri di Biciclette*. American distributors were reluctant to handle it, and when it eventually arrived in 1954 its sexual frankness was no longer a box-office factor. It was to be some years before Ophuls was recognised in America, despite his Hollywood films. In Britain, astonishingly, critics were

The Romantic World of
Max Ophuls

grudging about his next two films. Even with the success of *La Ronde* Ophuls found difficulty in getting backing for **Le Plaisir** (1952), which, following omnibus film versions of short stories by Maugham in Britain and O. Henry in the U.S., is made up of three tales by de Maupassant. 'Cynicism and sentimentality substitute for irony and melancholy,' noted Richard Winnington, but that is not true of either 'Le Masque', concerning a man who refuses to submit to old age, or 'Le Modèle', which follows the quarrels of an artist (Gélin) and his mistress (Mlle Simon). The long central story, 'La Maison de Madame Tellier', about a carriageful of whores who take an excursion to the country for a first communion, has a vivacity which defies criticism.

Madame de . . . (1953) is, wrote Karel Reisz in *Sight and Sound*, 'all stylishness . . . an uneven, often tedious film', but no matter how many times the camera of Matras glides full circle round d'Eaubonne's *fin de siècle* sets, the film is a masterpiece. These images are precisely correct for a wealthy, handsome society engaged in amorous intrigue, eventually more deeply snared by their hypocrisy than in any of Ophuls's other tales in the same vein. The character of Monsieur de . . . (Charles Boyer) is the archetype of his era, acknowledged to have a lover while his wife (Mlle Darrieux) may not; he allows her to flirt and lie, but because of his own double standard he is oblivious to the fact that she is playing with fire; and when she uses these deceits on the baron (Vittorio de Sica), in a love of genuine passion, he too rejects her. Thus society, frivolous and superficial, claims its victims, which is the theme of all of Ophuls's best films, from *Liebelei* through *Komedie om Geld*. Irony and melancholy are in *Le Plaisir* and *Madame de . . .*, as they are in *La Ronde*: but to find them you must perhaps be prepared to look beneath the surface.

Ophuls himself, working in an industry of vanities, was also a victim, his reputation constantly fluctuating. He was forced to return to Germany for what became his last film, **Lola Montès** (1955), the most expensive yet made on the Continent – and a failure of equal proportions. Like Paul Fejos, a quarter of a century earlier, a degree of success had made him (or his producers) overambitious, and the film

was made in three languages. Like Hitchcock with *Under Capricorn*, he was returning after many years to his native country with a subject which he admitted was unsuitable but which he felt was a worthy challenge. His initial objections to making a film about a nineteenth-century courtesan were silenced as he contemplated the romantic life of Zsa Zsa Gabor and the nervous disorders of Judy Garland. So he made the courtesan/star a victim, condemned to live out her life in the gaze of a contemptuous public, as indicated in the allegorical framing device of a circus, with Peter Ustinov as the ringmaster, 'exposing' Lola, but secretly sympathetic to her. This circus is as dazzling as anything Ophuls ever did, in itself a device similar to that used in *Komedie om Geld* and the compère introduced into *La Ronde*; but it so disturbed the earliest audiences of *Lola Montès* that the sequences were badly cut and reassembled at the end of the film by its producers, hoping to recoup their losses. The film failed equally in French, German and English. A version was eventually seen in New York in 1978, when the critic John Simon quite correctly observed that it 'sinks under the combined ballast of banality, sentimentality and pointlessness'. Ophuls retains only his visual style on this occasion; fatally lacking is his sense of humour, apparent even in such thankless chores as *The Exile*. Doubtless he was depressed by the wooden performance of Martine Carol, imposed upon him because she was supposed to be a popular star; he needed the wit of a Feuillère or Darrieux.

The French cinema was also the brighter for the return of another great film-maker, Jean Renoir, but in his case he went back reluctantly. His reputation, declining during his Hollywood years and with only *La Grande Illusion* then remembered from the earlier period, was restored when **The River** (1951) was acclaimed at the Venice Festival. He had, with her assistance, adapted Rumer Godden's novel about an English family living in Bengal, convinced that it would reopen the American studios to him. They wanted him to include either elephants or a tiger-hunt, as did Kenneth McEldowney, a Los Angeles florist who otherwise loved the book as much as he did; but the film went ahead without either after McEldowney had raised the money through his connections in India and in the film industry. The film is in the form of a diary kept by an adolescent girl – played by Patricia Walters, who had never acted before – and it is an affectionate documentary and a tale of the pangs of youth, which include her crush on an embittered ex-G.I. (Thomas E. Breen). Some of it is trite but all of it is beautiful, as photographed in Technicolor on locations found by Renoir's customary art director, Eugene Lourié. This is the East that Occidentals know, the ordinary among the extraordinary, with no dividing line between dream and reality; throughout there is the feeling that when the British have gone life will go on as before.

Renoir continued to live in California till the end of his life, but he had to go to Italy to get backing for his next film, **The Golden Coach** (1953). It is based on a one-act play by Mérimée about a *Commedia dell' Arte* troupe in a Spanish colony, whose

leading actress (Anna Magnani) has to choose between three suitors, including the viceroy (Duncan Lamont). Simultaneous versions were made in Italian, French and English, but when the English one was only moderately successful Renoir commuted to Paris to make – in French – his last half-dozen films. **French Cancan** (1955) is the story of a showman (Jean Gabin) whose instincts for theatre take precedence over his love life, even though, as he admits, the two are inseparable. In **Elena et les Hommes** (1956) an impoverished Polish princess (Ingrid Bergman) is persuaded by her lovers – who include Jean Marais and Mel Ferrer – that their passion for her might change the course of France's politics. Gaiety and high spirits pervade all three films, recalling *La Règle du Jeu* – for in a world in which masters chase maidservants, the theatre is the only reality. Except, of course, that it is

The last films of Jean Renoir are uneven in quality, but in sum they represent his life's ponderings on love, on art and the other matters that had often preoccupied him. The 'art' in *French Cancan* is that of the theatre, and since there are many pretty girls around, most of the male characters are in love with one or the other of them, while Renoir clearly rejoices in the cancan itself, since it was designed to shock the bourgeoisie.

not: in 1957 Renoir observed (in an interview in *Cahiers du Cinéma*) that 'the more honest approach to what we call a work of art would include the recognition that art is transitory . . . I wonder if the idea we have of a work isn't more important than the work itself, and if in turn the importance of this idea is not based on the good that this idea can do for men: a good which is absolutely undefinable, and which I refuse to catalogue. I refuse to say "This is good, that is bad".'

Yes, but in *The Golden Coach* and *French Cancan* a number of facts and factors jostle in a roundelay – success, poverty, promiscuity, prostitution, talent, art, roistering, wealth, failure, ambition. All may be forgotten when the curtain goes up – in the most transient of all the arts. In *Elena et les Hommes* all difficulties are solved by love, and that is the greatest illusion of them all. In the decade that culminated with *La Règle du Jeu*, Renoir was starkly realistic; in these three films, with their often stylised sets, he is, respectively, romantic, frivolous and facetious. They are all four, to an extent, the same film.

Elena et les Hommes, dubbed and rechristened – *Paris Does Strange Things*, by Warner Bros. – was a failure and Renoir never again flirted with international names or was so ambitious. In 1955 in Paris he directed a play he had written, 'Orvet', and arising from that he decided to examine further the nature of good and evil. He made a very personal adaptation of 'Dr Jekyll and Mr Hyde', called *Le Testament du Docteur Cordelier*, which he directed for television in 1959. It was shown in Paris cinemas two years later, and on the large screen is insubstantial and amateurish in appearance. Jean-Louis Barrault plays the double-role, but Renoir is fatally unable to be explicit about the exact nature of his evil. He so liked the working methods of television that he chose to film **Le Déjeuner sur l'Herbe** (1959) with five simultaneous cameras and in chronological order (in twenty-four days), using his father's home, Les Collettes, near Cagnes. As the title implies, he tried to render in screen terms the spirit of the early Impressionists – their discoveries with light, nature and sensuality. The wind rustles the leaves of the silvery Provençal trees, the goatherd blows his pipe and some picnickers embark on a bacchanal; a *savant*

(Paul Meurisse), usually preoccupied with European plans for artificial insemination, forgets everything in the arms of a farmer's daughter (Catherine Rouvel). We knew from *Dr Cordelier* that Renoir detested modern science, and this clash between nature and science is balanced the way he wanted it; it is the thesis of an old man imparting the lessons of a lifetime. Like his published memoir ten years later, it is neither penetrating nor provocative, but it is full of love and old truths. It is his last wholly personal statement.

That memoir does not mention **Le Caporal Epinglé** (1962), the only film of his later years which he did not initiate himself – clearly offered to him because he had made the most famous of P.O.W. films. He said at the time that the distributor had cut it, thereby distorting it, but it is a good film, somewhat different from his recent work. Of course, detention camps are ugly, yet something precious comes out of the German incarceration of the French in 1940 – camaraderie. When the two friends (Jean-Pierre Cassel, Claude Rich) say goodbye at the end, Renoir has gone further than in *La Grande Illusion*, in which the absurdity of war created mutual understanding. He made this statement again in his memoir, when he spoke of his love for Jacques Becker, noting that only chance had made it a non-sexual one. Clearly, when sex was not involved, love was no longer an illusion. The theme is repeated in his last screen work, **Le Petit Théâtre de Jean Renoir** (1969), in the episode 'Le Roi d'Yvetot', when the mutual love between husband, wife and best friend is only spoilt by the sexual act – or what society assumes to have been sexual. This four-part film was made for television, and apart from this sequence is negligible, with a Christmas Eve fantasy and an extended sketch about a house-proud wife. Renoir did not retire and did not give up the hope of making another film until just before his death. Despite the failure of *Elena* – in France also – his reputation had continued to grow in the Fifties and the restitution of the original version of *La Règle du Jeu* confirmed his position. Three years later *Le Caporal Epinglé* proved him as capable as any of making a youthful film. I do not know why the nouvelle vague directors, who admired Renoir so much, were unable to persuade their financiers to help him as they aided each other. I do know that his late films seem even better now than when they were made.

The strain sometimes evident in René Clair's two post-Hollywood movies may be found again in **Les Belles-de-Nuit** (1953), a tale of an impoverished musician (Gérard Philipe) who seeks relief from frustration, bureaucracy and the day's noises (pneumatic drills etc) in dreams – going back each time to a different generation, only to find that 'the good old days' were not so good after all. His dream adventures are mainly amorous, and as they turn sour he is pursued from epoch to epoch neither amusingly nor inventively. However, there is a pleasing tendency for everyone to burst into song, and Georges Van Parys's score is witty even if Clair's screenplay is not. No one else could have made it, and some of the sequences of the musician with his friends recall Clair's early films, which means that some of it at least is magical.

Putting aside whimsy, Clair made his most touching film, **Les Grandes Manoeuvres** (1955), about a philanderer (Philipe) who wagers with his fellow-officers that he can make any woman fall in love with him – and the woman chosen is a divorcée (Michèle Morgan) who is also the local milliner. The plot★ had seen valiant service in musical comedies, and the challenge to Clair was to make it work again, which he does in a splendid fusion of the players, the setting – a small garrison town before 1914 – and colour, predominantly pastel shades. The music of the period is wittily used and at least two sequences are of total enchantment. We had not seen Clair in this mood before, but **Porte des Lilas** (1957) has the same wistful quality – of chances lost and hopes unfulfilled. At the same time, like *Les Belles-de-Nuit*, it recalls the early films, for it shares a joy in the enterprise and loyalty of artisan chums – 'L'Artiste' (Georges Brassens) and the dreaming, drunken Ju-Ju (Pierre Brasseur), who shelter a gangster (Henri Vidal) on the run.

If none of these films has, when required, the gaiety of his early films they are nevertheless equally fresh, but with **Tout**

l'Or du Monde (1961) Clair was suddenly tired: some city-slickers, aided by the press and a publicity-seeking pop-singer, descend upon a village which they plan to turn into a skyscraper city – till it turns out that the country bumpkins are too smart for them. The targets are familiar ones from Clair's silent films onwards, but his jokes have become laboured. In the interim Hollywood, and Ealing, had tackled the situation with more zest, but there are some minor delights, including Bourvil as three different generations of yokel. One further film, **Les Fêtes Galantes** (1965), with Jean-Pierre Cassel, was considered so inferior to all the numerous historical romps which had followed in the wake of *Fanfan-la-Tulipe* that Clair retired. However, as with Renoir and Ophuls, a mellow decade followed his unsatisfactory experience in Hollywood.

Certainly the three of them were luckier than some of their contemporaries. Julien Duvivier made, in Italy, **Le Petit Monde de Don Camillo** (1952), which was so successful that a sequel was called for, **Le Retour de Don Camillo** (1953), made in Spain. The second seemed unnecessary at the time, and the first has dated, despite the fact that its subject – the clash of Church and Communism in postwar Italy – remains a factor in European life. Taking its

René Clair had not made a contemporary tale of his beloved Paris for over two decades when he filmed *Porte des Lilas*, and instead of the joyous, studio-created city of *Le Million* he filmed in one of the shabbier quartiers, under glum skies. However, his mood had hardly changed, and this a jolly, affectionate film; his heroes, Pierre Brasseur and Georges Brassens, are quite as enterprising as those of his earlier films.

★Clair's source was a novel by Georges Courteline, but the best-known version, 'Captain Jinx of the Horse Marines', is by Courteline's American contemporary, Clyde Fitch.

France: Before and After the Nouvelle Vague

The comic actor Fernandel had been popular in foreign art-houses for many years, but it was *Le Petit Monde de Don Camillo* which brought him a wider popularity, to the extent that after that every film he made was imported into Britain and the U.S., though with diminishing results, since few of them were as good. This was one of the last good films of the once-estimable Julien Duvivier; with Fernandel is Gino Cervi.

tone from the original novel by Giovanni Guareschi it offers no more than a series of comic compromises between the priest (Fernandel) and the mayor (Gino Cervi). The virtual dismissal everywhere of **Pot-Bouille** (1957) was an indication that Duvivier was no longer taken seriously. It is a good film, or seems so now: he was never a great director, but had on occasion fine material. Since Zola's book was not betrayed in Henri Jeanson's adaptation, and since the film is wholly amused and cynical about the sexual habits of the bourgeoisie it gives much pleasure, except towards the end when everyone suddenly seems tired of the venture. Gérard Philipe is the young philanderer from Aix whose arrival at the boarding house – the *potbouille* of the title – only increases the adultery being conducted therein. Dany Carrel is one of his victims and the more-than-fleeting glimpse of her bare breasts is instance of France still leading the way in screen frankness.

Duvivier continued making films till his death, but the results were at best undistinguished. The half-dozen features made by Marcel Carné during this period – the last in 1971 – were no more kindly received, but **Les Tricheurs** (1958) was very successful on its home territory. It was accepted as an authentic portrait of the French *jeunesse*, their morals and mores, but by the time it arrived in Britain and the

U.S. it seemed dowdy and cliché-ridden in comparison to *Les Cousins* (q.v.), which had preceded it. **Trois Chambres à Manhattan** (1958) is handled equally flatly, but Carné has retained some of the spirit of Simenon's original story, and it is engagingly played by Annie Girardot, Maurice Ronet and Gabriele Ferzetti.

Claude Autant-Lara, never as celebrated as Duvivier or Carné, fared much better and made some interesting films in the Fifties – even if, as before, the interest was often chiefly in the decor. Both **Le Rouge et le Noir** (1954) and **Le Joueur** (1958) are prettily designed in pastel shades. Gérard Philipe is wonderfully at home in both films, his Julien Sorel perfectly partnered by Danielle Darrieux's Mme de Renal and his Alexei by Françoise Rosay's aged countess. These are attractive and intelligent entertainments, but to be worthy of their originals – Stendhal and Dostoevsky – they need wit, bustle, energy, detail and intellectual strength. Autant-Lara's customary writers, Aurenche and Bost, gave him one of their rare original screenplays with **L'Auberge Rouge** (1951), and they were all more deft on this occasion. The inn of the title shelters a coachload of travellers, including a monk (Fernandel) and his accompanying novice (Didier d'Yd), who learn, but cannot report, that the innkeeper (Carette) and his wife (Mlle Rosay) are mass murderers whose customers never complete their journeys. Many Anglo-Saxons first learnt the expression *comédie noire* because of this film, which remains superior to most later examples of the genre.

Autant-Lara was one of several directors, including Rossellini and Yves Allégret, who contributed to **Les Sept Péchés Capitaux** (1952), and his episode is the best as well as the longest. It concentrates on two ladies, Rosay and Michèle Morgan, who are proud and impoverished, so that they surreptitiously steal food at a society gathering. Autant-Lara's instinct for emotional situations served Colette well in **Le Blé en Herbe** (1954), her story about a woman – played in the film by Edwige Feuillère – who, to relieve boredom during a long, hot summer, initiates an adolescent (Pierre-Michel Beck) into the pleasures of love-making. In **En Cas de Malheur** (1959) the same actress suffers heartbreak when her lawyer husband (Jean

Gabin) falls passionately in love with a hussy (Brigitte Bardot, q.v.) half his age. With more forceful material Autant-Lara made one of his best films, **La Traversée de Paris** (1956), which takes as its starting point Paris under the Occupation. That was a subject the French cinema had not yet confronted, and the exigencies of this plot required reference to the black market – for it is because of that that a painter (Gabin) and an unemployed cab driver (Bourvil) have to smuggle a pig across Paris in the blackout. Their series of adventures are mainly of a comic nature; although in Marcel Aymé's original story one murdered the other in exasperation, the ending used here is unusually moving, and it makes its own comment on the Nazis and the Occupation.

Jacqueline Audry (b. 1908) is a small-scale Autant-Lara, insofar as she was attracted to literary adaptations, preferably set in the recent past. Unlike him, she had little technical skill, being content to set her camera down before two people talking. In spite of this, her three films of Colette stories have a certain charm. Danièle Delorme, 'discovered' for **Gigi** (1949), is the star of all three, and she is absolutely right. She is marvellously partnered in that film by Frank Villard, a somewhat pasty and paunchy Gaston, growing younger as he falls in love, while Gaby Morlay as her tightmouthed aunt and Yvonne de Bray as her grandmother are also splendid. Audry had had difficulty setting up the film, but its success led to **L'Ingénue Libertine** (1950), with Delorme and Villard as the couple whose marriage founders in infidelity and boredom till a really good bout of love-making – but that was something even the French could not convey at this time. Again with her husband, Pierre Laroche, scripting, Audry made **Mitsou: ou, Comme l'Esprit vient aux Filles** (1957), with the welcome addition of colour. It falters on its thesis that a soldier would expect a cabaret artiste and kept woman (Delorme) to be a lady of taste, but is otherwise charming. It arrived in New York one month before M-G-M's icing-sugar *Gigi*, to which all three films are preferable.

The adolescent emotions in **Olivia** (1951) are lesbian, and this is the first major film since *Mädchen in Uniform*, also set in a girls' school, to handle the theme. The author of the pseudonymous novel was later revealed to be Dorothy Bussy, Lytton Strachey's sister, and it is an autobiographical account of her girlhood at a French school, where she was presumably the object who comes between the graceful, understanding headmistress (Feuillère) and her peevish, coquettish lover (Simone Simon). The film offers no more than a hand squeezed to bosom or lip to brow, but only once does it indicate that the love – not sexuality – permeating the school is unacceptable to society. Ophuls's designer, d'Eaubonne, had replaced Audry's earlier collaborator, and had clearly stimulated her to a more fluent style. There is a lesbian (Arletty) in **Huis Clos** (1955), closeted in a déclassé hotel room with a failed revolutionary (Villard) and a vapid Parisienne (Gaby Sylvia). This is a version of the play in which Sartre proposed '*L'enfer, c'est les autres*', and these three people are to irritate each other throughout eternity. By moving beyond the room in time and place, the film improves upon the play; but it is doubtful whether it is more worthwhile than adaptations of less distinguished dramatists.

It was still a long while after *Olivia* that the screen could suggest that schoolboys suffered similar passions, and **Les Amitiés Particulières** (1964) is based on a twenty-year-old novel of which producers had hitherto been wary. In the interim its author, Roger Peyrefitte, had become one of France's most respected writers – despite his hostility to the Church. Aurenche and Bost, who did the adaptation, have substituted for that a wry humour, though the picture of the Catholic seminary remains unflattering. Didier Haudepin and Francis Lacombrade are the unfortunate boys, with Michel Bouquet as an over-curious priest and Louis Seigner as the one whose meddling kindness leads to tragedy – the two of them as prejudiced as they are pious. The film indeed is an unexpected success, and a last major work by Jean Delannoy, whose historical films and literary adaptations had usually been inferior to those of Autant-Lara. However, he had directed two lively adaptations of Simenon, **Maigret tend un Piège** (1958) and **Maigret et l'Affaire Saint-Fiacre** (1959), both with Jean Gabin. He also made a visually exquisite but static version of **La Princesse de Clèves** (1961), with

Simone Signoret, centre, in *Casque d'Or*, Jacques Becker's romantic film, set in the Paris underworld just before the turn of the century. Much later this actress observed that it was the only *chef d'oeuvre* with which she had been associated and, if she is being unfair to the many other good films she has made, her pride in this one is understandable. On the left of her is Claude Dauphin and on the right Dominique Davray.

Marina Vlady and Jean Marais, thus resuming his collaboration with Jean Cocteau, who had prepared this version of Mme de Lafayette's novel some years earlier, but now felt disinclined to direct it himself.

Cocteau's own farewell to the cinema was **Le Testament d'Orphée** (1960), and in returning to the trickery of *Le Sang d'un Poète* he had come full circle. The reference in the title to his most celebrated work may be acknowledgement that it is the only one he created of lasting merit; the two films are not to be compared, despite the degree of cannibalism involved. Cocteau, whatever acclaim he had received, refused to see himself as part of the great world, since his penchant for fantasy and his private life were unsuited to it. His real-life lover, Edouard Dermithe, appears in that capacity and as Cégeste from *Orphée*; but although this is an arrogant film it resorts constantly to symbolism. George Steiner once wrote in *The New Yorker* that 'in Cocteau, homosexuality breeds ingenious tinsel', but the symbolism is far from ingenious. The film is a conceit, at once totally negative and totally narcissistic.

Among the younger French directors, Jacques Becker held the commanding place, though now it is hard to be amused by **Edouard et Caroline** (1951), which

made his name with Anglo-Saxon audiences. Marital, as opposed to bucolic, comedy was rare from France, inasmuch as the many similar French farces from the Thirties had not been exported; the quarrelling spouses here are Anne Vernon and Daniel Gélin, and the attempts at satire – at the expense of the bourgeoisie – are lacking in originality. Becker in fact is a puzzling talent, but he made one masterpiece, **Casque d'Or** (1952), and it is so perfectly crafted as to suggest that it was the only time he had complete control over his material. In taking this novel from the Thirties, based on a true underworld romance, his self-confessed task was to combine the worlds of Auguste Renoir and Eugène Sue; and quite probably the sequence of the lovers' rural happiness was inspired by *Partie de Campagne*. Much of it was filmed on location, in the wide cobbled streets of Montmartre and on the riverbanks of Arnet-sur-Marne; the art direction is by d'Eaubonne, surpassing himself, rendering his fine work for Ophuls and others as mere frou-frou. The details are unforgettable, such as Marie (Simone Signoret) knifing off slivers of cheese as she taunts her *mec* (Claude Dauphin), or her lover, Manda (Serge Reggiani), stuffing his casquette into his corduroy jacket as he prepares for the fight. Such moments are enveloped by Becker in a gathering narrative, like particles of dust shimmering in sunlight, triumphantly surmounting the major convention of underworld melodrama, in which the lovers cannot escape their tragic destiny. No praise can be too high for the playing: Signoret's hip-waggling, mocking whore is redeemed by an innate decency, and later transformed into a woman zealously in love, while Reggiani's meek, moustached carpenter finds sinew when that love is challenged. The film was poorly received in Paris and Brussels before winning golden opinions in London, as Mme Signoret recalled in 1973, when Paris flocked to a revival.

Touchez pas au Grisbi (1954) is a contemporary *Casque d'Or*, inasmuch as it is a gangster story; but this is more obviously B-picture material, if transformed by Becker's use of the milieu – plain little cafés, uncluttered hotel rooms. The movie re-introduced a theme of prewar French cinema, the undivided loyalty of two pals

France: Before and After the Nouvelle Vague

(Jean Gabin, Lino Ventura), and it was one to be repeated in virtually every gangster film that followed – chiefly because of the success* of this one, though its popularity had much to do with a catchy theme tune. Of Becker's last four films, only **Montparnasse 19** (1957) was widely seen abroad – despite its failure in France. It is dedicated to Max Ophuls, for whom the screenplay had been prepared, and Becker took it over when he died. We had learned to expect more from both of them than this conventional biography of an artist. He is Modigliani, and at first Gérard Philipe seems to want to play him as he was, prickly, cynical, cruel to women and determined to drink himself to death. But Philipe soon settles into his own customary charm; Anouk Aimée, gazing at him with cow's eyes, hardly suggests Jeanne Hébuterne's fierce devotion, while Lilli Palmer as Beatrice Hastings affects a mocking smile and a long cigarette holder as though she had just strayed in from a spy spoof. Nevertheless in a series of episodes the film does convey at least an impression of the difficulties of this artist's life, notably in a cruel scene in which he is persuaded to visit a prospective (American) patron at the Ritz. One sequence is a homage to *La Ronde*, with Lino Ventura as a death-watch art dealer hovering over the sick 'Modi', and it is an artistic intrusion on the honest style of the rest of the film. There is no screenplay credit, as Henri Jeanson took his name off the film after quarrels with Becker over cuts in his dialogue.

Le Trou (1960) is about four men who dig a tunnel out of the Santé prison, only to be betrayed at the last minute by a fifth. José Giovanni (q.v.) wrote a novel based on this factual incident, and turned it into a screenplay with Becker and Jean Aurel. The result is one of the best films made about prison life, and throughout Becker emphasises its strange rituals: being marshalled for 'promenade'; watching a guard cut into every item of a parcel; sharing out the grub; and there is a scene as two of the men peer out of a manhole at the Paris dawn, and it is full of wonder for them. The relationship of the men is somewhat too sweet, and Becker does not make the dénouement convincing. Despite the

*Not repeated in the U.S. or Britain, since it arrived after Dassin's *Du Rififi chez les Hommes* (q.v.) and was generally written down as inferior.

excitement of the escape sequences the film was not very popular, partly because it came out at the height of the nouvelle vague. He was even considered to be trying to adapt to the rising fashion, by using amateur actors (though three of them – Philippe Leroy, Michel Constantine and Marc Michel – all went on to successful film careers).

Like Becker, Henri-Georges Clouzot had a small output before a comparatively early death. He had two international successes to Becker's one, and they were of such proportions that they reached beyond the art-house audience, which tended to make reviewers both at home and abroad look askance at Clouzot, and may have in turn inhibited him. There is no doubt that **Le Salaire de la Peur** (1953) and **Les Diaboliques** (1954) succeed magnificently in their objective, which is to get the spectator on the edge of his seat – the first with events that are literally cliff-hanging and the second with some which are spine-chilling. *Les Diaboliques* is well named, for it is devilishly clever as adapted from the novel by Boileau and Narcejac. In a bleak boarding school, the headmaster (Paul Meurisse) ill-treats both his cowed wife (Vera Clouzot, the director's wife) and his confident mistress (Simone Signoret), who conspire to murder him; their scheme

Of the films so far illustrated in this chapter, *La Ronde*, *Don Camillo* and *Casque d'Or* were each notable in attracting new patrons to foreign-language films. The first two were particularly popular, but both were eclipsed by *Le Salaire de la Peur* – which had the advantage of very little dialogue for spectators unaccustomed to subtitles. The thrills they found were as unusual as they were plentiful, and here is one of the stickier moments for Yves Montand and Charles Vanel.

France: Before and After the Nouvelle Vague

René Clément's work went into decline after he started to make 'international' films, but the first of them, *Knave of Hearts/Monsieur Ripois*, made in London, seemed to prove the contrary. Gérard Philipe was the young Frenchman who considered every other English girl his natural prey, including Joan Greenwood. British morals have seldom been so well observed, despite what shocked British critics wrote at the time.

succeeds, until the body disappears . . . *Le Salaire de la Peur* starts in a sleazy Mexican village, where four derelicts (Yves Montand, Charles Vanel, Peter Van Eyck, Folco Lulli) agree to drive a consignment of nitroglycerine across treacherous mountain roads, for what – since only one of the lorries is expected to get through – is the paltry sum of $2,000. The journey is long – for once length is a virtue in a thriller – and you do not have to believe the premise, as taken from Georges Arnaud's novel, to find it full of tension. Because these people are exploited by greed and cynicism the film was regarded in some quarters as a comment on Capitalism.

Certainly that was as much as the French cinema wanted to say on any contemporary problem. In the years immediately

following the Occupation there had been references to the social and moral climate in France, but after Clément's *Les Jeux Interdits* the French cinema buried its head in the sand. It was not expected to compete with de Sica's exceptional films, while it had achieved a level of artistry which raised it above the even more moribund British cinema; but, by the end of the Fifties, Hollywood was turning out more films of social relevance than France had once made, and with more vitality. Clouzot hoped to rectify the situation, with the added incentive that Raoul Lévy, the promoter of Brigitte Bardot, was looking for a vehicle to prove that she could act; thus with five others Clouzot wrote the screenplay for **La Vérité** (1960), which, in the guise of a murder trial, examined the lifestyle of one of today's young – Bardot. Unfortunately, she was not typical, and if the portrait of *le jeune Paris* is more accurate than that in *Les Tricheurs* and less baroque than that in *Les Cousins* (q.v.), it is equally superficial. In Paris it was widely discussed, but elsewhere dismissed as unimportant. Bardot, incidentally, did not pass the test as an actress, but then most young stars would have looked amateur in the company of such players as Vanel, Meurisse and Louis Seigner.

One director who might have tackled contemporary problems was René Clément, but after *Les Jeux Interdits* he aimed for an international career. He set up **Knave of Hearts/Monsieur Ripois** (1954) in London, with Gérard Philipe as a clerk who, tired of filling forms in triplicate, turns to philandering. His boss (Margaret Johnston) is won over by a bottle of Chamade and some compliments; a nice suburban girl (Joan Greenwood), encountered with a cold and a copy of 'Gone with the Wind', refuses to go to his room in Westbourne Grove because of what Mummy might say but changes her mind after an offer of marriage; and a smart lady (Valerie Hobson), taking French lessons, converts him from 'J'irai Cracher Sur Vos Tombes' to Mallarmé. The real love of his life is woodenly played by Natasha Parry, but Hobson and Greenwood compensate, especially the latter as a dear little silly; Philipe's charm is formidable, whether running about like a puppy in Hobson's apartment, or refusing to spend a wet Sunday in a museum – and we never doubt the heartlessness beneath the smiling surface. London had not by a long chalk been better used – but that did not stop the British press, sensing an affront to British womanhood, from denouncing the film as 'immoral'.

Its failure sent Clément back to France, for **Gervaise** (1956), which was Zola's 'L'Assommoir' prepared by Aurenche and Bost, and directed with a Daumier-like intensity of feeling for the underside of Paris in the Second Empire. The film teems with life: the wedding party and its visit to the Louvre; the fight in the *blanchisserie*; the heroine's birthday; and a certain underlying coldness is offset by the director's narrative drive. He said himself that it was not the social problems of the novel, drunkenness, which interested him, but the fate of Gervaise, played by Maria Schell. She had been imposed on Clément, who intended to dub her with a French actress, but the film went with the original soundtrack to the Venice Festival so that she might be eligible for Best Actress prize – which she won. Thus the producers refused to dub, and Clément went into litigation to no avail. Since Gervaise is a noble spirit reduced by poverty, Fraulein Schell misconceives the role, smiling through tears as she hobbles from one disaster to another. It is a far cry from Lillian Gish, and in my opinion, this truly appalling performance is one reason why this otherwise fine film is seldom revived. François Périer is excellent as the husband, who, crippled, turns to drink, and Susy Delair is vivacious, if too vindictive, as Gervaise's rival.

Clément's reputation began to disintegrate when Dino de Laurentiis provided Italo-American backing for **The Sea Wall/La Diga sul Pacifico** (1958), based on Marguerite Duras's novel of a colonial family in Indo-China – a family strangely consisting of Jo Van Fleet, Anthony Perkins and Silvana Mangano, with Richard Conte as the girl's admirer. The film was taken from them by Alida Valli as the wealthy courtesan who seduces Perkins, and Nehemiah Persoff as Mangano's foolish, unwanted admirer. The locations are splendid, but this is another hybrid of a growing, and generally unwanted, breed. **Plein Soleil** (1960) was written with Paul Gégauff, who was to collaborate with Claude Chabrol on his more hedonistic

thrillers (q.v.), but neither he nor Clément seemed interested in putting flesh on the cardboard characters of Patricia Highsmith, on whose 'The Talented Mr Ripley' it is based. The portrait of aimless and cynical young people to be found in Mediterranean resorts is largely correct, but if this story of murder and impersonation offers a frisson or so, it is hard to accept Maurice Ronet and Alain Delon as Americans. The latter was also disastrously miscast as a young Italian rip in **Che Gioia Vivere** (1961), made in the peninsula, a rather glum comedy about the early days of Fascism. It was not a success, and Clément returned to the time and theme of *La Bataille du Rail* for **Le Jour et l'Heure** (1963), in which an ordinary housewife (Simone Signoret) conspires to help an American flyer (Stuart Whitman) over the border. In **Les Félins** (1965) two American women (Jane Fonda, Lola Albright), living on the Riviera, play cat and mouse with the vain, amatory crook (Alain Delon) who hides out in their mansion. Both were made in English versions – respectively as *The Day and the Hour* and *The Love Cage* or *The Joy House* – but without success. Both, purely as thrillers, deserved more, but **Paris Brûle-t-il?/Is Paris Burning?** (1966), which followed, was a misconceived, misdirected and overlong effort, based on a bestselling account of the last days of Paris under the Occupation. It was brought to the screen after the success of Darryl F. Zanuck's similarly structured *The Longest Day*. The screenplay by Gore Vidal and Francis Coppola has only a cursory connection with either the book or history, and substitutes confusion for complexity in an attempt to find cameos for its international cast – which includes Jean-Paul Belmondo, Orson Welles, Leslie Caron, Kirk Douglas, Jean-Louis Trintignant, Yves Montand and Simone Signoret. The credited French producer is Paul Graetz, who had backed Clément on the definitive film study of the Resistance, *La Bataille du Rail*. Between the two, Clément had had only two unqualified successes, *Les Jeux Interdits* and *Gervaise*; and certainly he deserved better with *Les Maudits, Knave of Hearts* and *Le Jour et l'Heure*. His decline is even more puzzling than that of de Sica (q.v.). In 1969 Clément resigned from an American film, *Play Dirty*, which would suggest that his principles remained intact, but he subsequently made two tales of skulduggery, **Passager de la Pluie/Rider on the Rain** (1969) with Charles Bronson and Marlène Jobert, and **La Maison sous les Arbres/ The Deadly Trap** (1971) with Faye Dunaway and Frank Langella – neither of which has the slightest merit. It would be too easy to say that he was left stranded by the nouvelle vague, but after using the movement's favourite photographer, Henri Decae, on *Plein Soleil*, he struggled against it, making the sort of films the new critic-directors had vowed to exterminate. It was foolish and self-destructive, for it is impossible to guess from these last two films that Clément had once been one of the best directors of his generation.

Of foreign directors who came to work in France, the most prolific was Jules Dassin, unable to work in Hollywood after the blacklistings of the early Fifties. After some years of silence he equalled his best Hollywood work with **Du Rififi chez les Hommes** (1954), based on Auguste le Breton's thriller about two underworld gangs who cross and double-cross each other for the sake of a fortune taken from the rue de la Paix branch of Mappin and Webb. The four thieves include Jean Servais and Dassin himself, acting under the pseudonym of Perlo Vita; and the thirty-minute heist sequence, done without music or dialogue – coming halfway through the picture – is rightly famous. The film's world-wide success enabled Dassin to film an ambitious allegory, **Celui qui Doit Mourir** (1957), from the novel by Kazantzakis. In Greece under Turkish domination the survivors of a devastated town arrive in a prosperous village where the only ones to welcome them are those about to take part in the annual Passion Play, and the man (Pierre Vaneck) playing Christ becomes a symbol of compassion. There are other symbols, but its points on religious intolerance could never be superfluous. Dassin's experience as a director of thrillers enabled him to push the film – brilliantly – in that direction.

Established as an art-house draw, he virtually destroyed his reputation with **La Loi** (1959), so that he was only able to raise a meagre $150,000 for **Never on Sunday** (1960), a star vehicle for his wife Melina Mercouri, the Greek actress who had been in his last two films. Recognising his own inadequacy, he was nevertheless forced into playing the male lead, an American who falls for her, in her role of Piraeus whore – and she is the happiest whore who ever lived, slapping down his idealism and puritanism. Dassin's own screenplay is the customary concept of young America versus old Europe, with borrowings from *Born Yesterday*, but it is the first ever to treat a prostitute as a creature *for* life and love. Movies had always loved the ladies of easy virtue, but the only full-scale studies had been of the tragic ones. Mercouri in *Never on Sunday* is realistic and unashamed, and by the standards of the time the film was erotic – if less in the bedroom scenes (by virtue of Dassin's performance) than those in which Mercouri joins the sailors to dance the sirtaki. The music of Manos Hadjidakis was one reason audiences adored the film; another was the sunshine, however murkily photographed. *Never on Sunday*, for all its naivety, is one of the great liberating films. Quite astonishingly, the years have not withered it.

Its unfortunate consequence was that it enabled Dassin to make **Phaedra** (1962), one of the legendary bad movies, though alas too solemn to laugh at. Made in English, it was nevertheless premiered in France, on the premise that the French would know their Racine if not their Euripides – though by setting the tale among the jet set Dassin has been able to load it with chic. At the climax, Phaedra (Mercouri) is preparing for suicide in a sleeping mask, with the aid of her lesbian servant; her husband (Raf Vallone) is trying to assuage the grief of the black-veiled women whose loved ones have gone down in one of his tankers; and the son (Anthony Perkins) is speeding to his death round the hairpin bends yelling 'Escorted out by Bach. Johann Sebastian in person. . . . Goodbye, Greek light; goodbye, sea . . . She loved me.' The mismatching of Perkins and Mercouri may be classic and there is a weird fascination in Dassin's overestimation of his own and his wife's talents. Dassin temporarily retrieved his reputation with **Topkapi** (1964), another caper movie, based on a novel by Eric Ambler, with generous glimpses of Istanbul in Technicolor; the cast includes Mercouri, Maximilian Schell, Robert Morley, and, most notably, Peter Ustinov as an expatriate who – in the actor's own words – 'hovers between the more reprehensible columns of the *News of the World* and oblivion'. The film was a respite in the pretension which had been growing since *Celui qui Doit Mourir*, but Dassin abjured serious consideration with **10.30 p.m. Summer** (1966), written with Marguerite Duras from one of her novels, which may, or may not, be about a couple (Mercouri, Peter Finch) who need a third (Romy Schneider) to make their marriage work. A number of subsequent films, made in France, Greece and the U.S., have been no better received.

Sadder – because his was a much greater talent – is the case of Preston Sturges who, unable to work in Hollywood, made one last film in France, **Les Carnets du Major Thompson** (1955), from the book by Pierre Daninos. This supposed memoir by a pukka Briton about his experiences in France had been a gigantic bestseller, and the producers hoped that signing Jack Buchanan to play the major would attract the international market. Sturges wrote the script, taking a long time in setting up obvious targets and with no degree of asperity; it is not even well directed – but it was popular in France, if nowhere else.

The same is true of another work by a major American film-maker, Orson Welles, who found backing for a version of Kafka, **Le Procès/The Trial** (1963), absurdly casting Anthony Perkins, tense and squirmy, as Joseph K. The film might have worked if set in the costume of the period, when the cosy bourgeoisie was first threatened by secret police and concentration camps; but filmed in the defunct Gare d'Orsay, dwarfing, both figuratively and literally, the events described, it hints less at the horrors of Nazi Germany and Soviet Russia than at what happened *L'Année Dernière à Marienbad* (q.v.). There was a guarded, kinder welcome outside France for **Histoire Immortelle** (1968), made for television and based on an Isak Dinesen short story about an aged man (Welles) who employs a virginal sailor (Norman Eshley) to make love to an experienced woman (Jeanne Moreau); notions about corruption, old age and loneliness move in such small concentric waves that they are soon lost, and the slight conviction available is ruined by Welles's every appearance, preposterous in make-up, performance and photography.

In the matter of serious film-making, Robert Bresson stood alone. Silent since 1945, his earlier films had not prepared us for **Le Journal d'un Curé de Campagne** (1951), one of the best realised achievements of cinema. Based on the novel by Georges Bernanos, who wrote of anguish

The career of Robert Bresson has been one of the most curious in films. He made his reputation with two melodramas in the Forties, and in the last two decades he has made many films equally silly – though melodrama might have brought some life to them. However, in the mid-Fifties he achieved a number of magnificent films, *Le Journal d'un Curé de Campagne*, with Claude Laydu, being pre-eminent among them – a study in solitude as effective as it is austere.

and doubt and torment, it is set in a hostile countryside – a bleak Normandy, where a lonely young priest (Claude Laydu) can die, unloved and forgotten, of consumption. Bresson imparts relevant images – a bottle of wine, a letter, a walk through the mud – to accompany the text of the diary, and he withholds what the diary withholds, thus not destroying the priest's delusions. This was, within its limitations, the first 'interior' movie. Remarkably, Bresson made a companion film, as absolute and austere, **Un Condamné à Mort s'est Echappé** (1956), whose source was a story by André Devigny, based on his own experiences in a wartime jail. The mechanics of the plan of escape, interesting in themselves and sprung with tension, are irrelevant to the record of this man's existence. If the film has a fault, it is too clinical, but in confronting the same subject for the third time – what Dilys Powell called 'the man who has to face a terrible predicament in human solitude' – Bresson has become romantic. In **Pickpocket** (1959) he feels no need to explain why his hero has become a thief, and invention runs no deeper than presenting a Dostoevskian inspector to play a cat-and-mouse game and a good woman for whom he reforms at the end.

If this film is banal but absorbing, the second adjective cannot be applied to **Le Procès de Jeanne d'Arc** (1962), which, like Dreyer and perhaps because of him, is based on the minutes of Joan's last trial. Although we had waited eagerly for the self-revelation that came to the country priest, the prisoner and the pickpocket, here we see only a burning, and an end to the mouse-like amateur actress whom Bresson chose because she looked like the only surviving portrait of Joan with any claim to authenticity. The film succeeds only in being austere to the point where passion is drained. One film later, Bresson returned to Bernanos with **Mouchette** (1967), the story of a gangling fourteen-year-old girl who finds salvation in heaven – to the strains of the Monteverdi Magnificat – leaving behind an alcoholic father, a dying mother, and the gamekeeper who rewarded her friendship with rape. Bresson fills in the detail of this poor child's world with his old unobtrusive skill, but the questioning and compassion of his earlier Bernanos film are missing. **Une Femme Douce** (1969) confirmed that,

like Dreyer, he no longer knew how people behaved. The first of two films based on Dostoevsky, it keeps to the plot, he says, while trying 'to communicate impressions that are mine and part of my experience' – which leads one to suppose that his impressions and experience belong to a world other than this. The plot is centred on an unlikely marriage, but at no point does Bresson come close to understanding either participant. **Lancelot du Lac** (1974) had been a pet project for years, but he had lacked financing: this reputedly cost $1 million, but Camelot consists of some smallish tents and an old castle wall, populated by the king and queen and approximately ten knights, all played by amateurs. Cinema, indeed, reached a nadir as the queen intoned such lines as '*Lancelot, tu es vivant et tu est là*' and '*Prends ce corps interdit*', to be followed by a tournament, which turns out to be a series of medium shots of horses's flanks, knights falling, the winner's flag being rung up, and a small section of the pavilion. Lack of funds need not be a drawback with a film-maker of skill and imagination, which Bresson had once been.

Since Bresson was never going to pander to the commercial dictates of the cinema, even his poor films have their admirers. There is also a coterie rooting for Jean-Pierre Melville, who similarly loved the medium but had difficulty in coming to terms with it. Having been branded an 'intellectual' director, he said, because of his first two films, he accepted **Quand tu Liras Cette Lettre** (1953) as a commercial assignment. It is a mediocre film, as taken from a story by Jacques Deval, but Melville responds warmly to the Nice bars and hotel rooms which are the natural habitat of his protagonist (Philippe Lemaire), a gigolo and would-be murderer, who is forced by a convent novice (Juliet Greco) to become engaged to her sister whom he has made pregnant. Earlier, Melville had planned a 'crook' melodrama on the Pigalle milieu which he knew so well, but he abandoned it after seeing *The Asphalt Jungle*, because of its similar plot. Huston's film, he always maintained, contained the nineteen elements (no more and no less) available to a cops-and-robbers story – and he was to use some of them in each of the crime films he wrote and directed. Some turned up in *Du Rififi chez les Hommes*, which he was to have made – despite its resemblance to *The Asphalt Jungle* – before finding that its producers preferred Dassin; others appear in **Bob le Flambeur** (1956), the tale of an ageing gambler (Roger Duchesne) whose debts encourage him to return to his former life of crime, organising a heist from the casino at Deauville. Melville asked Auguste le Breton to write the dialogue because of the success of *Rififi* but later thought it dated; the film has an air of melancholy which distinguishes it from other thrillers. Melville's love of Hollywood movies is not immediately apparent, but that is evident in **Deux Hommes à Manhattan** (1959), as the title may imply. Indeed, beyond a comment on journalistic ethics – the plot concerns a reporter (played by Melville himself) and a photographer (Pierre Grasset) searching for a missing French diplomat – the film has nothing to express apart from its fascination with New York.

Both movies were an influence on the nouvelle vague directors, but since their own films had begun to appear *Deux Hommes à Manhattan* seemed old fashioned and it was a failure. Melville was only able to film again when Jean-Paul Belmondo (b. 1933), the key actor of the movement, enabled him to get backing for **Léon Morin, Prêtre** (1961). Like Melville's first feature, it is set during the Occupation, and as written by him from a novel by Béatrix Beck the central situation is somewhat artificial; but it is blessed with life and two protagonists who are likeable and interesting. One is a young widow (Emmanuelle Riva), Communist, Jewish and atheist who, in the absence of young men from the town in which she lives, is sexually attracted towards a woman with whom she works; but after meeting a priest (Belmondo) who responds to her priest-baiting in kindly if idiosyncratic fashion, she tranfers her attentions to him. As in *Le Silence de la Mer*, a great deal is left unsaid, and the priest, finally, remains the more enigmatic of the two. In Belmondo's performance he is as appealing to us as to her.

It is a beautiful film, but the two that followed, both with Belmondo, are of only moderate interest. *Le Doulos* (1963) is a stealth-by-night gangster tale, and **L'Aîné des Ferchaux** (1963), relates the adventures of two Frenchmen as they travel from New York to New Orleans. One is a proud old man, a banker (Charles Vanel), seeking refuge from the police, and the other is a destitute boxer (Belmondo) who has taken on the job as his bodyguard; in their relationship the latter gradually assumes the dominant position –

France: Before and After the Nouvelle Vague

and that is something which Melville views romantically, despite the film's source, a novel by Simenon, and the detail of life in motels and diners. Melville claimed that his films were as far from realistic as possible, and it was the romanticism he now brought to **Le Deuxième Souffle** (1966) and **Le Samourai** (1967) which make them so superior to *Le Doulos*. They are again basically formula stories of the underworld, but transformed into masterly expositions of the thesis that the criminal is loyal, lonely and eventually horribly dead. The first, from a novel by José Giovanni, involves a master-crook (Lino Ventura) in one last heist and gang warfare; the second, from an American novel by Joan McLeod, transposed to Paris, follows the final days of a professional hit-man (Alain Delon).

Melville returned to the Occupation in **L'Armée des Ombres** (1969), as portrayed in a novel by Joseph Kessel, but despite his cast – Ventura, Signoret, Jean-Pierre Cassel, Paul Meurisse – and careful filming, this tale of failing nerves and divided loyalties among the Resistance adds little to our knowledge of the subject. Nor are his last two films, **Le Cercle Rouge** (1970) and **Un Flic** (1972), as good as the two which preceded it; it is clear from the episodic nature of both that they were devised to utilise some of the 'nineteen situations' that he had not yet attempted. Delon is in each, in the first as a crook who meets and teams up with another, Gian Maria Volonté, and an ex-cop, Yves Montand, for a heist, and in the second as a world-weary police inspector. As *Le Samourai* had been designed primarily in shades of grey, so the predominant colour of *Un Flic* is blue: but the matching of colour to the prevailing mood does not seem pretentious when the set-pieces, chiefly bank-raids and escapes, are so flawlessly executed.

The French cinema was not, however, all misery, period frills and gangsters; Fernandel continued to be extraordinarily popular – and for a brief while, after the Don Camillo films, was exportable – while Bourvil and later Louis de Funès kept local audiences laughing. The one French funny-man consistently welcome abroad was Jacques Tati (1908–82), a former cabaret artist and actor who turned clown, producing and directing himself in

Jour de Fête (1949), the selected adventures of a village policeman. His great success was **Les Vacances de M. Hulot** (1953), some adventures of a tourist in a small Channel coast resort. Much loving care has gone into the creation of Hulot – the *politesse* is Chaplin's, the hitched-up trousers are Larry Semon's, and the clumsiness that of any of the great Silent clowns without their nimbleness and wit. Most of Tati's gags are stolen from the Silents, but they come along slowly, without either the timing of the originals, or any relation to the gag before or the one after. Tati's quest for international attention is one reason why this film is so abysmal, for he tries to keep the dialogue to a minimum, making the action more self-conscious than is necessary. In the original, there was only one English couple at this Brittany pension, but in the 1977 re-issue print redubbing has made only the proprietor and Hulot French. The foreign market was important to Tati because of his high production costs: his later movies were unprofitable, and eventually his films (including this one) were impounded by creditors – thus restricting further income from them, which in turn would have enabled him to continue financing his own projects.

Pierre Etaix (b. 1928), a former assistant of Tati, also aped the Silent clowns. He made his debut with a short, **Heureux Anniversaire** (1961), written and directed with Jean-Claude Carrière (also beginning his own career as a screenwriter). This tale of the Parisian perils awaiting a little man hurrying home to an anniversary dinner is a total success. There are also some splendid moments in **Le Soupirant** (1963), the adventures of a young man pursuing a bride, whereas **Yoyo** (1965), the life story of a clown, only exposed Etaix's weaknesses. Etaix's physical resemblance to Max Linder was furthered by his sporting silk hats and spats in the earlier part of *Yoyo*, but he does not know how to use his appearance to make his loss of dignity funny; like Tati, he goes to elaborate lengths for gags which die in the process. Unlike Tati, he is good-hearted, but two subsequent features evidence a law of diminishing returns, as the gags became increasingly ponderous.

One other short should be mentioned, for it provides 36 minutes of pure pleasure:

Le Ballon Rouge (1956), a slight tale of a boy and his red balloon. Edmond Séchan photographed it, and Albert Lamorisse wrote and directed – not without a degree of obvious calculation – but the final moments, as the boy is wafted aloft by a bunch of coloured balloons over the grey roofs of Paris, constitute as pretty a time as may be had in a cinema.

Le Ballon Rouge and M. Hulot joined *Le Salaire de la Peur* and *Rififi* in moving out from the art-house circuit; but Brigitte Bardot (b. 1934) did more for the French film abroad than all four put together. She was the wife of Roger Vadim (b. 1928), a former assistant of Marc Allégret, and both Vadim and the producer Raoul Lévy recognised her potential as a sex symbol. Together they wrote **Et Dieu . . . Créa la Femme** (1956), from a news item Lévy found, '*trois frères, un village, une surprenante créature, un crime*', and with it Vadim was given a chance to direct. The brothers were to be played by Christian Marquand, Jean-Louis Trintignant and Curd Jürgens – the latter the 'name' imposed by Columbia Pictures if it was to finance colour and CinemaScope; but in the event Jürgens plays an American millionaire. The village became St Tropez and the crime never materialised (though a gun is waved about); the *surprenante créature* is Bardot. The film was sourly greeted in Paris, but went on to become by far the most successful French film yet shown in foreign markets. It is not a good one: despite occasional humour the direction is flat-footed, Bardot pouts, grins and sticks out her chest, but she is not much of an actress. Nevertheless she and Vadim changed the way we think about women in films – for by then most people had forgotten the equally blatant Clara Bow and Jean Harlow. Marilyn Monroe was reminding audiences of the female readiness to cooperate, but Bardot was even less inhibited, sunbathing naked, forgetting her wedding guests in her desire for her husband (Trintignant) and, a few days later, satisfying his brother (Marquand) in the rolling surf. If Vadim and Lévy were determined on eroticism, their attempt at myth-making is also evident in the plotting – and they did much for St Tropez, here a character in its own right.

Vadim and Bardot separated, privately and professionally, though he directed her

again when their careers needed a boost. He strove for a certain chic with **Sait-on Jamais?** (1957), a confused thriller set in Venice, with the Modern Jazz Quartet on the soundtrack, and **Les Liaisons Dangereuses** (1959), which uses the music of Thelonius Monk: but because of Vadim's complete lack of narrative sense both are dowdy. The latter is a modernisation of the eighteenth-century epistolary novel, otherwise faithful in outline except that the destructive protagonists are no longer lovers but husband and wife – of whom Jeanne Moreau has to carry the film since Gérard Philipe's range did not extend to profligacy. The government censor insisted on the addition of *1960* to the film's title to indicate its disapproval of the venture and banned it from export (though that was later rescinded) on the grounds that it showed the French diplomatic set in unflattering, i.e. promiscuous, light. Vadim's stock-in-trade remained sex through a number of pictures, including a

The makers of *Et Dieu . . . Créa la Femme* set out to exploit the nubile charms of Brigitte Bardot, and they proved delightfully exploitable. The director, Roger Vadim, had no hesitation in 'borrowing' the famous beach scene in *From Here to Eternity*, even if Bardot and her brother-in-law (Christian Marquand) could have fled to the bushes a few yards away. The point, of course, was that neither party could wait: and the screen's view of women would never be the same again.

remake of **La Ronde** (1964), flatly written by Jean Anouilh, and **Barbarella** (1968), a version of a science-fiction comic-strip, witlessly written by Terry Southern (and others), which starred his next wife, Jane Fonda. Vadim's direction is always vulgar, except in the matter of sex, when he may adopt any number of moods, from the frenetic to the limpid, though the love scenes in his films invariably emerge as quite asexual. And yet this meretricious film-maker was, if unwittingly, one of the precursors of the nouvelle vague, which revitalised the French cinema.

The nouvelle vague consisted of a number of young men, mostly acquainted with each other, who were besotted with films. Some of them were on the edge of the industry, some wrote film reviews, and several managed to make a number of shorts. Among the most vocal of them was Jean-Luc Godard (q.v.) who was to say much later (in 1980, to a reporter from *Variety*) that they did not have to become directors themselves to know that the so-called auteur theory was absurd: 'We invented it,' he said, 'to draw attention to ourselves.' Their rallying ground was *Cahiers du Cinéma*, an analytic buffs' magazine which, because of their subsequent success as working directors, was to have a disproportionate influence. They worshipped Hollywood and good commercial directors like Hitchcock; because their own first films were so impressive, it occurred to few critics to question whether their adulation for Hitchcock was not excessive. Most writers on film rejected their more idiosyncratic choices, but since we enjoyed Hitchcock – this then seemed his best period – we assumed that we had been missing something, instead of suspecting some perverse sets of values. On the subject of French directors the proponents of the movement were, understandably, more sound; they knew the tradition of French cinema had become stale. Certainly most film historians agreed with them that Renoir, whom they idolised, had been underrated – while Clair's reputation was unassailable. Chabrol once boasted that he had liked only *A Nous la Liberté* of Clair's films and Godard only *Quatorze Juillet*, while as far as he could recall Truffaut and Rohmer had not liked any – and these comments are worth contemplation in the light of the evident superiority of Clair's work to any of theirs as film-makers. Autant-Lara who, like Clair, was cold-shouldered as the film industry embraced the nouvelle vague, vehemently dismissed as worthless all the films it threw up, which is not quite fair. Those who, like myself, originally supported these young critics against most of the older, academic film-makers could not have foreseen how badly their own films would date – nor how benignly posterity would view many of those of Autant-Lara and his confrères.

There was a fervour in the way these young turks set about destroying the complacency surrounding both the industry and the medium itself. They had established their own credentials in a number of shorts, fiction and non-fiction, none of them indicating their love of Hollywood and most of them showing more intellectual sinew than the features they supported. The most important of the short-subject directors are Georges Franju (b. 1912) and Alain Resnais (b. 1922).

Franju was one of the founders, in 1936, of the Cinémathèque Scientifique, along with Jean Painlevé, the documentary film-maker, and it was there that he made **Le Sang des Bêtes** (1949), about slaughterhouses. In 1952 he was commissioned to make a documentary on the **Hôtel des Invalides**, which startled its sponsors by disapproving of that institution and all matters military. It was these two films, plus **Les Charmes de l'Existence** (1950), a witty study by Jean Grémillon and Pierre Kast of 'academic' painting, which are the primal seeds of the nouvelle vague. Short films flourished, since cinemas were forbidden by law to show double features. When that law was abolished, in 1953, the *Groupe des Trente* was formed to keep the documentary alive – its members including Franju, Painlevé, Alexandre Astruc, Nicole Vedrès and Resnais. Resnais made a slight reputation in 1950 with *Guernica*, an essay built around Picasso's painting, and he consolidated it in 1956 with **Nuit et Brouillard**, commissioned by the Comité de la Seconde Guerre Mondiale to mark the tenth anniversary of the liberation of the concentration camps. Resnais took an Eastmancolor camera to Auschwitz, to photograph the red-brick ruins languishing under a blue autumn sky, and as the camera begins to probe the commentato falls silent. Both he and the colour give way, so that newspaper newsreels and clippings tell something of what happened there between 1941 and 1945. The film's title derives from the order to destroy human beings, which became known as the 'Night and Fog' decree. The film is one epitaph on the Thousand Year Reich. Another was spoken by Hans Frank as he was led to the gallows at Nuremberg, 'A thousand years shall pass and Germany's guilt will not be expunged,' though the film's own final comment, 'Je ne suis pas responsable' is equally moving in context. Resnais's shattering half-hour film is essential to anyone trying to understand this century, yet it is still inadequate.

These shorts and the arguments in *Cahiers du Cinéma* coalesced to form a cultural climate in which cinema had a leading place: Melville★ and Bresson were heroes, as was Vadim, because he was one of the young people to make a mark in an ageing industry. All three of them rejected the stultifying studio art direction in favour of location shooting, in the manner of one of the more inexplicable heroes of the *Cahiers* group, Rossellini. Working in documentary, the young directors looked further back to the early Soviet film-makers, and Georges Sadoul coined an expression, *cinéma-vérité*, as a method to be recommended, requiring absolute honesty, to result in an immediate contact with the spectator. What was to be expressed was another matter: neither the always crumbling French political system nor De Gaulle's return to power in 1958 interested them, but in 1954 Françoise Sagan had published her first novel, 'Bonjour Tristesse' and its enormous success revealed a public for moral and sexual disorientation among the young.

That such a subject could be communicated in a movie was proved by another young film-maker, Louis Malle (b. 1932), former assistant to Jacques-Yves Cousteau, the marine documentary director, and to Bresson, when he found backing for **Ascenseur pour l'Echafaud** (1958) and **Les Amants** (1958), both starring his current mistress, Jeanne Moreau (b. 1928), then a second-rank star. Malle said at the

★Although Melville became friendly with most of the nouvelle vague directors, he dismissed their films as 'amateurish'; his own heroes were William Wyler and Robert Wise, whom they disliked, while he abhored many of their American favourites, such as Nicholas Ray.

time that watching films bored him, but that he enjoyed making them, and the paradox is evident, since he brought a fresh eye to everything – especially in *Ascenseur*, to Paris. Location shooting was to be a hallmark of the nouvelle vague, providing a contemporary portrait of Paris which would be virtually complete. *Ascenseur* also contained reference to current affairs – the troubles in Algeria and Indo-China; it had a first-class, if not airtight, thriller plot, from a novel by Henri Calef, about a man (Maurice Ronet) who murders the man who is both his boss and the husband of his mistress (Jeanne Moreau); and throughout it there broods the sexual intensity of Mlle Moreau. Such sexuality was the *raison d'être* of *Les Amants*, together with the love act itself. Louise de Vilmorin wrote the sparse dialogue for Malle's own adaptation of an eighteenth-century story about infidelity. This was the movies' most idealised version of a brief encounter; there is a reverie – in a garden, at night – before the lovers begin coupling, which was far less censored than predicted. By later standards the sequence is prudish rather than discreet, but what in fact made the film acceptable in the eyes of censors and critics was the witty manner in which Malle viewed his central triangle. Moreau decides that her husband (Alain Cuny) is odious and the prospective lover (Jean-Marc Bory) ridiculous: it is the ironic contrast of these three personalities which makes the film so entertaining.

Meanwhile, Claude Chabrol (b. 1930), a *Cahiers* critic, had used the inheritance of his (first) wife to make **Le Beau Serge** (1958), which he shortly followed with **Les Cousins** (1959). The first is a sombre and ultimately pointless bucolic drama about a wanderer (Jean-Claude Brialy) who returns to his roots to find that his old pal (Gérard Blain) has become a drunkard. The film bears two more hallmarks of the nouvelle vague – the arbitrary behaviour of its characters, and young acting talent. In *Les Cousins* Blain is the country mouse and Brialy the town mouse, or rather rat, whose Sorbonne set destroys his country cousin. The film is shallow but entertaining, and its ironic detachment was another new factor in movies. The point is made that Blain reads Balzac, neglected by all but provincial students, yet he is, in the end, as silly as any character within the

Balzac canon. André Bazin, so influential a critic for the nouvelle vague, had said that film-makers should learn from literature, and we ought to bear Balzac in mind when we learn that Chabrol's purpose, as he admitted, was to make us contemplate rather than identify.

Franju's first feature was **La Tête contre les Murs** (1958), adapted from Hervé Bazin's novel by an actor, Jean-Pierre Mocky, who had hoped to direct it himself. Mocky gives a surly performance as a high-living youngster committed by his father to a mental home, and the ambivalence of both characters, and of the chief doctor (Pierre Brasseur), gives a lift to an otherwise dull film. Franju never learnt to create mood or tension, which is why his Grand Guignol thriller, **Les Jeux sans Visage** (1959), confirmed him as one of the lesser members of the nouvelle vague. The most light-hearted member of the movement was Philippe de Broca (b. 1933), former assistant to Truffaut and Chabrol, whose company produced **Les Jeux de l'Amour** (1959), a rather old-fashioned comedy about a man (Jean-Pierre Cassel) who will neither marry his mistress (Geneviève Cluny) nor allow her to have a baby.

To an extent the nouvelle vague was a press invention, like the 'angry young men' in Britain two or three years earlier, but when three films by new or newish directors astounded the Cannes Festival in 1959, there was no longer any doubt that here was a vital new force in French cinema. One of the directors was Marcel Camus (1912–82) who hitherto and subsequently, in his few faltering films, showed little vitality. His first film, **Mort en Fraude** (1956), had been an uneven melodrama of a fugitive (Daniel Gélin) in Saigon; but the film that impressed at Cannes, **Orfeu Negro** (1959), if not really a nouvelle vague film, holds its charm better than some that are. It is set in Brazil at carnival time – the dialogue is in Portuguese – and as written by Jacques Viot, Camus and Vinitius de Moraes, from de Moraes's play, the screenplay is both simple-minded and strained. But that does not matter: if the picture were merely a travelogue with plot grafted on, its extended account of Rio and the carnival would justify its existence. The film is above all a celebration of both, with a score by

Antonio Carlos Jobim and Luis Bonfa which is one of the most haunting ever composed for a film.

The other two films at Cannes that year were Resnais's **Hiroshima Mon Amour** (1959) and *Les Quatre Cents Coups* (q.v.), directed by François Truffaut. Resnais's film was proposed by the Japanese, stipulating that it should be filmed in both countries. When Françoise Sagan refused the offer to write the screenplay, he turned to Marguerite Duras, who later said that both agreed that they could not imagine a film about Japan which did not deal with Hiroshima. But this surely cannot be why it starts with a prolonged bedroom scene, prelude to much musing by the lovers, a Japanese man (Eiji Okada) and a French woman (Emmanuelle Riva). Were you there, she asks. And he answers, Of course not. '*Une chance, quoi?*' she says, and he agrees. '*Une chance pour moi aussi,*' he replies, which may give you an idea of Mlle Duras' contribution. After that, you must accept that the film is not about Hiroshima at all, but about Riva's affair with a German soldier during the War, which branded her as a collaborator. This becomes, therefore, a film about memory and forgetfulness, and is minimal compared to *Nuit et Brouillard*, though it is, at least, beautifully constructed.

This method of combining past and present was new, since it was essential to the nouvelle vague to 'de-conventionalise' movies; but the theories of the movement were most effectively put into practice by Truffaut (b. 1932) in **Les Quatre Cents Coups**, significantly dedicated to André Bazin – who had bailed Truffaut out of reform school at the age of fourteen. One of Bazin's beliefs was that films should attempt the ambiguity and multiple levels of meaning to be found in literature – and it was this injection by the nouvelle vague which makes 1959 as important in cinema history as 1929 and the coming of Sound. In Italy, Antonioni (q.v.) was advancing in a more sophisticated manner, but though there was less scope in this simple autobiographical tale, Truffaut leaves conversations half heard or indeterminate, and reveals the inner identity of his young boy hero (Jean-Pierre Léaud) by a process of peeling off, like an onion skin, from reel to reel. The film is full of insights into the matters which pain a child, or amuse or bore him: his father hitting him in front of his classmates because he has lied; half-hearing a parental row when his mother gets in late; stealing a milk bottle at night from a Pigalle doorstep; being reminded to take down the garbage. If the film had not managed so complete a portrait of the world of this boy, the ending alone would have come as a revelation. As it is, it is simply perfect – the progression from the adventure with the stolen typewriter to reform school, and escape . . . The famous ending, by the sea, with the frozen frame. When Olmi uses it in *Il Posto*, it is more moving, since it suggests an even greater trap, but the point about *Les Quatre Cents Coups* is that the Bazin-dictated vocabulary was in full flower for the first time (not to mention a number of in-jokes). Truffaut himself said that the film was to be judged on its sincerity, rather than its technical quality, but it is a triumph on both counts.

Anything it lacked was available in **A Bout de Souffle** (1960), the last crest of the nouvelle vague, directed by Jean-Luc Godard (b. 1930), a fellow *Cahiers* critic of Truffaut, who ostensibly supervised the film. It is dedicated to Monogram Pictures, a sign of Godard's devotion to the American B-movies, which influence his young thug hero (Jean-Paul Belmondo), toting a gun, stealing money from his girlfriend's handbag, muttering 'Bogey' affectionately before a poster of Humphrey Bogart, facing death – as everything else – with a shrug. She (Jean Seberg) likes Mozart and Faulkner, and has a philosophy, 'Between grief and nothing, I would take grief.' They loaf about, play games, and since she is pregnant – a fact both refuse to face – we know that they have made love, but sex is second to their egotism. When she betrays him, it may be an *acte gratuit*, or mere practicality (to keep her work permit); or she may want to wake him from his lethargy. Godard's people say one thing and do another, they speak truth and deceive themselves at the same time. If life and people are wayward, Godard found an approach to fit: he said that he found it by cutting away everything not of prime importance, which is clearly not true, but if the jerky style is an accident, it is nevertheless a style. It was shot in chronological order, at a cost of approximately $100,000, and premiered just ten weeks after Godard met Belmondo,

whose passage to fame it was. Belmondo was certainly the most unusual and gifted of the nouvelle vague players – even if he moved into a star stereotype later – and his role here was said to characterise a generation. The film was described as 'anarchic' and 'challenging', but in fact it is highly moral. It is a superb analysis of the mentality of thugdom. It also communicates its love of the medium, and is as exciting to watch now as it was then.

It was not that the nouvelle vague was innovatory – at least, not consciously, as Antonioni was – but they were using with enthusiasm and intensity the tools which others had picked up and dropped, or used and only half understood. With one or two films each to their credit, Resnais, Truffaut, Godard and Chabrol were being discussed as eagerly as Eisenstein ever was. The French government stepped in: it was obvious that young film directors were beneficial for the industry, and in 1959 the decree called 'Avances sur Recettes' was promulgated, with an 8,000,000 million franc fund (later enlarged), to be dispensed by a committee after consideration of the proposed script and budget, and with up to one million francs available for an individual film, though the average amount advanced was usually just under that. In addition, French producers lent a ready ear to anyone under thirty who wanted to make a film. Of the results, it was estimated that for each one which received a Paris premiere another languished on the shelf. At the beginning of 1961 *Le Film Français* listed no less than sixty-seven directors who had made their first features within the past two years. Less than twenty of them made another, and less than a handful subsequently enjoyed a career as a director – the most notable being (q.v.) Claude Sautet, Michel Drach, Claude Lelouch and Eric Rohmer, of whom only the latter was linked with the nouvelle vague movement. Clearly a new generation of *cinéastes* did not emerge – the important ones had already arrived – but the euphoria within the industry resulted in a number of memorable films.

Roger Leenhardt, one of the heroes of the new directors, made his first feature in fourteen years, and his last to date – **Le Rendez-vous de Minuit** (1962), a film for the *cinéaste* if ever there was one, a Pirandello-like confection, haunting and

The five films that made the reputations of those five directors which we call the nouvelle vague – and the expression, 'the new wave', indicates the force with which each film knocked away the old standards of the French film. ABOVE FAR RIGHT, Louis Malle's *Les Amants*, with Jeanne Moreau and Jean-Marc Bory; ABOVE RIGHT, Claude Chabrol's *Les Cousins*, with Juliette Mayniel, Jean-Claude Brialy and Gérard Blain; BELOW FAR RIGHT, Alain Resnais's *Hiroshima Mon Amour*, with Emmanuelle Riva and Eiji Okada; BELOW RIGHT, François Truffaut's *Les Quatre Cents Coups*, with Jean-Pierre Léaud; and BELOW CENTRE, Jean-Luc Godard's *A Bout de Souffle* with Jean Seberg and Jean-Paul Belmondo. Interestingly, each of these films remains virtually as impressive as they did at the time, while the later work of their directors has varied. Resnais and Malle remain major film-makers, but Chabrol seems determined to make as many bad films as good while Godard and Truffaut have gone steadily downhill. Ironically, the work of many of the film-makers whom they as critics affected to despise is now more rewarding than their own films.

The Nouvelle Vague

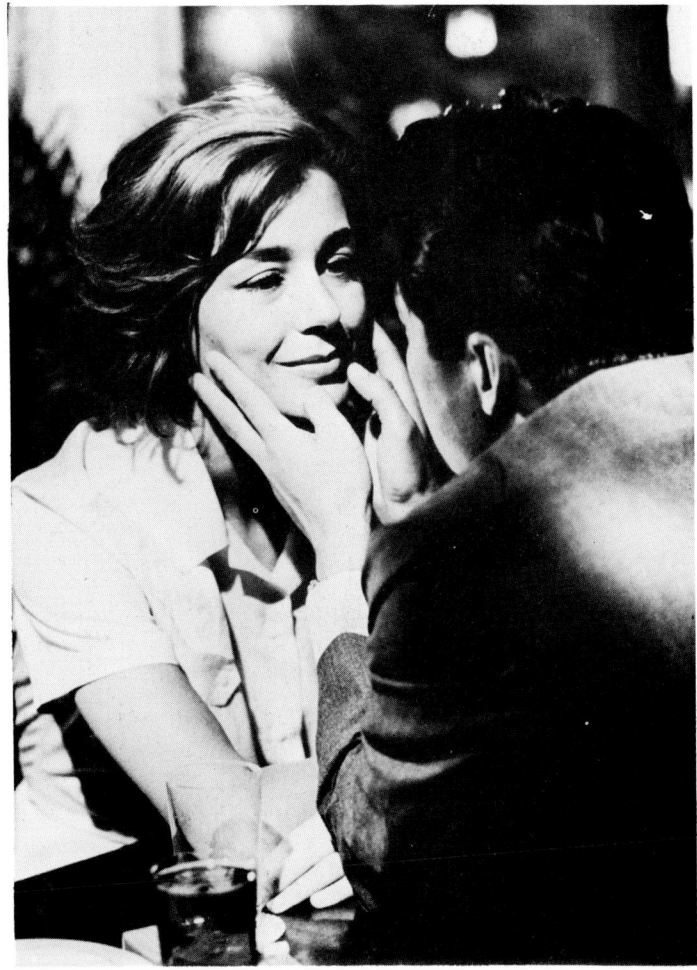

intricate. A poor, lonely woman is fascinated by a film about a rich, lonely woman – both played by Lilli Palmer, who later appears, tantalisingly, as herself; the poor woman's suicidal plans are interrupted by another cinemagoer (Michel Auclair) and then contrasted to the life of the rich woman, whose problems with her lover (Maurice Ronet) are wholly artificial. Life is shown to imitate art, but it would be wrong, I think, to regard the film as more than a sprightly *jeu*. It is 'one of the films requesting from their audiences a new standard of literacy', as Penelope Houston put it in *Sight and Sound*, though she was in fact discussing **La Proie pour l'Ombre** (1961), directed by a friend of Leenhardt, Alexandre Astruc. Astruc, a former *Cahiers* critic and occasional film-maker (though with only one popular film to his credit, *Le Rideau Cramoisi*) did not have the deserved success with this one. Admittedly both dialogue and the basic situation are banal: but in presenting yet again the eternal triangle Astruc offers a woman (Annie Girardot), caught in adultery, who never admits or concedes that it may be her fault. Predating Women's Lib, that is the film's subject, and virtually alone of all these films Astruc has eschewed Haussmann's Paris for the city of auto-routes and tower-blocks.

The British theatre director, Peter Brook, making his first film since *The Beggar's Opera*, adapted a novel by Marguerite Duras – with Gérard Jarlot and the author herself – **Moderato Cantabile** (1960), meant, he said, to please her and its star, Jeanne Moreau. The particular qualities and talents of Mlles Moreau and Girardot may be one reason for the preponderance of adultery as a subject in these films, but in this case Moreau only contemplates it. The setting is a small, bleak town on the Gironde, a lost waste of countryside: there has been a *crime passionel*, and the woman's fascination with it brings her into contact with one of her husband's employees (Belmondo). It is a love affair not only without sex but with no ecstasy; we never question that their meeting is the single most important event of her life, and that she will henceforth be even more miserable than before. Inevitably reminiscent of *Les Amants*, the film is, in Brook's own words, 'an attempt to tell a story with a *minimum* of fictional devices by using and

relying on the actors' power of characterisation'. Both players are superb. There is a moment when Moreau leans against a tree and rubs her head against it – and when Belmondo responds there is no better expression in all cinema of the need of one human for another.

The central situation of **Une Aussi Longue Absence** (1962) is similar: in a dusty suburb of Paris the owner (Alida Valli) of a bistro becomes convinced that a local vagabond (Georges Wilson) is the husband who disappeared years before. As with Brook's film, there are heavy emotions in a quiet setting, a yearning for a life that might have been. The situation was handled with dexterity by Henri Colpi (b. 1921), a former editor with Resnais, who in fact made a few further films: the accomplishment of this one makes their failure all the more surprising.

Jacques Doniol-Valcroze (b. 1920) was once a critic – with Bazin he was one of the founders of *Cahiers* – and occasional actor and director. His films have created no great stir, but **Le Coeur Battant** (1962) seems to me one of the most enchanting of comedies – *L'Avventura* (q.v.) in reverse, as a man (Jean-Louis Trintignant) and a woman (Françoise Brion) first squabble and fall in love while waiting for her lover to turn up. The setting is a small seaside resort, affectionately used as only the French seem able.

Robert Enrico (b. 1931) wrote and directed documentaries for cinema and television during the Fifties, eventually breaking away with **La Rivière du Hibou** (1961), which won the Palme d'Or at Cannes and an American Oscar for Best Live Action Short Subject. Between the two awards Enrico incorporated it into a feature, *Au Coeur de la Vie*, with two accompanying sections also based on short stories by Ambrose Bierce. This has not been shown complete in the U.S. or Britain, but *Rivière*, as *Incident at Owl Creek*, may be found at repertory cinemas, often dwarfing the feature. The incident depicted is of the War between the States, when a partisan escaped the hangman. Enrico has filmed the story with great simplicity, but credit should also go to the photographer, Jean Boffety, and to Roger Jacquet, the pursued man, whose expression may haunt one for days. Enrico went on to commercial films, with Bardot and

Belmondo among others, but of those I have seen, only one has merit, **Le Secret** (1974), a thriller written with Pascal Jardin from a novel by Francis Ryck about the adventures of an unworldly couple (Philippe Noiret, Marlène Jobert) and a possibly homicidal intruder (Trintignant). Among enigmatic 'twist' thrillers, it holds a high place, moving with surprise and without pretension; and if its political message is trite, it is worth recalling how many unsolved murders in France are rumoured to be politically motivated.

Jacques Rivette (b. 1928) has also managed a career since his first feature, **Paris Nous Appartient**, begun in 1957, completed in 1960, and finally shown in Paris in 1962, with friends such as Truffaut and Chabrol endorsing, on the posters, the director's personal vision. The film seemed remarkable then: a study of a group of people in Paris in August, the dog days, unable to come to terms with themselves and a world that includes the Bomb and Fascism – a world of unanswered telephones, bare apartments, rumoured organisations, and endless discussions. It may now be found to be as self-indulgent as its characters; the finale, set in a deserted garden in the country, was *the* cliché of the nouvelle vague, and the film now seems a parody of the movement.

Essentially, the movement was a matter of individual talent; and it was a matter for each member of the audience, each buff, to decide whether he wanted to continue the love affair with the director concerned. Buñuel once said of Godard 'I'll give him two years more, he's just a fashion' – speaking to Satyajit Ray, who observed some years later (in 1968, to *Sight and Sound*) how accurate Buñuel's prophecy had been.

Godard's work is exemplified thus: Anna Karina cavorting in a room; a montage of book jackets, postcards, advertisements; references to movies – usually bad ones (*Some Came Running, Hatari!, Viaggio in Italia*); long duologues, the camera darting to and fro, to be replaced in time with long muttered monologues to the camera, of even more stultifying banality . . . '*La photographie, c'est la vérité, le cinéma, c'est la vérité ving-quatre fois par seconde,*' says Michel Subor in **Le Petit Soldat**, but in Godard's case it is not enough. That was his second film, made in 1960, but because

of references to the Algerian situation it was not shown till 1963. It is a jigsaw about an O.A.S. man trying to escape his nemesis, and falling in love with a waif, played by Anna Karina, who became Mme Godard. Both **Une Femme est une Femme** (1961) and **Vivre sa Vie** (1962) are odes to her, the former a semi-musical re-hash of *Les Jeux de l'Amour*, with ill-advised references to Lubitsch and Gene Kelly, and the latter a sort of sentimentalised diary of a whore. It is dedicated to American B-pictures, to remind us of the critic Peter John Dyer's prescient comment on *A Bout de Souffle*: 'So one ends with a vague sense of infantilism, partly due to the film's violent repudiation of feeling, partly due to its mythomaniacal devotion to a washed-up, B-picture world which never existed in the first place. [It] is riveting enough in style and picaresque subject, and blessed with sufficient local insight, to prevent it deteriorating into the sort of dishonestly blown-up quickie, such as *Kiss Me Deadly*, on which it is undoubtedly dependent for its inspiration. But by eliminating meaning and feeling, Godard has merely trapped himself in that artistic cul-de-sac – the film all dressed up for rebellion, but with no real tangible territory on which to stand and fight.'

Les Carabiniers (1963) is about fighting in a mythical kingdom – symbolised by a rubbish dump – where two stupid young men volunteer for the army,

Jean-Luc Godard threw so many artefacts into his films that it took some time before audiences realised that most of them were devoid of content. Another reason why some remained faithful was the presence in many of his films of Anna Karina, and he certainly conveyed his own fascination with her. Here she is in the best of their collaborations, *Vivre sa Vie*, with Sady Rebbot.

dreaming of money, lust and power. A preface quotes from Borges, 'As times passes, I value simplicity more. I use the same metaphors . . .', but the film is less simple than nihilistic: there is little point in being anti-militarist and anti-capitalist if audiences are left as devoid of shock as the people in the film. It was an enormous failure, due, it was said, to its message being antipathetical to De Gaulle's France, but Godard's career was thought to revive with **Le Mépris** (1964), financed by Joseph Levine and produced by Carlo Ponti as well as Georges de Beauregard, who had backed several of the nouvelle vague films. Its source was a novel by Moravia, about the disintegration of a marriage within the movie industry, and Godard's consciously boring screenplay mocks his sponsors. He reduces Brigitte Bardot, Michel Piccoli and Jack Palance – as a Hollywood producer – to ciphers. The film failed everywhere, and may be best explained by Raoul Coutard, who photographed it, 'Godard is trying to explain something to his wife . . . It's a sort of letter – one that's costing [the backers] a million dollars.'

After that debacle, Godard disciplined himself to make three films which, if not as good as *A Bout de Souffle*, are at least as much fun as *Vivre sa Vie*. It might be that his good films were the result of some happy choices – in the case of **Bande à Part** (1964) the juxtaposition of the gazelle-like, sometimes incandescent Karina and the dreary suburb of Joinville, a hidden treasure and two impish, petty criminals (Sami Frey, Claude Brasseur). The reason for success with this *bande à part* may be found in a remark by Jean-Pierre Gorin, a later collaborator, 'With Jean-Luc and me, it was a love story; we really were deeply in love with each other, with no shame, no guilt. It was a deep, involved, sexual thing.' **Une Femme Mariée** (1964) – retitled from *La Femme Mariée* after the censor decreed it a slur on French womanhood – concerns adultery, with the smoky-faced Macha Méril as the lady concerned. The usual conceits are here, be they bursts of Beethoven, references to concentration camps or discussions on paradox, but Godard's style has become so beautifully honed that the film is a small pleasure. He moved from the white interiors of this to the harsh, cold boulevards

and towers of **Alphaville** (1965), a science-fiction caper that borrows from '1984', Cocteau's *Orphée*, Ian Fleming and Saul Steinberg – not to mention pulp fiction, as indicated by the subtitle, 'Une Etrange Aventure de Lemmy Caution'.

It was about this time that Godard made his oft-quoted remark that movies should have a beginning, a middle and an end, but not necessarily in that order – which did nothing to convince the increasing number of people who did not wish to stay to see the end of his films. Mindless confusion reigns from then on – anarchists, subversive agents, Hollywood references, high jinks, asides – through the next four films, each more trivial than the last. To an extent, **Weekend** (1968) is Alphaville revisited, a dream-fantasy of a brutal, technological future. It encompasses both the best and worst of Godard – the audacity, the insistence on breaking the rules, the witty, coruscating critic of a materialistic society who has no better answer for his failed revolutionaries than to have them resort to cannibalism. When he seesaws – dangerously, after the superb control in *Vivre sa Vie* – we must assume that he does it intentionally, though we may still find the blend of intelligence and irresponsibility irritating. Many artists have produced sloppy, uninteresting work when their technique has deserted them, but Godard is symptomatic of many in this period whose brilliance goes hand in hand with an equally startling childishness. Audiences will tolerate self-indulgence, but only while there are rewards, and it was at this point that they fell away – as did the financiers. Godard continued to make films, sometimes directed in collaboration, some on 16mm, but they attracted minimal attention. The early Godards, when they came out, were among the most stimulating experiences the cinema has ever offered me and, with reason, they influenced virtually every film-maker – certainly those of his own generation and younger.

The decline of François Truffaut has been much more gentle. After the achievement of *Les Quatre Cents Coups* he wrote a second film with Marcel Moussy, **Tirez sur la Pianiste** (1960), based on an American pulp fiction (a frequent source of his subsequent work). It sets a mild piano-player (Charles Aznavour) on the fringe of the underworld, whose denizens move in to destroy him – and the personality of the star, with his attractive combination of optimism and fatalism, gives, as Truffaut intended, a particular colour to what is a free-wheeling blend of satire, shoot-ups and *comédie noire*. **Jules et Jim** (1962) was designed for Jeanne Moreau, playing a 'free spirit' loved by, and loving two men (Oskar Werner, Henri Serre) simultaneously. The source was Henri-Pierre Roché's old novel, idiosyncratically observed by Truffaut, with an airy grace which finally degenerates into verbosity. It was one of the first films to emphasise the weaknesses of the nouvelle vague – its superficiality, as when the heroes watch a newsreel of Nazi book-burning, and its characters, often cases of arrested development: their individuality seems honest at first, but after a while one wonders why they cannot behave like other people. Moreau is particularly irritating – a selfish, wilful bitch, endowed by Truffaut with misguided charm.

The film was nonetheless for many years Truffaut's greatest success, both in France and elsewhere; but there was little liking anywhere for either **La Peau Douce** (1964), a grey tale of adultery between a podgy lecturer (Jean Desailly) and an air hostess, or **Fahrenheit 451** (1966), a mundane and finally embarrassing account of Ray Bradbury's novel, describing a society of the future in which the only surviving humanists turn themselves into books. It was one of several films Universal made in Britain at the time, of apparently highbrow interest or with prestigious names. Truffaut was so keen on the project that it was undertaken before his English was adequate to the task, but the result is so bad that it does not warrant making excuses. It was at about this time that Truffaut observed to Hitchcock that critics were unimaginative (which he did not think a bad thing) but that that lack of imagination 'might account for a predilection for films that are close to real life. On seeing *Ladri di Biciclette*, for instance, he's likely to think this is just the sort of thing he might have written himself, but that thought couldn't possibly occur to him in connection with *North by Northwest*. This being so, he's bound to attribute all kinds of merit to *Ladri di Biciclette* and none whatever to *North by Northwest*.' In fact *Ladri di Biciclette* was admired not because it was 'close'

to life, but because it made relevant and, indeed, moving comments on life, and because it was a marvellous example of what a sensitive director might do with his material – as opposed to *North by Northwest*, which is engineered fiction with cardboard characters. Truffaut went on to imitate Hitchcock, but not profitably. In his best films, he emulated Renoir, certainly as good a model as de Sica, and **Baisers Volés** (1968) was his last entirely acceptable film. He had returned to his young hero of *Les Quatre Cents Coups*, Antoine Doinel, in a sketch-film, *L'Amour à Vingt Ans* – an amusing anecdote about the boy, again played by Léaud, visiting the parents of his girlfriend. With sympathy and gentle ironic humour *Baisers Volés* follows Antoine from the end of his military service through a number of love affairs and mediocre jobs; but two later adventures of Antoine, **Domicile Conjugal** (1970) and **L'Amour en Fuite** (1979), both made after other films had been poorly received, are mild indeed.

They are nevertheless preferable to the imitations of Hitchcock, **La Mariée était en Noir** (1968) and **La Sirène du Mississippi** (1968), both based on novels by William Irish. The first is about a bride (Moreau) who sets out to murder the several men she thinks responsible for her husband's death, and the second involves a wealthy tobacco planter (Belmondo) who falls for the mysterious mail-order bride (Catherine Deneuve) who may be feeding him rat-poison. In this case the film emulated is *Vertigo*, indicating that Truffaut preferred to copy bad Hitchcock rather than good. He returned to a humanist theme with **L'Enfant Sauvage** (1970), based on a true story of the late eighteenth century, about a wild boy of the woods and the struggle to civilise him and prove that he has a soul. Truffaut himself plays the doctor trying to help the boy, but the film is less effective than the not dissimilar *The Miracle Worker* (q.v.). **Les Deux Anglaises et le Continent** (1971) is based on a novel by Roché which reverses the situation of *Jules et Jim*, with Jean-Pierre Léaud as the young man in love with two women. If, as Truffaut insists, his films take their personality from the leading player, that may be why this one and the later Antoine pictures are negative. Certainly **Une Belle Fille Comme Moi**

(1972), designed for Bernadette Lafont, is much more lively; it also recalls an earlier film, but more positively, for like *Tirez sur le Pianiste* it combines differing qualities, moving from sociological treatise to burlesque and thriller.

If Truffaut is happiest with a star player, to deflect attention from himself, that may be, as he himself admits, because he knows more about movies than life. That knowledge went into the screenplay of **La Nuit Américaine** (1973), in which he himself plays a director much like himself, involved in incidents recognisable to those who have followed his career. Consequently this is another filmed collection of memories, but without the invention and charm of Leterrier's similar *Projection Privée* (q.v.). It was a success in Britain and the U.S. but not in France, where the local branch of United Artists financed most of his films, with the option of purchasing world rights – to no great financial risk, since Truffaut is an economical film-maker. Foreign appreciation of his work had always been kinder than at home, but it was a French critic, Jean-Loup Bourget, writing in *The New Review*, who described **L'Argent de Poche** (1976), as 'offensively bad, as untrue as it is condescending' – an ironic judgment on a man reputed to have walked out of *Pather Panchali* and who, as a critic, loathed Clément, whose *Les Jeux Interdits* is also an infinitely better film about childhood. Among his next few films, **L'Homme qui Aimait les Femmes** (1978) most exposes his weaknesses. The man (Charles Denner) concerned uses women to gratify his sexual urges, and writes a book about them to exorcise the memory of his mother, which prevents him from fidelity and the experience of love. The moral point is there, but lost in trite philosophising, while the enterprise desperately needs humour or at least some resemblance to real life – if we are not to find it distasteful.

Truffaut's standing in his native land was restored by **Le Dernier Métro** (1980), which was not only his greatest commercial success to date but the winner of virtually every available César award, voted annually by the French film industry. It may be regarded either as his attempt at *Les Enfants du Paradis* or a theatrical companion piece to *La Nuit Américaine*. It is set during the Occupation, among theatre people including a Jewish impresario (Heinz Bennent), who is hidden in the cellar; his wife (Catherine Deneuve), who is under consequent strain; a new young actor (Gérard Depardieu), a secret member of the Resistance; a homosexual director (Jean Poiret); a lesbian designer (Andréa Ferréol); and a collaborationist critic/censor (Jean-Louis Richard). Truffaut does absolutely nothing with this potentially interesting group, and it is astonishing that anyone could have preferred this film to Resnais's *Mon Oncle d'Amérique* (q.v.) or Pialat's *Loulou* (q.v.), two of the other nominated films.★ Resnais and Pialat are astute observers, which cannot be said of Truffaut, whatever his other gifts. **La Femme d'à Côté** (1981) is a singularly unconvincing examination of adultery among the well-heeled suburbanites of Grenoble. The *amour fou* of the lovers (Gérard Depardieu, Fanny Ardant) bears the influence of *Vertigo* again and *Marnie*; indeed the film seems to belong to that era, with such outdated devices as telling stares and conversations summarising the past for audience convenience. Chabrol had not long before remarked that Truffaut was now making exactly the sort of films which he had condemned as a critic. It is therefore ironic that these two films show him now to be an infinitely inferior film-maker to even Clément in his decline.

The career of Claude Chabrol has a more complicated history, partly because he had no popular success immediately after *Les Cousins*. **A Double Tour** (1959) is a prettily coloured, rather vapid study of a Provençal family and its hangers-on, which evoked only mild enthusiasm. Although **Les Bonnes Femmes** (1960) was liked neither in France nor elsewhere, it seemed to me both then and now one of the triumphs of the nouvelle vague. One of its virtues, as with the best of the films of the movement, is that it is impossible to tell in which direction it will go – though a clue is provided by the cherished memento kept by the cashier in her handbag. For this is a black comedy about four shopgirls, with a particularly acrid tone and some brilliant detail of the daily grind in an electrical shop near the Place de la Bastille.

★The other film of the four was Godard's supposed return to 'commercial' film-making, *Sauve Qui Peut*, which made little impression elsewhere.

An epilogue explains the violent climax, asserting that a few hours' real happiness is worth the rest of the day's drab happenings. Chabrol's writer on both films was Paul Gégauff, who had also contributed to *Les Cousins* and was later to become a regular collaborator.

Les Godelureaux (1960) is a more bizarre variation on the themes of *Les Cousins*, but its interplay of character was to lead Chabrol to two more fine films, **L'Oeil du Malin** (1962) and **Ophélia** (1962). If *Les Bonnes Femmes* is the first mature demonstration of the malevolent Chabrol universe, these two films show this realm to be situated rather near to the *haute bourgeoisie*. The settings are respectively the home of a successful writer and the country estate of a landed family, their curiously calm existence about to be shattered by young men who are dreamers rather than schemers. In the first case destruction comes from without, from a journalist (Jacques Charrier) who is over-possessive towards both wife and husband, and in the other it comes from within, wrought by the son (André Jocelyn) who insists on re-enacting the situation of 'Hamlet' inside the family circle. The nature of evil was to preoccupy Chabrol, whose studies of its effects were to take him far deeper into psychology than his idol, Hitchcock. He would far surpass him as a film-maker, but at this stage of his career he made one film which approaches the standard of Truffaut's Hitchcock imitations. This is **Landru** (1963), but then this study of the mass-murderer has a particularly specious screenplay by Françoise Sagan. Despite the magnetic performance of Charles Denner in the title role, and the presence of Danielle Darrieux, Michèle Morgan and Hildegarde Neff among his victims, the film failed to attract audiences. It was the most publicised of Chabrol's failures, causing him to turn to solidly commercial products.

During this period he contributed to three of the numerous French omnibus films, among them **Les Sept Péchés Capitaux** (1961), a wholly nouvelle vague affair which did not demonstrate, as intended, its superiority over the film of the same name made by the old guard a decade earlier. He also made a conventional war film, **La Ligne de Démarcation** (1966), and three cinema equivalents of comic strips – *Le Tigre aime la Chair Fraîche, Marie-Chantal contre le Docteur Kha, Le Tigre se Parfume à la Dynamite* – all aiming, without much success, at the tongue-in-cheek high spirits of de Broca's *L'Homme de Rio* (q.v.). **La Route de Corinthe** (1967) was a slight move upwards, if only for some ambiguity in the murders, but Chabrol returned to more congenial territory in **Le Scandale/The Champagne Murders** (1967) – to look at the wealthy world of party-goers, gigolos and ladies who are not quite what they seem to be. It is a film of dubious standing, certainly not offering evidence that he would escape from the doldrums with his next film, **Les Biches** (1968). This was written with Gégauff, and its faults may be attributed to the fact that Chabrol wanted to make a commercial movie, but one less derisory than those he had been making. In setting the film partly in St Tropez he may have had in mind *Et Dieu . . . Créa la Femme* rather than his own studies set among the smart set, rich and destructive. The malicious character in this case is also the strongest, a lesbian, played by Stéphane Audran, the sleek and sensuous actress who was the second Mme Chabrol; the weak sides of the triangle are taken by Jacqueline Sassard and Jean-Louis Trintignant.

It was as his own writer that Chabrol began his unparalleled studies of bourgeois crime – predominantly murder – often derived from pulp fiction but in a way never contemplated by Truffaut or Godard. On one level Chabrol borrows from the glaring headlines of the French popular press, and his movies also depend for their effect on other movies – i.e. we are conditioned to expect the conventional pattern of the thriller, which he then proceeds to ignore. He uses suspense rather than guilt, and is compassionate only intermittently: the curiosity about the nature of the crime is matched by his interest in the equivocation of motive – not only on the part of the murderer but frequently by someone close who has guessed at the crime. Since most of these films are set, vividly, in the country, they might be subtitled 'Scenes From Provincial Life', and are all eloquently photographed by Jean Rabier. **La Femme Infidèle** (1968) concerns a mild husband (Michel Bouquet) who murders the lover (Maurice

France: Before and After the Nouvelle Vague

After a number of failures Chabrol became a purely 'commercial' director for a while, but emerging from what was clearly a trough in his career he embarked on a series of bourgeois murder stories which are among the most sustained group of films in all cinema – sustained, that is, when they are good, for there is at least one rotten apple in the barrel. Anyway, this picture is from the best of them, *Le Boucher*, with Stéphane Audran and Jean Yanne.

Ronet) of his wife (Stéphane Audran). **Que la Bête Meure!** (1969) centres on a journalist (Michel Duchaussoy) setting out to find the hit-and-run killer of his son. **La Rupture** (1970) is a group portrait of a Brussels family, Balzacian in its variety, its title referring to an L.S.D.-addicted man (Jean-Claude Drouot) who attacks his wife (Audran) and small son. **Juste Avant la Nuit** (1971) involves a successful businessman (Bouquet) who murders his mistress and feels bound to confess to both his wife (Audran), and his best friend (François Perier), husband of his victim – neither of whom wish to judge him. **Les Noces Rouges** (1973) reverts to adultery as its prime subject, with the wife (Audran) of the mayor (Claude Pieplu) sneaking off to the woods with a family friend (Michel Piccoli). Occasionally Chabrol uses a perfectly harmless object to create tension, manipulating his audience in the manner of minor directors of the thriller genre, but that he is capable of perfection is proved by **Le Boucher** (1970), a masterpiece depicting the relationship between the village schoolteacher (Audran) and the butcher (Jean Yanne), who happens to be a compulsive murderer.

The least pure and most conventional of the group is *Que la Bête Meure!*, and it is the

only one on which Chabrol had a script collaborator – once again, Paul Gégauff. It is surely no coincidence that Gégauff worked with him on his one dreadful film of this period – **La Décade Prodigieuse/ Ten Days' Wonder** (1971), a family saga from a novel by Ellery Queen, with any number of absurd undertones, including Moses and the House of Atreus, performed in a like manner by a cast including Orson Welles and Anthony Perkins. Gégauff also contributed to **Docteur Popaul** (1972), and that is not very good either. The ultra-chic furnishings of Chabrol's films, and their insistence on the 'games people play', often reveal a vulgarity just kept at bay. His instincts are invariably right on the films he makes alone, but when he pushes towards extravagance and excess that may be because the film concerned was designed as a lightweight entertainment. This one is *comédie noire*, the story of a philandering doctor (Jean-Paul Belmondo) whose marriage to a cripple (Mia Farrow) does not prevent him from bedding her sister (Laura Antonelli), with dire consequences to all concerned. When Chabrol creates his 'own' people, as it were, they are bitten by inhibitions and passions they cannot confess, but with Gégauff at this stage of his career they become no more than the cardboard figures of so many thrillers.

Gégauff's disastrous influence is borne out by **Une Partie de Plaisir** (1975), written solely by him and based on the break-up of his own marriage. The leading role was intended for Trintignant, but Chabrol felt that there was so much of Gégauff in it that he persuaded him to play it himself. His ex-wife plays his ex-wife, and their daughter their daughter; the premise is that Gégauff tells his wife that he is having an affair, and that she should feel free to do so, at which point the marriage falls apart – to his surprise and irritation. Gégauff offers a protagonist, trendy and wearing clothes twenty years too young, as dislikeable as any in movies. From Chabrol's point of view, this is another devastating attack on the bourgeoisie; but any other way it looks like the first major exhibitionist movie – of which there have since been a good number.

Gégauff was not, however, involved with two more 'game' stories, **Les Innocents aux Mains Sales** (1975), written by

1024

Chabrol alone, and **Folies Bourgeoises/ Twist** (1976), written with Norman Enfield. The first, set in a large house in St Tropez, examines a disintegrating marriage; the second, set in equally glamorous Paris apartments, is about infidelity, real or imagined, among the literary set. It is clear in each case that Chabrol set out to make a mordant comedy, but the jokes are laboured, the plotting absurd and his handling miscalculated. The stars of the one are Romy Schneider and Rod Steiger, while among those in the other are Bruce Dern and Ann-Margret; even more than *La Décade Prodigieuse* the films prove that Chabrol should avoid attempts at 'international' cinema. Both were poorly received, causing Chabrol to abandon the assaults on the bourgeoisie which had been one of the staples of his career. Instead, he has floundered in all directions, making only four respectable entertainments over the past decade and a half.

Nada (1974), written with Jean-Patrick Manchette from his own novel, is about a political kidnapping. Chabrol claimed that the piece was apolitical, perhaps because those responsible include cynics, neurotics and anarchists as well as leftists and idealists; but the opposite side is led by a kill-happy, fascist – and eventually ridiculous – detective, clearly one for spectators to dislike. **Violette Nozière** (1978) was a commissioned piece, based on a screenplay by other hands and the only Chabrol murder story, with *Landru* and *Les Noces Rouges*, with a foundation in fact. In 1933 Violette (Isabelle Huppert) administered poison to her parents (Mlle Audran, Jean Carmet), and although she became a heroine to the Surrealists she remains in this film as mysterious as many other ladies of scandal. For some critics, **Les Fantômes du Chapelier** (1982) showed Chabrol on form again, but the story, after Simenon, has to rely on devices familiar from Hitchcock (a dummy posing as a body) and Agatha Christie (the extraordinary coincidence involving the victims). The setting, a small coastal town, reaffirms Chabrol's gift for atmosphere, and there can be no doubt of the quality of Michel Serrault's performance as a mass murderer, a smug, dandified tradesman. The three films, however, if better than those made around the same time, use elements of sensationalism unworthy of the director of *Le*

Boucher. The fourth, **Le Cheval d'Orgueil** (1980), as a study of a Breton community in the manner of *L'Albero degli Zoccoli* (q.v.), suggests that his career might move in another direction.

Resnais was, and remains, the enigma of the nouvelle vague, his seven films since *Hiroshima, Mon Amour* being unequally daring and unequally rewarding. After that film he commissioned a screenplay from the novelist Alain Robbe-Grillet, **L'Année Dernière à Marienbad** (1961), which deals with a past either real or imagined. In a rococo grand hotel, a man (Giorgio Albertazzi) and a woman (Delphine Seyrig) touch and circle each other, with an effect at first hypnotic but soon soporific – a fact with which the expressionless playing is not unconnected. If Resnais and Robbe-Grillet intended allegory – we are Outward Bound, or in a womb, or a mental home – they should have offered something less bloodless, less redolent of the avant-garde films of the late Twenties. As written by Jean Cayrol, **Muriel, ou le Temps d'un Retour** (1963) is another riddle, but one of astonishing richness. It builds tension from the outset, as Seyrig waits at the station: the visitor is an old lover, the girl with him is a 'niece', and the boy at the subsequent dinner party is Seyrig's stepson. But as soon as the strands have come together, they are fragmented: images tumble on, days pass in a flash or are lingered upon. What matters is the disease and dissatisfaction of time passing – memories play false, and the newsreels from Algeria suggest that tomorrow promises no better. All that was here, is here, will be, are the cliffs and streets of Boulogne, divorced from thought and association – and even then, they deceive. The film exists because it exists, and this is what it chooses to say – in a manner as warm as *Marienbad* is frigid.

La Guerre est Finie (1966) confirmed Resnais as a full-blooded romantic. Jorge Semprun, a Spanish novelist living in France, contributed the screenplay about a Spanish exile (Yves Montand), half immersed in subversive activities relating to the Civil War, and uncertain whether or not he believes in the myths associated with it. Like *L'Avventura* (q.v.), the film is an insight into a man's soul, but where in that film each action sprang from the one before, the happenings of this film are arbitrary – as arbitrary as Montand's musings on his past, which may be imaginary. The enigma of memory was less agreeably worked over in **Je t'Aime, Je t'Aime** (1968), a science fiction, written by Jacques Sternberg, in which the hero (Claude Rich) is injected with a serum in order to make an odyssey into his past – which is also a search for the meaning of existence.

The film failed, and in 1971 a British project about the Marquis de Sade, with Dirk Bogarde, fell through. After a sojourn in the U.S., Resnais returned to France, where Semprun was preparing **Stavisky** (1974), mainly financed (without credit) by Jean-Paul Belmondo, who played the lead. It is not about the Stavisky affair, which began only with the death of the Russian-Jewish swindler: it is, said Resnais, 'a very sinister story about a crook . . . a fairy-tale, that's to say a cruel legend without any magic.' One expected more from this team: the film, as pretty as cake-frosting, is entertaining, but it constantly doles out historical facts without marshalling them. A subject more complex than *Citizen Kane* is made in the butterfly style of Ophuls, but without his control. Resnais is more dependent than most on his writers, and **Providence** (1977) by the British David Mercer, and filmed in English, is a melange of *Marienbad*, late Fellini and *Accident* (q.v.). According to one of its stars, Bogarde, no one in Britain wanted to show it, but after winning a number of French awards and golden opinions from some American critics, it opened to mildly respectful reviews. One American critic who disliked it was John Simon in *New York* magazine who called it Resnais's first unmitigated disaster. Mercer himself had explained 'I, myself, am bored with naturalism now, pissed-off with verisimilitude. As Francis Bacon said when someone asked him why he didn't paint realistic portraits, "I can do you one, but it would bore the arse off me" ' – a remark entirely in keeping with the content of the movie. The chief production company involved shortly afterwards went into bankruptcy.

Conversely **Mon Oncle d'Amérique** (1980) was Resnais's first popular success in France. Jean Gruault's screenplay evolved from Resnais's idea of a montage film, blending excerpts from old films with comments by Professor Henri Laborit, an expert in behaviour patterns (it was Gruault who had shown Resnais a number of American Silents, while Resnais and Laborit had already discussed a projected film on memory). The professor's comments, together with frequent shots of laboratory tests on rats, provide the framework, and clips of Danielle Darrieux, Jean Gabin and Jean Marais are shown to indicate the influence their screen activities had on the film's three chief protagonists (Roger Pierre, Nicole Garcia, Gérard Depardieu). The effect is amusing rather than serious, as the three characters explain themselves in terms of their childhood environment, in each case selective and becoming more detailed as they reach the present. Since what is shown to us is very much the real world, dealing in such matters as parental authority, infidelity and, most importantly, the choice of careers and the subsequent perils of earning a living, the professor's comments are often apposite, referring frequently to self-justification and self-protection. Despite the theorising this is not an intellectual film, though we may find it as clever as it is hypnotic. It serves Resnais's purpose better than any film since *Muriel*, for his aim has always been to question the nature of man and find what makes him behave in so mysterious a fashion. That questioning – which has led him into two disastrous movies – was never more explicit.

Like Resnais, it is only by an accident of timing that Louis Malle became associated with the nouvelle vague, and like him he was not to be greatly prolific or prone to any particular genre. **Zazie dans le Métro** (1960) is an adaptation of Raymond Queneau's novel of a small girl's crazy adventures in Paris: the outrageous puns and suchlike felicities are transcribed by a number of visual jokes, inspired, said Malle, by the Keystone Cops on one side and Buñuel and Dali on the other. In neither case does it show, and the film should be avoided except by those who like speeded-up photography and/or orgies of destruction. **Vie Privée** (1962) began as an M-G-M vehicle for Brigitte Bardot, and emerged as a film about her, i.e. a tale of a poor little rich little movie star. Bardot emerges as someone wanting only to be loved and admired, with no intellectual resources; but the views of Spoleto, photographed by Henri Decae, are splendid.

In both films the result was far from Malle's intention, but **Le Feu Follet** (1963) is one of the most perfectly realised of films. It is a cry of despair, and though there were to be many such in the years ahead, the only precedent was Antonioni. Like Antonioni's films, this is literary cinema, incisive and discursive, using the camera and a minimum of dialogue for the story – written in 1931 by Drieu la Rochelle, an imaginative account of a friend driven to suicide. La Rochelle later killed himself, and his own sexual torment is implied by Malle in the sequence where the hero (Maurice Ronet) returns for too long a young man's look in a *toilette* and leaves with sweat on his brow. The financial problems of the book have become a loan from a mistress; the drugs have become booze. The man is recovering from alcoholism and is bent on suicide; he says '*Demain je me tuerai*' and his visits to his old friends are an undertaking to find out why he should not; Ronet is as good in the role as Malle could conceivably have wished.

There is a golden rule that the quality of highly publicised movies is in inverse proportion to the publicity, and **Viva Maria!** (1965) was no exception. With United Artists money Malle directed two media favourites, Moreau and Bardot – and George Hamilton – in a burlesque set during a Mexican revolution. The musical numbers are charming, but the climactic battle has far less invention than the similar one in *The Beautiful Blonde from Bashful Bend*. **Le Voleur** (1967) has Belmondo as a turn-of-the-century burglar, in that always romantic French criminal milieu, but it was a second failure for Malle. He took a long while to prepare **Le Souffle au Coeur** (1971), a crafty, commercial, constructed film about growing up, about learning the variety of life and the importance of literature. It takes place in 1954, with many references to Dien Bien Phu, but as a background to more important matters, such as masturbation. To be fair, though, in this film the 'variety of life' in fact means sex, which means a session with mother, looking exactly like an Italian movie star – which she should, since she is played by Lea Massari. With the exception of the incest theme, the film is autobiographical, as Malle has admitted; the title refers to the boy's illness, a comparatively minor matter, and the film is, *faute de*

mieux, probably the best portrait we have of puberty. Lucien, in **Lacombe, Lucien** (1974), is somewhat older, a seventeen-year-old peasant who joins the French Gestapo; this is a study of him and his collaborators, and of a Jewish family living in hiding, paying dearly for the privilege of not being handed over to the Germans. Lucien is not intelligent – which is the whole point of the film. Collaboration was not a subject the French cinema had tackled before, and Malle's film was probably inspired by Marcel Ophuls's documentary, *Le Chagrin et la Pitié*. *Lacombe, Lucien* is an absorbing film, its only fault Malle's usual one of offering some minor point as though it were a great revelation.

After it, **Black Moon** (1975) is a particular aberration. Within minutes of it starting a series of enigmatic happenings and the presence of the military in a generally deserted countryside establish a cliché, for such matters had been used already as a metaphor for the world after nuclear destruction, usually by film-makers much Malle's inferior. Subsequent events, at an isolated house with a bedridden old lady and a brother and sister who may be her grandchildren, are resolutely obscure, and the final message, when it comes, is paltry. What little dialogue there is is in French, despite the title – not that either factor mattered, since the film was little seen.

Whether or not it was always advisable is uncertain, but Louis Malle is the only one of the nouvelle vague directors to have moved from genre to genre – proving in the process that he is at his best in the sort of intense, intimate dramas which at least to outsiders look more difficult to bring off than the burlesques he has also attempted. *Le Feu Follet* follows in perceptive detail the last days of a suicide, played by Maurice Ronet.

Pretty Baby (1978) is Malle's first film in English, backed by Paramount, and its subject is child prostitution in New Orleans some years ago. The film sprang both from his love of jazz and his admiration for the photographs taken by E.J. Bellocq in the cathouses of the New Orleans redlight district *circa* 1917. The scenario, by Polly Platt, is an unsurprising one, detailing the relationship of a photographer (Keith Carradine) with the daughter (Brooke Shields) of a prostitute, a child who at twelve is only too eager to follow Mama's profession. Malle, claiming that his approach is that of a film-maker rather than a moralist, adopts a matter-of-fact approach to the child's joy at losing her virginity or joining Mama with a client, the drugging of the madame, or men buying two women at once. Clearly, such matters are a long way from all the French prostitute films of Malle's youth: but his approach is the same – deeply romantic. Photographed in hushed tones by Sven Nykvist, the brothel is splendid to look at, a box of delights for the child, and an amusing place for us to spend an evening.

Malle did not want to return to French cinema because, as he said, he no longer found it stimulating. He arranged to make a film in Canada, but left the project after the producer did a deal with Disney, who never allows the director the final cut. The Canadians did back **Atlantic City** (1980), which Malle suggested to them after visiting the city with the dramatist John Guare, with whom he had said he wanted to work. Guare's screenplay is that of a convoluted thriller, like that of Malle's first film, centred on a bag of cocaine which interests a number of people, including the hippie couple who had found it, as well as a waitress (Susan Sarandon) and a supposedly retired gangster (Burt Lancaster). He, like Atlantic City, has seen better days, and the eccentricities of the place are not ignored as Malle pursues his aim of creating the tension and surprises necessary to this genre. The film came out at the same time as *Mon Oncle d'Amérique* and is equally satisfying. It was rewarding to find both directors so much on form after two decades of film-making.

Georges Franju was the least adventurous of the nouvelle vague directors. His best film is **Thérèse Desqueyroux** (1962), based on the novel by François Mauriac, and written with Mauriac's son

Georges Franju became associated with the nouvelle vague directors because, like some of them, he had made short documentaries – and he moved into features about the same time. His early full-length films were thrillers, and then he did a very successful literary adaptation, *Thérèse Desqueyroux*, after Mauriac, with Emmanuelle Riva and Philippe Noiret: it turned out to be the high spot of his career.

Claude. This is another attack on the *haute bourgeoisie* and its stifling way of life, exemplified in the tale of Thérèse (Emmanuelle Riva), who marries her best friend's brother (Philippe Noiret) to be near her, and then, a modern Emma Bovary – she also hates the country – proceeds to poison him. The same measured pace was adopted for **Judex** (1963), a homage to the director Feuillade that is quite as trivial and, less inevitably, almost as boring as the original, and also for **Thomas l'Imposteur** (1965), written with Jean Cocteau – his last work for the cinema – from his early autobiographical novel. Thomas (Fabrice Rouleau) is a dreamy adolescent who makes his way to the trenches, along the way posing as the nephew of a general, and as such is taken up by the Princess (Emmanuelle Riva). It lacks the necessary theatrical flourish but is, for all that, a respectable entertainment. However, Franju's lack of invention, and his inability to 'build' a narrative, make only melodrama from **La Faute de l'Abbé Mouret** (1970), based on Zola's novel about the young priest (Francis Huster) who goes from religious to sexual mania when he meets the Eve-like Albine (Gillian Hills). It seems typical of Franju that the bitterness and realism of Zola have been reduced to something that is pretty, whimsical, and rather dull.

Jacques Demy (b. 1931) is another of the incurable romantics of the French cinema, and his first feature, **Lola** (1961), is one of the most irresistible of films. In Nantes, a number of lives touch tangentially – especially those of Lola (Anouk Aimée), a prostitute, who goes to bed with sailors because she likes the uniform and dreams of the father of her child returning; of Roland (Marc Michel), not long out of adolescence, who dreams of her and of the South Seas; and of a widow (Elina Labourdette), whose aspirations include a suitor for her daughter and a knowledge of English. Mother and daughter are facets of Lola, and the sailor and lover are facets of Roland. Demy understands Roland best, for this is a film made by someone discovering that the adult world is made of lost ideals and lost loves. A number of themes recur in **La Baie des Anges** (1963) – the mysterious beau (Paul Guers), the sailors, an adoring hero (Claude Mann), an aggressively glamorous woman (Jeanne

Moreau) who happens to be a compulsive gambler and whose ups and downs are all the film has to offer in terms of plot. Demy returned to the Atlantic coast for **Les Parapluies de Cherbourg** (1964), which, since its characters include Roland from *Lola*, also reintroduces his theme, extended by Michel Legrand for a complete score – to which all the dialogue is sung. Furthermore, the film is pretty, with decor to match the jacket of hero and skirt of heroine. He (Nino Castelnuovo) works in a garage, and she (Catherine Deneuve) works in the umbrella shop of her mother (Anne Vernon): they are parted by his *service militaire*, and the threatening sentimentality gives way to a fatalism essentially and irrevocably French. Demy catches life on the wing, events half-glimpsed and half-understood; he has grown up since *Lola*. The film, which should not have worked, won a Grand Prix at Cannes, and went on to win hearts all round the world.

Basking in that success, Demy was rewarded with American backing and the presence of Gene Kelly for a follow-up, **Les Demoiselles de Rochefort** (1967), clear proof, after Clément and Truffaut, that French directors get worse in proportion to the American investment. (Vadim, for example, never a good director, was even worse when he set his sights on the international market.) Hollywood musicals have become an important factor in

Another failed director associated with the nouvelle vague is Jacques Demy, as if confirming the jinx on the movement – that they begin with excellence and then work downwards (to say nothing of the myriad other young directors given a chance by the industry at this time, who after a mediocre first picture and a terrible second one were not given a third chance). Demy's first feature, *Lola*, remains a pleasure – not least for the performance of Anouk Aimée. The sailor about to enjoy her favours is Alan Scott.

French culture, but they were not made by putting a moving camera among moving people who sing and dance. Rochefort responds less well than Cherbourg to a fresh paint job; Legrand's score is poor, and the choreography sub-Jerome Robbins; as the *demoiselles* Deneuve and Françoise Dorléac are limited musical performers, Danielle Darrieux is wasted as their mother and Kelly was simply too middle-aged for bare-armed dancing and twinkly smiles. Despite the film's failure, Columbia backed **Model Shop** (1969), which relocates Lola as an L.A. callgirl, loved by a loafer (Gary Lockwood), and the film becomes increasingly like trying to fight one's way through candy floss. Two fairy-tales, *Peau d'Ane*, and *The Pied Piper*, were even less successful, and a comedy about a pregnant man, *L'Evénement le Plus Important depuis que l'Homme a Marché sur la Lune*, is a fiasco. Demy's career is a sad example of starting at the top and working downwards, and **Lady Oscar** (1979) did not reverse the pattern. A Japanese film, based on a Japanese comic strip, it is set at the court of Marie Antoinette, with a cast of British unknowns. To find a plot, Demy evolved 'the kind of picaresque structure . . . already used in *Lola*: a host of characters whose paths cross, diverge, reappear, diverge once more': it proved to be highly unsuitable and the film itself has to date not been seen in France.

In 1962 Demy married Agnès Varda (b. 1928), who had made her own first feature about the same time as *Lola*. **Cléo de 5 à 7** (1962) is not as beguiling or original, but it is not unworthy of a director who had been one of the most distinguished of the short film-makers. Cléo (Corinne Marchand) is a singer who believes that she has a serious illness, which causes her to look at Paris anew – thus this film is another nouvelle vague love affair with the city. It also has odd mood changes and unfamiliar faces: in comparison **Le Bonheur** (1965) looks very conventional. It tells of a young carpenter (Jean-Claude Drouot), who loves equally his wife (Claire Drouot) and his new mistress (Marie-France Boyer). Moving from one to the other – from Fontenay-aux-Roses to Vincennes – enabled Varda's photographers, Rabier and Claude Beausoleil, to photograph every brightly coloured wall in both suburbs, and every brightly coloured lorry which

plies between the two. The lingering, lyrical shots of sunny meadows and of limbs in the throes of love-making, are further evidence of the detrimental effects of the nouvelle vague, though in fact this film is only a half-way mark between the movement's original use of such matters and the subsequent T.V. commercials based on them. Varda then moved into an artistic wilderness, not unlike that of her husband, to emerge charmingly with **L'Une Chante, l'Autre Pas** (1977), a study of two women friends from 1962 to the present. Both more feminist and more contrived than *Cléo*, it is a reminder that she can be both fond and funny on the subject of rather tacky people.

Among the *Cahiers* set, Eric Rohmer (b. 1920) took much longer to gain renown, but that was partly because of the failure of his first feature, **Le Signe de Lion**, in 1960. He began his series of *contes moraux* two years later, but it was not until the fourth, in 1969, that he became internationally known. The first two, **La Boulangère de Monceau** (1962) and **La Carrière de Suzanne** (1963), were shot on 16mm in black and white, and originally shown on television; both are quite short. They concern the love-pangs of students, and throughout the series Rohmer was looking at life through the eyes of a much younger man. His men and women on the brink of adult relationships are either introverted or complacent, hesitant in love or confident. They exist in deliberately beautiful images, the books around them seem to encase them, and the results are inconclusive: the would-be, could-be, might-have-been are set amidst the minutiae of daily life, and an accompanying commentary constantly suggests the possibility of a God-ordained world. Rohmer constructs like a novelist, embroidering seemingly real situations, and though these are usually sexual, intercourse usually remains only a probability. **La Collectionneuse** (1967) is a variation on the triangle of *La Carrière de Suzanne*, inasmuch as two friends share one girl, though not at the same time – and it should be emphasised that the relationships in these anecdotes are far from the usual course of movie love (one difference between the two films is that this one is set in a villa near St Trop', instead of around the Boul' Mich, and that it is in colour – since it was made for cinemas). **Ma Nuit chez Maud** (1969) takes place near Clermont-Ferrand, in winter, and presents Jean-Louis Trintignant as a returned emigrant caught between two women, with one of whom (Françoise Fabian) he mainly discusses Pascal, Marxist theory and Christian doctrine. **Le Genou de Claire** (1970) finds Jean-Claude Brialy, in a Cézanne-like beard, on the shores of Lake Annecy, meditating on the nature of love. Like its immediate predecessor, the piece is over-verbose; but Rohmer returned to his earlier theme of choice in **L'Amour, l'Après-Midi** (1972), when Frédéric (Bernard Verley) is tempted by the predatory Chloë (Zouzou) to desert his wife. These are rich films, inevitably minor, but as good a gloss on one aspect of modern life as we have.

The series concluded, Rohmer turned to period drama, in the shape of a story by Heinrich von Kleist, **Die Marquise von O . . .** (1976), about the unfortunate noble lady who finds herself pregnant some years after her husband's death. Filmed in the ossified style of the new German cinema (q.v.) it was, said Russell Davies in *The Observer* – knowing only too well what he was saying – 'destined to be a feature of art house repertory for some time to come.' Those critics subjected to the scattered showings of **Perceval de Galles** (1978) were considerably less kind. Rohmer accordingly announced a series of 'Comédies et Proverbes', which is clearly intended to be a continuation of his *contes moraux*. The first of them, **La Femme de l'Aviateur** (1981) is equally honest but completely lacking wit and insight. It is an anecdote about a married man who involves a passing – female – stranger in his musings about an affaire his mistress may be having.

Also belonging to the central group of nouvelle vague directors is Philippe de Broca, who followed *Les Jeux de l'Amour* with two more comedies with Jean-Pierre Cassel. **Cartouche** (1962), an oft-filmed subject – a French Robin Hood – is as light-hearted and entertaining as any swash-buckler that comes to mind, and with the same actor, Belmondo, **L'Homme de Rio** (1964) is simply the best of its genre, the chase spoof. It is a super-Tintin, neglecting no element of the adventure tales which it parodies, be it the crawl along the wall of the skyscraper, the stolen Aztec statuettes, the car(s) coming at the hero in the midst of the desert, or the jungle temple climax. It is a once-in-a-lifetime film, as was proved by the less successful **Les Tribulations d'un Chinois en Chine** (1965), substituting Hong Kong and the Himalayas for Rio and Brasilia, and said to be based on a tale by Jules Verne. In the same year de Broca made **Un Monsieur de Compagnie** (1965), a facetious and sometimes frenetic farce, with Cassel as a man who lives by his amatory wits. It was followed by the even more disappointing **Le Roi de Coeur** (1966), a piece of whimsy set at the end of World War One, in which the lunatics who take over the town – Senlis – are clearly more admirable than the Germans and British fighting over it. Tricked out with a number of processions and dances, not to mention some underscored jokes, this allegory on the folly of war is depressing – not least because it became a cult film in the U.S., running several years in some cities. De Broca admitted that because of that he was regarded as a commercial director in France.

His next two or three films did not cross boundaries, and **Le Magnifique** (1973) seemed to confirm a decline: it is another re-hash of *L'Homme de Rio*, with the ingenious addition of Belmondo also playing the meek writer who dreams up the adventures for the gentleman of the title. With **Chère Louise** (1972), de Broca turned serious, for this is the tale of a divorcée (Jeanne Moreau) who falls in love with a teddy-bear of a man (Julian Negulesco) half her age. In fact, de Broca proved incapable of exercising the requisite discipline for a serious subject: but he remains so inventive and affectionate throughout that the film did not deserve the dismissal it generally received. But then, few of the reviews of **Tendre Poulet** (1977) – or *Dear Detective* as it was splendidly retitled – gave any indication that it was one of the most amusing films in years. It is contrived, but the gags are as fresh as they are funny, and they are bountiful. Annie Girardot and Philippe Noiret had on other occasions proved a felicitous team, and here she is a detective of the Sûreté and he an unworldly professor, meeting for the first time since youth. The thrills are of the parody sort, in the manner of *L'Homme de Rio*, and there had not been a film

Anouk Aimée and Jean-Louis Trintignant in a typical scene from Lelouch's *Un Homme et une Femme* – or at least an almost typical scene, for much of the time the windscreen-wipers were working, to make rainswept compositions. The film itself may not be the best there is on a romance, but it is the best there is on a romance between a scriptgirl and a racing-driver.

with such good humour since that time.

For good commercial entertainments, de Broca is rivalled only by Claude Lelouch (b. 1937), who started making amateur films as a teenager. His first success was **Un Homme et une Femme** (1966), which created a stir at the Cannes Festival, and went on to win an Oscar (Best Foreign Language film) and break records for a French movie in the U.S. The man of the title is a racing-driver (Trintignant) and the woman a scriptgirl (Anouk Aimée), both of them grieving over dead spouses. Lelouch clearly started with only the personal charm of both players, adding to them Francis Lai's pulsating score, some rose-tinted views of Deauville beach in winter and, thankfully, some improvisation (or what seems like it). The film's popularity resulted in a critical reaction against Lelouch, who, consciously or not, has continued to offer ammunition to his critics. **Vivre pour Vivre** (1967), a similarly glossy love story, is intercut with scenes of violence in Vietnam on the premise that the protagonist (Yves Montand) is a television journalist; his mistress (Candice Bergen) is a model, another of the jet-set occupations. As we watch this pretty film – the best sequences are in Amsterdam in winter, where the wife (Mlle Girardot) has planned a second honeymoon – we may feel that it does not provide an appropriate occasion to remind us that men are dying elsewhere in the world. **La Vie, l'Amour, La Mort** (1969)

is a study of a meek murderer (Amidou) and a plea for the abolition of capital punishment: it is dazzlingly well made. By this time Lelouch – who is his own photographer and, usually with Pierre Uytterhoeven, his own scenarist – had mastered the tools of his trade better than anyone in the business, whether the camera lurks or stares hard in close-up, whether he chooses to cut off the sound or move into monochrome, or ignore chronology or move into flashback. His people fit easily into their settings, but it is hard to feel much sense of involvement. Amidou is both this film's prize and its chief drawback; he is sympathetic, so we feel for him when the whores – his victims – humiliate him, yet he is impassive as he watches a T.V. newsreel on his crimes. But with all his technical mastery Lelouch's patent manipulation of audiences destroys this film as the document it sets out to be. On the matter of crime and punishment he is less persuasive than Chabrol, and by far the lesser film-maker.

But if Lelouch is second-rate his films are not only technically adroit but beguiling and often charming. **Un Homme qui me Plaît** (1969) involves a French film star, played by Girardot, and a French composer (Belmondo) who start an affair while engaged on a film in Hollywood. These artists are two of the most likeable and talented working today, and what makes their affair singularly convincing is that they are put into an alien environment, i.e. tourist U.S.A., as cunningly and wittily observed as we are likely to get it. **Le Voyou** (1970), with Trintignant as a crook, is too clever by half, with its time ellipses, and on crime again **La Bonne Année** (1973) is best described as ingratiating. It may be more ephemeral than most films, but as Lino Ventura takes the Cannes branch of Van Cleef and Arpels for a fortune, or sweet-talks the beautiful Françoise Fabian, that is no matter. It begins with a clip from the director's most famous film, *Un Homme et une Femme*, which is then promptly and disarmingly disparaged. But I have to say that the last of Lelouch's films that I have seen,★ **Si C'Etait à Refaire** (1978), justifies all that

*Since writing this I have seen several more of Lelouch's films, including *Les Uns et les Autres* (1981), which was phenomenally successful on its home ground; it is hard to imagine a movie more ambitious and more banal.

his detractors have claimed. It has flashbacks within flashbacks and a glossy surface; it has dialogue constantly suggesting that the characters are on the verge of discovering the secret of life; and an idiotic story about an ex-convict (Catherine Deneuve), her adolescent son and a friend of hers (Anouk Aimée) who decides to seduce him.

Still, at its considerable worst it is more entertaining than **Détruire Dit-Elle** (1969) and **Nathalie Granger** (1972), written and directed by Marguerite Duras, presumably for her friends, or as Françoise Giroud put it of their confrères in her 1975 memoir, 'for the people they expect to meet at dinner'. I could not tell you what the former is about, other than that the eternal dialogue is of ineffable banality and inconsequence; the second concerns two zombie-like women (Moreau, Lucia Bosè) and a travelling salesman (Gérard Depardieu). As V. S. Pritchett once said of a novel by Samuel Beckett, 'All significance and no content.'

If there has to be pretension in films, it is better found in such as Jean Gabriel Albicocco's **La Fille aux Yeux d'Or** (1961), since it is a quality which sits better with triteness than wilful obscurity. This is a modernisation of one of Balzac's three stories in L'Histoire des Treize, and it emerges here as a tale of gothic horror. Balzac's contempt for the young and the idle rich is dissipated; the implied lesbian relationship has become explicit and is now set appropriately in the world of Paris *haute couture*. The updated plot, of a man who realises that his rival is a lesbian, is not derisory. The soundtrack, of Corelli and guitar, and the Cocteauesque decor, were entirely to the taste of Parisians, but the film's lack of success elsewhere did not augur well for Albicocco. He had one further success, also photographed by his father, Quinto Albicocco, **Le Grand Meaulnes** (1967), based on Alain Fournier's novel, and written by the director with Fournier's sister, who had refused till then to part with the screen rights. As it turned out, this was one of the last of the French screen transcriptions of literature, and the old tradition died in high visual style, vaseline on the lens, arc-lights and distortion, but like the earlier film, consistent in effect. The film sets out to be a portrait of a village some seventy years

earlier, of its schoolchildren and the charismatic Meaulnes (Jean Blaize), of his meeting, possibly imaginary, with the girl (Brigitte Fossey), and of the narrator's hero-worship.

La Fille aux Yeux d'Or belongs to that euphoric time when the French film industry was suddenly young, and also to that period belongs **Les Dimanches de Ville d'Avray** (1962), or *Sundays and Cybèle* as it was called when, by some chance, it was premiered in New York before Paris. It was the French art film *par excellence*: a score compounded of Handel, Albinoni and Maurice Jarre; florid photography by Henri Decae, never taking the normal view if he can find a mirror or a steamed-up window; and with a plot about the friendship between an amnesiac ex-pilot (Hardy Kruger) and a young girl (Patricia Gozzi). The setting, as with many of these films, is a wintry village, and this one is the supreme example of the great romantic French movie tradition dying in the wake of the nouvelle vague. It also demonstrates something else: in *The New York Times*, Bosley Crowther wrote, 'Heaven knows for what rare virtue New York has been rewarded with the first public exhibition of a French motion-picture masterpiece. But it has. And, what's more, this work . . . is almost by way of being a cinematic masterpiece.' When the film opened in Paris, with that and other U.S. praise quoted in the ads, both press and public were bemused; in Britain unanimously bad reviews despatched it at once.

A similar situation arose with both Claude Berri's **Le Vieil Homme et l'Enfant** (1964) and **La Vie devant Soi** (1977), directed by Moshe Mizrahi – the films known respectively in the U.S. as *The Two Of Us* and *Madame Rosa*. Each concerns childhood and old age: Berri's film is about an anti-semitic man (Michel Simon) who during the War grows to love a Jewish child, while in Mizrahi's a Jewish prostitute (Simone Signoret) shelters an Arab boy. Clearly both films had great appeal to New York audiences, at least, and **La Vieille Dame Indigne** (1965), also with an aged leading player (Sylvie), again found favour in the U.S. but not elsewhere outside France. Its appeal to American art house audiences is only too apparent: it is 'unusual', anti-bourgeois and slightly complex – which in fact here means muddled.

France: Before and After the Nouvelle Vague

The old lady behaves in unconventional manner on becoming a widow, and at the end we are informed that she finally blossomed after living her life as the chattel of another. The original story is by Brecht, but René Allio, the director, far from achieving any Brechtian alienation, attempts spontaneity. The result is merely careless; his later films are slapdash to the point of incomprehension.

Government intervention in the form of subsidy has brought forth a great many films from people who might be better employed making mindless commercial movies, but while there has been no restriction on subject matter in French cinema the brighter young film-makers continue to emulate the nouvelle vague – thus, for instance, the autobiographical films which pour out at the rate of half a dozen a year. It has become common in France in the last few years to say that the nouvelle vague was a disaster from which the French film industry has never recovered – and among those who have said so are Roman Polanski and the actor Daniel Gélin. In fact the movement revitalised the industry and it is only with hindsight that we might prefer the academic, historical and literary films which preceded it. It is also true that of the central nouvelle vague directors only Resnais and Malle have not declined. We have noted Chabrol's comment on Truffaut, of whom Godard dryly observed that he had forgotten all he ever knew about making a film, before adding that Chabrol had never known anything. He may be right, but Chabrol has at least a dozen fine films to his credit, which is more than Godard and Truffaut can muster between them.

So great, however, was the stir created by the nouvelle vague directors that despite decline or paucity of output they have overshadowed their successors, few of whom have established an international reputation. Though some have achieved both popularity and esteem within France, foreign audiences have seen only occasional films. From Clair's late Silents through Carné and Duvivier to the nouvelle vague, we have always been able to follow the careers of the leading French directors; but as the number of art houses has increased in the Seventies and Eighties so have the films imported from other film-producing countries. Now even the most ardent Francophile may have only a sketchy knowledge of recent French films.

He would almost certainly know that Maurice Pialat (b. 1925) is one of the outstanding directors of the present time, having worked in television before making his first feature, **L'Enfance Nue** (1978). Among his sponsors were Claude Berri and Truffaut, whose first features were also about childhood. François (Michel Tarrazon) is unwanted; he wets the bed, is vicious and wantonly destructive. One pair of foster parents return him to the authorities, who send him to an aged couple who between them – each had been married before – have a vast family of their own. They suffer under him, reaching out to him with love but not much understanding, because, as the old lady stubbornly puts it after he has been sent to reform school, 'Il a un bon coeur'. She, like the whole cast, is played by an amateur, Marie-Louise Thierry (and playing her husband is her husband), and she is memorable; but the boy, unlike those in *Ladri di Biciclette* or *Les 400 Coups*, could be any boy. The film is filled with moments of fresh observation, as when François instinctively gives the first foster mother a farewell gift. It is a rich piece, with as much insight and compassion as has been found since de Sica's great days.

Nous ne Vieillirons pas Ensemble (1972) portrays a couple (Jean Yanne, Marlène Jobert) whose six-year affair seldom looks less than temporary, and **La Gueule Ouverte** (1974) is about a family whose mother is dying. Like Chabrol's people, Pialat's are sexual beings; as in Renoir, life goes on; but more than any other director I can think of, Pialat finds humour in the grim facts of the everyday. Because both films refer to the same incidents, they may be autobiographical. In **Loulou** (1980), for the first time, Pialat is not wholly in command of his characters (it is therefore ironic that this was the first of his films to be publicly shown in Britain and the U.S.). He had said that he had a complex about starting to direct so late in life and then making so few films, which may be why he made this picture of a lout, nicknamed Loulou (Gérard Depardieu). It is an attempt to pin down today's young as rootless, shiftless, classless and apparently motivated mainly by sex, for example when the bourgeois Nelly (Isabelle Huppert) boasts to her rich cast-off lover of Loulou's prowess in bed. She patiently tolerates Loulou's constant drunkenness, his idiot family, occasional larceny, friends that move into their room to stay, even the termination of her pregnancy so that she can work to keep him. There have been hundreds of films about men obsessed with unworthy women, and the few taking the opposite as a starting-point have usually seen the men as either weaklings or philanderers. It is typical of Pialat that he takes a denser, more interesting approach: much is left mysterious or unexplained, but he does take us deep into the world of this sad couple.

It may be said that Pialat works in the tradition of Renoir, Chabrol and Rohmer in placing his characters in firm social context – as does Claude Sautet (b. 1924). A former collaborator of Franju, Sautet achieved a mild success with his second feature, **Classe Tous Risques** (1960), a *policier* in traditional manner, with Ventura and Belmondo as the loyal friends. It was not until 1970 that Sautet had a popular success, when he and Jean-Loup Dabadie – his usual writer – collaborated with Paul Guimard on an adaptation of Guimard's novel, *Les Choses de la Vie*, an unemotional account of events in the life of a man (Michel Piccoli), fatally injured in reel one. Still keeping to middle-aged reflections, Sautet offered **Vincent, François, Paul . . . et les Autres** (1974) and **Une Histoire Simple** (1978), the former built round a group of friends, including Yves Montand, Serge Reggiani, Stéphane Audran, Michel Piccoli, and the latter – which might have been called 'Marie et les Autres' – round Romy Schneider.

Sautet also contributed to the screenplay of **La Vie de Château** (1966), along with Jean-Paul Rappeneau, who directed, and Alain Cavalier, who has also directed his own scripts. This is a sunny comedy set during the Normandy landings of 1944, with Philippe Noiret as the squire and Catherine Deneuve as the wife who falls prey, in both senses, to a young hero of the Maquis. There is no other film quite like this, so it is a pity that Rappeneau's other films have been comparatively undistinguished.

Bertrand Tavernier (b. 1941) seems the most determined of his generation to inherit the mantle of his great predecessors, deliberately flouting the nouvelle vague

by choosing as his writers Aurenche and Bost. An adaptation of Simenon, **L'Horloger de Saint-Paul** (1974), about a mild-mannered man (Philippe Noiret) adjusting to the knowledge that his son is a murderer, was a quiet, and wholly assured, feature debut. However **Que la Fête Commence!** (1975), an historical romp looking at what we might call the worm under the Watteau, was reminiscent of the worst amateurish excesses of Allio's *Les Camisards*. **Le Juge et l'Assassin** (1976) is also historical, a study in contrasts between the judge (Noiret), who sees in the assassin a means to glory, and the murderer (Michel Galabru), who means, from stupidity or certified insanity, to achieve the same ends. Aurenche and Bost, with one of their rare original screenplays, have provided Tavernier with a plot in the manner of Costa-Gavras (q.v.), but without the passion – and the piece is ultimately pointless. Returning to the present-day, Tavernier in **Des Enfants Gâtés** (1977) indicated with irony, humour and emotion how a series of small events can illuminate the way society functions – the theme of the earlier films but far better expressed. This tale of a middle-aged film-maker (Piccoli) who leaves home to live in a tenement, and who finds himself involved both with a girl half his age and the indignant tenants, is a complete achievement.

Tavernier dedicates **Une Semaine de Vacances** (1980) to Aurenche, but the film is in the mainstream of contemporary French cinema, being realistic and civilised, but with too few of the insights which make Pialat so rewarding. In examining in detail the reasons why a young teacher (Nathalie Baye) should find herself on the verge of a nervous breakdown, Tavernier is often platitudinous, and only the sympathetic tone prevents it from being as irritating as those contemporary American films which similarly dispense their creators' wisdom. The setting is Lyon, but the picture postcard views which punctuate the action illuminate neither the narrative nor the characters. We knew from *L'Horloger de Saint-Paul* that Tavernier loves the city (he was born there), but when he re-introduces the protagonist from that film in a 'guest' appearance here, the effect is one of smugness – even if relieved by the pleasure of seeing

France: Before and After the Nouvelle Vague

M. Noiret. When at the end the teacher asks her pupils whether they saw *Casque d'Or* on T.V. we are reminded of how much the French cinema has lost since then – and how strong the force of the nouvelle vague was that even so confident a director as Tavernier is uncertain of his aims.

Death Watch/La Mort en Direct (1981) is further proof that with Hollywood names and/or the English language French directors go to pieces. Tavernier, with David Rayfiel, adapted a science fiction novel by David Compton, and the first hour of this long film is both obscure and nonsensical. It poses a very shabby Glasgow as a city of the future, and it has an excellent concept – a journalist (Harvey Keitel) has a television camera in his head and is therefore allowing viewers to watch, unbeknown to her, the antics of a dying woman (Romy Schneider). The film does improve in the second half, as they flee to the Scottish countryside and he develops a sense of guilt; and it is eventually brought to a respectable level by the authoritative presence of Max Von Sydow, as the woman's ex-husband.

Tavernier's best film to date is **Coup de Torchon** (1981), based on an undistinguished American thriller set in the Deep South – but which has become tropical Africa in 1938. That was the setting of many prewar romances, to which this film pays brief and amusing homage: but this is what the Colonies were really like, with the natives cowed and people in authority who would hardly have been employed as roadsweepers back home. Chief among them is the weak police chief (Philippe Noiret), who turns a blind eye to the affair that his slatternly wife (Stéphane Audran) is conducting with her 'brother'. One day, after a pep talk by a fascist-minded fellow-cop (Guy Marchand), this worm turns and shoots two pimps who have been taunting him. After that he does not know where to stop, and since he and his equally unprincipled mistress (Isabelle Huppert) are the most sympathetic people in the film Tavernier's intentions are questionable: the justification he offers is that of *Le Juge et l'Assassin*, itself borrowed from *Monsieur Verdoux*. Until that point it is a surprising and often amusing black comedy.

Another director who has shown a fondness for Simenon's psychological studies is Pierre Granier-Deferre (b. 1927),

who with **Le Chat** (1971) and **La Veuve Couderc** (1971) made two of his best films. Simone Signoret is in both, in the first with Jean Gabin as her husband, locked in mutual loathing in a dreary Paris suburb, and in the second as a country widow who hides a fugitive (Alain Delon) from the police. More ambitiously, in **Une Femme à sa Fenêtre** (1976) Granier-Deferre tackled Drieu la Rochelle's novel of the diplomatic set and certain moral causes between the wars. Scripted by him with Jorge Semprun – in mood closer to *Stavisky* than *La Guerre est Finie* – the film is hardly more than a prettily-coloured kaleidoscope, moving from Delphi to Athens and eventually dwindling into an account of Romy Schneider's love life. She is, as ever, incapable of displaying much emotion, but Philippe Noiret and Victor Lanoux present differing studies in conscience. **Une Etrange Affaire** (1981) is much more successful, though it is hard to agree with Granier-Deferre's own claim that the story, based on a novel by Jean-Marc Roberts, breaks new ground. It was one of several puzzle pictures popular in French cinema at this time, the puzzle being why a young department store employee (Gérard Lanvin) allows his boss (Michel Piccoli) and his cohorts to take over his life to the extent that his marriage disintegrates. For much of its length the film is brilliant, notably in its portrayal of the anxieties of office life, but it is much less brilliant in hinting at sexual ambiguity and then simply stopping with the question unresolved. It would have been too easy to make homosexuality the key to the mystery, but no other is offered.

Michel Deville (b. 1931) began with a series of inconsequential comedies, of which the most taking is **Adorable Menteuse** (1962), about a young Parisian (Marina Vlady) whose fantasy world takes on a sinister turn when she mistakenly suspects a neighbour (Michel Vitold) of wrong doing. The most striking of Deville's later films is **Le Dossier 51** (1978), based on a book which would seem to be a combination of Kafka and Eric Ambler's 'The Intercom Conspiracy'. Deville has filmed it in an appropriately impersonal manner which is nevertheless riveting; it is a pity that at the root of the mystery, which involves espionage, is the old bugbear of sexual deviation.

Alain Jessua (b. 1932) made a second feature, **La Vie à l'Envers** (1964), of wit and style, telling as it does of a man (Charles Denner) who begins to withdraw from the world, to the extent that he is quite, quite alone. Jessua's other attempts at parable were much less original, till in **Les Chiens** (1979) he combined *Alphaville*, *Invasion of the Body Snatchers* and several movies demanding sympathy for the underdog. François Leterrier (b. 1929) is another variable talent. After acting in Bresson's *Une Condamné à Mort* he became assistant to Malle and directed his first film with **Les Mauvais Coups** (1961), one of the soulful 'quiet lives' dramas of the time, based on a novel by Roger Vailland, about a woman (Signoret) who throws a younger woman in the way of her husband, in an attempt to rekindle his love. However it hardly prepares us for the invention and high spirits of **Projection Privée** (1973), a film about making a film, with a nod to Pirandello in the script and a wryly satirical look at the focal point of most French movies, *l'amour*.

Les Violons du Bal (1974), directed by Michel Drach (b. 1930) is also autobiographical. It starts similarly, with Drach as a Jewish film-maker trying to interest a backer in a project about his family during the Occupation; he metamorphoses into Trintignant for the modern part of the film. Marie-Josie Nat, Drach's wife, plays both herself and his mother, i.e. mother of the small boy hiding from the Nazis. The film has the grace, the sense of humanity and the superb narrative line of the best French cinema, qualities less discernible in **Le Passé Simple** (1977), one of the *Marienbad*-Kafkaesque movies which represent the worst: but if one cares to follow all the strands of the plot, they coalesce with logic. Mlle Nat is the frightened wife and the supposedly sinister husband is played by Victor Lanoux.

Lanoux is also in **Servante et Maîtresse** (1977), which may be the best of all the 'puzzle' movies which proliferated at this time. It is a rather bankrupt genre, with little reward except that which the spectator awards to himself, but as with Drach's film this one eventually plays fair. The director, Bruno Gantillon, and his writers, Dominique Fabre and Frantz-André Buruet, neither bore nor offer fake enigmas. Lanoux and Andréa Ferréol play

– brilliantly – the couple involved, but their game of Genet role-reversals soon involves other people, with tragic results.

In the same area of decadence is Joël Seria's delicious **Marie Poupée** (1976), whose hero (André Dussollier) has a fetish for early Twentieth-century dolls – to the extent that he marries a girl (Jeanne Goupil) who looks like them. Forced to dress like them, she eventually rebels, one twist among many which are as witty as they are economically treated.

Claude Miller's **La Meilleure Façon de Marcher** (1976) indicates, at first glance, a healthier society, taking place as it does at a boys' camp. That one of the guardians (Patrick Bouchity) wears lipstick and skirts in his own room is offset by the fact that he has a girlfriend, but neither factor is of benefit in his relationship with his best friend (Patrick Dewaere). Matters come to a head at a fancy-dress ball, as dramatically ineffective as it is unbelievable: from a tale of adolescent torment we are swept into a Cocteau-like enigma, for if the man is not gay the piece is pointless. The relationship of the two men, always improbable, resembles that of many similar movies, since the French, sometimes prudish, will often allow no hint of sexual consummation. Miller had been assistant to Truffaut, and may have emulated him in losing contact with reality in moulding what may be a fragment of autobiography. Pascal Thomas's **Les Zozos** (1973) is a better film in the same vein: the sexual urge this time is undoubtedly hetero-, and it is handled with a sense of sly satire. It is clear that Thomas had in mind both *Zero de Conduite* and *Les Quatre Cents Coups*, but although his vision is even fresher than Truffaut's it cannot be as touching fourteen years later.

Anthracite (1980) also concerns adolescence. This first feature written and directed by a former actor, Edouard Niermans, is sure of its setting – a Catholic boys' boarding school – if not of its style. It is really a film about cruelty, meted out to a withdrawn boy by his fellow-pupils and to one of the staff, despised by both the boys and his fellow priests.

Diane Kurys is somewhat less bitter about school in **Diabolo Menthe** (1977), another first feature, and she, too, is often funny about her teachers. The film, set in the early Sixties, is clearly autobiographical, and is one of the few about female

1037

Annie Girardot in Jean-Pierre Blanc's droll *La Vieille Fille*. She has the title role, a spinster alone on vacation who finds herself increasingly preoccupied with a more-than-friendly businessman of her own age – and Mlle Girardot's playing makes it clear why she has been the most popular female star in France for almost two decades.

puberty. Claude Berri's **La Première Fois** (1976) is set a decade earlier and is also about a Jewish family. Unlike Kurys, Berri stresses this aspect, quite openly offering the film as a tribute to his parents. The title gives a clear indication that growing up means having sex, and though Berri is somewhat prurient about it, he clearly believes that its pursuit finds us all at our most absurd. This theme recurs in **Un Moment d'Egarement** (1977), when an adolescent girl falls in love with the best friend (Jean-Pierre Marielle) of her father (Victor Lanoux), a potentially tragic situation which Berri treats cheerfully. He does not do so without strain, but the Côte d'Azur locations and the acting remind us of the great traditions of French cinema.

Jean-Pierre Blanc's **La Vieille Fille** (1972) is also resolutely old-fashioned and is also set by the sea, at a resort near the Spanish border. The spinster of the title, Annie Girardot, and a businessman, Philippe Noiret, find themselves placed at the same table; she keeps herself to herself while he is affable and insensitive – and the question is, after a while, will they or won't they? The two stars play marvellously together, the vignettes of hotel life are often funny, and the film is absolutely

successful on its chosen level. Jeanne Moreau, turning director, explored a similar territory, and it is pleasing to find her taste apparently unaffected by the increasingly arty movies in which she had been appearing. Her co-star in **Lumière** (1976) is Lucia Bosè, with whom she had endured *Nathalie Granger*, and they play actresses. The great heart of show business is found for once to be neither sobbing nor corroded, but a metier like any other. After this least egotistical of autobiographical films, Moreau, not this time appearing or writing her own screenplay, directed **L'Adolescente** (1979) with what was for the most part the same admirable objectivity. It is a tale of growing-up, in Pagnol territory, during the last summer of peace, in 1939. The film is even less ambitious, even more likeable than *Lumière*, and if Moreau blunders artistically in demanding sympathy for the Jewish doctor – beautifully played by Francis Huster – it is a fault on the right side.

Although a number of these films touch on social problems, they are clearly not the main preoccupations of French filmmakers. Tavernier once observed that to make good films one must be angry, yet I find less anger in him, even in *Des Enfants Gâtés*, than in Yves Boisset (b. 1939), whose films, though not distinguished, are nevertheless more closely related to contemporary France than many we have been discussing. **Dupont Lajoie** (1975) is a study of the average Frenchman – played by Jean Carmet – whom we see at his least attractive, on holiday in *le camping*. The film is much in the manner of *Bank Holiday*, observing a cross-section of holiday makers, until Lajoie becomes involved in a sex-murder, at which point the film veers towards Chabrol, and later, when local Arab workers are blamed, towards old Hollywood movies about racial prejudice. The film was enormously popular in France, and Boisset subsequently created a furore with **Le Juge Fayard Dit le Sheriff** (1977), because it suggested a connection between politicians and organised crime. It was based on a factual incident, and the young *juge* (Patrick Dewaere) who had discovered the connection becomes very dead. Boisset had earlier shown his expertise with the cops and robbers genre in **Folle à Tuer** (1975), an unpretentious kidnap drama. As one of the kidnappers, the usually amiable Victor Lanoux proves to be a villain as good as was Jules Berry; the other guilty parties turn out to be connected with big business and a charitable organisation.

L'Argent des Autres (1978) deals with a financial scandal and was directed by Christian de Chalonge from a screenplay written by him and Pierre Dumayet; unfortunately they were too clearly carried away with indignation at the fate meted out to the employee (Trintignant), who was forced to take the blame, to make their case watertight. The subject of a cover-up and the pursuit of truth had been the theme of *Cadaveri Eccellenti* (q.v.), and it is that film that de Chalonge has imitated. The grandiloquence of the settings on this occasion only serves to underline the banalities, but nevertheless, like *Le Juge Fayard Dit le Sheriff, Une Etrange Affaire, L'Horloger de Saint-Paul* and *Les Choses de la Vie*, this film was awarded the Prix Louis Delluc as the best film of the year.

Not one of them has repeated its success overseas – to many people the French cinema stopped with the nouvelle vague. In Italy and Japan a generation of great filmmakers similarly inhibited the succeeding one. In the case of France the nouvelle vague directors were less excellent than famous. Their successors drew the best from them – the 'fly on the wall' method of story telling, and slice-of-life stories that build neither to a flashy dénouement nor an anti-climax. Despite their faults these films are civilised and several have been very funny.

One of the two hugely successful French films of the Seventies, another Delluc prize-winner, **Cousin, Cousine** (1975), was directed by Jean-Charles Tacchella, his second film as director, after writing some of the more forgettable films of the Sixties. For audiences who loved *Un Homme et une Femme*, it was the same form of wish-fulfilment; those driven away by late Godard were now brought back. A nice woman (Marie-Christine Barrault) responds to her husband's frequent infidelities by taking a lover (Victor Lanoux), and they shack up cosily at every opportunity. This old situation of French farce is treated realistically, but at the same time we are supposed to sympathise with the lovers and, as of old, despise the bourgeoisie who disapprove; unlike previous

practitioners in the genre, Tacchella's manipulations of the plot and audience reaction are blatant.

The other greatly popular film was *La Cage aux Folles* (q.v.), directed by Edouard Molinaro (b. 1928), whose films have seldom lived up to the promise of his first, **Le Dos au Mur** (1957), a dark thriller with Jeanne Moreau as an adulteress. Whether tackling a cod thriller, **Arsène Lupin contre Arsène Lupin** (1962) or sex farce, **La Chasse à l'Homme** (1965), his approach is ponderous, and the success of **L'Emmerdeur** (1973) is mainly due to the situations of Francis Véber's original play, adapted for the screen by both of them. A contract killer (Lino Ventura) finds that he cannot carry out the job because of the antics of a sad sack (Jacques Brel) in the neighbouring hotel room. Their subsequent adventures may lack invention, but do offer suspense and amusement.

La Cage aux Folles (1978) has been more widely seen in Britain and the U.S. than any other foreign language film to the present time* – a matter of some interest, since it is neither good, nor, one would have supposed, a subject of wide appeal, dealing with the menage of a middle-aged gay couple. It was written by Jean Poiret for himself and Michel Serrault, a frequent collaboration in the boulevard comedies of the Paris theatre. In the film Poiret's role is taken by Ugo Tognazzi, while Serrault repeats his role as the drag-star half of the couple, who runs a transvestite nightclub in St Tropez. When Tognazzi's son invites his prospective in-laws to dinner Serrault decides to turn up as his 'mother', which does provide some riotous moments. 'Obvious' homosexuality is a legitimate subject for comedy, but elsewhere Molinaro's tendency to sentimentalise the central relationship is misjudged in this context, and his handling of Tognazzi's serious scenes with son and ex-wife only add to the general impression of feebleness. Since there are several genuinely comic moments, the public acceptance is understandable: but like *Cousin, Cousine* it would seem that sexuality becomes sophisticated and hence appealing if in French –

*It played well into its second year in cinemas in both London and New York, though a sequel, *La Cage aux Folles II*, came and went with speed – proof either of the power of the critics, who unanimously thought it inferior, or that the first film had satisfied audience curiosity for the humour to be derived from gay liaisons.

for the level of humour in both films is unremarkable (and both adultery and homosexuality had during these years become a staple of situation comedy on television).

In Belgium, André Delvaux (b. 1926) made documentaries on several movie-directors, and was backed by the Ministry of Education and the state television service to make his first feature, in Flemish, **The Man Who Had His Hair Cut Short** (1966), an anecdote about a schoolmaster with a crush on one of his pupils, and what happens when they meet again when she is a famous actress. Its success enabled him to get French backing and players for his next two films, **Un Soir . . . Un Train** (1968) with Yves Montand and Anouk Aimée, and **Rendezvous à Bray** (1971), with Mathieu Carrière and Anna Karina. Both are puzzle pictures, but whereas attention is held in the first by the performances of the leads and the increasing nightmare of the plot, the second only confirms that Delvaux is less interested in emotions than in decor and camera angles. As far as can be ascertained its theme is the unexpressed love of one young man for another, just before World War I, but as the characters mope on and on, one may prefer the vulgarity of *La Cage aux Folles*.

Nevertheless, Delvaux's is a subtle, if derivative, talent. The same must be said of the two Swiss directors, Alain Tanner and Claude Goretta, who worked for the British Film Institute in the Fifties and co-directed a pleasing documentary, *Nice Time*. Their first features were made very cheaply, with the backing of Swiss television. Though German is the predominant language in most of Switzerland, filming in French is more economic there, because the films may play in France and Belgium (the German-speaking films, in Schwyzer-deutsch, have to be dubbed for Germany and Austria.) Tanner's **Charles Mort ou Vif?** (1969) which he wrote himself, is inclined to be discursive, but is an otherwise affecting study of a middle-aged man (François Simon) given a new lease of life. His collaborator on **Le Salamandre** (1971) was the English expatriate author, John Berger, draining him, apparently, even of his minor insights and surprises. The young lady of the film, played by Bulle Ogier, bedding any

nearby man, is clearly the antithesis of the Swiss ethos, a nation renowned for conformity. **Le Retour d'Afrique** (1973), equally cold and grey yet equally in favour of life, is a portrait of a young married couple and of their sitting around bored and waiting when their plans to emigrate to Africa fall through. The audience gets bored too, for there is a 30-minute gap in the middle of the film when nothing happens.

Goretta is inclined to be more cheerful, and to acknowledge his sources – which in the case of both **Le Jour des Noces** (1970) and **L'Invitation** (1973) is Renoir. The former, about a wedding party, is homage to *Partie de Campagne*, and the latter, about a country-house party, to *La Règle du Jeu*. Both are more fluent than Tanner's work, but neither anticipates the mastery of **La Dentellière** (1977), written with Pascal Lainé from his Balzacian novel, but without the desolation of the original. Beatrice (Isabelle Huppert) is seduced by François (Yves Beneytoun) and they subsequently set up house together. But what, in the squally days of autumn in Cabourg had been heady, is only distressing in Paris; she is a hairdresser, he a student, and as they realise that she cannot fit into his world, she is destroyed. Goretta, offered a subject with substance, responded with empathetic sensitivity.

Delvaux is not specifically Belgian, nor Tanner and Goretta specifically Swiss. Two of these nine films – *Rendezvous à Bray* and *La Dentellière* – were filmed in France and all of them are quiet and thoughtful, qualities to be found in almost all the post-nouvelle vague films. The directors concerned have, to an extent, rejected the fascination with Hollywood melodrama which gave early Godard its vitality, and they have looked as one man to Renoir. The exception to prove the rule is another foreigner, Constantine Costa-Gavras (b. 1933), whose polemic thrillers have an audacity lacking in his colleagues. He arrived from Greece at the age of eighteen to study at the Sorbonne and subsequently became assistant to René Clair and Yves Allégret. Later he was assistant director on both *La Baie des Anges* and *Le Jour et l'Heure*, and we may assume from his subsequent work that Demy was less congenial than Clément's thriller. His first film, **Compartiment Tueurs** (1965), was set up by a collective which included Yves Montand and Simone Signoret and many of the rest of the cast – Trintignant, Pierre Mondy, Claude Mann, Daniel Gélin, Françoise Arnoul, Michel Piccoli and Jacques Perrin. Costa-Gavras wrote the screenplay from a thriller by Sébastien Japrisot, and it is best not to regard it as a whodunnit, since the dénouement is a cheat – though the territory is rich in signposts if you know how to recognise them. But it is smashing entertainment, wittily played by the cast, especially Signoret as a less-than-successful actress, and Montand as a Sûreté officer – with a head-cold. The detail throughout is brilliant under the racing camera, and the clutter and bustle of the police station was to be echoed frequently, in such films as *Madigan* (q.v.).

It was Costa-Gavras' third film, **Z** (1969), which made him world famous, and it is one of the most exciting ever made. With his screenwriter, Jorge Semprun, he signs a foreword to the effect that any resemblance of the characters to living people is intentional: their source is a novel by Vassili Vassilikos, based on the Lambrakis case of 1963, when a left-wing Greek deputy was killed in mysterious circumstances. It is the contention of the film that he was murdered, albeit accidentally, as the result of several right-wing alliances, with the police and the army secretly supporting organisations of fascist-minded thugs. A young and dedicated public prosecutor resists pressure to withhold details involving officials, but in the subsequent trial the two leading thugs receive light sentences – reduced further by good behaviour – and the officials are reprimanded. The resultant brouhaha brought about the fall of the government, and rather than see a left-wing one succeed it the Colonels stepped in. This corollary is presented to the audience as a postscript, which also lists the writers banned in Greece since the Colonels came to power; even as other countries were applauding this film Mikis Theodorakis, who composed the score, was in fact being held in a Greek prison without trial. The film rushes at its audience – mixing subtlety, deviousness, a joke or two – and is built dramatically, propelled by tension rather than chronology. Outrageously, it offers some conventional thrills – a man fleeing a killer in a car – and a reference to an earlier

miscarriage of justice, the Dreyfus case. Above all, *Z* has a sense of urgency, a reflection of the prosecutor's determination to get to the truth. He is played by Trintignant, and the deputy by Montand; Renato Salvatore and Marcel Bozzufi are the thugs; the deputy's wife is Irene Papas, Charles Denner a party member, Bernard Fresson a committed man of the left, and Perrin an inquisitive photographer.

Costa-Gavras stated publicly that he wanted to reach a mass audience with films about oppression and injustice, and in **L'Aveu** (1970) he and Semprun found both in Czechoslovakia, where the conspiracy trials of the Fifties, intended to disguise the regime's disastrous economic policy, were carried out, with a strong anti-Semite basis, on Stalin's orders. The historical background remains elusive, but as a dramatic reconstruction the film works powerfully, with the director exercising imagination to bring a comparable restlessness to a subject far more static than his earlier films. Montand is the primary accused and Signoret is his wife; as the principal interrogator Gabriele Ferzetti conveys the intelligence needed for that job, with the single mindedness typical of a Party hack.

Montand is the victim again in **Etat de Siège** (1973). An attaché at the American embassy in a South American country –

The 'political thriller' was not new when Costa-Gavras made *Z*, but he gave it a new excitement, and not only because he took a completely partisan view of recent events in his homeland, Greece. It could clearly not be made there, but the supposedly fictitious country in which it took place had Greek number plates on the cars and posters for Fix beer. (It was actually made in Algeria.) Yves Montand is in the centre of the picture, with Charles Denner, left.

identifiable as Chile – he is kidnapped by a terrorist group, the Tupamaros, who officially do not exist. Santore (Montand) claims that he is in the country for a peaceful organisation, Alliance for Progress, upon which the Tupamaros ask why the organisation has supplied the police force with 300 patrol cars. When Santore claims that his aims are the same as theirs – the end of corruption, chaos and public theft – they declare that he wants to preserve inequality and defend privilege; they say they want to balance the social order, but he replies that they are Communists out to destroy Western, Christian, civilisation. The film covers what turns out to be the last week of his life, taking in a number of other matters, such as the local allies of the Americans who, except for a misguided idealist or so, are professional agitators. 'I don't see why we need stand by and watch a country go communist due to the irresponsibility of its own people' said Henry Kissinger, on 27th June 1970, at a meeting of the National Security Council's 'committee of Forty', and though the remark is not quoted in the film, it was surely the mainspring for Costa-Gavras and Franco Solinas, his writer. Since this film is an unabashed attack on American imperialism, someone obviously blundered in choosing it to premiere for a charity in Washington.

Section Spéciale (1975) completes Costa-Gavras' political quartet in France – the only one with a French setting – written with Semprun from a novel by Hervé Villeré. The title refers to the unit formed by Vichy France to select and submit scapegoats to the Gestapo after a German naval cadet had been shot in the Métro. The accused are all criminals, and the French, enthusiastically working to gratify the Occupying power, have chosen either Jews or known communists. The French are shown with less bias than is the director's wont – depressed, befuddled, trying

to save their own skins – and as in *Z*, the sting is in the tail, with a printed comment that none of the parties involved was indicted or even accused in the collaborationist trials at the end of the War.

It is not only that *Section Spéciale* is set in the past which makes it the least of the quartet: there are times when Costa-Gavras' elliptical style overburdens the subject by incorporating flashbacks and tangential incidents. He can use the medium as eloquently as the Japanese directors, and sometimes does; that he is rabble-rousing is entirely to the point. It is probably because he has been so successful that he has been condemned by a minute coterie of critics,★ one of whom – not unconnected with the New York Film Festival – explained his dislike to me by observing that the discussion of left-wing causes should be confined to left-wing magazines. And that is all the justification that Costa-Gavras needs. It must be discomfiting to such critics to find that the only French directors to have made any public mark since the nouvelle vague are Lelouch (for a while) and Costa-Gavras, and the public is probably right in both cases. The latter's political beliefs are of no importance: he tries to make films which might illuminate the events of the time in which we live – and he has been uniquely successful in achieving his aims.

As far as the whole of French cinema of this period is concerned the verdict is not yet in. The dust still has not yet settled after the explosion of the nouvelle vague. Most of the work of Malle and Resnais would seem to be permanent and some of the films of Chabrol; with the exception of Costa-Gavras no director has contributed a body of work as satisfying as that of the older directors, Ophuls, Clair and Renoir.

★However, there was virtually blanket praise for his first American film, *Missing* (q.v.).

37

Occasional Bulletins from the Eastern Bloc

EVEN AT THE height of the wartime *entente* with Soviet Russia, its Western allies were in no haste to import its films about tractors and merry peasants. The art-houses remained content with revivals of Eisenstein and Donskoi's Gorki trilogy until the Iron Curtain descended in the late Forties – and with that went the prospect of programming any Soviet film but the classics. The U.S.S.R. continued to send films to the film festivals, and when **The Cranes Are Flying** (1957) won the Grand Prix at Cannes it became the first Russian film widely seen in the West since the war years. It was said to be significant in Russian cinema because it eschewed ideology, but probably most people responded to it because of its traditional elements – it is a tale of unrequited love, of life continuing, of a weak husband, a letter that is not read. It is set during the war and its aftermath, with a sketch of tenement life in Moscow and a more detailed study of commune life in Siberia. The troubled heroine is sensitively played by Tatiana Samoilova, who somewhat resembles Audrey Hepburn, and whose habit of staring into space reminded some of Garbo; she is more plebeian than either, and the scenes with her have a warmth rare in Soviet cinema. The veteran director, Mikhail Kalatozov, manages a number of virtuoso sequences, including a rape during an air-raid, with gun-fire, blowing curtains, startled eyes and movement in the dark.

The break-through established, the Russians began to send us films about the War, in which patriotism and heroism intermingled, and shots of peasants outlined against the sky proclaimed that little had changed in Soviet cinema. The heroes were as comely and idealised as ever, we found, as the cameras raked their features before moving on to river and meadow, marsh and spinney. The Western filmgoer again became familiar with the vastness of Russia and with its rail links, as in **Ballad of a Soldier** (1959). The soldier (Vladimir Ivashov) requests a trip home to see mother rather than a medal for his bravery – because, for one thing, the roof needs mending. His wish is granted, and equally naturally, a pretty girl stows away on the same freight car: but this contrivance can be forgiven since the director, Grigori Chukhrai, so obviously cares for his characters. As it happens, his first film, **The Forty First** (1956), dealt with a less likely relationship, between a Red partisan and the White Russian officer who is her prisoner, derived from Protazanov's Silent film of the same name. It follows the adventures of a Red patrol in the Turkestan desert at the time of the Civil War, and if only competently handled, is handsome to look at. It had received a few sporadic showings in the West before Kalatazov's film, but that and *Ballad of a Soldier* were almost the only Russian films of the Fifties to which audiences readily responded.

There had, however, already been some showings of **The Grasshopper** (1955), directed by Samson Samsonov from his own dramatisation of Tchekov's short story, with Sergei Bondarchuk as the doctor whose cheerful wife prefers artists – any artist – to his own modest achievements. The film itself is modest, and delightful; it proved to be the forerunner of some literary adaptations which would be much more welcome than the war stories. **The Lady with the Little Dog** (1960) was commissioned from the veteran director Josif Heifits to mark the centenary of

Occasional Bulletins from the Eastern Bloc

Tchekov's birth. Since dissolving his partnership with Alexander Zarkhi in 1950 Heifits had directed some contemporary subjects; none of his previous work prepares one for the perfection of this film. In the dying summer at Yalta, a Moscow banker (Alexei Batalov) engages the attention of a married lady (Ya Savvina), whom he is destined to seduce – in one of the most delicately handled sequences in all cinema. The fidelity to the spirit and the letter of the original are remarkable, but in adapting 'Ionych', retitled **In the Town of S** (1966), Heifits takes a number of liberties. The original is a portrait of a country doctor – played in the film by Anatoly Papanov – who falls mutely in love with the daughter of some very social friends in the nearest town, and Heifits has extended it with some amusing vignettes of their various *soirées*: it is as if we, the audience, were eavesdropping, and as that is the impression we receive with the plays and stories, it may be said that Tchekov in cinema has had no finer interpreter.

The Duel (1973) is the first of these films in colour, but on this occasion Heifits failed. This is one of Tchekov's Caucasian tales, based on the literary convention of conflict between two men of opposing principles: but whereas in the original each of their clashes has a precise order, in the film many seem arbitrary. The embellishments are a trifle vulgar and the duel itself is farcical rather than serio-comic. Heifits's feeling for people in their landscape is also evident in two contemporary subjects, **The One and Only** (1975) and **Married for the First Time** (1980). *The One and Only* is about a divorce – that of a truckdriver who returns from military service to find his wife unfaithful, and who cannot, even during a second, happy, marriage, get over her: but as he finally decides that where there's life there's hope, the propaganda for the Soviet way of life is again heavily with us. That, however, is absent from the second film, which follows an unwed mother from pregnancy to marriage – after a fortuitous meeting with her pen-pal, recently widowed. That takes place more than twenty years later, and the piece is often comic on the mother's difficulties and those of her daughter, who is courted by an ambitious young man working in movies. These three films have achieved only minimal showings in the West, which is a pity; but *The Lady with the Little Dog* and *In the Town of S* are unlikely ever to leave the international repertoire.

A more unexpected literary success was achieved by another veteran, Grigori Kozintsev, whose earlier films, as we have seen, were also made in collaboration. His last work with Trauberg was in 1945, after which he devoted himself chiefly to the theatre for some years. After a *Don Quixote* in 1957 (which I have not seen, as the only available version is dubbed) he made what is usually referred to as 'the Russian **Hamlet**' (1964) to distinguish it from Olivier's version – and it was, with that actor's stage Othello, the supreme celebration of Shakespeare in the quattrocentennial year. Kozintsev takes his key from the 'something rotten in the state of Denmark', with an Elsinore that is fortress rather than

Anastasia Vertinskaya as Ophelia and Innokenti Smoktunovski as the Prince in Kozintsev's *Hamlet*, as clear and as noble a version as Olivier's film, from which it borrows a number of details, including the melody for Ophelia's lament. It was made to mark the quatercentenary of Shakespeare's birth, an event celebrated worldwide – but not by either the British or American film industries.

palace, its drawbridge up, guarded by stormtroopers corrupt and menacing: it is a place from which Hamlet can only escape by death. He (Innokenti Smoktunovski) suggests despair, an inability to deal with tyranny; I have never found more moving 'What a piece of work is a man' – which obviously has less to do with his delivery than his drawn appearance. Constantly Kozintsev adds to our understanding of the tragedy – not least with the steely Ophelia – but his **King Lear** diminishes it. Again the translation is Boris Pasternak's, and the spare but superb score is by Shostakovich; again the period is indeterminate, the landscape savage and the concept of kingship socialist. Taken out to the heath, Lear is merely a tetchy old man brought low by court intrigue. Further, with the exception of an Edmund of barnstorming villainy, all the leading roles are undercast. In this case, there was no Olivier for guidance – and Kozintsev acknowledged that he had borrowed details from him: but if Kozintsev's *Hamlet* sometimes soars his *Lear* is resolutely earthbound.

We have an American version of Tolstoi's greatest novel, which I understand is preferred in Russia to the **War and Peace** (1967) directed by Bondarchuk and featuring himself as – a rather over-age – Pierre. Reputedly the most expensive film ever undertaken – at the rouble equivalent of $100 million – it originally lasted 507 minutes. The state export service offered it in various versions – in France, for instance, virtually whole, in four separate parts, shown when possible on the Cinerama screen. The version shown in the U.S. and Britain has an average running time of 365 minutes, usually played in two parts. In the dubbed version★ the Natasha (Ludmila Savelyeva) has Hepburn-like cadences to remind us of what we are missing; the Andrei is dull and the rest of the cast assembled as if for the lids of chocolate boxes. They are not so much dwarfed by the spectacle as hobbled by the most eclectic battery of shots ever accumulated. We may hope, after literally hours of battle,

★Unlike *Don Quixote* this film has been available in both Russian and English versions.

that human values reassert themselves, but this is not really Tolstoi: a random thought or so is transcribed, as the film settles for love, sentiment, heroism and gallantry.

I have also been disappointed by the Russian versions of Tchekov's plays that I have seen. In Yuli Karasik's **The Seagull** (1971) all the characters except Trigorin (Yuri Yakovlev) seem to disappear into the scenery; in Andrei Mikhalkov-Konchalovsky's **Uncle Vanya** (1971) they moon about in a sinister mansion, victims of some period *angst* rather than their own frustrations – and that *angst*, if I understand the opening correctly, has to do with guilt over the starving peasantry.

Mikhalkov-Konchalovsky is from a family of artists and writers; his brother Nikita Mikhalkov (b. 1945) is better known to us, since his second film, **A Slave of Love** (1976), has been widely seen outside the Soviet bloc. Mikhalkov-Konchalovsky and Friedrich Gorenstein were the writers of this promising satire, about the reaction of an irresponsible film unit to the Revolution of 1917. The American reviews were encouraging, indicating that the Russian cinema was finally escaping from fifty years of didactic, moribund material. So it has; but I watched this film with mixed feeling, caught between admiration for the variety and appositeness of the visuals and distaste for them, since they have been achieved at the expense of plot and narrative. Nor is **Unfinished Piece for Mechanical Piano** (1977) any more effective, as adapted from several of Tchekov's works, including the play 'Platonov' – unrecognisable in this manifestation. The plot is difficult to follow, perhaps because the actors were encouraged to improvise; the screenplay is credited to Mikhalkov himself and Alexander Adabashian, whose further collaborations would include two substantial works.

Adabashian adapted **Five Evenings** (1978) from a play by Alexander Volodin (he also plays the hero's friend, engagingly, and was one of the art directors). It is a comedy of tenement life, written and set in the late Fifties, and Mikhalkov has filmed it in the style of the movies of that period, without any propaganda for the Soviet way of life; instead there is wry humour and a spirit of enquiry in this tale of an easy-going man, missing since the War, who returns to confront his former fiancée, now a settled spinster and guardian of her student nephew. The collaboration of director and writer on **Oblomov** (1979) or *A Few Days of I.I. Oblomov's Life* is as successful as their Tchekov film was not. Aided by a commentary and a number of flashbacks, Goncharov's long novel has been compressed to show Oblomov's idyllic childhood and his youthful friendship with Stolz (Yuri Bogatyryov), devices which serve to demonstrate the sameness of life in old Russia. The film's length and pacing, with its limpid photography and meticulous period detail, also contribute to that effect. It is splendidly performed, especially by the three principals – Bogatyryov, Oleg Tabakov as the slothful Oblomov and Yelana Solovei as Olga, whom Stolz has designated to look after Oblomov, to the latter's surprised delight.

Autumn Marathon (1979) has an original screenplay by Volodin, concerning an academic translator who complicates his life by trying to share it with a mistress and a wife, who is unaware of the other's existence. The film has a few insights into the bureaucratic life which is the lot, apparently, of Leningrad's literary set, but it is bland – comment enough on the Soviet cinema since the director of this movie, Georgi Danielia, a Georgian, is reputed to be its leading satirist. The difficulty of commenting on the greatest factor of Russian life – those who control it – is partly overcome by the director Ilya Averbakh in **Declaration of Love** (1979), for the simple reason that it is set in the past. The source is 'Four Quartets', a novel by Evgeni Gabrilovich, a friend of Meyerhold and Eisenstein, and it follows the fluctuating love affair of Filippok (Mr Bogatyryov), a bespectacled bear of a man, and Zina (Eva Szikulska), a striking blonde with an illegitimate child. At their first meeting, before the Revolution, he claims to be an anarchist, and he later acquires fame for his studies of the collectives. The film presents only certain aspects of life during its fifty-year time span, but they are vividly portrayed – and if the final impression is of nostalgia, that was perhaps necessary.

Private Life (1982) deals with a middle-aged executive (Mikhail Ulyanov) in despair at suddenly being made redundant. The director is the octogenarian Yuli

Occasional Bulletins from the Eastern Bloc

Towards the end of his career the director Mark Donskoi returned to Gorki, whose autobiography had served him so memorably over three decades earlier. *The Orloffs* (1978) is the story of a drunken ikon-painter (Anatoly Semyonov) and his wife (Nina Ruslanova), and how their marriage disintegrates as she finds escape from poverty. That poverty is horrible was the theme of the earlier Donskoi-Gorki films, and if here Donskoi seemed keen to show off his knowledge of new cinema techniques he demonstrated too all his old feeling and ability to re-create the past.

Raizman, responsible for some of the great propaganda films of the Silent era, and it is interesting to see him managing not to question the Soviet way of life, yet give body and blood to the problem its bureaucracy has presented to his protagonist. Indeed, this group of films, considered with Heifits's two contemporary films and *Five Evenings*, do answer many of the questions most of us have about Russian life; and the warm sympathies expressed in them, coupled with impeccable craftsmanship, may mean that Russian cinema could be entering one of its richest periods. Curiously, **Moscow Does Not Believe in Tears** (1980) has much in common with *Married for the First Time*, following as it does the progress of an unmarried mother. It was awarded the Oscar for the Best Foreign Language film, and among the nominated entries it had not then been shown to the New York critics for their approval, usually a crucial matter for this particular award. I suspect that the Academicians liked it because it resembles several old Bette Davis vehicles. The director is Vladimir Menshov and Vera Alentova plays the leading character, whose life is detailed from her carefree days in a workers' dormitory to the stress of being a leading executive. As a young woman she is seduced while 'Bésame Mucho' plays on the turntable, by a man she regards as glamorous because he works in television; years later she is having an

affair with a married man when she meets a simple fitter (Alexei Batalov), who proves to her that though she may be a big wheel in the Union of Soviet Socialist Republics she is still a woman at heart. As in Davis's films, her fate is contrasted with that of some friends, while in middle-life she also has trouble with her daughter. It is a richly entertaining film, and was much liked in the U.S.; in Britain the title was changed to the less telling *Moscow Distrusts Tears*, and patrons showed their own distrust by not going to see it.

The British responded to *Oblomov* but not to *A Slave of Love*, both of which were relatively popular in the U.S. This leaves Andrei Tarkovsky (b. 1932) as the only Russian film-maker of the postwar period yet to gain any reputation in the West. In this regard the Americans have shown themselves wise in rejecting his films, some of which have been praised by European critics. His first feature, **Ivan's Childhood** (1962), also known as *My Name is Ivan*, is not only a paean to the Russian way of life, with heroism to match, but is filmed entirely according to the textbook theories of the film academies. It has exquisite photography which represents nothing but exquisite photography. Also, its story, the tutelage of a young boy by an experienced soldier, an old staple of films, has never been so unfeelingly projected. It was coolly received. So too was **Andrei Rublev** (1966) when it played in New York as *Rublyov* the year after it was made; but by the time it turned up in Britain in 1973 it was known that the Russians had banned domestic showings for some years. Its subject is a fifteenth-century ikon painter and his conflict between his art and his debt to society, told in eight seemingly interminable episodes from his life – episodes of pagan and Christian rites, of philosophising and merry-making, of battle and siege, during most of which gesticulating peasants are fleeing from cavalry. Despite this, the piece does not toe the Party line, but it is as barren of true content as its predecessor; for all the insight shown into the hero's art or times he might as well have been a gravedigger.

I am clearly not the person to criticise Tarkovsky, since I fled from **Solaris** (1972) after an hour, and was forced to leave **Mirror** (1974) even earlier. *Solaris*, which concerns a voyage to outer space, was originally shown in Britain to little favourable comment, but was revived after the success of *Andrei Rublev*; *Mirror*, in my opinion, was chiefly welcomed because it was also known that the Soviets had withheld its export for six years, either because they thought it decadent art, or because those examining it for subversion kept falling asleep. I could discern no plot in *Mirror*, nor the slightest resemblance to human behaviour or connection with imaginative thought. The soundtrack pounds with Bach and Pergolese, and at one point the film stops to examine a book of Renaissance prints. That Tarkovsky has a degree of culture should not fool anyone into supposing that he has an intellect. Of the film he himself has said 'There are no episodes to decipher like symbols . . . if one finds double meanings in it, that will be because we are not used to seeing truth on the screen.' I have read exhaustively Tarkovsky's interviews to try to find his intent, e.g. 'My objective is to create my own world and these images which we create mean nothing more than the images which they are. We have forgotten to relate emotionally to art.' I can only say that to move from the simplistic *Ivan's Childhood* through two mediocre movies to the impenetrable *Mirror* is progress of a peculiar sort.

Andrei Rublev may be compared with a magnificent film about an artist, **Pirosmani** (1971), directed by Georgy Shengelaya – though credit must surely be shared with the art director, Avtandil Varazi, since the film succeeds through being tableaux in slow motion. The difference between it and the earliest movies of all is, of course, enormous, and it should be said that Shengelaya adopted this form in an attempt to get at the truth behind the paintings, since they are virtually all we know of Pirosmani. He was an itinerant painter, a primitive – his subjects were usually animals and scenes of village life – and the film shows the hills of Georgia in which he wandered and the cafés of Tiflis in which he drank, as counterpoint to his work.

The film is so rewarding that I went to **The Eccentrics** (1974) because it was made by the director's brother, Eldar Shengelaya, but it is a filmed folk-tale of little distinction. The lively Georgian cinema is better represented by Otar Yossiliani (b. 1934). He made his first feature in 1967 and has made only two since: **A Thrush Once Sang** (1972) and **Pastorale** (1975), both with musical motifs. *Pastorale* is a mild group portrait of some youngsters who form a string quartet, with a slight narrative about their effect on the villagers with whom they are staying. It lacks the exuberance of the earlier film, which is about a young tympanist with the symphony orchestra in Tiflis, and what he does with those evenings when he has only a couple of drum-rolls. Yossiliani explains his inactivity in the studios by saying that he has difficulty in finding subjects agreeable to the bureaucrats who control the Soviet cinema, but he is more fortunate than his fellow Georgian, Sergei Paradzhanov (b. 1924), who has spent most of the past decade in prison (allegedly for incitement to suicide, homosexuality and currency offences). Both regard themselves as followers of Dovzhenko, but unlike his famous predecessor Paradzhanov is not patronising. The best known of his half-dozen films is **Shadows of Our Forgotten Ancestors** (1964), which is composed of extraordinary images – such as that of the farm-workers in their barn-like dormitory home, standing half-naked around the fire as they dry their shirts, wet from the rain which is literally cascading through the ceiling. The setting is that of a

There is only a handful of successful or even tolerable films on the lives of artists, and among the best of them is *Pirosmani*, made by the Georgian director Georgy Shengelaya, who followed both his father, Nikolai, and his brother, Eldar, into the film industry (all of them as directors). The beauty and simplicity of this film prove him a major film-maker and it is sad that we have had no further chance to sample his work.

Occasional Bulletins from the Eastern Bloc

Carpathian community in the early years of this century, and the story concerns a young man and his two women – the childhood sweetheart he loses to the river and the wealthy girl he unhappily weds. Paradzhanov's last film is **The Colour of Pomegranates** (1974), a biography of the Armenian poet Aruthin Sayadin; it may well be that Paradzhanov's real offence is in identifying himself with the traditional roots of Georgian culture, which is unlikely to be congenial to the authorities.

As I have implied, it is sad that we are not better acquainted with the films now being made in the Soviet Union. Other Russian bureaucrats, those at Sovexportfilm, have been assiduous in arranging weeks of Russian films, which are attended by the faithful, but with the exceptions noted art-house distributors have remained wary of those on offer. If the propaganda content has been drastically reduced in recent years, the subject matter remains limited. Melodrama is not permitted, as presumably too decadent, and the targets for comedy and satire are proscribed – which is a pity when we recall some of the Russian Silent comedies. Crime, the staple of much Western cinema,

is supposedly rare in the Communist utopias, but adultery★ and other forms of sexual behaviour are not to be regarded as common after more than fifty years of Communist inculcation. The behaviour of the authorities and their suppression of thought, independent culture and doctrine, etc., is potentially the richest imaginable subject – and clearly the most inconceivable.

The first Czech films we saw were the puppet films of Jiri Trnka, exported and welcomed precisely because of their lack of dogma. Karel Zeman (b. 1910) also began with puppet films, and moved into animation. With **Baron Munchhausen** (1962) he proved himself a true heir to Méliès, as live actors move against the Doré illustrations to Bürger's story, with animation to provide the special effects necessary to the fantasy. **A Jester's Tale** (1964) is repetitive and sometimes over-extended, but it is even more lighthearted and it has a sympathetic central character – the proverbial peasant caught up in the Thirty Years'

★The various seductions in the films I have mentioned are not destructive; as a general rule no one suffers because of them.

Milos Kopecky in Karel Zeman's version of *Baron Munchhausen*, a spirited rendering of the Baron's famous adventures. Although Gottfried Bürger's stories were published first in London they have never been as popular with Anglo-Saxon readers as on the Continent – and few of the several European film versions have found their way to our shores. However, it may be said with some confidence that none of them is as enchanting as this.

War; both films are breathlessly enjoyable. The fact that the latter is in black and white proved an obstacle, as *Variety* predicted, to Western appreciation, but that is clearly not the reason *Munchausen* is so little known. Though the original stories were first published in English (in 1785) none of the countless continental film versions has found an audience in the Anglo-Saxon countries; an animated version was begun in Canada in 1947, but abandoned. Zeman changed technique again in **The Tale of Honzik and Marenka** (1980), though I understand that he had used it earlier for *The Sorcerer's Apprentice*: his characters are cardboard cut-outs, wittily existing because they are two-dimensional. For a drawbridge that lowers, a dragon that turns, a winged horse, he uses true animation, and equally sparingly the camera rests on real water for a rainstorm or sea. The story, a synthesis of Czech fairy tales, is as captivating as Zeman's effects.

A more obvious inspiration for Czech film-makers is Kafka, and the unexpected aspect of **Joseph Kilián** (1963), a 40-minute feature directed by Pavel Juráček and Jan Schmidt, is that it approaches bureaucracy with a positive glee.. We do not know why the nondescript young man (Karel Vasicek) at its centre is searching for Joseph K., and anything and everything may have a double meaning – or no meaning at all, as in the sequence towards the end re-creating the inverted logic of an Escher drawing. A cat, literally, is let out of a bag, and two men discuss the difference between men and animals: 'Reasoning,' says one, but 'Obedience,' says the other. As bemused as this young protagonist are the guests in **The Party and the Guests** (1966), another gloss on the Communist state, and in simple-minded fashion the party of the title means the Party. The director, Jan Němec, was clearly influenced by Buñuel's *El Angel Exterminador*, which has wit, conviction, mystery and a blazing sense of what humanity is up to, qualities unknown to Němec. It was made during the Dubcek regime, when it was permissible to criticise the hold of Soviet Communism, and finished just before the Russians marched in to oust Dubcek. Němec's **Diamonds of the Night** (1964) is about two Jewish boys who have escaped from the train taking them to a concentration camp; different versions of

events are confusingly and boringly shown, but the film is a model of clarity beside Juro Jakubisko's **The Deserter and the Nomads** (1968), which tries to interpret the last two world wars and a future one in the style of folk painting. The cinema seems the wrong medium to attempt this approach, though such experimentation must seem laudable when subject matter is restricted; but as so often with obscure film-makers, the discernible message is trite. A subtitle wings across the screen: 'It is bad enough when people kill out of hate. It will be worse when they kill for the sake of killing.'

The aspect of war covered in **The Shop on the High Street** (1964) is the deportation of the Jews. The film was heralded from Prague by the critic Kenneth Tynan, who considered it 'the most moving film about anti-Semitism' that he had seen, before contemplating its fate at the Cannes Festival. In the event, the French critics considered it old-fashioned, which it is; but it is worth several of *The Deserter and the Nomads*. Tynan said 'The grand theme of the film – as of all good modern drama – can be simply stated: how much of a man belongs to authority and how much to himself? What demands can society legitimately make of a man without requiring him to sacrifice his selfhood?' The dilemma is that of a man divided between conscience and the demands of the state. He

Sometimes it seems that the only films imported from the Eastern bloc are, if not literary adaptations, about the War, but few of these on that subject have the quality of *The Shop on the High Street* or *The Shop on Main Street*, as it is known in America. Ida Kamińská and Jozef Króner were both memorable, she as the Jewish proprietor of a village shop, he as the 'Aryan controller' appointed to it by the authorities.

Occasional Bulletins from the Eastern Bloc

Of the three Czech directors who left their homeland to work in the West – the others are Ján Kadár and Ivan Passer – only Milos Forman has been greatly successful, a fact that may have been foretold by his early films, in which he brought freshness of observation to a number of everyday subjects. The dance-hall sequence of *A Blonde in Love* is both long and very funny; in fact the frustrations of these three soldiers in finding partners is extraneous to the main plot.

(Jozef Króner) is appointed 'Aryan controller' of a Jewish shop owned by a widow (Ida Kaminská) too senile to understand his function – let alone the turmoil wrought in this remote little town by the anti-Semitic insanity of a group of men living thousands of miles away. The film won the Best Foreign Language Oscar, which eventually severed the partnership of Ján Kadár (1918–79), the director, and Elmar Klos, the writer. After one more film together Kadár went to Hollywood from whence, after two indifferent films, he moved to Canada to make *Lies My Father Told Me* (1976), described by John Coleman in the *New Statesman* as 'benign, humorous, worldly and fraudulent'. The first three adjectives apply equally to *The Shop on the High Street*, and in view of its ghastly ending – in the manner of *Maytime* – the fourth and last is not surprising; but like all the best movies, it reverberates for days afterwards.

The Czech cinema received further impetus from Milos Forman (b. 1932), another director whose sense of humour survived film school training – not to men-

tion the death of his parents in a concentration camp. His first feature, **Peter and Pavla** (1964) recalls Olmi, and in particular *Il Posto*, since it is about a boy's first job – young Peter, working in a supermarket, is required to spot shoplifters. The blonde of **A Blonde in Love** (1965) goes to bed with a pianist she meets at a dance, and on a whim goes to his home in Prague where, finding him out, she spends a dull evening with his parents. The Saturday night dance of the first film becomes a 30-minute feature of the second, concentrating on three middle-aged soldiers who are doubtful of their chances with a hundred young conscripts as rivals.

This beautifully observed, hilarious sequence is developed into **The Firemen's Ball** (1967), a film which recalls another cinema commentator on the inarticulate, Humphrey Jennings; and, no more than he, does Forman require commendation for using physical characteristics as signposts to character. The difference between Jennings' firemen and Forman's is that the latter's are self-important and lecherous. They aim to

1052

dignify their dance with a 'Miss Fireman' conquest, and the degrees of vanity and ribaldry lead, to borrow a phrase, to 'a dithyramb of disaster'. Forman delights in walking on that knife-edge between truth and cinema convention; he is less instinctive and more impressionistic than either Olmi or Jennings, and he has, at the end of *The Firemen's Ball*, a vision blacker than either. Forman stated that he did not set out to make an allegory, but if the comedy was true it 'will automatically reveal an allegorical sense. That's a problem of all governments, of all committees, including firemen's committees – that they try and they pretend and they announce that they are preparing a happy, gay, amusing evening or life for the people. And everyone has the best intentions. And everybody's prepared to be happy, to help, but suddenly things turn out in such a catastrophic way.'

Since Forman left Czechoslovakia in the aftermath of the Russian take-over, we might digress to examine the genesis of *The Firemen's Ball*, as it provided him with his first important contacts outside his homeland. His first two films had been naturally state-funded, and they had so impressed Carlo Ponti that he offered Forman a project on American tourists. While preparing it with Ivan Passer and Jaroslav Papousek, his usual co-writers, they attended a firemen's ball which was 'such a nightmare that we couldn't stop talking until the next day about it.' They abandoned the American tourists and Ponti agreed to a film on the firemen, but only to approximately half its cost, i.e. $110,000. The contract specified a film of at least 80 minutes, and although Forman had shot 100 minutes of material, he felt that only 73 minutes of it would make a satisfactory film. It therefore became necessary to find a new sponsor, and he approached Claude Lelouch, who, like Ponti, had expressed a wish to sponsor a film of Forman's. Lelouch was unable to be in Paris for the screening of the material, but another French director, Claude Berri, arranged for the replacement of Ponti's investment. Passer, incidentally, followed Forman to Hollywood, where he was able to find work on the strength of *Intimate Lighting*, which he directed in 1966; but with the exception of *Cutter's Way* (q.v.), his American films were not as successful as those made by Forman (q.v.).

Hynek Bocan's **Private Hurricane** (1967) begins in the same way as Forman's early films, with a composite portrait of small town life, in this case the industrial town of Usti nad Laben. Contrast is established between a pretty factory worker, Bohunka, and her ox-like boyfriend, Standa, enjoying weekly sex while they wait to marry, with Standa's mild-mannered boss and his plump, pretty wife. In time the boss meets Bohunka, and his interest in sex is revived – at which point a pleasant 'slice of life' drama becomes black comedy, since Standa discovers their relationship and vows murder, though matters eventually turn to farce. The characters are small, ordinary and grubby, and their approach to sex and nudity is refreshing.

With this film and Forman's, and with Menzel's **Closely Observed Trains** (1966), the Czech cinema seemed to offer new impetus to proletarian cinema. *Closely Observed Trains*, based on a novel by Bohumil Hrabal and set during the War, also concerns a boy's first job – at a lonely railway station; it also relates his first fumbling attempts at sex, which are complicated by premature ejaculation. If we are startled that he seeks advice from the stationmaster's venerable wife, and sceptical when he eventually loses his virginity by an extremely glamorous Resistance heroine, we may rightly assume the director, Jiří Menzel (b. 1938), to be less able on the subject than Forman.

His **Capricious Summer** (1968), based on the novel by Vladislav Vančura – shot by the Nazis for his Communist beliefs – is centred on a freshwater bath-house, and concerns the effect of Anna from the circus on some local males. **Seclusion Near a Forest** (1976) takes a familiar situation, city folk renting a country home, and for much of its length simply represents the Czech equivalent of the events direly portrayed in *The Egg and I*. **Those Wonderful Movie Cranks** (1978) pours love and movie lore into a tale of the cinema's first days but is, unhappily, even less convincing than the films which preceded it. Several years' study at film school has apparently not quite equipped Menzel to portray the real world, which would seem to have been his mission in at least two of these films.

Reality hardly impinges on his best film,

'A film of contrived intensity' said David Denby in *New York Magazine* of the latest to date of István Szabó's films, *Confidence*, and that describes all but a handful of the films of the Eastern bloc that we have seen in the past three decades. One that is intense but not particularly contrived is Szabo's earlier *Father* – about a man's relationship with his son, played as a child by Dani Erdélyi, being pulled about here.

Cutting It Short (1980), although it is based on an autobiographical story by Hrabal, in this case about his own parents. Again they wrote the screenplay together, setting the story in a small rural brewery in the Twenties, managed by Francin (Jiří Schmitzer). The board of the brewery questions his competence, but its members adore his wife Marja (Magda Vašáryova) and her cooking. Apart from the arrival of his extrovert brother, little of real moment happens – Francin's motor-cycle side-car refuses to stop, Marja adopts the fashionable bobbed hair – but such details are beguilingly presented and Menzel's love of the countryside is given even more lyrical expression than in his earlier films.

He has also acted in some of the films directed by Vera Chytilová (b. 1929), whom he considers his mentor. To judge her from **Daisies** (1966) and **The Apple Game** (1976) she is relentlessly facetious, with social observation confined to movies she has seen. Czech cinema, as we know it, is devoted to a recognisable world, in which ordinary people, by virtue of pursuing a career or an obsession or sex, get caught up in extraordinary situations – but not impossible ones. They are situations such as Kafka might encounter had he to traverse modern Prague. Where Forman, observing human foibles, is affectionate and funny, Miss Chytilová is simply tricksy. For a while it seemed that Menzel

hovered between the two approaches, but *Cutting It Short* shows him marvellously closer to Forman.

Our knowledge of the Hungarian cinema is no more complete, but it seems to me to be even more polarised between the watchable and the unwatchable – sometimes within the work of one film-maker. István Szabó (b. 1938) is one such. **Father** (1966) contrasts the battles between the partisans and the Germans in Budapest in 1945 with the uprising against Russian domination twenty-one years later, as experienced by one person, boy and man. It is clearly a personal film, with its grown hero perhaps finding maturity in his relationship with a Jewish girl whose parents died at Auschwitz – a matter to be set against his father's experience in fighting the Germans, with the inference that the present, Communist state, is the inevitable result of the War. The fact that the father's heroism turns out to be imaginary makes a discordant note, but this is an extremely well-crafted film. A certain flashiness points towards **25, Fireman's Street** (1974), which pictures for us the dreams of the folks living at that address. This being a movie from the Eastern bloc, the dreams have mainly to do with the war: but a dream is a dream is a dream, and the film was barely seen outside the festival circuit. **Confidence** (1980) presents the situation of a married man and a married woman living in one room, pretending to be husband and wife because of the War; it is just another artificial war drama of the many sent to us by the Eastern bloc, and less convincingly motivated than the similar *How To Be Loved* (q.v.)

In contrast, **Mephisto** (1981) has been enormously popular with Western audiences, and was awarded an Oscar for the Best Foreign Language Film. Szabó wrote the screenplay with Péter Dobai from the novel by Klaus Mann, which is biographical inasmuch as its central character is based on Gustav Gründgens, who married Mann's sister Erika. Mann made him heterosexual since homosexuality was a weakness in the Manns themselves; the book, though written in 1936, was not thought safe to be published until twenty years later. The content of the film is not exceptional, as it follows an ambitious young actor, Hendrik Höfgen (Klaus

Maria Brandauer), from a left-wing theatre group in Hamburg in 1929 to the position of favourite player of the Nazis. There are hints of sexual ambiguity as he cavorts with a black dancing mistress and marries the daughter (Krystyna Janda) of a professor, but he later refuses to flee with his wife to pre-Occupation France because he is achieving success at home. Hendrik supports the Nazis because they support him; he is an opportunist. Szabó's period detail is often sloppy, and some sequences recall the worst of his earlier work. Yet each possesses an inner momentum and the film as a whole, with its dynamic leading performance, has an energy reminiscent of the films of Andrzej Wajda (q.v.).

The first Hungarian film to be widely seen in the West in the postwar period – and indeed it was one of the first films from the Soviet bloc – was **A Sunday Romance** (1957), a period piece in the style of Ophuls, about a serving maid and the aristocratic journalist with whom she takes up, in the belief that he is the army private whose uniform he borrows to wear once a week. The director, Imre Fehér, in his first film offers the romanticism and irony we associate with the Budapest school of dramatists – he is also a playwright – leading us then to expect other, similar films from Hungary. It is a pity that we have not seen Fehér's subsequent work, and that we know so little of István Gaál (b. 1933), though neither has been prolific. Gaál studied at the Centro Sperimentale in Rome, which may be why he is more accessible than his colleagues, being one of the very few Soviet-bloc film-makers to put feeling before form. **Dead Landscape** (1971) is a slight tale of a young couple (István Ferenczi, Mari Töröcsik) who elect to remain on their farm when the neighbours move away because of the impending industrialisation of the region; in the isolation, they begin to drink and quarrel, leading to an unhappy arbitrary ending – which is offset by Miss Töröcsik's glowing performance.

Most film-makers of the Eastern bloc show in their work the difficulties of working within a totalitarian regime; yet most seem afraid to criticise the authorities, and they are equally reluctant to confer respectability by treating them favourably. Hence the number of films set in the past or in remote parts of the country – and István Gaál's excellent *Dead Landscape* seems deliberately to be set in a backwater far from contemporary events. The mourning couple are Mari Töröcsik and István Ferenczi.

1055

Occasional Bulletins from the Eastern Bloc

The bleakness of a socialist Hungary is a feature of Károly Makk's *Love* (1971), since this old lady lives either in the past or in dreams about her son, whom she believes to be a successful film director in America. The screenplay by the veteran novelist Tibor Déry is eloquent on the quality of love, as experienced by son, wife and mother. The latter is beautifully played by an actress of Déry's generation, Lili Darvas – in life the widow of Ferenc Molnár.

The best-known Hungarian director is Miklós Jancsó (b. 1921), whose powerful visual style is unaccompanied by any positive narrative. In his early films he took his camera to the lonely wastes of the great Hungarian plain, its grasses changing pattern as the winds move them – and somewhere in the distance, or swooping down towards us, is the cavalry. Judging from **My Way Home** (1964) and **The Round-Up** (1965), Jancsó likes men in uniform and on horseback; he also likes them out of uniform, and if for every bevy of nude men there is a naked lady or so she is usually being subjected to some indignity – such as running between ranks of soldiers as they whip her. The first film concerns some young conscripts straggling home at the end of World War II, and the second the rounding-up of revolutionaries after the suppression of Kossuth's rebellion against Austria. In *Sight and Sound* the Hungarian-born critic Robert Vas suggested that Jancsó's work is 'Kafkaesque', that he 'invites his viewers to throw away the pleasant, comfortable dream of Hungary's romantic-heroic past and face up to reality', but Jancsó's subsequent films, shown abroad to diminishing returns, do not show much interest in reality.

It is a sad comment that Jancsó's work has been available to us while that of Gaál, for instance, has not. Jancsó's wife, Márta Mészáros, is a feminist, and those who share her views may be responsible for the circulation of her films in the West. **Adoption** (1975) was awarded the Golden Bear at the Berlin Film Festival, which suggests

that the feminist cause is more strongly supported than many suspected. In it, a forty-two-year-old widow (Kati Berek) adopts a baby when she fails to persuade her lover to father one; she also gives shelter to a younger woman, encouraging the girl's own romance to such a self-sacrificing extent that the movie becomes sentimental and unconvincing. **Nine Months** (1976), set in a small industrial town, confirms that Mészáros at least is interested in reality; but I am afraid that setting a romance in an iron foundry and having a plain, surly-looking heroine are no guarantee of honesty. She (Lili Monori) is pursued by the foreman (Jan Nowicki) who is somewhat perturbed to find that she already has a son; their miserable courtship is concluded by her giving birth to his child, in graphic detail. It is no surprise to learn that in the sequel, *The Two of Them*, they are unhappily married and he has become an alcoholic.

Similarly, I fail to share the enthusiasm for **Angi Vera** (1978), which has been praised by a number of critics, possibly because it portrays life under Communism as grim. Its heroine (Veronika Papp) is an assistant nurse selected by the State for special training, during the course of which she offers herself to a married instructor (Tamás Dunai) – daring behaviour for an eighteen-year-old virgin in 1948. However, she turns against him the following day in a public denunciation which leads to her further promotion. Pál Gábor, who wrote the screenplay – from a novel by Endre Vészi – and directed, says that the theme of the film is that society can only be manipulated to the extent that individuals are willing to be manipulated. However, he would have had a stronger case with a less inconsistent heroine. We assume that the girl is stupid enough to mix sex and politics because she lacks insight, but since Gábor himself is ambivalent on matters of human behaviour, sexual or social, we are unlikely to trust his views on political thought. He is talented, but the sequence of the social evening, influenced by Milos Forman, lacks Forman's humour and powers of observation, and as a critique of Communist rule the film is far less incisive than Wajda's *Man of Marble* (q.v.).

The weakening of the allegiance to the Warsaw Pact is not a subject confined to

Wajda and his Polish colleagues. **Duty Free Marriage** (1980), directed by János Zsombolyai, is on the surface less subversive than *Angi Vera*, but it reflects a fascination with the values and materialism of the Western democracies. It is a Hungarian-Finnish co-production, telling of a girl (Mari Kiss) who persuades a visiting Finnish businessman (Tom Wentzel) to propose marriage so that she can get out of Hungary and join her real boyfriend, who has defected. Once she and her girlfriends arrive in Finland the plot lacks direction, but the film is fresh and often funny, with an added charm for many of us, since its leading characters can only communicate in their limited English.

The joker of the Eastern bloc is Pál Sándor, whose best-known films, **Football of the Good Old Days** (1964) and **Improperly Dressed** (1976), are both set in the years following World War I. The first deals with sport and movie-going and the second, less promisingly, with transvestism, detailing the exploits of a young man who dons female attire to escape his enemies. Sándor is another film-maker not interested in probability or narrative form, which may be why his attempts at humour fail so completely.

We know even less of the films of Yugoslavia. Those that I have seen offer a generally unsavoury group of characters in an environment with which it is difficult to sympathise. They have been made with love and care, they are prodigal with conceits and concepts, but do not satisfy either as entertainments or works of art. Several of the films of Dušan Makavejev (b. 1932) have been exported, but the only one to make an impression is his second feature, **The Switchboard Operator** (1967), a slim story of a girl who ends up dead. She is picked up in a street in Skopje by Ahmed, the public ratcatcher. He leaves for a while and she, having as she says a passionate nature, gives in to a messenger boy. Ahmed returns, goes on a bender, and she is killed while trying to save him from suicide – it being an irony that he is arrested for her murder. Makavejev explained 'Men live their beautiful, wild lives quite close to magnificent ideas and progressive truths. My film is dedicated to those interesting, vague, in-between spaces.'

The photographer on this film was Aleksandar Petrović, whose third film as director, *I Even Met Happy Gypsies*, won the Grand Prix at Cannes in 1967, but that did not, in the event, qualify it for a successful international career. Emphasising Yugoslavia's independence of Russia, Petrović filmed **The Master and Margarita** (1972), Mikail Bugakov's posthumously published novel detailing his own frustration with the Soviet authorities. Since it is virtually unfilmable, this movie, a co-production with Italy and with Ugo Tognazzi as the maestro, was said to be based on 'ideas' contained within it. It wavers between satire, fantasy and polemic, failing at each because it connects with no known world.

Special Treatment (1980), directed by Goran Paskaljević, is a better example of the treatises so often offered by the Soviet bloc. It recounts an outing to a brewery of a group of patients of a sanitorium for alcoholics, guided by their doctor (Ljuba Tadić), who believes himself a liberal but is in fact a tyrant. The film is an allegory: thus any Communist regime, paternalistic but uncaring, its citizens seething with revolt but forced to be quiescent. The doctor's methods are supposed to liberate the patients, but in fact they do not have the freedom which is so much discussed.

Of all the countries behind the Iron Curtain, Poland is the only one which speaks to us directly – and frequently. Before the War the U.S.S.R. was the only Eastern European country to sell its films in the international market with any regularity. The establishment of film schools in the countries of the Soviet bloc brought about a confidence in producing and selling films, but there seems to have been a greater vitality at the academies in Cracow and Lodz than elsewhere. One man gave impetus to the Polish film industry, Aleksander Ford (b. 1908), who began making documentaries in 1928. His radical views and wartime military films with the Russians earned him the leading position in the state film industry when it was established in 1945; two years later he became production chief, and during the next two decades he made occasional films until 1968 when he quarrelled with the Party and emigrated to Israel.

Among his pupils is Andrzej Munk

(1921–61), best known for his last film, **The Passenger** (1963), a study of life in Auschwitz, and particularly the relationship between one of the overseers, a German woman, and one of the female prisoners. The film is told from the point of view of the German woman, twenty years later, a sequence told in commentary and still pictures as Munk had completed only the Auschwitz section when he was killed in an accident. Other Polish films seen at this time include **Mother Joan of the Angels** (1961), directed by Jerzy Kawalerowicz, an account of the incidents associated with the devils of Loudon but transferred to Poland, and a murky melodrama until it gathers intellectual strength towards the end, confident in its anticlericalism; and **The Knife in the Water** (1962), directed by Roman Polanski (b. 1933), a sterile exercise in games-playing by a married couple and the hitch-hiking youth they pick up on their way to their yacht.

Polanski used the international success of the film to move to the West, and one of his co-writers subsequently followed – Jerzy Skolimowski, though he waited till he had achieved some success as a director, notably in 1966 with *Barrier*. In Belgium he made **Le Départ** (1967), borrowing from Godard his cameraman on *Masculin-Féminin* and his two leading players, Catherine Duport and Jean-Pierre Léaud, as well as his passion for photographing motor vehicles and some of his style. After his next Polish film was banned by the authorities he worked in Germany and Britain, usually in English, but with uneven results. Too often Skolimowski is careless and self-indulgent, but **Deep End** (1971) is a free-wheeling achievement of the sort one might expect of an admirer of early Godard. It is clear from its visual style and lack of humanity that it is the work of an obsessive film-maker. The plot, if it exists at all, is wayward, culminating in one of those senseless deaths which solve nothing; but along the way there are some good jokes and some refreshing improvisation. The setting is a convincingly antiquated London municipal swimming-bath (though the film was made in Munich), where the new assistant (John Moulder-Brown) develops a passion for his opposite number (Jane Asher) in the female section. Their adventures are dreamlike, bizarre and unpretentious in turn, with an adolescent sexuality of extraordinary intensity.

If Skolimowski's later films have been disappointing, those of his fellow expatriate, Walerian Borowczyk (b. 1923) have been disastrous – which may be no surprise to those unimpressed with **Blanche** (1971), which he made in France after moving there in 1958. After many years working alternately in animation, in which he was trained, and live action shorts, Borowczyk turned to features, but it was the third, *Blanche*, which brought him some reputation. It is based on a nineteenth-century medieval tale by another expatriate, Juliusz Słowacki, and since Borowczyk wrote, directed, edited and was responsible for the art direction, we may suppose him misguided, since it is a tale of purple passion needing a more vital approach. Using the same arid style for **Story of a Sin** (1975), made in Poland, Borowczyk manages to be as entertaining as he is irritating. Based on a 1908 Polish novel influenced by Zola, it is about a woman's emancipation while searching throughout Europe for her one true love; it is typical that that emancipation has become almost wholly sexual, with sequences which move beyond voyeurism to pornography. The decor is vivid and glowing, but ultimately pointless because the film violates all precepts about the people of that era, who surely did not behave as if on the stage of a modern strip-club. Nevertheless, on this occasion Borowczyk communicates a real zest for medium and material, however degraded.

The film includes one of the cinema's more convincing rape scenes, with the man holding down his victim with one hand as he tears his clothes off with the other, and it is similar to the one in **How To Be Loved** (1962), although it is hard to imagine a director more diametrically opposed to Borowczyk's methods than Wojciech Has (b. 1925). Has has a self-discipline so daunting that his work has perfection but little conviction. This particular film has a strong situation, as a middle-aged actress (Barbara Krafftowna) recalls the war years and the actor (Zbigniew Cybulski) who was hidden in her room throughout. The War also features in **Farewells** (1958), for it separates a student and the dance hostess with whom he has been frittering away his time. Has's most celebrated film is more florid, **The Saragossa Manuscript** (1964), based on the catalogue of stories by Jan Potocki, centring on the Peninsula War and first published in Poland in 1847. From the introduction to the prints in foreign distribution we learn that Polish audiences were as bemused as we are likely to be; but with at least fifty minutes excised, the claim that all will be clear by the end is not justified. The piece is a melange of intrigue, amour, duels, gothic miracles and stories within stories, insufficiently incisive to maintain a level more than beguiling. Has's star is again Zbigniew Cybulski (1927–67), whose exceptional talent and charisma brought him a following in the West until his accidental death.

On the strength of **Hotel Pacific** (1975), the talent of Janusz Majewski (b. 1931) is more positive. It is much like that of Forman or Olmi, gently amused at the minutiae of everyday life – and equally discreet, seldom venturing beyond the confines of the hotel itself and refusing to capitalise on the period setting, which is the Thirties. It is a 'grand' hotel and we see it first through the eyes of the new help, who begins by washing dishes, and we leave it as he quits it, on the point of becoming head waiter. I know of no better film on the subject of hotel life. Marek Piwoski's **Excuse Me, Is It Here They Beat Up People?** (1976) is set in and around a department store. It is a competent, minor thriller, notable in the admission that Warsaw contains some petty crooks; but although the title would appear to refer to the police, they are as avuncular and professional as one would suppose of a Communist country.

There is one director who, if we discount the veterans still working in Russia, towers above all the others in the Soviet bloc, Andrzej Wajda (b. 1926). The son of an army officer, he worked with the Resistance and then studied painting and cinema at the Lodz Film School before making **A Generation** (1954) under 'the artistic supervision' of Aleksander Ford. The generous title refers to the youth of Warsaw who struggled surreptitiously against the Germans; and clearly a new day is dawning as they have forsaken religion for the teachings of 'a clever old boy with a beard' as the subtitle archly puts it.

Tadeusz Lomnicki plays the lead; whether or not the film is autobiographical is difficult to detect, for it is academic and with little of the feeling Clément brought to *La Bataille du Rail*. **Kanal** (1956), a tale of partisans forced into the sewers of Warsaw during the uprising of 1944, is less demonstrative of their desperation than its own craft; but **Ashes and Diamonds** (1958), Wajda's third film on the Resistance – sometimes called 'The Wajda Trilogy' – is something else again. The skills learnt at film school have given way to borrowings – from German expressionism, *The Wild One*, *Richard III*, *La Belle et la Bête*, from Buñuel. The symbols are heavy – the moth in the interrogator's flame, the crucifix upside-down – but here for the first time is that vitality which characterises almost all of Wajda's work. It is both more immature and more literary – its source is a novel by Jerzy Andrzejewski – than the two earlier films, and it was artless to clothe the hero, Maciek (Cybulski) in the duds of Brando and James Dean so that he is not only a Resistance hero but a representative of the generation that followed. He is also a modern Hamlet, undecided whether to live or die because, with the War over, he no longer has a cause. Cybulski's playing deliberately disguises Wajda's refusal to make Maciek anything more than cynical and confused, despite experience of love and mortality and with his own death probable. Equally imminent is the struggle for power between Maciek's side, the freedom-fighters, and the Communists whose motives are no clearer, since their leader longs only for the good old days, fighting in Spain. Everyone talks in large statements, but it is a film for which all can be forgiven, since it is consistent and all-encompassing until the last couples dance drunkenly towards the dawn, to a Chopin polonaise played hideously out of tune.

It established Wajda's reputation in the West, ensuring at least a muted welcome for **Lotna** (1959), which is built around an incident in 1939 when a Polish cavalry unit charged the German tanks. Wojciech Zukrowski, who had written a novel about the event, worked on the screenplay with Wadja, but if either of them had deep feelings on this foolish act of gallantry they are not communicated. Nevertheless the images are memorable: a soldier with a rifle pumping an organ; a bridal veil caught on bushes near some corpses; a stuffed eagle smouldering after a fire; children rushing to pick up a German cap. **Innocent Sorcerers** (1960) was praised for the wrong reasons, but understandably so: as Dilys Powell said in The (London) *Sunday Times*, it was 'fascinating to learn that young people in Warsaw may carry on in much the same way as young people anywhere else – mad about jazz, eager for chance encounters.' The film was made under the influence of *Les Cousins*, but the milieu is less affluent and there is a happy ending (forced upon Wajda by Film Polski). Above all, it is a film of *copains* – with Lomnicki as the protagonist, a young doctor, Polanski and Cybulski as his friends, and a screenplay by Andrzejewski and Skolimowski. In similar mood, Wajda contributed to an episode film, **L'Amour à Vingt Ans** (1962): his section, about a wealthy girl (Barbara Lass) who temporarily adopts a local government clerk (Cybulski), is a worthy companion to Truffaut's, but the others (German, Italian, Japanese) are poor.

In a surprising about-turn, Wajda moved to melodrama – to a tale by Nikolai Leskow which Shostakovitch had used for an opera, some extracts of which are heard on the soundtrack of **Siberian Lady Macbeth** (1961), filmed in Yugoslavia. It provides proof that Wajda was capable of making a superb film in this manner, a declaration of huge passions which must be played out, before witnesses, to the inevitable, tragic conclusion; but more importantly what the film has in common with Shakespeare are its ambiguous motivations. Katerina (Ljuba Tadic), deserted by her husband and despised by her father-in-law, is seduced – after barely a look has passed between them – by an itinerant swineherd, Sergei (Olivera Markovic). Carried away by lust, they progress towards murder – he unwillingly, for he had planned to move on before becoming trapped in her malice. Like Macbeth and his lady, guilt alienates them from society, leading at least one of them to madness and self-destruction. Wajda uses the wide screen with the acumen of Kurosawa, whose *Throne of Blood* was clearly the inspiration. He is blessed with his male interpreter, for Markovic's Sergei is one of the great screen performances, vaulting many devious emotions with ease; Miss

Tadic is rightly plump, and ripe, but a little too equable as events overtake them.

Wajda's ambitions tempted him to the four-hour *Ashes* in 1966, but it was hardly seen abroad, while *Gates of Paradise*, an account of the Children's Crusade of 1212, made in English for a British company, seems never to have been publicly shown. On his return to Poland he made **Everything for Sale** (1968), dedicated to Cybulski, whose death inspired it – an attempt to define Cybulski's place in the Polish cinema as well as his attitudes towards wife, mistress and friends. A film actor disappears: his director, simply called Andrzej (Andrzej Lapicki) casts the actor's wife as his wife in the film he is making, and his own wife as the actor's mistress; he replaces the actor with another (Daniel Olbrychski), physically unlike him – but who will, he predicts, become like him in time. This is not a film about stardom and only marginally is it about fame: the myths about Cybulski are examined in such a personal way that they spread to Wajda himself, till the piece is also partly auto-analysis. The same themes are evoked in **Hunting Flies** (1969), in which a mild librarian (Zygmunt Malanowicz) is enticed from his wife by a glamorous, high-spirited student (Malgorzata Braunek), determined to turn him into a celebrity at whatever cost. The film has a dual ending – one of the few successful ones of the several attempted over the years – and both movies propound that mixture of personal fantasy and intellectualism on which other directors have foundered. Wajda succeeds because he has a hold on the real world and an ability rare in Western cinema – the Japanese can achieve it – of matching his images to the prevailing mood and yet against it at the same time. Where others lack self-control, he has a dozen ideas simultaneously; but he can fall into the same traps which await his inferiors, as in **Landscape After Battle** (1970), which gathers power to little purpose. Its setting is an army barracks, sheltering detainees just released from a concentration camp – who are, they tell themselves, a 'great moral force'. A bishop preaches platitudes; an over-emotional American officer makes promises; and a bookish young man (Olbrychski) meets a girl (Stanislawa Celinska), uncertain of her identity and her Jewishness. At the Cannes

Festival the film was dismissed, not unreasonably, as just another well-meaning statement on the aftermath of war.

The Wedding (1972) recounts the nuptials undertaken by a poet and a peasant girl in Cracow in 1908. What attracted Wajda to the piece was the opportunity to show 'class conflict . . . though this may not be clear outside Poland because of the local colour'. The drunken fantasies which intersperse the action may be saying something about Poland's bloody past, but this would seem to be a work unsuitable for foreign audiences. Its screenwriter, Andrzej Kijowski, claimed great popularity for the story in Poland – at least in the original play by Stanislaw Wyspianski. Wajda had directed that on stage, as he had **November Night** (1978), which he made into a television film, with Wyspianski's own collaboration. This darts back and forth between revolutionaries and Tsarist rulers in Warsaw in 1830, with a commentary by the goddesses of Ancient Greece and with startling imagery but not, I think, much content.

Land of Promise (1974) must also be ranked as a failure, a long and chaotic study of Lodz under Tsarist rule, its population consisting equally of Poles, Germans and Jews, with a protagonist to represent each. The Pole (Olbrychski) is an impoverished nobleman but is able to move into the new class of factory-owners and is last seen defying the striking workers and trampling their red flag in the mud. The film's source is a novel by the Nobel prize-winner, Wladyslaw Stanislaw Reymont, clearly on the side of the oppressed; Wajda clouds his own attitude by making his heroes exponents of gratuitous sex and violence, less gentlemen of the last century than contemporaries of ours. That said, Wajda's sheer energy, as always, animates his subject and the film is still compelling. Conversely, **The Shadow Line** (1976) is well-crafted but rather dull, due in part to Marek Kondrat's performance as the young writer. He allows us no glimpse into his soul, surely essential in filming this particular novel by Conrad. He was presumably chosen because of his ability to speak English, for this was a co-production – made in Bulgaria – with British television. However, the mysterious, nightmarish voyage is handled so well that it is a pity that it is not better known.

Wajda was later to claim that most of his early films were only made after battles with the authorities over either the material or his approach to it, which may be why at this stage he chose to work on uncontroversial subjects. Some young film-makers were not prepared to be so circumspect, among them Krysztof Zanussi (b. 1939), also a graduate of the Lodz Film School, who regards Wajda as the major influence on his work. His early films made little impression, including **The Catamount Killing** (1974), a German movie made in English, in Vermont, about a bank raid in a small town. International attention came with **Camouflage** (1977), a tightly constructed and complex study of master-pupil relationships. An idealistic young lecturer (Piotr Garlicki) finds himself in conflict with a cynical older one, and has to stand by while a student prize is awarded to an essay far less advanced and talented than the one by the rumbustious Raczyk (Eugeniusz Priwieziencew). The students had looked to the lecturer as the one uncorrupt member of the faculty and therefore resent him when he proves unresponsive, of necessity, to their demands for reform. The film's thesis is that society only survives by relegating those whose radical approach suggests changes to it. It had been approved because on paper it had appeared to be a comedy about the stupidity of university life, and therefore anti-academic, but when it was shown, in Zanussi's words, 'my actors looked like some real-life people, allegories intervened, a certain fuss arose. But then the Ministry of Culture, which was forced to defend the film because it was guilty of having produced it, ran up against the Ministry of Propaganda, which greatly disliked it. Eventually it was shown, but no one was allowed to write about it, and the posters were torn down two days before the screening – I couldn't have had a better publicity campaign.'

That Zanussi was a writer-director of power and perception was confirmed by **The Constant Factor** (1980), whose hero, Witold (Tadeusz Bradecki) is another young idealist. The son of distinguished parents, his job as electrician-administrator gives him opportunities to travel abroad. He is startled to find that bribery is needed to obtain a better hospital bed for his mother, and it is his integrity which destroys him, when he refuses to 'fiddle' his expenses during one of his trips abroad. The title refers to the Polish predeliction – or necessity – for compromise. In his spare time Witold attends a course in advanced mathematics and devises a quicker and more efficient solution than that proposed by the teacher, who explains to him that for some problems the longer, more circuitous methods are best. **The Contract** (1980) is overtly critical of Polish society only in its portrait of a government dignitary able to confer favours, but even more than *The Constant Factor* it looks constantly towards the West and never towards the East. All of the characters have a smattering of English, and one of them (Leslie Caron) is a visitor from England. She is a guest at a wedding, and Altman's film on that subject obviously inspired this. It is a comedy, not without symbolism, showing the guests' behaviour while awaiting the return of the bride, who has fled from the church. Most of them ignore the disruption of events and, indeed, the trouble between the young couple, which remains unresolved at the end. It is as though all of them are reluctant to admit that they are on the brink of revolution.

Both of these films were made as Poland seemed to be moving towards a freer society, coincident with the founding of the trade union Solidarity at Gdansk in 1980. The Polish people were encouraged to believe that the stranglehold of the U.S.S.R. was being loosened due to the election of a Polish-born Pope and the accompanying acknowledgment that the Roman Catholic church remained a power in the land. Zanussi was approached by companies representing Italian and British television to make a film about the Pope, **From a Far Country** (1981), which he accepted as a challenge. With *E Venne un Uomo* (q.v.) in mind, he makes the Pope a subsidiary character, concentrating on some imagined friends of his youth, and their reaction to events in Poland from the War to the present day. Zanussi was given carte blanche, except that he was required to use British actors so that the film would be widely seen. They do not convince as Poles and the film itself is banal, which is particularly disappointing as its director is one of the most subtle currently working in films.

Zanussi appears as himself in **Camera Buff** (1979), directed by Krzysztof Kieslowski, and *Camouflage* is held up as an influence on the film's hero (Jerzy Stuhr), a factory worker whose obsession with amateur film-making leads to the break-up of his marriage. It also results in him becoming the factory's official film-maker, which leads him into conflict with the bosses. This is a tale of integrity and the right to free speech, and those in opposition are, like those in Zanussi's films, petty officials, not so much corrupt as tired and afraid to rock the boat. The film, which is nicely made, has dialogue by the director and his leading actor, and it shared the Grand Prix at the Moscow Film Festival, suggesting that the jury sided with its young hero. Jerzy Stuhr also played the lead in **Top Dog** (1979), directed by Feliks Falk, which is somewhat fiercer in its denunciation of the authorities, and indeed it created a furore in Poland, coming as it did before the liberalisation. Its subject is the wheeling and dealing of show business. Danielak (Stuhr), a small town compère of gigs and concerts, discovers that the officials who can make or break him are as corrupt as he; accordingly, in order to placate or best them, he moves from hypocrisy to deceit to betraying his friends. He is another protagonist who looks to the West; and we may say that this film would have created no stir had it emanated from Hollywood – but it is a brave film, rich in the details of small town life.

Wajda also chose to make two films discussing the responsibilities of the media, **Rough Treatment** (1978) and **The Conductor** (1979). There may be something of himself in the two leading characters, one a prominent television journalist (Zbigniew Zapasiewicz) and the other a world famous conductor (John Gielgud, unconvincingly dubbed when he has to speak Polish) returning to his native Poland after years in America. *Rough Treatment* deals with the break-up of the journalist's marriage due to the wife's infidelity, and it was made, Wadja said, 'in a blind rage', with no further explanation. *The Conductor* examines the strains on a marriage as the couple concerned are affected by this visitor, whom they heroworship. The first of the two films contains a number of comments on the authorities, especially in the peremptory

The Eloquence of Andrzej Wajda

Andrzej Wajda is the best-known of the Eastern bloc directors, and many of his films have had successful careers in the West, from *Ashes and Diamonds* TOP, with Ewa Krzyzanowska and Zbigniew Cybulski onwards. His work is eclectic and includes such a roaring melodrama, as *Siberian Lady Macbeth*, CENTRE, with Ljuba Tadic, Olivera Markovic and, being murdered, Miodrag Lazovic. One of his finest films is *Man of Iron*, BOTTOM, with Krystyna Janda and Jerzy Radziwilowicz.

transfer of officials; the second, a minor film, seems to be a-political until the end, when the young husband (Andrzej Seweryn) opts for duty and diplomacy rather than emotion, so that his wife (Krystyna Janda) screams at him 'Those who do not love what they are doing are not free.'

Wajda's vitality and roughness of approach are fitting companions to his passion, which is in full flood in two of his greatest films, **Man of Marble** (1976) and **Man of Iron** (1981). Again the leading characters are media personalities who become caught up in greater events, but as written by Aleksandor Ścibor-Rylski both are examinations of the forces which have shaped the recent events in Poland and are still shaping them. In *Man of Marble* a film student (Krystyna Janda) chooses to make her diploma piece on Birkut (Jerzy Radziwilowicz), a folk-hero of the Fifties who has been not only forgotten but discredited. She is both brave and foolhardy, undeterred by the atmosphere of guilt and suspicion around her as she forces confessions from those who knew Birkut or watches the propaganda film which made him the people's hero in the first place. He was 'the original hayseed', a Stakhanovite bricklayer, selected by the Party, and with a party man to guide him. But if, as is implied, he is destroyed by his best friend (Michael Tarkowski), why does this gentleman also disappear, to reappear as a high Party official? Wajda wonderfully recreates the period, throwing it into relief against today's changed circumstances and wickedly parodying the official movies of the time.

This was a film that Wajda had been wanting to make for thirteen years, and it was promptly shelved. Because of it and *Camouflage* the Minister of Culture, Josef Téchma, was dismissed (though he was later reinstated). Both films were nevertheless nominated for the industry's own annual awards, and were the only contenders in the absence of any other entries. They won jointly, but Zanussi was on location and could not receive his prize, and the television cameraman who photographed Wajda receiving his award on the back steps was fired. The city of Gdansk held a festival of the now proliferating films critical of the Communist regime just after the settlement between Solidarity and the Government, and it was while there that Wajda was asked to make a sequel to *Man of Marble* – naturally enough, for its ending had connected Birkut to the December massacres of 1970 in Gdansk.

Man of Iron is less complex than the earlier film, but typically bold in referring to the December massacres more directly. In 1980 a number of unfair dismissals have brought about more unrest among the workers; they have closed the dock gates and there is a spontaneous demonstration at the spot where some workers had died ten years earlier. A mediocre radio producer, Winkel (Marian Opania) is sent to Gdansk to prepare a report on the activities there, which must reveal the striking shipworkers as counter-revolutionaries, probably funded by the C.I.A. Winkel finds officials prepared to lie to him, he finds himself under surveillance, and in the world where 'bosses' can be replaced overnight – in dramatic contrast to the free, open world of the strikers, who have now been joined by the students (after initial doubts, because the shipworkers had not supported them during student unrest two years earlier). Winkel is craven, but he is increasingly drawn to the truth, especially when he meets Agnieska, whom we had last seen making her investigative film about the man of marble. She is now married to his son, the man of iron (also played by Mr Radziwilowicz), who is regarded as the chief dissident. Winkel slyly stamps 'Solidarity' on his press card, and his problems are partially solved by the signing of the agreement between the Government and Solidarity, represented by Lech Walesa, its leader, who has a small role in the film as himself.

Like *Man of Marble*, the film is eloquent on the responsibility of the media in representing the views of the people – who want freedom as the English wanted the Reform Bill in 1832, 'the bill, the whole bill and nothing but the bill'. Wajda hurried to finish work on the film, in order to get it to the Cannes Film Festival so that it would attract the maximum world attention. It won the Grand Prix, justifiable if only because it is, like its predecessor, a superb piece of film-making. Zanussi commented that it 'brings a nobility to the cinema it has not known before. In Poland people have always seen the film as an official medium.

Wajda's film is the first radical proof that it need not follow official policy but that it really can speak for the people.' In Britain the critic David Robinson made the salient point that 'rarely, even in the classic days of the Soviet revolutionary cinema, have film-makers felt themselves so much the instrument of history as in Poland's current political upheaval.'

In the euphoria surrounding the film's reception in the West Wajda and the Association of Polish Film Producers announced an annual film festival in Warsaw, in the hope of interesting the West in Polish cinema and so wresting control from its present chiefs. An 'honest partnership' was sought with Film Polski, 'no different from that of any other progressive film industry'. The actual shortage of film stock in Poland, plus the Western money brought in by the films of Wajda and Zanussi gave them leverage in arranging co-productions with the West. As I write both are working in the West because of the martial law which was imposed at the end of 1981 as the first step in abolishing Solidarity. I cannot help reflecting that Wajda would have been wiser to have had his conductor, Gielgud, returning from the U.S.S.R. rather than the U.S.A.

This outburst of socially critical films from Poland has not only been the outstanding event of the film industries within the Soviet bloc, but important in its own right. The reasons for it are enormous, but I find no parallel in the freer capitalist countries beyond the work of a few people like Rosi and Costa-Gavras, questioning the motives of those who rule our lives.

Further, one of the most rewarding experiences offered by the cinema in the last three decades is to have watched Wajda move to a study of his society after having raked over the coals of the Second World War, at one time the preoccupation of nine out of ten films made in the Soviet bloc. He is one of the few outstanding directors to have emerged from the state film academies, along with Zanussi and Milos Forman: he crashed through the limitations on subject matter with the voracity of his talent, while Zanussi did it with his meticulous intelligence and Forman with his sense of humour. They may not be alone in this, but they are the only ones whose work we have been allowed to see.

If we add Bulgaria, Roumania and East Germany, we may suppose that the Soviet Union and its satellites produce over five hundred films a year, and most of the few bad ones that we see are bad for the same reasons. Granted the restrictions on material and therefore the insistence on proletarian subjects, the films themselves too often are merely films made for their own sake. The camera moves from one exquisite image to another; characters wander in and out of close-up, caught at their most provocative and intense; and somehow the results are all alike – despite the separate cultural traditions of these countries, including the conglomeration of nation states within the Soviet Union itself. Occasionally, even in a film as poor as *Improperly Dressed*, there seems a voice crying to be free. What happened in Poland should have surprised none of us.

38

Italy: Traditions Maintained and Betrayed

DESPITE THE INTEREST caused by the so-called neo-realist films in the immediate postwar years, the number of Italian films widely seen overseas was not large. By the Fifties, however, the directors favoured by the art-houses were as likely to be Italian as French. The two countries reacted in different fashion. French film-makers, producers and directors alike, remained phlegmatic about the chances of foreign distribution, but their Italian counterparts became over-enthusiastic about the possibilities. The activity-zone, after thirty years, lies littered with the debris. Those directors whose flirtation with international fame destroyed their artistic credit soon retreated. The two most aggressive Italian entrepreneurs, Carlo Ponti and Dino de Laurentiis, moved their activities to the United States. Unlike, say, Pommer in the Silent era, neither of them has had the least artistic influence and, as their ratio of failures to successes shows, it is doubtful whether audiences have ever given more than a passing thought to their capability as producers. The Italian cinema has continued to reflect the preoccupations of its directors, who include at least one of genius and a few of great talent. There are as many again whose gifts have been woefully misused.

Roberto Rossellini was the first to fall and the cause was not a producer but an American star, Ingrid Bergman, who had seen *Roma, Città Aperta* and wrote to him asking whether he had a role for her in his next film. While making **Stromboli** (1950) they fell in love, and speculation that this enormously popular star might be an adulteress won the film more newspaper headlines than any yet made. R.K.O. were to release, and the

company's sales chief, Ned Depinset, urged Howard Hughes to buy out Bergman and Rossellini's shares in the film, anticipating a greater success than *Gone with the Wind*. R.K.O. fell short by thirteen days of getting the film out before the birth of Miss Bergman's baby (the imminence of which had been constantly denied), and after lethal reviews there were no profits for anyone. In the film Bergman is a Czech, a displaced person, who marries an Italian soldier (Mario Vitale) and goes to live with him in his fishing village which, though remote and primitive, has many English-speaking peasants. Because she is of a different class, she makes no attempt to please him or fit in, and she forfeits sympathy further by trying to seduce the priest and the lighthouse-keeper. A documentary sequence on tuna-fishing does little to elevate this gauche and obtuse melodrama; Rossellini himself claimed that it was butchered by R.K.O.'s editors, but we may suppose the fault lay in inept handling, which their customary expertise could not disguise.

The urgency and social concern of his earlier work resurfaced in **Europa '51** (1951), with Bergman as a wealthy manufacturer's wife who feels obliged to become the conscience of the world; but so great was the *Stromboli* debacle that its good intentions were not acknowledged. With more justification, Rossellini's reputation ebbed away with the films that followed. Although he had staged Honegger's oratorio, *Jeanne au Bucher* or **Giovanna d'Arco al Rogo** (1954), in several European opera houses, he achieved little in the film version beyond a camera moving amidst purple mist, pink lights and fairyland angels. The English dialogue of **Viaggio in Italia** (1954) is composed of phrase-book sentences, which would matter less if the story, about a doomed marriage, were told with a modicum of conviction or insight. Instead, Bergman, lacking her Hollywood radiance, is a comic figure plodding around Pompeii and the Phrygian Fields, while the film itself perpetuates the tourist's view of Italy, its inhabitants feckless, cute, argumentative and mandoline-playing.

The Bergman-Rossellini collaboration concluded with the even more disastrous **Angst/La Paura** (1955), made in Germany – not inappropriately, since it is based (although modified and simplified) on a story by Stefan Zweig. Bergman is a married woman blackmailed by her lover's girlfriend, a predicament in which she behaves absurdly and which is treated by Rossellini without the least tension. The revelation that it is the husband who has initiated the blackmail momentarily rouses the piece from its torpor and only then does it make any point – though inadvertently, being affected by the off-screen domestic situation: he was Italian and she Swedish, and this German film emphasises the difference in the marital imbalance in their own countries.

The *Cahiers du Cinéma* devotees continued to trumpet Rossellini's work, in the face of public indifference elsewhere. **Il Generale della Rovere** (1959) temporarily restored him to critical favour but his films for television, shown abroad in some specialised cinemas, only confirmed the impression left by this group of films.

The career of Vittoria de Sica is slightly less disastrous, but more disturbing, since he was the greater film-maker. When the Italian film industry and critics rejected *Umberto D* as decisively as they had *Ladri di Biciclette*, he succumbed to foreign blandishments. Zavattini wrote **Stazione Termini** or **Indiscretion of an American Wife** (1953), to prove his theory that one small situation can provide a complete drama – in this case the prolonged farewell between a married woman and her lover at Rome's central station. These roles were at one point to have been played by Ingrid Bergman and Gérard Philipe, but Rossellini was unwilling to have Bergman work for anyone else; David O. Selznick still wanted to work with de Sica, and he saw the woman's role as ideal for his wife, Jennifer Jones. He constantly interfered during filming and so detested the result that he cut it to just over an hour for the American release. The critics disliked this particular alliance – they underestimated the intensity of Montgomery Clift, as the lover – and the seemingly impulsive direction, designed to build tension as to whether or not the wife will board her train; but the chief flaw is the English dialogue by Truman Capote.

A second association with Hollywood proved no happier, when Paramount cut two episodes of **L'Oro di Napoli** (1954), which it released in English-speaking territories. Originally the film consisted of six sections – anecdotes on such aspects of Neapolitan life as a bourgeois funeral, a pizza-stall, a chess game, written by Zavattini. De Sica (who had been brought up in Naples) himself appeared in the film, together with other professional players, including Sophia Loren and Silvana Mangano. Its reception further determined de Sica and Zavattini to return to the spirit of their great films: **Il Tetto** (1956) is a study of the underprivileged, played by non-professional actors. With customary affection it tells of a young couple, tired of living with in-laws, who struggle to build a modest home of their own. But the motivations of the postwar period were no longer valid, and the attitudes seem assumed for their own sake. There was also some softening of pessimism, to appease local critics, but they did not like the film any more than the others; and this time de Sica found little consolation from the reviews of their foreign colleagues. Like Frank Capra before him, his vanity stung, this celebrant of the common man turned away from directing; and decided to devote himself exclusively to acting.

He said later that the heart had gone out of him, and that was apparent when he was prevailed upon by friends – Carlo Ponti and his wife, Sophia Loren – to direct **La Ciociara** (1961). Her American career had failed to bring prestige commensurate with its attendant publicity, so Ponti felt that Alberto Moravia's novel provided an ideal vehicle, detailing as it does the sad wanderings of a plucky woman and her daughter during the confusion of the War years. Zavattini worked on the adaptation, which shows little more involvement than

Italy: Traditions Maintained and Betrayed

The decline of Vittorio de Sica is perhaps the saddest in the history of cinema, since from making some of the greatest of all films he went on to make some of the worst. *La Ciociara* is among neither, but it was deservedly popular and has many excellent sequences, including those between Sophia Loren, as a homeless mother, and Jean-Paul Belmondo as the student who befriends her.

the direction; but, dubbed and rechristened *Two Women*, the film was particularly successful in the U.S., where it gained Miss Loren an Oscar for Best Actress. De Sica was again in demand as a director, and he elected to make **The Condemned of Altona** (1963), with an English script by Abby Mann, based on Jean-Paul Sartre's play. Its subject is German War guilt as it affects one German family; as its members are played by Loren, Fredric March, Maximilian Schell, Françoise Prévost and Robert Wagner the film may be seen to be internationalism run riot, and, therefore self-defeating.

De Sica fared little better with **Il Guidizio Universale** (1962), a whimsical confection by Zavattini, concerning the fun and pathos experienced by Neapolitans at the immediate prospect of the Last Judgment; taking part in the vignettes which comprise the film are Melina Mercouri, Ernest Borgnine, Anouk Aimée, Jimmy Durante, Lino Ventura, Akim Tamiroff, Jack Palance, Alberto Sordi, Fernandel, Vittorio Gassmann and others – but since their voices are dubbed the effect is less disturbing than in *Altona*. Zavattini also provided the impetus, and Ponti the backing, for **Boccaccio '70** (1961), with four different directors handling stories which Boccaccio might have written were he alive today. De Sica's episode, written by

Zavattini, does not recall former glories, but since it loves life, sex, Italy and Sophia Loren it is the only one that Boccaccio might have acknowledged. Its humour is sly, but it is nevertheless a *jeu d'esprit* about a shooting gallery attendant who offers herself in a raffle to pay for her sister's accouchement. Its joyful vulgarity has nothing to do with Loren shaking her breasts or adjusting her bra-straps, but she does so in such exuberant manner that it is astonishing that Visconti's flaccid episode should generally have been preferred by reviewers.

Ieri, Oggi e Domani (1964) and **Matrimonio all'Italiana** (1964) are costarring vehicles for Loren and Mastroianni, produced by Ponti and Joseph E. Levine (whose company had distributed *La Ciociara* in the U.S.). The former is another episode film – about the working-class in Naples, a wealthy woman and her less affluent lover in Milan, a call-girl and her client in Rome – and intermittently engaging. Eduardo de Filippo wrote the first of the three stories, while his comic play – known to us as 'Filumena' – is the basis of the second film. Mastroianni's performance in that is particularly brilliant – a seedy Lothario, moustached and cigarette-holdered, who takes his mistress so much for granted over the years that he is surprised when she determines to prevent him marrying another. It is a film as Italian as *panettone* or *fritto misto*, but like *Ieri, Oggi e Domani* was destroyed in the dubbed versions shown abroad. However, while the earlier film is a little more interesting in Italian, *Matrimonio* is transformed. It is not like de Sica's masterpieces, but it is well-constructed and hugely enjoyable.

De Sica and Zavattini announced the end of their collaboration at the time of *Ieri, Oggi e Domani*, and in view of the quality of **Woman Times Seven** (1967) it is a pity that they changed their minds. This episode piece might just have worked if filmed, as intended, in Italy with Loren; but made in English in Paris, with Shirley MacLaine and assorted leading men, it fails at every level. **I Girasole** (1970) seems to have begun as an uncompromising endeavour on the part of both writer and director, albeit a vehicle for Loren and Mastroianni; the story, based on fact, concerns a peasant couple separated by the

War and her refusal to acknowledge that he is dead – and later that he prefers to remain in Russia with the woman he has married. The situations always seem less real than concocted, and it is doubtful whether the film would be improved with the removal of the Henry Mancini score imposed by Ponti. De Sica may have felt that the pessimistic nature of the material made it appropriate for him, but this is basically a romantic film, whereas his great films were cries against social injustice.

His indifference shows, and he admitted at this time that he only worked to pay his gambling debts. However, two among his last handful of films show that he wanted to retrieve his reputation before he died. He came to **Il Giardino dei Finzi-Contini** (1971) at the invitation of Arthur Cohn, its American co-producer, who was struggling with one of the six completed scripts. Its tone is that of Giorgio Bassani's novel, discreet and well-bred, with murmurs of menace, as the well-heeled youngsters of Ferrara in 1938 realise that their world is to be shattered by Mussolini's legislation against Italian Jewry. When the film won an Oscar as Best Foreign Language Film, de Sica said that it was the only one of his late films that he himself thought could be set beside the early ones. He went on to make **Una Breva Vacanza** (1973), an equally simple film which Zavattini wrote for him: a Milan factory worker (Florinda Bolkan) is sent to a sanatorium in the mountains, where she realises for the first time that people have values other than those imposed by her family, including her male chauvinist husband; the doctors treat her as a human being and some of the other inmates, more privileged than she, regard her as an equal. There are faults, but the film's triumph, as superbly photographed by Ennio Guarino, is that every shot has been freshly thought out so that we can share the heroine's experience.

Zavattini's early work with de Sica convinced him that he no longer needed to work on pseudo-Carné subjects like *Au-delà des Grilles*, and in 1950 he worked with Luciano Emmer, a specialist in non-fiction subjects, on *Domenica d'Agosto*, a semi-documentary study of a day by the sea. His quest for realism led him to the anecdotal, which resulted in an omnibus film, **Amore in Città** (1953), which represents

the worst and best of neo-realism. Falsely claiming hidden cameras, Alberto Lattuada's leering study of Rome's pretty girls is patently artificial; Dino Risi's portrait of a Roman dance-hall is dull; and Michelangelo Antonioni's examination of suicidal young girls is pretentious in form (interviews in a film studio), and ineffectual except in its revelation of the director's concept of futility. However, the tale of an unwed mother and her unwanted baby, directed by Zavattini and Francesco Maselli, and an anecdote about a matrimonial agency and its attendant dangers, directed by Federico Fellini, are riveting short stories artfully told. Returning to the form, spurred by the success of a French episode film, Zavattini made **Le Italiane e l'Amore** (1962), again with young or unknown directors and an amateur cast: but the emphasis this time was closer to fiction than documentary.

Federico Fellini (b. 1920) moved from neo-realism to its antithesis: a former comedy writer and gag-man, he was writer and assistant director on Rossellini's three most original films – *Roma, Città Aperta, Paisà* and *Il Miracolo* – and his contribution to **Luci del Varietà** (1950), co-directed with Lattuada, is patently the paramount one. If it is better than Lattuada's later films, it is also better than those of Fellini; but we recognise Fellini's preoccupations – the tatty music-hall milieu, the invincible third-rate vaudevillians and their occasional exploitation by the wealthy. Remaining among the lower echelons of show business, he offered **Lo Sceicco Bianco** (1952), in which a young bride (Brunella Bovo) deserts her husband for the blandishments of a hero (Alberto Sordi) of the *fumetti* (i.e. photo-magazine fiction). Staying with the lost and lonely, he devised **I Vitelloni** (1953), about some young layabouts in a sleepy resort, their horizons bounded by carnival, music-hall, cinema, dance-hall, and a regard for themselves which exceeds, from sheer indolence, their desire for the opposite sex. Fellini was a gently amusing critic of provincial life, and his love of it is apparent in his night-time shots of deserted piazzas, with the only light and sound coming from a small bar, almost equally empty. **La Strada** (1954) is set in just this kind of rural environment, and on the endless open road which is home for two unlikely

Italy: Traditions Maintained and Betrayed

The portrait of rural Italy in Fellini's early films is quite remarkable. *La Strada* concerns two peripatetic street entertainers, a Strong Man and his assistant, Giulietta Masina – whose uncertain relationship does not improve when they meet up with an old rival of his, Richard Basehart.

people dependent on each other, the Strong Man (Anthony Quinn) and his subnormal companion, Gelsomina (Giulietta Masina). Despite the film's popularity, their adventures have always seemed to me too strenuously picaresque, and Signorina Masina (married to Fellini) less Chaplinesque, as intended, than a lugubrious Harpo Marx.

In her other films she had often played a rather wry whore, and it is nice to be reassured of her talent in Fellini's **Il Bidone** (1955), an engaging tale of conscience and retribution among con-men, with Broderick Crawford and Richard Basehart joining Franco Fabrizi as the schemers. Because *La Strada* had made Masina an international star he fashioned **Le Notti di Cabiria** (1956) for her, with some basic pathos and clowning. Again she is a prostitute, smiling back at all male injustice – and meant to be, at the end, after her 'respectable' sweetheart has stolen her savings, the embodiment of the indomitable human spirit.

La Strada's Oscar (for Best Foreign Language Film) encouraged Fellini to spend several years planning an elaborate and harsh panorama of Roman life, **La Dolce Vita** (1960), as witnessed by a reporter

(Marcello Mastroianni) who has been rendered emotionally bankrupt by it. He stumbles from a call-girl (Anouk Aimée) to a drunken movie star (Anita Ekberg), ending at a particularly joyless, unenthusiastic orgy, after trying to recapture true values with either his father or his intellectual mentor (Alain Cuny), who sits around playing the most commonly known Bach Toccata and Fugue. Fellini's striking visual sense and his ability to indict the foolish before they have uttered six words, now begin to desert him: there is no rule which decrees that a portrait must be realistic, but beyond a quality of incipient self-disgust the film seems fascinated by its own eccentrics. Outside Italy, in other European countries, it was regarded as trite and, at 178 minutes, self-indulgent – until, that is, it reached the U.S., where it confirmed the puritan suspicion that Europeans were irretrievably decadent. American tourists were just beginning to over-run Italy, and certainly at that time the Via Veneto at night did suggest that all manner of debaucheries were just around the corner.

As social critic, Fellini was best on the small and shabby, on the hypocritical: his episode in *Boccaccio '70* is splendid, an account of a moral campaigner (Peppino de Filippo), so upset at the prospect of a sexy lady on a poster advertising milk, removes his trousers to fling at it to prevent us seeing it. For a last time, the grotesques were held in check; henceforward, the director would publicly confess his nightmares and fantasies, so intermingled with reality and memory that no distinction could be made. Carried away by autocriticism, he no longer needed a plot, and **Otto e Mezzo** (1963) and **Giulietta delgi Spiriti** (1965) are, respectively, concerned with a film-maker (Mastroianni) who fears moral and mental bankruptcy, and a film-maker's wife (Masina) who fears she is losing her husband – both told as stream-of-consciousness conceits, with an occasional bold image. 'There would be little to say on this subject were it not for the nonsense that has been written about it,' said Namier, anticipating the theories expended on such films. Even fervent admirers fell away after two limp historical graffiti, **Fellini Satyricon** (1969) and **Casanova** (1977).

When Italian television offered *carte blanche* to a number of directors for a film of their choice, Fellini made **I Clowns** (1970), and where Antonioni chose China. Fellini showed that he had no desire to wrestle with the world's problems, or even those of the individual; he no longer wished to 'speak' to us but, as in his two memory films, **Roma** (1972) and **Amarcord** (1974), only to himself, and moreover, at inordinate length. *Roma* has motorway carnage, borrowed from *Weekend*, two minutes' intelligent comment from Gore Vidal and a number of very boring fantasies from the nether side of Roman life: it is a form of cinematic masturbation, with a music-hall sequence ten times longer than any in *Luce del Varietà* but without an iota of its charm or amused observation.

The uncertain reception of most of his earlier films, and the near-oblivion that enfolded Rossellini, surely convinced Fellini that he must be noticed at all costs; the abrupt switch from romantic reality to personal fantasy was surely dictated by the superiority of Luchino Visconti, whose *Rocco e i Suoi Fratelli* (q.v.) competed in 1960 with *La Dolce Vita* and Antonioni's *L'Avventura* (q.v.) in critical discussions of the renaissance of Italian cinema. When **Bellissima** (1951) opened in London and

New York it was the first of Visconti's films to do so, and since few reviewers had heard of *Ossessione* or *La Terra Trema* it was dismissed as merely a vehicle for Anna Magnani. As a mother fiercely determined that her child should become a movie-star she is in almost every frame. The screenplay is by Suso Cecchi d'Amico, Francesco Rosi and Visconti, from a story by Zavattini, whose preoccupations are recognisable: the exasperated artisans, the outrageously cunning con-men and women, the hangers-on; the innocence of childhood; the lonely people in the deserted streets; and the compromises forced on the poor. The conclusion is little different from that of *Ladri di Biciclette* – that love and honour transcend poverty – to remind us that de Sica's great artistic vision could render Zavattini's observations universal, whereas Visconti keeps them Roman. Zavattini, drawn to cinema, and Visconti, drawn to opera, were less able to avoid cliché, and a striving for significance tends to obscure the satiric intent.

Senso (1954) is Visconti's first historical film, and as such an excursion into the genre against which he had been rebelling when he made his debut. It owes much to such forerunners as Blasetti's *1860* and Soldati's *Piccolo Mondo Antico*, which is not to deny Visconti's own claim that the idea was born one evening at La Scala, Milan, with a desire to capture on film both opera and audience. Thus it begins at the Fenice in Venice during a performance of 'Il Trovatore' in 1848 – for Verdi had been adopted by the insurgents – and Visconti found a story about a Countess (Alida Valli) whose adulterous passion for a young Austrian officer (Farley Granger) shatters her emotional attachment to the Cause, the Risorgimento. The plan was 'to mount a whole tableau of Italian history . . . to tell a story of a war which ended in disaster and which was the work of a single class', but both the Government and the distributor objected to the script, forcing Visconti to play down the defeat at Custozza and to change the ending, which was to have shown the disillusioned Countess disappearing into the crowd and a drunken Austrian soldier crying 'Long live Austria'. The present ending – the execution of the officer, after betraying his mistress – is suitable enough for this sad tale. Visconti, aristocrat and communist, sought only a limited truth, and one that was determined further by his emotional nature. He worked all his life at extremes, from *La Terra Trema* to 'Die Rosenkavalier' in the opera house, and it is perhaps sensible to dismiss notions of artifice and to revel in the images. *Senso*, as photographed by G. R. Aldo and Robert Krasker, is one of the most beautiful of Italian films. It is obvious that the officer's cloak was planned to swing in a certain manner, that the Countess's veil would lift to reveal just this much anguish, but all artifice is valid in the spell cast by this panoply of nineteenth-century Italy, its manners, morals and expectations, its costumes and its landscapes.

Chopped to ribbons (though since restored), it was hardly a success in Italy: nor, dubbed, and retitled *The Wanton Countess*, was it much admired in London or New York – for which Visconti must share some blame, since its writers, Tennessee Williams and Paul Bowles, are credited on the original Italian print. The experience of making it strengthened Visconti's belief that 'neo-romanticism' was the logical development of neo-realism, and his version of Dostoevsky's **Le Notti Bianche** (1957) resembles nothing so much as a Griffith melodrama re-set in Carné's prewar Paris. The waif of Maria Schell makes Giulietta Masina seem both modern and full-blooded; Jean Marais is the man for whom she pines, and Mastroianni the man who entertains her while she waits. The film's failure caused Visconti to return to the mood of *La Terra Trema*, and **Rocco e i Suoi Fratelli** (1960), he claimed, was 'a kind of sequel'. The title is a reference to Thomas Mann's 'Joseph and his Brothers', and the brethren are from Lucania adjusting to life in the industrial north. Each has a 'chapter' but the film concentrates only on two – Rocco (Alain Delon) and Simone (Renato Salvatori) – which suggests great changes between original conception and what is finally on screen. If what is there suggests a leaning towards social history, the end result is soap opera. A myopic vision, an egotism and values acquired from staging Puccini and Tennessee Williams in the theatre, have been imposed upon the will that forged *La Terra Trema*, and the film is coarsened further by the passing-off of handsome nonentities as actors, a homosexual seduction scene and

a particularly misogynous rape. As an exercise in style, owing nothing to the innovations of Antonioni or the *nouvelle vague*, it is absolutely assured. This was Visconti's own favourite film.

That style, and Visconti's absorption in the nineteenth century, combined to make **Il Gattopardo** (1963), from Giuseppe Di Lampedusa's novel, as impressive as *Senso*. Though Visconti lacked de Sica's feeling for humanity, Antonioni's vision and Fellini's flair, he had great intelligence and taste, using the second to advance the first. One looks in his work for verisimilitude, for he never sacrificed authenticity to beauty but strove for both. His reputation sprang partly from the social undertones, supposedly leftist, in his films, but he was moralist rather than judge – and, like other careful, serious directors, he never had the courage really to disturb his audience. He was happiest in the past: the Milan of *Rocco* is risible, but his Sicily in *Il Gattopardo* is persuasive, from the credits onwards, as the camera moves towards the mansion on this particular morning, a light breeze disturbing the curtains as the family kneels at prayer. Carriages wind across a dusty landscape, hunters stalk through a field of yellow corn; a town nestles on a hill in the sunlight; birds fly in the morning air. The set pieces are unforgettable, including the picnic and the final dinner party, taking up the last forty minutes of the film and symbolising, as the battle-lines clear, the end of one era and the start of another. One is represented by a *nouveau riche* merchant (Paolo Stoppa), and the other by the Prince – a portrait limited by Burt Lancaster's too-often too-knowing smile, but conveying the man's wit, for instance, as he looks impatiently at his wasted daughters plying their embroidery. If in the end, the film is superficial on the Risorgimento, it is, we may feel, marvellous on the mood of the time. Physical beauty alone could not make it the enthralling experience it is: perhaps it was meant to be a dream, its characters cocooned, despite everything, against the pain of change, as was the case with Visconti's last four films.

Cut, dubbed and reprocessed in foul colour by 20th Century-Fox – its huge budget having required the participation of one of the major American companies – *Il Gattopardo* was a disaster in Britain and the U.S. Visconti, with reason, disowned

Visconti's Re-creation of the Past

Although Visconti set out to be the leading apostle of neo-realism it was clear from his first films that he was a full-blooded romantic – and he was able to combine both aspects of his talent in his period films. Perhaps the most striking of them are the two set at the time of the Risorgimento, *Senso*, LEFT, with Alida Valli and Farley Granger, and *Il Gattopardo*, BELOW, with Burt Lancaster, seated, and Rina Morelli, in the centre of the picture. The former is in fact romantic melodrama, and the latter, taken from the famous novel, a study of the effect of the Revolution on an aristocratic Sicilian family.

this version, whereas the original Italian version ran for over a year in Paris. After **Vaghe Stelle dell'Orsa** (1965), an operatic family melodrama, and **Lo Straniero** (1967), an off-centre version of Camus' 'L'Etranger', Visconti contributed to **Le Streghe** (1967), a sketch film prepared by de Laurentiis to re-launch his wife, Silvana Mangano, who had been in temporary retirement. Visconti's is the longest episode at forty-five minutes and is set in a house party in Kitzbühl where a movie star (Mangano) is a disruptive presence. The script by Giuseppe Patroni Griffi and Zavattini sets out to be satire, but is directed in such a manner as to take the rich and worldly at face value. The episode directed by Pasolini (q.v.) is equally dire, and that directed by de Sica, with Clint Eastwood as a husband no longer alive to his wife's sexual allure, only slightly better. The whole film is redolent of the worst of Italian cinema and despite bi-lingual credit-titles (in Italian and English) was hardly seen abroad.

Visconti himself took to filming in English, which is to say that English scripts were prepared for those of the international casts who could act in that language, while the rest did their best – for eventual dubbing. **The Damned** (1970) was backed by Warner Bros., since once again the budget was high; the subject was also supposedly of international appeal – an allegory of the rise and fall of Nazi Germany, as represented by a family presumably based on the Krupps. It comes to life briefly, in a re-creation of the Night of the Long Knives, a fetishistic orgy of uniforms and transvestism that surely resembles a sequence cut fifty years earlier from *The Four Horsemen of the Apocalypse* – except, that is, for the nude men and their blood-spattered bodies, all of which are most pictorial. The cast includes Dirk Bogarde, Ingrid Thulin, Florinda Bolkin, Umberto Orsini and, as the anti-hero, a young discovery of Visconti's, Helmut Berger, who moves from an impersonation of Marlene Dietrich in *The Blue Angel*, through child-molesting, to mother-rape. Berger, exuding all the chic of a second-rank male model, fascinated Visconti, to the extent that he became absorbed in Germanic culture: and his version of Thomas Mann's novella, **Death in Venice** (1971), atoned for the comic strip that is *The Damned*.

Except that the profession of Aschenbach has been changed from writer to composer (based on Gustav Mahler), and that a short tale has been extended to 130 minutes, the transcription is a literal one, even to the camera abandoned on its tripod as Aschenbach is dying. In that role, Bogarde is superb; and the use of the adagietto from Mahler's 5th Symphony as an accompaniment to the crossing of the Lagoon is one of the most emotional moments in cinema history. It was such deep-seated romanticism which caused many people to respond to this film, even those with little sympathy for an ageing man obsessed by the image of a fair youth. In the U.S., the art-house public, until then wary of Visconti, finally yielded. Americans felt happier with the obscurities of Fellini's fantasies than with the operatic and possibly decadent intrigues of the remote Visconti, but of the two the latter had been more successful in reaching the general public in Europe.

Ludwig (1973), was his first film in many a year to fail in Europe, and in New York, when it opened, it was a joke-of-the-month, along with the remake of *Lost Horizon*. M-G-M, who had taken distribution rights, cut it from three hours to two before abandoning hope, and refused to open it in Britain (they sold it later to an independent British distributor). Visconti wrote it with his customary collaborator, d'Amico, and Enrico Medioli, who joined them for Visconti's last films. Like Helmut Käutner's film on the same subject, this one starts with Ludwig's death and then proceeds to examine his life – in a manner which is dissertation rather than study. The original screenplay, lurching back and forth in time, was not only fragmentary, but so structured as to emphasise its own banality: by eventually assembling the material in chronological order the piece builds nobly enough to its final section – dealing with Ludwig's homosexuality, extravagance and insanity. The matter of homosexuality is the real trouble: whatever technical innovations Visconti might accept, he was unable to treat the subject except in the manner of a lady novelist of two decades earlier – as composed of coy voyeuristic glances or an all-guardsmen party as decorous as a church fête. As Wagner, Trevor Howard takes the film as the magnificent professional he is, but

Visconti's habitually weak casting goes beyond Berger as the King: Romy Schneider is a vulgar Sissi★ and Silvana Mangano a wraith-like Cosima. As in most of Visconti's late films, the costumes, by Piero Tosi, are splendid, and the locations are spectacular – as Käutner had already proved, also using Ludwig's own castles for interiors and exteriors.

During the film's making Visconti suffered a stroke, and directed his last two films from a wheelchair. **Conversation Piece** (1975) suffered a fate similar to *Ludwig* in New York, where it was laughed off the screen at the city's annual film festival. Nevertheless it proves to be, at least technically, the handiwork of a master, which is all the more refreshing since at this time most films showed scant respect for the old rules with nothing new to replace them. Burt Lancaster returned to work with Visconti, acting less studiously than in *Il Gattopardo* as an ageing professor confronted, in his Roman apartment, with the puzzling life-style of the young – as chiefly represented by Herr Berger, an unabashed gigolo. The film provides a detailed study of the professor's mentality and is also a tale of suspense in the manner of *The Servant* (q.v.): but the professor's fixation on the young man having been established, he is allowed only one carnal look in his direction. Since the professor clearly represents Visconti, it is sad that he, so artistically courageous in his early career, fails to confront his own homosexuality on screen. He seems to have wanted to but changed his mind, which may be why this film eventually fizzles out in a number of pointless scenes. He was a contradiction in private life, for instance, insisting that his menservants wore white gloves to serve his raffish retinue while he expounded his left-wing beliefs. His later films gave no indication of these, and most of them are disappointing compared to *La Terra Trema*. I believe that his rivalry with Fellini and Antonioni intensified after they became international names, and that he made the sort of films they would not, or could not, make. He certainly showed the weakness common to many eminent directors, in that every film he made had to be an 'event'.

★She had played Sissi, the Empress Elizabeth, several times in her teens, in some sugary German films.

His last film, **L'Innocente** (1976), carries less of that aura, and it is both less and more interesting than *Conversation Piece*. It is not remotely personal and the story, by d'Annunzio, merely states the obvious, that in his time there were different rules for men and women in sexual matters. The film is an exquisite portrait of a vanished age, its pictorial style once again derived from the Academic paintings. The grand flourish is missing, but otherwise the film is representative of Visconti's work as a whole, leading us to suppose that there is nothing more here than meets the eye; so his career, resplendent at its best, ends with a sigh.

Michelangelo Antonioni (b. 1912) is the greatest of the Italians: with *L'Avventura* (q.v.) he changed the language of the cinema. Born in Ferrara, he studied economics and film – at the Centro Sperimentale – and was also journalist, scriptwriter and documentary film-maker before directing his first feature, **Cronaca di un Amore** (1950). The affair of the title is adulterous and doomed, since, as the couple (Lucia Bosè and Massimo Girotti) are only too aware, because of the unexplained and accidental death of a friend, a private detective is spying on them. They decide to murder her husband, but he dies before they can do so, which does not contribute to their happiness. With great intensity Antonioni already deals with what were to become common themes in his work: the role of fate in our lives, and our sense of guilt in being unable to control either. They recur in **La Signora senza Camelie** (1953), a morality tale of a girl (Bosè) too sensitive to be a starlet, and not talented enough to be a star; a failure playing Joan of Arc, she begs her producer husband for a second chance and when that is denied settles for dustbin epics and the clandestine liaisons of the also-ran. Better focused than *Bellissima*, it has moments of amusing, if awkward symbolism, as in the matter of the stills – Davis, Hepburn and Garbo as she makes her way to greatness, and Hedy Lamarr and Virginia Mayo as she is put in her place.

Le Amiche (1955) is, true to the title, a study of a group of friends – the high bourgeoisie of Turin, directionless, whether locked in love or out of it – as adapted from a novel by Pavese, virtually the only time Antonioni has not provided his own source material. **Il Grido** (1957) is not a far cry from Camus' 'La Chute', about a man (Steve Cochran) who disintegrates when one love (Alida Valli) leaves him and he can find no consolation with another (Betsy Blair). Despite this progression to international star names, the four films met with little or no success. I should also mention a deserved failure, **I Vinti** (1953), filmed in three languages, the French and Italian versions concerning juvenile delinquency, and the English, ludicrously, an egomaniac killer (Peter Reynolds) and an ageing tart (Fay Compton). The catcalling and laughter that greeted *L'Avventura* at the Cannes Festival seemed to close the file on Antonioni, though there were some who, fortunately, recognised a masterpiece.

L'Avventura (1960) was, to many, mesmerising at first viewing, and I find it so after seeing it several times. It is, like *La Règle du Jeu*, which was also misunderstood by its original audiences, a novel written with a camera. Renoir's film was not revolutionary, but *L'Avventura* is, for it tells a tale of self-discovery and emotional change almost entirely in images. The dialogue is sparse, and the image itself is less important than the spatial relationships of figure to landscape, of these Roman people to the Sicilian environment. During a cruise a woman (Lea Massari) disappears on a barren island whereupon her lover (Gabriele Ferzetti), an architect, and her closest friend (Monica Vitti) undertake a search for her: as the search seems increasingly futile, they realise that they have fallen in love. The film probes the nature of loving itself, and that is the adventure of the title. Its starting point has a multitude of sources – a trip to Sicily, a love affair dying and another starting, impressions of friends. Events occur, of significance only to these people, moulded as they are by families, professions, friends and circumstances: yet they are not really aware till they are fully embarked on their emotional quest, which will lead them to a greater understanding but no greater happiness. We are sometimes ahead of them and sometimes not, depending on the image, always demanding a reconsideration of the one before, be it as they search for the lost girl on the volcanic island or meet in a hotel lobby. In *Signora senza Camelie* the audience is privy

to a telephone conversation, and only when it is over does the camera draw back to reveal another character in the room, causing a reassessment of what we had just heard. Withholding information had been a device available to novelists but not, seemingly, to film-makers, originating from stage production: it had been used in thrillers, perhaps with someone hiding, to create tension, but Antonioni was the first to use it to demand an intellectual response from his audience. True, he has one of the elements of a thriller – a disappearance – but the distinctive and growing menace devolves from the audience's awareness of Vitti's and Ferzetti's own growing awareness. That is one reason why *L'Avventura* is the cinema's most perfect matching of form and content.

The subject of **La Notte** (1961) is marital malaise, treated not as a narrative, but as another situation to be quarried in every direction. The husband (Mastroianni) is a novelist and it is only at the end, as he and his wife (Jeanne Moreau) stroll into the dawn after a smart party, that they acknowledge, albeit clumsily, that their marriage has disintegrated. She does say 'I feel like dying because I no longer love you', but her comment that he should take the job offered to him so that his life can be his own is not what one expects a writer's wife to say: it signals a defeat as hauntingly absurd as the lover's comment on his own career in *L'Avventura*. It was with *La Notte* that Antonioni exerted the most profound influence on his contemporaries, and it has tremendous force, unlike his imitators. They noted the chilly nightclub, the tower-blocks and wasteland of Milan and the platitudinous party guests, without understanding that at the heart of the film is a theme, and it concerns the self-doubts of an artist. *La Notte* is occasionally schematic, a charge to be levelled at all of **L'Eclisse** (1962) – once, that is, it has been established that its heroine (Vitti) is so bored by one affair that she is impelled to embark upon another. The title refers to the eclipse of feeling in modern life, and though elsewhere Antonioni was able to analyse contemporary *angst*, here he only sets it down, having, I think, over-intellectualised every line of dialogue, every set-up and every object seen on the screen. The air of improvisation apparent with *Le Amiche* and *L'Avventura* has been dissipated, but Antonioni's ability to communicate his excitement with the medium was to return in the next two films – though it is of the second, *Blow-Up* (q.v.), that he would claim, 'All the others I did with my stomach, this one I did with my brain.'

Il Deserto Rosso (1964) does convey a sense of having been laboured upon too long, especially in those scenes set in a street repainted in the required pastel shades. A year earlier, Bergman in *The Silence* had set his tortured ladies in a strange city, and the lady out of kilter here is Miss Vitti, then Antonioni's muse and chief protagonist. Because her life is bounded by her husband, his job and their child, she takes a lover (Richard Harris): 'There is something terrible about reality,' she tells him, 'and I don't know what it is' – which gives the film its title, though the red desert may also be the dreadful manufacturing town of Ravenna (significantly we do not see the mosaics), or the dreamed-of Patagonia, or bed, or a place of longings and frustrations, or any combination of these. It is an ambiguous title, too, because this is a very cold film, rewarding primarily to those prepared to be patient with its pessimism.

Like Bergman, Antonioni is more interesting when he is dealing with a male protagonist, and the one in **Blow-Up** (1967) is a successful London photographer (David Hemmings), who is plebeian, disgruntled and bored. Unlike the architect of *L'Avventura* and the novelist of *La Notte*, Antonioni does not seem to care for him, though he is sympathetic towards his dilemma in wanting to take 'real' pictures of vagrants instead of artful fashion stills. He claims to be confined, but his life is surely independent, able as he is to participate in an anti-war march or entertain two girls who throw themselves upon him. At one moment, in a park, he hops and skips, liberated at discovering that life holds something more, literally, than meets the eye. For his life has been galvanised by having taken, in that park, a series of photographs which may reveal a murder, and also, even less distinctly, the murderer: is he then no longer a purveyor of the real, but a conveyor of the illusion of reality (like a film director) . . . and does the final, even more symbolic sequence, mean that in future he will see? Like the

protagonists of *La Notte* and more particularly *L'Avventura*, he is an artist, disorientated in a worthless society, being pushed by new perceptions into a voyage of self-discovery.

It remains an astonishing film, too big an achievement to be dated by its portrait of 'swinging' London, though it was perhaps that which made it so popular at the time. Ponti, who had produced for M-G-M, had no difficulty in persuading that company to invest four million dollars in an American venture, **Zabriskie Point** (1970). Such plot as there is involves a student who, because he thinks he has killed a cop, steals a plane to fly to Death Valley; and such perceptions as there are are superficial – on the vulgarity of Los Angeles and the ready violence and despair of the young. American critics howled in execration and the film was only little better liked in Europe, to the gratification of some, for Antonioni could then be dismissed – like Bergman – as a bored man who made pictures about boring people.

Antonioni himself agreed that the film was a debacle, and he was only able to work with M-G-M again when, under a change of management, the company agreed to distribute **The Passenger** (1975), with Jack Nicholson in the title role as a reporter. It begins, hallucinatingly, in the North African desert, and moves to London, Munich and Barcelona, before settling in Southern Spain. Antonioni's use of his landscapes had become somewhat self-conscious, but this is, again, a film about seeing: Nicholson admits, after he has assumed the identity of another man, that he was blinkered before. When he and the girl (Maria Schneider) reach their final destination she asks what he sees, and he replies that he sees, exists and acts: therefore he is. As Kierkegaard expressed existentialism, he has re-created himself, in this specific situation and environment. Antonioni's co-authors were Mark Peploe and Peter Wollen, the latter author of a treatise on symbolism in film. The film's ultimate failure has less to do with that than with having opted for the form of a thriller, leaving too much unexplained. That might not have been a demerit, were not the characters so dehumanised – another tendency of Antonioni's which has increased over the years – so that Nicholson's natural warmth is subdued.

Antonioni the Innovator

Michelangelo Antonioni changed the language of cinema, the first director to do so since the Silent days. He may not have been the first to realise that the medium might follow literature rather than the theatre in being selective in deciding what to convey to an audience, but he was the first to do so in extended form – and often to demonstrate emotional content rather than advance the plot. He experimented with the form in some of his earlier films, and finally achieved a magnificent flowering with it in *L'Avventura*, ABOVE RIGHT, with Monica Vitti and Gabriele Ferzetti. At its most superficial the film could be described as a thriller with no solution, but it was also about the malaise of modern life, and that was a subject to which Antonioni returned in *La Notte*, ABOVE, with Jeanne Moreau and Marcello Mastroianni, and *Il Deserto Rosso*, RIGHT, with Signorina Vitti – often called upon by Antonioni to help him express his feelings upon the subject. When critics began to carp about his pessimism, he tried, in *The Passenger*, BOTTOM RIGHT, to incorporate more mysterious elements than in any of his films since *L'Avventura*: and since in the meantime others had been imitating his film language this movie is not as rewarding as that had been. But it was very entertaining, and Jack Nicholson was excellent as the man who assumes the identity of another.

Italy: Traditions Maintained and Betrayed

Though audiences were as enthusiastic as reviewers, they were insufficient to enable Antonioni to find backing for his next venture, said to be very expensive.★

Eventually he put aside a number of projects to make **Il Mistero di Oberwald** (1980) because, he said, he wanted to experiment with the video camera. It is possible that the choice of subject – it is a remake of *L'Aigle à Deux Têtes* – was that of Monica Vitti, who plays the lead, for, predictably, it seemed one with which he was not in sympathy. He regarded it as a minor work and it carried none of his hallmarks; so it was all the more intoxicating, after his long silence, to witness again his marvellously individual style in **Identificazione di una Donna** (1982), however much this is limited to the clever use of sets and locations and deliberate obfuscation. He has said that its preoccupations are Italian but also universal, being, as the title suggests, about the nature of the loved one. A film director (Tomas Milian), while searching for the ideal woman to play in his – vaguely planned – next movie, has affairs with two women, in the process of which he realises how little he knows about either. The disappearance of the first of the women is redolent of *L'Avventura*, but in this case she leaves deliberately and he is perplexed as to why; there are references to the other earlier films, and in view of the projects which had foundered since *The Passenger* we may wonder whether this return to old themes was undertaken in desperation. It would not be the first time a director, stuck for an idea, has made a film about a director stuck for an idea, but Antonioni is too much a film-maker not to fill his work with a thousand concepts, even if many of them appear as symbols. He wrote the screenplay with Gerard Brach (Polanski's sometime collaborator), and some of its aphorisms do not bear examination – and I am not sure that its thesis is 'universal', that we can never understand the one we love. That has always been one of his themes, but, as I said, his richest films are those in which the male protagonists embark on a voyage of self-discovery: they were all aspects of Antonioni himself. It is significant that in making a movie about a movie director for the first time his hero understands himself

no better at the end than at the beginning.

As I write, Antonioni is making the first of two films with American backing; it had been shameful that a great film-maker was denied an audience while lesser ones were finding backing. In Italy there is less dichotomy between talented film-makers and less gifted ones. If we accept the declines of de Sica and Fellini as owing to exceptional and personal circumstances, an examination of any other score of Italian directors will reveal one good film – hence one international success – and several bad ones. The disturbing factor is that they have had better raw material than film-makers in most European democracies – or, rather, they have a stronger tradition of socially concerned cinema, despite the restraining mantles of Fascism and the Church. The Vatican seems not to have minded the sex dramas of the Fifties, since these invariably held a moral, and seems to have considered it prudent to ignore the increasing attacks on its authority. The fact that the majority of Italian film-makers was militantly left-wing was not a matter to which attention should be drawn, particularly as the more serious they were the more likely was their work to be appreciated only by the intellectual coteries of Rome, Milan and Turin; the fact that many of them were also homosexual was also a matter best left unacknowledged. The dual advocacy of freedom from both clerical control and sexual constraint is a recurring theme, implicit in the films of Antonioni, concerned though they are with city sophisticates – and it is there, in galumphing form, in *La Dolce Vita*.

The richest field for such explorations is rural Italy, and in particular Calabria and Sicily – and Sicily is the setting of a small triumph, Pietro Germi's **Divorzio all' Italiana** (1961). A count (Mastroianni) is married to a podgy, moustached and amorous wife (Daniela Rocca), but is anxious to bed his pretty cousin: since that would only be possible after a wedding, and since divorce is impermissible, he decides on the unlikely course of finding another man who finds his wife attractive, and then shooting her, counting on the courts to be lenient. In these crumbling palazzi the girls have pasty faces and the men, always lecherous, dark moustaches: their sexual code is expressed in Germi's

★He was reported at one point as seeking finance in Australia.

follow-up, **Sedotta e Abbandonata** (1964), 'A man has the right to ask; a woman has the duty to refuse.' Agnese (Stefania Sandrelli) is the girl seduced – by Peppino her sister's fiancé; a new suitor, an impoverished *barone*, is found for the sister, but Peppino then refuses Agnese because he wants a chaste wife. Leader of the brouhaha is her father, played by an actor whose resemblance to Raimu is only physical, in which context we may be reminded that Mediterranean attitudes to sex are indeed hard to fathom. Whereas *Divorzio all'Italiana* developed its comment on Sicilian family honour logically and hilariously this one is strained – a proof that most bucolic sex comedies are strictly for local consumption.

Among Germi's writers were Age and Scarpelli, usually associated with Mario Monicelli (b. 1915), and their **I Soliti Ignoti** (1958) – *Big Deal on Madonna Street* in the U.S. – was, with *Divorzio all'Italiana*, one of the few Italian comedies to be widely popular abroad. Most of those that we see concern sex, but noticeable in the lighter moments of serious films are notions which amuse Italians about themselves: their ability to charm themselves out of situations, their predilection for idling and their cunning when the best-laid plans go awry. The vast difference between the people of the South and those of the North is another source of humour, and that is the one missing element in this film. It might be described as *Rififi* in the Ealing manner, inasmuch as it is about a heist attempted by a captivatingly incompetent band of crooks (Mastroianni, Gassmann, Toto, Salvatori). Monicelli attempted to combine comedy and social comment in both **La Grande Guerra** (1959) and his episode, cut from foreign release prints, of **Boccaccio '70**, the first an unsuccessful juxtaposition of World War I carnage and the antics of an Italian Quirt and Flagg (Gassmann, Alberto Sordi), and the second some misadventures of a young couple who marry though prohibited by her boss from doing so. Monicelli manages this with light irony, offering a milieu of neon lights and cold efficiency, of traffic and loneliness, boding well for **I Compagni** (1963), an account of strikers in Turin in the 1890s and the birth of Trade Unionism. Industrial unrest had been a favourite theme of Italian writers, painters

and film-makers until Mussolini came to power – but then for a long while it was a subject avoided by almost all national film industries. The only exception I know is Hochbaum's 1929 *Brüder*, which Monicelli could hardly have seen. *I Compagni* lacks the passion of that and of later films on the subject, but it handles the matter entertainingly, with exceptional performances by Mastroianni as the professional agitator, François Perier as the involved local schoolmaster, Salvatori as the voice of doubt and moderation, and, playing against cliché, Annie Girardot as a warm-hearted prostitute. It is all the more saddening that Monicelli's later films are, at best, undistinguished, including **Vogliamo i Colonnelli** (1973), a gross comedy which applies the situation of *I Soliti Ignoti* to a group of officers planning a Greek-style *coup d'état*.

A similar progression may be noted with Franco Rossi (b. 1919), who made his international reputation with **Amici per la Pelle** (1955), a perfect example of the film sensitive, concerning the friendship of two sub-teen boys and the misunderstandings which bring about its end. **Morte di un Amico** (1960) is, in contrast, unconcerned with the finer things in life, the relationship this time being between two layabouts (Spiros Fokas, Gianni Garko) who live off prostitution – and in this case it would not be perverse to speculate on the exact nature of the friendship. **Una Rosa**

The comedies which tumble copiously from the Italian studios are rarely exportable, though the few that have been of international standard have been very successful indeed. One of them is *I Soliti Ignoti*, directed by Mario Monicelli, about a gang of small-time hoods who experience every possible mishap in trying to pull off a burglary. Among the gang were Toto, behind the jet, Vittorio Gassmann, Memmo Carotenuto and Marcello Mastroianni.

Italy: Traditions Maintained and Betrayed

While many of Mauro Bolognini's compatriots have startled world audiences with ambitious and/or sensational movies, he has continued to make quiet, often absorbing films, usually with a social theme, many of them set in the recent past. His sense of period is remarkable, whether filming in the streets or indoors: here are Jean-Paul Belmondo and Claudia Cardinale inside a Florentine bordello in *La Viaccia*.

per Tutti (1967) concerns a prostitute (Claudia Cardinale) who behaves in Rio very much like Melina Mercouri in Athens, and is depressing evidence that Rossi had abandoned the realism of *Amici per la Pelle* to re-enter the White Telephone era.

Among the second-rank directors Mauro Bolognini (b. 1923) holds an honourable place, since he seems incapable of making either a very bad film or a magnificent one. He studied architecture and screen design, with the result that his modern films are impeccable in appearance, and the period subjects considerably more than stylish; his social concern reflects the legacy of realism, though clearly he works in the literary mood of many years earlier – an ironic detachment leaning slightly towards the emotional and melancholic. It is a detachment taken too far: he refuses to probe beneath the surface and, lacking the melodramatic energy of Visconti, his films are often attractive but bland. **Giovani Mariti** (1958) concerns a group of young men, married but unfit for matrimony; and **La Notte Brava** (1959) returns to the theme, except that they are younger, and more inclined to stealing and whoring – with one young man prepared to sell himself to another. The wealthy buyer is representative of Rome's *jeunesse dorée* – a suitable expression, since the screenplay by Pasolini is based on French models. The hero (Mastroianni) of **Il Bell'Antonio**

(1960) also has a sexual problem, in the form of impotence. Vitaliano Brancati's novel, published ten years earlier, had hitherto been rejected by the Censor, which may be why this adaptation fatally lacks the edge of *Divorzio all'Italiana*. This particular Sicilian male has had an entirely typical upbringing, leaving him with such an odd concept of women that, confronted with the one (Cardinale) to whom he is married, he can only stand aside and worship. Sexual discontent is also the subject of **La Viaccia** (1961) and **Senilità** (1962), companion pieces: respectively, a country lout (Jean-Paul Belmondo) becomes enamoured of a girl (Cardinale) who is one of the most contented inmates of a bordello; and a bourgeois (Anthony Franciosa) moves towards self-destruction by refusing to accept the fact that the girl (Cardinale) he adores is at least a semi-whore. The source of the latter is Italo Svevo's novel, 'As a Man Grows Older', updated from the turn of the century to the Twenties – perhaps to differentiate it from *La Viaccia*. The views of Florence in the one and Trieste in the other, photographed in the rain and in harsh monochrome, are memorable.

The setting of **Agostino** (1962), from Moravia's novel, has been transferred from Viareggio to Venice – which is typical of Bolognini's approach. However, Moravia liked the film, with reservations, and reviewing in *L'Espresso* he mentioned that the small boy hero (Paolo Colombo) 'knows nothing, either, of sex or class . . . his friends make him discover, with pain, in a short season at the seaside, what Marx demonstrated: that in the depths of social and family relations there is no innocence.' On the one hand, he discovers that his mother (Ingrid Thulin) is having an affair with a wealthy playboy (John Saxon); on the other, his companions accuse him of something similar with the fisherman (Mario Bartoletti) who is their idol – and it was bold, foolhardy and romantic to make this man so handsome, masculine and sympathetic.

The mainly bleak period which followed for Bolognini included a number of the omnibus films in which most of these directors participated, including **Le Bambole** (1965), which was perhaps the most notorious. These compendia were invariably sexual in nature – advancing in such

1082

matters as the exposure of the female torso – on the assumption that it was more practical to test censorship with part of a film than the whole, since the offending sequence could simply be removed if required: in the event, censorship, more often local than national, was less virulent than the headlines and the theoretically heavy fines would indicate.

Bolognini eventually escaped from such projects with **Metello** (1970), based on a novel by Vasco Pratolini, one of his series covering Italian history from the 1890s onwards and an attempt at understanding the present by an 'enchanted remembrance of things past'. Since Bolognini has always shown interest in such matters, we may wonder whether he was in fact rather more interested in decor than in the forces which move society. This film has a wonderful evocation of turn of the century Florence – in colour – and that overwhelms the struggles of its worker hero (Massimo Ranieri), made militant by injustice on the building sites. If the film lacks the conviction of *I Compagni*, it remains to Bolognini's credit, for labour unrest was an unpopular movie subject, even at this date, in most Western democracies; and he does achieve more passion in a loose sequel, **Libera . . . Amore Mio** (1975). The source this time is a memoir by Luciano Vincenzoni, writing about his mother, an outspoken opponent of Fascism. She is Libera (Cardinale) – and that is the name given at the end of *Metello* to the unborn baby; and just as Metello was influenced by the example of his father, an anarchist, so Libera lives by the example of hers (Adolfo Celli). As the mood darkens, with battles between the partisans and the Fascisti, Bolognini proves to be no polemicist, though he may be admired for being one of the first filmmakers prepared to examine that era. **Per e Antica Scala** (1975), is also set during that period, and it is an account of a madhouse where, unsurprisingly, the physicians are as mad as the patients. As the sexually-warped head of them, Mastroianni gives an exceptional performance, as does Françoise Fabian as the new doctor who clashes with him.

According to its French producers, Bolognini's **La Dame aux Camélias** (1981) is the twenty-second film version of this tale. It is almost certainly the best. It dispenses with the play by Dumas in prologue and epilogue, but he is seen as one of the admirers of Alphonsine Plessis (Isabelle Huppert), who was the model for his heroine. The film follows her from life with her drug-addicted father (Gian Maria Volonté) and poverty in Normandy to the demi-monde and death – which comes not a moment too soon in view of her debts. She is portrayed as a predatory bitch, stupid and without real feeling, while her companions are completely lacking in morals and scruples. An air of eroticism pervades the film, and there are hints of unnamed vices. As the strange man whom Alphonsine marries, Bruno Ganz is superb – and the adjective may be applied to the art direction of Mario Garbuglia and the costumes of Piero Tosi. Another collaborator of Visconti, Enrico Medioli, provided the story for the screenplay (by Jean Aurenche and Vladimir Pozner), and it may have been he who influenced Bolognini to make this the most full-blooded of his films. The world of *La Viaccia* is small and cosy in comparison.

Bolognini remains virtually unknown outside the continent; when *Per le Antiche Scala* was shown in London and New York in 1976 it went virtually unremarked by the press. It is far from being Bolognini's best film, but it is better than any made by Pier Paolo Pasolini (1922–75), who enjoyed, at least for a while, a measure of critical favour. He began in films as a writer, including collaboration on *Morte di un Amico* and several of Bolognini's, including *La Notte Brava* – and these were two films he particularly disliked. His first two films as a director, **Accattone** (1961) and **Mamma Roma** (1962) showed him to be less sensitive than Rossi (at that time) and Bolognini, but considerably more spirited than either. The first is little more than a hymn to the then amateur actor, Franco Citti, who plays the eponymous hero, and were his close-ups cut it would be at least fifteen minutes shorter. The second is also a star vehicle for Anna Magnani, playing a prostitute who has to go back on the game, and the ending in particular is as rigged as any star vehicle ever made. The accompaniment of Bach and Vivaldi to the action, like the use of suburban wasteland locations, was taken as evidence of high intent. There are isolated moments of honest observation, perhaps because Pasolini's involvement with the

Italy: Traditions Maintained and Betrayed

world of pimps and *putanas* was as personal as a Genet (Pasolini died at the hands of a homosexual drifter, on a suburban wasteland). His background (his father was an army officer), together with his outspoken Marxism and cultural references were already admired by Italian intellectuals when he contributed an anti-clerical sketch to **RoGoPaG** (1962), in the form of a movie director (Orson Welles) filming the Crucifixion. The film merely proves that Rossellini, Godard and Pasolini were among the most inept directors then working (the fourth episode was directed by Ugo Gregoretti and his sketch is no more than a minor jape). Nevertheless Pasolini was convicted of offending the Church and given a suspended sentence. His response was to make a film of the Crucifixion himself. **Il Vangelo Secondo Matteo** (1964) benefited immeasurably from its shoestring budget, for that seemed to prove that it was a labour of love; and its favourable reception was not unconnected with the hugely expensive and lifeless *Greatest Story Ever Told*. As against the myriad guest stars of that film, Pasolini's cast was composed solely of amateurs. The Christ looked like an El Greco, and the disciples might have been models for Caravaggio or Michelangelo, which was the nearest the film came to achieving any weight. That Christ may have been a poseur is hinted at, opposed to which his teachings are offered more or less complete. But the emotionalism surrounding Christ becomes a negative virtue in Pasolini's hands, not in the least compensated for by the incongruous use of 'Sometimes I Feel Like a Motherless Child'.

Pasolini's inability to put his camera at the service of his text was further demonstrated by another adaptation of an ancient text, the **Edipe Re** (1967) of Sophocles, which he regarded as his most autobiographical film. Presumably he identified with this elemental man in search of his destiny – and since it was not his way to offer Oedipus straight, there are a prologue and epilogue to remind us, impertinently, that this is a timeless story; and this timeless story turns out to be rather like a comic-strip.

The achievement of **Teorema** (1968) was to dragoon the male crotch into the realms of art, in the guise of offering a critique on the bourgeoisie: it gets many a close-up as a guest (Terence Stamp) affects a Milanese household in a manner which can only be described as disturbing. He has his way successively with maid, son, mother, daughter and father, after which each begins to behave oddly. Pasolini's approach puts the film in the 'heavy breathing' category, but when I originally saw it the audience began to titter as mother took to picking up boys and one of them peeled off his shirt before throwing himself upon her. As she progressed to picking up couples the sniggers turned to laughter, and the audience remained convulsed, cheering and clapping, as the maid began to levitate and father, after resisting the come-hither look of a young tough, disrobed on a Milan railway platform, to wander bare-arsed on the volcanic slopes of a conveniently nearby mountain. It was abundantly clear that Pasolini was 'played out', and with **Il Decamerone** (1970) he 'sold out', moving on to equally salacious versions of 'The Canterbury Tales' and 'The Thousand and One Nights'. Only a minor squeak of embarrassment greeted his posthumous version of de Sade updated to the Fascist era to serve, as he said, as a 'metaphor', **Salo, o le Centiventi Giornate di Sodoma** (1975). Great art has rarely derived from man's degradation, but this film is by turns risible, as small boys prepare for buggery; pole-axingly boring, during long discussions on masturbation, etc., and repugnant, in its graphic scatology. Banned virtually everywhere – few cinemas cared to show it, and those which did drew scant audiences – its defenders were, unsurprisingly few and muted.

The influence of Pasolini and Fellini on their weaker compatriots has been disastrous – not to mention some down market films which attracted world audiences: the 'spear-and-sandal' spectaculars and the made-in-Italy Westerns which followed them. No reputable director wished to make such films, but the showy, empty style of Serge Leone, acknowledged master director of 'spaghetti' Westerns seems to have found its way into other films. Even veteran directors like Lattuada bowed to the prevailing vulgarity, and I pass over a great many so-called comedies, every ancient wheeze heavily over-emphasised, and photographed appropriate bright colours and modish manner. I mention the dire **Dramma della Gelosia – Tutti i Particolari in Cronaca** (1970), a triangle mix-up with Mastroianni, Monica Vitti and Giancarlo Giannini, only to show that a director may improve – in this case Ettore Scola, whose **Una Giornata Particolare** (1977) is a neat attempt, in near-monochrome, to deal calmly with homosexuality, in the person of a radio-announcer (Mastroianni) whose private life has brought him into conflict with the Fascist authorities; at least at the moment of seduction by a – drab – housewife (Loren) he looks suitably abashed. In contrast to Scola, Elio Petri began directing with discretion but moved in the other direction. **L'Assassino** (1961) concerns an imprisoned murderer (Mastroianni), whose relationship with his victim (Micheline Presle) is laid painfully bare; in similar depth, and in the same time-jumping style, Petri offered another murderer in **Indagine su un Cittadino al di Sopra di Ogni Sospetto** (1970) – that is, a 'citizen above suspicion' (Gian Maria Volonté) because he happens to be head of homicide, now promoted to Chief of Political Intelligence. As Costa-Gavras has proved, flashiness is not necessarily a deterrent to the enjoyment of this kind of thriller, but in this case the behaviour examined is motivated entirely towards that flashiness.

A more extreme case of a once promising director is Lina Wertmuller, a former theatre and television writer who moved from assisting Fellini on *Otto e Mezzo* to directing. **I Basilischi** (1963) was made for less than $100,000 on location in a small town in Puglia, with amateur performers. One of her backers was the group called 22 Dicembre, to which Ermanno Olmi also belonged, and her study of this Southern community is not unlike his in *I Fidanzati* (q.v.), that is, in the pure style of neo-realism, without either the satire of Germi or the lyricism of Fellini's rural studies. Gianni Di Venanzo was the photographer, though one should think only of him to explain its superiority over the lady's later work, for this is very nicely made. In 1975 New York discovered Wertmuller, and her half dozen films followed each other into cinemas, to virtually unanimous rave reviews. However, she remained unknown in Britain and France since, as both

Time and *Variety* pointed out, critics of those countries had seen her films at festivals, and were not, to put it mildly, enthusiastic. Of course, Fellini is, or was, 'big' in New York, and it is he whom Wertmuller was pathetically emulating, with her grotesques, imprisoned in their gross bodies and subject to indignities – which by some chance are usually sexual. Two stories intertwine in **Pasqualino Settebellezze** (1976) – *Seven Beauties* – and it is hard to tell which is the less interesting, the one about the concentration camp internee (Giancarlo Giannini) who decides to make love to the huge mannish commandant (Shirley Stoler), or his memories of prewar Naples, murdering and chopping up the body of the man who turned his sister into a whore. John Coleman in the *New Statesman* noted its American success, and said it 'looks like shouting, gesticulating, postured rubbish to me', offering the additional indignity of a three-line review. In *The Observer*, Russell Davies took more trouble: 'This is another lady – Liliana Cavani was the last – who seems to think that the most pointed way of illustrating a moral decline is to stage it as a kind of nightclub parody of masochistic sexual relations . . . It is my belief that this kind of thing raises interest in nothing more political than itself: boots, boobs, thighs spilling over the top of stockings, and degradation in general; and whatever else Miss Wertmuller does with her Warner Bros. contract,* it is certain to involve her in reproducing the odd bit of comparable tatty sexual charade.' It did, too: and since the film concerned was in English, American critics were able to realise how appalling her films are. As they had turned on Fellini in English (*Casanova*), so they turned on her, bringing them, in both cases, in line with the majority of European critics. As for Miss Cavani, I have not seen *The Night Porter*, to which Mr Davies was referring, since I saw the earlier **I Cannibali** (1970), a showy triviality – though deadly serious – with aspirations towards being an Italian version of Bergman's *The Shame*. I would not have brought the matter up, but it is beyond comprehension how either lady – *I Basilischi* apart – ever found backers.

*It was annulled after one film. When American critics attacked Wertmuller's subsequent films, they referred to the earlier ones that they had liked as 'dated'.

Italy: Traditions Maintained and Betrayed

Bernardo Bertolucci (b. 1940) was assistant to Pasolini on *Accattone*, but his first two films as director, **Prima Della Rivoluzione** (1964) and **Partner** (1968) are a precocious blend of Antonioni and Godard, though, alas, tending more towards the latter – not that either director is free of misogyny or hints of perversion – with a hero, in the first film, who has an affair with an aunt. Supposedly he is trying to come to terms with his Marxism, and since the film is set in Bertolucci's birthplace, Parma, it may be autobiographical; I could not tell you the subject of the other film, since it remained obscure when I left after an hour. Both films make political allusions, and are lavish with cultural references – Verdi, Shakespeare, Howard Hawks, Nicholas Ray . . . One character has seen *Viaggio in Italia* fifteen times and anyone who could sit through it even twice is likely to make films as awful as these. Amazingly, the first won the Young Critics' prize at Cannes, which led to (minimal) foreign distribution. Bertolucci did not acquire a reputation till his fourth film, **Il Conformista** (1970), and **La Strategia del Ragno** (1970), made for television. Each is still immature and employs the enigmatic, time-jumping style fashionable at the time: the enormous advance on the earlier films is due to the stronger subjects involved. *Strategia*, based on a story by Borges – transcribed from Ireland in 1824 to the lower Po Valley in the post-Fascist period – is an examination of heroism, as undertaken by the dead man's son (Giulio Brogi); *Conformista* is a study of a Fascist (Jean-Louis Trintignant), his political attitudes conditioned by suppressed homosexuality – a dénouement unsurprising after *Agostino*, since this is also based on a novel by Moravia, who publicly announced his dislike of the film.

Bertolucci's bankruptcy, moral and intellectual, was again apparent in **Last Tango in Paris** (1972), a dreary piece about a girl (Maria Schneider) who regularly turns up to be sodomised, with the help of a pat of butter, in an empty apartment, by a man (Marlon Brando) whose name she does not know. With dialogue and trimmings of similar persuasion, this footnote to Freud caused a sensation, to the delight of United Artists, which had taken the film for world-wide release on the strength of Brando's participation. The company proclaimed that it would be the most financially successful film of all time, but the sensation lasted only a few weeks, dying at the box office despite much talk of suppression and praise from two expected critics in London and New York, who claimed it an earth-shattering masterpiece. Consequently, they had to say something similar about **Novecento** (1976), this time to more general ridicule. This was Bertolucci's way of topping *Last Tango*, dirtier and longer – to the extent of almost 5½ hours, and the longest film with which a Hollywood company had been associated since *The Wedding March*. I should say several Hollywood companies, since it passed from one to the other amidst threats of litigation; and although we may again find some Hollywood names in the cast – Burt Lancaster, Robert de Niro – it bears witness to Hollywood's fascination with European production when the content is mainly sexual.

Bertolucci's model was Visconti, but he was more ambitious, covering no less than half of this century as experienced by rich boy (de Niro) and poor (Gérard Depardieu). As a political tract it is, in the words of Frank Rich in *Time*, 'maddeningly simple-minded', while as an entertainment it hovers between late Joan Crawford and Pasolini's *Salo* – and it manages the considerable feat of being even less watchable than that. There is a wedding ceremony during which the aristocratic Amelia (Laura Betti) shouts four-letter words before rushing off to the woodshed where she performs fellatio on the Fascist Attila (Donald Sutherland): discovered by a small boy, he and then *she* sodomise him before killing him by swinging him by his legs so that his head is crushed by the four walls – for which the rich boy allows his best friend to be blamed, despite his being miles away at the time. This was another Bertolucci film I failed to see to the end – in common with many others. Tried out in Europe, cut to 4½ hours in two parts, it was discovered that less than half of those who saw the first part returned for the second. Despite the respectability conferred by some festival showings, 20th Century-Fox and Paramount (taking over from United Artists) had given up hope by the time they opened it in the Anglo-Saxon market, and it was just as well. It was surprise to no one that Bertolucci's nex film featured mother-son masturbation, incest and a father-fixation, as well as the usual homosexual longings.

Following such examples the Italian cinema has developed its own school of soft pornography, where ladies have their silk underwear torn off by gentlemen, and turn to other ladies for satisfaction when the spirit moves. It is apparently essential that these tales be set during the Fascist era, or before, and be prettily photographed in the manner of Visconti and Bolognini. Typical are **Mogliamante** (1977), directed by Mario Vicario, set in the foothills of the Dolomites, involving a husband (Mastroianni) who, hidden in an attic, watches his wife receive a succession of lovers; and **Ritratto di Borghesia in Nero** (1978) – or *A Nest of Vipers* – directed by Tonino Cervi, concerning a boy who seduces his friend's mother (Senta Berger), who, on his defection, then revenges herself by seducing his fiancée (Ornella Muti). Of the same standard is **Pane e Cioccolata** (1974), directed by Franco Brusati, which starts out as a bright satire on an Italian waiter (Nino Manfredi) and conditions in present-day Switzerland, but is soon throwing conviction aside for a number of feeble jokes.

Brusati has ideas above his station. At least this film has a creditable theme – the reaction of an Italian to 'abroad' – and it is always possible that its vulgarities were imposed upon him by Manfredi, star and producer; but **Dimenticare Venezia** (1979) proves them to be his own. The twin themes of a death in the family and the return to the country home are old, and their treatment here is none the worse for being influenced by Fellini and Carlos Saura (q.v.): and what is new and different here is that they are experienced by two homosexual couples, two women of the same age and a middle-aged man (Erland Josephson) and his younger partner. Brusati deals with their sexual behaviour in a way which violates all known patterns, so that he repeats the nudes prancing in the sylvan setting from *Pane e Cioccolata*, presumably on the grounds that from such repetitions are the reputations of auteurs made. The younger gay man proving himself capable of heterosexual sex (he looks down at his organ) provides the most unintentionally funny moment in cinema since *S. A. Mann Brand*. This is an 'art'

movie, i.e. one in which life is subservient to mood, and both are subservient to effect. The amount of female flesh on display suggests that Brusati is either opportunist or voyeur; if he is homosexual himself, he joins the other gay directors in being able only to handle the subject dishonestly.

That this film is reputed to have won awards in Italy must be depressing to those film-makers who have tried to make films entertaining without recourse to salaciousness or Fellini-like excess. These directors include Nanni Loy (b. 1925), who made his reputation with **Le Quattro Giornate di Napoli** (1963), a decent reconstruction of the battle resulting in the German withdrawal from Naples, and whose best film is probably **Detenuto in Attesa di Guidizio** (1971), the story of an innocent man (Alberto Sordi) imprisoned by bureaucratic error – Kafka in a recognisable setting. Dino Risi (b. 1917) also works agreeably in a commercial context, usually with Vittorio Gassmann – whose performances can make his films worthwhile. The best of their later films is **Profumo di Donna** (1974), the adventures of a blinded, one-armed ex-officer (Gassmann) and the army student detailed to look after him: the interplay of character is so felicitous that one regrets the tendency towards the conventional elsewhere. Another actor of ease and authority, under-appreciated outside Italy, is Gian Maria Volonté, whose proud, cold Vanzetti in **Sacco e Vanzetti** (1971) is to be treasured: Sacco is Riccardo Cucciolla, the director Giuliano Montaldo, and the film is probably the best possible cinematic account of one of the century's great *causes célèbres*. The exposition is clear, the approach unemotional, and the film can only be faulted in its attitude towards the events which brought the pair to trial: Montaldo is certain that socialism and radicalism are beneficial to society, but he hedges on the matter of anarchy, clearly because he does not want to lose sympathy for his heroes.

The tradition of the Italian political film has remained not only alive but kicking, due in part to Gillo Pontecorvo (b. 1919), a former journalist and documentary director. His second feature, **Kapo** (1959), is a superficial portrait of life in the German concentration camps. **Queimada!** (1970),

Italy: Traditions Maintained and Betrayed

The films of Gillo Pontecorvo have been few and far between, and they have been variable in quality, but *La Battaglia di Algeri* is the best film about a revolution since Eisenstein. Unlike the Soviet directors, however, Pontecorvo is fair to both sides.

an attempt to examine the roots of colonialism, is fatally flawed – possibly because of the need to change the locations from Colombia to Africa during shooting, and the publicised dissensions★ with the leading actor, Marlon Brando, in a narcissistic performance as an Englishman sent by his government to exploit the natives. But between the two, **La Battaglia di Algeri** (1966), is a perfect example of the political film, presenting the facts in enthralling fashion and leaving the audience to draw its own conclusions. It treats with dignity and sympathy both the Arab population and the harassed French 'occupiers', condemning only the far-away and indifferent government in Paris. It starts in

★The experience kept Pontecorvo away from films for five years, after which several projects came to nothing. He says that he would have been more prolific had he been a novelist or a painter, 'but with films the possibility of being true to yourself is that much harder'.

1957, with the capture of the last free member of the F.L.N., and then tracks back to show both his joining the Movement and the methods of its leader, Saari Kadar, whose terrorism, as the French colonel points out, is to revolution what guerrilla tactics are to war.

If the film was to influence Costa-Gavras, we may see that it was in turn influenced by Francesco Rosi (b. 1922), who unlike Pontecorvo has been reasonably prolific. A former law student and radio writer, he was an assistant to Visconti on *La Terra Trema*, and he collaborated with Zavattini and Antonioni, among others, as well as co-directing two films before making **La Sfida** (1958). He said, 'A director makes his first film with passion and without regard for what has gone before,' but this is in fact a reworking of *La Terra Trema*, with the Visconti arias replaced by Zavattini's naturalism. The setting is Naples, Rosi's native city, and his purpose was to expose certain business practices in what he calls 'the tomato war', with local racketeers controlling the price paid for fresh produce from the hinterland. A small-time operator tries to move into the big time, but unlike 'Ntoni in *La Terra Trema*, whose motives were philanthropic, his are selfish – and on that the film fails, since the role requires a stronger actor than it has. **I Magliari** (1959) also concerns racketeers, and they are rival con-men (Alberto Sordi, Renato Salvatori) preying on their compatriots, immigrant workers in Germany. Sordi, like the protagonist in *La Sfida*, manages to antagonise his colleagues more than his rivals – and this was to be a continuing theme in Rosi's films. For the moment it means that both films end dispiritedly, and they are further weakened by an uncertain grasp of narrative – though that is partially hidden in the vigorous handling of individual scenes and the photography of Gianni di Venanzo.

Rosi, aware of his chief fault, as he admitted, avoids narrative in **Salvatore Giuliano** (1961) and capitalises on these two virtues. There is a superb unity of the landscape and people of Sicily, and it was this dramatic but non-fictional examination of the Sicilian bandit that made Rosi's international reputation, which grew with **Le Mani sulla Citta** (1964), at once a return to Naples – though a city itself is never named – and the theme of corruption. A property speculator (Rod Steiger) is unconcerned with his methods, even when an unsafe building collapses and claims victims. He is made to show care because an election is imminent, and as a result of that the Right joins the Left in the enquiry that is ordered: but too much is at stake to allow any headway on the part of the idealists involved. Rosi explained his purpose: 'What interests me passionately is how a character behaves in relation to the collectivity of society. I'm not making a study of character but of society. To understand what a man is like in his private drama you must begin to understand him in his public life.'

The statement explains why a planned documentary of Spain became, instead, the story of a bullfighter (Miguel Mateo Miguelin), **Il Momento della Verità** (1965). Di Venanzo's superb pictures of the San Fermin fiesta in Pamplona and of the *penitentes* in Seville were incorporated into a portrait of a poor boy attracted to money and fame – at which point Rosi has little more to offer than a show business tale of a jet-setter, Linda Christian, playing 'herself', whose main interest is in seducing the bullfighter. The wide screen and colour footage of the *corrida* were incomparably superior to those seen outside Spain hitherto (the most honest accounts were in some black and white documentaries, and even they were censored in most countries; but by this time it was calculated that tourism had removed the horror from bullfighting). Also filmed in Spain was **C'era una Volta** (1967), among the brown hills, an appropriate setting for this tale of a peasant girl (Sophia Loren) who beats twelve princesses in a washing-up contest for the prince (Omar Sharif) – very much a Mediterranean fairy-tale and, as such, successful; but Anglo-Saxon audiences did not appreciate it. They did not get a chance to see **Uomini Contro** (1970), though the English title was already chosen – *Just Another War*: to which the response must be that it is just another war film. The cast is headed by Mark Frechette, from *Zabriskie Point*, and there is no reason why this semi-amateur American should play an Italian officer except that Rosi anticipated an international success; the cost, in any case, was such that he had had to seek Yugoslav collaboration. The Alpine battlefield has been imaginatively and bloodily re-created, and photographed in steely colours by Pasqualino de Santis, but Rosi's urge to say something important – doubtless intense after the last two films – resulted only in cliché: that military men are fanatics and war is hell.

Nevertheless, it had been clear from *Salvatore Giuliano* and *Mani sulla Città* that Rosi would one day make a great film. The occasion presented itself with **Il Caso Mattei** (1972), which again takes the form of an investigation into the nature of power and its ally, corruption. Like *Giuliano*, it is as much a quest into the man's death as his life. Enrico Mattei, played in the film by Gian Maria Volonté, was a socialist and idealist who persuaded the Government to make use of the oil deposits in the Po Valley (against its will, for it was committed to an agrarian society and that had been a Fascist policy). From his efforts grew AGIP, the vast state-owned refining company, ample proof of his belief that the state should own its country's assets. As a state industry it offered advantageous terms to the oil-producing countries of the Third World, thus incurring the wrath of the competing capitalist oil companies. Mattei's singleness of purpose was a match for their deviousness, but the implication that one or other of them was involved in his death, in a mysterious air crash, is the whole point of the film. Its enquiry consists of the necessity of half-truths, conjectures, events conveniently forgotten, and even a sequence involving Rosi himself, finding himself stone-walled as he prepared this film. His thesis is dazzlingly worked out with regard to explanations of the complicated business and political relationships – and their expression in visual terms. The film is, he said, 'a critique and a commentary', adding, 'I believe that power should be constantly renewed before it has a chance to corrupt. And by corruption I do not necessarily mean evil but also doing nothing that might interfere with the pursuit of power. Keeping quiet, hushing up, if you like. I believe profoundly that there is something wrong, not only in the West, between the ordinary people and those who exercise authority over them in their name. And what is wrong is not just political but economic, cultural, religious, and military too.' He also observed that although Mattei himself was incorruptible he 'created around him an enormous amount of corruption because he wanted to hold on to power for the sake of his vision of the future'. Mattei's beliefs become meaningless unless we believe, as Rosi intended, that it is because of them he was done away with. Only hints are offered of the involvement of the Mafia (which did not care for an impoverished society becoming self-sufficient) and the C.I.A., neither of which are mentioned, and their links with American capitalism.

The film opened in America not long after it was officially admitted that the C.I.A. had been involved in assassination plots against certain world figures in attempts to prevent the spread of Communism. It was an almost total failure, a puzzling matter explained to some extent when we know that the distributor had lopped off the film's last ten minutes in order to destroy its anti-American stance. I happened to see the idiotic potted review in *The New Yorker*,* particularly unfavourable towards the 'new' ending, and find it incredible that so influential a journal was apparently ignorant of the excision – especially as the film had attracted widespread comment in the world press when it had won the Grand Prix at Cannes. In Britain a number of reviewers, including the normally perceptive David Robinson in *The Times*, compared it with *Citizen Kane*, which is like comparing a well-loved novel with a report on one of the multi-national corporations – except of course that Rosi's film is considerably more riveting: but the actions of real-life press barons affect few of us, while the activities of the multi-nationals do. Rosi used the investigative form again in **Lucky Luciano** (1973), which has Volonté in the title role, Steiger in a sub-plot about another dubious Italo-American, and Edmond O'Brien as a U.N. man. The American names did not help the film in the States, nor did a commendation by Norman Mailer that this movie about the Mafia was 'the most careful, the most thoughtful, the truest, and the most sensitive to the paradoxes of a society of crime'. Actually the film damaged Rosi's reputation, since, by employing arbitrary time-shifts, he made it almost impossible to follow: Rosi's old narrative difficulty had returned in curious fashion.

Whether or not he has solved this problem, **Cadaveri Eccellenti** (1976) is a film so rich, so powerful and so absorbing that it leaves the spectator breathless. His visual style is extraordinary – as Russell Davies put it in *The Observer*: 'Few directors select their shots with such flamboyant intelligence as this.' The characters scurry in the shadows of the huge monuments of Church and state, dwarfed by baroque façades and grandiose staircases – undoubtedly in Italy though the setting is not identified. Police headquarters are vast and modern; the inspector (Lino Ventura) lives in a poky modern flat while the legal eagles

*This magazine has a reputation for being wrong about movies. Not only did it originally champion *Last Tango in Paris* and the films of Lina Wertmuller, all later discredited, but it had to withdraw its original annihilating caption review of *L'Avventura* as it became accepted as a classic. (In fact, *L'Avventura* has appeared in each of *Sight and Sound*'s once-in-a-decade polls of world critics of the Ten Best Films of all time since it was made.)

Italy: Traditions Maintained and Betrayed

The vagaries of foreign distribution – and, if it comes to that, foreign appreciation – are curious, and while Americans were applauding the films of Lina Wertmuller, regarded as worthless by virtually every European critic, they were given little or no chance to see either *Il Caso Mattei*, BELOW, with Gian Maria Volonté, or *Cadaveri Eccellenti*, LEFT, with Lino Ventura, standing. Both are 'political' film-makers, but where Wertmuller makes her few and very obvious points with the subtlety of a bulldozer, Rosi, in these two brilliant films, makes every line and detail politically allusive.

whose deaths he is investigating live in overstuffed apartments reeking, like the churches and halls of justice, of centuries past. This is a film, rare in the history of cinema, in which location – as opposed to decor – is a character in its own right, commenting upon the action. There is a sequence in Lina Wertmuller's *Pasqualino Settebelleze* which takes place in the Muzeo Nazionale in Naples, and like everything else in that film the setting is obtrusive, gimmicky and pointless: Rosi stages his finale in the same building, and it becomes relevant to the action. *Cadaveri* is slow-moving for a film which could be described as a thriller, but that suits Ventura's style as he doggedly pursues a homicidal maniac before realising that more important, political, forces are at work. From interviewing small-time crooks he moves to the bigwigs – a Minister (Fernando Rey), almost certainly involved in the later murders, and a High Court judge (Max von Sydow), denouncing Voltaire and denying the possibility of judicial error. Finally Ventura finds the responsible forces, and they belong not to the revolutionary party, as in the original novel by Leonardo Sciascia, but to the Communists.

Italy: Traditions Maintained and Betrayed

Rosi's starting point was the 'historical compromise', i.e. the alliance of the Christian Democrat and Communist Parties, and while he considered 'the C.P. the only uncorrupt party in power, the film shows that in the end it too has to take part in the maintenance of a certain political power.' When I expressed to him some disappointment that this merely meant that power corrupts, he responded that 'it has relevance to every European country with a strong Communist Party, for those Communists must, as in the film, find a democratic way to proceed.'

Invited by R.A.I., the state-owned television service, to select a subject for filming, Rosi chose the memoir by Carlo Levi, **Cristo si è Fermato a Eboli** (1979), cutting his four-part T.V. programme to a 141 minute movie of singular beauty, and since the form is experience-related rather than narrative no great harm seems to have been done. In moving from the political present to the past, Rosi has tried to explain the film as 'a journey through my own conscience', the experience of a backward rural region, Campania, by a city-bred intellectual (Volonté), exiled by Mussolini for his anti-Fascist views. Since this man is political, but impotently so, the film retains all the mystery of Rosi's best work – an enquiry where at least half the answers are withheld. In this enquiry there is a respect for the historical process, but the usual magisterial blend of art and dialectic is softened by a sympathy much deeper than that of *Il Momento della Verità*. The occasional self-conscious shot that we associate with peasantry cannot mar it.

Rosi remained in reflective mood in **Tre Fratelli** (1981), which concerns a Southern family, a subject which he had wanted to tackle for some time. Tonino Guerra, the customary co-author with him of his later films, suggested adapting a story by Platanov. In the film three brothers, a judge (Philippe Noiret), a factory-worker (Michele Placido) and a reform school teacher (Vittorio Mezzogiorno) return to visit their father (Charles Vanel) on the death of their mother. The reaction of the three men to their childhood environment is beautifully detailed, but Rosi's attempts to say something about urban terrorism, in the form of flashbacks and flash-forwards involving the judge, do not seem profound – though given the political situation in Italy at this time his urge to make some comment is understandable. These two last films, incidentally, have received some acclaim in the U.S., but his two masterpieces, *Il Caso Mattei* and *Cadaveri Eccellenti*, remain little known there.

The sponsorship by R.A.I. of some of the country's best film-makers may seem curious to television executives elsewhere, their thoughts seldom rising above cops and robbers. The network does not expect huge ratings at home or great profits from overseas distribution, but believes that it is spending public money in the public interest. When R.A.I. entered **Padre Padrone** (1977) in the Cannes Festival, it drew attention to the work of the Taviani brothers, Vittorio (b. 1930) and Paolo (b. 1932); they wrote and directed it from an autobiographical novel by the self-educated Gavino Ledda, whose working life began as a lad herding goats in the mountains for his father – who represents all the *padre padrones* of peasant stock, initially unfeeling and later simply incapable of understanding the boy's need for learning. As a study of a young man's odyssey, or of deprivation, in Sardinia, this film is in the great tradition of Italian cinema, but is sufficiently rough and direct to suggest that the Tavianis were not looking backwards. It is touching and appropriate that one of the last actions of Rossellini, as president of the Cannes Festival, was to fight, successfully, for this film to be awarded the Grand Prix; he died a week later.

The Tavianis had begun as neo-realists, but seem to have broken away at about the time of their fourth film, in 1969. Their other best-known films, **Allonsanfa'n** (1974) and **La Notte di San Lorenzo** (1982), are made in much more florid style – and it is one, common in some of their compatriots, in which conviction and narrative are sacrificed to visual imagery and immediacy of situation. To judge by the martial theme music of both these polemical pieces they are a pair, concerning as they do political activists after the Restoration of 1816 and during the German retreat of 1944. The earlier film, which centres on a traitor (Mastroianni), grew from despair with the political situation, producing a climate – said Vittorio Taviani – leading to two opposing movements, 'one towards regression, the loss of self and of the world, and the other towards desire and the need to live with the world'. The view may be discerned in both films, if in more muddled form in the later one, and, coupled with the vitality with which they are made, they are eminently watchable; but *La Notte di San Lorenzo* is a retrogression from the films on the same subject made soon after the War.

The films of Marco Bellochio (b. 1939) have also proved uneven. He studied philosophy and cinema at the Centro Sperimentale, and for a while held a scholarship to the Slade School of Fine Arts in London. Both **I Pugni in Tasca** (1965) and **Nel Nome del Padre** (1973) are intensely Italian and Catholic, though their subjects – the family in the one and school in the other – are common to all of us. The family in *I Pugni in Tasca* consists of a blind mother, a daughter who is quarrelsome and possibly mad, and two younger sons, one of whom is an epileptic and the other mentally retarded; there is also an elder son (Marino Masè), the breadwinner and 'normal' – and it is for him that Bellochio reserves his contempt. One virtue of his approach is that he is not, like others who have treated the family as divisive, nihilistic; he works from the inside outwards, and his misfits are individually and lovingly conceived. The same is true of pupils and teachers in *Nel Nome del Padre*, but instead of the sustained invective of the earlier film he builds tension in a series of small vignettes. One leaves the cinema believing that someone's adolescence was like this – and glad to have experienced it at one remove. Bellochio's views are not entirely in accordance with our best hopes for the human race, and it is hardly surprising that he was drawn to Tchekov, in a version of 'The Seagull' made for R.A.I., *Il Gabbiano* (1977) – dark, Italianate and, in his own words, 'depressing', but as perceptive an interpretation of this comedy as we are likely to see. He would have done better to have remained with the classics, for the strife-ridden families of **Salto nel Vuoto** (1980) and **Gli Occhi, la Bocca** (1982) seem to be so for their own sake. Since the characters of both behave in absurd fashion, Bellochio's customary mysteries do not connect with life. At his best his excoriation of the second-rate takes him near to Antonioni, but with these two films he is of the level of Brusati.

That leaves Antonioni and Rosi, both pessimists, in the forefront of living Italian directors, along with the more cheerful Ermanno Olmi (b. 1931), humanist rather than polemicist. He has said (in an interview in *Sight and Sound*, 1970), 'Many of our men of culture who wish to express their ideas through the cinema, end by debasing the medium in this way: they put over their "message" in thrillers, erotic stories, romantic fables. This is not serious, indeed it is dishonest. I believe that one of the fundamental examples of absolute purity of culture is to be found in the Gospels . . .' One cannot imagine any of his confrères reaching for the Gospels, and in fact the prevailing tone of Italian cinema is anti-clerical: the clergy in Italian films tend to be either comic or like the hellfire shouting bigot of Vicario's *Mogliamante* – a far cry from the gentle parish priest of Olmi's *L'Albero degli Zoccoli* (q.v.). Olmi is not typical of Italian film-makers for he is neither 'intellectual' nor well-born, and he lives in a small town in the North of the country, believing that one of his strengths lies in his isolation from Cinecittà. In the polarisation of Italian thought since the War, he is now the only cinema representative – though Rosi's films have become increasingly humanist – of his side, drawn by instinct and upbringing rather than 'the hope of prolonging the feeling of solidarity with the working-class experienced during the Resistance', as Adrian Lyttelton put it in the *New Statesman* in 1979, speaking of the artists of the previous generation. Olmi says he makes films 'because I desire to talk about the reality of the times in which I live, in other words I desire to express ideas and propose them to the largest number of people': in the first part of the sentence we can see Zavattini's creed made a quarter of a century before, 'The important thing is to see.'

Zavattini's primary themes of earning a living, of coping, recur in all of Olmi's films. While working as a clerk for Edison Volta Olmi had persuaded the company to let him become involved with its industrial shorts and while doing so he conceived the idea for his first feature, **Il Tempo si è Fermato** (1959), about two men in a small encampment high in the Alpine snows, watching over an unfinished dam till work can recommence in the spring. One is probably in his forties and the other is a

Olmi, the True Heir of Neo-realism

Ermanno Olmi lives and works away from the mainstream of the Italian film industry, which may be why, after twenty years, his vision remains so fresh – or that may have something to do with his entry in the film industry. He was a mere clerk with the Edison company when he was rewarded with the official gift of a 16mm camera for his work with the firm's dramatic society – and he persuaded the company to put him in charge of the company's documentary films. *Il Posto*, BELOW RIGHT, his first 'commercial' film, was based on his experiences with Edison, as was the office-party sequence in *I Fidanzati*, RIGHT. Among his superb later films is *Il Recuperanti*, BELOW FAR RIGHT, about two men scavenging for metal embedded in the hills after wartime battles there. All the players are amateurs.

newcomer, perhaps a student, since he says that he plans to spend the winter studying. The film's subject is no more than their reaction to each other, in this admittedly strange environment. Neither is very communicative, but it is the younger man who makes tentative gestures of friendliness. Since there is no plot, Olmi should not have a climax, but he manages one – a particularly wild stormy night when the boy thinks he has 'flu: and all that happens is that the older man begins to feel fatherly towards him. The delicacy with which the film is handled is remarkable, its humour slight but memorable – as when each of the men takes a surreptitious peep at the other's book to see what he is reading. Also astonishing is Olmi's confidence that we might treasure the least emotion, the least detail of the daily grind, if it is presented sympathetically.

Il Posto (1961) is precisely about one man's first job, and it is confessedly autobiographical, clearly the reason it captures so accurately adolescent fears of interviews, the boss, colleagues. The piece is primarily a comedy, ironic rather than satirical, especially in the brilliantly observed office party. A coda finds the boy moving upwards in the office hierarchy, probably never to lose either aspirations or frustrations. The malevolent universe of the de Sica-Zavattini films was leavened by humour since there was no hope for their peasants in this world and precious little in the next, but Olmi uses his humour to show that his characters neither start nor finish despairingly. His world is not especially harsh and contains nothing like the venal businessmen of *Miracolo a Milano*: but increasingly in his films, as in Rosi's, there is a tension between the mere fact of existence and a world in which so much is beyond comprehension. His subject is not character, but experience, and in **I Fidanzati** (1963) his hero, Giovanni, looks about him in the same puzzled attempt at understanding as the young hero of *Il Posto*: he is a Northerner sent to work in Sicily and to him it is, at first, a very strange place.

E Venne un Uomo (1964) is firstly about a boy's experience of learning and later becomes a study in vocation – of a man very much open to the thoughts of others; but this tribute to Pope John XXIII is Olmi's one failure. Working, for the

only time in his feature career, with a major collaborator – Vincenzo Labella, producer and co-scenarist – he devised a film part-documentary and part-dramatisation, with Rod Steiger, appearing humbly honoured to be present. But he remains a movie star, an unsuitable representative of John as priest or Pope: the commentary he speaks and the visuals which include him, move on different levels, and what should be a unifying force is in fact divisive, so that the spiritual struggles detailed in 'Journal of a Soul' – the source of the screenplay – remain resolutely beyond the film's grasp. Olmi blamed himself for the film's failure, believing the conception right but that it was a mistake to make a film which was 'all thought'. It was popular in Italy, but its failure elsewhere effectively closed most foreign markets to Olmi.

That failure may be the reason why in his subsequent films there is no longer any levity during the working day. Olmi refuses to satirise the advertising office which is the setting of **Un Certo Giorno** (1969): instead he concentrates on one man's quest for fulfilment – which means, firstly, an adjustment of his sense of guilt towards his wife and colleagues, and, secondly, attempts to avoid boredom. The theme, said Olmi, is 'that of a man responsible in the face of his own reality', and much of the film was improvised after he had watched the amateurs in the cast 're-creating' themselves; but it was, he said, not *cinéma vérité*, in which you accept whatever reality is thrown at you. I was at the disposition of this particular reality and I provoked it to carry forward the theme that interested me.' The theme of **I Recuperanti** (1970) is that of *Il Tempo si è Fermato*, developed further, with greater disparity between the ages of the two men. They are scavengers, working in the mountains in search of scrap metal left from the battles of the First World War – and that was what the older actor had done in life. He had, said Olmi, 'that baggage of experience which the character we had "invented" in our script should carry with him. The real Toni then took over from our literary creation.' Since *I Recuperanti* is an affirmation, after the doubt of *Un Certo Giorno*, the old man's experience may have coloured the finished film more than intended. The time is hard and the terrain wayward, but the working alliance between the old man and his young apprentice, an army veteran (of the Second World War) is as enlivening for us as for them – no Zorba-like confrontation, nor is the old man Boudu, though Renoir comes fleetingly to mind while watching Olmi's films. Olmi has 'an unmistakable leaning towards the positive qualities of man's condition in a world prone to cynicism and destructive violence' was *Variety*'s touching comment on **Durante l'Estate** (1971), which, after the earlier films, is something of a confection. Its protagonist is an elderly drop-out who colours maps to turn an honest lira, living in what he describes as a world of colours – and that is his downfall, since he feels the same way about people, or some of them, and is ready to cater to their fantasies. His reality has nothing to do with the Milanese who scurry around him, but his view is examined and found valid before he is returned to obscurity.

Olmi's films are about the ability to see and to feel, which is why so many of them feature encounters with strangers or unexpected meetings with old friends. In **La Circostanza** (1974) several members of a family are forced into new perceptions. In dealing again with people of the middle class, Olmi discards affection and humour, thus moving closer to Antonioni's work; he has adopted a similarly elliptical style, but hardly seems comfortable with it. He may have realised this, since **L'Albero degli Zoccoli** (1978) – *The Tree of Wooden Clogs* – is the most literal of his films. It is based on stories he heard as a boy, and its key 'is the permanence of the relationship between God's land and the people who farm it'. It portrays a way of life now being eroded (by television, by the refusal of youngsters to stay on the land). It is likely that it could not have been made later, since by then recollections would have become third hand, and it could not have been made earlier because the old film-stocks do require artificial lighting which would have imposed a certain theatricality. For all the basis in fact, the film's courtship recalls that in *Due Soldi di Speranza*, though that may be because of the similarity of wooing habits; the ending – the banishment of the family – which resembles the 'hopeless' endings of the early neo-realist films, does have its roots elsewhere; the solidarity of the peasants is like that of *Distant Thunder* (and Satyajit Ray has spoken of his debt to the neo-realists). The film, I think, lacks the flair of Sjöström's rural tales, but it is surely a beautiful counterpoint to most other retellings of the Italian past.

Frank Rich in *Time* was certain that Olmi was no fan of Bertolucci's *Novecento*, adding 'There is nothing wrong with Olmi's decision to avoid the contrivances of narrative and ideology, as long as he then goes on to reveal the truth about his characters. This he has not done.' Since that is something essential to Olmi's work up to then, he presumably had his reasons for not doing so on this occasion. He can be dangerously slow, and sometimes long-winded but, to use an analogy I think he might like, his films are like a church in which the lamps are being gradually lit: as the small lives he is examining will be illuminated. In *The New York Times*, Vincent Canby wrote a piece explaining why he could not yet be certain whether *L'Albero degli Zoccoli* was a masterpiece. I do not know either: but I have no reservations about *Il Posto*, *I Fidanzati*, *Un Certo Giorno*, *I Recuperanti* and *Durante l'Estate*. They are wonderful films.

Olmi had been backed, since *I Recuperanti*, by R.A.I., who were awarded a second consecutive Grand Prix at Cannes with *L'Albero degli Zoccoli* – thus ensuring distribution in the U.S. for Olmi for the first time after the failure of *E Venne un Uomo*. If America's lack of interest in Rosi's films has been because of their lack of sex – as John Francis Lane suggested in *Films and Filming* – then clearly Olmi would fare no better. It is easy enough to find sex in Fellini, Wertmuller and Bertolucci and easy enough to see that these are erratic film-makers. Their reputations, as I write, are no longer high: but if there are precedents for such judgments the reflection on the cinema culture of New York, crucial to the issue, is pretty damning.

One Italian director, Franco Zeffirelli (b. 1923) has made virtually all his films for American companies – or at least in English. A former assistant of Visconti, he was becoming established as an opera director when the Old Vic invited him to design and direct a production of 'Romeo and Juliet', which made his reputation. In 1967 he directed a film of *The Taming of the*

Franco Zeffirelli's
Romeo and Juliet,
with Michael York,
left, as Tybalt and
Leonard Whiting as
Romeo. One reason
that it was the best
screen version of this
particular play is that
the younger
generations of the
Montagues and
Capulets were
indeed young,
spirited and
non-actorish.

Shrew, which he followed with **Romeo and Juliet** (1968), the first of the three English-language film versions to see it as a play about adolescents, and Italian adolescents at that; the marauding bands of Montagues and Capulets had become Renaissance versions of the youths in films like *La Notte Brava*. The leading roles are poorly spoken and performed, but the Romeo (Leonard Whiting) has an appropriately pubescent, dreamy look, and Juliet (Olivia Hussey) is at least physically adorable, small, doll-like and piquant. In compensation, the handling of the action is inventive and vigorously imaginative: Zeffirelli has made the climax Juliet's intimations of mortality, a child clasping the vial of poison in front of a vast four-poster. The rest is played out as if in a dream, the child-lovers out of their depth, and good as

it is, it is inevitably a disappointment after the buoyancy of the first half. Danilo Donati's costumes and Renzo Mongiardino's decor – a huge piazza and muralled rooms effectively disguise the fact that little of the film was made on location – contribute mightily to the only Shakespeare film to rank with Olivier's as a critical and box-office success.

Zeffirelli was accordingly encouraged to embark on a youth-orientated view of St Francis of Assisi, **Brother Sun, Sister Moon** (1972), but in that context English dialogue (e.g. 'You pathetic little creep!') and actors proved an initial handicap. The camera has so lovingly photographed their faces – and the lyrical countryside – that a mood of sensuality has been asserted even before St Francis strips coyly in the town's main square. It is quite feasible for an

Italian film-maker to see St Francis in this manner (instead of as an ascetic), but making him an exponent of Sixties 'flower-power' completes the miscalculations. The film failed so completely that Paramount were not interested in backing Zeffirelli again, so that he confined his work to the theatre till approached by two television companies, R.A.I. and the British I.T.C., to make a six-hour **Jesus of Nazareth** (1977), to be televised in two parts. With Laurence Olivier consenting to take part, a starry cast was assembled, to support the relatively unknown Robert Powell as Jesus, evidently chosen for his visible sanctity.

Apart from an emphasis on the Jewishness of its characters, this film looks like Sunday School stamps, with an occasional excursion into Renaissance painting. In *The Observer*, Clive James said, 'There is no vulgarity. There is no sensationalism. In fact it gradually dawns on you that there is not much of anything, except good taste . . . On the whole it can be said that this was a project well worth trying, especially when you consider how lousy those Hollywood Biblical epics used to be.' Yes: but two of those lousy movies were made by Stevens and Wyler, using their idea of good taste, and Pasolini's used his idea of 'imagination'. There are moments here – the gold and purple of the Court, the portrait of a fishing community, passion in an olive grove – which transcended such considerations; and there were other occasions, mainly brought about by the English dialogue of Anthony Burgess, which seemed to undermine the whole enterprise. Nevertheless it restored Zeffirelli to favour, and coinciding with M-G-M's invitation to make a film, he happened to catch on television one made by that company in 1931 which he rather foolishly decided to remake, **The Champ** (1979).

The T.V. showing re-awakened childhood traumas, he said, for as a child he had been shoved from pillar to post like the boy in the film. His version is sunny and pretty, well acted by Jon Voight in the title role and Ricky Schroder as the boy, with a manipulation of audience emotions in the final scene so shameless that children are liable to emerge in floods of tears. One might have respected it more if Zeffirelli, on a tour to promote it, had not spoken disparagingly of some infinitely more worthwhile films – *Kramer vs. Kramer* (q.v.) and *The China Syndrome* (q.v.).

If, in truth, Zeffirelli belongs only marginally to a consideration of Italian cinema, he remains more central to the mainstream of Italian culture, certainly with his opera productions and their painterly compositions. Italy in the second half of the twentieth century is a country riven by contradictions, not least in its being the most communist of Catholic Western democracies. The hill towns of Tuscany and Umbria remain unspoilt, but the marvellous centres of the old cities have to fight the encroachment of neon light and traffic, and their new suburbs of surpassing ugliness. Thus the Italian cinema: one half opts for the traditional and the other for the trashy – and it is the former which is by far the more contemporary.

39

British Cinema:
A Matter of Collusion

WHEN KORDA DIED in 1956 the British cinema virtually expired with him. The few independents left concentrated on B-movies, for which there was apparently a market, since Hollywood had all but abandoned making them. Production was otherwise mainly in the hands of the Rank Organisation, whose executives seemed capable of initiating only programme pictures to play in the company's own cinemas – which constituted almost two-thirds of those in the country. Rank's popular films were confined to some war movies and the series begun by *Doctor in the House* (q.v.) with Dirk Bogarde. When in the early Sixties the company reduced its activity to a handful of films annually its 'stars' literally disappeared from the screens. Their names had glowed from the marquees of several hundred Gaumonts and Odeons, yet with the exception of Bogarde, Peter Finch and a few others those who chose to stay in the profession could do so only by taking supporting roles.

Hollywood summoned none of them, but film directors found work there or in the American-financed movies made in Britain. American financiers, producers, stars and writers arrived regularly in Elstree and Pinewood to make 'British' pictures of local appeal and a great many more of supposed world appeal. The success of *The Bridge on the River Kwai* (q.v.) and *Tom Jones* (q.v.) was responsible for much of Hollywood's interest in British talent, but the lower costs and the quality of supporting players were considerable factors when producing costume pictures, since it was clear that audiences more readily accepted historic characters with British accents. There remained the

advantage of the British quota system, so that the Hollywood companies continued to maintain distribution offices in London; and the British, from every point of view, were glad of the patronage.

The American influx did not kill the indigenous British film, but what remained was hardly worth preserving – war films, trivial thrillers and comedies. With Ealing Studios almost defunct, comedy was in a depressed state, and I at least never found any virtue in the 'Carry On' series which began a twenty-year run with **Carry On, Sergeant** (1958), a harmless service stage farce so renamed. A talented group of eccentric comedians was embroiled in increasingly salacious situations, devoid of wit but heavy with humour – not that much of that survived the clumsy handling.

Another military comedy, **Private's Progress** (1956), is a rehash of similar japes of the war years, complete to the gormless private (Ian Carmichael) parachuted behind German lines. But the picture was memorable among all the other officer-encrusted British movies by portraying for the first time the officers as just as venal and stupid as the men they commanded; they included Terry-Thomas, whose permanently outraged major is a thing of beauty. These two actors, together with Dennis Price and Richard Attenborough, played their roles again in **I'm All Right Jack** (1959), also adapted from a novel by Alan Hackney and produced by the Boultings, with brother John directing. This examined the further progress of the Carmichael character, in the postwar world, working in a factory and being manipulated by his former officers for their own selfish ends. Carmichael has been befriended by a union leader (Peter Sellers), who approves of 'intellectuals' like him and whose greatest wish is to go to Russia. Sellers is brilliant: his Kite is defensively shifty-eyed, uncertain of his vowels – and indeed of anything he says – as he attempts an accent which is not posh but which conceals his origins.

The Boultings were said to have 'taken on' the unions, but the film, though occasionally amusing, is smug, slackly scripted and conventional. The same may be said of their other attempts at satire, also supposedly at the expense of British authoritarian institutions. **Brothers in Law** (1957), directed by John Boulting, finds Carmichael, Attenborough and Terry-Thomas in the legal profession, and **Carleton-Browne of the F.O.** (1959), directed by Jeffrey Dell and Roy Boulting, pits Terry-Thomas, a particularly dense diplomat, against Sellers, the wily native prime minister of one of Britain's forgotten colonies. **Heavens Above!** (1963) has the charming idea of a parson – Sellers in another of his fine performances – whose innate goodness is mistaken for naivety by the worldly clerics and scheming local politicos who surround him; but the film offers the standard Boulting brothers' comic solution to the dilemmas of their earnest Capraesque heroes: the breakdown of law and order. They had used that effectively in their thriller, *Seven Days to Noon*, and to little purpose in *I'm All Right Jack*, which also portrays the usual band of smarty businessmen in league to bring down the proles. These are right-wing movies posing as left-wing movies, and the most shameful of them is **Lucky Jim** (1957), because its source is of different mettle from those of the other movies. Kingsley Amis's novel, a broadside taken at the academic world, was seminal, its hero – played in the film by Carmichael – caught in the crossfire of class and culture. Such predecessors as Orwell and Priestley had chosen to understate the dislike between the classes, but Lucky Jim responded by comforting himself with beer and inner sarcasm, and building a dream world in which the enemy – the phoneys and the pseuds on the faculty – falls flat on its collective face. That aspect of the novel was all that the Boultings understood, and they used it only too literally, so that the revolutionary literary movement of which

Amis was a part was not for the moment to affect the British film industry.

Launder and Gilliat made a cheery version of Amis's second novel, 'That Uncertain Feeling', retitled **Only Two Can Play** (1961) and directed by Gilliat from a screenplay by Bryan Forbes. It is clear that they were attracted to Amis's stereotypes, such as nagging landladies and local flirts, and the many jokes about breasts; the result is a sour, but accurate, portrait of provincial life. Peter Sellers is the disaffected hero, a librarian, and the pseuds this time are local literary men who write symbolic verse plays. Unhappily, the later films of Launder and Gilliat are disappointing, but they were responsible for **The Smallest Show on Earth** (1957), a pleasing and often hilarious comedy about a young couple (Virginia McKenna, Bill Travers) running a flea-pit cinema which shakes as the trains go by. Aided by the inebriated projectionist (Sellers) and the venerable cashier (Margaret Rutherford), they counter the attraction of the local supercinema with old flicks with such titles as 'Killer Riders of Wyoming'. William Rose and John Eldridge wrote it, from Rose's story, and Basil Dearden directed. The break-up of Ealing had pushed its alumni out into the cold, and it was Dearden's customary producer, Michael Relph, who had persuaded Launder and Gilliat to sponsor it.

Sellers was also seen to advantage in **The Wrong Arm of the Law** (1963), as a seedy London gang operator working under the cover of a French couturier. The film, however, belongs to Lionel Jeffries as a Scotland Yard man of sublime obtuseness, pleased as punch with his guile and his suspicions, and desperately sycophantic towards his superiors. This is one of the last and best of the variations on *The Lavender Hill Mob*, as directed by Cliff Owen, whose later attempts to put television comics through their screen paces have little of the finesse shown on this occasion.

Among the film's seven credited writers were Alan Simpson and Ray Galton, whose radio and television scripts had done so much to establish the comic persona of Tony Hancock (1924–68). They wrote, and Robert Day directed, **The Rebel** (1961), the only film to embody that persona – though, as *Call Me Genius*, it

British Cinema: A Matter of Collusion

The British comic Tony Hancock made his reputation in radio and television, and *The Rebel* is his only notable film appearance. It still is not quite right – note the bowler (on the table) instead of his usual déclassé, battered homberg, while the jokes about left-bank Paris are only one degree brighter than those in *Funny Face*: but it remains sufficient demonstration of his genius.

was a failure in the U.S. Intended as a satire on *The Moon and Sixpence*, the result is flatfooted – for instance, the regimentation of office life had been better done in many other movies – but Hancock is superb as a Sunday painter shakily convinced of his gifts. His landlady (Irene Handl) sees his daubs for what they are, but what would a landlady, detested breed, know of art? He nods sagely, if uncomprehendingly, at mention of Renoir or Cézanne, in turn not expecting his own idiotic comments on art to be any better understood; and thus with deceit practised on both sides he becomes the darling of the *rive gauche*. When praised, he offers a mock-modest shrug, certain that the world is finally coming to its senses; checked, he offers a fish-eye stare, desperately unsure as to whether the twerp before him is, after all, right. His fleeting doubts about his abilities, his subterfuges and his lies make him the most human of the self-obsessed. Offered an absurd price for a painting, he says 'Why resist fate?' – fate being as consistently fascinating as himself. Since he always expected to be exposed, he is not surprised to find his time in the sun so short, so he

retires to wait again for the world's call. In Hancock's only other starring film, **The Punch and Judy Man** (1963), directed by Jeremy Summers, he plays a resort entertainer married to a silly social climber – Sylvia Sims miscast in a role requiring the British equivalent of those ladies who played wife to W. C. Fields – which brings him into contact with a number of civic dignitaries. Whereas at other times he excelled at deflating the pompous, Hancock muffs it here; it is painful to see him struggling with this material, particularly as it cuts across the character Galton and Simpson created for him. He had rejected their script in favour of one by himself and the critic Philip Oakes; the film's failure, in conjunction with the American rejection of *The Rebel*, were factors which eventually led to his suicide.

Of the war films churned out by the plane load, the most popular were **The Dam Busters** (1955), directed by Michael Anderson, and **Reach for the Sky** (1956), directed by Lewis Gilbert. Both were adapted from factual R.A.F. exploits as put into book form by Paul Brickhill. The earlier movie details the experiments of

Barnes Wallis (Michael Redgrave) in devising a missile to bounce along the waters of the three dams which supplied the Ruhr, together with the subsequent bombing mission, led by Wing Commander Guy Gibson (Richard Todd); its superiority over other films of the genre is due to the intelligent and beautifully organised screenplay by R. C. Sherriff. It has a craftsmanship and a sense of pride lacking from *Reach for the Sky*, which does disservice to its hero, Squadron Leader Douglas Bader, a legless pilot readmitted to the R.A.F. on the outbreak of war, and a later inmate of Colditz. No one involved seems to understand what motivated him – except Kenneth More, playing Bader, and the film would be unbearable without him, with his breezy, easy way, his warm broad grin and his patent sincerity. The film may be bracketed with *Going My Way* and *The Sound of Music* as an instance of a likeable performer modifying mawkish intentions.

The biggest financial success of the decade was an Anglo-American war film, **The Bridge on the River Kwai** (1958), which was produced by Sam Spiegel, directed by David Lean and written by two Americans, Carl Foreman and Michael Wilson (though, since both were still on Hollywood's blacklist, the screenplay was credited to Pierre Boulle, author of the original novel). They were rewarded for their efforts by a total of seven Oscars, and, it would be nice to say, the contempt of the men who worked on the Kwai bridge and the Siam railway – but according to a B.B.C. documentary on the subject the survivors are unanimous in considering the film too unimportant to be repudiated. Sixteen thousand Europeans and one hundred thousand Asians died, a matter on which the film is completely silent; the malaria, beri-beri and cholera of reality are unmentioned in what appears to be an Eastern version of the *Club Méditerranée*. In fact the officers joined the men as white coolies, both because they felt it only right to do so and were threatened by machine guns if they did not: in the film the British commander (Alec Guinness) is prepared to die for the Geneva rule that P.O.W.s of commissioned rank must not do manual work and is cheered for his stand by the men – which reveals a profound ignorance of British service mentality. The cast includes William Holden and

Jack Hawkins, but the performances are uninteresting except for those by Sessue Hayakawa as the Japanese commander, digging beneath the yellow peril level of the writing, and James Donald, combining intelligence with the obligatory stiff upper lip. His famous final comment, 'Madness . . . madness', as the bridge is blown up, comes oddly after the schoolboy heroics and pretty jungle photography.

The great Japanese war films then being produced were not known in the West, but it is worth considering the extent to which the French and Italians had revitalised cinema by the time Lean and Spiegel made **Lawrence of Arabia** (1962) – especially as the notices throughout the world endorsed its makers' estimate of its importance. They had passed up Rattigan's recent play on Lawrence, 'Ross', for a screenplay by Robert Bolt,★ then best known for his play 'A Man for All Seasons'. Lawrence had fascinated film-makers since Lowell Thomas's magic lantern lectures during his lifetime, and in 1936 Korda, planning a film biography, had put the actor Walter Hudd under contract because of his physical resemblance. At another time Leslie Howard was to have played Lawrence, and twenty years later Rank projected a version with Dirk Bogarde, written by Rattigan – which became 'Ross' when the film was cancelled (that play was purchased during its West End run by Herbert Wilcox for £100,000, a fact which contributed to his bankruptcy, for Lean's film killed any prospect of his making it). During this time Richard Aldington's 1955 biography had somewhat tarnished the Lawrence legend, and Bolt's literal script pays lip-service to the revelations therein – that Lawrence was six-tenths poseur and even more partisan in the Arab cause after being sodomised in a Turkish jail. Such suggestions were heady among the empty spectacles of the time, but the film eventually concludes that Lawrence was a hero who became a nuisance to both the British and the Arabs – unless, that is, the grimaces in which Peter O'Toole indulges are meant to express paranoia. The action sequences are expertly handled and Lawrence's fascination with the desert is powerfully communicated by F. A. Young's colour photography.

★A decade later, Bolt's then-current play on Mary, Queen of Scots, was passed over as the source of a film (q.v.) on her.

British Cinema: A Matter of Collusion

Young's photography may be all you care to remember of **Doctor Zhivago** (1965), a further collaboration of Bolt and Lean, this time for Carlo Ponti and M-G-M. Boris Pasternak's novel had been a news item, a piece of merchandise, a holy tabernacle, its reception not uninfluenced in the West by its being banned in Russia, the author's incarceration and his reputation as heir to Tolstoi; but on screen his story emerges as a half-cocked version of *War and Peace*, shaping the Russian Revolution into the usual pattern of unrest, war and adjustment. Facile remarks are dropped about equality being best and of the necessity of sweeping away the old order; the 'people' seem composed of *tricoteurs* borrowed from antique movies about the French Revolution; and, in the end, none of the problems facing a capitalist film on this subject are resolved. Spain, Finland and Canada deputised for Russia, but Lean often settles for mere effect – as with the ice-house, as perfect in its way as Miss Havisham's cobwebbed dining room in *Great Expectations*. With the exception of Julie Christie, warm and spirited as Zhivago's true love, and Rod Steiger, as the commissar who vainly loves her, the performances are poor. In the title role Omar Sharif's spaniel-eyes mirror less centuries of suffering than a soppy bedside manner, while Ralph Richardson, shouting 'Oh no, not another purge!' is ludicrous. The film was even more popular than its predecessors, which meant that Lean had been responsible for drawing more money into the box office than any other individual director. Since his early films are so striking, it was sad to see him engaged on these museum pieces. At any given moment **Ryan's Daughter** (1970) is exquisitely made, but it is a terrible film. Its miscalculations start with Bolt's screenplay, a vehicle for his then wife, Sarah Miles, an inadequate actress. A wisp of a plot places her as the Scarlett O'Hara of the Emerald Isle, in 1916, being unfaithful to her schoolteacher husband (Robert Mitchum) with a British officer (Christopher Jones). The film lasts 3 hours 26 minutes, heavy with effects and 'atmosphere', some of it borrowed from German Silents, as when the villagers mock the woman or the village idiot (John Mills, who is embarrassing). Lean has let the old blarney interfere with his judgment, and this born film-maker is no longer able to recognise a cliché; a foolish screenplay encourages him to pander to his increasing proclivity towards grandiloquence. The film cost M-G-M $14 million, and brought in just over that amount at the American box office. Lean has not filmed since, due to the apparent cost of a project on the *H.M.S. Bounty* affair, which he had finally to abandon, but he is reported to be preparing *A Passage to India*.

His leading British contemporary, Carol Reed, emerged less fortunately from Hollywood backing. **The Key** (1958) continued his run of disappointing films, a trivial – and unatmospheric – wartime romance, with Sophia Loren as a girl whose doorkey is passed from one rescue boat captain to another. Carl Foreman's script makes small noises on the disillusion and degradation wrought by war but does not make its point; and it fails as a love story as neither Loren nor William Holden is interesting on this occasion. It is all the more regrettable therefore that Trevor Howard is killed at the end of the first hour. The sea sequences are magnificently handled, but with the inroads now being made by younger film-makers Reed's approach could be seen to be more impersonal than ever. Of his last half-dozen films he made only two of interest. **Our Man in Havana** (1959) lacks the élan of his earlier collaborations with Graham Greene, who adapted it from his own serio-comic novel about a vacuum-cleaner salesman inducted into the British secret service. In the role Alec Guinness substitutes Mr Polly for the drab and obsessive original, and the film is further weakened by Burl Ives, as a former Jewish refugee from Hitler, and Jo Morrow as the ingenue. But there are three superb performances: Noël Coward as the reptilian recruitment agent, Ralph Richardson as the dim, hide-bound Ministerial figure, and Ernie Kovacs as the local police chief; all of them bring a rare humour to the cat-and-mouse game. **Oliver!** (1968) is based on a British musical which succeeded on Broadway, a bastardisation of Dickens with a comic-lovable Fagin, given to ditties like 'You've Got to Pick a Pocket or Two', and orphans whose emaciated appearance and wistful rendering of 'Food, Glorious Food' is belied by their subsequent dance. The film won an Oscar for Best Picture and another for Best

Direction – the latter surprisingly justified. Reed's understanding of the medium and of Dickens are much in evidence; he had not been so artfully employed since *Kipps* almost twenty years earlier. He follows Lean's *Oliver Twist* only in his use of the decor, demonstrating a lighter touch and swinging easily back and forth from songs to dialogue. Unquestionably editing can help a director in these matters, but when a derivative score, tiresome choreography and a lacklustre cast can cheer an audience, that is as clear an evidence of a director's skill as one may find.

A few truly British films deserve mention before we look at the bulk of Anglo-American co-productions. One of the best is **A Night to Remember** (1958), at a cost of £640,000 the most expensive Rank film since *Caesar and Cleopatra*. John Davis, the head of Rank, was not enthusiastic about the project, but consented because Walter Lord's book had been a bestseller on both sides of the Atlantic. Using an understatement appropriate to the title, Lord had set down the details of that particular night when the unsinkable Titanic went down – a matter which caught the imagination of the world and has held it ever since. Eric Ambler's screenplay selects the most telling and ironic details, as well as adding some representative ones. Kenneth More was a sensible choice to play the first mate, Lightoller, who emerged from Lord's account as a natural hero and hugely likeable. 'I'll never be sure of anything again', are his last words. The film is never sufficiently nightmarish, but it is often moving, as when the ship's architect (Michael Goodliffe) realises that it is going to sink. Of the half-dozen films on this subject this remains the best, despite only workmanlike direction by Roy Baker.

Another untypical film to appear from Rank was **Victim** (1961), featuring Dirk Bogarde as a married lawyer forced to realise that an occasional fling does not make him an occasional gay: 'I wanted him, I tell you, I *wanted* him,' he screams at his wife. As in Proust, many of the characters are eventually revealed as homosexual, but what is most incredible is that it is not the affluent, eminent lawyer who is blackmailed but his young, impoverished lover. It was not unwise to present this particular subject for the first time to the British public as a thriller, following a

similar approach in *Sapphire*, a mystery with a race angle made by the same team – producer Michael Relph, director Basil Dearden and writer Janet Green, all of them earnest and glum. The subject was topical, in the light of the Wolfenden Report recommending changes in the laws against homosexuality, and Bogarde is on record as believing that the film was as much responsible as the report for the eventual change. That it was made at all was due to the new awareness in British films fostered by Woodfall (q.v.), but the subject matter was the only novelty in this well-intentioned but simplistic movie.

Alec Guinness also attempted, with the co-operation of director Ronald Neame and the backing of United Artists, to turn British films away from the War and footling comedy. Both **The Horse's Mouth** (1959) and **Tunes of Glory** (1960) are adaptations of novels, by, respectively, Joyce Cary, with a screenplay by Guinness himself, and James Kennaway, who wrote his own. Both are Ealing-influenced in their ardour for British eccentricity, and the tone of the Cary film may be judged from its frisky reworking of Prokofiev's already sprightly Lieutenant Kije Suite. Its thesis of an artist's right to indulgence in a philistine world provokes individual reaction – positively in the case of his paintings ('doubled' by John Bratby) but much less so in the case of Guinness's stubble-chinned painter, better at scrounging than expressing his love affair with the palette. *Tunes of Glory* is much more impressive. Beyond its Hugh Walpole-like conflict between two responsible men unable to understand each other, it is a nimble study of the military mind and such related matters as the mystique of the Regiment, in this case a Highland one in its peacetime mess. Guinness never immersed himself so deeply as in this role of the red-headed Scots colonel, with his bluster, his awkwardness, his goodness, his conceit and his lack of intelligence. The more interesting role is that of the university-trained disciplinarian, but John Mills so over-acts that he dissipates the conflict at the core of the film, to its consequent detriment.

Neame, not the toughest of directors, nevertheless has a certain grace when confronted with a congenial subject. **I Could Go On Singing** (1963) is the last screen work of Judy Garland, playing herself to an uncomfortable degree, a lady of accomplishment and fame, temperamental, selfish, unreliable, and treated as a spoilt child by her secretary (Aline MacMahon) and manager (Jack Klugman). That she makes us care is due to her extraordinary talent; the vulnerability of her youth has not left her, and though her one overriding resistible quality in life at this time was self-pity, she can tear at your heart with her denunciation of her life as entertainer. 'I can't be spread so thin . . . It's just not worth all the deaths I have to die.' Neame achieves, otherwise, a welcome informality in this dated tale of an American star trying to regain the love of her young, British son. And he might have got nearer the electricity of a Garland concert, in the Palladium sequences, had she had better songs. His weaknesses are more apparent in **The Prime of Miss Jean Brodie** (1969), in which Muriel Spark's serpent-beneath-the-velvet wit has been prettied up and conventionalised, admittedly with the help of Jay Presson Allen, who had made a hit play from Spark's novel. Miss Brodie (Maggie Smith) is a Scottish teacher believing passionately in art and fascism; her favouritism, her opinionated manner, her contempt for the curriculum and the headmistress (Celia Johnson) bring about her downfall – a matter of nuance in the book, and pure melodrama in this movie. Spark's Miss Brodie was oddly moving – as was Vanessa Redgrave in the stage version – but this one, nary a hair out of place, is not. The film is stolen by Celia Johnson, playing a waiting game with humour and little ticks of malevolence. The material is sufficiently unusual for one to be grateful that Neame was in charge, rather than a lesser director, but he shows little feeling for either the period (the Thirties) or Spark's ironies. And he should never have allowed an ending opposed to hers, which makes quite clear that Miss Brodie is not to be admired.

Acknowledgment should be made of Neame's greatest success, **The Poseidon Adventure** (1972), made in Hollywood for 20th Century-Fox. At first one suspects a remake, forty years on, of Fox's *Transatlantic*, which is a masterpiece compared with this screenplay as written by Stirling Silliphant and Wendell Mayes from a novel by Paul Gallico. It follows the adventures of a particularly uninteresting bunch of people (including Gene Hackman, Shelley Winters and Carol Lynley) trapped in a liner capsized on the ocean-bed, and is at once so old fashioned and unconvincing that its popularity surprised everyone, including its makers. It is not so much directed as organised.

Like Neame, Anthony Asquith continued to choose above-average material, and **Orders to Kill** (1958) is not only the best of his later films, but the best British war movie of the period. The material is slightly doubtful, for Donald Downes's original novel claimed to be based on fact, which is not entirely true; but in Paul Dehn's screenplay it makes both a good thriller and a drama of conscience, as a young American (Paul Massie) is secreted into Paris to assassinate a mild man suspected of being a traitor to the Resistance.

Returning to Shaw, Asquith made **The Doctor's Dilemma** (1959), the seventh full-length Shaw play to reach the screen. It concentrates on the Dubedats (Leslie Caron, Dirk Bogarde) at the expense of the medical profession, which is a pity in view of the faultless interpretations of Cutler Walpole (Alastair Sim), Sir Patrick (Felix Aylmer) and Dr Blenkinsop (Michael Gwynn). Anatole de Grunwald's adaptation omits the question of whether artists are subject to the same laws as other mortals, and we might have had guidance on the issue of whether humanity would be served by saving Louis, had we been shown even one of his paintings. De Grunwald also produced Asquith's last two features, **The V.I.P.s** (1963) and **The Yellow Rolls-Royce** (1964), which, written by another old colleague, Terence Rattigan, and with all-star Anglo-American casts, were by far the most successful they made. Both have episodic narratives, and the second of the two is feeble; but *The V.I.P.s*, a 'Grand Hotel' set at Heathrow airport, has its moments, most endurably with Rod Taylor and Maggie Smith, as an Australian businessman and his timid but ever-loving secretary. Reinforced by the confidence of these players, the writing and direction are surer than elsewhere in the film, while Margaret Rutherford is in her element as a batty duchess.

There are British directors of this period whose patronage by Hollywood is more curious, and we looked at some of their films in the last Hollywood chapter. The following are chiefly British, if not British-financed, and are listed here because of the success they achieved in the international market. **Those Magnificent Men in Their Flying Machines** (1965) is an aerial, period version of *It's a Mad, Mad, Mad, Mad World*, with a bunch of heavyweight comics, some American, with jokes to match. Its subject is a promising one – international rivalry to make the first London-Paris flight – and it is often visually rewarding. Despite a healthy profit (it cost $5 million and took almost three times that in the U.S. alone), 20th Century-Fox declined a second outing with director Ken Annakin and writer Jack Davies, which was eventually made by a Franco-Italian consortium and distributed by Paramount, who called it **Monte Carlo or Bust** (1969) in Britain and *Those Daring Young Men in Their Jaunty Jalopies* in the U.S. That it is marginally the better of the two films is due to the presence of Peter Cook and Dudley Moore as two Britons with unbounded confidence in the British; the joy of both films is Terry-Thomas as a dastardly baronet who will stop at nothing to win. Paramount withdrew from **The Battle of Britain** (1969) during pre-production, and as presented by United Artists there is little evidence of the reputed £12 million budget, except in the presence of a dozen leading stars, including Laurence Olivier, Kenneth More, Susannah York, Trevor Howard and Michael Caine. There is also little sense of period as directed by Guy Hamilton; in this case the film did not perform particularly well at the American box office.

One of its two producers was Harry Saltzman, the driving economic force behind Woodfall Films and, with Albert Broccoli, responsible for the movies featuring the adventures of Ian Fleming's secret-service man, James Bond. Saltzman is a Canadian and Broccoli an American who had also worked in Britain for some years, as a partner in Warwick Films. Warwick had resolutely sought popularity by importing rather *passé* Hollywood names to star in such 'action' movies as *Zarak*, *Interpol* and *Safari* and, in view of decreasing public interest, was about to give up the ghost when Broccoli and Saltzman signed an agreement with United Artists to make a series of films about Bond,

provided that the first one was successful. Although Fleming's snobbish thrillers had been praised and their sales were improving with each publication, other producers had hesitated. **Dr No** (1962) was made on a medium budget, and there was no indication during the first weeks of its release, to indifferent response, that business would pick up to make it the first of the most successful series in cinema history.★

Fleming's formula was as old as movies: an ersatz Mabuse, now prepared to use nuclear arms in his bid for world domination; a deadly tarantula or so borrowed from a modern Fu Manchu; and a hero for whom women fall like nine-pins. Bond is the sort of man who reads *Playboy*, with his taste in cocktails and clothes meticulously detailed. He is less fussy about his women, satisfying them quickly before jetting out to the next exotic locale and on occasion (like Sam Spade) bedding down with women he knows to be his mortal foes. Apart from its Caribbean setting, *Dr No* seemed one step up from a B picture, and dowdier than it might have been because of its Bond, Sean Connery, a minor actor chosen in desperation after a number of names had turned down the role. As long as he played the role he lacked suavity, but he was to gain greatly in authority and humour.

★Though we may now suppose it to be overtaken by *Star Wars* (q.v.) and its sequels.

James Bond in a typical situation, in *Diamonds are Forever* (1971), directed by Guy Hamilton, and the Bond, of course, is Sean Connery. Connery was Bond in the first film drawn from the secret agent thrillers by Ian Fleming, but after disputes with the producers about his fee was replaced for one film by George Lazenby, an Australian model, and permanently by Roger Moore. Moore is almost certainly closer to the Bond of Fleming, who publicly endorsed Connery while privately deploring the casting. But Connery is the only Bond: he grew into the role while Moore, in his own words, is a 'plastic' actor.

British Cinema: A Matter of Collusion

As popularity increased to a phenomenal degree, the Bond films became an annual event, each more expensive than the one before, and eventually having plots unconnected with the Fleming novels after which they were titled. Gimmickry was all, and probably the chief credit for the series belongs to Ken Adam, the production designer, or, in the case of **You Only Live Twice** (1967) John Stears, in charge of special effects. Bond, for instance, has a 'do it yourself' helicopter equipped with flame-throwers that can turn corners; the climax takes place in an atomic warship – claimed to be the largest set ever built for a movie – underneath a false lake in an extinct volcano. Any enthusiasm I, personally, felt was muted by the mercilessly methodical way the film was put together; as the mechanical devices abound and the killings mount, I sit glassy-eyed, wishing I were elsewhere, wondering about the dubious morality whereby named powers (Russia, China) struggle for control of the world with nuclear weapons. The success of the films perhaps reflects the paranoia of the nuclear age, with villains reduced to 'oily peril' types, and an intrepid, indestructible Britisher to put them in their place, which is of course the cold, cold ground. This particular Bond film was written by Roald Dahl, the only writer of any distinction to be employed on the series; the director was Lewis Gilbert, while Terence Young directed *Dr No*. Guy Hamilton is the other director most closely associated with the series, and it is not unkind to assume that they were employed less for their reputation as accomplished film-makers than for their ability to manipulate the weaponry involved.

Saltzman alone produced **The Ipcress File** (1965), from the novel by Len Deighton, whose Cockney secret agent, Harry Palmer (Michael Caine), was supposedly the antithesis of Bond. Sidney J. Furie directed this complot of red herrings, with more efficiency than most of the Bond directors managed. Two further Harry Palmer adventures failed to hold the public, but Bond marched on, with Roger Moore filling Connery's shoes after a conflict over his fee. Neither played Bond in **Casino Royale** (1967), based on the Fleming novel to which Broccoli and Saltzman did not hold the rights, since those were already owned by Charles K. Feldman.

When negotiations between both parties broke down it was found that most stars refused to invite comparison with Connery, so the film became a gigantic spoof with several stars, including David Niven and Woody Allen, sharing the role of Bond. The direction was shared between John Huston, Ken Hughes, Val Guest, Robert Parrish and Joe McGrath, but any competition between them was destructive, for the film belongs decisively in the category of those which tried to kill the cinema, along with *Candy* and *The Magic Christian*, its contemporaries.

Lewis Gilbert directed **The Greengage Summer** (1961), a likeable tale set, as the credits put it, in the green and gold champagne district of France. Based on Rumer Godden's novel, it tells of an abandoned adolescent (Susannah York), the debonair and mysterious Englishman (Kenneth More) on whom she gets a crush, and the lesbian-inclined hotel proprietress (Danielle Darrieux). **Alfie** (1966) concerns a Cockney tearaway (Michael Caine) who uses women as some people use Kleenex, until he gets his comeuppance, and is finally deserted. Bill McNaughton's dialogue shows the benificent influence of those scripts written by Galton and Simpson for Hancock: but if his original play was unexceptional in its morals the material makes an objectionable film, in which Gilbert's direction oscillates between *Carry On* salaciousness in the comic scenes and Aeschylian gloom to underline any point. The film's popularity was due in part to Caine probably the first true Cockney screen hero.

Among the films which have paved the way for the lack of morals evident in *Alfie* is **I Am a Camera** (1955), adapted from John van Druten's play based on 'Sally Bowles', one of Christopher Isherwood's Berlin stories. Despite the play's success in New York, Sally's alley-cat habits had prevented any Hollywood studio from buying the rights, so they were purchased by a British company, which, in an attempt to get the M.P.A.A. approval, to ensure showings in the U.S., decreed that Sally should change her mind and not go ahead with an abortion – but it was to no avail. Nevertheless, like *The Moon Is Blue*, some American theatres booked the film, but it is hardly better than that as directed by Henry Cornelius, showing little insight into the Berlin of the period or the character of the male lead, played by Laurence Harvey. As on Broadway, Julie Harris is Sally, extravagant, reckless and somewhat tatty; this movie would be unendurable without her.

A more elevated tale, **Sons and Lovers** (1960), was produced by an American, Jerry Wald, in his bid to bring culture to the masses; but since the novel in question does not exactly have a riveting plot, its justification would have to be the re-creation of Lawrence's world – which was entrusted to Jack Cardiff, directing, and Gavin Lambert and T. E. B. Clarke, who wrote the script. The mining village on the edge of the moors is well-found; there are some family snapshots – Christmas, father in the tin bath – and a whiff of the suffragette movement and contemporary attitudes to sex. As the father, even as diminished into a half-crusty lovable, Trevor Howard excels; but as Paul, Dean Stockwell is no more than a Hollywood leading man and as mother, Wendy Hiller signals her emotions as to a West End gallery.

Peter Ustinov's **Billy Budd** (1962) is technically one of the best of sea films, excellent on the physical details and balanced on the matter of above and below decks. As director and collaborator on the screenplay, Ustinov keeps soberly and thoughtfully to Melville, but weakens after the death of Claggart (Robert Ryan) because of a quirk of casting – his own performance as the captain, established as far too reasonable to stand by the letter of the law. (He only played the role as a way of getting another 'name' into the cast without paying much for it; Allied Artists, backing it to the tune of $1,400,000, remained unenthusiastic.) Of the excellent cast Terence Stamp is fittingly impressive as Billy, and nothing else in the film is quite as good as his night-time conversation with Claggart, where the purity of the one and the evil of the other are beautifully balanced, with Claggart's strange psychology only implied.

Another distinguished sea story, **A High Wind in Jamaica** (1965) was less fortunate, apparently due to loss of nerve on the part of the director, Alexander Mackendrick, and his writers. Richard Hughes's ecstatic adventure is about some children who, taken prisoner by pirates, not only retain their self-possession but take readily to cruelty since it has been part of their fantasy world and they are unable to separate that from reality. The eldest girl uses her sexuality, both knowingly and subconsciously, when she falls ill; but all of this has become a tale of a gruff old pirate captain (Anthony Quinn) stirred by a sick child.

The most famous American star to film in Britain was Marilyn Monroe, who started **The Prince and the Showgirl** (1957) in a blaze of publicity, having persuaded Laurence Olivier to direct and co-star with her in her own production, with Warners to distribute. Terence Rattigan's screenplay was adapted from his own mock-Ruritanian comedy, 'The Sleeping Prince', which on stage had been no more than a showcase for Sir Laurence and Vivien Leigh, whose role Monroe played – an American chorus girl hired to keep company with a visiting royal. The publicists' dream turned sour as her unpunctuality and rudeness to Olivier turned the set into one of hostility (years later he gallantly tried to explain her behaviour by saying that she loved being a model and star, but dreaded acting). It says much for him that she seldom acted more resourcefully or looked more beautiful, and his own performance is a triumph. The Prince is an ageing roué, a man with a heart for something beneath the call of duty, but not much of a heart – and it is a performance which calls to mind that of Gustav Gründgens in *Liebelei*, who at one point in his career had been known as Germany's Olivier. The film itself starts sparklingly, but it is hardly surprising that the final scenes seem perfunctorily treated. One begins to wonder how Lubitsch might have handled it, but it is only superficially Lubitsch material, since it is either anti-sex or very British on the subject, with the consummation between the prince and the showgirl almost an afterthought.

During the following decade Olivier was the director of Britain's National Theatre, where his successes included his Othello, Edgar in 'The Dance of Death' and a production of 'Three Sisters'. Filmed records of these were shown in cinemas, but in each case they give only an incomplete idea of what the original had been like. His screen appearances included the Mahdi in **Khartoum** (1966), with

British Cinema: A Matter of Collusion

Charlton Heston as 'Chinese' Gordon, who managed a fair British accent and the essential vanity, but lacked any hint of the desiccated, lonely visionary. Robert Ardrey's script is a history lesson, while Basil Dearden's direction hardly makes our pulses quicken – and nothing else is as good as the introduction, a potted history of the Nile, photographed by Eliot Elisofon. The film ends with an apologia, 'We cannot be sure how long his memory will live, but a world with no room for the Gordons will return to the sands.' The American producer, Julian Blaustein, had hoped to duplicate the success of *Lawrence of Arabia*.

The best historical film of the period was **The Trials of Oscar Wilde** (1960), written and directed by Ken Hughes, then known, if at all, for some undistinguished melodramas. Its true theme is that of a major literary figure ruined by his own foolhardiness, but it could not be done without reference to its protagonist's homosexuality. That remained prohibited as a screen subject but, as we have seen, a number of London and Broadway plays had touched on the matter during the last few years; and it was the acceptance of this particular film which gave rise to the later *Victim*. Making a film about Wilde was an idea whose time had come, for Gregory Ratoff was hastily directing a rival version in Britain. Hughes's film reached cinemas first (by three days) and reached it best, being especially good on the confused friendships and rivalries of the period; in a generally veracious account he omits Bosie's insistence on carrying out the family feud before the largest possible audience. That would have made Wilde (Peter Finch) a mere pawn, and Hughes sets him up as tragic hero brought low by love: given the nature of that love that was perhaps the wisest approach at that time, though we might have preferred him as dandy, wit or social lion. The respect accorded the film did not earn Hughes more interesting projects, so that it was ten years before he obtained backing for **Cromwell** (1970), which manages to be as inaccurate as the despised historicals of the past, and even duller. It turns on the sort of spurious confrontation thought to be a simple way of explaining complex historical questions, and is made the poorer since the Cromwell of Richard Harris is hardly a thinking man. Charles I, better acted by Alec Guinness, suffers by being saintly rather than scheming.

Becket (1964) also demonstrates the wrong approach to history. Anouilh's play, an irreverent chronicle of a friendship, has been smothered in cathedral-look gloom – except for the sex sequences, mostly involving Peter O'Toole's over-emotional Henry II. In the original each episode grew from the one before, but that is not true under Peter Glenville's direction, while Edward Anhalt's screenplay★ dampens what remains of the jokes about French misconceptions of the English and vice versa. Even in the first reel Richard Burton's Becket suffers from an overdose of piety, but oblivious to the stars and the direction John Gielgud and Pamela Brown act in the style Anouilh intended, he as a foxy King Louis and she as Queen Eleanor. The film enjoyed the same popularity as *Lawrence of Arabia*, *A Man for All Seasons* and *A Lion in Winter* (q.v.), which sent its producer, Hal Wallis, to search among old Broadway plays for another historical subject for Burton. He came up with Maxwell Anderson's 'Anne of the Thousand Days', but Charles Bluhdorn, then head of Paramount, refused to sanction any film with Burton (because Burton had agreed to speak the commentary of a Paramount film for a moderate sum, but changed his mind and asked instead for some diamond and emerald earrings to be given to his wife, Elizabeth Taylor). Wallis accordingly severed his twenty-five year association with Paramount, and moved to Universal. The film, with Burton as Henry VIII and Genevieve Bujold as Anne Boleyn, was mildly successful, but critics were unanimous in disliking the direction of Charles Jarrott, who was nevertheless retained for **Mary, Queen of Scots** (1971). He doggedly mishandles John Hale's screenplay, an adroit mixture of fact and fiction, historic dialogue and more specious speeches of his own devising. Given the approach, Vanessa Redgrave wisely interprets Mary as a storybook heroine but Glenda Jackson's Elizabeth I is a suburban harridan. Miss Jackson was more happily cast as a sluttish Emma Hamilton in **Bequest**

★Anhalt later wrote the book of a West End musical on Becket, which received about the worst notices in theatre history.

to the Nation (1973), directed by James Cellan Jones, with Peter Finch as Nelson; but both films were among the half dozen successive failures which led to Wallis's retirement in 1975.

The age of the wide screen spectacular was dying, and with it the historical drama. Both were expensive, and the adult and/or family audiences for whom they were intended were staying home with their television sets. Colour television was now available in many countries and the programmes shown had at last begun to rival the cinema in content and technique.

That the Hollywood studios had backed most of these films was proof of their continuing obsession with Britain – which would remain, for different reasons, long after it had ceased to be Hollywood's chief export market (indeed, it moved well down the list). As far as the British themselves were concerned, they were content to have their plays, novels and films dwell in the past, if only metaphorically. The British cinema was at its most hermetic, particularly when compared with some of the harshly observant Hollywood films of the late Fifties. The move towards a truly contemporary cinema began with **Room at the Top** (1959), if we are to judge from the admiring notices of the time. John Braine's original novel was the least of the three artefacts which most contributed to the upheaval in British culture, for the film of *Lucky Jim* had been contemptible, while that of *Look Back in Anger* (q.v.) was some months in the future. The tone of all three was anti-cant, but Braine's was the only one based on American models. Apart from Henry James and T. S. Eliot, American culture had impinged on the British only at the mundane level of thrillers or musicals. Braine's hero, a young man on the make, had been a constant in American fiction since Dreiser, if not before. He was also resolutely grammar-school, and, equally rare, tossed around brand names and openly indulged in sex as often as possible. The book's bestselling status interested two producers, John and James Woolf, most of whose films until then had been mediocre – none of them helped by the presence, as the critics pointed out, of an appalling actor, Laurence Harvey, who happened to be James's lover. *Room at the Top* contained a marvellous role for him, and it gave the Woolfs a chance to promote their associate producer, Jack Clayton (b. 1921), who had just directed an acclaimed short, *The Bespoke Overcoat*. Seen today, *Room at the Top* is specious, its portrait of provincial life ungenerous without being satiric; Neil Paterson's otherwise banal screenplay is against class-consciousness, and every reference is underscored in Clayton's direction. The acting is equally unsubtle, with the glowing exception of Simone Signoret, sensual and touching as the older woman grasping at love.

Meanwhile, the moribund local industry was receiving some impetus from the government-funded British Film Institute, whose journal, *Sight and Sound*, had been publishing a number of young critics with pronounced ideas on films. They included (q.v.) Lindsay Anderson, Tony Richardson and Karel Reisz, who were scraping up money to make documentary shorts. In 1956 the Institute's National Film Theatre presented a season called 'Free Cinema', which included an American documentary, *On the Bowery*, short films by Franju, Truffaut and Godard, plus British contributions by Anderson, Richardson, Reisz, Lorenza Mazzetti (unheard of again) and (q.v.) Claude Goretta and Alain Tanner. The preoccupations of Anderson's **O Dreamland** (1953), an account of a funfair, are reflected in Richardson's and Reisz's **Momma Don't Allow** (1955), a portrait of an evening at a suburban jazz club, which the B.F.I. financed. Walter Lassally was the photographer, as on so many films of the 'Free Cinema' movement, including Anderson's **Thursday's Children** (1953), about the teaching of deaf children, co-directed with Guy Brenton, and **Every Day Except Christmas** (1957), about the workers of Covent Garden market. Both films bear witness to Anderson's admiration for Humphrey Jennings, but as creative works – one of the declared aims of the movement – few of the films produced are important. However, as a record of the Fifties many of them are far more valuable than might have been suspected. That is especially true of *Momma Don't Allow* and a further collaboration of Reisz and Lassally, **We Are the Lambeth Boys** (1959), a study of a working-class boys' club. Financed by the Ford Motor Company and at 59 minutes the longest of these films, it also marked the end of the movement. It was difficult to see how any of these people could be assimilated into a local industry so opposed to their aims and methods, and yet some were – if not at the industry's instigation.

Tony Richardson (b. 1928) arrived there first, via the theatre, repeating on film his direction of John Osborne's **Look Back in Anger** (1959). The play had been staged at the Royal Court Theatre by the English Stage Company, whose aims were little different from those of New York's Group Theatre twenty years earlier, to offer drama of substance and a left-wing tinge: that the Royal Court's work seemed pioneering is comment enough on the state of the British theatre at the time. The British critical establishment as a whole were displeased with neither theatre nor cinema, and the damp critical reception accorded the film of *Look Back in Anger* was symptomatic: the play had really been liked only by a minority, but fortunately a vociferous one. That was sufficient to interest the moguls, including Harry Saltzman, a former producer in American television, whose only film was *The Iron Petticoat*, a terrible British imitation of *Ninotchka* written by Ben Hecht, with Katharine Hepburn and Bob Hope. In forming Woodfall Films with Osborne and Richardson, Saltzman allowed them the creative control they demanded, though in negotiating the distribution deal (with Associated British) they were forced to agree to some emasculation – thus Nigel Kneale's screenplay (with additional dialogue by Osborne) has little of Jimmy Porter's rantings against a class-divided society. Thus the young man is rebelling without any causes, and he is unlikeable as he hurls invective at his wife (Mary Ure) and beds her best friend (Claire Bloom), who had loathed him till a moment or two earlier. That may be wish-fulfilment on the part of the author, and it is certainly, in plot terms, not too far removed from *A Streetcar Named Desire*. Hollow and full of hatred as it is, and because it is, it is heartbreaking to see it now, knowing that Osborne, Richardson and Richard Burton – who uses his bark to superb effect as Jimmy – would never do anything better. Richardson may have studied Bazin and the Italian neo-realists but, unlike other British contemporaries working in features, he uses locations with understanding

and not only to prevent us from recalling the film's theatrical origins. He rejected the familiar 'character' playing, with its humour and overstatement – Edith Evans is superb as an interpolated character, Ma Tanner – and he gets a balance among the players that was missing from *Room at the Top*. The film is a worthy heir to the 'Free Cinema' movement, in being virtually the only British feature of the era to say something about that time.

For his second film Richardson chose **The Entertainer** (1960) (which he had also directed on stage), Osborne's study in disenchantment, a hotchpotch of anti-right bias, music-hall jokes, second-hand dreams and family strife. The allegorical aspect of the play – that the failed comic, Archie Rice, stood for a bankrupt Britain – has gone by now. The film is primarily a study of Archie, and thus of Archie's world, from dressing-room to saloon bar. It is Olivier, repeating his stage performance, who makes it a great experience, remodelling his Archie for one of the best performances ever given on film. A lesser actor might have managed the 'public' Archie, with his hail-fellow-well-met, his sniggering one-liners, his wheedling, high-pitched familiarity, his inability to feel a snub; some might manage the plebeian accent, falling into effeminacy; but no one else could have managed the inner Archie, which is an echoing hollow, who has devoted his life to chasing a will-o'-the-wisp – a dream of his own fame, his own success – and who in doing so has closed himself to any emotion other than the pleasure of a draught Bass or a quick lay. As his loving daughter, Joan Plowright brings more to the role than was written into it; and in small roles are Miriam Karlin (as an ageing, bad-tempered soubrette), Alan Bates, Daniel Massey and Albert Finney. Another virtue of Woodfall was its bringing fresh talent to the screen. With a couple of honourable exceptions, the press notices, except for praise for Olivier's own contribution, were worse than those for its predecessor, and the industry disliked it so much that a gala premiere was cancelled and the film sneaked out in the dead summer months. Yet the fact remains that the British cinema grew up because of these two films.

As far as the critics and the public were concerned, the breakthrough came with

Woodfall, Britain's New Wave

The British cinema was dying on its feet when it was injected with new blood by a group of theatre people, including John Osborne the dramatist and Tony Richardson the director, who helped to form a company called 'Woodfall', originally designed to film Osborne's plays. The second of these was *The Entertainer*, RIGHT, with Laurence Olivier repeating his much-acclaimed stage performance, supported by Joan Plowright, who took over the role of his daughter on the stage and repeated it in the film (and in real life she married him). Karel Reisz directed *Saturday Night and Sunday Morning*, BELOW, with Albert Finney and Shirley Field, and like Richardson he was connected with both film criticism and the movement called 'Free Cinema'.

British Cinema: A Matter of Collusion

The guiding force of the Woodfall films was to put the British working class on the screen honestly, and that had seldom even been attempted before. John Schlesinger may have succeeded even better, in *Billy Liar!* RIGHT, with Tom Courtenay and Rodney Bewes and *A Kind of Loving*, FAR RIGHT, with Alan Bates and June Ritchie. The films were so much discussed, as well as imitated, that it is a tribute to the care with which they were made that they remain still fresh today.

Saturday Night and Sunday Morning (1960), which Richardson and Saltzman produced for Karel Reisz (b. 1926) to direct, and **A Taste of Honey** (1961), directed by Richardson. Both tell as much about the England of those days as one may want to know. Each, like *Room at the Top*, goes North, to the industrial cities, and where Reisz finds some of the plainest, ugliest pubs and streets, Richardson uses canals, factory chimneys and winding streets. As we may have guessed from their earlier documentaries, they are very fond of dance-halls and pubs, i.e. places where 'the people' go, and these became the clichés of the Woodfall school. But I was astonished, recently, to find these films undated. Their strength lies in the subject matter and dialogue. *Saturday Night* was adapted by Alan Sillitoe from his own novel about a factory-worker (Albert Finney) who takes up with a married woman (Rachel Roberts). *A Taste of Honey* was written by Richardson and Shelagh Delaney (from the latter's play, on which it is a considerable improvement). Its subject was – and perhaps remains –

unusual in drama; a schoolgirl (Rita Tushingham) lives in mutual antagonism with her tarty mum (Dora Bryan), flitting from cheap apartment to cheap apartment as the rent becomes due. When Mum's latest fancy man (Robert Stephens) proposes, and doesn't want the girl, she lets her black sailor lover make her pregnant and with that predicament goes to live with a young homosexual misfit (Murray Melvin). Richardson's somewhat florid style is not unsuitable, since the crux of the matter is the girl's occasional moment of magic in a world all too familiarly hellish. Both films take a poor view of the working classes, but they were the first to take them seriously, finding pride, spirit and tenderness as integral as in any other milieu.

Richardson was patently anxious to give the lie to the customary British film view of Britain, and **The Loneliness of the Long Distance Runner** (1962) is light years ahead of another movie on a borstal institution, *Boys in Brown*, twelve years earlier. He is expectedly good on his young hero (Tom Courtenay), unexpectedly good on the governors and other do-gooders. Michael Redgrave, as the warden, an old codger with no understanding of the delinquents' mentalities, or indeed anything but the therapeutic joys of sport, gives one of his best performances and the film only fails – if significantly – in its suggestion that borstal boys and public schoolboys are brothers under the skin, finding a common ground in the lousy meals they are served.

The most sympathetic exponent of this 'stunted lives' syndrome was John Schlesinger (b. 1926), a former actor and documentary film-maker. Coming from a privileged background, like Richardson, he nevertheless feels much empathy with the working classes, and if his direction is even more studied it is also more confident. **A Kind of Loving** (1962) and **Billy Liar!** (1963) are the best films of this group, although the first was dismissed by British critics as just another kitchen-sink movie (perhaps because its production team was also responsible for the *Carry On* films), till it went on to win the Golden Bear at the Berlin Festival. That Schlesinger's films have wit is due in part to his

writers, Willis Hall and Keith Waterhouse, working in the first instance from Stan Barstow's novel, and in the second from their own play, based on Waterhouse's novel. In both cases they are acute on some fond and foolish aspects of British life. Humour begins with Barstow's title, which refers to the British kind of sex, with Vic (Alan Bates) turning either to a sex-manual or a book of nudes for help. The boredom of office life is relieved by the pursuit of Ingrid (June Ritchie), who succumbs in the front parlour one Sunday afternoon when Mum (Thora Hird) is out; and it is this lady who almost ruins the subsequent, shotgun marriage – a petty little Tory, incensed that Vic cares neither for T.V. quiz shows nor coats from Marks and Spencer. That terrain of suburban terrace houses is also the world of Billy the liar (Tom Courtenay), and infinitely sadder, since he longs to escape, from his mean-spirited employer (Leonard Rossiter), his irascible dad (Wilfred Pickles), and his grandmother (Ethel Griffies), a grumbling nonentity. Help arrives in the form of a liberated, highly up-to-the-minute and

British Cinema: A Matter of Collusion

very young Earth-mother (Julie Christie) – if only he can accept it. 'They're not worth it, the whole place isn't worth it,' she says.

The battle was won: British cinema had been released from its thrall to the upper and middle classes. Among those fighting the same fight on behalf of the stage was Joan Littlewood (b. 1916), whose East End Theatre Workshop had concentrated on plays about working people (including 'A Taste of Honey'). In the climate conditioned by the success of these films she was given the chance to direct a movie version of one of those plays, **Sparrows Can't Sing** (1963). She wrote the screenplay with its author, Stephen Lewis, but although she fought the studio at every step she cannot be exempted from perpetrating the myth of the East End as a haven of loveable Cockneys. As the most prominent of these, Barbara Windsor is more accurately cast than most actresses: she is found living in sin with a bus-driver (George Sewell) by her husband (James Booth) when he returns from sea, and the plot chiefly concerns his attempts to get her back. Littlewood's love for Stepney, with its barren pubs and rows of houses, is clear, and this makes the film refreshing. Penelope Gilliatt's lyrical review in *The Observer* was taken to task for inverted snobbery – but was understandable in view of her opinion that working-class films had for years been 'desolatingly bad'.

The prime recipient of overpraise was **This Sporting Life** (1963), directed by Lindsay Anderson in an attempt to turn David Storey's novel into a modern 'Wuthering Heights'. Since, as Anderson says, he has 'a very low opinion of the British film industry *and* the British public' (*The Sunday Times*, 9 June 1974), it is not surprising to find that this movie is somewhat second-hand: the rugger-playing hero (Richard Harris) is an amalgam of John Garfield and Marlon Brando; the frigid widow (Rachel Roberts) is a variation of the role played by this actress in *Saturday Night and Sunday Morning*; the oily, insinuating promoter (Alan Badel) is from *Rocco e i suoi Fratelli*; the predatory, rather cheap wife from Amis's 'That Uncertain Feeling', and the party from the film of that book; the vamp at that gathering is from *The Bachelor Party*; and the walk across the railway tracks at night from any six Hollywood dramas of the Forties.

It was nevertheless a welcome film to come from the Rank Organisation, which almost certainly had been encouraged by the fact that Karel Reisz was the producer. As across the Channel, this group of young film-makers emanating from Woodfall helped each other, and it was Richardson who produced **Girl with Green Eyes** (1964), directed by a former camera operator with Woodfall, Desmond Davis, from a screenplay and novel by Edna O'Brien. Its setting is Ireland, in itself a rarity, though its subject is not. That is the hopeless affair between a shop-girl (Rita Tushingham) and a suave, married, cosmopolitan writer (Peter Finch). But both players are superb, as is Lynn Redgrave, as the girl's sexually confident friend; the film is fresh, funny and poignant. Richardson's contribution may have been all-important, in view of **Smashing Time** (1967), with the same two actresses as Northern girls setting out to conquer 'swinging' London. The producer, Carlo Ponti, seems to have wanted a reflection of *Blow-Up*; George Melly contributed a horrendously unfunny script, and the film is less directed by Davis than assembled, with the aid of a sledge-hammer.

Another swift decline was that of Clive Donner, a former editor, who had made no mark as a director until **The Caretaker** (1964), an independent production whose slight budget – £30,000 – was collected from a group of people including Noël Coward, Richard Burton and Peter Hall. As adapted by Harold Pinter from his own play, it quickly disappeared from view, demonstrating the superior common sense of cinemagoers over theatrical devotees (in 1977 Bernard Levin, in *The Sunday Times*, was to fulminate against the play's 'emptiness, weightlessness and triviality . . . its terrible but complete absence of any subject matter or philosophical point.'). Donner really sprang into prominence with **Nothing But the Best** (1964), whose content was no more than that of *Room at the Top* restyled as black comedy, with a witty script by Frederic Raphael, adapted from Stanley Ellin's book. Alan Bates is the young man who will stop at literally nothing to achieve his goal, and Millicent Martin is the aristocratic girl who, fortunately for him, falls for him. The presence of this actress and a number of other artists from the B.B.C.'s 'That Was the Week

That Was' is evidence that this satiric, iconoclastic programme was another manifestation of the revolt against accepted British attitudes, and that programme's certainty that the wealthy and aristocratic were petty, self-satisfied and conscienceless was reflected in this film. This is virtually all it has in common with **Here We Go Round the Mulberry Bush** (1968), produced and directed by Donner, from a screenplay and novel by Hunter Davies. This is *Billy Liar!* worked over and transported south to one of the 'new' towns, Stevenage, and is an even more egregious example of the youth-orientated movie than *Smashing Time*. The additional dialogue is credited to the 'associate producer', an American, Larry Kramer, but its misinterpretation of contemporary life is too pervasive to be blamed on one man.

Suburbia is also the setting of **Live Now – Pay Later** (1962), whose subject, the association between corrupt businessmen and local politicians, was not uncommon in Hollywood but had hardly been touched upon by a British film. The hero, brilliantly played by Ian Hendry, epitomises the Sixties – a smooth-tongued heel, who works as a touting salesman required to get the goods into the home. He also tries to get into as many beds as possible, but that is typical of the approach, with anything thrown in for a laugh. Jack Trevor Story wrote the screenplay from a novel by Jack Lindsay, and the otherwise self-indulgent direction by Jay Lewis does at least move quickly. The industry by this time had managed to put aside its doubts about the two Osborne-Richardson films, unquestionably reassured by the popularity of the later Woodfall films, especially *Saturday Night and Sunday Morning*. It now proceeded to make its own working-class films but made sure that these were in the hands of talents more congenial to it.

The L-Shaped Room (1963) was directed and written by a former actor, Bryan Forbes, in which he employed the obligatory 'new' faces but could not prevent a number of them hamming it up. This account of a London rooming-house borrows only the trappings of new British cinema, being resolutely old-fashioned with its 'slice-of-life' vignettes. As adapted from the novel by Lynne Reid Banks, it strains for substance; what it achieves is the equivalent of a damned good read. **Term of Trial** (1962) does not even do that, rendering only drab the dilemma of a teacher (Laurence Olivier) accused of misconduct by a precocious adolescent (Sarah Miles); the director, Peter Glenville, wastes Simone Signoret as the teacher's contemptuous wife, but the care and detail of Olivier's work are clearly director-proof. **The Leather Boys** (1964), directed by Sidney J. Furie and written by Gillian Freeman (under a male pseudonym) is at least honest to its environment – the motor-cycle gangs, coming from the small terrace houses. It is a good study of a working-class marriage gone wrong and destroyed, when the husband (Colin Campbell) decides to leave his perky, discontented wife (Tushingham) for his easygoing homosexual friend (Dudley Sutton). The dénouement is decently handled, and if the men are the more sympathetically presented, that might be due to Mr Sutton's performance.

You would not have to like any of these films to appreciate that the British nouvelle vague did not roll in vain, but its aim was different from its brotherhood in France – it was to prise the British cinema loose from the influence of Shaftesbury Avenue. Hence its preoccupation with the working-classes; and as the movement died it gave birth to such films as *Here We Go Round the Mulberry Bush*, which saw Britain *only* in terms of working-class and upper crust. The demotic slant of these films made them more welcome in American cinemas than any British film since the heyday of the Ealing comedy. The Hollywood studios intervened more directly as their domestic audiences shrank and *The Bridge on the River Kwai* proved that a 'British' film was welcomed the world over – while the Oscar awarded to Simone Signoret for *Room at the Top* proved that prestige could be gained from an exclusively British film. The absolute confirmation, on both counts, was **Tom Jones** (1963), financed by United Artists when its cost, though low in comparison to most Hollywood-backed historical movies, proved too high for Woodfall's usual backers. It grossed over $17 million in the U.S. alone, and won Oscars for Best Picture, Best Direction for Tony Richardson and Best Screenplay for John Osborne, as adapted from Henry Fielding's classic novel. It is a tour of Merrie England with its pants down and a grimy face, the cinema equivalent of Hogarth after a lifetime of Gainsboroughs. Indeed, it rather overdoes its drunks and cripples. Its bawdry, so refreshing then, has been copied endlessly,★ and if few of Richardson's tricks were even then new – a speeded-up chase, the Silent screen parody, the wipes, the asides to the camera – they were then at least, bright and delightful. Like most critics turned directors, he was not interested in working either expensively or in academic mould, and if the film now seems tame and only mildly amusing, it has a springlike quality, a sense of happiness and of a nice cast having fun.

Richardson chose his subjects as boldly as his casts, but admiration for **The Loved One** (1965) is likely to go no further. Everything is overweighted and overloaded, and therefore quite inappropriate as a means of filming Evelyn Waugh. This is the only film made from one of his novels in his lifetime, a satire on American burial customs set mainly in a cemetery and funeral parlour. On the screen it has become a black comedy, as written by Christopher Isherwood and Terry Southern, with graftings from *Dr Strangelove* (q.v.) – to which Southern had contributed – in the form of a climax involving irresponsible military men and guided missiles. The piece is somewhat disadvantaged by Robert Morse, miscast as a Britisher and too knowing. (In an even worse film from a Waugh novel, 'Decline and Fall', Robin Phillips had the right Alice in Wonderland quality.) Richardson's earlier visit to Hollywood had been for 20th Century-Fox, to direct the film of an American novel, **Sanctuary** (1961), whose failure he blamed on studio interference. It is, nevertheless, more professional than most of his films, and its faults would seem to be due to the Production Code, not yet in its death throes, curtailing all the scenes which gave Faulkner's piece its meaning. The cast – not of Richardson's choosing – is also unfortunate, with the exception of Lee Remick, glowing at the carnal delights laid before her. Richardson's interest in unorthodox sexuality led to two disasters, **Mademoiselle** (1967) and **The Sailor from Gibraltar** (1967), both with Jeanne

Moreau, the former from a story by Jean Genet, the latter from a novel by Marguerite Duras, adapted by Richardson, Isherwood and Don Magner. The first concentrates on a schoolmistress whose frustration leads her to pyromania and humiliation, i.e. baying like a dog, while fornicating with an impossibly beautiful and strong Italian woodcutter (Ettore Manni). The second is about an Englishman (Ian Bannen) who joins a wealthy widow in the search for her sailor lover who may, or may not, be imaginary. The Genet is not only unpleasantly misogynist but a desperate quest for artiness, as it borrows from *Les Amants*, *La Terra Trema*, Pagnol, *Goupi Mains Rouges*, and Buñuel. The Duras has a line, 'It's like leaving a movie before the end' which, when I saw it, brought a loudly applauded *cri de coeur* from the audience, 'What a bloody good idea.'

The Charge of the Light Brigade (1968) recalls a song by Noël Coward, 'We cheered the Charge of the Light Brigade/ No Matter why they charged', because Richardson also does not care, though he is far from cheering. A good many years too late, he seems to want to get even with those Victorian generals. When Warners filmed the Charge, they added some fiction. Charles Wood's invented additions include a young bride (Vanessa Redgrave) who falls in love with her husband's best friend (David Hemmings), plus some heavy borrowings from Cecil Woodham-Smith's 'The Reason Why', as revealed in the credits. (Well into the project, Richardson had learned that Laurence Harvey owned the film rights to that book and part of the agreement with the actor was a lump sum to him and his appearance in a cameo role – which was cut from the final print.) Where Mrs Woodham-Smith was appalled but analytic, Wood is only scurrilous, but even so the antics of the lords – Cardigan (Trevor Howard), Raglan (John Gielgud) and Lucan (Harry Andrews) – are splendidly enjoyable. However, Richardson's faults are here in abundance. His indecision when to end a scene, meaningless shots and a lack of cohesive style contrast with the physical evocation of Victorian Britain which is superlative, and wonderfully complemented by Richard Williams's linking animation, encapsulating the graphic art of the period, and concise in

---

★Including Richardson himself, who returned to this novelist after a run of failures. But *Joseph Andrews* (1977) has all the vices of *Tom Jones* and none of its virtues.

its exposition of the Victorians' world. The final Charge is well managed; but it should be noted that the film neither presents nor considers the reason why.

Richardson tried to keep the film from the British critics, without success. It was poorly received, but quite justly did exceptional business in what the trade calls 'better class halls'. His subsequent films received even worse notices, and certainly **Laughter in the Dark** (1969) is very bad. What seems like spontaneity in the early films has become carelessness, but equally at fault with Richardson is the film's writer, Edward Bond, who did not know how to respond to Vladimir Nabokov's text with irony or implicit sophistication. Perhaps it was too large a task to transpose the action from Berlin in the Twenties to London in the present day, but that is no excuse for a subnormal vocabulary, even on the premise that it is appropriate to the tacky French couple (Anna Karina, Jean-Claude Drouot) who prey on the unfortunate Sir Edward. In the latter role Nicol Williamson conveys obsession as well as any actor since Jannings, and he is so persuasive that the final sequences, in which he is tormented in his blindness, are powerful.

One of the films that wrecked Richardson's reputation was *Ned Kelly*, and it was a film of that title that Reisz prepared after *Saturday Night and Sunday Morning*. When Columbia turned it down, Reisz accepted an offer from M-G-M to remake **Night Must Fall** (1964), with a screenplay by Clive Exton, which tries to provide a psycho-sexual attraction between Danny and the old lady's companion (now her daughter), which does not make sense, partly because Susan Hampshire is inadequate in the role. Albert Finney, however, pulls out all the stops as Danny, and the film does chill the spine. **Morgan – a Suitable Case for Treatment** (1966) concerns an impeccable young Marxist (David Warner) so hung up on animals that he confuses them with people, and after much discussion he is in a straitjacket at the end of the film. His fantasies are borrowed from *Billy Liar!*, except that he is the victim of the Fascists rather than their leader; his wife's very-U parents are Jimmy Porter's in-laws in person; and the feeling of pastiche in David Mercer's script is reinforced by resemblances to Ken

Kesey's 'One Flew Over the Cuckoo's Nest'. Richard Lester had recently made *The Knack* (q.v.) in a larky style, but Reisz proves not the man for a similar tactic. The film's greatest asset is Vanessa Redgrave, and for Reisz she became Isadora Duncan in **Isadora** (1969). As a former critic, Reisz was more aware than most of the pitfalls of film biography, which may be why this one, like *Salvatore Giuliano* (to go no further back) is an enquiry into the very nature of Miss Duncan, contrasting her last days with her youth, as it was and as it was imagined by her. Despite this ambition, the screenplay, by Exton, Melvyn Bragg and Margaret Drabble, does no more than pass on information. Miss Redgrave cannot prevent Isadora from being tiresome, nor Reisz rid his film from the stench of mothballs.

While making the film its producers, Universal, quoted him in their publicity as saying, 'Everything must spring from the moment, so that it seems fresh and alive', but this is something Reisz seems incapable of achieving, even in two contemporary tales, made in the U.S., **The Gambler** (1974) and **Who'll Stop the Rain?** (1978), though he responds as keenly as other foreign directors to the American scene. Both compare poorly with films on the same subjects. Unlike Altman with *California Suite* (q.v.), Reisz fails to tear through the more pretentious script of *The Gambler*, while *Who'll Stop the Rain?* is no more than an exploitation piece beside *Cutter's Way* (q.v.), with its heroin-running Vietnam veteran (Nick Nolte), vicious cops and other fashionable clichés.

Nor were Reisz's care and intelligence better served with **The French Lieutenant's Woman** (1981), based on John Fowles's novel. Fowles had retained control over the material, partly because of the terrible film made from another of his novels, *The Magus*. Both stories involve a young man puzzled by the behaviour of others, in the case of the later book an enigmatic young woman. It is a slight tale, made memorable by Fowles's witty asides on Victorian life and literature. The difficulty of wrenching a workable screenplay from the material had defeated half a dozen directors, including Fred Zinnemann. The problem appeared to be solved by replacing Fowles's commentary with a modern story about two actors (Meryl

Streep, Jeremy Irons) who play the Victorian couple in a film version; but as written by Harold Pinter it is vulgar in its own right, embarrassing to watch, and it wrecks the project. The book's dual ending is mentioned and then, foolishly, not used. The film's reviews were mixed, but it achieved a certain caché among cinema patrons, tired of the scifi and blood cluttering up so many screens.

It would be unjust also to label Lindsay Anderson disappointing, since *This Sporting Life* hardly raised expectations. **If . . .** (1968) is a moderately amusing portrait of public school life, but when it was described as 'a hatchet job', Anderson countered that the term was 'misleading . . . it is a timeless and non-specific metaphor for the basic tensions between hierarchy and anarchy, independence and tradition, liberty and law.' One might have hoped that a film about rebellion, or the flouting of authority would have concerned a section of society with a right to protest, e.g. miners or dockers; but Cheltenham College (the exteriors were filmed there, and it is where Anderson himself went to school) is not a microcosm of anything of any importance. The portrait of bumbling governors and other authoritarian figures is less incisive than that in *The Loneliness of the Long Distance Runner*, and the descent into anarchy less pointed than in its inspiration, *Zéro de Conduite*. **O Lucky Man!** (1973) is equally derivative and even more self-indulgent, taking almost three hours to recount the adventures of a salesman (Malcolm McDowell) in a Kafka-esque Britain. At one point he becomes involved with the rich and is told, 'Sir James's time is worth five hundred pounds a minute. Please keep it short', a line that exemplifies the film, heavy-handed, obvious and bludgeoning. It is a Brechtian film, despising its audience, and Anderson's comments, as usual, give ammunition to those who dislike his work. To him this is 'epic satire'. The O was added to the title for 'universality', and he hoped 'to entertain with a story that would continually surprise, continually amuse. And finally enlighten.' A number of respectful reviews hinted that he had succeeded, but the public knew better. The fact that Anderson has made a reputation on three poor films is a mystery, but probably not unconnected with a chronic disposition to

lash out publicly at anyone with whom he disagrees. He apparently told Joan Plowright that she was 'not politically mature' because she did not laugh at **Britannia Hospital** (1982), in which she appeared. The British critics agreed with her on this supposed satire on contemporary Britain, and were not at all amused or respectful.

Jack Clayton, on the other hand, seemed to have improved mightily over his first feature, *Room at the Top*, even if his version of James's 'The Turn of the Screw' seems unduly influenced by the 1944 *Jane Eyre*. **The Innocents** (1961), titled after William Archibald's dramatised version, is academically sound, sufficiently ambiguous and imaginative, and selective of its horrors. One of its few minor flaws is the declamatory tone adopted by Miss Giddens, played by Deborah Kerr, usually a subtle screen actress. Subtlety is not in evidence in **The Pumpkin Eater** (1964), an account of a nervous breakdown experienced by the perpetually pregnant wife (Anne Bancroft) of a philandering scriptwriter. The original novel by Penelope Mortimer was one of those which plundered friends and acquaintances for copy, with their Habitat kitchens and shopping expeditions to Harrods. The screenplay by Harold Pinter is observant of the idiotic remarks overheard on buses and at parties, but falters at content, intent on offering 'meaningful' pauses. Since Clayton's direction is subservient to these, the piece is as long-winded as it is inferior to Bergman's similar studies. **Our Mother's House** (1967) centres on seven young children who hide the fact of their mother's death from the world, which is not among the world's most familiar plots, but it had been used some years earlier by Torre Nilsson in *La Caida* (q.v.). The children in this case resemble some of those in 'Lord of the Flies', and the sense of *déjà-vu* is completed by Dirk Bogarde repeating his role in *The Servant* (q.v.).

The Great Gatsby (1974) was a mistake. The project was started by Ali MacGraw, then married to Paramount's production chief, Robert Evans, because she wanted to play Daisy. Paramount had filmed Fitzgerald's novel twice before, but had relinquished the rights on selling the 1949 version to M.C.A. Television. The company had to repurchase them, as well as paying $350,000 to the Fitzgerald estate, and when the cost rose to $6 million, it sold shares to independent brokers. Publicity was blamed for 'overkill' when the film failed, but the fact was simply that this bright, glancing, melancholy tale had become an ornate, funereal spectacular. The script by Francis Coppola (among those rejected was one by Truman Capote, for which he was paid $100,000) was over-reverential, and Clayton's direction was over-emphatic. Endlessly the parties roll (there are only two, but they seem like two hundred) and endlessly the feet tap, the skirts bob and the camera lingers on the rolled stockings. The film lasts 146 minutes, an achievement of sorts, since the book takes less than half that time to read. Robert Redford's Gatsby lacks the raffish and slightly sinister quality that Alan Ladd brought to the role (and he was not that good); Mia Farrow and Bruce Dern come off best as the Buchanans; Karen Black, the Shelley Winters *de nos jours*, plays Myrtle in familiar style. Scott would not have liked it, but he would have loved the ballyhoo. It is ironic that because of this movie the Twenties became referred to as 'The Gatsby era', and he would have loved that too, the poor son-of-a-bitch.

Clayton's career is unhappily typical of this group, with long pauses searching for the right property – viable, unusual, and above the ordinary run of material: not for him, Richardson or Reisz the pot-boilers that kept Chabrol going. It would be hard to say which approach was the wiser, since Chabrol did return to quality movies, with impressive results, while they foundered on their derivative prestige efforts or were swamped by Hollywood projects for which they were unsuited. It is in that context that the career of John Schlesinger must be considered. When he moved on from the working-class setting, it was to satire (a rare thing in British cinema) with an original screenplay by Frederic Raphael, who was later awarded an Oscar. The film, **Darling** (1965), also won the New York Critics' award as Best of the Year, but a number of dissenters found it as empty as the life it portrayed. Schlesinger himself said ten years later, 'I think it's a madly dated film; at the time we thought it was truthfully done.' It is certainly more truthful than *La Dolce Vita*, which it resembles in being about a world of journalists and models. The heroine, Diana, is an anthology of all the nit-witted models who ever made the headlines, though played by Julie Christie with engaging warmth. As she tells her tale (supposedly dictating for magazine serialisation) the action counterpoints her words with facile irony. 'It should be so easy to be happy,' she says. 'It should be the easiest thing in the world'; and her lover (Dirk Bogarde), rejecting her, cries, 'I don't take whores in taxis'. Both lines, changing the phraseology a little, could come from a Joan Crawford vehicle. I don't find the piece dated; it is amusingly done – from a parody of those man-in-the-street interviews to an embarrassed orgy in Paris, from Diana's gay photographer pal ogling the boys on the Piccola Marina to a theatrical audition.

Raphael, adapting Thomas Hardy for Schlesinger, has allowed the countryside to speak for itself. Hardy believed that man was moulded by his environment or, to use a word more common then, Nature. In **Far from the Madding Crowd** (1967) Dorset and Wiltshire are photographed plain; the supporting faces look neither like actors nor Flaherty-like posers. Best of all, Schlesinger believed we might share the pleasures and pains of rural England under the ageing Queen – bargaining in the corn-exchange, sheep-dipping and joining a workers' supper, saving the ricks from fire and celebrating the harvest festival. The story might be by any specialist in period romance – the self-willed girl (Christie) and her three suitors: the shepherd (Alan Bates), the squire (Peter Finch) and the soldier-deceiver (Terence Stamp); but there has never been a better film about the British countryside. The British press reacted as with *The Charge of the Light Brigade*, but this film also became a popular favourite and has remained so. In the U.S. it was liked by neither press nor public.

Schlesinger, nevertheless, found his next assignment in the U.S., **Midnight Cowboy** (1969), written by Waldo Salt, a Hollywood veteran, from the novel by James Leo Herlihy. It is, ultimately, about the love of two men, though neither of them is exactly, in the film's terminology, a fag. Joe Buck (Jon Voight), a hustler, is wistful American cousin to Billy Liar, and if there is a consistent theme in Schlesinger's films it is that since life is not what one expects as a child, a thought should be spared for those who cannot cope. He

The one British
director to go
from strength to
strength was John
Schlesinger, who at
his best shows both
wit and sympathy.
After making
Darling, RIGHT, with
Dirk Bogarde and
Julie Christie – who
with it became only
the third player to
win a Best Actress
Oscar for a non-
Hollywood film –
Schlesinger was
solicited by the
Americans to direct
Midnight Cowboy,
BELOW, with Jon
Voight and Dustin
Hoffman. The
Oscars this time
went to Schlesinger
for Best Direction
and to the film itself,
as that year's Best.

made his name with a documentary short, *Terminus*, about a lost child; and here both Joe and the shabby cripple, Ratso (Dustin Hoffman), are lost in New York. The film is not only about their relationship, but about the under-belly of the city: the 42nd Street hustlers and hand-me-down con-men; lonely men in hotel rooms; cinema balconies and cheap cafeterias; a man prostrate outside Tiffany's being ignored by passers-by; of a time and a town where sex buys money and money sex, and no one cares which is which any more. Schlesinger peddles dreams with regrettable razzle-dazzle – psychedelic lighting and quick cutting – but the American dream was never more sour. This is a remarkable movie, and was recognised as such by moviegoers, critics and the Academy Award voters.

Sunday, Bloody Sunday (1971) is also about the love of two men, though the younger (Murray Head) of them is unsure whether he cares more for the other (Peter Finch) or for a lonely divorcee (Glenda Jackson). Times Square has given way to Piccadilly, and Schlesinger's locations are, as usual, percipient and evocative. His continual obsession with the uneasy roots of his urban characters enables him to home in on detail – a pile of dishes in a sink, an office-block, a long-playing record – which builds into his fabric. He needs all his expertise for what is otherwise a pot-boiler, credited to Penelope Gilliatt, but by his own admission chiefly written by himself. The screenplay is about sex *only*; it is a sexual view of the universe. Undoubtedly much that is here is based on fact, but Schlesinger's own sympathies cannot bring it to life. *Midnight Cowboy* is optimistic, because its two leading characters, both losers, recognise one positive emotion, a love for each other. Schlesinger has said that *Bloody Sunday* is positive because it is about people coping. The older man is a doctor, but unlike the doctor in *Brief Encounter*, also involved in an emotional situation he could not control, this one fails to arouse sympathy.

Schlesinger returned to the U.S., with a screenplay by Waldo Salt, but despite the Oscars awarded to *Midnight Cowboy* there were no immediate takers for **The Day of the Locust** (1975). When Warners at the last minute backed out, Paramount stepped in, seemingly embarked on a series of

campus classics: but this film is even less successful than *The Great Gatsby*, and just as long, though from an equally short text. It is a travesty of Nathaniel West's novella of Hollywood misfits. Episode after episode in the film is drawn from the original, but with the point blunted or changed. West's book on characters trapped by situation and environment is a theme that excellently suits Schlesinger, but he misses the humour, the incongruities, the melancholy – finding only the grotesque, as is the way of less worthy directors.

Schlesinger made **Marathon Man** (1976) for Paramount to restore his bankability, though he commented later that it was not his favourite film; nor was it anybody's. His ability to create suspense goes for little in such situations as a pursuit in which Dustin Hoffman makes for the city freeways, instead of the bright lights and the nearest precinct. The screenwriter, questioned on its logicality, grunted, 'It's a thriller, for godsake.' He was William Goldman, writer of *Butch Cassidy and the Sundance Kid* (q.v.), and his work here is 'thin, flashy, oversold and opportunistic', to use the adjectives Russell Davies in *The* (London) *Observer* applied to the films of 1976 as a whole. What is so contemptible is that this film uses as its basis the Nazi persecution of the Jews – and we might note that it is mainly the work of Jewish talents. The only reason to see it is Laurence Olivier's performance as the head of New York's present-day coven of Nazis – and it is a sad comment on the movie industry that posterity will have a record of this tawdry monster and not of this actor's Macbeth.

Paramount turned down **Yanks** (1979), a pet project of Schlesinger's, and though Universal put up a sum for the American rights and United Artists another for the British, the bulk of the £3,000,000 budget came from Germany – ironically – since its subject is the effect of the G.I.s on the British, and *vice versa*, while stationed in England, en route for the invasion of Germany. Colin Welland – growing up in Lancashire when the Yanks were there – wrote it, with Walter Bernstein, brought from Hollywood to do the American dialogue. 'Ours is an intimate film,' Schlesinger said, but its trouble is that it is not. The score by Richard Rodney Bennett is grandiose; at 139 minutes the film is too long and though the cross section concept is unexceptionable, the necessary points on the subject are evident in the first reel, leaving no sense of urgency in what follows. However, if future generations want to know what it was like, this film will tell them. The reconstruction of the period is virtually faultless. There is one mistake (Christmas tree lights were banned during the War) and a few omissions (resentment over the G.I.s' smarter uniforms; nylons; the furtiveness of sex). There is also much that is excellent, including individual resentment of the intruding Yanks at a time of bereavement, British championing of black soldiers and a number of moments reminiscent of Schlesinger's early work, such as the busybody who takes over the queue for oranges. The film goes further back, to the days of *In Which We Serve*, with the lower orders having a 'Hokey Cokey' wedding and the lady of the manor (Vanessa Redgrave) an affair with an American officer (William Devane) that is discreet and frightfully well-conducted.

Honky Tonk Freeway (1981) is an American 'road' movie, another cross section tale, about a number of people making their way across country to a small town in Florida, whose leading inhabitants are in despair because the new freeway will bypass it. Edward Clinton's screenplay provided Schlesinger with an opportunity to make a companion picture to *Midnight Cowboy*, broader, funnier and more bitter, because middle-America does not inspire the same affection as Manhattan. The film reflects the consumer society of the good old U.S. of A., being exuberant, somewhat tacky, friendly and enterprising. American critics loathed it, possibly resenting a foreigner commenting on their country in this way. The British critics joined them in their scorn, but that is something which should be considered in the context of other Britishers working for Hollywood companies – a matter approved of only if they make cliquish, minority tales. In this case the money was provided by the British and American sections of E.M.I., and the amount of it was $30 million. I agree with those who failed to see where the money went on the screen, but this is otherwise an entertaining and often funny movie. It is by no means a great one, and is disappointing if compared to Schlesinger's early films –

but I cannot think of any more unfairly handled by the press.

Bryan Forbes followed *The L-Shaped Room* with **Seance on a Wet Afternoon** (1964), co-producing with Richard Attenborough in what seems to be a concerted attempt to draw attention to their virtuosity. The direction is as studied as Attenborough's busy performance – as the husband of a fake medium (Kim Stanley) who between them kidnap a small child. Unlike her co-star, Miss Stanley seems to have accepted that after the first clever scene there is nothing to 'act'. The performance of Edith Evans in **The Whisperers** (1967) is blessedly unlike those customarily given of pathetic old ladies in movies – gaunt, ungainly and unsmiling, her hooded eyes masking prejudice and fear. Eric Portman is also superb but, with the exception of Leonard Rossiter as a welfare man, the other performances are overdrawn. Forbes does not understand reticence and there is not a shot in the film not composed with an eye to the eyes of festival jurors. The two movies nevertheless belong to the aftermath of the Woodfall revolution, but Forbes had aspirations to Hollywood fame. He had an unhappy and unlucky two years as head of production when Associated British Pictures became E.M.I., at the start of which he failed with an American-backed film, **The Madwoman of Chaillot** (1969). He was called in by the producer Ely Landau, when John Huston quit after seventeen days' shooting. If, ideally, Jean Giraudoux's play deserved a fantasist of the order of Clair or Ophuls, Huston was at least an eclectic – but in the event Forbes is merely literal and slow. Edward Anhalt's updating of the original foolishly brings in the then topical subject of the Paris student riots, while Katharine Hepburn's performance as the recluse is one of her late film failures. She is merely an eccentric with 'concern' on her sleeve, whereas the role requires someone brought out of personal fantasy and indecision to represent the forces of right and common sense. Margaret Leighton, querulous and dotty, should have played the part, and of the all-star cast hers is the only successful performance. The largest role is that of the maid, first seen serving in the café, and then serving the Countess, though Giraudoux did not actually give her many lines. She appears constantly to the rear or side of other people's close-ups, and has a number of her own; she is in fact Nanette Newman, the wife of Mr Forbes.

When Forbes's friend Richard Attenborough became a director he showed a fondness for 'epic' films with messages. **Oh! What a Lovely War** (1969) had been a very moving stage piece in the form of an end-of-the-pier entertainment, built around the songs and statistics of the First World War. The casualty board, so eloquent on the stage, appears in the film but briefly, and it is difficult to believe that anyone concerned with this all-star effort really felt deeply about the waste, the criminality, the stupidity and pointlessness of that war – except Len Deighton, who wrote the screen adaptation but demanded that his name be removed from the credits after seeing the result. Joan Littlewood's original tight conception has been transmuted into a mish-mash of ill-digested ideas, many staged in an art director's dream decor, like the artful poppies popping into focus before the mud. American critics were much less impressed than the British, but it was an American, Joseph E. Levine, who chose Attenborough to direct **A Bridge Too Far** (1977). This is a study of one of the great debacles of the Second World War, the Battle of Arnhem, when 35,000 men were parachuted behind the German lines with the intention of taking the six strategic bridges across the Ruhr and thus shortening the war by three months. Cornelius Ryan had written a book on the subject as a follow-up to that on which *The Longest Day* was based, but the wherewithal for the operation, the tactics and the actual events seem to have been of little interest to either Attenborough or to the screenwriter, William Goldman. As the film draws to its overdue close – it lasts 175 minutes – it is clear that they, like Harlan in his wretched *Kolberg*, are trying to sell 'failure' to audiences; and they do it, incredibly, with sentimentality and artiness, borrowing an image from 'Mother Courage' and the spinning cartwheel from *Potemkin*. Of the names in the cast, Sean Connery and Anthony Hopkins impress, while the best performances are given by some lesser-known people, Frank Grimes, Edward Fox and John Stride.

It would seem from the evidence that Attenborough believes that the old-fashioned artefacts that he directs can become respectable or even 'art' if replete with liberal values – which is not to say that he is insincere. He was determined to make **Gandhi** (1982) from the moment he became a producer in the early Sixties, and the dream seemed to become a likelihood when Levine agreed to find the backing as a successor to *A Bridge Too Far*. The comparative failure of that film made him change his mind, but Attenborough had already sunk £60,000 of his own money into development. The film cost £9 million, the bulk of it coming from Goldcrest Films (q.v.), plus smaller amounts put up by an American investment company and, after an Indian maharaja had pulled out at the last minute, the Indian government. Since the film distorts what Gandhi said and believed, and since the greatest threat to Mrs Indira Gandhi's regime is from the Gandhians – with the Marxists a close second – it is not surprising that she wished to back it. At least, this is the view of the Indian critic Prabhu S. Guptara, who also objects to the presence in the film of an undue preponderance of Westerners in Gandhi's life, such as the American photographer (Candice Bergen) and reporter (Martin Sheen), a device imitative of *Lawrence of Arabia*. Guptara feels these people do not compensate for 'the major, central imbalance of the film, Gandhi's spiritual quest, which was at the centre of everything he attempted as a man and politician [and] is entirely and completely missing'; he has also pointed out that Gandhi was not against British rule but that he believed that it would not disappear until it was understood why foreigners were in power in the first place.

Gandhi is simply too important a figure for the film's distortions to pass unnoticed, particularly in the right-wing press, for the piece is violently against the Raj. Attenborough chose John Briley, an American, to write the screenplay on the basis of his work on *Pope Joan*, a film no one else seemed to like; and Briley claimed – at least before *Gandhi* won its many Oscars, including Best Picture, Best Direction and Best Actor – that what was on screen was not what he wrote. At 188 minutes it is an absurdly overlong entertainment, with none of the pretension which mars Attenborough's earlier work as a director; it has a slow, steady pace which recalls the discredited 'roadshow' epics of the Sixties. It

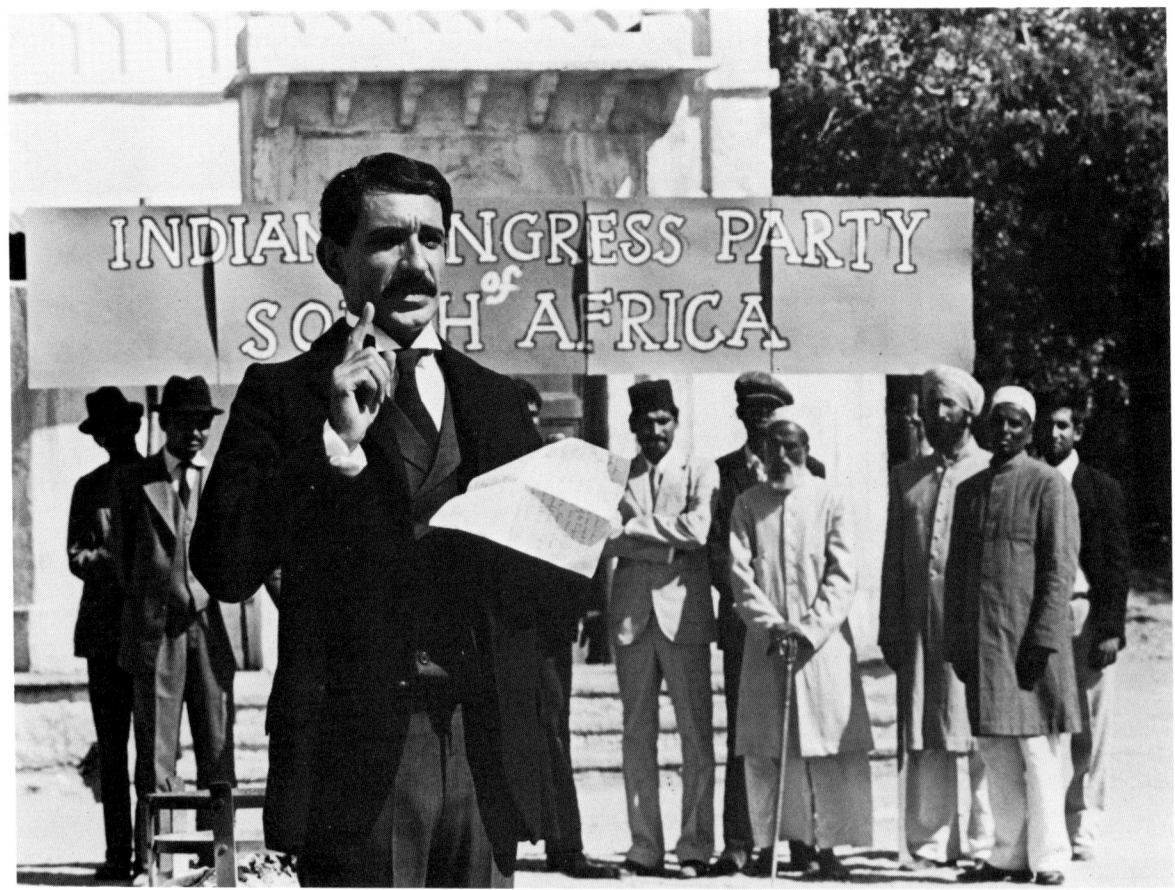

Ben Kingsley
in Richard
Attenborough's life
of *Gandhi*, which won
several Oscars and in
other ways justified
Attenborough's
twenty-year struggle
to complete the
project. This is the
young Gandhi,
during his South
African period, and
it has to be said
that Kingsley's
performance was a
vital factor in the
film's effectiveness.

is better than most of them because it has a strong subject – even if it is not the right one – injustice and one man's fight against it. It is a biography of a major twentieth-century figure who spent most of his life in dispute with the authorities set over him. It is therefore not dissimilar in several ways to its contemporary, *Reds* (q.v.), but where that has vitality and ambiguity this marshals its facts simply, though often with subtlety. Attenborough's respect for his subject and India is always apparent – in, for instance, hiring Ravi Shankar to compose the music – while Ben Kingsley's performance in the title role is often moving. The film's exposition of goodness may be one reason for its popularity – but it would be a pity if that encouraged a return to long, expensive movies.

Attenborough's other films as director include a story of Churchill's youth, *Young Winston*, which was not a success for its writer-producer Carl Foreman. Of the many films written and/or produced by Foreman, he himself directed only one, **The Victors** (1963), from his own script, declaring that in neither *The Bridge on the River Kwai* nor *The Guns of Navarone* had he been able 'to articulate the clear and forceful statement' that he wished to make on war. *The Victors*, like *Paisà*, offers episodes of army life from the invasion of Sicily upwards, and the gentlemen of the title are played by some young American actors, whose conquests are often restricted to a bevy of popular European female stars. Wars make nice girls whores, according to Foreman, but soldiers get dehumanised too. This particular platoon has the job of shooting a G.I. for desertion in 1943, as Frank Sinatra sings (anachronistically) 'Have Yourself a Merry Little Christmas', which is typical of Foreman's approach, as is the ending, a knife-fight between a G.I. (George Hamilton) and a Russian soldier (Albert Finney) – symbolic harbinger of the Cold War to come. The film lasts almost three hours, and never approaches the force of Wellman's *The Story of G.I. Joe*.

Another prominent black-listed American film-maker working in Britain, originally under a pseudonym, was Joseph Losey (b. 1909). A number of programmers under his own name occasioned no comment, but **Blind Date** (1959) gained several admirers in France – to the satisfaction of the Rank Organisation which, having abandoned hope of breaking into the American market, had turned to Europe, employing a number of continental stars. In this case they are Hardy Kruger and Micheline Presle, as suspect and victim in a particularly absurd murder mystery. Losey accepted an offer from France to film a pulp thriller by James Hadley Chase, but **Eva** (1962) emerged as art house fodder, helped by Gianni di Venanzo's grey-toned photography of Rome and Venice and borrowings from *L'Avventura*, not to mention Jeanne Moreau in her familiar role as *femme fatale*. Stanley Baker plays a writer obsessed by her. The film impressed a few, and picked up some further admirers (as is customary in such circumstances) when it became known that the producers, the Hakim brothers, had loathed it so much that they had cut it before distribution.

Losey returned to Britain, and at last achieved a considerable reputation with **The Servant** (1963), based on Robin Maugham's novel about a curious relationship between a rich young man (James Fox) and his valet (Dirk Bogarde). Losey and Bogarde had discussed filming it some years earlier, but in the meantime Michael Anderson had bought the rights and had found backing for a screenplay by Harold Pinter. Associated British became involved, and with the aid of the Grade Organisation, agent for some of the principals, the film was financed to the modest sum of £150,000. Pinter was the ideal choice for the script, since his first and best play, 'The Birthday Party', concerned a similar exercise in who might be doing what to whom. *The Servant* was like no other English-speaking movie. Only in Antonioni would one find this mocking, acrid view of the rich, and although Osborne, and others, had more broadly

characterised them as brainless nitwits, this film dropped large hints of lesbianism, drunkenness among the clergy and other decadent practices. Pinter offered, in the end, only a conundrum. The film works towards an affirmation of homosexual dependence – the whole point of Maugham's novel – and then up-ends it, in an epilogue tacked on by Losey and Pinter, who admitted that it was an attempt to deny the homosexual connotation.

For a mere £80,000 Losey made **King and Country** (1964), a drama of the trenches of World War One, with Tom Courtenay as a deserter and Bogarde as his defending officer. It is a film as heavy in irony and emotional bankruptcy as Foreman's *The Victors*. **Accident** (1967) sets a tale of interweaving loves, ambitions and jealousies against the minutiae of Oxford life, as adapted by Pinter from a novel by Nicholas Mosley, and it is a good example of the second-rate imitating its betters. In an interview in *Sight and Sound* Losey made it clear that he had seen *Muriel* and *Il Deserto Rosso*, but in his case the elliptical structure is used to confuse instead of illuminate – or to create enigma for its own sake, as in the sequence where the don (Dirk Bogarde) returns home to find another don in his dressing-gown, with a woman revealed to him, but not the audience (yet), as someone other than his wife.

M-G-M backed **The Go-Between** (1971) but disliked it so much that it sold the American rights to Columbia, just before it won the Grand Prix at Cannes, beating *Death in Venice* – to Visconti's professed annoyance. A number of theorists went to work to prove that it continued the Losey-Pinter exploration of the British class-structure, which it did, but only by violating L. P. Hartley's original novel, which concerns an affair between a young farmer (Alan Bates) and a well-born young lady (Julie Christie). She is the daughter of the manor-house, which becomes in the film the most stately of stately homes, a distance far more difficult to breach but in keeping with the film's overall vulgarity, with Michel Legrand's mock-Bach thundering on the soundtrack. Losey later observed that none of his British films – there were several others – had made money and, obviously aware that someone was trying to tell him something, decamped to France, where his reputation was less equivocally held. The first film of his sojourn, **Mr Klein** (1976), confirmed his craftsmanship, but also his relentless pursuit of an art house taste which did not exist outside his own imagination and that of the French. They awarded a César, i.e. their Oscar, to this modish piece about a Jew wanted by the Nazis for deportation, co-scripted with Franco Solinas, whose credits include *Salvatore Giuliano* and *La Battaglia di Algeri*. John Coleman's *New Statesman* review is an epitaph on Losey's work, 'God knows it is fashionable in some quarters to make puzzle-pictures, life being an enigma, etc . . . [but] after all, there was a real War, there were six million Jews killed, and super-chic, a kind of stoned mystification – however comforting to the prize-giving French – seem inapposite approaches to these facts: like running up a Dior shroud for a corpse.'

Another American working in Britain – and a former associate of Losey on British T.V. series – is Richard Lester (b. 1932), whose work on T.V. commercials developed into a fragmented, frenzied style which, added to his irreverent humour, made him an ideal director for the Sixties (and for the Beatles, the pop-group which left an indelible mark on that decade). His first film, a short, was *The Running, Jumping and Standing Still Film*, with Peter Sellers (with whom he had worked in T.V.), and he has the Beatles running, jumping and not standing still in his third feature and their first, **A Hard Day's Night** (1964). Indeed, everyone concerned seems to have St Vitus's dance, perhaps to divert us from the fact that our four heroes have no charisma as actors. A vague plot has them arriving in London for a concert, and on the assumption that audiences were curious to see *them*, it was just as well to let them play themselves. Alun Owen's inconsequential and theoretically Marxian script de-mythifies them. They are 'us', not 'them'. Their targets are the same as those of Lucky Jim, Hancock and Billy Liar – bowler-hatted gentlemen in railway-carriages, stuffed-shirt reporters, nervous shop-assistants, pompous hotel clerks and camp T.V. producers. All of these were easy targets, and the screenplay is humourless and sycophantic into the bargain.

Comment was inevitably centred on the Beatles, and it was not till **The Knack, and How To Get It** (1965) that Lester came into his own, a youthful lark about sex, and the graduation from fantasy to practice. This one has, however, dated even more horribly than *A Hard Day's Night*. We laughed then at Rita Tushingham running around London crying 'Rape'; at the journey of the new bed through the city; at the sight (or sound) of sacred cows on the soundtrack, e.g. the Queen, writers to the *Daily Telegraph*, senior citizens. They are old fogeys. Our young heroes are free spirits – literally, as they are wafted about London – and if they are preoccupied with sex, is that not because they are young and healthy? Lester does not seem really to know these emotions, but has borrowed them, with so much else, from Jean-Luc Godard. The high spirits aimed for are never comparable to such aged films as, say, *Le Million* or *Sonnenstrahl*, both of which, not coincidentally, had pleasing leading players. There were never three musketeers as lacklustre as Ray Brooks, Donal Donnelly and Michael Crawford, the latter in a particularly narcissistic performance.

A Funny Thing Happened on the Way to the Forum (1966) we owe first to Hal Prince (q.v.), creator extraordinary of Broadway musicals. Its 'anything-goes' comic-strip book, originally by Burt Shevelove and Larry Gelbart, required Lester's similar visual approach. Faced with the Beatles' lack of screen personality, he had broken their songs into fragments, and he does the same with Stephen Sondheim's songs, in keeping with the harum scarum quality of the enterprise. The final chariot race is no more inventive than that chase in *It's a Mad, Mad, Mad, Mad World*, but infinitely funnier, proving that Mack Sennett can be recycled if the spirit is right. Buster Keaton is around, if briefly. He, the flustered Michael Hordern and the ingratiating Jack Gilford take the piece from the two billed stars, Zero Mostel and Phil Silvers. Best of all is Patricia Jessel as the iron-jawed, iron-willed matron, innocently boasting to the incredulous commander that she entertained two hundred soldiers all by herself. More surprisingly, Lester proved adept at drama, or at least his frenetic handling was suitable for the special circumstances of **Petulia** (1968). The title role is played by Julie Christie, a young lady who leaves her sadistic husband (Richard Chamberlain) in search of an adulterous affair, which she achieves with a doctor (George C. Scott). Her sadness and the doctor's kindness are more important than the plot, and more important than either is the urban malaise suffocating them – specifically that of San Francisco. This was the first British film made in the U.S. since the days of the first Talkies. The camera, wielded by Nicolas Roeg (q.v.) is seldom still, and since Lawrence B. Marcus's sour screenplay is based on a novel called 'Me and the Arch Kook Petulia' it may be said that the film's visual style was appropriate for the kookiness.

On either side of *Petulia*, Lester made two comedies, *How I Won the War* and *The Bed Sitting Room*, so appallingly childish – the second concerned Britain after a nuclear attack – that his neglect over the next years was entirely understandable. He worked in Italian T.V., on commercials, until rescued by Alexander Salkind, who had envisaged **The Three Musketeers** (1973) for a new generation, with a great number of pratfalls and a kick in the groin as likely as a thrust with a sword. Lester's excesses and fussiness proved no substitute for the excitement engendered by previous versions, and Oliver Reed, Charlton Heston (Richelieu), Richard Chamberlain, Faye Dunaway, Raquel Welch, Geraldine Chaplin, Christopher Lee, Michael York and an unfunny comic, Spike Milligan, performed to less than expectations, which in most cases were not high to start with. They had, however, shot enough material for two films, and after re-negotiations involving salaries, *The Four Musketeers* turned up, to appreciably fewer spectators. Lester chose as his screenwriter George MacDonald Fraser, whose Victorian spoof novels about a character named Flashman he had been hoping to film for years. He finally did – *Royal Flash* – to no avail.

Undeterred, Lester tried once more for historical anachronism in **Robin and Marian** (1976). James Goldman provided the screenplay, with a number of thoughts on medieval kingship which he could not fit into *The Lion in Winter* (q.v.), in the process proving that more than realism, i.e. four-letter words and gallons of blood,★ was needed in attempting to redefine old

myths. The aged Robin Hood (Sean Connery) speaks as a modern radical; the peasants are merely oafish; and a number of talented people – Ian Holm, Ronnie Barker, Nicol Williamson, not to mention Audrey Hepburn as Maid Marian – are wasted. Warners offered **The Ritz** (1976) on the principle that Lester's characters are always leaping about, and this concerns a number of chases inside a gay New York bath-house, as adapted by Terence McNally from his own Broadway farce. The film features among others Jack Weston, escaping from his Mafia-minded brother-in-law, Rita Moreno as an untalented but temperamental chanteuse, and Treat Williams as a detective who only looks like Alan Ladd when he is fully clothed. There are good jokes for collectors of gay humour, and Lester's customary facetiousness gives way to that. His later work includes *Superman II* (q.v.).

His erstwhile photographer, Nicolas Roeg (who had also worked with Clive Donner and Schlesinger) became a director, but one less interested in situation and character than camera-angles and ostentatious locations. **Don't Look Now** (1973) and **The Man Who Fell to Earth** (1976) are splendid examples of mumbo-jumbo. The first, an elongation of a supernatural tale by Daphne du Maurier, takes place in a wintry Venice – much less sinister in this film, despite Roeg's tricks, than in reality – and concerns a child who might, or might not, be dead. The second is about an extraterrestrial being (David Bowie) stranded in the wilds of the U.S. and planning to take over control of the world. Paramount backed out from its involvement in the film on seeing it complete, and it was finally taken for America by a minor distributor, Cinema 5, whose president, Don Rugoff, said, 'I didn't understand the film, but the kids really do.' He cut it by 25 minutes, thereby causing Americans to wonder how many of the ambiguities were intentional.

Another director chiefly concerned with effect is John Boorman who, after a British pop film, found himself in the U.S. directing a heist tale with Lee Marvin, **Point Blank** (1967), which borrows all the tricks of Lester and Godard to such an extent that the plot is completely annihilated. One of its producers, Robert Chartoff, combined with Irwin Winkler to produce a similar

★Both elements were edited out of the television print, which I am told is quite pleasing.

movie, *The Split*, after which they backed Boorman's **Leo the Last** (1970), gallantly described by Chartoff as 'considerably ahead of its time' when it flopped with both press and public. It did, however, win the Director's Prize at Cannes, possibly because it can be seen to be directed – that is to say, derelict houses in Notting Hill Gate are painted black, the way Antonioni painted a street in *Il Deserto Rosso*, and the various orgies suggest Fellini. However, Boorman, under control, can direct, as Warners proved with **Deliverance** (1972), which offers the classic cinema suspense of chase and survival. As adapted by James Dickey from his own novel, four city men go canoeing in the Appalachian Mountains. 'The machines are gonna fail,' one (Burt Reynolds) says prophetically, 'the system's gonna fail,' and it is he who is first forced to kill – the mountain man who is raping one of his buddies. You may not care to trace the allegories, but this is the best man-against-nature thriller that films have yet done.

In the matter of showing-off, Boorman and Roeg are minor league compared with Ken Russell, who made the transition from T.V. to cinema with **Women in Love** (1969), written and produced by Larry Kramer with fidelity to its source, but also containing a subtle substitution of his own false premises for Lawrence's – most obviously in the matter of love, marital, carnal, platonic and in the nude wrestling scene between Gerald (Oliver Reed) and Rupert (Alan Bates). Apart from one lingering shot of a rearing horse (symbol of masculinity) over-emphasis is withheld till the final sequence in Zermatt, when the film goes completely off the rails, with Gudrun (Glenda Jackson) prancing round the room, while an ageing queen (Vladek Sheybal) proclaims himself Tchaikovsky. 'I'm a homosexual . . . You will be my wife and writhe on the floor of a railway carriage.' She did, too, for Miss Jackson played Tchaikovsky's wife in Russell's *The Music Lovers*, with Richard Chamberlain as the composer. Aided by some critics' quotes, United Artists was able to advertise the film as having 'raving and hysterical sex', while Russell's on-screen pyrotechnics and his penchant for publicity enabled his next film to arrive as 'Ken Russell's **The Devils**' (1971), the sort of billing it had taken other directors several years to earn. The film itself is a catalogue of violence, viciousness and sexuality built around the seventeenth century events in Loudon concerning diabolic possession. Not only did it confirm Russell's obsession with such matters, but it proved conclusively that he lacks virtually every requirement of a film-maker. He is capable of putting spectacular and *outré* images on the screen, but he has no gift for character, situation, pacing, rhythm, tension or tone. His subsequent movies, equally bizarre, created increasingly less controversy and less business at the box-office. He blamed the critics, adding that their opinions would not prevent him from making more films. As offers died away, he returned to television. After a three-year absence from films, however, he was invited to Hollywood to film **Altered States** (1980), the adventures of a scientist (William Hurt) who becomes obsessed with taking himself on psychedelic trips. Paddy Chayevsky, who had written the original novel, chose to use a pseudonym for his screenplay credit. Russell's contribution is leaden self-plagiarism, and if the film attracted some mild attention in the States, it was dismissed elsewhere.

For a while it looked as though the young Hungarian-born Peter Medak belonged to this school of showy filmmakers. **Negatives** (1970) consists of 'kinky' games-time between a particularly tedious trio (Glenda Jackson, Peter McEnery, Diane Cilento), and **The Ruling Class** (1972) is an overlong black comedy about an English milord (Peter O'Toole), who fancies himself first as Christ and then as Jack the Ripper, behaving accordingly. Peter Barnes adapted it from his own West End play, continuing to tilt at disused windmills, and Medak was no more able to make the jokes seem fresh than he was of controlling the star, O'Toole, who was also the producer. There was, however, some consolation in the butler (Arthur Lowe), whose servility masks communist sympathies and contempt for his employers. But with a better and more difficult piece, **A Day in the Death of Joe Egg** (1972), Medak proved to be the equal of almost any of his contemporaries. Peter Nichols, adapting his autobiographical play, moves in familiar fields – suburban send-up, nostalgia, family squabbles – but he moves confidently where others toil

If many of the British movies of the Sixties remain memorable all but a handful of those from the Seventies are best forgotten. That handful would include *A Day in the Death of Joe Egg*, with Alan Bates and Janet Suzman as a couple with a spastic child. Peter Nichols's play had been a success in both London and New York, and since Peter Medak's careful direction did justice to its difficulties its failure may be a comment on the differing sensibilities experienced in the theatre and the cinema.

and stumble. Since his purpose was to stimulate laughter in detailing the troubles of a couple with a helplessly spastic child, the stage production required the utmost delicacy. Moving in with close-up, Medak achieves an admirable reticence and sympathy which is admittedly aided by the performances of Janet Suzman and Alan Bates. It is a film made with love. Columbia, releasing it, did not love it – afraid, reasonably, of euthanasia as a movie subject. It could only have succeeded at the box office with rave notices, and, opening in the wake of *The Ruling Class*, it was dismissed, with virtually no acknowledgment of its subject or the fact that Nichols's play had been one of the most admired of the past decade.

Jack Gold, who has had more success directing for television than the cinema, made a good film from **The National Health** (1975), adapted by Peter Nichols from his own play. Nichols's virtues as humorist and social historian are evident in this realistic account of life in the ward of an antiquated hospital, its amenities contrasted with the fictional one – the scene of a parody of medical soap operas which cuts into the action. The best feature of the latter is Lynn Redgrave's joyful imitation of her sister Vanessa; the best of the rest of it are the character studies, headed by Jim Dale as the cheeky orderly, and Clive Swift, Colin Blakely and Bob Hoskins as assorted patients.

Another of Nichols's plays, **Privates on Parade** (1982), came to the screen in unfortunate manner, with some palm trees stuck in a sunny English field pretending to be Singapore in 1948. The small budget was also reflected in some historical inaccuracies, but John Cleese is funny as a C.O. magnificiently obtuse to the 'camping' all around him – as led by an outrageously effeminate Denis Quilley, repeating his clever and endearing stage performance. Michael Blakemore directed, as he had done for the Royal Shakespeare Company, and there are clear parallels with **The Virgin Soldiers**

(1969), directed by John Dexter, also best known for his work in the theatre. It is also set during the Malayan Emergency, in 1950; and it also has some amusement at the expense of young conscripts and their experience of sex and life in the service before becoming serious – and bloody – up country, to provide the expected antiwar message. As written by John Hopkins from the novel by Leslie Thomas, it is a much better film than *Privates on Parade*; it also reflects the changes wrought in British cinema by being almost the first accurate picture of British service life – marvellously so in its account of the monthly dance, from the hours spent before mirrors with combs and Brylcreem, to disillusion over the available ladies and the movement towards getting as drunk as possible. Hywel Bennett (the hero), Nigel Davenport (the sergeant), Michael Gwynn (the vague colonel), Jack Shepherd (the boastful corporal), Nigel Patrick (the R.S.M.), Rachel Kempson (his wife) and Lynn Redgrave (their daughter) are all splendidly right.

Nichols contributed to **Georgy Girl** (1966), writing the screenplay with Margaret Forster, author of the original novel. The Canadian-born director, Silvio Narizzano, has his predominantly young cast behave in the relentlessly facetious manner of those in the films of Richard Lester, but their antics otherwise are pleasing. The Georgy of the title is an ugly duckling, warmly and touchingly played by Lynn Redgrave, who finds herself permanent second fiddle to her glamorous and promiscuous room-mate (Charlotte Rampling). The latter spends most of her time in bed with Jos (Alan Bates) who, like Georgy's Daddy Long Legs (James Mason), gradually awakens to Georgy's considerable charms. The film was particularly popular in the U.S., where sexual activity was still more or less restricted to the comedies of Doris Day and Rock Hudson.

Narizzano directed **Loot** (1970), which arrived at the same time as **Entertaining Mr Sloane** (1970), directed by Douglas Hickox and also based on a play by Joe Orton. Of all those who cocked a snook at society in the wake of Amis and Osborne, Orton was the most individual, the most extreme and the wittiest, quietly advancing the most outrageous propositions on life behind the lace-curtains. *Mr Sloane*, briefly, concerns a middle-aged brother

(Harry Andrews) and sister (Beryl Reid) each with such lecherous intentions towards a young pick-up (Peter McEnery) that they are prepared to overlook his brutal murder of their father. *Loot* is a tale of two young thieves (Hywel Bennett, Roy Holder) prepared to do anything rather than surrender the swag they have hidden in the coffin of the mother of one of them, and a Scotland Yard man (Richard Attenborough) who has equally few scruples. On the understanding that Orton was a working-class writer, both films are burdened with pop-songs, garish suburban decor and a frenzied pace. They also dilute what was Orton's greatest strength, the Civil Servantese of his dialogue. That *Loot* is the better of the two only indicates the vulgarity of the other.

It may be typical of the British cultural climate that few critics pointed out how unworthy these two films were of their author; few complained at the inadequacy of *Privates on Parade*, and there were few to point out the virtues of *A Day in the Death of Joe Egg*; yet there was an outcry over **Charlie Bubbles** (1967), written by a much lesser figure than either Orton or Nichols, Shelagh Delaney. The film was rejected by the large London cinemas and the circuits, and the press as a whole came to the rescue – though fortunately not encouraging either the writer or the director, Albert Finney, to persevere in these occupations. The direction is, admittedly, observant, particularly on the experience of returning to once-familiar territory, now changed by circumstances and one's own experiences. Finney himself plays the lead and at the end, his problems unsolved, he grabs a balloon and floats out to sea – a final insult in a script of whoozy insignificance.

Even at this level it was clear that the sterility of the old British cinema had gone for ever. Certain talents moved ahead in their own fashion, unaffected by the American money poured into a number of projects, usually elephantine comedies, which tried and failed to unite traditional British humour with the new permissiveness. After its troubles at home at the end of the Sixties Hollywood became more selective in financing British pictures; E.M.I. had a few isolated successes, often with an American co-partner, while Rank and the television-owned I.T.C. limped along. The films of E.M.I. and I.T.C. were likely to be of supposed 'international' appeal, but Rank, too often burnt by like ambitions, backed predominately British films till deciding to quit production in 1980. The producers, directors and writers of the postwar period retired; and, as we have seen, few of those who came to prominence in the Woodfall period and afterwards had more than a precarious foothold. There were movie spin-offs from T.V. series, some very popular, and there were several one-of-a-kind films, symptomatic of an industry divided – sunk back into lethargy and desperate to know what next to put before the cameras.

20th Century-Fox financed **The Rocky Horror Picture Show** (1975), admittedly on a low budget and presumably because the original was then half way through what was to become its ten-year stage run. It is set in a Transylvanian castle where the men walk around in female underwear except for a leather-clad motor-cyclist and a robot fashioned from a physique magazine. A young American couple stumbles upon them, to the confusion of their own sexuality – but that promising idea is lost in timidity. The execution of the musical numbers is execrable and the overall lack of talent quite startling. Said the director, Jim Sharman, 'We've aimed for something tacky . . . It's trivia, but if you want to know what pop-culture in the Seventies is all about, this show will tell you.' He is apparently right: the attention paid to the stage show and the film was initially and at best dismissive, but it has become one of the most persistent items in the weekend midnight matinee repertory. A follow-up, **Shock Treatment** (1981), has not; this particular audience has available a large number of off-centre, low-budget, pornographic and scatological films more satisfying to its taste for camp.

British screen musicals have, with reason, a grim reputation, and **Bugsy Malone** (1976) is even more difficult to sit through than *The Rocky Horror Picture Show*, though made by more talented people. The idea of its writer-director, Alan Parker, was to re-create Chicago gang-warfare in terms of children, with guns firing custard-pies instead of bullets and with orange juice replacing booze; but his young cast was not accomplished enough to disguise the weakness of the

musical numbers and the intended satire. Parker, like most British directors of his generation, had graduated from television commercials to television films. The latter include **The Evacuees** (1975), an enchanting, honest and funny account, written by Jack Rosenthal, of two young Jewish boys billeted on a gentile Lancashire family during the War. *Bugsy Malone* came about when Parker realised that there were no films around to which he might take his children, but given the reluctance of British banks to finance local talent Parker did not find it easy to graduate from television to cinema. In this case the government-sponsored National Film Finance Corporation advanced some money, which encouraged Rank and Paramount to supply the rest needed, for the respective British and American rights (the supposition being, as in the case of *The Slipper and the Rose*, *Chitty-Chitty Bang-Bang* and others, that children's films provide an indefinite annuity, though the only proof has been provided by Disney and by M-G-M with *The Wizard of Oz*).

Parker and the producer David Puttnam were each offered **Midnight Express** (1978) by Columbia, and they decided to do it to prove that they could make the sort of action tale which appealed to American audiences. Oliver Stone's screenplay is based on the book by Billy Hayes (played in the film by Brad Davis) about his experiences in a Turkish jail for being in possession of two kilos of drugs. It was a dishonest book, as Puttnam (by his own admission) was increasingly aware, but the film compounds the matter by being rabidly racial. It implies that Hayes was innocent; it makes much of his escape, though he was in fact released under an amnesty agreement; homosexuality was practised by everyone (the commentary informs us) but in the film it is limited to the Turkish guards, who are brutal rapists as well. The Turks as a whole are shown to be hypocrites, only pretending to take a stand on drug-trafficking. Our hero tears out the one good eye and the tongue of a Turkish prisoner, said to be an informer, and we are expected to be sympathetic. The film was popular and considered to be powerful in some quarters, but it received its just deserts in others: *Time* called it 'repulsive' and Tom Milne in *The Observer* 'repellent'.

British Cinema: A Matter of Collusion

Working in television Parker had underplayed his situations, but he goes to the other extreme in movies, to the extent of killing whatever subtleties were in Bo Goldman's original script for **Shoot the Moon** (1982). This is one of the crop of Hollywood movies on divorce which followed *Kramer vs. Kramer* (q.v.) and the break-up in question occurs in Marin County between a writer (Albert Finney) and a wife (Diane Keaton) left with several small children. Finney's performance, without any reference to his English accent, and apparently modelled on Dracula, is as showy and heavy as the direction. There is hardly a scene which rings true, and when he goes berserk at the end it seems only too fitting.

Michael Apted has proved a more attentive student of the American scene. His British films are undistinguished, including **Agatha** (1979), a rather pointless investigation into the celebrated disappearance of the thriller writer Agatha Christie in 1926, with Vanessa Redgrave in that role and Dustin Hoffman as an American reporter. The film's thesis is that Ms Christie plans an elaborate plot to murder the mistress of her husband, whom she loathes so much, while the real truth seems to be that she accused her husband of intent to murder before she disappeared and hoped by staying hidden long enough that he would be convicted and hanged. The film is carefully made, but not the polished work that is **Coal Miner's Daughter** (1980), which follows the fortunes of Loretta Lynn from courtship in a Kentucky shack to coping with the stresses of fame as a popular Country and Western singer. Tom Rickman's screenplay, based on Miss Lynn's book, has the richer material in the first half, in its portrait of a primitive community and Lynn's realisation that fame might be at hand. That fame is handled, in the second part of the film, neither mawkishly nor with particular care for the two individuals concerned. They, Miss Lynn and her husband, are admirably played by Sissy Spacek (who was awarded an Oscar) and Tommy Lee Jones.

Agatha, like *Midnight Express*, was produced by David Puttnam, who said that he backed **Chariots of Fire** (1981) because it was the antithesis of the latter – and a more accurate example of the sort of movie he wanted to make. The director, Hugh Hud-

son, had done some second unit work on Parker's film, and before then had worked in commercials, as is evident from his style on this occasion. Colin Welland's screenplay is founded on what may be said to be false assumptions, since it was based on fact. Harold Abrahams (Ben Cross) was not motivated by his experience of anti-Semitism, but sibling rivalry; and Eric Lidell (Ian Charleson) had long decided to do what the film presents as a huge dilemma for him. But the film's faults are as nothing to its virtues – and, indeed, it was rewarding to find the British cinema, again moribund, making a statement on anti-Semitism and making a film about Cambridge University, about Scottish Presbyterianism and the two runners from each background who went on to triumph in the 1924 Paris Olympics. The film was part-financed by an American group, The Ladd Company, and when 20th Century-Fox (who released in Britain) lost its services, they let the film go with it to Warners. It was awarded a popular Best Picture Oscar and became the most successful 'British' film ever to play in American cinemas. With local production at its lowest level – films for television apart – within living memory, Puttnam became the man on whom the hopes of the British film industry rested, as he well knew: it was to him that aspiring directors and writers brought projects, in the knowledge that the American production companies had confidence in his judgment. He has said that he intends to remain a producer or an executive producer, only working on films to which he can give individual attention. He is encouraging on every aspect of the industry: it may be that he keeps a high profile (because of the Oscar), but I cannot recall in two decades a spokesman with such sound ideas on what British films should be doing.

The local industry was also cheered at this time by **The Long Good Friday** (1981), a corkscrew thriller about an East End gang leader (Bob Hoskins), expertly directed by John MacKenzie, and **Gregory's Girl** (1980), a naive but sweet comedy directed by Bill Forsyth. Forsyth's semi-amateur **That Sinking Feeling** (1979), the adventures of some Glaswegian teenagers, is pretentious, and derivative of Richard Lester's early films. However, the jokes in *Gregory's Girl* spring not from old movies but the whims and inconsistencies of life. Its young hero (Gordon John Sinclair) is a schoolboy in a new town near Glasgow, and his girl is a rather glamorous young lady (Dee Hepburn) who manages to get herself a place in the boys' football team. David Puttnam invited Forsyth to write and direct a film in the manner of Ealing comedy, and the result was **Local Hero** (1983), a pleasing entertainment which sets two smart American businessmen (Burt Lancaster, Peter Riegert) among some even cannier Scottish villagers, but it is not a very substantial one – at least in comparison with *The 'Maggie'*, but it is possible that Forsyth thought Ealing comedy should not be emulated at this stage.

Forsyth's obvious influences were the films of Ken Loach (b. 1936) and Tony Garnett (b. 1936), the dominant names at that point where British cinema and television meet. Loach made his name with a T.V. documentary in the B.B.C.'s 'Wednesday Play' series, 'Cathy Come Home', followed by another study of working-class life, 'Up the Junction', written by Nell Dunn. While inferior talents made a movie of the second, Joseph Janni – an old Rank hand best noted for finding the backing for Schlesinger's British films – got Loach and Dunn to collaborate on **Poor Cow** (1967), a further thesis on the deprived – in this case, the milieu of petty crooks and their women. This girl (Carol White) shacks up with a pal (Terence Stamp) of her husband's while the latter is in jail. She becomes a barmaid, poses for Sunday morning photographers and is both on the game and in the throes of divorce when the husband returns; they then settle down once more to domestic boredom. Loach was still reacting against films like *The Blue Lamp*, but the field had been long won and the flags run up.

The film is sterile, without the care that makes **Kes** (1970) exceptional. The producer here is Garnett, then a B.B.C. producer, and the director, Loach, is his most famous protégé. Together, with the backing of the short-lived American company, National General, they optioned a novel by Barry Hines and commissioned a screenplay from him, with the budget agreed at $400,000. National General then began to add overheads, etc. and changed its mind at the last minute. Tony Richard-

son, who had wanted Loach to work for Woodfall, took on the project and his clout was sufficient with United Artists for that company to back it. Set in Yorkshire, it is about a boy (David Bradley) and his pet kestrel, in the way that *The Great Adventure* was about a boy and his pet otter. It is also about the experiences of an English childhood, the morning paper-round, reading Desperate Dan, the squabbling family and above all, school – the boring soccer match, the bumptious games master, the sardonic head teacher. The lad himself is reasonably pessimistic, since the male members of the family traditionally go down the mines, and he is not sufficiently intelligent for an alternative job. His imagination has never been fired, he has never seen himself as an individual designated for special attention, and he does not know how to respond in kind to the well-meaning, platitudinous careers officer. Loach offers half-truths some of the time – the clichés of The Wednesday Play as derived jointly from Woodfall, the nouvelle vague and its off-shoot, *cinéma vérité* – but no other British film of the period is as rewarding as this.

British audiences reacted everywhere with glee, but the North Country accents were sufficiently heavy to limit appreciation in the U.S. **Family Life** (1971), however, quickly passed from sight, which is the fate it deserved. The source

Finally, the British cinema found some new talent, in the team of producer Tony Garnett and director Ken Loach, though they have worked mainly in television (and have now split, with Garnett turning director).

Admittedly, their few films for the cinema have been patchy, and the only memorable one is *Kes*, about a boy (David Bradley) and his kestrel. Significantly, the boy is less like a younger version of Billy Liar than a sour, English version of the youngster in Olmi's *Il Posto*.

was a T.V. play by David Mercer, doing his own adaptation, and his dialogue is bitingly accurate: but in its dual indictment of the institution of the title and the National Health Service it falters and fails. A nineteen-year-old girl succumbs to a nervous breakdown, and, finally losing the fight, is incarcerated; her quarrelling parents are apparently to blame, and the piece is such a scream of hatred against the suburbs that it flails out in every direction. The same is true of **Bleak Moments** (1971), financed – the cost was £18,000 – mainly by Albert Finney's company, with help from the B.F.I. and written and directed by Mike Leigh, whose work for T.V. and the theatre had been grounded in improvisation. He was responsible for 'Abigail's Party', a funny play about middle-class trendies, but **Grown-Ups** (1980) is again so biased against suburban people that it is boring as entertainment and useless as the social document it pretends to be. Leigh appears not to understand that all writers and film-makers who have successfully portrayed the deprived, be it physically, mentally or financially, have brought compassion to the task.

Tony Garnett does understand that, and turning director, he made **Prostitute** (1980) – which like *Grown-Ups* played a number of festivals but was designed for television audiences rather than the cinema. As a documentary *Prostitute* is impeccable, though Garnett's sympathies lead him not only into a discursive, plotless film, but into a number of schematic devices, so that the social worker (Kate Crutchley), responsible for the welfare of the lady of the title, is not only attached to her in sublimated lesbian fashion but has an affair with a weedy, jargon-spouting sociologist, as if to prove that they are sisters under the skin.

Working for Garnett and the B.B.C., Loach produced some of the best naturalistic work done in television, including the four-part **Days of Hope** (1975), written by Jim Allen, an account of the Labour movement from the Great War to the General Strike as experienced by a nucleus of agitators. This was followed by the two-part **The Price of Coal** (1977), written by Hines, a pertinent study of a mining community in present-day Britain. Garnett's influence on his team must be something of which other producers have only

dreamed: there may further be cited Roland Joffe's **The Spongers** (1978), written by Allen, an indictment of the welfare system, and Leslie Blair's four-part **Law and Order** (1978), written by G. F. Newman, an examination of Scotland Yard corruption. Both are of the same superlative quality. We may have doubts as to whether working-class solidarity is quite such a bulwark, or whether those set in authority over us are quite as venal and inefficient, but the best purpose of polemic is to question, and television – so prodigal with its mediocrity – is a good place for it. The standard of performance in Garnett's films is as extraordinary as their sympathies, and with them should be considered the pieces written by Jack Rosenthal, culminating in **The Knowledge** (1979), a study of London cab-drivers, directed by Bob Brooks, which as pure entertainment and social record is worth all the British cinema films made on either side of it.

Loach described **Looks and Smiles** (1981) as 'very gentle', observing that he is not interested in making propaganda films, since that is limiting. The subject to him is 'about kids coming to terms with the outside world', but to most of us it is about unemployment. The film is a timely reminder of Mrs Thatcher's Britain, with its three million out of work, and it is overly discreet in not mentioning either her or her government. The film looks at two North Country youngsters on the dole, a boy and a girl. The courtship shows how such matters have changed since *A Kind of Loving*. Otherwise these kids are inarticulate and aimless. If there is a danger in the Loach-Garnett approach it is that audiences may find the lack of literacy and the implied contempt of authority somewhat wearisome. They have become clichés among some less talented practitioners of the working-class genre, if I may call it such, though the examples I am thinking of have not left television for cinemas.

With these films in mind – to leave aside the Italian example of R.A.I. – it can only be promising that both the B.B.C. and the commercial television companies (via Channel Four, which began transmissions in 1982) are investing in films for the commercial cinema. The British cinema, otherwise, is virtually dead; but then it has been a long time a-dying. Apart from a period during the war years and just after, it produced little of note till the Woodfall revolt. Between the two it reverted, ethically and intellectually, to the Edwardian period. The Sixties, as a consequence of Woodfall, were enormously vital if leaving little of actual value. Take, for instance, 1967. If we include foreign directors working in Britain, the films include *A Countess from Hong Kong, Blow-Up, Two for the Road, The Deadly Affair* (q.v.), *Half-a-Sixpence, Accident, How I Won the War, Charlie Bubbles, The Whisperers, The Sailor from Gibraltar, Billion Dollar Brain, Far from the Madding Crowd, To Sir with Love, Our Mother's House, Smashing Time, Poor Cow* and *Pretty Polly*. You would have to go back twenty years to find the British industry coping with such confidence with so many themes, most of them rooted in the real world. But vitality proved insufficient. If we accept Chaplin's film as an aberration, *Blow-Up* is the only film by a major artist; and you may otherwise only care to remember *The Deadly Affair, Two for the Road* and *Far from the Madding Crowd*, three superior entertainments. The others strive to preach to us, without success, on the perils of old age, fame, loneliness, Soviet-West relations, war, race, juvenile delinquents, malaise, contemporary London and so on. It is little wonder that the films of the following decade had even less to say.

As the American companies began to pull out of Britain, the industry was left to the old duopoly of Rank and Associated British. At the time of Korda's death British Lion had been taken over by the National Film Finance Corporation, wiping out the debts he left, and for some years it successfully released many important independent productions, including those of the Boultings, Launder and Gilliat and Woodfall, but after the Conservative government decreed an injection of private money in 1963 it underwent a number of board changes and four years later its production was reduced to a trickle. In 1969 Associated British was bought by E.M.I., the giant recording/electronics conglomerate, and under the chairmanship of Bernard Delfont the initial policy was to make films primarily for the home market; when that policy failed (under the aegis of Bryan Forbes), E.M.I. aimed its product at the international market, often with American partnership involved. However, they had a number of expensive failures, such as *Honky Tonk Freeway, Can't Stop the Music* and the 1980 remake of *The Jazz Singer*, while turning down more essentially British projects – notably *Chariots of Fire* and *Gandhi*, Britain's biggest successes world wide since *Tom Jones* twenty years earlier (always excepting the Bond films). Delfont's brother, Lew Grade, the television peer, extended his activities to films, but his I.T.C. company again looked to the international market, with results at worst disastrous and at best unmemorable. Grade was relieved of his position in 1980 after the debacle of *Raise the Titanic*, reckoned to have lost most of its $22 million cost – understandably to those of us unfortunate to have seen it. The company was bought by the millionaire Australian entrepreneur, Robert Holmes a'Court, and it has since – like E.M.I. – proceeded with the utmost caution, usually in conjunction with an American partner. The Rank Organisation reduced its programme to moderate proportions in the early Sixties, sometimes producing less than half a dozen unambitious films in a year: imbued by the renewed competition of E.M.I. and I.T.C. in the late Seventies it began again to spend lavishly, but the public refused to go to see remakes of *The 39 Steps* and *The Lady Vanishes*, as well as *The Riddle of the Sands* and Roeg's *Bad Timing*. When all four failed within the same year, 1979, the company announced that it was quitting production entirely, but might invest in films it would distribute and show in its cinemas. Thus the duopoly of the British film industry was finally broken, and few alive could recall when it had not been there, since the predecessors of Rank and E.M.I. – respectively Gaumont-British and B.I.P. – had become rivals in the Twenties.

There had been, admittedly, a brief period during the War, when Associated British was quiescent and before the rise of Rank, which had seen a large number of independent producers operating, as in France or Italy; and this is the situation today, if we regard E.M.I. as no longer a dominant power. Unlike that time during the War, the Hollywood companies are investing in British movies, which may mean a more viable cinema – for the majority of films presented by I.T.C. and

British Cinema: A Matter of Collusion

E.M.I. in the late Seventies looked like and, indeed, were projects rejected by the American studios. That would seem to be the case of the Cannon group, making some British films after purchasing from Lew Grade the Classic circuit, but Cannon is Israeli-owned and also active in America; a remake of *The Wicked Lady*, directed by Michael Winner, with Faye Dunaway, was not an auspicious start.

And that brings us back to the two Oscar-winners, *Chariots of Fire* and *Gandhi*, both the products of Goldcrest Films, the company founded by a Canadian, John D. Eberts, originally as a sideline to find financing for movies. After four years of activity he obtained backing for an animated feature, *Watership Down*, chiefly from the Pearson-Longman conglomerate, whose subsidiary, Penguin Books, published the paperback edition of the original novel. In 1979 Pearson-Longman invested heavily in Goldcrest, and with the great successes of *Chariots of Fire* and *Gandhi* it may be said that Eberts never looked back. Whether or not he is the new Korda is up to him. He stresses that his team is as important as he is; that he wants his films, preferably, to be both optimistic and British in outlook; and made with British money. But after those two successes – Columbia released *Gandhi* – he has the confidence of Hollywood. The high financial risk involved can be shared with one of the major American companies and one of the American cable companies, such as Home Box Office, which will bring a much quicker return on investment than can be obtained from cinema showings.

But perhaps the most hopeful signal for the British film industry is Eberts's determination to work with as many major film talents as possible. One Puttnam and one Attenborough cannot be heirs to Korda, Balcon and del Guidice, but if a different order is required a sympathetic financier must be the next best thing. Who are to be Britain's film directors is another matter. Tony Garnett, who has an American wife, has moved to Los Angeles, and though his first American film, *Handgun*, was financed by E.M.I., it also has an American setting. Ken Loach may not adapt to the cinema as he should, and the same may be true of several others who have made reputations in television. As far as I am concerned, the jury is still out on such film-makers as Alan Parker and Ridley Scott, who made *The Duellists*, *Alien* and *Blade Runner*. Many of the directors whose work is discussed in the later part of this chapter are in theory active, even if the text implies that their credits ceased years ago. Many have not done interesting work. With the British cinema there have been too many lost chances.

1138

40

Movies Around the World

AS AN EXPERIENCE, the film festival is one of the most ghastly ever to be endured. The two exceptions are those held in London or New York, where a selection has been made of the films shown at other festivals, programmed in reasonable comfort and without undue ballyhoo – though I have never understood the stampede for tickets, since in both cities the foreign films that are distributed usually consist of festival entries, and many festival films are deservedly never seen again. The system is rich with anomalies: the festival organisers in both cities see it as their job to offer a representative selection of world cinema, while at the same time hoping to open up commercial possibilities. Such altruism aside, many of the entries should never have been made in the first place, while others have not had the subsequent showings they deserve. The choice of foreign or foreign-language films available to us depends on the festival organisers and the art-house managers, and no one has yet devised a better system: the later career of Buñuel, the international careers of Bergman, Ray and Kurosawa are all due to showings at festivals. Their works, hitherto considered too parochial, were exposed at those circuses which are the festivals of Cannes and Venice, and it is to these, and increasingly to Berlin, that many film-makers look for the key to international fame.

It is to the festivals that we owe our knowledge of the less prolific and less spectacular native industries – but it remains a partial knowledge. Most festival organisers reserve the right to select from the competing or submitting industries – a fact highlighted when Cannes initially refused *Bugsy Malone* as insufficiently 'esoteric' to justify its inclusion, surely the most foolish criterion ever to be applied to cinema. Secondly, a festival trophy often encourages the initiating producers to over-estimate prospects in the foreign market and ask for an advance which the distributors cannot meet. Eventually, however, the foreign films we see depend less on the vagaries of festival organisers and art-house exhibitors than on the qualities of the films themselves. An art-house distributor does not buy a film from Outer Mongolia to offer his clients a novelty: he hopes to establish a director and/or producer whose work he can profitably handle over the years. It seldom happens.

In 1953, at Cannes, a Brazilian film, **O Cangaciero** – *The Bandit* – attracted some attention. It is a conventional chase story which probably owed its foreign bookings to its catchy theme-tune. Though rather flatly directed by Lima Barreto (1910–82), he might have nevertheless had an international career on the strength of it; but he was so temperamental that his next film was never completed and for the next thirty years quarrels with producers kept his endless projects from being realised. No other Brazilian director attracted world attention till Glauber Rocha (1938–81) made **Antonio-das-Mortes** (1969), another tale of banditry. A burly, bearded trouble-shooter is hired to rid the region of some marauders who prey on the villagers, but, as he discovers, local politicians are using him as a cover to preserve the status quo. Rocha had founded the *cinema novo* movement with the aim of ridding Brazilian cinema of the apparently endless stream of carnival tales which dominated it; he wanted a cinema that acknowledged such realities of Brazilian life as illiteracy, unemployment and poverty. *Antonio* begins as an examination of the place of bandits in popular mythology, but then seems less interested in Brazilian life than in imitating Sergio Leone and Godard, or borrowing from *High Noon* and *The Wild Bunch*, whose bloody conclusion it follows. The film's worst excesses are repeated, with few of its virtues, in **Der Leone Have Sept Cabecas** (1970).

Among Rocha's followers the most exceptional would seem Ruy Guerra (b. 1931), whose more conventional approach is due to his training with Jean Delannoy in France. Born in Mozambique, he examines both the terrain of Brazil and its mythology with the same fascination as Rocha, but with less wilful obscurity. **Os Fuzis** (1963) is accordingly much more successful in demanding that political and religious leaders consider the plight of the peasants. The film is overlong and sometimes arid, which is a pity, for its theme is original and interesting – the interplay of a lonely army garrison and the apathetic peasantry, either of which might ignite the spark which sets off the explosion.

Dona Flor and her Two Husbands (1978) is a very different kettle of fish as written and directed by Bruno Barreto from a novel by Jorge Amado, which uses the situation of 'Blithe Spirit' without Coward's invention or any native wit. When Vadinho (José Winkler) drops dead returning from carnival, Dona Flor (Sonia Braga) later remembers both how he ill-treated her and how rapturous were their nights – in contrast to the hesitant, rhythmic love-making of her second husband, a stuffy, bourgeois chemist (Mauro Mendonça). Barreto's contrasting of the two marriages is as subtle as his handling of the sex sequences is not, and he fails to derive any humour from the situation of the first husband turning up as a ghost. Nevertheless, the American art-house public was much amused, but in Britain the critics' scorn quickly despatched the piece – which is sad because the local colour is pleasing.

The local colour in **Pixote** (1981) is urban and reminiscent of *Los Olvidados*. It is the third film made by Hector Babenco, a Chilean now living in Brazil, who appears at the outset to explain that Brazil has three million homeless children who are prey to adult criminals who coopt them

to work for them, since those under eighteen cannot be prosecuted. Pixote himself is twelve; he spends the earlier part of the film in reform school, where violence, sudden death, brutality and homosexual rape are everyday occurrences. The tradition of films about such institutions has accustomed us to the bullying, sadistic guards and the apathy of the rest of the staff: but the details are so degrading as to suggest Babenco did first-hand research in a just mood of reforming zeal. But after Pixote has escaped he carries on a life of crime involving drugs, pornography and prostitution – all aspects which movies have glamorised, and despite some squalor this one is not entirely free of that quality. When Pixote walks away at the end, a killer twice over, we do not know whether he goes to a bleak future or more prostitutes and pornography. The film would have been more honorable, and its moral better stated, had it been the second half, rather than the first, which had been wholly pessimistic; but then it might not have enjoyed its great success.

The best-known South American director remains the Argentinian, Leopoldo Torre Nilsson (1924–78), who expressed his dissatisfaction with society in very different terms. The Government on occasion took exception to his work, critical as it was of the bourgeoisie and the decadence that he found inseparable from it. In fact he seems to have been as much attracted as repelled by his subject matter. Torre Nilsson's world is of huge cloistered mansions, their curtains drawn, their furniture baroque, their conservatories stuffed with hot-house plants. It is a world in which the old are grasping and either gossiping or reminiscing about the past – and it is there that they seem to live, with the manners and clothes of their youth. The young go about their business with the calm of an earlier time, and that business is chiefly sexual. They dream and write love letters, reluctant to form permanent relationships. The girls indulge in fantasies of being deflowered by idealised men, who are the playboys who suggest – but never seem to experience – any number of perversions which they surely have the means to buy. They are all far less creatures of action than their cousins in Buñuel – and even more isolated from reality: it is not for nothing that a Torre Nilsson heroine may be found reading Proust, since an echo of the imprisoned Albertine reappears constantly in his work. That has a consistency almost unequalled in cinema – at least from 1957, when his eighth film attracted attention at the Cannes Film Festival. The first two were made in collaboration with his father, who was also a director; the year that Cannes made him an international figure he married the novelist Beatríz Guido, who was responsible for the screenplays and/or stories of most of his subsequent films.

It is conceivable that they were both influenced by Jean Anouilh, since the theme of youth corrupted or disillusioned by hypocritical elders surfaces so often. In **La Casa del Angel** (1957) and **La Caida** (1959) a charming and somewhat withdrawn blonde actress, Elsa Daniel, plays an adolescent whose life is restricted, in the first case by a prudish mother and a politically ambitious father, and in the second by a group of infant harpies. The chief protagonist of **Fin de Fiesta** (1960) is male, but also young, and, like her, he will eventually expiate the evils and mysteries of the grown-ups' world; he is caught between meaningless feuds – and, this being a Torre Nilsson film, is seduced in a chicken-house of all places. Miss Daniel plays a gauche girl in **La Mano en la Trampa** (1961), who finds that the contempt of her elders no longer matters when she becomes infatuated with an older stranger (Francisco Rabal); and since there is a secret in the attic you may think of 'Jane Eyre'. The gothic strain plays even more beautifully in **Piel de Verano** (1962). A wealthy girl is promised a trip to Paris by her grandmother if she will nurse the son, apparently fatally ill, of that lady's lover: but he is cured when they fall in love – or seem to fall in love; and she finds that she is the reason for his death as she was for his life.

Such tales hardly indicated great seriousness, yet Torre Nilsson was not only the one Argentine film-maker able to command world attention, but the only one to do so from the South American continent – and at that time, Buñuel apart, the only one to do so from Spanish-speaking territories. Important directors are expected to tackle weighty matters, which may be why Torre Nilsson turned to a study of a young revolutionary in **El**

Ojo de la Corradura (1965). He uses the labyrinth of Latin American politics as an occasion for comedy more sardonic than usual, and in moving from his familiar territory he reveals a remarkable aptitude for the form required. Martin – played by Stathis Giallelis, the young hero of Kazan's *America, America* – temporarily has to cease his activities with a Fascist terrorist organisation, and is forced to hole up in a decaying, claustrophobic hotel, accompanied by a childhood friend, Inês (Janet Margolin): in idleness, he manages to convince himself that the theatrical troupe down the hall are assassins, their victim to be a visiting dictator whom he particularly admires. Torre Nilsson expends on this misguided idealist his customary care when confronted with the abnormal or distorted psychology of the young: but this time the increasingly nightmarish world is one of the young man's own making – but not that far away from the 'normal' world we experience every day.

It is by far the most satisfying of Torre Nilsson's films, and till we can see the dozen or so subsequent films which were not exported we must conclude that the rest of his career was an anti-climax. He was not successful with a film made in English, in Puerto Rico, **Monday's Child** (1967), with Arthur Kennedy and Geraldine Page; and, as I have implied, the films that followed did not reach the major festivals. While we did not hear from him he had, like all film-makers, moved from

The films of the Argentinian director Leopoldo Torre Nilsson made an impact on the art-house circuit in the late Fifties and early Sixties and his present neglect is inexplicable. In suggesting decadence among the bourgeoisie he is not the master Buñuel is, but he is a master nevertheless, entirely consistent in his approach to the evils unshown and unnamed. In *La Casa del Angel* Elsa Daniel grows into adolescence dreaming of seduction by a political friend of her father, Lautaro Murua. It happens at her instigation, but the aftermath is not quite what she expected.

monochrome to colour, and strangely it did not suit him.

His powerful visual style had been a matter of dark shadows, tilted angles and the soft whites of girlhood; there were whispers, remarks half-heard and old gramophone records; his elliptical narrative style had preceded that of the European directors, but both **Boquitas Pintadas** (1974) and **Piedra Libre** (1976) seem not only old-fashioned but, compared with his other films, commonplace. The first, based on a strongly satiric novel by Manuel Puig, who wrote the screenplay with Torre Nilsson, deals with a group of friends over the years, and mostly the relationship of one (Marta Gonzales) with a cheap, tubercular Lothario (Alfredo Alcón); the second concerns another virginal girl (Marlina Ross), an orphan, who becomes in time a Becky Sharp-like intruder able to take over the household because of what she has learnt. It was the last in a series of skirmishes with authority, who banned it for 'immorality' and 'attacks on family, religion and class structure'. European and American critics, after an initial fascination, dismissed Torre Nilsson as a maker of women's weepies, which is certainly less than the truth. He is a minor master, believing absolutely in his own created world, and on that matter generally persuasive.

The only other South American country to have successfully exported film is Chile, but despite the title **Valparaiso Mi Amor** (1970) Aldo Francia's film reveals that, as he said, he speaks not only for his own country: 'Our social reality in Chile and Latin America is too horrible to be reproduced as pamphletarian caricature.' The voice is that which Buñuel used in *Los Olvidados*, but is somewhat less dispassionate, as befits his indebtedness to the nouvelle vague (evidenced by stills from their films stuck on an office wall). The setting is a shanty-town, and the subject the tribulations of one of its families, somewhat too thinly drawn but with compensation in Francia's rich portrait of the city. It is an accomplished movie for a film industry a year old. The first Chilean feature had been produced with the cooperation of one of the country's six universities – **El Chacal de Nahueltoro** (1969), directed by Miguel Littin, and it would be

a remarkable film under any circumstances. Based on fact, it is about a murderer, the jackal of the title: the cinema has a long history of sympathetic studies of murderers, and Littin is clever in completely avoiding sentiment, while extracting compassion for the peasantry – not, however, shown as other than illiterate and brutalised. But **La Tierra Prometida** (1974) contained all the pitfalls open to an inexperienced film-maker, and Littin fell into every one of them. His expressed undertaking was to side-step history as interpreted in 'the interests of the bourgeoisie' and 're-read the class struggle in the light of Marxism': his subject is a band of itinerant workers who, in 1932, attempted a cooperative on some acres of land which they hoped had been abandoned. The film was not started until after Allende came to power, and not finished till after the *putsch*: Littin had to flee, and in Mexico he found his favoured subject, 'the origins of the working class and the origins of Fascism and repression in Chile'. **Actas de Marusia** (1976), again based on fact, deals with an incident in 1907, when the inhumanly-treated workers in a saltpetre mine revolted against its British owners. Littin wrote the screenplay from information supplied by a fellow-Chilean, Patricio Mans, based on the 'letters' of the title, but the information he offers us is still not enough; he is too busy theorising. He has learnt to present an identifiable hero, played by Gian-Maria Volonté, but makes the mistake of assuming that we all share his view that policemen and soldiers are pigs.

The same incident serves as the source for a film by the Cuban Humberto Solás, already known for **Lucia** (1969), a prize-winner at the Moscow film festival. It conforms, alas, to stereotype, being again about revolution – though as this seems a staple of both Latin American cinema and the communist block it is perhaps inevitable in Cuba; and, as with many products of young film industries, it reflects influences – in the first section of this tripartite film, those of Buñuel, Renoir, Kurosawa, Welles and Visconti. This episode, set in 1895, is routine movie stuff, but the others, concerning later Lucias at other times of revolution, are, in contrast, concise, beautifully observed, and filmed with verve. Solás' film on the saltpetre workers,

Cantata de Chile (1976), is also based on material supplied by Patricio Mans; it too has its longueurs, as when the workers are proclaiming their solidarity or haranguing their colleagues – as always the fault of communist films, but Solás has more intelligence and imagination than most communist-bloc directors. He is violently didactic, but whereas with Littin one wants him to copy Costa-Gavras and hurl both narrative and propaganda at us simultaneously, Solás takes his own reasonable time. His exposition of the aspirations of the strikers and the moderation of their masters is exemplary. (The faces of the strikers disbelievingly comprehending that *their* government supports the *foreign* interests is one of the most eloquent images in cinema.) His purpose is to show the roots of totalitarianism in Chile from the conquistadores to the nineteenth-century presidents, and he uses any means that he thinks fit, be it tableaux, swirling mists, coloured lights or speeches addressed directly to the audience: his achievement is to have taken these theatrical devices and transformed them into pure – and very

exciting – cinema. The film was designed as 'an act of solidarity with the Chilean people', but, in the director's words, 'I feel that the film's significance could transcend Latin America and operate in the same way in any context of oppression and under-development.' For once a director's claims for significance in his own work are justified.

In 1981 there were retrospectives in Berlin and London of the Portuguese director Mañoël de Oliveira (b. 1908), plus a laudatory article by John Gillett in *Sight and Sound*. De Oliveira is an interesting figure, and he can be a film-maker of force and imagination, but I do not think he is of world class. He has spent most of his life working in the family's manufacturing plant and, until recently, made only an occasional film. His first short, a documentary, was filmed in 1931, and his first feature, **Aniki-Bobó** (1942), more than a decade later. It is nicely photographed in the streets and along the riverbanks of his native city, Oporto, and follows the adventures of some children,

Lucia won the Grand Prix at the 1969 Moscow Film Festival, which was not surprising since that particular festival tends to award prizes to films from other Communist countries – and in this case we may see the award as a pat on the back for a fledgling industry in a country not long converted to that way of life, Cuba. All the same, Humberto Solás's three-part epic has such verve that it is a pity that we have not seen more of his work. Playing the first of the three Lucias in the three episodes is Raquel Revuelta.

among them Carlitos, who steals a doll from a shop and then returns it when the shopkeeper proves that he is not to be blamed for an accident that befell one of his friends. De Oliveira did not film again till he made **The Passion of Christ** (1963), an account of the annual passion play which takes place in the village of Chaves, some fifty miles from Oporto. The scenes of village life are engaging, but some symbolism at the end, meant to remind audiences of the Cuba crisis of the previous year, looks merely jejune.

A decade later the Gulbenkian Foundation decided to subsidise the Portuguese cinema and de Oliveira took the opportunity to make **Past and Present** (1972), based on a comedy by Vincente Sanches that he particularly admired. In investigating the antics of some wealthy friends of the upper bourgeoisie the film has moments of sour humour, particularly in respect of their marital affairs, but as a whole the piece is less taking than Buñuel's similar Mexican films. It was successful enough for de Oliveira to accept an assignment (he had been his own producer on his earlier films), but **Benilde, Virgin and Mother** (1975) is no more than a photographed play – and not a very good one. Its heroine, a strange girl, is found to be pregnant, and the resolution is found in Act III, that she was 'taken advantage of' while sleepwalking; or else the father is the village idiot heard moaning off screen. That is about the level of it. That de Oliveira might one day make a first-rate movie was not confirmed by **Ill-Fated Love** (1978), a television serial adapted for cinema showings abroad. Based on a nineteenth-century novel of passion by Camilo Castelo Branco, noted for its exuberance (and already filmed twice), the film is anything but: the cardboard characters come and go before a motionless camera – so immobile, in fact, that it lingers on long after they have left any individual scene.

Any reflection on the small Portuguese film industry could be deflected across the Peninsula and along the Mediterranean, to Greece. Conditions there were equally inauspicious for movie-making: a sparse population, with few big cities, so that films were aimed at the mainly unsophisticated audiences of rural areas – thus limiting the prospects of overseas distribution.

Film production began in the early Twenties, and consisted chiefly of theatrical melodramas and light comedies with songs. The standard and output both declined in the late Thirties and during the German Occupation, but American aid in the postwar period brought a revival of Greek cinema, in subject matter deeply indebted to what was happening in Italy at that time. Nevertheless the first Greek film-maker to receive international attention was Michael Cacoyannis (b. 1922) – which is ironic, for he was born in Cyprus under British rule. He studied and worked in London during the War and afterwards, mainly as actor and producer under the name of Michael Yannis; it is perhaps because of his British connections that his first film was shown at the Edinburgh Festival in 1954.

Windfall in Athens (1953) is a slight film, and fresh, despite its debt to French and Italian comedies of the period. The locations are pleasing and the opening is delightful, showing the leading characters rising one Sunday morning and contemplating how to spend the day. The script, by Cacoyannis himself, is not as bright, telling as it does of a girl (Elli Lambetti) who has her clothes stolen while swimming and therefore loses the lottery ticket in a pocket; there are complications for the unhappily married man who has given her a lift from the beach and for the young man (Dimitri Horn) who has purchased the ticket from the thieves. **Stella** (1955) was sent to Cannes, where it was respectfully received, though it is even more derivative – relying heavily on the low life peasant melodramas emanating from Italy. Stella is a singer, wrongly identified in the subtitles as a whore: 'When she likes a man, she goes crazy' says someone, and as played by Melina Mercouri it is a vast understatement. When she throws over her gentleman for a footballer, it is like tigers mating, but when he forces her to marry herself she absents herself from the ceremony to spend the night dancing with a student: and then, rather than lose her freedom, she lets him stab her to death. Helped by the photography of Walter Lassally (who would frequently work in Greece in the years to come), Cacoyannis did much more complicated work in **A Girl in Black** (1955), based on his own, more confident, screenplay. A young writer

Most Greek films are for strictly local consumption, and those that appear abroad are usually heavy-breathing bucolic dramas, dubbed for their particular market. That leaves Michael Cacoyannis, a Cypriot, as the only Greek director of international renown (if we except Costa-Gavras, who has not directed in his native land). Cacoyannis has made some poor films, including the English-language *Zorba the Greek*, but he has made one film of high quality, *A Matter of Dignity*, a study of Athenian high society. Elli Lambetti is the girl in search of a wealthy husband, and she chooses Minas Christades, right, in preference to Michel Nikolinakos, whom she really loves.

(Dimitri Horn) goes to Hydra, where he is drawn into the feud between a girl (Miss Lambetti) and a local fisherman who has been persecuting her because she has rejected him.

Moving away from peasant drama, to Athenian high society, Cacoyannis made his best film, **A Matter of Dignity** (1957). The title refers to an impoverished aristocratic family trying to keep up appearances till the daughter (Miss Lambetti) has hooked a wealthy fiancé. The story is not unlike that of *Calle Mayor* and Cacoyannis responds as easily as Bardem to time and place – an empty house after a party, a seedy café, the streets above the town at night; both films share the suggestion that 'society' is basically as unhappy as it is worthless. **Our Last Spring** (1960) also has a familiar theme, that of adolescent responsibility to the adult world, as a group of boys grope their way to manhood; but the plot is indecipherable. Warners financed, which may be why Cacoyannis chose to film in English; but

he conformed to that rule by which European directors seem bound to make bad films when they have American backing.

He restored his reputation with **Electra** (1962), based on Euripides, and considered to be the first successful film of a classic Greek tragedy. In fact, the approach is desperate to make an effect, but Lassally's photography and the locations, in and around Mycenae, somewhat disguise that; and the face and presence of Irene Papas in the title-role are assets, though she hardly gives a performance. The moderate success of the film enabled Cacoyannis to embark on **Zorba the Greek** (1964), with the backing of 20th Century-Fox and the participation of Anthony Quinn as the male equivalent of the role Mercouri played in *Stella* – 'a life force', as the studio synopsis succinctly put it. As adapted from the novel by Kazantzakis, the life force introduces a prissy young Anglo-Greek (Alan Bates) to the joys of ouzo and the sirtaki, as well as into the bed of a young widow (Miss Papas), who is consequently stoned by the villagers. The film, aspiring to the 'realism' of *La Terra Trema*, is rather like nineteenth-century academic painting – predictable, sentimental, meticulous and empty. However, Cacoyannis knew what he was doing, and the easily-assimilated message found a large response, especially in the U.S., where, following *La Dolce Vita*, it confirmed prejudices about European life. In *The New York Times*, Bosley Crowther's fulsome notice referred to 'the meanness and ignorance of the people of Crete . . . [and] the hard, barren look of the island', thereby showing his own ignorance and unwittingly explaining why the film was as much loathed in Greece as it was admired elsewhere.

20th Century-Fox rewarded Cacoyannis by letting him film a subject of his own choosing, **The Day the Fish Came Out** (1967), a crypto-homosexual comic allegory, in English, about two atom bombs lost in the Aegean. The reviews were contemptuous and business minimal, forcing Cacoyannis back to classic tragedy again to retrieve his reputation. **The Trojan Women** (1971) uses Edith Hamilton's archaic translation, with some updating ('What's up?'), and Cacoyannis' own approach is no more consistent, free of whatever restraints had been imposed earlier by the Peloponnese (this was filmed in Spain). Katharine Hepburn, misled by critics who had hailed her as a tragedienne for her performance in *Long Day's Journey into Night* (q.v.), makes a querulous Hecuba. In 1977 Cacoyannis made his last film to date, *Iphigenia*, which passed unnoticed.

The house of Atreus is to be found again in **The Travelling Players** (1975), in the guise of a theatrical troupe in Greece between 1922 and 1952, but mostly during the war years. Such plot as there is might have been compressed into ten minutes, but the film lasts almost four hours as amateurishly directed by Theodor Angelopolos, whose other films have been poorly received: why this one escaped that fate is unfathomable.

Feature film production in Canada was sporadic till recent years; traditionally aspiring directors and artists sought work in London or, preferably, Hollywood. Documentaries have a stronger tradition, following the appointment of John Grierson as Film Commissioner in 1939 and the establishment of the National Film Board of Canada, which produced cartoons as well as non-fiction pieces. The Board's most prolific exponent was Norman McLaren, whose many experiments, like scratching patterns on celluloid, were too arid for most audiences. A one-time colleague, Claude Jutra (b. 1930), directed the first Canadian film widely seen abroad, **Mon Oncle Antoine** (1971), produced by l'Office National du Film du Canada. Set in a small, snow-covered town in Quebec Province, it is a familiar story of adolescence, with the customary sexual encounters. Jutra retrogressed rapidly with **Kamouraska** (1973), an attempt to blend the plot of 'Thérèse Raquin' with the vapourings of a Barbara Cartland – and filmed with greater fidelity to romantic fiction than the Zolaesque elements.

Jutra's two films were made as a consequence of the 1967 Act of Parliament setting up the Canadian Film Development Corporation, and after the mild success abroad of the first of them the Corporation became confident of success in world markets. Canadian-born artists were encouraged to return, but there was contention over the number of American and British players acceptable, especially as some of them were paid more than their usual fees and were, in any case, of doubtful box-office standing. With Government money, therefore, being injected either wholly or partially in a score or so films annually since 1970, it is disappointing that during that time only four have been made of more than passing interest.

The Apprenticeship of Duddy Kravitz (1974) was directed by Ted Kotcheff, who had made a handful of undistinguished British films, and it is based on a novel by Mordecai Richler, also a Canadian living in Britain. Richard Dreyfuss is the Duddy of the title, with some fellow Americans in support – Randy Quaid, Jack Warden and Joseph Wiseman (who was however born in Montreal) – and the British Denholm Elliott. Elliott repeats his performance of *Nothing but the Best*, but then the piece is itself a replication, a Montreal version of Budd Schulberg's 'What Makes Sammy Run?' with some bawdiness and an attempt to portray a Jewish community with less gloss than *Goodbye Columbus* (q.v.). Like *Mon Oncle Antoine* it is set in the recent past, as is **Why Shoot**

the Teacher? (1977), directed by Silvio Narizzano, another Canadian with some British (and American) credits. Yet again the source is an autobiographical book, by Max Braithwaite, played in the film by Bud Cort. In 1935 he left home to be a teacher to a small community on the Great Plains, clearly not a congenial place for that particular profession. The yokels seem in some perverse way to have modelled themselves on Ma and Pa Kettle and, again, the piece is consistently second-hand, even to the ending, when Max returns to fight back; but there is a nice moment when he and a farmer's wife (Samantha Eggar) read scenes from 'Private Lives'.

Outrageous (1977) features Craig Russell, a female impersonator, and the source is a story by Margaret Gibson, who lived with Russell at one point: we may therefore assume autobiography again, in this tale of a schizophrenic girl (Hollis McLaren), escaped from a mental home, who is befriended by a drag queen, and later reunited with him in the U.S. They are at home: 'There are eight million of us and we're all alive and sick and living in New York.' It is a naive film, and the equation of drag and homosexuality may be offensive to some; but it is honest and funny and, to use David Robinson's surprising but accurate adjective in *The Times*, endearing. The director is Richard Benner, from television and Toronto-based, who made it for $165,000 (Canadian). Zale Dalen, from Vancouver and with several successful shorts to his credit, made **Skip Tracer** (1977) for $20,000 less – and it would be a considerable achievement had it cost three times that amount. The title refers to the occupation of its protagonist (David Peterson), which is to exact payment for his employer, a finance company, or repossess, which may mean stripping the house to the last ashtray. When we meet him, he is the perfect company man, almost an automaton; when he eventually cracks the film becomes a study in conscience, but it is always as tight and taut as a thriller. Both films are about people leading offbeat lives, but they are genuinely illuminating and a sure guide to the direction that subsidised cinema should take.

The most successful Canadian feature to date is **Porky's**, released in 1982 and made in Florida with an American cast and mainly with American money. The others, in order, are *Quest for Fire, Meatballs, The Changeling, Murder by Decree, The Apprenticeship of Duddy Kravitz, Heavy Metal, Black Christmas, The Amateur* and *Why Shoot the Teacher?* It is not a list to give any Canadian self-respect, even though it does not reveal the fact that most of the subsidised films made in Canada are cheap, mindless, horror films. That can make no one proud, particularly when compared with what has been happening in Australia during this time.

The Australian film industry is much older than that of Canada, and it is reputed to have had a success during the war years with **40,000 Horsemen** (1940), directed by Charles Chauvel. His uncle had been commander of the Australian Light Horse in the Sinai desert campaign, a subject which so filled Chauvel with enthusiasm that he started this film in 1938, as another world war looked imminent: but he shot the bulk of it in 1940, when the outbreak of that war had given the project new meaning. The action scenes are well managed – some sand dunes near Sydney stood in for the desert – but almost everything else is lamentably amateurish, including the performances of assorted Turks, Germans and Arabs. The 'French' heroine (Betty Bryant) dons Arab garments for the sort of adventures unseen since the early Twenties, including an oasis meeting with the Anzac hero (Grant Taylor). If this film was not laughed at on its British and American showings (I can find record of only a few) it can only be because its heart is in the right place.

Consequently, it was not until the Seventies that Australia, like Canada, decided to confront the international market. There were similar reasons – the need for star names was disappearing and most people the world over watched movies in the English language in the first place. The Australians were too modest to suppose that the world was waiting for their films, but they could be cheaply made and there was also a possibility of a television sale abroad. And a number of Australians who had learnt their craft in television wished to try it out in movies made for the cinema. Show business was burgeoning with the population and local taste was thought to be much more sophisticated than it had been. Nevertheless, some broad and blunt-witted comedies were not initially intended for overseas consumption – those featuring the fictitious Alvin Purple and his non-fictitious counterpart Barry McKenzie, whose forte is the impersonation of typical cobbers; but their popularity at home aroused some scattered foreign bookings.

Those encouraged Michael Thornhill, a former critic and documentary filmmaker, to engage a British name, Corin Redgrave, to star in **Between Wars** (1974), written with Frank Moorhouse from the latter's account of Dr Edward Trenbow, whose experience in the First World War led to his becoming a specialist in nervous disorders and a campaigner against Australia's involvement in World War II. It was an intelligent choice of subject to offer to world audiences, and it impressed those who thought the Australian cinema consisted of comedies about Alvin and Barry; but seen ten years later, the material is mishandled, the period detail often absurd and the performances, except Redgrave's, stilted.

Thornhill made other films, each less well received than the one before, while Peter Weir (b. 1944) was the one Australian director to become well known abroad. He had been making documentaries with the Commonwealth Film Unit when given the chance to put into production **The Cars That Ate Paris** (1974), part-written by him and based on his own idea. Driving in the New South Wales outback two brothers are in a strange accident which is fatal for one of them. The survivor (Terry Camilleri) finds himself overcome by inertia, a 'vegie', as the population refers to the other, numerous victims of accidents. The affable mayor (John Meillon) is clearly lying when he claims that all is well, for the older citizens are just as clearly terrified of the strangely-garbed youths and their even stranger cars. It is not a successful film artistically; it seems to proclaim that it is not what was expected of an Australian film – which is both its strength and its weakness, its originality and its showing-off. Nor was it a success locally (though it would give rise to *Mad Max*, a not dissimilar tale, which has been one of Australia's biggest hits worldwide to date).

Nevertheless, the strangeness of the idea, coupled with Weir's skill, gained the film some bookings abroad, encouraging those factions in Sydney and Melbourne who were clamouring for an indigenous industry making worthwhile films. Its members were reckoned to be Socialist, and a Socialist Government had come to power in 1972 under the leadership of Gough Whitlam, who believed it was time for Australians to be proud of being Australians instead of relying on Britain and the U.S. for their culture. Accordingly the Australian Film Commission was established in 1975, to help commercial companies finance their product: by 1980 over fifty films had received Government money, of which approximately 38% was returned from box-office receipts – most of it from only eight films. Twenty-eight of the others were a total write-off.

Prior to the establishment of the A.F.C., the state of South Australia had decided to provide funds for film-makers, and New South Wales was to follow (both under Labour administrations); by the end of the decade most of the other states had followed suit. Virtually every Australian film since to find a welcome abroad has had public money contributing to its financing, and the results, though variable, are proof overall of Whitlam's theories. Alone, the first film of the South Australian Film Corporation (in this case the sole backer) is sufficient justification for state support: for **Sunday Too Far Away** (1974) is at the same time very Australian and very accomplished, as directed by Ken Hannam, who had worked in British and Australian television. It is an account of the sheep-shearers' strike in the outback in 1955, written by John Dingwall with a fine disregard for the clichés of other tales set in remote, enclosed communities; and its star is the fine actor Jack Thompson, who more than any of his colleagues has some of the heroic stature of the great Hollywood male stars.

The film made only a mild impact in the international market, unlike an Antonioni-like mystery, **Picnic at Hanging Rock** (1975). This proved to be *the* breakthrough for the Australian cinema in most countries, except in the U.S. where the public refused to be drawn to a mystery which remained unsolved at the end. The picnic of the title was held on St Valentine's Day,

1900, when three schoolgirls disappeared: only one was found (a week later) so that Cliff Green's script, from Joan Lindsay's factual novel, does not distort historical fact, but it is more inconclusive than it need be. The director, Peter Weir, is no Antonioni, able to examine either a relationship or a society in this context. Rather, his narrative is so consistent with the pregnant looks passed between the girls as they dress in the first scene that it is hardly compelling. Weir's ambitions go more awry in **The Last Wave** (1977), an attempt to translate to Sydney his own mystical experience while visiting Roman ruins in Tunisia. At a time of strange climatic omens, a young lawyer (Richard Chamberlain) dreams about an aborigine, whom he subsequently meets when asked to defend a group of them involved in a drunken brawl; through him he meets a tribal elder who tells the lawyer that he believes him to be the descendant of a South American race which had inhabited Australia in prehistoric times, and with him he goes to see paintings by his supposed ancestors, Mayan in design and predicting a cataclysmic disaster to precede spiritual renewal for the world. Like *The Cars That Ate Paris*, the film hopes to stun with its originality, but it too is confused when it thinks it is being profound. For all that, it is likeable and proof of an energetic and confident talent.

Meanwhile, the success of *Picnic at Hanging Rock* had established, for good or ill, a temporary pattern for Australian cinema: the stories were without melodramatics, they were set in the recent past and were often factual. The second of several school stories was **The Devil's Playground** (1976), an admittedly autobiographical account written and directed by Fred Schepisi, who had worked on commercials and documentaries. He had contributed to a three-part feature, *Libido*, working with the novelist Thomas Keneally, who appears in this film as a Catholic priest. The film is set in a Roman Catholic seminary in the autumn of 1953, skittering between the adolescent discontent of one boy (Simon Burke) and the misfit masters, including one going mad from (hetero)sexual abstinence and another whose beery approaches to women disguise his fear of them. The many references to masturbation serve to

underline the fact that all the school needs is an influx of women, but despite some sharp character sketches it adds up to very little.

Storm Boy (1976) also has a young hero (Greg Rowe), and it could be termed a boy-and-pelican film. The youngster lives with his dour hermit of a father (Peter Cummins) and as well as the pelican he is friendly with an aborigine (Gulpilil); their adventures, touching if a little banal, take place along the Cooring Beach of South Australia, whose Film Corporation produced. The film was such a great success Down Under that a follow-up was planned, **Blue Fin** (1978), with most of the same team, young Master Rowe, the screenwriter Sonia Berg (again working from a novel by Colin Thiele) and the cinematographer Geoff Burton. The French-born director of *Storm Boy*, Henri Safran, was replaced by Carl Schultz, and because that film had made little impact overseas the German actor Hardy Kruger was brought in to play Rowe's father, the

Not till the Sixties was the Australian cinema fit to travel, since it was hardly of a high standard. The breakthrough came with some comedies taking advantage of the new permissiveness and, to be fair, their crudeness was offset by an amused insight into the Aussies' innocence in such matters. There followed hard upon them a tale of the Outback, which might be supposed to be for local consumption only; but *Sunday Too Far Away*, directed by Ken Hannam and acted by Jack Thompson, is an absorbing drama.

captain of a small craft who despises the boy so much that he thinks him unworthy to follow in his footsteps. Uncredited, Bruce Beresford (q.v.) reshot some of Kruger's footage, using a double, to make him more sympathetic, but it was, deservedly, a failure in direct proportion to its predecessor.

Meanwhile, some more substantial films were being made. **The Mango Tree** (1977) was directed by Kevin Dobson, a newcomer from television, and adapted from a novel by Ronald McKie by the producer, Michael Pate, returning to his homeland after some years playing small roles in Hollywood. He also put his son Christopher in the lead, a rather uninteresting schoolboy who is taught the facts of life, apparently for his own good, by the French mistress – an action guessed at and approved of by his grandmother (Geraldine Fitzgerald). In other ways, too, the film contradicts our knowledge of the way people thought and behaved in 1915 (or thereabouts), so that this was another justified failure. The past was more respectfully re-created in **The Picture Show Man** (1977), directed by John Power, which follows the peregrinations of Pop (John Meillon), who, with his screen, projector, son and dog, goes from town to town hiring halls for his (Silent) movies. The film was written by Joan Long, who also wrote **Caddie** (1976) from an autobiography of a lady of that name, played in the film by Helen Morse. It details the vicissitudes endured by her from the time she runs out on her unfaithful husband, through love affairs with a bookie (Jack Thompson) and a Greek businessman (Takis Emmanuel) to working as a barmaid during the Depression. The director was Donald Crombie, whose work we shall examine again, along with a couple of other Australian directors, including Ken Hannam. But at this stage it can be said that following on *Sunday Too Far Away* Hannam's second film, **Break of Day** (1976), is a disappointment. Its subject is a Lawrentian affair between a young, married Gallipoli veteran (Andrew McFarlane) and a city-bred, 'new' woman, a painter (Sara Kestelman); possibly influenced by *Picnic at Hanging Rock* the film is far more inconclusive than it needs to be.

Despite their varying quality, these films justify a subsidised or an 'official'

cinema, affectionate towards the country's past and responsive to its landscape. They each suffer from an earnestness which has less to do with lack of humour than a pace which echoes the slowness of life, a fault which proves almost fatal to **Newsfront** (1978), which revives in otherwise heartening form the rivalry of newsreel companies as in *Too Hot to Handle*. It was directed by Philip Noyce and, set in the Forties and Fifties, it covers events fondly remembered by native audiences. Ironically the film is at its best at the end, when it gives way to Hollywood tradition in resolving the dilemma of the hero (Bill Hunter) by tempting him to give in to his natural enemy, television.

Amidst such nostalgic occasions, **End Play** (1975) was a tonic, as based on a contemporary thriller by Russell Braddon about a series of unexplained murders and two brothers (George Mallaby, John Waters), one of whom is in a wheelchair and one of whom – either one – is probably the killer. The dénouement has its weaknesses, but otherwise the film is handled with confidence by its writer-producer-director Tim Burstall, who made the Alvin Purple films. It is a pity that this 'veteran' of Australian films has since done such disappointing work.

The director of the Barry McKenzie films, Bruce Beresford (b. 1940) has been more fortunate. He also, for the moment, eschewed nostalgia by bringing to the screen **Don's Party** (1976), based on a play by David Williamson, who is considered Melbourne's leading playwright, if not of Australia as a whole (Burstall had earlier done a less successful version of one of Williamson's plays). Williamson wrote the screenplay for a piece which might be described as a variation on 'That Championship Season' with the wives along. It quite simply charts a drunken evening, with egos, flesh and neuroses exposed as the booze takes effect: the masochistic streak of humour is richer than in the American play, as each of the men falls on his face – a hail-fellow-well-met crew, cheery, naive, complacent, and more prone to boast of lechery than actually indulging in it.

Beresford then changed course to make his 'period' film, **The Getting of Wisdom** (1977), able to raise the financing because of the success of *Picnic at Hanging*

Rock – though there were doubts as to whether the public would want two films about an Australian girls' school at the turn of the century. Henry Handel (Ethel) Richardson's novel was autobiographical, telling of Laura, the daughter of a widowed postmistress who leaves home to board at the Presbyterian Ladies' College in Melbourne. As perfectly played by an amateur, Susannah Fowle, Laura's direct manner and extrovert personality make her unpopular; she is disliked by the headmistress; she has a crush on the new chaplain (John Waters) while a dumpy newcomer, who gets a crush on her, implies that he and Laura are having an affair – a rumour which Laura does not deny; finally she becomes friends with the head girl (Hilary Ryan), who, because of her beauty and her position, is an outsider like herself. The film is quietly and skilfully made, demonstrating Beresford's increasing confidence. He turned to a thriller, again as a change of pace, **The Money Movers** (1979), writing the screenplay himself after reading a book by Devon Minchin, who had founded one of Australia's commercial security services. The members of the film's security force lead a life of some excitement, since it involves an occasional cosh-or-be-coshed operation; they also appear to be corrupt. For that reason they are not sympathetic, nor are the villains – the gangsters – an interesting bunch; but Beresford moves between the two groups with exhilarating speed.

He became very serious with **'Breaker' Morant** (1980), written by himself with others from a number of sources – since Morant (who derived his nickname from horsebreaking) was an Australian folk hero. He was English-born, and saw the Boer War as a chance of being reunited with his family in England. Instead, he was courtmartialled and executed, and that is the subject of this film. He had taken the law into his own hands and killed some Boer prisoners and a German missionary – an action of considerable consequence, for it might have brought Germany into the War; Morant's defence was that the order came from Kitchener himself, through an intermediary, now dead. The direction is somewhat self-conscious, and if Beresford makes use of the unusual setting, the South African veldt – though the film was made in South Australia and could not deceive

Australians – he can do little with the British actor, Edward Woodward, who in the title role plays in vainglorious manner, denying any glimpse into Morant's character. This hollowness at the core of the film is somewhat offset by the clever performance of Jack Thompson as the defending counsel.

The Club (1980) is again based by Williamson on one of his plays, about a Melbourne rugby football club and the wrangling that ensues when a young player is acquired for a large sum, with the inference that the veteran coach (Thompson) is no longer helping the team to victory. As in *Don's Party*, the dialogue has bite, if still mainly of appeal to those interested in the Australian male: his swearing, drinking and relations with women. Beresford and Williamson make the team reasonably glamorous, but obviously do not care for the boys in the boardroom.

Overseas, **My Brilliant Career** (1979) was often bracketed with *The Getting of Wisdom*, for the good reason that both are based on autobiographical novels about growing up, written about the same time by women who published under male pseudonyms. In both cases the screenplays were written by Eleanor Witcombe, and this one is tellingly directed by Gillian Armstrong, a former art director. Miles Franklin's novel detailed her life with her impoverished family and her desire to escape into a world of what she calls culture and the arts. She does escape for a while to live with her comfortably-situated grandmother, and is proposed to by a handsome young man of a wealthy family: their relationship, beginning with teenage banter, develops into something deeper as they recognise in each other qualities of independence unlike those around them. She, Sybilla – splendidly played by Judy Davis – is tomboyish, unconventional and outspoken, but since Sam Neill's performance gives every reason why she should accept him, her rejection is clearly more faithful to the original than dramatically satisfying.

Donald Crombie, meanwhile, stayed with the past, and had been preparing **The Irishman** (1978) before the success of *Caddie*. He wrote the screenplay himself, from Elizabeth O'Connor's novel, about a teamster (Michael Craig) with twenty fine Clydesdale horses and little concern that

Movies Around the World

The new Australian cinema has made its aim clear, doubtless because there is government money in most of its projects: it is to be honest, unmelo-dramatic and, where possible, factual Consequently most of the films look at Australia's past, and since there isn't too much of that the films often seem alike – not surprisingly, since most of them are based on twentieth-century biographies or memoirs. Miles Franklin's story of her adolescence, *My Brilliant Career*, became unexpec-tedly the most rewarding of these films – due in large degree to the performances of Judy Davis and the New Zealand actor Sam Neill.

one of his rivals had brought the first motorised trucks to the area – North Queensland, with its sun, eucalyptus trees and jerry-built wooden towns. The film shows the effect of his drunkenness and fecklessness on the man's sons – but not entirely convincingly. It is hard to disagree with the Australian critic Romola Con-stantine, who wrote in the *Sun-Herald*, 'If this sensitive, beautiful film had come several years ago it would not have met the now predictable complaints: that Austra-lian pictures have now worked the 1920s Australian scene to death. And here's yet another one, taking its time showing the wide open spaces, the changing age, the young man growing up, country races, pub brawls, and old folk a-dying.' Whether or not Crombie took this to heart, **Cathy's Child** (1979) is set in the recent past as written by Ken Quinnell, a Sydney film critic, and based on a book by Dick Wordley, who had been involved in the Cathy Baikas affair of 1974. The film be-gins by suggesting that there is a story in

every newspaper item, which in this case is the abduction of a child from one parent by the other: this usually only makes head-lines when the child is spirited out of the country, and this child has been taken to Greece. A mother's anguish has been with us since movies began, but *Cathy's Child* is about much more than that, including governmental responsibility and press ethics – and it is made with richness of detail. The Maltese mother is flawlessly played by Michelle Fawden and Wordley by Alan Cassell, a man seemingly con-ditioned by too many cigarettes and too many late nights.

If *Cathy's Child* suggests that Crombie is one of the best of contemporary directors, the same might be said of **Summerfield** (1977) and Ken Hannam. Cliff Green wrote this exercise in the genre film, that of the stranger who arrives in town to meet with instant hostility. He (Nick Tate) is the new teacher in a sleepy coastal village (the outdoor scenes were filmed at Churchill Island, south of Melbourne), and there i something menacing in the very sunlight. In his book on the Australian cinema, 'The Last New Wave', David Stratton says that the film's problem was 'all too common among Australian films: an unusual location is found, exciting incidents are conceived, but not enough thought is given to character development, relationships between characters, and – more often than not – a satisfactory ending.' This last point is certainly true, but in general scariness and making us wonder what will happen next *Summerfield* holds a high place among the thrillers of the Seventies.

In the matter of comparisons, **The Odd Angry Shot** (1979) received a glowing one when it had its belated British premiere on B.B.C. television. Its subject is the Vietnam War, and Richard West, who was there, wrote in *The Spectator*, 'Unpublicised and unpretentious, it is nevertheless incomparably more true to Vietnam than Hollywood bores like *Apocalypse Now!* and *The Deer Hunter* . . . Above all, it is free of the whining self-pity that seems to accompany all American films and books on Vietnam.' There is talent in Tom Jeffrey's writing and directing, from a novel by William Nagle, but if, as I suspect, he was attempting to make a large statement he misses. There are a number of minor flaws, including the casting of a T.V. star, Graham Kennedy, as the unit veteran: he is convincing as an ordinary down-to-earth joe, but is unlikely as artist and thinker. The youngsters – John Hargreaves, Bryan Brown, John Jarratt – sit around bored and foul-mouthed, except when they go to the city for R and R, when they are drunk and foul-mouthed. Every so often they stalk other groups of young men, trying to kill them: these opponents have slant eyes, they open fire first and seem like creatures from another planet – but there seems no good reason why either side should be involved in undertaking this grisly operation.

Gallipoli (1981) makes its point about war more immediately and forcefully. The film was conceived and directed by Peter Weir, who commissioned David Williamson to write the screenplay, which falls into three parts. The first is about the acquaintanceship and subsequent friendship of a smiling blond boy (Mark Lee) from the Outback and a city – Perth – boy (Mel Gibson): since they are both runners

this part of the film resembles the concurrent *Chariots of Fire*, and it is not completely compelling. The middle section, with the troops in training near Cairo, is the best account I know of naive young white men coping with the deviousness of the pedlars of the East, and the film makes the telling point that it is because they are Australians that they are tough, proud and not to be monkeyed around with. The last section, at Gallipoli itself, has a night-before-battle sequence which is a tribute to Olivier's *Henry V*, but subsequently it neither emphasises the carnage nor explains (more than perfunctorily) the reason for battle – on the reasonable assumption that it was absurd in the first place. The decency, clarity and lack of pretentiousness make this film memorable; the mainly light-hearted dialogue underlines the strong relationships often formed between soldiers. The film's subject is not the mentality of soldiers but the waste of them, which may be why it does not equal the impact of the two similar films, *All Quiet on the Western Front* and *Paths of Glory*. The producer was a new company formed by two successful Australian tycoons, Rupert Murdoch and Robert Stigwood, and the latter's connections with Paramount was the reason for that company to undertake the requisite world distribution for the film to recover its costs. As a result, it was the most successful Australian film to date, despite

Norman Kaye and Wendy Hughes in *Lonely Hearts*, which won the Best Film prize when the Australian Film Awards were handed out in 1982 – and it is nice to know that such a quiet, civilised entertainment can gain recognition. It is about a couple, approaching middle-age, who meet through a marriage bureau, a relationship handled with wit and sensitivity by the director Paul Cox, who wrote the screenplay with John Clarke.

the initial publicity tag, 'From the place you've never heard of . . . the story you'll never forget', though that was quickly changed to 'From the place you may never have heard of . . .'

Buoyed by the international interest in this film and Government and state subsidies, the Australian film industry produced forty-nine films in 1981, but that was reduced to five the following year after some cunning entrepreneurs had found a means of making tax losses out of the industry. I should imagine that it would be healthy if annual production were to settle at somewhere between the two figures. There is talent to be exploited and a beautiful and varied country – aspects to be enjoyed in the least of these films. The best of them are among the best produced anywhere in the world in the Seventies, which says much for an industry which, if not young, had hitherto been insignificant for most of its life.

Despite its advantage of language, the Australian cinema has made smaller inroads into the consciousness of Anglo-Saxon movie-buffs than has the 'New German Cinema', so-called, which came along at the same time. Both the Australian film-makers and the 'new' Germans worked conscientiously but self-consciously, aware of a void in the past. In the case of the Australians, it is a true void; in the case of the Germans, it is a twenty-five year hiatus – or so it was described by one of the exponents of the new German cinema, Werner Herzog, explaining the recovery from 'an epoch of barbarism with the Nazis'. This is disingenuous: the Nazis did not rule for a quarter of a century, but by suggesting that the films of the post-Nazi era were poor Herzog implies that the new German cinema was all the more revolutionary.

In fact the Germans did produce a number of interesting films after the War, including **Tiefland** (1954), actually made during the War, with a history going even further back. Leni Riefenstahl had planned it in 1934, as a vehicle for Heinrich George, but his schedule and her nervous breakdown forced its cancellation. She later claimed that had she made it she would not have been forced into making *Triumph des Willens*, and that by resurrecting the subject on the outbreak of war she avoided making the propaganda films demanded by Goebbels at the time. The film's source is in an opera by Eugene d'Albert which had been popular in Berlin in the Twenties: the setting is nineteenth-century Spain and its hero an impoverished landlord (Bernhard Minetti) who marries a wealthy heiress although he is in love with a flamenco dancer (Miss Riefenstahl). The dancer marries a poor shepherd and when the landlord attempts to ravish her the two men fight with knives. It is a trumpery plot, but as with *Das Blaue Licht* the mountain scenery is superbly photographed and the direction accomplished. The film was not quite finished when the French confiscated it in 1945, and Riefenstahl did not manage to get it shown till after she had been deNazified in 1952; by that time it was considered old-fashioned and she withdrew it (and withheld it for over twenty years) though not, apparently, until it had recovered its cost. This had been considerable, bringing into question her standing with the upper echelons of the Nazi party. She said that both she and *Tiefland* were thought so unimportant that she was forced into filming the interiors in Prague, and Goebbels' diary confirms at least his own lack of interest; however, when she could no longer film the exteriors in Spain a Spanish town was constructed in Bavaria – and *Tiefland* became the most expensive film made by the Germans since the coming of Talkies. That fact, given the difficulties facing Germany in 1942, would not suggest that she was in disgrace, though there may well have been mutual disillusionment between her and the Party.

Only two German films made an international impact in the immediate post-war years. One of these is **Berliner Ballade** (1948), which is not good and could never have been good, but it was immensely cheering to the Germans themselves and interesting to the rest of the world as an entertainment rising literally from the rubble that was Berlin. It plants in those ruins a skinny soldier (Gert Fröbe), called Otto Normalverbraucher – or Otto Nobody in the English subtitles – who confronts shortages of food, jobs and housing while dreaming all the time of a café where a blonde serves him lashings of cream cakes. The film is little more than a series of revue sketches, of sophomoric humour, with a plea at the end for international harmony; but it wears a grin in the face of adversity, though one of slapstick rather than satire, after an excellent start showing the Prussian taste for militarism as more than usually absurd in the present circumstances. The director, Robert A. Stemmle, did little else of note in a twenty year career.

Die Mörder sind unter Uns (1946) was a co-production between East and West Germany taking a more serious view of the same situation, showing ordinary people coping with the horrifying living conditions and the Nazi sympathisers who believed that the overwhelming defeat was simply a setback. It is melodramatic, but handled with vigour by Wolfgang Staudte, who went on to make a good film from Heinrich Mann's 1918 satiric novel, **Der Untertan** (1951), about one Hessling (Werner Peters), a silly little man obsessed by all matters military. Hessling finds his own mediocrity assuaged by joining an absurd group of duellists, the New Teutonians, or confirmed by undertaking abject jobs as a soldier; later he only exists by kowtowing to authority or planning the further aggrandisement of the Kaiser; clearly this theme had singular relevance in the light of recent events. It was made under East German auspices, but without the smallest iota of the Soviet influence which was to seep into the East German cinema. Staudte himself went to West Germany in 1955, but succeeded in making only some increasingly flaccid films.

Helmut Käutner provided the West German film industry with a success when **Die Letzte Brücke** (1954) won the Palme d'Or and the International Critics' prize at the Cannes Festival, though it was actually an Austrian-Yugoslav co-production, and one of the few of the time to prove the feasibility of such cooperation. Käutner wrote the script with Norbert Kunze, which tells of a German doctor (Maria Schell) kidnapped by partisans to care for their wounded, and her difficulty in explaining to her fiancé (Carl Mohner) why her first loyalty is to them. Miss Schell avoids the cloying mannerisms we normally associate with her, but she remains a 'star' despite the circumstances; the partisans are too well groomed and the scenery too striking; and the approach is a mite sentimental.

Käutner's film on the mad king of Bavaria, **Ludwig II, Glanz und ende eines König** (1954), has only a few insights into its subject, a magnificent Wagner in Paul Bildt, an excellent Ludwig in O. W. Fischer and some pretty scenery photographed in colour by the British Douglas Slocombe; but **Der Hauptmann von Köpenick** (1956) is a less surefooted historical enterprise. Carl Zuckmayer wrote the screenplay from his own play, omitting practically nothing. He had been more selective in adapting it for Richard Oswald's 1931 version, to which the credits of this one acknowledge a debt. Käutner's treatment is far less invigorating; the original settings have been faithfully copied except when he seems to be imitating Clair's *Les Grandes Manoeuvres*; but period charm is not the prime requisite for Zuckmayer's biting anti-military satire. In other circumstances Heinz Rühmann might have made an excellent Wilhelm Voigt. Universal were so impressed with Käutner at this time that he was summoned to Hollywood to make two soap operas, of which I have seen **A Stranger in My Arms** (1959), a banal melodrama notable only for the performance of Mary Astor as a possessive mother.

It is not, perhaps, quite so depressing an experience as the films Fritz Lang made after returning to Germany. He later remarked that he did not consider them important, but was hoping for 'a great financial success so that I would again have the chance – as I had with *M* – to work without restrictions. It was my mistake.' It was also a gigantic miscalculation to suppose that audiences would want to see the childish fantasies of his very first film. **Der Tiger von Eschnapur** (1959) and its sequel, **Das Indische Grabmal** (1959) were based on scripts he had written with his wife in 1920. They are in colour and technically competent, but **Die Tausend Augen des Dr Mabuse** (1961) does not have even these advantages – nor indeed anything to indicate that it was made by a once formidable director. Pabst, on the other hand, made a partial return to form with **Der Letzte Akt** (1955), and it may be significant, given the preoccupations of the German industry up to this time, that, like *Die Letzte Brücke*, it is an Austrian production. It is an account of the last days of Hitler, played by Albin Skoda in a manner suggesting silliness rather than sickness.

The confined settings – most of it takes place inside the bunker – clearly did not inspire him, as if to confirm that he lost interest in realism at the time of *Kamaradschaft*. Despite the hysteria inherent in the subject, the piece comes to life only with the performance of Oskar Werner as the obligatory 'good' German. **Es Geschah am 20 Juli** (1955) retraces the plot to kill Hitler, but this second comment on the Nazi years is also made with momentary compassion but chiefly coldness.

Peter Lorre, a contemporary of Lang and Pabst, left Hollywood for Germany to make **Der Verlorene** (1951), not only as an actor, but as producer, director and part-writer. It is a psychological thriller in the manner of *M*, set during the War, but the regime under which its protagonist goes about his business might be any totalitarian one. I cannot agree with those who find in the film a condemnation of Nazi tactics, nor that its failure was due to Germany's refusal to face its recent past, since that is never an issue; I think, rather, that audiences found it old-fashioned, since its style so much resembles the films of the pre-Nazi era.

Die Brücke (1959) was one of the very few German films of the Fifties to be widely seen abroad. Its director, Bernhard Wicki, had played the partisan leader in *Die Letzte Brücke* for Käutner, whom he had assisted on a number of other films. These two films are alike in missing that element which can turn the well-made, well-intentioned into something beyond the mundane; their common subject is war, and though based on truth, both have the aura of reverentially created fictions – in this case about a group of schoolboys determined to defend the town bridge against the American advance. They are not sentimentalised, nor does the film strive too hard to condemn Nazism. As a result of its success, Wicki was invited to direct the German sequence of *The Longest Day* and then **The Visit** (1964), based on Friedrich Dürrenmatt's play. Ben Barzman's screenplay reduces the material, and the vengeful, infirm, aged lady becomes an inadequate, middle-aged Ingrid Bergman in the trappings of early Gloria Swanson, with Anthony Quinn on his usual form as the suitor who did her an injustice years before. The film is a companion to *The Condemned of Altona*, which

was also handled by 20th Century-Fox, with casts and production companies of several different nationalities.

The first German film on a contemporary subject to be extensively seen abroad was **Das Mädchen Rosemarie** (1958), and that was due to its content rather than Rolf Thiele's direction, which is rudimentary. Rosemarie Nitribitt, played in the film by Nadja Tiller, was a callgirl found murdered near Frankfurt, and subsequently revealed to have had among her clients some of Germany's most influential businessmen, several of whom she may have been blackmailing. Thiele attempts satire at the expense of the Mercedes set and strives for Brechtian significance by presenting two commentators who make sour remarks about Germany's economic miracle.

Similar motives on the part of foreign distributors brought a film by Veit Harlan to art-houses, **Anders als du und Ich** (1957). It is no less nondescript than his earlier films, but revives a subject dormant since the German Silent cinema, homosexuality. In this case, it is a false alarm, and a mother's worries have been in vain when the suspect *jugend* is caught chasing the housemaid. In the meantime we have been instructed by a number of legal and medical specialists, and amused, not intentionally, by a middle-aged gentleman whose home life consists of displays of wrestling by youths in satin swimsuits.

It was hardly to be expected that young German film buffs, fresh from watching the films of the nouvelle vague, would be empathetic to Harlan and Thiele. In 1962 a manifesto was launched to coincide with the Oberhausen Film Festival and signed by twenty-six young directors: 'The new cinema needs new forms of freedom: from the conventions and clichés of the established industry, from intervention by commercial partners, and finally freedom from . . . other vested interests.' The signatories were not part of the ramshackle German film industry, but they had been working on shorts and in television, thus creating a climate for Government discussions. In 1966 an awards system was announced, in which public money would be set aside for films and screenplays of quality. It was a system already adopted in a number of countries – primarily in Scandinavia – to encourage local production, which was always at the mercy of exhibitors preternaturally biased towards foreign, i.e. American, 'commercial' films. In Germany the situation had become critical as the state-run television channels devoured cinema patrons, and in 1974 the Government induced the two principal T.V. networks to commit the equivalent of $1.8 million to immediate film production, with control two years later over the films concerned, when their cinema career was deemed to be finished (the networks also bought seventeen existing films for $80,000 each). Two years earlier a tax had been placed on cinema attendances, to be ploughed back into the industry; a small annual fund was available to young directors; and a tax shelter scheme was devised to attract private investors – not, in fact, restricted to local film-makers and, as it turned out, of considerable benefit to a number of the more risky American productions.

Ironically, the first manifestations of the new German cinema appreciated abroad were of very limited appeal, *Abschied von Gestern*, directed by Alexander Kluge, and *Chronik der Anna Magdalena Bach*, directed by Jean-Marie Straub, both made in 1966. They impressed some on their festival showings, but, with reason, created no stir when shown in foreign art-houses, so that it was not until later that most film enthusiasts became aware that there was a new German cinema, when **Angst Essen Seele Auf** (1973) – *Fear Eats the Soul* – became a critical and popular success. It was the eighteenth film of Rainer Werner Fassbinder (1946–82), who had started making short films at the age of twenty, and who had also founded an *Anti-teater* movement. *Angst Essen Seele Auf* was not only a remarkable film to have come from Germany, hitherto untouched by any movement towards realism, but it also made a strong and subtle statement on racism: a middle-aged widow (Brigitte Mira), sheltering from the rain in a dreary prostitutes' bar, meets a young Arab *gastarbeiter*, Ali (El Hedi Ben Salem). Their eventual marriage is greeted with ridicule or scorn by her children and friends, but its destruction comes from within, when she begins to mother him. Fassbinder's unimaginative, Ozu-like style seemed right for his material, which includes aspects of the underbelly of life in Munich that few could have

imagined. The screenplay, which he wrote himself, was based on fact, and he had already used the incident in 1970 in **Der Amerikanische Soldat** as an anecdote told by a minor character. That film, according to *Sight and Sound*, is a revision of Douglas Sirk's *All That Heaven Allows*; and my own immediate desire after watching *Angst Essen Seele Auf* to see all of Fassbinder's early films was fulfilled by **Martha** (1974), a re-vamping of Sirk's *Sleep, My Love* and an excellent example of the second-rate imitating the third-rate. It was made for television and has not, with reason, been publicly seen in either Britain or the U.S.

Together *Angst Essen Seele Auf* and *Martha* showed a director capable of swinging from excellence to something worse than mediocrity. Later, I think, this polarisation became less apparent, but there were at this time two Fassbinders, the observant, lively one who had made **Händler der Vier Jahreszeiten** (1971), and the artificial, sterile director responsible for **Die Bitteren Tränen der Petra von Kant** (1972). If, as Fassbinder claimed, his movies were 'all self-contained discourses on human behaviour' the former is largely successful, losing some conviction on its insistence on cheap sexuality as it dwells on the affairs of Hans (Hans Hirschmüller), who sells fruit from a barrow, beats his wife and drinks himself

The 'new' German cinema, much discussed and written about, arouses strong passions – particularly among those who, having patronised two or three of its products, refuse to be subjected to like boredom again. The directors connected with this movement are not among the cinema's notable talents, being more concerned with effect than narrative form. Their acknowledged leader was the prolific Rainer Werner Fassbinder, who made his reputation with *Angst Essen Seele Auf*, where his compassion more than atoned for that deficiency. The leading players were Brigitte Mira and El Hedi Ben Salem, and their unlikely romance was very touching.

to death. In *Petra von Kant* a group of snake-like ladies squabble between themselves for bodily possession, and, except for that lack of inhibition, are the daughters of Sappho as movies ever presented them.

As he achieved international recognition Fassbinder announced 'About half the early films were "about" my discoveries in the American cinema . . . The others were investigations into German actualities. I thought then that if you brought people up against their own reality, they'd react against it. I now think that the primary need is to satisfy the audience, and then to deal with political comment. First, you have to make films that are seductive, beautiful, about love or whatever . . . That's the preliminary stage in a kind of political presentation.' If any of his films had any real political comment he hid it well; and if **Effi Briest** (1974) is about love, it is far from seductive. Theodor Fontane's classic novel proposes the not unfamiliar situation of a girl married to a much older man but attracted to a young one. Fassbinder attempts a visual style he supposes to be the cinema equivalent of 'literature', starting each sequence with a tableau unfreezing and finishing with a fade into white: but he succeeds in making this 148-minute film seem endless. He was too prolific, it seems, to develop any film sense. His early films are like radio with pictures, proceeding in a series of conversations either pretentious or pointless. Later he became obsessed with rather outré decor, featuring lamps, mirrors and furnishings of an Art Deco persuasion (even when inappropriate); his camera would circulate amidst it at least once in every sequence.

Bolwieser (1977) starts in this fashion, with characters glimpsed through dusty glass partitions or through lace curtains. The time and place – Bavaria in the dying days of the Weimar Republic – is well established, and the plot has possibilities, as Hanni (Elisabeth Trissenaar), married to the local stationmaster (Kurt Raab), moves from one lover (Bernhard Helfrich), the butcher, to another (Udo Kier), a hairdresser. The original novel by Oskar Maria Graf was published in 1931, and it is in the long German tradition of small town satire: but satire is not something Fassbinder understands, and the result is a betrayal

of the book. Admittedly the piece was made for television and shown in two separate hundred minute parts, but as cut to two hours for showings abroad it is certainly no better than **Despair/Eine Reise ins Licht**.(1978), a travesty of Vladimir Nabokov's clever novel as written in English by Tom Stoppard and acted in self-pitying, over-emphatic manner by Dirk Bogarde. Bogarde plays a chocolate manufacturer who is schizophrenic and getting no sexual satisfaction from his wife (Andréa Ferreol), so he arranges for his own disappearance by changing clothes with a tramp (Klaus Löwitsch). There is much more plot, and the film is conceivably meant to be a thriller, but beyond the fact that it is set at the same time as *Bolwieser* and has an ending stolen from *Sunset Boulevard* all point or purpose is withheld from us.

That the tramp stands around naked for much of the time and for no good reason is evidence of Fassbinder's sexual inclination – not that he tried to hide that, and indeed in **Faustrecht der Freiheit** (1975) he played a homosexual, a rather stupid carnival worker fleeced and dunned by the wealthy middle classes. This study of exploitation would be good enough to justify its own exploitation of the gay milieu did not most of the situations seem to come from old Joan Crawford movies, in which they were handled more honestly and dramatically. If Fassbinder abandoned his early obsession with Hollywood, the European cinema remained to be plundered: **Chinesisches Roulette** (1976) is a rehash of *La Règle du Jeu*, with a dash of *The Boys in the Band*, and **In Einem Jahr mit 13 Monden** (1979) a homosexual version of *Le Feu Follet*. **Die Zartlichkeit der Wölfe** (1973) is a homosexual version of *M*, based, admittedly, on the same source – Peter Kürten, the vampire of Düsseldorf; Fassbinder produced, for one of his actors, Ulli Lommel, to direct, which he does in the same manner as his master.

Despite occasional respectful and even enthusiastic notices Fassbinder did not become a name on the American art-house circuit till **Die Ehe der Maria Braun** (1979), undoubtedly his best film since *Angst Essen Seele Auf.* It is by turns stagey and imaginative, and Hanna Schygulla's performance in the leading role was gratifying to those who had not been exposed to Fassbinder's heroines with their slit skirts, net stockings and make-up and hair-styles of the Forties. Her costume is justified to an extent, for the film follows its heroine from the aftermath of war through the economic miracle. As in *Der Blaue Engel*, she is a lady of loose morals loved to the point of self-destruction by a respectable man – played by Ivan Desny with a professionalism not evident elsewhere in the film. He is a wealthy industrialist, and Maria Braun uses his devotion to make her way in the world, while still loving the man (Klaus Löwitsch) she married. It is not original of Fassbinder – credited with the original idea of the film – to suggest that Maria loves both men in different ways, but because she believes precisely that, the film has some weight. Her progress from poverty to power is as interesting as such matters often are in movies, and as a family saga, which is what this film really is, it is often unexpected. The film's success encouraged Fassbinder to make some more on the same theme before his early death from a combination of drugs and drink.

Werner Herzog (b. 1942) appears to have something more to say than Fassbinder, but since his way of saying it is equally debilitating few would agree with his own estimate that his films are ahead of their time. He achieved a degree of success in the international market with his fifth film, **Aguirre, der Zorn Gottes** (1972): its opening sequence alone would have justified that success, and actually did, for the rest is appalling. The setting is the Andes, forested and misty: down the mountainside, across the valley, files a troop of men, to unearthly sounding choral music. After that, the photography by Thomas Mauch finds a few more stunning images, but the screenplay, by Herzog, lacks both coherence and conviction as it follows the exploits of a megalomaniac conquistador (Klaus Kinski) hoping to establish his own empire. The large number of loose ends is due to the difficult conditions of filming in the jungle, with Herzog both extemporising and omitting much of what he intended at the outset. The original soundtrack in English was jettisoned, and the German one substituted is banal.

Reviewers gave the film only a muted welcome, but most surrendered to **Jeder für Sich und Gott Gegen Alle** (1974), the story of Kaspar Hauser, who in 1828 materialised in the main square of Nuremberg and was thought to have been kept in captivity since childhood. He is treated as a side-show and eventually murdered, in the meantime establishing an odd serenity and wisdom. This material, surely among the best that any film-maker ever had to work with, finds Herzog often didactic, complex and mysterious, but always prepared to sacrifice conviction for effect. **Woyzeck** (1979) begins with little conviction, since it violates all known concepts of military dress and behaviour, and as the errors accumulate a dull movie becomes an irritating one. Herzog turned to Büchner's astonishing play after the failure a year earlier of *Nosferatu*, a literal remake of Murnau's film, with another English track which had to be replaced (because audiences laughed). Herzog's adaptation of Büchner is framed with the device used by Carson McCullers in 'Reflections in a Golden Eye', suggesting that we alone are privy to reasons for the murder it speaks of, and that we should therefore cry out on behalf of the poor murderer. We do not care, for Herzog cannot move us, as did Georg Klarens in his less painstaking 1950 version.

The goalkeeper hero of **Die Angst des Tormanns beim Elfmeter** (1972) is a modern Woyzeck: with a similar mentality, but with less reason, he strangles the woman he has slept with. This is the second feature of Wim Wenders (b. 1945), and it is an excellent example of his intention that his films 'deal with the period of time in which they were made, the cities, the landscapes . . .' He and Peter Handke wrote it, from Handke's novel, and its chief fault is its lack of dimension, which is less than in Chabrol's lesser studies in crime. As a study of despair and desperation, **Alice in den Stadten** (1974) is mainly padding, and in this instance the film to be preferred is *Paper Moon*, also about a travelling man saddled with a precocious young girl. This is one of several films Wenders made in imitation of American 'road' movies; his admiration for Hollywood cinema was again apparent with **Der Amerikanische Freund** (1977), a very free adaptation of Patricia Highsmith's 'Ripley's Game', with Bruno Ganz as a Hamburg picture-framer who has leukemia and agrees to act as a hit-man in

Paris to provide for his widow and child. As in Hitchcock's *Strangers on a Train* the murder proposal takes place on a train – Hamburg's U-Bahn. And the cast includes two third-rate American film-makers, Samuel Fuller and Nicholas Ray, known to be admired by their European counterparts. In *Alice in den Stadten* there are several references to John Ford, but better Ford than Douglas Sirk.

And better Herzog than Hans Jürgen Syberberg, whose extensive films to date have been disquisitions on Ludwig II, the pulp writer Karl May, and Hitler, told in a mish-mash of fantasy, polemic, puppetry, monologue or whatever means are at hand. **Hitler** (1976) opened in Britain to the cautiously animated notices customarily given by critics confronted with the unusual: a handful were scornful, in contrast to the American press where Francis Coppola sponsored this seven-hour conglomeration. In the meantime British television critics had seen it, cut into four parts, and were unanimous. Clive James in *The Observer* called it 'a nonsense', going on, 'this trouncingly fatuous epic went only to prove that politics have changed immeasurably for the better. Hitler was a failed artist who took his revenge by wrecking as much of Europe as he could get his hands on [according to Syberberg]. Nowadays, thanks to State subsidies there is no such thing as a failed artist.' It is doubtful that without television and Government funds these four directors would ever have been heard of outside Germany, or, indeed, within. With a couple of exceptions the public's reception has been seldom higher than indifferent. Those exceptions belong to Fassbinder, while Herzog and Wenders, between moments of self-aggrandisement, have given evidence that they can direct. Even admirers find the new German cinema ponderous.

The one outstanding German director of this period does not really belong to the movement, for he made his first film in 1966. Volker Schlöndorff (b. 1939) studied in France with Melville, among others, returning to Germany to make his feature debut with **Der Junge Törless** (1966), a rather prosaic version of Robert Musil's novel of the sexual and brutal traumas awaiting sensitive students at military school. Schlöndorff's wife, Margarethe von Trotta, acted in several of his films and was co-writer and co-director of **Die Verlorene Ehre der Katharina Blum** (1975). Heinrich Böll's novel, an attack on the yellow press, provided Schlöndorff with international recognition, and the opening sequence – a young man on a Rhine steamer – shows that he has forgotten more about cinema than Fassbinder ever learnt. The film as a whole is an over-emphatic polemic, influenced by Costa-Gavras, and if ultimately not completely satisfactory that has something to do with the colourless performance of Angela Winkler as the girl pushed around by press and police for sheltering a man they refer to as an anarchist. Fräulein von Trotta plays the lead in **Der Fangschuss** (1976), a Countess who makes an unsuccessful pass at an officer (Matthias Habich), a young man with a undefined liaison in the past and a penchant for gazing at the sleeping figure of a colleague. The dénouement will come as no surprise to readers of Julien Green, but the source is in fact a novel by Marguerite Yourcenar, 'Coup de Grâce', turned into a feminist tract by von Trotta and two other women writers. Schlöndorff directed, alone, responding keenly to the setting, a castle near Riga during the First World War.

His greatest success has been **Die Blechtrommel** (1979), the first German film ever to win Hollywood's Oscar for the Best Foreign Language film. Its source is the influential novel by Gunter Grass that we know as 'The Tin Drum'. Schlöndorff was approached by the producer, Franz Seitz, after Grass had reserved the right to withdraw his own support if he disliked the final draft of the script, written by Schlöndorff and Jean-Claude Carrière. They begin as the book does, with the antecedents and birth of Oskar (David Bennent), who decides while a child to stop growing, observing at the same time the sexuality and mortality of those around him and the rise and fall of the Nazis. Reading the book it seemed to me that on these aspects of sex and death Grass was as imaginative as he was humourless and pointless; it required no perception to portray the Nazis as morons and clowns: but Schlöndorff treats this material with wit and insight, so that the film is by turns touching and disturbing. He did not feel that the film could stretch itself to include the last part of the book, taking Oskar through the Economic Miracle, which is a pity for, in my opinion, it is then that Grass shows his real power.

Schlöndorff was working on a second film with Grass about two young teachers who travel the world in an attempt to confront reality when Grass recommended to him **Die Falschung** (1981), a novel by a friend of his, Nicholas Born, who had based it on his experiences as a reporter during the Middle East crisis. The screenplay by the director, Von Trotta, Carrière and Kai Herrmann (a colleague of Born) focuses on a journalist (Bruno Ganz), who, reporting on the Civil War in Lebanon, becomes confused and then dismayed at the prospect of communicating its stupidity, cruelty and futility; on the sidelines are a failing marriage back home and an unsatisfactory affair with the German widow (Hanna Schygulla) of an Arab. Analogies are drawn between these problems and the conflict in the streets, and the unworthiness of this concept is admitted in a foreword which claims that what follows is a work of the imagination. Alternatively, that is Schlöndorff's way of advising audiences that, like his protagonist, he feels inadequate to the events he has to portray. The introduction further states that the film is not a documentary, but in that case is defensive for no good reason: at least forty per cent of the film consists of footage of the fighting in Beirut – the ruins, the wounded, the charred bodies, the partisans posing for pictures – and the compassion inherent in the selection is reason enough to admire this deeply flawed film.

Its failure highlights the dichotomy between Schlöndorff on the one hand and Fassbinder, Herzog and Wenders on the other: he works in traditional mould, liking literary adaptations or films of significance, while they try to find an original method of conveying their own personal fantasies, or those connected with their obsession with Hollywood. Both approaches are valid. But in the end his craftmanship, put at the service of the cinema's liberal values, is preferable to limited talents on their ego-trips. The Germans themselves have few doubts as to which they like best, and for some years the one great subsidised success was **Lina Braake** (1975). It united the critics and public, but has not to date been seen in the U.S., while its showings in Britain went virtually

ignored. Its writer-director, Bernhard Sinkel, a former lawyer making his first feature, shows much skill in detailing the cares of the lady of the title, who is eighty-two and trying to adjust to life in an old people's home. She is played by Lina Carstens and is magnificently matched by a white-maned fellow-inmate played by Fritz Rasp, the great villain of the Silent era. Lina's adventures include a trip to Sardinia which is not only implausible but too strong for this particular film – which nevertheless has heart, a rare quality in German cinema.

Angst Essen Seele Auf has it, as does **In der Fremde** (1975), directed by Sohrab Shahid Saless (b. 1944), an Iranian who had studied in Vienna and Paris before making shorts and documentaries for the Iranian Ministry of Culture. His first two features, made in Iran, are virtually motionless studies of two of the country's less affluent citizens, a railway-crossing keeper and a fisherman's small son. The second was awarded a prize at the Berlin Film Festival, which encouraged him to return to Germany for *In der Fremde*, written with Helga Houzer and concerning an immigrant Turkish worker, played by the Persian writer-actor Parviz Sayyad. It is better than Saless's earlier films, but some way below Tchekov, his avowed inspiration, since the aspirations of his hero remain barred to us beyond a desire for a woman and a vague wish to adapt to his environment.

Lina Carstens in *Lina Braake*, directed by Bernhard Sinkel, one of the most popular manifestations of the new German cinema, perhaps because it is one of the few with heart and feeling. Understandably, the cinema has seldom been interested in the problems of old age, and it would have to be said that this film is much less rigorous than *Umberto D*; but Miss Carstens gives a remarkable performance.

1161

Both Sinkel's film and Saless's are effortlessly superior to those of their more famous colleagues, while **Fabian** (1980) proves its director, Wolf Gremm, as talented as Fassbinder was not – and I make the analogy since its subject is that of *Bolwieser*, Germany on the brink of the Nazi take-over. Its source is a novel by Erich Kästner, and its eponymous hero (Hans Peter Hallwach) a young man too inert to care about the encroachment of Naziism. He is a copywriter for a tobacco firm, drifting from café to brothel, embarking on an affair with a movie starlet and seemingly indifferent to the suicide of his student friend and the 'removal' by the authorities of the professor he has befriended. Finally he returns to his home town and is drowned, for, as the end title explains, 'he couldn't swim'. In his home town he had been united with a childhood friend who has joined 'the steel helmets', and the man looks fierce till they are in a brothel together, when he suddenly appears mild. Gremm constantly demands readjustments in our attitudes from scene to scene; his period sense is impeccable and has been influenced, clearly, by a study of the films of the time; he has even 're-thought' his love scenes, so that entwined naked bodies break apart for the man to reach in a pocket for a cigarette. *Fabian* is in fact a considerable achievement: that it was turned down by the committee choosing films for the Cannes Film Festival only confirms my opinion of such bodies.

Its reception abroad has been mild, so it makes a rewarding comparison with **Taxi zum Klo** (1981), which won the Max Ophuls prize for comedy at the Berlin Film Festival; and after half a dozen other festival showings it went round the world to great acclaim and popularity. Its writer-director, Frank Ripploh, a former West Berlin schoolteacher, made it on his own and friends' money. Since it is autobiographical, it can be safely said that no film-maker had hitherto revealed so much of himself, so that we can see the blotches on his skin while engaged in various sexual acts – not to mention the various parts of the body essential to such acts. That the acts are homosexual would be of little consequence were the film not surfeited with self-loathing. It is misogynist, which is one thing, but Ripploh, who plays himself, felt compelled to tell us of his searches for sex in public lavatories and his inability to be faithful to the man who loves him – a role played by an ex-lover. He must surely have been aware that the Frank of the film indulges in practices that many gays privately abhor, whatever this film in toto does for their 'image' (in Germany, many gay groups protested). He emerges from the film less a happy homosexual than a sick one, and the final scene, of his pupils rioting as he sits before them in drag, is meant to imply that the logical conclusion of flamboyant homosexuality, i.e. the loss of the heterosexual role, the insistence on transvestism, leads to chaos. The sequences of driving around a night-and-neon Berlin are fairly intoxicating, and Ripploh, if he has anything else to say, may become a professional film-maker.

In the matter of frankness, the film makes laughable earlier German films on this subject, including **Die Konsequenz** (1977), a tragic but soppy love story between a prisoner and the warden's son. Its director, Wolfgang Petersen, would not on this evidence be a candidate for handling **Das Boot** (1981), the most expensive German film yet made – and the producer was able to raise the financing because of the popularity of Lother-Günther Buchheim's original novel. The film begins in 1943 in La Rochelle with an orgy, but the men are 'too drunk to fuck' (and the line is in English); the following morning we move out to sea with a U-boat and its crew, where their daily routine consists of profanity, proximity, fear, boredom and discipline. Petersen brings slickness to his material, but little insight, and the fact that the film actually made a profit in Germany alone on its huge investment is doubtless due to its view of the nation at a critical point in its history – courageous, desperate, defeated, pro-British to a degree (the crew sings 'Tipperary' in English) and no longer under any illusions about Nazi leadership. I believe that this merely conforms to what the Germans want to believe about themselves as they were then; but of course the same might have been said about the British when they flocked to *The Cruel Sea*, which was equally meretricious.

Britain was one of the few countries not to like *Das Boot*, but then its audiences did not greatly care for an infinitely better film about the War, **Aus einem Deutschen Leben** (1977). Perhaps the distributor was

The fact and experience of the Nazi concentration camps were too overwhelming for understanding, and it was not till the Seventies that many writers began to tackle the subject. Theodor Kotulla's *Aus Einem Deutschen Leben* is an honourable film, on the life of Rudolf Höss, the first commandant of Auschwitz, and it has become required viewing for German schoolchildren.

unwise to call it *Death is My Trade*, even if it is a literal translation of the title of the original novel by Robert Merle: it made it sound like a horror movie, and it is anything but – except by implication and in the cause of historical truth. Theodor Kotulla, the writer and director, has also used as source material the autobiographical notes left by Rudolf Höss, the first commandant of Auschwitz, and where appropriate he has found his style in *Nuit et Brouillard*. He takes his early events out of chronological order so that he can stress the irony of an averagely-intelligent German (Götz George, best known as the star of some action movies) becoming a non-fanatical Nazi functionary. It is because he is of minor importance that he is appointed commander of Auschwitz; it is because he regards himself as a disciplinarian that he accepts the institution of the Final Solution. His wife's acceptance of this, during a marital tiff, is the movie's most crass moment; otherwise this film is as much an expression of Germanness as *Der Untertan*, with a hero in love with uniforms, beer, the countryside and obedience. He may seem admirable to some until the final moments when an American officer states history's verdict with a lack of emotion which is nevertheless eloquent.

Perhaps the film says less than it should and too drily, but Kotulla's manner is preferable to the offensive splashiness of Wertmuller's *Pasqualino Settebelleze*. It is an important film and has become required viewing in German schools.

If the films from the minor film industries were poor for many years, amateurish and derivative, that is no longer the case, as film festivals demonstrate. During the last months of writing this book, I have seen excellent films from many countries whose movies were until then rarely up to festival standard. There is, however, only one other national industry that requires attention, the Chinese, if only because of the enormous population not only of the country itself but of the Chinese speaking world. Because of political differences, few Chinese films have found their way to the West; and not many of us would be naive enough to compare those that have with the Japanese. Yet both countries are not only neighbours, but the product of a long civilisation, in which the arts have played a pervasive role: we might therefore at least remark on the discrepancy between the standards of their films.

It is only recently that we have been able to see more than a small sample of Chinese cinema, and those organisers who have managed to bring Chinese films to the West have been guided by Jay Leyda's book on the subject. They have therefore to some extent chosen the films selected by Leyda as the cream of Chinese film production, which raises the question as to what the others must be like. Leyda is not always reliable. **Street Angel** (1937) is not a remake of the Borzage film, as he claims, for the only common factor in each is prostitution, or, rather, the threat of it. Initially the pleasure of seeing a film shot in the streets of Shanghai almost fifty years ago is immense: but the street scenes disappear quickly and we are left with an absurd story and screenplay by Yuan Muzhi, the director. It tries to say something about the oppressed poor, but is nothing more than a turgid melodrama, interspersed with crude slapstick and songs – accompanied by subtitles and a bouncing ball to enable the audience to join in. The other music is taken from Western records, lasting as long as it took to play one 78 r.p.m. 12″ side; and the acting is elementary – happy looks, coy looks, sad looks, and so on.

Crossroads (1937) is equally simple-minded but also rather sweet, with a stronger plot, most of it set in a run-down boarding-house, where a Box and Cox situation arises between hero and heroine. The title may refer to Shanghai – the film begins with a shot of the harbour – or to that awkward period between college and work. It focuses on four unemployed graduates, and life is not smooth: one commits suicide, one leaves for the country, one is relegated to the role of hero's friend – and the hero (Zhao Don) suffers a number of reversals before he and his sweetheart (Bai Yang) can face the future with hope. The director, Shen Xiling, had to rework the script constantly, for in the original one student went to fight, and Chiang Kai-shek's Kuomintang Government was unwilling to recognise that the country was at war with Japan until the fall of Shanghai. The War of course ruined the Chinese film industry, leaving these two films, apparently, as the most important and popular of their time.

Production ceased in Shanghai, and continued sporadically in Hankow and Chungking. The first notable post-war Chinese film was **8,000 Li of Cloud and Moon** (1947), produced by the Kun Lun company, formed by some of the personnel of the old Lianhua Film Company, one of the most important studios which had been forced to close in 1937. The story is autobiographical, for the writer-director Shi Dongshan had spent some years with an itinerant theatre company, first alerting the peasants to the Japanese menace by song and dance, and later putting on patriotic shows for the troops. In the film the troupe includes two lovers (Tao Jin, Bai Yang) who marry; the second part concerns their arrival in postwar Shanghai and their efforts to understand the wholesale corruption. At first they live with wealthy relatives, who have surrendered whole-heartedly and happily to blackmarketeering and bribery. The young couple leave, he teaching and she turning to journalism – till she is hurt in an accident. The leader of the theatrical troupe, now reunited, collects money from the members to pay for the operation, in a simple but emotional scene that has more force than any in any other Communist propaganda film that I know; the Civil War between Left and Right was in progress as this film was made, and is not mentioned; the director explained his theme as an attempt to understand why, after the Japanese surrender, he and his colleagues felt only defeat.

From this film grew another, much longer and more ambitious – and also much more naive, **The Spring River Flows East** (1947), made by Kun Lun with the same two popular players, Tao Jin and Bai Yang. Its model seems to have been either *Gone with the Wind* or *The Best Years of Our Lives*, being about men returning from the War; it begins as early as 1931, and was first shown in two parts, 'Wartime Separation' and 'Darkness and Dawn'. Zhang (Tao Jin) is a respected teacher, and a patriot inveighing against Japanese aggression; the War separates him and his wife Sufen (Bai Yang), whose family suffers atrocities at the hands of the invaders. Zhang is captured, but after escaping is taken up by the wealthy Miss Wang, who provides not only work but stylish suits and eventually a place beside her in bed. Zheng Junli and Cai Chuseng, the writer-directors, seem as certain as most filmmakers that vice is more entertaining than virtue, for while Zhang's adventures are freshly-observed, those of his now-forgotten wife are cliché-ridden. She becomes a servant in the mansion in which he now lives, the object of contention between two women: neither he nor they are pleased when she divulges herself as his wife and thereupon commits suicide. Her mother screams out that if there is a god, why does he allow such things to happen, which is an appropriately purple ending.

The film has great vitality, even if stylistically it is clumsy and frequently derivative. Zheng Junli, working alone for Kun Lun, made **Crows and Sparrows** (1949), the only one of these films of any real value, for it does appear to give a true portrait of Shanghai just before the fall of Chiang Kai-shek. As left-wing propaganda it is less obvious than the other films from this company, even if the Communists are nice and lovable while the supporters of the old regime are dastardly (as in the Soviet films of the Twenties). They are all to be found living in a boarding-house in Shanghai, and they include a schoolteacher (Sun Daolin) whose vacillations on the political situation would seem to be due to weakness of character: it says much for the film that his conversion to Communism, after being wrongly imprisoned by the villains, is at once apt and convincing. Also in the cast is Zhao Don, saddled with a nagging wife and striving to evolve schemes to defeat inflation: he is also one of the six credited writers, and said that the film was partly autobiographical.

By this time the Chinese film industry was again in full swing, but its product resembles those of the Soviet Union in being no more than simple-minded propaganda. When the subject is interesting, as with **Family** (1957), the treatment is not – and the direction, by Chen Xihe and Ye Ming, is at best uninspired. This is a family saga, one of a trilogy by Ba Jin, first published in 1933 and already filmed during the war years. Here we may justly invoke the Japanese cinema, for the subject is the resistance against oppression, at the end of feudalism, within the family circle. **Two Stage Sisters** (1964) takes another subject dear to Japanese cinemagoers, the adventures of a theatrical troupe – and these are at least pretty, in colour, and seeming to take us over vast stretches of beautiful countryside. They are also so melodramatic and predictable as to be relishable: two foster

sisters suffer deprivation and disaster, until they settle in the big city, where one becomes the mistress of a corrupt entrepreneur and the other the disciple of a worthy, culture-minded young Communist reporter. Come the Revolution and it is the latter, of course, who triumphs, while the other sinks into disgrace and dissolution; the film continues on its hysterical way as the actors, now in smart uniforms, take culture out to the provinces. The film was seen briefly before the Cultural Revolution, when it vanished; on its resurfacing, its makers, including the director, Xie Jin, sent it to the West as 'an example of their finest work'.

The Cultural Revolution brought imprisonment to both the leading players of **Red Crag** (1965), the actress Yu Lan and Zhao Don (1914–80). The film is the apotheosis of this popular and much-admired actor, but it must be said that he is somewhat self-conscious as a stoic and dedicated Communist leader. The film begins in the early Forties, when the country's leaders, the army and police officers, were bowing to their American allies. The action centres on two stalwart leaders of the underground Chinese Communist party, of their betrayal, imprisonment and torture – and of the celebrations which follow the resignation of Chiang Kai-shek. The material, once again, is fascinating: its execution, by the director Shui Hua, of no interest. It is, of course, an advance on *Street Angel* and *Crossroads*, but just as they

China's turbulent twentieth-century history was not conducive to a thriving film industry, but production continued even during the War. Not until the recent détente have we been able to sample China's cinema, which turned out to be disappointingly naive. That quality becomes a virtue in *The Spring River Flows East*, which lasts over three hours and is so prodigal of incident that one would not want to miss a single second. It concerns a married couple separated by war, and while she suffers every reversal known to screen waifs he, Tao Jin, loses his idealism when taken up by Shu Xiuwen, a wealthy lady of doubtful virtue – though on this occasion he seems to be caught up by his conscience.

were elementary compared to films coming from Japan – or France, or Britain, or Italy – so are *Family*, *Red Crag* and *Two Stage Sisters*. The three Kun Lun films of the Forties are at the very least interesting, and I would like to think that among the Chinese films that we have yet to see there are others of the quality of *Crows and Sparrows*.

So much is shadow. It was with confidence that I said, starting this book, that there would be nothing on the Mongolian cinema. Since then I have seen one Mongolian film and it demands inclusion, **Tsogt Taij** (1945). Of its fellows I know not, but I suspect it is the only good Mongolian film since the People's Republic of Mongolia sent it abroad in celebration of the country's Sixtieth Anniversary, when it was already aged. The Russians had made two films in the country, *Storm Over Asia* and *Son of Mongolia*, the latter in 1936. Just after this the Mongolians started turning out films themselves, at the rate of three or four a year. Clearly *Tsogt Taij* was an ambitious undertaking: the directors were M. Luysaniamts and M. Bold, and the authors of the screenplay Yury Tarich, also the artistic supervisor, and B. Rinchen, the historical adviser, both Russians. The time is the second quarter of the sixteenth century, when the Manchus were completing their conquest of Mongolia, and its hero is Prince Tsogt, an enlightened Northern chieftain and leading supporter of the claimant to the throne of Genghis Khan: he is not supported in return, which is why his heroism is so moving. The film has touches of naivety, but these are as nothing to those in the Chinese films of the period: the direction is accomplished and the film is magnificent in detailing the religious and military crosscurrents of a medieval society.

Festivals notwithstanding, we still have insufficient opportunity to see the new and re-emergent cinemas, the pleasures of which are not always due to technique or content. Before television became the window on the world, films introduced us to faraway places, and that was one of the joys of cinemagoing in the past. Of the films we have been discussing, vivid impressions remain: the dusty suburbs of Torre Nilsson's Buenos Aires, the Austrian village in *Die Angst des Tormanns beim Elfmeter*, the Athens of *A Matter of Dignity*, the Australian Outback, the dry small town of *Calle Mayor*. Tourism is an adjunct of subsidised cinema (who does not want to visit Venice after seeing *Summer Madness*?); in less commercial terms, as well, the portraits of their countries being offered by the Australian government and Italian television are to be wholeheartedly admired. In the end, the health of the minor film industries depends on the creative talents welcomed and nurtured. Buñuel rose above the limitations of the Mexican industry, Ray struck out in a direction never dreamt of by his colleagues in India – and both made films not intended for foreign audiences. The new German cinema would collapse overnight if subsidies were withdrawn, since local audiences shun it, and yet Borau, responsible for one of the best and most popular films ever made in Spain, said 'I am not interested in making films for minority groups. I believe that way is anti-social and wastes money. One cannot waste 15 million pesetas [approx. $200,000] to please oneself.' Nevertheless *Furtivos* is a personal work, infinitely more rewarding than *Diary of a Shinjuku Thief*, made by Oshima, a director who claims to make films about 'problems meaningful to anybody in the world'. It is a question of talent. As one great director said of another – both of them working in minor industries: 'He gives you so much. He has worked it out so beautifully.' That was Satyajit Ray, explaining why his favourite director is Ingmar Bergman.

41

In Hollywood the Director is King

VERY FEW AMERICAN movies of the last quarter century have dated. The television networks in the mid-Sixties often made it a policy to only programme movies in colour at prime time, with appropriate fees, and that was, effectively, the end of the black-and-white movie. At about the same time those movie-makers using the wide screen began to plan the scenes so that no action was lost in telecasting, and since there were no technical developments, it is only in matters of fashion and special effects that one can tell an American movie of the late Fifties from one of the late Seventies. Thus the Hollywood film-maker has been left to do what he had always done best: tell a story.

The content of films has also varied little. Two of the greatest changes accompanied the break up of the studios: the virtual extinction of artificial or high-flown melodrama under the onslaught of television realism (though that was not typical of T.V. drama as a whole), and the new permissiveness. Both were inevitable, since film has always followed in the wake of drama and literature. Earlier we noted how much admired Broadway plays and popular novels had contributed to the demise of the Production Code by forcing a new sexual frankness in films. That that frankness soon became explicit had much to do with the pedlars of pornography, but that it soon became widely acceptable was due to more respectable patrons than theirs, the art-house audience. At least since *Hiroshima, Mon Amour* that audience had been accustomed to gazing upon couples in ante- or post-coital poses, and with the advent in 1967 of a Swedish enquiry into sexuality, *I Am Curious – Yellow*, directed by Vilgot Sjöman, it

began to be accustomed to naked bodies humping on beds.

At the same time the 16mm films of the American pop artist Andy Warhol arrived on the scene, to be pondered over by the pseudo-intellectual. The so-called 'underground' amateur films of Kenneth Anger which preceded them had also had homosexual connotations, and since they were equally boring the idea was mooted that there must be some hidden significance. Warhol and the word 'underground' denoted a certain artistic integrity and, with the acceptance of the films associated with his name, the way was paved for the public exhibition of hard-core pornography. That remains, to date, banned in Britain (though violence, which is far more obscene, is not), but Warhol's **Flesh** (1968) achieved public exhibition in that country without much difficulty. Warhol's friend, Paul Morrissey, put together this parade of New York hustlers and transvestites, disregarding the fumblings and clumsiness of the amateur cast, not to mention the bloops on the soundtrack and the joins in the film. As improvisation it failed to catch an iota of the native wit of New Yorkers and as social commentary it did not begin to exist. In London the police seized a copy after a number of performances at an avant-garde theatre, but the Censor intervened by granting it a certificate for public showing and it opened in a Chelsea cinema at the same time as a Tate Gallery exhibition of Warhol's paintings. In *Sight and Sound* Richard Roud observed that Warhol was one of the most important film-makers to emerge in the last ten years, because he had 'pushed back the boundaries of boredom'.

The old morality was not the only

In Hollywood the Director is King

Dennis Hopper, Peter Fonda and Jack Nicholson in *Easy Rider*, three oddballs at the mercy of redneck America. Nicholson the lawyer tries to explain: 'This used to be a helluva country, I can't tell you what's wrong . . . They're scared not of you but of what you represent to them: freedom.' He apparently spoke for a lot of people, especially the young, for the film represented the feelings of its audience as few have done in the history of films. As far as Hollywood was concerned, the message was double-edged, for a mint was lost on other films hoping to find that audience again.

victim. Some prominent Americans were assassinated and there was an unpopular war in Vietnam; it was a time between two scandals, McCarthyism and Watergate, both exposing the blatant cynicism and corruption of the Establishment. Later, in July 1974, just before measures for his removal from office were instituted against President Nixon, a Gallup poll found that forty-one per cent of the population did not think Watergate important. It was a climate conducive to the so-called hippie movement and its reaction against materialistic values – even if it was a movement which attracted more than its fair share of fakes, and an easy cop-out for those who wanted to cop-out. The sexual revolution went hand in hand with disillusionment and, after Warhol's 'innocent', 'naive' sex films there appeared the Broadway musical, 'Hair', which included a sequence of hippies in the nude, and **Easy Rider** (1968). The message of *Easy Rider* was clear: 'Fuck you, America.' The film was written, with Terry Southern, by two not quite successful actors, Peter Fonda and Dennis Hopper, with Hopper directing; it has no plot and a one-sided point of

view. Wyatt (Fonda) and Billy (Hopper) sell drugs to a pusher near the Mexican border, before proceeding to New Orleans for Mardi Gras. They have no occupation, no ambition. Their journey, like the pilgrim's progress, is a series of encounters: with a hippie commune, with the hard-hats who are their natural enemies, and with an alcoholic lawyer, George (Jack Nicholson), who declines 'grass' because he has enough trouble with booze, but takes it all the same. If they are in trouble, he can get them off 'least if you haven't killed anyone. Killed anyone white, that is.' He is senselessly beaten to death by the men whose motivations he had hoped to explain: Wyatt and Billy move on, to a psychedelic drug trip with two whores in a cemetery, to their own ending, the slaughter of the innocents. It is not a good ending, but it is the one necessary to the film's makers, after its feeble acts of defiance and weaker apologia for the life-style of its heroes. If it is Nicholson's brilliant performance which holds the film together, credit should also be given to Laszlo Kovacs's photography and the editing of Henry Jaglom. It is a highly and incredibly romantic film, and that distorts its message, cloying, confused but worth making.

Columbia, which had backed the film on a medium budget, found the profits huge. The studio doors were thereupon opened to newcomers – with remarkably poor results; Hopper himself directed nothing else of interest. The industry wanted to cash in on the youth movement, and that was easy enough, in theory, with the flower-people on one side and the Establishment on the other. The great disillusionment came with the massacre of a group of innocent people by Charles Manson and his hippies in Los Angeles in 1969.

There is violence and murder in **Joe** (1970), as it concerns the two generations, allying the working-class with the affluent middle-class and making no distinction between the vicious drug-pushing young and their gentle brethren. The writer, Norman Wexler, and the director, John G. Avildsen, have no sympathy for either side. Their backers were two young men in their twenties, hitherto associated with mini-budget sexploitation movies: this one, rabble-rousing and horrendously lacking in any sort of subtlety, is only a hairsbreadth away, but its comment on American society is as valid as that in the far superior *Five Easy Pieces* (q.v.). Bill (Dennis Patrick) kills the drug-pusher who has corrupted his daughter, and in a drunken moment confesses to a hard-hat (Peter Boyle); the two men find they have much in common and later start a vigilante search for the girl, which takes them to a macrobiotic food bar, a joint for hippies where they are invited to group sex and 'grass', and to the hippie commune for the finale slaughter. The film stumbles from one improbability to another, but later variations – *Death Wish, Hardcore* (q.v.) – also failed to find a non-sensational way of showing the dilemma of the times.

Joe, though its acceptance was relative, joined *Easy Rider* and *M★A★S★H* (q.v.) as one of the free-wheeling, non-establishment movies which the predominantly young audiences preferred. The studios were willing to back such films, and if they had in some cases sold their producing facilities and abdicated much of their power as such, their distribution networks were still a prime attraction for filmmakers. Without long-term contracts, one

old problem became more acute – the near impossibility of following a flop with another project, and the young turks among the directors were as prone to these as were any of their predecessors. At this time there were approximately fifty American directors of more than passing interest, and there are many more reasons for their choice of subjects – but the principal driving force was a continuation of the Hollywood tradition – to entertain. A secondary consideration, and it was a more recent tradition, was a deliberate effort to wrest the artistic laurels from Europe's brow – which resulted in imitating, and imitating late. An important factor was the presence in the industry of Stanley Kubrick, whose career is an exemplar for every director in the industry.

Killer's Kiss (1955) represents the first time a major artist entered the industry by making his own film. Stanley Kubrick (b. 1928), a staff photographer for *Look*, had made two 16mm documentaries which R.K.O. handled. Joseph Burstyn, a foreign film distributor, suggested a feature, and Kubrick made *Fear and Desire* for $50,000, about four soldiers shot down behind enemy lines. When no Hollywood distributor would take it, Burstyn released it himself, but Kubrick then proposed *Killer's Kiss* to United Artists, who financed it together with money raised from his own family. He paid more attention to the requirements of the B-film than to logic – the title has no connection with the plot – filming in a small studio in New York and, memorably, on location. Self-confidence is evident, since he was co-producer, director, writer, editor and photographer; the plot involves a boxer, the girl he protects from the advances of her dance-hall boss (Frank Silvera) and the latter's attempt at revenge. The writing and direction of **The Killing** (1956) are even more manifest, but the style is no-nonsense and the plot – about a race-track heist, as based on a novel by Lionel White – a strong one. It was daring to present a B-picture with its events not set in chronological order, but that way it does expose the mechanics of the operation. The seedy and self-seeking world of crime had seldom been better portrayed and at a time when movies were getting wider and emptier it was rewarding to have a gaggle of crooks as varied as those in *The Asphalt Jungle* or *The Big Heat*.

The Films of Stanley Kubrick

It was with *The Killing*, FAR LEFT BELOW, with Jay C. Flippen, Sterling Hayden, Elisha Cook Jr, Ted de Corsia, Joe Sawyer and, on the bed, Marie Windsor, that Stanley Kubrick established himself as one of the most exciting young directors in years. He went on to make two powerful antiwar movies, a drama, *Paths of Glory*, FAR LEFT ABOVE, and a satire, *Dr Strangelove*, LEFT, with Peter Sellers (in the wheelchair). He next directed *2001: A Space Odyssey*, BELOW, by far the best science fiction film made up to that point. Indeed, it has not been surpassed, and it is in the light of these four films that his later work is doubly disappointing.

In Hollywood the Director is King

Jim Thompson, who wrote the screenplay with Kubrick, also collaborated on **Paths of Glory** (1957), together with Calder Willingham, who had worked with Kubrick on an abortive project at M-G-M. This film, based on the novel by Humphrey Cobb, was turned down by every Hollywood company until Kirk Douglas agreed to do it, at which point United Artists put up $900,000, of which Douglas's fee was $350,000 (Douglas later claimed that Kubrick then rewrote the script to make it more commercial, but he refused to do any but the script to which he had agreed). To economise the film was made in Munich, not unsuitably since its settings are a French château and the trenches of the First World War; the subject is a court martial and the events leading up to it – a mutiny in the French army, which had been omitted from the published French records. The idealistic motives of the defending officer (Douglas) are incomprehensible to his fellow officers. The film has three endings: the final confrontation between him and the cynical C.O. (Adolphe Menjou); the execution, with the Jew between the two other victims, an analogy which would be insupportable in a lesser film; and the soldiers singing in an 'all men are brothers' gesture. At first viewing the film is so overwhelming that it takes a second one to see its faults – the ostentatious camera-work, swirling images in the style of Ophuls, and some crude devices, such as the mouthing priest and the stupid generals. The fact that these men hold outrageous beliefs does not entirely excuse Kubrick from ridiculing them: yet, paradoxically, they are exactly what the film is about. The generals converse, eat and even waltz in the château, while the men slog it out in the trenches. The generals jockey for promotion, the 'paths of glory', while the men confess that it is not death they are afraid of, but dying. The acting in every instance is worthy of the occasion, one of the finest in Hollywood history. The film was warmly praised by a few critics, but was dismissed by as many more – the same critics who had a few weeks earlier been praising *The Bridge on the River Kwai* as a serious comment on war.

Nevertheless, **Spartacus** (1960) was considered important because of Kubrick's participation. He took it over from another director to show his gratitude to Douglas, whose pet project it was (and one entirely consistent with the ambitions of the star-producers of the time), hoping that the combination of spectacle and liberal views would meet with box-office and critical success. The liberal stance is only tentative: the film purports to examine the causes of revolt and the abuses of power, but as written by Dalton Trumbo (his first credited film after his blacklisting) it states only the obvious. The director's hand is nowhere evident, but the sequences in the gladiatorial school are exciting; and despite the reputed $12 million spent, the process shots are instantly recognisable. The fundamental mistake was to make the villains more interesting than the heroes – not because heroism is necessarily boring, but because in this film it is badly acted. As the patrician Crassus, Laurence Olivier beautifully crests the huge close-ups (they all get huge close-ups), by suggesting an arrogance, ambition and intellect not written into the script; and he is matched by Peter Ustinov as the wary opportunist slave-dealer and by Charles Laughton as the cunning and experienced senator Gracchus.

The original of **Lolita** (1962), a novel by Vladimir Nabokov, was originally issued in Paris, in English, by a company associated with pornography, since the author's usual publisher thought it risked prosecution for obscenity. Its protagonist is a middle-aged professor obsessed with pubescent girls, or nymphets, a word coined in the book itself. 'How did they ever make a film of *Lolita*?' asked M-G-M's publicity, a question answered at yawn-inducing length by the critics, who do not show the same enthusiasm for their task when it is a question of a classic novel or a historical subject. By making the girl (Sue Lyon) a couple of years older, and Humbert Humbert (James Mason) younger is to answer how they made a film of it. Nabokov incorporated many of his jokes into the screenplay, but Kubrick has adopted a style which is the reverse of his vitality and, since the film was made in Britain (for economy, since anticipated bannings in the U.S. were expected to restrict its profits) he fails to retain the book's major asset, its portrait of sub-topian America. The first half of the film is sustained by its situation, Humbert Humbert's marriage in order to be near the child, and the second by the juxtaposition of father-daughter/lover-mistress, a cultured man and a child whose idea of 'fun' is a lunch of French Fries and a malt. As the nemesis, Peter Sellers uses a battery of music-hall accents; and Shelley Winters is too broad as the vulgar but culture-addicted wife. Mason, all bland smiles for the world, his distaste and desperation saved for us, is now the sole reason why the piece should be seen.

Kubrick called **Dr Strangelove: or How I Learned to Stop Worrying and Love the Bomb** (1964) a 'nightmare comedy' but it is only superficially about the end of the world. It may be seen as a thriller – will-they won't-they press the right button in time? – but its purpose is less to warn of the nuclear pile-up than to expose the mentality in charge of our destinies. Like the generals in *Paths of Glory*, these scientists, politicians and high-ranking soldiers are unaware of the enormity of killing, and Kubrick, writing the screenplay with Terry Southern, from a novel by Peter George, has made the shift from drama to satire with gleaming brilliance. The visual interpretation of his thesis is perfect, and so is his cast, including Sellers in a triple role. Best of all is George C. Scott as General Buck Turgidson, a pyramid of cunning and self-satisfaction, followed by Sterling Hayden and Keenan Wynn as officers even more obtuse. The 'maybe' of the future fascinated Kubrick, but his predictions in **2001: A Space Odyssey** (1968), are trite, amusing and not very inspired – the space-station, the buttons to be pushed for phonevision, food, information, and the endless instructions. The film is visually magnificent, as 'designed and directed by' Kubrick, with a special credit; towards the end, 'the psychedelic trip', as *Variety* called it, sucks the viewer into a new dimension of sound, colour and movement, where conceptions of time and place are lost for all of its ten minutes' duration: 'Life has not many things better than this', as Dr Johnson said of travelling fast in a post-chaise. This is probably the first movie to use a simple fade to denote a time-lag of four million years, though in terms of plot, the mumbo-jumbo of the first half is preferable to that of the second. Kubrick wrote the screenplay with Arthur C. Clarke, author of the original novel; one witness, the science fiction writer, Michael Moorcock, has attested to their confusion at arriving at any ending at all. But as an abstract, *2001* is wonderful.

Unfortunately, **A Clockwork Orange** (1972) has a plot, taken from a novel by Anthony Burgess, which up-ends *Things to Come*: the people of the future are sex-obsessed, irrationally violent, and indifferent to squalor and litter. The distinction between cops and crooks has narrowed until they are interchangeable and, therefore, with all order gone, our hero (Malcolm McDowell) is of more value to society when pillaging, raping and killing than as reduced by society's more deliberate brain-washing to a vegetable. When he is sent to prison, you may think of another innocent transgressor, Paul Pennyfeather in 'Decline and Fall', a truer guide to the future than this puny, pretentious film.

Despite the fact that by this time Kubrick failed to get backing for an expensive film on Napoleon, he had achieved a position in the industry unparalleled since Capra. All his recent films had been ecstatically received, with the exception of *2001*, and that had become a great popular success – perhaps the most admired American film for a whole generation. Warners accordingly granted him complete autonomy on **Barry Lyndon** (1975), and even accepted his recommendations as to which cinema houses throughout the world it should be first offered (*Variety* reported that he employed a staff to keep track of such matters). The film opened to a panegyric in *Time* so impressive that its publicity referred to it as 'a 7-page cover story', and while *Time* undoubtedly hoped to attract those young people to whom Kubrick was a culture god, there was more than a sufficiency of hyperbole. A Warner executive was quoted as admiring Kubrick's slow methods, as that ensured a masterpiece at $11 million rather than a mediocre film at $8 million, while the article itself prophesied the 'inevitable' Oscar nominations, box-office takings to rival the record-breaking *Jaws* (q.v.) and spoke of qualities in the film 'that eluded Thackeray'. These apparently consisted of filming 'with as much beauty and grace as possible . . . all you can do is either pose questions or make truthful observations about human behaviour' – or so observed Kubrick himself, confirming his inability to understand Thackeray's malicious satire. Instead of a tale of the fashionable

In Hollywood the Director is King

world of the period, peopled by the naive and gullible, fleeced and conned by the greedy and cunning, most of them snobs and hypocrites, the film is a mild series of adventures. Thackeray's Barry is at best prevaricating, hitting notes of knavery, clod-hopping cruelty, conceit and, above all, self-deceit; Kubrick's Barry is a pale shadow of Errol Flynn. He is robbed by highwaymen instead of being 'taken' by confidence tricksters; he beats the child publicly instead of privately, thus exposing the true character he tries to hide; he escapes the army with a plan involving insanity, but Thackeray's Barry does not steal a uniform from an officer bathing (who is anachronistically whispering endearments to a fellow officer). The essential visual equivalents of the book are Rowlandson and Gillray, but Kubrick has chosen Fragonard, Boucher, Gainsborough and, of all painters, Georges de la Tour.

The film united the leading critics in condemnation, and failure at this expense brings into question the wisdom of allowing any director sole control. In *The New York Times*, John Hofses tried to counter the reviews by claiming that film reviewers were literary or drama critics in disguise, unable to 'appreciate qualities of form, composition, colour, mood, music, editing rhythms' but in most of these respects the film is less advanced than M-G-M's 1938 *Marie Antoinette*. The same article quoted Kubrick as saying 'the most important parts of a film are the mysterious parts – beyond the reach of reason and language', whereas most of us, I think, would suppose these to be those which connect with an audience. This film did not, as was soon made clear to Warners' accountants.

It is sad to see a director of Kubrick's record fail, but as this disaster was followed by **The Shining** (1980) it was hard to be sympathetic. This expensive and grandiose horror film broke records in the initial weeks of its engagement, but then attendances began to plummet, taking Kubrick's reputation with them.

At the time Kubrick made his first feature, audiences were admiring **A Time Out of War** (1954), a 30-minute short about two Northern soldiers and a Southern one who, one sunny afternoon on a river bank, call an unexpected truce. Not a word or a shot is superfluous as written

and directed with elegaic grace by Denis Sanders and photographed by his brother Terry. Unlike Kubrick, the Sanders brothers could not come to terms with the industry, and their later work was again done independently. United Artists, however, released **War Hunt** (1962), another slight study of men in battle, in this case the Korean War. It owes something to *A Walk in the Sun* in trying to be honest about the nature of warfare, but fails when its young hero searches for a meaning: this may be due to the actor – Robert Redford in his film debut – who gazes around with no more than an expression of wonder.

After *Shadows*, John Cassavetes accepted an invitation to work within the industry, but was happy with neither **Too Late Blues** (1961), made for Paramount, nor **A Child is Waiting** (1963), made for Stanley Kramer. The former, a trite tale of the tensions of a jazz man, has conventional leads – Bobby Darin and Stella Stevens – and only looks fresh when compared with such contemporaries as *Tender Is the Night*; but the second film has an exceptional subject, the education of retarded children, for which the director's naturalistic approach is exactly right. Abby Mann's screenplay is hardly more than a demonstration of teaching methods, interestingly focussing on the new teacher (Judy Garland), who has at last found something useful to do with her life, and whose easy emotionalism is withheld when she realises that the head teacher (Burt Lancaster) is right on the matter of strict discipline. The film appealed neither to those interested in the subject nor to whatever audience was left for weepies, a sad postscript to Cassavetes's on-set battles with Lancaster and later with Kramer, who, he claimed, re-edited to make it more sentimental. It must be said that Kramer and Lancaster always cared more for message, image and show business than Cassavetes, who in all his films seems only interested in setting down life as it is. Unfortunately, life for him is a grim business and his subsequent independent or semi-independent films showed the need for a controlling intelligence. Whether dealing with a working-class milieu, as in **A Woman Under the Influence** (1974) or small-time hoods and strippers, as in **The Killing of a Chinese Bookie** (1976), he lacks both real understanding of his people and the old Hollywood narrative flair. He failed even with the problems of an ageing actress, played by his wife, Gena Rowlands, in **Opening Night** (1977). There is some good stuff here, but buried in the customarily excessive verbiage. Too often he attempts a shot or situation simply because other film-makers have not done so before; his aims are admirable and the results usually abysmal.

Of all American directors, none has shown such consistent interest in the working-class – or at least in the matter of earning a living – as Martin Ritt (b. 1920), a former actor, stage director and teacher at the Actors' Studio, who was recommended by Robert Alan Aurthur for **Edge of the City** (1957), the film version of his T.V. play, 'A Man is Ten Feet Tall'. Combining two concepts popular at the time, waterfront thuggery and social misfits, the film is also melodrama – which Ritt's simple approach helps to conceal; he also gets excellent performances from Cassavetes as the misfit and Sidney Poitier as his fellow teamster; this was the first American film mainly concerned with an inter-racial friendship, clearly the reason why the black must die horribly at the hands of a minor racketeer (Jack Warden). The film established Ritt as a director capable of handling the harder-edged, more honest material with which Hollywood was now preparing to deal, such as **No Down Payment** (1957), produced for 20th Century-Fox by Jerry Wald. The film takes the then unusual view that suburbanites are mundane and less interested in community relations than enslaved to materialism; as in Wald's *Peyton Place*, they also tend toward promiscuity, and in one particular case to rape.

Wald's concept of a prestige picture was an adaptation from literature, and since Ritt had become an admired director he was assigned to two adaptations of Faulkner, **The Long, Hot Summer** and **The Sound and the Fury** (1958), the second of which is especially weird. It emerges as a mixture of Tennessee Williams and Emily Brontë; if Margaret Leighton is splendid as a Blanche du Bois type, Yul Brynner is absurd as a Heathcliff figure. **Adventures of a Young Man** (1962) added the prefix *Hemingway's* to the title when it began to flop – as it was bound to do, given Richard

Beymer's interpretation of Nick Adams, reacting as he does to all the Hemingway ethos on display with one expression – that of amazement.

Ritt's reputation was helped by neither *The Black Orchid* nor *Paris Blues*, but the two Faulkner films had introduced him to the husband and wife writing team of Irving Ravetch and Harriet Frank Jr. **Hud** (1963), based on a novel by Larry McMurty, was the best picture yet for any of them, even if the influence of Williams still hangs heavy on the scenes in which Hud (Paul Newman) sweet-talks the housekeeper (Patricia Neal) and tries to rape her. The setting is a small Texas town, where the talk is mainly of cattle and where social life is restricted to movie-shows and the diner. As photographed by James Wong Howe, everything is freshly observed, even the hero-worshipping but eventually disillusioned young observer, a role already played twice in other films by this actor, Brandon de Wilde. At the end, Hud finds himself justly deserted: 'Why pick on Hud?' asks the boy. 'Everyone round here's like him,' and if that is the film's thesis it is demonstrably untrue: no one round anywhere is quite like Paul Newman.

The reviews of *Hud* seem to have restored Ritt's confidence, and **The Spy Who Came in From the Cold** (1965) clearly demonstrates the extent of his skill. John le Carré's grey-toned thriller was well-timed, coming as it did when many people were weary of James Bond and the inferior imitations: as interpreted in the screenplay (by Paul Dehn and Guy Trosper), spies are pawns, in the business solely for money and grateful for some excitement, be it even a double-cross by their own side. Ritt has the London details not only right, rare enough in itself, but amusingly right, and his vivid cast of characters is headed by Richard Burton, in the title-role, supported by Claire Bloom, as the self-assured but lonely librarian who befriends him, and Oskar Werner as the East German contact. There is less action than dialogue, much of it stitched with surprises, but where most thrillers throw their surprises at the audience Ritt holds back, offering only such reaction shots as are vital. The result is a film worth all the Bonds.

Reunited with Newman, the Ravetches

In Hollywood the Director is King

Martin Ritt has never been a box-office director, as he has himself admitted, perhaps because he has always been attracted to the less sensational aspects of American society. His films are studies of environment, employment and the relationships between mundane people, in the honourable tradition of Capra; and though individually his films are not as good we may, eventually, find his work as valuable. Ritt's films lack heart rather than conviction, but that quality is present in *Conrack*, at least in Jon Voight's customary superb performance, in this case as a teacher dedicated to educating young black children.

and Wong Howe, Ritt made **Hombre** (1967), a not unworthy successor to *Stagecoach*, whose plot it resembles. He made his most serious films to that time with **The Molly Maguires** (1970) and **The Great White Hope** (1970), but both were inadequately scripted. The 'Molly Maguires' were a secret sect operating in the hard coal region of Pennsylvania in the 1870s and dedicated to improving the heinous conditions of the workers. The conditions are glossed over and Walter Bernstein's screenplay, after refusing to either clarify or take a stand against the capitalist bosses, becomes the usual story of an undercover man (Richard Harris). 'The Great White Hope' refers to the need for another prizefighter to best the first black to win the World Heavyweight title, Jack Johnson (here called Jefferson), considered an upstart – and the title is the only subtle aspect of the screenplay. Howard Sackler, who wrote it from his own Broadway play, was intent on tragedy in the Aristotelian sense and, at the height of Johnson's career, a black Tiresias appears in the crowd to harangue him for selling out to whitey's world. Sackler's viewpoint is so consistently of the Sixties that he neglects to tell us if Johnson simply ignored racial bigotry or why his white

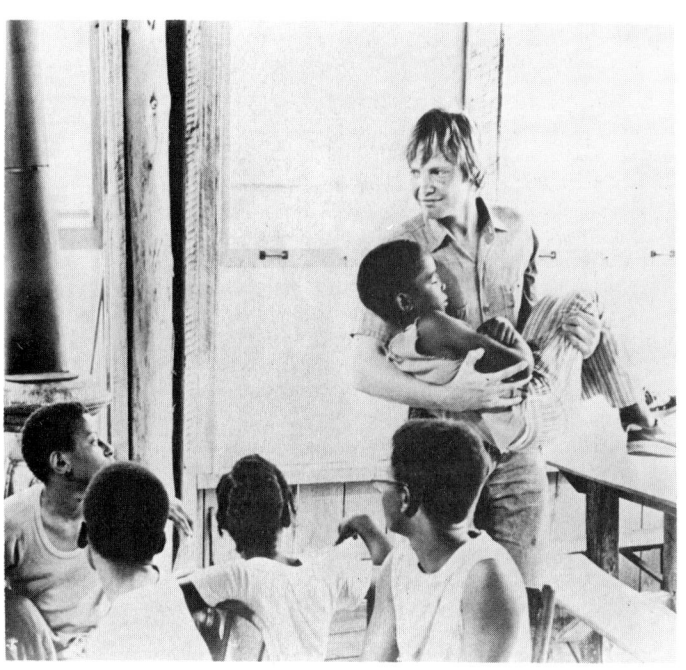

woman (Jane Alexander) defied society to be with him. Whether or not Johnson was a remarkable man he was in a remarkable situation, but it is left to the actor, James Earl Jones, to convey that, playing the joker or the clown.

Pete 'n' Tillie (1972) is one of Ritt's rare excursions into comedy, as written by Julius J. Epstein, from a novella by Peter de Vries, with more than a backward glance at *Penny Serenade*. Walter Matthau and Carol Burnett are much plainer, and hence more realistic, than Cary Grant and Irene Dunne. Their courtship is in a recognisable San Francisco, he punning, skittish and deliberate and she resigned: 'When you've reached my age, and your friends are beginning to worry you, blind dates are a way of life.' Ritt's detached approach is perfect, but as the material turns tragic he falters: clearly hoping for more honesty than was possible in the early Forties, the death of the child on this occasion leads not only to the break-up of the marriage but a nervous breakdown. But Hollywood had not in the meanwhile come to terms with bereavement (since audiences still did not wish to be confronted with it), and as the film strains to make any point within reach it is a pity that it left the comedy behind in reel three.

Sounder (1972) and **Conrack** (1974) are, on the other hand, splendidly brought off. *Sounder* is a story of growing-up in a black sharecropper family in the Thirties, but the script again falters, for it is no surprise that blacks have the same aspirations as the rest of us. *Conrack* concerns a young schoolteacher (Jon Voight) in an all-black community – of today, or at least a few years back – on an island just off the South Carolina coast. He is a liberal and his teachings are unorthodox, but the screenplay by the Ravetches, from Pat Conroy's autobiographical book, refuses to acknowledge that these situations have been done before, while Ritt's approach is fresher than in *Sounder*. He understates in his portrait of the community and in the teacher's battle to hold his job after meeting the disapproval of the school inspector (Hume Cronyn). And there is one sequence, as Voight's housekeeper comes to say goodbye, that is reminiscent of the first section of Satyajit Ray's *Three Daughters*.

Bernstein's screenplay for **The Front** (1976) is much better than his work on *The*

Molly Maguires, being quietly matter-of-fact on a matter which might justifiably have been handled with some hysteria – the blacklisting which operated in show business in the Fifties. Both he and Ritt had been on the list, together with other principals of the film, including Zero Mostel and Herschel Bernardi, the former playing a comic who finds that he is no longer in demand and the latter as a television executive too ineffectual to do anything about proscription. The network is shown to be avuncular, concerned but not concerned; the most telling remark in the script is spoken by the representative of the 'Freedom Information Agency', 'I don't hire, Mr Brown, I only report on Americanism.' Woody Allen plays the title-role, a cashier who passes off the work of blacklisted writers as his own.

Norma Rae (1979) is about unionisation in a backward factory in the South, and since the subject is a risky box-office prospect one may forgive Ritt and the Ravetches for indulging in a certain amount of convention and cleverness – especially in the relationship between Norma Rae (Sally Field) and the New York agitator (Ron Leibman) sent by his Union to do the organising. The relationship between the little hick girl and the city slicker – his being a Jew and cultured fascinate her – is freshly and amusingly observed, as well as being beautifully played (Miss Field won a Best Actress Oscar for her performance). The film otherwise views factory-workers without a hint of patronage and clearly expresses Ritt's own political views better than *The Molly Maguires*; its many virtues outweigh its faults.

Along with Ritt, Sidney Lumet (b. 1924) was one of the first directors to move from television into films, with **Twelve Angry Men** (1957). Henry Fonda had seen Reginald Rose's T.V. study of a dozen good men and true on jury duty, and bought it as a vehicle for himself, with Lumet redirecting. Fonda, Lee J. Cobb, E. G. Marshall, Martin Balsam, Jack Warden and George Voskovec are the leading actors in this gripping, amusing and finally too-pat drama: that their playing delights is due to the then rare practice of supposed naturalness – of overlapping dialogue, an occasional cough, of speaking off camera. Lumet's lively approach gave a lift to **Stage Struck** (1958), and as written by

Ruth and Augustus Goetz this remake of *Morning Glory* was less a tale of an aspiring actress than a witty portrait of Broadway mores and morals. Fonda is a producer and Joan Greenwood, hilariously, a temperamental star; as an ambitious young actress, Susan Strasberg offers a Juliet which in no way justifies the admiration it receives from the other characters.

That Kind of Woman (1959) was also based on old material, having reassigned the situation of *The Shopworn Angel* to World War II, with George Sanders as the wealthy businessman who almost loses his mistress, Sophia Loren, to a nice G.I., Tab Hunter. It was already clear that Lumet believed himself capable of switching from genre to genre and revitalising hoary situations, but in this case one suspected an element of mockery. He moved on to Tennessee Williams, with **That Fugitive Kind** (1960), based on the play 'Orpheus Descending'. Marlon Brando plays one of the drifters who also feature prominently in Williams's memoirs. He is one of four dreamers – together with the storekeeper's wife (Anna Magnani), the sheriff's wife (Maureen Stapleton) and the local rich girl (Joanne Woodward), dipsomaniac and nympho: and they are all threats to local red-necks (a situation to be given stronger expression, later, in *Easy Rider*). It takes a while for the piece to gather the emotional force of which Williams is capable, but Lumet is among the most successful cinema interpreters of this writer. Since he failed later, in *Blood Kin – né* 'The Seven Descents of Myrtle' – credit should perhaps be shared with Boris Kaufman, whose harsh, grainy photography had also helped to reduce the hot airs of *On the Waterfront* and *Baby Doll* to something approaching the realistic.

Lumet's reputation as an interpreter of contemporary drama increased with a television production of 'The Iceman Cometh' for Ely Landau, who subsequently produced **Long Day's Journey Into Night** (1962), also by Eugene O'Neill. The playwright's widow sold the rights only on condition that it was filmed in its entirety, which meant, among other things, no involvement by a major studio and a low budget – which was $400,000, with the four leading players getting $25,000 each, plus a percentage of the profits, if any. Consistently the best of

In Hollywood the Director is King

them is Jason Robards Jr, repeating his Broadway performance, self-loathing mixed with boozy good nature; as his younger brother, Dean Stockwell understandably looks as though he expects the others to eat him alive. Father Tyrone is completely self-assured, and no one is better than Ralph Richardson at behaving as though he is no longer of this world; as the drug-addicted mother, Katharine Hepburn is also theatrical, but when the role becomes demanding she grows with it. Kaufman did the photography, and Lumet, realising that the film could hardly be a true cinematic experience, allows this tortured family to move and breathe and talk amidst their waves of emotion.

However, as with the Williams piece, he transformed Arthur Miller's **A View From the Bridge** (1962), made in fact just before *Long Day's Journey*. It was financed in France, but photographed on New York locations by Michel Kelber. In the interiors Lumet manages the claustrophobia essential to this modern tragedy, and he brings homogeneity to his cast – Raf Vallone, Miss Stapleton and Carol Lawrence as the Italo-American family, and Jean Sorel and Raymond Pellegrin as the immigrants.

Turning to a contemporary problem for the first time, Lumet directed **Fail Safe** (1964), which starts with the premise of two pilots who, due to a mechanical error, are journeying towards Moscow to drop their nuclear weapons. This potentially frightening tale, told by Lumet in plain, urgent images, is notably acted by Walter Matthau as a German-Jewish professor of strong anti-communist views; but Walter Bernstein's screenplay adds nothing to the ideas expressed in the original novel (by Eugene Burdick and Harvey Wheeler), so that the result is a long way behind *Dr Strangelove*. Following Kubrick again, Lumet attempted his own analysis of the military mentality, choosing a British military prison in North Africa during the Second World War. In its more modest way **The Hill** (1965) is as good as *Paths of Glory*, and certainly there is no film by a British director as honest about the men who choose to spend their life in uniform. The source is a play by Ray Rigby and R. S. Allen, with a screenplay by the former; the plot is not too far removed from old prison movies – as one obstinate man, a

born kicker against the pricks, decides to fight the system. That the film works so well is due in large measure to the performance of Sean Connery in this role; equally good are Michael Redgrave as the doctor, one of life's more memorable failures, and Harry Andrews, Ian Hendry and Ian Bannen as the disciplinarians, virtually drunk – when not really drunk, which is every evening – on the smell of starch in their uniforms. **The Pawnbroker** (1965) also sets out to consider the seeds of fascism, by examining a New York Jew (Rod Steiger) permanently afflicted by his memories of the concentration camp and currently trapped, though he himself is an innocent, in the criminalities of Spanish Harlem. The screenplay, by David Friedkin and Morton Fine, from a novel by Edward Lewis Wallant, is so shadowy that Lumet moves through it with unwonted speed, untypically showy. The best scenes are those between the pawnbroker and the social worker (Geraldine Fitzgerald), and the worst those with the parade of junkies, racketeers, etc. These include the Black whore who bares her breasts – the first time this had been seen in an American non-ethnic film, and permitted in view of the film's respectability, even in, for instance, Italy (after months of discussion with the Censor). This was the first American film with a Jew as a leading character in over thirty years: the fact that it was also the first American film to refer to the suffering of the Jews in the War caused it to be greatly over-rated there.

British critics much preferred **The Group** (1966), based on Mary McCarthy's novel about a clique at Vassar and their later inability to cope with sex, careers and failing marriages. Among them is a lesbian (Candice Bergen) – and that was another aspect of life that Hollywood had avoided for over thirty years, though the screenplay thoughtfully omits the book's more 'daring' passages, such as the discussions of pessaries. The film was written by Sidney Buchman, brought out of retirement by the producer, Charles K. Feldman. Lumet had liked the script while disliking the novel, and his deft, one-take approach – typical of the T.V.-trained directors – punctured the pomposity and pretension that inevitably remained. His unfailing sense of timing was eminently suited to the episodic nature of the material, but its inherent flaws meant that the finished film could never have been more than superior soap opera.

The title nevertheless could be applied to almost all of Lumet's films. Although he prides himself on his eclecticism, enjoying the challenge of moving from an adaptation of a novel or a play to a semi-documentary study, virtually all his films have been about groups of people, either friends or co-workers, people confined to a particular milieu or with common aims. The New York literary Jewish society of **Bye Bye Braverman** (1968) is viewed much more incisively and satirically than Ms McCarthy's Vassar graduates. Herbert Sargent adapted the novel by Wallace Markfield, a memoir of growing up Jewish in New York (which Lumet had also done: his father was the distinguished Yiddish actor, Baruch Lumet). This is no teenage tale, but one about a funeral which draws a number of friends back to their shared past. The chief of these is played by George Segal, while Alan King's barbed cameo of a rabbi is a rare unflattering movie portrait of a religious leader.

The characters in **The Deadly Affair** (1967) are mainly Londoners engaged in espionage, and Lumet views both them and their setting as freshly as Ritt did in *The Spy Who Came in From the Cold*. Retained from those who worked on that film was the screenwriter, Paul Dehn, whose additions – a nymphomaniac wife and a beating-up sequence – were particularly disliked by the author of both books, John Le Carré. Le Carré did like the performance of Simone Signoret, as a suburban housewife who had survived the Nazi concentration camps, and there are also admirable portraits by James Mason as the secret agent Smiley (here called Dobbs) and Harry Andrews, Max Adrian and Maximilian Schell as civil servants who are communist sympathisers. While making the film, Lumet, Signoret and Mason decided to acquire backing for a version of Tchekov's **The Seagull** (1968), retaining also the services of Mr Andrews and David Warner, who plays Konstantin. Vanessa Redgrave unwisely portrays Nina as a Botticelli maiden, and Signoret's Arkadina is prim and selfish rather than superficial. Only James Mason, as Trigorin, valiantly attempts to bridge the gap between the various acting styles, and he is matched by Den-

holm Elliott and Eileen Herlie, but their roles are small. Only these three hint that the piece may be a comedy; perhaps the cold air of the Swedish locations led Lumet to his misinterpretation. Warner Bros.-Seven Arts financed, and regretted it.

It was the first of several failures for Lumet, which also include **The Appointment** (1969) and **Child's Play** (1972): both are inferior examples of currently fashionable models and miscalculations on the part of this usually intelligent director. *The Appointment*, which incited derisive laughter at the Cannes Film Festival, examines the *malaise* of some wealthy Italians, particularly Omar Sharif, who is dull as a man bewitched, bothered and bewildered by the enigmatic behaviour of Anouk Aimée, playing her customary role once too often. *Child's Play*, based on a Broadway play, is a rehash of Hugh Walpole's 'Mr Perrin and Mr Traill' with an injection of diabolism as borrowed from a best-selling novel, 'The Exorcist'; the schoolmaster protagonists are Mason and Robert Preston.

Lumet's standing within the industry was hardly affected by such films. His cast and crews adored him because he was and is the complete professional. He and his team arrive on the set knowing exactly what they are going to do, which is rare, and he invariably brings his films in under budget and under schedule. Since he enjoys working fast he is attracted to the thriller form, and he also thought Dehn's script for **Murder on the Orient Express** (1974) sufficiently good, provided that it was interpreted by stars of stature. Sean Connery, with whom he had worked before, also liked it, and he was subsequently joined by such names as Ingrid Bergman, Lauren Bacall, Richard Widmark, Miss Redgrave and John Gielgud. This old, tired Agatha Christie story deserved none of them, nor was Lumet's penchant for location shooting served, since almost all of it was set within the confines of a railway carriage: but it made a profit for its British producers, E.M.I., despite its being, at £1½ million, the most expensive film made in England for many years.

Network (1976) provided Lumet with a further success, and a more controversial one. Twenty years after they both had left television, he and Paddy Chayevsky joined forces to portray it as something

In Hollywood the Director is King

akin to the Black Death. Unfortunately, Chayevsky's gorge had so risen that he had forgotten that to explain evil it is necessary to understand it. In *The Hospital* (q.v.) he suggests that the staff and most of the patients are insane, but in *Network* his indictment extends from T.V. executives to the whole nation – that is, to all those who sit at home watching the small screen. At the end, an old T.V. hand (William Holden) rediscovers his humanity after being screwed both ways by his mistress (Faye Dunaway), who has taken his job, 'Like you, everything television touches is destroyed . . .' That is one of the more precise remarks in this combination of fantasy and hyperbole, and I should state that many within the television industry have confirmed the veracity of this film. The Academicians of Motion Picture Arts and Sciences, who should know, voted it a Best Screenplay Oscar – or were they donning their motion picture hats for a movie describing their friend/rival as a stream of mindless pap and vulgarity incarnate?

Lumet's questioning of the mentality of those set in authority over us had earlier been the subject of *The Hill* and one of his failures, **The Offence** (1972). The three films considered together confirm his strengths and weaknesses as commensurate to his material, and that of *The Offence* is poor, as based by John Hopkins on his play about a mentally-sick policeman (Connery). Hopkins had written several episodes of a much admired British T.V. series, 'Z Cars', showing the more admirable methods of police procedure, but in trying to show the other side of the coin he managed only a superficial and humourless piece about a cop who beats up a child molester (Ian Bannen) because he himself secretly yearns to be one. The scenes in which this revelation is made are typical of Lumet's films, being crude and overemphatic. But they are only shots, instances which are apparently the price we have to pay for Lumet's skill and craftsmanship in most of his work. The opening sequences of *The Offence*, grafted on to Hopkins's original play, demonstrate Lumet's continuing ability to look with fresh vision at virtually everything in sight. In this case we see the British countryside and the British police under several new guises; and he was to do something similar on his home territory.

Indeed, Lumet's three films on New York's Finest are among the best American films of the last twenty years – an achievement which gives us reason to digress for a moment, to examine his own thoughts on his career: 'I've never been a fashionable director. The whole *auteur* nonsense is repugnant to me. I won't take the billing "a Sidney Lumet film" or "Sidney Lumet's production" . . . When I go out shooting, I'm dependent on the weather, the sun, the 120 people around me knowing their work. And I don't want to settle into a particular style, because to me the style is determined by the material itself. I think this has left me in a vacuum from the critical point of view. It's nothing that disturbs me a great deal.' He is proud of his ability to give the impression of reality, and that is essential to these three films, which would lose force if we did not believe in them completely: for **Serpico** (1973) and **Prince of the City** (1981) deal with police corruption, and **Dog Day Afternoon** (1975) is about the public's relationship with the police. All three movies are based on actual events, and as far as the two films on corruption are concerned, we may wonder to what extent the New York Police Department cooperated on location facilities. In both cases the corruption seems not much less than a hundred per cent, so that the N.Y.P.D.

Treat Williams and Lindsay Crouse, playing his wife, in Sidney Lumet's *Prince of the City*, one of Lumet's three excellent films on New York's police force. Two of them, this one and *Serpico*, are about the corruption rife among New York's Finest, both based on factual books. The corruption in *Prince of the City* is a particularly complex matter, hardly simplified in the script, but that is only one reason why it is a particularly gripping film.

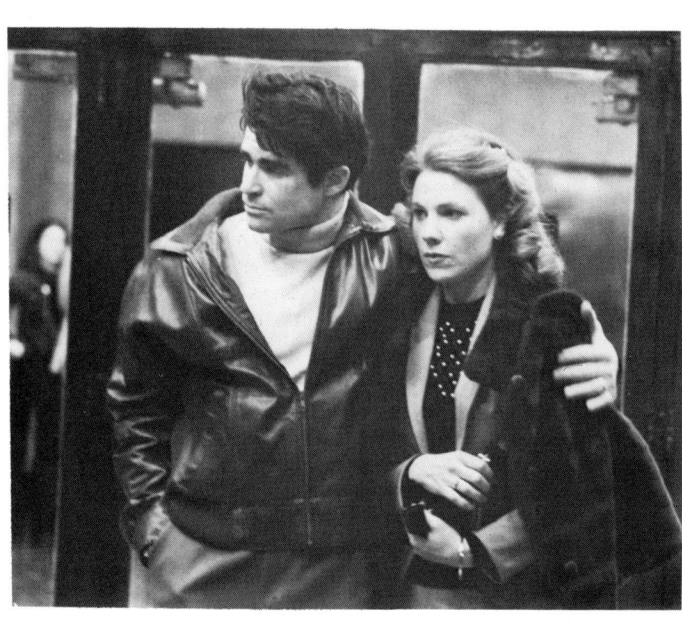

must have passed both scripts with a great degree of cynicism. Lumet himself has said of *Prince of the City* that as long as he lives he will never understand the motives of anyone involved, and quotes its real life protagonist, Robert Leuci, as saying that five per cent of the police will always be dishonest, as many again will be incorruptible and the other ninety per cent will follow whichever is the stronger.

Serpico is based on a book by Peter Maas and produced by Dino de Laurentiis, who had made his American production debut with *The Valachi Papers*, adapted from Maas's book about the Mafia. Frank Serpico (Al Pacino) is an honest cop, and is said to be further a-typical, with his macho moustache, his live-in women and his bijou apartment in the Village. He likes opera, ballet, dogs and wine, and laughs when falsely accused of going down on a colleague in the john. His colleagues have a hard-hat mentality, decent enough in their sense of humour, but firmly believing that the dope-pushers and other law-breakers can afford to pay and 'it's fair shares for all.' Lumet and Jay Presson Allen wrote *Prince of the City* from a novel by Robert Daley based on the experiences of Leuci, a dedicated cop who gave evidence to a Senate commission on the corruption rampant in the N.Y.P.D. He 'ratted' while demanding reassurances that his buddies would not be arrested, but since they and he were as guilty as anyone else he finds himself sucked into a whirlpool as dangerous as it is degrading. The moral issues involved are debated for almost three hours and every minute of them is riveting. Treat Williams achieves a blend of modesty and vitality as the cop based on Leuci – who, like Serpico, found that he was no longer wanted in the police.

Dog Day Afternoon was written by Frank Pierson from accounts of a raid on a Brooklyn bank one afternoon in 1972 by three nut-cases, one of whom chickened out within minutes. The other two holed themselves up with their hostages, and it transpired that they wanted money for a sex-change operation for the boyfriend of their leader, Sonny (Pacino) – an operation that was eventually paid for by Warners, in order to get cooperation for the film to be made. Despite the brilliant editing of Dede Allen, the film does sag when it wanders from its bizarre central situation and delves

back into Sonny's past. Whereas the excitement of the other two films springs from the threat to their heroes, here it is in the sly and sprightly observation of the behaviour of the hostages, the unprepossessing 'criminals', the waiting crowds and the spit-and-polish cops, only too human in their errors. The approach, as in *Network*, is satirical, but it is anecdotal instead of being hysterical.

John Frankenheimer (b. 1930) had at one time been Lumet's assistant in T.V., and had entered films at the same time. He had originally directed **The Young Stranger** (1957) on television, and we should be thankful for this transposition for it was, and remains, Hollywood's best study of adolescence. The boy (James MacArthur) is from a very comfortable home, and he is in no sense a delinquent: but when a minor incident brings him into contact with the police, he and his parents are in total conflict. He, looking for help, retreats into sarcasm; the father (James Daly), unthinking and unfeeling, does not hesitate to make matters worse; and the mother (Kim Hunter) stands weakly by, hoping the rot within her home will just go away. The happy ending robs the piece of its logic, though not of its position as one of the key films of the era; sadly, however, Frankenheimer's quiet creation of tension suggested a promise that has seldom been fulfilled. **The Young Savages** (1961) was the first deception, a meretricious

Among the best of the several interesting films of the Fifties which originated in television drama is *The Young Stranger*, with Eddie Ryder, James MacArthur, centre, and Jeff Silver, in which an incident in a movie theatre leads eventually to a crisis in a middle-class home. John Frankenheimer came from television to redirect the piece for the big screen, and he stayed; but only for a short while was the promise of this film borne out.

view of juvenile criminals, adapted from a novel by Evan Hunter. The understanding D.A. was played by Burt Lancaster, whose company called in Frankenheimer on two occasions, to replace Charles Crichton on **Birdman of Alcatraz** (1962) and Arthur Penn (q.v.) on **The Train** (1964). The latter is a banal blend of *La Bataille du Rail* and Ealing comedy, about the French Resistance attempting to save a cargo of paintings, 'our national heritage', from the Germans, with Lancaster at his most self-righteous as a French superman. However, in *Birdman* this variable actor is, like the film itself, beyond good and evil. 'Twelve years I've had to look at that frozen mug of yours' says the warder (Neville Brand), and the audience is offered little other option, as Lancaster, spending the rest of his natural life in jail, becomes the world's leading authority on caged bird diseases. In life, the man was Robert Stroud: his story was written down by Thomas E. Gaddis, and Guy Trosper was the screenwriter who collaborated with Frankenheimer to make a consciously humanist, social film. It was not a huge success in cinemas, but has always been popular on television, when audiences sympathise as Stroud helps to quell riots, and perhaps become indignant as a postscript says that he was still in jail after fifty-three years and still being refused parole.

The Manchurian Candidate (1962) was almost indecently well-received, being taken for a mordant satire on American politics: it is actually a melodrama involving political conniving, the Korean War and brainwashing (though this is irrelevant to the plot). As satire, the only point the film has to make is that unscrupulous politicians have used communist-baiting as a path to power; but the screenwriter, George Axelrod, working from Richard Condon's novel, has much fun with the senator (James Gregory), a man of goonish simplicity and with a taste for booze, and his wife (Angela Lansbury), a barracuda-like all-American mom. That she turns out to be a dedicated communist makes nonsense of all that has gone before, though as a thriller the film is fair. United Artists did not care for the film, and Paramount did not like **Seven Days in May** (1964), but Frankenheimer had independent financing and the backing of President Kennedy, who lent the White House

for filming. The tale, as derived by Rod Serling from a novel by Fletcher Nebel and Charles W. Bailey II, is about a plan to oust a U.S. president (Fredric March) because he plans to sign an anti-nuclear pact with the U.S.S.R.; the leader of the coup is a fanatic general (Lancaster), whose second-in-command (Kirk Douglas) throws in his lot with the beleaguered president. Frankenheimer restricts himself to the mechanics of plotting; and the film is more penetrating than its contemporary, *Fail Safe*.

It was not long afterwards that he began to lose his reputation. John Houseman's production of **All Fall Down** (1962) had shown Frankenheimer capable of sheer carelessness, but this family drama, a poor collage as scripted by William Inge from James Leo Herlihy's decent novel, was unlikely to inspire anyone. In Europe, after a number of failures, Frankenheimer made **The Fixer** (1968), a tale of anti-Semitism in old Russia, portentously scripted by Dalton Trumbo from Bernard Malamud's novel, and apart from Dirk Bogarde and Ian Holm as lawyers, poorly acted by a mainly British cast. Frankenheimer later called it 'a lousy movie, very boring', a description surely applying also to the failures which followed it, including one made in English in France,★ with French backing, which had no public showings in any English-speaking country till sold to television ten years later. Called back to Hollywood for **The French Connection II** (1975), Frankenheimer announced that he wanted to make good commercial movies in the future, but the movies he made, though commercial, were not widely liked. This one is the best. It could not be said that William Friedkin's original *French Connection* (q.v.) was worth a sequel, but this one had the excellent idea of setting down its pugnacious cop hero, 'Popeye' Doyle (Gene Hackman), in Marseille. Marseille is not the kindest city to a foreigner with no French, and both factors are extensively used; the film moves swiftly, only let down by its middle sequences, in which Doyle is forcibly turned junkie by the villain (Fernando Rey), and unconvincingly weaned 'cold turkey' by his French opposite number (Bernard Fresson).

Also coming from television was

★ *The Impossible Object.*

Arthur Penn (b. 1922), like Lumet and Frankenheimer also with theatre experience – and in that medium he was far more successful than they, continuing to direct on Broadway until 1964. His first film, **The Left-Handed Gun** (1958) was based on a T.V. play, by Gore Vidal, whose screenplay was rewritten by Leslie Stevens, at Penn's request (also dismayed by Penn's demands was the veteran photographer J. Peverell Marley, since Penn, accustomed to four cameras on a television set, insisted on two for this film). Anticipating Penn's most celebrated film, *Bonnie and Clyde* (q.v.), this one is an essay on the fusion of truth and myth, as a sycophantic journalist (Hurd Hatfield) is disappointed by the real Billy the Kid (Paul Newman), lout and psychopath. Symbolism abounds and, since there were rules governing Westerns – permitted only to be broken by the likes of *Shane* – the film was dismissed as pretentious. It was, however, liked by French critics, whose perceptions, for once, were not misplaced.

Penn was only able to return to films with **The Miracle Worker** (1962) because he had directed William Gibson's original play with success first on television and then on Broadway. There have been few American films with a theme so vital – the rescue of a human being from a state of savagery: this is the infant Helen Keller, deaf and blind, and her teacher is Annie Sullivan, from an orphanage, and with a slight affliction of her own. Gibson's writing is remarkably unsentimental, while offering some dramatic rigging in the form of opposition to Miss Sullivan's teaching methods, while Penn's loving direction errs only in allowing almost all the cast to overact – except his Annie, Anne Bancroft, and his Helen, Patty Duke, repeating their Broadway performances.

Penn has not been a prolific director, and his career might have finished with **Mickey One** (1965) had **The Chase** (1966) not already been in production. The former is a fanciful Kafkaesque fable with Warren Beatty which, unlike most of its breed, has apparently never drummed up a single supporter. As much may be said of *The Chase*, though it is at least the sort of film the industry understands. It was intended to be the definitive statement on Southern corruption, as produced by Sam Spiegel and written by Lillian Hellman – though

she expeditiously repudiated it. The attitudes towards the lynching of blacks are impeccable, but are entrenched in a story which seems of the same vintage as *They Won't Forget*: Penn manages a party sequence well, and also the atmosphere of sultry, boozy nights, but its many stars are merely stars, headed by Marlon Brando as the sheriff whose sufferings would, in another age, have brought him sainthood.

However, **Bonnie and Clyde** (1967) is one of the masterworks of the American cinema. A threnody of blood and violence, there had never been a film like it before – wholly itself, and still ahead of all other movies about America's criminals. The writers, David Newman and Robert Benton, then on the staff of *Esquire*, were movie-buffs, and patterned their screenplay on the early films of Truffaut and

The cinema's fascination with crime was never more evident than in *Bonnie and Clyde*, and only partly because it was the first of the many posthumous attempts to re-create the milieu of the gangsters of the past with anything like fidelity. Faye Dunaway played Bonnie Parker and Warren Beatty Clyde Barrow; and the film is the best of the infrequent ones directed by Arthur Penn.

In Hollywood the Director is King

Godard (both of whom, at one time, were asked to direct it), with a glance towards Hitchcock. Like Belmondo in *A Bout de Souffle*, a runt to everyone but a legend to himself, Bonnie Parker and Clyde Barrow believed in their own myth. Explaining their re-creation of these two gangsters, the writers suggest they were 'hung up' like many people today, which may explain why the film has no more depth than appears on the screen. It is a simple story brilliantly told. It does not tell the truth, but it works marvellously at that level where truth and legend meet – much better than in Penn's similar studies. Its only fault is Faye Dunaway, too film-starry in appearance and manner. And perhaps Clyde's impotence is unconvincing (used in preference, the writers said, to what they thought was the truth, that Barrow needed another man in the room). Warren Beatty – the film's producer, who invited Penn to direct – is sunny-insolent as Clyde, and is memorably supported by Gene Hackman as his brother, Estelle Parsons as the latter's giggly wife and Michael J. Pollard as the puppy-like gang member. There has never been a more awesome evocation of the U.S. during the Depression, of sleepy, dead little towns with ice-cream parlours, general stores that have not long had electric lights, and one, very surprised, bank.

Continuing his examination of the American past, Penn made **Alice's Restaurant** (1969), an inert fantasy, written by himself, built, paradoxically, around the life of a folk singer, Arlo Guthrie, son of Woody; and **Little Big Man** (1970), the story of a white man brought up as a Cheyenne, who was either 'the most neglected hero of his country or a liar of insane proportions' – a role played by Dustin Hoffman when it needs Brando or Jack Nicholson. As it happened, Penn paired these two actors in **The Missouri Breaks** (1976), and the sole virtue of Thomas McGuane's script would seem to be the provision of parts for their virtuosity. The cattle-rustler played by Nicholson is, at best, confused; the lawman played by Brando is, it would seem, a confusion of the actor's. Only the mood and tension remind us that Penn directed *Bonnie and Clyde*; the accretions are clearly the work of the man who made *Mickey One* and *Alice's Restaurant*. Penn later observed that

he would never again make a film for commercial reasons.

His last two films to date were also failures, unjustly so in the case of **Night Moves** (1975). Like *Bonnie and Clyde*, it uses people, time and place beautifully, finding nuances throughout the detailed script by the English novelist Alan Sharp. Harry Moseby (Gene Hackman) is a private eye hired to find a missing girl; he does, but she is killed and he is himself the subject of an attempted murder. 'You ask all the wrong questions' says someone to him, for he is, like America, a bit of a mess; he is also like Galahad, embarking on his own voyage of discovery as he seeks to solve the mystery. The theme and the use of symbols are reminiscent of Antonioni; the start of **Four Friends** (1981) is reminiscent of *Breaking Away* (q.v.), also written by Steve Tesich. Both films begin with amiable group portraits of adolescence, but where that one was content to stay that way this one sets out to chart the American experience of the Sixties, when conformity gave way to hippiedom, when people dropped out and/or took to drugs – as represented by the hero (Craig Wasson), who had arrived from Yugoslavia as a boy. The original script dealt with the cataclysmic assassinations of the Kennedys and Martin Luther King, but at Penn's request they have been replaced (though mentioned) by the boy's father-in-law going ape with a gun on his wedding day. It had already been clear that Penn was bent on hyperbole, so it is not the scene itself which is ludicrous; but as the survivors talk afterwards they show only movie emotions, not real ones, and the film never recovers.

Another director who came from T.V. is Robert Mulligan (b. 1925), whose score of films include only a few of note. The first, **Fear Strikes Out** (1957), is one of the quietly good T.V.-orientated dramas, based on the mental illness of the baseball-player Jim Piersall of the Boston Red Sox. He is played with neurotic intensity by Anthony Perkins, without his later mannerisms, and as his father – the villain of the piece – Karl Malden acts with unusual sympathy. The illness is schizophrenia, until then treated by Hollywood as an excuse for lovely ladies to go wandering on moonlit beaches. Mulligan – whose father was a New York cop – is most at ease with a proletarian background, and

Love with the Proper Stranger (1963) is even more freshly observed. This likeable film follows the ups and downs of a romance between a jazz musician (Steve McQueen) and a Macy's store clerk (Natalie Wood) who is pregnant by him. The matter-of-fact attitude to this situation was entirely new in an American film but, having progressed that far, it could not be expected that she would subject herself to the planned abortion, especially since it is a shabby back street business. **Up the Down Staircase** (1967) was written by Tad Mosel from a best-selling book by Bel Kaufman, based on her experiences as a teacher in New York; Mulligan manages a smell of chalk-dust and the undercurrent of violence. The piece juggles with a number of issues – parental apathy, bureaucratic stranglehold, the danger of walking a slum block if you are female and pretty, the fact that no black child can feel safe in a mixed school – without pushing any one of them forward, perhaps because none has an immediate solution. Sandy Dennis is not one of the dewy-eyed teachers of Hollywood's past, but obstinate, weary and vulnerable – and likely to become as bored and cynical as her colleagues.

Mulligan's most acclaimed film has been **To Kill a Mockingbird** (1962), one of the films which re-established Universal's lost esteem after a decade of programme pictures. His treatment perfectly reproduces the virtues and vices of Harper Lee's Pulitzer-prizewinning novel – though the former are evident to me only in its portrait of the special world of children. They while away the long hot summer days in a small town in the South, as a serious drama plays around them, involving a rape, an attempted lynching and a trial. But they are precious and goody-goody, like the lawyer father (Gregory Peck) of one of them and the material itself, which is equipped with unimpeachable stances on racialism – but they are only superficial and therefore lacking in tension.

The setting of **Inside Daisy Clover** (1965) is a particularly unreal Hollywood. Gavin Lambert's novel was a collection of Hollywood myths and truths, centring on an adolescent star not wholly unlike Judy Garland. Her Prince Charming flunks out on the wedding night because, she learns later, he prefers his own sex; her family feed on her fame and fortune, but she

adjusts to fame after a nervous breakdown. The book's many and witty references to the songs, people and events of the Thirties and Forties have been omitted from the screenplay written by Lambert himself; what was a tragicomedy has become an attempt at tragedy and a particularly pretentious one. The film might just as well have been set in Timbuktu; Natalie Wood and Robert Redford are only adequate in the leads. Mulligan's other films have been equally disappointing, but **Summer of '42** (1971) was, with some justification, very popular. It begins with pictures of sunset, breaking waves, seaside villas and wild flowers – and having thus announced its intentions it proceeds to fulfil them. The Andrews Sisters are heard on the radio, *Now, Voyager* is at the local cinema and at the over-stuffed village shop the boys buy condoms (another hitherto unmentionable matter in an American film). The central situation, as adapted from the novel by Herman Raucher, is a reworking of that in *Le Blé en Herbe*: an adolescent (Gary Grimes) is taught the facts of

Robert Mulligan's *Love with the Proper Stranger* has, like many films of its time, a theme song, but in this case heard only briefly on the radio before being turned off by Natalie Wood. 'That's what love is?' she asks, 'bells and banjoes?' That is typical of the movie, which has the old malarkey going on under the new realism. The man with whom Miss Wood falls in Love is Steve McQueen.

life by an older woman (Jennifer O'Neill). Michel Legrand's theme tune sounds not at all like the music of '42, but is otherwise appropriate.

Alan J. Pakula (b. 1928) was Mulligan's producer from their days in television till they split in 1968, after the failure of *The Stalking Moon*. As the films which he has directed have maintained a higher average quality than those on which they worked together, it is tempting to suppose that Pakula's was the major contribution. His first film as a director was **The Sterile Cuckoo** (1969), another consciously lyrical and amusing look at college sexuality, written by Alvin Sargent from a novel by John Nichols. The girl, having made all the running, is not about to give up easily when the boy (Wendell Burton) tires; she is played by Liza Minnelli, with much of the vulnerability of her mother, Judy Garland. As she yields her virginity one may like to recall that at that age Mama had not long walked along the Yellow Brick Road in her red shoes. **Klute** (1971) is graphic on the details of a whore's life, which includes, on this evidence, auditioning for an off-Broadway 'Saint Joan'. Success in that field or the love of the young detective (Donald Sutherland) might lead her (Jane Fonda) back to the straight and narrow – to which extent it is very much like the prostitute films of the Silent era. The piece

is on the level of a T.V. series-episode, though Pakula's control disguises the fact. He attempted a third unusual romance, between an English spinster (Maggie Smith) and a young American (Timothy Bottoms), but **Love and Pain and the Whole Damn Thing** (1973) is tepid.

Pakula then turned to the thriller, and **The Parallax View** (1974) suffered by being released at the same time as *Chinatown* (q.v.), which also resurrected once-familiar themes and combined them with political corruption. In this case the investigative journalist (Warren Beatty) joins, as of old, an undercover organisation to get his story; he even has a sceptical editor and a frightened lady to put him on to the story in the first place. Like many modern thrillers, this one withholds facts from the audience – and not only those unknown to the hero. People speak, unheard by us, beyond glass doors, but Pakula makes great use of his structures; just as every person glimpsed is a possible killer, so every rivet is bursting with menace. The screenplay is by David Giler and Lorenzo Semple Jr, based on a novel by Loren Singer, in turn inspired by rumours about the deaths and disappearances of various figures connected with the assassination of President Kennedy. Its implication of the U.S. as a trigger-happy country is more subtle than in some well-meaning films, and stronger. The film's virtue – apart from the fact that it is far more exciting than *Chinatown* – is that its level is blood and thunder and yet its aim to touch sore spots in the American conscience is entirely well-judged. Beatty is awkward and persistent, in the tradition of reporters in movies.

The man who directed him was obviously the man to handle **All the President's Men** (1976), or so thought Robert Redford, its star and producer. The film had its origins in a report in *The Washington Post* which connected a burglary at the National Democratic headquarters with the White House, and it is about that story as researched by two reporters, Bob Woodward, played in the film by Redford, and Carl Bernstein, played by Dustin Hoffman. The book they wrote on the subject was purchased by Redford for $450,000, and Warners put up the $8½ million cost on the basis of his drawing power. The studio was uncertain whether

Alan K. Pakula served his first decade in films as producer of those directed by Robert Mulligan. Turning director himself, he made some notable movies, including *All the President's Men*, which was in fact produced by Robert Redford, right. Redford and Dustin Hoffman play the two Washington reporters who helped to bring about the fall of Nixon, and the film's subject is, as one of them and Redford both put it, 'This is how we did it.'

the public would be interested in a tale familiar from newspaper reports, while the many and salient facts needed a screenwriter of the expertise of William Goldman to knock them into dramatic shape. Even so, the meticulous Pakula did a certain amount of improvisation, using *Z* as his model – and this movie is as violently partisan: Nixon is hardly mentioned, but as the reporters burrow away they are, even with their knowledge of him, stunned by the criminal cupidity, the sheer stupidity, the arrogance and deviousness of Nixon and the men around him. The film, unlike the book, plays down the role other newspapers took in the unmasking. One of its many virtues is that it uses unfamiliar players except for the *Post* staff. The subject would have made an enthralling film if only competently dealt with, but it is superlatively well done. It commends itself to posterity, which will surely think as highly of it as the audiences and reviewers of the time.

Rollover (1981) is about the world of high finance, which apparently deterred audiences from attending; but its purpose is that of *The Parallax View* and *All the President's Men*, to show how the lives of the humble are manipulated by the rich and powerful. Again Pakula shows that he has few peers in handling such conventions of the thriller as the apparently unmotivated crime, the unexpected clue, the frightened witness; but perhaps the chief virtue of David Shaber's screenplay is the ease of the plotting, via which Jane Fonda suspects the one man in the world she can trust, Kris Kristofferson, and vice versa. Pakula has made them glamorous ikons in the manner of Hollywood stars of old, and given their capabilities it is a device that works beautifully. I have a feeling that the film will revive better than **Sophie's Choice** (1982), despite the popularity and acclaim that has greeted it. Its source is a novel by William Styron, of whom I once observed that he wrote for the sake of writing. That is the impression given by this film, which has no discernible subject. A young Southern boy (Peter MacNicol) arrives in Brooklyn in 1947 and chums up with a Jewish biologist (Kevin Kline) and his mistress (Meryl Streep), a survivor of Auschwitz. The biologist turns out to be unworthy of the boy's hero-worship, while much of the rest of the time is taken

up with flashbacks to Auschwitz, when Miss Streep manages to be emotional and interesting, which she does not elsewhere. We have not yet come to grips with the concentration camp experience in drama and literature, and shall not do so by encasing it in meaningless fictions. Pakula wrote his own screenplay (for the first time), but at 157 minutes it serves only to remind us that old Hollywood made short, watchable films out of equally unpromising material.

Well before *All the President's Men* Nixon was a dirty word, if we are to believe **The Best Man** (1964), directed by Franklin J. Schaffner (b. 1920), and written by Gore Vidal from his own play. A former television director and producer, Schaffner had directed a Broadway version of 'Advise and Consent' which, in common with *The Best Man* concerns chicanery in Washington and homosexuality as the skeleton in the cupboard. The two chief contenders at a Presidential convention are Senator Russell (Henry Fonda), based on Adlai Stevenson, and Senator Cantwell (Cliff Robertson, who had recently played President Kennedy as a young man in *P.T. 109*), largely based on Nixon. It is Vidal's cruel joke that Cantwell lives to regret a youthful indiscretion, but this is not a drama *à clef*: Vidal does little to illuminate the minds and mentalities of those who seek power, clearly because he thinks little of their minds and mentalities. He loves the in-fighting, the hypocrisy, the difference between the public and private face. His text is witty and the cast of best quality: Schaffner lets both speak for themselves.

He had made his film debut with **The Stripper** (1963), in which his fresh handling concealed the tired elements in the plot – from William Inge's play, 'A Loss of Roses', concerning a showgirl (Joanne Woodward) in the suburbs, kindly seducing her old friend's adolescent son (Richard Beymer). It was not a success, nor was **The War Lord** (1965), for all its superiority to others of the genre – which may be left undefined, since there have been few enough movies set in the Dark Ages. The first and most striking quality is its understanding that man then lived by a different set of values – and the elemental tone of the piece is far closer to the sagas of the time than had been done before or

In Hollywood the Director is King

Franklin J. Schaffner's early films were modest in scale and completely realised, which led to offers to make immodest projects such as *Patton*, with George C. Scott. It was a considerable achievement, being both an excellent biographical study and a good war film, unlike many others offering some indication of how wars are planned from the battlefront.

since. In the title role, Charlton Heston plays a man of conscience, which is not an anachronism, since he alone is, and that provides the pivot of the plot. John Collier and Millard Kaufman wrote it, from a play by Leslie Stevens, and though there may be minor reservations these would not include the film's appearance – a watery, wintry world of reed and hedgerow, wattle and thatch buildings. Moving completely in the opposite direction, into the future, Heston and Schaffner made **Planet of the Apes** (1968), about some astronauts who journey not in space but time; it finishes, predictably, with the discovery of the Statue of Liberty half-buried in sand and Heston shrieking, with all the artificial anguish at his command, 'Maniacs!' – an antiwar message to remind us of the one at the end of *The Bridge on the River Kwai*, also the brainchild of Pierre Boulle. The make-up and other special effects are of outstanding quality, and there are enough good, horrific, moments to show why this spawned a number of sequels and a T.V. series.

Schaffner had a second success with

Patton (1970), controlling a large cast, a vast number of North African and European locations, and the complex character of the general himself – though written with little complexity, and requiring all George C. Scott's considerable skill to supply it. That they took a less than favourable view of its hero than is normal in such pictures undoubtedly helped the film to win a fistful of Oscars. And that brought the invitation to direct Sam Spiegel's production of **Nicholas and Alexandra** (1971), which is much more entertaining, but exactly the sort of historical epic seemingly rendered redundant by films like *Patton*. It has, moreover, a pallid, dead feel, and James Goldman's script is no more than a bland reduction of Robert K. Massie's moving biography. As the Tsar and Tsarina, Michael Jayston and Janet Suzman are dignified, humourless and somewhat unreal – which is as it should be; but if they never engage our sympathies, there are small insights, as in *Patton*, as to their inner lives. The parts of the film which do not involve the Romanovs are less satisfactory. Michael Bryant is a correct Lenin, and Brian Cox a decent Trotsky, but Tom Baker is insufficiently mesmeric as Rasputin. As Witte, Laurence Olivier alone is reason enough to see the film.

There is a superb performance by Dustin Hoffman as a myopic prisoner in **Papillon** (1973) as well as a good one by Steve McQueen in the title role, that of the Frenchman who escaped from Devil's Island and lived to tell the tale. Robert Dorfmann, another Frenchman, produced, but there was American interest because Henri Charrière's pseudo-autobiographical account had been a world bestseller. Some doubts were cast on its accuracy, which Schaffner acknowledges by using slow motion photography for one of the less credible incidents in Papillon's flight. He treats that as material for a superior adventure tale, and early strives for more authenticity – heat, sweat, proximity, deprivation, monotony – than the prison melodramas of forty years earlier.

Unjustly, the picture was not regarded as a major film by a major director, perhaps because it was designed to meet, even more than most, a popular market. Schaffner's reputation declined with **Islands in the Stream** (1977), admittedly not an entirely compelling version of Hemingway, and more reasonably with **The Boys from Brazil** (1978), based on a novel by Ira Levin. As an Austrian-Jewish Nazi hunter, Olivier has to say 'Whoever would believe such a preposterous story?' and the answer is unfathomable. The British producer, Lew Grade, had spent a fortune on a film without one believable scene, about Nazi clones growing up all over the world. The many locations show that at least one aspect of Schaffner's talent remains unimpaired.

Among the older directors, Don, or Donald, Siegel came into his own, finally fulfilling the promise of *Riot in Cell Block 11* and *Invasion of the Body Snatchers*. **Madigan** (1968) and **Coogan's Bluff** (1968) showed him to have few superiors in handling action scenes and a liking for irreverence and idiosyncrasy; the violence in both showed his antecedents to be in the thrillers of the late Fifties rather than those being made when he started his career. Both Madigan and Coogan are cops, the one, Richard Widmark, weary and resentful, the other, Clint Eastwood, wide-eyed from Arizona, but equally determined to clean New York of one particular criminal. With Eastwood, Siegel made **Two Mules for Sister Sara** (1970), about a whore (Shirley MacLaine), posing as a nun, who helps an American mercenary employed by Juarist revolutionaries; and **The Beguiled** (1971), about a wounded Union soldier sheltered in a seminary for young ladies. The latter, fastidiously made, propounds a very different view of such establishments than the one customary to nineteenth-century tales, and after wondering whether the combination of incest, lesbianism and mutilation is meant to be in emulation of lesser Jacobean tragedy, you may decide it is merely meant to be commercial – which it proved not to be. However, both **Dirty Harry** (1971) and **Charley Varrick** (1973) are so accomplished as to make one regret that Siegel has since been unable to find the same form. Charley (Walter Matthau) is a small time crook who, after a routine bank robbery, finds he has stirred up a hornet's nest, reaching right up to the Mafia; Harry (Eastwood) is a San Francisco cop hunting not the gangsters of yore but one tatty little sadist of a villain. Siegel's dual use of the city, as a place of light and space and sea,

and of scrap-dumps, seedy bars and liquor stores, was to be influential, as was the character of Harry – ruthless and cynical, a bruised, foul-tongued martyr.

If, with this handful of films, Siegel renewed the thriller genre, the transformation of the Western was the work of Sam Peckinpah (b. 1925), whose long term as director and writer of T.V. Westerns prompted him to attempt something other than the laundered version of the Old West which they offered. In **Ride the High Country** (1962) he kept to tradition by having his heroes (Joel McCrea, Randolph Scott) be true to their code; but they are ageing, paunchy and given to fond recall of the old days. And Peckinpah's mining town was not the usual constructed set, but a collection of tents, its only permanent structures the saloon and the brothel. The obligatory drunken judge is the obligatory Edgar Buchanan, but the girls all look like whores, and their boss is a gross redhead with quivering breasts. On the strength of the film's critical success, Peckinpah persuaded Columbia to put up a large budget for **Major Dundee** (1965),

Before he took to producing, and sometimes directing, his own films, Clint Eastwood appeared in a number of thrillers directed by Don Siegel, a veteran whose work took on new impetus with some cops-and-robbers films in the late Sixties. This is Eastwood in perhaps the most celebrated, *Dirty Harry*. Harry was a cop, ruthless and cynical, a bruised saint, a foul-tongued martyr – and very influential on the films and television series which followed in the wake of his success.

with Charlton Heston in the title role, chasing a bunch of Apaches into Mexico. After many rows, Columbia cut twenty minutes from the release print, and Peckinpah repudiated this rather sententious message about man's responsibility. It seemed to contradict the impression that he is a born film-maker, and **The Wild Bunch** (1969) proved conclusively that he is not. The locations are superbly chosen and photographed with all the professionalism of Lucien Ballard, and the portrait of Mexican life at the turn of the century seems authentic; but it is a boring film. So is **The Ballad of Cable Hogue** (1970), the tale of a good-natured man (Jason Robards) who survives his own stupidity and the hazards of Western life. Clichés of the new Western are in abundance: the sentimental ballad on the soundtrack and much larkiness, often consisting of the hero running around in longjohns and being bathed by the heroine, usually a somewhat bedraggled whore. The film failed at the box office; and Peckinpah resorted to the excessive and gratuitous violence which had made *The Wild Bunch* so much discussed and seen; but **Straw Dogs** (1971), made in Cornwall, England, was discussed and hardly seen. **Junior Bonner** (1972) tries for significance, in its sour portrait of contemporary America, through a story of a rodeo performer (Steve McQueen) visiting his family. Once again, Ballard did the photography, and the documentary footage of rodeos is entertaining: the rest is not, and the film's loss ($2 million) was a contributory factor in A.B.C. Pictures' abandoning film production. **The Getaway** (1972), a heist/chase movie with McQueen and Ali MacGraw, is again proof of Peckinpah's skill, making us regret that he has had few good opportunities in recent years, but it still left the impression that it might have been even better if the manifold killings and explosions had not been shown in such graphic, over-emphatic detail.

The Professionals (1966) has a similar plot to *The Wild Bunch*, concerning the expedition of a gang of mercenaries, and it is easily the better of the two films, as sharply directed and written by Richard Brooks. It opened to enthusiastic notices, but took some time to build to popular success – whereas *The Hallelujah Trail*, also with Burt Lancaster and launched at

similar expense, never got moving. The public was letting the Western die, but the faults were *sui generis*. The reasons were historical: the cattle-driving and wagon-speeding spectacles had become too difficult to mount and too costly; pro-Indian sentiment forbade the old cowboys *vs.* Indians conflict and few pro-Indian films were successful. Thus pioneering stories were out of the question, and demure gingham-clad girls now held no appeal. Lone strangers still rode into town, but like as not they were as corrupt as their opponents: we were supposed to admire their charm and strategy as they tricked their way to victory.

Brooks's best film remains **Elmer Gantry** (1960), which he adapted from Sinclair Lewis's novel, an ironic view of the mid-Western taste for revivalism. It was written not long after Aimee Semple Macpherson had been discredited, and the film's dominant virtue lies in not revealing the real ambitions of Sister Sharon (Jean Simmons) and her campaign manager (Dean Jagger). Both roles are magnificently acted, and in the compulsive first half they seem to be ardent in their mission, but realists: that she recognises Gantry (Burt Lancaster) as a charlatan and becomes his mistress does not contradict either fact. Neither the reporter (Arthur Kennedy) nor the prostitute (Shirley Jones) who conspire to bring them down is convincing: as Brooks increasingly fails to understand the motives of his characters he seems not to care what he puts on the screen as long as it is flashy.

Few of his later films were successful, including *Bite the Bullet*, one of the very few Westerns made in the Seventies. **In Cold Blood** (1967) deserved better, but unfortunately it came out at the same time as *Bonnie and Clyde*, which provided a more exciting view of old crime. People who had read Truman Capote's 'nonfiction novel' did not care to relive its grizzly matters; Conrad Hall's photography portrays Kansas only on grey days – appropriately, since its inhabitants seem to be grey; the cast is blessedly free of familiar faces. Brooks works competently in reconstructing the murder of the Clutter family, but fails to convey either its full horror or any understanding of the mentality of their killers. In the end he attempts a grim indictment of capital punishment;

withal, there have been few films on crime so honestly done.

Days of Wine and Roses (1963), directed by Blake Edwards, has an honourable place among harrowing films, as it charts the progress of a nice young couple toward alcoholism. He (Jack Lemmon) is in advertising, where boozing is used 'to entertain' and to relieve tension; she (Lee Remick) starts drinking along with him to make his drunkenness more tolerable. He can draw back, but she cannot. Lemmon, a patently honest actor, offers that Jack-in-the-box executive we had never previously seen in films, and Miss Remick refuses to allow his superb performance to overwhelm her. J. P. Miller wrote the screenplay, from his own T.V. play, and the film is as well made as Edwards's *Breakfast at Tiffany's*, which we looked at earlier.

The point about directorial quality has to be made, for Edwards's skill deteriorates when he handles his own material. He had written several of the films which Richard Quine had made for Columbia, and he began writing his own screenplays, always in collaboration, with *The Pink Panther* in 1964. This was the first of a series of so-called comedies with Peter Sellers as a bumbling French detective. I have not seen all of them, but the second one, **A Shot in the Dark** (1964), must be one of the worst-made films in cinema history. Edwards has no sense of the rhythm needed for comedy; his camera 'style', whether for one of Sellers's pratfalls or for two people in conversation is simply just to photograph them, with only an occasional close-up or long-shot. **The Great Race** (1965) is an elephantine twin to *Those Magnificent Men in their Flying Machines*, and equally unfunny, despite the presence of Jack Lemmon and Peter Falk as cod villains. The film's two set pieces, a Sennett-like custard-pie battle and a parody of *The Prisoner of Zenda*, are tedious. Given the cost and the high salaries of the stars (the others were Tony Curtis and Natalie Wood), the film, even at inflated seat prices, failed to turn a profit.

With *Darling Lili* (q.v.) Edwards began a decade of failures and near-misses, the latter including **The Tamarind Seed** (1974), a pleasing, old-fashioned cold war thriller, moving between Barbados, Paris and London. He restored his rating within the industry with another Pink Panther

film and more especially **'10'** (1979), the adventures of a bumbling lecher. The role was meant for George Segal, understandably, since both it and the situations were borrowed from *Loving* (q.v.) and *A Touch of Class*: Segal, also understandably, turned it down and the role was played by Dudley Moore, a British 'comic' whose sole claim to that description is his diminutive size. Even with Segal, these aged wheezes would have been offensive, being dragged out in a way which would have bewildered any half-decent practitioner of Hollywood comedy in the Thirties. **S.O.B.** (1981) is a satire on the movie industry, about a film director (Richard Mulligan) who turns a flop film into a hit by restaging a musical number with the girls in garter-belts and his lady-like star (Julie Andrews) baring her breasts. The film has a mildly amusing party scene, a great many unfunny scatological jokes and a dire second half, ending with a drawn-out funeral sequence. Since Miss Andrews is Edwards's lady-like wife – if far more talented than made to seem here – we did not need to be told that the film is partly autobiographical.

One of the flops it obliquely refers to is **Darling Lili** (1970), a costly musical

Blake Edwards started in films as a writer at Columbia, specialising in comedy, and as a director he is most renowned for some light-hearted entertainments, many of them lacking in both originality and wit. His few serious films have been much better, and especially *Days of Wine and Roses*, splendidly acted by Lee Remick and Jack Lemmon as a couple whose marriage is wrecked by too much booze.

whose failure was one reason why the industry looked askance at the genre. It has the enchanting idea of making Miss Andrews into a Mata Hari-type lady of World War I: but she and Henry Mancini's score are its sole virtues. As much may be said of **Victor/Victoria** (1982), in which Miss Andrews is an out-of-work British singer who becomes the toast of the Paris of the Thirties impersonating a female impersonator. Her mentor is a homosexual cabaret performer (Robert Preston), and there are homosexual complications when a gangster-type (James Garner) from Chicago falls in love with Andrews, believing her to be a boy. That aspect of the tale is only touched upon in Reinhold Schunzel's original, *Viktor und Viktoria*, made fifty years earlier, but much more subtly. Even when Edwards copies Schunzel, as in the night-club fight, and the final 'drag' number, he can only do so lumberingly. It is not to be expected that Edwards can reproduce the sheer vitality of Schunzel's film any more than we expect the finesse of a Lubitsch amidst the complications of the hotel bedrooms. *Darling Lili* and *Victor/ Victoria* run to two-and-a-quarter hours and I simply do not understand why Edwards, like many of today's directors, fails to understand the chief virtues of the films he is attempting to emulate – economy, pacing, brevity. *Victor/Victoria* was ecstatically received by most American critics, but was given short shrift by their British colleagues.

Miss Andrews had had a comic high spot earlier in her career, in **The Americanization of Emily** (1964), directed by Arthur Hiller (b. 1923), whose own favourite film it is. She plays a crisp English girl, a war widow, with advanced views about comforting military personnel, one of whom is Charlie (James Garner), a 'dog-robber', i.e. a rating who ensures that high-ranking officers lack for nothing in the way of comfort, be it edible, alcoholic or female. He is also a confirmed death-dodger, or coward. As written by Paddy Chayevsky from the novel by William Bradford Huie, the film makes its points far better than a number of more ambitious anti-war efforts. Hiller, from T.V., had already made a number of poor films, and there were more before **The Tiger Makes Out** (1967), Murray Schisgal's adaptation of his own play. A meek

postman (Eli Wallach) is so frustrated by his attempts at self-education and society's slights that, in revenge, he plans a kidnapping – taking, by mistake, a suburban housewife (Anne Jackson) equally discontented with her lot. This was one of the bright New York comedies of the time, more frenetic than most, but deeply alive to all sorts of human behaviour – particularly when that is conditioned by the rat race. **Popi** (1969) is about a New York Puerto Rican widower (Alan Arkin) so poor that he dreams up a scheme to get his two kids adopted as Cuban refugees. The first half is bitter, and the second bittersweet, but the whole film has Arkin extracting every ounce of penny-pinching pathos from the role.

Paddy Chayevsky turned to Hiller for his first original screenplay for more than a decade, **The Hospital** (1971) – an institution he portrays as a madhouse of weariness, fright, confusion and tension. Since the hospital itself is condemned, we may be certain of the allegory, but unlike the later *Network*, Chayevsky's observation is as keen as ever and he is marvellously served by George C. Scott as a doctor in trouble – impotent, ageing, with his wife just departed and his son 'building bombs in basements in the cause of universal brotherhood'. Hiller's tone is so much closer to *Marty* or *The Bachelor Party* than his other films, as if to prove Chayevsky's strength and his own weakness.

Hiller's box-office success with a slushy romantic drama, *Love Story*, was one reason why he was asked to direct the provocatively-titled **Making Love** (1982), regarded by the industry as a trailblazer because of its subject-matter. It was one of the many films on divorce made after the success of *Kramer vs. Kramer* (q.v.), but in this case the husband (Michael Ontkean), a doctor, leaves his wife (Kate Jackson) for another man (Harry Hamlin), a writer. Since both men are sort-of gay versions of the upright blacks Sidney Poitier used to play, the tale is little more than soap opera; but Barry Sandler's screenplay is convincing in the crucial scenes, as when the writer admits his homosexuality (a word, incidentally, never mentioned) in order to make the doctor confess that he is tempted by him. Wisely, the doctor is shown to have 'predilections' despite an apparently happy marriage –

which has no chance of surviving once they are realised.

Hiller's other films include two based on plays by Neil Simon. Filming this popular and prolific playwright is a major preoccupation for the industry – and not without reason he can be a box-office name in his own right. Admittedly, there are few adroit practitioners today of screen comedy, so that audiences gave a warm welcome to **Barefoot in the Park** (1967) and **The Odd Couple** (1968), both directed by Gene Saks from Simon's Broadway originals. They restored intimacy to Hollywood comedy, while bringing to it a new concept – that New York Jewish humour was best left to New York Jewish performers, even if gentile stars were sometimes necessary. *Barefoot* is an untidy piece about a honeymoon couple, at its best when imitative of Peter Arno, as when the bride (Jane Fonda) tries to embarrass her stuffy husband (Robert Redford) in the elevator of the Plaza Hotel, 'Mr Adams, you ever been with a fifteen-year-old girl before?' The 'odd couple' are a fastidious man (Jack Lemmon), rebounding from a broken marriage, and the slob (Walter Matthau) who gives him a home. It has some of Simon's best one-liners – 'He has 92 credit cards in his pocket. The moment he disappears America lights up' – and it teams the two most skilful light comedians in movies, even if, on this occasion, Lemmon has to work hard to make his role sympathetic. Saks's directorial method consists of little more than training his camera on the players.

As an actor, he played a supporting role in **The Prisoner of Second Avenue** (1974), the only film of Simon's work directed by one of the old guard, Melvin Frank. It is also one of Simon's failures, due perhaps to the subject, that of a man (Lemmon) who loses his job. At the end his wife (Anne Bancroft) has also lost her temporary employment, but they vow, as New Yorkers, that they will not let New York get them down. The humour is as desperate as the leading character, and its blend of the flip and the fatalistic – at the heart of all Jewish humour – goes for little in Frank's impersonal style.

Elaine May (b. 1930), the former cabaret artist, directed the best Simon film, **The Heartbreak Kid** (1972), though in this case her screenplay was based on a novel by Bruce Jay Friedman. It also poses a delicate situation, that of a honeymooner (Charles Grodin) who ditches his gauche bride (Jeannie Berlin, Miss May's daughter) for a beautiful Wasp (Cybill Shepherd). The result is iron hard, risking its laughs on our response to the heartlessness and superficiality of modern American speech. The traditional cruelty of American society goes back at least to Edith Wharton; it was treated lightheartedly in the screwball comedies of the Thirties, only to return to films in a more realistic manner with George Axelrod and Milos Forman – at least in his American film, *Taking Off* (q.v.). Miss May and Mike Nichols, in their dialogues for stage and disc, had brilliantly used the comedy of cruelty, but little of it had found its way into *The Graduate* (q.v.), with which Nichols made his reputation as a film director. On the other hand, there is a great deal of it in the first film Miss May directed, also about the country-club set, **A New Leaf** (1971), which she wrote from a story by Jack Ritchie. The Nichols-May sketches influenced the dialogue, as in the lawyer's gobbledygook about capital and income, before he gives up with: 'You have no money. I wish there was some other way of saying it.' The man who has no money is Henry Graham (Matthau), last of the New York playboys: 'All I am or was is rich,' he says, 'and that's all I ever wanted to be' – and since the only way to continue to be so is to make a wealthy match, he finds a painfully gauche spinster (May) – who happens to be the only character in the tale who is not mercenary.

Mike Nichols (b. 1931), after his cabaret work with Miss May, became one of Broadway's most successful directors, especially with Simon's plays. He made his film debut as director with **Who's Afraid of Virginia Woolf?** (1966), from Edward Albee's drama about the less endearing aspects of faculty life – drunken professors and their wives, whose screaming and shouting on this occasion permitted a number of four-letter words not heard before from the screen; and they sounded choice in the mouths of this particular husband and wife team, Richard Burton and Elizabeth Taylor. **The Graduate** (1967) also defied taboos as written by Calder Willingham and Buck Henry from a novel by Charles Webb, in showing the

In Hollywood the Director is King

brazen seduction of a minor (Dustin Hoffman) by an older woman (Anne Bancroft), a family friend and mother of one of his comrades. She is a self-confessed alcoholic and he is an Alice in a wonderland of the 'silent majority', a generation who had had it and lost it in a ceaseless ritual of martinis and barbecues. The film's second half betrays the sharp observation of the first, as the boy moons around the woman's daughter and then abducts her as an act of revenge. This curious morality is in keeping with the film's bitter attitude to the older generation and its portrait of the young as honest, deceived and manipulated. If that was intended as a blatant bid for the now mainly youthful cinema audiences, it was successful, for it became the third most profitable American film yet made, a position it held until overtaken by *Love Story* three years later. Simon and Garfunkel's pleasing soundtrack songs condemned us for some years to films with cars rolling along to similar melodies.

Nichols's reputation then made him claimant to a property eyed warily by Hollywood, **Catch-22** (1970), Joseph Heller's massive debunking of the military – which remained bursting out of Buck Henry's sloppily-packed screenplay. Nichols unfortunately made matters worse by trying to instil it with meaning, which was precisely what audiences did not want – especially after the irreverence of *M★A★S★H* (q.v.) a few months earlier. However, a much better cast realised a number of Heller's superior grotesques, headed by Alan Arkin as the perplexed Yossarian, with Jon Voight as the conniving Milo Minderbinder, Anthony Perkins as the ineffectual padre, Bob Newhart as Major Major, Richard Benjamin as the smooth Major Danby and Buck Henry himself as the acolyte Korn. Another contemporary satirist, the cartoonist Jules Feiffer, wrote **Carnal Knowledge** (1971), which strove for nothing less than a summary of the American male's sex-life, from college stimulation to middle-aged doubts about potency. If there was any point or wit, it escaped Nichols, who failed more interestingly with **The Fortune** (1975), written by Carole Eastman, who as Adrien Joyce wrote the brilliant *Five Easy Pieces* (q.v.). It is a comedy of cruelty in the manner of *A New Leaf*, with an heiress (Stockard Channing) pursued

by two small-time con-men (Jack Nicholson, Warren Beatty): but it is set in the Twenties, and always hopes to evoke the comedies of Hollywood's past. At one point facsimiles of Laurel and Hardy may be discerned in their jalopy, and a couple of their gags are borrowed; but despite the screaming and slapstick the film does not succeed because Nichols has not the courage to be vulgar. Its failure is sad, since Miss Channing is virtually the only actress today with the qualities of the great comediennes of the past.

Neither Nichols nor May★ has continued to work regularly in films; indeed the unexpected flowering of American comedy at the beginning of the Seventies soon died out. Other perpetrators proved to have little staying power, including Irvin Kershner (b. 1923), to whom we owe just two good films, **A Fine Madness** (1966) and **Loving** (1970), both concerning the artist as hero – and one to whom the fairer sex should not be denied. The former, written by Elliott Baker from his own novel, involves an irresponsible poet (Sean Connery), whose wife (Joanne Woodward), denied her alimony, puts him in the hands of a psychiatrist; the second, produced and written by Don Devlin from a novel by J. M. Ryan, is about a responsible commercial artist (George Segal), whose wife (Eva Marie Saint) is about to lose him to his mistress. Both films are devoted to New York; but that is not the metropolis of the films of the past, for these heroes and heroines are caught in its toils and go down fighting. The city in *A Fine Madness* is one of slum apartments and penthouses and in *Loving* it is seen from suburbia – the world of Updike and de Vries, novelists virtually ignored by the cinema. Kershner's understated reaction, catching the odd hint of absurdity, is absolutely correct.

Cy Howard (b. 1915), a former screenwriter, directed two films, of which **Lovers and Other Strangers** (1970) has merit, as written by Renée Taylor and Joseph Bologna from their play, with the aid of David Zelag Goodman. It is a pungent and funny account of a wedding, which must be one of the last times Jewish jokes were put into the mouths of Italians and/or Roman Catholics.

★In 1973 she made a film for Paramount, the subject of litigation between her and the company two years later: to date it has not been publicly shown.

A Jewish wedding is the highlight of **Goodbye, Columbus** (1969), the one good film made by Larry Peerce after *One Potato Two Potato* – and its strength is in Philip Roth's witty observation of the American Jewish milieu, as faithfully transcribed by Arnold Schulman. Undoubtedly the success of *The Graduate* caused Roth's book to be brought to the screen, since, unlike *The Pawnbroker* and *No Way to Treat a Lady* (q.v.), all the characters are Jewish, and the orientation of Howard's film indicates that the industry was not quite prepared for this. Simultaneously, each of the young Jewish heroes of *The Graduate*, *Goodbye, Columbus* and *The Heartbreak Kid* is entering an alien world, be it one of wealth, Wasps, or grown-ups, and I suspect their approach, through emotion or conviction, is the way many industry people like to refer to their past. Like Hoffman in *The Graduate*, Neil (Richard Benjamin) in *Goodbye, Columbus* observes the people with money, and is not sure that he likes them. He lives in Newark, works in a library, and is white and pasty; she (Ali MacGraw) is a Jewish princess, tanned and beautiful. His chutzpah gets him invited to stay, but the wedding – her brother's – proves her relatives no more refined than his. The implicit questioning of society's values, inherent in all the best of these films, is here; and the audiences who made this one so popular were undoubtedly refreshed by some more broken taboos – the girl hiding her diaphragm, the athlete brother washing his jockstrap, and the heroine's answer as to her summer activity, 'Growing a penis.'

Social virtues are hardly to be expected in **No Way to Treat a Lady** (1968), the best film directed by Jack Smight, otherwise well known for a slick private-eye thriller with Paul Newman, *Harper*. This one is a comedy-thriller, written by John Gay from a novel by William Goldman, and moving expertly between the antics of a camp mass-murderer (Rod Steiger) with a penchant for disguises, and the love affair of a Jewish detective (George Segal) and his gentile girl (Lee Remick). Although mother – 'I don't want to hear any more. Already I shan't sleep tonight' – is broadly acted by Eileen Heckart, she underplays compared with Ruth Gordon in **Where's Poppa?** (1970), whose whims ruin Segal's attempts at mutual seduction with his

nurse (Trish van Devere). Mother is such a menace that it is hard to understand why Segal should be catatonic at the prospect of putting her into a home, but brother Sidney (Ron Leibman) also spells trouble, running out to Central Park to be mugged and attempting rape on what turns out to be a cop in drag. Robert Kane wrote it, from his own novel, and Carl Reiner directed – poorly, clear evidence why he is best known as writer and performer. Reiner does a much smoother directorial job on **The One and Only** (1978), one of several comedies of this period, possibly autobiographical, about young Jewish guys on the make in the Fifties. This one (Henry Winkler) gives new meaning to the words 'brash' and 'extrovert', as he bounds from college to take Broadway by storm – but ends as a campy television wrestler. Neither Winkler nor Kim Darby, as his girlfriend, is quite good enough for the material, which has some marvellous satiric ideas and a few mild laughs as written by Steve Gordon, who as writer and director later had a success with *Arthur*.

Herbert Ross (b. 1927) has been an exponent of this aspect of New York, but his best and first film is very different, **Goodbye, Mr Chips** (1969). He came to it, a former choreographer, after working on the musical numbers in *Funny Lady*; like Sam Wood, director of the 1939 version, he is an American, and presumably immune from the pros and cons which surround the subject of public schools in Britain. The idea of a musical version of this particular tale was not appealing, and has been only partially solved; most of the songs are poor and they are either broken up, or used only on the soundtrack. The story itself does not especially matter: what does matter are the characters of Chips and the woman he marries, played by Peter O'Toole and Petula Clark, neither of whom ever did anything better. He is gawky, shy and stiff – and very touching, without moving into the areas of doddering lovability explored by Mr Donat. She – predictably a musical comedy star – is modest and warm and independent. The courtship between this awkward teacher and an extrovert soubrette is exquisitely rendered, against a background of Pompeii, Paestum and Naples, and beautifully written, by Terence Rattigan – who used

In Hollywood the Director is King

the occasion to add to his view of school-mastering in 'The Browning Version'. The film is one of the most unexpected of successes, but many critics, seeing only what they expected to see, trounced it: an honourable exception was John Simon, who admitted that it moved him to tears.

The coming together of two unlikely, lonely people occupied Ross again in both **The Owl and the Pussycat** (1970) and **T. R. Baskin** (1971). The couple in *Baskin* are Peter Boyle and Candice Bergen, who as the lady of the title, is possibly a high-class callgirl; in *Owl* Barbra Streisand is a low-class hooker, and George Segal is the shy writer drawn to her. The film was written by Buck Henry from Bill Manhoff's two-handed play, its black girl changed to a Jewish one, since Ray Stark produced (both play and film), and Streisand was under contract to him. 'Hey, you straight?' she yells at Segal, examining his bedroom, and if you do not think that is funny, you should hear her say it. 'Felix? Your name Felix? – That's a sort of ooghkie name.' Ross directed this actress again in a sequel to *Funny Girl* called **Funny Lady** (1975), and because Streisand had become, if anything, even less vulnerable with the years, it was a mistake to try and

turn the heroine, Fanny Brice, into a tragic figure. In the latter half, until that happens, the film has a splendid performance by James Caan as Fanny's second husband, the Jewish showman Billy Rose, and some funny parodies of old Follies numbers choreographed by Herbert Ross and his wife, Norah Kaye, a former ballet dancer.

Ross continued to film Broadway comedy, including **The Sunshine Boys** (1975), by Neil Simon. This aims to be the comedy of insult, and certainly the comedy of little else, as it details the attempts to reunite a vaudeville team renowned for their mutual loathing. Walter Matthau, expert in the sour, laser-beam wise-crack, is matched with George Burns, whose superb delivery reminds us of his long experience as a comic. He is the more likeable of the two, but in this context that means little. **The Goodbye Girl** (1977) has an original screenplay by Simon, and Ross's firm handling is directed towards achieving the aura of vintage romantic comedies. Unquestionably, our sympathies are being manipulated, yet not insultingly so, except in a roof dinner-party, with coloured lights: and at that point I was glad to be reminded of *Christmas in July* rather than the cliché-riddled movies which so often provide points of reference. The early part of the film, the bickering between this young mother (Marcia Mason) and her unwilling lodger (Richard Dreyfuss), resembles *The Owl and the Pussycat*: but their *détente* and *entente* make this the movies' most charming love story since *Goodbye, Mr Chips*. Dreyfuss won a Best Actor Oscar, and if the film was, in John Coleman's phrase, 'weirdly over-nominated' it was in every other category beaten by *Annie Hall* (q.v.), which merely aspires to be what this film is – much funnier, more touching and more professionally made.

The reviewer in *Variety* observed that **The Seven-Per-Cent Solution** (1976) was evidence that Ross had become one of the best directors working in films; but his talent was wasted on this Sherlock Holmes pastiche written by Nicholas Meyer. It is not to be compared to Billy Wilder's similar piece, while its borrowings – from James Bond, the Marx Brothers and *The Man with the Golden Arm* – were only too typical of the movies of this time. **The Turning Point** (1977) makes deliberate reference to *Old Acquaintance*, for in his screenplay Arthur Laurents has a character also called Deedee. Both films concern the friendship of two women whose lives have diverged, one of whom becomes an influence on the other's grown-up daughter. Here, Shirley MacLaine has settled into domesticity while Anne Bancroft has become a prima ballerina. As the first film about ballet since *The Red Shoes*, it could have used more of Ross's and Miss Kaye's experience of such matters as ego, temperament, ambition and others endemic to this milieu. Mikhail Baryshnikov is found to be bedding the corps de ballet one by one, but is also dancing at gratifying length.

Much was said about the film returning women's roles to the forefront; what its success more positively did was enable Ross to make **Nijinsky** (1980). Over the years the many attempts to film this subject had foundered during the lifetime of Romola Nijinsky, who threatened legal action at any suggestion of the relationship between her husband and Diaghilev. In the event Ross and his writer, Hugh Wheeler, approach it with timidity and so cannot achieve their aim – a study of the reasons for Nijinsky's descent into madness. But if

they omit the guilt he felt, they do show that the combined emotional and professional relationship was ruinous, since their ambitions made them play dangerous games with each other. As Diaghilev, Alan Bates offers little more than an inappropriate world-weariness, George de la Pena is a lacklustre Nijinsky and Leslie Brown gets no help in explaining the enigma of Romola, depicted here as an innocent society nobody. The famous sets and costumes have been reproduced with love, but while Ross correctly attempts to avoid a ballet version of *The Great Caruso* there seems little point in photographing de la Pena from only the waist upwards or in slow motion.

Ross's delight in musicals, an endangered species, tempted him into making **Pennies from Heaven** (1981), based on a B.B.C. series which had been a success in some quarters. Other people, myself included, thought it, without hyperbole, the worst programme to be seen on television. Its writer, Dennis Potter, in an attempt to tell the truth about the Thirties, in contrast to the myth, apparently found it represented in the songs, and had the cast mime them as recorded then: he failed to see, or at least to convey, the reasons for the optimism, while his plot was an irrelevant fable about a travelling salesman who leaves his wife for a nice young teacher who becomes a whore. Ross handles the numbers in the film with the old Hollywood pizzazz, and the American cast seems at ease miming to the sweet harmony singers (the British artists on the soundtrack were working in the American idiom). Steve Martin, imitating the more spineless leading men of the period, is likeable and more relaxed than Bob Hoskins was in the original; and in his cameo as an oily wolf, Christopher Walken does a striptease – to Cole Porter's 'Let's Misbehave' – borrowed from the stage musical, 'Chicago'. Potter's screenplay, with the action transferred to the mid-West, is so witless and humourless that the film's rapid failure was not surprising.

Another former dancer and choreographer, Bob Fosse (b. 1925), made his debut as a screen director with **Sweet Charity** (1969), after a number of Broadway successes. This had been a Broadway musical, based on *Notti di Cabiria*, but despite rave notices cinema audiences were

In Hollywood the Director is King

Liza Minnelli in *Cabaret*, virtually the only hugely popular film musical since *The Sound of Music* – and the reasons must include the star, the rousing score and, undoubtedly, fascination with the film's milieu – the louche nightclubs of Berlin at the time the Nazis took over the city. Bob Fosse's vigorous handling was also a contributory factor, reminding us that he had done something similar with *Sweet Charity*, though that failed precisely because it lacked the qualities in the latter half to send the audience out cheerful.

not prepared to buy the tale a third time around. Universal, which produced, blamed the star, Shirley MacLaine, and prepared a new advertising campaign omitting her name and bearing the slogan, 'The musical with the sound of Today' – but since the sole justification of that was the worst song in the score, sung by Sammy Davis Jr, it is hardly surprising that that made no difference. Audiences may have been tired of reverently treated Broadway musicals, and Fosse's direction was brilliant in the wrong way; numbers that needed the apparent spontaneity of Gene Kelly had been chopped up with jump-cuts, stop-cuts, and Miss MacLaine posed in another part of the set; the show-stopper, 'Hey, Big Spender', like most stage numbers directed at the audience, looks fossilised on the screen. And Miss MacLaine, an agreeable talent, has shoulders too frail to carry so long a film: she is *not* Judy Garland, whose *Star is Born* had much more going for it, including a degree of optimism, whereas the last thirty minutes of this piece are downhill all the way.

On the stage, **Cabaret** (1972) was, at least in the London production, one of the great musicals; and as Sally Bowles, Judi Dench, not a great singer, came as close to breaking the collective heart of an audience as Garland ever did: replacing her in the film with Liza Minnelli, with her little mouse face, was not a bad idea, and she won an Oscar. Nor was it a bad idea to restore Herr Issyvoo (Michael York) to bisexuality; but the rest is mild, beginning with the Emcee of Joel Grey repeating his Broadway role, and nowhere near as evil or as suggestive of unspecified vices as Barry Dennen in the London production. Jay Presson Allen's infantile screenplay omits characters and complexity from the original, and a brilliant score has been abbreviated. Miss Minnelli simply has not – or had not – the temperament for the title number, and the film concludes with that, rather than the original implication of a whole city somnambulantly dancing and making love as the Nazis prepare to turn the world upside down. Fosse's direction is enlivening and energetic, and is again in **All That Jazz** (1979), a semi-musical based on his own experience as a director of Broadway shows who almost died from a heart attack. If Roy Scheider in the film is giving an accurate portrait, he is as unpleasant as he is vain: this is the greatest ego trip in the history of movies, but entertaining till towards the end, when a musical number combining the fantasies of Busby Berkeley and Fellini is staged during open-heart surgery.

Harold Prince, who had directed *Cabaret* on the stage, has had no luck with either of the films he directed. **Something for Everyone** (1970) is a black comedy set in Bavaria in pre-Nazi days, with virtually the same plot as *Teorema* but with elements of *Kind Hearts and Coronets*. **A Little Night Music** (1977) is much better and made with love, for Prince had also directed this musical version of *Smiles of a Summer Night* on Broadway and in London. His leading ladies were respectively Glynis Johns and Jean Simmons and having seen them both it is clear that the piece stands or falls by the interpretation of their role. Despite Stephen Sondheim's charming pastiche-Ravel score, the show was a dull thing in New York; in London with the enchanting Jean Simmons it sparkled. The film has Elizabeth Taylor, who is dumpy, over made-up and lacking presence. Hermione Gingold, Len Cariou (both from the Broadway show) and Diana Rigg perform stylishly, and the film is prettily set in rococo drawing rooms and on dappled lawns. But only 'A Weekend in the Country' has been staged with style; and the film's losses were a contributing factor to its Austrian production company going out of business.

George Roy Hill (b. 1922) came from Broadway, after much success in television. After three films he had a fine chance when Fred Zinnemann resigned from **Hawaii** (1966), a high budgeted film based on a small portion of James A. Michener's huge novel encompassing one thousand years of Hawaiian history. The film restricts itself to the nineteenth century, and starts with an interesting premise, the destruction of a pagan civilisation by the crusading forces of Christianity: the three hour running time crushes the audience, not to mention fire, typhoon, and numerous births and deaths. The screenplay by Dalton Trumbo and Daniel Taradash is better than their combined screen credits would suggest, if only because it has humour – a quality also to be found in the performance of Julie Andrews, as the wife of the parson (Max von Sydow), a man who, in the tradition

of Victorian literature, regards himself as God's instrument on earth.

For Hill, Miss Andrews is **Thoroughly Modern Millie** (1967), to remind us that she made her American reputation in 'The Boy Friend', and where that was an affectionate spoof of the stage musicals of the Twenties, Richard Morris's screenplay does the same for the films of the era – though, of course, with songs, a number of which are charmingly staged. Few musicals of this era had so likeable a cast – apart from Miss Andrews, at her mock-innocent best, Beatrice Lillie, Carol Channing, Mary Tyler Moore, and, in emulation of Charles 'Buddy' Rogers or William Haines, James Fox and John Gavin: justly, the film was Universal's biggest money-maker to that time. It is also, like most of the films produced by Ross Hunter, often sloppy and occasionally vulgar. Hill said that he began on the wrong foot by barring Hunter from the set, 'but he got his own back by taking me off the picture as soon as I had finished shooting. Then he cut the film himself. Twenty minutes that I had discarded were put back in – just to make it up to roadshow length. It was like putting a soufflé back into the oven for another hour. The film became tacky and cute.'

Hill said of **Butch Cassidy and the Sundance Kid** (1969) 'The critics roasted the film. If it had been a play, we'd have closed in one night. Thank God for word of mouth and my scriptwriter [William Goldman] – he said "I gave you *Shane* and you gave me *Gunga Din*." What we really got was the Laurel and Hardy of Deadwood Gulch.' What they really got was a bloodless *Wild Bunch* crossed with *Jules et Jim*, prettily photographed by Conrad Hall and played in the same manner by Paul Newman and Robert Redford. They also appeared for Hill – to equal public approval, and in this case Oscars for Best Direction and Best Picture – in **The Sting** (1973), an excessively long joke, set in the Twenties, with red herrings inside red herrings.

In his sharpest film yet, **Slap Shot** (1977), Hill examined the world of professional ice-hockey players, aided by Nancy Dowd, whose screenplay was based on observation of her brother-in-law, who was involved in that world. She is not flattering: ice-hockey players are, apparently, simple-minded hulks, given to drinking and whoring and open to manipulation. They are meant to be a reflection of a society that is all too violent – a matter grossly overstated, since in the film the games are virtually homicidal: but the lady is trying to make a number of points, including, in her treatment of the team's owner, that capitalism can play havoc with our lives. Paul Newman, loud-mouthed and easygoing, gives one of his best performances as the coach; and Hill might only be faulted, as ever, for running on too long.

Norman Jewison (b. 1926) had experience in Canadian and British T.V. before joining C.B.S., from whence he moved to Universal, to make a few forgettable comedies for Ross Hunter; he showed himself of better mettle when asked to replace Peckinpah on **The Cincinnati Kid** (1965), set in New Orleans in the Thirties, concentrating on big-time poker players, as written by Ring Lardner Jr and Terry Southern, and with a cast equally rare, including Joan Blondell, Rip Torn, Tuesday Weld, Cab Calloway, Jack Weston, and, in the leads as rival gamblers, Edward G. Robinson and Steve McQueen. 'You're good, kid' says Robinson, 'but as long as I'm around you're second best.' **The Russians Are Coming, the Russians Are Coming** (1966) features a Soviet submarine that runs aground just off the coast of Maine, to subsequent local hysteria – a subject nearly akin to Ealing comedy, but William Rose, who knew much about that, is unfortunately nearer his later form on *It's a Mad, Mad, Mad, Mad World*. The film is mainly memorable for the performance of Alan Arkin as an enterprising Russian lieutenant.

Jewison managed a more subtle portrait of a rural community in **In the Heat of the Night** (1967) – a small Mississippi town where a murder has taken place. Sterling Silliphant wrote it, from a novel by John Ball, and it added new resonances to an overworked movie subject, tensions in a small Southern town – in this case exemplified by a bigoted white cop (Rod Steiger) and his black surrogate chief (Sidney Poitier). The latter is not merely a stranger passing through, but a homicide expert from the North, to whom the white man must unwillingly defer: it is the white man who is the shell, as he confesses, while the black man has it all together. This situation, and the accompanying conflict,

evoked a warm response from audiences, as did **The Thomas Crown Affair** (1968). Jewison used an appropriately jazzy style for this tale of a complicated heist with two comely and glamorous stars, McQueen and Faye Dunaway. A soundtrack song, · 'The Windmills of Your Mind', helped Jewison to his third consecutive success.

He has been less fortunate in his subsequent films, but was responsible for introducing a more reliable talent, Hal Ashby (b. 1936), with **The Landlord** (1970). He was scheduled to direct it himself but persuaded his backers, the Mirisch brothers, to reassign the project to Ashby, his associate producer and editor. Beau Bridges plays a wealthy innocent who decides to alleviate his idleness by going into real estate, in the black ghetto of Brooklyn, where his efforts to become involved with the inhabitants lead to dislocation and misery. As a portrait of the environment, the film is far less modern than, say, *Razzia in St Pauli*. As an attack on the mendacity of the American bourgeoisie, exemplified by the hero's family, Ashby employs the style of *Petulia* and Coppola's *You're a Big Boy Now*, and in the process almost wrecks the film. Another fey comedy, **Harold and Maude** (1971), has the greatest disparity in its stars' ages since Margaret O'Brien and Wallace Beery, except that this time they are in love. The boy (Bud Cort) has a lop-sided look and the mooning expression of Harry Langdon; the woman (Ruth Gordon) is witch-like, and in fact their romance is merely a climax to the events that have gone before, mainly about young Harold's attempts at suicide, since he is in love with easeful death. His mother – marvellously played by Vivian Pickles – is dismissive, and at such moments this becomes a marvellous *comédie noire*; however, a theme song ('If you want to sing out, sing out/If you want to be free, be free . . .') reveals that the piece is pandering to the half-baked philosophies of the time – and that was also the message of *Le Roi de Coeur*, another cult film. The writer was Colin Higgins, who later became a director.

The Last Detail (1974) was written by Robert Towne from a novel by Darryl Ponicsan about two petty officers escorting a simpleton of a sailor (Randy Quaid) from Norfolk, Virginia, to the brig at

In Hollywood the Director is King

Portsmouth, New Hampshire, and what they teach him on the way. It is about their isolation and guarded friendships – of the remoteness of civilian life, of forbearance towards another's peccadilloes (it would have been different had the sailor stolen from a colleague), of shared assumptions about women and language and beer. 'Best goddam drink in the world' says 'Bad-Ass', and as spoken by Jack Nicholson the remark is sheer poetry. There is not a facet of this character, from his basic insecurity to apparent *laissez-faire* that Nicholson has not understood, in a performance that is the crown of America's most honest study of service life. In **Shampoo** (1975) Towne and Ashby kick away the props that support Californian – if not American – society: the *dolce vita* of Los Angeles turns out to be a Vanity Fair where the puppets merely jig to a new tune – with no values and no concern, which is all that may be expected since the time is Election Night, 1968, and Nixon is mouthing platitudes on television. Its message aside, the film is rather dull, and surely mystifying to anyone not versed in the mores of California. The humour, mainly sexual, includes Julie Christie under the table at the election-party, at the fly of Warren Beatty, who elsewhere takes advantage of the fact that he is considered gay because he is a hairdresser by profession. **Coming Home** (1978) is equally frank, if not quite as explicit, its *raison d'être* the affair between an army wife (Jane Fonda) and a Vietnam veteran (Jon Voight), now a paraplegic. Waldo Salt and Robert C. Jones wrote the screenplay, from a story by Nancy Dowd, and though possibly all those responsible felt deeply about Vietnam, the film is no more than an updated and highly romantic variation on *The Men*.

Ashby's **Being There** (1979) was his most warmly welcomed film since *The Last Detail*, perhaps because there had been at this time a dearth of films with ideas. The central concept in this case was borrowed from Gogol – by Jerzy Kosinski, who wrote the script from his own novel. The question arises as to whether he can pull off the situations as well as does 'The Government Inspector': a reclusive, taciturn, stupid gardener (Peter Sellers) is sent out into the great world on the death of his employer and within hours is mingling with presidents and the like, all of whom

consider him an expert on economics, etc. But the film does not make us believe that he does, and Kosinski merely makes statements about American gullibility and the media instead of achieving satire.

Sydney Pollack (b. 1934) is, like Ashby, chiefly concerned with the problems of contemporary America, though he has made some films about its immediate past. He moved to films from television and made a promising debut with **The Slender Thread** (1965). More than thirteen years seem to separate it from *Coming Home*, and that is partly because it appears to belong to the modestly crusading films of the Fifties. Sterling Silliphant wrote the screenplay, which for much of the time is a duologue between a would-be suicide (Anne Bancroft) and the doctor (Sidney Poitier) in the 'Crisis Clinic', at the other end of the phone. **This Property Is Condemned** (1966) was produced by John Houseman for Seven Arts, Ray Stark and Paramount, to their eventual shame. Of the fourteen writers who are reported to have worked on the screenplay three are credited, including Fred Coe and Francis Ford Coppola, who later observed that he thought his script better than the one eventually used, 'but to take a really lovely one-act play and make it into a full-length film with movie-stars is a ridiculous idea in the first place.' The play was by Tennessee Williams, and it now provides only a framing device for some drama supposedly in the style of Williams, featuring Robert

Jack Nicholson and Randy Quaid in *The Last Detail*, directed by Hal Ashby. It belongs to that rare group of films which looks below the surface to find the emptiness of modern life – having looked where it might be found instead of where some polemic film-maker would like it to be: and if these sailors' lives are empty, it is significant that the sea is never mentioned.

In Hollywood the Director is King

Redford and an even more negative Natalie Wood. Neither seems to have been given help by Pollack, whose direction lurches all over the place.

It had improved considerably by the time he came to make **They Shoot Horses, Don't They?** (1969) and **Jeremiah Johnson** (1972). Both, nevertheless, are weak-kneed attempts to analyse the America of some years ago. The first, based on Horace McCoy's novel about a dance marathon during the Depression era, has a remarkable performance by Jane Fonda; the second is a tribute to the pioneer spirit written by an old Hollywood hand, Edward Anhalt, and a new one, John Milius. Its star again is Mr Redford, a buddy of Pollack's from his acting days, and it is the second of their several films together. Redford was teamed with Barbra Streisand in **The Way We Were** (1973), an exercise in more recent nostalgia, moving its stars from college in the Thirties to disillusion, fame, break-up and political activity in the Fifties. Arthur Laurents wrote it, with an eye more on star appeal than on honest comment. **The Electric Horseman** (1979) starts well, with its portraits of an over-the-hill rodeo star (Redford) and Las Vegas. He sells himself to some button-down-mind sponsors, and few films have managed to express so pungently the ambivalence of the world of hype, but as he lights out after his horse – his last link with integrity – and a female reporter (Jane Fonda) hopes to exploit him, one is reminded how far Hollywood can retrogress (for the situation was much better used in *Mr Deeds Goes to Town*).

Pollack's most accomplished film, **Absence of Malice** (1981), might be so because he is working from an excellent screenplay by Kurt Luedtke which, like several of the early Eighties, was based on fact. A reporter (Sally Field) on a Miami newspaper learns that an F.B.I. man (Bob Balaban) is trying to implicate Gallagher (Paul Newman) in the murder of the leader of the longshoremen's union; Gallagher has Mafia relations, but is otherwise a respectable warehouseman who is caused a great deal of grief by the tactics of the press and the F.B.I. The film confronts these less to question them than to create tension, and it is gratifying to see a thriller whose twists do not depend on murder or violence. The performances are superb,

though the film would undoubtedly have been effective with an actor of less heroic stature than Newman. Three epilogues were shot to show the development of his relationship with Miss Field – happy, unhappy and indeterminate; I cannot say that I liked the one chosen.★

Pollack's favourite interpreter, Robert Redford, turned director for **Ordinary People** (1980), which dishonourably confirmed Hollywood's misconceptions about itself by being awarded Oscars for Best Film and Best Direction. Alvin Sargent's screenplay, based on a novel by Judith Guest, probes beneath the surface of the apparent happiness of one 'average' upper-income bracket family and finds something rotten. That something is Mom (Mary Tyler Moore, known for her niceness in T.V. situation comedy), just as it was in some equally hollow plays and novels, e.g. 'All Fall Down', 'There Must Be a Pony', of the Fifties. The subject matter was presumably chosen as the least likely to have interested an actor considered one of the industry's golden boys.

Paul Newman has directed a number of films on similar themes, with more skill and an insight which proves that years of stardom had not impaired his observation – even if both **Rachel, Rachel** (1968) and **The Effect of Gamma Rays on Man-in-the-Moon Marigolds** (1972) were primarily designed as showcases for the considerable talents of his wife, Joanne Woodward. *Rachel, Rachel*, written by Stewart Stern from a novel by Margaret Laurence, is about a 35-year-old spinster schoolteacher (Miss Woodward) who feels 'This is my last ascending summer – everything from now on is just downhill . . . to the grave.' Accordingly she loses, with no particular emotion, her virginity to a city boy (James Olson); she says farewell to her lesbian friend (Estelle Parsons); and finds the courage to leave her aged, demanding mother. The title of the second film reveals its writer, Paul Zindel, as a follower of Tennessee Williams, and its monstrous mother makes the lady of 'The Glass Menagerie' seem like Snow White in comparison: but the role is well-sustained by

★The old practice of sneak-preview screenings was revived in the late Seventies, with alternative endings shown to test audience response. It was more expeditious to film several different conclusions than face the loss of the whole investment because prospective audiences left the cinema dissatisfied.

Miss Woodward until a disappointing ending. Both films are set in Connecticut and are alive to the continuity of rural life as well as such matters as earning a living and teacher-pupil relationships.

Gilbert Cates has intermittently shown himself as perceptive a director as Newman, and **Summer Wishes, Winter Dreams** (1973) has more than Miss Woodward in common with the two films in which Newman directed her. Stewart Stern wrote it, largely in the vein of his adaptation of *Rachel, Rachel*, though some jarring moments remind us that he also wrote *Rebel Without a Cause*. Rita (Woodward) suffers the death of her mother (Sylvia Sidney), and finds herself nearing a nervous breakdown on a trip to Europe with her husband (Martin Balsam). **I Never Sang for My Father** (1970) is an eloquent study of a man (Gene Hackman) attempting to come to terms with his father (Melvyn Douglas) at that delicate point when the old man has lost his wife. Robert Anderson adapted from his own play, which was indifferent on the stage. Cates brings compassion to the sad and serious themes with which he deals: the death of a parent; the discovery that an 'ordinary' person can be a failure; physical love between the middle-aged; the realisation that a son has grown up gay; the consequences of taking and giving nothing in return. Both films, unfortunately but understandably, failed to draw the public, and Cates has since worked mainly in T.V.

Robert Ellis Miller (b. 1927) has also worked chiefly in T.V., and to see most of his films is to understand why; but his version of Carson McCullers's **The Heart Is a Lonely Hunter** (1968) is very fine – as is the screenplay by Thomas C. Ryan, another gentleman with an otherwise unimposing list of credits. There are moments of stridency and self-consciousness, but the only other faults, in what must have been a difficult job of adaptation, stem from the novel itself. The small town – it was Selma, Alabama – is remarkably well rendered by James Wong Howe's camera; and Singer, the deaf-mute catalyst around whom these lonely, isolated people move, has a superlative interpreter in Alan Arkin, well supported by Sondra Locke as the plain and dreamy Mick, Stacy Keach as the drunk, Blount, and Chuck McCann as the 'dummy'. These characters have been

taken from the hothouse atmosphere of the book and out into the sunny air, and thereby becoming all the more touching.

Few claims can be made on behalf of William Friedkin (b. 1939), who caught attention with **The Night They Raided Minsky's** (1968), after some years in T.V. and two mediocre films. This one, which is enjoyable, proclaims itself a celebration of the famous burlesque house (except that the 'girls' were older and slower than in the film), and the plot about an Amish girl (Britt Ekland) taking refuge there is, to say the least, unusual. The direction appears to be frenetic, but its editor, Ralph Rosenblum, claims in his memoir that the film was dying on its feet until he rescued it in the cutting room. There are few movies more stagey than **The Boys in the Band** (1970), based on Mart Crowley's play about an all-gay New York birthday party, but **The French Connection** (1971) was awarded some justifiable Oscars – Best Picture, Best Direction and Best Actor (Gene Hackman). New York in this instance is wonderfully present, and its police department, rounding up a drugs syndicate, had seldom been so convincingly portrayed. Ernest Tidyman wrote it, from a novel based on fact, and one's chief reservations devolve upon the fact that thirty years earlier it would have made a suitable B-movie.

Paul Newman has directed his wife, Joanne Woodward, in a number of films remarkable for their quiet understanding of everyday life – all the more remarkable since it is doubtful whether either of them have been able to lead ordinary lives since they became Hollywood stars over twenty years ago. This is *Rachel, Rachel*, the only one of these films the public greatly liked, but then it says much for the Newmans that they made no attempt at box-office concessions – proving in that more adventurous than many younger talents.

Friedkin had an even bigger success with **The Exorcist** (1973), a sensational and silly account of demonic possession, and then followed it with a gigantic failure, **Sorcerer** (1977), a $21 million remake of *Le Salaire de la Peur*. He made an effort to regain favour by combining elements of two of his successful films with **Cruising** (1980), which, in fact, had been planned and then dropped ten years earlier by Philip D'Antoni, the producer of *The French Connection*. As in that film, its hero (Al Pacino) is a ruthless cop, and the boys in the band this time are the gays of the leather bars. Much shouting was heard from gay activists about its sensationalism, but I should have thought that the image presented is far healthier and better P.R. than the usual stereotyped drag queens of most films on this subject. The story, if exploitive, is no sillier than most thrillers about rough, tough New York of the present day, and it has a surrealistic ending as two men undress for either murder or sex, or both. Doubtless the effect was accidental, but since the cop gets 'corrupted' by the gay life, what are we to make of Friedkin's surely apocryphal Precinct, where a huge black cop sits around in jock-strap and Stetson just waiting to beat people up?

Mark Rydell (b. 1934) also has an uneven group of credits. None of his earlier films prepared us for the predominantly sour qualities of **The Rose** (1979), which was nevertheless partly devised to revive the musical form. More importantly it marked the first film vehicle for Bette Midler. It was not a traditional musical, since in recent years audiences had been far more sympathetic towards rock/pop concerts filmed as they were staged. Rose (Midler) is a lady in a whirlwind, or, as the latest of her casual lovers (Frederick Forrest) puts it, her 'life is like a grenade range'. Her highs are sex (including an innocent lesbian embrace), her audiences, singing in a drag club, and her lows innumerable: and to keep her going between the two, there are the pills and the booze, both responsible for many of the lows. Since she is simply unable to cope, we may recall Judy Garland, though the acknowledged source is the life of Janis Joplin; the villain of the piece is her conniving manager, who understands her well enough to play dangerously with her, but he is also

ripping her off – and it was a clever stroke to cast Alan Bates, looking cosily protective as he had done in *An Unmarried Woman* (q.v.). The film does not bother to tell us how she got this way, nor does it need to: Rydell is as completely in command of Rose's world as are Bill Kerby and Bo Goldman of her language. We are supposed to care, and we do: the sorrows of this suffering lady affected audiences as those of Mildred Pierce had done a generation earlier. This film is probably the more honest of the two, but in each case a certain mythologising is involved.

On Golden Pond (1981) proved Rydell's ability to change style as he sought different audiences, since this self-consciously lyrical film was very popular. The subject of Ernest Thompson's meretricious screenplay, from his own play, is old age, and all it really has to say is that old people are not as stuffy about sex and four-letter words as we all thought. Katharine Hepburn and Jane Fonda are mother and daughter; Henry Fonda, in his only film with his daughter – and the last that he made – won an Oscar, as did Miss Hepburn. He is superb as a crusty, querulous, outspoken old man, and so is Dabney Coleman as his daughter's lover.

Not least because of Miss Midler's performance, *The Rose* is an improvement on the last variation on the theme, **Lady Sings the Blues** (1972), in which a small, plastic Diana Ross tried to impersonate Billie Holliday. It stands halfway between *The Rose* and the artificial show business biopics of the past, and is interesting mainly because it is one of the few about a black artist (a considerable advance, for instance, on *St Louis Blues*, which in 1958 expended a superb black cast on a cheapjack biography of W. C. Handy); but, as produced by Motown the black-orientated record company, for Paramount, it is only too happy to distort in the case against whitey. Holliday did not, as far as is known, witness a lynching, as in the film, and she was not turned on to drugs by whites, but by her first, black husband. Sidney J. Furie directed, with a certain eye to period, the best of his uneven American films.

Of the British directors who have worked in Hollywood at this time, Peter Yates (b. 1929) most nearly qualifies as a native. After his third film, *Robbery*, he was offered **Bullitt** (1968), in which a San

Francisco cop (Steve McQueen) discovers the links between an underworld syndicate and a political boss (Robert Vaughn); McQueen's convincing performance and the car chases helped to make it enormously popular, and car chases, a staple of movie thrills from the very beginning, took on a new lease of life – with diminishing returns as every other film followed suit. Yates became a name director, so that much was expected of **John and Mary** (1969), since he was teamed with Dustin Hoffman, fresh from *The Graduate*, and Mia Farrow, from *Rosemary's Baby*. A respectful press was followed by public indifference, due partly to its leading players. Hoffman gives his customary impersonation of an amiable rabbit; she, playing a lovable kook, has baby-eyes, baby-voice and baby-haircut. Mervyn Jones's original novel was set in London, and it was a further mistake to have an English writer, John Mortimer, attempt the New York idiom. Yates's career went into diminuendo, but undeservedly so in the case of **The Friends of Eddie Coyle** (1973), whose bank raids and car crashes pall as they begin but which is otherwise admirable. Robert Mitchum as a petty hoodlum and fence is at his best, and Richard Jordan is equally brilliant as a plainclothes Treasury Agent. George V. Higgins, who wrote the original novel, is a Boston lawyer, and his view of crime has been honestly and unpretentiously rendered by Paul Monash, producer and writer. One thinks back to *Panic in the Streets* rather than to contemporaries like *Slither* or *The Sting*, but that is partly because of Yates's use of location – which in this case is Boston itself. The portrait of Bloomington, Indiana, in **Breaking Away** (1979) is treasurable, and one reason why the film attracted more audience affection than any in years. Bloomington seems a nice place to live, its principal drawback being that town and gown do not get on: of the four young heroes, one (Dennis Quaid) is openly resentful of the privileges accorded to the college boys. A number of clashes between the two sides suggests that Steve Tesich, the writer, may be on the verge of checking out the American class system as in no film since *Five Easy Pieces* (q.v.); he settles instead for the contrived and cute, but he is at least humorous with it – and since his umour is, if not original, likeable, and

since Yates approaches it in the manner of Capra rather than, say, Blake Edwards, all is permissible. Capra comes to mind, since audiences are rooting for the climactic cycle race to be won by the foremost (Dennis Christopher) of the young heroes.

Another British director whose films have been made chiefly in the U.S. is Anthony Harvey (b. 1931), and the first, though made in Britain, is set in the New York subway. **Dutchman** (1967) is based on LeRoi Jones's one act play about a smartly-dressed black man (Al Freeman Jr), who becomes prey to a loud-mouthed, loudly-dressed white girl (Shirley Knight). Since the piece is probably symbolical, and therefore significant, and since it is certainly well directed, Harvey was assigned to **The Lion in Winter** (1968), written by James Goldman from his play about the marriage of Henry II (Peter O'Toole) to Eleanor of Aquitaine (Katharine Hepburn). The tragic marriage has been reduced to a prolonged slanging match, and these complex people have become a wry prankster and an overemotional hell-cat, at their worst laughing over the wars they have waged against each other or bowing to the courtiers while trading insults *sotto voce* in the manner of the stars of the Thirties, e.g. Davis and Howard in *It's Love I'm After*. The public found this appealing, but if Harvey controls the wayward elements with skill, his subsequent films explain why he has since worked mostly in television.

Roman Polanski also made the transatlantic crossing, after a sojourn in Britain. Having left Poland he had paused in France, and we may assume both **Repulsion** (1965) and **Cul-de-Sac** (1966) to have been prepared in France, since Polanski's co-writer, Gerard Brach, and the leading ladies are French. *Repulsion* is a landmark in world cinema, if, intentionally, a repulsive one. It is the case-book history of a girl (Catherine Deneuve) who becomes mad and homicidal, with no one around to care, including apparently the director himself, and no probing of causes, beyond the final shot. It is Grand Guignol, the first horror film for grown-ups: we may never imagine ourselves being sucked of blood in Transylvania, but we may perhaps accept the departure from reality in a large, silent, untidy London flat. It is a film suitable only for psychopaths who do

In Hollywood the Director is King

Catherine Deneuve in *Repulsion*, directed by Roman Polanski, which confirmed his brilliance on his arrival from his native Poland. It was made in Britain, and he has since worked in the U.S., France and Italy, usually with American backing (he is no longer able to work in Hollywood after a misdemeanour caused a jail sentence passed by a California court). That did not prevent subsequent Oscar nominations for his last film to date, *Tess*, nor, probably, will it prevent Hollywood investing again in his remarkable talent.

not need it, and in the name of humanity should not see it: but its power could not be denied, nor the tension, nor the mastery with which it has been put together. *Cul-de-Sac* is a reversion to the mood of *A Knife in the Water*, slightly more humorous and perceptive, but eventually as lacking in real substance. It is also a Pinteresque fantasy, perhaps influenced by 'The Birthday Party', where two strangers turn up to menace an ordinary family. The two here are definitely crooks, and the menage consists of a bald, fussy, middle-aged man (Donald Pleasence) with transvestite tendencies and his luscious young wife (Françoise Dorléac): they, and the setting, Lindisfarne Island, are used cleverly.

Polanski was summoned to the U.S. by William Castle, producer of a number of cheap horror films, but **Rosemary's Baby** (1968), though of the same genre, is something more than that as based on Ira Levin's novel. It was a big success for all three of them, and not only with addicts of this particular form of mayhem. The pregnant heroine (Mia Farrow) is beset on all sides by people she believes to be witches, including her husband (John Cassavetes): that suspicion falls on him is perhaps the most cunning of Levin's inventions. The unthinkable impinges on the daily round to the extent that sanity is at stake: as in *Repulsion*, mundane walls have voices and therefore hidden terrors. The trump card is that everything is logically worked out:

our worst forebodings are realised. Only to be regretted is that the film's popularity caused an unending, unrewarding and relentless stream of imitations.

Polanski himself determined to film **Macbeth** (1972), with the cooperation of Kenneth Tynan, co-adapter, and *Playboy* magazine, financier. The visual conception is considerable, but as in Zeffirelli's *Romeo and Juliet* an ability to speak the verse was a talent denied the leads, Jon Finch and Francesca Annis, both chosen for their youth, but not, on this evidence, for any other qualities. The remainder of the cast, with the honourable exception of the Macduff of Terence Bayler, would seem more at home in your local bank. What attracted Polanski to the play, as might have been expected, were the dark forces, the supernatural, and the evil spirits; but there is more to the play than that. Recalled to the U.S. for **Chinatown** (1974), he ran for its producer, Robert Evans, a copy of *Che?*, that he had recently finished in Italy 'which he thought was terrific . . . [but] it was the worst picture★I ever saw in my life' said Evans, adding that Polanski could be brilliant 'if channelled properly.' Certainly Polanski responded to this material, with Jack Nicholson as the private eye who uncovers a nest of civic corruption. Robert Towne wrote it after *The Last Detail*, a film that owes nothing to old movies: this one owes everything. It was a huge success, but Polanski did not choose to be channelled further and went to France to make **The Tenant** (1976), written with Brach from a novel by the appropriately named Roland Topor. It defies description, if only because it is too painful to bear thinking about. The ad slogan, 'No one does it to you like Roman Polanski', turned out to be less inane than might have been supposed.

Polanski dedicated **Tess** (1979) to his dead wife Sharon Tate – murdered by the Manson gang in 1969 – because it was she who suggested that he make a film of Thomas Hardy's novel 'Tess of the d'Urbervilles'. In the meanwhile he had been searching for material to make a movie not unlike *Love Story*, and one may suppose that he thought that Hardy's novel might be an upmarket version: but in the event Polanski seems to have chosen it to

---

★I can think of only a few worse.

make his own version of *L'Albero degli Zoccoli*. It was made in France, since Britain has an extradition treaty with the U.S. and in 1977 Polanski had pleaded partial guilt to a sex-offence with a minor and had subsequently fled California while on bail: but while the terrain of Normandy and Brittany can look like Wessex, their buildings do not – and eventually the interiors look as French as the exteriors. As with his *Macbeth*, Polanski has undercast the leading roles – Nastassia Kinski as Tess, Leigh Lawson as Alexander Stoke-d'Urberville, her seducer, and Peter Firth as Angel Clare, the parson's son whom she marries. But far more crucial to the film's failure is Polanski's misunderstanding of Victorian England and the British class system. It is the latter which imbues Tess with her false pride, which causes her to accept seduction, leading therefore to her tragic conclusion. Tess has become only another film heroine, and Angel merely another priggish husband: and there is one horrendous interpolation, the slogan 'Blessed be the Merciful' painted on a gate as he bids farewell to her, as if audiences had failed to grasp the point. Nevertheless, the film is not the long slog it might have been and doubtless the popularity of the B.B.C.'s 'Classic Serial' – 'Masterpiece Theatre' in the U.S. – helped the film to a wider audience than Schlesinger's superior *Far From the Madding Crowd*.

Milos Forman, having left Czechoslovakia at the time of French investment in *The Firemen's Ball*, gravitated towards the American film industry but found himself in the midst of several years' negotiations before getting the backing for the film he wanted to do, **Taking Off** (1971), a comedy about the generation gap. He was originally interested in the subject from the point of view of the young, but made the film from the point of view of the parents – who are earnest, confused and well-meaning as they tentatively sample such habits as smoking marijuana, which they hope will give them an insight into the youngsters' world. The film was not sufficiently successful to guarantee the freedom essential to this director, and it was not until four years had passed that he directed another film, **One Flew Over the Cuckoo's Nest** (1975) – at the invitation of Michael Douglas, son of the actor Kirk Douglas. The latter had played in a

Broadway dramatisation of Ken Kesey's novel, but had been unable to find backers for a film of it; his son sought the support of Fantasy Records and the project advanced once Jack Nicholson agreed to play the lead. The screenplay is by Lawrence Hauben and Bo Goldman, though Forman's improvisatory methods are so extreme that the credited photographer, Haskell Wexler, quit before shooting ended. The film won every major Oscar – the first one to do so since *It Happened One Night*, forty-two years earlier – and became extremely popular, partly due to the cuckoo of the title, Randle P. McMurphy (Nicholson), and his battles to the death, virtually, with the ward-sister, Nurse Ratched (Louise Fletcher). Both players approach their roles by stealth: she, desiccated, unimaginative, claiming the support of discipline and her own conception of the silent majority and he a good Joe with malice towards none but with sharks' teeth when he smiles at her. He is one of the 'loonies' in this latter-day *Snake Pit*, an attempt to understand the confusions and ignominies of the mentally ill, though the film's appeal – if not the point of the original novel – seems to be its allegorical statement on the underprivileged and on authority's control over them.

Forman's sureness and energy are almost miraculous, an augury for his entanglement with the sticky subject of **Hair** (1979), a Broadway phenomenon of the

Jack Nicholson in Milos Forman's *One Flew Over the Cuckoo's Nest*, one of the most popular films of the Seventies, which proves, along with *All the President's Men* and maybe just a dozen others, that when the public is offered a film on the subject of sufficient importance, well-crafted and intelligently written, it could not care less about the feeble horror films and derivative comedies so much more often on offer. Two further examples are *The Rose* and *Melvin and Howard,* both of which, like Forman's film, have the name of Bo Goldman on the credits – and that may or may not be a coincidence.

1207

In Hollywood the Director is King

Sixties whose time had long since gone. There were considerable doubts about its merits at the time, seemingly confirmed when revivals in London and New York, not long before the film came out, disappeared with almost indecent speed. Critics were hardly more enthusiastic about the material in the film, though Forman and his collaborators, realising that that had dated, had done a considerable job of revamping; his work at least was much admired. However, neither the generation that had flocked to the theatrical production, nor the current movie audience, was interested.

Ragtime (1981) is based upon E. L. Doctorow's popular novel of life in America from 1905 to the First World War, a panoramic and fanciful blending of fiction and such people as Houdini, Stanford White and J. P. Morgan, many of whom have been dropped from the screenplay by Michael Weller. The rights were bought by Dino de Laurentiis, who engaged Robert Altman (q.v.) to direct, but changed his mind after the failure of *Buffalo Bill and the Indians*. In separate articles in *New York* magazine David Denby and William Wolf argued that Altman would have been a more suitable choice than Forman, who is a far greater director. But they are right in view of the result, which is unconvincing in historical detail, in situation and in virtually every respect. The chief theme concerns a white family and its involvement with a black pianist (Howard E. Rollins) who refuses to accept an inferior position in society and eventually becomes an urban terrorist – a not inappropriate term since most people behave as people do today. Forman, who has been alive to the nuances of American behaviour, on this occasion is not; he and the writer fought with de Laurentiis over the actual contents, and it is worth observing that of these three principals only Weller is American. Altman had earlier said that de Laurentiis had been primarily interested in the book because of its theme of black revenge. The film cost $25 million, but few went to see it, despite the return (after twenty years of retirement) of the eighty-year-old James Cagney to play the New York police chief.

The failure of *Ragtime* has not affected Hollywood's interest in Forman, who is making *Amadeus*, based on a popular London and Broadway play. Polanski also might get American backing for most projects which interest him. Probably both of them and Peter Yates have more in common with the next generation of American film-makers, but in this matter of chronology I have preferred to place them with those of their own age group, brought up on the movies of the Thirties. Whereas most of the directors we have discussed in this chapter came from television, which hardly existed when they were young, the American directors of the next generation probably saw their first movies on television. So it seems appropriate to pause and consider their current reputations as they were, in some instances, overtaken by the new influx of talent.

On past form Stanley Kubrick is more than likely to jump back after two failures, while Arthur Penn, currently unfashionable, will always be a more interesting director than the over-productive Blake Edwards. Like him, the veterans Don Siegel and Richard Brooks have an established pattern of failures and successes; Sam Peckinpah's career as a leading proponent of extreme violence – which ultimately repulsed audiences – is a special case. So are those (in films, that is) of Nichols and May and of Bob Fosse. George Roy Hill, Arthur Hiller, Norman Jewison, Frankenheimer, William Friedkin, Franklin Schaffner and Robert Mulligan have receded into the background somewhat; Herbert Ross, Hal Ashby, Alan J. Pakula, Martin Ritt and Sidney Lumet have not – and public acceptance of their work has been as varied as that of their contemporaries. Ross seems to be regarded as one of the few reliable directors of the lighter material, while Ritt and Lumet are held in esteem for the level of, and the social content in, most of their work. I have expressed my own admiration for the efforts, or some of them, of all these people. There were a number of 'arty' disasters; a number of commercial pictures have been discussed (and others ignored). Kubrick remains an unusual case: his last three feeble films cannot hide the enduring quality present in so many of his earlier ones.

42

The Movie Brats

THE EXPRESSION 'the movie brats' was coined to describe the young Hollywood film-makers who made such a splash in the late Seventies. I hope those who coined it will permit me to extend it to include the directors who were compulsive cinema-goers in childhood and went on to study at film school. That is no more true of all those to be discussed in this chapter than my statement at the end of the last chapter that the film-makers considered there had worked in television; but it is true enough.

It may be said that a new generation of American directors begins with Francis (Ford) Coppola (b. 1939). He was certainly for a time the most successful of them. Like many of the others he studied film (at U.C.L.A.) and entered the industry by way of one of its less eminent fringes, working for Roger Corman. In 1963 Corman arranged for him to direct *Dementia 13*, a low budget horror film, after which Coppola gained a slight reputation within the industry for helping on other people's scripts. Four years later he was sufficiently well known for Seven Arts to provide backing for **You're a Big Boy Now** (1967), which, apart from some established names, was to be made with friends on minimum pay and on New York locations – in place of the London of David Benedictus's original novel. The style came from Britain too, for it was derived from Richard Lester, but the film is nonetheless very taking, as it follows a sweet nineteen-year-old (Peter Kastner) trying to lose his virginity under the tutelage of a suave colleague (Tony Bill) at the Public Library. The girl (Elizabeth Hartman) he fancies is a kook, and virtually all the characters, including the monstrous parents (Geraldine Page, Rip Torn) exemplify the manners prevalent at the time.

Coppola became, in his own expression, a 'now' director, entrusted by Warner-Seven Arts with **Finian's Rainbow** (1968), a twenty-year-old Broadway musical whose mixture of whimsy and message had either defied adaptation or unnerved the various studios which had owned it. Although it is credited to the original authors, Coppola says that he wrote the screenplay; the piece is to some extent resistible, with Tommy Steele as a leprechaun and Petula Clark as a colleen. Keenan Wynn is good as a bigoted senator, as is Al Freeman as the black man (the hero's buddy) he is bigoted about. Fred Astaire could not be bad if he tried, but a puff of wind would have wafted him off screen; the little dancing which he does was spoilt by Warners, who liked the film so much that they blew it up to 70 mm. The critics agreed with Warners, but the public did not – because, Coppola considered, it was sent out to compete with the leaden *Funny Girl* and cost, in contrast, a mere $3½ million. The dances were improvised on the back lot, in sylvan settings, and the cast takes as naturally to those as to movement. The piece is also sunny and pretty, and it put what audiences there were into a cheery mood.

Warners were so pleased that they agreed to back Coppola's own company, a dream that became an occasional reality. Its first setback came when Warners withdrew after the failure of *THX 1138*, directed by Coppola's friend George Lucas (q.v.) and **The Rain People** (1969), directed by Coppola himself. Release of both was delayed, and *The Rain People* did not appear until after *Easy Rider* had started

The Movie Brats

Al Pacino, seated, and Marlon Brando in Coppola's *The Godfather*, a film about the Mafia that became the most financially successful ever made – calling, therefore, for a sequel. It seems a long time ago that these sequels started, undisguised and boldly proclaiming, as in this case, *Part II*. The conclusions to be drawn are not kind to the industry, suggesting poverty of ideas and a desire to turn a quick buck; and very few sequels have been remotely as good as the originals.

the vogue for 'road' movies. The message of this one is too heavily loaded and too simple: a girl (Shirley Knight) runs away from home and husband, but finds that she cannot escape responsibility when, out on the open road, she becomes involved with a brain-damaged hitch-hiker (James Caan) and a cop (Robert Duvall).

Coppola's work on the script of *Patton* was one reason he was assigned to the script and direction of **The Godfather** (1972), based on Mario Puzo's bestseller.★ Coppola could not turn its dross into gold, but he tightened the strands of this tenuous Mafia tale and made it watchable for three hours – with, admittedly, the excitements inherent in gang warfare, family vendettas, shoot-outs and such. The film's popularity – outstripping, at new admis-

★After the film came out the book's publisher complained to *Variety* that it had been well-received by book reviewers, but that film critics invariably referred to the novel as 'trashy'.

sion rates, any previous movie – occasioned a sequel, **The Godfather Part II** (1974), defended by Coppola on the ground that he knew from his own background that much more could be said about Italian immigration to the U.S. Thus, having covered the war years and just after, he had to go either forward or backwards for his saga, and he does both simultaneously, with Robert de Niro, in the flashbacks, preparing to become the aged Marlon Brando, who had played the Mafia chief in the first film. The film did so poorly in the U.S. that Paramount hoped that an Oscar or so would improve business, and it won a handful (this is the only time an original and a sequel have won Best Picture Oscars): but the response at the box office was only marginally improved thereby.

The screenplay for **The Conversation** (1974) had been prepared long before, and now that Coppola could get backing the topic was more timely – since the matter of wire-tapping and bugging had been brought into prominence by Watergate. Coppola himself said that he set out to make a film about privacy but found himself moving into that realm explored in *The Rain People*, i.e. responsibility. Despite their undoubted merits as director's films, each exposes an intellectual bankruptcy. *The Conversation* is as hollow as a drum. Its premise depends on a private operator (Gene Hackman) overhearing one particular, dull, conversation, and on the strength of one line – 'He'd kill us if he got the chance' – becoming obsessed with an impending murder. Conceivably a lot of conversations might lead to paranoia, but that would be moving too far from *Blow-Up*, the obvious model; instead the lone phrase leads to the wretched Hackman, being alone and unloved.

Apocalypse Now (1979) was another project which had waited for years: during its three years in production the cost rose to $31,100,000 – unsurpassed since *Cleopatra*, though some even more expensive films were in progress. A number of foreign market territories had been pre-sold, but none with an advance of more than a million dollars. United Artists put a ceiling of $20 million on their investment, which included a huge loan to Coppola, whose own involvement was $18 million – which meant placing most of his personal property at risk. The gist of his promotion was that the film is above criticism, since it is an honest endeavour to make a statement on the Vietnam War: 'I know the film is really rich and multi-levelled,' he told *Variety*, 'It's an experimental one-to-one relationship between the audience and the war. You can only dream about participating in a film like that. I feel I really showed that there could be a whole other kind of cinema . . . There are open questions in the film. The ending is like a Jungian exercise.' He lashed out at the lukewarm reception by American critics, but few would deny the salient point made by Vincent Canby in *The New York Times*: 'It's a serious attempt to deal with the manifold meanings of the American involvement in Vietnam but . . . is it to be a Philistine to suggest that though there is nothing wrong with personal movie-making, there is something slightly askew with personal movie-making on the grandiose scale of *Apocalypse Now*?' The source of the script, by Coppola and John Milius, is Conrad's 'The Heart of Darkness', but most of it is *The African Queen*, with an ending evocative of *The Black Watch* or any Tarzan movie where the hero stumbles across a mad ruler in the middle of the jungle. The character of the hero (Martin Sheen), sent on an assassination mission, is brother to some who have seen service with Graham Greene. Ichikawa's pacifist movies have also been plundered, as is, at one point, *Dersu Uzala*. What Coppola means by multi-levelled is that it is *Star Wars* (q.v.) with a message – since the cultural references within the script are to 'The Golden Bough', Eliot and Weston's 'From Ritual to Romance'; British critics, recognising them, were less flattered than amused. A photograph of Charles Manson reminds us of a time – 1968 – of American madness, of flower power and gutter-level philosophising. The ending is not, as far as I can see, a Jungian exercise, but a way of stopping a film which, having reached Kurtz's camp, has been getting gradually sillier. Up till then, it offered a number of powerful and imaginative sequences, and, it does hold our interest for most of its two and a half hours. It is an honest statement on Vietnam – on confusion, fear, a living nightmare, a world upended; and if Coppola is not, nor ever will be, Ichikawa, he is clearly to be attended to in preference to Michael Cimino and *The Deer Hunter* (q.v.).

The film's box-office performance was not such as to relieve Coppola entirely of the financial difficulties involved in its production, thus delaying (at least) his plans to help other film-makers. He had, however, already been instrumental in United Artists handling the first feature of a documentary director, Carroll Ballard, **The Black Stallion** (1979). Based on an apparently classic novel by Walter Farley, published in 1941, it starts with a fire at sea, which strands a boy and a horse on a desert island – and there they stay for the movie's first hour, which is as magical as anything in the history of movies. The second half, after they are rescued and transported home, is of necessity more conventional, but overall this is the best children's film since *The Wizard of Oz*.

Coppola's 'empire' collapsed as he filmed **One from the Heart** (1982), a musical about 'ordinary' people set in a grandiose, stylised and studio-recreated Las Vegas, which cost over $24 million. The film was completed through various loans, from companies and individuals, some arriving only on payday. In the face of industry indifference, Coppola himself booked the film into Radio City Music Hall for previews, but when public and critical reaction was the same Paramount dropped it. It was taken up by Columbia, but only by minor distributors in foreign territories. Something similar happened with **Hammett** (1982), also produced by Coppola's Zoetrope Studios, but he could have had little hope of that saving the situation, since after seeing a roughcut he observed (reputedly) that it was the worst film he had ever seen. The trouble starts with Zoetrope, since one of his colleagues bought Joe Gore's novel and offered the direction successively to Nicolas Roeg, François Truffaut and, on the basis of *Der Amerikanische Freund*, Wim Wenders. None of them, despite that American friend, would seem to be the obvious choice for a fast-moving Thirties-type thriller, but where the book, apart from being a good pastiche of Dashiell Hammett, was flashy, and second-rate, Wenders's film is flashy, ponderous, arty and sixth-rate. The plot has been thrown out and one borrowed from Chandler's 'The Little Sister'; and a latter-day Mr

The Movie Brats

Guttmann is introduced in the person of Roy Kinnear. As he insultingly offers a lengthy explanation of the word 'gunsel' one reflects how far movie thrillers have declined since *The Maltese Falcon*.

Another young director who entered films through the good graces of Roger Corman is Peter Bogdanovich (b. 1939), who had won a degree of national fame as a critic with a fond appreciation of old movies. **Targets** (1968) mixes old movies – including one of Corman's – with the type of subject of which Corman approved, i.e. horror, but Bogdanovich cleverly used a fool-proof modern topic. A foreword notes that '7000 Americans were killed by gun-fire in 1967', with a further reference to the Texas sniper of 1966 and a call for the reformation of the gun laws. The mingling of two separate stories, we learnt later, was due to expediency, but the equation between phoney 'gothic' horror movies and a young man berserk with a gun works well enough. There are a number of fairly good jokes in the sequences between the aged star, Boris Karloff, playing himself, and the young screenwriter, Bogdanovich – also, more or less, as himself. The sniper (Tim O'Kelly), in contrast, is the all-American jock, with short hair, in sneakers and pale-coloured chinos.

The two, star and sniper, come together in a drive-in cinema: Bogdanovich not only has fun with it but he makes the most concise of all movie statements on public violence. Paramount took over the film for distribution, proof to a movie-oriented generation that it was not only in France that movie lovers were able to make their own films. Bogdanovich had demonstrated a new way into the industry, which resulted in a number of imitators, including John Carpenter and Brian da Palma, who decided that they could draw attention to themselves by splashing the screen with blood.

Bogdanovich himself turned to the subject of growing up in a small Texas town in the Fifties, **The Last Picture Show** (1971), and then to a fairly witless piece of slapstick, **What's Up Doc?** (1972), written by David Newman, Robert Benton and Buck Henry, with Barbra Streisand and Ryan O'Neal vainly striving to imitate the great comedy players of the Thirties – and if any film can be said to have begun that soon-wearisome business of referring to old Hollywood, this is it. *The Last Picture Show* had been in black-and-white, in imitation of the old movies: and so is **Paper Moon** (1973), a film as beguiling as any ever made. It is set in the Thirties,

That directors are now as publicised and feted as the stars does have a reflex effect if a film fails, for Peter Bogdanovich's three successive flops were as much talked about – though obviously few went to see them – as the three hit movies which preceded them. It was in view of the publicity that Billy Wilder observed that he couldn't remember when Hollywood had been so united as over the failures – but few could have been pleased, recalling the pleasure Bogdanovich had given everyone with *Paper Moon*, featuring Tatum O'Neal.

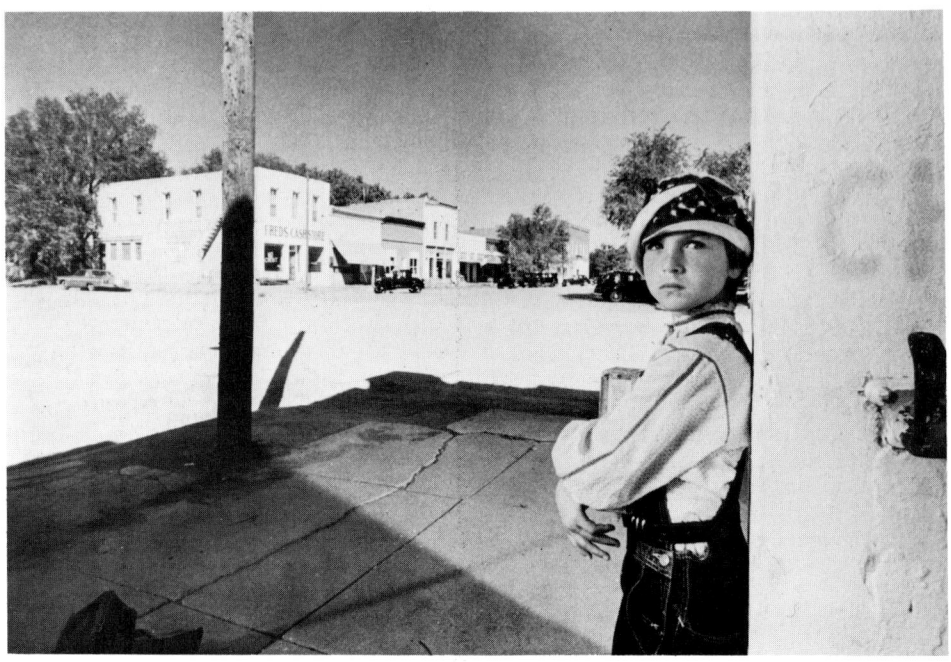

written by Alvin Sargent from a novel by Joe David Brown, and concerns a confidence trickster (O'Neal), who finds himself constantly outsmarted by the young child (Tatum O'Neal, the actor's daughter) he is taking to an aunt in St Joseph, Missouri. The two of them are so delightful, especially the child, that it by no means matters that the film is less a narrative than a series of confrontations. This was the director's third consecutive smash hit: and he threw it all away. **Daisy Miller** (1974) was only the fourth of Henry James's stories to be filmed, but one too short and too slight to be really suitable. Frederic Raphael wrote the screenplay, the locations were prettily found at Vevey and Rome, but Bogdanovich misdirects at every turn: of the entire cast only Mildred Natwick, as Daisy's snobbish aunt, seems to have read the script, let alone the book, and James's subtleties are entirely lost. **At Long Last Love** (1975) is set in the Thirties, in that favourite derivative setting of the era, Long Island; it also has a bevy of Cole Porter songs, none of which survives this treatment – and of the stars only Burt Reynolds and Madeline Kahn show glints of the gaiety and charm which are what it is supposed to be all about. One incident is taken from Hollywood lore, as set down in Bogdanovich's own book on movies, and by standards he established himself **Nickelodeon** (1976) is pure cannibalism. After a mauling by the press, it failed almost completely at the box office, though it might surely have found an audience in those unfamiliar with its anecdotes. Bogdanovich returned to Corman for **Saint Jack** (1979), not primarily to retrieve his reputation – though that was necessary – but to prove that American movies could be made on a restricted budget, and be profitable. Paul Theroux's novel is a series of anecdotes about a pimp (Ben Gazzara) in Singapore, and the film is likeable, with some excellent local colour. It lacks a certain conviction, most obviously at the end when Jack, hitherto without a single moral scruple of any kind, finds that he cannot 'shop' a homosexual U.S. senator (George Lazenby) to the C.I.A. The complexities of human behaviour, particularly necessary in what is intended as a character study, come a close second to elementary cinema technique, like cutting away from a funeral to a postcard view. Throughout

Bogdanovich's films, even the two good ones, arbitrary incident leads only to arbitrary incident by the most artificial means: it is curious that a man who has looked so hard at old Hollywood should have failed to grasp that that was not the way they did it.

In **An Unmarried Woman** (1978), at one moment the heroine and her friends sit around reminiscing about stars of the past, and like every scene in the film it rings true; but as they agree that there is no one around today to touch Davis, Garbo, Stanwyck and Jean Arthur, you know you would rather be watching one of them. This is not a film that could have been made in their heyday, for, as in all the films of this director, Paul Mazursky (b. 1938), the people are unglamorous, they move at life's pace, they mumble: unfortunately they still throw their dilemmas at us, and this particular one concerns the reactions of a woman (Jill Clayburgh) discovering that her husband prefers another woman. I was reminded of a remark of C. A. Lejeune's, that 'it dragged its slow pace along': the film was *Cobra Woman*, and there would be no worse condemnation than to say that I would rather have been watching Maria Montez. Mazursky, a former writer, made his name with **Bob and Carol and Ted and Alice** (1969), the first comedy – indeed the first film – about wife-swapping, and so somewhat daring at that time. The film starts with a sex-therapy group session handled seriously or, at least – which is equally startling – unfunnily, and much of its humour depends on marital reactions to such everyday problems as infidelity and not feeling up to sexual intercourse. When it comes to the actual wife-swapping, the two couples of the title do not feel up to that either, which makes you wonder why they abolished the Production Code; instead they go to listen to Tony Bennett, and all concerned sing 'What the World Needs Now is Love', which is supposed to be ironic and pointed at the same time. The audience which flocked to this avoided Mazursky's second film as director, **Alex in Wonderland** (1970), which is about a director who has made a successful first film and is stumped for an idea for a second – a plot not without resemblances to Fellini's *8½*, to which this is an overt homage. There is also a discussion on masturbation, to

The Movie Brats

Although critics were kind to *The Revolutionary*, the public in 1970 would have none of it – which is a pity, since it was flawlessly written by Hans Konigsberger (from his own novel) and finely directed by Paul Williams, with a performance to match by Jon Voight, centre, as a middle-class boy who takes to radicalism with fervour but with hardly a coherent thought in his well-meaning head. With him, at left, is Robert Duvall, as the factory worker who leads him towards the left, and Seymour Cassel as the nut who will take him from there to anarchy.

remind us that Mazursky in both these early films took advantage of the new permissiveness to discuss things hardly worth discussing – at least, not in this pointless manner; he was not, of course, the only one.

Michael Ritchie (b. 1939) is the social satirist which Mazursky would like to be, but it is possible that he is only as good as his script. That of **Downhill Racer** (1969) is quite literally only a study of a professional skier (Robert Redford), and we learn little about him beyond his monstrous and humourless devotion to his sport; the film was generally considered the best to date on a professional sport, a dubious compliment in view of the quality of most of the others. Ritchie's documentary approach was perfected, not without reference to *Taking Off* and *The Hospital*, by the time he directed **The Candidate** (1972) – a fragmentary, take-it-or-leave-it style particularly suitable for the purpose, which is an account of a senatorial campaign. As in *State of the Union* or *The Best Man* the details are fascinatingly set out – by Jeremy Larner, who had worked for Eugene McCarthy, and who won an Oscar for Best Original Screenplay. He is particularly adept at catching the non-committal committed remarks of both sides – which suggests satire, and that is exactly what the film is. 'There's got to be a better way' is one of the

slogans of the candidate, McKay (Redford), but he is not near to finding one: he feels deeply on a number of issues, notably pollution – but not deeply enough. He is young, ready, willing and able, but sufficiently mediocre to suggest that in thirty years' time he will be as much of a demagogue and a stereotype as his opponent. Preston Sturges would have approved of Ritchie, and **Smile** (1975) is about small-town life, an institution viewed favourably – at least by the movies – till the coming of Sturges. Ritchie himself admitted the film was influenced by *The Firemen's Ball*, but in this case we are watching a fairly dreadful group of people – though most of them are deliciously funny, as they plot and counterplot around a local beauty contest. They are also hurt and sad, given to odd revelations and moments of pomposity and pride – eventually not unlike a grown-up *American Graffiti* (q.v.), also a film of hopes and dreams. The film is so sure-footed that it is disappointing to find this director working on inferior material – in **The Bad News Bears** (1976) and **Semi-Tough** (1977), presumably offered, or taken, because they also are about forms of competition. The former involves a kids' baseball team, predictably foul-mouthed – though that is the film's only joke; – and the latter concerns two football-players (Burt Reynolds, Kris Kristofferson) with distinctly playful tastes and a yen for the same girl (Jill Clayburgh). *Bears* makes a point that baseball is not the ideal game for children, especially as the ideal is not playing but winning, and the parents' obsession with winning is unlikely to turn any of the children into good citizens; the other film is merciless on weirdo groups following the latest passing fads.

Bob Rafelson (b. 1935) has also taken as his theme contemporary America – if we except **Head** (1968), starring The Monkees, a pop-group which was, by Rafelson's own admission, his creation. They had made a lot of money for the records division of Columbia Pictures, and its television subsidiary, so Rafelson felt that he was entitled 'to make a picture that would in a sense expose the process', i.e. the manufacture of a pop group. It is soon clear that The Monkees have as little acting talent as The Beatles, so, as in *A Hard Day's Night*, this group is put through a series of cut-ups interspersed with songs – and not

even the semblance of a story-line. Parodies of other movies – and T.V. commercials – were not new, but they are done
here charmingly; even the jokes that fail
are buoyed by wit or imagination. *Head*
keeps its options open; it is a more accomplished witness to the fads and fancies of
the Sixties than any similar piece, and
one of the few non-narrative films which
offers hope for the genre. A small bonus is
a brief appearance by Jack Nicholson, co-
producer and co-writer. The co-sponsor
was Bert Schneider, and the three of them
were to be reunited on **Five Easy Pieces**
(1970), with a screenplay by Adrien Joyce.
(She and Nicholson had written a Western,
The Shooting, before he became a star, and
watching it I was uncertain whether they
or the director, Monte Hellman, were responsible for its pretension and consequent failure.) *Five Easy Pieces* is not unlike
Easy Rider, inasmuch as it is romantic
about disillusionment and decay; it is far
more honest, with points to make on the
rifts in American society and a man who
wants a better world and cannot find it – a
theme at one time rare in American culture, perhaps more cleverly treated here
than in any other version since the War.
Nicholson plays the man, a construction
worker, but in time we learn that he is
from a wealthy and cultured family. Says
his girl (Karen Black) to him, 'One thing I
don't understand – how you can have this
fantastic background of music and just
walk away from it without a second
thought', and he replies 'I did give it a
second thought.'

If for no other reason, the film would be
remarkable for the performance of Nicholson, who seems to *enjoy* himself as much as
any good actor since Walter Huston. The
theme is reprised in **The King of Marvin
Gardens** (1972), in which Nicholson has a
lonely night-time radio programme and
would like to come in from the cold – to his
family, as represented by his brother
(Bruce Dern). The behaviour of the latter
makes little sense, as written by Rafelson
and Jacob Brackman, but one of the other
players, Ellen Burstyn, explained why:
'Bob loves ambiguity. There was plenty in
the script to begin with, but then after the
first cut, which was about half-hour too
long as they always are, he cut it for further
ambiguity.' The film had little success and
the much better **Stay Hungry** (1976)

attracted only a cult following. Rafelson
said that he did not like Charles Gaines's
novel till he realised that its conclusion was
the same as that of *Five Easy Pieces* and
Marvin Gardens; the latter had come about
because 'the world was very despairing'.
Yet the screenplay of *Stay Hungry*, by
himself and Gaines, changes the novel's
end for an optimistic one – also perhaps an
arbitrary one, since he shoots in sequence
and did not, with these three films, decide
upon the ending until the last day of
filming. Reviewing the film in the *New
Statesman* John Coleman invoked 'Candide', since 'il faut cultiver notre jardin'
turns up as 'Stay hungry and you'll taste
life'; we may also invoke Satyajit Ray's
later films, with the young hero (Jeff
Bridges) searching for his identity in a
changing world; but like Rafelson's earlier
movies it is concerned with certain American values – those prevailing in Birmingham, Alabama. Rafelson may be the most
intuitive and optimistic director of his generation, and the two qualities may be interrelated: at least, I think the acclaim that
greeted *Five Easy Pieces* is reflected in this
film.

Rafelson's work has been infrequent,
since, as he observed, life can be happier
without the stress of directing a film. In
1979 he began to direct *Brubaker*, with
Robert Redford, but was removed by the

Bob Rafelson's *Five
Easy Pieces* is about a
hard-hat, Jack
Nicholson, who likes
to go bowling or to
sit around swilling
beer; and he has a
girlfriend, Karen
Black, with hardly
more aspirations
than he. When it
turns out that he
comes from a
cultured middle-
income family the
film has a comment
or so to make on class.

Jack Lemmon in John G. Avildsen's *Save the Tiger*, an executive in his forties who suddenly looks around him and doesn't like what he sees. The rumblings of Watergate had started to sound as the film was being made, but the film's pessimism is wider than that, covering a number of matters from business ethics to porno-houses.

producer; and then he and Nicholson revived **The Postman Always Rings Twice** (1981), which they had been discussing since 1973 – when Nicholson would have been the right age for the role. Hollywood is accustomed to remaking its successes rather than its failures, i.e. the good or excellent novels it mangled years ago, but in this case Rafelson should really have taken his tone from either James M. Cain's original novel or the M-G-M version of 1946. Instead, in restoring the sexual passion, he imitates the Visconti version of this story, *Ossessione*, but the reasonably explicit sex scenes have more of the flavour of cheap Italian movies like *Mogliamante* than the erotic tension Visconti achieved. Rafelson and David Mamet, his screenwriter, seem also to be in search of tragedy, and the postman now rings only once, leaving the Nicholson character crying for his lost love rather

than being accused of her murder. A further miscalculation is to have depicted the time – 1934 – as resolutely drab, confining period detail to clothes, cars, a couple of songs on the radio, and a breadline. But if the film is a disappointment from this star-director team, it has a small triumph in Jessica Lange, febrile, disturbing and far prettier and more appealing than any American film heroine in ages.

Redolent of Rafelson's best films is **Save the Tiger** (1973), with which John G. Avildsen (b. 1937) moved to the mainstream industry after the success of *Joe*. Its writer, a former assistant producer on a T.V. Tarzan series, was Steve Shagan, who adapted from his own novel: they interested Jack Lemmon but no one else, till Robert Evans at Paramount decided (in the manner of the old tycoons) that it should be made whether or not it earned a penny. It was shot in chronological order on location in Los Angeles, where Harry (Lemmon) works in the garment business. As Lemmon observed, Harry was once a nice, hustling kid who had surrendered to current values and, in the year of Watergate, is considering arson when his factory is threatened with closure: 'The Government has another word for arson and it's called fraud.' The film omits few of Harry's regrets, be they for forgotten jazz musicians or the ideals of the war years, and elsewhere it more overtly attacks the materialistic attitudes of American society. At one point there is a discussion on the ethics of Albert Speer, an indication that movies were beginning to reflect the conversations of reasonably intelligent people. Lemmon's performance won a deserved Best Actor Oscar.

Avildsen was awarded a Best Director Oscar for **Rocky** (1976), but it seems to me only marginally better than his subsequent films. The perceptions of *Save the Tiger* are largely absent in this tale of a punk (Sylvester Stallone), part-time boxer and part-time collector for a loan-shark. It was welcome to have an optimistic film in the year of *Taxi Driver* (q.v.), and since the climax is a prize-fight, with audiences rooting for Rocky, some reviewers invoked the name of Capra. Stallone wrote the screenplay as a vehicle for himself, and he has to date also directed two equally popular sequels.

Virtually all these film-makers have

been overshadowed by Robert Altman (b. 1922), who with **M★A★S★H** (1970) established himself as the most invigorating talent in the American cinema. There had not been an American film as free-wheeling and rambustious since *Shadows*, while its humour and irreverence suggested a contemporary *Duck Soup*. Ring Lardner Jr provided the dry martini cocktail script about a Mobile Army Surgical Hospital (hence the title) in Korea where, as in other recent service movies, everyone is obsessed with sex. The cast of then little-known names is headed by Donald Sutherland and Elliott Gould as medics, and the latter is very droll, given to mumbling insubordinate remarks with a knowing innocence. The lashings of blood in the operating theatre sequences give the impression that Altman was determined to be noticed at all costs, but do not detract from the circus-like effect of the film itself. It caught the mood of the anti-military young, sick of Vietnam, and there was considerable surprise when it was discovered that Altman was of another generation altogether. He had already made a number of disregarded movies, including one with a reasonably large budget, *That Cold Day in the Park*.

Altman's later work showed him youthful in his recklessness, using a seemingly rough-and-ready approach to retain his primary effect, spontaneity. Those who detected a polemic in *M★A★S★H* were not to find it again in his films, except glancingly, but they have a common theme, and it is that of Lumet (or Satyajit Ray) of people coming together and of their effect on each other. His ardour for his medium led him into a number of mindless art films, with the result that his career has been like a roller coaster. **Brewster McCloud** (1970), like Mazursky's *Alex in Wonderland*, made at the same time, is personal fantasy posing as serious or, if you like, anarchic comment, in this case on some citizens of Houston: and both films were contributory factors to the ruin of M-G-M. Its former chiefs must have been rotating in their graves since the film's major joke, repeated *ad nauseam*, is built around bird droppings, while what plot there is concerns a mild-mannered young man (Bud Cort) who yearns to be Icarus. **McCabe and Mrs Miller** (1971) is a pioneer tale set mainly in a brothel, and

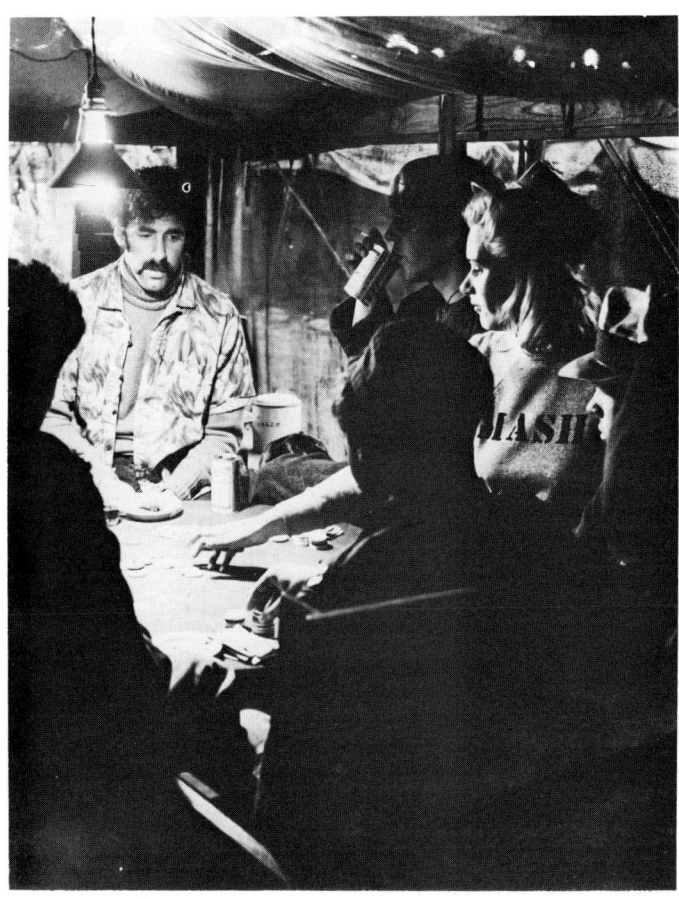

with many four-letter words exchanged between a hard-luck whore (Julie Christie) and a gambler (Warren Beatty). **Images** (1972) is about a woman (Susannah York) in the midst of a nervous breakdown, possibly from trying to sort out what is happening. Only the second of these had much success (and that was chiefly with the press). Although he was not assigned to the project, United Artists sought his advice as to the suitability of Elliott Gould playing Marlowe and Altman seized the opportunity to direct Raymond Chandler's story **The Long Goodbye** (1973) with a screenplay by Leigh Brackett. Altman suggested that by modernising it he could present a satire on modern-day California, which he has effectively done – but only at the expense of the original and a new and particularly foolish solution tagged on. And Gould is not Marlowe.

Altman hit his stride with his next three

Elliott Gould, left, Donald Sutherland, drinking from the can, and Sally Kellerman in Robert Altman's *M★A★S★H*, staff-members of a Mobile Army Surgical Hospital in Korea. Their misadventures, often hilarious, sexual and in defiance of authority, provided the basis of a television series, with different players, which ran for more than ten years and broke a number of records in that medium.

films. At moments it did occur to some that his main strength was his brilliant cinematographer, Vilmos Zsigmond, but he changed photographers, and his films remained startlingly vivid. **Thieves Like Us** (1974) is a new version of the novel once filmed as *They Live By Night*, with Keith Carradine and Shelley Duvall as the outlawed lovers; **California Split** (1974) concerns the oddball adventures of two inveterate gamblers (Gould, George Segal). Neither, despite warm notices, was successful, and he may have chosen **Nashville** (1975) because of the popularity of country and western music. The film did enable him to elaborate on the theme of *California Split* (and many other films of the time), of 'making it', of restless and funky people searching for pastures new. Those in *Nashville* aspire to political office or to a recording contract, and they are also searching for what may be described as a new lay or the ultimate in sexual satisfaction. Most of the dreams fade, or, once achieved, amount to little: the time had gone when movie heroes achieved goals or glory. We leave them more or less as we found them. One is dead, shot by a sniper at a concert, and although the atmosphere of violence had been created from the start, this cheap, cut-off ending reduces a film which for the last thirty minutes had already indicated that it did not know where to go. The first two hours are excellent, but the public failed to respond to the generally ecstatic reviews. Altman's standing had only been sustained by support from the press, but he lost that with **Buffalo Bill and the Indians** (1976) and the equally dire **Quintet** (1978), which disappeared from cinemas with uncommon rapidity, despite the presence in the cast of Paul Newman. Altman had always been prone to self-indulgence, and now it had overwhelmed him. He quarrelled with de Laurentiis, the producer of *Buffalo Bill*, and moved yet again, to 20th Century-Fox, for **The Wedding** (1978) which, like Tchekov's play and Wajda's film, is about nothing but a wedding, and **A Perfect Couple** (1979), the romance of a mismatched pair (Paul Dooley, Marta Heflin). Neither film was any more than a partial return to form, for the old energy was missing, and characters and situations of potential interest dither before disappearing altogether. As ventures in satire neither

may compare to *Stay Hungry* or *Smile*, but the cast of *A Wedding* includes Lillian Gish – Griffith's most famous actress being directed, almost seventy years later, by one who was for a while Hollywood's most stimulating film-maker.

Like Coppola, Altman has entrepreneurial ambitions and has sponsored a number of other directors, notably Robert Benton (b. 1932), who had written *Bonnie and Clyde* with David Newman. They also wrote *There Was a Crooked Man* and it was not a good idea to repeat its themes in **Bad Company** (1972) which Benton directed for producer Stanley Jaffe. In their West, there is no loyalty and no courage, and because their theme, the seduction of the young by crime, is of little dramatic interest, the film was a deserved failure. Altman enabled Benton to direct again by persuading Warners to put up the budget for **The Late Show** (1977), an improvement, as it happened, on *The Long Goodbye*, as Benton had written his own Chandleresque story, set in the present day and engagingly teaming a white-haired gammy-legged private eye (Art Carney) and a kooky dame (Lily Tomlin), a 'fruitcake' as he calls her. That again did not elicit further offers, but the producer, Jaffe, and star Dustin Hoffman decided to entrust Benton with the direction of **Kramer vs. Kramer** (1979): Benton also adapted the novel by Avery Corman, and, as David Castell observed in *Films Illustrated*, his credit, 'written for the screen' takes on 'a vivid new meaning'. The subject is a separation, a divorce, and the battle over the custody of the child (Justin Henry) – a small enough area and Benton stays rigidly within it, never straining either to move his audience or make them laugh, but succeeding simply with fresh observation. The husband (Hoffman) is in advertising, and his salary is underquoted for the purposes of the plot, since with a low-paid job he risks losing the child; but in that role Hoffman gives a magnificent, understated performance, justifying his own claim that he is 'demanding' to work with. Jane Alexander is the new lady in his life, radiant without make-up or Hepburn mannerisms; and Meryl Streep is rightly smug and unlikeable as the ex-wife. She, Hoffman, Benton and the film all won Oscars.

Hoffman has also been instrumental in furthering the career of Ulu Grosbard

(b. 1929), whom he had known when they worked together off Broadway. Grosbard's first film, **The Subject Was Roses** (1968) is an artless version of a prize-winning but derivative play, yet again unmasking the American family. Frank D. Gilroy wrote it, and the cast fortunately includes Patricia Neal, Jack Albertson and Martin Sheen. **Who Is Harry Kellerman and Why is He Saying Those Terrible Things About Me?** (1971) stars Hoffman as a Jewish, neurotic and famous pop singer. It moves uneasily from whimsy to satire (it is brilliant on his New Jersey boyhood), and Herb Gardner's screenplay reveals the same schisms as in his most famous work, *A Thousand Clowns*, that he is not as detached about New York and show business as he thinks he is. *Straight Time*, with Hoffman, was Grosbard's third failure, but he attracted favourable attention with his fourth film, **True Confessions** (1981), written by John Gregory Dunne and his wife, Joan Didion, from the former's novel. By this time Hollywood had attacked most of the institutions it had once revered, but this was the first time that it had roundly portrayed the Roman Catholic Church as having as its high ranking prelates men as greedy as they are ambitious. The film is, actually, a thriller, showing the effect on a monsignor (Robert de Niro) as his brother (Robert Duvall), a persistent L.A. cop, unmasks a wealthy supporter of the Church as the perpetrator of a particularly sadistic murder. Grosbard handles both the situations and the period detail (it is set in the Forties) with confidence, but the film is chiefly remarkable for the resource and attack of its leading players.

Grosbard may one day make a very interesting film, and so may Terrence Malick (b. 1945), a former student at the American Film Institute who entered the industry with the screenplay for an undistinguished cowboy tale, *Pocket Money*. He wrote and directed **Badlands** (1973) and **Days of Heaven** (1978), which do little more than establish that America is vast, beautiful and in places deserted (Malick was born in Texas). *Badlands* contains much spilling of blood, seemingly obligatory for directors making their first films, and though based on an actual shooting spree in Nebraska in 1958 it too often seems a combination of *Pretty Poison* and *Bonnie and Clyde*. *Days of Heaven* concentrates on immigrant farmhands in the Texas Panhandle of 1916, but in trying to come to terms with the rural past it is somewhat less successful than Richard Pearce's independently-made **Heartland** (1980), based on the autobiographical books of Elinore Randall Stewart, a widow who, in 1910, went to become housekeeper in the wilds of Wyoming to a dour Scot (Rip Torn). The hardships of her first year are told without sentimentality and in images of exceptional beauty, and she is warmly played by a stout, thirty-fiveish actress, Conchata Ferrell. Pearce, the director, had made a reputation and won the 1974 Oscar for feature documentary with his anti-Vietnam war film, *Hearts and Minds*.

John Landis may also surprise us. He had a huge success with his third film as a director, **National Lampoon's Animal House** (1978), a campus comedy which had the bright – but by now unoriginal – idea of turning the crewcut boys into prigs and villains and the slobs into heroes: but it had no other whatsoever and is at best lumberingly executed. However, **An American Werewolf in London** (1981) is a small triumph, engagingly welding together a parody of horror movies and real horror, the finale of *The Lost World* (or *King Kong*) and New York Jewish jokes with those depending on British understatement.

In the matter of humour we seem today to be dependent almost solely on the peurile and scatalogical fancies of Mel Brooks, though it is worth remarking that ever since **Blazing Saddles** (1974) broke records each of his films has been less successful at the box office. Compared to his 'anything goes' approach Woody Allen (b. 1935) seems erudite and disciplined, and he does offer four or five good lines per picture. The rest depends on recognising the references in the jokes – and his audiences of primarily young admirers are flattered at having heard of Strindberg, Zelda Fitzgerald and Marshall McLuan, not to mention his own frequent references to old movies. Most patrons, with good reasons, resisted his earlier films: **Annie Hall** (1977) was, however, enjoyed by people who normally could not stand Allen and his self-aware, self-deprecatory screen persona. We know from Ralph

The Movie Brats

You may well wonder why this particular number was staged in a saloon of the old, wild West, in *Blazing Saddles*, but then it is typical of Mel Brook's approach to comedy, which is not exactly disciplined. The lady is Madeline Kahn, who provided the film's more memorable moment.

Rosenblum's memoir that the film was a 'chaotic collection of bits and pieces' when he was asked to do the editing, 'and of all Allen's films, with the least promise for popular success.' It was he who suggested concentrating on the relationship with Annie (Diane Keaton), even though that meant shooting additional material. Allen observed 'It was originally a picture about me, exclusively . . . about my life, my thoughts, my ideas, my background,' a statement whose delusions of grandeur are perhaps only rivalled by those of his co-writer, Marshall Brickman, 'All that stuff I had written was cerebral, surreal, highly intellectual, overliterate, overeducated, self-conscious comedy.' Such revelations, of course, hardly make Allen appear disciplined and even with Rosenblum's help the film remains Hollywood's most ramshackle ego-trip since the days of Mae West.

Allen escaped from his self-absorption long enough to make **Interiors** (1978), a po-faced drama of a family, influenced by Ingmar Bergman and sporting would-be tart comments on literary society. It is as appalling as other Hollywood attempts at an art movie, and **Manhattan** (1979) dismays as much because it is virtually a remake of *Annie Hall*. It has more plot, and finally has a point to make about certain sections of New York society – or at least Allen's own quasi-literary, show-businessy set with its exhaustive egos and emotional demands. The soundtrack pounds with the melodies of Gershwin, who was never so demeaned; the film further strives for 'class' by being in black and white, but that only helps to distinguish it from *Annie Hall*. The title is not inappropriate, but they could have called it *Ants in My Pants of 1979*★ to remind us how much film humour has degenerated since the days of Preston Sturges.

The director James Frawley has displayed a more positive comic talent, at any rate in **Kid Blue** (1973) and **The Big Bus** (1976). The former is the first successful spoof Western (of many) since *Cat Ballou*, and the latter a parody of disaster movies. Frawley can pick over the bones of old

★Joel McCrea was making *Ants in My Pants of 1939* in *Sullivan's Travels*.

films and still be fresh and amusing, as few other practitioners of this particular proliferating genre, but **The Muppet Movie** (1979) indicates that something was very wrong. It may be that he had no control over those responsible for the dismally unoriginal story-line featuring the Muppets, the grotesque animal puppets, or he may have been defeated by the limitations set by the producers, I.T.C., who have an internationally famous penchant for wildly extravagant film disasters.

In the matter of humour, the actor Alan Alda has provided some sharply satirical thrusts in the two films he wrote for himself to appear in, **The Seduction of Joe Tynan** (1979), directed by Jerry Schatzberg, and **The Four Seasons** (1981), directed by Alda himself. Alda returns Hollywood comedy to its old level, less by wit than observation, capturing splendidly the smugness and sentimentality of the bourgeoisie. *Joe Tynan* charts the submission of a liberal senator (Alda) to the corruptions attendant on success in Washington, and *The Four Seasons* follows the fortunes of three married couples as they slip into middle-age.

Jonathan Demme, a protégé of Roger Corman, has directed two films in the same vein, **Citizens Band** (1977), written by Paul Brinkman, and **Melvin and Howard** (1980), written by Bo Goldman. Both celebrate the little folk out there in middle America, the first in its cross-section portrait of some small town people brought together by C.B. radio, and the second in its curious tale, based on fact, of a young man (Paul Le Mat) who believes that Howard Hughes (Jason Robards) has left him most of his fortune. Demme's affection for his milieux is matched by the playing of Mr Le Mat, who is in both films: his round-faced optimism and ingenuity recall some heroes of the Silent era, but the inference that he is essentially mediocre is new and touching. Neither film was popular, despite particularly enthusiastic reviews for the second of them.

Martin Scorsese (b. 1942) is, Coppola aside, the best-known of the film-makers sponsored by Corman. After his first, amateur film he was invited to make **Boxcar Bertha** (1972), virtually a copy of *Bonnie and Clyde* except that Scorsese is less romantic in re-creating the bloodletting gangsters of the Depression. The film was little seen, but Scorsese was encouraged to make **Mean Streets** (1973) by an independent producer, Jonathan T. Taplin, who raised its budget of $480,000 from private sources (or, according to Scorsese himself, $350,000). The only distributor willing to handle the film was Warners, which entered it for the New York Film Festival, but it was rarely shown until revived after Scorsese's later successes. It is a New York version of *I Vitelloni*, with much blood and violence, dialogue which is less explicit except in the matter of four-letter words, and no discernible point.

Scorsese established his reputation with a film which is the reverse of that, **Alice Doesn't Live Here Anymore** (1974). He was recommended for it by Coppola when its star, Ellen Burstyn, was determined that Robert Getchell's screenplay should become a film for cinemas rather than television. Her earlier Oscar nomination was sufficient warranty for Warners to finance the $2 million budget, and she was awarded an Oscar for her portrait of Alice, an ordinary housewife who, newly widowed, sets out to fulfil her ambition of returning to Monterey. She had been a band singer, so she resorts to that, finding kindness in Phoenix and then in Tucson. As she journeys on that road she is at one with all the other travellers in American films at this time, but plucky, gently sarcastic and self-mocking in a manner unlike

Martin Scorsese was one of the most talked-about directors of the Seventies, but few people, comparatively, actually went to see his films. The exception was *Alice Doesn't Live Here Anymore*, with Kris Kristofferson and Ellen Burstyn. Indeed, it was one of those films, like *Paper Moon* and *The Goodbye Girl*, which brought back people who had stopped going to the cinema years ago. One reason was that these films had the qualities of the films they used to like, but this was the only one of the three that did not particularly set out to be that way.

other screen heroines in many a year. Since she had been taken for granted by her husband, and is ill-treated by a lover (Harvey Keitel) in Phoenix, and as, in Miss Burstyn's words, she 'is a woman grappling with the change of consciousness we are all grappling with', the film was popular with supporters of Women's Lib, but more than the other 'road' films, its origins go back to *It Happened One Night*, with audiences wanting Alice to settle down with the gentle giant (Kris Kristofferson) who is attracted to her.

The film's success enabled Scorsese to find backing for **Taxi Driver** (1976), written by Paul Schrader (b. 1946). Schrader went on to direct two interesting films (q.v.), but we might pause to examine his antecedents since they are pertinent to this particularly unpleasant film. He had intended to become a minister in the Christian Reformed Church, and had not seen a film till he was eighteen. He subsequently studied film at U.C.L.A., and edited a movie magazine, in which he criticised some current screenwriters, 'their writing is flashy, brilliant and inherently unorganised. I am thinking primarily of certain scripts by such writers as John Milius (*Judge Roy Bean, Jeremiah Johnson*), Terry Malick (*Pocket Money*), Robert Dillon (*Prime Cut*), Walter Hill (*The Getaway*) and David Ward (*Steelyard Blues*). The premise of these scripts seems to be to create Great Scenes involving Great Characters, then stringing them together like beads on a rosary. The end result is not so much a well crafted script but a pastiche of touches, flashes of brilliance and momentary insights.' He might have been writing of *Taxi Driver*, which he wrote from his own experiences, according to *The Village Voice*, as 'a loner, sleeping days and wandering around Los Angeles at night. He was depressed. His nocturnal hours were spent riding aimlessly in taxicabs, drinking, and taking in an occasional porno flick': thus the protagonist (Robert de Niro) of *Taxi Driver*, except that he is a cabbie in New York, a city exclusively populated by what he calls 'garbage'. Foiled at assassinating a presidential candidate, he murders a twelve-year-old hooker and subsequently becomes a national hero, which is deeply and cheaply ironic, since audiences know that he is psychotic. The scene of the murder showed more blood (splattered on the walls and furniture of the room in which it takes place) than I think has ever been seen in a major Hollywood movie, and many spectators found it as offensive as it was unnecessary. Scorsese explained that he had seen an episode of a T.V. series in which twenty people were killed but 'not a drop of blood was shed. That's ridiculous. It's unrealistic. I don't do things that way.' It was no surprise to learn that the young psychopath who attempted to assassinate President Reagan in 1981 had seen this film several times and was obsessed by Jodie Foster, who plays the teenage whore.

Having failed to find the truth behind the malaise of contemporary New Yorkers, Scorsese set out in **New York, New York** (1977) to find the truth behind such old Hollywood movies as *Orchestra Wives*. This truth, it would seem, is that the musicians of the Forties were bores or boors: de Niro is objectionable when first seen and never becomes likeable, as he and his wife (Liza Minnelli) row for two and a half hours – undoubtedly the reason why the film failed to find a public. It originally ran for three hours, and what remains is so superficial that the mind boggles at the content of the missing material. The truth is in Miss Minnelli's performance and nowhere else.

Interviewed during this period, little emerged from Scorsese about his craft or the medium other than that he admired Powell and Pressburger, 'because they took a lot of chances and made movie magic'. He himself could never be accused of making movie magic, but he took chances with **Raging Bull** (1980) in that, apart from the most common four-letter word, the dialogue is virtually inaudible. In humourless and pretentious fashion it strains at recounting the career of Jake La Motta, a boxing champion of the Forties. Towards the end it manages at last to make an interesting point on the aftermath of celebrity, concluding with La Motta rehearsing Brando's taxicab speech from *On the Waterfront* – and in case we have missed the point of that, it is spelled out in a biblical quotation on the end title: 'Once I was blind and now I can see.' De Niro won an Oscar for his performance, presumably for managing to put on 250 pounds to play the middle-aged La Motta, a 'first' in the annals of this award. De Niro, in other circumstances, might have been able to illuminate some facet of La Motta's interesting career and personality, but the script and direction seem resolutely opposed to any such ideas.

Since Schrader worked on the screenplay it is rewarding to find considerable content in two of the films which he wrote for himself to direct, **Blue Collar** (1978) and **Hardcore** (1979). They are too schematic, and not entirely well constructed, but they are far more successful than *Taxi Driver* in examining the reasons for the undercurrent of violence in contemporary American life. *Blue Collar* follows the exploits of three Detroit factory workers – one white (Harvey Keitel) and two black (Richard Pryor, Yaphet Kotto) – as they, apathetically at first, realise the extent of union corruption. Their surroundings – the factory canteen, the cathouse, the suburban homes – are inventively portrayed, and a reminder that the world of the artisan had hardly been seen since *On the Waterfront*. Schrader provides a more convincing ending than Brando being martyred, but whereas the earlier film was outstanding in its day, and is still powerful, this is neither. *Hardcore* is forceful only in its portrait of the seedy porno parlours of Los Angeles; perhaps its most interesting aspect is the autobiographical section at the beginning, set in the religious community of Schrader's home town, Grand Rapids, Michigan. A teenage girl fails to return there after an expedition to California, and when her father (George C. Scott) finds that she is making pornographic films he sets out to find out why; along the way he makes friends with a girl (Season Hubley) who started selling her body at fifteen, ten years ago, and can still be bruised, though she tries not to show it. Unlike *Taxi Driver* these are moral films, but they do not give the impression of a sophisticated talent, one that can teach us something about life. That quality – so prevalent in the early Thirties films of, say, Frank Borzage, Leo McCarey, et al – has gone from American movies.

It is a quality especially absent from the films by friends and colleagues George Lucas (b. 1945) and Steven Spielberg (b. 1945). Lucas began as a protégé of Coppola, and they are linked professionally with Schrader and Scorsese, if only by John Milius, writer, producer and director,

who has worked (sometimes uncredited) with all of them. Lucas and Spielberg are the products of film schools and, it would seem, endless boyhood matinees watching Flash Gordon serials when not being indoctrinated by the Sunday comics. Spielberg acquired a reputation directing for television, especially with **Duel** (1971), a simple but tense account of a car driver menaced by a truck, based on a story by Richard Matheson. It was shown to some acclaim in cinemas abroad, causing Universal to promote him to a large-budgeted cinema feature, **The Sugarland Express** (1974). It might be termed *Dog Day Afternoon* on wheels, and like that, it is based on fact and concerns petty crooks: an escaped convict (William Atherton), his wife (Goldie Hawn), their hostage and the police. During both films a massive police force is immobilised, and Spielberg, like Lumet, has much fun with the serried ranks of cops and their autos with the flashing lights and screaming sirens. It is an enjoyable movie, as is **Jaws** (1975), expertly handled by Spielberg and then the most financially successful film in cinema history. Its takings exceeded *The Godfather* in just seventy-eight days, and like that – and *Love Story* and *The Exorcist* – it had started as a manufactured bestseller of dubious merit which as a film apparently everyone wanted to see. The books have in common writers all weaned in show business: this one, by Peter Benchley, concerned a small Long Island resort whose season is threatened with ruin by the presence of a killer shark in the waters.

Yaphet Kotto, left, Harvey Keitel and Richard Pryor relaxing after a hard day in the auto-factory in *Blue Collar*, written by Paul Schrader, who with it made his debut as a director. The three of them, and especially Keitel, find that they have bitten off more than they can chew in attempting to fight union malpractices.

The Movie Brats

Meanwhile, Lucas had had a success with **American Graffiti** (1973), which Coppola had managed to set up for him after his own success with *The Godfather*. *The Last Picture Show* and *Summer of '42* had recently demonstrated that audiences were interested in the youth of yesteryear, and *American Graffiti* went back only ten years, with as much affection, but without the drama of the one or the sentimentality of the other. The three films made a fetish of getting the period details right, as if to emphasise the changes, but little has changed: life in this small Californian town is much like that anywhere else – and except that there is less booze and the youngsters are from the proletariat, they are little different from those celebrated in 'The Beautiful and the Damned'.

Simultaneously Spielberg came up with **Close Encounters of the Third Kind** (1977) and Lucas with **Star Wars** (1977), both science fiction epics. Spielberg thought up his fancy while listening to the song 'When You Wish Upon a Star' from *Pinocchio*, and the use of that song at the end (though cut from the final print) reveals that Spielberg was going where Kubrick had already trod. *Dr Strangelove* is not the only source raided for this overblown space opera: *You Only Live Twice* is another, as well as any number of inept scifi movies of the Fifties; and the antiwar theme of *It Came from Outer Space* has been converted into a quasi-religious message. John Milius admires the film for its 'lack of pretension. Look at *Julia*. It's preachy, liberal preachy, a female macho film. *Close Encounters* is innocent, with wide-eyed, wonderful amazement.' This innocent creature was, however, considered sufficiently important to be reissued a couple of years later as *Close Encounters of the Third Kind: the Special Edition*, having become special by virtue of some minor changes made by Spielberg. This had not happened before in film history.

It is only slightly more bearable than the falsely naïve *Star Wars*, where the films of the past are supposedly parodied amidst the reigning gadgetry. Like *Nickelodeon*, it is stuffed with insider's conceits and no firm narrative to hold it together. The reviews outside the U.S. were bemused or unkind, but just as *Jaws* justified the enormous pre-release publicity budget, so *Star Wars* went on to take twice the money to date of any film yet made. Significantly the expensive and much-publicised sequel – the first of a projected series – was seen by only half the number who went to the original. In America, that is: elsewhere it did even worse, if that is a word to be used about a film which was nevertheless extremely profitable. Lucas had handed the direction over to Irvin Kershner, but to little benefit, except perhaps to sub-teenage audiences. In *Newsweek* David Ansen noted what the two films 'conspicuously lack: story (as opposed to action), characters (as opposed to cartoon figures) and any real emotional resonance'.

Spielberg indulged another fantasy with **1941** (1979), with Milius working on the script, which is incoherent, and one thinks of them besottedly devouring the carrion of old Hollywood. The initial idea is based on *The Russians Are Coming, The Russians Are Coming*, that of American panic at the thought of invasion of a foreign power; the vast cast of characters chasing all over Los Angeles recalls *It's a Mad, Mad, Mad, Mad World*, and since the time is 1941 we may note that the military are portrayed as even more blockheaded than in the movies of that time – recalled by the presence of John Belushi, whose likeness to Lou Costello is not the only resemblance; while the various scenes of planes and tanks out of control seem to have been meant to appeal to those who liked the 'trips' in *2001*. Columbia, which had made a sizeable profit on its investment of $18 million in *Close Encounters*, nevertheless baulked at the budget of $32 million, so shared the risk with Universal. Both companies lost heavily, but this has been the only failure in the Lucas-Spielberg parade of hits.

However, it was in the climate of failure that every studio passed up **Raiders of the Lost Ark** (1981), except Paramount, which sunk $20 million into its imbecilities. Spielberg directed and the producer was Lucas; who explained that it was 'based on the serials I loved when I was a kid: action movies set in exotic locales with a cliff-hanger every second. I wondered why they didn't make movies like that anymore. I still wanted to see them.' So apparently did many others, for this film was hugely popular, despite more illogicalities than ever appeared in a Republic or Monogram serial. The hero (Harrison Ford) is intrepid, but he is not (like Cooper in *High Noon* or Bogart in *The African*

Queen) vulnerable, or afraid. He is pushed into tight corners, but he escapes without conviction or ingenuity: guns or friendly natives materialise out of free air (he is even blown up at one point, but turns up unharmed a few minutes later). Worse, the piece is relentlessly solemn, unlike de Broca's infinitely superior *L'Homme de Rio*.

The film's popularity made Spielberg and Lucas even more the golden boys of the industry, but in the meantime Columbia dropped **E.T.: the Extra-Terrestrial** (1982) after spending $1 million in development. Universal picked it up only because it had turned down *Star Wars* (which went to 20th Century-Fox), and then saw *E.T.* become the quickest success in cinema history, overtaking all these other films at the box office. It is about the friendship of a young boy with a creature left here from another planet, and you have to believe, to start with, that small boys are not afraid of squidgey monsters. The relationship between the two is not developed, beyond a manipulative sequence where the boy at school 'feels' what E.T. is doing at home. The thinness of the plot suddenly gives way to a chase, when the scientists come for E.T., and the pursuit plagiarises that in *The Great Escape* and the end of *Miracolo in Milano*. Spielberg's now familiar style – serried rows of police cars, views of the city by night, the camera tracking back from lights mistily before it – is no consolation. In Britain, two weekly critics, John Coleman in the *New Statesman* and Peter Ackroyd in *The Spectator*, invoked Disney, and both used the word 'infantilism'. The broadcaster Kenneth Robinson called it 'the worst film I have ever seen . . . nauseating, sentimental rubbish', and I must confess that its popularity puzzles me: perhaps with so many sabre-rattlers in charge of our destinies it is nice to know that Out There are creatures who love children, while our scientists are the forces for destruction. The best that may be said for the film was put by Joseph L. Mankiewicz, 'charming, but as intellectually demanding as the old Lassie films.'

Both Mankiewicz and Elia Kazan have observed that today's films are like comic strips, so that the dialogue should ideally be in balloons. Another who agrees is the screenwriter William Goldman, who observed that few of them prompt new

The Superman pictures – there have been three to date – are the best of the spate of movies at this time based on comic strips (or seeming like it). This is a scene from the first, which has a turgid, long beginning in that planet, Krypton, which is supposed to be the home of Superman (Christopher Reeve). The film improves mightily as it establishes him as a gauche New York journalist and is even better when he gets into his gear to fly – in this case helping fellow reporter Lois Lane (Margot Kidder) to do like-wise, not that she recognises him as the guy from the office.

perceptions, specifically mentioning *Dumbo* as a film of the past which does. I am not sure whether the compliment might be paid to **Superman** (1978) or **Superman II** (1980), but, unlike the Lucas-Spielberg fantasies, you are likely to leave the cinema feeling much more cheerful. These two films are based on an old comic strip, and were produced by Alexander Salkind, who after a quarrel with Richard Donner, who had directed *Superman*, replaced him on the second film with Richard Lester (his director on *The Three Musketeers*). The two films are interchangeable, and in any case what matters are the special effects, which vary from the fair to the miraculous. The first film has a pretentious opening, and an inadequate villain (Gene Hackman), though this actor has the knack of the villainy in the second film – and is joined by some other relishable opponents for Superman (Christopher Reeve), who is, despite his name, occasionally vulnerable and in situations done with far more relish and wit than those in *Raiders of the Lost Ark*. The film is magical whenever he starts to fly; the second of the two films was even more popular than the first, and I imagine that they and *Superman III* will enchant successive generations of children.

The chief exponent of the comic strip film has been Michael Cimino (b. 1943), though in his case they have masqueraded as serious works. After beginning as a screenwriter he wrote and directed a derivative vehicle for Clint Eastwood, **Thunderbolt and Lightfoot** (1974). A British company, E.M.I., was virtually the only studio willing to back **The Deer Hunter** (1978), a three-hour movie on a subject Hollywood disliked, the Vietnam War, but Universal bought the American rights on the strength of Robert de Niro's participation. He plays a steelworker who is conscripted and goes to Vietnam, where his buddies play Russian roulette while he has some Errol Flynnish adventures; then he returns home disillusioned. The film particularly roused the ire of those war correspondents who had been in Vietnam: Gloria Emerson wrote in *The New York Times* that 'Cimino has cheapened and degraded the War as no one else had', and that journal reprinted John Pilger's attack in the *New Statesman*, '*The Deer Hunter* and its apologists insult the memory of every American who died in Vietnam.' In Hollywood the Academy voted Oscars to the film for Best Picture and Best Direction.

Those Oscars were responsible for the budget of **Heaven's Gate** (1980) escalating from an original $11 million to $36 million, since United Artists acceded to all Cimino's demands, such as transporting cast and crew to Oxford, England, which stands in for Harvard in the prologue. One set had to be dismantled and rebuilt since it was three feet out from Cimino's calculations; a skating sequence took six months of rehearsal. We may doubt whether the entire inhabitants of Western towns took to dancing on roller skates or whether they indulged in mooning (i.e. the practice of exposing their bare buttocks, in this case on the battle field). In fact, like *The Deer Hunter*, virtually every element of this film is there to make us marvel at the skill of its maker. Its subject is The Johnson County War, and certainly the film, rich in symbolism and set-pieces, is visually handsome. The photographer is Vilmos Zsigmond, who shot *McCabe and Mrs Miller* for Robert Altman, whose brothel scenes are reproduced here; one scene is borrowed from *Days of Heaven*; while the central situation is taken from Altman's film and *Jules et Jim*, with aspects added from Eastman's films. The film opened to lethal reviews, and since most of them called it incoherent, it was withdrawn and cut from 225 minutes to 148, with some refilming and changes adding a further $7 million to the cost. It reopened to equally poor reviews and such poor business that *The New York Times* observed that at the rate of attendance it had cost United Artists $4,800 for each customer. *Variety* announced that one in four Americans was needed to see this film before it could begin to recover its cost. There were discussions of further cuts, till someone observed that it would be cheaper to show the trailer.

The film's debacle was summed up by the magazine *American Film*, 'Cimino is now less a film-maker than a human bench-mark, as in "Post-Cimino Hollywood", the personification of the arrogant, profligate, irresponsible Young Movie Brat Director who has supposedly wrecked Hollywood's prosperity. The bitter words of veteran producer Pandro S. Berman speak for many: "When producers were supreme, Hollywood was at its peak. Now that the young director has taken over, Hollywood has gone to hell." ' This particular young director, in Cannes for a festival showing, told *Le Matin* that when Kennedy was killed many people felt better, since his brilliance reminded them that they had wasted their lives. He did not, he went on, compare himself with Kennedy, but certain journalists wanted to destroy him for not dissimilar reasons – since to them he represented success and talent.

Heaven's Gate is the most spectacular of Hollywood's follies in recent years, and it is possibly not quite the worst film. The industry which once produced entertainments for adults now caters to its teenage audiences with witless campus sex comedies and inane stories of the paranormal. There have been a few good American films in the past few years, including the enormously popular **Smokey and the Bandit** (1977), a Burt Reynolds vehicle directed by his friend Hal Needham, a former stuntman. It is clearly a committee film, and manipulative, but it is fresh and spontaneous – qualities unexpectedly found in what could have been yet another film with Reynolds as a good ol' boy involved in yet more car chases. He is a lawbreaker and a friend of whores, but withal a courtly Southerner, whereas his foe is a petty, stupid, fat sheriff (Jackie Gleason); the best of the film is in his relationship with a New York girl (Sally Field), whose cultural values centre on

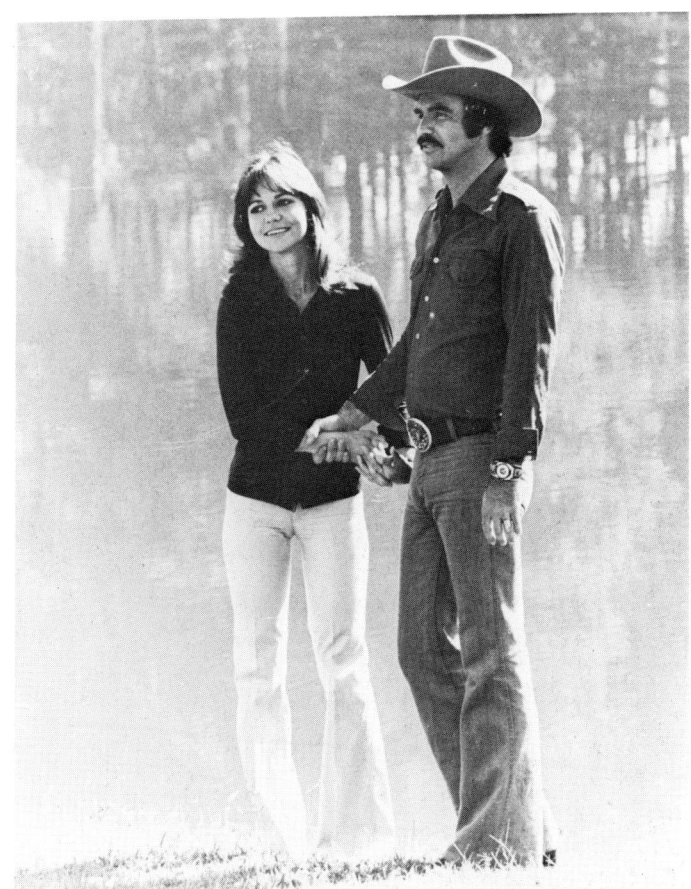

'A Chorus Line' and Stephen Sondheim, neither of which he has ever heard.

Body Heat (1981) is the first film directed by Lawrence Kasdan, who also wrote it after contributing to the scripts of *The Empire Strikes Back* and *Raiders of the Lost Ark*. I am not sure that it is an admirable movie, since it is another that feeds on the films of the past, but it does so more entertainingly than most. Kasdan's sources are *Double Indemnity* and the 1946 version of *The Postman Always Rings Twice*, but when taxed with plagiarising James M. Cain he observed, soundly, that the plot had been around since Aeschylus. After the wife (Kathleen Turner) and her lover (William Hurt) have successfully bumped off her ageing husband (Richard Crenna), Kasdan provides a hundred twists, some of which strain credibility. Hurt is excellent as bungler at his job, the law, and a stud in the sack; and the bright dia-

Burt Reynolds has worked long and hard at perfecting his image, that of the good ol' boy, fallible and only too human in his weaknesses. His popularity has been steadfast now for years, most understandably when teamed with the delightful Sally Field in *Smokey and the Bandit*, an unpretentious entertainment which attracted a large proportion of the world's population into its cinemas.

Michael Douglas and Jane Fonda, co-producers and stars of *The China Syndrome*, which hoped to alert us to the dangers inherent in manufacturing nuclear energy. Those who, in the film's plot, know of a potential breakdown try to hush it up, and would have succeeded but for the two investigative television reporters that you see here – not that the film is entirely sanguine about the power of T.V.

logue is at its best when two cops, friends of his, are not sure when and how to nab him.

The China Syndrome (1979) is a thriller on the dangers of nuclear power. A generating station may be on the verge of a breakdown, which would be fatal to the local population: two investigative reporters (Michael Douglas, Jane Fonda) need the proof necessary to present their evidence, and seek the cooperation of the plant supervisor (Jack Lemmon). The director, James Bridges, uses some of the cinema's oldest tricks to heighten tension. The screenplay by Mike Gray (who originated the project) and T. S. Cook is like that of *All the President's Men* in presenting its heroes as fearless investigators into the activities of the powerful; it is concerned to the proper degree, but never as fair as its supposedly impartial approach would imply. As Lemmon prepares to spill the beans, his boss decides that they cannot

just stand by and watch this idiot wash out a billion dollar investment. As Miss Fonda, who produced the film with Douglas, observed, its subject is greed. It is also about responsibility, by inference increasingly rare in an automated society; and as the film was premiered there was an accident at a nuclear power station in Harrisburg, Pennsylvania. The three leading players, especially Lemmon, are superb.

Warren Beatty is another star who has turned producer and director as well, starting with the impertinently titled **Heaven Can Wait** (1978), sharing the second job with Buck Henry and the writing with Elaine May. It is not a remake of Lubitsch's film, but of *Here Comes Mr Jordan*, of such poor quality as to expect little of **Reds** (1981), directed by Beatty and written by him with the British dramatist Trevor Griffiths. As filming of *Reds* stretched on for two years and the budget mounted to $43 million (provided by Barclays Bank, which then bought the film and leased it back to Paramount, both companies benefiting under British tax laws) many anticipated a second *Heaven's Gate*, but *Reds* turned out to be one of the most important and stimulating films for years. It is the story of Jack Reed (Beatty) and Louise Bryant (Diane Keaton), and certain sequences are deplorable – such as the dog which whines outside their door whenever they make love. As a love story, it is mediocre, but as an extended comment on American communism it is brave and sometimes illuminating. There is no doubt that Beatty regards Reed as the Alger Hiss of his day, American enemy to the American state: after publishing his book on the Russian Revolution Reed was militant in founding the American Communist Party, so that when he disappeared inside the U.S.S.R the State Department seized the chance to dismiss him as a non-person. The first half of the film is the better, with its portrait of a pseudo-intellectual set in New York and a literary clique at Cape Cod – with Jack Nicholson, as Eugene O'Neill, taking every scene in which he appears; the second half has impressive moments, if only in giving expression to the official view that Reed's political beliefs constituted subversion. Like Bryant's spirited defence of her agnosticism and the triumphant playing of the Internationale, this is something one never expected to find in an 'American' movie. In the end it hedges its bets, though remaining ambiguous as to whether Reed became disillusioned with Soviet communism or was merely tactful. The more romantic aspects of the plot are offset by those contemporaries of Reed who interrupt the action to offer sometimes irrelevant recollections; and in the same manner reservations about Beatty's boyish Reed are offset by his obvious dedication to the project. Miss Keaton's Bryant fails to sustain the three-hour running time and is a libel on a lady who was much sharper than made to appear. Beatty was awarded an Oscar for his direction.

I doubt whether the film recovered its costs, but the only one of these films to be a clear failure was *Cutter and Bone* or **Cutter's Way** (1981) as it was renamed in an effort to attract a public which had shunned it on its first appearance. Like *Who'll Stop the Rain?*, it is about Vietnam veterans in California who have gone to the bad – the feckless philanderer Bone (Jeff Bridges), his chum Cutter (John Heard), shorn of one eye, a leg and half an arm, plus Cutter's wife (Lisa Eichhorn), who has taken to drink. The two men make it their mission to bring to justice an oil tycoon they believe to be a murderer, but this film is less a thriller than a mood piece – and the mood is mysterious and not unlike that of the *films noirs* of the Forties. Jeffrey Alan Fiskin wrote it from a novel by Newton Thornburgh, and the director is Ivan Passer, who until this sharp upturn had made increasingly feeble movies after leaving Czechoslovakia.

Another European director, Costa-Gavras, was on more predictable form with his first American film, **Missing** (1982), which created an uproar in the States, since the news media in some parts of the country have been unforthcoming about C.I.A. involvement South of the Border. The film firmly states that the U.S. government connived at the killing of a young American during the 1973 right-wing coup in Chile. Edmund Horman, his father – played in the film by Jack Lemmon – later sued eleven high-ranking officials for $4 million, but though the case was thrown out for lack of evidence, no commentator was convinced by the three-page rebuttal by the State Department issued immediately after the film's premiere. Horman's lawyer, Thomas Hauser, wrote a book about the case, and it is that which the director and Donald Stewart drew upon for their screenplay. I did not care for the devices by which the hawkish father warms to his daughter-in-law (Sissy Spacek) and his dead son's radical views, but the facts are as persuasively presented as in *Etat de Siège*, Costa-Gavras's earlier piece about C.I.A. dirty work in Latin America. The movie is as compulsive as *Prince of the City*, which came out at the same time, and since after equally warm notices *Missing* was the more popular, we may suppose that stars, or at least names, are still a factor in audience appeal. I also make the analogy because Costa-Gavras, like Lumet, has always stressed that he is not a career director, but a 'film-maker who just gets on with the job'. In view of some of the films discussed in this chapter thank God for both of them.

Gratitude may be felt towards such films as are based on fact, like so many of the best of the early Eighties – *Reds*, *Gallipoli*, *Chariots of Fire* – even if these are only following recent European patterns. Being factual in itself is not a virtue, but since the industry cannot, or rather is unable, to return to making the sort of entertainments on which its greatness was founded, such movies are preferable to those which are no more than children's picture books. Those making films specifically aimed at the predominantly teenage audiences of today may not realise that the more intelligent films of recent years – *One Flew Over the Cuckoo's Nest*, *All the President's Men*, *Kramer vs. Kramer*, *Missing* – have all been enormously profitable. Lucas and Spielberg may be making themselves and their backers very wealthy: at the same time they are doing their medium a profound disservice.

Envoi

EVEN AS the bulk of this book was with the printer I was seeing new movies and I feel bound to include a word or so about those made by directors discussed in the text – together with a brief comment on some of the interesting new ones which have emerged.

As I do not wish to conclude this history on a graceless note I shall start with the disappointments and move on to those movies which seem to me to be successful. Ermanno Olmi, a great director, in *CamminaCammina* (1983), reconstructed the Journey of the Magi but without achieving much dramatic tension. The film is not, however, as misguided as Louis Malle's *My Dinner with André* (1981), a record of a particularly fatuous conversation between two minor New York theatre people. Nikita Mikhalkov's *Without Witnesses* (1983) is also a duologue, between a man and his ex-wife, but if it has more action it is equally devoid of humour – at least as far as this non-Soviet observer is concerned. Jerzy Skolimowski's *Moonlighting* (1982), about some Polish construction workers in London at the time of the crackdown on Solidarity, is lacking in content and in conviction, and the same is true of Martin Scorsese's *The King of Comedy* (1983), despite a typically resourceful performance by Robert de Niro as a New York schmuck with unorthodox methods of achieving fame in television. Francis Coppola followed the poor *The Outsiders* (1983) with the even worse *Rumble Fish* (1983), also based on a 'teenage' novel by S. E. Hinton – thus, as David Denby observed in *New York* magazine, signing away his reputation twice in one year.

My own expectations were less for Nagisa Oshima's *Merry Christmas, Mr Lawrence* (1983), an Anglo-Japanese production financed in New Zealand, and in the event they were met because the source, Laurens Van der Post's novel 'The Sower and the Seed', had been robbed of its point – that during the War the Japanese did not lose those qualities which were the reverse of their much-publicised barbarism. Just after I saw this thin enterprise I saw a good film with the same theme, Krzysztof Zanussi's *Wege in der Nacht* (1982), made for German television. The study of the relationship between conqueror and conquered – in this case the Germans and the Poles – is closer to *Le Silence de la Mer* than to Oshima's film, but this has intelligence as that has not.

Shyam Benegal was at less than his best with *Market Place* (1983), lingering for too long on the details of life within a *kotha* – which for the sake of brevity can be described as the Indian equivalent of a geisha house – then bringing in far too many strands of plot after the two-hour mark, which he cannot resolve in the remaining 50 minutes. Manuel Gutiérrez Aragón offered a further collaboration with his co-writer Luis Megino, *Demonios en el Jardin* (1982), which looks at a prosperous family of grocers in the Civil War and ten years later, but apart from some shafts of humour it would again seem to confirm that his best film, *Camada Negra*, owed its quality to Borau's contribution. *El Sur* (1983) is Victor Erice's first film since *El Espíritu de la Colmena*, which it too closely resembles. It is a quiet, civilised piece, but Erice's aim can only be pondered upon, since he intended a much longer film before leaving the project after a quarrel with the producer, Elias Quarejeta, who assembled what was shot into the resulting 94-

minute movie. Shohei Imamura's *The Ballad of Narayama* (1983) received the Grand Prix at the Cannes Film Festival: this remake of Kinoshita's similarly titled film included material from another novel by Fukasawa (also filmed before, by Ichikawa in 1958), but these additions turned out to be intractable, putting much of the film into the 'grunting peasants' genre. However, when Imamura remains with his central subject, the old lady who must be left on the hillside to die, he is at his magisterial best. Ichikawa himself did a new version of the novel by Junichiro Tanizaki, *The Makioka Sisters* (1983), filmed by Yutaka Abe in 1950 and Koji Shima in 1959; it is neatly told in the manner of the movies of the period when it is set, 1938, but too verbose.

Among other established directors, Wajda perhaps provided the most satisfactory work with *Danton* (1983), vividly presenting the conflicts between Danton, Robespierre and their factions; the film also has the most convincing French Revolution the cinema has given us – a time of hurry, scurry and confusion. Sidney Lumet believes that *Daniel* (1983) is his best film, which it conceivably is; but by choosing to film E. L. Doctorow's fictional account of what it was like to be the son of Jewish left-wing parents electrocuted for treachery he avoided any confrontation with the Rosenbergs and their guilt, thus bringing upon his head the wrath of American critics – not entirely without justice. However, the film deals intelligently with those who choose to be Communists in America, and passionately with the effect on children of their parents' 'aberrant' behaviour. It is its own film, going its own way, with more to say than most.

The public greatly appreciated *Tootsie* (1982), presumably because it has a cast of likeable characters played by talented people rather than because it is pointed or funny about its subject, that of an unemployed actor (Dustin Hoffman) who dons female attire to get a job in a soap opera. It is an amiable film, and with *Absence of Malice* confirms that Sidney Pollack has firm control of his directorial skills. As much may be said of George Roy Hill and *The World According to Garp* (1983), cleverly written by Steve Tesich in such a way that the confusions of John Irving's pseudo-Gunther Grass novel become

positive statements on nonconformity, fame and infidelity. Walter Hill's *48 HRS* (1983), though unforgivably foul-mouthed, is a fine audience-rousing thriller, easily exploiting the personality of a new star, Eddie Murphy. John Sayles proves himself only a competent director with *The Return of the Secaucus Seven* (1980), but his script, about some former peace protesters meeting again before the onslaught of middle age, is far better than might have been expected from the exploitation movies that he had written for other people. Woody Allen's *Zelig* (1983) is a beautifully done cod documentary on a famous figure of the Twenties and Thirties; it is not as funny as it might have been, but always likeable.

Any comments on *Daniel* may be applied to *The Ploughman's Lunch* (1983), though it is by no means as interesting. But it is such a heady experience to find a British movie even aware of politics that we may forgive some shortcomings in its story of a media figure (Jonathan Pryce) so ambitious that his integrity comes unstuck – if it was ever there. It is a first cinema movie for the director Richard Eyre and the writer Ian McEwan, even if designed to go quickly to television's Channel 4, partly responsible for its financing. Few of Channel 4's other movies have been notable but *Angel* (1982) deserved its cinema showings. Neil Jordan wrote and directed this Irish thriller in which the villains are probably IRA men, showing in his first feature a mastery of his medium. I am less sure about Geoff Murphy, the young New Zealand director of *Goodbye Pork Pie* (1981), especially as this 'road' movie is often derivative; but it is an exhilarating film, and one which uses the countryside eloquently. Australia continues to export superior works, notably Peter Weir's *The Year of Living Dangerously* (1983), a portrait of the world of the foreign correspondent as it existed in Djakarta at the time of the attempted Communist coup of 1965, and Igor Auzins's *We of the Never Never* (1982), set in the Outback at the turn of the century and based on yet another memoir by a courageous Australian lady.

I have also seen an exceptional film from Iran, *The Cycle* (1974), directed by Dariush Mehrjui, who made it clandestinely under the Shah's regime. Its subject is poverty, as

Envoi

Here is a scene from *Yol*, with Tarik Akan and Serif Sezer. One of the most moving statements about life in the Third World, the film was made despite a series of extraordinary difficulties and obstacles.

experienced by some down and outs who sell their blood to entrepreneurs who in turn sell it to the local hospital where, with the exception of one doctor, the staff are stuck in inertia and apathy. It is a film of great passion and contains images of such bleak beauty that it seems a wholly original work. These qualities it shares with the films of Yilmaz Güney (b. 1937), a former Turkish matinee idol who has directed movies the reverse of those in which he acted. Indeed, they were a new departure for the Turkish cinema, and since those that we have seen are critical of both the Turkish regime and feudal life as it is encouraged to persist it is not surprising that he has spent much of his recent life in

prison, reputedly for murder. While incarcerated he wrote and supervised *The Herd* (1978) and *Yol* (1982), both of which were directed for him by friends, respectively Zeki Ökten and Şerif Gören. Escaping into exile, he wrote and directed *Le Mur* (1983) with the aid of financing from the French government. The form of this film, a composite portrait from which emerged the dramas of certain individuals, is common to all three. It is the least of them – though still extraordinary – perhaps because of the limitations of making a film abroad, in Turkish, about conditions in a Turkish prison. *The Herd* is an exceptional piece about a fairly primitive tribesman confronted with life in modern Ankara; and *Yol*, a masterwork, follows the adventures of some prisoners allowed out on a two-week vacation. It, too, in an epic sequence, shows great compassion for the residue of feudalism.

The Pakistani director Jamil Dehlavi made *The Blood of Hossein* (1980) in his native land, but fled to Britain to complete it after the military government came to power in 1977. It is an ambitious film, criticising just such a government in a context which combines mysticism with the fates of two brothers (both played by Salmaan Peer), one caught up in the great world and the other remaining on the family estate. It could be said that the elements of soap opera were designed to appeal to an unsophisticated local population, but this is a wholly entertaining, partly magical movie by one who may be a major talent.

There are probably others now making films. There are new movies opening as I write this: perhaps it is time to quit the typewriter and look at them.

Select Bibliography

Over 5,000 films are listed in the text. Those discussed are those that I have seen (unless otherwise stated), while my viewings were supplemented by research into whatever memoirs, monographs or interviews were available. However, a list of the books consulted would run into thousands and its effectiveness accordingly diminished. What follows is a personal list, by no means exhaustive, of books for further reading.

REFERENCE AND HISTORY

Gifford, Denis: *The British Film Catalogue 1895–1970*, David & Charles, Newton Abbot, 1973
Subtitled 'A Guide to Entertainment Films' this is a listing of all of them, with casts and major credits, accompanied by a single-line plot summary – done with exemplary skill. It is not only an invaluable reference book but one to browse in, for hours and hours.

Jacobs, Lewis: *The Rise of the American Film*, Harcourt Brace, New York, 1939; Columbia University Press, New York, 1970
For many, the definitive film history, especially on early cinema, but it does stop in 1939. Jacobs's views stand the test of time much better than those of most of his contemporaries, but inevitably a few need readjustment. As I mentioned earlier, he devotes a chapter to Chaplin, but only mentions Keaton in passing.

Katz, Ephraim: *The International Film Encyclopedia*, T. Y. Crowell, New York, 1979; Macmillan, London, 1980
Without question the most informative and useful one-volume reference book on cinema, with complete credits for most directors, many producers and stars and intelligently selective credits for other movie-makers. When the author offers an opinion it tends to be conventional, but the details of individual careers are often telling; there are fewer errors than in any other book of this kind and only a couple of serious omissions.

Macgowan, Kenneth: *Behind the Screen*, Delacorte Press, New York, 1965
Subtitled 'The History and Techniques of the Motion Picture', this book is much more sound on the techniques than on the history, which is told not chronologically but as the author thinks fit – and, anyway, is chiefly concerned with Hollywood. One of the reasons the book is good is because it is told from the inside: Macgowan was a Hollywood producer.

Perry, George: *The Great British Picture Show*, Hart-Davis MacGibbon, London, 1974
A history of British cinema which manages to combine literate comments on most of the major films with splendidly researched details on financing, government intervention and many of the other minutiae involved.

René, Jeanne and Ford, Charles: *Dictionnaire du Cinéma Universel*, Robert Laffont, Paris, 1970
This, the fifth volume of the authors's *Histoire du Cinéma*, is an excellent reference work giving brief biographical and fuller filmographic details on some 4,000 directors, writers, producers, actors and technicians in the international film-making world. If not quite as accurate as it could be on the very early practitioners, it contains information on European directors not to be found elsewhere.

Robinson, David: *World Cinema, A Short History*, Eyre Methuen, London, 1973; Stein and Day, New York, 1974. Revised edition 1981
Concisely written and precisely what is claimed in its title. The first two chapters cover the cinema's pre-history with such excellence that it renders all others on the subject inadequate.

CRITICISM

Agee, James: *Agee on Film*, McDowell, Oblensky, New York, 1958; Grosset & Dunlap, 1968; Peter Owen, London, 1967
Most of the films which opened in New York between 1941 and 1948 are reviewed by a critic whose judgment is as trustworthy (still) as his writing is elegant.

Greene, Graham: *The Pleasure Dome: The Collected Film Criticism 1935–40*, Secker & Warburg, London; Oxford University Press, New York, 1980
An absorbing collection for several reasons, not least for an occasional revelation into the character of a man who would become a leading novelist. The book is a valuable insight into the mind of a serious movie-lover of the time; and it chronicles a number of films hardly written about elsewhere.

Lejeune, C. A.: *Chestnuts in Her Lap*, Phoenix House, London, 1948 (second edition)
The doyenne of London critics in her time, from 1936 (the earliest selection in this volume) till she retired in 1958. By the end she had rather lost her touch; however, she was able to analyse films brilliantly till a couple of years earlier.

Select Bibliography

These pieces from *The Observer* are a paradigm of what movie criticism should be.

Simon, John: *Movies into Film: Film Criticism 1967–70*, The Dial Press, New York, 1971. *Reverse Angle: A Decade of Films*, Clarkson S. Potter, New York, 1982

Together these two anthologies (taken from various publications) cover most of the important films shown in New York over a 15-year period, and they do so with erudition, wit, wisdom and a beautiful prose style. By the second of the two Simon has learned to curb his famous waspishness, which makes him less disturbing. He writes in the tradition of Woolcott, Agate and Tynan; there is only one critic today in Britain who might be said to be his equal and he has – as far as I know – no rivals in the U.S. These two books prove that contemporary American movie criticism does deserve to be reprinted in book form.

Winnington, Richard: *Drawn and Quartered*, The Saturn Press, London, 1948

A selection of Winnington's weekly writings on the film from 1943 to 1948 – witty, succinct and agreeably accurate by today's standards, forty years on. In 1975 Paul Rotha made a further selection of Winnington's writings on the cinema – till his death in 1953 – but it is disappointingly orthodox in choice, since Winnington could dispatch rubbish with more severity than most. What is needed is 'The Complete Winnington'.

INDIVIDUAL SURVEYS

Balio, Tino: *United Artists: The Company Built by the Stars*, University of Wisconsin, Madison, 1976

If Balio had written only a history of United Artists from published records and his viewings of the company's films this would still be a valuable book; but he had access to all the surviving papers from 1918 to 1951, when it finally lost the last of its two founders, Chaplin and Mary Pickford.

Behlmer, Rudy (editor): *Memo from David O. Selznick*, The Viking Press, New York, 1972; Macmillan, London, 1972

Selznick was a prodigious writer of memos on all aspects of the films with which he was dealing. These, selected by Mr Behlmer, take Selznick from M-G-M to Paramount to RKO to M-G-M again and finally to independent production. They provide an extraordinary portrait of the way the studio system functioned – and also, of course, the way that Selznick himself worked.

Bergan, Ronald: *Sports in the Movies*, Proteus, London and New York, 1982

One of the proliferating breed of movie books produced to meet the need for movie books, covering each of the famous sports – boxing, horse-racing – in a general essay featuring the most important films on the subject, followed by a checklist of some others. The fact that the book is livelier than most of its kind – indeed, is both enjoyable and informative – is due to a writer with an often malicious wit.

Brownlow, Kevin: *Hollywood – The Pioneers*, Collins, London, 1979; Alfred A. Knopf, New York, 1980. *The Parade's Gone By . . .*, Secker & Warburg, London, 1968; University of California Press, Berkeley and Los Angeles, 1976

The first is a beautifully illustrated book created to accompany the Thames Television series on the American Silent cinema, written by one whose knowledge of the subject is equalled by his considerable enthusiasm. The other book is described on the jacket as 'a vivid, affectionate portrait of the golden days of Hollywood', but this is only partly true, since it covers only the Silent era and there were some golden days after that. However, Brownlow's interviews with surviving veterans are riveting; and the illustrations are marvellous.

Chierichetti, David: *Hollywood Director: Mitchell Leisen*, Curtis Books, Philadelphia, 1973

A perceptive account of Leisen's career, with comments by many of the people who worked with him. As a text, not much better than competent, despite the author's love for his subject; but as a picture of the way Hollywood functioned – or used to – as valuable as the books listed here on Selznick or by Capra.

Dunne, John Gregory: *The Studio*, Farrar, Strauss and Giroux, New York, 1969; W. H. Allen, London, 1970

Mr Dunne was given access to the conferences and committees of 20th Century-Fox during one year in the late Sixties. What emerges is not as condemnatory of the mogul mentality as 'Picture', Lillian Ross's account of the making of *The Red Badge of Courage*, but it is illuminating, and chilling.

Eyles, Allen: *The Marx Brothers, Their World of Comedy*, Zwemmer, London, 1965; A. S. Barnes, New Jersey, 1966

The films are discussed in detail by a clear-sighted enthusiast; those who have seen them may laugh out loud at this book.

Fordin, Hugh: *The World of Entertainment*, Doubleday, New York, 1975

A film-by-film account of the work of Arthur Freed, with details of production costs and changes, together with interviews with the surviving participants: so far the indispensable source book on the M-G-M musical.

Hull, David Stewart: *Film in the Third Reich*, University of California Press, Berkeley and Los Angeles, 1969

A simply written study of the films made in Germany between 1933 and 1945, taken in chronological order, without an undue stress on opinion, little theorising and much fact about the production of the films, the personalities involved and the Nazi Party interference. But to be used with caution, for research reveals that, in some cases, the author has not always seen the film under discussion.

Leprohon, Pierre: *The Italian Cinema*, Editions Seghers, Paris, 1966; Secker & Warburg, London, 1972

As I considered this booklist over the years, it was my intention to mention at least one major or source book on all the leading film industries, but it simply isn't possible (for instance, the books I have on Russian and Japanese cinema are both factually inaccurate – to judge from the films I've seen – and badly organised). Leprohon's book is not ideal, since what it covers in most detail is the already better chronicled recent period, but it is still the best book available in English on the Italian cinema from 1895 to the neo-realists.

Mankiewicz, Joseph L.: *More About 'All About Eve'*, Random House, New York, 1972

This book describes itself as 'A colloquy by Gary Carey

with Joseph L. Mankiewicz', meaning that the long introduction consists of an interview by the erudite Mr Carey
with Mankiewicz about his most famous film, the screenplay of which follows. Mankiewicz speaks not only of the
genesis of the movie, fascinating matter in itself, but he
also has witty comments to make about Hollywood and its
denizens – chiefly, and appropriately, actresses.

Milne, Tom: *Mamoulian*, Thames and Hudson. London,
    1969
A detailed examination of the sixteen films directed by
Mamoulian by one of the best writers on the cinema.

Pratt, George C.: *Spellbound in Darkness: A History of the
    Silent Film*, University of Rochester Press, Rochester,
    1966; The New York Graphical Society, Greenwich,
    Connecticut, 1977
The subtitle is justified in only a loose sense, for this is a
collection of contemporary writings on movies from 1895
to 1929, with a commentary by George Pratt, master
archivist or archaeologist as you will. The material
gathered together here is invaluable for anyone wanting to
know how the press responded to early cinema.

Sinyard, Neil and Turner, Adrian: *A Journey Down Sunset
    Boulevard: The Films of Billy Wilder*, B.C.W./L.S.P.,
    1979
This is an excellent analysis of some of the best films ever
made by writers with an acute capacity for making one
agree with them. Theirs is a refreshing and persuasive
critical study of one of Hollywood's greatest directors.
While celebrating Wilder's famed wit, the authors place
particular emphasis on his European romanticism, which
in turn throws fresh light on his career.

Stratton, David: *The Last New Wave – The Australian Film
    Revival*, Angus & Robertson, Sydney, 1980
Ten years of the Australian cinema – an exciting time for
those in the film industry there, which is reflected in the
text. Stratton discusses all the major films in sections under
their individual directors, with a summary of the plot and
all relevant details from the inception of the project to the
critics' notices. One cannot imagine the subject better
handled.

FILM GUIDES

Bandmann, Christa and Hembus, Joe: *Klassiker des Deuts-
    chen Tonfilm, 1930–1960*, Goldman Verlag, Munich, 1980
Brennicke, Ilona and Hembus, Joe: *Klassiker des Deutschen
    Stummfilm, 1910–1930*, Goldman Verlag, Munich,
    1983
Both guides are fascinating reading, for the organisation of
the text enables the editors to present the highlights of each
year in selecting only the most outstanding films to be
thoroughly discussed and portrayed in stills. This is followed by an alphabetical list of almost every important
film in the years covered in each book, with production
details and plot summaries that are pleasurably compre-
hensive. The last section is devoted to an annual production survey and film production history and innovations.

Sadoul, Georges: *Dictionary of Films*, Editions du Seuil,
    Paris, 1965; University of California Press, Berkeley
    and Los Angeles, 1972
A discussion of 1,200 films in alphabetical order, with brief
production details and much common sense in the accompanying text. Sadoul's introduction mentions that he had

not seen some five per cent of the films and his original has
been amended in the English edition, 'translated, edited
and updated' by Peter Morris. Morris has made a beautiful
job of the translation – to judge it, anyway, from Sadoul's
French Film published by the Falcon Press in London in
1953, an exceptionally lucid and informative history of
French cinema, which I have not listed only because it does
stop in 1950. No translator is credited, but Morris has
successfully found the same style for the *Dictionary*.

INTERVIEWS

Bergman, Ingmar: *Bergman on Bergman*, P.A. Norstadt &
    Soners Forlag, Stockholm, 1970; London, Secker &
    Warburg, 1973; New York, Simon & Schuster, 1973
The great Swedish director discusses his films, his career
and cinema generally with three critics, Stig Björkman,
Torsten Manns and Jonas Sima.

Ciment, Michel: *Kazan on Kazan*, Secker & Warburg,
    London, in association with the British Film Institute,
    1973
Kazan talking – with insight, modesty and eloquence –
on his films and his career, with Ciment asking the questions likely to elicit the best responses.

Higham, Charles and Greenberg, Joel: *The Celluloid Muse:
    Hollywood Directors Speak*, Angus & Robertson, Lon-
    don, 1969; Henry Regnery Co, Chicago, 1971
Interviews with Robert Aldrich, Curtis Bernhardt,
George Cukor, John Frankenheimer, Alfred Hitchcock,
Fritz Lang, Rouben Mamoulian, Lewis Milestone, Vincente Minnelli, Jean Negulesco, Irving Rapper, Mark
Robson, Jacques Tourneur, King Vidor and Billy Wilder.
Most such collections are no more than gatherings from
journals, often with the subject discussing his current
project. The value of this particular book is that the
directors were encouraged to talk about each of their
films – those they considered worth analysing – in
chronological order, to build a portrait of their careers and
their feelings on those careers.

BIOGRAPHIES

Buñuel, Luis: *My Last Breath*, Editions Laffont, Paris,
    1982; Alfred A. Knopf, New York, 1983; Jonathan
    Cape, London, 1983
More about the life than the films, but given the life
involved we may not feel deprived. The tone is unexpectedly gentle, even if Buñuel is too honest to withhold
opinions which may not please everyone.

Capra, Frank: *The Name Above the Title*, Macmillan, New
    York, 1971; W. H. Allen, London, 1972
The most admired and acclaimed director of Hollywood's
golden years tells what it was like to be at the top of the
profession and in the process offers an important insight
into the way the American film industry once worked.

Dardis, Tom: *Buster Keaton, The Man Who Wouldn't Lie
    Down*, Andre Deutsch, London, 1979; Penguin
    Books, New York, 1980
Keaton's life together with his genius was so extraordinary
that it would be of interest if less than well told; he has had
two excellent biographers, and this one does contain more
material than was available earlier to Rudi Blesh.

Houseman, John: *Front and Center*, Simon and Schuster,
    New York, 1979

1235

Select Bibliography

Houseman continues his urbane account where he left off in his first book of reminiscences, 'Run Through' (published in New York by Simon and Schuster in 1972 and in London by Allen Lane in 1973); his arrival in Hollywood with Orson Welles. His lively and dispassionate style gives credibility to his opinions and anecdotes. Of all the many producers and directors who worked in Hollywood during and after World War II he was one of the most intellectual; and he furnishes the reader with an authoritative view of the industry.

Huston, John: *An Open Book*, Alfred A. Knopf, New York, 1980; Macmillan, London, 1981

Modest and frank in the manner of Buñuel's memoir, Huston writes amiably of his long career as a director. One is astonished at the range of the man's work and the standard of excellence which is evident in many of his films.

Kulik, Karol: *Alexander Korda: The Man Who Could Work Miracles*, W. H. Allen, London, 1975; Arlington House, New York, 1976

A clearly written and well researched biography with almost everything one needs to know about the films with which Korda was connected. Together with Sir Michael Balcon's memoir, 'A Lifetime of Films', it forms an almost complete history of the British cinema from the Thirties to the Fifties.

Kurosawa, Akira: *Something Like an Autobiography*, Random House, New York, 1983.

Kurosawa's account of his own life, with many revealing comments on his work and those of his colleagues.

Minnelli, Vincente, with Hector Arce: *I Remember It Well*, Doubleday, New York, 1974; Angus & Robertson, London, 1974

All that one might want to know about Minnelli's approach to the films he directed, with an incisive account of the manner in which M-G-M operated at the time.

Renoir, Jean: *My Life and My Films*, Collins, London, 1974; Atheneum, New York, 1974

I would commend the memoirs of any leading filmmaker, but Renoir's autobiography, translated by Norman Denny, is particularly interesting and it conveys the warmth and humanity that so imbue his films.

Taylor, John Russell: *Hitch: The Life and Work of Alfred Hitchcock*, Little Brown, Boston, 1978; Faber & Faber, London, 1978

A clearly written and sympathetic biography – and 'authorised', thus containing much essential information.

PICTORIAL HISTORIES

Blum, Daniel: *A Pictorial History of the Silent Screen*, Grosset and Dunlap, New York, 1953; Spring Books, London, 1961. *A Pictorial History of the Talkies*, Grosset and Dunlap, New York, 1958; Spring Books, London, 1961

A judicious selection of stills and portraits arranged year by year. It is devoted to Hollywood movies, and the occasional inclusion of foreign-language films – and British ones – comes oddly. Both books have been constantly reprinted in New York and London, but as the *Pictorial History of the Talkies* needed to be updated it was inexpertly savaged, by ripping out whole or half pages covering the years up to 1957. For anyone interested in the movies of the Thirties, Forties and Fifties it is worth searching for one of the original editions – which should not be too difficult, since the book was a vast seller.

Eames, John Douglas: *The M-G-M Story*, Octopus Books, London, 1975; Crown Publishers, New York, 1975

With very much an insider's knowledge (Eames had worked for M-G-M publicity in London) the author charts, with illustrations, every single film made by Metro-Goldwyn-Mayer after the three separate companies merged in 1924, managing in his text to mention producer, director, writer(s) and principal players. In the same format are *The Universal Story* and *The Warner Bros. Story*, both by Clive Hirschhorn, and *The RKO Story* by Richard B. Jewell and Vernon Harbin. Harbin had worked at RKO and had access to profit and loss figures on individual films as well as contract details. All the books in this series contain as much information about the history of the studios as anyone could hope for. Most of the stills in the M-G-M book are too small (in contrast to the full-page pictures, which could be said to be too big), but this fault has been rectified by the later books in the series.

Griffiths, Richard and Mayer, Arthur: *The Movies*, Simon and Schuster, New York, 1957; Spring Books, London, 1963

Along with Arthur Knight's now dated 'The Liveliest Art', published the same year, this is one of the pioneering books of film history. Since this is a picture book, it remains the more valuable of the two. The text is as packed with insights as it is debonair, but perhaps all the past fads of the movie industry should not be treated in this manner.

Hirschhorn, Clive: *The Hollywood Musical*, Octopus Books, London, 1981; Crown Publishers, New York, 1981

In the same format as the other Octopus series (see Eames: *The M-G-M Story*), covering over 1,300 musicals, with similar information about the principals involved, plus details of the musical numbers, written with enthusiasm, great good humour and erudition.

Index

Index

Index

1241

Index

Index

Index

Index

Index

Index

1248

Index

Index

Index

Index

Index

Index

Index

Index

Index

1268

Index

Index

Index

Index

1272

Index

Index

Index

Index